מחזור קורן ליום העצמאות וליום ירושלים

The Koren Maḥzor for Yom HaAtzma'ut and Yom Yerushalayim

נוסח אשכנז • Nusaḥ Ashkenaz

קוֹרֵן ירושלים

THE KRENGEL FAMILY WORLD MIZRACHI EDITION

מחזור קורן
ליום העצמאות וליום ירושלים

THE KOREN MAḤZOR FOR
YOM HAATZMA'UT AND YOM YERUSHALAYIM

KOREN PUBLISHERS JERUSALEM

The Koren Maḥzor for Yom HaAtzma'ut and Yom Yerushalayim
Second Hebrew/English Edition, 2016
Nusaḥ Ashkenaz

Koren Publishers Jerusalem Ltd.
POB 4044, Jerusalem 9104001, ISRAEL
POB 8531, New Milford, CT 06776, USA

www.korenpub.com

The creation of this Maḥzor was made possible with the generous support of
Torah Education in Israel.

Printed in the United States of America

Standard Size, Hardcover, ISBN 978 965 301 665 1
Compact Size, Hardcover, ISBN 978 965 301 824 2

YHASA2

WORLD MIZRACHI

*dedicates this page to our partners
in this wonderful project.*

*To all at Koren Publishers Jerusalem
for affording us this partnership opportunity;
your reinvigoration of the venerable Koren publishing house
in recent years is inspirational.*

*Our deepest gratitude to our friends and sponsors
from around the world, who appear in the dedication pages
and whose generosity has made this publication possible.*

A specific heartfelt thank you to

Zev Krengel

*for your generosity to this project and for your
outstanding leadership of the South African Jewish community,
and for the tireless efforts of you and your brother Avrom on many levels,
for the sake of Torah, Israel and the Jewish community.
How appropriate it is that this publication bears the Krengel name.*

Shalom and Iris Maidenbaum

and

Robert and Helene Rothenberg

*of New York,
for your generosity to this project and for your incredible
commitment to Torah learning, Israel and the Jewish People.
How fitting it is that the essay section bears
the Maidenbaum and Rothenberg names.*

Rav Doron Perez
Director-General

Kurt Rothschild
President

Harvey Blitz
Chairman

In memory
of
our beloved parents, grandparents and great-grandparents

Yacov and Pepy Eltes ז"ל

Leaders in the Mizrachi community
who personified the ideals
of religious Zionism

The Eltes Family
MONTREAL

The Rosenbaum Family
MIAMI BEACH · NEW YORK

The Meyer Family
TORONTO · TEL AVIV
MODIIN · HASHMONAIM

We remember
all the brave fallen soldiers
of the Israel Defense Forces
whose ultimate sacrifice affords us
the privilege of our precious
Medinat Yisrael.

Note to the Reader

For the accompanying essays please turn to the other end
of this volume.

The commentary to the Maḥzor is written by
Rabbi Moshe Taragin
except where indicated by initials:
BL – Rabbi Binyamin Lau
YR – Dr. Yoel Rappel

CONTENTS

For the essays on Yom HaAtzma'ut and Yom Yerushalayim
please turn to the other end of this volume.

I rejoiced when they said to me, "Let us go to the House of the LORD."
Our feet stood within your gates, Jerusalem. (Psalm 122)

God has an active presence in the world. Sometimes, with our human arrogance, we attempt to explain away the events of history, fail to recognize the miraculous nature of our survival, or deny the divine hand in our everyday existence.

Three years after the remnant of Europe's Jews emerged from the crematoria of Europe, months after a vote in the United Nations, weeks after the collective forces of six enemy countries grouped to destroy the tiny Yishuv in Mandate Palestine, the Jewish people prevailed and re-created the Jewish Commonwealth of Israel: the restoration of independence lost two thousand years previously.

Nineteen years later, faced once again with the collective aggression of our enemies, the young country triumphed, and the City of Jerusalem, the City of David and Solomon and Ezra and Nehemiah, was restored to Jewish sovereignty.

Sometimes, we need to step back and see the patterns of miracles. Not to recognize these is not to see the hand of God in this world.

It is fitting that the Rabbinate of Israel has established *tefillot* to express our thanks for these miracles and our national survival. Koren Publishers Jerusalem is proud to present the *Maḥzor for Yom HaAtzma'ut and Yom Yerushalayim*, designed to give spiritual expression and meaning to our celebration and thanksgiving.

Yom HaAtzma'ut is not yet a fixture in the Jewish consciousness in English-speaking countries. It is our hope that by providing this maḥzor, we will be able to further strengthen the bonds between the Jewish communities in Israel and the United States, Canada, Britain, Australia, South Africa and elsewhere.

The Challenge of Liturgical Innovation

The Rav, Rabbi Joseph B. Soloveitchik, one of the greatest Torah leaders of our generation, was well known for his ardent support of the State of Israel; he viewed the settling of the Land and the exercise of Jewish sovereignty in Israel as the fulfillment of a biblical commandment.

The Chief Rabbinate of Israel, upon whose structure of the *tefillot* this maḥzor is based, instituted the services for Yom HaAtzma'ut and Yom Yerushalayim; yet the Rav opposed these liturgical innovations. As Rabbi Menachem Genack wrote, "In general, [the Rav] was conservative regarding the structure of the service ... and was averse to changes in the traditional order and composition of the prayers." Nevertheless, Rav Soloveitchik agreed that the miraculous events of those days merited expression in the service. He allowed for the recitation of Hallel without blessings.

Customs vary widely as to what is added to Ma'ariv and Shaḥarit on Yom HaAtzma'ut and Yom Yerushalayim. Each community should follow the decisions of its own rabbinical authority.

Why this Maḥzor?

In recognition of the variations between communities, we offer the order of service as designated by the Chief Rabbinate of Israel, together with additional prayers, marked by shaded text, which some communities have chosen to adopt. Again, each community should follow its own rabbinic authority. But whether the community follows the standard order of the Rabbinate, or of Rav Soloveitchik, or indeed its own communal prayers, we say this: Observe these days. Commemorate, celebrate and give thanks. For the events of 1948 and 1967 are no less miraculous than those witnessed by Esther and Mordechai, or the Hasmoneans. "We thank You also for the miracles ... in those days, at this time."

In recognizing and praising and thanking God for these miracles, we can see, ever so faintly, that first flowering of the Redemption, may it come in our days.

ACKNOWLEDGMENTS

We are honored to have the Krengel family name grace this edition in acknowledgment of the outstanding support of Mr. Zev Krengel. We are also immensely grateful to Shalom and Iris Maidenbaum and Robert and Helene Rothenberg for their generosity in the creation of this maḥzor. Special thanks go to all those whose generous participation made this project possible.

We are delighted to extend our thanks to our partners, World Mizrachi, under the leadership of Rabbi Doron Perez, and to Young Israel. Their enthusiasm and active participation in this project launches it into hundreds of schools and synagogues throughout the English-speaking world.

This maḥzor is the fruit of the joint efforts of Rabbi Dr. Binyamin Lau, Rabbi Moshe Taragin and Dr. Yoel Rappel, whose thoughtful commentary brings special meaning to this volume. Rabbi Moshe Taragin in particular contributed greatly to this project and we thank him for his enthusiastic support as well as his scholarly and insightful words.

Rabbi Shmuel Katz of Jerusalem kindly reviewed the maḥzor and made helpful comments and suggestions. We are indebted to Rabbi Lord Jonathan Sacks for the beautifully elucidating translation of the *tefillot*. The introduction by Rabbi Shlomo Riskin deserves special mention. Without his direct influence, thousands of people (including the writer) would never have made *aliya* to our new and ancient home.

We thank the many contributors to the Essays section for their insights, for deepening our understanding of these special days and of the place of the State of Israel in Jewish law and thought.

Our wonderful team of professionals at Koren, Rabbi Reuven Ziegler, Editor Rachel Meghnagi and Designers Esther Be'er and Dena Landowne Bailey, consistently bring our textual and design standards to the highest level.

We hope that the united prayers of myriads of Jews will elevate each individual's prayers, enhancing the sense of gratitude to God, who lifted us up from the depths of exile and brought us here, to celebrate together. We have been granted a place in the process of redemption; may we merit a part in bringing about its completion swiftly, in our time.

Matthew Miller, Publisher
Koren Publishers Jerusalem Ltd.
Jerusalem, 5775

INTRODUCTION: THE SIGNIFICANCE OF
ISRAEL'S RETURN TO ZION

My First Lesson in Zionism

The most profound tragedy as well as the most uplifting confirmation of our faith were both experienced by the Jewish people within the very same decade of the last century: the shame of humanity that either cooperated with or silently permitted the decimation of the Jewish people and the diabolical atrocities of the Holocaust, and then – only three years after the suicide of Hitler – the newfound hope for humanity with the rebirth of the State of Israel confirmed by a vote in the United Nations.

To suggest that the Holocaust was the necessary price the Jews had to pay to return to their homeland after almost two thousand years of destruction, exile, and persecution, borders on the blasphemous. However, to overlook the inextricable juxtaposition of these two nationally defining events – the first bringing us down to the hellish depths of despair and the second raising us up to the dizzying heights of redemption – would be blinding oneself to the commanding voice of Jewish history. And so I begin this essay with my first lesson in Zionism, which emerged from the ashes of Auschwitz.

It was the Shabbat of the weekly portion *Ki Tavo*, toward the end of the summer of 1952. I had known that the Rebbe of Sanz-Klausenburg had taken over the Beth Moses Hospital (the place where I was born), where he had built a very large beit midrash-*beit knesset* (study hall-synagogue), as well as a printing press to teach his disciples a trade, and I wanted to pray with the Hasidim that Shabbat morning. I also wanted to wear my new bar mitzva suit, which had very recently arrived from the tailor.

I had to conduct a long, hard negotiation with my mother, who was reluctant for me to take such a long walk alone in what was not a very wholesome neighborhood, and was also adamantly opposed to my wearing the

◂ bar mitzva

bar mitzva suit close to a year before my bar mitzva (which was scheduled for the following year's portion of *Emor*). At length, my mother relented, but not until I promised not to get into any altercations with toughs who might start up, and not to partake of any Kiddush if there was one.

When I arrived at the beit midrash, I was amazed by the sea of black and white swaying figures that greeted my eyes, all newly immigrant Holocaust survivors. It was said about the Rebbe that although his wife and thirteen children had been murdered, he had not sat *shiva* for any of them; he preached that those still alive must be saved with exit visas before one could be allowed the luxury of mourning for the dead. The Rebbe himself was among the last to leave Europe, insisting that the captain does not leave the sinking ship before its passengers. I took a seat directly behind the Rebbe, who stood at his lectern facing the eastern wall and the Holy Ark, with his back to the congregation. The prayer was the most intense I had ever experienced, with no talking whatsoever, and chance individuals even bursting out in tears during varying parts of the service, apparently in response to a sudden association with a painful memory.

Then the Torah reader began to chant the weekly portion. When he came to the passage known as the *Tokheḥa*, consisting of the curses that would befall the Israelites, he began to read (in accordance with time-honored custom) in a whisper and very quickly. A sound suddenly came from the place of the Rebbe; he said only one word: "*Hecher*, louder."

The Torah reader immediately stopped reading, and seemed to hesitate for a few moments. I could almost hear him pondering. Did the Rebbe actually say "louder"? Would the Rebbe go against the custom of Israel in all congregations to chant the curses rapidly and in a barely audible voice? The reader apparently decided that he had been mistaken in what he thought the Rebbe had said, and continued reading in a whisper.

The Rebbe turned around to face the congregation, banged on the lectern, his eyes blazing: "*Ich hob gezogt hecher*, I said louder," he shouted out. "Let the Master of the Universe hear! We have nothing to be afraid of. We have already received all of the curses – and more. Let the Almighty hear, and let Him understand that the time has come to send the blessings!"

I was trembling, my body bathed in sweat. Many people around me were silently sobbing. The Rebbe turned back to his lectern, facing the

◄ wall

wall. The Torah reader continued to chant the curses loudly, and distinctively, and in a much slower cadence.

At the end of the additional prayers, after *Aleinu*, the Rebbe once again turned to his congregation, but this time with his eyes conveying deep love, "*Mein tayere shvestern un brider*, my beloved sisters and brothers, the blessings will come, but not from America. Indeed, God has promised the blessings after the curses, and He has already begun to fulfill His promise by bringing us home to Israel. May more blessings await us, but they will only come from Israel. Let us pack our bags for the last time. Our community is setting out for Kiryat Sanz, in Netanya, Israel."

God's Covenant with Abraham

As the founding patriarch of the Hebrew nation, Abraham enters world history with the "Covenant between the Pieces" (Gen. 15:1–21) in which God guarantees eternal continuity for his seed and the inheritance of the land from the Nile to the Euphrates. This is the covenant of the Jewish nation emanating from Abraham's loins and Sarah's womb. A nation is, after all, that which develops from a family "writ large," expanding into tribes that become geographically defined by clear borders. Generally, such a nation is forged by common historical experiences that are commemorated in days of celebration, characterized by unique foods and customs, and which have a compelling purpose and narrative that is transmitted from generation to generation.

The precursor to the Covenant between the Pieces is found three chapters earlier, at the very moment that God selects Abraham, a moment that is also centered on a specific, yet unspecified, land:

> The LORD said to Abram: "Go for yourself out of your [present] land [Ur of the Chaldees], out of your familial birthplace, and out of your father's house to the land that I will show you. I shall make of you a great nation; I shall bless you and make your name great and you shall be a blessing. I shall bless those who bless you, those who curse you I shall curse, and all the families of the earth shall be blessed through you." (Gen. 12:1–3)

Alongside the crucial importance of establishing Abraham's seed as a great nation on its own land is a divine charge, universal in import: "All

◀ the families

the families of the earth shall be blessed through you." We can understand this reference by looking at Genesis 18:18–19, wherein God reveals the reason for selecting Abraham:

> And Abraham is surely to become a great and mighty nation, and all the nations of the earth shall be blessed through him. For this reason, have I loved [chosen, appointed] him, because he commands his children, and his household after him, to keep the way of the LORD by doing compassionate righteousness and moral justice (*tzedaka umishpat*), in order that the LORD might bring upon Abraham that which He had spoken concerning him [to make him a great nation].

It appears that God's covenantal promise is a two-way street, a contractual agreement between two parties, God and Israel. In his breakthrough work *Created Equal*, Joshua Berman analyzes the covenants between God and Israel in the light of parallels with late Bronze Age Hittite suzerainty treaties. He concludes that the Bible expresses an "egalitarian theology" in which honor between suzerain and vassal is bestowed bilaterally if not with full mutuality. In imposing upon Israel the status of late Bronze Age vassalage, the Bible establishes a paradigm for the human-Divine encounter that places all the nation of Israel on an unprecedented pedestal; not only could Israel honor God, but God could honor Israel. The whole of Israel attains the status of a subordinate king – with benefits and obligations – entering into a treaty with a Sovereign King, God.

Since, according to the biblical narrative, our patriarch Jacob-Israel was the grandson of Abraham and Sarah, the Bible insists that the Children of Israel will never be destroyed and that the nation of Israel will eventually inherit the land of Canaan. These gifts, however, seem to be predicated upon Israel's dedication to compassionate righteousness (*tzedaka*) and moral justice (*mishpat*) and upon Israel's blessing the nations of the world with the moral imperatives that produce "compassionate righteousness and moral justice" throughout the world, i.e., ethical monotheism. Israel's mission is to become a "sacred nation and kingship of priest-teachers to all of humanity" (Ex. 19:5–6, Seforno ad loc.).

Is, then, Israel's covenant with God conditional? Yes and no. Our ability to conquer the Land and maintain Jewish habitation upon it *is* conditional upon proper comportment. Given the reason for which God selected Abraham, it is logical that God's purpose in making Abraham's seed a nation-state upon their own land is that they may become a nation among other nations, obligated to grapple with the national challenges of peace and war, economic struggles, issues of social and economic equality, educational opportunities for its citizens, as well as the universal challenges of ecology and international relations. Guided by the Torah teaching (chiefly of the Ten Commandments) that was revealed to Israel in the Sinai desert shortly after their freedom from Egyptian bondage, Israel must serve as a beacon and light for all the nations (Is. 42:6, 49:6). Israel will maintain its privilege to the Land only if the Jewish people are worthy of fulfilling its divine mission to demonstrate and teach compassionate righteousness and moral justice (Deut. 8:16–20).

However, from a theological perspective, just as God is eternal, so must His covenants be eternal and not subject to abrogation. Hence, despite the fact that the Israelites will be exiled from the Land if (when) they lose their moral worthiness, and will become persecuted strangers in foreign countries, a situation which will cause them to cease being active players on the world scene, *nevertheless* God guarantees the eventual restoration of Israel to their homeland, the eventual return to their calling, the eventual resumption of their historic destiny (Gen. 15:12–21; Deut. 4:26–31).

This is the symbolism of the three animals in the drama of the Abrahamic National Covenant (Gen. 15): the heifer, the goat, and the ram, symbolizing the powerful nations of the world, and the two birds, symbolizing Israel. The animals were bisected and each piece was placed facing its counterpart. Abraham, representing the future Hebrew people, walked between the severed parts, and a smoky furnace and a torch of fire, which represented the *Shekhina* or Divine Presence, also passed between the parts. These actions symbolize the mutuality of the covenant: God and Israel, each with their own respective commitment, each dependent on the other for mutual fulfillment. Yet, this also symbolizes Israel's eternal life and relationship to the Land, since each animal (nation with ascendancy over Israel) will ultimately be vanquished – bisected – and only the birds, symbolizing Israel, will remain alive and intact.

The paradox that the Bible reveals is that while some of Abraham's seed will be eternal and continuous, its relationship to the Land will be

◀ eternal

eternal but interrupted, dependent upon its moral worthiness. Abraham's seed will remain alive, but will not emerge from its exiles unscathed. Persecutions and assimilation will deplete its population, yet ultimately, the Jewish people will return to *tzedaka umishpat* and then to their Promised Land in perpetuity. God will forgive His repentant nation, their hearts will be purified, and their scattered compatriots will return home. The eternity and irrevocability of the covenant will be vindicated in historical time, when Israel will indeed be, and will remain, worthy (Deut. 30:1–10; Jer. 31:26–33). This is the Bible's philosophy-theology regarding the people of Israel and their relationship to Israel the Land.

Sinai: The Second Covenant

Against the backdrop of the Covenant between the Pieces in Genesis 15, we can better understand the religious, legally charged Covenant at Sinai (Ex. 24:1–11) between God and the descendants of Abraham, newly freed after 210 years of Egyptian enslavement. The Decalogue revealed at Sinai, together with the laws governing civil, capital, and personal status, and the ritual laws that follow (Ex. 20–23), flesh out the legal directives aimed at forging a sacred nation committed to compassionate and just relationships. Just as the Covenant between the Pieces emphasizes God's obligation to the Children of Israel, the Covenant of Laws at Sinai, the Second Covenant, emphasizes Israel's obligation to God.

Entering the Land: The Third Covenant

As the newly formed nation is about to enter the Promised Land after its forty-year sojourn in the desert, a Third Covenant with Israel is articulated: the "words of the covenant that the LORD commanded Moses to seal … in addition to the covenant which He sealed with them at Horeb [Sinai]" (Deut. 27–28). For the prior covenants, we had to be *worthy* of communicating our mission; this Third Covenant goes further and insists that we actually teach it, give witness to it, from the platform of our nation-state, Israel.

The Bible insists that this Third Covenant is to be "well clarified" (*be'er hetev*), which the Talmudic rabbis interpret to mean that the text had to be translated into seventy languages and written on twelve stones for everyone to see and understand whenever they entered or exited the

◀ of Israel

Land of Israel. This necessarily refers to the gentile nations, since the Israelites themselves would not have required translations into "the seventy languages of the nations" (Deut. 27:8, Rashi ad loc.).

The Third Covenant appears just as the Jewish people enters the Land, because only as a free nation that has power and that grapples with the stately challenges bound up with being a free nation, can the Jewish people influence other nations and help lead them in the challenges that every nation faces. In today's global village, threatened by nuclear warfare, only universal acceptance of a divinely endowed humankind, inviolate and free, will guarantee universal peace and security for all.

To summarize, the Third Covenant expresses the covenantal purpose and mission of Israel in the world: to teach ethical monotheism. This can only be done by example, by establishing a nation-state that is a model for others to emulate. And if you will ask, along with a large group of avowed anti-Semites, "How odd of God to choose the Jews," the biblical response must be (as we have seen in Gen. 18:18–19), "It is not at all odd, because Abraham chose God."

Persecution and the Confirmation of the Covenant

Why are the punishments of Deuteronomy 27–28 directed only toward the Israelites? Why is it the Jewish people that is to be exiled and persecuted – and by those very gentiles who also transgressed the universal laws of morality? The gentiles are warned, but then let off the hook of divine punishment.

If the Jewish people fail to become a sacred nation worthy of emulation, if they do not teach their message to the world, then they will be the first to suffer from the inhumanity of nations focused on power and domination rather than on peace and humanity. Gentile nations also suffer as a result of their inhumanity and immorality, but the Jewish people, who are responsible to teach others (Amos 3:20), suffer most. This is the interpretation of the final imprecation: "Cursed be he who does not cause the words of this Torah to be upheld" (Deut. 27:26), to be put into practice by all humanity. This applies to Jews, the "light to the nations," who fail in their covenantal mission.

And so, the first of the two *Tokheḥot*, the frightening chastisements in the Bible detailing the suffering and persecutions in exile that will

◂ overtake

overtake Israel, appears toward the end of Leviticus (26:14–45); the second appears toward the end of Deuteronomy (28:15–68), following the Third Covenant. The conclusion of the first list of horrific tragedies offers a note of optimism and redemption:

> I will remember My covenant with Jacob, and also My covenant with Isaac, and also My covenant with Abraham will I remember, and I will remember the Land.... And even despite their being in the land of their enemies, I will not have despised them or have been revolted by them to the point of obliterating them, of nullifying My covenant with them – for I am the LORD, their God. I shall remember for them the covenant of the original [Hebrews] whom I took out of the land of Egypt before the eyes of the nations to be God unto them; I am the LORD. (Lev. 26:42–45)

However, after the conclusion of the second chastisement, which contains almost twice as many punishments and curses as the first , there are no mitigating "remembrances" or blessings. This passage follows the last of the curses:

> These are the words of the covenant which the LORD commanded Moses to seal with the Children of Israel in the land of Moab, in addition to the covenant that He sealed with them in Horeb. (Deut. 28:69)

There are no words of comfort, no promise of redemption here. Will there be no relief or redemption following the second exile? What of the promises to become a great nation, of being a blessing to the world? If indeed the covenant is eternal, why is the second chastisement devoid of any promise of redemption?

According to the great biblical commentator Nahmanides, the second chastisement in Deuteronomy refers to the second exile, begun at the hands of Rome in 70 CE. In the Roman exile, the Jews were scattered to the "four corners of the earth," and that exile lasted nearly two thousand years until the Jewish return to the "born-again" State of Israel in 1948. The Deuteronomy chastisement makes no mention of comfort or return, since the return would take millennia; Jews would be bereft of their Temple and homeland for many more years than they had had them.

◄ Yet

Yet, two chapters later, in Deuteronomy 30:1–10, we do read of Jewish return, historically a near impossibility after two millennia:

> It will be that when all these things come upon you – the blessings and the curses that I have set before you – you shall cause yourself to return to your hearts within the midst of all the nations where the LORD your God has dispersed you. And you shall return unto the LORD your God and listen to His voice, in accordance with everything I command you this day, you and your children, with all your heart and all your soul. Then the LORD your God will return your exiles [captives in foreign lands] and have compassion upon you. He will return and He will gather you in from all the nations to where the LORD your God has scattered you. If your dispersed will be at the end of the heavens, from there will the LORD your God gather you in and from there He will take you. The LORD your God will bring you to the Land that your forefathers possessed and you shall inherit it. He will do good to you and make you more numerous than your forebears. The LORD your God will circumcise your heart and the heart of your seed to love the LORD your God with all your heart and with all your soul, that you may live.

There are two important aspects of the return promised in passage above. The return is a double one, a physical return to the Land of Israel "from within the midst of all the nations where the LORD your God has dispersed you," and a spiritual return to God and divine commandments. The context dictates that the spiritual return should be particularly to the universal laws emphasized by the Third Covenant. Critically, these physical and spiritual returns are to be initiated by Israel, and only after humans have taken the initiative will God aid in their conclusion. Only after Israel begins returning to the Land, will God restore its exiles, and only after Israel returns to God's voice, will God circumcise (i.e., purify) Israel's hearts (Jer. 31:30–33).

Nahmanides referred to this passage as "the portion of repentance," the source of God's commandment to Israel to repent. Maimonides saw these verses as God's guarantee that Israel *will* repent. This is crucial, because for Maimonides there could be no redemption without repentance, and like all the biblical prophets, Maimonides understood redemption

◄ to mean

to mean universal redemption, i.e., the time when through the seed of Abraham all the families of the earth will be blessed with freedom, morality, and peace.

As if in response to biblical demands, two unique events have occurred in recent Jewish history: (1) the Zionist movement toward the end of the nineteenth century, which signaled for the first time since Bar Kokhba's abortive rebellion against Rome in 135 CE the Jewish people's initiative to return to the Bible's covenantal land, without waiting passively for God or the Messiah to take them there, and (2) the widespread movement of *teshuva*, the return or repentance movement in which alienated Jews are finding their way back to God.

Until the early twentieth century, repentance was understood to apply nearly exclusively to religious Jews who had lapsed in their observance of one or another of the commandments. But the recent phenomenon of "born-again" Jews making a total change in their religious orientation (à la Franz Rosenzweig and, of course, the entire *ba'al teshuva* phenomenon), as well as the many thousands of Crypto-Jews in South America, "hidden" Jews in Eastern Europe and Germany, and the newly revealed tribes of Africa "coming out of the closet" and rediscovering their Jewish roots, are all products of our very special period of return.

I submit that the greatest significance of the Jewish return to Zion is its confirmation of the eternality of our covenant and the truth of the promises of our sacred Scriptures. In the words of Paul Johnson, "the creation of Israel was the quintessential event of the last century, and the only one that can fairly be called a miracle." This miracle has also brought in its wake the ingathering of Jewish exiles, from the forgotten tribe of Dan in Ethiopia to the lost tribe of Menashe in India; from the Jews of Persia and Kaifeng, China to the most recent return of the more than one million Jews of the former Soviet Union, who were hitherto "lost Jews" (see Is. 11:11).

This profound miracle illustrates the "dry bones" vision of Ezekiel, where he watched as the LORD put sinews and flesh upon dry bones in a valley in Babylon, coated them with skin, placed His Spirit within them, and enabled them to come to life and to acquire renewed faith and vigor as they walked upon the soil of Israel reborn (Ezek. 36). These are the dry bones of the *Muselmann* prisoners of Auschwitz, who rose from their

◀ graves

graves of the not-yet-dead and not-yet-quite-alive to miraculously fight in Israel's War of Independence and participate in her miraculous rebirth.

The Responsibility of the Jewish Return to Zion

The perseverance of the people of Israel during the past two thousand years – despite being bereft of their historic homeland and central Sanctuary, the two most tangible expressions of the Covenant of Abraham and the Covenant at Sinai – can only be explained by the ability of rabbinic Judaism's comprehensive religio-legal system (Halakha) to adapt to the cataclysmic changes wrought by the destruction of the Second Temple and the subsequent exile. It was the foresight of Rabban Yoḥanan ben Zakkai and the rabbinic scholars of Yavne in the first century CE that set the stage for the transition from a Land-and-Temple-centered priestly aristocracy to a rabbinically directed study-hall-and-synagogue-centered democratic "nomocracy." This system worked remarkably well until the European Emancipation at the end of the eighteenth century. Similarly, in our own post-Holocaust generation, our survival, return, and renewal demand no less a creative adaptation than the one achieved by the revolutionary generation of Yavne.

Using the prophetic "Return and Repentance" promise of Deuteronomy 30 as our guide, I would like to outline the most salient religious and national challenges and opportunities facing halakhic leadership in our return to Zion. To be sure, those voices opposed to change will argue that any significant deviation from our religio-legal practice will perforce lead to the weakening – and perhaps even to the obliteration – of the continuity of our time-honored tradition; nevertheless, it was a very carefully crafted dialectic between continuity and change that expressed the genius of the generation of Yavne. The leadership at that time was mindful of the tension that existed even in biblical times between the priest, whose task was to retain the continuity of the ritual from generation to generation, and the prophet, whose task was to bring the living God of compassionate righteousness into the contemporary ritual of his time.

Indeed, the Bible itself expresses this tension within the two commanding verses of religio-legal decision making: "Ask your father and he will tell you, your grandfather, and he will say unto you" (Deut. 32:7), that is to say, conduct your ritual lives precisely in the manner of your parents

◄ and grandparents

and grandparents; and, conversely, "When you are in a quandary as to how to make a judgment…you must go up to the judge in that time [the religio-legal authority who is sensitive to the changes in various historical periods and understands the zeitgeist of that particular time]…and in accordance with the Torah that he will teach you, you shall you conduct yourself" (17:8–11). The rabbinic sages of the Talmud even apply this last verse to a situation in which the contemporary judge is a person of lesser knowledge and authority than was the judge of the earlier period.

Surely, the period in which we are now privileged to live, which has experienced the two cataclysmic changes of the Holocaust and our return to Israel, deserves – and desperately requires – the invocation of this latter verse.

The leadership of Yavne succeeded in retaining the eternal sanctity and values of the Bible while hermeneutically reinterpreting the meaning of its words to cover a panoply of new conditions and issues. Similarly, our return to Zion requires us to once again adapt to a new reality, whether in the realm of halakha regarding marriage contracts and leniencies for *agunot*, the ritual sphere allowing women to attain "spiritual satisfaction" (*Ḥagiga* 16b), or as a sovereign host nation for the first time in two thousand years, as we seriously consider our policies towards minorities (Christians as well as Muslims) and non-Jews clamoring for Israeli citizenship.

To do all this and more, our government must promote a core curriculum for every Jewish citizen of the state, which will educate him or her as to the values of our Jewish civilization, the ethics that we must impart to ourselves and to the world, and the traditions that have expressed these ideals for the last four thousand years.

Returning to our national homeland also presents us with the opportunity to assume responsibility for the Jewish nation as a diverse people. If the covenantal obligation of the Jewish nation is to transmit "compassionate righteousness and moral justice," and if Jews are charged by divine commandment to be a sacred nation and a kingdom of priest-teachers to the world, then the elected leadership and religious authorities of the Jewish state must take a unique covenantal responsibility for every one of Israel's Jewish citizens.

◂ *A Promise Fulfilled*

A Promise Fulfilled

The time of my *aliya*, in 1983, was romantic and exciting – until I actually arrived in Efrat and reality set in. The streets weren't paved, there were no private telephones – only one public telephone that generally didn't work – and during that first rough winter we were often without heat or electricity, or both. Additionally, within a few months I realized that I had no clear means of earning a livelihood for my wife and four children. I would often wake up in the night in a cold sweat, thinking that I had made a terrible mistake.

In the midst of all these difficult thoughts came a knock on the door of our apartment. It was Yoni Ben-Ari, who was in charge of security for the young Efrat. "*Kevod HaRav*" (Honored Rabbi), he said, "take this Uzi. You have guard duty between two and six o'clock tomorrow morning."

My partner for this shift was Yussi, a fine young man from Holland who still lives in Efrat with his family. We walked in the stillness of the night, covering the periphery of Efrat every quarter of an hour. He asked me about my life prior to *aliya*, and I described it nostalgically, even lovingly and yearningly – perhaps all the more so because I was beginning to think that maybe I'd made a mistake by burning my bridges behind me.

When I asked him about his life before *aliya*, he answered:

"Believe it or not, I was a Christian. I went to church every Sunday with my parents and brother. But on June 7, 1967, when I was a young high-school boy, nineteen years ago, I read something that changed my life. It was on the front page of the Dutch daily newspaper, the magnificent story of the amazing Israeli victory in the Six-Day War. From that moment on, I became invested and involved – body and soul – in the State of Israel. I responded viscerally to the victory, to the salvation from enemy danger and destruction, to the gutsiness of a nation that emerged from the ashes of the Holocaust to recreate itself. When I had to write a senior paper for graduation from high school, I wrote on the burgeoning State of Israel. There was a compulsory draft in Holland, and everyone who was in the Dutch army is expected to talk to a clergyman of some kind. I found myself filling out the form with the request to talk to a rabbi, and I began learning how to read Hebrew.

"At home, one weekend, I was learning the Hebrew text of Grace after Meals. The rabbi had given me a prayer book, and as I was trying to make

◂ out

out the words, I saw my mother mouthing the words in Hebrew. Shocked, I asked how she knew this prayer. She smiled and explained that before the war she had worked as an au pair for a religious Jewish family. This seemingly inconsequential piece of information strengthened my resolve to learn even more about Judaism.

"When the Yom Kippur War came, I volunteered to help on the farms. The kibbutz members were all fighting on the front lines, and the fruits and vegetables needed to be gathered and harvested. Three Christian friends and I were sent to a secular kibbutz in the Galilee. I was sparked and excited. I fell in love with the land, and I fell in love with the people. Since I have an ear for languages, I picked up Hebrew easily. I read a great deal about Jewish history, Jewish philosophy, and Judaism. I decided then that I wanted to keep kosher and keep the Sabbath. Someone from the kibbutz suggested that I go to a special *ulpan giyur*, a school for converts. There was one in Kfar Etzion, a kibbutz right near what was to become Efrat. So I went there and joined the school for converts.

"After an intensive period of study, I was assigned a date to go to the ritual bath, the *mikve*, to immerse and to convert. The time had come then to tell my parents, since conversion was a momentous decision for a nineteen-year-old to make by himself. I called home and told my parents that I had an important matter to discuss with them. I announced that I wanted to convert to Judaism and live my life in Israel.

"My mother broke out in a cold sweat and fainted. After she revived, she told me, 'You don't have to convert. You are Jewish because I'm Jewish. I am the daughter of the *ḥazan*, the cantor, of the main synagogue in the town where my parents were murdered in front of my eyes. Before the Nazis shot my father dead, he cried out *Shema Yisrael Adonai Eloheinu Adonai Eḥad* (Listen, Israel: the Lord is Our God, the Lord is One), but to no avail. While being transported in the crowded, fetid cattle car to Theresienstadt, I felt that if one Holocaust was occurring, a second was even more likely, and I did not want my grandchildren or my great-grandchildren to suffer as I was suffering. I took an oath that if I ever go out of that hellhole, it would be as a Christian and not as a Jew.

"'I got out, I don't know how or why. I had no one to answer to because all of my relatives had been murdered in the Holocaust, so I became a Christian. Until now, the only person who knew my Jewish background

◄ was

was your father. But if you wish to rejoin the religion of my parents and their parents, may the God in whom I can no longer believe, bless you and keep you.'"

At that moment, during guard duty in the young city of Efrat in the depths of the night, all I could think of was the four-thousand-year-old promise that Moses gave to the Jewish people in God's name: Yes, you will be exiled. Yes, you will be persecuted. Yes, "you will be scattered to the ends of the heavens, for there the LORD your God will gather you, and from there will He take you up…and return you to the land of the your fathers" (Deut. 30:4–5).

The promise is being fulfilled now in our generation. Gone were all my questions. I understood that Israel was not only my destination, but was the destiny of my family and my people. I understood as deeply as anyone could understand that despite the unpaved streets, the lack of heat or electricity, the financial insecurity, I had come home.

My faith was strengthened in that momentous night of guard duty. As the prophets promised, the fulfillment of God's covenant, the security of the Jewish people, the final perfection of the world and world peace, will emanate from Israel and Jerusalem. The *coup de grâce* came more recently when I performed the marriage ceremony of Avishai, Yussi's oldest son, a member of the Israeli Air Force. As the young war hero stood before me, in army uniform and ritual fringes waving in the wind, I pictured Avishai's cantorial grandfather, looking down from his heavenly abode, smiling and declaring, "This is indeed the time of the coming of the Messiah."

If we've come this far since the Holocaust in realizing Moses' prophecy, we will surely come to the next stage and realize the vision of our prophets, that "From Zion shall come forth Torah and the word of the LORD from Jerusalem …. Nation will not lift up sword against nation and humanity will not learn war anymore" (Is. 2, Mic. 4).

Rabbi Shlomo Riskin

יום הזיכרון
YOM HAZIKARON

יום העצמאות
YOM HAATZMA'UT

שחרית ליום הזיכרון

SHAHARIT FOR YOM HAZIKARON

Memorial Day

*The service begins on page 150. At the end of Shaḥarit, after Full Kaddish (page 412),
the Ark is opened and the following is said by some congregations:*

לַמְנַצֵּחַ For the conductor of music. Upon the death of Labben. A psalm of   *Ps. 9*
David.

I will thank You, Lord, with all my heart; I will tell of all Your wonders.

I will rejoice and exult in You; I will sing praise to Your name, Most High.

My enemies retreat; they stumble and perish before You.

For You have upheld my case and my cause; You have sat enthroned as
righteous Judge.

You have rebuked nations and destroyed the wicked, blotting out their
name for ever and all time.

The enemy are finished, ruined forever; You have overthrown their cities;
even the memory of them is lost.

But the Lord abides forever; He has established His throne for judgment.

He will judge the world with righteousness, and try the cause of peoples
with justice.

The Lord is a refuge for the oppressed, a stronghold in times of trouble.

Those who know Your name trust in You, for You, Lord, do not forsake
those who seek You.

Sing praise to the Lord who dwells in Zion; tell the peoples of His deeds.

For He who avenges blood remembers; He does not forget the cry of the
afflicted.

Have mercy on me, Lord, see how my enemies afflict me. Lift me up from
the gates of death,

That in the gates of the Daughter of Zion I may tell all Your praises and
rejoice in Your deliverance.

The nations have fallen into the pit they dug; their feet are caught in the net
they hid.

The Lord is known by His justice; the wicked is ensnared by the work of
his own hands. Reflect on this, Selah.

---

who were brutally murdered by the enemies of our people, enemies who seek
to wipe Israel's name off the map.

   Evening and morning, a siren is sounded throughout the land. As the
siren wails, the entire country comes to a complete standstill: traffic stops;
all pause their work or studies, and join together in silence to commemorate

שחרית ליום הזיכרון

The service begins on page 151. At the end of שחרית, *after* קדיש שלם *(page 413),*
the ארון קודש *is opened and the following is said by some congregations:*

תהלים ט

לַמְנַצֵּחַ עַל־מוּת לַבֵּן מִזְמוֹר לְדָוִד:

אוֹדֶה יהוה בְּכָל־לִבִּי, אֲסַפְּרָה כָּל־נִפְלְאוֹתֶיךָ:

אֶשְׂמְחָה וְאֶעֶלְצָה בָךְ, אֲזַמְּרָה שִׁמְךָ עֶלְיוֹן:

בְּשׁוּב־אוֹיְבַי אָחוֹר, יִכָּשְׁלוּ וְיֹאבְדוּ מִפָּנֶיךָ:

כִּי־עָשִׂיתָ מִשְׁפָּטִי וְדִינִי, יָשַׁבְתָּ לְכִסֵּא שׁוֹפֵט צֶדֶק:

גָּעַרְתָּ גוֹיִם אִבַּדְתָּ רָשָׁע, שְׁמָם מָחִיתָ לְעוֹלָם וָעֶד:

הָאוֹיֵב תַּמּוּ חֳרָבוֹת לָנֶצַח, וְעָרִים נָתַשְׁתָּ, אָבַד זִכְרָם הֵמָּה:

וַיהוה לְעוֹלָם יֵשֵׁב, כּוֹנֵן לַמִּשְׁפָּט כִּסְאוֹ:

וְהוּא יִשְׁפֹּט־תֵּבֵל בְּצֶדֶק, יָדִין לְאֻמִּים בְּמֵישָׁרִים:

וִיהִי יהוה מִשְׂגָּב לַדָּךְ, מִשְׂגָּב לְעִתּוֹת בַּצָּרָה:

וְיִבְטְחוּ בְךָ יוֹדְעֵי שְׁמֶךָ, כִּי לֹא־עָזַבְתָּ דֹרְשֶׁיךָ, יהוה:

זַמְּרוּ לַיהוה יֹשֵׁב צִיּוֹן, הַגִּידוּ בָעַמִּים עֲלִילוֹתָיו:

כִּי־דֹרֵשׁ דָּמִים אוֹתָם זָכָר, לֹא־שָׁכַח צַעֲקַת עֲנָוִים:

חָנְנֵנִי יהוה רְאֵה עָנְיִי מִשֹּׂנְאָי, מְרוֹמְמִי מִשַּׁעֲרֵי־מָוֶת:

לְמַעַן אֲסַפְּרָה כָּל־תְּהִלָּתֶיךָ, בְּשַׁעֲרֵי בַת־צִיּוֹן אָגִילָה בִּישׁוּעָתֶךָ:

טָבְעוּ גוֹיִם בְּשַׁחַת עָשׂוּ, בְּרֶשֶׁת־זוּ טָמָנוּ נִלְכְּדָה רַגְלָם:

נוֹדַע יהוה מִשְׁפָּט עָשָׂה, בְּפֹעַל כַּפָּיו נוֹקֵשׁ רָשָׁע, הִגָּיוֹן סֶלָה:

YOM HAZIKARON – MEMORIAL DAY FOR FALLEN ISRAELI SOLDIERS AND VICTIMS OF TERROR

Yom HaZikaron, National Memorial Day, falls the day before Yom HaAtzma'ut, Independence Day. This day expresses our recognition of the sacrifice of those who gave their lives for the sake of our land and nation. Yom HaZikaron, originally instituted to commemorate the soldiers who fell for our country, has also become a day of commemoration for victims of terror

The wicked return to the grave, all the nations that forget God.
The needy will not be forgotten forever, nor the hope of the afflicted ever
    be lost.
Arise, LORD, let not man have power; let the nations be judged in Your
    presence.
Strike them with fear, LORD; let the nations know they are only men. Selah.

The Ark is closed.

Memorial Prayer for Fallen Israeli Soldiers

אָבִינוּ שֶׁבַּשָּׁמַיִם Heavenly Father, God, Source of the spirits of all flesh,
remember, we pray You, the pure souls of our sons and daughters
who heroically gave their lives
in defense of the people and the Land.
Swifter than eagles, stronger than lions,
they fought for the liberation of their people and homeland,
sacrificing their lives for Israel's rebirth in its holy land.
They breathed a spirit of strength and courage
into the whole house of Israel,
in the Land and the Diaspora,
inspiring it to go forward toward its redemption and liberation.
Remember them, our God, for good,
together with the myriad holy ones and heroes of Israel from ancient times.
May their souls be bound in the bonds of everlasting life,
may the Garden of Eden be their resting place,
may they rest in peace
and receive their reward at the End of Days.
Amen.

---

respects expresses a sense of national solidarity and mutual responsibility; a
source of strength and security for the entire Jewish nation.

The sirens mark the opening of memorial services held in educational
institutions, army bases and military cemeteries. The Israeli flag is lowered
to half-mast. The Chief Rabbis have always publicized the general obligation to stand during the siren as a mark of participating in the national
mourning.

Some have contested the idea of standing during the siren, contending that
this opposes halakha as it is a custom derived from non-Jewish culture – "And
you shall not follow their statutes" (Leviticus 18:3). However, leading figures

יָשׁוּבוּ רְשָׁעִים לִשְׁאוֹלָה, כָּל־גּוֹיִם שְׁכֵחֵי אֱלֹהִים:

כִּי לֹא לָנֶצַח יִשָּׁכַח אֶבְיוֹן, תִּקְוַת עֲנִיִּים תֹּאבַד לָעַד:

קוּמָה יהוה אַל־יָעֹז אֱנוֹשׁ, יִשָּׁפְטוּ גוֹיִם עַל־פָּנֶיךָ:

שִׁיתָה יהוה מוֹרָה לָהֶם, יֵדְעוּ גוֹיִם, אֱנוֹשׁ הֵמָּה סֶּלָה:

The ארון קודש is closed.

Memorial Prayer for Fallen Israeli Soldiers

אָבִינוּ שֶׁבַּשָּׁמַיִם, אֵל אֱלֹהֵי הָרוּחוֹת לְכָל בָּשָׂר

זְכֹר נָא אֶת הַנְּשָׁמוֹת הַזַּכּוֹת וְהַטְּהוֹרוֹת שֶׁל בָּנֵינוּ וּבְנוֹתֵינוּ

אֲשֶׁר הֵעֵרוּ אֶת נַפְשָׁם לָמוּת מוֹת גִּבּוֹרִים

בְּהֵחָלְצָם לְעֶזְרַת הָעָם וְהָאָרֶץ.

מִנְּשָׁרִים קַלּוּ מֵאֲרָיוֹת גָּבֵרוּ

בְּמִלְחַמְתָּם לְמַעַן שִׁחְרוּר עַמָּם וּמוֹלַדְתָּם.

בַּעֲלוֹתָם עַל מִזְבַּח תְּקוּמַת יִשְׂרָאֵל בְּאֶרֶץ קָדְשׁוֹ

הֵפִיחוּ רוּחַ עֹז וּגְבוּרָה בְּכָל בֵּית יִשְׂרָאֵל בָּאָרֶץ וּבַתְּפוּצוֹת

וַיִּתְעוֹרֵר לִקְרַאת גְּאֻלָּתוֹ וּפְדוּת נַפְשׁוֹ.

יִזָּכְרֵם אֱלֹהֵינוּ לְטוֹבָה

עִם רִבְבוֹת אַלְפֵי קְדוֹשֵׁי יִשְׂרָאֵל וְגִבּוֹרָיו מִימֵי עוֹלָם

בִּצְרוֹר הַחַיִּים יִצְרֹר אֶת נִשְׁמָתָם

בְּגַן עֵדֶן תְּהֵא מְנוּחָתָם

וְיָנוּחוּ בְשָׁלוֹם עַל מִשְׁכָּבָם

וְיַעַמְדוּ לְגוֹרָלָם לְקֵץ הַיָּמִין

אָמֵן.

those who, through their death, gave us life. Many have the custom of lighting memorial candles in their home.

During the day, many (not only the families of the fallen) visit the military cemeteries and hold memorial services. The great rush of people paying their

לְדָוִד Of David. Blessed is the Lᴏʀᴅ, my Rock, who trains my hands for war, *Ps. 144*
my fingers for battle. He is my Benefactor, my Fortress, my Stronghold and
my Refuge, my Shield in whom I trust, He who subdues nations under me.
Lᴏʀᴅ, what is man that You care for him, what are mortals that You think of
them? Man is no more than a breath, his days like a fleeting shadow. Lᴏʀᴅ,
part Your heavens and come down; touch the mountains so that they pour
forth smoke. Flash forth lightning and scatter them; shoot Your arrows and
panic them. Reach out Your hand from on high; deliver me and rescue me
from the mighty waters, from the hands of strangers, whose every word is
worthless, whose right hands are raised in falsehood. To You, God, I will sing
a new song; to You I will play music on a ten-stringed harp. He who gives
salvation to kings, who saved His servant David from the cruel sword: may
He deliver me and rescue me from the hands of strangers, whose every word
is worthless, whose right hands are raised in falsehood. Then our sons will be
like saplings, well nurtured in their youth. Our daughters will be like pillars
carved for a palace. Our barns will be filled with every kind of provision. Our
sheep will increase by thousands, even tens of thousands in our fields. Our
oxen will draw heavy loads. There will be no breach in the walls, no going into
captivity, no cries of distress in our streets. Happy are the people for whom
this is so; happy are the people whose God is the Lᴏʀᴅ.

For the Israeli soldiers:

אֵל מָלֵא רַחֲמִים God, full of mercy, who dwells on high, grant fitting rest on
the wings of the Divine Presence, in the heights of the holy, the pure and the
brave, who shine like the radiance of heaven, to the souls of the holy ones
who fought in any of Israel's battles, in clandestine operations and in Israel's
Defense Forces, who fell in battle and sacrificed their lives for the consecration of God's name, for the people and the land, and for this we pray for the
ascent of their souls. Therefore, Master of compassion, shelter them in the
shadow of Your wings forever, and bind their souls in the bond of everlasting life. The Lᴏʀᴅ is their heritage; may the Garden of Eden be their resting
place, may they rest in peace, may their merit stand for all Israel, and may they
receive their reward at the End of Days, and let us say: Amen.

Shaḥarit continues with Aleinu on page 414.

---

ing during the siren as "a holy mitzva that honors the martyrs" (*Tanḥumin*, 3,
p. 388). In 2001, Chief Rabbi Yisrael Meir Lau even cautioned the public to
take note of the siren, to be wary of dissent between sectors, and to adhere
carefully to this custom so as not to dishonor the memory of the fallen. ʙʟ

תהלים קמד

לְדָוִד בָּרוּךְ יהוה צוּרִי הַמְלַמֵּד יָדַי לַקְרָב, אֶצְבְּעוֹתַי לַמִּלְחָמָה: חַסְדִּי וּמְצוּדָתִי מִשְׂגַּבִּי וּמְפַלְטִי לִי מָגִנִּי וּבוֹ חָסִיתִי הָרוֹדֵד עַמִּי תַחְתָּי: יהוה מָה־אָדָם וַתֵּדָעֵהוּ, בֶּן־אֱנוֹשׁ וַתְּחַשְּׁבֵהוּ: אָדָם לַהֶבֶל דָּמָה יָמָיו כְּצֵל עוֹבֵר: יהוה הַט־שָׁמֶיךָ וְתֵרֵד גַּע בֶּהָרִים וְיֶעֱשָׁנוּ: בְּרוֹק בָּרָק וּתְפִיצֵם, שְׁלַח חִצֶּיךָ וּתְהֻמֵּם: שְׁלַח יָדֶיךָ מִמָּרוֹם פְּצֵנִי וְהַצִּילֵנִי מִמַּיִם רַבִּים מִיַּד בְּנֵי נֵכָר: אֲשֶׁר פִּיהֶם דִּבֶּר־שָׁוְא, וִימִינָם יְמִין שָׁקֶר: אֱלֹהִים שִׁיר חָדָשׁ אָשִׁירָה לָּךְ, בְּנֵבֶל עָשׂוֹר אֲזַמְּרָה־לָּךְ: הַנּוֹתֵן תְּשׁוּעָה לַמְּלָכִים הַפּוֹצֶה אֶת־דָּוִד עַבְדּוֹ מֵחֶרֶב רָעָה: פְּצֵנִי וְהַצִּילֵנִי מִיַּד בְּנֵי־נֵכָר אֲשֶׁר פִּיהֶם דִּבֶּר־שָׁוְא וִימִינָם יְמִין שָׁקֶר: אֲשֶׁר בָּנֵינוּ כִּנְטִעִים מְגֻדָּלִים בִּנְעוּרֵיהֶם בְּנוֹתֵינוּ כְזָוִיֹּת מְחֻטָּבוֹת תַּבְנִית הֵיכָל: מְזָוֵינוּ מְלֵאִים מְפִיקִים מִזַּן אֶל־זַן צֹאונֵנוּ מַאֲלִיפוֹת מְרֻבָּבוֹת בְּחוּצוֹתֵינוּ: אַלּוּפֵינוּ מְסֻבָּלִים אֵין פֶּרֶץ וְאֵין יוֹצֵאת וְאֵין צְוָחָה בִּרְחֹבֹתֵינוּ: אַשְׁרֵי הָעָם שֶׁכָּכָה לּוֹ אַשְׁרֵי הָעָם שֶׁיהוה אֱלֹהָיו:

For the Israeli soldiers:

אֵל מָלֵא רַחֲמִים, שׁוֹכֵן בַּמְּרוֹמִים, הַמְצֵא מְנוּחָה נְכוֹנָה עַל כַּנְפֵי הַשְּׁכִינָה, בְּמַעֲלוֹת קְדוֹשִׁים טְהוֹרִים וְגִבּוֹרִים, כְּזֹהַר הָרָקִיעַ מַזְהִירִים, לְנִשְׁמוֹת הַקְּדוֹשִׁים שֶׁנִּלְחֲמוּ בְּכָל מַעַרְכוֹת יִשְׂרָאֵל, בַּמַּחְתֶּרֶת וּבִצְבָא הַהֲגָנָה לְיִשְׂרָאֵל, וְשֶׁנָּפְלוּ בְּמִלְחַמְתָּם וּמָסְרוּ נַפְשָׁם עַל קְדֻשַּׁת הַשֵּׁם, הָעָם וְהָאָרֶץ, בַּעֲבוּר שֶׁאָנוּ מִתְפַּלְּלִים לְעִלּוּי נִשְׁמוֹתֵיהֶם. לָכֵן, בַּעַל הָרַחֲמִים יַסְתִּירֵם בְּסֵתֶר כְּנָפָיו לְעוֹלָמִים, וְיִצְרוֹר בִּצְרוֹר הַחַיִּים אֶת נִשְׁמוֹתֵיהֶם, יהוה הוּא נַחֲלָתָם, בְּגַן עֵדֶן תְּהֵא מְנוּחָתָם, וְיָנוּחוּ בְשָׁלוֹם עַל מִשְׁכְּבוֹתֵיהֶם וְתַעֲמֹד לְכָל יִשְׂרָאֵל זְכוּתָם, וְיַעַמְדוּ לְגוֹרָלָם לְקֵץ הַיָּמִין, וְנֹאמַר אָמֵן.

שחרית *continues with* עָלֵינוּ *on page 415.*

---

of the past few generations have dismissed this argument, proving that this verse only applies to a non-Jewish custom of no substance that is based entirely on non-Jewish beliefs. Standing during the siren has nothing to do with such beliefs – rather, it is an expression of the emotion of the great sacrifices which have upheld the land and nation (see Rabbi Yaakov Ariel's answer in his book *Ohola shel Torah* 1:23). Rabbi Tzvi Yehuda Kook perceived stand-

מנחה ליום הזיכרון

MINḤA FOR YOM HAZIKARON

Minḥa for Yom HaZikaron

אַשְׁרֵי Happy are those who dwell in Your House;   *Ps. 84*
they shall continue to praise You, Selah!
Happy are the people for whom this is so;   *Ps. 144*
happy are the people whose God is the LORD.

A song of praise by David.   *Ps. 145*
> I will exalt You, my God, the King, and bless Your name for
> ever and all time. Every day I will bless You, and praise Your
> name for ever and all time. Great is the LORD and greatly to be
> praised; His greatness is unfathomable. One generation will
> praise Your works to the next, and tell of Your mighty deeds.
> On the glorious splendor of Your majesty I will meditate, and
> on the acts of Your wonders. They shall talk of the power of
> Your awesome deeds, and I will tell of Your greatness. They
> shall recite the record of Your great goodness, and sing with
> joy of Your righteousness. The LORD is gracious and compas-
> sionate, slow to anger and great in loving-kindness. The LORD
> is good to all, and His compassion extends to all His works.
> All Your works shall thank You, LORD, and Your devoted ones
> shall bless You. They shall talk of the glory of Your kingship,
> and speak of Your might. To make known to mankind His
> mighty deeds and the glorious majesty of His kingship. Your
> kingdom is an everlasting kingdom, and Your reign is for all
> generations. The LORD supports all who fall, and raises all who

---

In preparation for the festival, one should shave and change into festive
clothing. Although Yom HaAtzma'ut falls during the Omer, Chief Rabbis
Yitzḥak Nissim, Isser Yehuda Unterman, and Shlomo Goren, as well as the
Chief Rabbi of Jerusalem Tzvi Pesach Frank, have all ruled that one should
cut one's hair and shave in honor of this day.   BL

מנחה ליום הזיכרון
לחללי מערכות ישראל ולנפגעי פעולות האיבה

תהלים פד

אַשְׁרֵי יוֹשְׁבֵי בֵיתֶךָ, עוֹד יְהַלְלוּךָ סֶּלָה:

תהלים קמד

אַשְׁרֵי הָעָם שֶׁכָּכָה לּוֹ, אַשְׁרֵי הָעָם שֶׁיהוה אֱלֹהָיו:

תהלים קמה

תְּהִלָּה לְדָוִד

אֲרוֹמִמְךָ אֱלוֹהַי הַמֶּלֶךְ, וַאֲבָרְכָה שִׁמְךָ לְעוֹלָם וָעֶד:

בְּכָל־יוֹם אֲבָרְכֶךָּ, וַאֲהַלְלָה שִׁמְךָ לְעוֹלָם וָעֶד:

גָּדוֹל יהוה וּמְהֻלָּל מְאֹד, וְלִגְדֻלָּתוֹ אֵין חֵקֶר:

דּוֹר לְדוֹר יְשַׁבַּח מַעֲשֶׂיךָ, וּגְבוּרֹתֶיךָ יַגִּידוּ:

הֲדַר כְּבוֹד הוֹדֶךָ, וְדִבְרֵי נִפְלְאֹתֶיךָ אָשִׂיחָה:

וֶעֱזוּז נוֹרְאֹתֶיךָ יֹאמֵרוּ, וּגְדוּלָּתְךָ אֲסַפְּרֶנָּה:

זֵכֶר רַב־טוּבְךָ יַבִּיעוּ, וְצִדְקָתְךָ יְרַנֵּנוּ:

חַנּוּן וְרַחוּם יהוה, אֶרֶךְ אַפַּיִם וּגְדָל־חָסֶד:

טוֹב־יהוה לַכֹּל, וְרַחֲמָיו עַל־כָּל־מַעֲשָׂיו:

יוֹדוּךָ יהוה כָּל־מַעֲשֶׂיךָ, וַחֲסִידֶיךָ יְבָרְכוּכָה:

כְּבוֹד מַלְכוּתְךָ יֹאמֵרוּ, וּגְבוּרָתְךָ יְדַבֵּרוּ:

לְהוֹדִיעַ לִבְנֵי הָאָדָם גְּבוּרֹתָיו, וּכְבוֹד הֲדַר מַלְכוּתוֹ:

מַלְכוּתְךָ מַלְכוּת כָּל־עֹלָמִים, וּמֶמְשַׁלְתְּךָ בְּכָל־דּוֹר וָדֹר:

סוֹמֵךְ יהוה לְכָל־הַנֹּפְלִים, וְזוֹקֵף לְכָל־הַכְּפוּפִים:

If one prays Minḥa earlier in the day (*Minḥa Gedola*), one should say regular *Taḥanun*. If one prays right before sundown *Taḥanun* should not be said, following the laws of festival eves.

are bowed down. All raise their eyes to You in hope, and You give them their food in due season. You open Your hand, and satisfy every living thing with favor. The LORD is righteous in all His ways, and kind in all He does. The LORD is close to all who call on Him, to all who call on Him in truth. He fulfills the will of those who revere Him; He hears their cry and saves them. The LORD guards all who love Him, but all the wicked He will destroy. ‣ My mouth shall speak the praise of the LORD, and all creatures shall bless His holy name for ever and all time.

We will bless the LORD now and for ever. Halleluya!   *Ps. 115*

HALF KADDISH

Leader: יִתְגַּדַּל Magnified and sanctified may His great name be,
in the world He created by His will.
May He establish His kingdom
in your lifetime and in your days,
and in the lifetime of all the house of Israel,
swiftly and soon –
and say: Amen.

All: May His great name be blessed for ever and all time.

Leader: Blessed and praised,
glorified and exalted,
raised and honored,
uplifted and lauded
be the name of the Holy One,
blessed be He,
beyond any blessing,
song, praise and consolation
uttered in the world –
and say: Amen.

עֵינֵי־כֹל אֵלֶיךָ יְשַׂבֵּרוּ, וְאַתָּה נוֹתֵן־לָהֶם אֶת־אָכְלָם בְּעִתּוֹ:

פּוֹתֵחַ אֶת־יָדֶךָ, וּמַשְׂבִּיעַ לְכָל־חַי רָצוֹן:

צַדִּיק יהוה בְּכָל־דְּרָכָיו, וְחָסִיד בְּכָל־מַעֲשָׂיו:

קָרוֹב יהוה לְכָל־קֹרְאָיו, לְכֹל אֲשֶׁר יִקְרָאֻהוּ בֶאֱמֶת:

רְצוֹן־יְרֵאָיו יַעֲשֶׂה, וְאֶת־שַׁוְעָתָם יִשְׁמַע, וְיוֹשִׁיעֵם:

שׁוֹמֵר יהוה אֶת־כָּל־אֹהֲבָיו, וְאֵת כָּל־הָרְשָׁעִים יַשְׁמִיד:

‹ תְּהִלַּת יהוה יְדַבֶּר פִּי, וִיבָרֵךְ כָּל־בָּשָׂר שֵׁם קָדְשׁוֹ לְעוֹלָם וָעֶד:

וַאֲנַחְנוּ נְבָרֵךְ יָהּ מֵעַתָּה וְעַד־עוֹלָם, הַלְלוּיָהּ:

תהלים קטו

חצי קדיש

שׁ״ץ: יִתְגַּדַּל וְיִתְקַדַּשׁ שְׁמֵהּ רַבָּא (קהל: אָמֵן)

בְּעָלְמָא דִּי בְרָא כִרְעוּתֵהּ

וְיַמְלִיךְ מַלְכוּתֵהּ

בְּחַיֵּיכוֹן וּבְיוֹמֵיכוֹן וּבְחַיֵּי דְּכָל בֵּית יִשְׂרָאֵל

בַּעֲגָלָא וּבִזְמַן קָרִיב

וְאִמְרוּ אָמֵן. (קהל: אָמֵן)

קהל
ושׁ״ץ: יְהֵא שְׁמֵהּ רַבָּא מְבָרַךְ לְעָלַם וּלְעָלְמֵי עָלְמַיָּא.

שׁ״ץ: יִתְבָּרַךְ וְיִשְׁתַּבַּח וְיִתְפָּאַר וְיִתְרוֹמַם וְיִתְנַשֵּׂא

וְיִתְהַדָּר וְיִתְעַלֶּה וְיִתְהַלָּל

שְׁמֵהּ דְּקֻדְשָׁא בְּרִיךְ הוּא (קהל: בְּרִיךְ הוּא)

לְעֵלָּא מִן כָּל בִּרְכָתָא וְשִׁירָתָא, תֻּשְׁבְּחָתָא וְנֶחֱמָתָא

דַּאֲמִירָן בְּעָלְמָא

וְאִמְרוּ אָמֵן. (קהל: אָמֵן)

THE AMIDA

The following prayer, until "in former years" on page 28, is said silently, standing
with feet together. If there is a minyan, the Amida is repeated aloud by the Leader.
Take three steps forward and at the points indicated by ˇ, bend the knees at the
first word, bow at the second, and stand straight before saying God's name.

When I proclaim the LORD's name, give glory to our God.   *Deut. 32*
O LORD, open my lips, so that my mouth may declare Your praise.   *Ps. 51*

PATRIARCHS

ˇבָּרוּךְ Blessed are You, LORD our God and God of our fathers,
God of Abraham, God of Isaac and God of Jacob;
the great, mighty and awesome God, God Most High,
who bestows acts of loving-kindness and creates all,
who remembers the loving-kindness of the fathers
and will bring a Redeemer to their children's children
for the sake of His name, in love.
King, Helper, Savior, Shield:
ˇBlessed are You, LORD, Shield of Abraham.

DIVINE MIGHT

אַתָּה גִּבּוֹר You are eternally mighty, LORD.
You give life to the dead and have great power to save.

In Israel: He causes the dew to fall.

He sustains the living with loving-kindness,
and with great compassion revives the dead.
He supports the fallen, heals the sick,
sets captives free,
and keeps His faith with those who sleep in the dust.
Who is like You, Master of might,
and to whom can You be compared,
O King who brings death and gives life,
and makes salvation grow?
Faithful are You to revive the dead.
Blessed are You, LORD, who revives the dead.

עמידה

The following prayer, until קַדְמֹנִיּוֹת *on page 29, is said silently, standing with feet together. If there is a* מִנְיָן*, the* עמידה *is repeated aloud by the* שְׁלִיחַ צִבּוּר*. Take three steps forward and at the points indicated by* ׳*, bend the knees at the first word, bow at the second, and stand straight before saying God's name.*

כִּי שֵׁם יהוה אֶקְרָא, הָבוּ גֹדֶל לֵאלֹהֵינוּ:
אֲדֹנָי, שְׂפָתַי תִּפְתָּח, וּפִי יַגִּיד תְּהִלָּתֶךָ:

דברים לב
תהלים נא

אבות

יּבָּרוּךְ אַתָּה יהוה, אֱלֹהֵינוּ וֵאלֹהֵי אֲבוֹתֵינוּ
אֱלֹהֵי אַבְרָהָם, אֱלֹהֵי יִצְחָק, וֵאלֹהֵי יַעֲקֹב
הָאֵל הַגָּדוֹל הַגִּבּוֹר וְהַנּוֹרָא, אֵל עֶלְיוֹן
גּוֹמֵל חֲסָדִים טוֹבִים, וְקֹנֵה הַכֹּל, וְזוֹכֵר חַסְדֵי אָבוֹת
וּמֵבִיא גוֹאֵל לִבְנֵי בְנֵיהֶם לְמַעַן שְׁמוֹ בְּאַהֲבָה.
מֶלֶךְ עוֹזֵר וּמוֹשִׁיעַ וּמָגֵן.
יּבָּרוּךְ אַתָּה יהוה, מָגֵן אַבְרָהָם.

גבורות

אַתָּה גִּבּוֹר לְעוֹלָם, אֲדֹנָי
מְחַיֵּה מֵתִים אַתָּה, רַב לְהוֹשִׁיעַ
בארץ ישראל: מוֹרִיד הַטָּל

מְכַלְכֵּל חַיִּים בְּחֶסֶד, מְחַיֵּה מֵתִים בְּרַחֲמִים רַבִּים
סוֹמֵךְ נוֹפְלִים, וְרוֹפֵא חוֹלִים, וּמַתִּיר אֲסוּרִים
וּמְקַיֵּם אֱמוּנָתוֹ לִישֵׁנֵי עָפָר.
מִי כָמוֹךָ, בַּעַל גְּבוּרוֹת, וּמִי דּוֹמֶה לָךְ
מֶלֶךְ, מֵמִית וּמְחַיֶּה וּמַצְמִיחַ יְשׁוּעָה.
וְנֶאֱמָן אַתָּה לְהַחֲיוֹת מֵתִים.
בָּרוּךְ אַתָּה יהוה, מְחַיֵּה הַמֵּתִים.

When saying the Amida silently, continue with "You are holy" below.

___

KEDUSHA
> *During the Leader's Repetition, the following is said standing*
> *with feet together, rising on the toes at the words indicated by ˄.*

Cong. then
Leader:
נְקַדֵּשׁ We will sanctify Your name on earth, as they sanctify it in the highest heavens, as is written by Your prophet, "And they [the angels] call to one another saying: *Is. 6*

Cong. then
Leader:
˄Holy, ˄holy, ˄holy is the LORD of hosts the whole world is filled with His glory." Those facing them say "Blessed – "

Cong. then
Leader:
˄"Blessed is the LORD's glory from His place."   *Ezek. 3*
And in Your holy Writings it is written thus:

Cong. then
Leader:
˄"The LORD shall reign for ever. He is your God, Zion,   *Ps. 146*
from generation to generation, Halleluya!"

Leader: From generation to generation we will declare Your greatness, and we will proclaim Your holiness for evermore. Your praise, our God, shall not leave our mouth forever, for You, God, are a great and holy King. Blessed are You, LORD, the holy God.

The Leader continues with "You grace humanity" below.

___

HOLINESS

אַתָּה קָדוֹשׁ You are holy and Your name is holy,
and holy ones praise You daily, Selah!
Blessed are You, LORD, the holy God.

KNOWLEDGE

אַתָּה חוֹנֵן You grace humanity with knowledge
and teach mortals understanding.
Grace us with the knowledge, understanding
and discernment that come from You.
Blessed are You, LORD, who graciously grants knowledge.

REPENTANCE

הֲשִׁיבֵנוּ Bring us back, our Father, to Your Torah.
Draw us near, our King, to Your service.
Lead us back to You in perfect repentance.
Blessed are You, LORD, who desires repentance.

When saying the עמידה *silently, continue with* אַתָּה קָדוֹשׁ *below.*

קדושה

During the חזרת הש״ץ, *the following is said standing
with feet together, rising on the toes at the words indicated by* ᵔ.

קהל
then
ש״ץ
נְקַדֵּשׁ אֶת שִׁמְךָ בָּעוֹלָם, כְּשֵׁם שֶׁמַּקְדִּישִׁים אוֹתוֹ בִּשְׁמֵי מָרוֹם
ישעיהו ו
כַּכָּתוּב עַל יַד נְבִיאֶךָ: וְקָרָא זֶה אֶל־זֶה וְאָמַר

קהל
then
ש״ץ
ᵔקָדוֹשׁ, ᵔקָדוֹשׁ, ᵔקָדוֹשׁ, יהוה צְבָאוֹת, מְלֹא כָל־הָאָרֶץ כְּבוֹדוֹ:
לְעֻמָּתָם בָּרוּךְ יֹאמֵרוּ

קהל
then
ש״ץ
ᵔבָּרוּךְ כְּבוֹד־יהוה מִמְּקוֹמוֹ:
יחזקאל ג
וּבְדִבְרֵי קָדְשְׁךָ כָּתוּב לֵאמֹר

קהל
then
ש״ץ
ᵔיִמְלֹךְ יהוה לְעוֹלָם, אֱלֹהַיִךְ צִיּוֹן לְדֹר וָדֹר, הַלְלוּיָהּ:
תהלים קמו

ש״ץ
לְדוֹר וָדוֹר נַגִּיד גָּדְלֶךָ, וּלְנֵצַח נְצָחִים קְדֻשָּׁתְךָ נַקְדִּישׁ, וְשִׁבְחֲךָ
אֱלֹהֵינוּ מִפִּינוּ לֹא יָמוּשׁ לְעוֹלָם וָעֶד, כִּי אֵל מֶלֶךְ גָּדוֹל וְקָדוֹשׁ אָתָּה.
בָּרוּךְ אַתָּה יהוה, הָאֵל הַקָּדוֹשׁ.

The שליח ציבור *continues with* אַתָּה חוֹנֵן *below.*

קדושת השם

אַתָּה קָדוֹשׁ וְשִׁמְךָ קָדוֹשׁ, וּקְדוֹשִׁים בְּכָל יוֹם יְהַלְלוּךָ סֶּלָה.
בָּרוּךְ אַתָּה יהוה, הָאֵל הַקָּדוֹשׁ.

דעת

אַתָּה חוֹנֵן לְאָדָם דַּעַת, וּמְלַמֵּד לֶאֱנוֹשׁ בִּינָה.
חָנֵּנוּ מֵאִתְּךָ דֵּעָה בִּינָה וְהַשְׂכֵּל.
בָּרוּךְ אַתָּה יהוה, חוֹנֵן הַדָּעַת.

תשובה

הֲשִׁיבֵנוּ אָבִינוּ לְתוֹרָתֶךָ, וְקָרְבֵנוּ מַלְכֵּנוּ לַעֲבוֹדָתֶךָ
וְהַחֲזִירֵנוּ בִּתְשׁוּבָה שְׁלֵמָה לְפָנֶיךָ.
בָּרוּךְ אַתָּה יהוה, הָרוֹצֶה בִּתְשׁוּבָה.

FORGIVENESS

Strike the left side of the chest at °.

סְלַח לָנוּ Forgive us, our Father, for we have °sinned.
Pardon us, our King, for we have °transgressed;
for You pardon and forgive.
Blessed are You, LORD,
the gracious One who repeatedly forgives.

REDEMPTION

רְאֵה Look on our affliction, plead our cause,
and redeem us soon for Your name's sake,
for You are a powerful Redeemer.
Blessed are You, LORD,
the Redeemer of Israel.

HEALING

רְפָאֵנוּ Heal us, LORD, and we shall be healed.
Save us and we shall be saved, for You are our praise.
Bring complete recovery for all our ailments,

The following prayer for a sick person may be said here:
May it be Your will, O LORD my God and God of my ancestors, that You
speedily send a complete recovery from heaven, a healing of both soul and
body, to the patient (*name*), son/daughter of (*mother's name*) among the
other afflicted of Israel.

---

for You, God, King, are a faithful and compassionate Healer.
Blessed are You, LORD,
Healer of the sick of His people Israel.

PROSPERITY

בָּרֵךְ Bless this year for us, LORD our God,
and all its types of produce for good.
Grant blessing on the face of the earth,
and from its goodness satisfy us,
blessing our year as the best of years.
Blessed are You, LORD, who blesses the years.

סליחה

Strike the left side of the chest at °.

סְלַח לָנוּ אָבִינוּ כִּי °חָטָאנוּ

מְחַל לָנוּ מַלְכֵּנוּ כִּי °פָשָׁעְנוּ

כִּי מוֹחֵל וְסוֹלֵחַ אָתָּה.

בָּרוּךְ אַתָּה יהוה, חַנּוּן הַמַּרְבֶּה לִסְלֹחַ.

גאולה

רְאֵה בְעָנְיֵנוּ, וְרִיבָה רִיבֵנוּ

וּגְאָלֵנוּ מְהֵרָה לְמַעַן שְׁמֶךָ, כִּי גּוֹאֵל חָזָק אָתָּה.

בָּרוּךְ אַתָּה יהוה, גּוֹאֵל יִשְׂרָאֵל.

רפואה

רְפָאֵנוּ יהוה וְנֵרָפֵא, הוֹשִׁיעֵנוּ וְנִוָּשֵׁעָה

כִּי תְהִלָּתֵנוּ אָתָּה, וְהַעֲלֵה רְפוּאָה שְׁלֵמָה לְכָל מַכּוֹתֵינוּ

_____

The following prayer for a sick person may be said here:

יְהִי רָצוֹן מִלְּפָנֶיךָ יהוה אֱלֹהַי וֵאלֹהֵי אֲבוֹתַי, שֶׁתִּשְׁלַח מְהֵרָה רְפוּאָה שְׁלֵמָה

מִן הַשָּׁמַיִם רְפוּאַת הַנֶּפֶשׁ וּרְפוּאַת הַגּוּף לַחוֹלֶה/לַחוֹלָה   *name of patient*

בֶּן/בַּת   *mother's name*   בְּתוֹךְ שְׁאָר חוֹלֵי יִשְׂרָאֵל.

_____

כִּי אֵל מֶלֶךְ רוֹפֵא נֶאֱמָן וְרַחֲמָן אָתָּה.

בָּרוּךְ אַתָּה יהוה, רוֹפֵא חוֹלֵי עַמּוֹ יִשְׂרָאֵל.

ברכת השנים

בָּרֵךְ עָלֵינוּ יהוה אֱלֹהֵינוּ אֶת הַשָּׁנָה הַזֹּאת

וְאֶת כָּל מִינֵי תְבוּאָתָהּ, לְטוֹבָה

וְתֵן בְּרָכָה עַל פְּנֵי הָאֲדָמָה

וְשַׂבְּעֵנוּ מִטּוּבָהּ, וּבָרֵךְ שְׁנָתֵנוּ כַּשָּׁנִים הַטּוֹבוֹת.

בָּרוּךְ אַתָּה יהוה, מְבָרֵךְ הַשָּׁנִים.

INGATHERING OF EXILES

תְּקַע Sound the great shofar for our freedom,
raise high the banner to gather our exiles,
and gather us together
from the four quarters of the earth.
Blessed are You, LORD,
who gathers the dispersed of His people Israel.

JUSTICE

הָשִׁיבָה Restore our judges as at first,
and our counselors as at the beginning,
and remove from us sorrow and sighing.
May You alone, LORD, reign over us
with loving-kindness and compassion, and vindicate us in justice.
Blessed are You, LORD,
the King who loves righteousness and justice.

AGAINST INFORMERS

וְלַמַּלְשִׁינִים For the slanderers let there be no hope,
and may all wickedness perish in an instant.
May all Your people's enemies swiftly be cut down.
May You swiftly uproot, crush, cast down
and humble the arrogant swiftly in our days.
Blessed are You, LORD,
who destroys enemies and humbles the arrogant.

THE RIGHTEOUS

עַל הַצַּדִּיקִים To the righteous, the pious,
the elders of Your people the house of Israel,
the remnant of their scholars, the righteous converts, and to us,
may Your compassion be aroused, LORD our God.
Grant a good reward to all who sincerely trust in Your name.
Set our lot with them, so that we may never be ashamed,
for in You we trust.
Blessed are You, LORD,
who is the support and trust of the righteous.

קבוץ גלויות
תְּקַע בְּשׁוֹפָר גָּדוֹל לְחֵרוּתֵנוּ, וְשָׂא נֵס לְקַבֵּץ גָּלֻיּוֹתֵינוּ
וְקַבְּצֵנוּ יַחַד מֵאַרְבַּע כַּנְפוֹת הָאָרֶץ.
בָּרוּךְ אַתָּה יהוה, מְקַבֵּץ נִדְחֵי עַמּוֹ יִשְׂרָאֵל.

השבת המשפט
הָשִׁיבָה שׁוֹפְטֵינוּ כְּבָרִאשׁוֹנָה וְיוֹעֲצֵינוּ כְּבַתְּחִלָּה
וְהָסֵר מִמֶּנּוּ יָגוֹן וַאֲנָחָה
וּמְלֹךְ עָלֵינוּ אַתָּה יהוה לְבַדְּךָ בְּחֶסֶד וּבְרַחֲמִים,
וְצַדְּקֵנוּ בַּמִּשְׁפָּט.
בָּרוּךְ אַתָּה יהוה
מֶלֶךְ אוֹהֵב צְדָקָה וּמִשְׁפָּט.

ברכת המינים
וְלַמַּלְשִׁינִים אַל תְּהִי תִקְוָה, וְכָל הָרִשְׁעָה כְּרֶגַע תֹּאבֵד
וְכָל אוֹיְבֵי עַמְּךָ מְהֵרָה יִכָּרֵתוּ
וְהַזֵּדִים מְהֵרָה תְעַקֵּר וּתְשַׁבֵּר וּתְמַגֵּר וְתַכְנִיעַ בִּמְהֵרָה בְיָמֵינוּ.
בָּרוּךְ אַתָּה יהוה, שׁוֹבֵר אוֹיְבִים וּמַכְנִיעַ זֵדִים.

על הצדיקים
עַל הַצַּדִּיקִים וְעַל הַחֲסִידִים, וְעַל זִקְנֵי עַמְּךָ בֵּית יִשְׂרָאֵל
וְעַל פְּלֵיטַת סוֹפְרֵיהֶם, וְעַל גֵּרֵי הַצֶּדֶק, וְעָלֵינוּ
יֶהֱמוּ רַחֲמֶיךָ יהוה אֱלֹהֵינוּ
וְתֵן שָׂכָר טוֹב לְכָל הַבּוֹטְחִים בְּשִׁמְךָ בֶּאֱמֶת
וְשִׂים חֶלְקֵנוּ עִמָּהֶם
וּלְעוֹלָם לֹא נֵבוֹשׁ כִּי בְךָ בָּטָחְנוּ.
בָּרוּךְ אַתָּה יהוה, מִשְׁעָן וּמִבְטָח לַצַּדִּיקִים.

REBUILDING JERUSALEM

וְלִירוּשָׁלַיִם To Jerusalem, Your city,
may You return in compassion,
and may You dwell in it as You promised.
May You rebuild it rapidly in our days
as an everlasting structure,
and install within it soon the throne of David.
Blessed are You, LORD, who builds Jerusalem.

KINGDOM OF DAVID

אֶת צֶמַח May the offshoot of Your servant David soon flower,
and may his pride be raised high by Your salvation,
for we wait for Your salvation all day.
Blessed are You, LORD, who makes the glory of salvation flourish.

RESPONSE TO PRAYER

שְׁמַע קוֹלֵנוּ Listen to our voice, LORD our God.
Spare us and have compassion on us,
and in compassion and favor accept our prayer,
for You, God, listen to prayers and pleas.
Do not turn us away, O our King,
empty-handed from Your presence,
for You listen with compassion
to the prayer of Your people Israel.
Blessed are You, LORD, who listens to prayer.

TEMPLE SERVICE

רְצֵה Find favor, LORD our God,
in Your people Israel and their prayer.
Restore the service to Your most holy House,
and accept in love and favor
the fire-offerings of Israel and their prayer.
May the service of Your people Israel
always find favor with You.

בניין ירושלים

וְלִירוּשָׁלַיִם עִירְךָ בְּרַחֲמִים תָּשׁוּב
וְתִשְׁכֹּן בְּתוֹכָהּ כַּאֲשֶׁר דִּבַּרְתָּ
וּבְנֵה אוֹתָהּ בְּקָרוֹב בְּיָמֵינוּ בִּנְיַן עוֹלָם
וְכִסֵּא דָוִד מְהֵרָה לְתוֹכָהּ תָּכִין.
בָּרוּךְ אַתָּה יהוה, בּוֹנֵה יְרוּשָׁלָיִם.

משיח בן דוד

אֶת צֶמַח דָּוִד עַבְדְּךָ מְהֵרָה תַצְמִיחַ
וְקַרְנוֹ תָּרוּם בִּישׁוּעָתֶךָ
כִּי לִישׁוּעָתְךָ קִוִּינוּ כָּל הַיּוֹם.
בָּרוּךְ אַתָּה יהוה, מַצְמִיחַ קֶרֶן יְשׁוּעָה.

שומע תפלה

שְׁמַע קוֹלֵנוּ יהוה אֱלֹהֵינוּ
חוּס וְרַחֵם עָלֵינוּ
וְקַבֵּל בְּרַחֲמִים וּבְרָצוֹן אֶת תְּפִלָּתֵנוּ
כִּי אֵל שׁוֹמֵעַ תְּפִלּוֹת וְתַחֲנוּנִים אָתָּה
וּמִלְּפָנֶיךָ מַלְכֵּנוּ רֵיקָם אַל תְּשִׁיבֵנוּ
כִּי אַתָּה שׁוֹמֵעַ תְּפִלַּת עַמְּךָ יִשְׂרָאֵל בְּרַחֲמִים.
בָּרוּךְ אַתָּה יהוה, שׁוֹמֵעַ תְּפִלָּה.

עבודה

רְצֵה יהוה אֱלֹהֵינוּ בְּעַמְּךָ יִשְׂרָאֵל, וּבִתְפִלָּתָם
וְהָשֵׁב אֶת הָעֲבוֹדָה לִדְבִיר בֵּיתֶךָ
וְאִשֵּׁי יִשְׂרָאֵל וּתְפִלָּתָם בְּאַהֲבָה תְקַבֵּל בְּרָצוֹן
וּתְהִי לְרָצוֹן תָּמִיד עֲבוֹדַת יִשְׂרָאֵל עַמֶּךָ.

וְתֶחֱזֶינָה And may our eyes witness Your return
to Zion in compassion.
Blessed are You, LORD, who restores His Presence to Zion.

THANKSGIVING *Bow at the first nine words.*

מוֹדִים We give thanks to You,
for You are the LORD our God
and God of our ancestors
for ever and all time.
You are the Rock of our lives,
Shield of our salvation
from generation to generation.
We will thank You and
declare Your praise for our lives,
which are entrusted into Your hand;
for our souls,
which are placed in Your charge;
for Your miracles
which are with us every day;
and for Your wonders and favors
at all times, evening,
morning and midday.
You are good –
for Your compassion never fails.
You are compassionate –
for Your loving-kindnesses never cease.
We have always placed our hope in You.

During the Leader's Repetition,
the congregation says quietly:

מוֹדִים We give thanks to You,
for You are the LORD our God
and God of our ancestors,
God of all flesh,
who formed us
and formed the universe.
Blessings and thanks
are due to Your great
and holy name for giving us
life and sustaining us.
May You continue
to give us life and sustain us;
and may You gather our
exiles to Your holy courts,
to keep Your decrees,
do Your will and serve You
with a perfect heart,
for it is for us
to give You thanks.
Blessed be God to whom
thanksgiving is due.

וְעַל כֻּלָּם For all these things may Your name be blessed and
exalted, our King, continually, for ever and all time.
Let all that lives thank You, Selah! and praise Your name in truth,
God, our Savior and Help, Selah!
▸Blessed are You, LORD,
whose name is "the Good" and to whom thanks are due.

וְתֶחֱזֶינָה עֵינֵינוּ בְּשׁוּבְךָ לְצִיּוֹן בְּרַחֲמִים.
בָּרוּךְ אַתָּה יהוה, הַמַּחֲזִיר שְׁכִינָתוֹ לְצִיּוֹן.

הוֹדָאָה

Bow at the first five words.

מוֹדִים אֲנַחְנוּ לָךְ
שָׁאַתָּה הוּא יהוה אֱלֹהֵינוּ
וֵאלֹהֵי אֲבוֹתֵינוּ לְעוֹלָם וָעֶד.
צוּר חַיֵּינוּ, מָגֵן יִשְׁעֵנוּ
אַתָּה הוּא לְדוֹר וָדוֹר.
נוֹדֶה לְּךָ וּנְסַפֵּר תְּהִלָּתֶךָ
עַל חַיֵּינוּ הַמְּסוּרִים בְּיָדֶךָ
וְעַל נִשְׁמוֹתֵינוּ הַפְּקוּדוֹת לָךְ
וְעַל נִסֶּיךָ שֶׁבְּכָל יוֹם עִמָּנוּ
וְעַל נִפְלְאוֹתֶיךָ וְטוֹבוֹתֶיךָ
שֶׁבְּכָל עֵת
עֶרֶב וָבֹקֶר וְצָהֳרָיִם.
הַטּוֹב, כִּי לֹא כָלוּ רַחֲמֶיךָ
וְהַמְרַחֵם, כִּי לֹא תַמּוּ חֲסָדֶיךָ
מֵעוֹלָם קִוִּינוּ לָךְ.

During the חזרת הש״ץ,
the קהל *says quietly:*

מוֹדִים אֲנַחְנוּ לָךְ
שָׁאַתָּה הוּא יהוה אֱלֹהֵינוּ
וֵאלֹהֵי אֲבוֹתֵינוּ
אֱלֹהֵי כָל בָּשָׂר
יוֹצְרֵנוּ, יוֹצֵר בְּרֵאשִׁית.
בְּרָכוֹת וְהוֹדָאוֹת
לְשִׁמְךָ הַגָּדוֹל וְהַקָּדוֹשׁ
עַל שֶׁהֶחֱיִיתָנוּ וְקִיַּמְתָּנוּ.
כֵּן תְּחַיֵּנוּ וּתְקַיְּמֵנוּ
וְתֶאֱסֹף גָּלֻיּוֹתֵינוּ
לְחַצְרוֹת קָדְשֶׁךָ
לִשְׁמֹר חֻקֶּיךָ
וְלַעֲשׂוֹת רְצוֹנֶךָ וּלְעָבְדְּךָ
בְּלֵבָב שָׁלֵם
עַל שֶׁאֲנַחְנוּ מוֹדִים לָךְ.
בָּרוּךְ אֵל הַהוֹדָאוֹת.

וְעַל כֻּלָּם יִתְבָּרַךְ וְיִתְרוֹמַם שִׁמְךָ מַלְכֵּנוּ תָּמִיד לְעוֹלָם וָעֶד.
וְכֹל הַחַיִּים יוֹדוּךָ סֶּלָה, וִיהַלְלוּ אֶת שִׁמְךָ בֶּאֱמֶת
הָאֵל יְשׁוּעָתֵנוּ וְעֶזְרָתֵנוּ סֶלָה.
בָּרוּךְ אַתָּה יהוה, הַטּוֹב שִׁמְךָ וּלְךָ נָאֶה לְהוֹדוֹת.

PEACE

שָׁלוֹם רָב Grant great peace to Your people Israel for ever,
for You are the sovereign LORD of all peace;
and may it be good in Your eyes to bless Your people Israel
at every time, at every hour, with Your peace.
Blessed are You, LORD, who blesses His people Israel with peace.

The following verse concludes the Leader's Repetition of the Amida.
Some also say it here as part of the silent Amida.

May the words of my mouth and the meditation of my heart   *Ps. 19*
find favor before You, LORD, my Rock and Redeemer.

אֱלֹהַי My God,   *Berakhot*
guard my tongue from evil and my lips from deceitful speech.   *17a*
To those who curse me, let my soul be silent;
may my soul be to all like the dust.
Open my heart to Your Torah
and let my soul pursue Your commandments.
As for all who plan evil against me,
swiftly thwart their counsel and frustrate their plans.
　　Act for the sake of Your name; act for the sake of Your right hand;
　　　act for the sake of Your holiness; act for the sake of Your Torah.
That Your beloved ones may be delivered,   *Ps. 60*
save with Your right hand and answer me.
May the words of my mouth and the meditation of my heart   *Ps. 19*
find favor before You, LORD, my Rock and Redeemer.

Bow, take three steps back, then bow, first left, then right, then center, while saying:
May He who makes peace in His high places,
make peace for us and all Israel – and say: Amen.

יְהִי רָצוֹן May it be Your will, LORD our God and God of our ancestors,
that the Temple be rebuilt speedily in our days,
and grant us a share in Your Torah.
And there we will serve You with reverence,
as in the days of old and as in former years.
Then the offering of Judah and Jerusalem will be pleasing to the LORD   *Mal. 3*
as in the days of old and as in former years.

ברכת שלום

שָׁלוֹם רָב עַל יִשְׂרָאֵל עַמְּךָ תָּשִׂים לְעוֹלָם

כִּי אַתָּה הוּא מֶלֶךְ אָדוֹן לְכָל הַשָּׁלוֹם.

וְטוֹב בְּעֵינֶיךָ לְבָרֵךְ אֶת עַמְּךָ יִשְׂרָאֵל

בְּכָל עֵת וּבְכָל שָׁעָה בִּשְׁלוֹמֶךָ.

בָּרוּךְ אַתָּה יהוה, הַמְבָרֵךְ אֶת עַמּוֹ יִשְׂרָאֵל בַּשָּׁלוֹם.

The following verse concludes the חזרת הש״ץ.
Some also say it here as part of the silent עמידה.

תהלים יט

יִהְיוּ לְרָצוֹן אִמְרֵי־פִי וְהֶגְיוֹן לִבִּי לְפָנֶיךָ, יהוה צוּרִי וְגֹאֲלִי:

ברכות יז

אֱלֹהַי

נְצֹר לְשׁוֹנִי מֵרָע וּשְׂפָתַי מִדַּבֵּר מִרְמָה

וְלִמְקַלְלַי נַפְשִׁי תִדֹּם, וְנַפְשִׁי כֶּעָפָר לַכֹּל תִּהְיֶה.

פְּתַח לִבִּי בְּתוֹרָתֶךָ, וּבְמִצְוֹתֶיךָ תִּרְדֹּף נַפְשִׁי.

וְכָל הַחוֹשְׁבִים עָלַי רָעָה

מְהֵרָה הָפֵר עֲצָתָם וְקַלְקֵל מַחֲשַׁבְתָּם.

עֲשֵׂה לְמַעַן שְׁמֶךָ, עֲשֵׂה לְמַעַן יְמִינֶךָ

עֲשֵׂה לְמַעַן קְדֻשָּׁתֶךָ, עֲשֵׂה לְמַעַן תּוֹרָתֶךָ.

תהלים ס

לְמַעַן יֵחָלְצוּן יְדִידֶיךָ, הוֹשִׁיעָה יְמִינְךָ וַעֲנֵנִי:

תהלים יט

יִהְיוּ לְרָצוֹן אִמְרֵי־פִי וְהֶגְיוֹן לִבִּי לְפָנֶיךָ, יהוה צוּרִי וְגֹאֲלִי:

Bow, take three steps back, then bow, first left, then right, then center, while saying:

עֹשֶׂה שָׁלוֹם בִּמְרוֹמָיו

הוּא יַעֲשֶׂה שָׁלוֹם עָלֵינוּ וְעַל כָּל יִשְׂרָאֵל, וְאִמְרוּ אָמֵן.

יְהִי רָצוֹן מִלְּפָנֶיךָ יהוה אֱלֹהֵינוּ וֵאלֹהֵי אֲבוֹתֵינוּ

שֶׁיִּבָּנֶה בֵּית הַמִּקְדָּשׁ בִּמְהֵרָה בְיָמֵינוּ, וְתֵן חֶלְקֵנוּ בְּתוֹרָתֶךָ

וְשָׁם נַעֲבָדְךָ בְּיִרְאָה כִּימֵי עוֹלָם וּכְשָׁנִים קַדְמֹנִיּוֹת.

מלאכי ג

וְעָרְבָה לַיהוה מִנְחַת יְהוּדָה וִירוּשָׁלָ͏ִם כִּימֵי עוֹלָם וּכְשָׁנִים קַדְמֹנִיּוֹת:

If Minḥa is said in the middle of the day, Taḥanun is said.
If Minḥa is said before evening, the Leader says Full Kaddish on page 32 as on festive evenings.

TAHANUN

LOWERING THE HEAD

Say while sitting; in the presence of a Torah scroll say until "in sudden shame,"
leaning forward and resting one's head on the left arm.

וַיֹּאמֶר דָּוִד David said to Gad, "I am in great distress. Let us fall into God's hand, for His mercy is great; but do not let me fall into the hand of man." *II Sam. 24*

Compassionate and gracious One, I have sinned before You.
LORD, full of compassion, have compassion on me and accept my pleas.

LORD, do not rebuke me in Your anger or chastise me in Your wrath. Be *Ps. 6*
gracious to me, LORD, for I am weak. Heal me, LORD, for my bones are
in agony. My soul is in anguish, and You, O LORD – how long? Turn,
LORD, set my soul free; save me for the sake of Your love. For no one
remembers You when he is dead. Who can praise You from the grave? I
am weary with my sighing. Every night I drench my bed, I soak my couch
with my tears. My eye grows dim from grief, worn out because of all my
foes. Leave me, all you evildoers, for the LORD has heard the sound of
my weeping. The LORD has heard my pleas. The LORD will accept my
prayer. All my enemies will be shamed and utterly dismayed. They will
turn back in sudden shame.

Sit upright.

שׁוֹמֵר יִשְׂרָאֵל Guardian of Israel, guard the remnant of Israel,
        and let not Israel perish, who declare, "Listen, Israel."
Guardian of a unique nation, guard the remnant of a unique people,
        and let not that unique nation perish, who proclaim the unity of
        Your name [saying], "The LORD is our God, the LORD is One."
Guardian of a holy nation, guard the remnant of that holy people,
        and let not the holy nation perish, who three times repeat
        the threefold declaration of holiness to the Holy One.
You who are conciliated by calls for compassion and placated by pleas,
        be conciliated and placated toward an afflicted generation,
        for there is no other help.
Our Father, our King, be gracious to us and answer us,
        though we have no worthy deeds;
        act with us in charity and loving-kindness and save us.

If מנחה is said in the middle of the day, תחנון is said.
If מנחה is said before evening, the שליח ציבור says קדיש שלם on page 33 as on festive evenings.

סדר תחנון

נפילת אפיים

*Say while sitting; in the presence of a ספר תורה say until יֵבֹשׁוּ רָגַע,
leaning forward and resting one's head on the left arm.*

שמואל ב׳ כד

וַיֹּאמֶר דָּוִד אֶל־גָּד, צַר־לִי מְאֹד

נִפְּלָה־נָּא בְיַד־יהוה, כִּי־רַבִּים רַחֲמָו, וּבְיַד־אָדָם אַל־אֶפֹּלָה:

רַחוּם וְחַנּוּן, חָטָאתִי לְפָנֶיךָ. יהוה מָלֵא רַחֲמִים, רַחֵם עָלַי וְקַבֵּל תַּחֲנוּנָי.

תהלים ו

יהוה, אַל־בְּאַפְּךָ תוֹכִיחֵנִי, וְאַל־בַּחֲמָתְךָ תְיַסְּרֵנִי: חָנֵּנִי יהוה, כִּי אֻמְלַל
אָנִי, רְפָאֵנִי יהוה, כִּי נִבְהֲלוּ עֲצָמָי: וְנַפְשִׁי נִבְהֲלָה מְאֹד, וְאַתָּ יהוה, עַד־
מָתָי: שׁוּבָה יהוה, חַלְּצָה נַפְשִׁי, הוֹשִׁיעֵנִי לְמַעַן חַסְדֶּךָ: כִּי אֵין בַּמָּוֶת
זִכְרֶךָ, בִּשְׁאוֹל מִי יוֹדֶה־לָּךְ: יָגַעְתִּי בְּאַנְחָתִי, אַשְׂחֶה בְכָל־לַיְלָה מִטָּתִי,
בְּדִמְעָתִי עַרְשִׂי אַמְסֶה: עָשְׁשָׁה מִכַּעַס עֵינִי, עָתְקָה בְּכָל־צוֹרְרָי: סוּרוּ
מִמֶּנִּי כָּל־פֹּעֲלֵי אָוֶן, כִּי־שָׁמַע יהוה קוֹל בִּכְיִי: שָׁמַע יהוה תְּחִנָּתִי, יהוה
תְּפִלָּתִי יִקָּח: יֵבֹשׁוּ וְיִבָּהֲלוּ מְאֹד כָּל־אֹיְבָי, יָשֻׁבוּ יֵבֹשׁוּ רָגַע:

Sit upright.

שׁוֹמֵר יִשְׂרָאֵל, שְׁמֹר שְׁאֵרִית יִשְׂרָאֵל, וְאַל יֹאבַד יִשְׂרָאֵל
הָאוֹמְרִים שְׁמַע יִשְׂרָאֵל.

שׁוֹמֵר גּוֹי אֶחָד, שְׁמֹר שְׁאֵרִית עַם אֶחָד, וְאַל יֹאבַד גּוֹי אֶחָד
הַמְיַחֲדִים שִׁמְךָ, יהוה אֱלֹהֵינוּ יהוה אֶחָד.

שׁוֹמֵר גּוֹי קָדוֹשׁ, שְׁמֹר שְׁאֵרִית עַם קָדוֹשׁ, וְאַל יֹאבַד גּוֹי קָדוֹשׁ
הַמְשַׁלְּשִׁים בְּשָׁלֹשׁ קְדֻשּׁוֹת לְקָדוֹשׁ.

מִתְרַצֶּה בְּרַחֲמִים וּמִתְפַּיֵּס בְּתַחֲנוּנִים, הִתְרַצֵּה וְהִתְפַּיֵּס לְדוֹר עָנִי
כִּי אֵין עוֹזֵר.

אָבִינוּ מַלְכֵּנוּ, חָנֵּנוּ וַעֲנֵנוּ, כִּי אֵין בָּנוּ מַעֲשִׂים
עֲשֵׂה עִמָּנוּ צְדָקָה וָחֶסֶד וְהוֹשִׁיעֵנוּ.

Stand at ▲.

וַאֲנַחְנוּ We do not know ▲what to do, but our eyes are turned to You. *II Chr. 12*
Remember, LORD, Your compassion and loving-kindness, for they are *Ps. 25*
everlasting. May Your loving-kindness, LORD, be with us, for we have put *Ps. 33*
our hope in You. Do not hold against us the sins of those who came before *Ps. 79*
us. May Your mercies meet us swiftly, for we have been brought very low.
Be gracious to us, LORD, be gracious to us, for we are sated with contempt. *Ps. 123*
In wrath, remember mercy. He knows our nature; He remembers that *Hab. 3*
                                                                        Ps. 103
we are dust. ▸ Help us, God of our salvation, for the sake of the glory of *Ps. 79*
Your name. Save us and grant atonement for our sins for Your name's sake.

FULL KADDISH

Leader: יִתְגַּדַּל Magnified and sanctified may His great name be,
in the world He created by His will.
May He establish His kingdom
in your lifetime and in your days,
and in the lifetime of all the house of Israel,
swiftly and soon – and say: Amen.

All: May His great name be blessed for ever and all time.

Leader: Blessed and praised,
glorified and exalted, raised and honored,
uplifted and lauded be
the name of the Holy One, blessed be He,
beyond any blessing, song, praise and consolation
uttered in the world – and say: Amen.

May the prayers and pleas of all Israel
be accepted by their Father in heaven – and say: Amen.

May there be great peace from heaven,
and life for us and all Israel – and say: Amen.

Bow, take three steps back, as if taking leave of the Divine Presence,
then bow, first left, then right, then center, while saying:
May He who makes peace in His high places,
make peace for us and all Israel – and say: Amen.

Stand at ^.

דברי
הימים ב׳ י״ב
תהלים כ״ה
וַאֲנַחְנוּ לֹא נֵדַע מַה־נַּעֲשֶׂה, כִּי עָלֶיךָ עֵינֵינוּ: זְכֹר־רַחֲמֶיךָ יהוה

תהלים ל״ג
וַחֲסָדֶיךָ, כִּי מֵעוֹלָם הֵמָּה: יְהִי־חַסְדְּךָ יהוה עָלֵינוּ, כַּאֲשֶׁר יִחַלְנוּ לָךְ:

תהלים ע״ט
תהלים קכ״ג
חבקוק ג׳
תהלים ק״ג
תהלים ע״ט
אַל־תִּזְכָּר־לָנוּ עֲוֹנֹת רִאשֹׁנִים, מַהֵר יְקַדְּמוּנוּ רַחֲמֶיךָ, כִּי דַלּוֹנוּ מְאֹד:
חָנֵּנוּ יהוה חָנֵּנוּ, כִּי־רַב שָׂבַעְנוּ בוּז: בְּרֹגֶז רַחֵם תִּזְכּוֹר: כִּי־הוּא יָדַע
יִצְרֵנוּ, זָכוּר כִּי־עָפָר אֲנָחְנוּ: ◂ עָזְרֵנוּ אֱלֹהֵי יִשְׁעֵנוּ עַל־דְּבַר כְּבוֹד־שְׁמֶךָ,
וְהַצִּילֵנוּ וְכַפֵּר עַל־חַטֹּאתֵינוּ לְמַעַן שְׁמֶךָ:

קדיש שלם

ש״ץ: יִתְגַּדַּל וְיִתְקַדַּשׁ שְׁמֵהּ רַבָּא (קהל: אָמֵן)
בְּעָלְמָא דִּי בְרָא כִרְעוּתֵהּ, וְיַמְלִיךְ מַלְכוּתֵהּ
בְּחַיֵּיכוֹן וּבְיוֹמֵיכוֹן וּבְחַיֵּי דְכָל בֵּית יִשְׂרָאֵל
בַּעֲגָלָא וּבִזְמַן קָרִיב, וְאִמְרוּ אָמֵן. (קהל: אָמֵן)

קהל
 וש״ץ: יְהֵא שְׁמֵהּ רַבָּא מְבָרַךְ לְעָלַם וּלְעָלְמֵי עָלְמַיָּא.

ש״ץ: יִתְבָּרַךְ וְיִשְׁתַּבַּח וְיִתְפָּאַר
וְיִתְרוֹמַם וְיִתְנַשֵּׂא וְיִתְהַדָּר וְיִתְעַלֶּה וְיִתְהַלָּל
שְׁמֵהּ דְּקֻדְשָׁא בְּרִיךְ הוּא (קהל: בְּרִיךְ הוּא)
לְעֵלָּא מִן כָּל בִּרְכָתָא וְשִׁירָתָא, תֻּשְׁבְּחָתָא וְנֶחֱמָתָא
דַּאֲמִירָן בְּעָלְמָא וְאִמְרוּ אָמֵן. (קהל: אָמֵן)

תִּתְקַבֵּל צְלוֹתְהוֹן וּבָעוּתְהוֹן דְּכָל יִשְׂרָאֵל
קֳדָם אֲבוּהוֹן דִּי בִשְׁמַיָּא, וְאִמְרוּ אָמֵן. (קהל: אָמֵן)

יְהֵא שְׁלָמָא רַבָּא מִן שְׁמַיָּא
וְחַיִּים, עָלֵינוּ וְעַל כָּל יִשְׂרָאֵל, וְאִמְרוּ אָמֵן. (קהל: אָמֵן)

Bow, take three steps back, as if taking leave of the Divine Presence,
then bow, first left, then right, then center, while saying:

עֹשֶׂה שָׁלוֹם בִּמְרוֹמָיו
הוּא יַעֲשֶׂה שָׁלוֹם עָלֵינוּ וְעַל כָּל יִשְׂרָאֵל, וְאִמְרוּ אָמֵן. (קהל: אָמֵן)

Stand while saying Aleinu. Bow at ˅.

עָלֵינוּ It is our duty to praise the Master of all,
and ascribe greatness to the Author of creation,
who has not made us like the nations of the lands
nor placed us like the families of the earth;
who has not made our portion like theirs,
nor our destiny like all their multitudes.
(For they worship vanity and emptiness,
and pray to a god who cannot save.)
˅But we bow in worship
and thank the Supreme King of kings,
the Holy One, blessed be He,
who extends the heavens and establishes the earth,
whose throne of glory is in the heavens above,
and whose power's Presence is in the highest of heights.
He is our God; there is no other.
Truly He is our King, there is none else,
as it is written in His Torah:
"You shall know and take to heart this day   *Deut. 4*
that the LORD is God,
in heaven above and on earth below.
There is no other."

Therefore, we place our hope in You, LORD our God,
that we may soon see the glory of Your power,
when You will remove abominations from the earth,
and idols will be utterly destroyed,
when the world will be perfected
under the sovereignty of the Almighty,
when all humanity will call on Your name,
to turn all the earth's wicked toward You.
All the world's inhabitants will realize and know
that to You every knee must bow
and every tongue swear loyalty.

Stand while saying עָלֵינוּ. Bow at ˇ.

עָלֵינוּ לְשַׁבֵּחַ לַאֲדוֹן הַכֹּל, לָתֵת גְּדֻלָּה לְיוֹצֵר בְּרֵאשִׁית

שֶׁלֹּא עָשָׂנוּ כְּגוֹיֵי הָאֲרָצוֹת

וְלֹא שָׂמָנוּ כְּמִשְׁפְּחוֹת הָאֲדָמָה

שֶׁלֹּא שָׂם חֶלְקֵנוּ כָּהֶם וְגֹרָלֵנוּ כְּכָל הֲמוֹנָם.

(שֶׁהֵם מִשְׁתַּחֲוִים לְהֶבֶל וָרִיק וּמִתְפַּלְלִים אֶל אֵל לֹא יוֹשִׁיעַ.)

ˇוַאֲנַחְנוּ כּוֹרְעִים וּמִשְׁתַּחֲוִים וּמוֹדִים

לִפְנֵי מֶלֶךְ מַלְכֵי הַמְּלָכִים, הַקָּדוֹשׁ בָּרוּךְ הוּא

שֶׁהוּא נוֹטֶה שָׁמַיִם וְיוֹסֵד אָרֶץ

וּמוֹשַׁב יְקָרוֹ בַּשָּׁמַיִם מִמַּעַל

וּשְׁכִינַת עֻזּוֹ בְּגָבְהֵי מְרוֹמִים.

הוּא אֱלֹהֵינוּ, אֵין עוֹד.

אֱמֶת מַלְכֵּנוּ, אֶפֶס זוּלָתוֹ

כַּכָּתוּב בְּתוֹרָתוֹ

וְיָדַעְתָּ הַיּוֹם וַהֲשֵׁבֹתָ אֶל-לְבָבֶךָ

דברים ד

כִּי יהוה הוּא הָאֱלֹהִים בַּשָּׁמַיִם מִמַּעַל וְעַל-הָאָרֶץ מִתַּחַת

אֵין עוֹד:

עַל כֵּן נְקַוֶּה לְּךָ יהוה אֱלֹהֵינוּ

לִרְאוֹת מְהֵרָה בְּתִפְאֶרֶת עֻזֶּךָ

לְהַעֲבִיר גִּלּוּלִים מִן הָאָרֶץ

וְהָאֱלִילִים כָּרוֹת יִכָּרֵתוּן

לְתַקֵּן עוֹלָם בְּמַלְכוּת שַׁדַּי.

וְכָל בְּנֵי בָשָׂר יִקְרְאוּ בִשְׁמֶךָ לְהַפְנוֹת אֵלֶיךָ כָּל רִשְׁעֵי אָרֶץ.

יַכִּירוּ וְיֵדְעוּ כָּל יוֹשְׁבֵי תֵבֵל

כִּי לְךָ תִּכְרַע כָּל בֶּרֶךְ, תִּשָּׁבַע כָּל לָשׁוֹן.

Before You, Lord our God, they will kneel and bow down
and give honor to Your glorious name.
They will all accept the yoke of Your kingdom,
and You will reign over them soon and for ever.
For the kingdom is Yours,
and to all eternity You will reign in glory,
as it is written in Your Torah:
"The Lord will reign for ever and ever."   *Ex. 15*

▸ And it is said:
"Then the Lord shall be King over all the earth;   *Zech. 14*
on that day the Lord shall be One and His name One."

Some add:
Have no fear of sudden terror or of the ruin when it overtakes the wicked.   *Prov. 3*
Devise your strategy, but it will be thwarted; propose your plan,   *Is. 8*
but it will not stand, for God is with us.
When you grow old, I will still be the same.   *Is. 46*
When your hair turns gray, I will still carry you.
I made you, I will bear you, I will carry you, and I will rescue you.

MOURNER'S KADDISH

*The following prayer, said by mourners, requires the presence of a minyan.
A transliteration can be found on page 667.*

Mourner: יִתְגַּדַּל Magnified and sanctified
may His great name be,
in the world He created by His will.
May He establish His kingdom
in your lifetime and in your days,
and in the lifetime
of all the house of Israel,
swiftly and soon –
and say: Amen.

All: May His great name be blessed
for ever and all time.

לְפָנֶיךָ יהוה אֱלֹהֵינוּ יִכְרְעוּ וְיִפֹּלוּ

וְלִכְבוֹד שִׁמְךָ יְקָר יִתֵּנוּ

וִיקַבְּלוּ כֻלָּם אֶת עֹל מַלְכוּתֶךָ

וְתִמְלֹךְ עֲלֵיהֶם מְהֵרָה לְעוֹלָם וָעֶד .

כִּי הַמַּלְכוּת שֶׁלְּךָ הִיא וּלְעוֹלְמֵי עַד תִּמְלֹךְ בְּכָבוֹד

שמות טו כַּכָּתוּב בְּתוֹרָתֶךָ, יהוה יִמְלֹךְ לְעֹלָם וָעֶד :

זכריה יד ◂ וְנֶאֱמַר, וְהָיָה יהוה לְמֶלֶךְ עַל־כָּל־הָאָרֶץ

בַּיּוֹם הַהוּא יִהְיֶה יהוה אֶחָד וּשְׁמוֹ אֶחָד :

Some add:

משלי ג אַל־תִּירָא מִפַּחַד פִּתְאֹם וּמִשֹּׁאַת רְשָׁעִים כִּי תָבֹא :

ישעיה ח עֻצוּ עֵצָה וְתֻפָר, דַּבְּרוּ דָבָר וְלֹא יָקוּם, כִּי עִמָּנוּ אֵל :

ישעיה מו וְעַד־זִקְנָה אֲנִי הוּא, וְעַד־שֵׂיבָה אֲנִי אֶסְבֹּל

אֲנִי עָשִׂיתִי וַאֲנִי אֶשָּׂא וַאֲנִי אֶסְבֹּל וַאֲמַלֵּט :

קדיש יתום

The following prayer, said by mourners, requires the presence of a מנין.
A transliteration can be found on page 667.

אבל: יִתְגַּדַּל וְיִתְקַדַּשׁ שְׁמֵהּ רַבָּא (קהל: אָמֵן)

בְּעָלְמָא דִּי בְרָא כִרְעוּתֵהּ

וְיַמְלִיךְ מַלְכוּתֵהּ

בְּחַיֵּיכוֹן וּבְיוֹמֵיכוֹן

וּבְחַיֵּי דְכָל בֵּית יִשְׂרָאֵל

בַּעֲגָלָא וּבִזְמַן קָרִיב

וְאִמְרוּ אָמֵן. (קהל: אָמֵן)

קהל
ואבל: יְהֵא שְׁמֵהּ רַבָּא מְבָרַךְ לְעָלַם וּלְעָלְמֵי עָלְמַיָּא.

Mourner: Blessed and praised,
glorified and exalted,
raised and honored,
uplifted and lauded
be the name of the Holy One,
blessed be He,
beyond any blessing,
song, praise and consolation
uttered in the world –
and say: Amen.

May there be great peace from heaven,
and life for us and all Israel –
and say: Amen.

Bow, take three steps back, as if taking leave of the Divine Presence,
then bow, first left, then right, then center, while saying:

May He who makes peace in His high places,
make peace for us and all Israel –
and say: Amen.

For Ma'ariv of Yom Yerushalayim turn to page 514.

Hearing a presentation from family members of the fallen.
Hearing a presentation (from the Rabbi or community member)
about the significance of the transition from Yom HaZikaron to
Yom HaAtzma'ut.
Raising the flag to full mast for the singing of the national anthem,
"HaTikva."

After singing "HaTikva" and *Ani Ma'amin*, the congregation returns to the
synagogue for the evening prayer.   BL

אבל: יִתְבָּרֵךְ וְיִשְׁתַּבַּח וְיִתְפָּאַר
וְיִתְרוֹמַם וְיִתְנַשֵּׂא וְיִתְהַדָּר וְיִתְעַלֶּה וְיִתְהַלָּל
שְׁמֵהּ דְּקֻדְשָׁא בְּרִיךְ הוּא (קהל: בְּרִיךְ הוּא)
לְעֵלָּא מִן כָּל בִּרְכָתָא
וְשִׁירָתָא, תֻּשְׁבְּחָתָא וְנֶחֱמָתָא
דַּאֲמִירָן בְּעָלְמָא
וְאִמְרוּ אָמֵן. (קהל: אָמֵן)

יְהֵא שְׁלָמָא רַבָּא מִן שְׁמַיָּא
וְחַיִּים, עָלֵינוּ וְעַל כָּל יִשְׂרָאֵל
וְאִמְרוּ אָמֵן. (קהל: אָמֵן)

*Bow, take three steps back, as if taking leave of the Divine Presence,
then bow, first left, then right, then center, while saying:*

עֹשֶׂה שָׁלוֹם בִּמְרוֹמָיו
הוּא יַעֲשֶׂה שָׁלוֹם עָלֵינוּ וְעַל כָּל יִשְׂרָאֵל
וְאִמְרוּ אָמֵן. (קהל: אָמֵן)

For מעריב *of* יום ירושלים *turn to page 515.*

THE TRANSITION FROM YOM HAZIKARON TO YOM HAATZMA'UT

Some congregations gather in the synagogue hall following Minḥa in order
to mark the transition from Yom HaZikaron to Yom HaAtzma'ut by one or
more of the following customs:

Learning a tractate of Mishna and reciting psalms in memory
of the fallen.

Mentioning the names of fallen members of the community.

תפילת מעריב ליום העצמאות

MA'ARIV FOR YOM HAATZMA'UT

Ma'ariv for Yom HaAtzma'ut

In Israel and many communities outside Israel the following is said before Ma'ariv:

הֹדוּ Thank the LORD for He is good; His loving-kindness is for ever.   *Ps. 107*
Let those the LORD redeemed say this –
those He redeemed from the enemy's hand,
those He gathered from the lands,
from east and west, from north and south.
Some lost their way in desert wastelands,
finding no way to a city where they could live.
They were hungry and thirsty, and their spirit grew faint.
Then they cried out to the LORD in their trouble,
and He rescued them from their distress.
He led them by a straight path to a city where they could live.
> Let them thank the LORD for His loving-kindness
> and His wondrous deeds for humankind,
for He satisfies the thirsty and fills the hungry with good.

Some sat in darkness and the shadow of death,
cruelly bound in iron chains,
for they had rebelled against God's words
and despised the counsel of the Most High.
He humbled their hearts with hard labor;
they stumbled, and there was none to help.
Then they cried to the LORD in their trouble,
and He saved them from their distress.
He brought them out from darkness and the shadow of death
and broke open their chains.
> Let them thank the LORD for His loving-kindness
> and His wondrous deeds for humankind,
for He shattered gates of bronze and broke their iron bars.

Some were fools with sinful ways,
and suffered affliction because of their iniquities.
They found all food repulsive, and came close to the gates of death.

מעריב ליום העצמאות

In ארץ ישראל *and many communities in* חוץ לארץ *the following is said before* מעריב:

תהלים קז

הֹדוּ לַיהוה כִּי־טוֹב, כִּי לְעוֹלָם חַסְדּוֹ:

יֹאמְרוּ גְּאוּלֵי יהוה, אֲשֶׁר גְּאָלָם מִיַּד־צָר:

וּמֵאֲרָצוֹת קִבְּצָם, מִמִּזְרָח וּמִמַּעֲרָב, מִצָּפוֹן וּמִיָּם:

תָּעוּ בַמִּדְבָּר, בִּישִׁימוֹן דָּרֶךְ, עִיר מוֹשָׁב לֹא מָצָאוּ:

רְעֵבִים גַּם־צְמֵאִים, נַפְשָׁם בָּהֶם תִּתְעַטָּף:

וַיִּצְעֲקוּ אֶל־יהוה בַּצַּר לָהֶם, מִמְּצוּקוֹתֵיהֶם יַצִּילֵם:

וַיַּדְרִיכֵם בְּדֶרֶךְ יְשָׁרָה, לָלֶכֶת אֶל־עִיר מוֹשָׁב:

יוֹדוּ לַיהוה חַסְדּוֹ, וְנִפְלְאוֹתָיו לִבְנֵי אָדָם:

כִּי־הִשְׂבִּיעַ נֶפֶשׁ שֹׁקֵקָה, וְנֶפֶשׁ רְעֵבָה מִלֵּא־טוֹב:

יֹשְׁבֵי חֹשֶׁךְ וְצַלְמָוֶת, אֲסִירֵי עֳנִי וּבַרְזֶל:

כִּי־הִמְרוּ אִמְרֵי־אֵל, וַעֲצַת עֶלְיוֹן נָאָצוּ:

וַיַּכְנַע בֶּעָמָל לִבָּם, כָּשְׁלוּ וְאֵין עֹזֵר:

וַיִּזְעֲקוּ אֶל־יהוה בַּצַּר לָהֶם, מִמְּצוּקוֹתֵיהֶם יוֹשִׁיעֵם:

יוֹצִיאֵם מֵחֹשֶׁךְ וְצַלְמָוֶת, וּמוֹסְרוֹתֵיהֶם יְנַתֵּק:

יוֹדוּ לַיהוה חַסְדּוֹ, וְנִפְלְאוֹתָיו לִבְנֵי אָדָם:

כִּי־שִׁבַּר דַּלְתוֹת נְחֹשֶׁת, וּבְרִיחֵי בַרְזֶל גִּדֵּעַ:

אֱוִלִים מִדֶּרֶךְ פִּשְׁעָם, וּמֵעֲוֺנֹתֵיהֶם יִתְעַנּוּ:

כָּל־אֹכֶל תְּתַעֵב נַפְשָׁם, וַיַּגִּיעוּ עַד־שַׁעֲרֵי מָוֶת:

הֹדוּ *Psalm 107.* For commentary on this psalm see Rabbi Yoel Bin-Nun's essay on page 147 in the Essay section.

Then they cried to the Lord in their trouble,
and He saved them from their distress.
He sent His word and healed them;
He rescued them from their destruction.
> Let them thank the Lord for His loving-kindness
> and His wondrous deeds for humankind.
Let them sacrifice thanksgiving-offerings
and tell His deeds with songs of joy.

Those who go to sea in ships, plying their trade in the mighty waters,
have seen the works of the Lord, His wondrous deeds in the deep.
He spoke and stirred up a tempest that lifted high the waves.
They rose to the heavens and plunged down to the depths;
their souls melted in misery.
They reeled and staggered like drunkards; all their skill was to no avail.
Then they cried to the Lord in their trouble,
and He brought them out of their distress.
He stilled the storm to a whisper, and the waves of the sea grew calm.
They rejoiced when all was quiet,
then He guided them to their destination.
> Let them thank the Lord for His loving-kindness
> and His wondrous deeds for humankind.
Let them exalt Him in the assembly of the people
and praise Him in the council of the elders.

He turns rivers into a desert, springs of water into parched land,
fruitful land into a salt marsh,
because of the wickedness of its inhabitants.
He turns the desert into pools of water,
parched land into flowing springs;
He brings the hungry to live there,
they build themselves a town in which to live.

---

the highest happiness. And this is the State of Israel – the earthly foot of
God's throne. For all its desire is that God shall be One and His name One;
and this is in truth the very highest happiness.

(Rav A.I. Kook, *Orot HaKodesh* 3, "*Musar HaKodesh*," 136)

וַיִּזְעֲקוּ אֶל־יהוה בַּצַּר לָהֶם, מִמְּצֻקוֹתֵיהֶם יוֹשִׁיעֵם:

יִשְׁלַח דְּבָרוֹ וְיִרְפָּאֵם, וִימַלֵּט מִשְּׁחִיתוֹתָם:

יוֹדוּ לַיהוה חַסְדּוֹ, וְנִפְלְאוֹתָיו לִבְנֵי אָדָם:

וְיִזְבְּחוּ זִבְחֵי תוֹדָה וִיסַפְּרוּ מַעֲשָׂיו בְּרִנָּה:

יוֹרְדֵי הַיָּם בָּאֳנִיּוֹת, עֹשֵׂי מְלָאכָה בְּמַיִם רַבִּים:

הֵמָּה רָאוּ מַעֲשֵׂי יהוה, וְנִפְלְאוֹתָיו בִּמְצוּלָה:

וַיֹּאמֶר, וַיַּעֲמֵד רוּחַ סְעָרָה, וַתְּרוֹמֵם גַּלָּיו:

יַעֲלוּ שָׁמַיִם, יֵרְדוּ תְהוֹמוֹת, נַפְשָׁם בְּרָעָה תִתְמוֹגָג:

יָחוֹגּוּ וְיָנוּעוּ כַּשִּׁכּוֹר, וְכָל־חָכְמָתָם תִּתְבַּלָּע:

וַיִּצְעֲקוּ אֶל־יהוה בַּצַּר לָהֶם, וּמִמְּצוּקֹתֵיהֶם יוֹצִיאֵם:

יָקֵם סְעָרָה לִדְמָמָה, וַיֶּחֱשׁוּ גַּלֵּיהֶם:

וַיִּשְׂמְחוּ כִי־יִשְׁתֹּקוּ, וַיַּנְחֵם אֶל־מְחוֹז חֶפְצָם:

יוֹדוּ לַיהוה חַסְדּוֹ, וְנִפְלְאוֹתָיו לִבְנֵי אָדָם:

וִירֹמְמוּהוּ בִּקְהַל־עָם, וּבְמוֹשַׁב זְקֵנִים יְהַלְלוּהוּ:

יָשֵׂם נְהָרוֹת לְמִדְבָּר, וּמֹצָאֵי מַיִם לְצִמָּאוֹן:

אֶרֶץ פְּרִי לִמְלֵחָה, מֵרָעַת יוֹשְׁבֵי בָהּ:

יָשֵׂם מִדְבָּר לַאֲגַם־מַיִם, וְאֶרֶץ צִיָּה לְמֹצָאֵי מָיִם:

וַיּוֹשֶׁב שָׁם רְעֵבִים, וַיְכוֹנְנוּ עִיר מוֹשָׁב:

THE STATE OF ISRAEL – THE FOUNDATION OF GOD'S THRONE

"The state is not the highest happiness of man" – This may be said of any ordinary state, which does not rise to any higher value than that of a great Welfare State; which has many ideals, the crowning glory of humanity's being, hovering over it, never touching.

But this is not true of a state that is at its very foundation idealistic; that has engraved in its being the most elevated idealistic content, which is in truth the greatest happiness an individual can know. Such a state is in truth

They sow fields and plant vineyards that yield a fruitful harvest;
He blesses them, and they increase greatly, their herds do not decrease:

Though they had been few
and brought low by oppression, adversity and sorrow.
He pours contempt on nobles
and makes them wander in a pathless waste.
‣ He lifts the destitute from poverty
and enlarges their families like flocks.
The upright see and rejoice,
but the mouth of all wrongdoers is stopped.
Whoever is wise, let him lay these things to heart,
and reflect on the loving-kindness of the Lord.

יהוה מָלָךְ The Lord reigns, let the earth be glad.   *Ps. 97*
Let the many islands rejoice.
Clouds and thick darkness surround Him;
righteousness and justice are the foundation of His throne.
Fire goes ahead of Him, consuming His enemies on every side.
His lightning lights up the world; the earth sees and trembles.
Mountains melt like wax before the Lord,
before the Lord of all the earth.
The heavens proclaim His righteousness,
and all the peoples see His glory.
All who worship images and boast in idols are put to shame.
Bow down to Him, all you heavenly powers.
Zion hears and rejoices, and the towns of Judah are glad
because of Your judgments, Lord.
For You, Lord, are supreme over all the earth;
You are exalted far above all heavenly powers.
Let those who love the Lord hate evil,
for He protects the lives of His devoted ones,
delivering them from the hand of the wicked.
‣ Light is sown for the righteous, and joy for the upright in heart.
Rejoice in the Lord, you who are righteous,
and give thanks to His holy name.

וַיִּזְרְעוּ שָׂדוֹת, וַיִּטְּעוּ כְרָמִים, וַיַּעֲשׂוּ פְּרִי תְבוּאָה:

וַיְבָרְכֵם וַיִּרְבּוּ מְאֹד, וּבְהֶמְתָּם לֹא יַמְעִיט:

וַיִּמְעֲטוּ וַיָּשֹׁחוּ, מֵעֹצֶר רָעָה וְיָגוֹן:

שֹׁפֵךְ בּוּז עַל־נְדִיבִים, וַיַּתְעֵם בְּתֹהוּ לֹא־דָרֶךְ:

וַיְשַׂגֵּב אֶבְיוֹן מֵעוֹנִי, וַיָּשֶׂם כַּצֹּאן מִשְׁפָּחוֹת:

יִרְאוּ יְשָׁרִים וְיִשְׂמָחוּ, וְכָל־עַוְלָה קָפְצָה פִּיהָ:

מִי־חָכָם וְיִשְׁמָר־אֵלֶּה, וְיִתְבּוֹנְנוּ חַסְדֵי יהוה:

תהלים צו

יהוה מָלָךְ תָּגֵל הָאָרֶץ, יִשְׂמְחוּ אִיִּים רַבִּים:

עָנָן וַעֲרָפֶל סְבִיבָיו, צֶדֶק וּמִשְׁפָּט מְכוֹן כִּסְאוֹ:

אֵשׁ לְפָנָיו תֵּלֵךְ, וּתְלַהֵט סָבִיב צָרָיו:

הֵאִירוּ בְרָקָיו תֵּבֵל, רָאֲתָה וַתָּחֵל הָאָרֶץ:

הָרִים כַּדּוֹנַג נָמַסּוּ מִלִּפְנֵי יהוה, מִלִּפְנֵי אֲדוֹן כָּל־הָאָרֶץ:

הִגִּידוּ הַשָּׁמַיִם צִדְקוֹ, וְרָאוּ כָל־הָעַמִּים כְּבוֹדוֹ:

יֵבֹשׁוּ כָּל־עֹבְדֵי פֶסֶל הַמִּתְהַלְלִים בָּאֱלִילִים הִשְׁתַּחֲווּ־לוֹ כָּל־אֱלֹהִים:

שָׁמְעָה וַתִּשְׂמַח צִיּוֹן, וַתָּגֵלְנָה בְּנוֹת יְהוּדָה לְמַעַן מִשְׁפָּטֶיךָ יהוה:

כִּי־אַתָּה יהוה עֶלְיוֹן עַל־כָּל־הָאָרֶץ מְאֹד נַעֲלֵיתָ עַל־כָּל־אֱלֹהִים:

אֹהֲבֵי יהוה שִׂנְאוּ רָע, שֹׁמֵר נַפְשׁוֹת חֲסִידָיו מִיַּד רְשָׁעִים יַצִּילֵם:

אוֹר זָרֻעַ לַצַּדִּיק, וּלְיִשְׁרֵי־לֵב שִׂמְחָה:

שִׂמְחוּ צַדִּיקִים בַּיהוה, וְהוֹדוּ לְזֵכֶר קָדְשׁוֹ:

Each of the following verses is recited aloud by the Leader followed by the congregation.

מִזְמוֹר A Psalm. Sing a new song to the Lord,   Ps. 98
for He has done wondrous things;
He has saved by His right hand and His holy arm.
The Lord has made His salvation known;
He has displayed His righteousness in the sight of the nations.
He remembered His loving-kindness
and faithfulness to the house of Israel;
all the ends of the earth have seen the victory of our Lord.
Shout for joy to the Lord, all the earth;
burst into song, sing with joy, play music.
Play music to the Lord on the harp –
on the harp with the sound of singing.
With trumpets and the sound of the shofar,
shout for joy before the Lord, the King.
‣ Let the sea and all that is in it thunder,
the world and all who live in it.
Let the rivers clap their hands,
the mountains sing together for joy –
before the Lord, for He is coming to judge the earth.
He will judge the world with justice,
and the peoples with equity.

The same midrash cites an intriguing verse in Yirmiyahu which describes Israel with two phonetically similar terms which connote apparently different meanings. The Land of Israel is described as "*tzvi*" or enviable, and also "*tzivot goyim*" or the target of international armies. Presumably Yirmiyahu associates the historical armed presence in Israel to its being desirable and thus hotly contested throughout the centuries.

This condition certainly has persisted in modern times. Our country, and particularly our attempts to settle her, have attracted non-stop attention, disproportionate to her size and presumed influence. Our return has excited Messianic fervor in some, and violent opposition in others. Worldwide events appear to be influenced by local dynamics. The Land of Israel continues to function as *Afsei Aretz*.

תהלים צח

Each of the following verses is recited aloud by the שליח ציבור *followed by the* קהל.

מִזְמוֹר, שִׁירוּ לַיהוה שִׁיר חָדָשׁ, כִּי־נִפְלָאוֹת עָשָׂה
הוֹשִׁיעָה־לּוֹ יְמִינוֹ וּזְרוֹעַ קָדְשׁוֹ:
הוֹדִיעַ יהוה יְשׁוּעָתוֹ, לְעֵינֵי הַגּוֹיִם גִּלָּה צִדְקָתוֹ:
זָכַר חַסְדּוֹ וֶאֱמוּנָתוֹ לְבֵית יִשְׂרָאֵל
רָאוּ כָל־אַפְסֵי־אָרֶץ אֵת יְשׁוּעַת אֱלֹהֵינוּ:
הָרִיעוּ לַיהוה כָּל־הָאָרֶץ, פִּצְחוּ וְרַנְּנוּ וְזַמֵּרוּ:
זַמְּרוּ לַיהוה בְּכִנּוֹר, בְּכִנּוֹר וְקוֹל זִמְרָה:
בַּחֲצֹצְרוֹת וְקוֹל שׁוֹפָר, הָרִיעוּ לִפְנֵי הַמֶּלֶךְ יהוה:
יִרְעַם הַיָּם וּמְלֹאוֹ, תֵּבֵל וְיֹשְׁבֵי בָהּ:
נְהָרוֹת יִמְחֲאוּ־כָף, יַחַד הָרִים יְרַנֵּנוּ:
לִפְנֵי־יהוה כִּי בָא לִשְׁפֹּט הָאָרֶץ
יִשְׁפֹּט־תֵּבֵל בְּצֶדֶק, וְעַמִּים בְּמֵישָׁרִים:

___

אַפְסֵי־אָרֶץ *Ends of the earth.* The literal meaning of the term "*Afsei Aretz*" refers to the edges of the earth. The Divine Redemption will be so vast that the entire world will notice. The term "*Afsei Aretz*" first appears in the blessing delivered by Moshe to the tribe of Yosef. They are promised weaponry with which the entire land will be defeated. The Midrash asserts that Yosef is equipped with weaponry to assist in the Jewish conquest of the Land of Israel. Even though the "lone" country of Israel is being considered, the term *Afsei Aretz* is applied, as this small territory encompasses the edges of the earth. Though undersized, it occupies and attracts global interest and involvement. It may not be defined as *Afsei Aretz geographically,* but it does provide a global "stretch," historically and politically.

The Midrash describes that even in ancient times every nation sought representative presence in Israel. Recognizing its supernatural significance and unearthly beauty, every ancient monarch jostled to acquire a toehold in Israel. The long-running wars between at least nine local sovereigns – described in *Bereshit* 14 – highlight the pivotal role which Israel played in ancient times, and the disproportionate interest in this land.

It is customary to sing:

הִתְעוֹרְרִי Wake up, wake up,
For your light has come: rise, shine!
Awake, awake, break out in song,
For the LORD's glory is revealed on you.

This is the day the LORD has made;   *Ps. 118*
let us rejoice and be glad in it.

---

books of Jewish communities all over the world, despite an already well-established liturgy. This testifies to the power of this impressive poem, which operates both on the dimensions of *peshat* (the plain meaning of the text) and *sod* ("secret," that is, Kabbalistic meanings) simultaneously. It has become the most central prayer of *Kabbalat Shabbat*; a song that welcomes the Shabbat and the redemption of Zion into the hearts of those who sing it. *Lekha Dodi* marks the transition between the secular and the holy, accompanying the departing moments of the weekday and the arrival of the sanctity of Shabbat.   YR

כִּי בָא אוֹרֵךְ קוּמִי אוֹרִי *For your light has come: rise, shine!* The Holy One, blessed be He, said to Israel: As My light is yours, and your light is Mine – let us go and light up Zion together, as it says (Isaiah 60:1), "Rise, shine, for your light has come" (*Yalkut Shimoni*, Isaiah, 499).

Based on a prophecy of consolation in Isaiah (60:1), the word "rise" in this stanza expresses the idea of redemption, and is reminiscent of the word *aliya*, "ascension," used to describe our people's most recent return to Zion. The *Zohar* teaches that the people of Israel during Isaiah's time had fallen so low that only the redemptive God, "your Light," could raise them to their former glory.

Each line of this stanza is based on a different verse:

"Wake up, wake up, arise, Jerusalem" – Isaiah 51:17.
"Rise, shine, for your light has come,
     and the glory of the LORD rises upon you" – Isaiah 60:1.
"Awake, awake, Deborah, awake,
     awake, break out in song" – Judges 5:12.
"And the LORD's glory is revealed,
     and all flesh shall see it together" – Isaiah 40:5.

It is customary to sing:

הִתְעוֹרְרִי הִתְעוֹרְרִי

כִּי בָא אוֹרֵךְ קוּמִי אְוֹרִי

עְוּרִי עְוּרִי, שִׁיר דַּבֵּרִי

כְּבוֹד יהוה עָלַיִךְ נִגְלָה.

תהלים קיח

זֶה־הַיּוֹם עָשָׂה יהוה

נָגִילָה וְנִשְׂמְחָה בוֹ:

THE INCLUSION OF VERSES FROM LEKHA DODI

The stanzas from *Lekha Dodi* and the refrain "This is the day the LORD has made; let us rejoice and be glad in it" were selected by Rabbi Shaul Israeli and Rabbi M.Z. Neriya, who first proposed a dedicated prayer service for Yom HaAtzma'ut to the Chief Rabbinate of Israel. Their suggested service incorporated prayers from the liturgy of Shabbat, the Days of Awe, Ḥanukka, and the Pesaḥ Haggada. The Religious Affairs Committee of the Religious Kibbutz Movement objected to these selections on the basis that such prayers deny the unique spirit of Yom HaAtzma'ut; for example, *Lekha Dodi* is inherently connected to the spirit of Shabbat. Ultimately, the prayers of the current service were carefully chosen to express our acknowledgment that Yom HaAtzma'ut is only the beginning of the redemption process. We give thanks to God for the milestones we recognize on the path to redemption, as we continue to yearn for and anticipate the final redemption and the coming of the *Mashiaḥ*. As an example of the careful consideration given to what should be included in this service, Rabbi Shaul Israeli points out the deliberate decision not to institute new blessings for this service, in order to avoid the issues associated with saying God's name. (For a broader discussion of this topic, see Rabbi Shmuel Katz's essay on page 187 in the Essay section.)

YR

LEKHA DODI

This poem was written in the mid-sixteenth century by Rabbi Shlomo HaLevi Alkabetz of the Safed Kabbalists, and it was rapidly integrated into the prayer

לֹא תֵבְשִׁי Do not be ashamed, do not be confounded.
Why be downcast? Why do you mourn?
In you the needy of My people find shelter,
And the city shall be rebuilt on its hill.

This is the day the Lᴏʀᴅ has made;
let us rejoice and be glad in it.

יָמִין Right and left you shall spread out,
And God you will revere.
Through the descendant of Peretz,
We shall rejoice and we shall be glad.

This is the day the Lᴏʀᴅ has made;
let us rejoice and be glad in it.

The Leader and the congregation sing:
The Lᴏʀᴅ is my strength and my song;
He has become my salvation.
Sounds of song and salvation
resound in the tents of the righteous:
"The Lᴏʀᴅ's right hand has done mighty deeds.
The Lᴏʀᴅ's right hand is lifted high.
The Lᴏʀᴅ's right hand has done mighty deeds.

Ps. 118

Rabbi Aba Serungia said: "And light dwells with him," this is the king, the
Messiah, as it says: "Rise, shine, etc." (*Bereshit Raba*, Vilna ed. 1:6), "and
there was light" – the light of the future was already created during the six
days of creation, as it says, "Rise, shine" (ibid. 2:5).   YR

לֹא תֵבֹשִׁי וְלֹא תִכָּלְמִי

מַה תִּשְׁתּוֹחֲחִי וּמַה תֶּהֱמִי

בָּךְ יֶחֱסוּ עֲנִיֵּי עַמִּי

וְנִבְנְתָה עִיר עַל תִּלָּהּ.

זֶה־הַיּוֹם עָשָׂה יהוה

נָגִילָה וְנִשְׂמְחָה בוֹ:

יָמִין וּשְׂמֹאל תִּפְרֹצִי

וְאֶת יהוה תַּעֲרִיצִי

עַל יַד אִישׁ בֶּן פַּרְצִי

וְנִשְׂמְחָה וְנָגִילָה.

זֶה־הַיּוֹם עָשָׂה יהוה

נָגִילָה וְנִשְׂמְחָה בוֹ:

תהלים קיח

The שליח ציבור *and the* קהל *sing:*

קוֹל רִנָּה וִישׁוּעָה בְּאָהֳלֵי צַדִּיקִים

יְמִין יהוה עֹשָׂה חָיִל:

יְמִין יהוה רוֹמֵמָה

יְמִין יהוה עֹשָׂה חָיִל:

Each verse contributes to the unique quality of the stanza. The Midrash discusses these verses in the context of the future redemption, and interprets the word "light" as a metaphor for redemption:

Some say "who has given us life".

Blessed are You, LORD our God,
King of the Universe,
who has given us life, sustained us,
and brought us to this time.

---

it is said on all festivals, including Ḥanukka and Purim. He believes the *Sheheḥeyanu* blessing is an expression of joy, and therefore one who is not especially joyful on Yom HaAtzma'ut is permitted to recite *Sheheḥeyanu*, but not required to; whereas one who is joyful on the anniversary of Israel's reestablishment is required to recite *Sheheḥeyanu*. (See also Rabbi Ḥ.D. HaLevi's article, "Yom HaAtzma'ut: Its Significance and Laws," in his book *Religion and State*.)

5. Others have refuted this opinion, stating that *Sheheḥeyanu* should not be said on Yom HaAtzma'ut because the sages instituted the blessing for festivals on which it is forbidden to work, namely the Three Festivals, Rosh HaShana, and Yom Kippur. On Ḥanukka and Purim, when there is no prohibition to do work, the blessing is recited over the special mitzva of each festival: the lighting of the candles and reading the Megilla, respectively. Since on Yom HaAtzma'ut work is permitted and there is no unique mitzva associated with this day, reciting *Sheheḥeyanu*, according to this opinion, would not be appropriate.

6. If one wishes to honor the day and still adhere to the opinion above, one may wear a new item of clothing and recite *Sheheḥeyanu* over the clothing, whilst having the day in mind as well. A *Ḥazan* leading a congregation in prayer should bless *Sheheḥeyanu* on his new clothing before *Hallel*, so that the congregation can fulfill this mitzva by answering *Amen*.   BL

Some say שהחיינו.

בָּרוּךְ אַתָּה יהוה אֱלֹהֵינוּ מֶלֶךְ הָעוֹלָם
שֶׁהֶחֱיָנוּ וְקִיְּמָנוּ, וְהִגִּיעָנוּ לַזְּמַן הַזֶּה.

RECITING THE SHEHEḤEYANU BLESSING ON YOM HAATZMA'UT

1. The Talmud (*Eiruvin* 40b) teaches that reciting the *Sheheḥeyanu* blessing is not restricted to Kiddush or the Three Festivals. The blessing is
   also recited on Rosh HaShana and Yom Kippur because just like the
   Three Festivals, the Days of Awe also occur at a regular, fixed time
   every year.

2. Halakha prescribes that *Sheheḥeyanu* should also be said on rabbinically ordained festivals – on Ḥanukka and Purim. While the blessing
   on Ḥanukka is said in conjunction with candle lighting, and the blessing on Purim is said before the Megilla reading, Halakha has already
   permitted the reciting of this blessing at any time during the day (see
   the *Mishna Berura* 676; *Biur Halakha* and *Sha'ar HaTziyun*, 3).

3. The *Sheheḥeyanu* blessing is also considered an optional blessing. This
   explains the Talmudic passage (ibid.) that tells of an *Amora* who would
   recite *Sheheḥeyanu* as an optional blessing over seasonal vegetables.
   Based on this passage, the Rivash wrote a responsum (505) on reciting *Sheheḥeyanu* on the second day of Rosh HaShana: "Since [the
   second day] recurs at a regular time, it is renewed like a new veg-
   etable, and therefore [*Sheheḥeyanu*] is not considered a superfluous
   blessing."

4. The first Minister of Religious Affairs, Rabbi Y.L. Maimon asked
   Rabbi Meshulam Rath whether the blessing should be recited on
   Yom HaAtzma'ut, and his answer can be found in Rav Rath's book
   Kol Mevaser (part 1, 21). In his opinion, as Yom HaAtzma'ut is a day
   which marks Israel's salvation, it is fitting to bless *Sheheḥeyanu*, just as

Ma'ariv for Weekdays in the Yom Tov melody.

וְהוּא רַחוּם He is compassionate.

He forgives iniquity and does not destroy.

Repeatedly He suppresses His anger, not rousing His full wrath.

LORD, save! May the King, answer us on the day we call.

Ps. 78

Ps. 20

BLESSINGS OF THE SHEMA

*The Leader says the following, bowing at "Bless," standing straight
at "the LORD"; the congregation, followed by the Leader, responds,
bowing at "Bless," standing straight at "the LORD":*

Leader: # BLESS

the LORD, the blessed One.

Congregation: Bless the LORD, the blessed One,
for ever and all time.

Leader: Bless the LORD, the blessed One,
for ever and all time.

He begins to return, at which point the Temple Mount is miraculously and temporarily repositioned toward the north to spare Yaakov the effort of returning all the way to Yerushalayim.

Beyond the personal elements of Yaakov's prayer, he also prayed on behalf of Jewish history and, in particular, for the redemption from our final exile. As the third "Father" to pray, and as someone who prayed toward the end of the day, he is cast as praying for the Final Redemption at the end of history. The imagery of a ladder positioned on the ground, but towering towards the heavens with angels ascending and descending, merely affirms its eschatological symbolism.

In this context the sequence of Yaakov's initiating the process by starting back toward Yerushalayim – and God reciprocating by miraculously relocating the mountain – is figurative. Our final redemption – for which Yaakov

יום טוב *is said, in the* מעריב לחול *melody.*

וְהוּא רַחוּם, יְכַפֵּר עָוֹן וְלֹא־יַשְׁחִית
וְהִרְבָּה לְהָשִׁיב אַפּוֹ, וְלֹא־יָעִיר כָּל־חֲמָתוֹ:
יהוה הוֹשִׁיעָה, הַמֶּלֶךְ יַעֲנֵנוּ בְיוֹם־קָרְאֵנוּ:

קריאת שמע וברכותיה

The שליח ציבור *says the following, bowing at* בָּרְכוּ*, standing straight at* ה'*; the* קהל*, followed by the* שליח ציבור*, responds, bowing at* בָּרוּךְ*, standing straight at* ה':

ש״ץ: **בָּרְכוּ**

אֶת יהוה הַמְבֹרָךְ.

קהל: בָּרוּךְ יהוה הַמְבֹרָךְ לְעוֹלָם וָעֶד.

ש״ץ: בָּרוּךְ יהוה הַמְבֹרָךְ לְעוֹלָם וָעֶד.

PRAYER AND REDEMPTION

The Gemara (*Berakhot* 26b) attributes the three daily *Tefillot* to the original prayers offered by our forefathers. Avraham was the first to *daven* Shaḥarit, Yitzḥak the first to *daven* Minḥa, and Yaakov the first to *daven* Maariv – during his initial flight from his father's house, as narrated in the opening section of *Vayetzeh* (*Bereshit* 28:11).

The geography of this episode is confusing. The opening section portrays Yaakov as arriving in Ḥaran (in the north of Israel) while the ensuing section has him visiting the Temple Mount in Jerusalem, and then ultimately giving the name Beit El to his current location. To help synchronize these coordinates, Ḥazal describe him as initially traveling outside of Israel, only to remember that he has passed the Temple Mount and neglected to pray.

בָּרוּךְ Blessed are You, Lord our God, King of the Universe,
who by His word brings on evenings,
by His wisdom opens the gates of heaven,
with understanding makes time change and the seasons rotate,
and by His will
orders the stars in their constellations in the sky.
He creates day and night,
rolling away the light before the darkness,
and darkness before the light.
‣ He makes the day pass and brings on night,
distinguishing day from night:
the Lord of hosts is His name.
May the living and forever enduring God rule over us for all time.
Blessed are You, Lord,
who brings on evenings.

אַהֲבַת עוֹלָם With everlasting love
have You loved Your people, the house of Israel.
You have taught us Torah and commandments,
decrees and laws of justice.
Therefore, Lord our God, when we lie down and when we rise up
we will speak of Your decrees, rejoicing in the words of Your Torah
and Your commandments for ever.
‣ For they are our life and the length of our days;
on them will we meditate day and night.
May You never take away Your love from us.
Blessed are You, Lord,
who loves His people Israel.

---

return. Finally he sees an apparition which spurs his return. His delayed
return to Israel presages his children's struggle to return. In the days of Ezra,
most of the Jewish population didn't return. In our day we have yet to merit
a full return to our Land.

בָּרוּךְ אַתָּה יהוה אֱלֹהֵינוּ מֶלֶךְ הָעוֹלָם

אֲשֶׁר בִּדְבָרוֹ מַעֲרִיב עֲרָבִים

בְּחָכְמָה פּוֹתֵחַ שְׁעָרִים

וּבִתְבוּנָה מְשַׁנֶּה עִתִּים וּמַחֲלִיף אֶת הַזְּמַנִּים

וּמְסַדֵּר אֶת הַכּוֹכָבִים בְּמִשְׁמְרוֹתֵיהֶם בָּרָקִיעַ כִּרְצוֹנוֹ.

בּוֹרֵא יוֹם וָלָיְלָה

גּוֹלֵל אוֹר מִפְּנֵי חֹשֶׁךְ וְחֹשֶׁךְ מִפְּנֵי אוֹר

◦ וּמַעֲבִיר יוֹם וּמֵבִיא לָיְלָה

וּמַבְדִּיל בֵּין יוֹם וּבֵין לָיְלָה

יהוה צְבָאוֹת שְׁמוֹ.

אֵל חַי וְקַיָּם תָּמִיד, יִמְלֹךְ עָלֵינוּ לְעוֹלָם וָעֶד.

בָּרוּךְ אַתָּה יהוה, הַמַּעֲרִיב עֲרָבִים.

אַהֲבַת עוֹלָם בֵּית יִשְׂרָאֵל עַמְּךָ אָהָבְתָּ

תּוֹרָה וּמִצְוֹת, חֻקִּים וּמִשְׁפָּטִים, אוֹתָנוּ לִמַּדְתָּ

עַל כֵּן יהוה אֱלֹהֵינוּ בְּשָׁכְבֵנוּ וּבְקוּמֵנוּ נָשִׂיחַ בְּחֻקֶּיךָ

וְנִשְׂמַח בְּדִבְרֵי תוֹרָתֶךָ וּבְמִצְוֹתֶיךָ לְעוֹלָם וָעֶד

◦ כִּי הֵם חַיֵּינוּ וְאֹרֶךְ יָמֵינוּ, וּבָהֶם נֶהְגֶּה יוֹמָם וָלָיְלָה.

וְאַהֲבָתְךָ אַל תָּסִיר מִמֶּנּוּ לְעוֹלָמִים.

בָּרוּךְ אַתָּה יהוה, אוֹהֵב עַמּוֹ יִשְׂרָאֵל.

prayed during this episode – will also be a product of human initiative –
augmented by divine intercession.

Furthermore, Yaakov delays his return to Israel after an absence of twenty-
two years. Though he left with every intention of returning swiftly, the complications of family life as well as financial pressures appear to thwart his

The Shema must be said with intense concentration.
When not with a minyan, say:
God, faithful King!

The following verse should be said aloud, while covering the eyes with the right hand:

Listen, Israel: the LORD is our God, the LORD is One.

Deut. 6

Quietly: Blessed be the name of His glorious kingdom for ever and all time.

וְאָהַבְתָּ Love the LORD your God with all your heart, with all your *Deut. 6* soul, and with all your might. These words which I command you today shall be on your heart. Teach them repeatedly to your children, speaking of them when you sit at home and when you travel on the way, when you lie down and when you rise. Bind them as a sign on your hand, and they shall be an emblem between your eyes. Write them on the doorposts of your house and gates.

וְהָיָה If you indeed heed My commandments with which I charge *Deut. 11* you today, to love the LORD your God and worship Him with all your heart and with all your soul, I will give rain in your land in its season, the early and late rain; and you shall gather in your grain, wine and oil. I will give grass in your field for your cattle, and you shall eat and be satisfied. Be careful lest your heart be tempted and you go astray and worship other gods, bowing down to them. Then

---

even if a person *only* achieves these basics, he has led a religiously successful life and will enter the next world. Among these basics are reciting *Shema* and living in Israel.

Unfortunately Rabbi Meir was forced to depart from Israel with his *Rebbe* – Rabbi Akiva – in the aftermath of the waves of Roman persecutions which the Jews endured in the generation immediately after the destruction of the Temple. He also died outside of Israel, but had instructed that until his body was transported to Israel it be left on a beach so at least the same waters which lapped Israel could skim his body until its eventual burial.

The שמע *must be said with intense concentration.*

When not with a מנין, *say:*

אֵל מֶלֶךְ נֶאֱמָן

The following verse should be said aloud, while covering the eyes with the right hand:

דברים ו

שְׁמַע יִשְׂרָאֵל, יְהוָה אֱלֹהֵינוּ, יְהוָה ׀ אֶחָֽד:

Quietly

בָּרוּךְ שֵׁם כְּבוֹד מַלְכוּתוֹ לְעוֹלָם וָעֶד.

דברים ו

וְאָהַבְתָּ אֵת יְהוָה אֱלֹהֶיךָ, בְּכָל־לְבָבְךָ וּבְכָל־נַפְשְׁךָ וּבְכָל־מְאֹדֶֽךָ: וְהָיוּ הַדְּבָרִים הָאֵלֶּה, אֲשֶׁר אָנֹכִי מְצַוְּךָ הַיּוֹם, עַל־לְבָבֶךָ: וְשִׁנַּנְתָּם לְבָנֶיךָ וְדִבַּרְתָּ בָּם, בְּשִׁבְתְּךָ בְּבֵיתֶךָ וּבְלֶכְתְּךָ בַדֶּרֶךְ, וּֽבְשָׁכְבְּךָ וּבְקוּמֶֽךָ: וּקְשַׁרְתָּם לְאוֹת עַל־יָדֶךָ וְהָיוּ לְטֹטָפֹת בֵּין עֵינֶֽיךָ: וּכְתַבְתָּם עַל־מְזֻזוֹת בֵּיתֶךָ וּבִשְׁעָרֶֽיךָ:

דברים יא

וְהָיָה אִם־שָׁמֹעַ תִּשְׁמְעוּ אֶל־מִצְוֹתַי אֲשֶׁר אָנֹכִי מְצַוֶּה אֶתְכֶם הַיּוֹם, לְאַהֲבָה אֶת־יְהוָה אֱלֹהֵיכֶם וּלְעָבְדוֹ, בְּכָל־לְבַבְכֶם וּבְכָל־נַפְשְׁכֶם: וְנָתַתִּי מְטַר־אַרְצְכֶם בְּעִתּוֹ, יוֹרֶה וּמַלְקוֹשׁ, וְאָסַפְתָּ דְגָנֶךָ וְתִירֹשְׁךָ וְיִצְהָרֶךָ: וְנָתַתִּי עֵשֶׂב בְּשָׂדְךָ לִבְהֶמְתֶּךָ, וְאָכַלְתָּ וְשָׂבָֽעְתָּ: הִשָּׁמְרוּ לָכֶם פֶּן־יִפְתֶּה לְבַבְכֶם, וְסַרְתֶּם וַעֲבַדְתֶּם אֱלֹהִים אֲחֵרִים

_____

KERIAT SHEMA AND LIVING IN ISRAEL.

Rabbi Meir would comment: "Whoever lives permanently in the Land of Israel, eats only halakhically pure food, speaks *Lashon HaKodesh*, and recites *Keriat Shema* twice daily, is guaranteed to enter the next world" (*Yerushalmi Shabbat* 1:3). In this statement Rabbi Meir couples living in Israel with several other *basic* elements of a successful religious lifestyle. Undoubtedly a person should strive for more: he should strive to study more Torah rather than merely reciting *Keriat Shema* twice daily. Speaking *Lashon HaKodesh* and eating pure food are relatively easy challenges compared to more complex aspects of religious behavior. Rabbi Meir is merely establishing a baseline:

the LORD's anger will flare against you and He will close the heavens so that there will be no rain. The land will not yield its crops, and you will perish swiftly from the good land that the LORD is giving you. Therefore, set these, My words, on your heart and soul. Bind them as a sign on your hand, and they shall be an emblem between your eyes. Teach them to your children, speaking of them

---

reading] and by reading the language, Torah comprehension is [ultimately] improved."

A second halakhic application emerges from the laws of oaths, which typically must be pronounced while grasping a sacred item such as a *Sefer Torah*. The *Shulḥan Arukh* claims that any material written in Hebrew can substitute for a *Sefer Torah*, presumably because the language possesses inherent sanctity.

The *Shulḥan Arukh* (*Oraḥ Ḥayyim* 85:2) allows discussing non-Torah material in a washroom. Yet the *Mishna Berura* comments that some are careful not to speak in *Lashon HaKodesh at all* in a washroom – to preserve the sanctity of *Lashon HaKodesh*. These examples indicate that the halakhic system acknowledged the inherent sanctity of Hebrew, and shaped normative practice based on its holiness.

There is an intriguing debate as to why the language possesses holiness. In his comments to *Shemot* 30:13, the Ramban claims that it is a language in which HaKadosh Barukh Hu communicates with His prophets and delivers the Torah to His People. It is also the language in which the Divine names and attributes are expressed. Rashi (*Bereshit* 11:1) claims that *Lashon HaKodesh* was the original universal language before the diversification of language after the Tower of Bavel incident. Support for the metaphysical significance of Hebrew can be found in a Gemara in *Ḥagiga* (16a) which acknowledges that celestial angels speak in Hebrew. This position ascribes intrinsic importance and sanctity to the Hebrew language. By contrast, the Rambam (*Guide for the Perplexed* 3:8) claims that this language is holy simply because it allows idioms for sexual activities rather than direct references. This holiness would appear to be "*incidental*" rather than essential.

Tzefania (3:9) prophesied: "For at that time I will change the speech of the peoples to a pure speech, that all of them may call upon the name of Hashem and serve Him with one accord," leading the Midrash (*Tanḥuma Noaḥ* 19) to assert that in the Messianic Era the entire world will return to its universal language of *Lashon HaKodesh*.

וְהִשְׁתַּחֲוִיתֶם לָהֶם: וְחָרָה אַף־יְהוָה בָּכֶם, וְעָצַר אֶת־הַשָּׁמַיִם
וְלֹא־יִהְיֶה מָטָר, וְהָאֲדָמָה לֹא תִתֵּן אֶת־יְבוּלָהּ, וַאֲבַדְתֶּם מְהֵרָה
מֵעַל הָאָרֶץ הַטֹּבָה אֲשֶׁר יְהוָה נֹתֵן לָכֶם: וְשַׂמְתֶּם אֶת־דְּבָרַי
אֵלֶּה עַל־לְבַבְכֶם וְעַל־נַפְשְׁכֶם, וּקְשַׁרְתֶּם אֹתָם לְאוֹת עַל־יֶדְכֶם,
וְהָיוּ לְטוֹטָפֹת בֵּין עֵינֵיכֶם: וְלִמַּדְתֶּם אֹתָם אֶת־בְּנֵיכֶם לְדַבֵּר בָּם,

---

לְדַבֵּר בָּם *Speaking of them.* Our status as a "selected" nation expresses itself
through historical mission, national identity, and distinctive language. The
Midrash (*Mekhilta Parashat Bo*) says that the Jewish slaves in Egypt neglected
much of their cultural past, their monotheistic practices, and various other
rituals. However, they kept their language (among other basic mores), and
thereby maintained their core identity. In contrast, when the Jews were exiled to Babylonia after the destruction of the first Temple, evidently Hebrew
language usage faded. As a result, the book of Daniel which portrays that era
is written in the spoken language of the day – Aramaic.

Two interesting comments suggest that speaking Hebrew is actually considered a halakhic mitzva, and not just a cultural value. The second section of
Keriat Shema instructs us to teach our children to "speak *in it.*" Commenting
on this verse, Rashi describes the process of training children to study Torah:
When a child reaches the age of speech, teach him Torah and speak with
him in *Lashon HaKodesh.* Though this mandate is cited in various sources,
it is omitted from our version of the Talmud Bavli, and hence isn't cited in
mainstream halakhic works.

Commenting on a Mishna which cautions us to adhere to both taxing
and effortless mitzvot, the Rambam lists speaking in *Lashon HaKodesh* as an
undemanding mitzva. Evidently he categorized speaking in Hebrew as an
actual mitzva, and not merely a cultural convention.

Though mainstream halakhic works – such as those which list the 613
mitzvot – didn't incorporate speaking in Hebrew as a formal mitzva, the
value of *Lashon HaKodesh* is evident in three interesting halakhic applications. In *Oraḥ Ḥayyim* chapter 307, which discusses the laws of Shabbat, the *Shulḥan Arukh* bans reading empty stories on Shabbat (the application of this prohibition in modern contexts is highly debated). Yet
the Rema notes that books written in *Lashon HaKodesh* are permitted. As explained by one of the commentators to the *Shulḥan Arukh,*
"This language is inherently holy [and thereby appropriate for Shabbat

when you sit at home and when you travel on the way, when you lie down and when you rise. Write them on the doorposts of your house and gates, so that you and your children may live long in the land that the LORD swore to your ancestors to give them, for as long as the heavens are above the earth.

וַיֹּאמֶר The LORD spoke to Moses, saying: Speak to the Israelites *Num. 15* and tell them to make tassels on the corners of their garments for all generations. They shall attach to the tassel at each corner a thread of blue. This shall be your tassel, and you shall see it

---

The Torah describes the four corners of *tzitzit*-suitable clothing with the word "*kanaf.*" The same phrase appears in a messianic prophecy delivered by Zekharia about universal recognition of HaKadosh Barukh Hu in the Messianic Era. The concluding verses of the eighth chapter of the book portray worldwide pilgrimages to Yerushalayim to discover the word of God. The final verse depicts throngs of people "grasping on to the clothing of Jewish people," adhering to them upon acknowledging us as God's chosen: So said the LORD of hosts: "In those days it shall come to pass, that ten men shall take hold, out of all the languages of the nations, shall even take hold of the skirt of him that is a Jew, saying: 'We will go with you, for we have heard that God is with you.'" (*Zekharia* 8:23). Not only will the *city* of Yerushalayim serve as a magnet for those thirsting for divine instruction, but Jews as well will be actively pursued and associated with. The image of ten people clutching the clothing of a single Jew indicates the degree of desperation of those pursuing the word of God, but perhaps unable to identify it on their own. Wearing *tzitzit* – clothing so clearly identified as Jewish – accentuates this messianic role of extending the divine word to all of humanity.

The term *kanaf*, aside from meaning corner, more literally means "a wing." Consequently, Jews adorn themselves in *four* wings – in contrast to angels, who only possess two. The winged image of *tzitzit* suggests a rapid, airborne return to Israel as opposed to a slow, ground-based return. In fact, one of the more familiar verses describing ingathering from the four corners of the earth employs the very same word *kanaf* to describe quadrants of our planet – reinforcing both the redemptive metaphor of *tzitzit* as well as the suggestion of winged return. Yeshayahu also captures the aerial nature of our return to

בִּשְׁבְתְּךָ בְּבֵיתֶ֫ךָ וּבְלֶכְתְּךָ בַדֶּ֫רֶךְ, וּֽבְשָׁכְבְּךָ וּבְקוּמֶֽךָ: וּכְתַבְתָּ֛ם
עַל־מְזוּזֹ֥ות בֵּיתֶ֖ךָ וּבִשְׁעָרֶ֑יךָ: לְמַ֨עַן יִרְבּ֤וּ יְמֵיכֶם֙ וִימֵ֣י בְנֵיכֶ֔ם עַ֚ל
הָ֣אֲדָמָ֔ה אֲשֶׁ֨ר נִשְׁבַּ֤ע יְהֹוָה֙ לַאֲבֹ֣תֵיכֶ֔ם לָתֵ֖ת לָהֶ֑ם, כִּימֵ֥י הַשָּׁמַ֖יִם
עַל־הָאָֽרֶץ:

במדבר טו

וַיֹּ֥אמֶר יְהֹוָ֖ה אֶל־מֹשֶׁ֥ה לֵּאמֹֽר: דַּבֵּ֞ר אֶל־בְּנֵ֤י יִשְׂרָאֵל֙ וְאָמַרְתָּ֣
אֲלֵהֶ֔ם, וְעָשׂ֨וּ לָהֶ֥ם צִיצִ֛ת עַל־כַּנְפֵ֥י בִגְדֵיהֶ֖ם לְדֹרֹתָ֑ם, וְנָֽתְנ֛וּ עַל־
צִיצִ֥ת הַכָּנָ֖ף פְּתִ֥יל תְּכֵֽלֶת: וְהָיָ֣ה לָכֶם֮ לְצִיצִת֒, וּרְאִיתֶ֣ם אֹת֗ו

לָתֵת לָהֶם, כִּימֵי הַשָּׁמַיִם עַל־הָאָרֶץ *"To give them, for as long as the heavens are above the earth."* The Torah qualifies the Land of Israel as a "land which God swore to your fathers to *give them (latet lahem).*" Conceivably, as the Torah is addressing a nation about to enter the actual land, the oath should have been described as God swearing to our fathers to deliver the land to *you.* By concluding with the phrase "to give *them*" the verse implies that the forefathers themselves – the recipients of the oath – will one day receive the land. As they had already passed on, evidently they would one day be resurrected and receive the Land of Israel.

The Gemara (*Sanhedrin* 90a) lists this verse as one of the many veiled references to resurrection. Though resurrection constitutes a principle of faith, it isn't articulated explicitly. There are numerous intimations which confirm its importance. By embedding one of these references within the oath to deliver the Land of Israel to the Jewish people, the Torah reaffirms our historical license. The land was awarded to us because of the covenant with our fathers, and they themselves will one day arise to participate in our joint claim to this land. In several places the Gemara derives actual halakhot from the reality that *Eretz Yisrael* was already monetarily owned by the *Avot.* This reference to their ultimate resurrection affirms that they will also reside on this land in our joint future.

TZITZIT AND REDEMPTION
Though the primary symbolism of the *tzitzit* evokes awareness of mitzvot in general, several features conjure redemptive images.

and remember all of the LORD's commandments and keep them, not straying after your heart and after your eyes, following your own sinful desires. Thus you will be reminded to keep all My commandments, and be holy to your God. I am the LORD your God, who brought you out of the land of Egypt to be your God. I am the LORD your God.

True –

The Leader repeats:

▸ The LORD your God is true –

וֶאֱמוּנָה – and faithful is all this,
      and firmly established for us
      that He is the LORD our God,
      and there is none besides Him,
      and that we, Israel, are His people.
      He is our King, who redeems us from the hand of kings
      and delivers us from the grasp of all tyrants.
      He is our God,
      who on our behalf repays our foes
      and brings just retribution on our mortal enemies;
      who performs great deeds beyond understanding
      and wonders beyond number;
      who kept us alive, not letting our foot slip;   *Ps. 66*

---

flights home. Indeed, it was the dove that, at the conclusion of the biblical flood, indicated to the whole of creation that it was time to return "home."

    Finally, the recent rediscovery of *tekhelet* – the blue dye associated with *tzitzit* – has profoundly enhanced the performance of this mitzva, and contributed to the redemptive process. The Ḥafetz Ḥayyim – who authored a well-known article about the redemptive era entitled "*Ikvita DiMeshiḥa*" (the footprints of the Messiah) – wrote that the Jews who will witness the end of history will be particularly committed to the mitzva of *tzitzit*. Our ability to fulfill the mitzva in its original, enhanced form indicates our progression toward the close of history.

וּזְכַרְתֶּם אֶת־כָּל־מִצְוֹת יהוה וַעֲשִׂיתֶם אֹתָם, וְלֹא תָתֻוּרוּ אַחֲרֵי לְבַבְכֶם וְאַחֲרֵי עֵינֵיכֶם, אֲשֶׁר־אַתֶּם זֹנִים אַחֲרֵיהֶם: לְמַעַן תִּזְכְּרוּ וַעֲשִׂיתֶם אֶת־כָּל־מִצְוֹתָי, וִהְיִיתֶם קְדֹשִׁים לֵאלֹהֵיכֶם: אֲנִי יהוה אֱלֹהֵיכֶם, אֲשֶׁר הוֹצֵאתִי אֶתְכֶם מֵאֶרֶץ מִצְרַיִם, לִהְיוֹת לָכֶם לֵאלֹהִים, אֲנִי יהוה אֱלֹהֵיכֶם:

אֱמֶת

The שליח ציבור repeats:

‹ יהוה אֱלֹהֵיכֶם אֱמֶת

וֶאֱמוּנָה כָּל זֹאת וְקַיָּם עָלֵינוּ
כִּי הוּא יהוה אֱלֹהֵינוּ וְאֵין זוּלָתוֹ
וַאֲנַחְנוּ יִשְׂרָאֵל עַמּוֹ.
הַפּוֹדֵנוּ מִיַּד מְלָכִים
מַלְכֵּנוּ הַגּוֹאֲלֵנוּ מִכַּף כָּל הֶעָרִיצִים.
הָאֵל הַנִּפְרָע לָנוּ מִצָּרֵינוּ
וְהַמְשַׁלֵּם גְּמוּל לְכָל אֹיְבֵי נַפְשֵׁנוּ.
הָעוֹשֶׂה גְדוֹלוֹת עַד אֵין חֵקֶר, וְנִפְלָאוֹת עַד אֵין מִסְפָּר
הַשָּׂם נַפְשֵׁנוּ בַּחַיִּים, וְלֹא־נָתַן לַמּוֹט רַגְלֵנוּ:

תהלים סו

Israel, by comparing our arrival to floating clouds and soaring birds: "Who are these that fly as a cloud, and as the doves to their cotes?" (*Yeshayahu* 60:8).

Mass immigration to Israel surged in the second half of the past century, as civilian air flight became common. The availability of air travel facilitated more rapid and efficient relocation, and has also enabled Jews who have not yet emigrated to be frequent visitors. The concluding imagery of the aforementioned verse in *Yeshayahu* describes doves returning to their nests; doves are often involved in frequent patterns of repeated excursions and return

who led us on the high places of our enemies,
raising our pride above all our foes;
who did miracles for us
and brought vengeance against Pharaoh;
who performed signs and wonders
in the land of Ham's children;
who smote in His wrath all the firstborn of Egypt,
and brought out His people Israel from their midst
into everlasting freedom;
who led His children through the divided Reed Sea,
plunging their pursuers and enemies into the depths.
When His children saw His might,
they gave praise and thanks to His name,
‣ and willingly accepted His Sovereignty.
Moses and the children of Israel
then sang a song to You with great joy,
and they all exclaimed:

מִי־כָמֹכָה "Who is like You, LORD, among the mighty?   *Ex. 15*
Who is like You, majestic in holiness,
awesome in praises, doing wonders?"

‣ Your children beheld Your majesty
as You parted the sea before Moses.
"This is my God!" they responded,
and then said:

"The LORD shall reign for ever and ever."   *Ex. 15*

---

the process is fundamentally sound but currently inadvisable. Evidently there
will be a period of history in which human initiative will be appropriate. One
of the signs of the Messianic Era suggested by the Gemara (*Sota* 49b) is the
preponderance of audacity. This impudence will be apt and will prove invalu-
able to press toward our redemption." In general, Hasidic writing endorsed
the notion of "appropriate human audacity" when petitioning on behalf of
national needs, and on behalf of redemption in particular.

הַמַּדְרִיכֵנוּ עַל בָּמוֹת אוֹיְבֵינוּ

וַיָּרֶם קַרְנֵנוּ עַל כָּל שׂוֹנְאֵינוּ.

הָעוֹשֶׂה לָנוּ נִסִּים וּנְקָמָה בְּפַרְעֹה

אוֹתוֹת וּמוֹפְתִים בְּאַדְמַת בְּנֵי חָם.

הַמַּכֶּה בְעֶבְרָתוֹ כָּל בְּכוֹרֵי מִצְרָיִם

וַיּוֹצֵא אֶת עַמּוֹ יִשְׂרָאֵל מִתּוֹכָם לְחֵרוּת עוֹלָם.

הַמַּעֲבִיר בָּנָיו בֵּין גִּזְרֵי יַם סוּף

אֶת רוֹדְפֵיהֶם וְאֶת שׂוֹנְאֵיהֶם בִּתְהוֹמוֹת טִבַּע

וְרָאוּ בָנָיו גְּבוּרָתוֹ, שִׁבְּחוּ וְהוֹדוּ לִשְׁמוֹ

‹ וּמַלְכוּתוֹ בְּרָצוֹן קִבְּלוּ עֲלֵיהֶם.

מֹשֶׁה וּבְנֵי יִשְׂרָאֵל, לְךָ עָנוּ שִׁירָה בְּשִׂמְחָה רַבָּה

וְאָמְרוּ כֻלָּם

שמות טו

מִי־כָמֹכָה בָּאֵלִם יהוה

מִי כָּמֹכָה נֶאְדָּר בַּקֹּדֶשׁ

נוֹרָא תְהִלֹּת עֹשֵׂה פֶלֶא:

‹ מַלְכוּתְךָ רָאוּ בָנֶיךָ, בּוֹקֵעַ יָם לִפְנֵי מֹשֶׁה

זֶה אֵלִי עָנוּ, וְאָמְרוּ

שמות טו

יהוה יִמְלֹךְ לְעֹלָם וָעֶד:

REDEMPTION THROUGH JEWISH ACTIVISM

Often the biblical story of the *Ma'apilim* is cited as evidence *against* advancing the resettling of Israel through natural means. After the debacle of the spies, a band of Jews attempted an unsanctioned entry into Israel. Their efforts were met with blistering defeat. Moshe himself forewarned them, "Why are you disobeying the LORD's command? This will not succeed" (*Bemidbar* 14:41). Commenting upon Moshe's admonition Rabbi Tzaddok HaKohen of Lublin, one of the great Hasidic Masters, writes: "Moshe's comments indicate that

▸ And it is said,

> "For the LORD has redeemed Jacob
> and rescued him from a power stronger than his own."

Jer. 31

Blessed are You, LORD, who redeemed Israel.

---

the pursuit by his murderous brother, he was particularly vexed about the prospect of departing the Land. When he embeds in his *Tefilla* the dream of "I will return to my father's house and the LORD will once again be my God," he is praying for his return to the Land. The Tosefta (*Avoda Zara* 5:2) questions the inclusion of the hope that "The LORD will once again be my God" in his prayer. The Tosefta comments that life in the Diaspora is equivalent to a weakened encounter with God. Yaakov is the first to recognize the theological *fading* of the divine encounter while in *Ḥutz LaAretz*, and he prays for its eventual restoration when he will one day return (see also the *Zohar* to *Vayetzeh* 1:150 page 2).

In fact when he does ultimately return, he is frightened by the upcoming confrontation with his heavily armed brother. The Midrash (*Bereshit Raba* 76:2) highlights that he fretted that his brother would triumph based on his having resided in Israel during the intervening years of Yaakov's absence. Though Yaakov accrued many merits during his sojourn in Lavan's homestead, he did not amass the elusive but potentially convincing merit of residence in the Land of Israel.

PREFACING *TEFILLA* WITH *GEULA*

The Gemara (*Berakhot* 4b) stresses the importance of introducing *Tefilla* with imagery of redemption: Whoever prefaces *geula* to *Tefilla* is assured entry in the afterlife. Based on this directive we introduce *Shemoneh Esreh* – both morning and evening – by both citing features of our initial redemption, and praying for future salvation.

There are several benefits to this sequencing:

1. Setting a Blissful Mood for *Tefilla*: The Gemara suggests that *Tefilla* should be engaged in with happiness and hopefulness rather than depression or gloominess. One way to induce confident optimism is to invoke memories of our redemptive past. Even when Jews faced incalculable national adversity or overwhelming personal travail they could look to their past glory and take consolation in a national salvation

‹ וְנֶאֱמַר
כִּי־פָדָה יהוה אֶת־יַעֲקֹב
וּגְאָלוֹ מִיַּד חָזָק מִמֶּנּוּ:
בָּרוּךְ אַתָּה יהוה, גָּאַל יִשְׂרָאֵל.

THE "END OF THE DAY"

Zekharia asserts "It will be a unique day – a day known only to the LORD – with no distinction between day and night. When evening comes, there will be light" (14:7). This imagery describing sudden light at the conclusion of the day or evening resonates with redemptive imagery. It indicates a redemptive process which is delayed until the latter stages of history. David writes, "My days are like the evening shadow; I wither away like grass" (*Tehillim* 102:11). The similar images of lives shrouded in shadows convey a sense of redemption deferred until the latter stages of a day – when the shadows are long.

Conventionally each of our three *Tefillot* is associated with a different one of the three *Avot* and a different redemption respectively.

Avraham instituted Shaḥarit, and this *tefilla* elaborates upon the first redemption from Egypt. Particularly the sections immediately after *Keriat Shema* expound upon the liberation from Egypt.

Yitzḥak was the first to introduce Minḥa, and his career is often associated with the return from Bavel. Minḥa doesn't contain unique liturgy, and hence includes no direct reference to the return from Bavel.

In his legendary dream of the heavenly ladder, Yaakov witnessed both the extended exile as well as the ultimate redemption. His establishment of Maariv, offered in the dark precincts of Yerushalayim, symbolizes the redemption which will occur at one of the darkest periods of history. The section after *Keriat Shema* primarily discusses our future Messianic victories. The final section prays for a divine protective dome extended over Yerushalayim.

וְנֶאֱמַר, כִּי־פָדָה יהוה אֶת־יַעֲקֹב, וּגְאָלוֹ מִיַּד חָזָק מִמֶּנּוּ *And it is said, For the* LORD *has redeemed Jacob and rescued him from a power stronger than his own.* Before departing the Land of Israel for the first time, Yaakov dreams of a ladder lodged on the ground and scaling the heavens. When he awakens he erects a *matzeva*, monument, prays about his future, and pledges to return and offer a gift to God. Though he was frightened by his general uncertainty and

הַשְׁכִּיבֵנוּ Help us lie down, O Lᴏʀᴅ our God, in peace,
and rise up, O our King, to life.
Spread over us Your canopy of peace.
Direct us with Your good counsel,
and save us for the sake of Your name.

---

inadequacy in shaping history, and reinforce our reliance on divine intervention. Humbled by the force of Divine Providence, we submit to His wisdom. To establish the tone of submission, we introduce our *Tefillot* with imagery of past intervention and dreams of historic intercession in the future.

3. Establishing a Baseline of Faith: Prayer to God presupposes a belief that He listens and alters His decisions based on human petitioning. Prefacing prayer with faith fortifies our belief and allows prayer to evolve. King David is thankful that "He has caused His wonderful works to be remembered; God is gracious and compassionate" (*Tehillim* 111:4). He is grateful that we possess "festival days" to commemorate past miracles, because these experiences bolster our faith. Revisiting past miracles consolidates our belief in a God who actively intervenes in history on our behalf.

   In particular, remembering past redemptions reminds us that our prayers can actively *effect geula* and likewise "persuade" HaKadosh Barukh Hu to accede to our personal prayers.

4. Rav Soloveitchik addressed the ennobling impact of geula as a preface to *Tefilla*. Stripped of any context, *Tefilla* can develop into an egotistical or self-centered experience. Standing in the presence of God and lodging parochial requests can become petty and even trivial. In the larger cosmic scheme, personal needs are dwarfed in importance by "loftier" necessities. To ensure the "purity" of *Tefilla* it is encased in a larger national narrative of *geula*. Before standing before HaKadosh Barukh Hu proposing personal wants, a Jew attaches to the larger story of Jewish history and redemption, and casts his own experience within that broader storyline. Personal requests are necessary to help advance a wider national endpoint. *Tefilla*, in this context, has become ennobled, and cleansed of narcissism or self-interest.

הַשְׁכִּיבֵנוּ יהוה אֱלֹהֵינוּ לְשָׁלוֹם
וְהַעֲמִידֵנוּ מַלְכֵּנוּ לְחַיִּים
וּפְרֹשׂ עָלֵינוּ סֻכַּת שְׁלוֹמֶךָ, וְתַקְּנֵנוּ בְּעֵצָה טוֹבָה מִלְּפָנֶיךָ
וְהוֹשִׁיעֵנוּ לְמַעַן שְׁמֶךָ.

---

soon to be granted. This historical journey allowed enthusiastic *Tefilla* even in the face of hardship.

2. Enabling *Tefilla* of Submission: *Tefilla* is referred to as "*Avoda ShebaLev*" (emotional exertion), and like an actual *korban* (sacrifice) includes human submission to the divine will. Submission forms the basis of *Tefilla*, as a person surrenders his hopes and prayers to divine authority. When entering the *Mikdash*, King David acknowledges (*Tehillim* 5:8): "But I can enter Your house because of Your great kindness, I will bow down toward Your holy Temple in reverence for You," declaring his obedience and punctuating it by fully prostrating himself. Without embracing divine authority and recognizing HaKadosh Barukh Hu as solely empowered to consider and grant our *Tefillot*, the process of prayer is futile.

Submission is also necessary after prayer. The Gemara (*Berakhot* 32b) speaks critically of someone who prays protractedly and scrutinizes his *Tefillot*. Rashi comments that he is scrutinizing his requests, and confidently expects a favorable response. God doesn't always respond to our prayers in the manner we long for, or in a manner we can easily understand. Submitting to the divine wisdom and accepting His answers should also influence our behavior as we conclude *Tefilla*.

Since submission is indispensable to *Tefilla*, we begin our prayers by revisiting the source of this experience. By unilaterally freeing us from a house of slavery, HaKadosh Barukh Hu acquired us as His people, and established the right and ability to impose His will upon us. Numerous mitzvot are suffixed by the phrase "I am your God who extracted you from Egypt," reminding us of the historical mandate underlying His authority and our expected submission. Additionally, redemptive moments – apocalyptic in nature – remind us of human

Shield us and remove from us every enemy,
plague, sword, famine and sorrow.
Remove the adversary from before and behind us.
Shelter us in the shadow of Your wings,
for You, God, are our Guardian and Deliverer;
You, God, are a gracious and compassionate King.

▸ Guard our going out and our coming in,
for life and peace, from now and for ever.
Blessed are You, LORD,
who guards His people Israel for ever.

In Israel the service continues with Half Kaddish on page 78.

בָּרוּךְ Blessed be the LORD for ever. Amen and Amen.   *Ps. 89*
Blessed from Zion be the LORD   *Ps. 135*
who dwells in Jerusalem. Halleluya!
Blessed be the LORD, God of Israel,   *Ps. 72*
who alone does wondrous things.
Blessed be His glorious name for ever,
and may the whole earth be filled with His glory. Amen and Amen.
May the glory of the LORD endure for ever;   *Ps. 104*
may the LORD rejoice in His works.
May the name of the LORD be blessed now and for all time.   *Ps. 113*
For the sake of His great name   *1 Sam. 12*
the LORD will not abandon His people,
for the LORD vowed to make you a people of His own.
When all the people saw [God's wonders]   *1 Kings 18*
they fell on their faces
and said: "The LORD, He is God; the LORD, He is God."
Then the LORD shall be King over all the earth;   *Zech. 14*
on that day the LORD shall be One and His name One.
May Your love, LORD, be upon us,   *Ps. 33*
as we have put our hope in You.

וְהָגֵן בַּעֲדֵנוּ, וְהָסֵר מֵעָלֵינוּ אוֹיֵב, דֶּבֶר וְחֶרֶב וְרָעָב וְיָגוֹן

וְהָסֵר שָׂטָן מִלְּפָנֵינוּ וּמֵאַחֲרֵינוּ

וּבְצֵל כְּנָפֶיךָ תַּסְתִּירֵנוּ

כִּי אֵל שׁוֹמְרֵנוּ וּמַצִּילֵנוּ אָתָּה

כִּי אֵל מֶלֶךְ חַנּוּן וְרַחוּם אָתָּה.

‹ וּשְׁמֹר צֵאתֵנוּ וּבוֹאֵנוּ לְחַיִּים וּלְשָׁלוֹם

מֵעַתָּה וְעַד עוֹלָם.

בָּרוּךְ אַתָּה יהוה, שׁוֹמֵר עַמּוֹ יִשְׂרָאֵל לָעַד.

In ארץ ישראל the service continues with חצי קדיש on page 79.

תהלים פט	בָּרוּךְ יהוה לְעוֹלָם, אָמֵן וְאָמֵן:
תהלים קלה	בָּרוּךְ יהוה מִצִּיּוֹן, שֹׁכֵן יְרוּשָׁלָיִם, הַלְלוּיָהּ:
תהלים עב	בָּרוּךְ יהוה אֱלֹהִים אֱלֹהֵי יִשְׂרָאֵל, עֹשֵׂה נִפְלָאוֹת לְבַדּוֹ:
	וּבָרוּךְ שֵׁם כְּבוֹדוֹ לְעוֹלָם
	וְיִמָּלֵא כְבוֹדוֹ אֶת־כָּל־הָאָרֶץ, אָמֵן וְאָמֵן:
תהלים קד	יְהִי כְבוֹד יהוה לְעוֹלָם, יִשְׂמַח יהוה בְּמַעֲשָׂיו:
תהלים קיג	יְהִי שֵׁם יהוה מְבֹרָךְ מֵעַתָּה וְעַד־עוֹלָם:
שמואל א, יב	כִּי לֹא־יִטֹּשׁ יהוה אֶת־עַמּוֹ בַּעֲבוּר שְׁמוֹ הַגָּדוֹל
	כִּי הוֹאִיל יהוה לַעֲשׂוֹת אֶתְכֶם לוֹ לְעָם:
מלכים א, יח	וַיַּרְא כָּל־הָעָם וַיִּפְּלוּ עַל־פְּנֵיהֶם:
	וַיֹּאמְרוּ, יהוה הוּא הָאֱלֹהִים, יהוה הוּא הָאֱלֹהִים:
זכריה יד	וְהָיָה יהוה לְמֶלֶךְ עַל־כָּל־הָאָרֶץ
	בַּיּוֹם הַהוּא יִהְיֶה יהוה אֶחָד וּשְׁמוֹ אֶחָד:
תהלים לג	יְהִי־חַסְדְּךָ יהוה עָלֵינוּ, כַּאֲשֶׁר יִחַלְנוּ לָךְ:

Save us, Lord our God, gather us

and deliver us from the nations,

to thank Your holy name, and glory in Your praise.

All the nations You made shall come and bow before You, Lord,

and pay honor to Your name,

for You are great and You perform wonders:

You alone are God.

We, Your people, the flock of Your pasture, will praise You for ever.

For all generations we will relate Your praise.

Ps. 106

Ps. 86

Ps. 79

בָּרוּךְ Blessed is the Lord by day, blessed is the Lord by night.

Blessed is the Lord when we lie down;

blessed is the Lord when we rise.

For in Your hand are the souls of the living and the dead,

[as it is written:] "In His hand is every living soul,

and the breath of all mankind."

Into Your hand I entrust my spirit:

You redeemed me, Lord, God of truth.

Our God in heaven, bring unity to Your name,

establish Your kingdom constantly

and reign over us for ever and all time.

Job 12

Ps. 31

יִרְאוּ May our eyes see, our hearts rejoice,

and our souls be glad in Your true salvation,

when Zion is told, "Your God reigns."

The Lord is King, the Lord was King,

the Lord will be King for ever and all time.

‣ For sovereignty is Yours,

and to all eternity You will reign in glory,

for we have no king but You.

Blessed are You, Lord,

the King who in His constant glory will reign over us

and all His creation for ever and all time.

תהלים קו
הוֹשִׁיעֵנוּ יהוה אֱלֹהֵינוּ, וְקַבְּצֵנוּ מִן־הַגּוֹיִם
לְהֹדוֹת לְשֵׁם קָדְשֶׁךָ, לְהִשְׁתַּבֵּחַ בִּתְהִלָּתֶךָ:

תהלים פו
כָּל־גּוֹיִם אֲשֶׁר עָשִׂיתָ, יָבְוֹאוּ וְיִשְׁתַּחֲווּ לְפָנֶיךָ, אֲדֹנָי
וִיכַבְּדוּ לִשְׁמֶךָ:
כִּי־גָדוֹל אַתָּה וְעֹשֵׂה נִפְלָאוֹת, אַתָּה אֱלֹהִים לְבַדֶּךָ:

תהלים עט
וַאֲנַחְנוּ עַמְּךָ וְצֹאן מַרְעִיתֶךָ, נוֹדֶה לְּךָ לְעוֹלָם
לְדוֹר וָדֹר נְסַפֵּר תְּהִלָּתֶךָ:

בָּרוּךְ יהוה בַּיּוֹם, בָּרוּךְ יהוה בַּלָּיְלָה
בָּרוּךְ יהוה בְּשָׁכְבֵנוּ, בָּרוּךְ יהוה בְּקוּמֵנוּ.
כִּי בְיָדְךָ נַפְשׁוֹת הַחַיִּים וְהַמֵּתִים.

איוב יב
אֲשֶׁר בְּיָדוֹ נֶפֶשׁ כָּל־חָי, וְרוּחַ כָּל־בְּשַׂר־אִישׁ:

תהלים לא
בְּיָדְךָ אַפְקִיד רוּחִי, פָּדִיתָה אוֹתִי יהוה אֵל אֱמֶת:
אֱלֹהֵינוּ שֶׁבַּשָּׁמַיִם, יַחֵד שִׁמְךָ וְקַיֵּם מַלְכוּתְךָ תָּמִיד
וּמְלֹךְ עָלֵינוּ לְעוֹלָם וָעֶד.

יִרְאוּ עֵינֵינוּ וְיִשְׂמַח לִבֵּנוּ
וְתָגֵל נַפְשֵׁנוּ בִּישׁוּעָתְךָ בֶּאֱמֶת
בֶּאֱמֹר לְצִיּוֹן מָלַךְ אֱלֹהָיִךְ.
יהוה מֶלֶךְ, יהוה מָלָךְ, יהוה יִמְלֹךְ לְעֹלָם וָעֶד.
‹ כִּי הַמַּלְכוּת שֶׁלְּךָ הִיא, וּלְעוֹלְמֵי עַד תִּמְלֹךְ בְּכָבוֹד
כִּי אֵין לָנוּ מֶלֶךְ אֶלָּא אָתָּה.
בָּרוּךְ אַתָּה יהוה
הַמֶּלֶךְ בִּכְבוֹדוֹ תָּמִיד, יִמְלֹךְ עָלֵינוּ לְעוֹלָם וָעֶד
וְעַל כָּל מַעֲשָׂיו.

HALF KADDISH

Leader: יִתְגַּדַּל Magnified and sanctified
may His great name be,
in the world He created by His will.
May He establish His kingdom
in your lifetime and in your days,
and in the lifetime of all the house of Israel,
swiftly and soon –
and say: Amen.

All: May His great name be blessed for ever and all time.

Leader: Blessed and praised, glorified and exalted,
raised and honored, uplifted and lauded
be the name of the Holy One,
blessed be He,
beyond any blessing,
song, praise and consolation
uttered in the world –
and say: Amen.

THE AMIDA

*The following prayer, until "in former years" on page 98, is said silently, standing with feet
together. Take three steps forward and at the points indicated by ּ, bend the knees at
the first word, bow at the second, and stand straight before saying God's name.*

O Lord, open my lips,   *Ps. 51*
so that my mouth may declare Your praise.

PATRIARCHS

בָּרוּךְּ Blessed are You, Lord our God and God of our fathers,
God of Abraham, God of Isaac and God of Jacob;
the great, mighty and awesome God, God Most High,
who bestows acts of loving-kindness and creates all,

חצי קדיש

ש״ץ: יִתְגַּדַּל וְיִתְקַדַּשׁ שְׁמֵהּ רַבָּא (קהל: אָמֵן)

בְּעָלְמָא דִּי בְרָא כִרְעוּתֵהּ

וְיַמְלִיךְ מַלְכוּתֵהּ

בְּחַיֵּיכוֹן וּבְיוֹמֵיכוֹן וּבְחַיֵּי דְכָל בֵּית יִשְׂרָאֵל

בַּעֲגָלָא וּבִזְמַן קָרִיב

וְאִמְרוּ אָמֵן. (קהל: אָמֵן)

קהל
וש״ץ: יְהֵא שְׁמֵהּ רַבָּא מְבָרַךְ לְעָלַם וּלְעָלְמֵי עָלְמַיָּא.

ש״ץ: יִתְבָּרַךְ וְיִשְׁתַּבַּח וְיִתְפָּאַר וְיִתְרוֹמַם וְיִתְנַשֵּׂא

וְיִתְהַדָּר וְיִתְעַלֶּה וְיִתְהַלָּל

שְׁמֵהּ דְּקֻדְשָׁא בְּרִיךְ הוּא (קהל: בְּרִיךְ הוּא)

לְעֵלָּא מִן כָּל בִּרְכָתָא וְשִׁירָתָא, תֻּשְׁבְּחָתָא וְנֶחֱמָתָא

דַּאֲמִירָן בְּעָלְמָא

וְאִמְרוּ אָמֵן. (קהל: אָמֵן)

עמידה

The following prayer, until קְדֻשָּׁה on page 99, is said silently, standing with feet together. Take three steps forward and at the points indicated by ּ, bend the knees at the first word, bow at the second, and stand straight before saying God's name.

תהלים נא

אֲדֹנָי, שְׂפָתַי תִּפְתָּח, וּפִי יַגִּיד תְּהִלָּתֶךָ:

אבות

יָּבָּרוּךְ אַתָּה יהוה, אֱלֹהֵינוּ וֵאלֹהֵי אֲבוֹתֵינוּ

אֱלֹהֵי אַבְרָהָם, אֱלֹהֵי יִצְחָק, וֵאלֹהֵי יַעֲקֹב

הָאֵל הַגָּדוֹל הַגִּבּוֹר וְהַנּוֹרָא, אֵל עֶלְיוֹן

גּוֹמֵל חֲסָדִים טוֹבִים, וְקֹנֵה הַכֹּל

who remembers the loving-kindness of the fathers
and will bring a Redeemer to their children's children
for the sake of His name, in love.
King, Helper, Savior, Shield:
▾Blessed are You, Lord, Shield of Abraham.

DIVINE MIGHT

אַתָּה גִּבּוֹר You are eternally mighty, Lord.
You give life to the dead and have great power to save.

In Israel: He causes the dew to fall.

He sustains the living with loving-kindness,
and with great compassion revives the dead.
He supports the fallen, heals the sick, sets captives free,
and keeps His faith with those who sleep in the dust.
Who is like You, Master of might,
and to whom can You be compared,
O King who brings death and gives life,
and makes salvation grow?
Faithful are You to revive the dead.
Blessed are You, Lord, who revives the dead.

HOLINESS

אַתָּה קָדוֹשׁ You are holy and Your name is holy,
and holy ones praise You daily, Selah!
Blessed are You, Lord, the holy God.

---

time he thinks of or inquires about a child, he remembers and inquires about
the caregiver. As the three children of HaKadosh Barukh Hu were jointly
raised in, and by, the Land of Israel, every time He mentions the merits of
our Fathers, He mentions the merits of the Land of Israel."

Our benefit from *Zekhut Avot* is dependent upon our identification with
their Land. After the failure of the spies, Moshe prays on behalf of the people.
He employs the thirteen Divine Attributes which HaKadosh Barukh Hu
Himself had previously taught him. Yet he doesn't petition based on *Zekhut*

וְזוֹכֵר חַסְדֵי אָבוֹת

וּמֵבִיא גוֹאֵל לִבְנֵי בְנֵיהֶם לְמַעַן שְׁמוֹ בְּאַהֲבָה.

מֶלֶךְ עוֹזֵר וּמוֹשִׁיעַ וּמָגֵן.

בָּרוּךְ אַתָּה יהוה, מָגֵן אַבְרָהָם.

גבורות

אַתָּה גִבּוֹר לְעוֹלָם, אֲדֹנָי

מְחַיֵּה מֵתִים אַתָּה, רַב לְהוֹשִׁיעַ

בארץ ישראל: מוֹרִיד הַטָּל

מְכַלְכֵּל חַיִּים בְּחֶסֶד, מְחַיֵּה מֵתִים בְּרַחֲמִים רַבִּים

סוֹמֵךְ נוֹפְלִים, וְרוֹפֵא חוֹלִים, וּמַתִּיר אֲסוּרִים

וּמְקַיֵּם אֱמוּנָתוֹ לִישֵׁנֵי עָפָר.

מִי כָמְוֹךָ, בַּעַל גְּבוּרוֹת, וּמִי דּוֹמֶה לָּךְ

מֶלֶךְ, מֵמִית וּמְחַיֶּה וּמַצְמִיחַ יְשׁוּעָה.

וְנֶאֱמָן אַתָּה לְהַחֲיוֹת מֵתִים.

בָּרוּךְ אַתָּה יהוה, מְחַיֵּה הַמֵּתִים.

קדושת השם

אַתָּה קָדוֹשׁ וְשִׁמְךָ קָדוֹשׁ

וּקְדוֹשִׁים בְּכָל יוֹם יְהַלְלוּךָ סֶּלָה.

בָּרוּךְ אַתָּה יהוה, הָאֵל הַקָּדוֹשׁ.

ERETZ YISRAEL AND ZEKHUT AVOT

Commenting on a verse in *Beḥukotai* which mentions the merits of our Fathers alongside the merits of the Land of Israel, the Midrash (*Vayikra Raba* 36:5) comments, "It is similar to a king whose three children were raised by a common caregiver. She is so deeply associated with his children that every

KNOWLEDGE

אַתָּה חוֹנֵן You grace humanity with knowledge
and teach mortals understanding.
Grace us with the knowledge, understanding
and discernment that come from You.
Blessed are You, LORD,
who graciously grants knowledge.

REPENTANCE

הֲשִׁיבֵנוּ Bring us back, our Father, to Your Torah.
Draw us near, our King, to Your service.
Lead us back to You in perfect repentance.
Blessed are You, LORD,
who desires repentance.

FORGIVENESS

Strike the left side of the chest at °.

סְלַח לָנוּ Forgive us, our Father, for we have °sinned.
Pardon us, our King, for we have °transgressed;
for You pardon and forgive.
Blessed are You, LORD,
the gracious One who repeatedly forgives.

REDEMPTION

רְאֵה Look on our affliction, plead our cause,
and redeem us soon for Your name's sake,
for You are a powerful Redeemer.
Blessed are You,
LORD, the Redeemer of Israel.

---

during their moments of crisis. The seventh and final invocation speaks of
David and Shlomo, who prayed on behalf of Yerushalayim. The *berakha*
concludes with the phrase "*Meraḥem al HaAretz*" – "Who has mercy on the
Land." After basing our *Tefillot* upon the *Zekhut* of previous *Tzaddikim*, the
berakha concludes by capturing our longing for the Land of Israel.

דעת

אַתָּה חוֹנֵן לְאָדָם דַּעַת, וּמְלַמֵּד לֶאֱנוֹשׁ בִּינָה.

חָנֵּנוּ מֵאִתְּךָ דֵּעָה בִּינָה וְהַשְׂכֵּל.

בָּרוּךְ אַתָּה יהוה, חוֹנֵן הַדָּעַת.

תשובה

הֲשִׁיבֵנוּ אָבִינוּ לְתוֹרָתֶךָ, וְקָרְבֵנוּ מַלְכֵּנוּ לַעֲבוֹדָתֶךָ

וְהַחֲזִירֵנוּ בִּתְשׁוּבָה שְׁלֵמָה לְפָנֶיךָ.

בָּרוּךְ אַתָּה יהוה, הָרוֹצֶה בִּתְשׁוּבָה.

סליחה

Strike the left side of the chest at °.

סְלַח לָנוּ אָבִינוּ כִּי °חָטָאנוּ

מְחַל לָנוּ מַלְכֵּנוּ כִּי °פָשָׁעְנוּ

כִּי מוֹחֵל וְסוֹלֵחַ אָתָּה.

בָּרוּךְ אַתָּה יהוה, חַנּוּן הַמַּרְבֶּה לִסְלֹחַ.

גאולה

רְאֵה בְעָנְיֵנוּ, וְרִיבָה רִיבֵנוּ

וּגְאָלֵנוּ מְהֵרָה לְמַעַן שְׁמֶךָ

כִּי גּוֹאֵל חָזָק אָתָּה.

בָּרוּךְ אַתָּה יהוה, גּוֹאֵל יִשְׂרָאֵל.

Avot. The Ramban (*Bemidbar* 14:17) comments: By scorning the land which our *Avot* received as a gift and so coveted, the spies were in effect betraying their *Avot*; hence they abdicated the right to receive mercy based on *Zekhut Avot.*

The special prayers of a public fast day invoke several different precedents in which God answered the prayers of various prophets and righteous people

HEALING

רְפָאֵנוּ Heal us, LORD, and we shall be healed.
Save us and we shall be saved, for You are our praise.
Bring complete recovery for all our ailments,

The following prayer for a sick person may be said here:
May it be Your will, O LORD my God and God of my ancestors, that You
speedily send a complete recovery from heaven, a healing of both soul and
body, to the patient (*name*), son/daughter of (*mother's name*) among the
other afflicted of Israel.

---

for You, God, King, are a faithful and compassionate Healer.
Blessed are You, LORD, Healer of the sick of His people Israel.

PROSPERITY

בָּרֵךְ Bless this year for us, LORD our God,
and all its types of produce for good.
Grant blessing on the face of the earth,
and from its goodness satisfy us,
blessing our year as the best of years.
Blessed are You, LORD, who blesses the years.

INGATHERING OF EXILES

תְּקַע Sound the great shofar for our freedom,
raise high the banner to gather our exiles, and gather us together
from the four quarters of the earth.
Blessed are You, LORD,
who gathers the dispersed of His people Israel.

---

day that our city was destroyed and its nation cast into exile. I suspect that
the angels appointed over the Sanctuary of Song erased the sounds of my
dreams in the night when I awoke in the morning, for fear that if I were
to sing the songs of my dreams, my fellow brothers would not be able to
withstand the sorrow that would resonate from their realization of all the
goodness they have lost.

In order to recompense me for the songs they prevented me from singing with my voice, they granted me to write songs instead.
(S.Y. Agnon, from his acceptance speech for the Nobel Prize in Literature)

רְפוּאָה

רְפָאֵנוּ יהוה וְנֵרָפֵא, הוֹשִׁיעֵנוּ וְנִוָּשֵׁעָה, כִּי תְהִלָּתֵנוּ אָתָּה
וְהַעֲלֵה רְפוּאָה שְׁלֵמָה לְכָל מַכּוֹתֵינוּ

The following prayer for a sick person may be said here:

יְהִי רָצוֹן מִלְּפָנֶיךָ יהוה אֱלֹהַי וֵאלֹהֵי אֲבוֹתַי, שֶׁתִּשְׁלַח מְהֵרָה רְפוּאָה שְׁלֵמָה
מִן הַשָּׁמַיִם רְפוּאַת הַנֶּפֶשׁ וּרְפוּאַת הַגּוּף לַחוֹלֶה/לַחוֹלָה *name of patient*
בֶּן/בַּת *mother's name* בְּתוֹךְ שְׁאָר חוֹלֵי יִשְׂרָאֵל.

כִּי אֵל מֶלֶךְ רוֹפֵא נֶאֱמָן וְרַחֲמָן אָתָּה.
בָּרוּךְ אַתָּה יהוה, רוֹפֵא חוֹלֵי עַמּוֹ יִשְׂרָאֵל.

בִּרְכַּת הַשָּׁנִים

בָּרֵךְ עָלֵינוּ יהוה אֱלֹהֵינוּ אֶת הַשָּׁנָה הַזֹּאת
וְאֶת כָּל מִינֵי תְבוּאָתָהּ, לְטוֹבָה
וְתֵן בְּרָכָה עַל פְּנֵי הָאֲדָמָה
וְשַׂבְּעֵנוּ מִטּוּבָהּ, וּבָרֵךְ שְׁנָתֵנוּ כַּשָּׁנִים הַטּוֹבוֹת.
בָּרוּךְ אַתָּה יהוה, מְבָרֵךְ הַשָּׁנִים.

קִבּוּץ גָּלֻיּוֹת

תְּקַע בְּשׁוֹפָר גָּדוֹל לְחֵרוּתֵנוּ, וְשָׂא נֵס לְקַבֵּץ גָּלֻיּוֹתֵינוּ
וְקַבְּצֵנוּ יַחַד מֵאַרְבַּע כַּנְפוֹת הָאָרֶץ.
בָּרוּךְ אַתָּה יהוה, מְקַבֵּץ נִדְחֵי עַמּוֹ יִשְׂרָאֵל.

THE SONGS OF EXILE

Because of historical catastrophe – the destruction of Jerusalem at the
hands of King Titus of Rome – Israel was exiled from its land, and I was
born in a city of the Diaspora. But at all times, I always considered myself
as one born in Jerusalem. In a dream, in a night-vision, I saw myself standing with my brother Levites in the Temple, together singing the songs of
King David of Israel. No ear has rung with these sweet sounds since the

JUSTICE

הָשִׁיבָה Restore our judges as at first,
and our counselors as at the beginning,
and remove from us sorrow and sighing.
May You alone, Lᴏʀᴅ, reign over us
with loving-kindness and compassion, and vindicate us in justice.
Blessed are You, Lᴏʀᴅ,
the King who loves righteousness and justice.

AGAINST INFORMERS

וְלַמַּלְשִׁינִים For the slanderers let there be no hope,
and may all wickedness perish in an instant.
May all Your people's enemies swiftly be cut down.
May You swiftly uproot, crush, cast down
and humble the arrogant swiftly in our days.
Blessed are You, Lᴏʀᴅ,
who destroys enemies and humbles the arrogant.

---

family upon the virtues of charity: "For I have chosen him, that he may command his children and his household after him to keep the way of the Lᴏʀᴅ by doing righteousness and justice" (*Bereshit* 18:19). Through our charitable behavior we continue to educate the world in the legacy of Avraham, and we advance our redemptive process.

Though Jews at both a personal and communal level have always excelled at charity, the development of the modern communities of Israel has instigated an unprecedented level of *tzedaka*. From the inception of Jewish Settlement in the late eighteenth century the population was dependent upon foreign assistance. Jewish communities the world over bestowed significant sums to support the pioneers who returned to our collective homeland. Often the transfer of monies was performed illegally and at great risk, as local governments banned the removal of currency from their respective empires.

As the modern State was born, taxation as well as a modern economy alleviated the level of dependence upon philanthropy. However, our State has attracted a level of *tzedaka* unparalleled in history, as worldwide Jewry participates from afar in the rebuilding and renovation of our joint homeland. We are literally witnessing a prophetic fulfillment: the Land and People of Israel have been rebuilt through charity.

השבת המשפט

הָשִׁיבָה שׁוֹפְטֵינוּ כְּבָרִאשׁוֹנָה, וְיוֹעֲצֵינוּ כְּבַתְּחִלָּה
וְהָסֵר מִמֶּנּוּ יָגוֹן וַאֲנָחָה
וּמְלֹךְ עָלֵינוּ אַתָּה יהוה לְבַדְּךָ בְּחֶסֶד וּבְרַחֲמִים
וְצַדְּקֵנוּ בַּמִּשְׁפָּט.
בָּרוּךְ אַתָּה יהוה, מֶלֶךְ אוֹהֵב צְדָקָה וּמִשְׁפָּט.

ברכת המינים

וְלַמַּלְשִׁינִים אַל תְּהִי תִקְוָה, וְכָל הָרִשְׁעָה כְּרֶגַע תֹּאבֵד
וְכָל אוֹיְבֵי עַמְּךָ מְהֵרָה יִכָּרֵתוּ
וְהַזֵּדִים מְהֵרָה תְעַקֵּר וּתְשַׁבֵּר וּתְמַגֵּר וְתַכְנִיעַ בִּמְהֵרָה בְיָמֵינוּ.
בָּרוּךְ אַתָּה יהוה, שׁוֹבֵר אוֹיְבִים וּמַכְנִיעַ זֵדִים.

AWAITING GOD'S KINGSHIP

[Our forefathers] said before Him: Master of the World, what if our children are never to return? He said to them: Do not say that! If a generation
awaits My kingship, they are immediately redeemed.

(*Yalkut Shimoni, Eikha* 997)

מֶלֶךְ אוֹהֵב צְדָקָה וּמִשְׁפָּט *The King who loves righteousness and justice.* A verse
in *Yeshayahu* reaffirms the function of righteousness (charity) in advancing
our redemption: "Tziyon will be redeemed by justice, and those in her who
repent, by righteousness" (1:27).

Based on this verse the Gemara (*Sanhedrin* 98a) stresses that charity is
necessary to rebuild Yerushalayim. Slightly altering this Gemara, the Rambam claimed that our nation at large and the Land of Israel are restored
through charity.

Charity ennobles personal human virtue just as it stabilizes social progress.
We live in an era of "welfare" governments which attempt to relieve suffering through ambitious socialist platforms. Though these achievements are
impressive, society continues to rely upon charitable assistance at both the
personal and organizational level. The charitable tradition is part of the Jewish legacy. Avraham was credited by HaKadosh Barukh Hu for raising his

THE RIGHTEOUS

עַל הַצַּדִּיקִים To the righteous, the pious,
the elders of Your people the house of Israel,
the remnant of their scholars, the righteous converts, and to us,
may Your compassion be aroused, Lᴏʀᴅ our God.
Grant a good reward to all who sincerely trust in Your name.
Set our lot with them, so that we may never be ashamed,
for in You we trust.
Blessed are You, Lᴏʀᴅ,
who is the support and trust of the righteous.

REBUILDING JERUSALEM

וְלִירוּשָׁלַיִם To Jerusalem, Your city, may You return in compassion,
and may You dwell in it as You promised.
May You rebuild it rapidly in our days as an everlasting structure,
and install within it soon the throne of David.
Blessed are You, Lᴏʀᴅ,
who builds Jerusalem.

KINGDOM OF DAVID

אֶת צֶמַח May the offshoot of Your servant David soon flower,
and may his pride be raised high by Your salvation,
for we wait for Your salvation all day.
Blessed are You, Lᴏʀᴅ,
who makes the glory of salvation flourish.

---

personal affront as well as mutiny against the Supreme Monarch – HaKadosh
Barukh Hu.

This dissonance evolves into a well-known dispute between the Rambam,
who strongly approved of Jewish monarchy, and Abarbanel, who assumed
it represents a concession to feeble human nature, incapable of revering a
Divine Monarch. Our Messianic image incorporates a human king, though
the syntax of the *berakha* of Justice implies the exclusivity of our true King –
"May You alone, Lᴏʀᴅ, reign over us with loving-kindness and compassion"
(see previous page).

על הצדיקים

עַל הַצַּדִּיקִים וְעַל הַחֲסִידִים, וְעַל זִקְנֵי עַמְּךָ בֵּית יִשְׂרָאֵל
וְעַל פְּלֵיטַת סוֹפְרֵיהֶם, וְעַל גֵּרֵי הַצֶּדֶק, וְעָלֵינוּ
יֶהֱמוּ רַחֲמֶיךָ יהוה אֱלֹהֵינוּ
וְתֵן שָׂכָר טוֹב לְכָל הַבּוֹטְחִים בְּשִׁמְךָ בֶּאֱמֶת
וְשִׂים חֶלְקֵנוּ עִמָּהֶם
וּלְעוֹלָם לֹא נֵבוֹשׁ כִּי בְךָ בָּטָחְנוּ.
בָּרוּךְ אַתָּה יהוה, מִשְׁעָן וּמִבְטָח לַצַּדִּיקִים.

בניין ירושלים

וְלִירוּשָׁלַיִם עִירְךָ בְּרַחֲמִים תָּשׁוּב, וְתִשְׁכֹּן בְּתוֹכָהּ כַּאֲשֶׁר דִּבַּרְתָּ
וּבְנֵה אוֹתָהּ בְּקָרוֹב בְּיָמֵינוּ בִּנְיַן עוֹלָם
וְכִסֵּא דָוִד מְהֵרָה לְתוֹכָהּ תָּכִין.
בָּרוּךְ אַתָּה יהוה, בּוֹנֵה יְרוּשָׁלָיִם.

משיח בן דוד

אֶת צֶמַח דָּוִד עַבְדְּךָ מְהֵרָה תַצְמִיחַ, וְקַרְנוֹ תָּרוּם בִּישׁוּעָתֶךָ
כִּי לִישׁוּעָתְךָ קִוִּינוּ כָּל הַיּוֹם.
בָּרוּךְ אַתָּה יהוה, מַצְמִיחַ קֶרֶן יְשׁוּעָה.

אֶת צֶמַח דָּוִד עַבְדְּךָ *May the offshoot of Your servant David.* Though modern society has established democracy as the most equitable form of governance, we
pray for the restoration of Jewish monarchy. We anticipate a benevolent monarchy as potential abuses of the crown are checked by the king's fear of Heaven.

There is some discrepancy between the sections in *Shofetim* describing
the mitzva to appoint a king and the narrative in *1 Shmuel* in which the first
Jewish king, Shaul, is appointed. The Torah's description presents monarchy
in a favorable light, asserting it as a positive mitzva. By contrast, Shmuel is
highly critical of the choice of monarchy, and perceives this request as a

RESPONSE TO PRAYER

שְׁמַע קוֹלֵנוּ Listen to our voice, Lᴏʀᴅ our God.
Spare us and have compassion on us,
and in compassion and favor accept our prayer,
for You, God, listen to prayers and pleas.
Do not turn us away, O our King,
empty-handed from Your presence,
for You listen with compassion to the prayer of Your people Israel.
Blessed are You, Lᴏʀᴅ, who listens to prayer.

TEMPLE SERVICE

רְצֵה Find favor, Lᴏʀᴅ our God,
in Your people Israel and their prayer.
Restore the service to Your most holy House,
and accept in love and favor
the fire-offerings of Israel and their prayer.
May the service of Your people Israel always find favor with You.

---

dole out justice independent of classic halakhic parameters. In this respect
he provided a complementary agency to the court system.

עבודה *Temple service.* Even though the *Shemoneh Esreh* has already included
prayers to restore Jewish sovereignty and establish a Kingdom of God, a
specific *berakha* about the rebuilding of the *Mikdash* is inserted. In fact the
Midrash (*Midrash Shmuel* chapter 13) records that redemption can only arrive
once Jews have prayed for the Kingdom of Heaven, for the Davidic dynasty,
and for the restoration of the *Mikdash*.

As the Midrash comments (see *Bereshit Raba* 13:2), "Jews are constantly
talking about their *Mikdash*, asking HaKadosh Barukh Hu to rebuild the
Mikdash, and requesting of Him the date on which it will be rebuilt." In addition to formally praying for the rebuilding of the *Mikdash*, Jews constantly
have the *Mikdash* on their minds; even informal or colloquial conversation
centers upon a structure we have never actually seen, but whose renovation
we anxiously await.

Constantly conversing about the *Mikdash* transcends praying for its
reconstruction. The *Kohanim* were tasked with guarding the *Mikdash* (as
described in the opening sections of *Massekhet Tamid*). These sentinels

שומע תפלה

שְׁמַע קוֹלֵנוּ יהוה אֱלֹהֵינוּ, חוּס וְרַחֵם עָלֵינוּ
וְקַבֵּל בְּרַחֲמִים וּבְרָצוֹן אֶת תְּפִלָּתֵנוּ
כִּי אֵל שׁוֹמֵעַ תְּפִלּוֹת וְתַחֲנוּנִים אָתָּה
וּמִלְּפָנֶיךָ מַלְכֵּנוּ רֵיקָם אַל תְּשִׁיבֵנוּ
כִּי אַתָּה שׁוֹמֵעַ תְּפִלַּת עַמְּךָ יִשְׂרָאֵל בְּרַחֲמִים.
בָּרוּךְ אַתָּה יהוה, שׁוֹמֵעַ תְּפִלָּה.

עבודה

רְצֵה יהוה אֱלֹהֵינוּ בְּעַמְּךָ יִשְׂרָאֵל, וּבִתְפִלָּתָם
וְהָשֵׁב אֶת הָעֲבוֹדָה לִדְבִיר בֵּיתֶךָ
וְאִשֵּׁי יִשְׂרָאֵל וּתְפִלָּתָם בְּאַהֲבָה תְקַבֵּל בְּרָצוֹן
וּתְהִי לְרָצוֹן תָּמִיד עֲבוֹדַת יִשְׂרָאֵל עַמֶּךָ.

The halakhic functions of a monarch include three mitzvot: conquering
the Land of Israel, constructing a *Mikdash*, and destroying Amalek. Beyond
these *specific* halakhically mandated functions, he supervises all affairs of
state: military, economic, social and political. Educationally he serves as national *teacher* of Torah. Toward this occupation he must pen a personal *Sefer
Torah* which must accompany him wherever he travels. Though each Jew is
commanded to draft a *Sefer Torah,* a King must write an additional one. By
carrying this *Sefer* on his person he is enabled to teach Torah.

His role as teacher was accentuated every seven years when he directed a
national Torah reading at the *Hak'hel* ceremonies. Typically he would also
convene public learning sessions during the national pilgrimage over the
three Ḥagim. Shlomo named his *Sefer* "Kohelet," in part because he would
gather the nation to teach them Torah (perhaps even teaching the book of
Kohelet) during these weeklong celebrations.

A Jewish king also provides recourse for those who have been unjustly
exploited. Though the official court system handles most litigation, various
legal loopholes may allow criminals to escape unpunished, and the weak to
be exploited by the powerful. The king has the authority to intercede and

And may our eyes witness Your return to Zion in compassion.
Blessed are You, LORD, who restores His Presence to Zion.

THANKSGIVING
Bow at the first nine words.
מוֹדִים We give thanks to You,
for You are the LORD our God and God of our ancestors
for ever and all time.
You are the Rock of our lives,
Shield of our salvation from generation to generation.
We will thank You and declare Your praise for our lives,
which are entrusted into Your hand;
for our souls, which are placed in Your charge;
for Your miracles which are with us every day;
and for Your wonders and favors at all times,
evening, morning and midday.
You are good – for Your compassion never fails.
You are compassionate – for Your loving-kindnesses never cease.
We have always placed our hope in You.

Prayers for the rebuilding of the *Mikdash* are so important that even
HaKadosh Barukh Hu actively prays for it. The name Yerushalayim is a conjugation of the term *yera'eh* (it should appear) and *shalem* (perfect). According to the Midrash (*Bereshit Raba* 56:10) this conjugated name – *yearning for
perfection* – captures a Divine longing for the ultimate reconstruction of the
Mikdash: Rabbi Berekhia cites Rabbi Ḥelbo, "God erects a temporary *sukka*
and prays for the ultimate rebuilding of the *Mikdash*." The word Yerushalayim
forms the content of God's prayer. He prays for the appearance of a perfect
and complete city, in place of the current unfinished and flawed city. Renovation of the *Mikdash* is the only agenda which both humans and HaKadosh
Barukh Hu pray for.

SENDING A TELEGRAM TO THE KOTEL 1967
After the Kotel was liberated during the Six Day War this telegram was sent:
    To: The Western Wall, Yerushalayim
    We thank HaKadosh Barukh Hu for His Miracles and Salvation
    Signed: The Jewish Community of Antwerp

וְתֶחֱזֶינָה עֵינֵינוּ בְּשׁוּבְךָ לְצִיּוֹן בְּרַחֲמִים.
בָּרוּךְ אַתָּה יהוה, הַמַּחֲזִיר שְׁכִינָתוֹ לְצִיּוֹן.

הודאה

Bow at the first five words.

מוֹדִים אֲנַחְנוּ לָךְ
שָׁאַתָּה הוּא יהוה אֱלֹהֵינוּ וֵאלֹהֵי אֲבוֹתֵינוּ לְעוֹלָם וָעֶד.
צוּר חַיֵּינוּ, מָגֵן יִשְׁעֵנוּ, אַתָּה הוּא לְדוֹר וָדוֹר.
נוֹדֶה לְּךָ וּנְסַפֵּר תְּהִלָּתֶךָ, עַל חַיֵּינוּ הַמְּסוּרִים בְּיָדֶךָ
וְעַל נִשְׁמוֹתֵינוּ הַפְּקוּדוֹת לָךְ, וְעַל נִסֶּיךָ שֶׁבְּכָל יוֹם עִמָּנוּ
וְעַל נִפְלְאוֹתֶיךָ וְטוֹבוֹתֶיךָ שֶׁבְּכָל עֵת, עֶרֶב וָבֹקֶר וְצָהֳרָיִם.
הַטּוֹב, כִּי לֹא כָלוּ רַחֲמֶיךָ, וְהַמְרַחֵם, כִּי לֹא תַמּוּ חֲסָדֶיךָ
מֵעוֹלָם קִוִּינוּ לָךְ.

were not stationed merely to prevent theft from the *Mikdash*. A verse in
II *Melakhim* (11:6) describes various sentries of *Kohanim* and concludes, "so
shall you keep the watch of the house, so that it is not broken down." The
final word suggests that their watch is intended to assure that the *Mikdash*
isn't *ignored*. While the general population may temporarily overlook the
Mikdash, a regiment of *Kohanim* maintains constant consciousness of it.
Having squandered the *Mikdash*, our constant referencing of the *Mikdash* in
our prayers bolsters this consciousness.

Jewish tradition has allocated a unique *tefilla* for the rebuilding of the
Mikdash. The Gemara (*Bava Batra* 60b) records initial responses to the
trauma of the destruction of the *Mikdash*. Many considered a complete ban
on eating meat and drinking wine. This prohibition was deemed too harsh
and was discarded. Despite the lack of official prohibitions, the *Shulḥan
Arukh* (*Oraḥ Ḥayyim* 1:3) encourages a pious person to be distraught and
agonize about the loss of the *Mikdash*. Beginning in medieval times a practice known as *Tikun Ḥatzot* developed. A special prayer incorporating *kinot*
(laments) upon the loss of the *Mikdash* and prayers for its renewal, it is
designed to be recited at the mid-way point of the night.

*At this point in the silent Amida it is permitted to add a rabbinically
formulated "Al HaNissim." The following was written by Rabbi Neria
(alternative versions can be found on pages 656–659).*

עַל הַנִּסִּים [We thank You also] for the miracles, the redemption, the
mighty deeds, the salvations, and the victories in battle which You
performed for our ancestors in those days, at this time.

When the armies of the Middle East rose up against Your people
Israel and sought to destroy, slay and exterminate the inhabitants of
Your Land, young and old, children and women, and among them
those who had survived the sword and were saved from the horror
of Your enemies' flames, one from a city, two from a family, hoping
to find a resting place for the soles of their feet in Your land that You
had promised them; then You in Your great compassion stood by us
in our time of distress, thwarted their counsel and frustrated their
plans, raised us upright and established our liberty, championed our
cause, judged our claim, avenged our wrong, delivered the strong
into the hands of the weak, the many into the hands of the few, the
impure into the hands of the holy. You made for Yourself great and
holy renown in Your world, and for Your people Israel You performed
a great salvation and redemption as of this day. You subjugated peoples
under us, nations beneath our feet, and You gave us our inheritance,
the Land of Canaan to its borders, and returned us to the place of
Your holy Sanctuary.

(In the same way, make us a miracle and a glorious wonder, thwart
the counsel of our enemies, have us prosper in the pastures of our
Land, and gather in our scattered ones from the four corners of the
earth, and we will rejoice in the rebuilding of Your city and in the
establishment of Your Sanctuary and in the flourishing of the pride
of Your servant David, speedily in our days, and we will give thanks
to Your great name.)   *Continue with "For all these things."*

Some dispute the addition of *Al HaNissim* in the final three blessings
of the Amida, in light of the *Shulḥan Arukh* (*Oraḥ Ḥayyim* 119:1): "If one
wishes to add any blessing among the middle blessings, one may add." From
here, some have inferred that additional passages may only be added in the

*At this point in the silent עמידה it is permitted to add a rabbinically
formulated עַל הַנִּסִּים. The following was written by Rabbi Neria
(alternative versions can be found on pages 656–659).*

עַל הַנִּסִּים וְעַל הַפֻּרְקָן וְעַל הַגְּבוּרוֹת וְעַל הַתְּשׁוּעוֹת וְעַל הַמִּלְחָמוֹת
שֶׁעָשִׂיתָ לַאֲבוֹתֵינוּ בַּיָּמִים הָהֵם בַּזְּמַן הַזֶּה.

כְּשֶׁעָמְדוּ צִבְאוֹת עֲרָב עַל עַמְּךָ יִשְׂרָאֵל, וּבִקְשׁוּ לְהַשְׁמִיד לַהֲרֹג וּלְאַבֵּד אֶת
יוֹשְׁבֵי אַרְצֶךָ, מִנַּעַר וְעַד זָקֵן טַף וְנָשִׁים, וּבָהֶם עַם שְׂרִידֵי חֶרֶב אֲשֶׁר נִצְּלוּ
מִתֻּפֶת הָאֵשׁ שֶׁל שׂוֹנְאֶיךָ, אֶחָד מֵעִיר וּשְׁנַיִם מִמִּשְׁפָּחָה, וְשָׁבְרוּ לִמְצֹא
מָנוֹחַ לְכַף רַגְלָם בְּאַרְצְךָ אֲשֶׁר הִבְטַחְתָּ לָהֶם. וְאַתָּה בְּרַחֲמֶיךָ הָרַבִּים
עָמַדְתָּ לָנוּ בְּעֵת צָרָתֵנוּ, הֲפַרְתָּ אֶת עֲצָתָם וְקִלְקַלְתָּ אֶת מַחֲשַׁבְתָּם, זָקַפְתָּ
קוֹמָתֵנוּ וְקוֹמַמְתָּ אֶת חֻרְבוֹתֵינוּ, רַבְתָּ אֶת רִיבֵנוּ, דַּנְתָּ אֶת דִּינֵנוּ, נָקַמְתָּ אֶת
נִקְמָתֵנוּ, מָסַרְתָּ רַבִּים בְּיַד מְעַטִּים, טְמֵאִים בְּיַד קְדוֹשִׁים, וְעָשִׂיתָ לְּךָ שֵׁם
גָּדוֹל וְקָדוֹשׁ בְּעוֹלָמֶךָ, וּלְעַמְּךָ יִשְׂרָאֵל עָשִׂיתָ תְּשׁוּעָה גְדוֹלָה וּפֻרְקָן כְּהַיּוֹם
הַזֶּה, הִדְבַּרְתָּ עַמִּים תַּחְתֵּנוּ וּלְאֻמִּים תַּחַת רַגְלֵנוּ, וְנָתַתָּ לָנוּ אֶת נַחֲלָתֵנוּ,
אֶרֶץ כְּנַעַן לִגְבוּלוֹתֶיהָ, וַהֲחֱזַרְתָּנוּ אֶל מְקוֹם מִקְדַּשׁ הֵיכָלֶךָ.

(כֵּן עֲשֵׂה עִמָּנוּ נֵס וָפֶלֶא לְטוֹבָה, הָפֵר עֲצַת אוֹיְבֵינוּ, וְדַשְּׁנֵנוּ בִּנְאוֹת אַרְצֶךָ,
וּנְפוּצוֹתֵינוּ מֵאַרְבַּע כַּנְפוֹת הָאָרֶץ תְּקַבֵּץ, וְנִשְׂמַח בְּבִנְיַן עִירֶךָ וּבְתִקּוּן
הֵיכָלֶךָ וּבִצְמִיחַת קֶרֶן לְדָוִד עַבְדֶּךָ בִּמְהֵרָה בְּיָמֵינוּ, וְנוֹדֶה לְשִׁמְךָ הַגָּדוֹל).

Continue with וְעַל כֻּלָּם.

_____

עַל הַנִּסִּים *Al HaNissim.* The *Al HaNissim* prayer, "[We thank You also] for
the Miracles," is incorporated into and completes the thanksgiving blessing
that begins with *Modim.* It is recited on Ḥanukka and Purim, on days that
we thank God for His open miracles that saved the nation of Israel from
physical and spiritual annihilation. This addition is already mentioned in
the *Tosefta* (*Megilla* 3, 4) which determines that "on Ḥanukka and Purim, the
event should be recounted in the blessings of thanksgiving." The text of *Al
HaNissim* that features in our prayer books today first appears in the prayer
books of the Geonim.

In this vein, a version of *Al HaNissim* that similarly "recounts the event"
has been composed for Yom HaAtzma'ut, printed here above.

וְעַל כֻּלָם For all these things may Your name be blessed and
exalted, our King, continually, for ever and all time.
Let all that lives thank You, Selah!
and praise Your name in truth,
God, our Savior and Help, Selah!
▸Blessed are You, LORD, whose name is "the Good"
and to whom thanks are due.

PEACE
שָׁלוֹם רָב Grant great peace to Your people Israel for ever,
for You are the sovereign LORD of all peace;
and may it be good in Your eyes
to bless Your people Israel
at every time, at every hour, with Your peace.
Blessed are You, LORD,
who blesses His people Israel with peace.

Some say the following verse:
May the words of my mouth and the meditation of my heart   Ps. 19
find favor before You, LORD, my Rock and Redeemer.

_____

tute a new prayer of thanksgiving based on the classical *Al HaNissim* format (see Rabbi David's *Ufros Aleha Sukkat Shelomekha*, Afula 2000, pages
49–51).

In the prayer book of the Religious Kibbutz Movement (the 1968 edition),
it says: "Some say *Al HaNissim* in the Amida and in Grace after Meals," based
on the custom of the Italian synagogue in Jerusalem, and also on the words
of Rabbi E.Z. Melamed (in his book *Minhag VeHalakha*, Jerusalem 1960, 192).
This comment was omitted in later versions of the prayer book, presumably
because this addition was not taken up by the congregation. Whether it was
felt that the proposed version of *Al HaNissim* was too long, or perhaps for
some other reason, this prayer generally appears in prayer books under the
rubric "Some say," and is commonly omitted.   BL

וְעַל כֻּלָּם יִתְבָּרַךְ וְיִתְרוֹמַם שִׁמְךָ מַלְכֵּנוּ תָּמִיד לְעוֹלָם וָעֶד.

וְכֹל הַחַיִּים יוֹדוּךָ סֶּלָה

וִיהַלְלוּ אֶת שִׁמְךָ בֶּאֱמֶת

הָאֵל יְשׁוּעָתֵנוּ וְעֶזְרָתֵנוּ סֶלָה.

יָבָרוּךְ אַתָּה יהוה, הַטּוֹב שִׁמְךָ וּלְךָ נָאֶה לְהוֹדוֹת.

בִּרְכַּת שָׁלוֹם

שָׁלוֹם רָב עַל יִשְׂרָאֵל עַמְּךָ תָּשִׂים לְעוֹלָם

כִּי אַתָּה הוּא מֶלֶךְ אָדוֹן לְכָל הַשָּׁלוֹם.

וְטוֹב בְּעֵינֶיךָ לְבָרֵךְ אֶת עַמְּךָ יִשְׂרָאֵל

בְּכָל עֵת וּבְכָל שָׁעָה בִּשְׁלוֹמֶךָ.

בָּרוּךְ אַתָּה יהוה, הַמְבָרֵךְ אֶת עַמּוֹ יִשְׂרָאֵל בַּשָּׁלוֹם.

Some say the following verse:

תהלים יט יִהְיוּ לְרָצוֹן אִמְרֵי־פִי וְהֶגְיוֹן לִבִּי לְפָנֶיךָ, יהוה צוּרִי וְגֹאֲלִי:

---

middle blessings of the Amida, but not in its opening or concluding blessings. However, in his work *Beit Yosef* (*Oraḥ Ḥayyim* 693), Rabbi Yosef Karo responds to those who claim the recitation of *Al HaNissim* on the 15th of Adar (Shushan Purim) is prohibited: "I do not know what prohibition there is in reciting *Al HaNissim*." That is, if a person uses a formula that the sages instituted, it is not considered a disruption in prayer. However, the *Aḥaronim* disagreed, and established that *Al HaNissim* should not be recited after Purim (in walled cities, where they lived) and the *Mishna Berura* also holds (108:38) that reciting *Al HaNissim* constitutes a disruption in the prayer as if one were making conversation.

Rabbi Shmuel David, the Rabbi of Afula (and previously the Rabbi of Kibbutz Rosh Tzurim) responded to those who disagree by asserting that there is no basis to forbid this addition, and it is even fitting to insti-

אֱלֹהַי My God,
guard my tongue from evil and my lips from deceitful speech.
To those who curse me, let my soul be silent;
may my soul be to all like the dust.
Open my heart to Your Torah
and let my soul pursue Your commandments.
As for all who plan evil against me,
swiftly thwart their counsel and frustrate their plans.

Berakhot 17a

    Act for the sake of Your name;
     act for the sake of Your right hand;
     act for the sake of Your holiness;
     act for the sake of Your Torah.

That Your beloved ones may be delivered,
save with Your right hand and answer me.

Ps. 60

May the words of my mouth
and the meditation of my heart find favor before You,
LORD, my Rock and Redeemer.

Ps. 19

Bow, take three steps back, then bow, first left, then right, then center, while saying:

May He who makes peace in His high places,
make peace for us and all Israel –
and say: Amen.

יְהִי רָצוֹן May it be Your will, LORD our God and God of our ancestors,
that the Temple be rebuilt speedily in our days,
and grant us a share in Your Torah.
And there we will serve You with reverence,
as in the days of old and as in former years.
Then the offering of Judah and Jerusalem
will be pleasing to the LORD as in the days of old and as in former years.

Mal. 3

ברכות יז

אֱלֹהַי

נְצֹר לְשׁוֹנִי מֵרָע וּשְׂפָתַי מִדַּבֵּר מִרְמָה

וְלִמְקַלְלַי נַפְשִׁי תִדֹּם, וְנַפְשִׁי כֶּעָפָר לַכֹּל תִּהְיֶה.

פְּתַח לִבִּי בְּתוֹרָתֶךָ, וּבְמִצְוֹתֶיךָ תִּרְדֹּף נַפְשִׁי.

וְכָל הַחוֹשְׁבִים עָלַי רָעָה

מְהֵרָה הָפֵר עֲצָתָם וְקַלְקֵל מַחֲשַׁבְתָּם.

עֲשֵׂה לְמַעַן שְׁמֶךָ

עֲשֵׂה לְמַעַן יְמִינֶךָ

עֲשֵׂה לְמַעַן קְדֻשָּׁתֶךָ

עֲשֵׂה לְמַעַן תּוֹרָתֶךָ.

תהלים ס
לְמַעַן יֵחָלְצוּן יְדִידֶיךָ, הוֹשִׁיעָה יְמִינְךָ וַעֲנֵנִי:

תהלים יט
יִהְיוּ לְרָצוֹן אִמְרֵי פִי וְהֶגְיוֹן לִבִּי לְפָנֶיךָ, יהוה צוּרִי וְגֹאֲלִי:

Bow, take three steps back, then bow, first left, then right, then center, while saying:

עֹשֶׂה שָׁלוֹם בִּמְרוֹמָיו

הוּא יַעֲשֶׂה שָׁלוֹם עָלֵינוּ וְעַל כָּל יִשְׂרָאֵל

וְאִמְרוּ אָמֵן.

יְהִי רָצוֹן מִלְּפָנֶיךָ יהוה אֱלֹהֵינוּ וֵאלֹהֵי אֲבוֹתֵינוּ

שֶׁיִּבָּנֶה בֵּית הַמִּקְדָּשׁ בִּמְהֵרָה בְיָמֵינוּ, וְתֵן חֶלְקֵנוּ בְּתוֹרָתֶךָ.

וְשָׁם נַעֲבָדְךָ בְּיִרְאָה כִּימֵי עוֹלָם וּכְשָׁנִים קַדְמֹנִיּוֹת.

מלאכי ג
וְעָרְבָה לַיהוה מִנְחַת יְהוּדָה וִירוּשָׁלָ͏ִם כִּימֵי עוֹלָם וּכְשָׁנִים קַדְמֹנִיּוֹת:

Hallel

*In some communities the Full Hallel is said on the eve of Yom HaAtzma'ut,
and many add the blessing before*

בָּרוּךְ Blessed are You, LORD our God, King of the Universe,
who has made us holy through His commandments
and has commanded us to recite the Hallel.

---

be said. Rabbeinu Tam (*Tosafot, Berakhot* 14a), and in his wake, all
Ashkenazic authorities and some Sephardic and North African authorities, hold that one does make a blessing on a custom. According
to Sephardim from Eastern communities (Maimonides, *The Laws of
Ḥanukka*, 83:5–7) one does not make a blessing on a custom. (See
sources and discussion about this dispute in Rabbi Shmuel David's
"Collection of Questions and Answers Regarding the Laws of Yom
HaAtzma'ut," Afula: 2000; Rabbi Uri Sherki, *Siddur Beit Melukha*;
the pamphlet *"Ba Orekh"* which supports reciting the blessing even
in Eastern communities.)

Many of those who came to Israel from North Africa and the
East did not struggle with issues of Zionist philosophy and religious
practice. The community considered themselves an inherent part of
the fulfillment of the vision of returning to Zion, experiencing the
redemption firsthand; and thus saw no contradiction between the
world of the synagogue and the redemptive process. In a short, sharp
response to the question of whether one should recite Hallel on Yom
HaAtzma'ut, Rabbi Yosef Messas answered: "Don't meddle in such
affairs. You are a devout Sephardi – do what we do. Celebrate the festival with complete Hallel, with gratitude to the glorious King, blessed
be He; eat, drink and be merry, and we have no business with others"
(*Otzar HaMikhtavim*, 3, 2009:1).

4. Some hold that though we must praise and thank God on Yom
   HaAtzma'ut, this should be in the form of Half Hallel and a blessing
   should not be said. Some authorities hold that Hallel can only be recited with a blessing when a miracle is performed for all of Israel, and

סדר הלל

In some communities the הלל שלם *is said on* יום העצמאות *night,*
and many add the blessing before

בָּרוּךְ אַתָּה יהוה אֱלֹהֵינוּ מֶלֶךְ הָעוֹלָם
אֲשֶׁר קִדְּשָׁנוּ בְּמִצְוֹתָיו וְצִוָּנוּ לִקְרֹא אֶת הַהַלֵּל.

HALLEL ON YOM HAATZMA'UT

1. According to Talmudic tradition, the prophets instituted the recitation
    of Hallel "for every [appropriate] occasion and for every trouble, may
    it not come upon the Jewish people. And when they are redeemed,
    they recite it over their redemption" (*Pesaḥim* 117a). Hallel was also
    instituted after the era of prophecy: the sages of the generation af-
    ter the Hasmonean Rebellion introduced the recitation of Hallel on
    Ḥanukka. The prophets had conferred authority upon the leaders of
    future generations to determine whether the events of their own time
    were considered redemptions from crisis, thus requiring the recitation
    of Hallel.

2. Opinions are divided with regard to the recitation of Hallel on Yom
    HaAtzma'ut. Some hold that it is obligatory, based on the decision
    of Rabbi Herzog and Rabbi Uziel of the Chief Rabbinate in the first
    years of the State, who are considered the "sages of the generation"
    (just as the Hasmonean sages were). Some say that the source of the
    obligation is not a rabbinic decision but stems from the established
    custom of reciting Hallel in the synagogue, which, over the years, has
    acquired the binding status of "an old custom" (*minhag vatikin*).

3. Whether or not to recite the introductory blessing is also a matter
    of debate. If Hallel is based on the prophetic institution, its recital
    on Yom HaAtzma'ut is of equal standing with the Hallel recited on
    Ḥanukka, and, as the blessing is recited on all eight days of Ḥanukka,
    the blessing should similarly be recited on Yom HaAtzma'ut. However,
    if the recitation of Hallel on Yom HaAtzma'ut is based on a long-
    established custom, then it is questionable whether a blessing should

הַלְלוּיָהּ Halleluya! Servants of the LORD, give praise; praise **Ps. 113** the name of the LORD. Blessed be the name of the LORD now and for evermore. From the rising of the sun to its setting, may the LORD's name be praised. High is the LORD above all nations; His glory is above the heavens. Who is like the LORD our God, who sits enthroned so high, yet turns so low to see the heavens and the earth? ▸ He raises the poor from the dust and the needy from the refuse heap, giving them a place alongside princes, the princes of His people. He makes the woman in a childless house a happy mother of children. Halleluya!

asked: If a person can disrupt his prayer to "greet a king" during the Shema, which is a Torah-prescribed mitzva, then surely he can disrupt Hallel, which is a rabbinically prescribed mitzva – or is publicizing the miracle more important? The asker of this question makes two assertions: firstly, that Hallel is rabbinically prescribed; and secondly, that Hallel publicizes the miracle. The significance of Hallel "publicizing the miracle" also emerges from a discussion in *Megilla* 3a: "Priests at their service, the Levites on their platform, and the Israelites at their post – all leave their work and come to hear the Megilla reading." From here, the sages justified putting their Torah studies on hold in order to hear the Megilla. The *Tosafot* (ibid.) raise the possibility that they must first finish their work, and then they may read the Megilla by themselves (rather than with the congregation), but come to the conclusion that "it is best to read with the congregation because it serves to publicize the miracle."

Whoever is familiar with the prayer service of Yom HaAtzma'ut knows that the miracle is mainly publicized during the evening prayers, when men, women and children, arrayed in blue and white, flock to the synagogue in order to usher in the festival. Reciting Hallel with most of the congregation present truly "publicizes the miracle," and indeed, there is special significance, and a special atmosphere, in the recitation of Hallel at night, as the festival begins.   BL

מוֹשִׁיבִי עֲקֶרֶת הַבַּיִת, אֵם־הַבָּנִים שְׂמֵחָה *He makes the woman in a childless house a happy mother of children.* Our land is described as our home or house, and

הַלְלוּיָהּ, הַלְלוּ עַבְדֵי יהוה, הַלְלוּ אֶת־שֵׁם יהוה: יְהִי שֵׁם
יהוה מְבֹרָךְ, מֵעַתָּה וְעַד־עוֹלָם: מִמִּזְרַח־שֶׁמֶשׁ עַד־מְבוֹאוֹ,
מְהֻלָּל שֵׁם יהוה: רָם עַל־כָּל־גּוֹיִם יהוה, עַל הַשָּׁמַיִם כְּבוֹדוֹ:
מִי כַּיהוה אֱלֹהֵינוּ, הַמַּגְבִּיהִי לָשֶׁבֶת: הַמַּשְׁפִּילִי לִרְאוֹת,
בַּשָּׁמַיִם וּבָאָרֶץ: ‹ מְקִימִי מֵעָפָר דָּל, מֵאַשְׁפֹּת יָרִים אֶבְיוֹן:
לְהוֹשִׁיבִי עִם־נְדִיבִים, עִם נְדִיבֵי עַמּוֹ: מוֹשִׁיבִי עֲקֶרֶת הַבַּיִת,
אֵם־הַבָּנִים שְׂמֵחָה, הַלְלוּיָהּ:

only a small percentage of the nation was in the Land of Israel in 1948. Some hold that Hallel should only be said in the case of an open or revealed miracle (*nes galui*), such as the miracle of the oil on Ḥanukka. Some would class the establishment of the State as a *nes tiv'i*, a miracle through more natural means. These doubts were taken into account by the members of the Chief Rabbinate in its early years. However, in 1974, following the miraculous deliverance during the Yom Kippur War, the Rabbinate, headed by Rabbi Shlomo Goren, ruled that that year, Hallel should be said with a blessing.

5. The Rabbinate instituted the recitation of Hallel in the morning prayers, but not in the evening prayers. Some communities also recite Hallel on the evening of Yom HaAtzma'ut, as they do on Pesaḥ. The main source for this recitation comes from Rabbi Shlomo Goren (in his book *Torat HaShabbat VeHaMoed*.) He holds that reciting Hallel in the evening is obligatory, because a miracle that takes place at night (such as the exodus from Egypt) requires the recitation of Hallel at night, and most of the miracles of the War of Independence took place at night. Many disagreed with his argument, and communities differ. Most do not say Hallel at night, some recite Hallel without a blessing, and a few communities do say Hallel in the spirit of Rabbi Goren. Each congregation must fix their own custom, in accordance with their communities.

Rabbi Goren's opinion is supported by another argument, that of "publicizing the miracle." In tractate *Berakhot* 14a, Rabbi Ḥiyya is

בְּצֵאת When Israel came out of Egypt, the house of Jacob *Ps. 114*
from a people of foreign tongue, Judah became His sanctuary,
Israel His dominion. The sea saw and fled; the Jordan turned
back. The mountains skipped like rams, the hills like lambs. ‣
Why was it, sea, that you fled? Jordan, why did you turn back?
Why, mountains, did you skip like rams, and you, hills, like
lambs? It was at the presence of the LORD, Creator of the earth,
at the presence of the God of Jacob, who turned the rock into
a pool of water, flint into a flowing spring.

לֹא לָנוּ Not to us, LORD, not to us, but to Your name give glory, *Ps. 115*
for Your love, for Your faithfulness. Why should the nations
say, "Where now is their God?" Our God is in heaven; what-

Perhaps the *type* of sin determines our ability to remain in our Land. We
were first expelled due to cardinal sins; chief among them idol worship.
Outright theological rebellion shatters our historical contract with our Land,
and prompts our expulsion. During the Second Temple Era our society was
fractured by internecine struggle and ideological hatred. A frayed nation
lost its mandate to reside as a unified nation in its homeland. In the absence
of these conditions – even under conditions of religious malfunction – the
Land embraces her children.

Alternatively, conscious rebels aren't tolerated by the Land, while innocent
wayward children are embraced. The generations of the First and Second
Temples were exposed to revelation and miracles, and lived close enough
to the exodus to vividly recall those events. Their mutiny is offensive to the
Land and cannot be countenanced. Modern secular Jews who have returned
to Israel lack religious education and may not operate under the demands
of previous generations. Their entry into the Land isn't preconditioned on
religious awakening; they are welcomed home, despite religious malfunction,
with the hope that their return will one day awaken religious interest.

A NATION OF MONOTHEISM – PSALM 115
The great task of the Jewish People is to disseminate the message of monotheism to an entire world. The predominantly monotheistic environment which
we inhabit reflects the success of the Jewish mission. Christianity and Islam
each lifted Jewish ideas of monotheism, and helped propagate these concepts

בְּצֵאת יִשְׂרָאֵל מִמִּצְרָיִם, בֵּית יַעֲקֹב מֵעַם לֹעֵז: הָיְתָה יְהוּדָה לְקָדְשׁוֹ, יִשְׂרָאֵל מַמְשְׁלוֹתָיו: הַיָּם רָאָה וַיָּנֹס, הַיַּרְדֵּן יִסֹּב לְאָחוֹר: הֶהָרִים רָקְדוּ כְאֵילִים, גְּבָעוֹת כִּבְנֵי־צֹאן: מַה־לְּךָ הַיָּם כִּי תָנוּס, הַיַּרְדֵּן תִּסֹּב לְאָחוֹר: הֶהָרִים תִּרְקְדוּ כְאֵילִים, גְּבָעוֹת כִּבְנֵי־צֹאן: מִלִּפְנֵי אָדוֹן חוּלִי אָרֶץ, מִלִּפְנֵי אֱלֽוֹהַּ יַעֲקֹב: הַהֹפְכִי הַצּוּר אֲגַם־מָיִם, חַלָּמִישׁ לְמַעְיְנוֹ־מָיִם:

לֹא לָנוּ יהוה לֹא לָנוּ, כִּי־לְשִׁמְךָ תֵּן כָּבוֹד, עַל־חַסְדְּךָ עַל־אֲמִתֶּךָ: לָמָּה יֹאמְרוּ הַגּוֹיִם אַיֵּה־נָא אֱלֹהֵיהֶם: וֵאלֹהֵינוּ

our return as a homecoming. Though our warrant to remain in our Land is dependent upon our religious and moral behavior, our actual presence in Israel has meaning – flawed meaning – but meaning, even without complete religious fidelity.

Yeḥezkel captures this concept when he describes "when the people of Israel were living in their own Land, they defiled it by their conduct and their actions. Their conduct was like a woman's monthly uncleanness in My sight" (36:17). The *pasuk* presents a strange formulation: Jewish residence in Israel which, in effect, contaminates the Land. The prophet censures this tragedy, but *Ḥazal* invert the meaning of this verse. In *Eikha Raba* (3:7) the *pasuk* depicts a wistful God, longing for the return of His rebellious children: "I wish My children would return *even if* they contaminate the Land by their infidelity." A parallel midrash actually presents HaKadosh Barukh Hu as nostalgic for His errant children: "Would it be that My aberrant children would be united with Me, as we were in the desert."

It is difficult to reconcile this nostalgia with verses which attribute our expulsion from Israel to our wayward behavior. Among the numerous verses, the most graphic is the *pasuk* in *Vayikra* (18:28) which portrays our expulsion as a national spewing: "And if you defile the Land, it will vomit you out as it vomited out the nations that were before you." Under which conditions are we welcomed in our Land despite our betrayal, and under which conditions are we expelled?

ever He wills He does. Their idols are silver and gold, made by human hands. They have mouths but cannot speak; eyes but cannot see. They have ears but cannot hear; noses but cannot smell. They have hands but cannot feel; feet but cannot walk. No sound comes from their throat. Those who make them become like them; so will all who trust in them. ▸ Israel, trust in the LORD – He is their Help and their Shield. House of Aaron, trust in the LORD – He is their Help and their Shield. You who fear the LORD, trust in the LORD – He is their Help and their Shield.

יהוה זְכָרָנוּ The LORD remembers us and will bless us. He will bless the house of Israel. He will bless the house of Aaron. He will bless those who fear the LORD, small and great alike. May the LORD give you increase: you and your children. May you be blessed by the LORD, Maker of heaven and earth. ▸ The heavens are the LORD's, but the earth He has given over to

---

Throughout history, regardless of overall religious commitment, Jews have steadfastly and courageously avoided any humanizing imageries of HaKadosh Barukh Hu, while preserving our pure blend of monotheism. For two thousand years Jews have heroically confronted aggressive attempts to sway us from our unadulterated concept of God – even to the point of death. This great miracle of history warrants our redemption, even if certain segments of our people have abandoned classical religious performance. Despite this unfortunate regression, Jews across the world continue to represent pure monotheism, and this calling is loyal to our original covenant with HaKadosh Barukh Hu, whose terminus is national redemption.

The right for redemption based solely on our heroic adherence to monotheism is stressed in three verses of *Tehillim*:

If we had forgotten the name of our God or spread out our hands to a foreign god, would not God have discovered it, since He knows the secrets of the heart?

Yet for Your sake we face death all day long; we are considered as sheep to be slaughtered. (*Tehillim* 44:21–23)

בַּשָּׁמָיִם, כֹּל אֲשֶׁר־חָפֵץ עָשָׂה: עֲצַבֵּיהֶם כֶּסֶף וְזָהָב, מַעֲשֵׂה
יְדֵי אָדָם: פֶּה־לָהֶם וְלֹא יְדַבֵּרוּ, עֵינַיִם לָהֶם וְלֹא יִרְאוּ: אָזְנַיִם
לָהֶם וְלֹא יִשְׁמָעוּ, אַף לָהֶם וְלֹא יְרִיחוּן: יְדֵיהֶם וְלֹא יְמִישׁוּן,
רַגְלֵיהֶם וְלֹא יְהַלֵּכוּ, לֹא־יֶהְגּוּ בִּגְרוֹנָם: כְּמוֹהֶם יִהְיוּ עֹשֵׂיהֶם,
כֹּל אֲשֶׁר־בֹּטֵחַ בָּהֶם: ◄ יִשְׂרָאֵל בְּטַח בַּיהוה, עֶזְרָם וּמָגִנָּם
הוּא: בֵּית אַהֲרֹן בִּטְחוּ בַיהוה, עֶזְרָם וּמָגִנָּם הוּא: יִרְאֵי
יהוה בִּטְחוּ בַיהוה, עֶזְרָם וּמָגִנָּם הוּא:

יהוה זְכָרָנוּ יְבָרֵךְ, יְבָרֵךְ אֶת־בֵּית יִשְׂרָאֵל, יְבָרֵךְ אֶת־בֵּית
אַהֲרֹן: יְבָרֵךְ יִרְאֵי יהוה, הַקְּטַנִּים עִם־הַגְּדֹלִים: יֹסֵף יהוה
עֲלֵיכֶם, עֲלֵיכֶם וְעַל־בְּנֵיכֶם: בְּרוּכִים אַתֶּם לַיהוה, עֹשֵׂה
שָׁמַיִם וָאָרֶץ: ◄ הַשָּׁמַיִם שָׁמַיִם לַיהוה, וְהָאָרֶץ נָתַן לִבְנֵי־

---

to a world audience. Even though each religion corrupted our pure brand of
monotheism, they still succeeded in transitioning humanity from ancient
idolatry into modern monotheism. One of the basic tenets of monotheism
is that HaKadosh Barukh Hu has absolutely no physical likeness or imagery.
Here we will outline the absurdity of casting God in physical form.

A pivotal moment in the history of monotheism occurred after the destruction of the First *Mikdash*. Nebuchadnezzar gathered emissaries from across the
globe to kneel before his six-story idol which was ablaze with fire. One by one
each culture submitted to his indomitable authority, and worshiped his statue.
Only three relatively unknown Jews defied his authority, refused his command,
and championed the cause of monotheism. Ḥananya, Misha'el, and Azarya
were forcibly thrust into Nebuchadnezzar's fiery furnace, while reciting the
phrases of this chapter, and reinforcing the presence of monotheism during an
otherwise dark period. The era of the First Temple had been marred by widespread idol worship. Though believing in God, most Jews also deified pagan
idols. This hypocrisy exiled ten tribes and ultimately destroyed the *Mikdash*.
The defiance of these three martyrs not only debunked Nebuchadnezzar's faith,
but it also reestablished the Jewish mission of monotheism.

mankind. It is not the dead who praise the Lord, nor those who go down to the silent grave. But we will bless the Lord, now and for ever. Halleluya!

אָהַבְתִּי I love the Lord, for He hears my voice, my pleas. *Ps. 116* He turns His ear to me whenever I call. The bonds of death encompassed me, the anguish of the grave came upon me, I was overcome by trouble and sorrow. Then I called on the name of the Lord: "Lord, I pray, save my life." Gracious is the Lord, and righteous; our God is full of compassion. The Lord protects the simple hearted. When I was brought low, He saved me. My soul, be at peace once more, for the Lord has been good to you. For You have rescued me from death, my eyes from weeping, my feet from stumbling. ‣ I shall walk in the presence of the Lord in the land of the living. I had faith, even when I said, "I am greatly afflicted," even when I said rashly, "All men are liars."

מָה־אָשִׁיב How can I repay the Lord for all His goodness to me? I will lift the cup of salvation and call on the name of the Lord. I will fulfill my vows to the Lord in the presence of all His people. Grievous in the Lord's sight is the death of His devoted ones. Truly, Lord, I am Your servant; I am Your servant, the son of Your maidservant. You set me free from my chains. ‣ To You I shall bring a thanksgiving-offering and call on the Lord by name. I will fulfill my vows to the Lord in the presence of all His people, in the courts of the House of the Lord, in your midst, Jerusalem. Halleluya!

---

verse reminds us, "My Beloved is like a gazelle or a young stag, look! There He stands behind our wall, gazing through the windows, peering through the lattice" (*Shir HaShirim* 2:9).

The reference to His lingering behind our walls is an allusion to the part of the *Mikdash* which was never abandoned by HaKadosh Barukh Hu – the

אָדָם: לֹא הַמֵּתִים יְהַלְלוּ־יָהּ, וְלֹא כָּל־יֹרְדֵי דוּמָה: וַאֲנַחְנוּ
נְבָרֵךְ יָהּ, מֵעַתָּה וְעַד־עוֹלָם, הַלְלוּיָהּ:

תהלים קטז

אָהַבְתִּי, כִּי־יִשְׁמַע יהוה, אֶת־קוֹלִי תַּחֲנוּנָי: כִּי־הִטָּה אָזְנוֹ
לִי, וּבְיָמַי אֶקְרָא: אֲפָפוּנִי חֶבְלֵי־מָוֶת, וּמְצָרֵי שְׁאוֹל מְצָאוּנִי,
צָרָה וְיָגוֹן אֶמְצָא: וּבְשֵׁם־יהוה אֶקְרָא, אָנָּה יהוה מַלְּטָה
נַפְשִׁי: חַנּוּן יהוה וְצַדִּיק, וֵאלֹהֵינוּ מְרַחֵם: שֹׁמֵר פְּתָאִים
יהוה, דַּלּוֹתִי וְלִי יְהוֹשִׁיעַ: שׁוּבִי נַפְשִׁי לִמְנוּחָיְכִי, כִּי־יהוה
גָּמַל עָלָיְכִי: כִּי חִלַּצְתָּ נַפְשִׁי מִמָּוֶת, אֶת־עֵינִי מִן־דִּמְעָה,
אֶת־רַגְלִי מִדֶּחִי: ◂ אֶתְהַלֵּךְ לִפְנֵי יהוה, בְּאַרְצוֹת הַחַיִּים:
הֶאֱמַנְתִּי כִּי אֲדַבֵּר, אֲנִי עָנִיתִי מְאֹד: אֲנִי אָמַרְתִּי בְחָפְזִי,
כָּל־הָאָדָם כֹּזֵב:

מָה־אָשִׁיב לַיהוה, כָּל־תַּגְמוּלוֹהִי עָלָי: כּוֹס־יְשׁוּעוֹת
אֶשָּׂא, וּבְשֵׁם יהוה אֶקְרָא: נְדָרַי לַיהוה אֲשַׁלֵּם, נֶגְדָה־נָּא
לְכָל־עַמּוֹ: יָקָר בְּעֵינֵי יהוה, הַמָּוְתָה לַחֲסִידָיו: אָנָּה יהוה
כִּי־אֲנִי עַבְדֶּךָ, אֲנִי־עַבְדְּךָ בֶּן־אֲמָתֶךָ, פִּתַּחְתָּ לְמוֹסֵרָי:
◂ לְךָ־אֶזְבַּח זֶבַח תּוֹדָה, וּבְשֵׁם יהוה אֶקְרָא: נְדָרַי לַיהוה
אֲשַׁלֵּם, נֶגְדָה־נָּא לְכָל־עַמּוֹ: בְּחַצְרוֹת בֵּית יהוה, בְּתוֹכֵכִי
יְרוּשָׁלָיִם, הַלְלוּיָהּ:

בְּחַצְרוֹת בֵּית יהוה *In the courts of the House of the Lord.* A verse in *Shir HaShir-im* describes our Redeemer bounding over mountains and leaping over cliffs. This imagery implies the excitement, energy and enthusiasm of our *geula.* The following verse reminds us that although He appears during the redemptive experience, He was always *present,* though not noticeably observable. As the

הַלְלוּ Praise the LORD, all nations;
acclaim Him, all you peoples;
for His loving-kindness to us is strong,
and the LORD's faithfulness is everlasting.
Halleluya!

The following verses are chanted by the Leader.
At the end of each verse, the congregation responds, "Thank the LORD
for He is good; His loving-kindness is for ever."

הוֹדוּ Thank the LORD

for He is good; His loving-kindness is for ever.
Let Israel say   His loving-kindness is for ever.
Let the house of Aaron say   His loving-kindness is for ever.
Let those who fear the LORD say   His loving-kindness is for ever.

מִן־הַמֵּצַר In my distress I called on the LORD. The LORD answered me and set me free. The LORD is with me; I will not be afraid. What can man do to me? The LORD is with me. He is my Helper. I will see the downfall of my enemies. It is better to take refuge in the LORD than to trust in man. It is better to take refuge in the LORD than to trust in princes. The nations all surrounded me, but in the LORD's name I drove

Ps. 117
Ps. 118

כָּל־גּוֹיִם סְבָבוּנִי *The nations all surrounded me.* In the Diaspora, Jews were often persecuted and discriminated against. Lacking a homeland, we were expelled or contained in ghettos, but rarely did we experience being "surrounded." Additionally we were typically oppressed by a *particular* nation or tyrant. We rarely if ever faced a situation of being encircled by "*all the nations.*"

Returning to Israel and establishing our State we encounter this menace. We are literally surrounded by enemies bent on our destruction, and we look to HaKadosh Barukh Hu as our only prospect. We face both military threats and diplomatic threats lodged by alliances of nations. This scenario clearly describes a Messianic event in Israel.

Ḥazal associated this experience of being helplessly surrounded with the great wars of Gog and Magog. The war will be centered upon a surrounded Yerushalayim and an international force will be mustered. The three verses

הַלְלוּ אֶת־יהוה כָּל־גּוֹיִם, שַׁבְּחוּהוּ כָּל־הָאֻמִּים:
כִּי גָבַר עָלֵינוּ חַסְדּוֹ, וֶאֱמֶת־יהוה לְעוֹלָם
הַלְלוּיָהּ:

The following verses are chanted by the שליח ציבור.
At the end of each verse, the קהל *responds:* הוֹדוּ לַיהוה כִּי־טוֹב, כִּי לְעוֹלָם חַסְדּוֹ.

הוֹדוּ לַיהוה כִּי־טוֹב	כִּי לְעוֹלָם חַסְדּוֹ:
יֹאמַר־נָא יִשְׂרָאֵל	כִּי לְעוֹלָם חַסְדּוֹ:
יֹאמְרוּ־נָא בֵית־אַהֲרֹן	כִּי לְעוֹלָם חַסְדּוֹ:
יֹאמְרוּ־נָא יִרְאֵי יהוה	כִּי לְעוֹלָם חַסְדּוֹ:

מִן־הַמֵּצַר קָרָאתִי יָּהּ, עָנָנִי בַמֶּרְחָב יָהּ: יהוה לִי לֹא אִירָא, מַה־
יַּעֲשֶׂה לִי אָדָם: יהוה לִי בְּעֹזְרָי, וַאֲנִי אֶרְאֶה בְשֹׂנְאָי: טוֹב לַחֲסוֹת
בַּיהוה, מִבְּטֹחַ בָּאָדָם: טוֹב לַחֲסוֹת בַּיהוה, מִבְּטֹחַ בִּנְדִיבִים:
כָּל־גּוֹיִם סְבָבְוּנִי, בְּשֵׁם יהוה כִּי אֲמִילַם: סַבְּוּנִי גַם־סְבָבְוּנִי, בְּשֵׁם

Western Wall. Though this wall formed only the outer perimeter of the original *Mikdash*, it outlasted the destruction of the rest of the *Mikdash*, and continues to house the Divine Presence which still dwells "behind our wall." Though the *Shekhina* may have departed from the overall compound of the *Mikdash*, it remained secreted behind the *Kotel*, preserving the Temple Mount for Jewish settlement.

The prominent role of the *Kotel* in reviving Jewish spirit is a redemptive indicator. Though denied the Jewish people in 1948, the *Kotel* was recovered in 1967 and immediately became the epicenter of Jewish spiritual and national experience. Jews who had previously been hostile toward religion experienced revelational epiphanies upon visiting the Wall. World Jewry discerns in the Wall the last vestige of our wrecked *Mikdash*, but also the starting point for its rebuilding. The iconic images of paratroopers visiting the Wall they had fought so spiritedly to recover remain forever etched in our national consciousness.

them off. They surrounded me on every side, but in the LORD's name
I drove them off. They surrounded me like bees, they attacked me as
fire attacks brushwood, but in the LORD's name I drove them off. They
thrust so hard against me, I nearly fell, but the LORD came to my help.
The LORD is my strength and my song; He has become my salvation.
Sounds of song and salvation resound in the tents of the righteous:
"The LORD's right hand has done mighty deeds. The LORD's right hand
is lifted high. The LORD's right hand has done mighty deeds." I will not
die but live, and tell what the LORD has done. The LORD has chastened
me severely, but He has not given me over to death. ‣ Open for me the
gates of righteousness that I may enter them and thank the LORD. This
is the gateway to the LORD; through it, the righteous shall enter.

אוֹדְךָ I will thank You, for You answered me, and became my salvation.
I will thank You, for You answered me, and became my salvation.

The stone the builders rejected has become the main cornerstone.
The stone the builders rejected has become the main cornerstone.

This is the LORD's doing; it is wondrous in our eyes.
This is the LORD's doing; it is wondrous in our eyes.

This is the day the LORD has made; let us rejoice and be glad in it.
This is the day the LORD has made; let us rejoice and be glad in it.

However, when personal conduct may not merit that passage, he may pass
through a national entry point – the Gates of Faith.

Commenting on the Gates of Faith, the Midrash (*Mekhilta DeRabbi Yishmael Masekhta DeVayehi* chapter 6) describes entry for all who have maintained their belief in HaKadosh Barukh Hu throughout history. Implicit in
the midrash is the notion that even those whose behavior may not merit
entry through the gates of the righteous are granted passage through the
national gates of faith. Highlighting the value of faith as a national experience,
the midrash cites the original faith expressed by Avraham which warranted
his selection and license to the Land of Israel. The midrash also stresses the
faith experienced at the banks of the Reed Sea as the catalyst for subsequent
national *shira*.

A parallel Gemara toward the end of *Makkot* describes various prophets

יְהוה כִּי אֲמִילַם: סַבּוּנִי כִדְבֹרִים, דֹּעֲכוּ כְּאֵשׁ קוֹצִים, בְּשֵׁם יְהוה
כִּי אֲמִילַם: דָּחֹה דְחִיתַנִי לִנְפֹּל, וַיהוה עֲזָרָנִי: עָזִּי וְזִמְרָת יָהּ,
וַיְהִי־לִי לִישׁוּעָה: קוֹל רִנָּה וִישׁוּעָה בְּאָהֳלֵי צַדִּיקִים, יְמִין יְהוה
עֹשָׂה חָיִל: יְמִין יְהוה רוֹמֵמָה, יְמִין יְהוה עֹשָׂה חָיִל: לֹא־אָמוּת
כִּי־אֶחְיֶה, וַאֲסַפֵּר מַעֲשֵׂי יָהּ: יַסֹּר יִסְּרַנִּי יָּהּ, וְלַמָּוֶת לֹא נְתָנָנִי:
◆ פִּתְחוּ־לִי שַׁעֲרֵי־צֶדֶק, אָבֹא־בָם אוֹדֶה יָהּ: זֶה־הַשַּׁעַר לַיהוה,
צַדִּיקִים יָבֹאוּ בוֹ:

אוֹדְךָ כִּי עֲנִיתָנִי, וַתְּהִי־לִי לִישׁוּעָה:
אוֹדְךָ כִּי עֲנִיתָנִי, וַתְּהִי־לִי לִישׁוּעָה:

אֶבֶן מָאֲסוּ הַבּוֹנִים, הָיְתָה לְרֹאשׁ פִּנָּה:
אֶבֶן מָאֲסוּ הַבּוֹנִים, הָיְתָה לְרֹאשׁ פִּנָּה:

מֵאֵת יְהוה הָיְתָה זֹּאת, הִיא נִפְלָאת בְּעֵינֵינוּ:
מֵאֵת יְהוה הָיְתָה זֹּאת, הִיא נִפְלָאת בְּעֵינֵינוּ:

זֶה־הַיּוֹם עָשָׂה יְהוה, נָגִילָה וְנִשְׂמְחָה בוֹ:
זֶה־הַיּוֹם עָשָׂה יְהוה, נָגִילָה וְנִשְׂמְחָה בוֹ:

describing the "surrounding" imply three different waves of attacks during this war. Only at the final stage will God fully redeem us.

The final "surrounding" is portrayed as bees circling a hive. Bees are frightening, but ultimately produce honey and improve the hive. The Messianic resolution won't merely be the rescuing of Jews from their enemies. The outcome of the surrounding of Yerushalayim will be an enhanced city, both materially and spiritually. The wars will – in some fashion – contribute to the Messianic utopia.

שַׁעֲרֵי־צֶדֶק *Gates of righteousness.* The verse in Hallel announces entry for the righteous. A parallel verse in *Yeshayahu* (26:2) invites a nation of believers to enter the gates. Ideally a Jew passes through the gates of the *Tzaddikim.*

Leader followed by congregation:

אָנָּא LORD, please, save us.
LORD, please, save us.
LORD, please, grant us success.
LORD, please, grant us success.

בָּרוּךְ Blessed is one who comes in the name of the LORD;
we bless you from the House of the LORD.
Blessed is one who comes in the name of the LORD;
we bless you from the House of the LORD.

The LORD is God; He has given us light. Bind the festival
offering with thick cords [and bring it] to the horns of the altar.
The LORD is God; He has given us light. Bind the festival offering
with thick cords [and bring it] to the horns of the altar.

You are my God and I will thank You;
You are my God, I will exalt You.
You are my God and I will thank You; You are my God, I will exalt You.

Thank the LORD for He is good;
His loving-kindness is for ever.
Thank the LORD for He is good; His loving-kindness is for ever.

יְהַלְלוּךָ All Your works will praise You, LORD our God, and Your
devoted ones – the righteous who do Your will, together with all
Your people the house of Israel – will joyously thank, bless, praise,
glorify, exalt, revere, sanctify, and proclaim the sovereignty of
Your name, our King. ▸ For it is good to thank You and fitting to
sing psalms to Your name, for from eternity to eternity You are
God. Blessed are You, LORD, King who is extolled with praises.

Despite the inability of many Jews to fully sustain the entire Jewish experience, our steadfast faith in HaKadosh Barukh Hu and in our national mission
still remains robust. The national gates of faith admit all those whose *emuna*
outlasted the travails of history.

קָהָל followed by שליח ציבור:

אָנָּא יהוה הוֹשִׁיעָה נָּא:

אָנָּא יהוה הוֹשִׁיעָה נָּא:

אָנָּא יהוה הַצְלִיחָה נָא:

אָנָּא יהוה הַצְלִיחָה נָא:

בָּרוּךְ הַבָּא בְּשֵׁם יהוה, בֵּרַכְנוּכֶם מִבֵּית יהוה:

בָּרוּךְ הַבָּא בְּשֵׁם יהוה, בֵּרַכְנוּכֶם מִבֵּית יהוה:

אֵל יהוה וַיָּאֶר לָנוּ, אִסְרוּ־חַג בַּעֲבֹתִים עַד־קַרְנוֹת הַמִּזְבֵּחַ:

אֵל יהוה וַיָּאֶר לָנוּ, אִסְרוּ־חַג בַּעֲבֹתִים עַד־קַרְנוֹת הַמִּזְבֵּחַ:

אֵלִי אַתָּה וְאוֹדֶךָּ, אֱלֹהַי אֲרוֹמְמֶךָּ:

אֵלִי אַתָּה וְאוֹדֶךָּ, אֱלֹהַי אֲרוֹמְמֶךָּ:

הוֹדוּ לַיהוה כִּי־טוֹב, כִּי לְעוֹלָם חַסְדּוֹ:

הוֹדוּ לַיהוה כִּי־טוֹב, כִּי לְעוֹלָם חַסְדּוֹ:

יְהַלְלוּךָ יהוה אֱלֹהֵינוּ כָּל מַעֲשֶׂיךָ, וַחֲסִידֶיךָ צַדִּיקִים עוֹשֵׂי רְצוֹנֶךָ, וְכָל עַמְּךָ בֵּית יִשְׂרָאֵל בְּרִנָּה, יוֹדוּ וִיבָרְכוּ וִישַׁבְּחוּ וִיפָאֲרוּ וִירוֹמְמוּ, וְיַעֲרִיצוּ וְיַקְדִּישׁוּ וְיַמְלִיכוּ אֶת שִׁמְךָ מַלְכֵּנוּ, ◂ כִּי לְךָ טוֹב לְהוֹדוֹת וּלְשִׁמְךָ נָאֶה לְזַמֵּר, כִּי מֵעוֹלָם וְעַד עוֹלָם אַתָּה אֵל. בָּרוּךְ אַתָּה יהוה, מֶלֶךְ מְהֻלָּל בַּתִּשְׁבָּחוֹת.

who reduced Judaism to core values. Recognizing the inability of the masses to fully comply with the extensive halakhic system, each prophet attempted to reduce the experience to several seminal values. The final "reducer" was Ḥavakkuk who claimed, "See, the enemy is puffed up; his desires are not upright – but the righteous person will live by his faithfulness" (2:4) – the core of Judaism is faith.

FULL KADDISH

Leader: יִתְגַּדַּל Magnified and sanctified may His great name be,
in the world He created by His will.
May He establish His kingdom
in your lifetime and in your days,
and in the lifetime of all the house of Israel,
swiftly and soon –
and say: Amen.

All: May His great name be blessed for ever and all time.

Leader: Blessed and praised,
glorified and exalted,
raised and honored,
uplifted and lauded be
the name of the Holy One,
blessed be He, beyond any blessing,
song, praise and consolation
uttered in the world –
and say: Amen.

May the prayers and pleas of all Israel
be accepted by their Father in heaven –
and say: Amen.

May there be great peace from heaven,
and life for us and all Israel –
and say: Amen.

*Bow, take three steps back, as if taking leave of the Divine Presence,
then bow, first left, then right, then center, while saying:*

May He who makes peace in His high places,
make peace for us and all Israel –
and say: Amen.

קדיש שלם

ש״ץ: יִתְגַּדַּל וְיִתְקַדַּשׁ שְׁמֵהּ רַבָּא (קהל: אָמֵן)

בְּעָלְמָא דִּי בְרָא כִרְעוּתֵהּ

וְיַמְלִיךְ מַלְכוּתֵהּ

בְּחַיֵּיכוֹן וּבְיוֹמֵיכוֹן וּבְחַיֵּי דְכָל בֵּית יִשְׂרָאֵל

בַּעֲגָלָא וּבִזְמַן קָרִיב, וְאִמְרוּ אָמֵן. (קהל: אָמֵן)

קהל
 וש״ץ: יְהֵא שְׁמֵהּ רַבָּא מְבָרַךְ לְעָלַם וּלְעָלְמֵי עָלְמַיָּא.

ש״ץ: יִתְבָּרַךְ וְיִשְׁתַּבַּח וְיִתְפָּאַר וְיִתְרוֹמַם וְיִתְנַשֵּׂא

וְיִתְהַדָּר וְיִתְעַלֶּה וְיִתְהַלָּל

שְׁמֵהּ דְּקֻדְשָׁא בְּרִיךְ הוּא (קהל: בְּרִיךְ הוּא)

לְעֵלָּא מִן כָּל בִּרְכָתָא

וְשִׁירָתָא, תֻּשְׁבְּחָתָא וְנֶחֱמָתָא

דַּאֲמִירָן בְּעָלְמָא, וְאִמְרוּ אָמֵן. (קהל: אָמֵן)

תִּתְקַבַּל צְלוֹתְהוֹן וּבָעוּתְהוֹן דְּכָל יִשְׂרָאֵל

קֳדָם אֲבוּהוֹן דִּי בִשְׁמַיָּא, וְאִמְרוּ אָמֵן. (קהל: אָמֵן)

יְהֵא שְׁלָמָא רַבָּא מִן שְׁמַיָּא

וְחַיִּים, עָלֵינוּ וְעַל כָּל יִשְׂרָאֵל, וְאִמְרוּ אָמֵן. (קהל: אָמֵן)

Bow, take three steps back, as if taking leave of the Divine Presence,
then bow, first left, then right, then center, while saying:

עֹשֶׂה שָׁלוֹם בִּמְרוֹמָיו

הוּא יַעֲשֶׂה שָׁלוֹם

עָלֵינוּ וְעַל כָּל יִשְׂרָאֵל, וְאִמְרוּ אָמֵן. (קהל: אָמֵן)

The Ark is opened
and the following is said responsively by the Leader and congregation.

Listen, Israel: the Lᴏʀᴅ is our God, the Lᴏʀᴅ is One. *Deut. 6*

The following is said three times responsively:

The Lᴏʀᴅ, He is God.

The Leader says the following which is repeated by the congregation.

מִי שֶׁעָשָׂה May He who performed miracles
for our ancestors and for us,
redeeming us from slavery to freedom,
grant us a complete redemption soon,
and gather in our dispersed people
from the four quarters of the earth,
so that all Israel may be united in friendship,
and let us say: Amen.

The Ark is closed.

The Leader continues:

וְכִי־תָבֹאוּ When you go into battle in your land against an enemy who *Num. 10*
is attacking you, sound a staccato blast on the trumpets. Then you
will be remembered by the Lᴏʀᴅ your God and you will be delivered
from your enemies. On your days of rejoicing – your festivals and new
moon celebrations – you shall sound a note on the trumpets over your
burnt- and peace-offerings, and they will be a remembrance for you
before your God. I am the Lᴏʀᴅ your God.

---

now ongoing and we hope that its culmination is imminent, rather than
distant in time and place.   YR

ISRAEL AND ITS LAND

The Holy One, blessed be He, said to Moses: The land is beloved to Me, as
it says [Deuteronomy 11:12]: "A land which God continually wants"; and
Israel is beloved to Me, as it says [ibid. 7:8]: "Out of the Lᴏʀᴅ's love for
you." The Holy One, blessed be He, said: I will bring Israel, who is beloved
to Me, to the land that is beloved to Me, as it says (Numbers 34:2): "For
you are coming to the land of Canaan." (*Bemidbar Raba* 23:7)

דברים ו

The ארון קודש *is opened*
and the following is said responsively by the שליח ציבור *and the* קהל.

שְׁמַע יִשְׂרָאֵל, יהוה אֱלֹהֵינוּ, יהוה אֶחָד:

The following is said three times responsively:

יהוה הוּא הָאֱלֹהִים.

The שליח ציבור *says the following which is repeated by the* קהל.

מִי שֶׁעָשָׂה נִסִּים לַאֲבוֹתֵינוּ וְלָנוּ
וּגְאָלֵנוּ מֵעַבְדוּת לְחֵרוּת
הוּא יִגְאָלֵנוּ גְּאֻלָּה שְׁלֵמָה בְּקָרוֹב
וִיקַבֵּץ נִדָּחֵינוּ מֵאַרְבַּע כַּנְפוֹת הָאָרֶץ
חֲבֵרִים כָּל יִשְׂרָאֵל, וְנֹאמַר אָמֵן.

The ארון קודש *is closed.*

The שליח ציבור *continues:*

במדבר י

וְכִי־תָבֹאוּ מִלְחָמָה בְּאַרְצְכֶם עַל־הַצַּר הַצֹּרֵר אֶתְכֶם, וַהֲרֵעֹתֶם
בַּחֲצֹצְרֹת, וְנִזְכַּרְתֶּם לִפְנֵי יהוה אֱלֹהֵיכֶם, וְנוֹשַׁעְתֶּם מֵאֹיְבֵיכֶם:
וּבְיוֹם שִׂמְחַתְכֶם וּבְמוֹעֲדֵיכֶם וּבְרָאשֵׁי חָדְשֵׁכֶם, וּתְקַעְתֶּם
בַּחֲצֹצְרֹת עַל עֹלֹתֵיכֶם וְעַל זִבְחֵי שַׁלְמֵיכֶם, וְהָיוּ לָכֶם לְזִכָּרוֹן
לִפְנֵי אֱלֹהֵיכֶם, אֲנִי יהוה אֱלֹהֵיכֶם:

מִי שֶׁעָשָׂה נִסִּים *May He who performed miracles.* This passage is adapted from
the blessing recited in the morning prayers on the Shabbat preceding Rosh
Ḥodesh. The most striking differences are related to the root גאל, "redeem."
The Shabbat prayer is phrased וגאל אותם – "and redeemed them" – referring
to our ancestors, while here it says וגאלנו – "redeeming *us*." Similarly, the word
ולנו, "and for us," is added to the opening "May He who performed miracles
for our ancestors *and for us.*" We also add the phrase "a complete redemption" to the original prayer "redeem us soon." The redemption process is

The shofar is sounded with a Tekia Gedola and the following is said aloud:

Next year in Jerusalem rebuilt.

All:

May it be Your will, Lord our God and God of our fathers,
That as we have merited to witness the beginning of redemption,
So may we merit to hear the sound of the shofar
of our righteous anointed one, swiftly in our days.

All sing:

שִׁיר הַמַּעֲלוֹת A song of ascents. When the Lord brought back the ex- *Ps. 126* iles of Zion we were like people who dream. Then were our mouths filled with laughter, and our tongues with songs of joy. Then was it said among the nations, "The Lord has done great things for them." The Lord did do great things for us and we rejoiced. Bring back our exiles, Lord, like streams in a dry land. May those who sowed in tears, reap in joy. May one who goes out weeping, carrying a bag of seed, come back with songs of joy, carrying his sheaves.

---

the redemption of Israel and Jerusalem in the days of the return to Zion, and the sense of joy which envelops the redeemed. The first words, "When the Lord brought back the exiles of Zion we were like people who dream," present a picture of a people who cannot believe what is unfolding before their eyes. This verse is contrasted with "Then was it said among the nations" – the nations are the first to recognize the magnitude of the event – "The Lord has done great things for them."

Rabbi Elḥanan Samet, in his commentary on Psalms, writes:

No other psalm…expresses the national experience related to the establishment of the State and the days that followed. In the days of the establishment of the State, we fulfilled the description "we were like people who dream," joy abounded throughout the Jewish nation, and we all declared, "The Lord did do great things for us." Immediately afterward, the newborn State, which held about six hundred thousand Jews within it, was plunged into fierce war with the enemies who surrounded it…but the prayers of the returnees to Zion (the founders of the State), "Bring back our exiles, Lord, like streams in a dry land," were answered. A great surge of immigrants flooded the State after its establishment, and in the years that followed.

The שופר *is sounded with a* תקיעה גדולה *and the following is said aloud:*

לְשָׁנָה הַבָּאָה בִּירוּשָׁלַיִם הַבְּנוּיָה.

All:

יְהִי רָצוֹן מִלְּפָנֶיךָ יהוה אֱלֹהֵינוּ וֵאלֹהֵי אֲבוֹתֵינוּ
שֶׁכְּשֵׁם שֶׁזָּכִינוּ לְאַתְחַלְתָּא דִגְאֻלָּה
כֵּן נִזְכֶּה לִשְׁמְעַ קוֹל שׁוֹפָרוֹ שֶׁל מָשִׁיחַ צִדְקֵנוּ בִּמְהֵרָה בְיָמֵינוּ.

All sing:

תהלים קכו

שִׁיר הַמַּעֲלוֹת, בְּשׁוּב יהוה אֶת־שִׁיבַת צִיּוֹן, הָיִינוּ כְּחֹלְמִים: אָז
יִמָּלֵא שְׂחוֹק פִּינוּ וּלְשׁוֹנֵנוּ רִנָּה, אָז יֹאמְרוּ בַגּוֹיִם הִגְדִּיל יהוה
לַעֲשׂוֹת עִם־אֵלֶּה: הִגְדִּיל יהוה לַעֲשׂוֹת עִמָּנוּ, הָיִינוּ שְׂמֵחִים:
שׁוּבָה יהוה אֶת־שְׁבִיתֵנוּ, כַּאֲפִיקִים בַּנֶּגֶב: הַזֹּרְעִים בְּדִמְעָה
בְּרִנָּה יִקְצֹרוּ: הָלוֹךְ יֵלֵךְ וּבָכֹה נֹשֵׂא מֶשֶׁךְ־הַזָּרַע, בֹּא־יָבֹא בְרִנָּה
נֹשֵׂא אֲלֻמֹּתָיו:

JERUSALEM IS THE HIGHEST JOY

All of Israel rejoice "when the LORD brings back the exiles of Zion," and "Jerusalem is set above my highest joy." Jerusalem is the highest. We have returned to our Land, to our place, and all of us rejoice. But the central joy is in Jerusalem. "Then will our mouths be filled with laughter." We have arrived at that "then," when our mouths will fill with laughter and our tongues with songs of joy. "Then it will be said among the nations..." Thank God, we have arrived, and the nations around us are saying, "The LORD has done great things for them." And so we too say, "The LORD has done great things for us," and rejoice. And we pray, "Bring back our exiles, LORD, like streams in a dry land… May they come back with songs of joy, carrying their sheaves." Thank God, the sheaves are already beginning to show in the fields, as the LORD brings back the exiles of Zion, finally, wholly, greatly.

(Rabbi A.I. Kook, *The Redemptive Torah*, 4, 100–108)

שִׁיר הַמַּעֲלוֹת *A song of ascents.* The connection between Yom HaAtzma'ut and Psalm 126 is apparent from the content of the psalm itself, which is related to

COUNTING OF THE OMER

Some say the following meditation before the blessing:
For the sake of the unification of the Holy One, blessed be He,
and His Divine Presence, in reverence and love,
to unify the name *Yod-Heh* with *Vav-Heh*
in perfect unity in the name of all Israel.

הִנְנִי I am prepared and ready to fulfill the positive commandment of Counting the Omer, as is written in the Torah, "You shall count seven complete   *Lev. 23*
weeks from the day following the [Pesaḥ] rest day, when you brought the
Omer as a wave-offering. To the day after the seventh week you shall count
fifty days. Then you shall present a meal-offering of new grain to the Lord."
May the pleasantness of the Lord our God be upon us. Establish for us the   *Ps. 90*
work of our hands, O establish the work of our hands.

בָּרוּךְ Blessed are You, Lord our God, King of the Universe,
who has made us holy through His commandments,
and has commanded us about counting the Omer.

3 Iyar   Today is the eighteenth day,
making two weeks and four days of the Omer.

4 Iyar   Today is the nineteenth day,
making two weeks and five days of the Omer.

5 Iyar   Today is the twentieth day,
making two weeks and six days of the Omer.

6 Iyar   Today is the twenty-first day,
making three weeks of the Omer.

הָרַחֲמָן May the Compassionate One restore the Temple service
to its place speedily in our days. Amen, Selah.

COUNTING OF THE OMER
The official date of Yom HaAtzma'ut is the 5th of Iyar, but it can fall anytime
between the 3rd and the 6th of Iyar.   YR

סדר ספירת העומר

Some say the following meditation before the blessing:

לְשֵׁם יִחוּד קֻדְשָׁא בְּרִיךְ הוּא וּשְׁכִינְתֵּהּ בִּדְחִילוּ וּרְחִימוּ
לְיַחֵד שֵׁם י״ה בו״ה בְּיִחוּדָא שְׁלִים בְּשֵׁם כָּל יִשְׂרָאֵל.

הִנְנִי מוּכָן וּמְזֻמָּן לְקַיֵּם מִצְוַת עֲשֵׂה שֶׁל סְפִירַת הָעֹמֶר. כְּמוֹ שֶׁכָּתוּב בַּתּוֹרָה,
וּסְפַרְתֶּם לָכֶם מִמָּחֳרַת הַשַּׁבָּת, מִיּוֹם הֲבִיאֲכֶם אֶת־עֹמֶר הַתְּנוּפָה, שֶׁבַע   _{ויקרא כג}
שַׁבָּתוֹת תְּמִימֹת תִּהְיֶינָה: עַד מִמָּחֳרַת הַשַּׁבָּת הַשְּׁבִיעִת תִּסְפְּרוּ חֲמִשִּׁים
יוֹם, וְהִקְרַבְתֶּם מִנְחָה חֲדָשָׁה לַיהוה: וִיהִי נֹעַם אֲדֹנָי אֱלֹהֵינוּ עָלֵינוּ, וּמַעֲשֵׂה   _{תהלים צ}
יָדֵינוּ כּוֹנְנָה עָלֵינוּ, וּמַעֲשֵׂה יָדֵינוּ כּוֹנְנֵהוּ:

בָּרוּךְ אַתָּה יהוה אֱלֹהֵינוּ מֶלֶךְ הָעוֹלָם
אֲשֶׁר קִדְּשָׁנוּ בְּמִצְוֹתָיו וְצִוָּנוּ עַל סְפִירַת הָעֹמֶר.

ג׳ באייר: הַיּוֹם שְׁמוֹנָה עָשָׂר יוֹם

שֶׁהֵם שְׁנֵי שָׁבוּעוֹת וְאַרְבָּעָה יָמִים בָּעֹמֶר.   _{נצח שבתפארת}

ד׳ באייר: הַיּוֹם תִּשְׁעָה עָשָׂר יוֹם

שֶׁהֵם שְׁנֵי שָׁבוּעוֹת וַחֲמִשָּׁה יָמִים בָּעֹמֶר.   _{הוד שבתפארת}

ה׳ באייר: הַיּוֹם עֶשְׂרִים יוֹם

שֶׁהֵם שְׁנֵי שָׁבוּעוֹת וְשִׁשָּׁה יָמִים בָּעֹמֶר.   _{יסוד שבתפארת}

ו׳ באייר: הַיּוֹם אֶחָד וְעֶשְׂרִים יוֹם

שֶׁהֵם שְׁלֹשָׁה שָׁבוּעוֹת בָּעֹמֶר.   _{מלכות שבתפארת}

הָרַחֲמָן הוּא יַחֲזִיר לָנוּ עֲבוֹדַת בֵּית הַמִּקְדָּשׁ לִמְקוֹמָהּ
בִּמְהֵרָה בְיָמֵינוּ, אָמֵן סֶלָה.

Rabbi Y.L. Maimon, Israel's first Minister of Religion, suggested this psalm
as the national anthem. It seems that this is the source of the custom of singing Psalm 126 on Yom HaAtzma'ut to the tune of "HaTikva."

Some add:

לַמְנַצֵּחַ For the conductor of music. With stringed instruments. A psalm, a song. *Ps. 67*
May God be gracious to us and bless us. May He make His face shine on us, Selah.
Then will Your way be known on earth, Your salvation among all the nations. Let
the peoples praise You, God; let all peoples praise You. Let nations rejoice and
sing for joy, for You judge the peoples with equity, and guide the nations of the
earth, Selah. Let the peoples praise You, God; let all peoples praise You. The earth
has yielded its harvest. May God, our God, bless us. God will bless us, and all the
ends of the earth will fear Him.

אָנָּא Please, by the power of Your great right hand, set the captive nation free.
Accept Your people's prayer. Strengthen us, purify us, You who are revered. Please,
Mighty One, guard like the pupil of the eye those who seek Your unity. Bless them,
cleanse them, have compassion on them, grant them Your righteousness always.
Mighty One, Holy One, in Your great goodness guide Your congregation. Only
One, Exalted One, turn to Your people, who proclaim Your holiness. Accept our
plea and heed our cry, You who know all secret thoughts. Blessed be the name
of His glorious kingdom for ever and all time.

רִבּוֹנוֹ שֶׁל עוֹלָם Master of the Universe, You commanded us through Your servant
Moses to count the Omer, to cleanse our carapaces and impurities, as You have
written in Your Torah: "You shall count seven complete weeks from the day *Lev. 23*
following the [Pesaḥ] rest day, when you brought the Omer as a wave-offering. To
the day after the seventh week, you shall count fifty days." This is so that the souls
of Your people Israel may be purified from their uncleanliness. May it also be
Your will, Lord our God and God of our ancestors, that in the merit of the Omer
count that I have counted today, there may be rectified any defect on my part in
the counting of (*insert the appropriate sefira for each day*). May I be cleansed and
sanctified with Your holiness on high, and through this may there flow a rich
stream through all worlds, to rectify our lives, spirits and souls from any dross
and defect, purifying and sanctifying us with Your sublime holiness. Amen, Selah.

Stand while saying Aleinu. Bow at ˙.

עָלֵינוּ It is our duty to praise the Master of all,
and ascribe greatness to the Author of creation,
who has not made us like the nations of the lands
nor placed us like the families of the earth;
who has not made our portion like theirs,
nor our destiny like all their multitudes.
(For they worship vanity and emptiness,
and pray to a god who cannot save.)

תהילים סו

לַמְנַצֵּחַ בִּנְגִינֹת, מִזְמוֹר שִׁיר: אֱלֹהִים יְחָנֵּנוּ וִיבָרְכֵנוּ, יָאֵר פָּנָיו אִתָּנוּ סֶלָה:
לָדַעַת בָּאָרֶץ דַּרְכֶּךָ, בְּכָל־גּוֹיִם יְשׁוּעָתֶךָ: יוֹדוּךָ עַמִּים אֱלֹהִים, יוֹדוּךָ עַמִּים
כֻּלָּם: יִשְׂמְחוּ וִירַנְּנוּ לְאֻמִּים, כִּי־תִשְׁפֹּט עַמִּים מִישֹׁר, וּלְאֻמִּים בָּאָרֶץ תַּנְחֵם
סֶלָה: יוֹדוּךָ עַמִּים אֱלֹהִים, יוֹדוּךָ עַמִּים כֻּלָּם: אֶרֶץ נָתְנָה יְבוּלָהּ, יְבָרְכֵנוּ
אֱלֹהִים אֱלֹהֵינוּ: יְבָרְכֵנוּ אֱלֹהִים, וְיִירְאוּ אוֹתוֹ כָּל־אַפְסֵי־אָרֶץ:

אָנָּא, בְּכֹחַ גְּדֻלַּת יְמִינְךָ, תַּתִּיר צְרוּרָה. קַבֵּל רִנַּת עַמְּךָ, שַׂגְּבֵנוּ, טַהֲרֵנוּ,
נוֹרָא. נָא גִבּוֹר, דּוֹרְשֵׁי יִחוּדְךָ כְּבָבַת שָׁמְרֵם. בָּרְכֵם, טַהֲרֵם, רַחֲמֵם, צִדְקָתְךָ
תָּמִיד גָּמְלֵם. חֲסִין קָדוֹשׁ, בְּרֹב טוּבְךָ נַהֵל עֲדָתֶךָ. יָחִיד גֵּאֶה, לְעַמְּךָ פְּנֵה,
זוֹכְרֵי קְדֻשָּׁתֶךָ. שַׁוְעָתֵנוּ קַבֵּל וּשְׁמַע צַעֲקָתֵנוּ, יוֹדֵעַ תַּעֲלוּמוֹת. בָּרוּךְ שֵׁם
כְּבוֹד מַלְכוּתוֹ לְעוֹלָם וָעֶד.

רִבּוֹנוֹ שֶׁל עוֹלָם, אַתָּה צִוִּיתָנוּ עַל יְדֵי מֹשֶׁה עַבְדְּךָ לִסְפֹּר סְפִירַת הָעֹמֶר,
ויקרא כג
כְּדֵי לְטַהֲרֵנוּ מִקְּלִפּוֹתֵינוּ וּמִטֻּמְאוֹתֵינוּ. כְּמוֹ שֶׁכָּתַבְתָּ בְּתוֹרָתֶךָ: וּסְפַרְתֶּם
לָכֶם מִמָּחֳרַת הַשַּׁבָּת, מִיּוֹם הֲבִיאֲכֶם אֶת־עֹמֶר הַתְּנוּפָה, שֶׁבַע שַׁבָּתוֹת
תְּמִימֹת תִּהְיֶינָה: עַד מִמָּחֳרַת הַשַּׁבָּת הַשְּׁבִיעִת תִּסְפְּרוּ חֲמִשִּׁים יוֹם:
כְּדֵי שֶׁיִּטָּהֲרוּ נַפְשׁוֹת עַמְּךָ יִשְׂרָאֵל מִזֻּהֲמָתָם. וּבְכֵן יְהִי רָצוֹן מִלְּפָנֶיךָ יהוה
אֱלֹהֵינוּ וֵאלֹהֵי אֲבוֹתֵינוּ, שֶׁבִּזְכוּת סְפִירַת הָעֹמֶר שֶׁסָּפַרְתִּי הַיּוֹם, יְתֻקַּן
מַה שֶּׁפָּגַמְתִּי בִּסְפִירָה (insert appropriate ספירה for each day) וְאֶטָּהֵר וְאֶתְקַדֵּשׁ
בִּקְדֻשָּׁה שֶׁל מַעְלָה, וְעַל יְדֵי זֶה יֻשְׁפַּע שֶׁפַע רַב בְּכָל הָעוֹלָמוֹת, לְתַקֵּן
אֶת נַפְשׁוֹתֵינוּ וְרוּחוֹתֵינוּ וְנִשְׁמוֹתֵינוּ מִכָּל סִיג וּפְגָם, וּלְטַהֲרֵנוּ וּלְקַדְּשֵׁנוּ
בִּקְדֻשָּׁתְךָ הָעֶלְיוֹנָה, אָמֵן סֶלָה.

Stand while saying עָלֵינוּ. Bow at ˅.

עָלֵינוּ לְשַׁבֵּחַ לַאֲדוֹן הַכֹּל, לָתֵת גְּדֻלָּה לְיוֹצֵר בְּרֵאשִׁית
שֶׁלֹּא עָשָׂנוּ כְּגוֹיֵי הָאֲרָצוֹת, וְלֹא שָׂמָנוּ כְּמִשְׁפְּחוֹת הָאֲדָמָה.
שֶׁלֹּא שָׂם חֶלְקֵנוּ כָּהֶם וְגוֹרָלֵנוּ כְּכָל הֲמוֹנָם.
(שֶׁהֵם מִשְׁתַּחֲוִים לְהֶבֶל וָרִיק וּמִתְפַּלְלִים אֶל אֵל לֹא יוֹשִׁיעַ.)

˅But we bow in worship and thank the Supreme King of kings,
  the Holy One, blessed be He,
  who extends the heavens and establishes the earth,
  whose throne of glory is in the heavens above,
  and whose power's Presence is in the highest of heights.
  He is our God; there is no other.
  Truly He is our King, there is none else,
  as it is written in His Torah:
"You shall know and take to heart this day   *Deut. 4*
  that the Lᴏʀᴅ is God,
  in heaven above and on earth below. There is no other."

Therefore, we place our hope in You, Lᴏʀᴅ our God,
  that we may soon see the glory of Your power,
  when You will remove abominations from the earth,
  and idols will be utterly destroyed,
  when the world will be perfected
  under the sovereignty of the Almighty,
  when all humanity will call on Your name,
  to turn all the earth's wicked toward You.
  All the world's inhabitants will realize and know
  that to You every knee must bow and every tongue swear loyalty.
  Before You, Lᴏʀᴅ our God, they will kneel and bow down
  and give honor to Your glorious name.
  They will all accept the yoke of Your kingdom,
  and You will reign over them soon and for ever.
  For the kingdom is Yours, and to all eternity You will reign in glory,
  as it is written in Your Torah: "The Lᴏʀᴅ will reign for ever and ever."   *Ex. 15*
▸ And it is said: "Then the Lᴏʀᴅ shall be King over all the earth;   *Zech. 14*
  on that day the Lᴏʀᴅ shall be One and His name One."

Some add:

Have no fear of sudden terror or of the ruin when it overtakes the wicked.   *Prov. 3*
Devise your strategy, but it will be thwarted; propose your plan,   *Is. 8*
but it will not stand, for God is with us.
When you grow old, I will still be the same.   *Is. 46*
When your hair turns gray, I will still carry you.
I made you, I will bear you, I will carry you, and I will rescue you.

וַאֲנַחְנוּ כּוֹרְעִים וּמִשְׁתַּחֲוִים וּמוֹדִים

לִפְנֵי מֶלֶךְ מַלְכֵי הַמְּלָכִים, הַקָּדוֹשׁ בָּרוּךְ הוּא

שֶׁהוּא נוֹטֶה שָׁמַיִם וְיוֹסֵד אָרֶץ

וּמוֹשַׁב יְקָרוֹ בַּשָּׁמַיִם מִמַּעַל, וּשְׁכִינַת עֻזּוֹ בְּגָבְהֵי מְרוֹמִים.

הוּא אֱלֹהֵינוּ, אֵין עוֹד.

אֱמֶת מַלְכֵּנוּ, אֶפֶס זוּלָתוֹ

כַּכָּתוּב בְּתוֹרָתוֹ

דברים ד

וְיָדַעְתָּ הַיּוֹם וַהֲשֵׁבֹתָ אֶל־לְבָבֶךָ

כִּי יהוה הוּא הָאֱלֹהִים בַּשָּׁמַיִם מִמַּעַל וְעַל־הָאָרֶץ מִתָּחַת, אֵין עוֹד:

עַל כֵּן נְקַוֶּה לְךָ יהוה אֱלֹהֵינוּ, לִרְאוֹת מְהֵרָה בְּתִפְאֶרֶת עֻזֶּךָ

לְהַעֲבִיר גִּלּוּלִים מִן הָאָרֶץ, וְהָאֱלִילִים כָּרוֹת יִכָּרֵתוּן

לְתַקֵּן עוֹלָם בְּמַלְכוּת שַׁדַּי.

וְכָל בְּנֵי בָשָׂר יִקְרְאוּ בִשְׁמֶךָ לְהַפְנוֹת אֵלֶיךָ כָּל רִשְׁעֵי אָרֶץ.

יַכִּירוּ וְיֵדְעוּ כָּל יוֹשְׁבֵי תֵבֵל

כִּי לְךָ תִּכְרַע כָּל בֶּרֶךְ, תִּשָּׁבַע כָּל לָשׁוֹן.

לְפָנֶיךָ יהוה אֱלֹהֵינוּ יִכְרְעוּ וְיִפֹּלוּ, וְלִכְבוֹד שִׁמְךָ יְקָר יִתֵּנוּ

וִיקַבְּלוּ כֻלָּם אֶת עֹל מַלְכוּתֶךָ

וְתִמְלֹךְ עֲלֵיהֶם מְהֵרָה לְעוֹלָם וָעֶד.

כִּי הַמַּלְכוּת שֶׁלְּךָ הִיא וּלְעוֹלְמֵי עַד תִּמְלֹךְ בְּכָבוֹד

שמות טו

כַּכָּתוּב בְּתוֹרָתֶךָ, יהוה יִמְלֹךְ לְעֹלָם וָעֶד:

זכריה יד

‹ וְנֶאֱמַר, וְהָיָה יהוה לְמֶלֶךְ עַל־כָּל־הָאָרֶץ

בַּיּוֹם הַהוּא יִהְיֶה יהוה אֶחָד וּשְׁמוֹ אֶחָד:

Some add:

משלי ג

אַל־תִּירָא מִפַּחַד פִּתְאֹם וּמִשֹּׁאַת רְשָׁעִים כִּי תָבֹא:

ישעיה ח

עֻצוּ עֵצָה וְתֻפָר, דַּבְּרוּ דָבָר וְלֹא יָקוּם, כִּי עִמָּנוּ אֵל:

ישעיה מו

וְעַד־זִקְנָה אֲנִי הוּא, וְעַד־שֵׂיבָה אֲנִי אֶסְבֹּל אֲנִי עָשִׂיתִי וַאֲנִי אֶשָּׂא וַאֲנִי אֶסְבֹּל וַאֲמַלֵּט:

MOURNER'S KADDISH

The following prayer, said by mourners, requires the presence of a minyan.
A transliteration can be found on page 667.

Mourner: יִתְגַּדַּל Magnified and sanctified
may His great name be,
in the world He created by His will.
May He establish His kingdom
in your lifetime and in your days,
and in the lifetime of all the house of Israel,
swiftly and soon –
and say: Amen.

All: May His great name be blessed for ever and all time.

Mourner: Blessed and praised, glorified and exalted,
raised and honored,
uplifted and lauded
be the name of the Holy One,
blessed be He, beyond any blessing,
song, praise and consolation
uttered in the world –
and say: Amen.

May there be great peace from heaven,
and life for us and all Israel –
and say: Amen.

Bow, take three steps back, as if taking leave of the Divine Presence,
then bow, first left, then right, then center, while saying:

May He who makes peace in His high places,
make peace for us and all Israel –
and say: Amen.

In Israel, the person saying Kaddish adds:
Bless the Lord, the blessed One.

and the congregation responds:
Bless the Lord, the blessed One, for ever and all time.

קדיש יתום

The following prayer, said by mourners, requires the presence of a מנין.
A transliteration can be found on page 667.

אבל: יִתְגַּדַּל וְיִתְקַדַּשׁ שְׁמֵהּ רַבָּא (קהל: אָמֵן)
בְּעָלְמָא דִּי בְרָא כִרְעוּתֵהּ
וְיַמְלִיךְ מַלְכוּתֵהּ
בְּחַיֵּיכוֹן וּבְיוֹמֵיכוֹן וּבְחַיֵּי דְּכָל בֵּית יִשְׂרָאֵל
בַּעֲגָלָא וּבִזְמַן קָרִיב, וְאִמְרוּ אָמֵן. (קהל: אָמֵן)

קהל
ואבל: יְהֵא שְׁמֵהּ רַבָּא מְבָרַךְ לְעָלַם וּלְעָלְמֵי עָלְמַיָּא.

אבל: יִתְבָּרַךְ וְיִשְׁתַּבַּח וְיִתְפָּאַר
וְיִתְרוֹמַם וְיִתְנַשֵּׂא וְיִתְהַדָּר וְיִתְעַלֶּה וְיִתְהַלָּל
שְׁמֵהּ דְּקֻדְשָׁא בְּרִיךְ הוּא (קהל: בְּרִיךְ הוּא)
לְעֵלָּא מִן כָּל בִּרְכָתָא
וְשִׁירָתָא, תֻּשְׁבְּחָתָא וְנֶחֱמָתָא
דַּאֲמִירָן בְּעָלְמָא, וְאִמְרוּ אָמֵן. (קהל: אָמֵן)

יְהֵא שְׁלָמָא רַבָּא מִן שְׁמַיָּא
וְחַיִּים, עָלֵינוּ וְעַל כָּל יִשְׂרָאֵל, וְאִמְרוּ אָמֵן. (קהל: אָמֵן)

Bow, take three steps back, as if taking leave of the Divine Presence,
then bow, first left, then right, then center, while saying:

עֹשֶׂה שָׁלוֹם בִּמְרוֹמָיו
הוּא יַעֲשֶׂה שָׁלוֹם
עָלֵינוּ וְעַל כָּל יִשְׂרָאֵל, וְאִמְרוּ אָמֵן. (קהל: אָמֵן)

In ארץ ישראל, the person saying קדיש adds:
בָּרְכוּ אֶת יהוה הַמְבֹרָךְ.
and the קהל responds:
בָּרוּךְ יהוה הַמְבֹרָךְ לְעוֹלָם וָעֶד.

Great is the living God and praised.
    He exists, and His existence is beyond time.
He is One, and there is no unity like His.
    Unfathomable, His oneness is infinite.
He has neither bodily form nor substance;
    His holiness is beyond compare.
He preceded all that was created.
    He was first: there was no beginning to His beginning.
Behold He is Master of the Universe; and every creature
    shows His greatness and majesty.
The rich flow of His prophecy He gave
    to His treasured people in whom He gloried.
Never in Israel has there arisen another like Moses,
    a prophet who beheld God's image.
God gave His people a Torah of truth
    by the hand of His prophet, most faithful of His House.
God will not alter or change His law
    for any other, for eternity.
He sees and knows our secret thoughts;
    as soon as something is begun, He foresees its end.
He rewards people with loving-kindness according to their deeds;
    He punishes the wicked according to his wickedness.
At the end of days He will send our Messiah
    to redeem those who await His final salvation.
God will revive the dead in His great loving-kindness.
    Blessed for evermore is His glorious name!

All sing:

אֲנִי מַאֲמִין I believe with perfect faith
    in the coming of the Messiah,
        and though he may delay,
        I wait daily for his coming.

It is customary to greet each other with the following phrase:
Happy festival; to a complete redemption!

יִגְדַּל אֱלֹהִים חַי וְיִשְׁתַּבַּח, נִמְצָא וְאֵין עֵת אֶל מְצִיאוּתוֹ.

אֶחָד וְאֵין יָחִיד כְּיִחוּדוֹ, נֶעְלָם וְגַם אֵין סוֹף לְאַחְדּוּתוֹ.

אֵין לוֹ דְּמוּת הַגּוּף וְאֵינוֹ גוּף, לֹא נַעֲרֹךְ אֵלָיו קְדֻשָּׁתוֹ.

קַדְמוֹן לְכָל דָּבָר אֲשֶׁר נִבְרָא, רִאשׁוֹן וְאֵין רֵאשִׁית לְרֵאשִׁיתוֹ.

הִנּוֹ אֲדוֹן עוֹלָם, וְכָל נוֹצָר יוֹרֶה גְדֻלָּתוֹ וּמַלְכוּתוֹ.

שֶׁפַע נְבוּאָתוֹ נְתָנוֹ אֶל־אַנְשֵׁי סְגֻלָּתוֹ וְתִפְאַרְתּוֹ.

לֹא קָם בְּיִשְׂרָאֵל כְּמֹשֶׁה עוֹד נָבִיא וּמַבִּיט אֶת תְּמוּנָתוֹ.

תּוֹרַת אֱמֶת נָתַן לְעַמּוֹ אֵל עַל יַד נְבִיאוֹ נֶאֱמַן בֵּיתוֹ.

לֹא יַחֲלִיף הָאֵל וְלֹא יָמִיר דָּתוֹ לְעוֹלָמִים לְזוּלָתוֹ.

צוֹפֶה וְיוֹדֵעַ סְתָרֵינוּ, מַבִּיט לְסוֹף דָּבָר בְּקַדְמָתוֹ.

גּוֹמֵל לְאִישׁ חֶסֶד כְּמִפְעָלוֹ, נוֹתֵן לְרָשָׁע רַע כְּרִשְׁעָתוֹ.

יִשְׁלַח לְקֵץ יָמִין מְשִׁיחֵנוּ לִפְדּוֹת מְחַכֵּי קֵץ יְשׁוּעָתוֹ.

מֵתִים יְחַיֶּה אֵל בְּרֹב חַסְדּוֹ, בָּרוּךְ עֲדֵי עַד שֵׁם תְּהִלָּתוֹ.

All sing:

אֲנִי מַאֲמִין בֶּאֱמוּנָה שְׁלֵמָה בְּבִיאַת הַמָּשִׁיחַ
וְאַף עַל פִּי שֶׁיִּתְמַהְמֵהַּ
עִם כָּל זֶה אֲחַכֶּה לּוֹ בְּכָל יוֹם שֶׁיָּבוֹא.

It is customary to greet each other with the following phrase:

מוֹעֲדִים לְשִׂמְחָה לִגְאֻלָּה שְׁלֵמָה

It is customary to have a festive meal on the night of Yom HaAtzma'ut. See page 147.

HATIKVA

The service continues with HaTikva.

כָּל עוֹד As long as in the heart, within,
A Jewish soul still yearns,
And onward, towards the ends of the east,
An eye still gazes toward Zion;

Our hope is not yet lost,
The hope of two thousand years,
To be a free people in our land,
The land of Zion and Jerusalem.

The transliteration of HaTikva:

Kol od balevav penima
Nefesh yehudi homiya,
Ulfa'atei mizraḥ, kadima,
Ayin letziyon tzofiya;

Od lo av'da tikvatenu,
Hatikva bat sh'not alpayim,
Lihyot am ḥofshi b'artzenu,
Eretz tziyon virushalayim.

התקווה

The service continues with התקווה.

כָּל עוֹד
בַּלֵּבָב פְּנִימָה
נֶפֶשׁ יְהוּדִי הוֹמִיָּה
וּלְפַאֲתֵי מִזְרָח, קָדִימָה
עַיִן לְצִיּוֹן צוֹפִיָּה

עוֹד לֹא אָבְדָה תִּקְוָתֵנוּ
הַתִּקְוָה בַּת שְׁנוֹת אַלְפַּיִם
לִהְיוֹת עַם חָפְשִׁי בְּאַרְצֵנוּ
אֶרֶץ צִיּוֹן וִירוּשָׁלַיִם.

BLESSING OF THE NEW MOON

Kiddush Levana, the Blessing of the New Moon, is said between the third day and the middle day of each month, under the open sky, and in the presence of a minyan.

הַלְלוּיָהּ Halleluya! Praise the LORD from the heavens, praise Him in *Ps. 148* the heights. Praise Him, all His angels; praise Him, all His hosts. Praise Him, sun and moon; praise Him, all shining stars. Praise Him, highest heavens and the waters above the heavens. Let them praise the name of the LORD, for He commanded and they were created. He established them for ever and all time, issuing a decree that will never change.

כִּי־אֶרְאֶה When I see Your heavens, the work of Your fingers, the moon *Ps. 8* and the stars which You have set in place: What is man that You are mindful of him, the son of man that You care for him?

---

to recite the blessing on Motza'ei Shabbat, the optimum night, and therefore one should not postpone the blessing.

Blessing the New Moon has come to express more than a blessing of praise over the renewal of the moon. The version of the blessing in the Jerusalem Talmud (*Berakhot* 9:2) only expresses praise to the Creator for the renewal of the month, and some manuscripts of the Babylonian Talmud (*Berakhot* 59b) also reflect this focus on praise to God for the might of creation. However, more accepted printed versions of the Babylonian Talmud (*Sanhedrin* 42a) already conceive of the blessing over the New Moon as a festive, public ceremony, which completely changes the status of the blessing. The Talmud adds a comparison between the nation of Israel and the moon: "A crown of beauty for those He carried from the womb [Israel], for they are destined to be renewed like [the moon]." The sages who instituted this blessing perceived the cycle of the moon as a symbol for the nation of Israel, who in exile become diminished and distant from the source of light, but in the time of redemption return and illuminate the world in renewed splendor. This perspective resulted in the blessing over the New Moon becoming a public ceremony in which the entire congregation, decked in their Shabbat attire, stands together and expresses their yearning for the renewal of God's sovereignty over the world as embodied by the house of David. The readings that accompany this special ceremony include "David, King of Israel, lives and endures" (*Rosh HaShana* 25a); "The voice of my beloved – I hear him coming"

קידוש לבנה

קידוש לבנה, *the Blessing of the New Moon, is said between the third day and the middle day of each month, under the open sky, and in the presence of a* מנין.

תהלים קמח הַלְלוּיָהּ, הַלְלוּ אֶת־יהוה מִן־הַשָּׁמַיִם, הַלְלוּהוּ בַּמְּרוֹמִים: הַלְלוּהוּ כָל־מַלְאָכָיו, הַלְלוּהוּ כָּל־צְבָאָו: הַלְלוּהוּ שֶׁמֶשׁ וְיָרֵחַ, הַלְלוּהוּ כָּל־כּוֹכְבֵי אוֹר: הַלְלוּהוּ שְׁמֵי הַשָּׁמָיִם, וְהַמַּיִם אֲשֶׁר מֵעַל הַשָּׁמָיִם: יְהַלְלוּ אֶת־שֵׁם יהוה, כִּי הוּא צִוָּה וְנִבְרָאוּ: וַיַּעֲמִידֵם לָעַד לְעוֹלָם, חָק־נָתַן וְלֹא יַעֲבוֹר:

תהלים ח כִּי־אֶרְאֶה שָׁמֶיךָ מַעֲשֵׂה אֶצְבְּעֹתֶיךָ, יָרֵחַ וְכוֹכָבִים אֲשֶׁר כּוֹנָנְתָּה: מָה־אֱנוֹשׁ כִּי־תִזְכְּרֶנּוּ, וּבֶן־אָדָם כִּי תִפְקְדֶנּוּ:

BLESSING THE NEW MOON ON YOM HAATZMA'UT EVENING

According to Talmudic tradition, the blessing over the New Moon should be recited soon after its renewal. Yemenite Jews, following the ruling of Maimonides (*Laws of Blessings* 10:17), recite this blessing from the first of the month. Ashkenazic and Lithuanian custom (according to the ruling of the students of Rabbeinu Yona in *Berakhot* 21b) holds that one should wait until the third night of the month in order to enjoy the light of the New Moon (which is too weak when it first appears). Following Kabbalistic tradition, many wait until the seventh of the month (see *Shulḥan Arukh, Oraḥ Ḥayyim* 426:2).

It is the custom of most congregations to recite the blessing of the New Moon on Motza'ei Shabbat, when the synagogue is full of congregants dressed in their Shabbat best. This tradition originates in *Massekhet Soferim* (19:10): "The moon should only be blessed on Motza'ei Shabbat, when [the congregant] is perfumed, wearing fine clothing."

In the book *Terumat HaDeshen* (part 35), the author discusses the linking of the blessing of the New Moon to Motza'ei Shabbat. In his answer, he differentiates between Motza'ei Shabbat that falls during the first three days of the month and a much later Motza'ei Shabbat in winter, where there is concern that the moon will be covered with clouds, thereby prohibiting the blessing from being recited. He posits that such a concern overrides the preference

Look at the moon, then say:

בָּרוּךְ Blessed are You, LORD our God, King of the Universe who by His word created the heavens, and by His breath all their host. He set for them laws and times, so that they should not deviate from their appointed task. They are joyous and glad to perform the will of their Owner, the Worker of truth whose work is truth. To the moon He said that it should renew itself as a crown of beauty for those He carried from the womb [Israel], for they are destined to be renewed like it, and to praise their Creator for the sake of His glorious majesty. Blessed are You, LORD, who renews the months.

Israel does a *Beit Din* enjoy full legislative ability, and calendar adjustments are therefore limited to there.

However the Midrash (*Yalkut Shimoni Bereshit* chapter 5) describes our *Avot* adjusting the calendar. When Yaakov attempts to adjust it in exile he is stopped by HaKadosh Barukh Hu, who reminds him that this activity is limited to the Land of Israel. Evidently there is an *inherent* limitation to the Land irrespective of the status of *Beit Din* outside of Israel. In altering the calendar, our *Avot* did not assume the status of *Beit Din*, and yet Yaakov was denied this ability when in exile.

Manipulating the calendar by adding a month was necessary to modulate climatic factors which could adversely affect society. For example a month was added if limited rainfall threatened the availability of grains for Pesaḥ. Of course these socioeconomic factors are only significant enough to warrant calendar adjustment in Israel.

The more subtle adjustment of the monthly schedule (by adding an extra day) was based on witnessing lunar patterns. Though the moon is visible across the globe, only its primary vector – and hence its primary audience – is stationed in Israel. Only lunar data collected in Israel can factor into calendar modification.

Beyond the *logistics* and *function* of calendar being limited to the Land of Israel, there is a separate reason that only Israel-based courts can manipulate the calendar. "Adjusting" time is an expression of man's empowerment to interact with a divinely created universe. HaKadosh Barukh Hu created immutable planets and set them into inexorable orbit. Typically, human beings merely translate these fixed patterns into marked and quantified

Look at the moon, then say:

בָּרוּךְ אַתָּה יהוה אֱלֹהֵינוּ מֶלֶךְ הָעוֹלָם, אֲשֶׁר בְּמַאֲמָרוֹ בָּרָא שְׁחָקִים, וּבְרוּחַ פִּיו כָּל צְבָאָם, חֹק וּזְמַן נָתַן לָהֶם שֶׁלֹּא יְשַׁנּוּ אֶת תַּפְקִידָם. שָׂשִׂים וּשְׂמֵחִים לַעֲשׂוֹת רְצוֹן קוֹנָם, פּוֹעֵל אֱמֶת שֶׁפְּעֻלָּתוֹ אֱמֶת. וְלַלְּבָנָה אָמַר שֶׁתִּתְחַדֵּשׁ, עֲטֶרֶת תִּפְאֶרֶת לַעֲמוּסֵי בָטֶן, שֶׁהֵם עֲתִידִים לְהִתְחַדֵּשׁ כְּמוֹתָהּ וּלְפָאֵר לְיוֹצְרָם עַל שֵׁם כְּבוֹד מַלְכוּתוֹ. בָּרוּךְ אַתָּה יהוה, מְחַדֵּשׁ חֳדָשִׁים.

(Song of Songs 2:8), and others, which were added to the blessing of the New Moon in the time of Rabbi Yehuda HeḤasid, one of the first harbingers of Zionism.

In light of all this, it seems only natural to conclude the festive prayer service of Yom HaAtzma'ut with the recital of the blessing of the New Moon, with the entire congregation, in festive clothing, and with special joy. The very essence of this blessing reflects our nation's yearning for the renewal of Israel's independence and return to Zion. Now, as we stand together to thank God for the establishment of the State, we can recite the blessing of the New Moon with abundant joy, thanksgiving, and praise.   BL

ALTERING TIME IN THE LAND OF ISRAEL

Regulating the Lunar Calendar and scheduling Jewish Holidays is a unique Jewish capacity. Unlike other religions our calendar isn't fixed but can be flexible. Minute changes to the duration of each month and larger alterations such as adding an extra month can affect the calendar and our experience of time. The mathematically and intellectually gifted tribe of Issachar excelled in this field, and according to some positions these astronomical calculations entail an actual mitzva. Aside from being necessary to enable the manipulation of the calendar, these computations expose the clockwork nature of God's universe, and the vast infinity of His handiwork.

This calendar engineering can only be performed by a *Beit Din* in Israel. In fact an episode of altering the calendar which occurred outside of Israel came under sharp criticism, as recounted by the Gemara (*Berakhot* 63a), which likened this non-licensed activity to heresy. Presumably the limitation to the Land of Israel is based on the need for a fully operational *Beit Din*. Only in

The following five verses are each said three times:

Blessed is He who formed you; blessed is He who made you; blessed is He who owns you; blessed is He who created you.

The following verse is said rising on the toes.

Just as I leap toward you but cannot touch you, so may none of my enemies be able to touch me to do me harm.

May fear and dread fall upon them; *Ex. 15* by the power of Your arm may they be still as stone.

May they be still as stone through the power of Your arm, when dread and fear fall upon them.

David, King of Israel, lives and endures.

Turn to three people and say to each:

Peace upon you.

They respond:

Upon you, peace.

Say three times:

May it be a good sign and a good omen for us and all Israel. Amen.

קוֹל Hark! My beloved! Here he comes, leaping over the mountains, *Song. 2* bounding over the hills. My beloved is like a gazelle, like a young deer. There he stands outside our wall, peering in through the windows, gazing through the lattice.

שִׁיר לַמַּעֲלוֹת A song of ascents. I lift my eyes up to the hills; from where *Ps. 121* will my help come? My help comes from the LORD, Maker of heaven and earth. He will not let your foot stumble; He who guards you does not slumber. See: the Guardian of Israel neither slumbers nor sleeps. The LORD is your Guardian; the LORD is your Shade at your right hand.

---

a status which surpasses typical human identity. Jews living in Israel are fulfilling a divine program, and one manifestation is their ability to effect "independent time."

The following five verses are each said three times:

בָּרוּךְ יוֹצְרֶךְ, בָּרוּךְ עוֹשֵׂךְ, בָּרוּךְ קוֹנֶךְ, בָּרוּךְ בּוֹרְאֶךְ.

The following verse is said rising on the toes.

כְּשֵׁם שֶׁאֲנִי רוֹקֵד כְּנֶגְדֶּךְ וְאֵינִי יָכוֹל לִנְגֹּעַ בָּךְ
כָּךְ לֹא יוּכְלוּ כָּל אוֹיְבַי לִנְגֹּעַ בִּי לְרָעָה.

שמות טו   תִּפֹּל עֲלֵיהֶם אֵימָתָה וָפַחַד, בִּגְדֹל זְרוֹעֲךָ יִדְּמוּ כָּאָבֶן:

כָּאָבֶן יִדְּמוּ זְרוֹעֲךָ בִּגְדֹל, וָפַחַד אֵימָתָה עֲלֵיהֶם תִּפֹּל.

דָּוִד מֶלֶךְ יִשְׂרָאֵל חַי וְקַיָּם.

Turn to three people and say to each:

שָׁלוֹם עֲלֵיכֶם.

They respond:

עֲלֵיכֶם שָׁלוֹם.

Say three times:

סִימָן טוֹב וּמַזָּל טוֹב יְהֵא לָנוּ וּלְכָל יִשְׂרָאֵל, אָמֵן.

שיר   קוֹל דּוֹדִי הִנֵּה־זֶה בָּא, מְדַלֵּג עַל־הֶהָרִים, מְקַפֵּץ עַל־הַגְּבָעוֹת:
השירים ב   דּוֹמֶה דוֹדִי לִצְבִי אוֹ לְעֹפֶר הָאַיָּלִים, הִנֵּה־זֶה עוֹמֵד אַחַר כָּתְלֵנוּ,
מַשְׁגִּיחַ מִן־הַחַלֹּנוֹת, מֵצִיץ מִן־הַחֲרַכִּים:

תהלים קכא   שִׁיר לַמַּעֲלוֹת, אֶשָּׂא עֵינַי אֶל־הֶהָרִים, מֵאַיִן יָבֹא עֶזְרִי: עֶזְרִי מֵעִם
יהוה, עֹשֵׂה שָׁמַיִם וָאָרֶץ: אַל־יִתֵּן לַמּוֹט רַגְלֶךָ, אַל־יָנוּם שֹׁמְרֶךָ: הִנֵּה
לֹא־יָנוּם וְלֹא יִישָׁן, שׁוֹמֵר יִשְׂרָאֵל: יהוה שֹׁמְרֶךָ, יהוה צִלְּךָ עַל־יַד

---

time. Jews don't merely translate planetary orbit into time – they actively
manipulate time, independently of planetary realities. This empowerment
is only attainable when Jews inhabit their homeland and are endowed with

The sun will not strike you by day, nor the moon by night. The LORD will guard you from all harm; He will guard your life. The LORD will guard your going and coming, now and for evermore.

הַלְלוּיָהּ Halleluya! Praise God in His holy place; praise Him in the heavens of His power. Praise Him for His mighty deeds; praise Him for His surpassing greatness. Praise Him with blasts of the ram's horn; praise Him with the harp and lyre. Praise Him with timbrel and dance; praise Him with strings and flute. Praise Him with clashing cymbals; praise Him with resounding cymbals. Let all that breathes praise the LORD. Halleluya! Let all that breathes praise the LORD. Halleluya! *Ps. 150*

תָּנָא In the academy of Rabbi Yishmael it was taught: Were the people of Israel privileged to greet the presence of their heavenly Father only once a month, it would have been sufficient for them. Abaye said: Therefore it [the blessing of the moon] should be said standing. Who is this coming up from the desert, leaning on her beloved? *Sanhedrin 42a* *Song. 8*

וִיהִי May it be Your will, LORD my God and God of my ancestors, to make good the deficiency of the moon, so that it is no longer in its diminished state. May the light of the moon be like the light of the sun and like the light of the seven days of creation as it was before it was diminished, as it says, "The two great luminaries." And may there be fulfilled for us the verse: "They shall seek the LORD their God, and David their king." Amen. *Gen. 1* *Hos. 3*

---

presumably the dimming of these celestial bodies serves a military function. There is an additional theological purpose to the shaming of the sun and the dimming of the moon. As they were historically worshiped as deities, by disgracing them the associated pagan beliefs are debunked. As part of landscaping a world of pure monotheism, objects of pagan worship are demoted. In as much as celestial bodies were the *first* objects to be deified, this description may refer to *all* objects of worship. They will all be disgraced in order to discredit them and the systems of worship they symbolize.

Interestingly, though the sun and moon are attacked, the *stars* aren't affected. Again this may serve as a metaphor to the rise of the Jewish nation which is likened to the stars. While the rest of the universe is leveled, or at the very least humbled, the Jewish nation retains its radiance and historical significance.

יְמִינֶךָ: יוֹמָם הַשֶּׁמֶשׁ לֹא־יַכֶּכָּה, וְיָרֵחַ בַּלֶּיְלָה: יהוה יִשְׁמָרְךָ מִכָּל־רָע, יִשְׁמֹר אֶת־נַפְשֶׁךָ: יהוה יִשְׁמָר־צֵאתְךָ וּבוֹאֶךָ, מֵעַתָּה וְעַד־עוֹלָם:

תהלים קנ

הַלְלוּיָהּ, הַלְלוּ־אֵל בְּקָדְשׁוֹ, הַלְלוּהוּ בִּרְקִיעַ עֻזּוֹ: הַלְלוּהוּ בִגְבוּרֹתָיו, הַלְלוּהוּ כְּרֹב גֻּדְלוֹ: הַלְלוּהוּ בְּתֵקַע שׁוֹפָר, הַלְלוּהוּ בְּנֵבֶל וְכִנּוֹר: הַלְלוּהוּ בְתֹף וּמָחוֹל, הַלְלוּהוּ בְּמִנִּים וְעֻגָב: הַלְלוּהוּ בְצִלְצְלֵי־שָׁמַע, הַלְלוּהוּ בְּצִלְצְלֵי תְרוּעָה: כֹּל הַנְּשָׁמָה תְּהַלֵּל יָהּ, הַלְלוּיָהּ:

סנהדרין מב.

תָּנָא דְּבֵי רַבִּי יִשְׁמָעֵאל: אִלְמָלֵי לֹא זָכוּ יִשְׂרָאֵל אֶלָּא לְהַקְבִּיל פְּנֵי אֲבִיהֶם שֶׁבַּשָּׁמַיִם פַּעַם אַחַת בַּחֹדֶשׁ, דַּיָּם. אָמַר אַבַּיֵי: הִלְכָּךְ צָרִיךְ לְמֵימְרָא מְעֻמָּד. מִי זֹאת עֹלָה מִן־הַמִּדְבָּר, מִתְרַפֶּקֶת עַל־דּוֹדָהּ:

שיר
השירים ח

וִיהִי רָצוֹן מִלְּפָנֶיךָ יהוה אֱלֹהַי וֵאלֹהֵי אֲבוֹתַי, לְמַלֹּאת פְּגִימַת הַלְּבָנָה וְלֹא יִהְיֶה בָהּ שׁוּם מִעוּט. וִיהִי אוֹר הַלְּבָנָה כְּאוֹר הַחַמָּה וּכְאוֹר שִׁבְעַת יְמֵי בְרֵאשִׁית, כְּמוֹ שֶׁהָיְתָה קֹדֶם מִעוּטָהּ, שֶׁנֶּאֱמַר: אֶת־שְׁנֵי הַמְּאֹרֹת הַגְּדֹלִים: וְיִתְקַיֵּם בָּנוּ מִקְרָא שֶׁכָּתוּב: וּבִקְשׁוּ אֶת־יהוה אֱלֹהֵיהֶם וְאֵת דָּוִיד מַלְכָּם: אָמֵן.

בראשית א

הושע ג

לְמַלֹּאת פְּגִימַת הַלְּבָנָה *Make good the deficiency of the moon.* Yeshayahu (24:23) describes the dimming of the moon and the defaming of the sun when HaKadosh Barukh Hu rules in Yerushalayim and His elders receive honor. Quite possibly this can be understood entirely metaphorically: the glory showered upon the elders of the Jewish people surrounding God in Yerushalayim will be so radiant that it will shame the glow of the sun and moon. No actual cosmic interruption occurs, but metaphorically the light of these celestial bodies is diminished.

The more literal reading implies that an *actual* disruption or eclipse will accompany one stage or aspect of the Messianic process. The most direct, literal reading suggests an eclipse, darkening the sky during the wars of Gog and Magog and thereby foiling the military intentions of our enemies. The two preceding verses portray the assembly of armies to battle Yerushalayim during this war. God is cast as a Commander of Heavenly forces (*Yeshayahu* 24:21) and

לַמְנַצֵּחַ For the conductor of music. With stringed instruments, a psalm. *Ps. 67*
A song. May God be gracious to us and bless us. May He make His face
shine on us, Selah. Then will Your way be known on earth, Your salvation
among all the nations. Let the peoples praise You, God; let all peoples
praise You. Let nations rejoice and sing for joy, for You judge the peoples
with equity, and guide the nations of the earth, Selah. Let the peoples
praise You, God; let all peoples praise You. The earth has yielded its
harvest. May God, our God, bless us. God will bless us, and all the ends
of the earth will fear Him.

Stand while saying Aleinu. Bow at ˅.

עָלֵינוּ It is our duty to praise the Master of all, and ascribe greatness to the
Author of creation, who has not made us like the nations of the lands nor
placed us like the families of the earth; who has not made our portion like
theirs, nor our destiny like all their multitudes. (For they worship vanity and
emptiness, and pray to a god who cannot save.) ˅But we bow in worship and
thank the Supreme King of kings, the Holy One, blessed be He, who extends
the heavens and establishes the earth, whose throne of glory is in the heavens
above, and whose power's Presence is in the highest of heights. He is our God;
there is no other. Truly He is our King, there is none else, as it is written in
His Torah: "You shall know and take to heart this day that the Lord is God, *Deut. 4*
in heaven above and on earth below. There is no other."

Therefore, we place our hope in You, Lord our God, that we may soon see
the glory of Your power, when You will remove abominations from the earth,
and idols will be utterly destroyed, when the world will be perfected under
the sovereignty of the Almighty, when all humanity will call on Your name, to
turn all the earth's wicked toward You. All the world's inhabitants will realize
and know that to You every knee must bow and every tongue swear loyalty.
Before You, Lord our God, they will kneel and bow down and give honor to
Your glorious name. They will all accept the yoke of Your kingdom, and You
will reign over them soon and for ever. For the kingdom is Yours, and to all
eternity You will reign in glory, as it is written in Your Torah: "The Lord will *Ex. 15*
reign for ever and ever." ˅ And it is said: "Then the Lord shall be King over all *Zech. 14*
the earth; on that day the Lord shall be One and His name One."

Some add:

Have no fear of sudden terror or of the ruin when it overtakes the wicked. Devise *Prov. 3*
your strategy, but it will be thwarted; propose your plan, but it will not stand, for God *Is. 8*
is with us. When you grow old, I will still be the same. When your hair turns gray, I *Is. 46*
will still carry you. I made you, I will bear you, I will carry you, and I will rescue you.

MOURNER'S KADDISH

The following prayer, said by mourners, requires the presence of a minyan.
A transliteration can be found on page 667.

Mourner: יִתְגַּדַּל Magnified and sanctified
may His great name be,
in the world He created by His will.
May He establish His kingdom
in your lifetime and in your days,
and in the lifetime of all the house of Israel,
swiftly and soon –
and say: Amen.

All: May His great name be blessed
for ever and all time.

Mourner: Blessed and praised,
glorified and exalted,
raised and honored,
uplifted and lauded
be the name of the Holy One,
blessed be He,
beyond any blessing,
song, praise and consolation
uttered in the world –
and say: Amen.

May there be great peace from heaven,
and life for us and all Israel –
and say: Amen.

Bow, take three steps back, as if taking leave of the Divine Presence,
then bow, first left, then right, then center, while saying:
May He who makes peace in His high places,
make peace for us and all Israel –
and say: Amen.

קדיש יתום

The following prayer, said by mourners, requires the presence of a מנין.
A transliteration can be found on page 667.

אבל: יִתְגַּדַּל וְיִתְקַדַּשׁ שְׁמֵהּ רַבָּא (קהל: אָמֵן)

בְּעָלְמָא דִּי בְרָא כִרְעוּתֵהּ

וְיַמְלִיךְ מַלְכוּתֵהּ

בְּחַיֵּיכוֹן וּבְיוֹמֵיכוֹן וּבְחַיֵּי דְּכָל בֵּית יִשְׂרָאֵל

בַּעֲגָלָא וּבִזְמַן קָרִיב

וְאִמְרוּ אָמֵן. (קהל: אָמֵן)

קהל
ואבל: יְהֵא שְׁמֵהּ רַבָּא מְבָרַךְ לְעָלַם וּלְעָלְמֵי עָלְמַיָּא.

אבל: יִתְבָּרַךְ וְיִשְׁתַּבַּח וְיִתְפָּאַר

וְיִתְרוֹמַם וְיִתְנַשֵּׂא וְיִתְהַדָּר וְיִתְעַלֶּה וְיִתְהַלָּל

שְׁמֵהּ דְּקֻדְשָׁא בְּרִיךְ הוּא (קהל: בְּרִיךְ הוּא)

לְעֵלָּא מִן כָּל בִּרְכָתָא

וְשִׁירָתָא, תֻּשְׁבְּחָתָא וְנֶחֱמָתָא

דַּאֲמִירָן בְּעָלְמָא

וְאִמְרוּ אָמֵן. (קהל: אָמֵן)

יְהֵא שְׁלָמָא רַבָּא מִן שְׁמַיָּא

וְחַיִּים, עָלֵינוּ וְעַל כָּל יִשְׂרָאֵל

וְאִמְרוּ אָמֵן. (קהל: אָמֵן)

Bow, take three steps back, as if taking leave of the Divine Presence,
then bow, first left, then right, then center, while saying:

עֹשֶׂה שָׁלוֹם בִּמְרוֹמָיו

הוּא יַעֲשֶׂה שָׁלוֹם עָלֵינוּ וְעַל כָּל יִשְׂרָאֵל

וְאִמְרוּ אָמֵן. (קהל: אָמֵן)

All sing:

טוֹבִים Good are the radiant stars our God created;
He formed them with knowledge,
understanding and deliberation.
He gave them strength and might
to rule throughout the world.

Full of splendor, radiating light,
beautiful is their splendor throughout the world.
Glad as they go forth, joyous as they return,
they fulfill with awe their Creator's will.

Glory and honor they give to His name,
jubilation and song at the mention of His majesty.
He called the sun into being and it shone with light.
He looked and fashioned the form of the moon.

Kiddush at the beginning of the meal. I traced this custom to a ruling made by Rabbi Elimelekh bar Shaul, of blessed memory, who was the halakhic authority for Kibbutz Yavne during its first years.

I have since become acquainted with the custom of Rabbi Yoel Bin-Nun's father, Dr. Yeḥiel Bin-Nun, of blessed memory, who would open this festive meal with the reading of the verses of the *Bikkurim*, the First Fruits (Deuteronomy 26) instead of *Kiddush*. This passage is found in the Pesaḥ Haggada without the final verse, "And He shall bring us to this place and give us this land flowing with milk and honey" (ibid. 26:9). It may well be that during Israel's exile, this joyous verse was omitted, and now, with our return to the Land of Israel, it is fitting to restore it to its place. After reciting the verses of the *Bikkurim*, he would recite the blessing over wine and *Sheheḥeyanu*.

Rabbi Yoel Bin-Nun added the custom of eating matza together with leavened bread to express the transitional nature of this festival, which falls between Pesaḥ and Shavuot.

Out of all of these customs, the only halakhic question is in regard to the *Sheheḥeyanu* blessing – as we have seen, this has been discussed by the greatest contemporary authorities (see page 55). In any case, if one makes this blessing in the synagogue, it should not be repeated at home.　　BL

All sing:

טוֹבִים מְאוֹרוֹת שֶׁבָּרָא אֱלֹהֵינוּ

יְצָרָם בְּדַעַת בְּבִינָה וּבְהַשְׂכֵּל

כֹּחַ וּגְבוּרָה נָתַן בָּהֶם

לִהְיוֹת מוֹשְׁלִים בְּקֶרֶב תֵּבֵל.

מְלֵאִים זִיו וּמְפִיקִים נֹגַהּ

נָאֶה זִיוָם בְּכָל הָעוֹלָם

שְׂמֵחִים בְּצֵאתָם וְשָׂשִׂים בְּבוֹאָם

עוֹשִׂים בְּאֵימָה רְצוֹן קוֹנָם.

פְּאֵר וְכָבוֹד נוֹתְנִים לִשְׁמוֹ

צָהֳלָה וְרִנָּה לְזֵכֶר מַלְכוּתוֹ

קָרָא לַשֶּׁמֶשׁ וַיִּזְרַח אוֹר

רָאָה וְהִתְקִין צוּרַת הַלְּבָנָה.

THE YOM HAATZMA'UT FESTIVE MEAL – A FAMILY TRADITION

My parents have the custom of serving a festive meal upon their return from the synagogue on Yom HaAtzma'ut night. The table is set and decorated with little flags, my mother lights the candles and makes a *Sheheḥeyanu* blessing, we wash our hands and sit down for the meal. Over the years, my father developed the custom, taking his cues from the Pesaḥ Seder, of "וְהִגַּדְתָּ לְבִנְךָ and you shall tell your children." He tells his children, grandchildren, and great-grandchildren, how the nation of Israel has fared over the previous generations, and how far they have come today. The holiday songs we sing are songs of the Land of Israel, both old and new.

When I arrived at Kibbutz Sa'ad in the South, I experienced this custom on a communal scale. All members of the kibbutz would leave the evening prayers in joyous dance, and arrive at the communal dining hall for a festive meal. This meal was similar in spirit to the one I was accustomed to from my parents' home, with one difference: the members of the kibbutz made

תפילת שחרית

SHAḤARIT

Shaḥarit

The following order of prayers and blessings, which departs from that of most prayer books,
is based on the consensus of recent halakhic authorities.

ON WAKING

On waking, our first thought should be that we are in the presence of God. Since
we are forbidden to speak God's name until we have washed our hands, the
following prayer is said, which, without mentioning God's name, acknowledges
His presence and gives thanks for a new day and for the gift of life.

מוֹדֶה I thank You, living and eternal King,
for giving me back my soul in mercy.
Great is Your faithfulness.

Wash hands and say the following blessings.
Some have the custom to say "Wisdom begins" on page 156 at this point.

בָּרוּךְ Blessed are You, Lᴏʀᴅ our God, King of the Universe,
who has made us holy through His commandments,
and has commanded us about washing hands.

בָּרוּךְ Blessed are You, Lᴏʀᴅ our God, King of the Universe,
who formed man in wisdom
and created in him many orifices and cavities.
It is revealed and known before the throne of Your glory
that were one of them to be ruptured or blocked,
it would be impossible to survive
and stand before You.
Blessed are You, Lᴏʀᴅ,
Healer of all flesh who does wondrous deeds.

שחרית

The following order of prayers and blessings, which departs from that of most prayer books,
is based on the consensus of recent halakhic authorities.

השכמת הבוקר

On waking, our first thought should be that we are in the presence of God. Since
we are forbidden to speak God's name until we have washed our hands, the
following prayer is said, which, without mentioning God's name, acknowledges
His presence and gives thanks for a new day and for the gift of life.

מוֹדֶה/ *women* מוֹדָה/ אֲנִי לְפָנֶיךָ מֶלֶךְ חַי וְקַיָּם
שֶׁהֶחֱזַרְתָּ בִּי נִשְׁמָתִי בְּחֶמְלָה
רַבָּה אֱמוּנָתֶךָ.

Wash hands and say the following blessings.
Some have the custom to say רֵאשִׁית חָכְמָה on page 157 at this point.

בָּרוּךְ אַתָּה יהוה אֱלֹהֵינוּ מֶלֶךְ הָעוֹלָם
אֲשֶׁר קִדְּשָׁנוּ בְּמִצְוֹתָיו וְצִוָּנוּ עַל נְטִילַת יָדָיִם.

בָּרוּךְ אַתָּה יהוה אֱלֹהֵינוּ מֶלֶךְ הָעוֹלָם
אֲשֶׁר יָצַר אֶת הָאָדָם בְּחָכְמָה
וּבָרָא בוֹ נְקָבִים נְקָבִים, חֲלוּלִים חֲלוּלִים.
גָּלוּי וְיָדוּעַ לִפְנֵי כִסֵּא כְבוֹדֶךָ
שֶׁאִם יִפָּתֵחַ אֶחָד מֵהֶם אוֹ יִסָּתֵם אֶחָד מֵהֶם
אִי אֶפְשָׁר לְהִתְקַיֵּם וְלַעֲמֹד לְפָנֶיךָ.
בָּרוּךְ אַתָּה יהוה, רוֹפֵא כָל בָּשָׂר וּמַפְלִיא לַעֲשׂוֹת.

אֱלֹהַי My God,
the soul You placed within me is pure.
You created it,
You formed it,
You breathed it into me,
and You guard it while it is within me.
One day You will take it from me,
and restore it to me in the time to come.
As long as the soul is within me,
I will thank You,
Lord my God and God of my ancestors,
Master of all works, Lord of all souls.
Blessed are You, Lord,
who restores souls to lifeless bodies.

TZITZIT

*The following blessing is said before putting on tzitzit. Neither it nor the subsequent prayer
is said by those who wear a tallit. The blessing over the latter exempts the former.*

בָּרוּךְ Blessed are You, Lord our God, King of the Universe,
who has made us holy through His commandments,
and has commanded us
about the command of tasseled garments.

After putting on tzitzit, say:

יְהִי רָצוֹן May it be Your will,
Lord my God and God of my ancestors,
that the commandment of the tasseled garment
be considered before You
as if I had fulfilled it in all its specifics,
details and intentions,
as well as the 613 commandments dependent on it,
Amen, Selah.

אֱלֹהַי

נְשָׁמָה שֶׁנָּתַתָּ בִּי טְהוֹרָה הִיא.

אַתָּה בְרָאתָהּ, אַתָּה יְצַרְתָּהּ, אַתָּה נְפַחְתָּהּ בִּי

וְאַתָּה מְשַׁמְּרָהּ בְּקִרְבִּי

וְאַתָּה עָתִיד לִטְּלָהּ מִמֶּנִּי

וּלְהַחֲזִירָהּ בִּי לֶעָתִיד לָבוֹא.

כָּל זְמַן שֶׁהַנְּשָׁמָה בְקִרְבִּי, מוֹדֶה/ *women* מוֹדָה/ אֲנִי לְפָנֶיךָ

יהוה אֱלֹהַי וֵאלֹהֵי אֲבוֹתַי

רִבּוֹן כָּל הַמַּעֲשִׂים

אֲדוֹן כָּל הַנְּשָׁמוֹת.

בָּרוּךְ אַתָּה יהוה, הַמַּחֲזִיר נְשָׁמוֹת לִפְגָרִים מֵתִים.

לבישת ציצית

The following blessing is said before putting on a טלית קטן. *Neither it nor* יְהִי רָצוֹן *is said by those who wear a* טלית. *The blessing over the latter exempts the former.*

בָּרוּךְ אַתָּה יהוה אֱלֹהֵינוּ מֶלֶךְ הָעוֹלָם

אֲשֶׁר קִדְּשָׁנוּ בְּמִצְוֹתָיו

וְצִוָּנוּ עַל מִצְוַת צִיצִית.

After putting on the טלית קטן, *say:*

יְהִי רָצוֹן מִלְּפָנֶיךָ, יהוה אֱלֹהַי וֵאלֹהֵי אֲבוֹתַי

שֶׁתְּהֵא חֲשׁוּבָה מִצְוַת צִיצִית לְפָנֶיךָ

כְּאִלּוּ קִיַּמְתִּיהָ בְּכָל פְּרָטֶיהָ וְדִקְדּוּקֶיהָ וְכַוָּנוֹתֶיהָ

וְתַרְיַ״ג מִצְוֹת הַתְּלוּיוֹת בָּהּ

אָמֵן סֶלָה.

BLESSINGS OVER THE TORAH

In Judaism, study is greater even than prayer. So, before beginning to pray, we engage in a
miniature act of study, preceded by the appropriate blessings. The blessings are followed by
brief selections from Scripture, Mishna and Gemara, the three foundational texts of Judaism.

בָּרוּךְ Blessed are You, Lord our God, King of the Universe,
who has made us holy through His commandments,
and has commanded us to engage in study of the words of Torah.
Please, Lord our God,
make the words of Your Torah sweet in our mouths
and in the mouths of Your people, the house of Israel,
so that we, our descendants (and their descendants)
and the descendants of Your people, the house of Israel,
may all know Your name
and study Your Torah for its own sake.
Blessed are You, Lord, who teaches Torah to His people Israel.

בָּרוּךְ Blessed are You, Lord our God, King of the Universe,
who has chosen us from all the peoples
and given us His Torah.
Blessed are You, Lord, Giver of the Torah.

יְבָרֶכְךָ May the Lord bless you and protect you. *Num. 6*
May the Lord make His face shine on you and be gracious to you.
May the Lord turn His face toward you and grant you peace.

As a selected people we were given the Torah and mitzvot to enable a lifestyle
reflective of His will. Making a blessing prior to Torah study acknowledges
the connection between the Torah and God's selection of the Jewish people.
In fact the Gemara (*Berakhot* 11b) records that Rav Hamnuna codified the
blessing of *"Asher baḥar banu…"* which highlights our being chosen through
the delivery of the Torah.

By omitting the *berakha*, Torah was no longer viewed as part of our selection. As our status as "selected" waned, our license to *Eretz Yisrael* expired,
and we were exiled.

ברכות התורה

In Judaism, study is greater even than prayer. So, before beginning to pray, we engage in a miniature act of study, preceded by the appropriate blessings. The blessings are followed by brief selections from תנ״ך *,* משנה *and* גמרא *, the three foundational texts of Judaism.*

בָּרוּךְ אַתָּה יהוה אֱלֹהֵינוּ מֶלֶךְ הָעוֹלָם

אֲשֶׁר קִדְּשָׁנוּ בְּמִצְוֹתָיו וְצִוָּנוּ לַעֲסֹק בְּדִבְרֵי תוֹרָה.

וְהַעֲרֶב נָא יהוה אֱלֹהֵינוּ אֶת דִּבְרֵי תוֹרָתְךָ

בְּפִינוּ וּבְפִי עַמְּךָ בֵּית יִשְׂרָאֵל

וְנִהְיֶה אֲנַחְנוּ וְצֶאֱצָאֵינוּ (וְצֶאֱצָאֵי צֶאֱצָאֵינוּ)

וְצֶאֱצָאֵי עַמְּךָ בֵּית יִשְׂרָאֵל

כֻּלָּנוּ יוֹדְעֵי שְׁמֶךָ וְלוֹמְדֵי תוֹרָתְךָ לִשְׁמָהּ.

בָּרוּךְ אַתָּה יהוה, הַמְלַמֵּד תּוֹרָה לְעַמּוֹ יִשְׂרָאֵל.

בָּרוּךְ אַתָּה יהוה אֱלֹהֵינוּ מֶלֶךְ הָעוֹלָם

אֲשֶׁר בָּחַר בָּנוּ מִכָּל הָעַמִּים וְנָתַן לָנוּ אֶת תּוֹרָתוֹ.

בָּרוּךְ אַתָּה יהוה, נוֹתֵן הַתּוֹרָה.

במדברו

יְבָרֶכְךָ יהוה וְיִשְׁמְרֶךָ:

יָאֵר יהוה פָּנָיו אֵלֶיךָ וִיחֻנֶּךָּ:

יִשָּׂא יהוה פָּנָיו אֵלֶיךָ וְיָשֵׂם לְךָ שָׁלוֹם:

ברכות התורה *Blessings over the Torah.* מִי־הָאִישׁ הֶחָכָם וְיָבֵן (*Yirmiyahu* 9:11–12): Yirmiyahu blames the destruction of Land of Israel and the ensuing Exile upon the people abandoning the Torah. The Gemara (*Nedarim* 81a) claims that the sin was more subtle. Although the people studied Torah, they didn't recite *Birkat HaTorah*. The punishment of National Exile appears disproportionate to the crime!

Our connection to the Land of Israel is based on our historical selection to represent HaKadosh Barukh Hu in this world and disseminate His message.

אֵלּוּ These are the things for which there is no fixed measure:
      the corner of the field, first-fruits,
      appearances before the Lord [on festivals, with offerings],
      acts of kindness and the study of Torah.

Mishna
Pe'ah 1:1

אֵלּוּ These are the things whose fruits we eat in this world
but whose full reward awaits us in the World to Come:
      honoring parents; acts of kindness;
      arriving early at the house of study morning and evening;
      hospitality to strangers; visiting the sick;
      helping the needy bride; attending to the dead;
      devotion in prayer;
      and bringing peace between people –
but the study of Torah is equal to them all.

Shabbat
127a

Some say:

רֵאשִׁית חָכְמָה Wisdom begins in awe of the Lord;
all who fulfill [His commandments] gain good understanding;
His praise is ever-lasting.
The Torah Moses commanded us is the heritage of the congregation of Jacob.
Listen, my son, to your father's instruction,
and do not forsake your mother's teaching.
May the Torah be my faith and Almighty God my help.
Blessed be the name of His glorious kingdom for ever and all time.

Ps. 111
Deut. 33
Prov. 1

---

    those of a prince who has long been expelled from his country. Upon his
    return he may lay natural claim, "I have returned to claim my legacy." The
    license to Torah study and the Land isn't disqualified through neglect.

3.   The Jerusalem Talmud (*Bava Batra* 8:2) associates the word "*morasha*"
    with the word "*diha*" which means struggle. The sweep and difficulty of
    Torah study dictate that the initial process can be frustrating, ultimately
    yielding greater satisfaction as study progresses. Similarly our initial
    acquisition of the Land of Israel may be contentious and laborious but
    ultimately will be more straightforward and trouble-free.

Beyond the similar features alluded to by the term *morasha,* the common
designation reinforces the inseparability of Torah and the Land of Israel.

משנה,
פאה א׳א

אֵלּוּ דְבָרִים שֶׁאֵין לָהֶם שִׁעוּר

הַפֵּאָה וְהַבִּכּוּרִים וְהָרֵאָיוֹן וּגְמִילוּת חֲסָדִים וְתַלְמוּד תּוֹרָה.

שבת קכז.

אֵלּוּ דְבָרִים שֶׁאָדָם אוֹכֵל פֵּרוֹתֵיהֶם בָּעוֹלָם הַזֶּה

וְהַקֶּרֶן קַיֶּמֶת לוֹ לָעוֹלָם הַבָּא

וְאֵלּוּ הֵן

כִּבּוּד אָב וָאֵם, וּגְמִילוּת חֲסָדִים

וְהַשְׁכָּמַת בֵּית הַמִּדְרָשׁ שַׁחֲרִית וְעַרְבִית

וְהַכְנָסַת אוֹרְחִים, וּבִקּוּר חוֹלִים

וְהַכְנָסַת כַּלָּה, וּלְוָיַת הַמֵּת

וְעִיּוּן תְּפִלָּה, וַהֲבָאַת שָׁלוֹם בֵּין אָדָם לַחֲבֵרוֹ

וְתַלְמוּד תּוֹרָה כְּנֶגֶד כֻּלָּם.

Some say:

תהלים קיא
דברים לג
משלי א

רֵאשִׁית חָכְמָה יִרְאַת יהוה, שֵׂכֶל טוֹב לְכָל־עֹשֵׂיהֶם, תְּהִלָּתוֹ עֹמֶדֶת לָעַד:

תּוֹרָה צִוָּה־לָנוּ מֹשֶׁה, מוֹרָשָׁה קְהִלַּת יַעֲקֹב:

שְׁמַע בְּנִי מוּסַר אָבִיךָ וְאַל־תִּטֹּשׁ תּוֹרַת אִמֶּךָ:

תּוֹרָה תְּהֵא אֱמוּנָתִי, וְאֵל שַׁדַּי בְּעֶזְרָתִי:

בָּרוּךְ שֵׁם כְּבוֹד מַלְכוּתוֹ לְעוֹלָם וָעֶד.

מוֹרָשָׁה קְהִלַּת יַעֲקֹב *The heritage of the congregation of Jacob.* Torah and *Eretz Yisrael* are each designated as "*Morasha*" – our heritage (*Devarim* 33:4; *Shemot* 6:8). This draws our attention to several similarities between the two:

1. We inherit both Torah and the Land of Israel. Our faith is delivered throughout the generations based upon the mass revelation at *Har Sinai*. Similarly, our license to the Land has been delivered as an inheritance from our ancestors. To merit the Land we must display fidelity to the lifestyle of our ancestors.

2. Even if an individual has deserted Torah, he can always return and stake a claim to his rightful legacy. The Midrash (*Shemot Raba* 33:7) portrays our rights to Torah – and by extension to *Eretz Yisrael* – as similar to

TALLIT

*Say the following meditation before putting on the tallit. Meditations before
the fulfillment of mitzvot are to ensure that we do so with the requisite intention
(kavana). This particularly applies to mitzvot whose purpose is to induce in
us certain states of mind, as is the case with tallit and tefillin, both of which are
external symbols of inward commitment to the life of observance of the mitzvot.*

בָּרְכִי נַפְשִׁי **Bless the** LORD, **my soul.** LORD, **my God, You are very great,** *Ps. 104*
clothed in majesty and splendor, wrapped in a robe of light, spreading
out the heavens like a tent.

Some say:

For the sake of the unification of the Holy One, blessed be He, and His Divine Presence,
in reverence and love, to unify the name *Yod-Heh* with *Vav-Heh* in perfect unity in the
name of all Israel.

I am about to wrap myself in this tasseled garment (tallit). So may my soul, my 248
limbs and 365 sinews be wrapped in the light of the tassel (*hatzitzit*) which amounts to
613 [commandments]. And just as I cover myself with a tasseled garment in this world,
so may I be worthy of rabbinical dress and a fine garment in the World to Come in the
Garden of Eden. Through the commandment of tassels may my life's-breath, spirit,
soul and prayer be delivered from external impediments, and may the tallit spread its
wings over them like an eagle stirring up its nest, hovering over its young. May the *Deut. 32*
commandment of the tasseled garment be considered before the Holy One, blessed
be He, as if I had fulfilled it in all its specifics, details and intentions, as well as the 613
commandments dependent on it, Amen, Selah.

Before wrapping oneself in the tallit, say:

בָּרוּךְ **Blessed are You,** LORD **our God, King of the Universe,**
who has made us holy through His commandments,
and has commanded us to wrap ourselves in the tasseled garment.

*According to the Shela (R. Isaiah Horowitz), one should say
these verses after wrapping oneself in the tallit:*

מַה־יָּקָר **How precious is Your loving-kindness, O God,** and the chil- *Ps. 36*
dren of men find refuge under the shadow of Your wings. They are
filled with the rich plenty of Your House. You give them drink from
Your river of delights. For with You is the fountain of life; in Your light,
we see light. Continue Your loving-kindness to those who know You,
and Your righteousness to the upright in heart.

---

maintain intense Torah study, to assure successful acquisition of Israel (see
Yehoshua 1:1–15 especially verse 8).

עֲטִיפַת טַלִּית

Say the following meditation before putting on the טלית. Meditations before
the fulfillment of מצוות are to ensure that we do so with the requisite intention
(כוונה). This particularly applies to מצוות whose purpose is to induce in us certain
states of mind, as is the case with תפילין and טלית, both of which are external
symbols of inward commitment to the life of observance of the מצוות.

תהלים קד

בָּרְכִי נַפְשִׁי אֶת־יהוה, יהוה אֱלֹהַי גָּדַלְתָּ מְּאֹד, הוֹד וְהָדָר לָבָשְׁתָּ:
עֹטֶה־אוֹר כַּשַּׂלְמָה, נוֹטֶה שָׁמַיִם כַּיְרִיעָה:

Some say:

לְשֵׁם יִחוּד קֻדְשָׁא בְּרִיךְ הוּא וּשְׁכִינְתֵּהּ בִּדְחִילוּ וּרְחִימוּ, לְיַחֵד שֵׁם י"ה בו"ה
בְּיִחוּדָא שְׁלִים בְּשֵׁם כָּל יִשְׂרָאֵל.

הֲרֵינִי מִתְעַטֵּף בַּצִּיצִית. כֵּן תִּתְעַטֵּף נִשְׁמָתִי וְרַמַ"ח אֵבָרַי וְשַׁסַ"ה גִידַי בְּאוֹר
הַצִּיצִית הָעוֹלָה תַּרְיַ"ג. וּכְשֵׁם שֶׁאֲנִי מִתְכַּסֶּה בְּטַלִּית בָּעוֹלָם הַזֶּה, כָּךְ אֶזְכֶּה
לַחֲלוּקָא דְרַבָּנָן וּלְטַלִּית נָאָה לָעוֹלָם הַבָּא בְּגַן עֵדֶן. וְעַל יְדֵי מִצְוַת צִיצִית
תִּנָּצֵל נַפְשִׁי רוּחִי וְנִשְׁמָתִי וּתְפִלָּתִי מִן הַחִיצוֹנִים. וְהַטַּלִּית תִּפְרֹשׂ כְּנָפֶיהָ עֲלֵיהֶם
וְתַצִּילֵם, כְּנֶשֶׁר יָעִיר קִנּוֹ, עַל גּוֹזָלָיו יְרַחֵף; וּתְהֵא חֲשׁוּבָה מִצְוַת צִיצִית לִפְנֵי
הַקָּדוֹשׁ בָּרוּךְ הוּא, כְּאִלּוּ קִיַּמְתִּיהָ בְּכָל פְּרָטֶיהָ וְדִקְדּוּקֶיהָ וְכַוָּנוֹתֶיהָ וְתַרְיַ"ג
מִצְוֹת הַתְּלוּיוֹת בָּהּ, אָמֵן סֶלָה.

Before wrapping oneself in the טלית, say:

בָּרוּךְ אַתָּה יהוה אֱלֹהֵינוּ מֶלֶךְ הָעוֹלָם
אֲשֶׁר קִדְּשָׁנוּ בְּמִצְוֹתָיו וְצִוָּנוּ לְהִתְעַטֵּף בַּצִּיצִית.

According to the Shela (R. Isaiah Horowitz), one should say
these verses after wrapping oneself in the טלית:

תהלים לו

מַה־יָּקָר חַסְדְּךָ אֱלֹהִים, וּבְנֵי אָדָם בְּצֵל כְּנָפֶיךָ יֶחֱסָיוּן: יִרְוְיֻן
מִדֶּשֶׁן בֵּיתֶךָ, וְנַחַל עֲדָנֶיךָ תַשְׁקֵם: כִּי־עִמְּךָ מְקוֹר חַיִּים, בְּאוֹרְךָ
נִרְאֶה־אוֹר: מְשֹׁךְ חַסְדְּךָ לְיֹדְעֶיךָ, וְצִדְקָתְךָ לְיִשְׁרֵי־לֵב:

Without the former, we have no license to the latter. When HaKadosh Barukh
Hu encourages Yehoshua to conquer the land, He intersperses reminders to

TEFILLIN

Some say the following meditation before putting on the tefillin.

For the sake of the unification of the Holy One, blessed be He, and His Divine Presence, in reverence and love, to unify the name *Yod-Heh* with *Vav-Heh* in perfect unity in the name of all Israel.

By putting on the tefillin I hereby intend to fulfill the commandment of my Creator who commanded us to wear tefillin, as it is written in His Torah: "Bind them as a sign on your hand, and they shall be an emblem *Deut. 6* on the center of your head." They contain these four sections of the Torah: one beginning with *Shema* [Deut. 6:4–9]; another with *Vehaya im shamo'a* [ibid. 11:13–21]; the third with *Kadesh Li* [Ex. 13:1–10]; and the fourth with *Vehaya ki yevi'akha* [ibid. 13:11–16]. These proclaim the uniqueness and unity of God, blessed be His name in the world. They also remind us of the miracles and wonders which He did for us when He brought us out of Egypt, and that He has the power and the dominion over the highest and the lowest to deal with them as He pleases. He commanded us to place one of the tefillin on the arm in memory of His "outstretched arm" (of redemption), setting it opposite the heart, to subject the desires and designs of our heart to His service, blessed be His name. The other is to be on the head, opposite the brain, so that my mind, whose seat is in the brain, together with my other senses and faculties, may be subjected to His service, blessed be His name. May the spiritual influence of the commandment of the tefillin be with me so that I may have a long life, a flow of holiness, and sacred thoughts, free from any suggestion of sin or iniquity. May the evil inclination neither incite nor entice us, but leave us to serve the LORD, as it is in our hearts to do.

And may it be Your will, LORD our God and God of our ancestors, that the commandment of tefillin be considered before You as if I had fulfilled it in all its specifics, details and intentions, as well as the 613 commandments dependent on it, Amen, Selah.

---

experiential advantage to Torah study in Israel, as the Midrash on *Tehillim* (chapter 105) comments: Rabbi Yose bar Ḥalafta instructed his son Shmuel, "If you want to experience the *Shekhina* in this world, study Torah in Israel!"

הנחת תפילין

Some say the following meditation before putting on the תפילין.

לְשֵׁם יִחוּד קֻדְשָׁא בְּרִיךְ הוּא וּשְׁכִינְתֵּהּ בִּדְחִילוּ וּרְחִימוּ, לְיַחֵד שֵׁם י״ה בו״ה בְּיִחוּדָא שְׁלִים בְּשֵׁם כָּל יִשְׂרָאֵל.

הִנְנִי מְכַוֵּן בַּהֲנָחַת תְּפִלִּין לְקַיֵּם מִצְוַת בּוֹרְאִי, שֶׁצִּוָּנוּ לְהָנִיחַ תְּפִלִּין, כַּכָּתוּב בְּתוֹרָתוֹ: וּקְשַׁרְתָּם לְאוֹת עַל יָדֶךָ, וְהָיוּ לְטֹטָפֹת בֵּין עֵינֶיךָ: דברים ו וְהֵן אַרְבַּע פָּרָשִׁיּוֹת אֵלּוּ, שְׁמַע, וְהָיָה אִם שָׁמֹעַ, קַדֶּשׁ לִי, וְהָיָה כִּי יְבִאֲךָ, שֶׁיֵּשׁ בָּהֶם יִחוּדוֹ וְאַחְדוּתוֹ יִתְבָּרַךְ שְׁמוֹ בָּעוֹלָם, וְשֶׁנִּזְכֹּר נִסִּים וְנִפְלָאוֹת שֶׁעָשָׂה עִמָּנוּ בְּהוֹצִיאוֹ אוֹתָנוּ מִמִּצְרַיִם, וַאֲשֶׁר לוֹ הַכֹּחַ וְהַמֶּמְשָׁלָה בָּעֶלְיוֹנִים וּבַתַּחְתּוֹנִים לַעֲשׂוֹת בָּהֶם כִּרְצוֹנוֹ. וְצִוָּנוּ לְהָנִיחַ עַל הַיָּד לְזִכְרוֹן זְרוֹעַ הַנְּטוּיָה, וְשֶׁהִיא נֶגֶד הַלֵּב, לְשַׁעְבֵּד בָּזֶה תַּאֲווֹת וּמַחְשְׁבוֹת לִבֵּנוּ לַעֲבוֹדָתוֹ יִתְבָּרַךְ שְׁמוֹ. וְעַל הָרֹאשׁ נֶגֶד הַמֹּחַ, שֶׁהַנְּשָׁמָה שֶׁבְּמֹחִי עִם שְׁאָר חוּשַׁי וְכֹחוֹתַי כֻּלָּם יִהְיוּ מְשֻׁעְבָּדִים לַעֲבוֹדָתוֹ, יִתְבָּרַךְ שְׁמוֹ. וּמִשֶּׁפַע מִצְוַת תְּפִלִּין יִתְמַשֵּׁךְ עָלַי לִהְיוֹת לִי חַיִּים אֲרוּכִים וְשֶׁפַע קֹדֶשׁ וּמַחְשָׁבוֹת קְדוֹשׁוֹת בְּלִי הִרְהוּר חֵטְא וְעָוֹן כְּלָל, וְשֶׁלֹּא יְפַתֵּנוּ וְלֹא יִתְגָּרֶה בָּנוּ יֵצֶר הָרַע, וְיַנִּיחֵנוּ לַעֲבֹד אֶת יהוה כַּאֲשֶׁר עִם לְבָבֵנוּ.

וִיהִי רָצוֹן מִלְּפָנֶיךָ, יהוה אֱלֹהֵינוּ וֵאלֹהֵי אֲבוֹתֵינוּ, שֶׁתְּהֵא חֲשׁוּבָה מִצְוַת הֲנָחַת תְּפִלִּין לִפְנֵי הַקָּדוֹשׁ בָּרוּךְ הוּא, כְּאִלּוּ קִיַּמְתִּיהָ בְּכָל פְּרָטֶיהָ וְדִקְדּוּקֶיהָ וְכַוָּנוֹתֶיהָ וְתַרְיַ״ג מִצְוֹת הַתְּלוּיוֹת בָּהּ, אָמֵן סֶלָה.

Alternatively, though Torah study can be conducted outside of Israel, its highest achievement is only realized in Israel. The Gemara in *Bava Batra* records Rabbi Zeira changing his opinion about a halakhic dispute after relocating to Israel. He commented that the "air" of Israel had made him wiser (*avira d'Eretz Yisrael maḥkim*) allowing him to discern the correct ruling. Beyond intellectual achievements in Torah, Ḥazal recognized an

Stand and place the hand-tefillin on the biceps of the left arm (or right arm if you
are left-handed), angled toward the heart, and before tightening the strap, say:

בָּרוּךְ Blessed are You, Lᴏʀᴅ our God,
King of the Universe,
who has made us holy through His commandments,
and has commanded us to put on tefillin.

Wrap the strap of the hand-tefillin seven times around the arm.
Place the head-tefillin above the hairline, centered between the eyes, and say quietly:

בָּרוּךְ Blessed are You, Lᴏʀᴅ our God,
King of the Universe,
who has made us holy through His commandments,
and has commanded us about the commandment of tefillin.

Adjust the head-tefillin and say:
בָּרוּךְ Blessed be the name of His glorious kingdom for ever and all time.

> *Some say:*
> From Your wisdom, God most high, grant me [wisdom], and from Your
> understanding, give me understanding. May Your loving-kindness be
> greatly upon me, and in Your might may my enemies and those who rise
> against me be subdued. Pour Your goodly oil on the seven branches of
> the menora so that Your good flows down upon Your creatures. You   *Ps. 145*
> open Your hand, and satisfy every living thing with favor.

Wind the strap of the hand-tefillin three times around the middle finger, saying:

וְאֵרַשְׂתִּיךְ I will betroth you to Me for ever;   *Hos. 2*
I will betroth you to Me in righteousness and justice,
loving-kindness and compassion;
I will betroth you to Me in faithfulness;
and you shall know the Lᴏʀᴅ.

After putting on the tefillin, say the following:
וַיְדַבֵּר The Lᴏʀᴅ spoke to Moses, saying, "Consecrate to Me every   *Ex. 13*
firstborn male. The first offspring of every womb among the
Israelites, whether man or beast, belongs to Me." Then Moses said
to the people, "Remember this day on which you left Egypt, the

Stand and place the תפילין של יד *on the biceps of the left arm (or right arm if you are left-handed), angled toward the heart, and before tightening the strap, say:*

בָּרוּךְ אַתָּה יהוה אֱלֹהֵינוּ מֶלֶךְ הָעוֹלָם
אֲשֶׁר קִדְּשָׁנוּ בְּמִצְוֹתָיו
וְצִוָּנוּ לְהָנִיחַ תְּפִלִּין.

Wrap the strap of the תפילין של יד *seven times around the arm.*
Place the תפילין של ראש *above the hairline, centered between the eyes, and say quietly:*

בָּרוּךְ אַתָּה יהוה אֱלֹהֵינוּ מֶלֶךְ הָעוֹלָם
אֲשֶׁר קִדְּשָׁנוּ בְּמִצְוֹתָיו
וְצִוָּנוּ עַל מִצְוַת תְּפִלִּין.

Adjust the תפילין של ראש *and say:*
בָּרוּךְ שֵׁם כְּבוֹד מַלְכוּתוֹ לְעוֹלָם וָעֶד

Some say:

וּמֵחָכְמָתְךָ אֵל עֶלְיוֹן תַּאֲצִיל עָלַי, וּמִבִּינָתְךָ תְּבִינֵנִי, וּבְחַסְדְּךָ
תַּגְדִּיל עָלַי, וּבִגְבוּרָתְךָ תַּצְמִית אוֹיְבַי וְקָמַי. וְשֶׁמֶן הַטּוֹב תָּרִיק
עַל שִׁבְעָה קְנֵי הַמְּנוֹרָה, לְהַשְׁפִּיעַ טוּבְךָ לִבְרִיּוֹתֶיךָ. פּוֹתֵחַ אֶת־יָדֶךָ
וּמַשְׂבִּיעַ לְכָל־חַי רָצוֹן:

תהלים
קמה

Wind the strap of the תפילין של יד *three times around the middle finger, saying:*

הושע ב

וְאֵרַשְׂתִּיךְ לִי לְעוֹלָם
וְאֵרַשְׂתִּיךְ לִי בְּצֶדֶק וּבְמִשְׁפָּט וּבְחֶסֶד וּבְרַחֲמִים:
וְאֵרַשְׂתִּיךְ לִי בֶּאֱמוּנָה, וְיָדַעַתְּ אֶת־יהוה:

After putting on the תפילין, *say the following:*

שמות יג

וַיְדַבֵּר יהוה אֶל־מֹשֶׁה לֵּאמֹר: קַדֶּשׁ־לִי כָל־בְּכוֹר, פֶּטֶר כָּל־רֶחֶם
בִּבְנֵי יִשְׂרָאֵל, בָּאָדָם וּבַבְּהֵמָה, לִי הוּא: וַיֹּאמֶר מֹשֶׁה אֶל־הָעָם,
זָכוֹר אֶת־הַיּוֹם הַזֶּה, אֲשֶׁר יְצָאתֶם מִמִּצְרַיִם מִבֵּית עֲבָדִים, כִּי

slave-house, when the LORD brought you out of it with a mighty hand. No leaven shall be eaten. You are leaving on this day, in the month of Aviv. When the LORD brings you into the land of the Canaanites, Hittites, Amorites, Hivites and Jebusites, the land He swore to your ancestors to give you, a land flowing with milk and honey, you are to observe this service in this same month. For seven days you shall eat unleavened bread, and make the seventh day a festival to the LORD. Unleavened bread shall be eaten throughout the seven days. No leavened bread may be seen in your possession, and no leaven shall be seen anywhere within your borders. On that day you shall tell your son, 'This is because of what the LORD did for me when I left Egypt.' [These words] shall also be a sign on your hand, and a reminder above your forehead, so that the LORD's Torah may always be in your mouth, because with a mighty hand the LORD brought you out of Egypt. You shall therefore keep this statute at its appointed time from year to year."

וְהָיָה After the LORD has brought you into the land of the Canaanites, as He swore to you and your ancestors, and He has given it to you, you shall set apart for the LORD the first offspring of every womb. All the firstborn males of your cattle belong to the LORD. Every firstling donkey you shall redeem with a lamb. If you do not redeem it, you must break its neck. Every firstborn among your sons you must redeem. If, in time to come, your son asks you, "What does this mean?" you shall say to him, "With a mighty hand the LORD brought us out of Egypt, out of the slave-house. When Pharaoh stubbornly refused to let us leave, the LORD killed all the firstborn in the land of Egypt, both man and beast. That is why I sacrifice to the LORD the first male offspring of every womb, and redeem all the firstborn of my sons." [These words] shall be a sign on your hand and as an emblem above your forehead, that with a mighty hand the LORD brought us out of Egypt.

בְּחֹזֶק יָד הוֹצִיא יהוה אֶתְכֶם מִזֶּה, וְלֹא יֵאָכֵל חָמֵץ: הַיּוֹם אַתֶּם
יֹצְאִים, בְּחֹדֶשׁ הָאָבִיב: וְהָיָה כִי־יְבִיאֲךָ יהוה אֶל־אֶרֶץ הַכְּנַעֲנִי
וְהַחִתִּי וְהָאֱמֹרִי וְהַחִוִּי וְהַיְבוּסִי, אֲשֶׁר נִשְׁבַּע לַאֲבֹתֶיךָ לָתֶת
לָךְ, אֶרֶץ זָבַת חָלָב וּדְבָשׁ, וְעָבַדְתָּ אֶת־הָעֲבֹדָה הַזֹּאת בַּחֹדֶשׁ
הַזֶּה: שִׁבְעַת יָמִים תֹּאכַל מַצֹּת, וּבַיּוֹם הַשְּׁבִיעִי חַג לַיהוה:
מַצּוֹת יֵאָכֵל אֵת שִׁבְעַת הַיָּמִים, וְלֹא־יֵרָאֶה לְךָ חָמֵץ וְלֹא־יֵרָאֶה
לְךָ שְׂאֹר, בְּכָל־גְּבֻלֶךָ: וְהִגַּדְתָּ לְבִנְךָ בַּיּוֹם הַהוּא לֵאמֹר, בַּעֲבוּר
זֶה עָשָׂה יהוה לִי בְּצֵאתִי מִמִּצְרָיִם: וְהָיָה לְךָ לְאוֹת עַל־יָדְךָ
וּלְזִכָּרוֹן בֵּין עֵינֶיךָ, לְמַעַן תִּהְיֶה תּוֹרַת יהוה בְּפִיךָ, כִּי בְּיָד חֲזָקָה
הוֹצִאֲךָ יהוה מִמִּצְרָיִם: וְשָׁמַרְתָּ אֶת־הַחֻקָּה הַזֹּאת לְמוֹעֲדָהּ,
מִיָּמִים יָמִימָה:

וְהָיָה כִּי־יְבִאֲךָ יהוה אֶל־אֶרֶץ הַכְּנַעֲנִי כַּאֲשֶׁר נִשְׁבַּע לְךָ
וְלַאֲבֹתֶיךָ, וּנְתָנָהּ לָךְ: וְהַעֲבַרְתָּ כָל־פֶּטֶר־רֶחֶם לַיהוה, וְכָל־
פֶּטֶר שֶׁגֶר בְּהֵמָה אֲשֶׁר יִהְיֶה לְךָ הַזְּכָרִים, לַיהוה: וְכָל־פֶּטֶר
חֲמֹר תִּפְדֶּה בְשֶׂה, וְאִם־לֹא תִפְדֶּה וַעֲרַפְתּוֹ, וְכֹל בְּכוֹר אָדָם
בְּבָנֶיךָ תִּפְדֶּה: וְהָיָה כִּי־יִשְׁאָלְךָ בִנְךָ מָחָר, לֵאמֹר מַה־זֹּאת,
וְאָמַרְתָּ אֵלָיו, בְּחֹזֶק יָד הוֹצִיאָנוּ יהוה מִמִּצְרַיִם מִבֵּית עֲבָדִים:
וַיְהִי כִּי־הִקְשָׁה פַרְעֹה לְשַׁלְּחֵנוּ, וַיַּהֲרֹג יהוה כָּל־בְּכוֹר בְּאֶרֶץ
מִצְרַיִם, מִבְּכֹר אָדָם וְעַד־בְּכוֹר בְּהֵמָה, עַל־כֵּן אֲנִי זֹבֵחַ לַיהוה
כָּל־פֶּטֶר רֶחֶם הַזְּכָרִים, וְכָל־בְּכוֹר בָּנַי אֶפְדֶּה: וְהָיָה לְאוֹת
עַל־יָדְכָה וּלְטוֹטָפֹת בֵּין עֵינֶיךָ, כִּי בְּחֹזֶק יָד הוֹצִיאָנוּ יהוה
מִמִּצְרָיִם:

PREPARATION FOR PRAYER

On entering the synagogue:

HOW GOODLY

Num. 24

are your tents, Jacob, your dwelling places, Israel.
As for me,
in Your great loving-kindness,
I will come into Your House.
I will bow down to Your holy Temple
in awe of You.
Lord, I love the habitation of Your House,
the place where Your glory dwells.

Ps. 5

Ps. 26

As for me,
I will bow in worship;

> I will bend the knee
> before the Lord my Maker.

As for me,
may my prayer come to You, Lord,

Ps. 69

> at a time of favor.
> God, in Your great loving-kindness,
> answer me with Your faithful salvation.

הכנה לתפילה

On entering the בית כנסת:

במדבר כד

מַה־טֹּבוּ

אֹהָלֶיךָ יַעֲקֹב, מִשְׁכְּנֹתֶיךָ יִשְׂרָאֵל:

תהלים ה

וַאֲנִי בְּרֹב חַסְדְּךָ אָבוֹא בֵיתֶךָ
אֶשְׁתַּחֲוֶה אֶל־הֵיכַל־קָדְשְׁךָ
בְּיִרְאָתֶךָ:

תהלים כו

יהוה אָהַבְתִּי מְעוֹן בֵּיתֶךָ
וּמְקוֹם מִשְׁכַּן כְּבוֹדֶךָ:

וַאֲנִי אֶשְׁתַּחֲוֶה

וְאֶכְרָעָה
אֲבָרְכָה לִפְנֵי יהוה עֹשִׂי.

תהלים סט

וַאֲנִי תְפִלָּתִי־לְךָ יהוה

עֵת רָצוֹן
אֱלֹהִים בְּרָב־חַסְדֶּךָ
עֲנֵנִי בֶּאֱמֶת יִשְׁעֶךָ:

*The following poems, on this page and the next, both from the Middle Ages,
are summary statements of Jewish faith, orienting us to the spiritual contours
of the world that we actualize in the mind by the act of prayer.*

LORD OF THE UNIVERSE,
who reigned before the birth of any thing –

When by His will all things were made
then was His name proclaimed King.

And when all things shall cease to be
He alone will reign in awe.

He was, He is, and He shall be
glorious for evermore.

He is One, there is none else,
alone, unique, beyond compare;

Without beginning, without end,
His might, His rule are everywhere.

He is my God; my Redeemer lives.
He is the Rock on whom I rely –

My banner and my safe retreat,
my cup, my portion when I cry.

Into His hand my soul I place,
when I awake and when I sleep.

The LORD is with me, I shall not fear;
body and soul from harm will He keep.

The following poems, on this page and the next, both from the Middle Ages,
are summary statements of Jewish faith, orienting us to the spiritual contours
of the world that we actualize in the mind by the act of prayer.

אֲדוֹן עוֹלָם

אֲשֶׁר מָלַךְ בְּטֶרֶם כָּל־יְצִיר נִבְרָא.

לְעֵת נַעֲשָׂה בְחֶפְצוֹ כֹּל אֲזַי מֶלֶךְ שְׁמוֹ נִקְרָא.

וְאַחֲרֵי כִּכְלוֹת הַכֹּל לְבַדּוֹ יִמְלֹךְ נוֹרָא.

וְהוּא הָיָה וְהוּא הֹוֶה וְהוּא יִהְיֶה בְּתִפְאָרָה.

וְהוּא אֶחָד וְאֵין שֵׁנִי לְהַמְשִׁיל לוֹ לְהַחְבִּירָה.

בְּלִי רֵאשִׁית בְּלִי תַכְלִית וְלוֹ הָעֹז וְהַמִּשְׂרָה.

וְהוּא אֵלִי וְחַי גּוֹאֲלִי וְצוּר חֶבְלִי בְּעֵת צָרָה.

וְהוּא נִסִּי וּמָנוֹס לִי מְנָת כּוֹסִי בְּיוֹם אֶקְרָא.

בְּיָדוֹ אַפְקִיד רוּחִי בְּעֵת אִישַׁן וְאָעִירָה.

וְעִם רוּחִי גְּוִיָּתִי יהוה לִי וְלֹא אִירָא.

GREAT
is the living God and praised.
He exists, and His existence is beyond time.

He is One, and there is no unity like His.
Unfathomable, His oneness is infinite.

He has neither bodily form nor substance;
His holiness is beyond compare.

He preceded all that was created.
He was first: there was no beginning to His beginning.

Behold He is Master of the Universe; and every creature
shows His greatness and majesty.

The rich flow of His prophecy He gave
to His treasured people in whom He gloried.

Never in Israel has there arisen another like Moses,
a prophet who beheld God's image.

God gave His people a Torah of truth
by the hand of His prophet, most faithful of His House.

God will not alter or change His law
for any other, for eternity.

He sees and knows our secret thoughts;
as soon as something is begun, He foresees its end.

He rewards people with loving-kindness according to their deeds;
He punishes the wicked according to his wickedness.

At the end of days He will send our Messiah
to redeem those who await His final salvation.

God will revive the dead in His great loving-kindness.
Blessed for evermore is His glorious name!

יִגְדַּל

אֱלֹהִים חַי וְיִשְׁתַּבַּח, נִמְצָא וְאֵין עֵת אֶל מְצִיאוּתוֹ.

אֶחָד וְאֵין יָחִיד כְּיִחוּדוֹ, נֶעְלָם וְגַם אֵין סוֹף לְאַחְדּוּתוֹ.

אֵין לוֹ דְּמוּת הַגּוּף וְאֵינוֹ גוּף, לֹא נַעֲרֹךְ אֵלָיו קְדֻשָּׁתוֹ.

קַדְמוֹן לְכָל דָּבָר אֲשֶׁר נִבְרָא, רִאשׁוֹן וְאֵין רֵאשִׁית לְרֵאשִׁיתוֹ.

הִנּוֹ אֲדוֹן עוֹלָם, וְכָל נוֹצָר יוֹרֶה גְדֻלָּתוֹ וּמַלְכוּתוֹ.

שֶׁפַע נְבוּאָתוֹ נְתָנוֹ אֶל־אַנְשֵׁי סְגֻלָּתוֹ וְתִפְאַרְתּוֹ.

לֹא קָם בְּיִשְׂרָאֵל כְּמֹשֶׁה עוֹד נָבִיא וּמַבִּיט אֶת תְּמוּנָתוֹ.

תּוֹרַת אֱמֶת נָתַן לְעַמּוֹ אֵל עַל יַד נְבִיאוֹ נֶאֱמַן בֵּיתוֹ.

לֹא יַחֲלִיף הָאֵל וְלֹא יָמִיר דָּתוֹ לְעוֹלָמִים לְזוּלָתוֹ.

צוֹפֶה וְיוֹדֵעַ סְתָרֵינוּ, מַבִּיט לְסוֹף דָּבָר בְּקַדְמָתוֹ.

גּוֹמֵל לְאִישׁ חֶסֶד כְּמִפְעָלוֹ, נוֹתֵן לְרָשָׁע רָע כְּרִשְׁעָתוֹ.

יִשְׁלַח לְקֵץ יָמִין מְשִׁיחֵנוּ לִפְדּוֹת מְחַכֵּי קֵץ יְשׁוּעָתוֹ.

מֵתִים יְחַיֶּה אֵל בְּרֹב חַסְדּוֹ, בָּרוּךְ עֲדֵי עַד שֵׁם תְּהִלָּתוֹ.

MORNING BLESSINGS

The following blessings are said aloud by the Leader, but each individual should say them quietly as well. It is our custom to say them standing.

בָּרוּךְ Blessed are You, LORD our God,
King of the Universe,
who gives the heart understanding
to distinguish day from night.

Blessed are You, LORD our God,
King of the Universe,
who has not made me a heathen.

Blessed are You, LORD our God,
King of the Universe,
who has not made me a slave.

Blessed are You, LORD our God,
King of the Universe,
men: who has not made me a woman.
women: who has made me according to His will.

Blessed are You, LORD our God,
King of the Universe,
who gives sight to the blind.

Blessed are You, LORD our God,
King of the Universe,
who clothes the naked.

Blessed are You, LORD our God,
King of the Universe,
who sets captives free.

Blessed are You, LORD our God,
King of the Universe,
who raises those bowed down.

Blessed are You, LORD our God,
King of the Universe,
who spreads the earth above the waters.

בִּרְכוֹת הַשַּׁחַר

The following blessings are said aloud by the שליח ציבור, but each individual should say them quietly as well. It is our custom to say them standing.

בָּרוּךְ אַתָּה יהוה אֱלֹהֵינוּ מֶלֶךְ הָעוֹלָם
אֲשֶׁר נָתַן לַשֶּׂכְוִי בִינָה
לְהַבְחִין בֵּין יוֹם וּבֵין לַיְלָה.

בָּרוּךְ אַתָּה יהוה אֱלֹהֵינוּ מֶלֶךְ הָעוֹלָם
שֶׁלֹּא עָשַׂנִי גּוֹי.

בָּרוּךְ אַתָּה יהוה אֱלֹהֵינוּ מֶלֶךְ הָעוֹלָם
שֶׁלֹּא עָשַׂנִי עָבֶד.

בָּרוּךְ אַתָּה יהוה אֱלֹהֵינוּ מֶלֶךְ הָעוֹלָם
men שֶׁלֹּא עָשַׂנִי אִשָּׁה. / *women* שֶׁעָשַׂנִי כִּרְצוֹנוֹ.

בָּרוּךְ אַתָּה יהוה אֱלֹהֵינוּ מֶלֶךְ הָעוֹלָם
פּוֹקֵחַ עִוְרִים.

בָּרוּךְ אַתָּה יהוה אֱלֹהֵינוּ מֶלֶךְ הָעוֹלָם
מַלְבִּישׁ עֲרֻמִּים.

בָּרוּךְ אַתָּה יהוה אֱלֹהֵינוּ מֶלֶךְ הָעוֹלָם
מַתִּיר אֲסוּרִים.

בָּרוּךְ אַתָּה יהוה אֱלֹהֵינוּ מֶלֶךְ הָעוֹלָם
זוֹקֵף כְּפוּפִים.

בָּרוּךְ אַתָּה יהוה אֱלֹהֵינוּ מֶלֶךְ הָעוֹלָם
רוֹקַע הָאָרֶץ עַל הַמָּיִם.

Blessed are You, LORD our God,
King of the Universe,
who has provided me with all I need.

Blessed are You, LORD our God,
King of the Universe,
who makes firm the steps of man.

Blessed are You, LORD our God,
King of the Universe,
who girds Israel with strength.

Blessed are You, LORD our God,
King of the Universe,
who crowns Israel with glory.

Blessed are You, LORD our God,
King of the Universe,
who gives strength to the weary.

בָּרוּךְ Blessed are You, LORD our God, King of the Universe, who removes sleep from my eyes and slumber from my eyelids. And may it be Your will, LORD our God and God of our ancestors, to accustom us to Your Torah, and make us attached to Your commandments. Lead us not into error, transgression, iniquity, temptation or disgrace. Do not let the evil instinct dominate us. Keep us far from a bad man and a bad companion. Help us attach ourselves to the good instinct and to good deeds and bend our instincts to be subservient to You. Grant us, this day and every day, grace, loving-kindness and compassion in Your eyes and in the eyes of all who see us, and bestow loving-kindness upon us. Blessed are You, LORD, who bestows loving-kindness on His people Israel.

יְהִי רָצוֹן May it be Your will, LORD my God and God of my ancestors, to save me today and every day, from the arrogant and from arrogance itself, from a bad man, a bad friend, a bad neighbor, a bad mishap, a destructive adversary, a harsh trial and a harsh opponent, whether or not he is a son of the covenant.

Berakhot 16b

בָּרוּךְ אַתָּה יהוה אֱלֹהֵינוּ מֶלֶךְ הָעוֹלָם
שֶׁעָשָׂה לִי כָּל צָרְכִּי.

בָּרוּךְ אַתָּה יהוה אֱלֹהֵינוּ מֶלֶךְ הָעוֹלָם
הַמֵּכִין מִצְעֲדֵי גָבֶר.

בָּרוּךְ אַתָּה יהוה אֱלֹהֵינוּ מֶלֶךְ הָעוֹלָם
אוֹזֵר יִשְׂרָאֵל בִּגְבוּרָה.

בָּרוּךְ אַתָּה יהוה אֱלֹהֵינוּ מֶלֶךְ הָעוֹלָם
עוֹטֵר יִשְׂרָאֵל בְּתִפְאָרָה.

בָּרוּךְ אַתָּה יהוה אֱלֹהֵינוּ מֶלֶךְ הָעוֹלָם
הַנּוֹתֵן לַיָּעֵף כֹּחַ.

בָּרוּךְ אַתָּה יהוה אֱלֹהֵינוּ מֶלֶךְ הָעוֹלָם, הַמַּעֲבִיר שֵׁנָה מֵעֵינַי
וּתְנוּמָה מֵעַפְעַפָּי. וִיהִי רָצוֹן מִלְּפָנֶיךָ יהוה אֱלֹהֵינוּ וֵאלֹהֵי
אֲבוֹתֵינוּ, שֶׁתַּרְגִּילֵנוּ בְּתוֹרָתֶךָ, וְדַבְּקֵנוּ בְּמִצְוֹתֶיךָ, וְאַל תְּבִיאֵנוּ
לֹא לִידֵי חֵטְא, וְלֹא לִידֵי עֲבֵרָה וְעָוֹן, וְלֹא לִידֵי נִסָּיוֹן וְלֹא לִידֵי
בִזָּיוֹן, וְאַל תַּשְׁלֶט בָּנוּ יֵצֶר הָרָע, וְהַרְחִיקֵנוּ מֵאָדָם רָע וּמֵחָבֵר רָע,
וְדַבְּקֵנוּ בְּיֵצֶר הַטּוֹב וּבְמַעֲשִׂים טוֹבִים, וְכֹף אֶת יִצְרֵנוּ לְהִשְׁתַּעְבֶּד
לָךְ, וּתְנֵנוּ הַיּוֹם וּבְכָל יוֹם לְחֵן וּלְחֶסֶד וּלְרַחֲמִים, בְּעֵינֶיךָ, וּבְעֵינֵי
כָל רוֹאֵינוּ, וְתִגְמְלֵנוּ חֲסָדִים טוֹבִים. בָּרוּךְ אַתָּה יהוה, גּוֹמֵל
חֲסָדִים טוֹבִים לְעַמּוֹ יִשְׂרָאֵל.

ברכות טז יְהִי רָצוֹן מִלְּפָנֶיךָ יהוה אֱלֹהַי וֵאלֹהֵי אֲבוֹתַי, שֶׁתַּצִּילֵנִי הַיּוֹם וּבְכָל יוֹם
מֵעַזֵּי פָנִים וּמֵעַזּוּת פָּנִים, מֵאָדָם רָע, וּמֵחָבֵר רָע, וּמִשָּׁכֵן רָע, וּמִפֶּגַע רָע,
וּמִשָּׂטָן הַמַּשְׁחִית, מִדִּין קָשֶׁה, וּמִבַּעַל דִּין קָשֶׁה בֵּין שֶׁהוּא בֶן בְּרִית וּבֵין
שֶׁאֵינוֹ בֶן בְּרִית.

THE BINDING OF ISAAC

*On the basis of Jewish mystical tradition, some have the custom of saying daily
the biblical passage recounting the Binding of Isaac, the supreme trial of faith
in which Abraham demonstrated his love of God above all other loves.*

Our God and God of our ancestors, remember us with a favorable memory,
and recall us with a remembrance of salvation and compassion from the
highest of high heavens. Remember, Lord our God, on our behalf, the love
of the ancients, Abraham, Isaac and Yisrael Your servants; the covenant, the
loving-kindness, and the oath You swore to Abraham our father on Mount
Moriah, and the Binding, when he bound Isaac his son on the altar, as is
written in Your Torah:

It happened after these things that God tested Abraham. *Gen. 22*
He said to him, "Abraham!" "Here I am," he replied. He said,
"Take your son, your only son, Isaac, whom you love, and go
to the land of Moriah and offer him there as a burnt-offering
on one of the mountains which I shall say to you." Early the
next morning Abraham rose and saddled his donkey and
took his two lads with him, and Isaac his son, and he cut
wood for the burnt-offering, and he set out for the place
of which God had told him. On the third day Abraham
looked up and saw the place from afar. Abraham said to his
lads, "Stay here with the donkey while I and the boy go on

---

adjoining the *Mikdash* known as "*Lishkat HaGazit*." Prior to the codification
of the *Torah Shebe'al Peh*, entry into the *Mikdash* area to visit the *Sanhedrin*
was necessary both to arbitrate halakhic issues and to study Torah from the
great sages.

A different position claims that "*Moriya*" reflects the term "*Yira*," awe.
The *Mikdash* showcased monotheism to an ancient world which still con-
ceived of religion in pagan imagery. The absence of visual depictions of
HaKadosh Barukh Hu in the *Mikdash* reinforced the tenets of monotheism.
Yirat Hashem constitutes the acceptance of His transcendence. The *Mikdash*
underscored *Yira* – "*Nora Elokim MiMikdashekha!*" (*Tehillim* 68).

פרשת העקדה

On the basis of Jewish mystical tradition, some have the custom of saying daily
the biblical passage recounting the Binding of Isaac, the supreme trial of faith
in which Abraham demonstrated his love of God above all other loves. .

אֱלֹהֵינוּ וֵאלֹהֵי אֲבוֹתֵינוּ, זָכְרֵנוּ בְּזִכָּרוֹן טוֹב לְפָנֶיךָ, וּפָקְדֵנוּ בִּפְקֻדַּת יְשׁוּעָה
וְרַחֲמִים מִשְּׁמֵי שְׁמֵי קֶדֶם, וּזְכָר לָנוּ יהוה אֱלֹהֵינוּ, אַהֲבַת הַקַּדְמוֹנִים אַבְרָהָם
יִצְחָק וְיִשְׂרָאֵל עֲבָדֶיךָ, אֶת הַבְּרִית וְאֶת הַחֶסֶד וְאֶת הַשְּׁבוּעָה שֶׁנִּשְׁבַּעְתָּ
לְאַבְרָהָם אָבִינוּ בְּהַר הַמּוֹרִיָּה, וְאֶת הָעֲקֵדָה שֶׁעָקַד אֶת יִצְחָק בְּנוֹ עַל גַּבֵּי
הַמִּזְבֵּחַ, כַּכָּתוּב בְּתוֹרָתֶךָ:

בראשית כב

וַיְהִי אַחַר הַדְּבָרִים הָאֵלֶּה, וְהָאֱלֹהִים נִסָּה אֶת־אַבְרָהָם,
וַיֹּאמֶר אֵלָיו אַבְרָהָם, וַיֹּאמֶר הִנֵּנִי: וַיֹּאמֶר קַח־נָא אֶת־בִּנְךָ
אֶת־יְחִידְךָ אֲשֶׁר־אָהַבְתָּ, אֶת־יִצְחָק, וְלֶךְ־לְךָ אֶל־אֶרֶץ
הַמֹּרִיָּה, וְהַעֲלֵהוּ שָׁם לְעֹלָה עַל אַחַד הֶהָרִים אֲשֶׁר אֹמַר
אֵלֶיךָ: וַיַּשְׁכֵּם אַבְרָהָם בַּבֹּקֶר, וַיַּחֲבֹשׁ אֶת־חֲמֹרוֹ, וַיִּקַּח
אֶת־שְׁנֵי נְעָרָיו אִתּוֹ וְאֵת יִצְחָק בְּנוֹ, וַיְבַקַּע עֲצֵי עֹלָה, וַיָּקָם
וַיֵּלֶךְ אֶל־הַמָּקוֹם אֲשֶׁר־אָמַר־לוֹ הָאֱלֹהִים: בַּיּוֹם הַשְּׁלִישִׁי
וַיִּשָּׂא אַבְרָהָם אֶת־עֵינָיו וַיַּרְא אֶת־הַמָּקוֹם מֵרָחֹק: וַיֹּאמֶר
אַבְרָהָם אֶל־נְעָרָיו, שְׁבוּ־לָכֶם פֹּה עִם־הַחֲמוֹר, וַאֲנִי וְהַנַּעַר

בְּהַר הַמּוֹרִיָּה *On Mount Moriah.* The name *Har HaMoriya* predated the
construction of the *Mikdash.* HaKadosh Barukh Hu instructs Avraham
to sacrifice his son Yitzḥak upon the mountain *already* referred to as
"*Moriya.*"

The Gemara (*Ta'anit* 16a) asserts that this name foreshadowed different
functions of the *Mikdash* which was located on the mountain.

One position claims that "*Moriya*" reflects the word "*Hora'a*" which refers
to the teaching of Torah. In addition to facilitating *korbanot,* the *Mikdash*
also serviced the delivery of Torah. The Great *Sanhedrin* was located in a hall

ahead. We will worship and we will return to you." Abraham took the wood for the burnt-offering and placed it on Isaac his son, and he took in his hand the fire and the knife, and the two of them went together. Isaac said to Abraham his father, "Father?" and he said "Here I am, my son." And he said, "Here are the fire and the wood, but where is the sheep for the burnt-offering?" Abraham said, "God will see to the sheep for the burnt-offering, my son." And the two of them went together. They came to the place God had told him about, and Abraham built there an altar and arranged the wood and bound Isaac his son and laid him on the altar on top of the wood. He reached out his hand and took the knife to slay his son. Then an angel of the LORD called out to him from heaven, "Abraham! Abraham!" He said, "Here I am." He said, "Do not reach out your hand against the boy; do not do anything to him, for now I know that you fear God, because you have not held back your son, your only son, from Me." Abraham looked up and there he saw a ram caught in a thicket by its horns, and Abraham went and took the ram and offered it as a burnt-offering instead of his son. Abraham called that place "The LORD will see," as is said to this day, "On the mountain of the LORD He will be seen." The angel of the LORD called to Abraham a second time from heaven, and said, "By Myself I swear, declares the LORD, that

_____

Bein HaBetarim which forecast the immediate and pending Egyptian exile, the *Akeda* portrayed the longer odyssey of Jewish history, and the multiple confrontations which this journey would pose. This frightful foreshadowing was delivered on *Har HaMoriya* – the very sight of the original covenant, and the birthplace of Jewish history. The entanglement of the ram in the "brush" of history will only be resolved by the sound of its horn to announce the End of Days: God will sound the shofar, and the lost Jews of Ashur will return (*Zekharia* 9:14).

נֵלְכָה עַד־כֹּה, וְנִשְׁתַּחֲוֶה וְנָשׁוּבָה אֲלֵיכֶם: וַיִּקַּח אַבְרָהָם
אֶת־עֲצֵי הָעֹלָה וַיָּשֶׂם עַל־יִצְחָק בְּנוֹ, וַיִּקַּח בְּיָדוֹ אֶת־הָאֵשׁ
וְאֶת־הַמַּאֲכֶלֶת, וַיֵּלְכוּ שְׁנֵיהֶם יַחְדָּו: וַיֹּאמֶר יִצְחָק אֶל־
אַבְרָהָם אָבִיו, וַיֹּאמֶר אָבִי, וַיֹּאמֶר הִנֶּנִּי בְנִי, וַיֹּאמֶר, הִנֵּה
הָאֵשׁ וְהָעֵצִים, וְאַיֵּה הַשֶּׂה לְעֹלָה: וַיֹּאמֶר אַבְרָהָם, אֱלֹהִים
יִרְאֶה־לּוֹ הַשֶּׂה לְעֹלָה, בְּנִי, וַיֵּלְכוּ שְׁנֵיהֶם יַחְדָּו: וַיָּבֹאוּ אֶל־
הַמָּקוֹם אֲשֶׁר אָמַר־לוֹ הָאֱלֹהִים, וַיִּבֶן שָׁם אַבְרָהָם אֶת־
הַמִּזְבֵּחַ וַיַּעֲרֹךְ אֶת־הָעֵצִים, וַיַּעֲקֹד אֶת־יִצְחָק בְּנוֹ, וַיָּשֶׂם
אֹתוֹ עַל־הַמִּזְבֵּחַ מִמַּעַל לָעֵצִים: וַיִּשְׁלַח אַבְרָהָם אֶת־יָדוֹ,
וַיִּקַּח אֶת־הַמַּאֲכֶלֶת, לִשְׁחֹט אֶת־בְּנוֹ: וַיִּקְרָא אֵלָיו מַלְאַךְ
יהוה מִן־הַשָּׁמַיִם, וַיֹּאמֶר אַבְרָהָם אַבְרָהָם, וַיֹּאמֶר הִנֵּנִי:
וַיֹּאמֶר אַל־תִּשְׁלַח יָדְךָ אֶל־הַנַּעַר, וְאַל־תַּעַשׂ לוֹ מְאוּמָה,
כִּי עַתָּה יָדַעְתִּי כִּי־יְרֵא אֱלֹהִים אַתָּה, וְלֹא חָשַׂכְתָּ אֶת־בִּנְךָ
אֶת־יְחִידְךָ מִמֶּנִּי: וַיִּשָּׂא אַבְרָהָם אֶת־עֵינָיו, וַיַּרְא וְהִנֵּה־אַיִל,
אַחַר נֶאֱחַז בַּסְּבַךְ בְּקַרְנָיו, וַיֵּלֶךְ אַבְרָהָם וַיִּקַּח אֶת־הָאַיִל,
וַיַּעֲלֵהוּ לְעֹלָה תַּחַת בְּנוֹ: וַיִּקְרָא אַבְרָהָם שֵׁם־הַמָּקוֹם
הַהוּא יהוה יִרְאֶה, אֲשֶׁר יֵאָמֵר הַיּוֹם בְּהַר יהוה יֵרָאֶה:
וַיִּקְרָא מַלְאַךְ יהוה אֶל־אַבְרָהָם שֵׁנִית מִן־הַשָּׁמָיִם: וַיֹּאמֶר,
בִּי נִשְׁבַּעְתִּי נְאֻם־יהוה, כִּי יַעַן אֲשֶׁר עָשִׂיתָ אֶת־הַדָּבָר הַזֶּה,

---

נֶאֱחַז בַּסְּבַךְ בְּקַרְנָיו *Caught in a thicket by its horns.* This apparently irrelevant detail of the *Akeda* is highlighted because it is a metaphor for Jewish history. The ram thrashed violently and unsuccessfully to release itself from the thicket. Historically the Jewish nation would struggle to release itself from foreign rule and discriminatory persecution. Successful release from one crisis would ultimately yield a new crisis and a new enemy. Unlike the *Berit*

because you have done this and have not held back your son, your only son, I will greatly bless you and greatly multiply your descendants, as the stars of heaven and the sand of the seashore, and your descendants shall take possession of the gates of their enemies. Through your descendants, all the nations of the earth will be blessed, because you have heeded My voice." Then Abraham returned to his lads, and they rose and went together to Beersheba, and Abraham stayed in Beersheba.

Master of the Universe, just as Abraham our father suppressed his compassion to do Your will wholeheartedly, so may Your compassion suppress Your anger from us and may Your compassion prevail over Your other attributes. Deal with us, LORD our God, with the attributes of loving-kindness and compassion, and in Your great goodness may Your anger be turned away from Your people, Your city, Your land and Your inheritance. Fulfill in us, LORD our God, the promise You made in Your Torah through the hand of Moses Your servant, as it is said: "I *Lev. 26* will remember My covenant with Jacob, and also My covenant with Isaac, and also My covenant with Abraham I will remember, and the land I will remember."

ACCEPTING THE SOVEREIGNTY OF HEAVEN

לְעוֹלָם A person should always be God-fearing, privately and publicly, *Tanna* acknowledging the truth and speaking it in his heart. *DeVei* He should rise early and say: *Eliyahu,* *ch. 21*

> Master of all worlds,
> not because of our righteousness *Dan. 9*
> do we lay our pleas before You,
> but because of Your great compassion.

What are we? What are our lives?
What is our loving-kindness?
What is our righteousness? What is our salvation?
What is our strength? What is our might?

וְלֹא חָשַׂכְתָּ אֶת־בִּנְךָ אֶת־יְחִידֶךָ: כִּי־בָרֵךְ אֲבָרֶכְךָ, וְהַרְבָּה
אַרְבֶּה אֶת־זַרְעֲךָ כְּכוֹכְבֵי הַשָּׁמַיִם, וְכַחוֹל אֲשֶׁר עַל־שְׂפַת
הַיָּם, וְיִרַשׁ זַרְעֲךָ אֵת שַׁעַר אֹיְבָיו: וְהִתְבָּרְכוּ בְזַרְעֲךָ כֹּל
גּוֹיֵי הָאָרֶץ, עֵקֶב אֲשֶׁר שָׁמַעְתָּ בְּקֹלִי: וַיָּשָׁב אַבְרָהָם אֶל־
נְעָרָיו, וַיָּקֻמוּ וַיֵּלְכוּ יַחְדָּו אֶל־בְּאֵר שָׁבַע, וַיֵּשֶׁב אַבְרָהָם
בִּבְאֵר שָׁבַע:

רִבּוֹנוֹ שֶׁל עוֹלָם, כְּמוֹ שֶׁכָּבַשׁ אַבְרָהָם אָבִינוּ אֶת רַחֲמָיו לַעֲשׂוֹת רְצוֹנְךָ
בְּלֵבָב שָׁלֵם, כֵּן יִכְבְּשׁוּ רַחֲמֶיךָ אֶת כַּעַסְךָ מֵעָלֵינוּ וְיִגֹּלּוּ רַחֲמֶיךָ עַל מִדּוֹתֶיךָ.
וְתִתְנַהֵג עִמָּנוּ יהוה אֱלֹהֵינוּ בְּמִדַּת הַחֶסֶד וּבְמִדַּת הָרַחֲמִים, וּבְטוּבְךָ הַגָּדוֹל
יָשׁוּב חֲרוֹן אַפְּךָ מֵעַמְּךָ וּמֵעִירְךָ וּמֵאַרְצְךָ וּמִנַּחֲלָתֶךָ. וְקַיֶּם לָנוּ יהוה אֱלֹהֵינוּ
אֶת הַדָּבָר שֶׁהִבְטַחְתָּנוּ בְּתוֹרָתֶךָ עַל יְדֵי מֹשֶׁה עַבְדֶּךָ, כָּאָמוּר: וְזָכַרְתִּי   ויקרא כו
אֶת־בְּרִיתִי יַעֲקוֹב וְאַף אֶת־בְּרִיתִי יִצְחָק וְאַף אֶת־בְּרִיתִי אַבְרָהָם אֶזְכֹּר,
וְהָאָרֶץ אֶזְכֹּר:

קבלת עול מלכות שמים

תנא דבי
אליה,
פרק כא לְעוֹלָם יְהֵא אָדָם יְרֵא שָׁמַיִם בְּסֵתֶר וּבְגָלוּי
וּמוֹדֶה עַל הָאֱמֶת, וְדוֹבֵר אֱמֶת בִּלְבָבוֹ
וְיַשְׁכֵּם וְיֹאמַר

רִבּוֹן כָּל הָעוֹלָמִים

דניאל ט לֹא עַל־צִדְקוֹתֵינוּ אֲנַחְנוּ מַפִּילִים תַּחֲנוּנֵינוּ לְפָנֶיךָ
כִּי עַל־רַחֲמֶיךָ הָרַבִּים:

מָה אָנוּ, מֶה חַיֵּינוּ

מֶה חַסְדֵּנוּ, מַה צִּדְקוֹתֵינוּ

מַה יְשׁוּעָתֵנוּ, מַה כֹּחֵנוּ, מַה גְּבוּרָתֵנוּ

What shall we say before You,
Lord our God and God of our ancestors?
Are not all the mighty like nothing before You,
the men of renown as if they had never been,
the wise as if they know nothing,
and the understanding as if they lack intelligence?
For their many works are in vain,
and the days of their lives like a fleeting breath before You.
The pre-eminence of man over the animals is nothing,
for all is but a fleeting breath.

Eccl. 3

אֲבָל Yet we are Your people, the children of Your covenant,
the children of Abraham, Your beloved,
to whom You made a promise on Mount Moriah;
the offspring of Isaac his only one who was bound on the altar;
the congregation of Jacob Your firstborn son
whom – because of the love with which You loved him
and the joy with which You rejoiced in him –
You called Yisrael and Yeshurun.

לְפִיכָךְ Therefore it is our duty to thank You, and to praise, glorify,
bless, sanctify and give praise and thanks to Your name.
Happy are we, how good is our portion,
how lovely our fate, how beautiful our heritage.

▸ Happy are we who, early and late, evening and morning,
say twice each day –

> Listen, Israel: the Lord is our God, the Lord is One.　*Deut. 6*
>
> *Quietly:* Blessed be the name of His glorious kingdom for ever and all time.
>
> *Some congregations say the entire first paragraph of the Shema (below) at this point.*
> *If there is a concern that the Shema will not be recited within the*
> *prescribed time, then all three paragraphs should be said.*

Love the Lord your God with all your heart, with all your soul, and with all your
might. These words which I command you today shall be on your heart. Teach them
repeatedly to your children, speaking of them when you sit at home and when you
travel on the way, when you lie down and when you rise. Bind them as a sign on your
hand, and they shall be an emblem between your eyes. Write them on the doorposts
of your house and gates.

מַה נֹּאמַר לְפָנֶיךָ, יהוה אֱלֹהֵינוּ וֵאלֹהֵי אֲבוֹתֵינוּ
הֲלֹא כָּל הַגִּבּוֹרִים כְּאַיִן לְפָנֶיךָ, וְאַנְשֵׁי הַשֵּׁם כְּלֹא הָיוּ
וַחֲכָמִים כִּבְלִי מַדָּע, וּנְבוֹנִים כִּבְלִי הַשְׂכֵּל
כִּי רֹב מַעֲשֵׂיהֶם תֹּהוּ, וִימֵי חַיֵּיהֶם הֶבֶל לְפָנֶיךָ

קהלת ג

וּמוֹתַר הָאָדָם מִן־הַבְּהֵמָה אָיִן, כִּי הַכֹּל הָבֶל:

אֲבָל אֲנַחְנוּ עַמְּךָ בְּנֵי בְרִיתֶךָ
בְּנֵי אַבְרָהָם אֹהַבְךָ שֶׁנִּשְׁבַּעְתָּ לּוֹ בְּהַר הַמּוֹרִיָּה
זֶרַע יִצְחָק יְחִידוֹ שֶׁנֶּעֱקַד עַל גַּבֵּי הַמִּזְבֵּחַ
עֲדַת יַעֲקֹב בִּנְךָ בְּכוֹרֶךָ
שֶׁמֵּאַהֲבָתְךָ שֶׁאָהַבְתָּ אוֹתוֹ, וּמִשִּׂמְחָתְךָ שֶׁשָּׂמַחְתָּ בּוֹ
קָרָאתָ אֶת שְׁמוֹ יִשְׂרָאֵל וִישֻׁרוּן.

לְפִיכָךְ אֲנַחְנוּ חַיָּבִים לְהוֹדוֹת לְךָ וּלְשַׁבֵּחֲךָ וּלְפָאֶרְךָ
וּלְבָרֵךְ וּלְקַדֵּשׁ וְלָתֵת שֶׁבַח וְהוֹדָיָה לִשְׁמֶךָ.
אַשְׁרֵינוּ, מַה טּוֹב חֶלְקֵנוּ, וּמַה נָּעִים גּוֹרָלֵנוּ, וּמַה יָּפָה יְרֻשָּׁתֵנוּ.

◂ אַשְׁרֵינוּ, שֶׁאֲנַחְנוּ מַשְׁכִּימִים וּמַעֲרִיבִים עֶרֶב וָבֹקֶר
וְאוֹמְרִים פַּעֲמַיִם בְּכָל יוֹם

דברים ו

שְׁמַע יִשְׂרָאֵל, יהוה אֱלֹהֵינוּ, יהוה אֶחָד:
Quietly
בָּרוּךְ שֵׁם כְּבוֹד מַלְכוּתוֹ לְעוֹלָם וָעֶד.

Some congregations say the entire first paragraph of the שמע (below) at this point.
If there is a concern that the שמע will not be recited within the
prescribed time, then all three paragraphs should be said.

וְאָהַבְתָּ אֵת יהוה אֱלֹהֶיךָ, בְּכָל־לְבָבְךָ, וּבְכָל־נַפְשְׁךָ, וּבְכָל־מְאֹדֶךָ: וְהָיוּ הַדְּבָרִים
הָאֵלֶּה, אֲשֶׁר אָנֹכִי מְצַוְּךָ הַיּוֹם, עַל־לְבָבֶךָ: וְשִׁנַּנְתָּם לְבָנֶיךָ, וְדִבַּרְתָּ בָּם, בְּשִׁבְתְּךָ
בְּבֵיתֶךָ, וּבְלֶכְתְּךָ בַדֶּרֶךְ, וּבְשָׁכְבְּךָ וּבְקוּמֶךָ: וּקְשַׁרְתָּם לְאוֹת עַל־יָדֶךָ וְהָיוּ לְטֹטָפֹת
בֵּין עֵינֶיךָ: וּכְתַבְתָּם עַל־מְזֻזוֹת בֵּיתֶךָ וּבִשְׁעָרֶיךָ:

אַתָּה הוּא It was You who existed before the world was created,
it is You now that the world has been created.
It is You in this world
and You in the World to Come.
▸ Sanctify Your name through those who sanctify Your name,
and sanctify Your name throughout Your world.
By Your salvation may our pride be exalted;
raise high our pride.
Blessed are You, Lord,
who sanctifies His name among the multitudes.

אַתָּה הוּא You are the Lord our God
in heaven and on earth,
and in the highest heaven of heavens.
Truly, You are the first
and You are the last,
and besides You there is no god.
Gather those who hope in You
from the four quarters of the earth.
May all mankind recognize and know
that You alone are God
over all the kingdoms on earth.

You made the heavens and the earth,
the sea and all they contain.
Who among all the works of Your hands, above and below,
can tell You what to do?

Heavenly Father, deal kindly with us
for the sake of Your great name by which we are called,
and fulfill for us, Lord our God, that which is written:
"At that time I will bring you home,   *Zeph. 3*
and at that time I will gather you,
for I will give you renown and praise
among all the peoples of the earth
when I bring back your exiles before your eyes, says the Lord."

אַתָּה הוּא עַד שֶׁלֹּא נִבְרָא הָעוֹלָם
אַתָּה הוּא מִשֶּׁנִּבְרָא הָעוֹלָם.
אַתָּה הוּא בָּעוֹלָם הַזֶּה
וְאַתָּה הוּא לָעוֹלָם הַבָּא.

◂ קַדֵּשׁ אֶת שִׁמְךָ עַל מַקְדִּישֵׁי שְׁמֶךָ
וְקַדֵּשׁ אֶת שִׁמְךָ בְּעוֹלָמֶךָ, וּבִישׁוּעָתְךָ תָּרוּם וְתַגְבִּיהַּ קַרְנֵנוּ.
בָּרוּךְ אַתָּה יהוה, הַמְקַדֵּשׁ אֶת שְׁמוֹ בָּרַבִּים.

אַתָּה הוּא יהוה אֱלֹהֵינוּ
בַּשָּׁמַיִם וּבָאָרֶץ, וּבִשְׁמֵי הַשָּׁמַיִם הָעֶלְיוֹנִים.
אֱמֶת, אַתָּה הוּא רִאשׁוֹן, וְאַתָּה הוּא אַחֲרוֹן
וּמִבַּלְעָדֶיךָ אֵין אֱלֹהִים.
קַבֵּץ קֹוֶיךָ מֵאַרְבַּע כַּנְפוֹת הָאָרֶץ.
יַכִּירוּ וְיֵדְעוּ כָּל בָּאֵי עוֹלָם
כִּי אַתָּה הוּא הָאֱלֹהִים לְבַדְּךָ לְכֹל מַמְלְכוֹת הָאָרֶץ.

אַתָּה עָשִׂיתָ אֶת הַשָּׁמַיִם וְאֶת הָאָרֶץ
אֶת הַיָּם וְאֶת כָּל אֲשֶׁר בָּם
וּמִי בְּכָל מַעֲשֵׂי יָדֶיךָ בָּעֶלְיוֹנִים אוֹ בַתַּחְתּוֹנִים
שֶׁיֹּאמַר לְךָ מַה תַּעֲשֶׂה.

אָבִינוּ שֶׁבַּשָּׁמַיִם עֲשֵׂה עִמָּנוּ חֶסֶד
בַּעֲבוּר שִׁמְךָ הַגָּדוֹל שֶׁנִּקְרָא עָלֵינוּ
וְקַיֶּם לָנוּ יהוה אֱלֹהֵינוּ מַה שֶּׁכָּתוּב:

צפניה ג
בָּעֵת הַהִיא אָבִיא אֶתְכֶם, וּבָעֵת קַבְּצִי אֶתְכֶם
כִּי־אֶתֵּן אֶתְכֶם לְשֵׁם וְלִתְהִלָּה בְּכֹל עַמֵּי הָאָרֶץ
בְּשׁוּבִי אֶת־שְׁבוּתֵיכֶם לְעֵינֵיכֶם, אָמַר יהוה:

OFFERINGS

The sages held that, in the absence of the Temple, studying the laws of sacrifices is the equivalent of offering them. Hence the following texts. There are different customs as to how many passages are to be said, and one should follow the custom of one's congregation. The minimum requirement is to say the verses relating to The Daily Sacrifice on the next page.

THE BASIN

The LORD spoke to Moses, saying: Make a bronze basin, with *Ex. 30* its bronze stand for washing, and place it between the Tent of Meeting and the altar, and put water in it. From it, Aaron and his sons are to wash their hands and feet. When they enter the Tent of Meeting, they shall wash with water so that they will not die; likewise when they approach the altar to minister, presenting a fire-offering to the LORD. They must wash their hands and feet so that they will not die. This shall be an everlasting ordinance for Aaron and his descendants throughout their generations.

TAKING OF THE ASHES

The LORD spoke to Moses, saying: Instruct Aaron and his sons, *Lev. 6* saying, This is the law of the burnt-offering. The burnt-offering shall remain on the altar hearth throughout the night until morning, and the altar fire shall be kept burning on it. The priest shall then put on his linen garments, and linen breeches next to his body, and shall remove the ashes of the burnt-offering that the fire has consumed on the altar and place them beside the altar. Then he shall take off these clothes and put on others, and carry the ashes outside the camp to a clean place. The fire on the altar must be kept burning; it must not go out. Each morning the priest shall burn wood on it, and prepare on it the burnt-offering and burn the fat of the peace-offerings. A perpetual fire must be kept burning on the altar; it must not go out.

May it be Your will, LORD our God and God of our ancestors, that You have compassion on us and pardon us all our sins, grant atonement for all our iniquities and forgive all our transgressions. May You rebuild the Temple swiftly in our days so that we may offer You the continual-offering that it may atone for us as You have prescribed for us in Your Torah through Moses Your servant, from the mouthpiece of Your glory, as it is said:

סדר הקרבנות

חז״ל *held that, in the absence of the Temple, studying the laws of sacrifices is the equivalent of offering them. Hence the following texts. There are different customs as to how many passages are to be said, and one should follow the custom of one's congregation. The minimum requirement is to say the verses relating to the* קרבן תמיד *on the next page.*

פרשת הכיור

שמות ל

וַיְדַבֵּר יהוה אֶל־מֹשֶׁה לֵּאמֹר: וְעָשִׂיתָ כִּיּוֹר נְחֹשֶׁת וְכַנּוֹ נְחֹשֶׁת לְרָחְצָה, וְנָתַתָּ אֹתוֹ בֵּין־אֹהֶל מוֹעֵד וּבֵין הַמִּזְבֵּחַ, וְנָתַתָּ שָׁמָּה מָיִם: וְרָחֲצוּ אַהֲרֹן וּבָנָיו מִמֶּנּוּ אֶת־יְדֵיהֶם וְאֶת־רַגְלֵיהֶם: בְּבֹאָם אֶל־אֹהֶל מוֹעֵד יִרְחֲצוּ־מַיִם, וְלֹא יָמֻתוּ, אוֹ בְגִשְׁתָּם אֶל־הַמִּזְבֵּחַ לְשָׁרֵת, לְהַקְטִיר אִשֶּׁה לַיהוה: וְרָחֲצוּ יְדֵיהֶם וְרַגְלֵיהֶם וְלֹא יָמֻתוּ, וְהָיְתָה לָהֶם חָק־עוֹלָם, לוֹ וּלְזַרְעוֹ לְדֹרֹתָם:

פרשת תרומת הדשן

ויקרא ו

וַיְדַבֵּר יהוה אֶל־מֹשֶׁה לֵּאמֹר: צַו אֶת־אַהֲרֹן וְאֶת־בָּנָיו לֵאמֹר, זֹאת תּוֹרַת הָעֹלָה, הִוא הָעֹלָה עַל מוֹקְדָה עַל־הַמִּזְבֵּחַ כָּל־הַלַּיְלָה עַד־הַבֹּקֶר, וְאֵשׁ הַמִּזְבֵּחַ תּוּקַד בּוֹ: וְלָבַשׁ הַכֹּהֵן מִדּוֹ בַד, וּמִכְנְסֵי־בַד יִלְבַּשׁ עַל־בְּשָׂרוֹ, וְהֵרִים אֶת־הַדֶּשֶׁן אֲשֶׁר תֹּאכַל הָאֵשׁ אֶת־הָעֹלָה, עַל־הַמִּזְבֵּחַ, וְשָׂמוֹ אֵצֶל הַמִּזְבֵּחַ: וּפָשַׁט אֶת־בְּגָדָיו, וְלָבַשׁ בְּגָדִים אֲחֵרִים, וְהוֹצִיא אֶת־הַדֶּשֶׁן אֶל־מִחוּץ לַמַּחֲנֶה, אֶל־מָקוֹם טָהוֹר: וְהָאֵשׁ עַל־הַמִּזְבֵּחַ תּוּקַד־בּוֹ, לֹא תִכְבֶּה, וּבִעֵר עָלֶיהָ הַכֹּהֵן עֵצִים בַּבֹּקֶר בַּבֹּקֶר, וְעָרַךְ עָלֶיהָ הָעֹלָה, וְהִקְטִיר עָלֶיהָ חֶלְבֵי הַשְּׁלָמִים: אֵשׁ, תָּמִיד תּוּקַד עַל־הַמִּזְבֵּחַ, לֹא תִכְבֶּה:

יְהִי רָצוֹן מִלְּפָנֶיךָ יהוה אֱלֹהֵינוּ וֵאלֹהֵי אֲבוֹתֵינוּ, שֶׁתְּרַחֵם עָלֵינוּ, וְתִמְחָל לָנוּ עַל כָּל חַטֹּאתֵינוּ וּתְכַפֶּר לָנוּ עַל כָּל עֲוֹנוֹתֵינוּ וְתִסְלַח לָנוּ עַל כָּל פְּשָׁעֵינוּ, וְתִבְנֶה בֵּית הַמִּקְדָּשׁ בִּמְהֵרָה בְיָמֵינוּ, וְנַקְרִיב לְפָנֶיךָ קָרְבַּן הַתָּמִיד שֶׁיְּכַפֵּר בַּעֲדֵנוּ, כְּמוֹ שֶׁכָּתַבְתָּ עָלֵינוּ בְּתוֹרָתֶךָ עַל יְדֵי מֹשֶׁה עַבְדֶּךָ מִפִּי כְבוֹדֶךָ, כָּאָמוּר

THE DAILY SACRIFICE

וַיְדַבֵּר The LORD said to Moses, "Command the Israelites and tell *Num. 28*
them: 'Be careful to offer to Me at the appointed time My food-
offering consumed by fire, as an aroma pleasing to Me.' Tell them:
'This is the fire-offering you shall offer to the LORD – two lambs
a year old without blemish, as a regular burnt-offering each day.
Prepare one lamb in the morning and the other toward evening,
together with a meal-offering of a tenth of an ephah of fine flour
mixed with a quarter of a hin of oil from pressed olives. This is
the regular burnt-offering instituted at Mount Sinai as a pleasing
aroma, a fire-offering made to the LORD. Its libation is to be a quarter of a hin [of wine] with each lamb, poured in the Sanctuary as a
libation of strong drink to the LORD. Prepare the second lamb in
the afternoon, along with the same meal-offering and libation as in
the morning. This is a fire-offering, an aroma pleasing to the LORD.'"

"Fortunate are the Jewish people; in front of whom do you achieve purity and
who purifies you? Our Father in Heaven!" (*Yoma* 86b).

An additional example of location-based absolution is the intriguing phenomenon of "*Tzitz Meratze.*" If a *korban* became impure during processing,
it may still be considered valid because the golden head ornament of the
Kohen Gadol "repairs" the deficiency and validates the *korban*. However if
the *korban* exited from the precincts of the *Mikdash* (and is thereby invalid
because it is considered "*yotzei*"), the *Tzitz* cannot compensate. As the
Gemara (*Menaḥot* 25a) comments, this unique repair of invalid sacrifices
only applies to mistakes which occur "*lifnei Hashem,*" but not to errors which
remove the *korban* from this vicinity. *Korbanot* which still remain within the
confines of the *Mikdash* can be processed despite incorrect procedures, but
a *korban* which is dislocated remains invalid.

In this spirit Ḥazal stress the "geographic" atonement conferred on those
who live closer to the *Mikdash*, within Yerushalayim. In a broader sense
referring to residents of greater Israel, the Gemara (*Ketuvot* 111a) cites Rabbi
Eliezer: "Whoever lives in Israel, lives without sin!"

Although Judaism shuns the notion of vicarious atonement, and full repentance is a product of scrupulous *teshuva*, residing in Israel or in Yerushalayim
facilitates the process of *teshuva*, and contributes toward the achievement
of *kapara*.

פרשת קרבן התמיד

במדבר כח

וַיְדַבֵּר יהוה אֶל־מֹשֶׁה לֵּאמֹר: צַו אֶת־בְּנֵי יִשְׂרָאֵל וְאָמַרְתָּ
אֲלֵהֶם, אֶת־קָרְבָּנִי לַחְמִי לְאִשַּׁי, רֵיחַ נִיחֹחִי, תִּשְׁמְרוּ לְהַקְרִיב
לִי בְּמוֹעֲדוֹ: וְאָמַרְתָּ לָהֶם, זֶה הָאִשֶּׁה אֲשֶׁר תַּקְרִיבוּ לַיהוה,
כְּבָשִׂים בְּנֵי־שָׁנָה תְמִימִם שְׁנַיִם לַיּוֹם, עֹלָה תָמִיד: אֶת־
הַכֶּבֶשׂ אֶחָד תַּעֲשֶׂה בַבֹּקֶר, וְאֵת הַכֶּבֶשׂ הַשֵּׁנִי תַּעֲשֶׂה בֵּין
הָעַרְבָּיִם: וַעֲשִׂירִית הָאֵיפָה סֹלֶת לְמִנְחָה, בְּלוּלָה בְּשֶׁמֶן
כָּתִית רְבִיעִת הַהִין: עֹלַת תָּמִיד, הָעֲשֻׂיָה בְּהַר סִינַי, לְרֵיחַ
נִיחֹחַ אִשֶּׁה לַיהוה: וְנִסְכּוֹ רְבִיעִת הַהִין לַכֶּבֶשׂ הָאֶחָד,
בַּקֹּדֶשׁ הַסֵּךְ נֶסֶךְ שֵׁכָר לַיהוה: וְאֵת הַכֶּבֶשׂ הַשֵּׁנִי תַּעֲשֶׂה
בֵּין הָעַרְבָּיִם, כְּמִנְחַת הַבֹּקֶר וּכְנִסְכּוֹ תַּעֲשֶׂה, אִשֶּׁה רֵיחַ
נִיחֹחַ לַיהוה:

פרשת קרבן התמיד *The Daily Sacrifice.* The Midrash (*Tanḥuma Pinḥas, Bemidbar Raba* 19) asserts that no resident of Yerushalayim ever went to sleep without expiation of sins. The morning daily sacrifice atoned for sins committed at night, while the afternoon offering atoned for sins perpetrated during the day. This unique atonement is derived from a verse in the opening chapter of Yeshayahu which describes Yerushalayim as a city in which "righteousness resides" (*tzedek yalin ba*). Typically the public daily offerings are meant to provide "national" coverage – without any distinction between inhabitants of Yerushalayim and residents of other cities. Evidently – according to this midrash – proximity to the *Mikdash* affords a unique and more immediate atonement of sin.

Though forgiveness is typically a product of rigorous *teshuva*, often it is achieved by mere consciousness of national identity, or sensitivity to the Divine Presence. Famously, the Rambam (*Hilkhot Teshuva* 1:2) claimed that the *experience* of Yom Kippur itself atones for most transgressions, even in the absence of personal *teshuva*. In a similar vein – though not intending halakhic consequences – Rabbi Akiva reminded the generation traumatized by the destruction of the second *Beit HaMikdash* that the very *encounter* with HaKadosh Barukh Hu, rather than *Mikdash* rituals, purifies us of our sins:

וְשָׁחַט He shall slaughter it at the north side of the altar before *Lev. 1*
the Lord, and Aaron's sons the priests shall sprinkle its blood
against the altar on all sides.

May it be Your will, Lord our God and God of our ancestors, that this recitation be
considered accepted and favored before You as if we had offered the daily sacrifice at
its appointed time and place, according to its laws.

It is You, Lord our God, to whom our ancestors offered fragrant incense when the
Temple stood, as You commanded them through Moses Your prophet, as is written
in Your Torah:

THE INCENSE

The Lord said to Moses: Take fragrant spices – balsam, onycha, *Ex. 30*
galbanum and pure frankincense, all in equal amounts – and make
a fragrant blend of incense, the work of a perfumer, well mixed, pure
and holy. Grind it very finely and place it in front of the [Ark of]
Testimony in the Tent of Meeting, where I will meet with you. It
shall be most holy to you.

And it is said:

Aaron shall burn fragrant incense on the altar every morning when
he cleans the lamps. He shall burn incense again when he lights the
lamps toward evening so that there will be incense before the Lord
at all times, throughout your generations.

The rabbis taught: How was the incense prepared? It weighed 368 manehs, 365 *Keritot 6a*
corresponding to the number of days in a solar year, a maneh for each day, half
to be offered in the morning and half in the afternoon, and three additional
manehs from which the High Priest took two handfuls on Yom Kippur. These
were put back into the mortar on the day before Yom Kippur and ground again
very thoroughly so as to be extremely fine. The incense contained eleven kinds
of spices: balsam, onycha, galbanum and frankincense, each weighing seventy
manehs; myrrh, cassia, spikenard and saffron, each weighing sixteen manehs;
twelve manehs of costus, three of aromatic bark; nine of cinnamon; nine kabs
of Carsina lye; three seahs and three kabs of Cyprus wine. If Cyprus wine was
not available, old white wine might be used. A quarter of a kab of Sodom salt,
and a minute amount of a smoke-raising herb. Rabbi Nathan the Babylonian
says: also a minute amount of Jordan amber. If one added honey to the mixture,
he rendered it unfit for sacred use. If he omitted any one of its ingredients, he is
guilty of a capital offence.

וְשָׁחַט אֹתוֹ עַל יֶרֶךְ הַמִּזְבֵּחַ צָפֹנָה לִפְנֵי יהוה, וְזָרְקוּ בְּנֵי ויקרא א
אַהֲרֹן הַכֹּהֲנִים אֶת־דָּמוֹ עַל־הַמִּזְבֵּחַ, סָבִיב:

יְהִי רָצוֹן מִלְּפָנֶיךָ, יהוה אֱלֹהֵינוּ וֵאלֹהֵי אֲבוֹתֵינוּ, שֶׁתְּהֵא אֲמִירָה זוֹ חֲשׁוּבָה
וּמְקֻבֶּלֶת וּמְרֻצָּה לְפָנֶיךָ, כְּאִלּוּ הִקְרַבְנוּ קָרְבַּן הַתָּמִיד בְּמוֹעֲדוֹ וּבִמְקוֹמוֹ וּכְהִלְכָתוֹ.

אַתָּה הוּא יהוה אֱלֹהֵינוּ שֶׁהִקְטִירוּ אֲבוֹתֵינוּ לְפָנֶיךָ אֶת קְטֹרֶת הַסַּמִּים בִּזְמַן
שֶׁבֵּית הַמִּקְדָּשׁ הָיָה קַיָּם, כַּאֲשֶׁר צִוִּיתָ אוֹתָם עַל יְדֵי מֹשֶׁה נְבִיאֶךָ, כַּכָּתוּב
בְּתוֹרָתֶךָ:

פרשת הקטורת

וַיֹּאמֶר יהוה אֶל־מֹשֶׁה, קַח־לְךָ סַמִּים נָטָף וּשְׁחֵלֶת וְחֶלְבְּנָה, סַמִּים שמות ל
וּלְבֹנָה זַכָּה, בַּד בְּבַד יִהְיֶה: וְעָשִׂיתָ אֹתָהּ קְטֹרֶת, רֹקַח מַעֲשֵׂה רוֹקֵחַ,
מְמֻלָּח, טָהוֹר קֹדֶשׁ: וְשָׁחַקְתָּ מִמֶּנָּה הָדֵק, וְנָתַתָּה מִמֶּנָּה לִפְנֵי הָעֵדֻת
בְּאֹהֶל מוֹעֵד אֲשֶׁר אִוָּעֵד לְךָ שָׁמָּה, קֹדֶשׁ קָדָשִׁים תִּהְיֶה לָכֶם:

וְנֶאֱמַר

וְהִקְטִיר עָלָיו אַהֲרֹן קְטֹרֶת סַמִּים, בַּבֹּקֶר בַּבֹּקֶר בְּהֵיטִיבוֹ אֶת־הַנֵּרֹת
יַקְטִירֶנָּה: וּבְהַעֲלֹת אַהֲרֹן אֶת־הַנֵּרֹת בֵּין הָעַרְבַּיִם יַקְטִירֶנָּה, קְטֹרֶת
תָּמִיד לִפְנֵי יהוה לְדֹרֹתֵיכֶם:

תָּנוּ רַבָּנָן: פִּטּוּם הַקְּטֹרֶת כֵּיצַד, שְׁלֹשׁ מֵאוֹת וְשִׁשִּׁים וּשְׁמוֹנָה מָנִים הָיוּ בָהּ. כריתות ו
שְׁלֹשׁ מֵאוֹת וְשִׁשִּׁים וַחֲמִשָּׁה כְּמִנְיַן יְמוֹת הַחַמָּה, מָנֶה לְכָל יוֹם, פְּרַס בְּשַׁחֲרִית
וּפְרַס בֵּין הָעַרְבַּיִם, וּשְׁלֹשָׁה מָנִים יְתֵרִים שֶׁמֵּהֶם מַכְנִיס כֹּהֵן גָּדוֹל מְלֹא חָפְנָיו
בְּיוֹם הַכִּפּוּרִים, וּמַחֲזִירָן לְמַכְתֶּשֶׁת בְּעֶרֶב יוֹם הַכִּפּוּרִים וְשׁוֹחֲקָן יָפֶה יָפֶה, כְּדֵי
שֶׁתְּהֵא דַקָּה מִן הַדַּקָּה. וְאַחַד עָשָׂר סַמָּנִים הָיוּ בָהּ, וְאֵלּוּ הֵן: הַצֳּרִי, וְהַצִּפֹּרֶן,
וְהַחֶלְבְּנָה, וְהַלְּבוֹנָה מִשְׁקַל שִׁבְעִים שִׁבְעִים מָנֶה, מֹר, וּקְצִיעָה, שִׁבֹּלֶת נֵרְדְּ,
וְכַרְכֹּם מִשְׁקַל שִׁשָּׁה עָשָׂר שִׁשָּׁה עָשָׂר מָנֶה, הַקֹּשְׁטְ שְׁנֵים עָשָׂר, קִלּוּפָה שְׁלֹשָׁה,
קִנָּמוֹן תִּשְׁעָה, בֹּרִית כַּרְשִׁינָה תִּשְׁעָה קַבִּין, יֵין קַפְרִיסִין סְאִין תְּלָת וְקַבִּין תְּלָתָא,
וְאִם לֹא מָצָא יֵין קַפְרִיסִין, מֵבִיא חֲמַר חִוַּרְיָן עַתִּיק. מֶלַח סְדוֹמִית רֹבַע, מַעֲלֶה
עָשָׁן כָּל שֶׁהוּא. רַבִּי נָתָן הַבַּבְלִי אוֹמֵר: אַף כִּפַּת הַיַּרְדֵּן כָּל שֶׁהוּא, וְאִם נָתַן בָּהּ
דְּבַשׁ פְּסָלָהּ, וְאִם חִסַּר אַחַד מִכָּל סַמָּנֶיהָ, חַיָּב מִיתָה.

Rabban Simeon ben Gamliel says: "Balsam" refers to the sap that drips from the balsam tree. The Carsina lye was used for bleaching the onycha to improve it. The Cyprus wine was used to soak the onycha in it to make it pungent. Though urine is suitable for this purpose, it is not brought into the Temple out of respect.

It was taught, Rabbi Nathan says: While it was being ground, another would say, "Grind well, well grind," because the [rhythmic] sound is good for spices. If it was mixed in half-quantities, it is fit for use, but we have not heard whether this applies to a third or a quarter. Rabbi Judah said: The general rule is that if it was made in the correct proportions, it is fit for use even if made in half-quantity, but if he omitted any one of its ingredients, he is guilty of a capital offence.

It was taught, Bar Kappara says: Once every sixty or seventy years, the accumu- *JT Yoma 4:5* lated surpluses amounted to half the yearly quantity. Bar Kappara also taught: If a minute quantity of honey had been mixed into the incense, no one could have resisted the scent. Why did they not put honey into it? Because the Torah says, "For you are not to burn any leaven or honey in a fire-offering made to the LORD." *Lev. 2*

> *The following three verses are each said three times:*
> The LORD of hosts is with us; the God of Jacob is our stronghold, Selah. *Ps. 46*
> LORD of hosts, happy is the one who trusts in You. *Ps. 84*
> LORD, save! May the King answer us on the day we call. *Ps. 20*

You are my hiding place; You will protect me from distress and surround me *Ps. 32* with songs of salvation, Selah.
Then the offering of Judah and Jerusalem will be pleasing to the LORD as in *Mal. 3* the days of old and as in former years.

---

city, its name, and religion in general. True perfection of the human condition can only be achieved by an encounter with a monotheistic God based on divine will – not human instinct or conventions. His visit is a symbolic transition – he receives the traditions of the city of *Shalem*, but is destined to augment this formula with divine elements of religion. This augmentation is deferred to the end of his career when he revisits the city and ascends *Har HaMoriya* to perform the *Akeda*. This challenge demands that he sublimate his morality, reason, paternal love, and prospects for future succession – all to fulfill the indecipherable command of the unknowable Divine Wisdom. By embracing this challenge, Avraham encounters God, and this moment of Divine revelation is characterized as the "moment that the Presence of God was 'seen' upon the mountain." Man cannot see God, and that recognition is, in and of itself, the truest *perception* of the Divine. Acknowledging inability

רַבָּן שִׁמְעוֹן בֶּן גַּמְלִיאֵל אוֹמֵר: הַצֳרִי אֵינוֹ אֶלָּא שְׂרָף הַנּוֹטֵף מֵעֲצֵי הַקְּטָף. בֹּרִית כַּרְשִׁינָה שֶׁשָּׁפִין בָּהּ אֶת הַצִּפֹּרֶן כְּדֵי שֶׁתְּהֵא נָאָה, יֵין קַפְרִיסִין שֶׁשּׁוֹרִין בּוֹ אֶת הַצִּפֹּרֶן כְּדֵי שֶׁתְּהֵא עַזָּה, וַהֲלֹא מֵי רַגְלַיִם יָפִין לָהּ, אֶלָּא שֶׁאֵין מַכְנִיסִין מֵי רַגְלַיִם בַּמִּקְדָּשׁ מִפְּנֵי הַכָּבוֹד.

תַּנְיָא, רַבִּי נָתָן אוֹמֵר: כְּשֶׁהוּא שׁוֹחֵק אוֹמֵר, הָדֵק הֵיטֵב הֵיטֵב הָדֵק, מִפְּנֵי שֶׁהַקּוֹל יָפֶה לַבְּשָׂמִים. פִּטְּמָהּ לַחֲצָאִין כְּשֵׁרָה, לִשְׁלִישׁ וְלִרְבִיעַ לֹא שָׁמָעְנוּ. אָמַר רַבִּי יְהוּדָה: זֶה הַכְּלָל, אִם כְּמִדָּתָהּ כְּשֵׁרָה לַחֲצָאִין, וְאִם חִסַּר אֶחָד מִכָּל סַמָּנֶיהָ חַיָּב מִיתָה.

תַּנְיָא, בַּר קַפָּרָא אוֹמֵר: אַחַת לְשִׁשִּׁים אוֹ לְשִׁבְעִים שָׁנָה הָיְתָה בָאָה שֶׁל שִׁירַיִם לַחֲצָאִין. וְעוֹד תָּנֵי בַּר קַפָּרָא: אִלּוּ הָיָה נוֹתֵן בָּהּ קוֹרְטוֹב שֶׁל דְּבַשׁ אֵין אָדָם יָכוֹל לַעֲמוֹד מִפְּנֵי רֵיחָהּ, וְלָמָּה אֵין מְעָרְבִין בָּהּ דְּבַשׁ, מִפְּנֵי שֶׁהַתּוֹרָה אָמְרָה: כִּי כָל שְׂאֹר וְכָל דְּבַשׁ לֹא תַקְטִירוּ מִמֶּנּוּ אִשֶּׁה לַיהוה:

The following three verses are each said three times:

יהוה צְבָאוֹת עִמָּנוּ, מִשְׂגָּב לָנוּ אֱלֹהֵי יַעֲקֹב סֶלָה:

יהוה צְבָאוֹת, אַשְׁרֵי אָדָם בֹּטֵחַ בָּךְ:

יהוה הוֹשִׁיעָה, הַמֶּלֶךְ יַעֲנֵנוּ בְיוֹם־קָרְאֵנוּ:

אַתָּה סֵתֶר לִי, מִצַּר תִּצְּרֵנִי, רָנֵּי פַלֵּט תְּסוֹבְבֵנִי סֶלָה:

וְעָרְבָה לַיהוה מִנְחַת יְהוּדָה וִירוּשָׁלָ͏ִם כִּימֵי עוֹלָם וּכְשָׁנִים קַדְמֹנִיֹּת:

מִנְחַת יְהוּדָה וִירוּשָׁלַיִם *The offering of Judah and Jerusalem.* At this stage – after the *Akeda* – Yerushalayim receives its complete name. It had previously been labelled as "*Shalem*" – a city of perfection. Malkitzedek, a mysterious Canaanite priest-king, had already assembled a community seeking perfection through religion. The name "*Shalem*" captured their belief that religion could perfect the human condition. Their moral disposition is evident as they host Avraham upon his return from battle. They provide refreshment and even deliver tithes to Avraham, who is perceived as a religious minister.

As pagans, however, they lacked the notion of an encounter with the *Other*. Religion can perfect the human condition through conventions of morality and charity.

Avraham's visit to this community (*Bereshit* 14) effects a transition for this

THE ORDER OF THE PRIESTLY FUNCTIONS

Abaye related the order of the daily priestly functions in the name *Yoma 33a*
of tradition and in accordance with Abba Shaul: The large pile [of
wood] comes before the second pile for the incense; the second
pile for the incense precedes the laying in order of the two logs of
wood; the laying in order of the two logs of wood comes before the
removing of ashes from the inner altar; the removing of ashes from
the inner altar precedes the cleaning of the five lamps; the cleaning of
the five lamps comes before the blood of the daily offering; the blood
of the daily offering precedes the cleaning of the [other] two lamps;
the cleaning of the two lamps comes before the incense-offering; the
incense-offering precedes the burning of the limbs; the burning of
the limbs comes before the meal-offering; the meal-offering precedes
the pancakes; the pancakes come before the wine-libations; the wine-
libations precede the additional offerings; the additional offerings
come before the [frankincense] censers; the censers precede the daily
afternoon offering; as it is said, "On it he shall arrange burnt-offerings, *Lev. 6*
and on it he shall burn the fat of the peace-offerings" – "on it" [the
daily offering] all the offerings were completed.

Please, by the power of Your great right hand, set the captive nation free.
Accept Your people's prayer. Strengthen us, purify us, You who are revered.
Please, Mighty One, guard like the pupil of the eye those who seek Your unity.
Bless them, cleanse them, have compassion on them,
grant them Your righteousness always.
Mighty One, Holy One, in Your great goodness guide Your congregation.
Only One, Exalted One, turn to Your people, who proclaim Your holiness.
Accept our plea and heed our cry, You who know all secret thoughts.
Blessed be the name of His glorious kingdom for ever and all time.

Master of the Universe, You have commanded us to offer the daily sacrifice at
its appointed time with the priests at their service, the Levites on their platform, and the Israelites at their post. Now, because of our sins, the Temple
is destroyed and the daily sacrifice discontinued, and we have no priest at
his service, no Levite on his platform, no Israelite at his post. But You said:
"We will offer in place of bullocks [the prayer of] our lips." Therefore may it *Hos. 14*
be Your will, LORD our God and God of our ancestors, that the prayer of our
lips be considered, accepted and favored before You as if we had offered the
daily sacrifice at its appointed time and place, according to its laws.

סדר המערכה

יומא לג. אַבַּיֵי הֲוָה מְסַדֵּר סֵדֶר הַמַּעֲרָכָה מִשְּׁמָא דִּגְמָרָא, וְאַלִּבָּא דְאַבָּא
שָׁאוּל: מַעֲרָכָה גְּדוֹלָה קוֹדֶמֶת לְמַעֲרָכָה שְׁנִיָּה שֶׁל קְטֹרֶת, וּמַעֲרָכָה
שְׁנִיָּה שֶׁל קְטֹרֶת קוֹדֶמֶת לְסִדּוּר שְׁנֵי גִּזְרֵי עֵצִים, וְסִדּוּר שְׁנֵי גִּזְרֵי עֵצִים
קוֹדֵם לְדִשּׁוּן מִזְבֵּחַ הַפְּנִימִי, וְדִשּׁוּן מִזְבֵּחַ הַפְּנִימִי קוֹדֵם לַהֲטָבַת
חָמֵשׁ נֵרוֹת, וַהֲטָבַת חָמֵשׁ נֵרוֹת קוֹדֶמֶת לְדַם הַתָּמִיד, וְדַם הַתָּמִיד
קוֹדֵם לַהֲטָבַת שְׁתֵּי נֵרוֹת, וַהֲטָבַת שְׁתֵּי נֵרוֹת קוֹדֶמֶת לִקְטֹרֶת, וּקְטֹרֶת
קוֹדֶמֶת לָאֵבָרִים, וְאֵבָרִים לְמִנְחָה, וּמִנְחָה לַחֲבִתִּין, וַחֲבִתִּין לִנְסָכִין,
וּנְסָכִין לְמוּסָפִין, וּמוּסָפִין לְבָזִיכִין, וּבָזִיכִין קוֹדְמִין לְתָמִיד שֶׁל בֵּין
ויקרא ו הָעַרְבָּיִם. שֶׁנֶּאֱמַר: וְעָרַךְ עָלֶיהָ הָעֹלָה, וְהִקְטִיר עָלֶיהָ חֶלְבֵי הַשְּׁלָמִים:
עָלֶיהָ הַשְׁלֵם כָּל הַקָּרְבָּנוֹת כֻּלָּם.

אָנָּא, בְּכֹחַ גְּדֻלַּת יְמִינְךָ, תַּתִּיר צְרוּרָה.
קַבֵּל רִנַּת עַמְּךָ, שַׂגְּבֵנוּ, טַהֲרֵנוּ, נוֹרָא.
נָא גִבּוֹר, דּוֹרְשֵׁי יִחוּדְךָ כְּבָבַת שָׁמְרֵם.
בָּרְכֵם, טַהֲרֵם, רַחֲמֵם, צִדְקָתְךָ תָּמִיד גָּמְלֵם.
חֲסִין קָדוֹשׁ, בְּרֹב טוּבְךָ נַהֵל עֲדָתֶךָ.
יָחִיד גֵּאֶה, לְעַמְּךָ פְּנֵה, זוֹכְרֵי קְדֻשָּׁתֶךָ.
שַׁוְעָתֵנוּ קַבֵּל וּשְׁמַע צַעֲקָתֵנוּ, יוֹדֵעַ תַּעֲלוּמוֹת.
בָּרוּךְ שֵׁם כְּבוֹד מַלְכוּתוֹ לְעוֹלָם וָעֶד.

רִבּוֹן הָעוֹלָמִים, אַתָּה צִוִּיתָנוּ לְהַקְרִיב קָרְבַּן הַתָּמִיד בְּמוֹעֲדוֹ וְלִהְיוֹת כֹּהֲנִים
בַּעֲבוֹדָתָם וּלְוִיִּם בְּדוּכָנָם וְיִשְׂרָאֵל בְּמַעֲמָדָם, וְעַתָּה בַּעֲוֹנוֹתֵינוּ חָרַב בֵּית
הַמִּקְדָּשׁ וּבֻטַּל הַתָּמִיד וְאֵין לָנוּ לֹא כֹהֵן בַּעֲבוֹדָתוֹ וְלֹא לֵוִי בְּדוּכָנוֹ וְלֹא
הושע יד יִשְׂרָאֵל בְּמַעֲמָדוֹ, וְאַתָּה אָמַרְתָּ: וּנְשַׁלְּמָה פָרִים שְׂפָתֵינוּ: לָכֵן יְהִי רָצוֹן
מִלְּפָנֶיךָ יהוה אֱלֹהֵינוּ וֵאלֹהֵי אֲבוֹתֵינוּ, שֶׁיְּהֵא שִׂיחַ שִׂפְתוֹתֵינוּ חָשׁוּב וּמְקֻבָּל
וּמְרֻצֶּה לְפָנֶיךָ, כְּאִלּוּ הִקְרַבְנוּ קָרְבַּן הַתָּמִיד בְּמוֹעֲדוֹ וּבִמְקוֹמוֹ וּכְהִלְכָתוֹ.

---

to see is the closest approximation of actual perception of God. At this stage
the mountain receives its fully conjugated name – "Yera'eh Shalem" – God is
encountered and humans achieve authentic perfection – Yerushalayim!

LAWS OF OFFERINGS, MISHNA ZEVAḤIM

אֵיזֶהוּ מְקוֹמָן What is the location for sacrifices? The holiest offerings were slaugh- *Zevaḥim*
tered on the north side. The bull and he-goat of Yom Kippur were slaughtered *Ch. 5*
on the north side. Their blood was received in a sacred vessel on the north side,
and had to be sprinkled between the poles [of the Ark], toward the veil [screen-
ing the Holy of Holies], and on the golden altar. [The omission of] one of these
sprinklings invalidated [the atonement ceremony]. The leftover blood was to be
poured onto the western base of the outer altar. If this was not done, however,
the omission did not invalidate [the ceremony].

The bulls and he-goats that were completely burnt were slaughtered on the north
side, their blood was received in a sacred vessel on the north side, and had to be
sprinkled toward the veil and on the golden altar. [The omission of] one of these
sprinklings invalidated [the ceremony]. The leftover blood was to be poured onto
the western base of the outer altar. If this was not done, however, the omission
did not invalidate [the ceremony]. All these offerings were burnt where the altar
ashes were deposited.

The communal and individual sin-offerings – these are the communal sin-offerings: the he-goats offered on Rosh Ḥodesh and Festivals were slaughtered on
the north side, their blood was received in a sacred vessel on the north side, and
required four sprinklings, one on each of the four corners of the altar. How was
this done? The priest ascended the ramp and turned [right] onto the surrounding ledge. He came to the southeast corner, then went to the northeast, then to
the northwest, then to the southwest. The leftover blood he poured onto the
southern base. [The meat of these offerings], prepared in any manner, was eaten
within the [courtyard] curtains, by males of the priest-hood, on that day and the
following night, until midnight.

The burnt-offering was among the holiest of sacrifices. It was slaughtered on
the north side, its blood was received in a sacred vessel on the north side, and
required two sprinklings [at opposite corners of the altar], making four in all. The
offering had to be flayed, dismembered and wholly consumed by fire.

The communal peace-offerings and the guilt-offerings – these are the guilt-
offerings: the guilt-offering for robbery; the guilt-offering for profane use of a
sacred object; the guilt-offering [for violating] a betrothed maidservant; the
guilt-offering of a Nazirite [who had become defiled by a corpse]; the guilt-
offering of a leper [at his cleansing]; and the guilt-offering in case of doubt. All
these were slaughtered on the north side, their blood was received in a sacred
vessel on the north side, and required two sprinklings [at opposite corners of the
altar], making four in all. [The meat of these offerings], prepared in any manner,
was eaten within the [courtyard] curtains, by males of the priesthood, on that
day and the following night, until midnight.

דיני זבחים

אֵיזֶהוּ מְקוֹמָן שֶׁל זְבָחִים. קָדְשֵׁי קָדָשִׁים שְׁחִיטָתָן בַּצָּפוֹן. פַּר וְשָׂעִיר
שֶׁל יוֹם הַכִּפּוּרִים, שְׁחִיטָתָן בַּצָּפוֹן, וְקִבּוּל דָּמָן בִּכְלִי שָׁרֵת בַּצָּפוֹן,
וְדָמָן טָעוּן הַזָּיָה עַל בֵּין הַבַּדִּים, וְעַל הַפָּרֹכֶת, וְעַל מִזְבַּח הַזָּהָב.
מַתָּנָה אַחַת מֵהֶן מְעַכָּבֶת. שְׁיָרֵי הַדָּם הָיָה שׁוֹפֵךְ עַל יְסוֹד מַעֲרָבִי
שֶׁל מִזְבֵּחַ הַחִיצוֹן, אִם לֹא נָתַן לֹא עִכֵּב.

פָּרִים הַנִּשְׂרָפִים וּשְׂעִירִים הַנִּשְׂרָפִים, שְׁחִיטָתָן בַּצָּפוֹן, וְקִבּוּל דָּמָן
בִּכְלִי שָׁרֵת בַּצָּפוֹן, וְדָמָן טָעוּן הַזָּיָה עַל הַפָּרֹכֶת וְעַל מִזְבַּח הַזָּהָב.
מַתָּנָה אַחַת מֵהֶן מְעַכָּבֶת. שְׁיָרֵי הַדָּם הָיָה שׁוֹפֵךְ עַל יְסוֹד מַעֲרָבִי שֶׁל
מִזְבֵּחַ הַחִיצוֹן, אִם לֹא נָתַן לֹא עִכֵּב. אֵלּוּ וָאֵלּוּ נִשְׂרָפִין בְּבֵית הַדֶּשֶׁן.

חַטֹּאת הַצִּבּוּר וְהַיָּחִיד. אֵלּוּ הֵן חַטֹּאת הַצִּבּוּר: שְׂעִירֵי רָאשֵׁי חֳדָשִׁים
וְשֶׁל מוֹעֲדוֹת. שְׁחִיטָתָן בַּצָּפוֹן, וְקִבּוּל דָּמָן בִּכְלִי שָׁרֵת בַּצָּפוֹן, וְדָמָן
טָעוּן אַרְבַּע מַתָּנוֹת עַל אַרְבַּע קְרָנוֹת. כֵּיצַד, עָלָה בַכֶּבֶשׁ, וּפָנָה
לַסּוֹבֵב, וּבָא לוֹ לְקֶרֶן דְּרוֹמִית מִזְרָחִית, מִזְרָחִית צְפוֹנִית, צְפוֹנִית
מַעֲרָבִית, מַעֲרָבִית דְּרוֹמִית. שְׁיָרֵי הַדָּם הָיָה שׁוֹפֵךְ עַל יְסוֹד דְּרוֹמִי.
וְנֶאֱכָלִין לִפְנִים מִן הַקְּלָעִים, לְזִכְרֵי כְהֻנָּה, בְּכָל מַאֲכָל, לְיוֹם וָלַיְלָה
עַד חֲצוֹת.

הָעוֹלָה קֹדֶשׁ קָדָשִׁים. שְׁחִיטָתָהּ בַּצָּפוֹן, וְקִבּוּל דָּמָהּ בִּכְלִי שָׁרֵת
בַּצָּפוֹן, וְדָמָהּ טָעוּן שְׁתֵּי מַתָּנוֹת שֶׁהֵן אַרְבַּע, וּטְעוּנָה הֶפְשֵׁט
וְנִתּוּחַ, וְכָלִיל לָאִשִּׁים.

זִבְחֵי שַׁלְמֵי צִבּוּר וַאֲשָׁמוֹת. אֵלּוּ הֵן אֲשָׁמוֹת: אֲשַׁם גְּזֵלוֹת, אֲשַׁם
מְעִילוֹת, אֲשַׁם שִׁפְחָה חֲרוּפָה, אֲשַׁם נָזִיר, אֲשַׁם מְצֹרָע, אָשָׁם
תָּלוּי. שְׁחִיטָתָן בַּצָּפוֹן, וְקִבּוּל דָּמָן בִּכְלִי שָׁרֵת בַּצָּפוֹן, וְדָמָן טָעוּן
שְׁתֵּי מַתָּנוֹת שֶׁהֵן אַרְבַּע. וְנֶאֱכָלִין לִפְנִים מִן הַקְּלָעִים, לְזִכְרֵי כְהֻנָּה,
בְּכָל מַאֲכָל, לְיוֹם וָלַיְלָה עַד חֲצוֹת.

The thanksgiving-offering and the ram of a Nazirite were offerings of lesser holiness. They could be slaughtered anywhere in the Temple court, and their blood required two sprinklings [at opposite corners of the altar], making four in all. The meat of these offerings, prepared in any manner, was eaten anywhere within the city [Jerusalem], by anyone during that day and the following night until midnight. This also applied to the portion of these sacrifices [given to the priests], except that the priests' portion was only to be eaten by the priests, their wives, children and servants.

Peace-offerings were [also] of lesser holiness. They could be slaughtered anywhere in the Temple court, and their blood required two sprinklings [at opposite corners of the altar], making four in all. The meat of these offerings, prepared in any manner, was eaten anywhere within the city [Jerusalem], by anyone, for two days and one night. This also applied to the portion of these sacrifices [given to the priests], except that the priests' portion was only to be eaten by the priests, their wives, children and servants.

The firstborn and tithe of cattle and the Pesaḥ lamb were sacrifices of lesser holiness. They could be slaughtered anywhere in the Temple court, and their blood required only one sprinkling, which had to be done at the base of the altar. They differed in their consumption: the firstborn was eaten only by priests, while the tithe could be eaten by anyone. Both could be eaten anywhere within the city, prepared in any manner, during two days and one night. The Pesaḥ lamb had to be eaten that night until midnight. It could only be eaten by those who had been numbered for it, and eaten only roasted.

(one afflicted with *tzara'at*) was barred entry. Ultimately, when the *Mikdash* was constructed, these regional levels of *kedusha* were preserved. The general *Har HaBayit* grounds were designated as *Maḥaneh Levi,* while the city of Yerushalayim was infused with the status of *Maḥaneh Yisrael.*

Though Yerushalayim is endowed with metaphysical holiness, its halakhic status stems from its designation as *Maḥaneh Yisrael.* Without serving as a zone of actual Jewish residence, it would be absent of halakhic status.

Judaism resists the common division between the sacred world and the mundane reality. Unlike other religions, which station their shrines at a safe distance from the population to preserve the sanctity of the religious sphere, Judaism positions the *Mikdash* in the heart of our national capital of Yerushalayim, firmly entrenched in the daily intercourse of human experience. Religion embraces and ennobles reality, instead of shrinking from it. Classifying Yerushalayim as *Maḥaneh Yisrael* reaffirms the integration between transcendent holiness and immanent reality.

הַתּוֹדָה וְאֵיל נָזִיר קָדָשִׁים קַלִּים. שְׁחִיטָתָן בְּכָל מָקוֹם בָּעֲזָרָה, וְדָמָן טָעוּן שְׁתֵּי מַתָּנוֹת שֶׁהֵן אַרְבַּע, וְנֶאֱכָלִין בְּכָל הָעִיר, לְכָל אָדָם, בְּכָל מַאֲכָל, לְיוֹם וָלַיְלָה עַד חֲצוֹת. הַמּוּרָם מֵהֶם כַּיּוֹצֵא בָהֶם, אֶלָּא שֶׁהַמּוּרָם נֶאֱכָל לַכֹּהֲנִים, לִנְשֵׁיהֶם, וְלִבְנֵיהֶם וּלְעַבְדֵּיהֶם.

שְׁלָמִים קָדָשִׁים קַלִּים. שְׁחִיטָתָן בְּכָל מָקוֹם בָּעֲזָרָה, וְדָמָן טָעוּן שְׁתֵּי מַתָּנוֹת שֶׁהֵן אַרְבַּע, וְנֶאֱכָלִין בְּכָל הָעִיר, לְכָל אָדָם, בְּכָל מַאֲכָל, לִשְׁנֵי יָמִים וְלַיְלָה אֶחָד. הַמּוּרָם מֵהֶם כַּיּוֹצֵא בָהֶם, אֶלָּא שֶׁהַמּוּרָם נֶאֱכָל לַכֹּהֲנִים, לִנְשֵׁיהֶם, וְלִבְנֵיהֶם וּלְעַבְדֵּיהֶם.

הַבְּכוֹר וְהַמַּעֲשֵׂר וְהַפֶּסַח קָדָשִׁים קַלִּים. שְׁחִיטָתָן בְּכָל מָקוֹם בָּעֲזָרָה, וְדָמָן טָעוּן מַתָּנָה אֶחָת, וּבִלְבַד שֶׁיִּתֵּן כְּנֶגֶד הַיְסוֹד. שִׁנָּה בַּאֲכִילָתָן, הַבְּכוֹר נֶאֱכָל לַכֹּהֲנִים וְהַמַּעֲשֵׂר לְכָל אָדָם, וְנֶאֱכָלִין בְּכָל הָעִיר, בְּכָל מַאֲכָל, לִשְׁנֵי יָמִים וְלַיְלָה אֶחָד. הַפֶּסַח אֵינוֹ נֶאֱכָל אֶלָּא בַלַּיְלָה, וְאֵינוֹ נֶאֱכָל אֶלָּא עַד חֲצוֹת, וְאֵינוֹ נֶאֱכָל אֶלָּא לִמְנוּיָיו, וְאֵינוֹ נֶאֱכָל אֶלָּא צָלִי.

קָדָשִׁים קַלִּים *Offerings of lesser holiness.* The array of sacrifices is divided into two basic categories: *Kodshei Kodsahim* (more extreme holiness) and *Kodashim Kalim* (less severe sanctity). The basic difference between these is the region within which the *korban* may be consumed. The former must be consumed within the *Mikdash* complex, while the latter can be eaten outside the *Mikdash,* within the walls of Yerushalayim.

This feature of Yerushalayim was merely an extension of the sanctity which inhabited the Jewish encampment in the desert. The *Mishkan* was surrounded by two concentric rings of encampment. The proximate encircling was provided by the various Levite families – each dwelling on a different flank. This inner ring formed *Mahaneh Levi,* a region forbidden to moderately impure individuals such as post-natal women and *zavim.* The outer ring was comprised of the twelve tribes arranged in the original lineup which Yaakov had choreographed surrounding his death bed. The outer zone constituted *Mahaneh Yisrael,* which possessed reduced sanctity, but to which a *Metzora*

THE INTERPRETIVE PRINCIPLES OF RABBI YISHMAEL

רַבִּי יִשְׁמָעֵאל Rabbi Yishmael says:

The Torah is expounded by thirteen principles:

1. An inference from a lenient law to a strict one, and vice versa.
2. An inference drawn from identical words in two passages.
3. A general principle derived from one text or two related texts.
4. A general law followed by specific examples
   [where the law applies exclusively to those examples].
5. A specific example followed by a general law
   [where the law applies to everything implied in the general statement].
6. A general law followed by specific examples
   and concluding with a general law:
   here you may infer only cases similar to the examples.
7. When a general statement requires clarification by a specific example,
   or a specific example requires clarification by a general statement
   [then rules 4 and 5 do not apply].
8. When a particular case, already included in the general statement,
   is expressly mentioned to teach something new,
   that special provision applies to all other cases included
   in the general statement.
9. When a particular case, though included in the general statement,
   is expressly mentioned with a provision similar to the general law,
   such a case is singled out to lessen the severity of the law,
   not to increase it.
10. When a particular case, though included in the general statement,
    is explicitly mentioned with a provision differing from the general law,
    it is singled out to lessen in some respects, and in others to increase,
    the severity of the law.
11. When a particular case, though included in the general statement,
    is explicitly mentioned with a new provision,
    the terms of the general statement no longer apply to it,
    unless Scripture indicates explicitly that they do apply.
12. A matter elucidated from its context, or from the following passage.
▸13. Also, when two passages [seem to] contradict each other,
    [they are to be elucidated by] a third passage that reconciles them.

May it be Your will, LORD our God and God of our ancestors, that the Temple be speedily rebuilt in our days, and grant us our share in Your Torah. And may we serve You there in reverence, as in the days of old and as in former years.

בְּרַיְתָא דְרַבִּי יִשְׁמָעֵאל

רַבִּי יִשְׁמָעֵאל אוֹמֵר: בִּשְׁלֹשׁ עֶשְׂרֵה מִדּוֹת הַתּוֹרָה נִדְרֶשֶׁת

א מִקַּל וָחֹמֶר

ב וּמִגְּזֵרָה שָׁוָה

ג מִבִּנְיַן אָב מִכָּתוּב אֶחָד, וּמִבִּנְיַן אָב מִשְּׁנֵי כְתוּבִים

ד מִכְּלָל וּפְרָט

ה מִפְּרָט וּכְלָל

ו כְּלָל וּפְרָט וּכְלָל, אִי אַתָּה דָן אֶלָּא כְּעֵין הַפְּרָט

ז מִכְּלָל שֶׁהוּא צָרִיךְ לִפְרָט, וּמִפְּרָט שֶׁהוּא צָרִיךְ לִכְלָל

ח כָּל דָּבָר שֶׁהָיָה בִכְלָל, וְיָצָא מִן הַכְּלָל לְלַמֵּד
לֹא לְלַמֵּד עַל עַצְמוֹ יָצָא
אֶלָּא לְלַמֵּד עַל הַכְּלָל כֻּלּוֹ יָצָא

ט כָּל דָּבָר שֶׁהָיָה בִכְלָל, וְיָצָא לִטְעֹן טְעַן אֶחָד שֶׁהוּא כְעִנְיָנוֹ
יָצָא לְהָקֵל וְלֹא לְהַחֲמִיר

י כָּל דָּבָר שֶׁהָיָה בִכְלָל, וְיָצָא לִטְעֹן טְעַן אַחֵר שֶׁלֹּא כְעִנְיָנוֹ
יָצָא לְהָקֵל וּלְהַחֲמִיר

יא כָּל דָּבָר שֶׁהָיָה בִכְלָל, וְיָצָא לִדּוֹן בַּדָּבָר הֶחָדָשׁ
אִי אַתָּה יָכוֹל לְהַחֲזִירוֹ לִכְלָלוֹ
עַד שֶׁיַּחֲזִירֶנּוּ הַכָּתוּב לִכְלָלוֹ בְּפֵרוּשׁ

יב דָּבָר הַלָּמֵד מֵעִנְיָנוֹ, וְדָבָר הַלָּמֵד מִסּוֹפוֹ

יג וְכֵן שְׁנֵי כְתוּבִים הַמַּכְחִישִׁים זֶה אֶת זֶה
עַד שֶׁיָּבוֹא הַכָּתוּב הַשְּׁלִישִׁי וְיַכְרִיעַ בֵּינֵיהֶם.

יְהִי רָצוֹן מִלְּפָנֶיךָ, יְהוָה אֱלֹהֵינוּ וֵאלֹהֵי אֲבוֹתֵינוּ, שֶׁיִּבָּנֶה בֵּית הַמִּקְדָּשׁ בִּמְהֵרָה בְיָמֵינוּ, וְתֵן חֶלְקֵנוּ בְּתוֹרָתֶךָ, וְשָׁם נַעֲבָדְךָ בְּיִרְאָה כִּימֵי עוֹלָם וּכְשָׁנִים קַדְמוֹנִיּוֹת.

THE RABBIS' KADDISH

The following prayer, said by mourners, requires the presence of a minyan.
A transliteration can be found on page 666.

Mourner: יִתְגַּדַּל Magnified and sanctified
may His great name be,
in the world He created by His will.
May He establish His kingdom in your lifetime
and in your days,
and in the lifetime of all the house of Israel,
swiftly and soon –
and say: Amen.

All: May His great name be blessed
for ever and all time.

Mourner: Blessed and praised,
glorified and exalted,
raised and honored,
uplifted and lauded
be the name of the Holy One, blessed be He,
beyond any blessing, song,
praise and consolation
uttered in the world –
and say: Amen.

To Israel, to the teachers,
their disciples and their disciples' disciples,
and to all who engage in the study of Torah,
in this (*in Israel add:* holy) place or elsewhere,
may there come to them and you great peace,
grace, kindness and compassion,
long life, ample sustenance and deliverance,
from their Father in Heaven –
and say: Amen.

קדיש דרבנן

The following prayer, said by mourners, requires the presence of a מנין.
A transliteration can be found on page 666.

אבל: יִתְגַּדַּל וְיִתְקַדַּשׁ שְׁמֵהּ רַבָּא (קהל: אָמֵן)

בְּעָלְמָא דִּי בְרָא כִרְעוּתֵהּ

וְיַמְלִיךְ מַלְכוּתֵהּ

בְּחַיֵּיכוֹן וּבְיוֹמֵיכוֹן וּבְחַיֵּי דְכָל בֵּית יִשְׂרָאֵל

בַּעֲגָלָא וּבִזְמַן קָרִיב

וְאִמְרוּ אָמֵן. (קהל: אָמֵן)

קהל
ואבל: יְהֵא שְׁמֵהּ רַבָּא מְבָרַךְ לְעָלַם וּלְעָלְמֵי עָלְמַיָּא.

אבל: יִתְבָּרַךְ וְיִשְׁתַּבַּח וְיִתְפָּאַר וְיִתְרוֹמַם וְיִתְנַשֵּׂא

וְיִתְהַדָּר וְיִתְעַלֶּה וְיִתְהַלָּל

שְׁמֵהּ דְּקֻדְשָׁא בְּרִיךְ הוּא (קהל: בְּרִיךְ הוּא)

לְעֵלָּא מִן כָּל בִּרְכָתָא וְשִׁירָתָא, תֻּשְׁבְּחָתָא וְנֶחֱמָתָא

דַּאֲמִירָן בְּעָלְמָא

וְאִמְרוּ אָמֵן. (קהל: אָמֵן)

עַל יִשְׂרָאֵל וְעַל רַבָּנָן

וְעַל תַּלְמִידֵיהוֹן וְעַל כָּל תַּלְמִידֵי תַלְמִידֵיהוֹן

וְעַל כָּל מָאן דְּעָסְקִין בְּאוֹרַיְתָא

דִּי בְאַתְרָא (בארץ ישראל: קַדִּישָׁא) הָדֵין, וְדִי בְכָל אֲתַר וַאֲתַר

יְהֵא לְהוֹן וּלְכוֹן שְׁלָמָא רַבָּא

חִנָּא וְחִסְדָּא, וְרַחֲמֵי, וְחַיֵּי אֲרִיכֵי, וּמְזוֹנֵי רְוִיחֵי

וּפֻרְקָנָא מִן קֳדָם אֲבוּהוֹן דִּי בִשְׁמַיָּא

וְאִמְרוּ אָמֵן. (קהל: אָמֵן)

May there be great peace from heaven,
and (good) life for us and all Israel –
and say: Amen.

Bow, take three steps back, as if taking leave of the Divine Presence,
then bow, first left, then right, then center, while saying:
May He who makes peace in His high places,
in His compassion make peace
for us and all Israel –
and say: Amen.

A PSALM BEFORE VERSES OF PRAISE

מִזְמוֹר שִׁיר A psalm of David. A song for the dedication of the House.   *Ps. 30*
I will exalt You, Lᴏʀᴅ, for You have lifted me up,
and not let my enemies rejoice over me.
Lᴏʀᴅ, my God, I cried to You for help and You healed me.
Lᴏʀᴅ, You lifted my soul from the grave;
You spared me from going down to the pit.
Sing to the Lᴏʀᴅ, you His devoted ones,
and give thanks to His holy name.
For His anger is for a moment, but His favor for a lifetime.
At night there may be weeping, but in the morning there is joy.
When I felt secure, I said, "I shall never be shaken."
Lᴏʀᴅ, when You favored me,
You made me stand firm as a mountain,
but when You hid Your face, I was terrified.
To You, Lᴏʀᴅ, I called; I pleaded with my Lᴏʀᴅ:
"What gain would there be if I died and went down to the grave?
Can dust thank You? Can it declare Your truth?
Hear, Lᴏʀᴅ, and be gracious to me; Lᴏʀᴅ, be my help."
‣ You have turned my sorrow into dancing.
You have removed my sackcloth and clothed me with joy,
so that my soul may sing to You and not be silent.
Lᴏʀᴅ my God, for ever will I thank You.

יְהֵא שְׁלָמָא רַבָּא מִן שְׁמַיָּא
וְחַיִּים (טוֹבִים) עָלֵינוּ וְעַל כָּל יִשְׂרָאֵל
וְאִמְרוּ אָמֵן. (קהל: אָמֵן)

Bow, take three steps back, as if taking leave of the Divine Presence,
then bow, first left, then right, then center, while saying:

עֹשֶׂה שָׁלוֹם בִּמְרוֹמָיו
הוּא יַעֲשֶׂה בְרַחֲמָיו שָׁלוֹם עָלֵינוּ וְעַל כָּל יִשְׂרָאֵל
וְאִמְרוּ אָמֵן. (קהל: אָמֵן)

מזמור לפני פסוקי דזמרה

תהלים ל

מִזְמוֹר שִׁיר־חֲנֻכַּת הַבַּיִת לְדָוִד:
אֲרוֹמִמְךָ יהוה כִּי דִלִּיתָנִי, וְלֹא־שִׂמַּחְתָּ אֹיְבַי לִי:
יהוה אֱלֹהָי, שִׁוַּעְתִּי אֵלֶיךָ וַתִּרְפָּאֵנִי:
יהוה, הֶעֱלִיתָ מִן־שְׁאוֹל נַפְשִׁי, חִיִּיתַנִי מִיָּרְדִי־בוֹר:
זַמְּרוּ לַיהוה חֲסִידָיו, וְהוֹדוּ לְזֵכֶר קָדְשׁוֹ:
כִּי רֶגַע בְּאַפּוֹ, חַיִּים בִּרְצוֹנוֹ, בָּעֶרֶב יָלִין בֶּכִי וְלַבֹּקֶר רִנָּה:
וַאֲנִי אָמַרְתִּי בְשַׁלְוִי, בַּל־אֶמּוֹט לְעוֹלָם:
יהוה, בִּרְצוֹנְךָ הֶעֱמַדְתָּה לְהַרְרִי עֹז
הִסְתַּרְתָּ פָנֶיךָ הָיִיתִי נִבְהָל:
אֵלֶיךָ יהוה אֶקְרָא, וְאֶל־אֲדֹנָי אֶתְחַנָּן:
מַה־בֶּצַע בְּדָמִי, בְּרִדְתִּי אֶל שָׁחַת, הֲיוֹדְךָ עָפָר, הֲיַגִּיד אֲמִתֶּךָ:
שְׁמַע־יהוה וְחָנֵּנִי, יהוה הֱיֵה־עֹזֵר לִי:
◂ הָפַכְתָּ מִסְפְּדִי לְמָחוֹל לִי, פִּתַּחְתָּ שַׂקִּי, וַתְּאַזְּרֵנִי שִׂמְחָה:
לְמַעַן יְזַמֶּרְךָ כָבוֹד וְלֹא יִדֹּם, יהוה אֱלֹהָי, לְעוֹלָם אוֹדֶךָּ:

MOURNER'S KADDISH

The following prayer, said by mourners, requires the presence of a minyan.
A transliteration can be found on page 667.

Mourner: יִתְגַּדַּל Magnified and sanctified
may His great name be,
in the world He created by His will.
May He establish His kingdom
in your lifetime and in your days,
and in the lifetime of all the house of Israel,
swiftly and soon –
and say: Amen.

All: May His great name be blessed
for ever and all time.

Mourner: Blessed and praised,
glorified and exalted,
raised and honored,
uplifted and lauded
be the name of the Holy One,
blessed be He,
beyond any blessing,
song, praise and consolation
uttered in the world –
and say: Amen.

May there be great peace from heaven,
and life for us and all Israel –
and say: Amen.

Bow, take three steps back, as if taking leave of the Divine Presence,
then bow, first left, then right, then center, while saying:
May He who makes peace in His high places,
make peace for us and all Israel –
and say: Amen.

קדיש יתום

The following prayer, said by mourners, requires the presence of a מנין.
A transliteration can be found on page 667.

אבל: יִתְגַּדַּל וְיִתְקַדַּשׁ שְׁמֵהּ רַבָּא (קהל: אָמֵן)
בְּעָלְמָא דִּי בְרָא כִרְעוּתֵהּ
וְיַמְלִיךְ מַלְכוּתֵהּ
בְּחַיֵּיכוֹן וּבְיוֹמֵיכוֹן וּבְחַיֵּי דְכָל בֵּית יִשְׂרָאֵל
בַּעֲגָלָא וּבִזְמַן קָרִיב
וְאִמְרוּ אָמֵן. (קהל: אָמֵן)

קהל
ואבל: יְהֵא שְׁמֵהּ רַבָּא מְבָרַךְ לְעָלַם וּלְעָלְמֵי עָלְמַיָּא.

אבל: יִתְבָּרַךְ וְיִשְׁתַּבַּח וְיִתְפָּאַר
וְיִתְרוֹמַם וְיִתְנַשֵּׂא וְיִתְהַדָּר וְיִתְעַלֶּה וְיִתְהַלָּל
שְׁמֵהּ דְּקֻדְשָׁא בְּרִיךְ הוּא (קהל: בְּרִיךְ הוּא)
לְעֵלָּא מִן כָּל בִּרְכָתָא וְשִׁירָתָא
תֻּשְׁבְּחָתָא וְנֶחֱמָתָא
דַּאֲמִירָן בְּעָלְמָא
וְאִמְרוּ אָמֵן. (קהל: אָמֵן)

יְהֵא שְׁלָמָא רַבָּא מִן שְׁמַיָּא
וְחַיִּים, עָלֵינוּ וְעַל כָּל יִשְׂרָאֵל
וְאִמְרוּ אָמֵן. (קהל: אָמֵן)

Bow, take three steps back, as if taking leave of the Divine Presence,
then bow, first left, then right, then center, while saying:

עֹשֶׂה שָׁלוֹם בִּמְרוֹמָיו
הוּא יַעֲשֶׂה שָׁלוֹם עָלֵינוּ וְעַל כָּל יִשְׂרָאֵל
וְאִמְרוּ אָמֵן. (קהל: אָמֵן)

PESUKEI DEZIMRA

The following introductory blessing to the Pesukei DeZimra (Verses of Praise)
is said standing, while holding the two front tzitziot of the tallit. They are
kissed and released at the end of the blessing at "songs of praise". From the
beginning of this prayer to the end of the Amida, conversation is forbidden.

Some say:

I hereby prepare my mouth to thank, praise and laud my Creator, for the sake of the unification of the Holy One, blessed be He, and His Divine Presence, through that which is hidden and concealed, in the name of all Israel.

BLESSED IS HE WHO SPOKE

and the world came into being, blessed is He.

Blessed is He who creates the universe.
Blessed is He who speaks and acts.
Blessed is He who decrees and fulfills.
Blessed is He who shows compassion to the earth.
Blessed is He who shows compassion to all creatures.
Blessed is He who gives a good reward
to those who fear Him.
Blessed is He who lives for ever
and exists to eternity.
Blessed is He who redeems and saves.
Blessed is His name.

Blessed are You, Lord our God, King of the Universe, God, compassionate Father, extolled by the mouth of His people, praised and glorified by the tongue of His devoted ones and those who serve Him. With the songs of Your servant David we will praise You, O Lord our God. With praises and psalms we will magnify and praise You, glorify You, Speak Your name and proclaim Your kingship, our King, our God, ‣ the only One, Giver of life to the worlds the King whose great name is praised and glorified to all eternity. Blessed are You, Lord, the King extolled with songs of praise.

פסוקי דזמרה

The following introductory blessing to the פסוקי דזמרה is said standing, while holding the two front ציצית of the טלית. They are kissed and released at the end of the blessing at בְּתִשְׁבָּחוֹת. From the beginning of this prayer to the end of the עמידה, conversation is forbidden.

Some say:

הֲרֵינִי מְזַמֵּן אֶת פִּי לְהוֹדוֹת וּלְהַלֵּל וּלְשַׁבֵּחַ אֶת בּוֹרְאִי, לְשֵׁם יִחוּד קֻדְשָׁא בְּרִיךְ הוּא וּשְׁכִינְתֵּהּ עַל יְדֵי הַהוּא טָמִיר וְנֶעְלָם בְּשֵׁם כָּל יִשְׂרָאֵל.

בָּרוּךְ שֶׁאָמַר

וְהָיָה הָעוֹלָם, בָּרוּךְ הוּא.

בָּרוּךְ עוֹשֶׂה בְרֵאשִׁית

בָּרוּךְ אוֹמֵר וְעוֹשֶׂה

בָּרוּךְ גּוֹזֵר וּמְקַיֵּם

בָּרוּךְ מְרַחֵם עַל הָאָרֶץ

בָּרוּךְ מְרַחֵם עַל הַבְּרִיּוֹת

בָּרוּךְ מְשַׁלֵּם שָׂכָר טוֹב לִירֵאָיו

בָּרוּךְ חַי לָעַד וְקַיָּם לָנֶצַח

בָּרוּךְ פּוֹדֶה וּמַצִּיל

בָּרוּךְ שְׁמוֹ

בָּרוּךְ אַתָּה יהוה אֱלֹהֵינוּ מֶלֶךְ הָעוֹלָם, הָאֵל הָאָב הָרַחֲמָן הַמְהֻלָּל בְּפִי עַמּוֹ, מְשֻׁבָּח וּמְפֹאָר בִּלְשׁוֹן חֲסִידָיו וַעֲבָדָיו, וּבְשִׁירֵי דָוִד עַבְדֶּךָ נְהַלֶּלְךָ יהוה אֱלֹהֵינוּ. בִּשְׁבָחוֹת וּבִזְמִירוֹת נְגַדֶּלְךָ וּנְשַׁבֵּחֲךָ וּנְפָאֶרְךָ, וְנַזְכִּיר שִׁמְךָ וְנַמְלִיכְךָ מַלְכֵּנוּ אֱלֹהֵינוּ, ◄ יָחִיד חֵי הָעוֹלָמִים, מֶלֶךְ, מְשֻׁבָּח וּמְפֹאָר עֲדֵי עַד שְׁמוֹ הַגָּדוֹל, בָּרוּךְ אַתָּה יהוה, מֶלֶךְ מְהֻלָּל בַּתִּשְׁבָּחוֹת.

הוֹדוּ Thank the LORD, call on His name, make His acts known 1 Chr. 16 among the peoples. Sing to Him, make music to Him, tell of all His wonders. Glory in His holy name; let the hearts of those who seek the LORD rejoice. Search out the LORD and His strength; seek His presence at all times. Remember the wonders He has done, His miracles, and the judgments He pronounced. Descendants of Yisrael His servant, sons of Jacob His chosen ones: He is the LORD our God. His judgments are throughout the earth. Remember His covenant for ever, the word He commanded for a thousand generations. He made it with Abraham, vowed it to Isaac, and confirmed it to Jacob as a statute and to Israel as an everlasting covenant, saying, "To you I will give the land of Canaan as your allotted heritage." You were then small in number, few, strangers there, wandering from nation to nation, from one kingdom to another, but He let no man oppress them, and for their sake He rebuked kings: "Do not touch My anointed ones, and do My prophets no harm." Sing to the LORD, all the earth; proclaim His salvation daily. Declare His glory among the nations, His marvels among all the peoples. For great is the LORD and greatly to be praised; He is awesome beyond all heavenly powers. ▸ For all the gods of the peoples are mere idols; it was the LORD who made the heavens.

The second verse in this couplet also reinforces a personal relationship with the Land. Although the Land was earmarked as part of Jewish historical heritage, it was delivered to individuals *before* an entire population inhabited it. This is quite atypical, as most lands are imbued with national identity only *after* a population with national consciousness settles it. For the original settlers of Israel, the Land was not just a future prophetic narrative; it was a personal home, measured and tailored to the individual.

The Torah writes: "When the LORD brings you to the land of the Canaanite, as He swore to you and to your fathers, and He gave it to you" (*Shemot* 13:11). After describing Israel as a land which HaKadosh Barukh Hu swore to deliver to the *Avot*, the verse concludes, "*untana lakh* – and He gave it to you." Though it was awarded to the *Avot*, it was also presented to each common individual. As the *Mekhilta* comments to this verse, "It should not be treated [merely] as a national inheritance."

(See Rav Kook in *Olat Re'iya* for elaboration on this theme.)

הוֹדוּ לַיהוה קִרְאוּ בִשְׁמוֹ, הוֹדִיעוּ בָעַמִּים עֲלִילֹתָיו: שִׁירוּ לוֹ,
זַמְּרוּ־לוֹ, שִׂיחוּ בְּכָל־נִפְלְאוֹתָיו: הִתְהַלְלוּ בְּשֵׁם קָדְשׁוֹ, יִשְׂמַח לֵב
מְבַקְשֵׁי יהוה: דִּרְשׁוּ יהוה וְעֻזּוֹ, בַּקְּשׁוּ פָנָיו תָּמִיד: זִכְרוּ נִפְלְאֹתָיו
אֲשֶׁר עָשָׂה, מֹפְתָיו וּמִשְׁפְּטֵי־פִיהוּ: זֶרַע יִשְׂרָאֵל עַבְדּוֹ, בְּנֵי יַעֲקֹב
בְּחִירָיו: הוּא יהוה אֱלֹהֵינוּ, בְּכָל־הָאָרֶץ מִשְׁפָּטָיו: זִכְרוּ לְעוֹלָם
בְּרִיתוֹ, דָּבָר צִוָּה לְאֶלֶף דּוֹר: אֲשֶׁר כָּרַת אֶת־אַבְרָהָם, וּשְׁבוּעָתוֹ
לְיִצְחָק: וַיַּעֲמִידֶהָ לְיַעֲקֹב לְחֹק, לְיִשְׂרָאֵל בְּרִית עוֹלָם: לֵאמֹר,
לְךָ אֶתֵּן אֶרֶץ־כְּנָעַן, חֶבֶל נַחֲלַתְכֶם: בִּהְיוֹתְכֶם מְתֵי מִסְפָּר,
כִּמְעַט וְגָרִים בָּהּ: וַיִּתְהַלְּכוּ מִגּוֹי אֶל־גּוֹי, וּמִמַּמְלָכָה אֶל־עַם
אַחֵר: לֹא־הִנִּיחַ לְאִישׁ לְעָשְׁקָם, וַיּוֹכַח עֲלֵיהֶם מְלָכִים: אַל־תִּגְּעוּ
בִמְשִׁיחָי, וּבִנְבִיאַי אַל־תָּרֵעוּ: שִׁירוּ לַיהוה כָּל־הָאָרֶץ, בַּשְּׂרוּ
מִיּוֹם־אֶל־יוֹם יְשׁוּעָתוֹ: סַפְּרוּ בַגּוֹיִם אֶת־כְּבוֹדוֹ, בְּכָל־הָעַמִּים
נִפְלְאֹתָיו: כִּי גָדוֹל יהוה וּמְהֻלָּל מְאֹד, וְנוֹרָא הוּא עַל־כָּל־
אֱלֹהִים: ‹ כִּי כָּל־אֱלֹהֵי הָעַמִּים אֱלִילִים, וַיהוה שָׁמַיִם עָשָׂה:

לְךָ אֶתֵּן אֶרֶץ־כְּנָעַן, חֶבֶל נַחֲלַתְכֶם: בִּהְיוֹתְכֶם מְתֵי מִסְפָּר, כִּמְעַט וְגָרִים בָּהּ *To you I will*
give the land of Canaan as your allotted heritage. You were then small in num-
ber, few, strangers there. These two verses appear in both *Tehillim* (105:11–12)
and 1 *Divrei HaYamim* (16:18–19). In each instance the first verse begins by
addressing an *individual* – I have delivered *to you* – while it concludes by
describing Israel as our collective inheritance – *your national* heritage. Our
relationship to the Land must be founded upon both a historical appreciation
and national identity. However, the relationship must also be *personalized*. If
the relationship remains "national" or "historical," it may not compel an individual to incorporate it as a practical part of their life. By beginning the verse
in the singular, David HaMelekh compels us to personalize our relationship
with the Land. The metaphor of ḥevel naḥalatkhem, *your allotted heritage,*
evokes the image of "roping off" parcels of land (the word ḥevel shares its
root with the word for rope). Roping off land is a method of mapping out
personal property, both geographically and experientially.

Before Him are majesty and splendor; there is strength and beauty in His holy place. Render to the LORD, families of the peoples, render to the LORD honor and might. Render to the LORD the glory due to His name; bring an offering and come before Him; bow down to the LORD in the splendor of holiness. Tremble before Him, all the earth; the world stands firm, it will not be shaken. Let the heavens rejoice and the earth be glad; let them declare among the nations, "The LORD is King." Let the sea roar, and all that is in it; let the fields be jubilant, and all they contain. Then the trees of the forest will sing for joy before the LORD, for He is coming to judge the earth. Thank the LORD for He is good; His loving-kindness is for ever. Say: "Save us, God of our salvation; gather us and rescue us from the nations, to acknowledge Your holy name and glory in Your praise. Blessed is the LORD, God of Israel, from this world to eternity." And let all the people say "Amen" and "Praise the LORD."

‣ Exalt the LORD our God and bow before His footstool: He is *Ps. 99* holy. Exalt the LORD our God and bow at His holy mountain; for holy is the LORD our God.

He is compassionate. He forgives iniquity and does not destroy. *Ps. 78* Repeatedly He suppresses His anger, not rousing His full wrath. You, *Ps. 40* LORD: do not withhold Your compassion from me. May Your loving-kindness and truth always guard me. Remember, LORD, Your acts of *Ps. 25* compassion and love, for they have existed for ever. Ascribe power *Ps. 68* to God, whose majesty is over Israel and whose might is in the skies. You are awesome, God, in Your holy places. It is the God of Israel who gives might and strength to the people, may God be blessed. God of retribution, LORD, God of retribution, appear. Arise, Judge of *Ps. 94* the earth, to repay the arrogant their just deserts. Salvation belongs *Ps. 3*

---

people and their history. The heavens convey how formidable, unknowable, and unreachable God is.

A second and complementary implication of the phrase "*al Yisrael ga'avato*" hints at the pride the Jewish people themselves bear as the nation of HaKadosh Barukh Hu. Just as the heavens brim with God's

הוֹד וְהָדָר לְפָנָיו, עֹז וְחֶדְוָה בִּמְקֹמוֹ: הָבוּ לַיהוה מִשְׁפְּחוֹת
עַמִּים, הָבוּ לַיהוה כָּבוֹד וָעֹז: הָבוּ לַיהוה כְּבוֹד שְׁמוֹ, שְׂאוּ
מִנְחָה וּבְאוּ לְפָנָיו, הִשְׁתַּחֲווּ לַיהוה בְּהַדְרַת־קֹֽדֶשׁ: חִֽילוּ מִלְּפָנָיו
כָּל־הָאָֽרֶץ, אַף־תִּכּוֹן תֵּבֵל בַּל־תִּמּוֹט: יִשְׂמְחוּ הַשָּׁמַֽיִם וְתָגֵל
הָאָֽרֶץ, וְיֹאמְרוּ בַגּוֹיִם יהוה מָלָךְ: יִרְעַם הַיָּם וּמְלֹאוֹ, יַעֲלֹץ
הַשָּׂדֶה וְכָל־אֲשֶׁר־בּוֹ: אָז יְרַנְּנוּ עֲצֵי הַיָּֽעַר, מִלִּפְנֵי יהוה, כִּי־בָא
לִשְׁפּוֹט אֶת־הָאָֽרֶץ: הוֹדוּ לַיהוה כִּי טוֹב, כִּי לְעוֹלָם חַסְדּוֹ:
וְאִמְרוּ, הוֹשִׁיעֵֽנוּ אֱלֹהֵי יִשְׁעֵֽנוּ, וְקַבְּצֵֽנוּ וְהַצִּילֵֽנוּ מִן־הַגּוֹיִם,
לְהֹדוֹת לְשֵׁם קָדְשֶֽׁךָ, לְהִשְׁתַּבֵּֽחַ בִּתְהִלָּתֶֽךָ: בָּרוּךְ יהוה אֱלֹהֵי
יִשְׂרָאֵל מִן־הָעוֹלָם וְעַד־הָעֹלָם, וַיֹּאמְרוּ כָל־הָעָם אָמֵן, וְהַלֵּל
לַיהוה:

‹ רוֹמְמוּ יהוה אֱלֹהֵֽינוּ וְהִשְׁתַּחֲווּ לַהֲדֹם רַגְלָיו, קָדוֹשׁ הוּא: תהלים צט
רוֹמְמוּ יהוה אֱלֹהֵֽינוּ וְהִשְׁתַּחֲווּ לְהַר קָדְשׁוֹ, כִּי־קָדוֹשׁ יהוה
אֱלֹהֵֽינוּ:

וְהוּא רַחוּם, יְכַפֵּר עָוֹן וְלֹא־יַשְׁחִית, וְהִרְבָּה לְהָשִׁיב אַפּוֹ, תהלים עח
וְלֹא־יָעִיר כָּל־חֲמָתוֹ: אַתָּה יהוה לֹא־תִכְלָא רַחֲמֶֽיךָ מִמֶּֽנִּי, חַסְדְּךָ תהלים מ
וַאֲמִתְּךָ תָּמִיד יִצְּרֽוּנִי: זְכֹר־רַחֲמֶֽיךָ יהוה וַחֲסָדֶֽיךָ, כִּי מֵעוֹלָם תהלים כה
הֵֽמָּה: תְּנוּ עֹז לֵאלֹהִים, עַל־יִשְׂרָאֵל גַּאֲוָתוֹ, וְעֻזּוֹ בַּשְּׁחָקִים: תהלים סח
נוֹרָא אֱלֹהִים מִמִּקְדָּשֶֽׁיךָ, אֵל יִשְׂרָאֵל הוּא נֹתֵן עֹז וְתַעֲצֻמוֹת
לָעָם, בָּרוּךְ אֱלֹהִים: אֵל־נְקָמוֹת יהוה, אֵל נְקָמוֹת הוֹפִֽיעַ: הִנָּשֵׂא תהלים צד
שֹׁפֵט הָאָֽרֶץ, הָשֵׁב גְּמוּל עַל־גֵּאִים: לַיהוה הַיְשׁוּעָה, עַל־עַמְּךָ תהלים ג

עַל־יִשְׂרָאֵל גַּאֲוָתוֹ, וְעֻזּוֹ בַּשְּׁחָקִים. *Whose majesty is over Israel and whose might is in the skies.* The glory of HaKadosh Barukh Hu, which can be discerned in the heavens, is compared to His strength which can be witnessed in the Jewish

to the LORD; may Your blessing rest upon Your people, Selah! ▸ The *Ps. 46*
LORD of hosts is with us, the God of Jacob is our stronghold, Selah!
LORD of hosts, happy is the one who trusts in You. LORD, save! May *Ps. 84* *Ps. 20*
the King answer us on the day we call.

Save Your people and bless Your heritage; tend them and carry *Ps. 28*
them for ever. Our soul longs for the LORD; He is our Help and *Ps. 33*
Shield. For in Him our hearts rejoice, for in His holy name we have
trusted. May Your loving-kindness, LORD, be upon us, as we have
put our hope in You. Show us, LORD, Your loving-kindness and grant *Ps. 85*
us Your salvation. Arise, help us and redeem us for the sake of Your *Ps. 44*
love. I am the LORD your God who brought you up from the land of *Ps. 81*
Egypt: open your mouth wide and I will fill it. Happy is the people *Ps. 144*
for whom this is so; happy is the people whose God the LORD. ▸ As *Ps. 13*
for me, I trust in Your loving-kindness; my heart rejoices in Your
salvation. I will sing to the LORD for He has been good to me.

The custom is to say it standing.

מִזְמוֹר A psalm of thanksgiving. Shout joyously to the LORD, *Ps. 100*
all the earth. Serve the LORD with joy. Come before Him with
jubilation. Know that the LORD is God. He made us and we
are His. We are His people and the flock He tends. Enter His
gates with thanksgiving, His courts with praise. Thank Him
and bless His name. ▸ For the LORD is good, His loving-kindness is everlasting, and His faithfulness is for every generation.

Messianic Era will usher in a utopia without moral failure and with little need
for prayer or *korbanot*. In a perfect world no prayers are necessary, and living
in a realm of moral clarity without confusion or sin, mankind will have little
need for sacrifices.

Gratitude as expressed through prayers of thanksgiving and *Korban Toda*
will endure, and accrue greater significance. Experiencing the perfect Kingdom of God, man will be grateful for having merited that reality.

Lack of gratitude in general is a grave moral flaw. Rabbeinu Baḥye Ibn

תהלים מו בְּרִכָּתֶךָ סֶּלָה: › יהוה צְבָאוֹת עִמָּנוּ, מִשְׂגָּב לָנוּ אֱלֹהֵי יַעֲקֹב

תהלים פד
תהלים כ סֶלָה: יהוה צְבָאוֹת, אַשְׁרֵי אָדָם בֹּטֵחַ בָּךְ: יהוה הוֹשִׁיעָה,
הַמֶּלֶךְ יַעֲנֵנוּ בְיוֹם־קָרְאֵנוּ:

תהלים כח הוֹשִׁיעָה אֶת־עַמֶּךָ, וּבָרֵךְ אֶת־נַחֲלָתֶךָ, וּרְעֵם וְנַשְּׂאֵם עַד־

תהלים לג הָעוֹלָם: נַפְשֵׁנוּ חִכְּתָה לַיהוה, עֶזְרֵנוּ וּמָגִנֵּנוּ הוּא: כִּי־בוֹ יִשְׂמַח
לִבֵּנוּ, כִּי בְשֵׁם קָדְשׁוֹ בָטָחְנוּ: יְהִי־חַסְדְּךָ יהוה עָלֵינוּ, כַּאֲשֶׁר

תהלים פה
תהלים מד יִחַלְנוּ לָךְ: הַרְאֵנוּ יהוה חַסְדֶּךָ, וְיֶשְׁעֲךָ תִּתֶּן־לָנוּ: קוּמָה עֶזְרָתָה
לָּנוּ, וּפְדֵנוּ לְמַעַן חַסְדֶּךָ: אָנֹכִי יהוה אֱלֹהֶיךָ הַמַּעַלְךָ מֵאֶרֶץ

תהלים פא
תהלים קמד מִצְרָיִם, הַרְחֶב־פִּיךָ וַאֲמַלְאֵהוּ: אַשְׁרֵי הָעָם שֶׁכָּכָה לּוֹ, אַשְׁרֵי
הָעָם שֶׁיהוה אֱלֹהָיו: › וַאֲנִי בְּחַסְדְּךָ בָטַחְתִּי, יָגֵל לִבִּי בִּישׁוּעָתֶךָ,

תהלים יג אָשִׁירָה לַיהוה, כִּי גָמַל עָלָי:

The custom is to say it standing.

תהלים ק מִזְמוֹר לְתוֹדָה, הָרִיעוּ לַיהוה כָּל־הָאָרֶץ: עִבְדוּ אֶת־יהוה
בְּשִׂמְחָה, בֹּאוּ לְפָנָיו בִּרְנָנָה: דְּעוּ כִּי־יהוה הוּא אֱלֹהִים,
הוּא עָשָׂנוּ וְלוֹ אֲנַחְנוּ, עַמּוֹ וְצֹאן מַרְעִיתוֹ: בֹּאוּ שְׁעָרָיו
בְּתוֹדָה, חֲצֵרֹתָיו בִּתְהִלָּה, הוֹדוּ לוֹ, בָּרְכוּ שְׁמוֹ: › כִּי־טוֹב
יהוה, לְעוֹלָם חַסְדּוֹ, וְעַד־דֹּר וָדֹר אֱמוּנָתוֹ:

_____

strength, so the Jewish nation experiences pride as they represent Him in this world.

בֹּאוּ שְׁעָרָיו בְּתוֹדָה, חֲצֵרֹתָיו בִּתְהִלָּה *Enter His gates with thanksgiving, His courts with praise.* Rabbi Pinḥas quotes Rabbi Levi, and Rabbi Yoḥanan quoted Rabbi Menaḥem of Galilee: "During the Messianic Era all prayers will be voided with the exception of a prayer of gratitude. Similarly all *korbanot* will be suspended with the exception of a *Korban Toda*" (*Vayikra Raba* 27). The

לַמְנַצֵּחַ For the conductor of music. A psalm of David. The heavens *Ps. 19* declare the glory of God; the skies proclaim the work of His hands. Day to day they pour forth speech; night to night they communicate knowledge. There is no speech, there are no words, their voice is not heard. Yet their music carries throughout the earth, their words to the end of the world. In them He has set a tent for the sun. It emerges like a groom from his marriage chamber, rejoicing like a champion about to run a race. It rises at one end of the heaven and makes its circuit to the other: nothing is hidden from its heat. The LORD's Torah is perfect, refreshing the soul. The LORD's testimony is faithful, making the simple wise. The LORD's precepts are just, gladdening the heart. The LORD's commandment is radiant, giving light to the eyes. The fear of the LORD is pure, enduring for ever. The LORD's judgments are true, altogether righteous. More precious than gold, than much fine gold. They are sweeter than honey, than honey from the comb. Your servant, too, is careful of them, for in observing them there is great reward. Yet who can discern his errors? Cleanse me of hidden faults. Keep Your servant also from willful sins; let them not have dominion over me. Then shall I be blameless, and innocent of grave sin. ‣ May the words of my mouth and the meditation of my heart find favor before You, LORD, my Rock and my Redeemer.

לְדָוִד Of David. When he pretended to be insane before Abimelech, *Ps. 34* who drove him away, and he left.
I will bless the LORD at all times; His praise will be always on my lips.
My soul will glory in the LORD; let the lowly hear this and rejoice.

---

level we fall victim to sin and our prayers are primarily penitential. Among the roster of *korbanot*, the sacrifices which respond to sin and general human failure are the most dominant.

As we shift to a utopian state, the tone of our *Tefilla* and the texture of our *korbanot* shift towards *hoda'a* and gratitude. Living in a world without need, our primary emotion toward God is gratitude.

תהלים יט

לַמְנַצֵּחַ מִזְמוֹר לְדָוִד: הַשָּׁמַיִם מְסַפְּרִים כְּבוֹד־אֵל, וּמַעֲשֵׂה
יָדָיו מַגִּיד הָרָקִיעַ: יוֹם לְיוֹם יַבִּיעַ אֹמֶר, וְלַיְלָה לְּלַיְלָה יְחַוֶּה־
דָּעַת: אֵין־אֹמֶר וְאֵין דְּבָרִים, בְּלִי נִשְׁמָע קוֹלָם: בְּכָל־הָאָרֶץ
יָצָא קַוָּם, וּבִקְצֵה תֵבֵל מִלֵּיהֶם, לַשֶּׁמֶשׁ שָׂם־אֹהֶל בָּהֶם: וְהוּא
כְּחָתָן יֹצֵא מֵחֻפָּתוֹ, יָשִׂישׂ כְּגִבּוֹר לָרוּץ אֹרַח: מִקְצֵה הַשָּׁמַיִם
מוֹצָאוֹ, וּתְקוּפָתוֹ עַל־קְצוֹתָם, וְאֵין נִסְתָּר מֵחַמָּתוֹ: תּוֹרַת יהוה
תְּמִימָה, מְשִׁיבַת נָפֶשׁ, עֵדוּת יהוה נֶאֱמָנָה, מַחְכִּימַת פֶּתִי:
פִּקּוּדֵי יהוה יְשָׁרִים, מְשַׂמְּחֵי־לֵב, מִצְוַת יהוה בָּרָה, מְאִירַת
עֵינָיִם: יִרְאַת יהוה טְהוֹרָה, עוֹמֶדֶת לָעַד, מִשְׁפְּטֵי־יהוה אֱמֶת,
צָדְקוּ יַחְדָּו: הַנֶּחֱמָדִים מִזָּהָב וּמִפָּז רָב, וּמְתוּקִים מִדְּבַשׁ וְנֹפֶת
צוּפִים: גַּם־עַבְדְּךָ נִזְהָר בָּהֶם, בְּשָׁמְרָם עֵקֶב רָב: שְׁגִיאוֹת מִי־
יָבִין, מִנִּסְתָּרוֹת נַקֵּנִי: גַּם מִזֵּדִים חֲשֹׁךְ עַבְדֶּךָ, אַל־יִמְשְׁלוּ־בִי
אָז אֵיתָם, וְנִקֵּיתִי מִפֶּשַׁע רָב: ◄ יִהְיוּ לְרָצוֹן אִמְרֵי־פִי וְהֶגְיוֹן לִבִּי
לְפָנֶיךָ, יהוה, צוּרִי וְגֹאֲלִי:

תהלים לד

לְדָוִד, בְּשַׁנּוֹתוֹ אֶת־טַעְמוֹ לִפְנֵי אֲבִימֶלֶךְ, וַיְגָרְשֵׁהוּ וַיֵּלַךְ:
אֲבָרְכָה אֶת־יהוה בְּכָל־עֵת, תָּמִיד תְּהִלָּתוֹ בְּפִי:
בַּיהוה תִּתְהַלֵּל נַפְשִׁי, יִשְׁמְעוּ עֲנָוִים וְיִשְׂמָחוּ:

Pekuda, who authored the well-known sefer "Ḥovot Halevavot," positioned gratitude as the foundation of Jewish theology. To those who experience redemption, gratitude is even more imperative. Inability to be
grateful at divine redemption is both morally appalling and historically
blind.

In a non-redeemed reality the primary voices of *Tefilla* are petitioning and
imploring. We live in a fallen and challenging reality, and we appeal to
HaKadosh Barukh Hu to rescue us and redeem our state. On a personal

Magnify the Lord with me; let us exalt His name together.
I sought the Lord, and He answered me;
 He saved me from all my fears.
Those who look to Him are radiant; Their faces are never downcast.
This poor man called, and the Lord heard;
 He saved him from all his troubles.
The Lord's angel encamps around those who fear Him,
 and He rescues them.
Taste and see that the Lord is good;
 happy is the man who takes refuge in Him.
Fear the Lord, you His holy ones, for those who fear Him lack nothing.
Young lions may grow weak and hungry,
 but those who seek the Lord lack no good thing.
Come, my children, listen to me; I will teach you the fear of the Lord.
Who desires life, loving each day to see good?
Then guard your tongue from evil and your lips from speaking deceit.
Turn from evil and do good; seek peace and pursue it.
The eyes of the Lord are on the righteous
 and His ears attentive to their cry;
The Lord's face is set against those who do evil,
 to erase their memory from the earth.
The righteous cry out, and the Lord hears them;
 delivering them from all their troubles.
The Lord is close to the brokenhearted,
 and saves those who are crushed in spirit.
Many troubles may befall the righteous,
 but the Lord delivers him from them all;
He protects all his bones, so that none of them will be broken.
Evil will slay the wicked;
 the enemies of the righteous will be condemned.
▸ The Lord redeems His servants;
 none who take refuge in Him shall be condemned.

תְּפִלָּה לְמֹשֶׁה A prayer of Moses, the man of God. Lord, You have *Ps. 90*
been our shelter in every generation. Before the mountains were born,
before You brought forth the earth and the world, from everlasting to

גַּדְּלוּ לַיהוה אִתִּי, וּנְרוֹמְמָה שְׁמוֹ יַחְדָּו:

דָּרַשְׁתִּי אֶת־יהוה וְעָנָנִי, וּמִכָּל־מְגוּרוֹתַי הִצִּילָנִי:

הִבִּיטוּ אֵלָיו וְנָהָרוּ, וּפְנֵיהֶם אַל־יֶחְפָּרוּ:

זֶה עָנִי קָרָא, וַיהוה שָׁמֵעַ, וּמִכָּל־צָרוֹתָיו הוֹשִׁיעוֹ:

חֹנֶה מַלְאַךְ־יהוה סָבִיב לִירֵאָיו, וַיְחַלְּצֵם:

טַעֲמוּ וּרְאוּ כִּי־טוֹב יהוה, אַשְׁרֵי הַגֶּבֶר יֶחֱסֶה־בּוֹ:

יְראוּ אֶת־יהוה קְדֹשָׁיו, כִּי־אֵין מַחְסוֹר לִירֵאָיו:

כְּפִירִים רָשׁוּ וְרָעֵבוּ, וְדֹרְשֵׁי יהוה לֹא־יַחְסְרוּ כָל־טוֹב:

לְכוּ־בָנִים שִׁמְעוּ־לִי, יִרְאַת יהוה אֲלַמֶּדְכֶם:

מִי־הָאִישׁ הֶחָפֵץ חַיִּים, אֹהֵב יָמִים לִרְאוֹת טוֹב:

נְצֹר לְשׁוֹנְךָ מֵרָע, וּשְׂפָתֶיךָ מִדַּבֵּר מִרְמָה:

סוּר מֵרָע וַעֲשֵׂה־טוֹב, בַּקֵּשׁ שָׁלוֹם וְרָדְפֵהוּ:

עֵינֵי יהוה אֶל־צַדִּיקִים, וְאָזְנָיו אֶל־שַׁוְעָתָם:

פְּנֵי יהוה בְּעֹשֵׂי רָע, לְהַכְרִית מֵאֶרֶץ זִכְרָם:

צָעֲקוּ וַיהוה שָׁמֵעַ, וּמִכָּל־צָרוֹתָם הִצִּילָם:

קָרוֹב יהוה לְנִשְׁבְּרֵי־לֵב, וְאֶת־דַּכְּאֵי־רוּחַ יוֹשִׁיעַ:

רַבּוֹת רָעוֹת צַדִּיק, וּמִכֻּלָּם יַצִּילֶנּוּ יהוה:

שֹׁמֵר כָּל־עַצְמֹתָיו, אַחַת מֵהֵנָּה לֹא נִשְׁבָּרָה:

תְּמוֹתֵת רָשָׁע רָעָה, וְשֹׂנְאֵי צַדִּיק יֶאְשָׁמוּ:

‹ פּוֹדֶה יהוה נֶפֶשׁ עֲבָדָיו, וְלֹא יֶאְשְׁמוּ כָּל־הַחֹסִים בּוֹ:

תהלים צ

תְּפִלָּה לְמֹשֶׁה אִישׁ־הָאֱלֹהִים, אֲדֹנָי, מָעוֹן אַתָּה הָיִיתָ לָּנוּ בְּדֹר

וָדֹר: בְּטֶרֶם הָרִים יֻלָּדוּ, וַתְּחוֹלֵל אֶרֶץ וְתֵבֵל, וּמֵעוֹלָם עַד־עוֹלָם

אַתָּה אֵל: תָּשֵׁב אֱנוֹשׁ עַד־דַּכָּא, וַתֹּאמֶר שׁוּבוּ בְנֵי־אָדָם: כִּי

everlasting You are God. You turn men back to dust, saying, "Return, you children of men." For a thousand years in Your sight are like yesterday when it has passed, like a watch in the night. You sweep men away; they sleep. In the morning they are like grass newly grown: in the morning it flourishes and is new, but by evening it withers and dries up. For we are consumed by Your anger, terrified by Your fury. You have set our iniquities before You, our secret sins in the light of Your presence. All our days pass away in Your wrath, we spend our years like a sigh. The span of our life is seventy years, or if we are strong, eighty years; but the best of them is trouble and sorrow, for they quickly pass, and we fly away. Who can know the force of Your anger? Your wrath matches the fear due to You. Teach us rightly to number our days, that we may gain a heart of wisdom. Relent, O Lᴏʀᴅ! How much longer? Be sorry for Your servants. Satisfy us in the morning with Your loving-kindness, that we may sing and rejoice all our days. Grant us joy for as many days as You have afflicted us, for as many years as we saw trouble. Let Your deeds be seen by Your servants, and Your glory by their children. ▸ May the pleasantness of the Lᴏʀᴅ our God be upon us. Establish for us the work of our hands, O establish the work of our hands.

These opinions *limit* the Messianic experience to a relatively reduced interval. Functionally *Mashiah* is meant to *compensate* the Jewish nation for past suffering, and briefly introduce a Kingdom of God in our world. This relatively brief interlude prepares conditions for a different reality which can only be realized in *Olam Haba* – the World to Come.

In contrast, many opinions in the Gemara interpret the term as referring to the days of our "subjugation" or inferiority. Some claim it will endure for exactly the same period as pre-Messianic history, while others believe it will last for seven thousand years. Parallel positions cited by various *Midrashim* assert that the period may last one or possibly two millennia.

Conceivably these exaggerated figures can be taken metaphorically rather than literally. These positions viewed the Messianic Era as more than an adjustment period, or compensation for past national anguish. The Messianic Era will entail a re-creation and revamping of history, allowing humanity to experience physical and spiritual utopia, and to repair past errors and failures. It doesn't merely set the stage for resurrection and afterlife, but provides a

אֶלֶף שָׁנִים בְּעֵינֶיךָ, כְּיוֹם אֶתְמוֹל כִּי יַעֲבֹר, וְאַשְׁמוּרָה בַלָּיְלָה:
זְרַמְתָּם, שֵׁנָה יִהְיוּ, בַּבֹּקֶר כֶּחָצִיר יַחֲלֹף: בַּבֹּקֶר יָצִיץ וְחָלָף,
לָעֶרֶב יְמוֹלֵל וְיָבֵשׁ: כִּי־כָלִינוּ בְאַפֶּךָ, וּבַחֲמָתְךָ נִבְהָלְנוּ: שַׁתָּ
עֲוֺנֺתֵינוּ לְנֶגְדֶּךָ, עֲלֻמֵנוּ לִמְאוֹר פָּנֶיךָ: כִּי כָל־יָמֵינוּ פָּנוּ בְעֶבְרָתֶךָ,
כִּלִּינוּ שָׁנֵינוּ כְמוֹ־הֶגֶה: יְמֵי־שְׁנוֹתֵינוּ בָהֶם שִׁבְעִים שָׁנָה, וְאִם
בִּגְבוּרֹת שְׁמוֹנִים שָׁנָה, וְרָהְבָּם עָמָל וָאָוֶן, כִּי־גָז חִישׁ וַנָּעֻפָה:
מִי־יוֹדֵעַ עֹז אַפֶּךָ, וּכְיִרְאָתְךָ עֶבְרָתֶךָ, לִמְנוֹת יָמֵינוּ כֵּן הוֹדַע,
וְנָבִא לְבַב חָכְמָה: שׁוּבָה יהוה עַד־מָתָי, וְהִנָּחֵם עַל־עֲבָדֶיךָ:
שַׂבְּעֵנוּ בַבֹּקֶר חַסְדֶּךָ, וּנְרַנְּנָה וְנִשְׂמְחָה בְּכָל־יָמֵינוּ: שַׂמְּחֵנוּ
כִּימוֹת עִנִּיתָנוּ, שְׁנוֹת רָאִינוּ רָעָה: יֵרָאֶה אֶל־עֲבָדֶיךָ פָעֳלֶךָ,
וַהֲדָרְךָ עַל־בְּנֵיהֶם: ◂ וִיהִי נֹעַם אֲדֹנָי אֱלֹהֵינוּ עָלֵינוּ, וּמַעֲשֵׂה
יָדֵינוּ כּוֹנְנָה עָלֵינוּ, וּמַעֲשֵׂה יָדֵינוּ כּוֹנְנֵהוּ:

ADDITIONAL PESUKEI DEZIMRA FOR YOM HAATZMA'UT

Adding supplementary psalms to *Pesukei DeZimra* poses no halakhic problem, falling under the category of "whoever adds is praiseworthy." In order to validate the special nature of Yom HaAtzma'ut through its prayer service, the Chief Rabbinate ruled that we recite the *Pesukei DeZimra* of Shabbat and festivals.

BL

שַׂמְּחֵנוּ כִּימוֹת עִנִּיתָנוּ *Grant us joy for as many days as You have afflicted us.* Although the duration of the Messianic Era is unknown, two different patterns emerge – each derived from this verse which promises that HaKadosh Barukh Hu will one day provide bliss "as the days of our suffering." One approach in the Gemara (*Sanhedrin* 99a) is that the Messianic Era will compensate for difficult periods in Jewish History. In this respect the phrase "as the days of our suffering" is interpreted quite literally. Some claim it will last forty years, commensurate to the period of drifting in the desert. Others believe it will last four hundred years, corresponding to the overall time spent in Egypt. Yet a third opinion suggests seventy years, based on a verse in *Yeshayahu*.

יֹשֵׁב בְּסֵתֶר He who lives in the shelter of the Most High dwells in the shadow of the Almighty. I say of the LORD, my Refuge and Stronghold, my God in whom I trust, that He will save you from the fowler's snare and the deadly pestilence. With His pinions He will cover you, and beneath His wings you will find shelter; His faithfulness is an encircling shield. You need not fear terror by night, nor the arrow that flies by day; not the pestilence that stalks in darkness, nor the plague that ravages at noon. A thousand may fall at your side, ten thousand at your right hand, but it will not come near you. You will only look with your eyes and see the punishment of the wicked. Because you said "The LORD is my Refuge," taking the Most High as your shelter, no harm will befall you, no plague will come near your tent, for He will command His angels about you, to guard you in all your ways. They will lift you in their hands, lest your foot stumble on a stone. You will tread on lions and vipers, you will trample on young lions and snakes. [God says] "Because he loves Me, I will rescue him; I will protect him, because he acknowledges My name. When he calls on Me, I will answer him, I will be with him in distress, I will deliver him and bring him honor. ▸ With long life I will satisfy him, and show him My salvation. With long life I will satisfy him, and show him My salvation." *Ps. 91*

הַלְלוּיָהּ Halleluya! Praise the name of the LORD. Praise Him, you servants of the LORD who stand in the LORD's House, in the courtyards of the House of our God. Praise the LORD, for the LORD is good; sing praises to His name, for it is lovely. For the LORD has chosen Jacob as His own, Israel as his treasure. For I know that the LORD is great, that our LORD is above all heavenly powers. Whatever pleases the LORD, He does, in heaven and on earth, in the seas and all the depths. He raises clouds from the ends of the earth; He sends lightning with the rain; He brings out the wind from His storehouses. He struck down the firstborn of Egypt, of both man and animals. He sent signs and wonders into your *Ps. 135*

In practical terms some have suggested that the Messianic Era will comprise two separate periods – an introductory shorter period, and a more extended utopia.

יֹשֵׁב בְּסֵתֶר עֶלְיוֹן, בְּצֵל שַׁדַּי יִתְלוֹנָן: אֹמַר לַיהוה מַחְסִי וּמְצוּדָתִי, אֱלֹהַי אֶבְטַח־בּוֹ: כִּי הוּא יַצִּילְךָ מִפַּח יָקוּשׁ, מִדֶּבֶר הַוּוֹת: בְּאֶבְרָתוֹ יָסֶךְ לָךְ, וְתַחַת־כְּנָפָיו תֶּחְסֶה, צִנָּה וְסֹחֵרָה אֲמִתּוֹ: לֹא־תִירָא מִפַּחַד לָיְלָה, מֵחֵץ יָעוּף יוֹמָם: מִדֶּבֶר בָּאֹפֶל יַהֲלֹךְ, מִקֶּטֶב יָשׁוּד צָהֳרָיִם: יִפֹּל מִצִּדְּךָ אֶלֶף, וּרְבָבָה מִימִינֶךָ, אֵלֶיךָ לֹא יִגָּשׁ: רַק בְּעֵינֶיךָ תַבִּיט, וְשִׁלֻּמַת רְשָׁעִים תִּרְאֶה: כִּי־אַתָּה יהוה מַחְסִי, עֶלְיוֹן שַׂמְתָּ מְעוֹנֶךָ: לֹא־תְאֻנֶּה אֵלֶיךָ רָעָה, וְנֶגַע לֹא־יִקְרַב בְּאָהֳלֶךָ: כִּי מַלְאָכָיו יְצַוֶּה־לָּךְ, לִשְׁמָרְךָ בְּכָל־דְּרָכֶיךָ: עַל־כַּפַּיִם יִשָּׂאוּנְךָ, פֶּן־תִּגֹּף בָּאֶבֶן רַגְלֶךָ: עַל־שַׁחַל וָפֶתֶן תִּדְרֹךְ, תִּרְמֹס כְּפִיר וְתַנִּין: כִּי בִי חָשַׁק וַאֲפַלְּטֵהוּ, אֲשַׂגְּבֵהוּ כִּי־יָדַע שְׁמִי: יִקְרָאֵנִי וְאֶעֱנֵהוּ, עִמּוֹ אָנֹכִי בְצָרָה, אֲחַלְּצֵהוּ וַאֲכַבְּדֵהוּ: ‹ אֹרֶךְ יָמִים אַשְׂבִּיעֵהוּ, וְאַרְאֵהוּ בִּישׁוּעָתִי:

אֹרֶךְ יָמִים אַשְׂבִּיעֵהוּ, וְאַרְאֵהוּ בִּישׁוּעָתִי:

הַלְלוּיָהּ, הַלְלוּ אֶת־שֵׁם יהוה, הַלְלוּ עַבְדֵי יהוה: שֶׁעֹמְדִים בְּבֵית יהוה, בְּחַצְרוֹת בֵּית אֱלֹהֵינוּ: הַלְלוּיָהּ כִּי־טוֹב יהוה, זַמְּרוּ לִשְׁמוֹ כִּי נָעִים: כִּי־יַעֲקֹב בָּחַר לוֹ יָהּ, יִשְׂרָאֵל לִסְגֻלָּתוֹ: כִּי אֲנִי יָדַעְתִּי כִּי־גָדוֹל יהוה, וַאֲדֹנֵינוּ מִכָּל־אֱלֹהִים: כֹּל אֲשֶׁר־חָפֵץ יהוה עָשָׂה, בַּשָּׁמַיִם וּבָאָרֶץ, בַּיַּמִּים וְכָל־תְּהֹמוֹת: מַעֲלֶה נְשִׂאִים מִקְצֵה הָאָרֶץ, בְּרָקִים לַמָּטָר עָשָׂה, מוֹצֵא־רוּחַ מֵאוֹצְרוֹתָיו: שֶׁהִכָּה בְּכוֹרֵי מִצְרָיִם, מֵאָדָם עַד־בְּהֵמָה: שָׁלַח אוֹתֹת וּמֹפְתִים

---

historical redo. Ultimately the debate about the period of the Messianic Era is not merely an issue of duration. It speaks to the function and purpose of this period as well.

midst, Egypt – against Pharaoh and all his servants. He struck down many nations and slew mighty kings: Siḥon, King of the Amorites, Og, King of Bashan, and all the kingdoms of Canaan, giving their land as a heritage, a heritage for His people Israel. Your name, LORD, endures for ever; Your renown, LORD, for all generations. For the LORD will bring justice to His people, and have compassion on His servants. The idols of the nations are silver and gold, the work of human hands. They have mouths, but cannot speak; eyes, but cannot see; ears, but cannot hear; there is no breath in their mouths. Those who make them will become like them: so will all who trust in them. ‣ House of Israel, bless the LORD. House of Aaron, bless the LORD. House of Levi, bless the LORD. You who fear the LORD, bless the LORD. Blessed is the LORD from Zion, He who dwells in Jerusalem. Halleluya!

The custom is to stand for the following psalm.

הודו Thank the LORD for He is good;	His loving-kindness is for ever.	Ps. 136
Thank the God of gods,	His loving-kindness is for ever.	
Thank the LORD of lords,	His loving-kindness is for ever.	
To the One who alone works great wonders,	His loving-kindness is for ever.	
Who made the heavens with wisdom,	His loving-kindness is for ever.	
Who spread the earth upon the waters,	His loving-kindness is for ever.	
Who made the great lights,	His loving-kindness is for ever.	
The sun to rule by day,	His loving-kindness is for ever.	
The moon and the stars to rule by night;	His loving-kindness is for ever.	

---

inheritance. For this reason, immediately after Yitzḥak's birth, local opposition to "Jewish" settlement surfaces. This resistance is evident in the arduous negotiations which Avraham endures to acquire a burial site for Sara. It is also on display in the skirmishes between Yitzḥak and Avimelekh over water cisterns excavated by Avraham, and subsequently spoiled by the Pelishtim. Due to these "soft" hostilities the 400-year predicted exile commences with the birth of Yitzḥak. At this stage our sovereignty over the Land of Israel was first challenged. Weakened sovereignty entails the first stage of Jewish exile. This period lasted 190 years, after which we descended to Egypt for

225

בְּתוֹכֵכִי מִצְרָיִם, בְּפַרְעֹה וּבְכָל־עֲבָדָיו: שֶׁהִכָּה גּוֹיִם רַבִּים, וְהָרַג
מְלָכִים עֲצוּמִים: לְסִיחוֹן מֶלֶךְ הָאֱמֹרִי, וּלְעוֹג מֶלֶךְ הַבָּשָׁן, וּלְכֹל
מַמְלְכוֹת כְּנָעַן: וְנָתַן אַרְצָם נַחֲלָה, נַחֲלָה לְיִשְׂרָאֵל עַמּוֹ: יהוה
שִׁמְךָ לְעוֹלָם, יהוה זִכְרְךָ לְדֹר־וָדֹר: כִּי־יָדִין יהוה עַמּוֹ, וְעַל־
עֲבָדָיו יִתְנֶחָם: עֲצַבֵּי הַגּוֹיִם כֶּסֶף וְזָהָב, מַעֲשֵׂה יְדֵי אָדָם: פֶּה־
לָהֶם וְלֹא יְדַבֵּרוּ, עֵינַיִם לָהֶם וְלֹא יִרְאוּ: אָזְנַיִם לָהֶם וְלֹא יַאֲזִינוּ,
אַף אֵין־יֶשׁ־רוּחַ בְּפִיהֶם: כְּמוֹהֶם יִהְיוּ עֹשֵׂיהֶם, כֹּל אֲשֶׁר־בֹּטֵחַ
בָּהֶם: ‹ בֵּית יִשְׂרָאֵל בָּרְכוּ אֶת־יהוה, בֵּית אַהֲרֹן בָּרְכוּ אֶת־
יהוה: בֵּית הַלֵּוִי בָּרְכוּ אֶת־יהוה, יִרְאֵי יהוה בָּרְכוּ אֶת־יהוה:
בָּרוּךְ יהוה מִצִּיּוֹן, שֹׁכֵן יְרוּשָׁלָ͏ִם, הַלְלוּיָהּ:

The custom is to stand for the following psalm.

תהלים קלו

הוֹדוּ לַיהוה כִּי־טוֹב   כִּי לְעוֹלָם חַסְדּוֹ:
הוֹדוּ לֵאלֹהֵי הָאֱלֹהִים   כִּי לְעוֹלָם חַסְדּוֹ:
הוֹדוּ לַאֲדֹנֵי הָאֲדֹנִים   כִּי לְעוֹלָם חַסְדּוֹ:
לְעֹשֵׂה נִפְלָאוֹת גְּדֹלוֹת לְבַדּוֹ   כִּי לְעוֹלָם חַסְדּוֹ:
לְעֹשֵׂה הַשָּׁמַיִם בִּתְבוּנָה   כִּי לְעוֹלָם חַסְדּוֹ:
לְרֹקַע הָאָרֶץ עַל־הַמָּיִם   כִּי לְעוֹלָם חַסְדּוֹ:
לְעֹשֵׂה אוֹרִים גְּדֹלִים   כִּי לְעוֹלָם חַסְדּוֹ:
אֶת־הַשֶּׁמֶשׁ לְמֶמְשֶׁלֶת בַּיּוֹם   כִּי לְעוֹלָם חַסְדּוֹ:
אֶת־הַיָּרֵחַ וְכוֹכָבִים לְמֶמְשְׁלוֹת בַּלָּיְלָה   כִּי לְעוֹלָם חַסְדּוֹ:

כִּי לְעוֹלָם חַסְדּוֹ *His loving-kindness is for ever.* Yitzḥak's birth signaled the fulfillment of the divine oath to deliver the Land of Israel to Avraham *and his descendants.* Prior to Yitzḥak's birth Avraham's revolution, as well as his presence in his newly Chosen Land, could have been perceived as transient. Once Yitzḥak is born, Avraham's legacy is assured and the Land becomes an

Who struck Egypt
        through their firstborn,   His loving-kindness is for ever.
And brought out Israel
        from their midst,   His loving-kindness is for ever.
With a strong hand
        and outstretched arm,   His loving-kindness is for ever.
Who split the Reed Sea into parts,   His loving-kindness is for ever.
And made Israel pass through it,   His loving-kindness is for ever.
Casting Pharaoh and his army
        into the Reed Sea;   His loving-kindness is for ever.
Who led His people
        through the wilderness;   His loving-kindness is for ever.
Who struck down great kings,   His loving-kindness is for ever.
And slew mighty kings,   His loving-kindness is for ever.
Siḥon, King of the Amorites,   His loving-kindness is for ever.
And Og, King of Bashan,   His loving-kindness is for ever.
And gave their land as a heritage,   His loving-kindness is for ever.
A heritage for His servant Israel;   His loving-kindness is for ever.
Who remembered us in our lowly state, His loving-kindness is for ever.
And rescued us from our tormentors,   His loving-kindness is for ever.
▸ Who gives food to all flesh,   His loving-kindness is for ever.
Give thanks to the God of heaven.   His loving-kindness is for ever.

---

amount of land, or as the Torah refers to it, "*me'a she'arim*." Drawing such abundance from the land demonstrated its relationship with Yitzḥak and his descendants. Only to the chosen people would the Land of Israel offer its fertility so freely.

As significant as this settlement and agricultural success was, Yitzḥak was unable to repeat this in the center of the country – the corridor spanning Beit El in the north to Ḥevron in the south, where the primary encounters with HaKadosh Barukh Hu had occurred. He developed his farmstead along the coast – near the city of Gerar; the coastal land proved easier to settle than the center of the country. So it was then and so it continues to be in our day.

לְמַכֵּה מִצְרַיִם בִּבְכוֹרֵיהֶם כִּי לְעוֹלָם חַסְדּוֹ:
וַיּוֹצֵא יִשְׂרָאֵל מִתּוֹכָם כִּי לְעוֹלָם חַסְדּוֹ:
בְּיָד חֲזָקָה וּבִזְרוֹעַ נְטוּיָה כִּי לְעוֹלָם חַסְדּוֹ:
לְגֹזֵר יַם־סוּף לִגְזָרִים כִּי לְעוֹלָם חַסְדּוֹ:
וְהֶעֱבִיר יִשְׂרָאֵל בְּתוֹכוֹ כִּי לְעוֹלָם חַסְדּוֹ:
וְנִעֵר פַּרְעֹה וְחֵילוֹ בְיַם־סוּף כִּי לְעוֹלָם חַסְדּוֹ:
לְמוֹלִיךְ עַמּוֹ בַּמִּדְבָּר כִּי לְעוֹלָם חַסְדּוֹ:
לְמַכֵּה מְלָכִים גְּדֹלִים כִּי לְעוֹלָם חַסְדּוֹ:
וַיַּהֲרֹג מְלָכִים אַדִּירִים כִּי לְעוֹלָם חַסְדּוֹ:
לְסִיחוֹן מֶלֶךְ הָאֱמֹרִי כִּי לְעוֹלָם חַסְדּוֹ:
וּלְעוֹג מֶלֶךְ הַבָּשָׁן כִּי לְעוֹלָם חַסְדּוֹ:
וְנָתַן אַרְצָם לְנַחֲלָה כִּי לְעוֹלָם חַסְדּוֹ:
נַחֲלָה לְיִשְׂרָאֵל עַבְדּוֹ כִּי לְעוֹלָם חַסְדּוֹ:
שֶׁבְּשִׁפְלֵנוּ זָכַר לָנוּ כִּי לְעוֹלָם חַסְדּוֹ:
וַיִּפְרְקֵנוּ מִצָּרֵינוּ כִּי לְעוֹלָם חַסְדּוֹ:
‹ נֹתֵן לֶחֶם לְכָל־בָּשָׂר כִּי לְעוֹלָם חַסְדּוֹ:
הוֹדוּ לְאֵל הַשָּׁמָיִם כִּי לְעוֹלָם חַסְדּוֹ:

the second stage of exile – 210 years of geographic dislocation, punctuated by slavery and persecution.

Unlike his father and his son who were both shepherds, Yitzḥak was the only Father of our nation to harvest the land as a farmer. Shepherds lead nomadic lifestyles, wandering from one pasture land to another to feed their grazing herds. They establish no permanence and build no homestead; their lifestyles mirrored our unformed and flimsy hold upon the land. By founding the first farmstead, Yitzḥak fortified our grip on our land. His first agricultural venture netted one hundred times the crops typically harvested from that

רַנְּנוּ Sing joyfully to the Lᴏʀᴅ, you righteous, for praise from the *Ps. 33*
upright is seemly. Give thanks to the Lᴏʀᴅ with the harp; make music
to Him on the ten-stringed lute. Sing Him a new song, play skillfully
with shouts of joy. For the Lᴏʀᴅ's word is right, and all His deeds are
done in faith. He loves righteousness and justice; the earth is full of the
Lᴏʀᴅ's loving-kindness. By the Lᴏʀᴅ's word the heavens were made,
and all their starry host by the breath of His mouth. He gathers the
sea waters as a heap, and places the deep in storehouses. Let all the
earth fear the Lᴏʀᴅ, and all the world's inhabitants stand in awe of
Him. For He spoke, and it was; He commanded, and it stood firm. The
Lᴏʀᴅ foils the plans of nations; He thwarts the intentions of peoples.
The Lᴏʀᴅ's plans stand for ever, His heart's intents for all generations.
Happy is the nation whose God is the Lᴏʀᴅ, the people He has chosen
as His own. From heaven the Lᴏʀᴅ looks down and sees all mankind;
from His dwelling place He oversees all who live on earth. He forms
the hearts of all, and discerns all their deeds. No king is saved by the
size of his army; no warrior is delivered by great strength. A horse is
a vain hope for deliverance; despite its great strength, it cannot save.
The eye of the Lᴏʀᴅ is on those who fear Him, on those who place
their hope in His unfailing love, to rescue their soul from death, and
keep them alive in famine. Our soul waits for the Lᴏʀᴅ; He is our Help
and Shield. ▸ In Him our hearts rejoice, for we trust in His holy name.
Let Your unfailing love be upon us, Lᴏʀᴅ, as we have put our hope
in You.

מִזְמוֹר שִׁיר A psalm. A song for the Sabbath day. It is good to thank *Ps. 92*
the Lᴏʀᴅ and sing psalms to Your name, Most High – to tell of Your
loving-kindness in the morning and Your faithfulness at night, to the
music of the ten-stringed lyre and the melody of the harp. For You
have made me rejoice by Your work, O Lᴏʀᴅ; I sing for joy at the
deeds of Your hands. How great are Your deeds, Lᴏʀᴅ, and how very
deep Your thoughts. A boor cannot know, nor can a fool understand,
that though the wicked spring up like grass and all evildoers flourish, it is only that they may be destroyed for ever. But You, Lᴏʀᴅ,

רַנְּנוּ צַדִּיקִים בַּיהוה, לַיְשָׁרִים נָאוָה תְהִלָּה: הוֹדוּ לַיהוה בְּכִנּוֹר,

בְּנֵבֶל עָשׂוֹר זַמְּרוּ־לוֹ: שִׁירוּ־לוֹ שִׁיר חָדָשׁ, הֵיטִיבוּ נַגֵּן בִּתְרוּעָה:

כִּי־יָשָׁר דְּבַר־יהוה, וְכָל־מַעֲשֵׂהוּ בֶּאֱמוּנָה: אֹהֵב צְדָקָה וּמִשְׁפָּט,

חֶסֶד יהוה מָלְאָה הָאָרֶץ: בִּדְבַר יהוה שָׁמַיִם נַעֲשׂוּ, וּבְרוּחַ פִּיו

כָּל־צְבָאָם: כֹּנֵס כַּנֵּד מֵי הַיָּם, נֹתֵן בְּאוֹצָרוֹת תְּהוֹמוֹת: יִירְאוּ

מֵיהוה כָּל־הָאָרֶץ, מִמֶּנּוּ יָגוּרוּ כָּל־יֹשְׁבֵי תֵבֵל: כִּי הוּא אָמַר

וַיֶּהִי, הוּא־צִוָּה וַיַּעֲמֹד: יהוה הֵפִיר עֲצַת־גּוֹיִם, הֵנִיא מַחְשְׁבוֹת

עַמִּים: עֲצַת יהוה לְעוֹלָם תַּעֲמֹד, מַחְשְׁבוֹת לִבּוֹ לְדֹר וָדֹר:

אַשְׁרֵי הַגּוֹי אֲשֶׁר־יהוה אֱלֹהָיו, הָעָם בָּחַר לְנַחֲלָה לוֹ: מִשָּׁמַיִם

הִבִּיט יהוה, רָאָה אֶת־כָּל־בְּנֵי הָאָדָם: מִמְּכוֹן־שִׁבְתּוֹ הִשְׁגִּיחַ,

אֶל כָּל־יֹשְׁבֵי הָאָרֶץ: הַיֹּצֵר יַחַד לִבָּם, הַמֵּבִין אֶל־כָּל־מַעֲשֵׂיהֶם:

אֵין־הַמֶּלֶךְ נוֹשָׁע בְּרָב־חָיִל, גִּבּוֹר לֹא־יִנָּצֵל בְּרָב־כֹּחַ: שֶׁקֶר

הַסּוּס לִתְשׁוּעָה, וּבְרֹב חֵילוֹ לֹא יְמַלֵּט: הִנֵּה עֵין יהוה אֶל־יְרֵאָיו,

לַמְיַחֲלִים לְחַסְדּוֹ: לְהַצִּיל מִמָּוֶת נַפְשָׁם, וּלְחַיּוֹתָם בָּרָעָב: נַפְשֵׁנוּ

חִכְּתָה לַיהוה, עֶזְרֵנוּ וּמָגִנֵּנוּ הוּא: ◀ כִּי־בוֹ יִשְׂמַח לִבֵּנוּ, כִּי בְשֵׁם

קָדְשׁוֹ בָטָחְנוּ: יְהִי־חַסְדְּךָ יהוה עָלֵינוּ, כַּאֲשֶׁר יִחַלְנוּ לָךְ:

מִזְמוֹר שִׁיר לְיוֹם הַשַּׁבָּת: טוֹב לְהֹדוֹת לַיהוה, וּלְזַמֵּר לְשִׁמְךָ

עֶלְיוֹן: לְהַגִּיד בַּבֹּקֶר חַסְדֶּךָ, וֶאֱמוּנָתְךָ בַּלֵּילוֹת: עֲלֵי־עָשׂוֹר

וַעֲלֵי־נָבֶל, עֲלֵי הִגָּיוֹן בְּכִנּוֹר: כִּי שִׂמַּחְתַּנִי יהוה בְּפָעֳלֶךָ, בְּמַעֲשֵׂי

יָדֶיךָ אֲרַנֵּן: מַה־גָּדְלוּ מַעֲשֶׂיךָ יהוה, מְאֹד עָמְקוּ מַחְשְׁבֹתֶיךָ:

אִישׁ־בַּעַר לֹא יֵדָע, וּכְסִיל לֹא־יָבִין אֶת־זֹאת: בִּפְרֹחַ רְשָׁעִים

כְּמוֹ עֵשֶׂב, וַיָּצִיצוּ כָּל־פֹּעֲלֵי אָוֶן, לְהִשָּׁמְדָם עֲדֵי־עַד: וְאַתָּה

מָרוֹם לְעֹלָם יהוה: כִּי הִנֵּה אֹיְבֶיךָ יהוה, כִּי־הִנֵּה אֹיְבֶיךָ יֹאבֵדוּ,

are eternally exalted. For behold Your enemies, Lord, behold Your enemies will perish; all evildoers will be scattered. You have raised my pride like that of a wild ox; I am anointed with fresh oil. My eyes shall look in triumph on my adversaries, my ears shall hear the downfall of the wicked who rise against me. ‣ The righteous will flourish like a palm tree and grow tall like a cedar in Lebanon. Planted in the Lord's House, blossoming in our God's courtyards, they will still bear fruit in old age, and stay vigorous and fresh, proclaiming that the Lord is upright: He is my Rock, in whom there is no wrong.

יהוה מָלָךְ The Lord reigns. He is robed in majesty. The Lord is robed, *Ps. 93* girded with strength. The world is firmly established; it cannot be moved. Your throne stands firm as of old; You are eternal. Rivers lift up, Lord, rivers lift up their voice, rivers lift up their Crashing waves. ‣ Mightier than the noise of many waters, than the mighty waves of the sea is the Lord on high. Your testimonies are very sure; holiness adorns Your House, Lord, for evermore.

יְהִי כְבוֹד May the Lord's glory be for ever; may the Lord rejoice *Ps. 104* in His works. May the Lord's name be blessed, now and for ever. *Ps. 113* From the rising of the sun to its setting, may the Lord's name be praised. The Lord is high above all nations; His glory is above the heavens. Lord, Your name is for ever. Your renown, Lord, *Ps. 135* is for all generations. The Lord has established His throne in *Ps. 103* heaven; His kingdom rules all. Let the heavens rejoice and the *1 Chr. 16* earth be glad. Let them say among the nations, "The Lord is King." The Lord is King, the Lord was King, the Lord will be King for ever and all time. The Lord is King for ever and all *Ps. 10* time; nations will perish from His land. The Lord foils the plans *Ps. 33* of nations; He frustrates the intentions of peoples. Many are *Prov. 19* the intentions in a person's mind, but the Lord's plan prevails. The Lord's plan shall stand for ever, His mind's intent for all *Ps. 33* generations. For He spoke and it was; He commanded and it stood firm. For the Lord has chosen Zion; He desired it for His *Ps. 132* dwelling. For the Lord has chosen Jacob, Israel as His special *Ps. 135*

יִתְפָּרְדוּ כָּל־פֹּעֲלֵי אָוֶן: וַתָּרֶם כִּרְאֵים קַרְנִי, בַּלֹּתִי בְּשֶׁמֶן רַעֲנָן:
וַתַּבֵּט עֵינִי בְּשׁוּרָי, בַּקָּמִים עָלַי מְרֵעִים תִּשְׁמַעְנָה אָזְנָי: ‹ צַדִּיק
כַּתָּמָר יִפְרָח, כְּאֶרֶז בַּלְּבָנוֹן יִשְׂגֶּה: שְׁתוּלִים בְּבֵית יְהוָה, בְּחַצְרוֹת
אֱלֹהֵינוּ יַפְרִיחוּ: עוֹד יְנוּבוּן בְּשֵׂיבָה, דְּשֵׁנִים וְרַעֲנַנִּים יִהְיוּ: לְהַגִּיד
כִּי־יָשָׁר יְהוָה, צוּרִי, וְלֹא־עַוְלָתָה בּוֹ:

תהלים צג
יְהוָה מָלָךְ, גֵּאוּת לָבֵשׁ, לָבֵשׁ יְהוָה עֹז הִתְאַזָּר, אַף־תִּכּוֹן תֵּבֵל
בַּל־תִּמּוֹט: נָכוֹן כִּסְאֲךָ מֵאָז, מֵעוֹלָם אָתָּה: נָשְׂאוּ נְהָרוֹת יְהוָה,
נָשְׂאוּ נְהָרוֹת קוֹלָם, יִשְׂאוּ נְהָרוֹת דָּכְיָם: ‹ מִקֹּלוֹת מַיִם רַבִּים,
אַדִּירִים מִשְׁבְּרֵי־יָם, אַדִּיר בַּמָּרוֹם יְהוָה: עֵדֹתֶיךָ נֶאֶמְנוּ מְאֹד
לְבֵיתְךָ נַאֲוָה־קֹדֶשׁ, יְהוָה לְאֹרֶךְ יָמִים:

תהלים קד
תהלים קיג
יְהִי כְבוֹד יְהוָה לְעוֹלָם, יִשְׂמַח יְהוָה בְּמַעֲשָׂיו: יְהִי שֵׁם
יְהוָה מְבֹרָךְ, מֵעַתָּה וְעַד־עוֹלָם: מִמִּזְרַח־שֶׁמֶשׁ עַד־
מְבוֹאוֹ, מְהֻלָּל שֵׁם יְהוָה: רָם עַל־כָּל־גּוֹיִם יְהוָה, עַל
תהלים קלה
הַשָּׁמַיִם כְּבוֹדוֹ: יְהוָה שִׁמְךָ לְעוֹלָם, יְהוָה זִכְרְךָ לְדֹר־וָדֹר:
תהלים קג
דברי הימים
א' טז
יְהוָה בַּשָּׁמַיִם הֵכִין כִּסְאוֹ, וּמַלְכוּתוֹ בַּכֹּל מָשָׁלָה: יִשְׂמְחוּ
הַשָּׁמַיִם וְתָגֵל הָאָרֶץ, וְיֹאמְרוּ בַגּוֹיִם יְהוָה מָלָךְ: יְהוָה מֶלֶךְ,
תהלים י
יְהוָה מָלָךְ, יְהוָה יִמְלֹךְ לְעוֹלָם וָעֶד: יְהוָה מֶלֶךְ עוֹלָם וָעֶד,
תהלים לג
אָבְדוּ גוֹיִם מֵאַרְצוֹ: יְהוָה הֵפִיר עֲצַת־גּוֹיִם, הֵנִיא מַחְשְׁבוֹת
משלי יט
עַמִּים: רַבּוֹת מַחֲשָׁבוֹת בְּלֶב־אִישׁ, וַעֲצַת יְהוָה הִיא תָקוּם:
תהלים לג
עֲצַת יְהוָה לְעוֹלָם תַּעֲמֹד, מַחְשְׁבוֹת לִבּוֹ לְדֹר וָדֹר: כִּי
תהלים קלב
הוּא אָמַר וַיֶּהִי, הוּא־צִוָּה וַיַּעֲמֹד: כִּי־בָחַר יְהוָה בְּצִיּוֹן,
תהלים קלה
אִוָּה לְמוֹשָׁב לוֹ: כִּי־יַעֲקֹב בָּחַר לוֹ יָהּ, יִשְׂרָאֵל לִסְגֻלָּתוֹ:

treasure. For the LORD will not abandon His people; nor will He forsake His heritage. ▸ He is compassionate. He forgives iniquity and does not destroy. Repeatedly He suppresses His anger, not rousing His full wrath. LORD, save! May the King answer us on the day we call.

Ps. 94
Ps. 78
Ps. 20

Jews in Israel are rescued because we are His nation and because of His inheritance or land. Jews in the Diaspora are rescued for the sake of His name. Those who reside in His land merit unique intervention for the sake of, and based on the merit of, His land. When Jews are absent from Israel, the land *itself* grieves, and to avert this tragedy Jews are rescued – even if they are otherwise undeserving.

UNLIKELY RESCUERS

וְנַחֲלָתוֹ לֹא יַעֲזֹב *Nor will He forsake His heritage.* During the First *Mikdash* era, as the Northern and Southern Kingdoms split, the Northern monarchs became increasingly impious. One of the most notorious kings was Yeravam ben Nevat, who banned the *Aliya LaRegel* pilgrimage and incited mass idolatry. His successor was Yorovam ben Yo'ash, who is likened to his predecessor in his behavior and policies.

Surprisingly he leads a massive military victory which had been prophesied by Yona: "He was the one who restored the boundaries of Israel from *Levo Ḥamat* to the Dead Sea, in accordance with the word of the LORD God of Israel, spoken through His servant Yona son of Amitai, the prophet from *Gat Ḥefer*" (*II Melakhim* 14:25). It is odd that such a wicked king be the divine agent for wholesale redemption and geographic expansion. The continuation of the report supplies the rationale, "there was no one to help them. And since the LORD had not said He would blot out the name of Israel from under heaven, He saved them by the hand of Yorovam ben Yo'ash" (ibid., 26–27). The state of the Jewish people was too desperate, as we lacked any allies or any other forms of support. The urgency to aid the Jewish people "compelled" HaKadosh Barukh Hu to employ an iniquitous agent for our national redemption.

A similar drama unfolded years later during the reign of Aḥav, who in additional to pagan crimes was guilty of the horrific murder of numerous prophets, as well as intermarriage with a heathen wife. Yet when the armies of Aram amass, he and his paltry regiment of seven thousand emerge victorious.

כִּי לֹא־יִטֹּשׁ יהוה עַמּוֹ, וְנַחֲלָתוֹ לֹא יַעֲזֹב: ‹ וְהוּא רַחוּם,
יְכַפֵּר עָוֹן וְלֹא־יַשְׁחִית, וְהִרְבָּה לְהָשִׁיב אַפּוֹ, וְלֹא־יָעִיר

כָּל־חֲמָתוֹ: יהוה הוֹשִׁיעָה, הַמֶּלֶךְ יַעֲנֵנוּ בְיוֹם־קָרְאֵנוּ:

כִּי לֹא־יִטֹּשׁ יהוה עַמּוֹ *For the* LORD *will not abandon His people.* The phrase "For the LORD will not abandon His people" appears twice in Tanakh. This verse is lifted from *Tehillim* 94:14, while the parallel verse appears in *1 Shmuel* 12:22. This verse roots divine loyalty in the fact that we are His inheritance – *naḥalato.* The parallel verse in *Shmuel* professes that He will not forsake us because of His great name.

Recognizing this disparity, Ḥazal (*Rut Raba* 2:11) provided two different schemes. Rabbi Shmuel bar Naḥmeni suggests that when we deserve deliverance, we receive it on merit, whereas an undeserving nation is only rescued for the sake of His name. This model of redemption is driven by a concern for Ḥillul Hashem. As a chosen people we reflect the Divine Presence in the world. As the Jewish fate declines, the presence of HaKadosh Barukh Hu in the world regresses. Even though we may not merit redemption, we often benefit from a larger concern of the "name of God." Chapter 20 of *Yeḥezkel* portrays the exodus from Egypt in this fashion. Though we didn't earn our liberation, God declares, "But for the sake of My name, I brought them out of Egypt. I did it to keep My name from being profaned in the eyes of the nations among whom they lived and in whose sight I had revealed Myself to the Israelites" (*Yeḥezkel* 20:9).

After the *Egel* (golden calf) fiasco Moshe prays on behalf of a nation of sinners. Yet he pleads with HaKadosh Barukh Hu, "Why should the Egyptians say, 'It was with evil intent that He brought them out, to kill them in the mountains and to wipe them off the face of the earth'? Turn from Your fierce anger; relent and do not bring disaster on Your people" (*Shemot* 32:12), and succeeds in staving off a national calamity because of the repercussions to the presence of God in our world. In fact Shmuel the prophet formulates this concept when he responds to a nation which has rebelled against the Divine King by requesting a human monarch. He assures them that despite their infidelity they are still a chosen nation whose fate reflects upon the Divine Presence.

Rabbi Ivo offers a different resolution for the disparity between the verses.

*The line beginning with "You open Your hand" should be said with special
concentration, representing as it does the key idea of this psalm, and of
Pesukei DeZimra as a whole, that God is the creator and sustainer of all.*

אַשְׁרֵי Happy are those who dwell in Your House;
they shall continue to praise You, Selah!

Ps. 84

Happy are the people for whom this is so;
happy are the people whose God is the LORD.

Ps. 144

A song of praise by David.

Ps. 145

I will exalt You, my God, the King, and bless Your name for ever
and all time. Every day I will bless You, and praise Your name for
ever and all time. Great is the LORD and greatly to be praised;
His greatness is unfathomable. One generation will praise Your
works to the next, and tell of Your mighty deeds. On the glorious
splendor of Your majesty I will meditate, and on the acts of Your
wonders. They shall talk of the power of Your awesome deeds,
and I will tell of Your greatness. They shall recite the record of
Your great goodness, and sing with joy of Your righteousness. The
LORD is gracious and compassionate, slow to anger and great in
loving-kindness. The LORD is good to all, and His compassion
extends to all His works. All Your works shall thank You, LORD,
and Your devoted ones shall bless You. They shall talk of the glory
of Your kingship, and speak of Your might. To make known to
mankind His mighty deeds and the glorious majesty of His kingship. Your kingdom is an everlasting kingdom, and Your reign is
for all generations. The LORD supports all who fall, and raises
all who are bowed down. All raise their eyes to You in hope, and
You give them their food in due season. You open Your hand,
and satisfy every living thing with favor. The LORD is righteous
in all His ways, and kind in all He does. The LORD is close to all
who call on Him, to all who call on Him in truth. He fulfills the

Twice during the First *Mikdash* era unlikely and sinful agents of redemption were dispatched by God to rescue the Jewish people from untenable
conditions. After the Holocaust our pitiful state warranted divine intervention even through unlikely agents, including followers of other faiths or those

The line beginning with פּוֹתֵחַ אֶת יָדֶךָ should be said with special concentration, representing as it does the key idea of this psalm, and of פסוקי דזמרה as a whole, that God is the creator and sustainer of all.

תהלים פד

אַשְׁרֵי יוֹשְׁבֵי בֵיתֶךָ, עוֹד יְהַלְלוּךָ סֶּלָה:

תהלים קמד

אַשְׁרֵי הָעָם שֶׁכָּכָה לּוֹ, אַשְׁרֵי הָעָם שֶׁיהוה אֱלֹהָיו:

תהלים קמה

תְּהִלָּה לְדָוִד

אֲרוֹמִמְךָ אֱלוֹהַי הַמֶּלֶךְ, וַאֲבָרְכָה שִׁמְךָ לְעוֹלָם וָעֶד:

בְּכָל־יוֹם אֲבָרְכֶךָ, וַאֲהַלְלָה שִׁמְךָ לְעוֹלָם וָעֶד:

גָּדוֹל יהוה וּמְהֻלָּל מְאֹד, וְלִגְדֻלָּתוֹ אֵין חֵקֶר:

דּוֹר לְדוֹר יְשַׁבַּח מַעֲשֶׂיךָ, וּגְבוּרֹתֶיךָ יַגִּידוּ:

הֲדַר כְּבוֹד הוֹדֶךָ, וְדִבְרֵי נִפְלְאֹתֶיךָ אָשִׂיחָה:

וֶעֱזוּז נוֹרְאֹתֶיךָ יֹאמֵרוּ, וּגְדוּלָּתְךָ אֲסַפְּרֶנָּה:

זֵכֶר רַב־טוּבְךָ יַבִּיעוּ, וְצִדְקָתְךָ יְרַנֵּנוּ:

חַנּוּן וְרַחוּם יהוה, אֶרֶךְ אַפַּיִם וּגְדָל־חָסֶד:

טוֹב־יהוה לַכֹּל, וְרַחֲמָיו עַל־כָּל־מַעֲשָׂיו:

יוֹדוּךָ יהוה כָּל־מַעֲשֶׂיךָ, וַחֲסִידֶיךָ יְבָרְכוּכָה:

כְּבוֹד מַלְכוּתְךָ יֹאמֵרוּ, וּגְבוּרָתְךָ יְדַבֵּרוּ:

לְהוֹדִיעַ לִבְנֵי הָאָדָם גְּבוּרֹתָיו, וּכְבוֹד הֲדַר מַלְכוּתוֹ:

מַלְכוּתְךָ מַלְכוּת כָּל־עֹלָמִים, וּמֶמְשַׁלְתְּךָ בְּכָל־דּוֹר וָדֹר:

סוֹמֵךְ יהוה לְכָל־הַנֹּפְלִים, וְזוֹקֵף לְכָל־הַכְּפוּפִים:

עֵינֵי־כֹל אֵלֶיךָ יְשַׂבֵּרוּ, וְאַתָּה נוֹתֵן־לָהֶם אֶת־אָכְלָם בְּעִתּוֹ:

פּוֹתֵחַ אֶת־יָדֶךָ, וּמַשְׂבִּיעַ לְכָל־חַי רָצוֹן:

צַדִּיק יהוה בְּכָל־דְּרָכָיו, וְחָסִיד בְּכָל־מַעֲשָׂיו:

קָרוֹב יהוה לְכָל־קֹרְאָיו, לְכֹל אֲשֶׁר יִקְרָאֻהוּ בֶאֱמֶת:

Once again, to confirm that this is a divine intervention, a prophet – in this instance Mikhayhu – announces the pending triumph.

will of those who revere Him; He hears their cry and saves them. The LORD guards all who love Him, but all the wicked He will destroy. ▸ My mouth shall speak the praise of the LORD, and all creatures shall bless His holy name for ever and all time.

We will bless the LORD now and for ever. Halleluya!   *Ps. 115*

הַלְלוּיָהּ Halleluya! Praise the LORD, my soul. I will praise the LORD   *Ps. 146*
all my life; I will sing to my God as long as I live. Put not your trust in princes, or in mortal man who cannot save. His breath expires, he returns to the earth; on that day his plans come to an end. Happy is he whose help is the God of Jacob, whose hope is in the LORD his God who made heaven and earth, the sea and all they contain; He who keeps faith for ever. He secures justice for the oppressed. He gives food to the hungry. The LORD sets captives free. The LORD gives sight to the blind. The LORD raises those bowed down. The LORD loves the righteous. The LORD protects the stranger. He gives

---

relax the rigorous standards for conversion, it may relax the level of evidence necessary to prove proper conversion. Perhaps this statement was made during a period in which life in Israel was overwhelmingly challenging. Anyone who claimed to have converted was probably telling the truth; life as a Jew was so arduous that no one would unnecessarily invite it.

In a broader sense this statement underscores an enduring challenge. Without sovereignty or national identity Judaism only attracts converts interested in halakhic lifestyles. When Jews prosper in their land, Judaism draws many who are interested in our national destiny, but who are not necessarily committed to the lifestyle required for actual conversion. This phenomenon first occurred during the exodus from Egypt as the "*erev rav*" – local Egyptian nationals – joined the Jewish march from Egypt. This group – numbering between 1.2 million to 3.6 million people – did not formally or halakhically convert. A similar occurrence took place in the days of Yehoshua as *Givoni* nationals affiliated themselves with the Jewish nation. Once again during the Jewish Renaissance in Persia as described in the Megilla, many of the local inhabitants "became Jews because fear of the Jews had seized them" (*Esther* 8:17).

רְצוֹן־יְרֵאָיו יַעֲשֶׂה, וְאֶת־שַׁוְעָתָם יִשְׁמַע, וְיוֹשִׁיעֵם:
שׁוֹמֵר יהוה אֶת־כָּל־אֹהֲבָיו, וְאֵת כָּל־הָרְשָׁעִים יַשְׁמִיד:
‹ תְּהִלַּת יהוה יְדַבֶּר פִּי, וִיבָרֵךְ כָּל־בָּשָׂר שֵׁם קָדְשׁוֹ לְעוֹלָם וָעֶד:
וַאֲנַחְנוּ נְבָרֵךְ יָהּ מֵעַתָּה וְעַד־עוֹלָם, הַלְלוּיָהּ:

תהלים קטו

תהלים קמו

הַלְלוּיָהּ, הַלְלִי נַפְשִׁי אֶת־יהוה: אֲהַלְלָה יהוה בְּחַיָּי, אֲזַמְּרָה לֵאלֹהַי
בְּעוֹדִי: אַל־תִּבְטְחוּ בִנְדִיבִים, בְּבֶן־אָדָם שֶׁאֵין לוֹ תְשׁוּעָה: תֵּצֵא
רוּחוֹ, יָשֻׁב לְאַדְמָתוֹ, בַּיּוֹם הַהוּא אָבְדוּ עֶשְׁתֹּנֹתָיו: אַשְׁרֵי שֶׁאֵל
יַעֲקֹב בְּעֶזְרוֹ, שִׂבְרוֹ עַל־יהוה אֱלֹהָיו: עֹשֶׂה שָׁמַיִם וָאָרֶץ, אֶת־הַיָּם
וְאֶת־כָּל־אֲשֶׁר־בָּם, הַשֹּׁמֵר אֱמֶת לְעוֹלָם: עֹשֶׂה מִשְׁפָּט לַעֲשׁוּקִים,
נֹתֵן לֶחֶם לָרְעֵבִים, יהוה מַתִּיר אֲסוּרִים: יהוה פֹּקֵחַ עִוְרִים, יהוה
זֹקֵף כְּפוּפִים, יהוה אֹהֵב צַדִּיקִים: יהוה שֹׁמֵר אֶת־גֵּרִים, יָתוֹם

---

who did not believe in divine intervention themselves. Whilst I draw no comparison between these unlikely agents and the aforementioned kings, I wish to illustrate how redemption is often packaged in ways which defy our expectation.

שֹׁמֵר אֶת־גֵּרִים *Protects the stranger.* Judaism is unique in its non-missionary agenda. We are meant to model a lifestyle predicated upon monotheism and morality, but not to convert others to Judaism. Judaism is the only one of the three major religions whose eschatological endpoint does not include conversion or elimination of the "other."

Yet the Torah constantly instructs us to be kind to a convert. In addition to the obvious moral imperatives driving this behavior, it is essential because Judaism began as a religion of converts and we collectively shared the experience of being the "other" in Egypt.

A provocative statement by *Ḥazal* highlights the unique relationship between converts and the Land of Israel: "The Land of Israel is cherished because she certifies converts; if a person in Israel announces that they have converted, we immediately embrace them, whereas outside of Israel they must provide evidence and corroboration." Though this statement does not

courage to the orphan and widow. He thwarts the way of the wicked. ▸
The LORD shall reign for ever. He is your God, Zion, for all generations. Halleluya!

הַלְלוּיָהּ Halleluya! How good it is to sing songs to our God; how *Ps. 147*
pleasant and fitting to praise Him. The LORD rebuilds Jerusalem. He
gathers the scattered exiles of Israel. He heals the brokenhearted and
binds up their wounds. He counts the number of the stars, calling
each by name. Great is our LORD and mighty in power; His understanding has no limit. The LORD gives courage to the humble, but
casts the wicked to the ground. Sing to the LORD in thanks; make
music to our God on the harp. He covers the sky with clouds. He
provides the earth with rain and makes grass grow on the hills. He
gives food to the cattle and to the ravens when they cry. He does
not take delight in the strength of horses nor pleasure in the fleet-
ness of man. The LORD takes pleasure in those who fear Him, who
put their hope in His loving care. Praise the LORD, Jerusalem; sing
to your God, Zion, for He has strengthened the bars of your gates
and blessed your children in your midst. He has brought peace to
your borders, and satisfied you with the finest wheat. He sends His
commandment to earth; swiftly runs His word. He spreads snow

needy, release for the imprisoned, and food and general support for the
disadvantaged. The chapter concludes by announcing to *Tziyon* that its God
will reign for eternity – *Yimlokh Hashem le'olam Elohayich Tziyon ledor vador
Halleluya*. It is one of only two instances in all of Scripture in which this association is drawn.

Divine morality extends beyond time and place. At a human level we both
strive, and are commanded, to act morally at every stage of history. Despite
persistent experimentation with various social structures, a perfect moral
reality and an absolute ethical city have each proven elusive. We yearn for a
day in which – with divine intervention – we partner in creating that reality
surrounding *Tziyon*. In this context *Tziyon* is cast as the moral center of the
world, with its God the source of a universal moral impulse.

בּוֹנֵה יְרוּשָׁלַם יהוה, נִדְחֵי יִשְׂרָאֵל יְכַנֵּס *The LORD rebuilds Jerusalem. He gathers the
scattered exiles of Israel.* Commenting on this verse – which associates the

וְאַלְמָנָה יְעוֹדֵד, וְדֶרֶךְ רְשָׁעִים יְעַוֵּת: ◄ יִמְלֹךְ יהוה לְעוֹלָם, אֱלֹהַיִךְ צִיּוֹן לְדֹר וָדֹר, הַלְלוּיָהּ:

תהלים קמז

הַלְלוּיָהּ, כִּי־טוֹב זַמְּרָה אֱלֹהֵינוּ, כִּי־נָעִים נָאוָה תְהִלָּה: בּוֹנֵה יְרוּשָׁלַםִ יהוה, נִדְחֵי יִשְׂרָאֵל יְכַנֵּס: הָרוֹפֵא לִשְׁבוּרֵי לֵב, וּמְחַבֵּשׁ לְעַצְּבוֹתָם: מוֹנֶה מִסְפָּר לַכּוֹכָבִים, לְכֻלָּם שֵׁמוֹת יִקְרָא: גָּדוֹל אֲדוֹנֵינוּ וְרַב־כֹּחַ, לִתְבוּנָתוֹ אֵין מִסְפָּר: מְעוֹדֵד עֲנָוִים יהוה, מַשְׁפִּיל רְשָׁעִים עֲדֵי־אָרֶץ: עֱנוּ לַיהוה בְּתוֹדָה, זַמְּרוּ לֵאלֹהֵינוּ בְכִנּוֹר: הַמְכַסֶּה שָׁמַיִם בְּעָבִים, הַמֵּכִין לָאָרֶץ מָטָר, הַמַּצְמִיחַ הָרִים חָצִיר: נוֹתֵן לִבְהֵמָה לַחְמָהּ, לִבְנֵי עֹרֵב אֲשֶׁר יִקְרָאוּ: לֹא בִגְבוּרַת הַסּוּס יֶחְפָּץ, לֹא־בְשׁוֹקֵי הָאִישׁ יִרְצֶה: רוֹצֶה יהוה אֶת־יְרֵאָיו, אֶת־הַמְיַחֲלִים לְחַסְדּוֹ: שַׁבְּחִי יְרוּשָׁלַםִ אֶת־יהוה, הַלְלִי אֱלֹהַיִךְ צִיּוֹן: כִּי־חִזַּק בְּרִיחֵי שְׁעָרָיִךְ, בֵּרַךְ בָּנַיִךְ בְּקִרְבֵּךְ: הַשָּׂם־גְּבוּלֵךְ שָׁלוֹם, חֵלֶב חִטִּים יַשְׂבִּיעֵךְ: הַשֹּׁלֵחַ אִמְרָתוֹ אָרֶץ, עַד־מְהֵרָה יָרוּץ דְּבָרוֹ:

During the period of Jewish exile this phenomenon receded. By and large, only those interested in halakhic behavior migrated to Judaism. With the rebirth of national identity and the prosperity of the Jewish state this issue has once again resurfaced. Though this creates halakhic challenges, the phenomenon itself is the outcome of the revitalization of Jewish national identity.

In a foreword to a *sefer* listing and celebrating converts to Judaism in pre-war Palestine, Rav Kook writes "The ultimate spiritual rhapsody which the Jewish people will one day provide for the entire world is hinted at in each generation by scattered converts to Judaism who sense this awakening."

יִמְלֹךְ יהוה לְעוֹלָם, אֱלֹהַיִךְ צִיּוֹן לְדֹר וָדֹר, הַלְלוּיָהּ *The Lord shall reign for ever. He is your God, Zion, for all generations. Halleluya!* Chapter 146 is the first of five similarly labeled chapters which conclude the book of *Tehillim*. It details the moral activities of HaKadosh Barukh Hu, who is both Creator and also Provider for the needy. He provides justice for the exploited, food for the

like fleece, sprinkles frost like ashes, scatters hail like crumbs. Who can stand His cold? He sends His word and melts them; He makes the wind blow and the waters flow. ‣ He has declared His words to Jacob, His statutes and laws to Israel. He has done this for no other nation; such laws they do not know. Halleluya!

הַלְלוּיָהּ Halleluya! Praise the Lord from the heavens, praise Him *Ps. 148* in the heights. Praise Him, all His angels; praise Him, all His hosts. Praise Him, sun and moon; praise Him, all shining stars. Praise Him, highest heavens and the waters above the heavens. Let them praise the name of the Lord, for He commanded and they were created. He established them for ever and all time, issuing a decree that will never change. Praise the Lord from the earth: sea monsters and all the deep seas; fire and hail, snow and mist, storm winds that obey His word; mountains and all hills, fruit trees and all cedars; wild animals and all cattle, creeping things and winged birds; kings of the earth and all nations, princes and all judges on earth; youths and maidens, old and young. ‣ Let them praise the name of the Lord, for His name alone is sublime; His majesty is above earth and heaven. He has raised the pride of His people, for the glory of all His devoted ones, the children of Israel, the people close to Him. Halleluya!

---

and birds are listed. There is one particular bird vested with Messianic symbolism. *Zekharia* (10:8) announces "I will signal for them and gather them in," describing a whistling or hooting signal announcing redemption. This sound – meant to collect Jews from the Diaspora – parallels the fulminating sound of a shofar described in various redemptive prophecies. As opposed to an earsplitting heavenly shofar, this invitation is more "coded," and may not be understood by those who are ignorant of redemptive storylines.

The Gemara (*Ḥullin* 63a) discusses a non-kosher bird dually named as *sherakrak* and *raḥum*. Considering the second name, which in other contexts means *merciful,* the Gemara imputes historical importance to this bird. It will arrive prior to *Mashiaḥ* and herald a more compassionate world. Commenting on its other name – *sherakrak* – the Gemara claims this refers to the bird's

הַנֹּתֵן שֶׁלֶג כַּצֶּמֶר, כְּפוֹר כָּאֵפֶר יְפַזֵּר: מַשְׁלִיךְ קַרְחוֹ כְפִתִּים, לִפְנֵי
קָרָתוֹ מִי יַעֲמֹד: יִשְׁלַח דְּבָרוֹ וְיַמְסֵם, יַשֵּׁב רוּחוֹ יִזְּלוּ־מָיִם: ‹ מַגִּיד
דְּבָרָיו לְיַעֲקֹב, חֻקָּיו וּמִשְׁפָּטָיו לְיִשְׂרָאֵל: לֹא עָשָׂה כֵן לְכָל־גּוֹי,
וּמִשְׁפָּטִים בַּל־יְדָעוּם, הַלְלוּיָהּ:

תהלים קמח

הַלְלוּיָהּ, הַלְלוּ אֶת־יהוה מִן־הַשָּׁמַיִם, הַלְלוּהוּ בַּמְּרוֹמִים: הַלְלוּהוּ
כָל־מַלְאָכָיו, הַלְלוּהוּ כָּל־צְבָאָו: הַלְלוּהוּ שֶׁמֶשׁ וְיָרֵחַ, הַלְלוּהוּ כָּל־
כּוֹכְבֵי אוֹר: הַלְלוּהוּ שְׁמֵי הַשָּׁמָיִם, וְהַמַּיִם אֲשֶׁר מֵעַל הַשָּׁמָיִם:
יְהַלְלוּ אֶת־שֵׁם יהוה, כִּי הוּא צִוָּה וְנִבְרָאוּ: וַיַּעֲמִידֵם לָעַד לְעוֹלָם,
חָק־נָתַן וְלֹא יַעֲבוֹר: הַלְלוּ אֶת־יהוה מִן־הָאָרֶץ, תַּנִּינִים וְכָל־
תְּהֹמוֹת: אֵשׁ וּבָרָד שֶׁלֶג וְקִיטוֹר, רוּחַ סְעָרָה עֹשָׂה דְבָרוֹ: הֶהָרִים
וְכָל־גְּבָעוֹת, עֵץ פְּרִי וְכָל־אֲרָזִים: הַחַיָּה וְכָל־בְּהֵמָה, רֶמֶשׂ וְצִפּוֹר
כָּנָף: מַלְכֵי־אֶרֶץ וְכָל־לְאֻמִּים, שָׂרִים וְכָל־שֹׁפְטֵי אָרֶץ: בַּחוּרִים
וְגַם־בְּתוּלוֹת, זְקֵנִים עִם־נְעָרִים: ‹ יְהַלְלוּ אֶת־שֵׁם יהוה, כִּי־נִשְׂגָּב
שְׁמוֹ לְבַדּוֹ, הוֹדוֹ עַל־אֶרֶץ וְשָׁמָיִם: וַיָּרֶם קֶרֶן לְעַמּוֹ, תְּהִלָּה לְכָל־
חֲסִידָיו, לִבְנֵי יִשְׂרָאֵל עַם קְרֹבוֹ, הַלְלוּיָהּ:

ingathering of exiles with the reconstruction of Yerushalayim – the Midrash (*Tanḥuma Noaḥ*) comments that the capital city will only be restored once the Jewish population returns. Historically, Jerusalem remained relatively unpopulated until the return of a Jewish population under the modern State of Israel. More specifically the reunification of the city after the War of 1967 prompted major *aliya*.

הַלְלוּיָהּ *Psalm 148:* This psalm envisions all of nature and man harmoniously exulting the presence of God. Though nature involuntarily glorifies HaKadosh Barukh Hu with its ceaseless and wondrous cycles, humanity has yet to fully embrace the divine presence. That is inevitably deferred to the Messianic Era.

Among the components of nature embracing God, the crawling creatures

הַלְלוּיָה Halleluya! Sing to the LORD a new song, His praise in the *Ps. 149*
assembly of the devoted. Let Israel rejoice in its Maker; let the
children of Zion exult in their King. Let them praise His name with
dancing; sing praises to Him with timbrel and harp. For the LORD
delights in His people; He adorns the humble with salvation. Let
the devoted revel in glory; let them sing for joy on their beds. Let
high praises of God be in their throats, and a two-edged sword in
their hand: to impose retribution on the nations, punishment on
the peoples, ‣ binding their kings with chains, their nobles with
iron fetters, carrying out the judgment written against them. This
is the glory of all His devoted ones. Halleluya!

הַלְלוּיָה Halleluya! Praise God in His holy place; *Ps. 150*
    praise Him in the heavens of His power.
Praise Him for His mighty deeds;
    praise Him for His surpassing greatness.
Praise Him with blasts of the shofar;
    praise Him with the harp and lyre.
Praise Him with timbrel and dance;
    praise Him with strings and flute.
‣ Praise Him with clashing cymbals;
    praise Him with resounding cymbals.
Let all that breathes praise the LORD. Halleluya!
Let all that breathes praise the LORD. Halleluya!

בָּרוּךְ Blessed be the LORD for ever. Amen and Amen. *Ps. 89*
Blessed from Zion be the LORD *Ps. 135*
who dwells in Jerusalem. Halleluya!
Blessed be the LORD, God of Israel, *Ps. 72*
who alone does wonders.
‣ Blessed be His glorious name for ever,
and may all the earth be filled with His glory.
Amen and Amen.

תהלים קמט

הַלְלוּיָהּ, שִׁירוּ לַיהוה שִׁיר חָדָשׁ, תְּהִלָּתוֹ בִּקְהַל חֲסִידִים: יִשְׂמַח
יִשְׂרָאֵל בְּעֹשָׂיו, בְּנֵי־צִיּוֹן יָגִילוּ בְמַלְכָּם: יְהַלְלוּ שְׁמוֹ בְמָחוֹל, בְּתֹף
וְכִנּוֹר יְזַמְּרוּ־לוֹ: כִּי־רוֹצֶה יהוה בְּעַמּוֹ, יְפָאֵר עֲנָוִים בִּישׁוּעָה:
יַעְלְזוּ חֲסִידִים בְּכָבוֹד, יְרַנְּנוּ עַל־מִשְׁכְּבוֹתָם: רוֹמְמוֹת אֵל
בִּגְרוֹנָם, וְחֶרֶב פִּיפִיּוֹת בְּיָדָם: לַעֲשׂוֹת נְקָמָה בַּגּוֹיִם, תּוֹכֵחוֹת
בַּלְאֻמִּים: ◄ לֶאְסֹר מַלְכֵיהֶם בְּזִקִּים, וְנִכְבְּדֵיהֶם בְּכַבְלֵי בַרְזֶל:
לַעֲשׂוֹת בָּהֶם מִשְׁפָּט כָּתוּב, הָדָר הוּא לְכָל־חֲסִידָיו, הַלְלוּיָהּ:

תהלים קנ

הַלְלוּיָהּ, הַלְלוּ־אֵל בְּקָדְשׁוֹ, הַלְלוּהוּ בִּרְקִיעַ עֻזּוֹ:
הַלְלוּהוּ בִגְבוּרֹתָיו, הַלְלוּהוּ כְּרֹב גֻּדְלוֹ:
הַלְלוּהוּ בְּתֵקַע שׁוֹפָר, הַלְלוּהוּ בְּנֵבֶל וְכִנּוֹר:
הַלְלוּהוּ בְּתֹף וּמָחוֹל, הַלְלוּהוּ בְּמִנִּים וְעֻגָב:
◄ הַלְלוּהוּ בְצִלְצְלֵי־שָׁמַע, הַלְלוּהוּ בְּצִלְצְלֵי תְרוּעָה:
כֹּל הַנְּשָׁמָה תְּהַלֵּל יָהּ, הַלְלוּיָהּ:
כֹּל הַנְּשָׁמָה תְּהַלֵּל יָהּ, הַלְלוּיָהּ:

תהלים פט

בָּרוּךְ יהוה לְעוֹלָם, אָמֵן וְאָמֵן:

תהלים קלה

בָּרוּךְ יהוה מִצִּיּוֹן, שֹׁכֵן יְרוּשָׁלָ͏ִם, הַלְלוּיָהּ:

תהלים עב

בָּרוּךְ יהוה אֱלֹהִים אֱלֹהֵי יִשְׂרָאֵל, עֹשֵׂה נִפְלָאוֹת לְבַדּוֹ:
◄ וּבָרוּךְ שֵׁם כְּבוֹדוֹ לְעוֹלָם, וְיִמָּלֵא כְבוֹדוֹ אֶת־כָּל־הָאָרֶץ
אָמֵן וְאָמֵן:

---

whistling tendencies. Based on the aforementioned prophecy from Zekharia,
the Gemara claims that this bird will whistle and announce the *Mashiaḥ*. The
tooting signal described in the prophecy is attributed to this bird.

The outcome of this Talmudic overlay is the odd image of redemption

Stand until "May Your name be praised" on page 256.

וַיְבָרֶךְ David blessed the LORD in front of the entire assembly.   *1 Chr. 29*
David said, "Blessed are You, LORD, God of our father Yisrael, for
ever and ever. Yours, LORD, are the greatness and the power, the
glory, majesty and splendor, for everything in heaven and earth is
Yours. Yours, LORD, is the kingdom; You are exalted as Head over
all. Both riches and honor are in Your gift and You reign over all
things. In Your hand are strength and might. It is in Your power
to make great and give strength to all. Therefore, our God, we
thank You and praise Your glorious name."   You alone are   *Neh. 9*
the LORD. You made the heavens, even the highest heavens, and
all their hosts, the earth and all that is on it, the seas and all they
contain. You give life to them all, and the hosts of heaven worship
You. ‹ You are the LORD God who chose Abram and brought him
out of Ur of the Chaldees, changing his name to Abraham. You
found his heart faithful toward You, ‹ and You made a covenant
with him to give to his descendants the land of the Canaanites,

───────────────────────────────

וְכָרוֹת עִמּוֹ הַבְּרִית לָתֵת אֶת־אֶרֶץ הַכְּנַעֲנִי *And You made a covenant with him to give
to his descendants the land of the Canaanites.* After resoundingly defeating the
four formidable kings in battle, Avraham is visited by HaKadosh Barukh
Hu as he dreams. He wonders about his future as he is currently childless.
Perhaps his slave will ultimately inherit his estate and continue his legacy.
God assures him that he will bear children. Furthermore his nation will one
day outnumber the heavenly stars. Though these promises appear remote,
Avraham summons the faith to embrace them, and HaKadosh Barukh Hu
credits this conviction, as the Torah concludes "and He reckoned it to him
as righteousness" (*Bereshit* 15:6).

    In the ensuing verse God switches topics and guarantees Avraham that He
will grant him the Land of Israel. To this prophecy Avraham is incredulous,
and asks, "O LORD God, how may I know that I will possess it?" (ibid. 15:8).
Evidently the prospects for inheriting this land are so illogical that even
Avraham, who has continuously demonstrated unflinching belief in divine
promises, questions its validity. This interchange merely emphasizes how
much faith is necessary to believe in our rights to Israel and in our eventual
return to sovereignty in our Land.

Stand until יִשְׁתַּבַּח *on page 257.*

דברי
הימים א׳
כט

וַיְבָרֶךְ דָּוִיד אֶת־יהוה לְעֵינֵי כָּל־הַקָּהָל, וַיֹּאמֶר דָּוִיד, בָּרוּךְ אַתָּה יהוה, אֱלֹהֵי יִשְׂרָאֵל אָבִינוּ, מֵעוֹלָם וְעַד־עוֹלָם: לְךָ יהוה הַגְּדֻלָּה וְהַגְּבוּרָה וְהַתִּפְאֶרֶת וְהַנֵּצַח וְהַהוֹד, כִּי־כֹל בַּשָּׁמַיִם וּבָאָרֶץ, לְךָ יהוה הַמַּמְלָכָה וְהַמִּתְנַשֵּׂא לְכֹל לְרֹאשׁ: וְהָעֹשֶׁר וְהַכָּבוֹד מִלְּפָנֶיךָ, וְאַתָּה מוֹשֵׁל בַּכֹּל, וּבְיָדְךָ כֹּחַ וּגְבוּרָה, וּבְיָדְךָ לְגַדֵּל וּלְחַזֵּק לַכֹּל: וְעַתָּה אֱלֹהֵינוּ מוֹדִים אֲנַחְנוּ לָךְ, וּמְהַלְלִים לְשֵׁם תִּפְאַרְתֶּךָ:

נחמיה ט

אַתָּה־הוּא יהוה לְבַדֶּךָ, אַתְּ עָשִׂיתָ אֶת־הַשָּׁמַיִם, שְׁמֵי הַשָּׁמַיִם וְכָל־צְבָאָם, הָאָרֶץ וְכָל־אֲשֶׁר עָלֶיהָ, הַיַּמִּים וְכָל־אֲשֶׁר בָּהֶם, וְאַתָּה מְחַיֶּה אֶת־כֻּלָּם, וּצְבָא הַשָּׁמַיִם לְךָ מִשְׁתַּחֲוִים: ◂ אַתָּה הוּא יהוה הָאֱלֹהִים אֲשֶׁר בָּחַרְתָּ בְּאַבְרָם, וְהוֹצֵאתוֹ מֵאוּר כַּשְׂדִּים, וְשַׂמְתָּ שְּׁמוֹ אַבְרָהָם: וּמָצָאתָ אֶת־לְבָבוֹ נֶאֱמָן לְפָנֶיךָ, ◂ וְכָרוֹת עִמּוֹ הַבְּרִית לָתֵת אֶת־אֶרֶץ הַכְּנַעֲנִי

---

being delivered by impure birds rather than kosher ones. Rabbi Teichtel viewed this unconventional vision as a presage to an unconventional redemption, heralded by ritually impure agents. Our state may seem secular and its leadership ritually unfaithful, but this is the predicted divine mechanism.

וּמָצָאתָ אֶת־לְבָבוֹ נֶאֱמָן לְפָנֶיךָ, וְכָרוֹת עִמּוֹ הַבְּרִית *You found his heart faithful toward You, and You made a covenant.* The Torah doesn't describe Avraham's defiance of paganism and his heroism in risking his life to defend his faith. The story of the *kivshan ha'esh* and his being miraculously spared isn't recorded by the text.

This prayer cites verses from Neḥemya that juxtapose the fact that HaKadosh Barukh Hu discovered Avraham's heart to be true with the covenant about Israel. The Covenant of the Land of Israel was only facilitated by Avraham's act of *Kiddush Hashem* and his true heart. Even though his heroism in *Ur Kasdim* happened years before the *actual* covenant (the *Berit Bein HaBetarim*) these verses in *Neḥemya* stress Avraham's *Kiddush Hashem* as the basis for the Covenant of the Land (see Mabit, *Beit Elokim*, chapter 32).

Hittites, Amorites, Perizzites, Jebusites and Girgashites. You fulfilled Your promise for You are righteous. You saw the suffering of
our ancestors in Egypt. You heard their cry at the Sea of Reeds. You
sent signs and wonders against Pharaoh, all his servants and all the
people of his land, because You knew how arrogantly the Egyptians
treated them. You created for Yourself renown that remains to this
day. ‣ You divided the sea before them, so that they passed through
the sea on dry land, but You cast their pursuers into the depths, like
a stone into mighty waters.

---

supernatural conditions, when we fulfill the divine expectations, the Land of
Israel is freely awarded by the international community. Often the reigning
inhabitants submit to fear and freely allow Jewish sovereignty. This hope was
asserted by the Jews themselves at the splitting of the Sea, when they sang,
"The chiefs of Edom were dismayed, Moab's leaders were seized with trembling, the people of Canaan melted away." This condition was also evident in
the report issued by Raḥav, who harbored the two spies of Yeshoshua. She
speaks of a demoralized population whose courage has dissolved based on
the miracles which the Jews enjoyed in their desert march.

In the instance of Canaan, apparently their emigration wasn't conducted out
of fear but out of recognition of the divine warrant which the Jews possess to
this land. In either situation our license to the Land of Israel is unchallenged.

In 1948, as we declared Independence, we were attacked by Arab armies
seeking to dislodge us from our homeland. Without any justifiable cause
Arabs fled their homes, yielding to the emerging State of Israel and its inhabitants. Though the "issue" of these former residents remains a politically charged concern, their voluntary emigration is reminiscent of earlier
phenomena.

We haven't yet merited a reality in which our license to this land is undisputed. In the end of History our claim will once again remain uncontested,
as Yerushalayim is recognized as the center of the world, and the Jews as the
providers of Torah and moral instruction to the entire planet, newly reborn
as "Malkhut Shadai."

לָתֵת *To give.* Rabbi Simcha Bunim of Pashischa – the Rebbe of the famed
Kotzker Rebbe – was an ardent supporter of the modern return to the Land
of Israel. He noted that the term *"latet"* (to give) is repeated twice in the verse

הַחִתִּי הָאֱמֹרִי וְהַפְּרִזִּי וְהַיְבוּסִי וְהַגִּרְגָּשִׁי, לָתֵת לְזַרְעוֹ, וַתָּקֶם אֶת־דְּבָרֶיךָ, כִּי צַדִּיק אָתָּה: וַתֵּרֶא אֶת־עֳנִי אֲבֹתֵינוּ בְּמִצְרָיִם, וְאֶת־זַעֲקָתָם שָׁמַעְתָּ עַל־יַם־סוּף: וַתִּתֵּן אֹתֹת וּמֹפְתִים בְּפַרְעֹה וּבְכָל־עֲבָדָיו וּבְכָל־עַם אַרְצוֹ, כִּי יָדַעְתָּ כִּי הֵזִידוּ עֲלֵיהֶם, וַתַּעַשׂ־ לְךָ שֵׁם כְּהַיּוֹם הַזֶּה: ‹ וְהַיָּם בָּקַעְתָּ לִפְנֵיהֶם, וַיַּעַבְרוּ בְתוֹךְ־ הַיָּם בַּיַּבָּשָׁה, וְאֶת־רֹדְפֵיהֶם הִשְׁלַכְתָּ בִמְצוֹלֹת כְּמוֹ־אֶבֶן, בְּמַיִם עַזִּים:

Unable to accept the fact that Avraham actually *questioned* the divine promise, many commentators suggest that he was merely soliciting HaKadosh Barukh Hu for an omen to assure him of a notion which was already secured as an article of faith. Others claim that he worried that his own misdeeds may torpedo the divine promise.

Yet despite the mitigating circumstances – this was still a miscue. Our belief in Israel as our license *independent of our conduct,* and an assured destiny *even without omens* is seminal to our religious consciousness. According to one position in the Gemara (*Nedarim* 32a) our eventual descent to Egypt and subsequent enslavement was a punishment for this error. Our relationship with the Land of Israel is so sensitive that even nuanced insults – such as Avraham's questioning – require departure from the Land to allow us to recalibrate our affiliation with our homeland.

לָתֵת אֶת־אֶרֶץ הַכְּנַעֲנִי הַחִתִּי הָאֱמֹרִי וְהַפְּרִזִּי וְהַיְבוּסִי וְהַגִּרְגָּשִׁי, לָתֵת לְזַרְעוֹ *To give to his descendants the land of the Canaanites, Hittites, Amorites, Perizzites, Jebusites and Girgashites.* Though the Land of Israel was previously inhabited by six nations (those listed in this *pasuk* in Neḥemya as well as the Ḥivi), the Torah constantly refers to the land as Canaan. The *Mekhilta* (*Bo, Masekhta DePisḥa, parasha* 18) suggests that the tribe of Canaan, on hearing about the approaching Jewish nation, *voluntarily* emigrated to allow the Jewish entry. As a reward for this deed the land was referred to as Canaan and this tribe was awarded a different country. The root of the word Canaan is similar to the Hebrew word "*keni'a*" which connotes surrender. Alternate versions have the tribe of Girgashi willfully vacating the land for Jewish inhabitance.

This decision is significant because it hints to a more comprehensive vision of international cooperation in the Jewish return to Israel. Under ideal and

וַיּוֹשַׁע That day the Lord saved Israel from the hands of the Egyptians, *Ex. 14*
and Israel saw the Egyptians lying dead on the seashore. ‣ When
Israel saw the great power the Lord had displayed against the Egyptians, the people feared the Lord, and believed in the Lord and in
His servant, Moses.

אָז יָשִׁיר־מֹשֶׁה Then Moses and the Israelites sang this song to the *Ex. 15*
    Lord, saying:
      I will sing to the Lord, for He has triumphed gloriously;
      horse and rider He has hurled into the sea.
The Lord is my strength and song; He has become my salvation.
      This is my God, and I will beautify Him,
      my father's God, and I will exalt Him.
The Lord is a Master of war; Lord is His name.
Pharaoh's chariots and army He cast into the sea;
      the best of his officers drowned in the Sea of Reeds.
The deep waters covered them;
      they went down to the depths like a stone.
Your right hand, Lord, is majestic in power.
      Your right hand, Lord, shatters the enemy.
In the greatness of Your majesty, You overthrew those who rose
      against You.
      You sent out Your fury; it consumed them like stubble.
By the blast of Your nostrils the waters piled up.
      The surging waters stood straight like a wall;
      the deeps congealed in the heart of the sea.
The enemy said, "I will pursue. I will overtake. I will divide the spoil.
      My desire shall have its fill of them.
      I will draw my sword. My hand will destroy them."
You blew with Your wind; the sea covered them.
      They sank in the mighty waters like lead.

אָז יָשִׁיר־מֹשֶׁה וּבְנֵי יִשְׂרָאֵל *Then Moses and the Israelites sang.* The *Zohar*
(*Beshallaḥ* 54:2) notes that *Az Yashir* contains allusions to the final Messianic
redemptions as well as to the afterlife. Its content is everlasting, and those

שמות יד

וַיּוֹשַׁע יהוה בַּיּוֹם הַהוּא אֶת־יִשְׂרָאֵל מִיַּד מִצְרָיִם, וַיַּרְא יִשְׂרָאֵל אֶת־מִצְרַיִם מֵת עַל־שְׂפַת הַיָּם: ‹ וַיַּרְא יִשְׂרָאֵל אֶת־הַיָּד הַגְּדֹלָה אֲשֶׁר עָשָׂה יהוה בְּמִצְרַיִם, וַיִּירְאוּ הָעָם אֶת־יהוה, וַיַּאֲמִינוּ בַּיהוה וּבְמֹשֶׁה עַבְדּוֹ:

שמות טו

אָז יָשִׁיר־מֹשֶׁה וּבְנֵי יִשְׂרָאֵל אֶת־הַשִּׁירָה הַזֹּאת לַיהוה, וַיֹּאמְרוּ לֵאמֹר, אָשִׁירָה לַיהוה כִּי־גָאֹה גָּאָה, סוּס וְרֹכְבוֹ רָמָה בַיָּם: עָזִּי וְזִמְרָת יָהּ וַיְהִי־לִי לִישׁוּעָה, זֶה אֵלִי וְאַנְוֵהוּ, אֱלֹהֵי אָבִי וַאֲרֹמְמֶנְהוּ: יהוה אִישׁ מִלְחָמָה, יהוה שְׁמוֹ: מַרְכְּבֹת פַּרְעֹה וְחֵילוֹ יָרָה בַיָּם, וּמִבְחַר שָׁלִשָׁיו טֻבְּעוּ בְיַם־סוּף: תְּהֹמֹת יְכַסְיֻמוּ, יָרְדוּ בִמְצוֹלֹת כְּמוֹ־אָבֶן: יְמִינְךָ יהוה נֶאְדָּרִי בַּכֹּחַ, יְמִינְךָ יהוה תִּרְעַץ אוֹיֵב: וּבְרֹב גְּאוֹנְךָ תַּהֲרֹס קָמֶיךָ, תְּשַׁלַּח חֲרֹנְךָ יֹאכְלֵמוֹ כַּקַּשׁ: וּבְרוּחַ אַפֶּיךָ נֶעֶרְמוּ מַיִם, נִצְּבוּ כְמוֹ־נֵד נֹזְלִים, קָפְאוּ תְהֹמֹת בְּלֶב־יָם: אָמַר אוֹיֵב אֶרְדֹּף, אַשִּׂיג, אֲחַלֵּק שָׁלָל, תִּמְלָאֵמוֹ נַפְשִׁי, אָרִיק חַרְבִּי תּוֹרִישֵׁמוֹ יָדִי: נָשַׁפְתָּ בְרוּחֲךָ כִּסָּמוֹ יָם, צָלֲלוּ כַּעוֹפֶרֶת בְּמַיִם אַדִּירִים: מִי־כָמֹכָה בָּאֵלִם יהוה, מִי

Who is like You, LORD, among the mighty?
> Who is like You – majestic in holiness, awesome in glory,
> working wonders?
You stretched out Your right hand, the earth swallowed them.
In Your loving-kindness, You led the people You redeemed.
> In Your strength, You guided them to Your holy abode.
Nations heard and trembled;
> terror gripped Philistia's inhabitants.

---

creation, and may have fueled hopes for a future gathering of humanity in Yerushalayim, around the Temple, in the end of days.

Their unexpected conjuring of the concept of *Mikdash* while passing through the Sea is underlined by a Midrash which tethers this miracle to the future *Mikdash* in Yerushalayim. Before the Sea actually splits, Moshe prays fervently to HaKadosh Barukh Hu to rescue the cornered people. At this stage God responds to him. The Midrash comments that HaKadosh Barukh Hu assured Moshe that no prayers were necessary, since their safe passage was assured due to the merits of one day constructing a *Mikdash* in Yerushalayim!

According to the *Zohar* (*Midrash HaNe'elam*) hundreds of years later King David authored a psalm about constructing the *Mikdash* based on the image of waters gathering during creation. In Chapter 24, when dreaming of ascending to the mountain of God (מִי־יַעֲלֶה בְהַר־ה') David HaMelekh begins by noting that the world was founded on water (,כִּי־הוּא עַל־יַמִּים יְסָדָהּ וְעַל־נְהָרוֹת יְכוֹנְנֶהָ). Elsewhere (Chapter 93) he refers to the *Mikdash* as נָאֲוָה קֹדֶשׁ – similar to the term נְוֵה קָדְשֶׁךָ employed at the Sea. The *Zohar* (*Midrash HaNe'elam*, page 12, side 3) asserts that David requested that God confine His *Shekhina* to the *Mikdash* in the same manner that the waters were restrained during Creation.

The image of original waters being confined appeared to David as a metaphor for the divine circumscription, and may have also inspired a nation to first conceive of this *Mikdash*.

שָׁמְעוּ עַמִּים יִרְגָּזוּן *Nations heard and trembled.* The basic meaning of the word *yirgazun*, "trembled," implies fear and anxiety about the advancing Israelite nation. This fear is palpable both in the manner in which Bilam and Balak conspire to halt the advancing nation, and in the reports which Raḥav delivers to the spies she accommodates.

כְּמֹכָה נֶאְדָּר בַּקֹּדֶשׁ,   נוֹרָא תְהִלֹּת עֹשֵׂה

פֶּלֶא: נָטִיתָ יְמִינְךָ תִּבְלָעֵמוֹ אָרֶץ: נָחִיתָ

בְחַסְדְּךָ עַם־זוּ גָּאֶלְתָּ,   נֵהַלְתָּ בְעָזְּךָ אֶל־נְוֵה

קָדְשֶׁךָ:   שָׁמְעוּ עַמִּים יִרְגָּזוּן,   חִיל

אָחַז יֹשְׁבֵי פְּלָשֶׁת: אָז נִבְהֲלוּ אַלּוּפֵי

---

who assimilate it in this world will once again experience it in those foretold futures.

נֵהַלְתָּ בְעָזְּךָ אֶל־נְוֵה קָדְשֶׁךָ *In Your strength, You guided them to Your holy abode.* The term *Neveh Kodshekha* refers to the *Beit HaMikdash*. In particular it addresses the aesthetic qualities of the structure, as the word *neveh* evokes the word "*noi*" or "*na'eh*," describing something attractive or pleasant. The Rambam (*Hilkhot Beit HaBeḥira* 1:11) describes a mitzva to build the *Mikdash* as strong, as high, and as attractive as possible. When Yirmiyahu (10:25) laments the destruction of the Temple, he wails about the devastation of Yaakov and the demolition of "*naveihu*" – his *Mikdash*. The first employment of this term relating to *Mikdash* occurred at the splitting of the Sea.

The idea of a *Mikdash* was actually alluded to in the beginning of the *Shira*. The nation sang "*Zeh Eli v'anveihu*" – "This is my God, and I will beautify Him" The first part of this verse refers to the Jews encountering HaKadosh Barukh Hu at the Sea and exclaiming "This is my God." The last word – *v'anveihu* – is unclear. One of the interpretations offered by Ḥazal (see *Mekhilta*) interprets the term *v'anveihu* as referring to "*neveh*" – they beheld God splitting the Sea, and coveted a future opportunity to build a shelter for the Divine Presence.

Some aspect of the splitting of the Sea triggered the first human consciousness about the idea of a *Mikdash*. Perhaps it was the confidence that divine intervention would endure long enough to ferry them to Israel and not just rescue them from Egypt. Imagining this future with confidence for the first time conjured up ideas of a Temple.

Yirmiyahu (3:17) describes the *ingathering* of all nations to Jerusalem in the end of time with imagery which evokes the "*gathering*" of waters during creation. He portrays the final gathering with the verb וְנִקְווּ (*venikvu*) which is the same expression used to describe the collection of waters during Genesis – יִקָווּ הַמַּיִם. Standing at the sea and watching the waters collect into one area may have evoked memories of the original gathering of waters during

The chiefs of Edom were dismayed,
> Moab's leaders were seized with trembling,
> the people of Canaan melted away.

Fear and dread fell upon them.
> By the power of Your arm, they were still as stone –
> until Your people crossed, LORD,
> until the people You acquired crossed over.

You will bring them and plant them on the mountain of Your
> heritage –
> the place, LORD, You made for Your dwelling,

---

the Second Temple was destined to never achieve the miraculous nature of the First Temple (*Yoma* 9b).

Due to this unenthusiastic return, the Jewish people are described as "the nation God had acquired" and possessed a *legal* responsibility to redeem, rather than the "Nation of God" whom He lovingly redeemed. Even at this stage of history, at the Sea, the shortcomings of the Second Temple era were introduced.

מָכוֹן לְשִׁבְתְּךָ פָּעַלְתָּ יהוה *The place, LORD, You made for Your dwelling.* One of the names for the *Mikdash* is *Makhon* – literally place or location. Yet this unusual noun (it is only employed one additional time in Tanakh: *I Melakhim* 8:13) captures additional features of the *Mikdash*. By adding an extra *"vav"* the word can be rendered as *"mekhuvan"* or aligned. As the Jerusalem Talmud (*Berakhot* 4:8) illustrates, the terrestrial *Mikdash* was aligned with a heavenly *Mikdash*. The alignment of a human epicenter with a divine palace was already sensed by Yaakov when he recognized that the Mountain upon which he slept was, in truth "the House of God … the gateway to Heaven."

Aligning the earthly *Mikdash* with a celestial counterpart highlights the metaphysical and cosmic effect of the *Mikdash* and its rituals. Sacrifices and ceremonies performed on the earth's surface impacted higher worlds – as these activities were reflected in similar events in Heaven. By extension the destruction of the *Mikdash* is a cosmic tragedy, not merely a national calamity. Of particular note is the *Kaporet* – a gold cover which plated the Holy Ark. It was shaped to evoke the *Kiseh HaKavod* – God's metaphysical throne.

Similar ideas are expressed about an earthly Yerushalayim aligned with a Heavenly one. The Gemara in *Ta'anit* comments upon the meaning of the

אָז נִבְהֲלוּ אַלּוּפֵי אֱדוֹם, אֵילֵי מוֹאָב יֹאחֲזֵמוֹ רָעַד, נָמֹגוּ
כֹּל יֹשְׁבֵי כְנָעַן: תִּפֹּל עֲלֵיהֶם אֵימָתָה
וָפַחַד, בִּגְדֹל זְרוֹעֲךָ יִדְּמוּ כָּאָבֶן, עַד־
יַעֲבֹר עַמְּךָ יהוה, עַד־יַעֲבֹר עַם־זוּ
קָנִיתָ: תְּבִאֵמוֹ וְתִטָּעֵמוֹ בְּהַר נַחֲלָתְךָ, מָכוֹן

However, *yirgazun* can also connote anger or rage. The Midrash (*Mekhilta Beshallaḥ Masekhta deShira*, chapter 9) describes the rage and antagonism which the Jewish march toward Israel created amongst the reigning nations. Sensing this resistance, HaKadosh Barukh Hu protests to these nations: "Throughout the centuries you have enjoyed numerous kings and monarchies without any Jewish challenge, and the moment the Jews begin to exert sovereignty you protest!" Due to this behavior, the Midrash continues, God will one day upend those who opposed the Jewish passage to Canaan.

The Midrash (*Sifri Devarim* 333) claims that a similar phenomenon will occur during our final redemption. Indeed, this trend has repeated itself in modern times. For close to two millennia Jews have wandered the planet without enjoying statehood, while every culture, religion, and nationality has experienced self-determination. Yet when the Jews finally assert their national identity in their natural homeland, much of the international community rises in protest. HaKadosh Barukh Hu will ultimately topple those who contest this process, while He will recompense those who assist and support it.

עַד־יַעֲבֹר עַמְּךָ יהוה, עַד־יַעֲבֹר עַם־זוּ קָנִיתָ *Until Your people crossed, Lord, until the people You acquired crossed over.* The repetition of the image of a nation passing through to Israel alludes to two distinct "passages" of the Jewish nation into the Land of Israel – once with Yehoshua after completing the forty-year journey through the desert, and a second time with Ezra, returning from a seventy year sojourn in Bavel. Interestingly, the third and final "passage" is not referenced – perhaps because the ingathering will be phased, and cannot be described as a national journey.

The first passage is undertaken by "Your people / the people of God" whereas the second passage is experienced by the people "You acquired." The latter portrayal – clearly less affectionate – may correspond to the flawed status of the Second Redemption. Only 42,000 Jews returned to Israel with Ezra, while most chose to remain in Bavel. Because of this tepid response,

the Sanctuary, LORD, Your hands established.
The LORD will reign for ever and all time.

The LORD will reign for ever and all time.
The LORD's kingship is established for ever and to all eternity.

When Pharaoh's horses, chariots and riders went into the sea,
the LORD brought the waters of the sea back over them,
but the Israelites walked on dry land through the sea.

אֲדֹנָי כּוֹנְנוּ יָדֶיךָ. If this is true, the earlier sentiments about humans crafting the Temple characterize the first two natural or common *Batei Mikdash* but not the latter, Divinely constructed *Mikdash*.

Notably, the Rambam (*Hilkhot Melakhim* 11:1) describes the construction of the *Mikdash* among the many tasks of *Mashiah* himself. The Gemara (*Sukka* 52b) cites a verse in *Zekharia* describing four carpenters and names *Mashiah* as one of the four. This is one of the many sources which support the Rambam's minority opinion.

Another Gemara (*Megilla* 17b) describes *Mashiah* as arriving after the *Mikdash* has been assembled. This would imply that it precedes the arrival of *Mashiah*. A similar statement in the Talmud Yerushalmi (*Ma'aser Sheni* 5:2) is quite clear that the construction of the third *Mikdash* precedes the re-establishment of Davidic monarchy.

Some have suggested that these varying timelines represent different models of final redemption. Rashi's model of a Divinely constructed and delivered *Mikdash* implies a terrestrially driven process imposed from above. Its pace, texture, and authors are supernatural. The Rambam's model suggests a human-powered redemptive process, subject to human influences and shaped by human initiative.

As with many redemptive narratives, these two strategies can represent coexistent truths. Some have suggested (see Maharim Shik *Yoreh De'a* 213) that a more righteous generation will be more deserving of a supernaturally driven and thereby more accelerated process. A less deserving nation may endure a more arduous process, hampered by human limitations.

Alternatively, redemption may be a hybrid of supernatural forces fused with human effort.

יהוה יִמְלֹךְ לְעֹלָם וָעֶד *The LORD shall reign for ever and ever. Shirat HaYam* concludes with a verse exclaiming the authority of HaKadosh Barukh Hu

לְשִׁבְתְּךָ פָּעַלְתָּ יהוה, מִקְּדָשׁ אֲדֹנָי כּוֹנֲנוּ
יָדֶיךָ:   יהוה יִמְלֹךְ לְעֹלָם וָעֶד:

יהוה יִמְלֹךְ לְעֹלָם וָעֶד.

יהוה מַלְכוּתֵהּ קָאֵם לְעָלַם וּלְעָלְמֵי עָלְמַיָּא.

כִּי
בָא סוּס פַּרְעֹה בְּרִכְבּוֹ וּבְפָרָשָׁיו בַּיָּם, וַיָּשֶׁב יהוה עֲלֵהֶם אֶת־מֵי
הַיָּם,   וּבְנֵי יִשְׂרָאֵל הָלְכוּ בַיַּבָּשָׁה בְּתוֹךְ   הַיָּם:

---

name Yerushalayim as a city which unites and connects (*Tehillim* 122). This refers to the fusion between "lower" Yerushalayim and its "upper" counterpart. HaKadosh Barukh Hu announces that He will only enter the celestial Yerushalayim after the terrestrial one is inhabited, further demonstrating the cosmic influence of events in Yerushalayim and the *Mikdash*.

However the original word "*makhon*" can also be construed as "*mukhan*," prepared or formulated (*Midrash Sekhel Tov, Shemot* 15). The concept of *Mikdash* was already predestined from the start of history. The Gemara (*Pesaḥim* 54) asserts that the *Mikdash* was one of the many items created before our world was fashioned. Without a *Mikdash* to enable the encounter between Man and God, and the rituals which mediate this encounter, human experience is incomplete.

Additionally, this allusion to "prepared" suggests that the *Mikdash* will be prefabricated in Heaven, as asserted by many commentators (see below).

מָכוֹן לְשִׁבְתְּךָ פָּעַלְתָּ יהוה, מִקְּדָשׁ אֲדֹנָי כּוֹנֲנוּ יָדֶיךָ *The place, LORD, You made for Your dwelling, the Sanctuary, LORD, Your hands established.* This final reference to the *Mikdash* in *Shirat HaYam* describes it as the handiwork of God. The terminology is very graphic, even referring to the "hand of God." It leaves no question as to the divine construction of the *Mikdash*. As mentioned above, the phrase זֶה אֵלִי וְאַנְוֵהוּ is interpreted as a national hope to one day build a *Mikdash* through human endeavor.

The first two *Batei Mikdash* were constructed through human enterprise, reflecting the sentiments of זֶה אֵלִי וְאַנְוֵהוּ. Many Rishonim (see Rashi on *Sukka* 41a s.v. אי נמי and on *Rosh HaShana* 30a s.v. לֹא) claim that the final *Mikdash* will be assembled in Heaven based on the concluding phrase מִקְּדָשׁ

‣ For kingship is the Lord's and He rules over the nations. *Ps. 22*
Saviors shall go up to Mount Zion to judge Mount Esau, *Ob. 1*
and the Lord's shall be the kingdom.
Then the Lord shall be King over all the earth; *Zech. 14*
on that day the Lord shall be One and His name One,

(as it is written in Your Torah, saying:
Listen, Israel: the Lord is our God, the Lord is One.) *Deut. 6*

יִשְׁתַּבַּח May Your name be praised for ever, our King,
the great and holy God, King in heaven and on earth.
For to You, Lord our God and God of our ancestors,
it is right to offer song and praise, hymn and psalm,
strength and dominion, eternity, greatness and power,
song of praise and glory, holiness and kingship,
‣ blessings and thanks, from now and for ever.
Blessed are You, Lord,
God and King, exalted in praises,
God of thanksgivings, Master of wonders,
who delights in hymns of song,
King, God, Giver of life to the worlds.

---

as King, this is the first example of communal consciousness of His monarchy. This realization lives on eternally and warrants divine love for the Jews,
regardless of future behavior.

The Jewish people would advance beyond the Sea and transform this *general* notion of kingship into a more mature and comprehensive acceptance of
authority, centered around the Law of the Torah delivered six weeks after the
splitting of the Sea. Ideally a Jew cannot merely accept the divine authority in
a general sense, but must submit to that authority through practice and study.
However, even Jews who no longer exhibit fidelity to the system delivered at
Sinai still receive that divine attention, when they perceive His authority as
a King. In the State of Israel we haven't yet merited an entire nation subject
to the laws of Sinai. However, an overwhelming majority intuitively sense
God's presence and general authority, and, like our ancestors, subscribe to
the verse, "Hashem will rule for eternity."

תהלים כב ‹ כִּי לַיהוה הַמְּלוּכָה וּמֹשֵׁל בַּגּוֹיִם:

עובדיה א וְעָלוּ מוֹשִׁעִים בְּהַר צִיּוֹן, לִשְׁפֹּט אֶת־הַר עֵשָׂו
וְהָיְתָה לַיהוה הַמְּלוּכָה:

זכריה יד וְהָיָה יהוה לְמֶלֶךְ עַל־כָּל־הָאָרֶץ
בַּיּוֹם הַהוּא יִהְיֶה יהוה אֶחָד וּשְׁמוֹ אֶחָד:

דברים ו (וּבְתוֹרָתְךָ כָּתוּב לֵאמֹר, שְׁמַע יִשְׂרָאֵל, יהוה אֱלֹהֵינוּ יהוה אֶחָד:)

יִשְׁתַּבַּח שִׁמְךָ לָעַד, מַלְכֵּנוּ

הָאֵל הַמֶּלֶךְ הַגָּדוֹל וְהַקָּדוֹשׁ בַּשָּׁמַיִם וּבָאָרֶץ

כִּי לְךָ נָאֶה, יהוה אֱלֹהֵינוּ וֵאלֹהֵי אֲבוֹתֵינוּ

שִׁיר וּשְׁבָחָה, הַלֵּל וְזִמְרָה

עֹז וּמֶמְשָׁלָה, נֶצַח, גְּדֻלָּה וּגְבוּרָה

תְּהִלָּה וְתִפְאֶרֶת, קְדֻשָּׁה וּמַלְכוּת

‹ בְּרָכוֹת וְהוֹדָאוֹת, מֵעַתָּה וְעַד עוֹלָם.

בָּרוּךְ אַתָּה יהוה

אֵל מֶלֶךְ גָּדוֹל בַּתִּשְׁבָּחוֹת

אֵל הַהוֹדָאוֹת, אֲדוֹן הַנִּפְלָאוֹת

הַבּוֹחֵר בְּשִׁירֵי זִמְרָה, מֶלֶךְ, אֵל, חֵי הָעוֹלָמִים.

as an eternal Monarch. Though many verses throughout Tanakh amplify and elaborate upon His kingship, this verse asserts it in an unqualified and straightforward fashion.

The Midrash cites a conversation between Moshe Rabbeinu and God, in which Moshe effectively wonders why so many commandments and communications surround the Jewish People. God responds that He will never forget this moment when for the first time a human community embraced His authority. Though Avraham already introduced HaKadosh Barukh Hu

HALF KADDISH

Leader: יִתְגַּדַּל Magnified and sanctified may His great name be,
in the world He created by His will.
May He establish His kingdom
in your lifetime and in your days,
and in the lifetime of all the house of Israel,
swiftly and soon – and say: Amen.

All: May His great name be blessed for ever and all time.

Leader: Blessed and praised, glorified and exalted,
raised and honored, uplifted and lauded
be the name of the Holy One,
blessed be He,
beyond any blessing, song,
praise and consolation
uttered in the world – and say: Amen.

BLESSINGS OF THE SHEMA

*The following blessing and response are said only in the presence of a minyan.
They represent a formal summons to the congregation to engage in an act of collective
prayer. The custom of bowing at this point is based on 1 Chronicles 29:20, "David said
to the whole assembly, 'Now bless the Lord your God.' All the assembly blessed the
Lord God of their fathers and bowed their heads low to the Lord and the King."*

*The Leader says the following, bowing at "Bless," standing straight at "the Lord."
The congregation, followed by the Leader, responds, bowing at "Bless,"
standing straight at "the Lord."*

Leader: # BLESS
the Lord, the blessed One.

Congregation: Bless the Lord, the blessed One,
for ever and all time.

Leader: Bless the Lord, the blessed One,
for ever and all time.

חצי קדיש

ש"ץ: יִתְגַּדַּל וְיִתְקַדַּשׁ שְׁמֵהּ רַבָּא (קהל: אָמֵן)

בְּעָלְמָא דִּי בְרָא כִרְעוּתֵהּ

וְיַמְלִיךְ מַלְכוּתֵהּ

בְּחַיֵּיכוֹן וּבְיוֹמֵיכוֹן וּבְחַיֵּי דְּכָל בֵּית יִשְׂרָאֵל

בַּעֲגָלָא וּבִזְמַן קָרִיב, וְאִמְרוּ אָמֵן. (קהל: אָמֵן)

קהל
ושׁ"ץ: יְהֵא שְׁמֵהּ רַבָּא מְבָרַךְ לְעָלַם וּלְעָלְמֵי עָלְמַיָּא.

ש"ץ: יִתְבָּרַךְ וְיִשְׁתַּבַּח וְיִתְפָּאַר וְיִתְרוֹמַם וְיִתְנַשֵּׂא

וְיִתְהַדָּר וְיִתְעַלֶּה וְיִתְהַלָּל

שְׁמֵהּ דְּקֻדְשָׁא בְּרִיךְ הוּא (קהל: בְּרִיךְ הוּא)

לְעֵלָּא מִן כָּל בִּרְכָתָא וְשִׁירָתָא, תֻּשְׁבְּחָתָא וְנֶחֱמָתָא

דַּאֲמִירָן בְּעָלְמָא, וְאִמְרוּ אָמֵן. (קהל: אָמֵן)

קריאת שמע וברכותיה

The following blessing and response are said only in the presence of a מנין.
They represent a formal summons to the קהל to engage in an act of collective prayer.
The custom of bowing at this point is based on דברי הימים א׳ כט, כ, "David said
to the whole assembly, 'Now bless the Lord your God.' All the assembly blessed the
Lord God of their fathers and bowed their heads low to the Lord and the King."

The שליח ציבור says the following, bowing at בָּרְכוּ, standing straight at ה׳. The קהל,
followed by the שליח ציבור, responds, bowing at בָּרוּךְ, standing straight at ה׳.

ש"ץ:

אֶת יהוה הַמְבֹרָךְ.

קהל: בָּרוּךְ יהוה הַמְבֹרָךְ לְעוֹלָם וָעֶד.

ש"ץ: בָּרוּךְ יהוה הַמְבֹרָךְ לְעוֹלָם וָעֶד.

*The custom is to sit from this point until the Amida, since the predominant
emotion of this section of the prayers is love rather than awe.
Conversation is forbidden until after the Amida.*

בָּרוּךְ Blessed are You, LORD our God,
King of the Universe,
who forms light and creates darkness,   *Is. 45*
makes peace and creates all.

הַמֵּאִיר In compassion He gives light to the earth
and its inhabitants,
and in His goodness continually renews the work of creation,
day after day.
How numerous are Your works, LORD;   *Ps. 104*
You made them all in wisdom;
the earth is full of Your creations.
He is the King exalted alone since the beginning of time –
praised, glorified and elevated since the world began.
Eternal God,
               in Your great compassion, have compassion on us,
               LORD of our strength, Rock of our refuge,
               Shield of our salvation,
               You are our stronghold.
The blessed God,
great in knowledge,
prepared and made the rays of the sun.
He who is good formed glory for His name,
surrounding His power with radiant stars.
The leaders of His hosts, the holy ones,
exalt the Almighty,
constantly proclaiming God's glory and holiness.
Be blessed, LORD our God,
for the magnificence of Your handiwork
and for the radiant lights You have made.
May they glorify You, Selah!

The custom is to sit from this point until the עמידה, since the predominant
emotion of this section of the prayers is love rather than awe.
Conversation is forbidden until after the עמידה.

בָּרוּךְ אַתָּה יהוה אֱלֹהֵינוּ מֶלֶךְ הָעוֹלָם

ישעיה מה

יוֹצֵר אוֹר וּבוֹרֵא חֹשֶׁךְ

עֹשֶׂה שָׁלוֹם וּבוֹרֵא אֶת הַכֹּל.

הַמֵּאִיר לָאָרֶץ וְלַדָּרִים עָלֶיהָ בְּרַחֲמִים

וּבְטוּבוֹ מְחַדֵּשׁ בְּכָל יוֹם תָּמִיד מַעֲשֵׂה בְרֵאשִׁית.

תהלים קד

מָה־רַבּוּ מַעֲשֶׂיךָ יהוה, כֻּלָּם בְּחָכְמָה עָשִׂיתָ

מָלְאָה הָאָרֶץ קִנְיָנֶךָ:

הַמֶּלֶךְ הַמְרוֹמָם לְבַדּוֹ מֵאָז

הַמְשֻׁבָּח וְהַמְפֹאָר וְהַמִּתְנַשֵּׂא מִימוֹת עוֹלָם.

אֱלֹהֵי עוֹלָם

בְּרַחֲמֶיךָ הָרַבִּים רַחֵם עָלֵינוּ

אֲדוֹן עֻזֵּנוּ, צוּר מִשְׂגַּבֵּנוּ

מָגֵן יִשְׁעֵנוּ, מִשְׂגָּב בַּעֲדֵנוּ.

אֵל בָּרוּךְ גְּדוֹל דֵּעָה

הֵכִין וּפָעַל זָהֳרֵי חַמָּה

טוֹב יָצַר כָּבוֹד לִשְׁמוֹ

מְאוֹרוֹת נָתַן סְבִיבוֹת עֻזּוֹ

פִּנּוֹת צְבָאָיו קְדוֹשִׁים

רוֹמְמֵי שַׁדַּי

תָּמִיד מְסַפְּרִים כְּבוֹד אֵל וּקְדֻשָּׁתוֹ.

תִּתְבָּרַךְ יהוה אֱלֹהֵינוּ, עַל שֶׁבַח מַעֲשֵׂה יָדֶיךָ.

וְעַל מְאוֹרֵי אוֹר שֶׁעָשִׂיתָ, יְפָאֲרוּךָ סֶּלָה.

תִּתְבָּרַךְ May You be blessed,
our Rock, King and Redeemer, Creator of holy beings.
May Your name be praised for ever,
our King, Creator of the ministering angels,
all of whom stand in the universe's heights,
proclaiming together, in awe, aloud,
the words of the living God, the eternal King.
They are all beloved, all pure, all mighty,
and all perform in awe and reverence the will of their Maker.
‣ All open their mouths in holiness and purity,
with song and psalm,
and bless, praise, glorify,
revere, sanctify and declare the sovereignty of – ‹
The name of the great, mighty and awesome God and King,
holy is He.
‣ All accept on themselves, one from another,
the yoke of the kingdom of heaven,
granting permission to one another
to sanctify the One who formed them, in serene spirit,
pure speech and sweet melody.
All, as one, proclaim His holiness, saying in awe:

All say aloud:

Holy, holy, holy is the LORD of hosts;
the whole world is filled with His glory.

Is. 6

בְּשָׂפָה בְרוּרָה וּבִנְעִימָה *Pure speech and sweet melody.* This phrase may be simply
characterizing the song of angels as smooth and mellifluous. However the
source of this phrase is a verse in *Tzefania* describing a common and united
"language":

For then I will change the peoples, so that they will have pure lips,
to call on the name of the LORD, all of them,
and serve Him with one accord [lit. one shoulder]. (*Tzefania* 3:9)

The general meaning of this verse is simply that the entire world will one day

תִּתְבָּרֵךְ

צוּרֵנוּ מַלְכֵּנוּ וְגוֹאֲלֵנוּ, בּוֹרֵא קְדוֹשִׁים

יִשְׁתַּבַּח שִׁמְךָ לָעַד

מַלְכֵּנוּ, יוֹצֵר מְשָׁרְתִים

וַאֲשֶׁר מְשָׁרְתָיו כֻּלָּם עוֹמְדִים בְּרוּם עוֹלָם

וּמַשְׁמִיעִים בְּיִרְאָה יַחַד בְּקוֹל

דִּבְרֵי אֱלֹהִים חַיִּים וּמֶלֶךְ עוֹלָם.

כֻּלָּם אֲהוּבִים, כֻּלָּם בְּרוּרִים, כֻּלָּם גִּבּוֹרִים

וְכֻלָּם עוֹשִׂים בְּאֵימָה וּבְיִרְאָה רְצוֹן קוֹנָם

‹ וְכֻלָּם פּוֹתְחִים אֶת פִּיהֶם בִּקְדֻשָּׁה וּבְטָהֳרָה

בְּשִׁירָה וּבְזִמְרָה

וּמְבָרְכִים וּמְשַׁבְּחִים וּמְפָאֲרִים

וּמַעֲרִיצִים וּמַקְדִּישִׁים וּמַמְלִיכִים ›

אֶת שֵׁם הָאֵל הַמֶּלֶךְ הַגָּדוֹל, הַגִּבּוֹר וְהַנּוֹרָא

קָדוֹשׁ הוּא.

‹ וְכֻלָּם מְקַבְּלִים עֲלֵיהֶם עֹל מַלְכוּת שָׁמַיִם זֶה מִזֶּה

וְנוֹתְנִים רְשׁוּת זֶה לָזֶה

לְהַקְדִּישׁ לְיוֹצְרָם בְּנַחַת רוּחַ

בְּשָׂפָה בְרוּרָה וּבִנְעִימָה

קְדֻשָּׁה כֻּלָּם כְּאֶחָד

עוֹנִים וְאוֹמְרִים בְּיִרְאָה

All say aloud

קָדוֹשׁ, קָדוֹשׁ, קָדוֹשׁ יהוה צְבָאוֹת

מְלֹא כָל־הָאָרֶץ כְּבוֹדוֹ:

ישעיה ו

▸ Then the Ophanim and the Holy Ḥayyot,
with a roar of noise,
raise themselves toward the Seraphim and,
facing them, give praise, saying:

> *All say aloud:*
> Blessed is the Lord's glory from His place.   *Ezek. 3*

לְאֵל To the blessed God they offer melodies.
To the King, living and eternal God,
they say psalms and proclaim praises.

> For it is He alone
> who does mighty deeds
> and creates new things,
> who is Master of battles,
> and sows righteousness,
> who makes salvation grow
> and creates cures,
> who is revered in praises,
> Lord of wonders,

who in His goodness,
continually renews the work of creation, day after day,
as it is said:

> "[Praise] Him who made the great lights,   *Ps. 136*
> for His love endures for ever."

---

only speak Hebrew, and have difficulty understanding other languages such as Aramaic.

This view of the eventual supremacy of *Lashon HaKodesh* suggests a degree of cultural homogeny in the messianic age. Judaism is the only major religion which doesn't preach conversion or elimination of the others. Our endgame consists merely of exposing humanity to a pure blend of monotheism and morality. This interpretation asserts that, at least linguistically, non-Jewish cultures will undergo conversion.

‮‭וְהָאוֹפַנִּים וְחַיּוֹת הַקֹּֽדֶשׁ‬‬

בְּרַעַשׁ גָּדוֹל מִתְנַשְּׂאִים לְעֻמַּת שְׂרָפִים

לְעֻמָּתָם מְשַׁבְּחִים וְאוֹמְרִים

All say aloud

יחזקאל ג

בָּרוּךְ כְּבוֹד־יהוה מִמְּקוֹמוֹ:

לְאֵל בָּרוּךְ נְעִימוֹת יִתֵּֽנוּ

לְמֶֽלֶךְ אֵל חַי וְקַיָּם

זְמִירוֹת יֹאמֵֽרוּ וְתִשְׁבָּחוֹת יַשְׁמִֽיעוּ

כִּי הוּא לְבַדּוֹ

פּוֹעֵל גְּבוּרוֹת, עוֹשֶׂה חֲדָשׁוֹת

בַּֽעַל מִלְחָמוֹת, זוֹרֵֽעַ צְדָקוֹת

מַצְמִֽיחַ יְשׁוּעוֹת, בּוֹרֵא רְפוּאוֹת

נוֹרָא תְהִלּוֹת, אֲדוֹן הַנִּפְלָאוֹת

הַמְחַדֵּשׁ בְּטוּבוֹ בְּכָל יוֹם תָּמִיד מַעֲשֵׂה בְרֵאשִׁית

כָּאָמוּר

תהלים קלו

לְעֹשֵׂה אוֹרִים גְּדֹלִים, כִּי לְעוֹלָם חַסְדּוֹ:

recognize the divine presence in a manner which is no longer adulterated by vestigial paganism. *Safa Berura* would imply an undistorted understanding.

Yet many commentators (see Ibn Ezra) claim that the phrase in *Tzefania* is literal: In the Messianic Era the entire world will communicate in *Lashon HaKodesh*. It is only by communicating in this language that humanity can achieve a fully accurate comprehension of HaKadosh Barukh Hu. The unity of actual language is mirrored by the conclusion of the verse, which describes a different anatomical unity: one shoulder to bear the worship of God. In this context the description of angels conversing in *Safa Berura* is consistent with the report of the Gemara (*Shabbat* 12a) that these celestial beings can

‣ May You make a new light shine over Zion,
and may we all soon be worthy of its light.
Blessed are You, LORD, who forms the radiant lights.

אַהֲבָה You have loved us with great love, LORD our God,
and with surpassing compassion
have You had compassion on us.

---

described through the metaphor of the Jewish people illuminating a world of darkness:

> God says, "Where is your mother's divorce document which I gave her when I divorced her? Or: to which of My creditors did I sell you? You were sold because of your sins;
>
> Because of your crimes was your mother divorced. Why was no one here when I came?
>
> Why, when I called, did nobody answer? Is My arm too short to redeem? Have I too little power to save? With My rebuke I dry up the sea; I turn rivers into desert, their fish rot for lack of water and they die of thirst; I dress the heavens in black to mourn and make their covering sackcloth." (*Yeshayahu* 50:1–3)

Based on these verses the Gemara describes Yerushalayim as a radiant city illuminating the entire world – "*Yerushalayim ora shel olam.*" The radiance is supernatural and drawn from HaKadosh Barukh Hu – as the midrash concludes, "Who is the light of Yerushalayim? HaKadosh Barukh Hu!" This prophecy and the associated midrash employ light, not merely to describe the *process* of redemption, but also to depict a post-redemptive utopian world bathed in the light of Yerushalayim and the presence of the *Shekhina*.

It is in the spirit of all these light images and metaphors that we pray "*Or ḥadash al Tziyon ta'ir.*"

אַהֲבָה רַבָּה אֲהַבְתָּנוּ, יהוה אֱלֹהֵינוּ *You have loved us with great love, LORD our God.* This section describes the love HaKadosh Barukh Hu feels for His people. The two emotions which we are commanded to generate toward Him are love and awe. Though these mitzvot apply equally in Israel and in the Diaspora, the *Zohar* already sensed that in Israel love is a more natural emotion, whereas in the Diaspora awe is more instinctive.

Our love for HaKadosh Barukh Hu stems from our ability to understand His providence, His *midot* and His Torah. By understanding Him we also

‹ אוֹר חָדָשׁ עַל צִיּוֹן תָּאִיר וְנִזְכֶּה כֻלָּנוּ מְהֵרָה לְאוֹרוֹ.
בָּרוּךְ אַתָּה יהוה, יוֹצֵר הַמְּאוֹרוֹת.

אַהֲבָה רַבָּה אֲהַבְתָּנוּ, יהוה אֱלֹהֵינוּ
חֶמְלָה גְדוֹלָה וִיתֵרָה חָמַלְתָּ עָלֵינוּ.

אוֹר חָדָשׁ עַל צִיּוֹן תָּאִיר וְנִזְכֶּה כֻלָּנוּ מְהֵרָה לְאוֹרוֹ *May You make a new light shine over Zion, and may we all soon be worthy of its light.* Having described the divine dominion over the planetary realm, the conclusion of the *berakha* applies the image of light towards the redemption of *Tziyon*. In general, light signifies deliverance and salvation, whereas darkness signifies persecution and suffering. In a well-known prayer in which we petition on behalf of Jews who suffer persecution, we ask that they be delivered from darkness to light and from bondage to redemption – מֵאֲפֵלָה לְאוֹרָה, וּמִשִׁעְבּוּד לִגְאֻלָּה – stressing the imagery of light and darkness as a metaphor for the different states of human experience.

Light also serves as a metaphor for redemption for a different reason. The Jerusalem Talmud (*Yoma* 3:2) records that Rabbi Ḥiyya and Rabbi Shimon ben Ḥalafta were traveling near the Kinneret when they gazed upon a sunrise. Rabbi Ḥiyya saw in the sunrise a symbol for Jewish redemption: first isolated rays gradually break the horizon; ultimately as the sun climbs the heaven its full radiance is displayed. This imagery reminds us to temper our sometimes unrealistic expectations of redemption. We assume that it will follow an apocalyptic pace, occurring almost instantaneously. Rav Ḥiyya reminded us that – at least in its initial stages – it unfolds gradually.

Perhaps the imagery of light also explains the *reason* for gradual or evolutionary redemption. Having resided in "*darkness*" for so many centuries, the Jewish people may be unable to absorb a fully redeemed reality. The process expands gradually, affording us the opportunity to familiarize ourselves with the newfound reality of statehood, sovereignty, and historical identity.

Based on this midrash and a parallel reference in the *Zohar*, the phrase "*kim'a kim'a*" (little by little) has become a slogan for both the desire for expanded redemption and the patience necessary to receive its full benefits.

A well-known prophecy of Yeshayahu describes a messianic reality in which the entire world acknowledges the Jewish people as the People of God, and they yearn to follow the wisdom of the Torah. This desire is

Our Father, our King,
for the sake of our ancestors who trusted in You,
and to whom You taught the laws of life,
be gracious also to us and teach us.
Our Father, compassionate Father, ever compassionate,
have compassion on us.
Instill in our hearts the desire to understand and discern,
to listen, learn and teach, to observe, perform and fulfill
all the teachings of Your Torah in love.
Enlighten our eyes in Your Torah
and let our hearts cling to Your commandments.
Unite our hearts to love and revere Your name,
so that we may never be ashamed.
And because we have trusted in Your holy, great and revered name,
may we be glad and rejoice in Your salvation.

In contrast, under the unexplainable conditions of Diaspora we feel less empowered historically and are less able to sense the divine providence. This condition more readily evokes awe – standing back in surrender to the Divine Mystery.

An example of *Ahavat Hashem* attributed specifically to residents of Israel can be found in *Yalkut Shimoni* to *Yitro*, chapter 292, in which Rabbi Natan interprets the verse in the Ten Commandments referring to those "*who love Me and keep My mitzvot.*" He asserts that this refers particularly to those who adhere to mitzvot in Israel. However this text may be interpreted as a limited reference to the Jewish population which adhered to mitzvot during the Roman Oppression, toward the end of the second Temple and immediately after its destruction. Mitzva adherence came at a steep price – often the price of death. Under *these* conditions, fulfillment of mitzvot was an expression of unconditional love for God.

נָגִילָה וְנִשְׂמְחָה בִּישׁוּעָתֶךָ *May we be glad and rejoice in Your salvation*. When envisioning redemption, the *berakha* voices the hope that the Jewish people will rejoice in "Your salvation" (*biyeshuatekha*). A similar phraseology appears in Psalms chapter 20, which we recite daily toward the end of *Tefilla*. The more natural phrase would have been "we will rejoice at *our* salvation

אָבִינוּ מַלְכֵּנוּ
בַּעֲבוּר אֲבוֹתֵינוּ שֶׁבָּטְחוּ בְךָ
וַתְּלַמְּדֵם חֻקֵּי חַיִּים
כֵּן תְּחָנֵּנוּ וּתְלַמְּדֵנוּ.
אָבִינוּ, הָאָב הָרַחֲמָן, הַמְרַחֵם
רַחֵם עָלֵינוּ
וְתֵן בְּלִבֵּנוּ לְהָבִין וּלְהַשְׂכִּיל
לִשְׁמֹעַ, לִלְמֹד וּלְלַמֵּד, לִשְׁמֹר וְלַעֲשׂוֹת, וּלְקַיֵּם
אֶת כָּל דִּבְרֵי תַלְמוּד תּוֹרָתֶךָ בְּאַהֲבָה.
וְהָאֵר עֵינֵינוּ בְּתוֹרָתֶךָ, וְדַבֵּק לִבֵּנוּ בְּמִצְוֹתֶיךָ
וְיַחֵד לְבָבֵנוּ לְאַהֲבָה וּלְיִרְאָה אֶת שְׁמֶךָ
וְלֹא נֵבוֹשׁ לְעוֹלָם וָעֶד.
כִּי בְשֵׁם קָדְשְׁךָ הַגָּדוֹל וְהַנּוֹרָא בָּטָחְנוּ
נָגִילָה וְנִשְׂמְחָה בִּישׁוּעָתֶךָ.

discover the ennobling nature of religion, and the manner in which it enriches human prosperity. We thereby love Him because we understand the manner in which our relationship with Him enhances our lives.

In contrast, *yira* or awe represents the inability to *fully* comprehend the mystery of the Divine. We are baffled by His will and cannot discern the beneficial impact of His will toward human welfare. Recognizing the indescribable difference between Man and God, we submit to that mystery, acknowledging the divine will as a higher ethic.

These two emotions govern the inner life of a Jew, and modulate the emotional interface between Man and God. They are equally vital in Israel and in the Diaspora.

Yet life in Israel – particularly during redemptive phases of history – more easily facilitates love, since we more readily understand the divine plan in history, and view ourselves as partners to HaKadosh Barukh Hu in shaping that history. This sense of partnership amplifies the emotion of love.

At this point, gather the four tzitziot of the tallit, holding them in the left hand.

Bring us back in peace from the four quarters of the earth
and lead us upright to our land.
▸ For You are a God who performs acts of salvation,
and You chose us from all peoples and tongues,
bringing us close to Your great name for ever in truth,
that we may thank You
and proclaim Your oneness in love.
Blessed are You, LORD, who chooses His people Israel in love.

*The Shema must be said with intense concentration. In the first paragraph one
should accept, with love, the sovereignty of God; in the second, the mitzvot as
the will of God. The end of the third paragraph constitutes fulfillment of the
mitzva to remember, morning and evening, the exodus from Egypt.*

When not praying with a minyan, say:

God, faithful King!

The following verse should be said aloud, while covering the eyes with the right hand:

Listen, Israel: the LORD is our God,
the LORD is One.

Deut. 6

Quietly: Blessed be the name of His glorious kingdom for ever and all time.

The Midrash associates this "tethering" with the symbolism of flags. Only
after we are assigned flags (as were the tribes of Israel in the opening chapters
of *Bemidbar*) does our national fate become bound to God. The Divine fate
cannot be fastened to *an individual*. National identity – symbolized by a flag –
can be fused with the Divine Presence in our world. As the aforementioned
verse in Psalms concludes, "we will rejoice in *Your* salvation, and in the name
of God we will raise our *flag.*"

SEEING *SHEMA* IN A DREAM

The Gemara in *Berakhot* interprets a dream in which a person is reciting *Keriat Shema*. This person "deserves" to receive the *Shekhina* but his
generation hasn't merited it. The inability to disseminate the *Shekhina* to
others isn't merely an incidental or peripheral flaw. The failure to facilitate

At this point, gather the four ציציות of the טלית, holding them in the left hand.

וַהֲבִיאֵנוּ לְשָׁלוֹם מֵאַרְבַּע כַּנְפוֹת הָאָרֶץ
וְתוֹלִיכֵנוּ קוֹמְמִיּוּת לְאַרְצֵנוּ.

‹ כִּי אֵל פּוֹעֵל יְשׁוּעוֹת אָתָּה, וּבָנוּ בָחַרְתָּ מִכָּל עַם וְלָשׁוֹן
וְקֵרַבְתָּנוּ לְשִׁמְךָ הַגָּדוֹל סֶלָה, בֶּאֱמֶת
לְהוֹדוֹת לְךָ וּלְיַחֶדְךָ בְּאַהֲבָה.
בָּרוּךְ אַתָּה יהוה, הַבּוֹחֵר בְּעַמּוֹ יִשְׂרָאֵל בְּאַהֲבָה.

The שמע must be said with intense concentration. In the first paragraph one should accept, with love, the sovereignty of God; in the second, the מצוות as the will of God. The end of the third paragraph constitutes fulfillment of the מצווה to remember, morning and evening, the exodus from Egypt.

When not praying with a מנין, say:

אֵל מֶלֶךְ נֶאֱמָן

The following verse should be said aloud, while covering the eyes with the right hand:

דברים ו

שְׁמַע יִשְׂרָאֵל, יהוה אֱלֹהֵינוּ, יהוה ׀ אֶחָד:

Quietly בָּרוּךְ שֵׁם כְּבוֹד מַלְכוּתוֹ לְעוֹלָם וָעֶד.

(*biyeshuateinu*). Commenting on this difference, the Midrash (*Bemidbar Raba* 2:2) claims that our redemption also constitutes a Divine redemption – when we are rescued, HaKadosh Barukh Hu experiences salvation as well.

Though He is transcendent and unalterable, God tethered His Presence in our world to the fate of the Jewish people. When the Jewish nation suffers, His Presence is obscured; when Jews experience redemption, His Presence is redeemed as well.

This doctrine, known as "*Shekhinta beGaluta*" was first outlined to Yaakov upon his descent to Egypt to be reunited with his son Yosef. Having once been exiled, and having struggled to return to Israel, Yaakov agonizes over his current departure. HaKadosh Barukh Hu assures him, "I will descend with you to Egypt, and I will also leave with you," thereby assuring him that the exile will not be interminable.

Touch the hand-tefillin at ° and the head-tefillin at °°.

וְאָהַבְתָּ Love the LORD your God with all your heart, with all your   *Deut. 6*
soul, and with all your might. These words which I command you
today shall be on your heart. Teach them repeatedly to your children, speaking of them when you sit at home and when you travel
on the way, when you lie down and when you rise. °Bind them as
a sign on your hand, and °°they shall be an emblem between your
eyes. Write them on the doorposts of your house and gates.

Touch the hand-tefillin at ° and the head-tefillin at °°.

וְהָיָה If you indeed heed My commandments with which I charge   *Deut. 11*
you today, to love the LORD your God and worship Him with all
your heart and with all your soul, I will give rain in your land in its

---

THE ROLE OF AGRICULTURE IN THE MODERN STATE

In the past three centuries, thoughts of returning to the Land of Israel
prompted a renewed interest in agriculture in general, and the unique agricultural challenges of the Land of Israel in particular.

As reported in a *sefer* written by one of his disciples, the Vilna Gaon saw
agricultural activity in Israel not merely as an omen of redemption, but as
a catalyst. Redemption can be hastened by spiritual revival, extreme international pressure, and persecution; or alternatively by a mass return to, and
agricultural investment in, the Land of Israel. King David (*Tehillim* 102:14–15)
describes the return to *Tziyon* and the craving for the stones and dirt of
Tziyon. Traditionally this craving of stones was attributed to the longing for
redemption. The Gemara records many sages who would display physical
affection for the actual dirt and stones of Israel, to demonstrate their love of
the land and their desire for ultimate redemption. To the Vilna Gaon, *Tehillim*
forecasts not only craving the stones and dirt of Israel, but actively improving
it by building and planting. This behavior doesn't merely express a desire for
redemption, but stimulates it.

As Jews returned to Israel they faced daunting challenges. European Jews
in particular hadn't participated extensively in large scale agricultural ven-
tures. Additionally, a different climate and harsh landscapes provided unprecedented obstacles. A verse in *Bereshit* (36:20) contrasts the descendants
of Eisav who were "dwellers of the land," with the family of Yaakov (who

Touch the תפילין של יד at ° and the תפילין של ראש at °°.

דברים ו

וְאָהַבְתָּ אֵת יהוה אֱלֹהֶיךָ, בְּכָל־לְבָבְךָ וּבְכָל־נַפְשְׁךָ וּבְכָל־מְאֹדֶךָ: וְהָיוּ הַדְּבָרִים הָאֵלֶּה, אֲשֶׁר אָנֹכִי מְצַוְּךָ הַיּוֹם, עַל־לְבָבֶךָ: וְשִׁנַּנְתָּם לְבָנֶיךָ וְדִבַּרְתָּ בָּם, בְּשִׁבְתְּךָ בְּבֵיתֶךָ וּבְלֶכְתְּךָ בַדֶּרֶךְ, וּבְשָׁכְבְּךָ וּבְקוּמֶךָ: °וּקְשַׁרְתָּם לְאוֹת עַל־יָדֶךָ °°וְהָיוּ לְטֹטָפֹת בֵּין עֵינֶיךָ: וּכְתַבְתָּם עַל־מְזֻזוֹת בֵּיתֶךָ וּבִשְׁעָרֶיךָ:

Touch the תפילין של יד at ° and the תפילין של ראש at °°.

דברים יא

וְהָיָה אִם־שָׁמֹעַ תִּשְׁמְעוּ אֶל־מִצְוֹתַי אֲשֶׁר אָנֹכִי מְצַוֶּה אֶתְכֶם הַיּוֹם, לְאַהֲבָה אֶת־יהוה אֱלֹהֵיכֶם וּלְעָבְדוֹ, בְּכָל־לְבַבְכֶם וּבְכָל־ נַפְשְׁכֶם: וְנָתַתִּי מְטַר־אַרְצְכֶם בְּעִתּוֹ, יוֹרֶה וּמַלְקוֹשׁ, וְאָסַפְתָּ

---

encounters with the *Shekhina* in others is a defect in our personal encounter with HaKadosh Barukh Hu. The *Shema* isn't conjugated as a personal affirmation of belief, but rather as an announcement to an entire nation – aiming to inspire others toward similar appreciation.

The more unified our embrace of His authority, the more resonant our message of monotheism. An entire *unified* people announcing His Oneness is far more convincing than isolated acceptances; our solidarity of faith reflects His indivisibility. In the section of *Shmuel* in which God informs King David that he will not construct the *Mikdash*, He asserts the uniqueness of the Jewish people: "Who can be compared with Your people, with Israel? What other nation on earth did God set out to redeem and make into a people for Himself?" (II *Shmuel* 7:23). The Gemara (*Berakhot* 6a) claims that this verse is housed in the *tefillin* of HaKadosh Barukh Hu. Essentially, our *tefillin* contain the sections of the *Shema* which mention the Oneness of God, while reciprocally His *tefillin* avow the uniqueness of His people.

The Gemara in *Yoma* describes the morning recital of the *Shema* in the *Mikdash*. A chandelier was hung, and when the first rays of sunrise ricocheted off its buffed metal the entire assembled congregation began to recite the *Shema*. Great efforts were made to assure a unified and joint recital. This is the source of the custom for the *Shaliaḥ Tzibbur* to recite the first verse aloud so the entire congregation can coordinate a joint recital.

season, the early and late rain; and you shall gather in your grain, wine and oil. I will give grass in your field for your cattle, and you shall eat and be satisfied. Be careful lest your heart be tempted and you go astray and worship other gods, bowing down to them. Then the LORD's anger will flare against you and He will close the heavens so that there will be no rain. The land will not yield its crops, and you will perish swiftly from the good land that the LORD is

---

skills, and numerous kings and prophets functioned as shepherds in the early stages of their "careers." However, shepherding does not enable true and permanent bonding with the land. Shepherds and their flocks draw nutrition from the land but do not improve it, or in any way establish a presence on the land. Despite all his adventures, Avraham passes away without clear ownership over any parcel of land save the Cave of the Patriarchs. Ironically, he has been generously hosted by various colleagues and partners, but hasn't really rooted himself in the land. Yaakov struggles even more doggedly to establish a presence in the land, but concludes his life in Egypt with the status of his homestead unclear. Yitzḥak is the only one of the three *Avot* who succeeds – through agricultural investment – to clutch the actual land: "Yitzḥak planted crops in that land, and reaped that year a hundred times as much as he had sowed. God had blessed him" (*Bereshit* 26:12). Despite and perhaps because of his relatively unspectacular sedentary lifestyle, Yitzḥak establishes an estate in Gerar and a farmstead named Me'a She'arim ("a hundred-fold") to indicate the dramatic success he had achieved.

In 1873, due to overcrowding, housing prices in Yerushalayim were exorbitant. To solve this issue the first community outside of the walls of the Old City of Yerushalayim was founded. It was ultimately named Me'a She'arim, since the organization which spearheaded the effort consolidated in the week of *Parashat Toledot*, during which the aforementioned verse is read.

THE STATUS OF COMMANDMENTS OUTSIDE THE LAND OF ISRAEL
This section of *Keriat Shema* presents eviction from the Land of Israel as the punishment for transgressing mitzvot. Immediately following the description of expulsion, the Torah writes: "Therefore you shall store up these, My words, in your heart and in your soul, and you shall bind them for a sign upon your hand, and they shall be for frontlets between your eyes" (*Devarim* 11:18). Based on the juxtaposition of the description of expulsion with the verse

דְּגָנֶךָ וְתִירשְׁךָ וְיִצְהָרֶךָ: וְנָתַתִּי עֵשֶׂב בְּשָׂדְךָ לִבְהֶמְתֶּךָ, וְאָכַלְתָּ
וְשָׂבָעְתָּ: הִשָּׁמְרוּ לָכֶם פֶּן־יִפְתֶּה לְבַבְכֶם, וְסַרְתֶּם וַעֲבַדְתֶּם
אֱלֹהִים אֲחֵרִים וְהִשְׁתַּחֲוִיתֶם לָהֶם: וְחָרָה אַף־יהוה בָּכֶם, וְעָצַר
אֶת־הַשָּׁמַיִם וְלֹא־יִהְיֶה מָטָר, וְהָאֲדָמָה לֹא תִתֵּן אֶת־יְבוּלָהּ,
וַאֲבַדְתֶּם מְהֵרָה מֵעַל הָאָרֶץ הַטֹּבָה אֲשֶׁר יהוה נֹתֵן לָכֶם:

---

had spent upwards of twenty years in exile in the house of Lavan), who were less familiar with the agricultural norms of the Land of Israel. The Gemara (*Shabbat* 85a) comments that these dwellers knew the land so well that they could smell and taste the actual land to determine appropriate agricultural strategy.

On their return to a land they had been absent from for close to two thousand years, the early pioneers acknowledged their need to learn the local norms of agriculture. Rav Tzvi Kalisher, one of the Rabbis most ardently urging a return to Israel, actually encouraged the formation of a *Beit Midrash* to study the "*Ḥokhmat Ha'aretz*" to train students in agricultural tactics. Many Rabbinic leaders encouraged their disciples to persist, despite the innate difficulties of tilling an unfamiliar land. As Rav Yitzḥak Elḥanan assured his students, "the special spirit of the land will assist us gradually in this agricultural endeavor."

The centrality of agriculture accrued great significance for Secular Zionists searching for a secular ideal to anchor their pioneering struggle. For those inspired by Socialism and class equality, farming was a great equalizer against the class divisions created by capitalism. As well as the egalitarianism within agricultural activity, the mere return to nature offered both spiritual experience as well as reunification between returning exiles and their homeland. A.D. Gordon, who emigrated to Palestine in 1904, and who articulated a religion of labor, wrote that, "The Jewish people has been completely cut off from nature and imprisoned within city walls these two thousand years.... We lack the habit of labor – not labor performed out of external compulsion, but labor to which one is attached in a natural and organic way. This kind of labor binds a people to its soil and to its national culture."

THE FIRST JEWISH FARMER OF ISRAEL
Avraham and Yaakov were shepherds who lived nomadic lifestyles, roaming from one pastureland to another. This vocation fosters various leadership

giving you. Therefore, set these, My words, on your heart and soul. °Bind them as a sign on your hand, °°and they shall be an emblem between your eyes. Teach them to your children, speaking of them when you sit at home and when you travel on the way, when you lie down and when you rise. Write them on the doorposts of your house and gates, so that you and your children may live long in the

---

discuss *Tefillin* are prefaced with a reference to our entry into the Land of Israel (*Shemot* 13:5 and 13:11). Halakhically, donning *Tefillin* is a mitzva which is not anchored to residence in Israel, and applies equally in the Diaspora. Yet given these prefaces, the Gemara in *Kiddushin* announces that performance of this mitzva assures entry into the Land of Israel.

A Jew's interaction with HaKadosh Barukh Hu is often internal, cognitive, or emotional. Study, prayer, and ritual all forge a profound and intimate interaction with an infinite and invisible Being. Donning *Tefillin* is a more experiential encounter; by wrapping ourselves with major sections of the Torah, we encircle ourselves with the divine word. *Tefillin* originally were worn for the entire day – even during periods of labor or general daily routine. Wrapping *Tefillin* wasn't intended to enable greater study; rather it facilitates an uninterrupted holistic encounter with God throughout the entire human experience. Ideally the enveloping of the body is complemented by a physical stationing in God's chosen land. Wrapping a body with *Tefillin* and residing in a land of direct divine proximity can allow one to achieve full experiential enclosure.

Tefillin are also meant to broadcast our national religious agenda. The Torah describes this effect (*Devarim* 28:10), suggesting that *Tefillin* are meant to be seen as they transmit this message. The *Tefillin* include the three letters of God's name – "שַׁדַּי" – and they convey this awareness of God. The effect of this message is at its peak when broadcast on a national scale, fully realizable only in the Land of Israel.

וּכְתַבְתָּם עַל־מְזוּזוֹת בֵּיתֶךָ וּבִשְׁעָרֶיךָ *Write them on the doorposts of your house and gates.* The Torah juxtaposes the mitzva of *mezuza* to the goal of "living on the land which HaKadosh Barukh Hu swore to our fathers." Despite this alignment, the obligation of *mezuza* isn't a *mitzva hateluya baAretz* (a commandment that is dependent on the Land), and applies equally in the Diaspora. There is one halakhic scenario which differentiates between homes in Israel

וְשַׂמְתֶּם֙ אֶת־דְּבָרַ֣י אֵ֔לֶּה עַל־לְבַבְכֶ֖ם וְעַֽל־נַפְשְׁכֶ֑ם, °וּקְשַׁרְתֶּ֨ם
אֹתָ֤ם לְאוֹת֙ עַל־יֶדְכֶ֔ם, °°וְהָי֥וּ לְטֽוֹטָפֹ֖ת בֵּ֣ין עֵֽינֵיכֶֽם: וְלִמַּדְתֶּ֤ם
אֹתָ֣ם אֶת־בְּנֵיכֶ֔ם לְדַבֵּ֣ר בָּ֑ם, בְּשִׁבְתְּךָ֤ בְּבֵיתֶ֨ךָ֙ וּבְלֶכְתְּךָ֣ בַדֶּ֔רֶךְ,
וּֽבְשָׁכְבְּךָ֖ וּבְקוּמֶֽךָ: וּכְתַבְתָּ֛ם עַל־מְזוּז֥וֹת בֵּיתֶ֖ךָ וּבִשְׁעָרֶֽיךָ: לְמַ֨עַן

mandating mitzva performance, the Midrash (*Sifrei Eikev* 43:17) comments: "HaKadosh Barukh Hu instructs us that even though you are expelled from the land, *practice* mitzvot, so that when you return to Israel you will be familiar with their performance." The term *metzuyanim* instructs us to rehearse mitzvot even when expelled from the Land of Israel. This phrase, describing mitzvot outside of Israel as practice sessions for our ultimate return, is borrowed from a verse in *Yirmiyahu* (31:20) which promotes the establishments of markers and signs (*tziyunim*) to expedite our eventual homecoming.

Most assume that the midrash refers to land-based commandments which fundamentally do not apply outside of Israel. These mitzvot must still be practiced, to maintain familiarity and facilitate our return. Despite the absence of a biblical injunction for these mitzvot outside of Israel, the Rabbis retained these practices to preserve tradition and ensure actual fulfillment when we are repatriated. Most mitzvot which are not land based – known in Halakha as *Ḥovat HaGuf* – apply equally in, and outside of, the Land of Israel.

Rabbi Moshe ben Naḥman (Ramban), however, argued that *all* mitzvot are intended solely for performance in the Land of Israel. Since the final sentences of this section discuss the mitzvot of *Tefillin* and *Mezuza*, obviously the midrashic overlay is addressing those mitzvot which are considered *ḥovat haguf!* Yet the midrash classifies these commandments (and others like these) as rehearsals for actual fulfillment when we are redeemed. Practically, mitzvot must still be performed outside of Israel since the Torah itself mandates them. However, the mitzvot possess less inherent value, and are merely tools to sustain our familiarity. Aside from some of his disciples, most did not accept the Ramban's unique position. Mitzva performance transcends place, and has preserved Jewish identity even as we were absent from our homeland.

TEFILLIN AND THE LAND OF ISRAEL

Tefillin are mentioned in four different sections of the Torah, and each of these sections is encased in the actual *Tefillin*. Two of the sections which

land that the Lᴏʀᴅ swore to your ancestors to give them, for as long
as the heavens are above the earth.

Transfer the tzitziot to the right hand, kissing them at °.

וַיֹּאמֶר The Lᴏʀᴅ spoke to Moses, saying: Speak to the Israelites   *Num. 15*
and tell them to make °tassels on the corners of their garments

---

they already partially contain a status similar to the Land of Israel itself.
Hence frequenting these locations may be compared to life in Israel, which
would grant extended longevity.

Although this conversation assumed a literal reading of long life, the divine
promise could also be read figuratively. In particular in this verse at the end of
the second section of *Keriat Shema* the Torah may be referring to *continuity
and heritage* and not personal longevity. The verse concludes with a reference to children, and in particular it promises days as endless as Heaven and
earth. Presumably, as no one individual lives as long as nature, this reward
refers to continuity and tradition achieved through successive generations.
The natural manner of assuring generational continuity is living upon the
same land. This better facilitates sustaining common heritage and customs.
Without this geographical basis, we require the study of Torah to maintain
generational continuity.

וְעָשׂוּ לָהֶם צִיצִת *To make tassels.* The mitzva of *tzitzit* is delivered to the Jewish
People immediately after the *meraglim* (spies) debacle – at the end of *Parashat
Shelaḥ*. When sentencing the Israelites to a forty-year journey in the desert,
HaKadosh Barukh Hu criticizes the nation for their infidelity (*zenuteikhem*)
toward the Land of Israel. *Tzitzit* is designed to prevent "illicit" eyes (*aḥarei ei-
neikhem asher atem zonim aḥareihem*). Additionally God accuses the *meraglim*
of having "explored" the land – (*asher tartem et ha'aretz*). Perhaps they are being faulted for "excess" curiosity supplanting faith in a divine promise. *Tzitzit*
are also meant to stem unhealthy curiosity – *Velo taturu aḥarei levavkhem....*

The symbolism of *Tzitzit* is meant to remind one of all 613 mitzvot –
uzkhartem et kol mitzvot Hashem. Similarly living in Israel is considered
equivalent to fulfilling the entire body of mitzvot. The Gemara comments
that by gazing at the original blue-colored string, a person ponders the
similar blue glint of the ocean and by extension the deep blue pigment of
the sky. Ultimately this color association helps direct our imagination to the

יִרְבּוּ יְמֵיכֶם וִימֵי בְנֵיכֶם עַל הָאֲדָמָה אֲשֶׁר נִשְׁבַּע יהוה לַאֲבֹתֵיכֶם
לָתֵת לָהֶם, כִּימֵי הַשָּׁמַיִם עַל־הָאָרֶץ:

Transfer the ציציות *to the right hand, kissing them at* °.

וַיֹּאמֶר יהוה אֶל־מֹשֶׁה לֵּאמֹר: דַּבֵּר אֶל־בְּנֵי יִשְׂרָאֵל וְאָמַרְתָּ
אֲלֵהֶם, וְעָשׂוּ לָהֶם °כַּנְפֵי עַל־כַּנְפֵי בִגְדֵיהֶם לְדֹרֹתָם, וְנָתְנוּ

---

and those abroad. A rental unit doesn't require a *mezuza* until thirty days have elapsed. If, however, the unit is rented in Israel, a *mezuza* must be affixed immediately. The Gemara (*Menaḥot* 44a) attributes this more immediate obligation to the goal of *yishuv haAretz* – settling the Land. It is unclear how compelling a speedy performance of the mitzva of *mezuza* will increase settlement of the Land. The *Sefat Emet* suggests that the protective function of the *mezuza* will be realized immediately in homes in Israel, thereby encouraging settlement. Alternatively the mere performance of a mitzva may showcase the significance of living in Israel by stressing the opportunity to perform additional mitzvot. Ideally, the opportunity for added mitzva performance should inspire settlement of the Land of Israel.

עַל הָאֲדָמָה *In the land.* The Gemara (*Berakhot* 8a) retells the following conversation between Rabbi Yoḥanan and his students. The students inquired as to whether there were elderly people in Bavel. Since the Torah promises extended years for those who reside "upon the land which HaKadosh Barukh Hu swore to the *Avot*," presumably those who don't, die prematurely. With only one exception (*Devarim* 6:2), whenever the Torah extends long life as a reward for mitzva performance, it qualifies it as an experience "upon the land I have delivered to you," or "upon the land I have delivered to your fathers." Rabbi Yoḥanan assured them that they have an alternative method for achieving longevity – Torah study and prayer in synagogues and study halls.

Interestingly, this query may have possessed personal urgency for Rabbi Yoḥanan, who resided in Israel and dispatched his only remaining son (Rabbi Matna) to study Torah in Bavel with Shmuel. Having suffered the loss of nine previous children, he was anxious to assure his remaining son's future.

Furthermore, the Gemara (*Megilla* 29a) comments that the synagogues and study halls of the Diaspora will be one day relocated to Israel. Perhaps

for all generations. They shall attach to the °tassel at each corner a thread of blue. This shall be your °tassel, and you shall see it and remember all of the LORD's commandments and keep them, not straying after your heart and after your eyes, following your own sinful desires. Thus you will be reminded to keep all My commandments, and be holy to your God. I am the LORD your God, who brought you out of the land of Egypt to be your God. I am the LORD your God.

°True –

The Leader repeats:

‣ The LORD your God is true –

---

feet was something like a sapphire stone pavement, as clear as the sky itself" (*Shemot* 24:10). By gazing at the blue strings of *tekhelet*, a person – through creative analogy – encounters HaKadosh Barukh Hu, and is inspired toward overall religious improvement. A variant of this visualization is described in a midrash on *Tehillim* (chapter 90) which concludes by instructing a Jew to view his *Tzitzit* not merely as blue strings, but as a *direct* encounter with God. The Torah concludes the above verse with the phrase: you should see "*it*" or "*Him*" rather than the more suitable phrase "you should see *them*" (which would refer to the *Tzitzit* themselves). This indicates that by observing the *Tzitzit* a person is, in effect, embracing the *Shekhina*.

For thousands of years the identity of *tekhelet* was obscured, and with it our ability to fulfill the complete mitzva vanished. The past century has witnessed a revived interest in *tekhelet* as well as significant effort at its recovery. After thousands of years of neglect, the reinvigoration of a mitzva which enables a firmer encounter between the human imagination and HaKadosh Barukh Hu can be perceived as a feature of redemption.

Beyond the visual impact of *tekhelet*, its function in redemption stems from its use in the *Mikdash*. Being that it was the dye of royalty, it was widely used in the *Mikdash* in both the priestly attire as well as many of the fabrics of the *Mikdash* itself. Without this dye, reconstructing the priestly attire is inconceivable. With it, one more obstacle toward rebuilding the *Mikdash* has been removed.

°עַל־צִיצִת הַכָּנָף פְּתִיל תְּכֵלֶת: וְהָיָה לָכֶם °לְצִיצִת, וּרְאִיתֶם
אֹתוֹ וּזְכַרְתֶּם אֶת־כָּל־מִצְוֹת יהוה וַעֲשִׂיתֶם אֹתָם, וְלֹא תָתוּרוּ
אַחֲרֵי לְבַבְכֶם וְאַחֲרֵי עֵינֵיכֶם, אֲשֶׁר־אַתֶּם זֹנִים אַחֲרֵיהֶם: לְמַעַן
תִּזְכְּרוּ וַעֲשִׂיתֶם אֶת־כָּל־מִצְוֹתָי, וִהְיִיתֶם קְדֹשִׁים לֵאלֹהֵיכֶם: אֲנִי
יהוה אֱלֹהֵיכֶם, אֲשֶׁר הוֹצֵאתִי אֶתְכֶם מֵאֶרֶץ מִצְרַיִם, לִהְיוֹת לָכֶם
לֵאלֹהִים, אֲנִי יהוה אֱלֹהֵיכֶם:
°אֱמֶת

The שליח ציבור *repeats:*

› יהוה אֱלֹהֵיכֶם אֱמֶת

Divine Throne, typically positioned in Heaven. Having been punished and
denied entry into the land, the Jews were deprived of a national station in
Yerushalayim directly beneath the Divine Throne. *Tzitzit* allowed them to
direct their imaginations back to that Divine Throne even when dislocated
from the Land of Israel.

These two mitzvot are so basic that they aren't accomplished by an *additional* activity. Merely wearing *tzitzit* and living in Israel yield the performance
of mitzvot. Distinct activity-based mitzvot allow an intense but limited
interaction with HaKadosh Barukh Hu. Living in Israel and wearing *tzitzit*
reflect a more holistic experience of interaction with God, independent of
framed activities.

TEKHELET AND GEULA

The Torah describes *Tzitzit* as a mitzva which bolsters general consciousness
of *all mitzvot*: "for you to look at and thereby remember all of God's mitzvot and obey them" (*Bemidbar* 15:39).

In several places the Gemara cites Rabbi Meir who claimed that the unique
tekhelet coloration of *Tzitzit* gives the mitzva this extraordinary feature. He
claimed that the color *tekhelet* is reminiscent of the ocean, which itself is
evocative of the sky (to which the ocean connects at the horizon), which in
turn conjures visions of the Divine Throne which is situated in Heaven, and
is also rendered in blueish hues: "And they saw the God of Israel. Under His

וְיַצִּיב **And firm,** established and enduring, right, faithful,
beloved, cherished, delightful, pleasant,
awesome, mighty, perfect, accepted,
good and beautiful
is this faith for us for ever.

True is the eternal God, our King,
Rock of Jacob, Shield of our salvation.
He exists and His name exists
through all generations.
His throne is established,
His kingship and faithfulness endure for ever.

At °, kiss the tzitziot and release them.

His words live and persist, faithful and desirable
°for ever and all time.

‣ So they were for our ancestors,
so they are for us,
and so they will be for our children
and all our generations
and for all future generations
of the seed of Israel, Your servants. ‣

For the early and the later generations
this faith has proved good and enduring for ever –

True and faithful, an irrevocable law.

True You are the LORD:
our God and God of our ancestors,
‣ our King and King of our ancestors,
our Redeemer and Redeemer of our ancestors,
our Maker,
Rock of our salvation,
our Deliverer and Rescuer:
this has ever been Your name.
There is no God but You.

וְיַצִּיב, וְנָכוֹן וְקַיָּם, וְיָשָׁר וְנֶאֱמָן

וְאָהוּב וְחָבִיב, וְנֶחְמָד וְנָעִים

וְנוֹרָא וְאַדִּיר, וּמְתֻקָּן וּמְקֻבָּל

וְטוֹב וְיָפֶה

הַדָּבָר הַזֶּה עָלֵינוּ לְעוֹלָם וָעֶד.

אֱמֶת אֱלֹהֵי עוֹלָם מַלְכֵּנוּ, צוּר יַעֲקֹב מָגֵן יִשְׁעֵנוּ

לְדוֹר וָדוֹר הוּא קַיָּם וּשְׁמוֹ קַיָּם

וְכִסְאוֹ נָכוֹן

וּמַלְכוּתוֹ וֶאֱמוּנָתוֹ לָעַד קַיָּמֶת.

At °, kiss the ציצית and release them.

וּדְבָרָיו חָיִים וְקַיָּמִים, נֶאֱמָנִים וְנֶחֱמָדִים

°לָעַד וּלְעוֹלְמֵי עוֹלָמִים

‹ עַל אֲבוֹתֵינוּ וְעָלֵינוּ

עַל בָּנֵינוּ וְעַל דּוֹרוֹתֵינוּ

‹ וְעַל כָּל דּוֹרוֹת זֶרַע יִשְׂרָאֵל עֲבָדֶיךָ. ›

עַל הָרִאשׁוֹנִים וְעַל הָאַחֲרוֹנִים

דָּבָר טוֹב וְקַיָּם לְעוֹלָם וָעֶד

אֱמֶת וֶאֱמוּנָה, חֹק וְלֹא יַעֲבֹר.

אֱמֶת שָׁאַתָּה הוּא יהוה אֱלֹהֵינוּ וֵאלֹהֵי אֲבוֹתֵינוּ

‹ מַלְכֵּנוּ מֶלֶךְ אֲבוֹתֵינוּ

גּוֹאֲלֵנוּ גּוֹאֵל אֲבוֹתֵינוּ

יוֹצְרֵנוּ צוּר יְשׁוּעָתֵנוּ

פּוֹדֵנוּ וּמַצִּילֵנוּ מֵעוֹלָם שְׁמֶךָ

אֵין אֱלֹהִים זוּלָתֶךָ.

עֶזְרַת You have always been the help of our ancestors,
Shield and Savior of their children after them
in every generation.
Your dwelling is in the heights of the universe,
and Your judgments and righteousness
reach to the ends of the earth.
Happy is the one who obeys Your commandments
and takes to heart Your teaching and Your word.

True   You are the Master of Your people
and a mighty King who pleads their cause.

True   You are the first and You are the last.
Besides You, we have no king,
redeemer or savior.

Rabbeinu Sa'adia Gaon (*Emunot VeDeot Ma'amar Shelishi*) and Ramban (*Shir HaShirim* 8:13), and forms the baseline of our conviction that the modern State is a Messianic event. Even though it originated from various geopolitical currents, it is the launch of our redemption. Just as Koresh was dispatched by HaKadosh Barukh Hu as an "agent," similarly the Balfour declaration and the UN declaration are divine instruments to return our people to our land.

The Gemara (*Sanhedrin* 98a) contrasted two different imageries of the arrival of *Mashiaḥ*. Daniel the prophet envisions him hovering upon heavenly clouds, whereas Zekharia pictures him journeying upon an unsteady donkey. The Gemara reconciles these divergent narratives as referring to two different redemptive schemes. If we merit redemption, the process is likened to celestial clouds; if *Mashiaḥ* arrives despite our unworthiness, it is likened to a donkey. One of the differences between these images is whether redemption is supernatural (heavenly clouds) or natural (as in a donkey ride). The less we deserve redemption, the more natural its packaging.

עֶזְרַת אֲבוֹתֵינוּ אַתָּה הוּא מֵעוֹלָם
מָגֵן וּמוֹשִׁיעַ לִבְנֵיהֶם אַחֲרֵיהֶם בְּכָל דּוֹר וָדוֹר.
בְּרוּם עוֹלָם מוֹשָׁבֶךָ
וּמִשְׁפָּטֶיךָ וְצִדְקָתְךָ עַד אַפְסֵי אָרֶץ.
אַשְׁרֵי אִישׁ שֶׁיִּשְׁמַע לְמִצְוֹתֶיךָ
וְתוֹרָתְךָ וּדְבָרְךָ יָשִׂים עַל לִבּוֹ.

אֱמֶת אַתָּה הוּא אָדוֹן לְעַמֶּךָ
וּמֶלֶךְ גִּבּוֹר לָרִיב רִיבָם.

אֱמֶת אַתָּה הוּא רִאשׁוֹן וְאַתָּה הוּא אַחֲרוֹן
וּמִבַּלְעָדֶיךָ אֵין לָנוּ מֶלֶךְ גּוֹאֵל וּמוֹשִׁיעַ.

NATURAL AND SUPERNATURAL REDEMPTION

One of the central questions regarding our final redemption is whether it will be launched through human convention or be completely driven by supernatural forces. The simple reading of this verse implies that humans cannot provide redemption, and only God can be relied upon for this event. Rabbi David Kimchi (Radak) inverts the literal meaning of this verse: Without divine authorization, redemption cannot occur. However HaKadosh Barukh Hu can affect *geula* through human initiation.

Human initiation can occur in two different fashions – a Jewish initiative, and/or an international effort. Rabbi Kimchi addresses the second form – a redemption which is prompted by international or political events. He cites the return from Bavel through the authorization of Koresh as a precedent for an internationally driven redemptive process. In fact Koresh is referred to as *Mashiaḥ* (*Yeshayahu* 45:1), further strengthening the idea that redemption can be triggered by political forces. This belief was also asserted by both

From Egypt You redeemed us,
Lᴏʀᴅ our God,
and from the slave-house You delivered us.
All their firstborn You killed,
but Your firstborn You redeemed.
You split the Sea of Reeds
and drowned the arrogant.
You brought Your beloved ones across.
The water covered their foes;
not one of them was left.

Ps. 106

For this, the beloved ones praised and exalted God,
the cherished ones sang psalms, songs and praises,
blessings and thanksgivings to the King,
the living and enduring God.
High and exalted, great and awesome,

---

was told that if/when Pharaoh would refuse, HaKadosh Barukh Hu would execute Pharaoh's firstborn. Though this plague only occurred on the night of the exodus, an ominous sense of inevitability was tangible from the outset.

Aside from threatening the Egyptians, this warning and eventual realization introduced the Jewish people to a new feature of their relationship with God. The *Avot* had discovered Him as Creator, appreciated Him as Judge, and revered Him as King. They had never viewed Him as a Father. By announcing His interest in and protection of His "firstborn child," HaKadosh Barukh Hu encouraged His people to view Him as a Father.

Furthermore, by referring to us as *"firstborn"* we are reminded that we are not alone as children of God, but share that status with all human beings. We are chosen for added responsibility in the same fashion that a firstborn child has additional duties to the family.

As Rabbi Akiva articulated so clearly (Mishna *Avot* 3:14), "Man is beloved since he was created in the Divine image…. Jews are especially cherished since they are referred to as children of God."

מִמִּצְרַיִם גְּאַלְתָּנוּ, יהוה אֱלֹהֵינוּ
וּמִבֵּית עֲבָדִים פְּדִיתָנוּ
כָּל בְּכוֹרֵיהֶם הָרָגְתָּ, וּבְכוֹרְךָ גָּאָלְתָּ
וְיַם סוּף בָּקַעְתָּ
וְזֵדִים טִבַּעְתָּ
וִידִידִים הֶעֱבַרְתָּ
וַיְכַסּוּ־מַיִם צָרֵיהֶם, אֶחָד מֵהֶם לֹא נוֹתָר:

תהלים קו

עַל זֹאת שִׁבְּחוּ אֲהוּבִים, וְרוֹמְמוּ אֵל
וְנָתְנוּ יְדִידִים זְמִירוֹת, שִׁירוֹת וְתִשְׁבָּחוֹת
בְּרָכוֹת וְהוֹדָאוֹת לְמֶלֶךְ אֵל חַי וְקַיָּם
רָם וְנִשָּׂא, גָּדוֹל וְנוֹרָא

כָּל בְּכוֹרֵיהֶם הָרָגְתָּ, וּבְכוֹרְךָ גָּאָלְתָּ *All their firstborn You killed, but Your firstborn You redeemed.* This *berakha* contains an extensive list of exploits which HaKadosh Barukh Hu performed on behalf of the Jewish people during the exodus from Egypt. Particularly noteworthy are the actual liberation and the splitting of the Sea, seven days later. These two events bracket the entire process, and they dominate the first and last days of Pesaḥ respectively. The list also mentions *Makkat Bekhorot* (the slaying of the firstborn), and the Tur (*Oraḥ Ḥayyim* 66) claims that our *Tefilla* must include a mention of this plague. Additionally the syntax of Maariv also includes a prominent reference to the last plague of *Bekhorot*: "Who smote in His wrath all the firstborn of Egypt, and brought out His people Israel from their midst."

The prominence of this plague is due to its serving as the climax, as well as the back breaker. After this plague Pharaoh was devastated and demoralized, and could no longer resist Moshe's requests.

Ironically, although it was the final plague, it was the first to be reported. When God originally dispatched Moshe to approach Pharaoh He told him to warn Pharaoh to release "*My child the People of Israel*." Furthermore, Moshe

He humbles the haughty
and raises the lowly,
freeing captives
and redeeming those in need,
helping the poor
and answering His people when they cry out to Him.

Stand in preparation for the Amida.
Take three steps back before beginning the Amida.

▸ Praises to God Most High,
the Blessed One who is blessed.
Moses and the children of Israel
recited to You a song with great joy,
and they all exclaimed:

"Who is like You, Lᴏʀᴅ, among the mighty?   *Ex. 15*
Who is like You, majestic in holiness,
awesome in praises, doing wonders?"

▸ With a new song, the redeemed people praised
Your name at the seashore.
Together they all gave thanks,
proclaimed Your kingship,
and declared:

"The Lᴏʀᴅ shall reign for ever and ever."   *Ex. 15*

Congregants should end the following blessing together
with the Leader so as to be able to move directly from the words
"redeemed Israel" to the Amida, without the interruption of saying Amen.

▸ צוּר יִשְׂרָאֵל Rock of Israel!
Arise to the help of Israel.
Deliver, as You promised, Judah and Israel.
Our Redeemer, the Lᴏʀᴅ of hosts is His name,   *Is. 47*
the Holy One of Israel.
Blessed are You, Lᴏʀᴅ,
who redeemed Israel.

מַשְׁפִּיל גֵּאִים וּמַגְבִּיהַּ שְׁפָלִים

מוֹצִיא אֲסִירִים, וּפוֹדֶה עֲנָוִים וְעוֹזֵר דַּלִּים

וְעוֹנֶה לְעַמּוֹ בְּעֵת שַׁוְּעָם אֵלָיו.

Stand in preparation for the עמידה.
Take three steps back before beginning the עמידה.

‹ תְּהִלּוֹת לְאֵל עֶלְיוֹן, בָּרוּךְ הוּא וּמְבֹרָךְ

מֹשֶׁה וּבְנֵי יִשְׂרָאֵל

לְךָ עָנוּ שִׁירָה בְּשִׂמְחָה רַבָּה

וְאָמְרוּ כֻלָּם

שמות טו   מִי־כָמֹכָה בָּאֵלִם, יהוה

מִי כָּמֹכָה נֶאְדָּר בַּקֹּדֶשׁ

נוֹרָא תְהִלֹּת, עֹשֵׂה פֶלֶא:

‹ שִׁירָה חֲדָשָׁה שִׁבְּחוּ גְאוּלִים

לְשִׁמְךָ עַל שְׂפַת הַיָּם

יַחַד כֻּלָּם הוֹדוּ וְהִמְלִיכוּ

וְאָמְרוּ

שמות טו   יהוה יִמְלֹךְ לְעֹלָם וָעֶד:

The קהל *should end the following blessing together with the* שליח ציבור
so as to be able to move directly from the words גָּאַל יִשְׂרָאֵל *to*
the עמידה, *without the interruption of saying* אמן.

‹ צוּר יִשְׂרָאֵל

קוּמָה בְּעֶזְרַת יִשְׂרָאֵל

וּפְדֵה כִנְאֻמֶךָ יְהוּדָה וְיִשְׂרָאֵל.

ישעיה מז   גֹּאֲלֵנוּ יהוה צְבָאוֹת שְׁמוֹ, קְדוֹשׁ יִשְׂרָאֵל:

בָּרוּךְ אַתָּה יהוה, גָּאַל יִשְׂרָאֵל.

THE AMIDA

The following prayer, until "in former years" on page 324, is said standing with feet together in imitation of the angels in Ezekiel's vision (Ezek. 1:7). The Amida is said silently, following the precedent of Hannah when she prayed for a child (1 Sam. 1:13). If there is a minyan, it is repeated aloud by the Leader. Take three steps forward, as if formally entering the place of the Divine Presence. At the points indicated by ˋ, bend the knees at the first word, bow at the second, and stand straight before saying God's name.

O Lord, open my lips,   Ps. 51
so that my mouth may declare Your praise.

PATRIARCHS

בָּרוּךְˋ Blessed are You, Lord our God and God of our fathers,
God of Abraham, God of Isaac and God of Jacob;
the great, mighty and awesome God, God Most High,
who bestows acts of loving-kindness and creates all,
who remembers the loving-kindness of the fathers
and will bring a Redeemer to their children's children
for the sake of His name, in love.
King, Helper, Savior, Shield:
ˋBlessed are You, Lord, Shield of Abraham.

---

mission, considerable struggle, but also a terminus of redemption. Though the merits of our Fathers may not influence particular phases of this process, the overall arc cannot be altered. Redemption is inevitable and we are expected to invoke the *Avot* as we petition for the conclusion of that arc of history. Hence we conclude the first paragraph of the first *berakha* of the *Shemoneh Esreh* by reminding HaKadosh Barukh Hu of the virtues of the *Avot* with the expectation that in turn He will produce a redeemer for their descendants.

Similarly we invoke the inevitability of redemption in our added sections on Rosh HaShana. Before mentioning the holiness of the day we insert a phrase attesting to the reliability and durability of the divine promise, "and Your word is true and endures for ever."

Rabbi Yosef Karo in his work the *Beit Yosef* (*Oraḥ Ḥayyim* 581) interprets this phrase to refer to the inevitability of an unconditional redemption. His word – *particularly about redemption* – is reliable precisely because it will materialize regardless of human cooperation or deservedness.

עמידה

The following prayer, until קָדְמֹנִיּוֹת *on page 325, is said standing with feet together*
*in imitation of the angels in Ezekiel's vision (*יחזקאל א, ז*). The* עמידה *is said silently,*
*following the precedent of Hannah when she prayed for a child (*שמואל א׳ א, יג*). If there*
is a מניין*, it is repeated aloud by the* שליח ציבור*. Take three steps forward, as if formally*
entering the place of the Divine Presence. At the points indicated by ׳*, bend the knees*
at the first word, bow at the second, and stand straight before saying God's name.

תהלים נא

אֲדֹנָי, שְׂפָתַי תִּפְתָּח, וּפִי יַגִּיד תְּהִלָּתֶךָ:

אבות

יבָּרוּךְ אַתָּה יהוה, אֱלֹהֵינוּ וֵאלֹהֵי אֲבוֹתֵינוּ

אֱלֹהֵי אַבְרָהָם, אֱלֹהֵי יִצְחָק, וֵאלֹהֵי יַעֲקֹב

הָאֵל הַגָּדוֹל הַגִּבּוֹר וְהַנּוֹרָא, אֵל עֶלְיוֹן

גּוֹמֵל חֲסָדִים טוֹבִים, וְקֹנֵה הַכֹּל

וְזוֹכֵר חַסְדֵי אָבוֹת

וּמֵבִיא גוֹאֵל לִבְנֵי בְנֵיהֶם לְמַעַן שְׁמוֹ בְּאַהֲבָה.

מֶלֶךְ עוֹזֵר וּמוֹשִׁיעַ וּמָגֵן.

יבָּרוּךְ אַתָּה יהוה, מָגֵן אַבְרָהָם.

Who remembers the וְזוֹכֵר חַסְדֵי אָבוֹת, וּמֵבִיא גוֹאֵל לִבְנֵי בְנֵיהֶם לְמַעַן שְׁמוֹ בְּאַהֲבָה
loving-kindness of the fathers, and will bring a Redeemer to their children's children,
for the sake of His name, in love. The Gemara (*Shabbat* 55a) comments that the
merits or virtues of our forefathers have already expired. Throughout earlier
generations HaKadosh Barukh Hu redeemed us based on debts owed to our
Avot for their faith and sacrifice. Though the Gemara is ambiguous about
when these merits were depleted, it was pretty clear to the later *Amora'im*
(c. second–third century) that the assets had already expired.

Many commentators question this Gemara since we constantly evoke the
merit of our forefathers when we pray. In his halakhic work, the *Tur* – Rabbi
Yaakov Ben Asher (c. twelfth–thirteenth century) asserts that there is one
area of national experience for which the merits of our Fathers is interminable.
God enacted a pact with the founders of our people which included a historical

DIVINE MIGHT

אַתָּה גִּבּוֹר You are eternally mighty, LORD.
You give life to the dead
and have great power to save.

In Israel: He causes the dew to fall.

He sustains the living with loving-kindness,
and with great compassion revives the dead.
He supports the fallen, heals the sick,
sets captives free,
and keeps His faith with those who sleep in the dust.
Who is like You, Master of might,
and to whom can You be compared,
O King who brings death and gives life,
and makes salvation grow?
Faithful are You to revive the dead.
Blessed are You, LORD,
who revives the dead.

When saying the Amida silently, continue with "You are holy" on page 296.

---

as well as burial. In fact, Ulla wept upon realizing that he would pass away outside of Israel. When attempts were made to console him based on assurances that he would be buried in Israel, he agonized, "I am still sad that I am losing a pearl (an idiom for passing away) in an impure land. You cannot compare ejecting [that pearl] in a mother's womb to ejecting it in a foreign land" (*Yerushalmi Kilayim* 9).

One statement is even critical of the burial of Jews who didn't ever reside in the Land. Rabbi Barkira challenged Rabbi Eliezer: "What is the value of these [people who live outside of Israel and are buried here]? They have rendered my land an abomination by neglecting it, and now they impurify it – by being buried here!" (The actual quote of the verse in *Yirmiyahu* 2:7 reads, "I brought you into a fertile land to eat its fruit and rich produce. But you came and defiled My land and made My inheritance detestable.")

In response to Rabbi Barkira's admonition, Rabbi Eliezer assures him that when these bodies arrive for burial, some earth from the Land of Israel

גבורות

אַתָּה גִּבּוֹר לְעוֹלָם, אֲדֹנָי

מְחַיֵּה מֵתִים אַתָּה, רַב לְהוֹשִׁיעַ

מוֹרִיד הַטָּל בארץ ישראל

מְכַלְכֵּל חַיִּים בְּחֶסֶד, מְחַיֵּה מֵתִים בְּרַחֲמִים רַבִּים

סוֹמֵךְ נוֹפְלִים, וְרוֹפֵא חוֹלִים, וּמַתִּיר אֲסוּרִים

וּמְקַיֵּם אֱמוּנָתוֹ לִישֵׁנֵי עָפָר.

מִי כָמוֹךָ, בַּעַל גְּבוּרוֹת

וּמִי דּוֹמֶה לָּךְ

מֶלֶךְ, מֵמִית וּמְחַיֶּה וּמַצְמִיחַ יְשׁוּעָה.

וְנֶאֱמָן אַתָּה לְהַחֲיוֹת מֵתִים.

בָּרוּךְ אַתָּה יהוה, מְחַיֵּה הַמֵּתִים.

When saying the עמידה silently, continue with אַתָּה קָדוֹשׁ on page 297.

_____

וְנֶאֱמָן אַתָּה לְהַחֲיוֹת מֵתִים *Faithful are You to revive the dead.* The significance
of burial in the Land of Israel isn't explicitly mentioned in the Torah but is
evident from both Yaakov and Yosef's concern for this opportunity. In each
instance considerable resources were invested in achieving this goal.

The primary benefit of burial in Israel is implied by a *pasuk* which asserts
that "His land will atone for His people" (*Devarim* 32:43). Based upon this
concept Rabbi Levi claimed that "Whoever dwells in the Land of Israel and
dies there is guaranteed entry into the next world." Rabbi Neḥemya added
that "The Land of Israel atones for all sins of those who die there" (*Midrash
Mishlei* 17). This interpretation highlights living and dying, but not necessarily
burial, in Israel as an apparatus of atonement. A similar statement based on
the aforementioned *pasuk* remarks that "Whoever is buried in the Land of
Israel is considered buried underneath the altar" (*Ketubot* 111a) – suggesting
that *burial* provides atonement, just as a sacrifice upon an altar.

Apparently Ḥazal placed great emphasis both on actually *dying* in Israel

KEDUSHA

During the Leader's Repetition, the following is said standing
with feet together, rising on the toes at the words indicated by ▲.

Cong. then נְקַדֵּשׁ We will sanctify Your name on earth,
Leader: as they sanctify it in the highest heavens,
    as is written by Your prophet,
    "And they [the angels] call to one another saying: *Is. 6*

Cong. then ▲Holy, ▲holy, ▲holy is the LORD of hosts
Leader: the whole world is filled with His glory."
    Those facing them say "Blessed – "

Cong. then ▲"Blessed is the LORD's glory from His place."   *Ezek. 3*
Leader: And in Your holy Writings it is written thus:

Cong. then ▲"The LORD shall reign for ever. He is your God, Zion, *Ps. 146*
Leader: from generation to generation, Halleluya!"

Leader: From generation to generation
   we will declare Your greatness,
   and we will proclaim Your holiness for evermore.
   Your praise, our God, shall not leave our mouth forever,
   for You, God, are a great and holy King.
   Blessed are You, LORD,
   the holy God.

The Leader continues with "You grace humanity" on page 298.

---

adjusts his opinion claiming that those buried outside of Israel must experience "*gilgul*" (a cycling); they will spin back to Israel, and after arrival become resurrected. The Gemara admits that the righteous who are buried outside of Israel merit passage through supernatural shafts to eliminate the pain of "*gilgul*." The uncertainty of being granted these "shafts" worried both Yaakov and Yosef, and compelled them to request burial or re-interment in Israel.

 Tragically the two greatest leaders to be denied burial in Israel were Aharon and Moshe. HaKadosh Barukh Hu comforts them by tasking them with assisting Jews buried outside the Land of Israel in their more challenging

קדושה

During חזרת הש״ץ, *the following is said standing*
with feet together, rising on the toes at the words indicated by ▲.

קהל <br> then
 ש״ץ: נְקַדֵּשׁ אֶת שִׁמְךָ בָּעוֹלָם

כְּשֵׁם שֶׁמַּקְדִּישִׁים אוֹתוֹ בִּשְׁמֵי מָרוֹם

ישעיה ו כַּכָּתוּב עַל יַד נְבִיאֶךָ, וְקָרָא זֶה אֶל־זֶה וְאָמַר

קהל <br> then
 ש״ץ: ▲קָדוֹשׁ, ▲קָדוֹשׁ, ▲קָדוֹשׁ, יהוה צְבָאוֹת, מְלֹא כָל־הָאָרֶץ כְּבוֹדוֹ:

לְעֻמָּתָם בָּרוּךְ יֹאמֵרוּ

קהל <br> then
 ש״ץ: יחזקאל ג ▲בָּרוּךְ כְּבוֹד־יהוה מִמְּקוֹמוֹ:

וּבְדִבְרֵי קָדְשְׁךָ כָּתוּב לֵאמֹר

קהל <br> then
 ש״ץ: תהלים קמו ▲יִמְלֹךְ יהוה לְעוֹלָם, אֱלֹהַיִךְ צִיּוֹן לְדֹר וָדֹר, הַלְלוּיָהּ:

ש״ץ: לְדוֹר וָדוֹר נַגִּיד גָּדְלֶךָ

וּלְנֵצַח נְצָחִים קְדֻשָּׁתְךָ נַקְדִּישׁ

וְשִׁבְחֲךָ אֱלֹהֵינוּ מִפִּינוּ לֹא יָמוּשׁ לְעוֹלָם וָעֶד

כִּי אֵל מֶלֶךְ גָּדוֹל וְקָדוֹשׁ אָתָּה.

בָּרוּךְ אַתָּה יהוה, הָאֵל הַקָּדוֹשׁ.

The שליח ציבור *continues with* אַתָּה חוֹנֵן *on page 299.*

---

is placed upon the coffin to fulfill the verse "and His Land will atone for His people." Based on this response a *minhag* developed to place earth from Israel alongside the coffin even for those who are buried in Ḥutz LaAretz.

A second advantage of burial in Israel surrounds resurrection. In *Tehillim* 116 David HaMelekh aspires, "I will walk in the presence of God in the land of life." The future tense of this statement suggests that he is referring to resurrection, and more so, the term "land of life" indicates that there may be a specific set of coordinates for this future event. In fact the Gemara in *Ketubot* records the initial opinion of Rabbi Elazar that those who are buried in Ḥutz LaAretz aren't resurrected. Unwilling to accept this exclusion the Gemara

HOLINESS

אַתָּה קָדוֹשׁ You are holy and Your name is holy,
and holy ones praise You daily, Selah!
Blessed are You, Lord, the holy God.

The Gemara (*Pesaḥim* 50b) announces that "*harugei malkhut*" – those who are murdered or executed because of their Jewish identity – ascend to a surpassing level in the afterlife (literally "no one can reside in their midst"). The term "*harugei malkhut*" extends martyr status beyond those who defied pressure to surrender religious values or violate religious practice. This status as "sacred martyr" has been applied throughout Jewish history to all those who were murdered based on their Jewish identity – even those who had no option to be saved by denouncing their religion (see Maharil response 99 and Ḥatam Sofer *Yoreh De'a* 333).

After introducing the general term "*harugei malkhut*" the Gemara specifically refers to the "martyrs of Lod." This episode concerns two brothers who voluntarily admitted – falsely – that they had murdered a Roman girl. The Roman authorities had accused the entire city of Lod, and had threatened to exact retribution. By offering their own guilt, these two brothers rescued numerous Jews. For this act of heroism they were designated holy martyrs. By extension those who die while protecting other Jews are clearly part of this category of *harugei malkhut*. Israeli soldiers who fall while protecting our country would obviously be considered *harugei malkhut*.

Beyond performing *Kiddush Hashem* in this classic sense, Israeli soldiers fulfill a broader level of sanctifying His name. The Midrash (*Sifrei Zuta* 10:33) contrasts the military tactics of Jewish soldiers battling for the Land of Israel with classic military approaches. Typically, even fervent and eager soldiers are frightened when entering the battlefield. Jewish soldiers who battle for Israel readily and fearlessly enter battle, stirred by the prospect of entering or defending the Land of Israel. They reason that even if they die immediately on the battlefield their lives have been substantiated by encountering or protecting the land which Moshe was denied.

Unlike some cultures which lionize death and martyrdom, Judaism celebrates life, and Halakha is generally discarded when it clashes with danger of death. With the exception of the three cardinal sins, any halakha should be

קדושת השם

אַתָּה קָדוֹשׁ וְשִׁמְךָ קָדוֹשׁ
וּקְדוֹשִׁים בְּכָל יוֹם יְהַלְלוּךָ סֶּלָה.
בָּרוּךְ אַתָּה יהוה, הָאֵל הַקָּדוֹשׁ.

---

resurrection. From a metaphoric standpoint, their love and commitment to Jewish *people* supersedes their desire for the *Land*.

KEDUSHAT HASHEM AND KIDDUSH HASHEM

Kiddush Hashem – to disseminate the presence of HaKadosh Barukh Hu – is our purpose in this world, both individually and as a nation. When the Jewish people are denuded of national identity and common united experience, we are unable to fully represent Him as a nation. When we return to our homeland and build a Jewish state, we possess an opportunity to broadcast our message at a national level.

Kiddush Hashem is expressed primarily by the lifestyles we lead and the societies we create. The mitzva also demands that we sacrifice our lives on behalf of His will – if called upon. The ethic of Jewish martyrdom was established through two experiences of our founding father Avraham: his defiance of pagan culture and being cast into a furnace, and his willingness to obey the divine will and sacrifice his son. These two formative moments established the paradigm of *Kiddush Hashem* within the Jewish consciousness.

After the destruction of the first *Beit HaMikdash* three prophets – Ḥananya, Misha'el, and Azaria – reinforced this value by defying Nebuchadnezzar and refusing to bow to his towering idol. At this critical juncture – the first Jewish foray into exile – the ethic of *Kiddush Hashem* was reanimated.

Hundreds of years later Rabbi Akiva and the Ten Martyrs faced Roman brutality and forfeited their lives in God's name. On the eve of our 2000-year exile, these heroes shaped an experience which would buoy Jewish survival during the long journey through the Diaspora. The Jewish people faced unparalleled discrimination and persecution, but defied the entire world by maintaining their commitment to pure monotheism and to our historic covenant with God, even at the threat of death.

KNOWLEDGE

אַתָּה חוֹנֵן You grace humanity with knowledge
and teach mortals understanding.
Grace us with the knowledge, understanding
and discernment that come from You.
Blessed are You, LORD,
who graciously grants knowledge.

---

the Land of Israel and that, by extension, prophecy can only be attained
within the confines of Israel.

Our Sages were sensitive to this advantage, and displayed clear preference
to the Torah Sages of the Land of Israel. The Gemara in *Bava Metzia* speaks
of Rabbi Zeira (who first coined the phrase *Avira d'Eretz Yisrael Maḥkim*)
fasting one hundred fasts when he moved to Israel, to help purge his intellect of the inferior Torah he had studied outside the Land. Similarly Abaye is
recorded (*Ketubot* 85a) as claiming that one scholar from Israel is equivalent
in knowledge to two scholars from abroad.

The scholars in Israel were also known to study more harmoniously, while
their counterparts in Bavel studied more contentiously (*Sanhedrin* 24a).
Some attributed the more direct and succinct style of Israel-based sages to
this more amicable process.

Ultimately life in Israel under Roman rule became incompatible with
widespread quality Torah study, and the epicenter of Torah shifted to Bavel.
This shift conferred supremacy to the *Talmud Bavli*, which comprises the
main body of Talmudic study.

Modern times have witnessed the renaissance of the Land of Israel as a
Torah center. The return of Israel to its original status signifies a redemptive
aspect of our national return.

Additionally the return to Israel has ignited a debate surrounding the style
of Torah study, and its possible adjustment to be better aligned with the perceived original style of learning in Israel. Rav Kook in particular examined
several differences between Torah study in Israel and abroad. His primary
distinction addressed the manner in which Torah study in Israel was more
holistic, and was pollinated both from prophetic and mystical elements, as
well as from broader cultural elements.

דעת
אַתָּה חוֹנֵן לְאָדָם דַּעַת
וּמְלַמֵּד לֶאֱנוֹשׁ בִּינָה.
חָנֵּנוּ מֵאִתְּךָ דֵּעָה בִּינָה וְהַשְׂכֵּל.
בָּרוּךְ אַתָּה יהוה, חוֹנֵן הַדָּעַת.

violated to preserve life. However, martyrdom – when imposed – is a central ingredient of Jewish history and has allowed our people to miraculously survive our long exile. Having returned to our Land, this experience still lends sanctity to our redemptive process.

דעת *Knowledge.* The Gemara (*Kiddushin* 49b) describes ten components of wisdom which were allocated to our world – nine of which were distributed within Israel. Interestingly, the Gemara doesn't merely accentuate the superior Torah knowledge potential within Israel, but also addresses general knowledge and wisdom. In a similar vein the Torah describes one of the four mystical rivers to emanate from Eden as circumscribing a land of gold whose gold is "good." The Midrash (*Bereshit Raba* 16:12) views this is as a reference to the Land of Israel which possesses superior and golden Torah knowledge.

The idea that the Land of Israel enabled greater access to both Torah knowledge and general wisdom was attributed to its being directly aligned with the celestial presence of God (see commentary on *Az Yashir*, page 252). The Gemara (*Bava Batra* 158a) introduces a phrase "*Avira d'Eretz Yisrael Maḥkim,*" that the air of Israel delivers greater intelligence. This phrase – which has become an often quoted adage, possibly implies a superior '"spiritual" quality to the Land, which enables greater acumen. Rabbi Moshe Isserles (the Rema) wrote that the higher intelligence available in Israel is due to genuine mitzva performance, which is only possible in this Land. Mitzvot aren't just opportunities to fulfill divine will; they enhance human intelligence (*Torah HaOla* 3:38).

Beyond the superior access to Torah knowledge and general wisdom, prophetic capacity can only be realized in the Land of Israel. The Gemara (*Mo'ed Katan* 25a) implies that the *Shekhina* cannot be encountered outside

REPENTANCE

הֲשִׁיבֵנוּ Bring us back, our Father, to Your Torah.
Draw us near, our King, to Your service.
Lead us back to You in perfect repentance.
Blessed are You, LORD,
who desires repentance.

Similarly, the Egyptian redemption is often attributed to the desire to avoid a *Ḥillul Hashem*. The Jewish people represent monotheism and morality, and when our nation declines, the presence of HaKadosh Barukh Hu regresses from view, and a *Ḥillul Hashem* develops. In Egypt the redemption occurred to *avoid* the regression of HaKadosh Barukh Hu; our *geula* may be partially in response to the desecration of God's presence produced by centuries of persecution of Jews, capped by the Holocaust.

A third factor which may contribute toward "non-*teshuva*" based redemption is the Jewish commitment to monotheism and disdain for idolatry. Despite lethargy in mitzva performance, our aversion to paganism remains steadfast and has re-landscaped the world from idolatry to monotheism.

Finally we are redeemed unconditionally due to the original covenants and oaths offered to our forefathers. As mentioned earlier (page 291) these assurances are immutable.

Even if redemption will occur without *teshuva* as a prerequisite, *teshuva* can certainly affect the schedule, pace and caliber of redemption. The Gemara (*Sanhedrin* 98a) notes an oxymoron describing the final redemption: "I am your God and will accelerate redemption in its time" (*Yeshayahu* 60:22). The Gemara comments on this paradox: "If we merit we will receive acceleration; if we don't, it will be delayed until its natural schedule."

A similar contradiction is raised by the Gemara when considering two different metaphors for the arrival of *Mashiaḥ*. One suggests an arrival upon a heavenly Chariot, whereas the alternative image describes a poor man wobbling upon a donkey. These two metaphors also depict alternative options of *geula*. A meritorious generation will enjoy a supernaturally driven redemption, whereas a less deserving population receives a slower redemption, powered by humans and packaged in human convention.

תשובה

הֲשִׁיבֵנוּ אָבִינוּ לְתוֹרָתֶךָ
וְקָרְבֵנוּ מַלְכֵּנוּ לַעֲבוֹדָתֶךָ
וְהַחֲזִירֵנוּ בִּתְשׁוּבָה שְׁלֵמָה לְפָנֶיךָ.
בָּרוּךְ אַתָּה יהוה, הָרוֹצֶה בִּתְשׁוּבָה.

הֲשִׁיבֵנוּ אָבִינוּ לְתוֹרָתֶךָ *Bring us back, our Father, to Your Torah.* Is *geula* (redemption) dependent upon *teshuva* (repentance)?

There is great ambiguity in Tanakh as to whether repentance will precede redemption as a necessary precondition, or whether redemption will occur unconditionally, prompting in its wake a mass repentance. This textual uncertainty yields a well-known dispute (*Sanhedrin* 97b) between Rabbi Elazar, who claimed that *teshuva* is a precondition of *geula*, and Rabbi Yehoshua, who claimed that redemption will occur independently.

Most major authorities supported Rabbi Yehoshua's position that our people will be redeemed even without a massive religious revival. A notable exception is the Rambam who claimed that *teshuva* is necessary for *ultimate* redemption. Even the Rambam believed that eventual mass *teshuva* is prophetically guaranteed – thereby assuring ultimate redemption, even if repentance serves as a prerequisite. Additionally the Rambam speaks of the *Mashiaḥ* as tasked with inciting a mass *teshuva*, while others assign this role to Eliyahu or to a preliminary *Mashiaḥ* referred to as *Mashiaḥ ben Yosef* (descending from the tribe of Yosef rather than the tribe of Yehuda). Regardless of the individual catalyzing mass *teshuva*, it appears that an initial redemptive personality can emerge even without prior *teshuva*, and motivate ultimate *teshuva*.

Several factors are identified as responsible for *geula* according to the opinions that it occurs independently of *teshuva*. One factor facilitating redemption is the *teshuva* and general religiosity of the righteous Jews – the *Tzaddikim*. Interestingly, the Midrash imputes the original redemption from Egypt to the virtuous conduct of the minority of righteous Jews. As the exodus from Egypt serves as a template for the final redemption, we might expect a similar dynamic.

FORGIVENESS

Strike the left side of the chest at °.

סְלַח לָנוּ Forgive us, our Father, for we have °sinned.

Pardon us, our King, for we have °transgressed;

for You pardon and forgive.

Blessed are You, LORD, the gracious One who repeatedly forgives.

REDEMPTION

רְאֵה Look on our affliction, plead our cause,

and redeem us soon for Your name's sake,

---

seventy-seven male lambs and, as a sin offering, twelve male goats…" (*Ezra* 8:35). Typically only non-intentional sins can be exonerated through sacrifices. Additionally there is no classic precedent for offering such numbers. Commenting on these anomalies the Gemara (*Horayot* 6a) claims that this process qualifies as "*hora'at sha'a*" or a special case with unique dispensations. Returning to Israel provides mitigating circumstances validating even non-conventional and partial forms of *teshuva*.

REDEMPTION FOR AN UNDESERVING WORLD

The Gemara (*Sanhedrin* 98a) claims that *Mashiaḥ ben David* will only arrive amidst a generation of surpassing merit or within a generation of complete moral and religious breakdown. Indeed, various depictions of the generation in which *Mashiaḥ* arrives describe moral decay and religious deterioration. Some of the images include the dwindling of Torah scholarship, isolation and scorning of the handful of righteous people, and the emergence of heretical leaders.

Presumably, a religiously malfunctioning generation doesn't *merit* the arrival of *Mashiaḥ*, but compels a divine response. History isn't open ended. If human behavior declines too severely, HaKadosh Barukh Hu must respond by delivering redemption even to undeserving people. The first redemption – from Egypt – was prompted by a national descent into the forty-ninth level of impurity – demanding an immediate and rapid extraction before it was too late. Of course the caliber and the pace of our final redemption might be negatively affected if it is pressured by a corrupt generation.

Some have understood that the redemptive scheme based on moral breakdown refers to unqualified animosity toward the Jewish people. If redemption isn't produced through Jewish merit, it can also stem from excessive

סְלִיחָה

Strike the left side of the chest at °.

סְלַח לָנוּ אָבִינוּ כִּי °חָטָאנוּ
מְחַל לָנוּ מַלְכֵּנוּ כִּי °פָשָֽׁעְנוּ
כִּי מוֹחֵל וְסוֹלֵחַ אָתָּה.
בָּרוּךְ אַתָּה יהוה, חַנּוּן הַמַּרְבֶּה לִסְלֹחַ.

גְּאוּלָה

רְאֵה בְעָנְיֵֽנוּ, וְרִיבָה רִיבֵֽנוּ
וּגְאָלֵֽנוּ מְהֵרָה לְמַֽעַן שְׁמֶֽךָ

RESIDENCE IN ISRAEL AND ATONEMENT OF SINS

Our license to this land is based on our being a chosen people, naturally suited to reside in a selected land. As we return to this land we are obliged to improve our personal state and national condition through *teshuva*. Part of the *Mashiaḥ*'s task includes awakening a national penitence.

Yet complete and authentic *teshuva* is sometimes beyond our immediate national capability. As Ezra and his faction return to Israel and near its borders, he launches a collective fast, in part to stimulate a national *teshuva*. Subsequently, he is informed that the returning Jews did not divorce the gentile wives they had married in Bavel. He is stunned by this heartbreaking news, and commences a heartfelt confessional on behalf of his people. It is unclear how successful this confessional was in redirecting Jewish marital conduct.

The first round of *Tokhaḥa* – embedded in *Parashat Beḥukotai* – is presumed to be a narration of the first exile and Ezra's recovery from this seventy-year interlude. The Torah describes the recovery: "But if they will confess their sins and the sins of their ancestors… I will remember my covenant… and I will remember the land" (*Vayikra* 26:40–42). The Ramban detects that the prophetic description doesn't include *actual* repentance, merely confession. The Jews did not succeed in comprehensive *teshuva* but their frank and genuine confession still succeeded in enabling their entry to Israel. Apparently even incomplete forms of *teshuva* are effective as we return to our land.

Additionally, the returnees accompanying Ezra offered a non-conventional sacrifice: "Then the exiles who had returned from captivity sacrificed burnt offerings to the God of Israel: twelve bulls for all Israel, ninety-six rams,

for You are a powerful Redeemer.
Blessed are You, LORD, the Redeemer of Israel.

HEALING

רְפָאֵנוּ Heal us, LORD, and we shall be healed.
Save us and we shall be saved, for You are our praise.
Bring complete recovery for all our ailments,

The following prayer for a sick person may be said here:

May it be Your will, O LORD my God and God of my ancestors, that You
speedily send a complete recovery from heaven, a healing of both soul and
body, to the patient (*name*), son/daughter of (*mother's name*) among the
other afflicted of Israel.

---

for You, God, King, are a faithful and compassionate Healer.
Blessed are You, LORD, Healer of the sick of His people Israel.

---

shifts the focus of the *berakha*. Subsequent *berakhot* in the *Amida* will address future and final redemption (for example the *berakha* of "*Et Tzemaḥ
David*" or the blessing of *VeLiYerushalayim*). However this *berakha* considers the innumerable moments in history in which God rescued His people
from peril.

This position – first asserted by Rashi (on *Megilla* 17b) – affirms a remarkable truth about redemptive history. God forged a covenant with the Jews.
History isn't open ended and it will be redeemed, along with His chosen
people, in His selected Land. However redemption is not a *singular* event
limited to location or to a specific formative event. Throughout history Jews
face stiff encounters with those who bristle at our message. In each generation
many rise up against us. By rescuing us from their threat, God is redeeming
His people, and allowing history to continue its inevitable redemptive arc.

A similar notion emerges from the conclusion of *Shemot* – known to Ḥazal
as the book of redemption. Although it begins with our liberation from Egypt,
it concludes *outside the boundaries of the Land of Israel*, when the Divine Presence finally nestles within the *Mishkan*. Enabling this encounter between
God and His people through the interface of the *Mishkan* is an ingredient
of the redemptive process, even if it is geographically dislocated from the
Land of Israel. Redemption is a lengthy process of creating divine presence
in our world, which culminates with the Jewish people residing in Israel, and
presiding over a world re-landscaped in the image of God.

כִּי גוֹאֵל חָזָק אָתָּה.
בָּרוּךְ אַתָּה יהוה, גּוֹאֵל יִשְׂרָאֵל.

רפואה

רְפָאֵנוּ יהוה וְנֵרָפֵא
הוֹשִׁיעֵנוּ וְנִוָּשֵׁעָה, כִּי תְהִלָּתֵנוּ אָתָּה
וְהַעֲלֵה רְפוּאָה שְׁלֵמָה לְכָל מַכּוֹתֵינוּ

The following prayer for a sick person may be said here:

יְהִי רָצוֹן מִלְּפָנֶיךָ יהוה אֱלֹהַי וֵאלֹהֵי אֲבוֹתַי, שֶׁתִּשְׁלַח מְהֵרָה רְפוּאָה שְׁלֵמָה
מִן הַשָּׁמַיִם רְפוּאַת הַנֶּפֶשׁ וּרְפוּאַת הַגּוּף לַחוֹלֶה/לַחוֹלָה *name of patient*
בֶּן/בַּת *mother's name* בְּתוֹךְ שְׁאָר חוֹלֵי יִשְׂרָאֵל.

כִּי אֵל מֶלֶךְ רוֹפֵא נֶאֱמָן וְרַחֲמָן אָתָּה.
בָּרוּךְ אַתָּה יהוה, רוֹפֵא חוֹלֵי עַמּוֹ יִשְׂרָאֵל.

hostility toward the Jewish people or their national state. The annihilation of the Jewish people would entail an intolerable *Hillul Hashem* or desecration of God's name. At this point HaKadosh Barukh Hu would intervene, and reorient history by redeeming them.

גּוֹאֵל יִשְׂרָאֵל *The Redeemer of Israel.* The *berakha* which most directly addresses our redemption concludes with an ambiguous phrase: "*Go'el Yisrael.*" Instead of referring to a past redemption, we proclaim that HaKadosh Barukh Hu "*redeems Israel,*" implying a current process. This syntax is in striking contrast with the terminology of the final *berakha* after *Keriat Shema* which concludes with the phrase "*Ga'al Yisrael*" – "who *redeemed* Israel [from Egypt]."

The obvious basis for this change is the specific context of *Shemoneh Esreh*. The *berakhot* after *Keriat Shema* offer an opportunity to relive our original redemption and draw strength for future *geula*. After iterating the various elements of the original redemption we conclude the *berakha* with the recognition of God as our past Redeemer. By contrast the *Shemoneh Esreh* is a list of prayerful requests, and in the seventh *berakha* we actively petition for future redemption. Instead of reviewing past events, we describe an attribute of HaKadosh Barukh Hu – that He is the Redeemer.

Some claim that the employment of the phrase *Go'el Yisrael* dramatically

PROSPERITY

בָּרֵךְ Bless this year for us, LORD our God,
and all its types of produce for good.
Grant blessing on the face of the earth,
and from its goodness satisfy us,
blessing our year as the best of years.
Blessed are You, LORD, who blesses the years.

INGATHERING OF EXILES

תְּקַע Sound the great shofar for our freedom,
raise high the banner to gather our exiles,

wither its fertility rather than benefit the intruders who had inhabited the land because of Jewish disloyalty. The land indeed diminished its output, reserving its full abundance for its natural residents.

In 1867, Mark Twain visited Palestine and famously captured the wretchedness of the landscape:

We traversed some miles of desolate country whose soil is rich enough but is given wholly to weeds – a silent mournful expanse [...] A desolation is here that not even imagination can grace with the pomp of life and action.

We reached Tabor safely...We never saw a human being on the whole route [...]

We pressed on toward the goal of our crusade, renowned Jerusalem. The further we went the hotter the sun got, and the more rocky and bare...the landscape became...There was hardly a tree or a shrub any where. Even the olive and the cactus, those fast friends of a worthless soil, had almost deserted the country. [...]

Palestine sits in sackcloth and ashes. Over it broods the spell of a curse that has withered its fields and fettered its energies. [...]

Palestine is desolate and unlovely. And why should it be otherwise? Can the curse of the Deity beautify a land?

Palestine is no more of this work-day world. It is sacred to poetry and tradition – it is dream-land.

(*The Innocents Abroad*. American Publishing Co., 1869)

תְּקַע בְּשׁוֹפָר גָּדוֹל לְחֵרוּתֵנוּ, וְשָׂא נֵס לְקַבֵּץ גָּלֻיּוֹתֵינוּ *Sound the great shofar for our freedom, raise high the banner to gather our exiles.* There is much debate as to

ברכת השנים

בָּרֵךְ עָלֵינוּ יהוה אֱלֹהֵינוּ אֶת הַשָּׁנָה הַזֹּאת
וְאֶת כָּל מִינֵי תְבוּאָתָהּ, לְטוֹבָה
וְתֵן בְּרָכָה עַל פְּנֵי הָאֲדָמָה
וְשַׂבְּעֵנוּ מִטּוּבָהּ, וּבָרֵךְ שְׁנָתֵנוּ כַּשָּׁנִים הַטּוֹבוֹת.
בָּרוּךְ אַתָּה יהוה, מְבָרֵךְ הַשָּׁנִים.

קבוץ גלויות

תְּקַע בְּשׁוֹפָר גָּדוֹל לְחֵרוּתֵנוּ
וְשָׂא נֵס לְקַבֵּץ גָּלֻיּוֹתֵינוּ

AGRICULTURAL SUCCESS AS AN OMEN OF REDEMPTION

וְתֵן בְּרָכָה עַל פְּנֵי הָאֲדָמָה *Grant blessing on the face of the earth.* The Gemara announces, "In the future [even] barren trees in Israel will produce fruit" (*Ketuvot* 112b). The dramatic resurgence in agricultural success signals the return of Israel's children to their homeland and the redemptive era. The Gemara in *Megilla* studies the sequence of blessings in the *Shemoneh Esreh*, placing the blessing for material and agricultural prosperity immediately prior to the blessing of Ingathering of Exiles. Inasmuch as the blossoming of our Land heralds the return to Yerushalayim and final redemption, structuring the *berakhot* in this manner reflects the final course of history.

In fact the final sections of *Massekhet Ketuvot* describe the immense abundance which the Land of Israel will one day yield. Though many of these descriptions seem hyperbolic, the overall image of bounty and plenty reminds us of the supernatural potency of the land which will once again be unlocked. To bolster their predictions many *Tanna'im* and *Amora'im* described actual situations in which they encountered such abundance – even after the *Mikdash* was destroyed. The land's fertility was so prodigious that its residue outlasted the destruction of the *Mikdash*.

Many have seen the blossoming of the Land of Israel in modern times as a signal of the redemptive nature of our return. For thousands of years the land remained fallow and desolate, unwilling to lend its fecundity to foreign populations. The Gemara records Rabbi Yehoshua ben Levi visiting a site in Israel and witnessing the outsized abundance. He implored the land to

and gather us together from the four quarters of the earth.
Blessed are You, LORD,
who gathers the dispersed of His people Israel.

---

the outcasts of Israel, 'I will collect them upon those [already] collected'"
(*Yeshayahu* 56:8). This final phrase, "I will collect them upon those [already]
collected," strongly suggests different phases of ingathering.

One of the metaphors for the arrival of *Mashiaḥ* is that of a "poor man atop
a donkey" (*Sanhedrin* 98a). This inelegant image of redemption will ensue if
the Jewish People don't merit the "express" form of redemption symbolized
by "Heavenly clouds." In his comments to the aforementioned Gemara Rashi
comments that a donkey ride is slow, awkward, and occurs in stages – the
ingathering will be slow and gradual. Similar themes are conveyed by the
Ramban in his comments to Yeshayahu's prophecy (see Chapter 56) that
HaKadosh Barukh Hu will "gather the outcasts of Israel … collect them upon
those [already] collected." Collecting those who have been collected portrays
an initial amassing followed by a subsequent collection (see Ramban on
Shir HaShirim 8:13).

Indeed, Jewish return to the Second Temple was also staged. Initially
the first wave of Jews returned and began to construct the foundations of
the *Mikdash*. Ultimately their efforts were blunted, and only eighteen years
afterwards did the next (final) wave arrive, fully construct the *Mikdash*, and
rebuild Yerushalayim.

Envisioning a staged ingathering allows the initial stages to precede the
arrival of *Mashiaḥ*. The process can begin without Messianic appearance,
leaving the concluding stages to be led by the individual described by the
Rambam.

JEWISH POPULATION EXPANSION
When Jewish history is launched, Avraham is assured that his children will
multiply as the dust of the earth (*Bereshit* 13:15–16). Subsequent promises
liken Jewish population to the stars of the heavens.

Presumably this promise is a metaphor to the eventual size, and perhaps
even caliber, of the Jewish people. Even as a metaphor the prophecy hasn't
materialized, as Jews rarely composed a significant percentage of the world
population. In fact Moshe warns the people of their inevitable exile and di-
minishing population: "The LORD will scatter you among the peoples, and
only a few of you will survive among the nations to which the LORD will

וְקַבְּצֵנוּ יַחַד מֵאַרְבַּע כַּנְפוֹת הָאָרֶץ.
בָּרוּךְ אַתָּה יהוה, מְקַבֵּץ נִדְחֵי עַמּוֹ יִשְׂרָאֵל.

whether the Ingathering of Exiles will precede *Mashiaḥ* or occur after his arrival and primarily through his efforts.

The Rambam (*Hilkhot Melakhim* 11:1) describes the *Mashiaḥ* as a king who "retrieves the exiled," suggesting that the ingathering must occur *after* his arrival. Yet his comments about renewing the original but lost tradition of *Semikha* imply that the assembly of the Jewish population in the Land of Israel may precede the *Mashiaḥ* and contribute toward his arrival.

This question is also addressed in a famous parable cited by Rashi. The seventieth chapter of *Tehillim* begins with the phrase, "For David to be remembered," implying that David is pleading a personal matter. Rashi elaborates by providing a parable about a king who, in a fury, dismantled his sheepfold, drove out his sheep and dismissed his shepherd. When his anger subsides he rebuilds the fold and returns his sheep. At this point the lonely shepherd pleads, "The fold is rebuilt, the sheep have returned, but I am excluded." David prays for his descendant who will feel similarly discounted. This parable portrays the return of the sheep (ingathering of exiles) and the rebuilding of the sheepfold (reconstruction of *Beit HaMikdash*) as occurring prior to the arrival of *Mashiaḥ*.

The body of this *berakha* describes "*galuyoteinu*" (a general term referencing all who are exiled), but the conclusion addresses those who are "*nidhei amo Yisrael*" – referring to those who are *forcibly* thrust from Israel or denied the ability to immigrate. At this point in history almost all the Jews who were "*nidhei*" – trapped in countries barring them immigration to Israel – have been released and have immigrated. Many Jews who live outside of Israel possess the "right" to immigrate but have chosen not to. Essentially, the *nidhei Yisrael* have *already been collected*, suggesting that this process is part of the divine prophecy of *Geula*.

This issue of "sequencing" forms a major point of dispute between those who view the modern State as redemptive and those who deny its redemptive nature. If the ingathering only occurs *after Mashiaḥ* arrives, the return of millions of Jews cannot be considered an omen of redemption.

In response to this claim some have suggested that the ingathering will occur in stages – with the final phases being authored by *Mashiaḥ*. A well-known verse cites the divine promise: "So says the LORD God, who gathers

JUSTICE

הָשִׁיבָה Restore our judges as at first,
and our counselors as at the beginning,
and remove from us sorrow and sighing.
May You alone, LORD,
reign over us with loving-kindness and compassion,
and vindicate us in justice.
Blessed are You, LORD,
the King who loves righteousness and justice.

AGAINST INFORMERS

וְלַמַּלְשִׁינִים For the slanderers let there be no hope,
and may all wickedness perish in an instant.
May all Your people's enemies swiftly be cut down.
May You swiftly uproot, crush, cast down
and humble the arrogant swiftly in our days.
Blessed are You, LORD,
who destroys enemies and humbles the arrogant.

---

societies upheld justice, inevitably the absence of social fraternity eroded general social fitness.

As representatives of God we are tasked with promoting justice and morality. Though we can model these traits in our personal and communal behavior, our primary national challenge is to construct a society in our homeland which is founded upon these values.

Life in the modern State presents new and unique moral challenges. Primary among them is the goal to create an army capable of defending us against vicious and cruel enemies while still adhering to a moral code. In our efforts to face ruthless enemies we must also protect the dignity of human life.

Having founded a Jewish State we continue to host a large Arab population of Israeli citizens. How do we democratically ensure the rights of this minority without compromising the nature of a Jewish State?

A healthy modern economy is a strategic asset to the State of Israel. Without a robust economy our national existence is vulnerable. Successful modern economies are built upon capitalist and free market strategies. How can we

השבת המשפט

הָשִׁיבָה שׁוֹפְטֵינוּ כְּבָרִאשׁוֹנָה וְיוֹעֲצֵינוּ כְּבַתְּחִלָּה
וְהָסֵר מִמֶּנּוּ יָגוֹן וַאֲנָחָה
וּמְלֹךְ עָלֵינוּ אַתָּה יהוה לְבַדְּךָ בְּחֶסֶד וּבְרַחֲמִים
וְצַדְּקֵנוּ בַּמִּשְׁפָּט.
בָּרוּךְ אַתָּה יהוה, מֶלֶךְ אוֹהֵב צְדָקָה וּמִשְׁפָּט.

ברכת המינים

וְלַמַּלְשִׁינִים אַל תְּהִי תִקְוָה
וְכָל הָרִשְׁעָה כְּרֶגַע תֹּאבֵד
וְכָל אוֹיְבֵי עַמְּךָ מְהֵרָה יִכָּרֵתוּ
וְהַזֵּדִים מְהֵרָה תְעַקֵּר וּתְשַׁבֵּר וּתְמַגֵּר וְתַכְנִיעַ בִּמְהֵרָה בְיָמֵינוּ.
בָּרוּךְ אַתָּה יהוה, שׁוֹבֵר אוֹיְבִים וּמַכְנִיעַ זֵדִים.

---

drive you" (*Devarim* 4:27). Evidently the *size* of the Jewish population is a factor of our general historical condition, and more specifically our presence in the Land of Israel.

The original prophecy of abundance like the sand of the earth is tethered to the promise to deliver the Land of Israel to the Jewish people, further reinforcing the relationship between residence in the Land of Israel and population growth. The image of sand may also suggest a deferral of this prophecy to the Messianic Era. As some have commented, this metaphor conveys that at the very stage that the Jewish people reach a nadir and decline as the dust of the earth, redemption will appear and they will multiply like that very dust.

MORAL CHALLENGES

The two national exiles were prompted in part by general moral decay. Yeshayahu (1:21) laments about a city, known for justice, which had deteriorated into a den of iniquity and murder. The anarchic reality could not sustain a *Mikdash* which should ideally be perched upon principles of morality. The second exile was due in large measure to internecine struggle. Though their

THE RIGHTEOUS

עַל הַצַּדִּיקִים To the righteous, the pious,
the elders of Your people the house of Israel,
the remnant of their scholars,
the righteous converts, and to us,
may Your compassion be aroused,
LORD our God.
Grant a good reward to all who sincerely trust in Your name.
Set our lot with them,
so that we may never be ashamed, for in You we trust.
Blessed are You, LORD,
who is the support and trust of the righteous.

---

bala which expects man to be an *activist* in both cosmic as well as national redemption. Although that activism need not be expressed solely through geographic relocation to Israel, it can *include* such efforts. Many sensed that the political turmoil at the turn of the eighteenth century signaled the start of the Messianic Era, which should naturally be followed by efforts to accelerate the final process.

More importantly, Ḥasidut preached an overarching concern for and love of *every* Jew, regardless of their level of religious commitment. This ideology is certainly independent of a common homeland, but becomes even more compelling in the context of a common state. Forming an organized nationality of Jews creates a common framework to integrate the joint experiences of different types of Jews. Originally many strains of Ḥasidut advocated and supported the growing organized efforts to resettle Israel and form a national entity.

As the Zionist movement developed it became clear that for many Jews secular nationalism replaced their classic religious identity. Fearing this calamity the Hasidic world overwhelmingly rejected mainstream Zionism. In the modern context Chabad Ḥasidut has been more outspoken than any other branch of Ḥasidut in endorsing participation in state building, even if not subscribing to Zionist ideology. This shift occurred, in large part, due to the late Lubavitcher Rebbe – Rabbi Manachem Mendel Schneerson – reversing the views of his grandfather.

על הצדיקים
עַל הַצַּדִּיקִים וְעַל הַחֲסִידִים, וְעַל זִקְנֵי עַמְּךָ בֵּית יִשְׂרָאֵל
וְעַל פְּלֵיטַת סוֹפְרֵיהֶם, וְעַל גֵּרֵי הַצֶּדֶק, וְעָלֵינוּ
יֶהֱמוּ רַחֲמֶיךָ יהוה אֱלֹהֵינוּ
וְתֵן שָׂכָר טוֹב לְכָל הַבּוֹטְחִים בְּשִׁמְךָ בֶּאֱמֶת
וְשִׂים חֶלְקֵנוּ עִמָּהֶם
וּלְעוֹלָם לֹא נֵבוֹשׁ כִּי בְךָ בָּטָחְנוּ.
בָּרוּךְ אַתָּה יהוה, מִשְׁעָן וּמִבְטָח לַצַּדִּיקִים.

---

blend these policies with an overarching concern for the welfare of the less fortunate?

We have the opportunity, oftentimes the privilege, of wresting with newly encountered national and social dilemmas. Our ability to face these with moral fortitude advances our redemption. As we build a country in the divine image of "justice and charity," we inch closer to a Messianic Kingdom of God.

עַל הַצַּדִּיקִים וְעַל הַחֲסִידִים *The righteous, the pious.* The Hasidic movement evolved in the early part of the eighteenth century in Poland and Hungary. Viewed as a response to the ossification of conventional Judaism, it gained increasing popularity under the charismatic leadership of Hasidic "Masters" or "Rebbes." As the Hasidic movement was evolving, unrelated events destabilized the Jewish world and raised anew the prospect of emigration to the Land of Israel. Political instability in Poland and the Napoleonic War were the two most influential events which catalyzed renewed interest in *aliya.* Unlike previous periods of interest, this era witnessed well-organized attempts to build Jewish communities in Israel. These efforts preceded the birth of modern Zionism, which is generally assumed to have occurred in the latter half of the nineteenth century.

Initially many Hasidic Rebbes encouraged these organized attempts at resettling Israel – even with the knowledge that many of their partners were non-religious Jews. Ideologically the attempt to resettle Israel resonated with two very important Hasidic principles. *Hasidut* is based on a system of Kab-

REBUILDING JERUSALEM

וְלִירוּשָׁלַיִם To Jerusalem, Your city, may You return in compassion,
and may You dwell in it as You promised.
May You rebuild it rapidly in our days
as an everlasting structure,
and install within it soon the throne of David.
Blessed are You, LORD, who builds Jerusalem.

KINGDOM OF DAVID

אֶת צֶמַח May the offshoot of Your servant David soon flower,
and may his pride be raised high by Your salvation,
for we wait for Your salvation all day.
Blessed are You, LORD, who makes the glory of salvation flourish.

---

watched over you and have seen" (*Shemot* 3:16) – repeating the term "*pakod*"
and insinuating that the process would have *two* launches. Indeed Moshe's
initial efforts were at first only moderately successful, and finally boomer-
anged into failure. Pharaoh scoffs at him while the Jews – burdened with an
increased workload – ridicule and denigrate him. According to the Midrash,
he retreats back to Midian and his father-in-law's home for three months.
Only afterwards is he reinserted into Egypt, re-empowered by HaKadosh
Barukh Hu, and only after the second launch can redemption climb toward
its climactic conclusion. By employing the image of *tzemah* twice, similar notions are implied about our final redemption. It will not happen immediately,
and it will be propelled by multiple launches.

Secondly, the image invites the notion of a process nurtured by God but
cultivated by human effort as well. The rising sun was also cast as a metaphor
for a staged process of redemption, because like a plant it unfolds gradually.
However, unlike a sunrise which transpires automatically, a plant must be
tended to by human care. Redemption is a bilateral process, combining
divine initiative with human provision. The bilateral nature of a redemption
resembling a plant is underscored by a verse in *Zekharia* 6:12, "Here is the
man whose name is the *Branch*, and he will *branch* out from his place and
build the temple of the LORD" This is the *only* verse in Scripture which uses
the word "*tzemah*" as a verb of human endeavor. HaKadosh Barukh Hu announces the emergence of "*tzemah*," but the *Mashiah* himself blossoms into
his historic role.

בניין ירושלים

וְלִירוּשָׁלַיִם עִירְךָ בְּרַחֲמִים תָּשׁוּב
וְתִשְׁכֹּן בְּתוֹכָהּ כַּאֲשֶׁר דִּבַּרְתָּ
וּבְנֵה אוֹתָהּ בְּקָרוֹב בְּיָמֵינוּ בִּנְיַן עוֹלָם
וְכִסֵּא דָוִד מְהֵרָה לְתוֹכָהּ תָּכִין.
בָּרוּךְ אַתָּה יהוה, בּוֹנֵה יְרוּשָׁלָיִם.

מלכות בית דוד

אֶת צֶמַח דָּוִד עַבְדְּךָ מְהֵרָה תַצְמִיחַ, וְקַרְנוֹ תָּרוּם בִּישׁוּעָתֶךָ
כִּי לִישׁוּעָתְךָ קִוִּינוּ כָּל הַיּוֹם.
בָּרוּךְ אַתָּה יהוה, מַצְמִיחַ קֶרֶן יְשׁוּעָה.

JERUSALEM – THE HEART OF THE STATE OF ISRAEL

We see an obligation to declare that Jewish Jerusalem is an organic and inextricable part of the State of Israel… Just as she is an inextricable part of Israeli history, of Israeli faith, of the soul of its nation. Jerusalem is the heart of the State of Israel… a nation that for two and a half thousand years faithfully kept the oath the exiles swore by the rivers of Babylon not to forget Jerusalem – this nation will never accept the separation of Jerusalem. (David Ben-Gurion, from a speech in the Knesset, 22nd of Kislev, 1950)

אֶת צֶמַח דָּוִד עַבְדְּךָ מְהֵרָה תַצְמִיחַ *May the offshoot of Your servant David soon flower.* The image of "*tzemaḥ*" or "plant" as a metaphor for redemption is borrowed from several verses which describe the Davidic dynasty and/or *Mashiaḥ* with this term. The image conveys the concept of a "process" – just as vegetation grows gradually, similarly the restoration of Jewish monarchy and sovereignty develops in stages.

In fact several verses use the word *tzemaḥ* twice (*Yirmiyahu* 33:15 and *Zekharia* 6:12), and this phraseology is embedded in the *berakha* of the *Shemoneh Esreh* which states, "*May the offshoot (צֶמַח)… soon flower (תַצְמִיחַ).*" This repetition suggests that not only is redemption a *gradual* process, but that it is also punctuated by multiple onsets. When HaKadosh Barukh Hu dispatched Moshe to liberate the Jews from Egypt He assured them, "*I have*

RESPONSE TO PRAYER

שְׁמַע קוֹלֵנוּ Listen to our voice, LORD our God.
Spare us and have compassion on us,
and in compassion and favor accept our prayer,
for You, God, listen to prayers and pleas.
Do not turn us away, O our King, empty-handed from Your presence,
for You listen with compassion to the prayer of Your people Israel.
Blessed are You, LORD, who listens to prayer.

TEMPLE SERVICE

רְצֵה Find favor, LORD our God,
in Your people Israel and their prayer.
Restore the service to Your most holy House,
and accept in love and favor
the fire-offerings of Israel and their prayer.
May the service of Your people Israel always find favor with You.
And may our eyes witness Your return to Zion in compassion.
Blessed are You, LORD, who restores His Presence to Zion.

הַמַּחֲזִיר שְׁכִינָתוֹ לְצִיּוֹן *Who restores His Presence to Zion.* Though the Land of
Israel possesses timeless, metaphysical importance, its actual halakhic *kedusha* is a product of human installation. The first cycle of "legal" *kedusha* was
installed by conquest. The Jews entered Israel, seized the land, and thereby
conferred on it legal holiness. This consequently triggered a range of mitzvot
which had previously not existed due to its lack of legal status. This *kedusha*
status terminated when the land was subsequently conquered and the Jews
were exiled.

The return to Israel was marked not by military acquisition but international authorization. Koresh requisitioned the return to Israel and construction of the *Mikdash.* Our legal reacquisition of the land installed the second
round of *kedusha,* and reinstated the various halakhot dependent upon this
status. There is significant debate as to whether this *kedusha* expired when
we were exiled. Exile does not ultimately affect our legal rights to our land in
the manner that it cancelled national sovereignty during the first exile. Some
claim that the second installed *kedusha is* eternal, but most believe that also
this *kedusha* expired.

Although he agrees that the *general kedusha* elapsed, the Rambam asserts

שומע תפלה
שְׁמַע קוֹלֵנוּ יהוה אֱלֹהֵינוּ
חוּס וְרַחֵם עָלֵינוּ, וְקַבֵּל בְּרַחֲמִים וּבְרָצוֹן אֶת תְּפִלָּתֵנוּ
כִּי אֵל שׁוֹמֵעַ תְּפִלּוֹת וְתַחֲנוּנִים אֶתָּה
וּמִלְּפָנֶיךָ מַלְכֵּנוּ רֵיקָם אַל תְּשִׁיבֵנוּ
כִּי אַתָּה שׁוֹמֵעַ תְּפִלַּת עַמְּךָ יִשְׂרָאֵל בְּרַחֲמִים.
בָּרוּךְ אַתָּה יהוה, שׁוֹמֵעַ תְּפִלָּה.

עבודה
רְצֵה יהוה אֱלֹהֵינוּ בְּעַמְּךָ יִשְׂרָאֵל, וּבִתְפִלָּתָם
וְהָשֵׁב אֶת הָעֲבוֹדָה לִדְבִיר בֵּיתֶךָ
וְאִשֵּׁי יִשְׂרָאֵל וּתְפִלָּתָם בְּאַהֲבָה תְקַבֵּל בְּרָצוֹן
וּתְהִי לְרָצוֹן תָּמִיד עֲבוֹדַת יִשְׂרָאֵל עַמֶּךָ.
וְתֶחֱזֶינָה עֵינֵינוּ בְּשׁוּבְךָ לְצִיּוֹן בְּרַחֲמִים.
בָּרוּךְ אַתָּה יהוה, הַמַּחֲזִיר שְׁכִינָתוֹ לְצִיּוֹן.

Finally the metaphor evokes images of a land regaining its lost fertility as the redemptive process evolves. One of the promised signs for redemption is the blooming of our land after years of desolation. Describing the return of dynasty as agricultural growth reminds us that simultaneous to this figurative growth, we will witness *actual* growth.

Based on this image of "*tzemaḥ*," the phrase "*Reshit Tzemiḥat Geulateinu*" – the first flowering of our redemption – was incorporated into the text of the Prayer for the State of Israel, authored by the first two Chief Rabbis of Israel – Rabbi Yitzchak Isaac HaLevi Herzog and Rabbi Ben Tziyon Chai Uziel. This phrase captures the Messianic nature of the return to the State of Israel.

KIM'A KIM'A

In 1947 when the Gerrer Rebbe was informed that the UN had decided to partition Palestine and create a Jewish State, he responded, "such is Jewish redemption – *kim'a kim'a* (little by little)."

THANKSGIVING

Bow at the first nine words.

מוֹדִים We give thanks to You,
for You are the LORD our God
and God of our ancestors
for ever and all time.
You are the Rock of our lives,
Shield of our salvation
from generation to generation.
We will thank You and
declare Your praise for our lives,
which are entrusted into Your hand;
for our souls,
which are placed in Your charge;
for Your miracles
which are with us every day;
and for Your wonders and favors
at all times, evening,
morning and midday.
You are good –
for Your compassion never fails.
You are compassionate –
for Your loving-
kindnesses never cease.
We have always
placed our hope in You.

*During the Leader's Repetition,
the congregation says quietly:*

מוֹדִים We give thanks to You,
for You are the LORD
our God
and God of our ancestors,
God of all flesh,
who formed us
and formed the universe.
Blessings and thanks are due
to Your great and holy name
for giving us life
and sustaining us.
May You continue
to give us life and sustain us;
and may You gather
our exiles
to Your holy courts,
to keep Your decrees,
do Your will and serve You
with a perfect heart,
for it is for us
to give You thanks.
Blessed be God
to whom thanksgiving is due.

---

debate was addressed in Rabbi Tzvi Hirsh Kalisher's well-known book *Derishat Tziyon* about Modern Zionism. Supporting the renewal of the *Korban Pesaḥ* even prior to the construction of *Mikdash*, he cites this position of the Rambam as the baseline of his endorsement. Even among those who disagree, much of the opposition is based on secondary issues, such as the absence of pedigreed *Kohanim*, or the inability to manufacture authentic priestly garb due to lack of certain materials.

הודאה

Bow at the first five words.

יְמוֹדִים אֲנַחְנוּ לָךְ
שָׁאַתָּה הוּא יהוה אֱלֹהֵינוּ
וֵאלֹהֵי אֲבוֹתֵינוּ לְעוֹלָם וָעֶד.
צוּר חַיֵּינוּ, מָגֵן יִשְׁעֵנוּ
אַתָּה הוּא לְדוֹר וָדוֹר.
נוֹדֶה לְךָ וּנְסַפֵּר תְּהִלָּתֶךָ
עַל חַיֵּינוּ הַמְּסוּרִים בְּיָדֶךָ
וְעַל נִשְׁמוֹתֵינוּ הַפְּקוּדוֹת לָךְ
וְעַל נִסֶּיךָ שֶׁבְּכָל יוֹם עִמָּנוּ
וְעַל נִפְלְאוֹתֶיךָ וְטוֹבוֹתֶיךָ
שֶׁבְּכָל עֵת
עֶרֶב וָבֹקֶר וְצָהֳרָיִם.
הַטּוֹב, כִּי לֹא כָלוּ רַחֲמֶיךָ
וְהַמְרַחֵם, כִּי לֹא תַמּוּ חֲסָדֶיךָ
מֵעוֹלָם קִוִּינוּ לָךְ.

חֲזָרַת הש״ץ, During
the קהל says quietly:

יְמוֹדִים אֲנַחְנוּ לָךְ
שָׁאַתָּה הוּא יהוה אֱלֹהֵינוּ
וֵאלֹהֵי אֲבוֹתֵינוּ
אֱלֹהֵי כָל בָּשָׂר
יוֹצְרֵנוּ, יוֹצֵר בְּרֵאשִׁית.
בְּרָכוֹת וְהוֹדָאוֹת
לְשִׁמְךָ הַגָּדוֹל וְהַקָּדוֹשׁ
עַל שֶׁהֶחֱיִיתָנוּ וְקִיַּמְתָּנוּ.
כֵּן תְּחַיֵּנוּ וּתְקַיְּמֵנוּ
וְתֶאֱסוֹף גָּלֻיּוֹתֵינוּ
לְחַצְרוֹת קָדְשֶׁךָ
לִשְׁמוֹר חֻקֶּיךָ
וְלַעֲשׂוֹת רְצוֹנֶךָ וּלְעָבְדְּךָ
בְּלֵבָב שָׁלֵם
עַל שֶׁאֲנַחְנוּ מוֹדִים לָךְ.
בָּרוּךְ אֵל הַהוֹדָאוֹת.

(Hilkhot Beit HaBeḥira 6:16) that the condensed kedusha surrounding the Temple Mount itself is eternal, and outlasted the destruction of the physical Mikdash. According to the Rambam the phrase "return Your Shekhina to Tziyon" must be read in a broader sense as referring to the physical rebuilding of the Mikdash on the site which continues to house the Shekhina.

This position of the Rambam spurs an interesting debate about the feasibility of renewing sacrifices even prior to the construction of the Mikdash. The primary focus surrounded the Pesaḥ sacrifice, which unlike most is offered from private funds. Public sacrifices are thwarted by the absence of the Maḥatzit HaShekel, which is necessary to collect public funds. This

> At this point in the silent Amida it is permitted to add a rabbinically
> formulated "Al HaNissim." The following was written by Rabbi Neria
> (alternative versions can be found on pages 656–659).
>
> עַל הַנִּסִּים [We thank You also] for the miracles, the redemption, the mighty
> deeds, the salvations, and the victories in battle which You performed for our
> ancestors in those days, at this time.
>
> When the armies of the Middle East rose up against Your people Israel and
> sought to destroy, slay and exterminate the inhabitants of Your Land, young
> and old, children and women, and among them those who had survived the
> sword and were saved from the horror of Your enemies' flames, one from a
> city, two from a family, hoping to find a resting place for the soles of their feet
> in Your land that You had promised them; then You in Your great compassion
> stood by us in our time of distress, thwarted their counsel and frustrated their
> plans, raised us upright and established our liberty, championed our cause,
> judged our claim, avenged our wrong, delivered the strong into the hands
> of the weak, the many into the hands of the few, the impure into the hands

Similarly the colossal miracles surrounding the establishment of the State
of Israel were not pointless, but influence and contribute to an ultimate and
comprehensive redemption. That a fledgling nation, including many Holocaust
refugees, could survive a seething Arab onslaught during the War of Independence was a divine miracle. That nineteen years later we were saved from the
dastardly designs of three of our enemies was a wondrous manifestation of
divine intervention. That we returned to the heartland of Jewish history and
resettled the "corridor of Jewish history," stretching from Shekhem in the
North to Ḥevron in the South, rendered these events Messianic. Events of
this magnitude aren't rendered purposelessly – they augur future redemption!

DELAYING FULL REDEMPTION UNTIL THE LAND IS READY
A fascinating midrash (*Shemot Raba* 20:16) questions the need for the forty-
year period of wandering through the desert. Typically this period is viewed
as a punishment for the betrayal of the spies. Yet this midrash attributes a
different purpose. Upon hearing the news of the exodus, the indigenous nations of Canaan plundered their *own* land to discourage Jewish settlement.
HaKadosh Barukh Hu delayed our entry for forty years to allow the land
to recover its fertility, and for the infrastructure to be rebuilt. Full redemption can only ensue once the land is fully developed and cultivated. As we
continue to renovate our homeland after an absence of 1900 years, we edge
closer to the full redemption.

At this point in the silent עמידה it is permitted to add a rabbinically
formulated עַל הַנִּסִּים. The following was written by Rabbi Neria
(alternative versions can be found on pages 656–659).

עַל הַנִּסִּים וְעַל הַפֻּרְקָן וְעַל הַגְּבוּרוֹת וְעַל הַתְּשׁוּעוֹת וְעַל הַמִּלְחָמוֹת
שֶׁעָשִׂיתָ לַאֲבוֹתֵינוּ בַּיָּמִים הָהֵם בַּזְּמַן הַזֶּה.

כְּשֶׁעָמְדוּ צִבְאוֹת עֲרָב עַל עַמְּךָ יִשְׂרָאֵל, וּבִקְשׁוּ לְהַשְׁמִיד לַהֲרֹג וּלְאַבֵּד אֶת
יוֹשְׁבֵי אַרְצֶךָ, מִנַּעַר וְעַד זָקֵן טַף וְנָשִׁים, וּבָהֶם עַם שְׂרִידֵי חֶרֶב אֲשֶׁר נִצְּלוּ מִתְּפַת
הָאֵשׁ שֶׁל שׂוֹנְאֶיךָ, אֶחָד מֵעִיר וּשְׁנַיִם מִמִּשְׁפָּחָה, וְשָׁבְרוּ לִמְצֹא מָנוֹחַ לְכַף
רַגְלָם בְּאַרְצְךָ אֲשֶׁר הִבְטַחְתָּ לָהֶם. וְאַתָּה בְּרַחֲמֶיךָ הָרַבִּים עָמַדְתָּ לָנוּ
בְּעֵת צָרָתֵנוּ, הֵפַרְתָּ אֶת עֲצָתָם וְקִלְקַלְתָּ אֶת מַחֲשַׁבְתָּם, זָקַפְתָּ קוֹמָתֵנוּ
וְקוֹמַמְתָּ אֶת חֻרְבוֹתֵינוּ, רַבְתָּ אֶת רִיבֵנוּ, דַּנְתָּ אֶת דִּינֵנוּ, נָקַמְתָּ אֶת נִקְמָתֵנוּ,
מָסַרְתָּ רַבִּים בְּיַד מְעַטִּים, טְמֵאִים בְּיַד קְדוֹשִׁים, וְעָשִׂיתָ לְךָ שֵׁם גָּדוֹל

AL HANISSIM

For a discussion on the addition of *Al HaNissim* to the silent Amida, see
page 95.

MIRACLES HAVE A PURPOSE

Prior to the birth of Shimshon and the redemptive potential which evolved,
his parents were twice visited by an angel and informed of his birth. Furthermore, they witnessed a miraculous ascent of this angel as their sacrifice
was consumed. Yet Shimshon's father was rattled, and feared for his and his
wife's safety. He was assured by his wife "If the LORD had meant to kill us, He
would not have accepted a burnt offering and grain offering from our hands,
nor shown us all these things or now told us this" (*Shofetim* 13:23). Miracles
don't occur *needlessly*. God would not have intervened without some larger
plan for them, as parents of a potential national savior.

Witnessing miracles on a grand scale reassures us that we will behold and
benefit from future providence of HaKadosh Barukh Hu. The experience of
the Jewish people – the great miracle of human history – confirms that we
haven't been forsaken, and will one day merit final redemption. That a nation
could survive almost two thousand years without common language, flag,
currency, army or any other national symbol is extraordinary. That the Jewish people survived this period under conditions of constant discrimination,
persecution, and hostility is nothing short of miraculous. It is the greatest
testament to our future redemption.

of the holy. You made for Yourself great and holy renown in Your world, and for Your people Israel You performed a great salvation and redemption as of this day. You subjugated peoples under us, nations beneath our feet, and You gave us our inheritance, the Land of Canaan to its borders, and returned us to the place of Your holy Sanctuary.

(In the same way, make us a miracle and a glorious wonder, thwart the counsel of our enemies, have us prosper in the pastures of our Land, and gather in our scattered ones from the four corners of the earth, and we will rejoice in the rebuilding of Your city and in the establishment of Your Sanctuary and in the flourishing of the pride of Your servant David, speedily in our days, and we will give thanks to Your great name.) *Continue with "For all these things."*

וְעַל כֻּלָּם For all these things may Your name be blessed and exalted, our King, continually, for ever and all time.
Let all that lives thank You, Selah! and praise Your name in truth, God, our Savior and Help, Selah!
▸Blessed are You, LORD,
whose name is "the Good" and to whom thanks are due.

The following is said by the Leader during the Repetition of the Amida.
In Israel, if Kohanim bless the congregation, turn to page 660.

Our God and God of our fathers, bless us with the threefold blessing in the Torah, written by the hand of Moses Your servant and pronounced by Aaron and his sons the priests, Your holy people, as it is said:
May the LORD bless you and protect you.   *Num. 6*
Cong: May it be Your will.
May the LORD make His face shine on you and be gracious to you.
Cong: May it be Your will.
May the LORD turn His face toward you, and grant you peace.
Cong: May it be Your will.

PEACE

שִׂים שָׁלוֹם Grant peace, goodness and blessing,
grace, loving-kindness and compassion
to us and all Israel Your people.
Bless us, our Father, all as one, with the light of Your face,
for by the light of Your face You have given us, LORD our God,
the Torah of life and love of kindness,
righteousness, blessing, compassion, life and peace.

וְקָדוֹשׁ בְּעוֹלָמֶךְ, וּלְעַמְּךָ יִשְׂרָאֵל עָשִׂיתָ תְּשׁוּעָה גְדוֹלָה וּפֻרְקָן כְּהַיּוֹם הַזֶּה, הַדְבַּרְתָּ עַמִּים תַּחְתֵּנוּ וּלְאֻמִּים תַּחַת רַגְלֵנוּ, וְנָתַתָּ לָנוּ אֶת נַחֲלָתֵנוּ, אֶרֶץ כְּנַעַן לִגְבוּלוֹתֶיהָ, וְהֶחֱזַרְתָּנוּ אֶל מְקוֹם מִקְדַּשׁ הֵיכָלֶךָ.

(כֵּן עֲשֵׂה עִמָּנוּ נֵס וָפֶלֶא לְטוֹבָה, הָפֵר עֲצַת אוֹיְבֵינוּ, וְדַשְּׁנֵנוּ בִּנְאוֹת אַרְצֶךָ, וּנְפוּצוֹתֵינוּ מֵאַרְבַּע כַּנְפוֹת הָאָרֶץ תְּקַבֵּץ, וְנִשְׂמַח בְּבִנְיַן עִירֶךָ וּבְתִקּוּן הֵיכָלֶךָ וּבִצְמִיחַת קֶרֶן לְדָוִד עַבְדֶּךָ בִּמְהֵרָה בְיָמֵינוּ, וְנוֹדֶה לְשִׁמְךָ הַגָּדוֹל).

Continue with וְעַל כֻּלָם.וְעַל כֻּלָּם

וְעַל כֻּלָּם יִתְבָּרַךְ וְיִתְרוֹמַם שִׁמְךָ מַלְכֵּנוּ תָּמִיד לְעוֹלָם וָעֶד.
וְכֹל הַחַיִּים יוֹדוּךָ סֶּלָה, וִיהַלְלוּ אֶת שִׁמְךָ בֶּאֱמֶת
הָאֵל יְשׁוּעָתֵנוּ וְעֶזְרָתֵנוּ סֶלָה.
בָּרוּךְ אַתָּה יהוה, הַטּוֹב שִׁמְךָ וּלְךָ נָאֶה לְהוֹדוֹת.

The following is said by the שליח ציבור during חזרת הש״ץ.
In ארץ ישראל if כהנים say ברכת כהנים turn to page 661.

אֱלֹהֵינוּ וֵאלֹהֵי אֲבוֹתֵינוּ, בָּרְכֵנוּ בַּבְּרָכָה הַמְשֻׁלֶּשֶׁת בַּתּוֹרָה, הַכְּתוּבָה עַל יְדֵי מֹשֶׁה עַבְדֶּךָ, הָאֲמוּרָה מִפִּי אַהֲרֹן וּבָנָיו כֹּהֲנִים עַם קְדוֹשֶׁיךָ, כָּאָמוּר

במדבר ו

יְבָרֶכְךָ יהוה וְיִשְׁמְרֶךָ: קהל: כֵּן יְהִי רָצוֹן
יָאֵר יהוה פָּנָיו אֵלֶיךָ וִיחֻנֶּךָּ: קהל: כֵּן יְהִי רָצוֹן
יִשָּׂא יהוה פָּנָיו אֵלֶיךָ וְיָשֵׂם לְךָ שָׁלוֹם: קהל: כֵּן יְהִי רָצוֹן

שלום
שִׂים שָׁלוֹם טוֹבָה וּבְרָכָה
חֵן וָחֶסֶד וְרַחֲמִים עָלֵינוּ וְעַל כָּל יִשְׂרָאֵל עַמֶּךָ.
בָּרְכֵנוּ אָבִינוּ כֻּלָּנוּ כְּאֶחָד בְּאוֹר פָּנֶיךָ
כִּי בְאוֹר פָּנֶיךָ נָתַתָּ לָנוּ יהוה אֱלֹהֵינוּ
תּוֹרַת חַיִּים וְאַהֲבַת חֶסֶד
וּצְדָקָה וּבְרָכָה וְרַחֲמִים וְחַיִּים וְשָׁלוֹם.

May it be good in Your eyes to bless Your people Israel
at every time, in every hour, with Your peace.
Blessed are You, LORD, who blesses His people Israel with peace.

The following verse concludes the Leader's Repetition of the Amida.
Some also say it here as part of the silent Amida.
May the words of my mouth and the meditation of my heart   Ps. 19
find favor before You, LORD, my Rock and Redeemer.

אֱלֹהַי My God,   Berakhot
guard my tongue from evil and my lips from deceitful speech.   17a
To those who curse me, let my soul be silent;
may my soul be to all like the dust.
Open my heart to Your Torah and let my soul
pursue Your commandments.
As for all who plan evil against me,
swiftly thwart their counsel and frustrate their plans.
     Act for the sake of Your name; act for the sake of Your right hand;
         act for the sake of Your holiness; act for the sake of Your Torah.
That Your beloved ones may be delivered,   Ps. 60
save with Your right hand and answer me.
May the words of my mouth and the meditation of my heart   Ps. 19
find favor before You, LORD, my Rock and Redeemer.

Bow, take three steps back, then bow, first left, then right, then center, while saying:
May He who makes peace in His high places,
make peace for us and all Israel – and say: Amen.

יְהִי רָצוֹן May it be Your will, LORD our God and God of our ancestors,
that the Temple be rebuilt speedily in our days,
and grant us a share in Your Torah.
And there we will serve You
with reverence, as in the days of old and as in former years.
Then the offering of Judah and Jerusalem will be pleasing to the LORD   Mal. 3
as in the days of old and as in former years.

When praying with a minyan,
the Amida is repeated aloud by the Leader.

וְטוֹב בְּעֵינֶיךָ לְבָרֵךְ אֶת עַמְּךָ יִשְׂרָאֵל

בְּכָל עֵת וּבְכָל שָׁעָה בִּשְׁלוֹמֶךָ.

בָּרוּךְ אַתָּה יהוה, הַמְבָרֵךְ אֶת עַמּוֹ יִשְׂרָאֵל בַּשָּׁלוֹם.

The following verse concludes the חזרת הש״ץ.
Some also say it here as part of the silent עמידה.

תהלים יט

יִהְיוּ לְרָצוֹן אִמְרֵי־פִי וְהֶגְיוֹן לִבִּי לְפָנֶיךָ, יהוה צוּרִי וְגֹאֲלִי:

ברכות יז.

אֱלֹהַי

נְצֹר לְשׁוֹנִי מֵרָע וּשְׂפָתַי מִדַּבֵּר מִרְמָה

וְלִמְקַלְלַי נַפְשִׁי תִדֹּם, וְנַפְשִׁי כֶּעָפָר לַכֹּל תִּהְיֶה.

פְּתַח לִבִּי בְּתוֹרָתֶךָ, וּבְמִצְוֹתֶיךָ תִּרְדֹּף נַפְשִׁי.

וְכָל הַחוֹשְׁבִים עָלַי רָעָה, מְהֵרָה הָפֵר עֲצָתָם וְקַלְקֵל מַחֲשַׁבְתָּם.

עֲשֵׂה לְמַעַן שְׁמֶךָ, עֲשֵׂה לְמַעַן יְמִינֶךָ

עֲשֵׂה לְמַעַן קְדֻשָּׁתֶךָ, עֲשֵׂה לְמַעַן תּוֹרָתֶךָ.

תהלים ס

לְמַעַן יֵחָלְצוּן יְדִידֶיךָ, הוֹשִׁיעָה יְמִינְךָ וַעֲנֵנִי:

תהלים יט

יִהְיוּ לְרָצוֹן אִמְרֵי־פִי וְהֶגְיוֹן לִבִּי לְפָנֶיךָ, יהוה צוּרִי וְגֹאֲלִי:

Bow, take three steps back, then bow, first left, then right, then center, while saying:

עֹשֶׂה שָׁלוֹם בִּמְרוֹמָיו

הוּא יַעֲשֶׂה שָׁלוֹם עָלֵינוּ וְעַל כָּל יִשְׂרָאֵל, וְאִמְרוּ אָמֵן.

יְהִי רָצוֹן מִלְּפָנֶיךָ יהוה אֱלֹהֵינוּ וֵאלֹהֵי אֲבוֹתֵינוּ

שֶׁיִּבָּנֶה בֵּית הַמִּקְדָּשׁ בִּמְהֵרָה בְיָמֵינוּ

וְתֵן חֶלְקֵנוּ בְּתוֹרָתֶךָ

וְשָׁם נַעֲבָדְךָ בְּיִרְאָה כִּימֵי עוֹלָם וּכְשָׁנִים קַדְמֹנִיּוֹת.

מלאכי ג

וְעָרְבָה לַיהוה מִנְחַת יְהוּדָה וִירוּשָׁלָ͏ִם כִּימֵי עוֹלָם וּכְשָׁנִים קַדְמֹנִיּוֹת:

When praying with a מנין,
the עמידה is repeated aloud by the שליח ציבור.

Hallel

The Full Hallel is said. Some say the Hallel with a Blessing and some do not.
There is also a custom to say Half Hallel.

בָּרוּךְ Blessed are You, LORD our God, King of the Universe,
who has made us holy through His commandments
and has commanded us to recite the Hallel.

הַלְלוּיָהּ Halleluya! Servants of the LORD, give praise; praise the   Ps. 113
name of the LORD. Blessed be the name of the LORD now and
for evermore. From the rising of the sun to its setting, may the

---

The *Midrash* associates his silence with the phrase, "Sing to the LORD, for
He has done glorious things; let this be known to all the world" (*Yeshayahu*
12:5). Ḥizkiyahu assumed that the divine glory was apparent, and declined
the opportunity to broadcast it through *shira*. Though a transcendent God
has no need for human assistance, HaKadosh Barukh Hu desires human
initiative in redemption, and through human participation His glory is
heightened.

An intriguing Gemara (*Pesaḥim* 117a) suggests that Ḥizkiyahu *did* recite
Hallel in response to this victory. Evidently reciting was insufficient, and *shira*
was required. Hallel confirms our historical reliance upon God to deliver us
from our enemies. Exclaiming Hallel in response to a miracle frames that
event in the broader context of Jewish history and divine intervention. It
lacks the immediacy and spontaneity of *shira*, which is a direct response of
praise to a national success. Hallel is a composed appreciation of a miracle,
whereas *shira* is a *passionate* song in response to a divine encounter which
the miracle has enabled.

Whatever the reason for Ḥizkiyahu's oversight, it cost the Jewish people
an early opportunity for messianic closure. Inability to recite Hallel or *shira*
in the face of a redemptive process stalls that very process.

מִמִּזְרַח־שֶׁמֶשׁ עַד־מְבוֹאוֹ *From the rising of the sun to its setting.* This phrase is
employed in this section to describe an expansive all-encompassing praise
offered to HaKadosh Barukh Hu. A parallel verse claims "The Mighty One,

סדר הלל

הלל שלם is said. Some say the הלל with the Blessing and some do not.
There is also a custom to say only הלל בדילוג.

בָּרוּךְ אַתָּה יהוה אֱלֹהֵינוּ מֶלֶךְ הָעוֹלָם
אֲשֶׁר קִדְּשָׁנוּ בְּמִצְוֹתָיו וְצִוָּנוּ לִקְרֹא אֶת הַהַלֵּל.

תהלים קיג

הַלְלוּיָהּ, הַלְלוּ עַבְדֵי יהוה, הַלְלוּ אֶת־שֵׁם יהוה: יְהִי שֵׁם יהוה
מְבֹרָךְ, מֵעַתָּה וְעַד־עוֹלָם: מִמִּזְרַח־שֶׁמֶשׁ עַד־מְבוֹאוֹ, מְהֻלָּל,

---

HALLEL

For a discussion on the recitation of Hallel on Yom HaAtzma'ut see page 101.

ḤIZKIYAHU'S MESSIANIC POTENTIAL

Though he was raised by his wicked father Aḥaz, Ḥizkiyahu was a righteous monarch who eradicated idol worship and enjoyed several military triumphs. Chief among them was a miraculous victory over Sanḥerev's invading armies, which after conquering much of Northern and Central Israel, laid siege to Yerushalayim. On the very day of Pesaḥ – when the Jews had, hundreds of years earlier, been liberated from Egypt – a divine plague destroyed over 185,000 soldiers of Sanḥerev's army, forcing a retreat and rescuing Yerushalayim from almost certain collapse and conquest. This was clearly a divine redemption!

Yet, for some unexplained reason, Ḥizkiyahu didn't recite Hallel, or *shira* – singing praises to God. The Gemara (*Sanhedrin* 94b) claims that HaKadosh Barukh Hu originally intended Ḥizkiyahu as *Mashiaḥ*, but this plan was cancelled because he didn't recite *shira* in response to this miracle.

Ḥizkiyahu's historical failure to recite *shira* may have been due to the imperfect and incomplete nature of the redemption. Though Yerushalayim was spared, hundreds of Israeli cities were despoiled, and ten tribes were exiled. Redemption can sometimes occur in *stages*, and each stage warrants appreciation and the recital of *shira*.

LORD's name be praised. High is the LORD above all nations; His glory is above the heavens. Who is like the LORD our God, who sits enthroned so high, yet turns so low to see the heavens and the earth? ‣ He raises the poor from the dust and the needy from the refuse heap, giving them a place alongside princes, the princes of His people. He makes the woman in a childless house a happy mother of children. Halleluya!

בְּצֵאת When Israel came out of Egypt, the house of Jacob from   *Ps. 114*
a people of foreign tongue, Judah became His sanctuary, Israel His dominion. The sea saw and fled; the Jordan turned back. The mountains skipped like rams, the hills like lambs. ‣ Why was it, sea, that you fled? Jordan, why did you turn back? Why, mountains, did you skip like rams, and you, hills, like lambs? It was at the presence of the LORD, Creator of the earth, at the presence of the God of Jacob, who turned the rock into a pool of water, flint into a flowing spring.

Mount in particular, served as the basis for the created world, which radiated from its hub.

Another opinion asserts that the Land of Israel was created *last*, only *after* the rest of the earth. This sequencing casts Israel as the land of destiny and historical providence. History evolves towards a messianic terminus centered upon the Land of Israel and the People of Israel.

This image is consistent with messianic prophecies which cast Israel in general and Yerushalayim in particular as the epicenter of the entire world. Nations will flock to Yerushalayim to be inspired by the word of God as mediated by the Jewish people. The book of *Shir HaShirim,* which narrates the historical journey, describes "daughters of Yerushalayim" who find the female narrator searching for her male counterpart. The Gemara claims that one day every city will become a "daughter of Yerushalayim" or a suburb to the international hub which Yerushalayim will become.

THE GOLDEN ERA OF JEWISH HISTORY
Our honeymoon with HaKadosh Barukh Hu lasted a mere three months. Liberated from Egypt, we received the divine word, and were poised to

שֵׁם יהוה: רָם עַל־כָּל־גּוֹיִם יהוה, עַל הַשָּׁמַיִם כְּבוֹדוֹ: מִי כַּיהוה
אֱלֹהֵינוּ, הַמַּגְבִּיהִי לָשָׁבֶת: הַמַּשְׁפִּילִי לִרְאוֹת, בַּשָּׁמַיִם וּבָאָרֶץ:
‹ מְקִימִי מֵעָפָר דָּל, מֵאַשְׁפֹּת יָרִים אֶבְיוֹן: לְהוֹשִׁיבִי עִם־נְדִיבִים,
עִם נְדִיבֵי עַמּוֹ: מוֹשִׁיבִי עֲקֶרֶת הַבַּיִת, אֵם־הַבָּנִים שְׂמֵחָה,
הַלְלוּיָהּ:

תהלים קיד

בְּצֵאת יִשְׂרָאֵל מִמִּצְרָיִם, בֵּית יַעֲקֹב מֵעַם לֹעֵז: הָיְתָה יְהוּדָה
לְקָדְשׁוֹ, יִשְׂרָאֵל מַמְשְׁלוֹתָיו: הַיָּם רָאָה וַיָּנֹס, הַיַּרְדֵּן יִסֹּב לְאָחוֹר:
הֶהָרִים רָקְדוּ כְאֵילִים, גְּבָעוֹת כִּבְנֵי־צֹאן: ‹ מַה־לְּךָ הַיָּם כִּי
תָנוּס, הַיַּרְדֵּן תִּסֹּב לְאָחוֹר: הֶהָרִים תִּרְקְדוּ כְאֵילִים, גְּבָעוֹת
כִּבְנֵי־צֹאן: מִלִּפְנֵי אָדוֹן חוּלִי אָרֶץ, מִלִּפְנֵי אֱלוֹהַּ יַעֲקֹב: הַהֹפְכִי
הַצּוּר אֲגַם־מָיִם, חַלָּמִישׁ לְמַעְיְנוֹ־מָיִם:

God, the LORD, speaks and summons the earth, from the rising of the sun to where it sets" (*Tehillim* 50:1). The image of God summoning a land from amidst the entire planet is a reference to the land upon which the entire creation is pivoted.

The Gemara (*Ta'anit* 10a) claims that the Land of Israel was created prior to the rest of the cosmos. This sequencing implies that the quality or caliber of the land is superior to other lands. In fact the continuation of the Gemara speaks of the Land of Israel being prioritized in daily maintenance. This chronology also implies that the land is not governed by typical natural realities. It was created first and *apart from* the rest of the universe, and isn't subject to the physical and metaphysical laws which administer creation.

Another Gemara (*Yoma* 54b) highlights a slightly different nuance. In commenting on the phrase "From the rising of the sun to its setting" the Gemara suggests that the entire planet was fashioned *from* the Land of Israel. In this view Israel is the core, and it radiates life and meaning to the entire planet. The large boulder embedded in the *Kodesh HaKodashim* (and today housed in the Dome of the Rock) is termed the *Even HaShetiya* or the Rock of Foundation. This implies that Israel in general, and the Temple

לֹא לָֽנוּ Not to us, LORD, not to us, but to Your name give glory, ^{Ps. 115} for Your love, for Your faithfulness. Why should the nations say, "Where now is their God?" Our God is in heaven; whatever He wills He does. Their idols are silver and gold, made by human hands. They have mouths but cannot speak; eyes but cannot see. They have ears but cannot hear; noses but cannot smell. They have hands but cannot feel; feet but cannot walk. No sound comes from their throat. Those who make them become like them; so will all who trust in them. ‣ Israel, trust in the LORD – He is their Help and their Shield. House of Aaron, trust in the LORD – He is their Help and their Shield. You who fear the LORD, trust in the LORD – He is their Help and their Shield.

---

perfect state, nature enthusiastically cooperated with him in the service of God. As man represented the pinnacle of creation, assisting him was nature's method of consecrating creation. As he fell from *Gan Eden*, nature was rendered less compliant to rebellious man. Initially Adam is cursed to earn his bread by the sweat of his brow, and subsequently Kayin is condemned to plant thorns and bristles. In each instance human moral decay ruins the amenability of nature. As man's lot declines, nature can no longer serve God solely by cooperating with man.

Having left Egypt, the Jews briefly achieved a perfected state, and nature happily restored her trust and support. Of course our national fall signaled a universal failure, once again deterring a fully harmonious relationship with nature. When *Mashiah* closes history, mankind will once again achieve a state of perfection, inviting nature to once again serve man unconditionally. Various prophecies describing the healing powers of nature, as well as the lack of predation in the Messianic Era, reinforce the prospect of a fully restored relationship with nature.

לֹא לָֽנוּ יהוה לֹא לָֽנוּ, כִּי־לְשִׁמְךָ תֵּן כָּבוֹד *Not to us, LORD, not to us, but to Your name give glory. Yeḥezkel* chapter 20 provides a very different narrative to *Yetziat Mitzrayim* (the exodus from Egypt). The account in *Shemot* doesn't indicate that anything was expected from the Jewish people. This alternate version highlights God's expectations of them. To help jumpstart the redemption

לֹא לָנוּ יהוה לֹא לָנוּ, כִּי־לְשִׁמְךָ תֵּן כָּבוֹד, עַל־חַסְדְּךָ עַל־
אֲמִתֶּךָ: לָמָּה יֹאמְרוּ הַגּוֹיִם אַיֵּה־נָא אֱלֹהֵיהֶם: וֵאלֹהֵינוּ בַשָּׁמָיִם,
כֹּל אֲשֶׁר־חָפֵץ עָשָׂה: עֲצַבֵּיהֶם כֶּסֶף וְזָהָב, מַעֲשֵׂה יְדֵי אָדָם:
פֶּה־לָהֶם וְלֹא יְדַבֵּרוּ, עֵינַיִם לָהֶם וְלֹא יִרְאוּ: אָזְנַיִם לָהֶם וְלֹא
יִשְׁמָעוּ, אַף לָהֶם וְלֹא יְרִיחוּן: יְדֵיהֶם וְלֹא יְמִישׁוּן, רַגְלֵיהֶם וְלֹא
יְהַלֵּכוּ, לֹא־יֶהְגּוּ בִּגְרוֹנָם: כְּמוֹהֶם יִהְיוּ עֹשֵׂיהֶם, כֹּל אֲשֶׁר־בֹּטֵחַ
בָּהֶם: ‹ יִשְׂרָאֵל בְּטַח בַּיהוה, עֶזְרָם וּמָגִנָּם הוּא: בֵּית אַהֲרֹן
בִּטְחוּ בַיהוה, עֶזְרָם וּמָגִנָּם הוּא: יִרְאֵי יהוה בִּטְחוּ בַיהוה, עֶזְרָם
וּמָגִנָּם הוּא:

march into the Land of Israel and usher in the Kingdom of God and utopia.
An eleven-day walk is all that separated us from this potential. Unfortunately
our dual mutinies of the Golden Calf and the spies condemned us to a historical struggle fraught with exile and persecution. All of history has been
an attempt to recapture the bliss of those first three months of national
experience.

This chapter in *Tehillim* portrays that era by describing a nation marching
through the desert as God's dominion. Even nature recognized our enchanted status by unnaturally but happily yielding to our advance. The chapter
condenses three supernatural events – all of which include supernatural
anomalies which aided the Jewish people's evolution: the splitting of the sea,
the delivery of the Torah, and the crossing of the Jordan River thirty-nine
years afterwards, upon our eventual entry to the Land of Israel. In each instance nature is personified or animated. The sea *perceives* the nation and flees,
while the Jordan River retreats from our chosen trail. During the delivery of
the Torah the mountains cheerfully dance at the thrill of a human community
accepting the divine word. Though these events are all authored by God, they
are described from the vantage point of nature willfully cooperating with the
Jewish agenda.

These images capture the Eden-like nature of that golden era, and the
prospect for similar collaboration in the Messianic Era. In man's original

יהוה זְכָרָנוּ The Lord remembers us and will bless us. He will bless
the house of Israel. He will bless the house of Aaron. He will bless
those who fear the Lord, small and great alike. May the Lord give
you increase: you and your children. May you be blessed by the
Lord, Maker of heaven and earth. ‣ The heavens are the Lord's,
but the earth He has given over to mankind. It is not the dead who
praise the Lord, nor those who go down to the silent grave. But
we will bless the Lord, now and for ever. Halleluya!

The Holocaust represented the single greatest desecration of His name
since the destruction of the First Temple. Though history is littered with
pogroms, inquisitions, and expulsions, the attempt to eliminate anything
and everything Jewish from the streets of Europe was an attack against His
presence, and not just the Jewish nation. A Ḥillul Hashem of that magnitude
required some response to restore His presence in our world. No human
can fully wrap his mind around the horror of the Holocaust. Offsetting the
horror of the Holocaust against the triumph of the State of Israel is not morally acceptable, nor intellectually accurate. Yet the juxtaposition of the two
events provides an additional insight into our peculiar form of redemption.
We may not have deserved to be redeemed in 1948. However, just as we undeserving people were redeemed from Egypt to protect the dignity of His
name, similarly we were redeemed in our homeland to restore the luster of
His presence in our world.

JEWISH POPULATION GROWTH IN THE STATE OF ISRAEL
יֹסֵף יהוה עֲלֵיכֶם, עֲלֵיכֶם וְעַל־בְּנֵיכֶם *May the Lord give you increase: you and your
children.* Throughout the period of exile, the population of Jews in Israel was
meager. As late as the mid-eighteenth century, prior to great waves of *aliya*,
Jews in Israel numbered as low as a couple of thousand. Steadily the population grew to around 65,000 in 1914 and to around 425,000 by the end of the
1930s. Interestingly, the Jewish population numbered approximately 650,000
when the State was declared in 1948 – around the same number of Jews who
exited Egypt and received the Torah at Sinai. An intriguing midrash (*Yalkut
Shimoni Hoshea* 2:918) comments that the same population size that left
Egypt and entered the Land of Israel – namely 600,000 – will return during

יהוה זְכָרָנוּ יְבָרֵךְ, יְבָרֵךְ אֶת־בֵּית יִשְׂרָאֵל, יְבָרֵךְ אֶת־בֵּית אַהֲרֹן:
יְבָרֵךְ יִרְאֵי יהוה, הַקְּטַנִּים עִם־הַגְּדֹלִים: יֹסֵף יהוה עֲלֵיכֶם,
עֲלֵיכֶם וְעַל־בְּנֵיכֶם: בְּרוּכִים אַתֶּם לַיהוה, עֹשֵׂה שָׁמַיִם וָאָרֶץ:
‹ הַשָּׁמַיִם שָׁמַיִם לַיהוה, וְהָאָרֶץ נָתַן לִבְנֵי־אָדָם: לֹא הַמֵּתִים
יְהַלְלוּ־יָהּ, וְלֹא כָּל־יֹרְדֵי דוּמָה: וַאֲנַחְנוּ נְבָרֵךְ יָהּ, מֵעַתָּה וְעַד־
עוֹלָם, הַלְלוּיָהּ:

_____

they were asked to retreat from the pagan culture by which they had become
captivated: "And I said to them: Cast away, every man, the detestable things
of his eyes, and do not defile yourselves with the idols of Egypt; I am the
LORD your God" (*Yeḥezkel* 20:7). The Jewish response is uninspired: "But
they rebelled against Me, and would not hearken unto Me; every man did
not cast away the detestable things of their eyes, neither did they forsake the
idols of Egypt" (ibid. 8). HaKadosh Barukh Hu intended to annihilate the
nation and begin the historical process afresh: "…then I said I would pour out
My fury upon them, to spend My anger upon them in the midst of the land
of Egypt" (ibid.). The phrase "*shefokh Ḥamatekha*" or "pour Your wrath" is
familiar from the *Seder Haggada* in which we ask God to dispense His anger
upon iniquitous nations. Originally, however, this warning was hurled at the
Jewish people, threatening them with extinction.

Why did HaKadosh Barukh Hu recant His intentions, and redeem an
otherwise undeserving people? *Yeḥezkel* provides the answer: "But I wrought
for My name's sake, that it should not be profaned in the sight of the nations,
among whom they were, in whose sight I made Myself known to them, so
as to bring them forth out of the land of Egypt" (ibid. 9). Hundreds of years
had been invested in exposing mankind to a monotheistic God, through
the prism of the Jewish nation. Through the tireless efforts of our *Avot*, the
concept of an unknowable but moral God began to percolate through the
human imagination. Eliminating the people at this stage would have led to a
reversal of this process, a regression of the presence of HaKadosh Barukh Hu
in our world, and an intolerable *Ḥillul Hashem*. We were redeemed in Egypt
– not necessarily because we deserved it – but as part of a larger narrative to
sanctify His name in our world.

אָהַבְתִּי I love the LORD, for He hears my voice, my pleas. He turns *Ps. 116* His ear to me whenever I call. The bonds of death encompassed me, the anguish of the grave came upon me, I was overcome by trouble and sorrow. Then I called on the name of the LORD: "LORD, I pray, save my life." Gracious is the LORD, and righteous; our God is full of compassion. The LORD protects the simple hearted. When I was brought low, He saved me. My soul, be at peace once more, for the LORD has been good to you. For You have rescued me from death,

---

During the period preceding the war women and children were dispatched to "safe havens" in Europe and the United States to place them out of harm's way. For weeks on end children attending school simply recited *Tehillim* for a few hours and returned home. Tests, projects, and curriculums seemed pointless.

Much of the political and military planning was couched in terms of absorbing significant and inevitable casualties but hopefully, under optimal conditions, being able to conserve a remnant of the State of Israel. As the well-known "gallows humor" went, the last person to leave the country was instructed to shut off the lights in the Ben Gurion airport.

Suddenly the miraculous occurred: people exited basements after the first night of battle to hear that the Egyptian air force had been eliminated. Most homes or building did not even have bomb shelters, rendering the inhabitants exposed to the predicted Egyptian strafing. For weeks we had begged King Hussein of Jordan to stay out of the war; we had no grievance with him as we battled the Egyptians to the South and the Syrians to the North. Astonishingly he was duped into joining the war by a false telegram sent by General Nasser. As the latter's tank divisions were being surrounded in the Sinai desert he conveyed a message to the monarch of Jordan that Egyptian divisions were marching on Ashdod and he was invited to join and take his share in the ultimate spoils of victory. Beyond anyone's wildest dreams, within days we were strolling in the streets of Jerusalem, and we had returned to the "Biblical Homeland" of Israel – the land in which our forefathers crafted Jewish history. The return to these lands was completely unexpected, unplanned for, and a secondary consequence of Jordan's entry into the war.

תהלים קטז

אָהַבְתִּי, כִּי־יִשְׁמַע יהוה, אֶת־קוֹלִי תַּחֲנוּנָי: כִּי־הִטָּה אָזְנוֹ לִי,
וּבְיָמַי אֶקְרָא: אֲפָפוּנִי חֶבְלֵי־מָוֶת, וּמְצָרֵי שְׁאוֹל מְצָאוּנִי, צָרָה
וְיָגוֹן אֶמְצָא: וּבְשֵׁם־יהוה אֶקְרָא, אָנָּה יהוה מַלְּטָה נַפְשִׁי: חַנּוּן
יהוה וְצַדִּיק, וֵאלֹהֵינוּ מְרַחֵם: שֹׁמֵר פְּתָאִים יהוה, דַּלּוֹתִי וְלִי
יְהוֹשִׁיעַ: שׁוּבִי נַפְשִׁי לִמְנוּחָיְכִי, כִּי־יהוה גָּמַל עָלָיְכִי: כִּי חִלַּצְתָּ

the Messianic Era. In truth this "magic number" represents the number of males over the age of twenty who left Egypt. At the time of the Six Day War the census showed that number of Jews residing in Israel. This number is institutionalized in Halakha, as several practices require an encounter with this size of Jewish population.

Subsequent to the formation of the State, Jewish population grew exponentially, swelled by dramatic absorption of Jews from Arabic lands in the fifties, Ethiopian Jews in the late eighties, and finally Russian Jews in the nineties. In the seventy years since its formation, the Jewish population in Israel has multiplied more than tenfold. Successfully admitting and integrating so many different ethnicities, cultures, and dialects has been a great achievement of the State.

THE SIX DAY WAR

אֲפָפוּנִי חֶבְלֵי־מָוֶת *The bonds of death encompassed me.* The events of 1967 have undergone significant and unfortunate historical revisionism. Due to the current political struggle surrounding Judea and Samaria, this war has been cast as an operation surrounding the conquest of land and territory. Nothing could be further from the truth. In 1967 General Nasser of Egypt evicted the United Nations forces from the Suez Canal (which served then as the border between Israel and Egypt) and launched his infamous threat to "hurl the Jews into the sea." In retrospect this threat seems cartoonish, but when it was announced it was extremely intimidating and frightening. The nineteen intervening years between 1948 and 1967 were not robust years of growth and expansion, but stark years of economic austerity and diplomatic isolation. Forced to wage continuing battles against our Arab neighbors, we were almost constantly in a state of war.

The nation feared a continuation and culmination of Hitler's Holocaust.

my eyes from weeping, my feet from stumbling. ‣ I shall walk in
the presence of the Lᴏʀᴅ in the land of the living. I had faith, even
when I said, "I am greatly afflicted," even when I said rashly, "All
men are liars."

מָה־אָשִׁיב How can I repay the Lᴏʀᴅ for all His goodness to me?
I will lift the cup of salvation and call on the name of the Lᴏʀᴅ. I
will fulfill my vows to the Lᴏʀᴅ in the presence of all His people.
Grievous in the Lᴏʀᴅ's sight is the death of His devoted ones.
Truly, Lᴏʀᴅ, I am Your servant; I am Your servant, the son of Your
maidservant. You set me free from my chains. ‣ To You I shall bring
a thanksgiving-offering and call on the Lᴏʀᴅ by name. I will fulfill
my vows to the Lᴏʀᴅ in the presence of all His people, in the courts
of the House of the Lᴏʀᴅ, in your midst, Jerusalem. Halleluya!

---

historically conscious Jew (see *Bereshit Raba* 39:8). Some claim (see *Sefer
Haredim* page 196) that even initially Avraham visits the Land of Israel but
is instructed to return to his homeland. Only after five years of waiting does
HaKadosh Barukh Hu allow him to return. He too learns to covet the Land
in a manner that only distance can generate.

Sadly we have been distant from our land for close to two millennia. This
absence has rendered our national heart fonder of our land and more willing
to sacrifice on her behalf.

HELPLESSNESS AND DISPLACEMENT
Having been pursued relentlessly by Shaul, David HaMelekh was forced
to temporarily vacate the Land of Israel and resettle on the East Bank of
the Jordan. This exile exacerbates his sense of vulnerability – not only is
he pursued but he is also evicted. The chapter is dominated by images portraying this vulnerability: David is surrounded by "enemies of death" and
engulfed by the "confines of the grave." He recognizes that his soul has been
"spared from death" and his eye has been safeguarded from tears. He values HaKadosh Barukh Hu as the protector of the innocent and defense-
less. Amidst this suffering and defenselessness he yearns for a return to
his homeland: "That I may walk before the Lᴏʀᴅ in the land of the living"

נַפְשִׁי מִמָּוֶת, אֶת־עֵינִי מִן־דִּמְעָה, אֶת־רַגְלִי מִדֶּחִי: ‹ אֶתְהַלֵּךְ
לִפְנֵי יהוה, בְּאַרְצוֹת הַחַיִּים: הֶאֱמַנְתִּי כִּי אֲדַבֵּר, אֲנִי עָנִיתִי
מְאֹד: אֲנִי אָמַרְתִּי בְחָפְזִי, כָּל־הָאָדָם כֹּזֵב:

מָה־אָשִׁיב לַיהוה, כָּל־תַּגְמוּלוֹהִי עָלָי: כּוֹס־יְשׁוּעוֹת אֶשָּׂא,
וּבְשֵׁם יהוה אֶקְרָא: נְדָרַי לַיהוה אֲשַׁלֵּם, נֶגְדָה־נָּא לְכָל־עַמּוֹ:
יָקָר בְּעֵינֵי יהוה, הַמָּוְתָה לַחֲסִידָיו: אָנָּה יהוה כִּי־אֲנִי עַבְדֶּךָ,
אֲנִי־עַבְדְּךָ בֶּן־אֲמָתֶךָ, פִּתַּחְתָּ לְמוֹסֵרָי: ‹ לְךָ־אֶזְבַּח זֶבַח תּוֹדָה,
וּבְשֵׁם יהוה אֶקְרָא: נְדָרַי לַיהוה אֲשַׁלֵּם, נֶגְדָה־נָּא לְכָל־עַמּוֹ:
בְּחַצְרוֹת בֵּית יהוה, בְּתוֹכֵכִי יְרוּשָׁלָםִ, הַלְלוּיָהּ:

ABSENCE MAKES THE HEART GROW FONDER

אֶתְהַלֵּךְ... בְּאַרְצוֹת הַחַיִּים *I shall walk... in the land of the living.* Having been
temporarily exiled, King David yearns for a return to the Land of Israel.
Having been forcibly removed from the land he hungers for it even more
intensely. Similar conditions befell our *Avot*: though they had settled in
Israel, circumstances led to their departure, affecting greater desire for a
return.

Yaakov had been dispatched to Aram Naharaim for twenty-two years and
his return to the land wasn't straightforward. An apparition visits him in
a dream and compels his return. His father-in-law pursues him, hoping to
blunt that return. When he arrives, his murderous brother awaits him with
four hundred mercenaries. His absence from the land has only whetted his
appetite for resettlement. When he finally does arrive he assumes that his
struggles have ended and he can enjoy serenity in the Land of Israel. Unfortunately HaKadosh Barukh Hu presented alternate plans, and he was forced
to descend into a second Egyptian exile.

According to several versions, Avraham experienced a brief removal from
Israel to animate his desire for the land. One version of the Midrash describes
him returning to his foreign homeland after embracing the *Berit Bein HaBetarim* and the historical mission of Judaism. Having accepted this historical
pact he is forced to once again journey back to Israel – this time as a fully

הַלְלוּ Praise the Lord, all nations; acclaim Him, all you peoples;   *Ps. 117*
for His loving-kindness to us is strong,
and the Lord's faithfulness is everlasting.
Halleluya!

---

disconsolate community that these verbal efforts at debunking our faith would collapse. One day these taunts will be replaced by a hymn to the Jewish people.

In fact the continuing derision of the Jews and their faith during the Second *Mikdash* era was cited by the Ramban as evidence that this era was not Messianic. These expectations of worldwide acclaim for the Jews had yet to be realized.

In the Modern era we are under a verbal assault of a very different nature. In a post-ideological world, debating various religions has become outmoded. However, we are assailed for our moral conduct in the Land of Israel. Heroically, and at great cost, we maintain our moral code while we defend ourselves against suicidal enemies. Our license to the Land of Israel is based on our selection as His people and our duty to reflect His moral values. If we compromise this platform we abdicate that license. Yet despite our efforts we are internationally lambasted and verbally condemned in the court of public opinion. As Yeshayahu prophesied, we face tongues which arise to challenge us regarding *justice*. These tongues will also one day be quieted when the presence of HaKadosh Barukh Hu becomes unmistakable, and our mission undeniable. These verbal indictments will be replaced by a chorus of approval and admiration.

הַלְלוּ אֶת־יהוה כָּל־גּוֹיִם, שַׁבְּחוּהוּ כָּל־הָאֻמִּים: *Praise the Lord, all nations; acclaim Him, all you peoples.* This verse presents an unusual image of Gentile nations praising HaKadosh Barukh Hu because of Jewish triumph and God's kindness in enabling our redemption. An even more strident image is found in *Devarim* (32:43): "Rejoice, O nations, with His people; for He will avenge the blood of His servants, and will render vengeance on His adversaries, and will atone for His land and His people." This verse describes divine vengeance upon those who have previously persecuted the Jews. The universal response to this vengeance is praise for God. Evidently, as history closes, all of humanity will acknowledge HaKadosh Barukh Hu, as well as the unique Jewish role in reflecting His presence in our world for so many

הַלְלוּ אֶת־יהוה כָּל־גּוֹיִם, שַׁבְּחוּהוּ כָּל־הָאֻמִּים:
כִּי גָבַר עָלֵינוּ חַסְדּוֹ, וֶאֱמֶת־יהוה לְעוֹלָם
הַלְלוּיָהּ:

(*Tehillim* 116:9). The state of being distant from the Land of Israel aggravates feelings of vulnerability, and the return bolsters a sense of security and tranquility.

Though these verses describe generic suffering and deliverance, they provide specific representation of the experience of suffering in exile, and release upon returning to the land of life. Referring to Israel as *Artzot HaḤayyim* – the Land of the Living – the Midrash notes that Israel shares this qualifier with nine other entities, among them God, Torah and *Gan Eden,* all of which are referred to as "Ḥayyim."

THE WORLD WILL ACCLAIM THE JEWS

A Messianic world which acknowledges the dominion of HaKadosh Barukh Hu will also applaud the Jewish nation as His representatives. Our function in disseminating monotheism will be universally recognized, and our presence in His Chosen Land will be internationally approved. Moshe promises: "Rejoice, you nations, with His people, for He will avenge the blood of His servants; He will take vengeance on His enemies and make atonement for His land and people" (*Devarim* 32:43), asserting that we will be celebrated for the mission we served. This verse declares that humanity at large will praise God when He provides overwhelming kindness to His people. Our national redemption will be appreciated as a universal redemption.

Throughout our exile we were physically persecuted, but also verbally assailed. In the twelfth century the Rambam authored a communique to the demoralized Jewish community in Yemen. They had encountered a false messiah, followed by an Islamic fundamentalist movement attempting to forcibly convert them. He cited a verse in *Yeshayahu*, "No weapon forged against you will prevail, and you will refute every tongue that accuses you. This is the heritage of the servants of the LORD..." (54:17). He reminded the community that Jews had perennially encountered violent aggression but also had faced verbal assaults – as implied by this verse. Throughout the exile our religion and its tenets were constantly under attack. Our religion and belief was cast as heresy or outdated. The Rambam assured this

The following verses are chanted by the Leader.
At the end of each verse, the congregation responds, "Thank the LORD
for He is good; His loving-kindness is for ever."

הוֹדוּ Thank the LORD for He is good;   Ps. 118
HIS LOVING-KINDNESS IS FOR EVER.

Let Israel say
HIS LOVING-KINDNESS IS FOR EVER.

Let the house of Aaron say
HIS LOVING-KINDNESS IS FOR EVER.

Let those who fear the LORD say
HIS LOVING-KINDNESS IS FOR EVER.

מִן־הַמֵּצַר In my distress I called on the LORD. The LORD answered me and set me free. The LORD is with me; I will not be afraid. What can man do to me? The LORD is with me. He is my Helper. I will see the downfall of my enemies. It is better to take refuge in the

---

recur in history. Studying the evolution of this bondage yields a better sense of the rhythm of future events.

However, the word "*meitzar*" primarily connotes a condition of confinement or narrowness. The conclusion of the verse supports this image by asking HaKadosh Barukh Hu to "set me free," literally "answer me, God, with expansiveness." Confinement of space and expansion of space become both metaphors for redemption as well as part of its mechanics. During redemptive moments, Jewish sovereignty expands without external limitation. During moments of struggle we are confined to cramped areas.

The first person to experience this dynamic was Yitzḥak, who was confined in the Land of Israel partly due to local political conflicts with the coast-dwelling Pelishtim. When the pressure was finally relieved he named his city Reḥovot, to convey the newfound ability to expand without opposition. Based on this name and concept, the modern city of Reḥovot received its name.

Similarly, HaKadosh Barukh Hu promises the Jewish people that upon entering Israel, "When the LORD your God has expanded your territory as

The following verses are chanted by the שליח ציבור.
At the end of each verse, the קהל *responds:* הוֹדוּ לַיהוה כִּי־טוֹב, כִּי לְעוֹלָם חַסְדּוֹ.

תהלים קיח

הוֹדוּ לַיהוה כִּי־טוֹב   כִּי לְעוֹלָם חַסְדּוֹ:

יֹאמַר־נָא יִשְׂרָאֵל   כִּי לְעוֹלָם חַסְדּוֹ:

יֹאמְרוּ־נָא בֵית־אַהֲרֹן   כִּי לְעוֹלָם חַסְדּוֹ:

יֹאמְרוּ־נָא יִרְאֵי יהוה   כִּי לְעוֹלָם חַסְדּוֹ:

מִן־הַמֵּצַר קָרָאתִי יָּהּ, עָנָנִי בַמֶּרְחָב יָהּ: יהוה לִי לֹא אִירָא, מַה־
יַּעֲשֶׂה לִי אָדָם: יהוה לִי בְּעֹזְרָי, וַאֲנִי אֶרְאֶה בְשֹׂנְאָי: טוֹב לַחֲסוֹת

---

centuries. Rashi comments that mankind will be particularly impressed by
the Jewish dedication to monotheism despite repeated harassments and
oppressions. Recognizing God's authority will render them grateful for
Jewish commitment throughout the millennia. They will not only praise
God, but be grateful for the Jewish role, and for HaKadosh Barukh Hu both
protecting us and avenging us against our enemies.

Similar sentiments are expressed in the opening section to *Tefilla* on Rosh
HaShana, when we envision a messianic future in which "all that have breath
in their mouths will declare: The LORD, God of Israel is King, and His kingship has dominion over all."

In his book *Sefer HaGeula*, the Rambam employs these verses and the
associated imagery as proof that a third redemption will still occur. The
Second Temple didn't usher an era of universal acceptance of the unique
status of the Jewish people. We were still subjugated and many nations still
possessed an adversarial attitude toward us. We are still awaiting that future
vision.

CONFINED AND SUFFERING

מִן־הַמֵּצַר *In my distress.* The word *meitzar* evokes the word "*tzara*" or persecution. Additionally the conjugation conjures the name *Mitzrayim*. The
Midrash (*Vayikra Raba* 13:4) senses this association, and concludes that the
oppression in Egypt was an archetype for all future Jewish suffering. The
same patterns which contributed towards our eventual enslavement will

LORD than to trust in man. It is better to take refuge in the LORD than to trust in princes. The nations all surrounded me, but in the LORD's name I drove them off. They surrounded me on every side, but in the LORD's name I drove them off. They surrounded me like bees, they attacked me as fire attacks brushwood, but in the LORD's name I drove them off. They thrust so hard against me, I nearly fell, but the LORD came to my help. The LORD is my strength and my song; He has become my salvation. Sounds of song and salvation resound in the tents of the righteous: "The LORD's right hand has done mighty deeds. The LORD's right hand is lifted high. The LORD's right hand has done mighty deeds." I will not die but live, and tell what the LORD has done. The LORD has chastened me severely, but He has not given me over to death. ‣ Open for me the gates of righteousness that I may enter them and thank the LORD. This is the gateway to the LORD; through it, the righteous shall enter.

Often Jews were barred from moving to Israel because *local* gates were closed. Rules against immigration to Israel weren't necessarily intended to prevent Jewish return to their homeland. Instead local restrictions existed against emigration. Many believe that the MaHaram of Rothenburg, who was legendarily imprisoned in France, was arrested because of his plans to make *aliya*.

As Jewish interest in returning to their homeland increased, oftentimes stiff quotas curbed this movement. A notorious policy paper was published by the British government in 1939, setting severe quotas on Jewish immigration into Palestine, and effectively assuring an Arab majority. Great efforts were made to circumvent these quotas and create alternate gates of passage. Shortly after achieving independence, in 1950 the Law of Return or *Hok HaShevut* was enacted, assuring unconditional entry and citizenship in the Jewish State to every Jew worldwide.

Towards the end of the twentieth century, Jews living under Soviet rule were barred from emigrating in general, and in particular from going to Israel. With great courage and tenacity the "Prisoners of Zion" movement defied the erstwhile indomitable regime, and forced open the gates to Israel. Ultimately the efforts at prying open these gates led to the felling of the Iron curtain and the fall of the Soviet Empire.

בַּיהוה, מִבְּטֹחַ בָּאָדָם: טוֹב לַחֲסוֹת בַּיהוה, מִבְּטֹחַ בִּנְדִיבִים:
כָּל־גּוֹיִם סְבָבְוּנִי, בְּשֵׁם יהוה כִּי אֲמִילַם: סַבְּוּנִי גַם־סְבָבְוּנִי, בְּשֵׁם
יהוה כִּי אֲמִילַם: סַבְּוּנִי כִדְבֹרִים, דֹּעֲכוּ כְּאֵשׁ קוֹצִים, בְּשֵׁם יהוה
כִּי אֲמִילַם: דָּחֹה דְחִיתַנִי לִנְפֹּל, וַיהוה עֲזָרְנִי: עָזִּי וְזִמְרָת יָהּ,
וַיְהִי־לִי לִישׁוּעָה: קוֹל רִנָּה וִישׁוּעָה בְּאָהֳלֵי צַדִּיקִים, יְמִין יהוה
עֹשָׂה חָיִל: יְמִין יהוה רוֹמֵמָה, יְמִין יהוה עֹשָׂה חָיִל: לֹא־אָמוּת
כִּי־אֶחְיֶה, וַאֲסַפֵּר מַעֲשֵׂי יָהּ: יַסֹּר יִסְּרַנִּי יָּהּ, וְלַמָּוֶת לֹא נְתָנָנִי:
‹ פִּתְחוּ־לִי שַׁעֲרֵי־צֶדֶק, אָבֹא־בָם אוֹדֶה יָהּ: זֶה־הַשַּׁעַר לַיהוה,
צַדִּיקִים יָבֹאוּ בוֹ:

He promised you, and you crave meat and say, 'I would like some meat,' then you may eat as much of it as you want" (*Devarim* 12:20), restating the natural and uncontested expansion which a redeemed people will experience.

Throughout our history in the Diaspora Jews were often restricted to constrained living areas. The establishment of Jewish ghettos dates as far back as the eleventh century, and was common both in European communities as well as Arabic countries.

Ultimately Avraham was guaranteed "Your descendants will be like the dust of the earth, and you will spread out to the west and to the east, to the north and to the south. All peoples on earth will be blessed through you and your offspring" (*Bereshit* 28:14), depicting a utopian state in which Jews and their influence suffuse a world thirsting for the divine word, as disseminated by the Jewish nation.

THE GATES OF ISRAEL

פִּתְחוּ־לִי שַׁעֲרֵי־צֶדֶק *Open for me the gates of righteousness.* Entering through open gates is a metaphor for passage into a previously impassable area. A parallel verse in *Yeshayahu* (26:2) frames the return to Yerushalayim with this metaphor of unlocked gates: "Open the gates that the righteous nation may enter, the nation that keeps faith." Throughout history the "gates" to Israel haven't always been accessible. As redemption advances, the gates become unlocked.

אוֹדְךָ I will thank You, for You answered me,
and became my salvation.
I will thank You, for You answered me,
and became my salvation.

The stone the builders rejected
has become the main cornerstone.
The stone the builders rejected
has become the main cornerstone.

---

even tragic ultimately amplified our triumph. Acknowledging these sudden turns of events, we praise HaKadosh Barukh Hu for what appeared to be a punishment.

DIVINE MAKEOVER

אֶבֶן מָאֲסוּ *The stone ... rejected.* The transformation of the Jewish people in Egypt was stunning. A nation which had been suppressed and subjugated for over two hundred years was suddenly soaring on Heavenly clouds. Astounded by this sudden change, the Egyptians inquired as to our secret. Equally astonished, the Jewish people responded that they themselves were left speechless. At which point HaKadosh Barukh Hu Himself replied, "This is the LORD's doing; it is wondrous in our eyes." Some shifts in human history are too dramatic to be explained as anything other than divine providence.

The state of the Jewish people in the middle of the past century was forlorn and bleak. Ravaged by poverty, scattered across the globe, Jewish identity was vulnerable. An unprecedented and merciless attack upon our people destroyed nearly a third of us.

Close to seventy years later, our nation is flourishing as never before. We have crafted a modern state which in many ways is the envy of the entire world. There is more Torah being studied than at any point since the First *Mikdash* era. Jewish identity has attained unparalleled heights, as Jews the world over actively participate in shaping our world in the image of our traditions of morality and respect for others. The meteoric rise of our national condition surpasses even the revolutionary transformation in Egypt. We can easily hear the echo of God's earlier comments about our own experiences: "This is the LORD's doing; it is wondrous in our eyes."

אוֹדְךָ כִּי עֲנִיתָנִי, וַתְּהִי־לִי לִישׁוּעָה:
אוֹדְךָ כִּי עֲנִיתָנִי, וַתְּהִי־לִי לִישׁוּעָה:

אֶבֶן מָאֲסוּ הַבּוֹנִים, הָיְתָה לְרֹאשׁ פִּנָּה:
אֶבֶן מָאֲסוּ הַבּוֹנִים, הָיְתָה לְרֹאשׁ פִּנָּה:

כִּי עֲנִיתָנִי *For You answered me.* The phrase "*ki anitani*" can mean "for You answered me," or, entirely differently, it can mean "even though You tormented me." Obviously these diametrically opposed phrases radically alter the meaning of this verse. A similar dichotomy appears in a verse in *Yeshayahu*: "On that day you will say: 'I will praise You, LORD, even though/because You were angry with me, Your anger has turned away and You have comforted me'" (12:1).

The simpler meaning would translate "*ki*" in each of these verses as "even though." Consequently the verse in Hallel announces our praise for HaKadosh Barukh Hu *even though* He punished us. Ultimately though, He redeemed us. Though we suffered at certain historical stages, our final redemption will dwarf those dark moments. Similarly in *Yeshayahu* we thank God "*even though*" He was angry; He rejected that anger and rescued us. Taken in this form these verses attest to the inevitability of final redemption: we may suffer, and God may be angered by our behavior. However, when history is resolved, our redemptive state will yield a praise which surpasses those dismal experiences.

But the term "*ki*" can also mean "because." We thank HaKadosh Barukh Hu *because* we suffered and *because* He was angry. Oftentimes events which appear detrimental and which cause us distress ultimately yield unimagined benefits. Several events in the history of our State initially appeared devastating, but ultimately proved to be beneficial. Had our Arab neighbors accepted the partition plan, our original State would have been much smaller in size than the ultimate State based on the Armistice agreements after the War of Independence. Arab disgust with a Jewish State and their fierce attack on the young State led to the expansion of our borders.

Similarly, during the Six Day War, initial attempts for a ceasefire were rejected by the Arabs. Ultimately the continuation of the war yielded the restoration of the historical corridor of Israel stretching from Shekhem in the north to Ḥevron in the south. Events which initially seemed unfortunate and

This is the LORD's doing.
It is wondrous in our eyes.
This is the LORD's doing.
It is wondrous in our eyes.

---

bear their names. Sadly most of the population remained in Bavel due to economic hardships and security concerns in the Land of Israel. Those who did return were of dubious religious character. Ezra himself is exasperated at the repeated but ultimately failed attempts to improve the national religious character. Chief among their offenses was widespread intermarriage. Twenty years into the redemptive period the nation still maintained their foreign wives, forcing Ezra into a dramatic personal fast and public mission to rid the people of this transgression. Sadly the ninth chapter of Ezra describes the leadership as setting a damaging model for the rest of the population.

Beyond particular religious corrosion, apparently their basic pedigree was disoriented. Ezra 2:59 portrays this confusion: "The following came up from the towns of Tel Melaḥ, Tel Ḥarsha, Keruv, Adan and Immer, but they could not show that their families were descended from Israel." Apparently the assimilation in Bavel was so severe that basic Jewish identity was muddled and family lineage was scrambled. In fact Ezra was forced to sort the population clutter by arranging the various factions into separate classes. The first Mishna of the fourth *perek* of *Kiddushin* portrays this process by announcing: "Ten [familial] genealogical lineages went up [with Ezra] from [the] Babylon [exile]." Some claim that he *intentionally* relocated these dubious classes so that they would not remain behind in Bavel and infiltrate the pedigreed population. Under his supervision in Israel he could better protect the purity of the pedigreed population. Either way the return to Israel was piloted by an ethnically tainted population.

For his part, Neḥemya describes widespread Shabbat desecration: "I rebuked the nobles of Judah and said to them, 'What is this wicked thing you are doing –desecrating the Shabbat day? Didn't your ancestors do the same things, so that God brought all this calamity on us and on this city? Now you are stirring up more wrath against Israel by desecrating the Shabbat'" (*Neḥemya* 13:17–18). Commenting on this overall religious and national decay, the Gemara (*Kiddushin* 70a) likens the behavior of this generation to the population of Sedom.

Yet despite their defects, this company, few in number and flawed in

מֵאֵת יהוה הָיְתָה זֹּאת, הִיא נִפְלָאת בְּעֵינֵינוּ: מֵאֵת יהוה הָיְתָה זֹּאת, הִיא נִפְלָאת בְּעֵינֵינוּ:

GOD ALONE PERFORMS MIRACLES

מֵאֵת יהוה הָיְתָה זֹּאת, הִיא נִפְלָאת בְּעֵינֵינוּ *This is the* Lord's *doing; it is wondrous in our eyes.* We conclude the first part of the Pesah *Seder* with a *berakha* praising HaKadosh Barukh Hu for His miracles. The syntax of the blessing concludes in an atypical fashion: we recite praise to *The One* who performed (*leMi She'asa*) miracles for our fathers and for us. The Gemara (*Berakhot* 50a) questions this composition; it is rarely employed since the term may indicate *multiple* sources – a heretical notion, as everything stems from God. The Gemara responds that when referencing miracles, this term can be employed since it is obvious that *only* HaKadosh Barukh Hu is the source of miracles. Major interventions in nature cannot be attributed to any other source. As there is no alternative option we can refer to *The One* who delivered miracles.

This theological premise – that miracles can only be performed by God – hasn't always been obvious. Moshe's impressive miracles were attributed to black magic, since the original ones were reproduced by Pharaoh's magicians. As the ten plagues unfolded, it became evident that the interferences were divine acts, and that HaKadosh Barukh Hu alone is the source for major interventions.

Similar concerns haunted Eliyahu as he stood atop Har HaCarmel, in his attempts to debunk the ancient prophets of the pagan Baal. The Gemara (*Berakhot* 9b) records that he implored God on two fronts: that his demonstration against paganism should be successful, and that it should not be misinterpreted as sorcery.

As we have experienced continuing miracles in our return to Israel, some have misinterpreted it as a mirage effected by non-divine forces, meant to dupe our people into anti-redemptive behavior. This attitude that major miracles can stem from non-divine sources runs contrary to the Gemara's affirmation that such thought is inconceivable. As we chant in the Hallel, "This is the Lord's doing; it is wondrous in our eyes."

UNLIKELY AGENTS OF REDEMPTION

הִיא נִפְלָאת בְּעֵינֵינוּ *It is wondrous in our eyes.* The Return from Bavel was spearheaded by Ezra and Nehemya and is described primarily in the books which

This is the day the Lord has made.
Let us rejoice and be glad in it.
This is the day the Lord has made.
Let us rejoice and be glad in it.

Leader followed by congregation:

אָנָּא Lord, please, save us.
Lord, please, save us.
Lord, please, grant us success.
Lord, please, grant us success.

---

forward. The Torah establishes the paradigm of a generic fast day in response to a particular crisis. These days include fasting, extra prayer, and an agenda of *teshuva*. Ḥazal applied this model not just in response to *current* crises, but also in memory of past events. The four fasts were all incorporated to mourn and memorialize past tragedies. Throughout the Exile, unique fast days were initiated in response to major tragedies. Perhaps the most well known is the twentieth day of Sivan which was established as a fast day in the twelfth century in response to brutal pogroms. Though the fast day was forgotten, it was reinstituted in the seventeenth century, after the pogroms surrounding the Khmelnitsky rebellion. Other days were added in response to local catastrophes.

For the past two millennia no redemptive event warranted the institution of a new festival. The formation of the State of Israel was the first national event of salvation or redemption in close to 2500 years. Sensing this occasion, Yom HaAtzma'ut was added as a national day of celebration. Lacking a *Sanhedrin* we are unable to insert actual halakhot to fully develop this day as a classic *ḥag*.

The Midrash (*Tanḥuma Pinḥas* chapter 16) cites a discussion between HaKadosh Barukh Hu and the Jewish people in which we reaffirm our commitment to the existing holidays and the sacrifices we are asked to deliver. In response God promises, "I won't dismiss any of the holidays you have so carefully maintained: I will add new holidays for you to rejoice."

We have commenced this process by inserting Yom HaAtzma'ut into our calendar. We hope to one day witness the completion of this day as a comprehensive *ḥag* in fulfillment of the midrash.

זֶה־הַיּוֹם עָשָׂה יהוה, נָגִילָה וְנִשְׂמְחָה בוֹ:
זֶה־הַיּוֹם עָשָׂה יהוה, נָגִילָה וְנִשְׂמְחָה בוֹ:

קהל followed by שליח ציבור:

אָנָּא יהוה הוֹשִׁיעָה נָּא:
אָנָּא יהוה הוֹשִׁיעָה נָּא:
אָנָּא יהוה הַצְלִיחָה נָּא:
אָנָּא יהוה הַצְלִיחָה נָּא:

character, facilitated our redemption. HaKadosh Barukh Hu chooses unlikely heroes to redeem His people and His land. Sometimes they are righteous, and neatly accommodate our visions of divine redemption. More often they are flawed heroes who serve as divine agents in rerouting our national history.

Many of these returnees possessed odd names. Both Ezra and Neḥemya describe people with names which don't resonate as Jewish, for example, Bakbuk, Hakupha, Harhur, Bazluth, Mehida, Harsha… (Ezra 2:51–53; Neḥemya 7:53–55). Commenting on these bizarre names the Midrash concedes, "Some have revolting names but striking accomplishments." Effectively this midrash is endorsing a redemption brokered by otherwise unsuitable agents. The desire and commitment to return to Israel is heroic and historical, even when expressed by those who don't possess complementary ritualistic commitment.

ADDING NEW FESTIVALS

The Torah establishes three Ḥagim to mark great miracles which occurred during the prophetic era and advanced the arc of Jewish History. The miracle of Purim, though occurring during Exile, was canonized in Tanakh and justified being incorporated as an additional holiday. Hundreds of years later the miracle of Ḥanukka occurred in the post-prophetic era after Tanakh had been sealed. The presence of an active Anshei Keneset HaGedola enabled the institutionalization of a new Holiday, complete with ritual and Hallel recital. Having lost the Sanhedrin we lack the machinery to create new festivals with distinct halakhic practices.

By contrast, the addition of new fast days is logistically more straight-

בָּרוּךְ Blessed is one who comes in the name of the Lord;
we bless you from the House of the Lord.

Blessed is one who comes in the name of the Lord;
we bless you from the House of the Lord.

The Lord is God; He has given us light. Bind the festival offering
with thick cords [and bring it] to the horns of the altar.

The Lord is God; He has given us light. Bind the festival offering
with thick cords [and bring it] to the horns of the altar.

You are my God and I will thank You;
You are my God, I will exalt You.

You are my God and I will thank You;
You are my God, I will exalt You.

Thank the Lord for He is good;
His loving-kindness is for ever.

Thank the Lord for He is good;
His loving-kindness is for ever.

יְהַלְלוּךָ All Your works will praise You, Lord our God,
and Your devoted ones – the righteous who do Your will,
together with all Your people the house of Israel –
will joyously thank, bless, praise, glorify, exalt, revere, sanctify,
and proclaim the sovereignty of Your name, our King.
‣ For it is good to thank You
and fitting to sing psalms to Your name,
for from eternity to eternity You are God.
Blessed are You, Lord, King who is extolled with praises.

*On Yom Yerushalayim the service continues on page 578 on
a Monday, and on page 598 on all other days.*

בָּרוּךְ הַבָּא בְּשֵׁם יהוה, בֵּרַכְנוּכֶם מִבֵּית יהוה:

בָּרוּךְ הַבָּא בְּשֵׁם יהוה, בֵּרַכְנוּכֶם מִבֵּית יהוה:

אֵל יהוה וַיָּאֶר לָנוּ, אִסְרוּ־חַג בַּעֲבֹתִים עַד־קַרְנוֹת הַמִּזְבֵּחַ:

אֵל יהוה וַיָּאֶר לָנוּ, אִסְרוּ־חַג בַּעֲבֹתִים עַד־קַרְנוֹת הַמִּזְבֵּחַ:

אֵלִי אַתָּה וְאוֹדֶךָּ, אֱלֹהַי אֲרוֹמְמֶךָּ:

אֵלִי אַתָּה וְאוֹדֶךָּ, אֱלֹהַי אֲרוֹמְמֶךָּ:

הוֹדוּ לַיהוה כִּי־טוֹב, כִּי לְעוֹלָם חַסְדּוֹ:

הוֹדוּ לַיהוה כִּי־טוֹב, כִּי לְעוֹלָם חַסְדּוֹ:

יְהַלְלוּךָ יהוה אֱלֹהֵינוּ כָּל מַעֲשֶׂיךָ
וַחֲסִידֶיךָ צַדִּיקִים עוֹשֵׂי רְצוֹנֶךָ
וְכָל עַמְּךָ בֵּית יִשְׂרָאֵל
בְּרִנָּה יוֹדוּ וִיבָרְכוּ וִישַׁבְּחוּ
וִיפָאֲרוּ וִירוֹמְמוּ וְיַעֲרִיצוּ וְיַקְדִּישׁוּ
וְיַמְלִיכוּ אֶת שִׁמְךָ מַלְכֵּנוּ
◂ כִּי לְךָ טוֹב לְהוֹדוֹת וּלְשִׁמְךָ נָאֶה לְזַמֵּר
כִּי מֵעוֹלָם וְעַד עוֹלָם אַתָּה אֵל.
בָּרוּךְ אַתָּה יהוה, מֶלֶךְ מְהֻלָּל בַּתִּשְׁבָּחוֹת.

On יום ירושלים the service continues on page 579 on a
Monday, and on page 599 on all other days.

HALF KADDISH

Leader: יִתְגַּדַּל Magnified and sanctified may His great name be,
in the world He created by His will.
May He establish His kingdom
in your lifetime and in your days,
and in the lifetime of all the house of Israel,
swiftly and soon – and say: Amen.

All: May His great name be blessed for ever and all time.

Leader: Blessed and praised, glorified and exalted,
raised and honored, uplifted and lauded
be the name of the Holy One, blessed be He,
beyond any blessing,
song, praise and consolation
uttered in the world – and say: Amen.

REMOVING THE TORAH FROM THE ARK

Before taking the Torah out of the Ark, some add:

אֵין־כָּמוֹךָ There is none like You among the heavenly powers,   Ps. 86
LORD, and there are no works like Yours.
Your kingdom is an eternal kingdom,   Ps. 145
and Your dominion is for all generations.

The LORD is King, the LORD was King,
the LORD shall be King for ever and all time.
The LORD will give strength to His people;   Ps. 29
the LORD will bless His people with peace.

---

2. When Yom HaAtzma'ut falls on a Tuesday or Wednesday, the same
   passage from *Ekev* is read. Most congregations do not divide the reading into *aliyot*, although some have the custom of calling three people
   to the Torah, with blessings, on these days as well.

3. Some congregations only read from the Torah if Yom HaAtzma'ut falls
   on a Thursday.   YR

חצי קדיש

ש״ץ: יִתְגַּדַּל וְיִתְקַדַּשׁ שְׁמֵהּ רַבָּא (קהל: אָמֵן)
בְּעָלְמָא דִּי בְרָא כִרְעוּתֵהּ
וְיַמְלִיךְ מַלְכוּתֵהּ
בְּחַיֵּיכוֹן וּבְיוֹמֵיכוֹן וּבְחַיֵּי דְּכָל בֵּית יִשְׂרָאֵל
בַּעֲגָלָא וּבִזְמַן קָרִיב, וְאִמְרוּ אָמֵן. (קהל: אָמֵן)

קהל   יְהֵא שְׁמֵהּ רַבָּא מְבָרַךְ לְעָלַם וּלְעָלְמֵי עָלְמַיָּא.
 וש״ץ:

ש״ץ: יִתְבָּרַךְ וְיִשְׁתַּבַּח וְיִתְפָּאַר וְיִתְרוֹמַם וְיִתְנַשֵּׂא
וְיִתְהַדָּר וְיִתְעַלֶּה וְיִתְהַלָּל
שְׁמֵהּ דְּקֻדְשָׁא בְּרִיךְ הוּא (קהל: בְּרִיךְ הוּא)
לְעֵלָּא מִן כָּל בִּרְכָתָא וְשִׁירָתָא, תֻּשְׁבְּחָתָא וְנֶחֱמָתָא
דַּאֲמִירָן בְּעָלְמָא, וְאִמְרוּ אָמֵן. (קהל: אָמֵן)

הוצאת ספר תורה

Before taking the תורה *ספר out of the* ארון קודש, *some add:*

תהלים פו   אֵין־כָּמוֹךָ בָאֱלֹהִים, אֲדֹנָי, וְאֵין כְּמַעֲשֶׂיךָ:
תהלים קמה   מַלְכוּתְךָ מַלְכוּת כָּל־עֹלָמִים, וּמֶמְשַׁלְתְּךָ בְּכָל־דּוֹר וָדֹר:
יהוה מֶלֶךְ, יהוה מָלָךְ, יהוה יִמְלֹךְ לְעֹלָם וָעֶד:
תהלים כט   יהוה עֹז לְעַמּוֹ יִתֵּן, יהוה יְבָרֵךְ אֶת־עַמּוֹ בַשָּׁלוֹם:

THE TORAH READING

Yom HaAtzma'ut always falls on Tuesday, Wednesday, or Thursday. Different customs have emerged in relation to the Torah reading:

1. When Yom HaAtzma'ut falls on a Thursday, the weekly Torah portion is read (Yom HaAtzma'ut may fall during the week of the one of the following *parashot*: *Tazria, Aḥarei Mot, Kedoshim, Emor, Behar*). Some congregations add a reading from *Parashat Ekev* (Deuteronomy 11:22–25), without the blessings of the *oleh*.

Father of compassion,
favor Zion with Your goodness; rebuild the walls of Jerusalem.
For we trust in You alone, King, God,
high and exalted, Master of worlds.

Ps. 51

The Ark is opened and the congregation stands. All say:

וַיְהִי בִּנְסֹעַ Whenever the Ark set out, Moses would say,
"Arise, LORD, and may Your enemies be scattered.
May those who hate You flee before You."
For the Torah shall come forth from Zion,
and the word of the LORD from Jerusalem.
Blessed is He who in His holiness
gave the Torah to His people Israel.

Num. 10

Is. 2

Blessed is the name of the Master of the Universe. Blessed is Your crown and
Your place. May Your favor always be with Your people Israel. Show Your people
the salvation of Your right hand in Your Temple. Grant us the gift of Your good
light, and accept our prayers in mercy. May it be Your will to prolong our life
in goodness. May I be counted among the righteous, so that You will have
compassion on me and protect me and all that is mine and all that is Your people
Israel's. You feed all; You sustain all; You rule over all; You rule over kings, for
sovereignty is Yours. I am a servant of the Holy One, blessed be He, before whom
and before whose glorious Torah I bow at all times. Not in man do I trust, nor
on any angel do I rely, but on the God of heaven who is the God of truth, whose
Torah is truth, whose prophets speak truth, and who abounds in acts of love and
truth. ▸ In Him I trust, and to His holy and glorious name I offer praises. May it
be Your will to open my heart to the Torah, and to fulfill the wishes of my heart
and of the hearts of all Your people Israel for good, for life, and for peace.

Zohar,
Vayak-hel

be centered upon accepting the Torah. Each entry into the land was accentuated by a public ceremony reacquiring Torah.

Immediately upon arriving at Gilgal, the first station in Israel, Yehoshua
constructs the monument of twelve stones and inscribes the Torah on them.
It is unclear as to whether the *entire* Torah was engraved or merely a list of
mitzvot. Either way the construction provided a visible monument of our

תהילים נא

אַב הָרַחֲמִים
הֵיטִיבָה בִרְצוֹנְךָ אֶת־צִיּוֹן תִּבְנֶה חוֹמוֹת יְרוּשָׁלָ͏ִם:
כִּי בְךָ לְבַד בָּטָחְנוּ, מֶלֶךְ אֵל רָם וְנִשָּׂא, אֲדוֹן עוֹלָמִים.

The ארון קודש *is opened and the* קהל *stands. All say:*

במדבר י

וַיְהִי בִּנְסֹעַ הָאָרֹן וַיֹּאמֶר מֹשֶׁה
קוּמָה יהוה וְיָפֻצוּ אֹיְבֶיךָ וְיָנֻסוּ מְשַׂנְאֶיךָ מִפָּנֶיךָ:

ישעיה ב

כִּי מִצִּיּוֹן תֵּצֵא תוֹרָה וּדְבַר־יהוה מִירוּשָׁלָ͏ִם:
בָּרוּךְ שֶׁנָּתַן תּוֹרָה לְעַמּוֹ יִשְׂרָאֵל בִּקְדֻשָּׁתוֹ.

זוהר ויקהל

בְּרִיךְ שְׁמֵהּ דְּמָרֵא עָלְמָא, בְּרִיךְ כִּתְרָךְ וְאַתְרָךְ. יְהֵא רְעוּתָךְ עִם עַמָּךְ יִשְׂרָאֵל
לְעָלַם, וּפֻרְקַן יְמִינָךְ אַחֲזֵי לְעַמָּךְ בְּבֵית מַקְדְּשָׁךְ, וּלְאַמְטוֹיֵי לָנָא מִטּוּב נְהוֹרָךְ,
וּלְקַבֵּל צְלוֹתַנָא בְּרַחֲמִין. יְהֵא רַעֲוָא קֳדָמָךְ דְּתוֹרִיךְ לַן חַיִּין בְּטִיבוּ, וְלֶהֱוֵי אֲנָא
פְּקִידָא בְּגוֹ צַדִּיקַיָּא, לְמִרְחַם עֲלַי וּלְמִנְטַר יָתִי וְיָת כָּל דִּי לִי וְדִי לְעַמָּךְ יִשְׂרָאֵל.
אַנְתְּ הוּא זָן לְכֹלָּא וּמְפַרְנֵס לְכֹלָּא, אַנְתְּ הוּא שַׁלִּיט עַל כֹּלָּא, אַנְתְּ הוּא דְּשַׁלִּיט
עַל מַלְכַיָּא, וּמַלְכוּתָא דִּילָךְ הִיא. אֲנָא עַבְדָּא דְּקֻדְשָׁא בְּרִיךְ הוּא, דְּסָגֵדְנָא
קַמֵּהּ וּמִקַּמֵּי דִּיקַר אוֹרַיְתֵהּ בְּכָל עִדָּן וְעִדָּן. לָא עַל אֱנָשׁ רָחִיצְנָא וְלָא עַל בַּר
אֱלָהִין סָמִיכְנָא, אֶלָּא בֶּאֱלָהָא דִשְׁמַיָּא, דְּהוּא אֱלָהָא קְשׁוֹט, וְאוֹרַיְתֵהּ קְשׁוֹט,
וּנְבִיאוֹהִי קְשׁוֹט, וּמַסְגֵּא לְמֶעְבַּד טָבְוָן וּקְשׁוֹט. ◂ בֵּהּ אֲנָא רָחִיץ, וְלִשְׁמֵהּ קַדִּישָׁא
יַקִּירָא אֲנָא אֵמַר תֻּשְׁבְּחָן. יְהֵא רַעֲוָא קֳדָמָךְ דְּתִפְתַּח לִבַּאי בְּאוֹרַיְתָא, וְתַשְׁלִים
מִשְׁאֲלִין דְּלִבַּאי וְלִבָּא דְכָל עַמָּךְ יִשְׂרָאֵל לְטַב וּלְחַיִּין וְלִשְׁלָם.

KERIAT HATORAH AND OUR ENTRY INTO ISRAEL

The first recorded public recital of the Torah is attributed to Moshe in the weeks prior to *Matan Torah*. Though the actual text in its current format wasn't yet delivered, Moshe launched the practice of public recital every three days (*Bava Kama* 82a).

As our claim to the Land of Israel is historical, our entry into the land must

The Leader takes the Torah scroll in his right arm. Leader then congregation:
Listen, Israel: the LORD is our God, the LORD is One.   *Deut. 6*

Leader then congregation:
One is our God; great is our Master; holy is His name.

The Leader takes the Torah scroll in his right arm, bows toward the Ark and says: *Ps. 34*
Magnify the LORD with me, and let us exalt His name together.

The Ark is closed. The Leader carries the Torah scroll to the bima and the congregation says:
לְךָ Yours, LORD, are the greatness and the power, the glory and the   *1 Chr. 29*
majesty and splendor, for everything in heaven and earth is Yours.
Yours, LORD, is the kingdom; You are exalted as Head over all.

רוֹמְמוּ Exalt the LORD our God and bow to His footstool; He is holy.   *Ps. 99*
Exalt the LORD our God, and bow at His holy mountain, for holy is
the LORD our God.

אַב הָרַחֲמִים May the Father of compassion have compassion on the
people borne by Him. May He remember the covenant with the mighty
[patriarchs], and deliver us from evil times. May He reproach the evil
instinct in the people carried by Him, and graciously grant that we be
an everlasting remnant. May He fulfill in good measure our requests
for salvation and compassion.

---

the slow erosion of Torah knowledge, Ezra, who was a *Sofer,* reengineered
the ceremony of *Keriat HaTorah.* He set the modern-day schedule of Torah
reading, and instituted the number of people who are called to the Torah as
well as the quota of *pesukim* which must be read. Finally he introduced the
recital of *Targum* to assist those who could not understand Hebrew.

The Jewish people cannot return to Israel without reenacting the events at
Har Sinai; without reaffirming the embrace of the Torah. In our final redemptive process we haven't yet experienced this event. The great renaissance of
personal Torah study in our generation is both a *function* of our return to the
land and a *basis* for our return. We await the public ceremony of Torah which
will undoubtedly accompany our final redemption.

דברים ו

קהל then שליח ציבור takes the ספר תורה in his right arm. The שליח ציבור:

שְׁמַע יִשְׂרָאֵל, יהוה אֱלֹהֵינוּ, יהוה אֶחָד:

קהל then שליח ציבור:

אֶחָד אֱלֹהֵינוּ, גָּדוֹל אֲדוֹנֵינוּ, קָדוֹשׁ שְׁמוֹ.

תהלים לד

The שליח ציבור takes the ספר תורה in his right arm, bows toward the ארון קודש and says:

גַּדְּלוּ לַיהוה אִתִּי וּנְרוֹמְמָה שְׁמוֹ יַחְדָּו:

The ארון קודש is closed. The שליח ציבור carries the ספר תורה to the בימה and the קהל says:

דברי הימים א, כט

לְךָ יהוה הַגְּדֻלָּה וְהַגְּבוּרָה וְהַתִּפְאֶרֶת וְהַנֵּצַח וְהַהוֹד, כִּי־כֹל בַּשָּׁמַיִם וּבָאָרֶץ, לְךָ יהוה הַמַּמְלָכָה וְהַמִּתְנַשֵּׂא לְכֹל לְרֹאשׁ:

תהילים צט

רוֹמְמוּ יהוה אֱלֹהֵינוּ וְהִשְׁתַּחֲווּ לַהֲדֹם רַגְלָיו, קָדוֹשׁ הוּא: רוֹמְמוּ יהוה אֱלֹהֵינוּ וְהִשְׁתַּחֲווּ לְהַר קָדְשׁוֹ, כִּי־קָדוֹשׁ יהוה אֱלֹהֵינוּ:

אַב הָרַחֲמִים הוּא יְרַחֵם עַם עֲמוּסִים, וְיִזְכֹּר בְּרִית אֵיתָנִים, וְיַצִּיל נַפְשׁוֹתֵינוּ מִן הַשָּׁעוֹת הָרָעוֹת, וְיִגְעַר בְּיֵצֶר הָרָע מִן הַנְּשׂוּאִים, וְיָחֹן אוֹתָנוּ לִפְלֵיטַת עוֹלָמִים, וִימַלֵּא מִשְׁאֲלוֹתֵינוּ בְּמִדָּה טוֹבָה יְשׁוּעָה וְרַחֲמִים.

license to the Land of Israel. A similar structure was erected in the vicinity of the twin mountains of Gerizim and Eval, upon which a related ceremony was conducted. The population was equally divided between the two mountains and responded to the *Levi'im* who announced rewards for mitzva observance and penalties for various infractions. These two ceremonies provided visual expression of Torah as our warrant for entering Israel.

Hundreds of years later Ezra returned with the exiles of Bavel. On the first Rosh HaShana of their return he gathered the nation near the water channel and publicly read from the Torah. This experience extended two weeks, as the Torah was publicly read during the eight days of Sukkot as well. Recognizing

The Torah scroll is placed on the bima and the Gabbai calls a Kohen to the Torah. .

May His kingship over us be soon revealed and made manifest. May He be gracious to our surviving remnant, the remnant of His people the house of Israel in grace, loving-kindness, compassion and favor, and let us say: Amen. Let us all render greatness to our God and give honor to the Torah. *Let the Kohen come forward. Arise (*name* son of *father's name*), the Kohen.

*If no Kohen is present, a Levi or Yisrael is called up as follows:
/As there is no Kohen, arise (*name* son of *father's name*) in place of a Kohen./

Blessed is He who, in His holiness, gave the Torah to His people Israel.

Congregation followed by the Gabbai:
You who cling to the LORD your God are all alive today.   *Deut. 4*

The appropriate Torah portions are to be found from page 364.

The Reader shows the oleh the section to be read.
The oleh touches the scroll at that place with the tzitzit of his tallit,
which he then kisses. Holding the handles of the scroll, he says:

Oleh: Bless the LORD, the blessed One.

Cong: Bless the LORD, the blessed One,
for ever and all time.

Oleh: Bless the LORD, the blessed One,
for ever and all time.

Blessed are You, LORD our God,
King of the Universe,
who has chosen us from all peoples
and has given us His Torah.
Blessed are You, LORD, Giver of the Torah.

After the reading, the oleh says:

Oleh: Blessed are You, LORD our God,
King of the Universe,
who has given us the Torah of truth,
planting everlasting life in our midst.
Blessed are You, LORD, Giver of the Torah.

The ספר תורה *is placed on the* שולחן *and the* גבאי *calls a* כהן *to the* תורה.

וְתִגָּלֶה וְתֵרָאֶה מַלְכוּתוֹ עָלֵינוּ בִּזְמַן קָרוֹב, וְיָחֹן פְּלֵיטָתֵנוּ וּפְלֵיטַת עַמּוֹ בֵּית יִשְׂרָאֵל לְחֵן וּלְחֶסֶד וּלְרַחֲמִים וּלְרָצוֹן וְנֹאמַר אָמֵן. הַכֹּל הָבוּ גֹדֶל לֵאלֹהֵינוּ וּתְנוּ כָבוֹד לַתּוֹרָה. *כֹּהֵן קְרָב, יַעֲמֹד (פלוני בן פלוני) הַכֹּהֵן.

If no כהן *is present, a* לוי *or* ישראל *is called up as follows:*

/אֵין כָּאן כֹּהֵן, יַעֲמֹד (פלוני בן פלוני) בִּמְקוֹם כֹּהֵן./

בָּרוּךְ שֶׁנָּתַן תּוֹרָה לְעַמּוֹ יִשְׂרָאֵל בִּקְדֻשָּׁתוֹ.

קהל *followed by the* גבאי:

דברים ד

וְאַתֶּם הַדְּבֵקִים בַּיהוה אֱלֹהֵיכֶם חַיִּים כֻּלְּכֶם הַיּוֹם:

The appropriate תורה *portions are to be found from page 365.*

The קורא *shows the* עולה *the section to be read.*
The עולה *touches the* ספר תורה *at that place with the* ציצית *of his* טלית, *which he then kisses. Holding the handles of the* ספר תורה, *he says:*

עולה: בָּרְכוּ אֶת יהוה הַמְבֹרָךְ.

קהל: בָּרוּךְ יהוה הַמְבֹרָךְ לְעוֹלָם וָעֶד.

עולה: בָּרוּךְ יהוה הַמְבֹרָךְ לְעוֹלָם וָעֶד.
בָּרוּךְ אַתָּה יהוה, אֱלֹהֵינוּ מֶלֶךְ הָעוֹלָם
אֲשֶׁר בָּחַר בָּנוּ מִכָּל הָעַמִּים
וְנָתַן לָנוּ אֶת תּוֹרָתוֹ.
בָּרוּךְ אַתָּה יהוה, נוֹתֵן הַתּוֹרָה.

After the קריאת התורה, *the* עולה *says:*

עולה: בָּרוּךְ אַתָּה יהוה אֱלֹהֵינוּ מֶלֶךְ הָעוֹלָם
אֲשֶׁר נָתַן לָנוּ תּוֹרַת אֱמֶת
וְחַיֵּי עוֹלָם נָטַע בְּתוֹכֵנוּ.
בָּרוּךְ אַתָּה יהוה, נוֹתֵן הַתּוֹרָה.

One who has survived a situation of danger says:
Blessed are You, LORD our God, King of the Universe,
who bestows good on the unworthy,
who has bestowed on me much good.

The congregation responds:
Amen. May He who bestowed much good on you
continue to bestow on you much good, Selah.

After a Bar Mitzva boy has finished the Torah blessing, his father says aloud:
Blessed is He who has released me
from the responsibility for this child.

FOR AN OLEH

May He who blessed our fathers, Abraham, Isaac and Jacob, bless (*name,
son of father's name*) who has been called up in honor of the All-Present, in
honor of the Torah, and in honor of Yom HaAtzma'ut. As a reward for this,
may the Holy One, blessed be He, protect and deliver him from all trouble
and distress, all infection and illness, and send blessing and success to all
the work of his hands, together with all Israel, his brethren, and let us say:
Amen.

FOR A SICK MAN

May He who blessed our fathers, Abraham, Isaac and Jacob, Moses and
Aaron, David and Solomon, bless and heal one who is ill, (*sick person's name,
son of mother's name*), on whose behalf (*name of the one making the offering*)
is making a contribution to charity. As a reward for this, may the Holy One,
blessed be He, be filled with compassion for him, to restore his health, cure
him, strengthen and revive him, sending him a swift and full recovery from
heaven to all his 248 organs and 365 sinews, amongst the other sick ones in
Israel, a healing of the spirit and a healing of the body, may healing be quick
to come – now, swiftly and soon, and let us say: Amen.

FOR A SICK WOMAN

May He who blessed our fathers, Abraham, Isaac and Jacob, Moses and
Aaron, David and Solomon, bless and heal one who is ill, (*sick person's name,
daughter of mother's name*), on whose behalf (*name of the one making the
offering*) is making a contribution to charity. As a reward for this, may the
Holy One, blessed be He, be filled with compassion for her, to restore her
health, cure her, strengthen and revive her, sending her a swift and full

One who has survived a situation of danger says:

בָּרוּךְ אַתָּה יהוה אֱלֹהֵינוּ מֶלֶךְ הָעוֹלָם הַגּוֹמֵל לְחַיָּבִים טוֹבוֹת
שֶׁגְּמָלַנִי כָּל טוֹב.

The קהל *responds:*

אָמֵן. מִי שֶׁגְּמָלְךָ כָּל טוֹב הוּא יִגְמָלְךָ כָּל טוֹב, סֶלָה.

After a בר מצוה *has finished the* תורה *blessing, his father says aloud:*

בָּרוּךְ שֶׁפְּטָרַנִי מֵעָנְשׁוֹ שֶׁלָּזֶה.

מי שברך לעולה לתורה

מִי שֶׁבֵּרַךְ אֲבוֹתֵינוּ אַבְרָהָם יִצְחָק וְיַעֲקֹב, הוּא יְבָרֵךְ אֶת (פלוני בן פלוני),
בַּעֲבוּר שֶׁעָלָה לִכְבוֹד הַמָּקוֹם וְלִכְבוֹד הַתּוֹרָה וְלִכְבוֹד יוֹם הָעַצְמָאוּת.
בִּשְׂכַר זֶה הַקָּדוֹשׁ בָּרוּךְ הוּא יִשְׁמְרֵהוּ וְיַצִּילֵהוּ מִכָּל צָרָה וְצוּקָה וּמִכָּל
נֶגַע וּמַחֲלָה, וְיִשְׁלַח בְּרָכָה וְהַצְלָחָה בְּכָל מַעֲשֵׂה יָדָיו עִם כָּל יִשְׂרָאֵל
אֶחָיו, וְנֹאמַר אָמֵן.

מי שברך לחולה

מִי שֶׁבֵּרַךְ אֲבוֹתֵינוּ אַבְרָהָם יִצְחָק וְיַעֲקֹב, מֹשֶׁה וְאַהֲרֹן דָּוִד וּשְׁלֹמֹה
הוּא יְבָרֵךְ וִירַפֵּא אֶת הַחוֹלֶה (פלוני בן פלונית) בַּעֲבוּר שֶׁ(פלוני בן פלוני)
נוֹדֵר צְדָקָה בַּעֲבוּרוֹ. בִּשְׂכַר זֶה הַקָּדוֹשׁ בָּרוּךְ הוּא יִמָּלֵא רַחֲמִים עָלָיו
לְהַחֲלִימוֹ וּלְרַפֹּאתוֹ וּלְהַחֲזִיקוֹ וּלְהַחֲיוֹתוֹ וְיִשְׁלַח לוֹ מְהֵרָה רְפוּאָה שְׁלֵמָה
מִן הַשָּׁמַיִם לִרְמַ"ח אֵבָרָיו וּשְׁסַ"ה גִּידָיו בְּתוֹךְ שְׁאָר חוֹלֵי יִשְׂרָאֵל, רְפוּאַת
הַנֶּפֶשׁ וּרְפוּאַת הַגּוּף וּרְפוּאָה קְרוֹבָה לָבוֹא, הַשְׁתָּא בַּעֲגָלָא וּבִזְמַן קָרִיב,
וְנֹאמַר אָמֵן.

מי שברך לחולה

מִי שֶׁבֵּרַךְ אֲבוֹתֵינוּ אַבְרָהָם יִצְחָק וְיַעֲקֹב, מֹשֶׁה וְאַהֲרֹן דָּוִד וּשְׁלֹמֹה
הוּא יְבָרֵךְ וִירַפֵּא אֶת הַחוֹלָה (פלונית בת פלונית) בַּעֲבוּר שֶׁ(פלוני בן פלוני)
נוֹדֵר צְדָקָה בַּעֲבוּרָהּ. בִּשְׂכַר זֶה הַקָּדוֹשׁ בָּרוּךְ הוּא יִמָּלֵא רַחֲמִים עָלֶיהָ
לְהַחֲלִימָהּ וּלְרַפֹּאתָהּ וּלְהַחֲזִיקָהּ וּלְהַחֲיוֹתָהּ וְיִשְׁלַח לָהּ מְהֵרָה רְפוּאָה

recovery from heaven to all her organs and sinews, amongst the other sick ones in Israel, a healing of the spirit and a healing of the body, may healing be quick to come – now, swiftly and soon, and let us say: Amen.

ON THE BIRTH OF A SON

May He who blessed our fathers, Abraham, Isaac and Jacob, Moses and Aaron, David and Solomon, Sarah, Rebecca, Rachel and Leah, bless the woman (*name*, daughter of *father's name*) who has given birth, and her son who has been born to her as an auspicious sign. Her husband, the child's father, is making a contribution to charity. As a reward for this, may father and mother merit to bring the child into the covenant of Abraham and to a life of Torah, to the marriage canopy and to good deeds, and let us say: Amen.

ON THE BIRTH OF A DAUGHTER

May He who blessed our fathers, Abraham, Isaac and Jacob, Moses and Aaron, David and Solomon, Sarah, Rebecca, Rachel and Leah, bless the woman (*name*, daughter of *father's name*) who has given birth, and her daughter who has been born to her as an auspicious sign; and may her name be called in Israel (*baby's name*, daughter of *father's name*). Her husband, the child's father, is making a contribution to charity. As a reward for this, may father and mother merit to raise her to a life of Torah, to the marriage canopy, and to good deeds, and let us say: Amen.

FOR A BAR MITZVA

May He who blessed our fathers, Abraham, Isaac and Jacob, bless (*name*, son of *father's name*) who has completed thirteen years and attained the age of the commandments, who has been called to the Torah to give praise and thanks to God, may His name be blessed, for all the good He has bestowed on him. May the Holy One, blessed be He, protect and sustain him and direct his heart to be perfect with God, to walk in His ways and keep the commandments all the days of his life, and let us say: Amen.

FOR A BAT MITZVA

May He who blessed our fathers, Abraham, Isaac and Jacob, Sarah, Rebecca, Rachel and Leah, bless (*name*, daughter of *father's name*) who has completed twelve years and attained the age of the commandments, and gives praise and thanks to God, may His name be blessed, for all the good He has bestowed on her. May the Holy One, blessed be He, protect and sustain her and direct her heart to be perfect with God, to walk in His ways and keep the commandments all the days of her life, and let us say: Amen.

שְׁלֵמָה מִן הַשָּׁמַיִם לְכָל אֵבָרֶיהָ וּלְכָל גִּידֶיהָ בְּתוֹךְ שְׁאָר חוֹלֵי יִשְׂרָאֵל, רְפוּאַת הַנֶּפֶשׁ וּרְפוּאַת הַגּוּף וּרְפוּאָה קְרוֹבָה לָבוֹא, הַשְׁתָּא בַּעֲגָלָא וּבִזְמַן קָרִיב, וְנֹאמַר אָמֵן.

מי שברך ליולדת בן

מִי שֶׁבֵּרַךְ אֲבוֹתֵינוּ אַבְרָהָם יִצְחָק וְיַעֲקֹב, מֹשֶׁה וְאַהֲרֹן דָּוִד וּשְׁלֹמֹה, שָׂרָה רִבְקָה רָחֵל וְלֵאָה הוּא יְבָרֵךְ אֶת הָאִשָּׁה הַיּוֹלֶדֶת (פלונית בת פלוני) וְאֶת בְּנָהּ שֶׁנּוֹלַד לָהּ לְמַזָּל טוֹב בַּעֲבוּר שֶׁבַּעְלָהּ וְאָבִיו נוֹדֵר צְדָקָה בַּעֲדָם. בִּשְׂכַר זֶה יִזְכּוּ אָבִיו וְאִמּוֹ לְהַכְנִיסוֹ בִּבְרִיתוֹ שֶׁל אַבְרָהָם אָבִינוּ וּלְגַדְּלוֹ לַתּוֹרָה וּלְחֻפָּה וּלְמַעֲשִׂים טוֹבִים, וְנֹאמַר אָמֵן.

מי שברך ליולדת בת

מִי שֶׁבֵּרַךְ אֲבוֹתֵינוּ אַבְרָהָם יִצְחָק וְיַעֲקֹב, מֹשֶׁה וְאַהֲרֹן דָּוִד וּשְׁלֹמֹה, שָׂרָה רִבְקָה רָחֵל וְלֵאָה הוּא יְבָרֵךְ אֶת הָאִשָּׁה הַיּוֹלֶדֶת (פלונית בת פלוני) וְאֶת בִּתָּהּ שֶׁנּוֹלְדָה לָהּ לְמַזָּל טוֹב וְיִקָּרֵא שְׁמָהּ בְּיִשְׂרָאֵל (פלונית בת פלוני), בַּעֲבוּר שֶׁבַּעְלָהּ וְאָבֶיהָ נוֹדֵר צְדָקָה בַּעֲדָן. בִּשְׂכַר זֶה יִזְכּוּ אָבֶיהָ וְאִמָּהּ לְגַדְּלָהּ לַתּוֹרָה וּלְחֻפָּה וּלְמַעֲשִׂים טוֹבִים, וְנֹאמַר אָמֵן.

מי שברך לבר מצווה

מִי שֶׁבֵּרַךְ אֲבוֹתֵינוּ אַבְרָהָם יִצְחָק וְיַעֲקֹב הוּא יְבָרֵךְ אֶת (פלוני בן פלוני) שֶׁמָּלְאוּ לוֹ שְׁלֹשׁ עֶשְׂרֵה שָׁנָה וְהִגִּיעַ לְמִצְוֹת, וְעָלָה לַתּוֹרָה, לָתֵת שֶׁבַח וְהוֹדָיָה לְהַשֵּׁם יִתְבָּרֵךְ עַל כָּל הַטּוֹבָה שֶׁגְּמָל אִתּוֹ. יִשְׁמְרֵהוּ הַקָּדוֹשׁ בָּרוּךְ הוּא וִיחַיֵּהוּ, וִיכוֹנֵן אֶת לִבּוֹ לִהְיוֹת שָׁלֵם עִם יהוה וְלָלֶכֶת בִּדְרָכָיו וְלִשְׁמֹר מִצְוֹתָיו כָּל הַיָּמִים, וְנֹאמַר אָמֵן.

מי שברך לבת מצווה

מִי שֶׁבֵּרַךְ אֲבוֹתֵינוּ אַבְרָהָם יִצְחָק וְיַעֲקֹב, שָׂרָה רִבְקָה רָחֵל וְלֵאָה, הוּא יְבָרֵךְ אֶת (פלונית בת פלוני) שֶׁמָּלְאוּ לָהּ שְׁתֵּים עֶשְׂרֵה שָׁנָה וְהִגִּיעָה לְמִצְוֹת, וְנוֹתֶנֶת שֶׁבַח וְהוֹדָיָה לְהַשֵּׁם יִתְבָּרֵךְ עַל כָּל הַטּוֹבָה שֶׁגְּמָל אִתָּהּ. יִשְׁמְרָהּ הַקָּדוֹשׁ בָּרוּךְ הוּא וִיחַיֶּהָ, וִיכוֹנֵן אֶת לִבָּהּ לִהְיוֹת שָׁלֵם עִם יהוה וְלָלֶכֶת בִּדְרָכָיו וְלִשְׁמֹר מִצְוֹתָיו כָּל הַיָּמִים, וְנֹאמַר אָמֵן.

TAZRIA

The Lord spoke to Moses, saying: Speak to the children of Israel, and say: If a woman conceives and gives birth to a male, she shall be impure for seven days; she shall be impure as at the time of her menstrual impurity. And on the eighth day, the flesh of his foreskin shall be circumcised. Then she must wait thirty-three days while her pure blood flows ; she may not touch anything sacred nor may she enter the Temple until the days of her purification are completed. And if she gives birth to a female, she shall be impure for two weeks in which she shall conduct herself as during the period of her menstrual impurity, and she shall wait while her pure blood flows for sixty-six days. And when the days of her purification are completed, whether for a son or a daughter, she shall bring a yearling lamb as a burnt offering and a dove or turtle-dove as a sin-offering to the entrance of the Tent of Meeting, to the priest. And he shall offer it before the Lord and he shall atone for her and she will be purified of the source of her bloods; this is the law of a woman who has given birth, whether it is to a male or a female. And if she cannot afford the price of a lamb, she may take two doves or two turtle-doves, one for a burnt offering and the other for a sin-offering, and the priest shall atone for her, and she shall be pure.

Lev.
12:1–13:5

LEVI

The Lord spoke to Moses and Aaron saying: Should there be on a person's skin a swelling or a rash or a bright spot which erupted on his skin as a leprous plague, he shall be brought to Aaron the priest or to one of his sons, the priests. And the priest shall examine the eruption upon the skin: if the hair in the eruption has turned white and the appearance of the eruption seems to be deeper than the skin, it is a leprous plague; the priest shall examine it and then declare it impure. But if there is a white spot on his skin and its appearance does not seem deeper than the skin, and its hair has not turned white, then the priest shall confine the person with the eruption for seven days. And on the seventh day, the priest shall examine it; if the eruption remains the same and has not spread upon the skin, then the priest shall confine him for an additional seven days.

YISRAEL

AḤAREI MOT

After the deaths of Aaron's two sons, when they had drawn close to the Lord and died, the Lord spoke to Moses. And the Lord said to Moses: speak to Aaron your brother, that he come not at any time to the holiest place – behind the curtain, to the presence of the *kaporet* that covers the Ark – so that he does not die; for I shall be revealed in the cloud above the *kaporet*.

Lev.
16:1–17

תזריע

ויקרא
יב:א-יג:ה

וַיְדַבֵּר יהוה אֶל־מֹשֶׁה לֵּאמֹר: דַּבֵּר אֶל־בְּנֵי יִשְׂרָאֵל לֵאמֹר אִשָּׁה כִּי
תַזְרִיעַ וְיָלְדָה זָכָר וְטָמְאָה שִׁבְעַת יָמִים כִּימֵי נִדַּת דְּוֺתָהּ תִּטְמָא:
וּבַיּוֹם הַשְּׁמִינִי יִמּוֹל בְּשַׂר עָרְלָתוֹ: וּשְׁלֹשִׁים יוֹם וּשְׁלֹשֶׁת יָמִים תֵּשֵׁב
בִּדְמֵי טָהֳרָה בְּכָל־קֹדֶשׁ לֹא־תִגָּע וְאֶל־הַמִּקְדָּשׁ לֹא תָבֹא עַד־מְלֹאת
יְמֵי טָהֳרָהּ: *וְאִם־נְקֵבָה תֵלֵד וְטָמְאָה שְׁבֻעַיִם כְּנִדָּתָהּ וְשִׁשִּׁים יוֹם   לוי
וְשֵׁשֶׁת יָמִים תֵּשֵׁב עַל־דְּמֵי טָהֳרָה: וּבִמְלֹאת ׀ יְמֵי טָהֳרָהּ לְבֵן אוֹ
לְבַת תָּבִיא כֶּבֶשׂ בֶּן־שְׁנָתוֹ לְעֹלָה וּבֶן־יוֹנָה אוֹ־תֹר לְחַטָּאת אֶל־
פֶּתַח אֹהֶל־מוֹעֵד אֶל־הַכֹּהֵן: וְהִקְרִיבוֹ לִפְנֵי יהוה וְכִפֶּר עָלֶיהָ וְטָהֲרָה
מִמְּקֹר דָּמֶיהָ זֹאת תּוֹרַת הַיֹּלֶדֶת לַזָּכָר אוֹ לַנְּקֵבָה: וְאִם־לֹא תִמְצָא
יָדָהּ דֵּי שֶׂה וְלָקְחָה שְׁתֵּי־תֹרִים אוֹ שְׁנֵי בְּנֵי יוֹנָה אֶחָד לְעֹלָה וְאֶחָד
לְחַטָּאת וְכִפֶּר עָלֶיהָ הַכֹּהֵן וְטָהֵרָה:

וַיְדַבֵּר יהוה אֶל־מֹשֶׁה וְאֶל־אַהֲרֹן לֵאמֹר: אָדָם כִּי־יִהְיֶה בְעוֹר־   ישראל
בְּשָׂרוֹ שְׂאֵת אוֹ־סַפַּחַת אוֹ בַהֶרֶת וְהָיָה בְעוֹר־בְּשָׂרוֹ לְנֶגַע צָרָעַת
וְהוּבָא אֶל־אַהֲרֹן הַכֹּהֵן אוֹ אֶל־אַחַד מִבָּנָיו הַכֹּהֲנִים: וְרָאָה הַכֹּהֵן
אֶת־הַנֶּגַע בְּעוֹר־הַבָּשָׂר וְשֵׂעָר בַּנֶּגַע הָפַךְ ׀ לָבָן וּמַרְאֵה הַנֶּגַע עָמֹק
מֵעוֹר בְּשָׂרוֹ נֶגַע צָרַעַת הוּא וְרָאָהוּ הַכֹּהֵן וְטִמֵּא אֹתוֹ: וְאִם־בַּהֶרֶת
לְבָנָה הִוא בְּעוֹר בְּשָׂרוֹ וְעָמֹק אֵין־מַרְאֶהָ מִן־הָעוֹר וּשְׂעָרָה לֹא־
הָפַךְ לָבָן וְהִסְגִּיר הַכֹּהֵן אֶת־הַנֶּגַע שִׁבְעַת יָמִים: וְרָאָהוּ הַכֹּהֵן בַּיּוֹם
הַשְּׁבִיעִי וְהִנֵּה הַנֶּגַע עָמַד בְּעֵינָיו לֹא־פָשָׂה הַנֶּגַע בָּעוֹר וְהִסְגִּירוֹ
הַכֹּהֵן שִׁבְעַת יָמִים שֵׁנִית:

אחרי מות

ויקרא
טז:א-טז

וַיְדַבֵּר יהוה אֶל־מֹשֶׁה אַחֲרֵי מוֹת שְׁנֵי בְּנֵי אַהֲרֹן בְּקָרְבָתָם לִפְנֵי־יהוה
וַיָּמֻתוּ: וַיֹּאמֶר יהוה אֶל־מֹשֶׁה דַּבֵּר אֶל־אַהֲרֹן אָחִיךָ וְאַל־יָבֹא בְכָל־
עֵת אֶל־הַקֹּדֶשׁ מִבֵּית לַפָּרֹכֶת אֶל־פְּנֵי הַכַּפֹּרֶת אֲשֶׁר עַל־הָאָרֹן וְלֹא
יָמוּת כִּי בֶּעָנָן אֵרָאֶה עַל־הַכַּפֹּרֶת: בְּזֹאת יָבֹא אַהֲרֹן אֶל־הַקֹּדֶשׁ בְּפַר

This is how Aaron shall come to the holiest place: he shall bring a young bull for a sin offering, and a ram for a burnt offering. He shall wear a consecrated linen tunic, and trousers of linen shall cover his skin; he shall tie a linen sash about him and bind a linen miter on his head. These are the consecrated garments; he shall wash his skin in water and then put them on. From the congregation of Israel he shall take two young goats as a sin offering, and a ram as a burnt offering. And Aaron shall offer up the sin-offering bullock that is his, as atonement for him and for his family.

He shall take the two goats and stand them before the Lᴏʀᴅ at the opening LEVI of the Tent of Meeting. And for these two goats, Aaron shall draw lots – one lot for the Lᴏʀᴅ and one lot for Azazel. And Aaron shall offer up the goat whose lot falls to the Lᴏʀᴅ, and make it a sin offering. And the goat whose lot falls to Azazel shall be left to stand alive before the Lᴏʀᴅ, to be an atonement – to be sent away to Azazel, into the wastelands.

Aaron shall offer up the sin-offering bullock that is his, as atonement for him and for his family; he shall slaughter the sin-offering bullock that is his. Then he shall take a pan full of burning coals from the altar, from the YISRAEL presence of the Lᴏʀᴅ, and with his cupped handsful of finest incense, bring them within the curtain. He shall place the incense into the fire in the presence of the Lᴏʀᴅ, and a cloud of incense will engulf the *kaporet* over the [Ark of] Testimony – then he shall not die.

He shall take of the bullock's blood and sprinkle with his finger onto the *kaporet* before him – and in front of the *kaporet*, he shall sprinkle seven times from the blood with his finger. And he shall slaughter the sin-offering goat that is the people's, and bring its blood behind the curtain, and do with its blood as he did with the blood of the bullock: he shall sprinkle it onto the *kaporet* and in front of the *kaporet*. So shall he bring atonement to the holiest place, for the impurities of Israel, for their rebellions and for all their sins. And so shall he do also for the Tent of Meeting, which abides with them, in the midst of their impurities. No man shall be in the Tent of Meeting when [Aaron] comes to make atonement in the holiest place, until he leaves; and he shall atone himself and his family and all the community of Israel.

KEDOSHIM

The Lᴏʀᴅ spoke to Moses saying: "Speak to the entire congregation of *Lev.* the children of Israel and tell them: You shall be holy, for I, the Lᴏʀᴅ your *19:1–14* God, am holy. Each person must revere his mother and father, and keep my

בֶּן־בָּקָר לְחַטָּאת וְאַיִל לְעֹלָה: כְּתֹנֶת־בַּד קֹדֶשׁ יִלְבָּשׁ וּמִכְנְסֵי־בַד
יִהְיוּ עַל־בְּשָׂרוֹ וּבְאַבְנֵט בַּד יַחְגֹּר וּבְמִצְנֶפֶת בַּד יִצְנֹף בִּגְדֵי־קֹדֶשׁ
הֵם וְרָחַץ בַּמַּיִם אֶת־בְּשָׂרוֹ וּלְבֵשָׁם: וּמֵאֵת עֲדַת בְּנֵי יִשְׂרָאֵל יִקַּח
שְׁנֵי־שְׂעִירֵי עִזִּים לְחַטָּאת וְאַיִל אֶחָד לְעֹלָה: וְהִקְרִיב אַהֲרֹן אֶת־פַּר
הַחַטָּאת אֲשֶׁר־לוֹ וְכִפֶּר בַּעֲדוֹ וּבְעַד בֵּיתוֹ: *וְלָקַח אֶת־שְׁנֵי הַשְּׂעִירִם לוי
וְהֶעֱמִיד אֹתָם לִפְנֵי יְהוָה פֶּתַח אֹהֶל מוֹעֵד: וְנָתַן אַהֲרֹן עַל־שְׁנֵי
הַשְּׂעִירִם גֹּרָלוֹת גּוֹרָל אֶחָד לַיהוָה וְגוֹרָל אֶחָד לַעֲזָאזֵל: וְהִקְרִיב
אַהֲרֹן אֶת־הַשָּׂעִיר אֲשֶׁר עָלָה עָלָיו הַגּוֹרָל לַיהוָה וְעָשָׂהוּ חַטָּאת:
וְהַשָּׂעִיר אֲשֶׁר עָלָה עָלָיו הַגּוֹרָל לַעֲזָאזֵל יָעֳמַד־חַי לִפְנֵי יְהוָה לְכַפֵּר
עָלָיו לְשַׁלַּח אֹתוֹ לַעֲזָאזֵל הַמִּדְבָּרָה: וְהִקְרִיב אַהֲרֹן אֶת־פַּר הַחַטָּאת
אֲשֶׁר־לוֹ וְכִפֶּר בַּעֲדוֹ וּבְעַד בֵּיתוֹ וְשָׁחַט אֶת־פַּר הַחַטָּאת אֲשֶׁר־לוֹ:
*וְלָקַח מְלֹא־הַמַּחְתָּה גַּחֲלֵי־אֵשׁ מֵעַל הַמִּזְבֵּחַ מִלִּפְנֵי יְהוָה וּמְלֹא ישראל
חָפְנָיו קְטֹרֶת סַמִּים דַּקָּה וְהֵבִיא מִבֵּית לַפָּרֹכֶת: וְנָתַן אֶת־הַקְּטֹרֶת
עַל־הָאֵשׁ לִפְנֵי יְהוָה וְכִסָּה ׀ עֲנַן הַקְּטֹרֶת אֶת־הַכַּפֹּרֶת אֲשֶׁר עַל־
הָעֵדוּת וְלֹא יָמוּת: וְלָקַח מִדַּם הַפָּר וְהִזָּה בְאֶצְבָּעוֹ עַל־פְּנֵי הַכַּפֹּרֶת
קֵדְמָה וְלִפְנֵי הַכַּפֹּרֶת יַזֶּה שֶׁבַע־פְּעָמִים מִן־הַדָּם בְּאֶצְבָּעוֹ: וְשָׁחַט
אֶת־שְׂעִיר הַחַטָּאת אֲשֶׁר לָעָם וְהֵבִיא אֶת־דָּמוֹ אֶל־מִבֵּית לַפָּרֹכֶת
וְעָשָׂה אֶת־דָּמוֹ כַּאֲשֶׁר עָשָׂה לְדַם הַפָּר וְהִזָּה אֹתוֹ עַל־הַכַּפֹּרֶת
וְלִפְנֵי הַכַּפֹּרֶת: וְכִפֶּר עַל־הַקֹּדֶשׁ מִטֻּמְאֹת בְּנֵי יִשְׂרָאֵל וּמִפִּשְׁעֵיהֶם
לְכָל־חַטֹּאתָם וְכֵן יַעֲשֶׂה לְאֹהֶל מוֹעֵד הַשֹּׁכֵן אִתָּם בְּתוֹךְ טֻמְאֹתָם:
וְכָל־אָדָם לֹא־יִהְיֶה ׀ בְּאֹהֶל מוֹעֵד בְּבֹאוֹ לְכַפֵּר בַּקֹּדֶשׁ עַד־צֵאתוֹ
וְכִפֶּר בַּעֲדוֹ וּבְעַד בֵּיתוֹ וּבְעַד כָּל־קְהַל יִשְׂרָאֵל:

קדושים

וַיְדַבֵּר יְהוָה אֶל־מֹשֶׁה לֵּאמֹר: דַּבֵּר אֶל־כָּל־עֲדַת בְּנֵי־יִשְׂרָאֵל וְאָמַרְתָּ ארקיו
די־א־טי
אֲלֵהֶם קְדֹשִׁים תִּהְיוּ כִּי קָדוֹשׁ אֲנִי יְהוָה אֱלֹהֵיכֶם: אִישׁ אִמּוֹ וְאָבִיו

Sabbaths, for I am the LORD your God. Do not turn to false deities, and do not make molten gods for yourselves, for I am the LORD your God. If you should bring a peace-offering to the LORD, you must offer it in such a way that it will be accepted from you. It shall be eaten on the day it is offered and on the next day; whatever is left over until the third day must be burned in fire. And if it is eaten on the third day, it is a foul thing – it will not be accepted. One who eats it will bear his sin, for he has defiled the LORD's holy offering; that soul shall be cut off from its people. When you reap the grain of your land, do not complete reaping the corner of your field, and do not collect the remnants of your harvest. Do not glean your vineyard and do not gather the fallen grapes of your vineyard; you must leave them for the poor and for the stranger – I am the LORD your God. Do not steal, do not deceive, and do not act fraudulently with one another. And do not swear falsely in My name, thereby profaning the name of your God – I am the LORD. Do not oppress your fellow man and do not rob; do not withhold a worker's wages until the following morning. Do not curse the deaf and do not place a stumbling block in front of the blind; you shall hold your God in awe – I am the LORD."

LEVI

YISRAEL

EMOR

The LORD said to Moses: Speak to the priests, the sons of Aaron, and say to them: none of them may become impure for a corpse of one of his people . He may only become impure for one of his close relatives, his flesh and blood: for his mother, his father, his son, his daughter or his brother. Or for his virgin sister who is closely related to him, who has not been with a man – for her, he may become impure. A husband among the priestly people may not become impure; he may not desecrate his priesthood. The priests may not make a bald spot on their heads and they may not shave the corners of their beards; upon their flesh they shall make no incision [as a rite of mourning]. They shall be sanctified to their God and they must not desecrate the name of their God, for it is they who bring the offerings of the LORD, the bread of their God; they shall be holy. They may not take a harlot or a desecrated woman [as a wife], nor may they take a woman who was divorced from her husband, for he is sanctified to his God. And you shall sanctify him, for it is he who offers the bread of your God; he shall be holy to you, because I, the LORD who sanctifies you, am holy. And the daughter of a priest who begins to commit fornication – she is desecrating her father's honor ; she shall be burned in fire.

Lev. 21:1–15

LEVI

תִּירָאוּ וְאֶת־שַׁבְּתֹתַי תִּשְׁמֹרוּ אֲנִי יְהוָה אֱלֹהֵיכֶם: אַל־תִּפְנוּ אֶל־
הָאֱלִילִם וֵאלֹהֵי מַסֵּכָה לֹא תַעֲשׂוּ לָכֶם אֲנִי יְהוָה אֱלֹהֵיכֶם: *וְכִי ^{יול}
תִזְבְּחוּ זֶבַח שְׁלָמִים לַיהוָה לִרְצֹנְכֶם תִּזְבָּחֻהוּ: בְּיוֹם זִבְחֲכֶם יֵאָכֵל
וּמִמָּחֳרָת וְהַנּוֹתָר עַד־יוֹם הַשְּׁלִישִׁי בָּאֵשׁ יִשָּׂרֵף: וְאִם הֵאָכֹל יֵאָכֵל
בַּיּוֹם הַשְּׁלִישִׁי פִּגּוּל הוּא לֹא יֵרָצֶה: וְאֹכְלָיו עֲוֹנוֹ יִשָּׂא כִּי־אֶת־קֹדֶשׁ
יְהוָה חִלֵּל וְנִכְרְתָה הַנֶּפֶשׁ הַהִוא מֵעַמֶּיהָ: וּבְקֻצְרְכֶם אֶת־קְצִיר
אַרְצְכֶם לֹא תְכַלֶּה פְּאַת שָׂדְךָ לִקְצֹר וְלֶקֶט קְצִירְךָ לֹא תְלַקֵּט: וְכַרְמְךָ
לֹא תְעוֹלֵל וּפֶרֶט כַּרְמְךָ לֹא תְלַקֵּט לֶעָנִי וְלַגֵּר תַּעֲזֹב אֹתָם אֲנִי יְהוָה
אֱלֹהֵיכֶם: *לֹא תִּגְנֹבוּ וְלֹא־תְכַחֲשׁוּ וְלֹא־תְשַׁקְּרוּ אִישׁ בַּעֲמִיתוֹ: ^{ישראל}
וְלֹא־תִשָּׁבְעוּ בִשְׁמִי לַשָּׁקֶר וְחִלַּלְתָּ אֶת־שֵׁם אֱלֹהֶיךָ אֲנִי יְהוָה:
לֹא־תַעֲשֹׁק אֶת־רֵעֲךָ וְלֹא תִגְזֹל לֹא־תָלִין פְּעֻלַּת שָׂכִיר אִתְּךָ עַד־
בֹּקֶר: לֹא־תְקַלֵּל חֵרֵשׁ וְלִפְנֵי עִוֵּר לֹא תִתֵּן מִכְשֹׁל וְיָרֵאתָ מֵּאֱלֹהֶיךָ
אֲנִי יְהוָה:

אמור

^{ויקרא}
^{כא:א-טו}
וַיֹּאמֶר יְהוָה אֶל־מֹשֶׁה אֱמֹר אֶל־הַכֹּהֲנִים בְּנֵי אַהֲרֹן וְאָמַרְתָּ אֲלֵהֶם
לְנֶפֶשׁ לֹא־יִטַּמָּא בְּעַמָּיו: כִּי אִם־לִשְׁאֵרוֹ הַקָּרֹב אֵלָיו לְאִמּוֹ וּלְאָבִיו
וְלִבְנוֹ וּלְבִתּוֹ וּלְאָחִיו: וְלַאֲחֹתוֹ הַבְּתוּלָה הַקְּרוֹבָה אֵלָיו אֲשֶׁר לֹא־
הָיְתָה לְאִישׁ לָהּ יִטַּמָּא: לֹא יִטַּמָּא בַּעַל בְּעַמָּיו לְהֵחַלּוֹ: לֹא־יִקְרְחָה ^{יקרחו}
קָרְחָה בְּרֹאשָׁם וּפְאַת זְקָנָם לֹא יְגַלֵּחוּ וּבִבְשָׂרָם לֹא יִשְׂרְטוּ שָׂרָטֶת:
קְדֹשִׁים יִהְיוּ לֵאלֹהֵיהֶם וְלֹא יְחַלְּלוּ שֵׁם אֱלֹהֵיהֶם כִּי אֶת־אִשֵּׁי יְהוָה
לֶחֶם אֱלֹהֵיהֶם הֵם מַקְרִיבִם וְהָיוּ קֹדֶשׁ: *אִשָּׁה זֹנָה וַחֲלָלָה לֹא יִקָּחוּ ^{לוי}
וְאִשָּׁה גְּרוּשָׁה מֵאִישָׁהּ לֹא יִקָּחוּ כִּי־קָדֹשׁ הוּא לֵאלֹהָיו: וְקִדַּשְׁתּוֹ
כִּי־אֶת־לֶחֶם אֱלֹהֶיךָ הוּא מַקְרִיב קָדֹשׁ יִהְיֶה־לָּךְ כִּי קָדוֹשׁ אֲנִי יְהוָה
מְקַדִּשְׁכֶם: וּבַת אִישׁ כֹּהֵן כִּי תֵחֵל לִזְנוֹת אֶת־אָבִיהָ הִיא מְחַלֶּלֶת
בָּאֵשׁ תִּשָּׂרֵף: וְהַכֹּהֵן הַגָּדוֹל מֵאֶחָיו אֲשֶׁר־יוּצַק עַל־

As for the priest who is exalted above his brethren, the one upon whose head the anointing oil has been poured and who has been charged with wearing the priestly garments – he may not let his hair grow nor may he rend his garments [as a rite of mourning]. And he may not come near the dead body of any person; he may not defile himself even for his father or mother. He may not leave the Temple; he must not desecrate his God's Temple, for the consecration of his God's anointing oil is upon him; I am the Lord. *He must take a wife who is a virgin. A widow, divorcee, des- YISRAEL ecrated woman or harlot – he may not take any of these; rather, he must take a virgin of his people as a wife. He must not desecrate his seed among his people, for I am the Lord who sanctifies him.

BEHAR

The Lord spoke to Moses at Mount Sinai, saying: Speak to the children *Lev. 25:1–13* of Israel, say to them: When you enter the land which I am giving to you, the land shall rest, a Sabbath for the Lord. Six years you shall plant your field and six years you shall prune your vineyard, gathering in its crops. But LEVI the seventh year shall be a Sabbath of Sabbaths for the land, a Sabbath for the Lord; you may not plant your field nor may you prune your vineyard. Do not harvest the growth of your spilled kernels and do not harvest your finest grapes ; it shall be a Sabbath of Sabbaths for the land. But you may eat the [produce of] the Sabbath of the land – you and your male slave and your female slave and your hired laborer and the sojourner who live among you. And your domesticated animals and the wild animals in your land may eat all of its yield.

You shall count for yourself seven weeks of years – seven years, seven YISRAEL times – until the period of the seven weeks of years amounts to forty-nine years. You shall then make a proclamation with a shofar blast in the seventh month on the tenth of the month; on the Day of Atonement shall you make a proclamation with a shofar throughout your land. And you shall sanctify the fiftieth year, proclaiming freedom in the land for all its inhabitants; it shall be a jubilee for you: each of you shall return to his land and to his family. It shall be a jubilee for you – lasting the entire fiftieth year – you may not plant and you may not harvest the growth of spilled kernels nor may you harvest your finest grapes. For it is a jubilee, it shall be sacred to you; you shall eat its crops from the field. During this jubilee you shall return, each man to his own land.

רֹאשׁוֹ ׀ שֶׁמֶן הַמִּשְׁחָה וּמִלֵּא אֶת־יָדוֹ לִלְבֹּשׁ אֶת־הַבְּגָדִים אֶת־רֹאשׁוֹ
לֹא יִפְרָע וּבְגָדָיו לֹא יִפְרֹם: וְעַל כָּל־נַפְשֹׁת מֵת לֹא יָבֹא לְאָבִיו וּלְאִמּוֹ
לֹא יִטַּמָּא: וּמִן־הַמִּקְדָּשׁ לֹא יֵצֵא וְלֹא יְחַלֵּל אֵת מִקְדַּשׁ אֱלֹהָיו כִּי
נֵזֶר שֶׁמֶן מִשְׁחַת אֱלֹהָיו עָלָיו אֲנִי יְהוָה: יְוְהוּא אִשָּׁה בִבְתוּלֶיהָ יִקָּח: **ישראל**
אַלְמָנָה וּגְרוּשָׁה וַחֲלָלָה זֹנָה אֶת־אֵלֶּה לֹא יִקָּח כִּי אִם־בְּתוּלָה מֵעַמָּיו
יִקַּח אִשָּׁה: וְלֹא־יְחַלֵּל זַרְעוֹ בְּעַמָּיו כִּי אֲנִי יְהוָה מְקַדְּשׁוֹ:

בהר

וַיְדַבֵּר יְהוָה אֶל־מֹשֶׁה בְּהַר סִינַי לֵאמֹר: דַּבֵּר אֶל־בְּנֵי יִשְׂרָאֵל וְאָמַרְתָּ **ויקרא**
אֲלֵהֶם כִּי תָבֹאוּ אֶל־הָאָרֶץ אֲשֶׁר אֲנִי נֹתֵן לָכֶם וְשָׁבְתָה הָאָרֶץ שַׁבָּת **כה:א–יג**
לַיהוָה: שֵׁשׁ שָׁנִים תִּזְרַע שָׂדֶךָ וְשֵׁשׁ שָׁנִים תִּזְמֹר כַּרְמֶךָ וְאָסַפְתָּ
אֶת־תְּבוּאָתָהּ: יוּבַשָּׁנָה הַשְּׁבִיעִת שַׁבַּת שַׁבָּתוֹן יִהְיֶה לָאָרֶץ שַׁבָּת **לוי**
לַיהוָה שָׂדְךָ לֹא תִזְרָע וְכַרְמְךָ לֹא תִזְמֹר: אֵת סְפִיחַ קְצִירְךָ לֹא
תִקְצוֹר וְאֶת־עִנְּבֵי נְזִירֶךָ לֹא תִבְצֹר שְׁנַת שַׁבָּתוֹן יִהְיֶה לָאָרֶץ:
וְהָיְתָה שַׁבַּת הָאָרֶץ לָכֶם לְאָכְלָה לְךָ וּלְעַבְדְּךָ וְלַאֲמָתֶךָ וְלִשְׂכִירְךָ
וּלְתוֹשָׁבְךָ הַגָּרִים עִמָּךְ: וְלִבְהֶמְתְּךָ וְלַחַיָּה אֲשֶׁר בְּאַרְצֶךָ תִּהְיֶה
כָל־תְּבוּאָתָהּ לֶאֱכֹל: יְוְסָפַרְתָּ לְךָ שֶׁבַע שַׁבְּתֹת שָׁנִים **ישראל**
שֶׁבַע שָׁנִים שֶׁבַע פְּעָמִים וְהָיוּ לְךָ יְמֵי שֶׁבַע שַׁבְּתֹת הַשָּׁנִים תֵּשַׁע
וְאַרְבָּעִים שָׁנָה: וְהַעֲבַרְתָּ שׁוֹפַר תְּרוּעָה בַּחֹדֶשׁ הַשְּׁבִעִי בֶּעָשׂוֹר
לַחֹדֶשׁ בְּיוֹם הַכִּפֻּרִים תַּעֲבִירוּ שׁוֹפָר בְּכָל־אַרְצְכֶם: וְקִדַּשְׁתֶּם אֵת
שְׁנַת הַחֲמִשִּׁים שָׁנָה וּקְרָאתֶם דְּרוֹר בָּאָרֶץ לְכָל־יֹשְׁבֶיהָ יוֹבֵל הִוא
תִּהְיֶה לָכֶם וְשַׁבְתֶּם אִישׁ אֶל־אֲחֻזָּתוֹ וְאִישׁ אֶל־מִשְׁפַּחְתּוֹ תָּשֻׁבוּ:
יוֹבֵל הִוא שְׁנַת הַחֲמִשִּׁים שָׁנָה תִּהְיֶה לָכֶם לֹא תִזְרָעוּ וְלֹא תִקְצְרוּ
אֶת־סְפִיחֶיהָ וְלֹא תִבְצְרוּ אֶת־נְזִרֶיהָ: כִּי יוֹבֵל הִוא קֹדֶשׁ תִּהְיֶה לָכֶם
מִן־הַשָּׂדֶה תֹּאכְלוּ אֶת־תְּבוּאָתָהּ: בִּשְׁנַת הַיּוֹבֵל הַזֹּאת תָּשֻׁבוּ אִישׁ
אֶל־אֲחֻזָּתוֹ:

HALF KADDISH

After the Reading of the Torah, the Reader says Half Kaddish:

Reader: יִתְגַּדַּל Magnified and sanctified
may His great name be,
in the world He created by His will.
May He establish His kingdom
in your lifetime and in your days,
and in the lifetime of all the house of Israel,
swiftly and soon –
and say: Amen.

All: May His great name be blessed for ever and all time.

Reader: Blessed and praised, glorified and exalted,
raised and honored,
uplifted and lauded
be the name of the Holy One,
blessed be He,
beyond any blessing,
song, praise and consolation
uttered in the world –
and say: Amen.

HAGBAHA AND GELILA

The Torah scroll is lifted and the congregation says:

וְזֹאת הַתּוֹרָה This is the Torah   *Deut. 4*
that Moses placed before the children of Israel,
at the LORD's commandment, by the hand of Moses.   *Num. 9*

Some add:
It is a tree of life to those who grasp it,   *Prov. 3*
and those who uphold it are happy.
Its ways are ways of pleasantness, and all its paths are peace.
Long life is at its right hand; at its left, riches and honor.
It pleased the LORD for the sake of [Israel's] righteousness,   *Is. 42*
to make the Torah great and glorious.

חצי קדיש

קריאת התורה, the קורא says חצי קדיש: After the התורה

קורא: יִתְגַּדַּל וְיִתְקַדַּשׁ שְׁמֵהּ רַבָּא (קהל: אָמֵן)

בְּעָלְמָא דִּי בְרָא כִרְעוּתֵהּ

וְיַמְלִיךְ מַלְכוּתֵהּ

בְּחַיֵּיכוֹן וּבְיוֹמֵיכוֹן וּבְחַיֵּי דְּכָל בֵּית יִשְׂרָאֵל

בַּעֲגָלָא וּבִזְמַן קָרִיב

וְאִמְרוּ אָמֵן. (קהל: אָמֵן)

קורא
וקהל: יְהֵא שְׁמֵהּ רַבָּא מְבָרַךְ לְעָלַם וּלְעָלְמֵי עָלְמַיָּא.

קורא: יִתְבָּרַךְ וְיִשְׁתַּבַּח וְיִתְפָּאַר וְיִתְרוֹמַם וְיִתְנַשֵּׂא

וְיִתְהַדָּר וְיִתְעַלֶּה וְיִתְהַלָּל

שְׁמֵהּ דְּקֻדְשָׁא בְּרִיךְ הוּא (קהל: בְּרִיךְ הוּא)

לְעֵלָּא מִן כָּל בִּרְכָתָא וְשִׁירָתָא

תֻּשְׁבְּחָתָא וְנֶחֱמָתָא

דַּאֲמִירָן בְּעָלְמָא

וְאִמְרוּ אָמֵן. (קהל: אָמֵן)

הגבהה וגלילה

ספר תורה is lifted and the קהל says: The

דברים ד   וְזֹאת הַתּוֹרָה אֲשֶׁר־שָׂם מֹשֶׁה לִפְנֵי בְּנֵי יִשְׂרָאֵל:

במדבר ט   עַל־פִּי יהוה בְּיַד־מֹשֶׁה:

Some add:

משלי ג   עֵץ־חַיִּים הִיא לַמַּחֲזִיקִים בָּהּ וְתֹמְכֶיהָ מְאֻשָּׁר:
דְּרָכֶיהָ דַרְכֵי־נֹעַם וְכָל־נְתִיבֹתֶיהָ שָׁלוֹם:
אֹרֶךְ יָמִים בִּימִינָהּ, בִּשְׂמֹאולָהּ עֹשֶׁר וְכָבוֹד:

ישעיה מב   יהוה חָפֵץ לְמַעַן צִדְקוֹ יַגְדִּיל תּוֹרָה וְיַאְדִּיר:

READING FOR YOM HAATZMA'UT (*from the second Torah scroll*)

Those who read this as a Torah portion, divide the reading into three aliyot: Kohen, Levi and Yisrael. Those who read this as an addition to the Torah reading do not divide it.

If you obey these laws and safeguard them and observe them, the LORD your God shall also safeguard the covenant and the kindness which he swore to your ancestors. And he will love you and bless you and multiply you; he will bless the fruit of your wombs and the fruit of your land, your grains and wine and olive oil, the offspring of your herds and the young of your sheep upon the land which He swore to your ancestors to give to you. You shall be the most blessed of all nations; no man or woman among your people will be barren, nor shall any of your livestock be barren. The LORD will remove from among you every type of illness; he will not afflict you with any of the terrible diseases known to you from Egypt; instead, he will cast them upon all of your enemies. And you will devour all of the nations [whose land] the LORD your God is giving to you ; do not show them any pity, and do not worship their gods, for it shall surely ensnare you.

Deut. 7:12–8:18

Should you say to yourself: these nations are more numerous than I, how might I possibly dispossess them [of the land]? You must not fear them; recall all that the LORD your God did to Pharaoh and to all of Egypt. All those great trials which you witnessed, and the signs and wonders and the mighty hand and the outstretched

---

THE MITZVA OF LIVING IN THE LAND

We were commanded to inherit the land that the blessed and exalted God gave to our forefathers, to Abraham, Isaac and Jacob, and it was not left in the hands of the surrounding nations, or left to waste. And His saying to them, "And you shall inherit the land and you shall dwell in it, for to you I have given the land to inherit, and you shall settle the land" (Numbers 33:53–54) … is what the sages refer to as *milhemet mitzva* – a holy war.

קריאה ליום העצמאות (ספר תורה from the second)

Those who read this as a תורה portion, divide the reading into three עליות: כהן, לוי and ישראל.
Those who read this as an addition to the תורה reading do not divide it.

דברים
ג,יב – ח,יח

וְהָיָה ׀ עֵקֶב תִּשְׁמְעוּן אֵת הַמִּשְׁפָּטִים הָאֵלֶּה וּשְׁמַרְתֶּם
וַעֲשִׂיתֶם אֹתָם וְשָׁמַר יהוה אֱלֹהֶיךָ לְךָ אֶת־הַבְּרִית וְאֶת־
הַחֶסֶד אֲשֶׁר נִשְׁבַּע לַאֲבֹתֶיךָ: וַאֲהֵבְךָ וּבֵרַכְךָ וְהִרְבֶּךָ וּבֵרַךְ
פְּרִי־בִטְנְךָ וּפְרִי־אַדְמָתֶךָ דְּגָנְךָ וְתִירשְׁךָ וְיִצְהָרֶךָ שְׁגַר־אֲלָפֶיךָ
וְעַשְׁתְּרֹת צֹאנֶךָ עַל הָאֲדָמָה אֲשֶׁר־נִשְׁבַּע לַאֲבֹתֶיךָ לָתֶת
לָךְ: בָּרוּךְ תִּהְיֶה מִכָּל־הָעַמִּים לֹא־יִהְיֶה בְךָ עָקָר וַעֲקָרָה
וּבִבְהֶמְתֶּךָ: וְהֵסִיר יהוה מִמְּךָ כָּל־חֹלִי וְכָל־מַדְוֵי מִצְרַיִם
הָרָעִים אֲשֶׁר יָדַעְתָּ לֹא יְשִׂימָם בָּךְ וּנְתָנָם בְּכָל־שֹׂנְאֶיךָ:
וְאָכַלְתָּ אֶת־כָּל־הָעַמִּים אֲשֶׁר יהוה אֱלֹהֶיךָ נֹתֵן לָךְ לֹא־
תָחֹס עֵינְךָ עֲלֵיהֶם וְלֹא תַעֲבֹד אֶת־אֱלֹהֵיהֶם כִּי־מוֹקֵשׁ
הוּא לָךְ:   כִּי תֹאמַר בִּלְבָבְךָ רַבִּים הַגּוֹיִם הָאֵלֶּה
מִמֶּנִּי אֵיכָה אוּכַל לְהוֹרִישָׁם: לֹא תִירָא מֵהֶם זָכֹר תִּזְכֹּר
אֵת אֲשֶׁר־עָשָׂה יהוה אֱלֹהֶיךָ לְפַרְעֹה וּלְכָל־מִצְרָיִם: הַמַּסֹּת
הַגְּדֹלֹת אֲשֶׁר־רָאוּ עֵינֶיךָ וְהָאֹתֹת וְהַמֹּפְתִים וְהַיָּד הַחֲזָקָה

TORAH READING FOR YOM HAATZMA'UT

The festival of Yom HaAtzma'ut is certainly worthy of a special Torah reading
that is thematically linked to the meaning of the day, similar to the readings
instituted by our sages for Ḥanukka and Purim. This passage from *Parashat
Ekev* is a fitting reminder of to whom we owe our gratitude for the Land and
all its blessings, as well as how we are responsible, through our own behavior,
for whether or not we merit to live peacefully in our own land and to enjoy
its bounty.

YR

arm with which the LORD your God took you out [of their land], so too shall the LORD your God do to all of the nations you now fear. He, the LORD your God, shall also send hornets upon them until all those who are left in hiding perish before you. Do not tremble before them, for the LORD your God is with you, a great, awesome God. The LORD your God shall clear away these nations before you little by little; you will not be able to destroy them swiftly, lest the wild beasts of the field multiply against you. The LORD your God shall deliver them to you, throwing them into a great confusion until they are destroyed. He shall deliver their kings into your hand and you shall obliterate their names from under the heavens; no man shall stand up against you until you they are destroyed. Burn the images of their gods in fire; do not covet the silver and gold that adorns them, taking it for yourself, lest it ensnare you, for it is an abomination to the LORD your God. And do not bring an abomination into your house, lest you become deserving of annihilation as they were; you shall treat it as a detested and abhorred thing, for it is banned.

LEVI

Take care to observe all the commandments I am commanding you today so that you might live and multiply and enter and possess the land the LORD swore to your ancestors. Remember the entire journey on which the LORD your God has led you in the wilderness these past forty years, in order to afflict you and test you, to know what is in your heart- would you or would you not observe his commandments. He afflicted you and allowed you to go hungry and then fed you the manna, which neither you nor your ancestors had ever known, in order to make it known

---

outside of Israel should be considered as idol worshipers (*Sifra, Behar* 5:4) … all of this is derived from this positive commandment, in which we are commanded to inherit the land and dwell in it. If so, it is a positive commandment for the generations, one that obligates each individual, even in times of exile, and this is mentioned many times in the Talmud."

(Nahmanides, *Positive Mitzvot Omitted by Maimonides* 4)

וְהַזֶּרַע הַנְּטוּיָה אֲשֶׁר הוֹצִאֲךָ יהוה אֱלֹהֶיךָ כֵּן־יַעֲשֶׂה יהוה
אֱלֹהֶיךָ לְכָל־הָעַמִּים אֲשֶׁר־אַתָּה יָרֵא מִפְּנֵיהֶם: וְגַם אֶת־
הַצִּרְעָה יְשַׁלַּח יהוה אֱלֹהֶיךָ בָּם עַד־אֲבֹד הַנִּשְׁאָרִים
וְהַנִּסְתָּרִים מִפָּנֶיךָ: לֹא תַעֲרֹץ מִפְּנֵיהֶם כִּי־יהוה אֱלֹהֶיךָ
בְּקִרְבֶּךָ אֵל גָּדוֹל וְנוֹרָא: ^{לוי}וְנָשַׁל יהוה אֱלֹהֶיךָ אֶת־הַגּוֹיִם
הָאֵל מִפָּנֶיךָ מְעַט מְעָט לֹא תוּכַל כַּלֹּתָם מַהֵר פֶּן־תִּרְבֶּה
עָלֶיךָ חַיַּת הַשָּׂדֶה: וּנְתָנָם יהוה אֱלֹהֶיךָ לְפָנֶיךָ וְהָמָם מְהוּמָה
גְדֹלָה עַד הִשָּׁמְדָם: וְנָתַן מַלְכֵיהֶם בְּיָדֶךָ וְהַאֲבַדְתָּ אֶת־שְׁמָם
מִתַּחַת הַשָּׁמָיִם לֹא־יִתְיַצֵּב אִישׁ בְּפָנֶיךָ עַד הִשְׁמִדְךָ אֹתָם:
פְּסִילֵי אֱלֹהֵיהֶם תִּשְׂרְפוּן בָּאֵשׁ לֹא־תַחְמֹד כֶּסֶף וְזָהָב עֲלֵיהֶם
וְלָקַחְתָּ לָךְ פֶּן תִּוָּקֵשׁ בּוֹ כִּי תוֹעֲבַת יהוה אֱלֹהֶיךָ הוּא: וְלֹא־
תָבִיא תוֹעֵבָה אֶל־בֵּיתֶךָ וְהָיִיתָ חֵרֶם כָּמֹהוּ שַׁקֵּץ ׀ תְּשַׁקְּצֶנּוּ
וְתַעֵב ׀ תְּתַעֲבֶנּוּ כִּי־חֵרֶם הוּא:
כָּל־הַמִּצְוָה אֲשֶׁר אָנֹכִי מְצַוְּךָ הַיּוֹם תִּשְׁמְרוּן לַעֲשׂוֹת לְמַעַן
תִּחְיוּן וּרְבִיתֶם וּבָאתֶם וִירִשְׁתֶּם אֶת־הָאָרֶץ אֲשֶׁר־נִשְׁבַּע יהוה
לַאֲבֹתֵיכֶם: וְזָכַרְתָּ אֶת־כָּל־הַדֶּרֶךְ אֲשֶׁר הוֹלִיכֲךָ יהוה אֱלֹהֶיךָ
זֶה אַרְבָּעִים שָׁנָה בַּמִּדְבָּר לְמַעַן עַנֹּתְךָ לְנַסֹּתְךָ לָדַעַת אֶת־
אֲשֶׁר בִּלְבָבְךָ הֲתִשְׁמֹר מִצְוֹתָו אִם־לֹא: וַיְעַנְּךָ וַיַּרְעִבֶךָ וַיַּאֲכִלְךָ
אֶת־הַמָּן אֲשֶׁר לֹא־יָדַעְתָּ וְלֹא יָדְעוּן אֲבֹתֶיךָ לְמַעַן הוֹדִיעֲךָ כִּי

And it says thus in Tractate *Sota* (44b): "Rabbi Yehuda said: Joshua's war
to conquer – all agree it is obligatory; David's war to expand – all agree
it is voluntary…understand that this law refers to conquering…and I say
that the mitzva that the sages are in dispute over is that of living in the
land, there are even those who say that whoever leaves [the land] and lives

to you that man shall not live by bread alone; he shall live by all the decrees of the LORD. Your garments have not worn out [and fallen] from upon you and your feet have not swollen these past forty years. Bear in mind that just as a man disciplines his son, so too is the LORD your God disciplining you. So that you might observe the commandments of the LORD your God; following His ways and fearing Him. For the LORD your God is bringing you to a good land: a land of streams of water, springs and deep waters flowing through valleys and upon mountains. A land of wheat and barley, of vines, fig trees and pomegranate trees; a land of olive-oil yielding trees and honey. A land in which you shall not eat bread in poverty, where you shall lack nothing; a land whose stones are iron and from whose mountains you shall mine copper. And you shall eat and be satiated and bless the LORD your God for the good land he gave you. Take care lest you forget the LORD your God, and fail to observe His commandments, His statutes and His laws which I am commanding you today. Lest you eat and become satiated and build good houses and dwell in them. Lest your cattle and sheep multiply and you accumulate much silver and gold, and all that you possess becomes abundant. So that your heart grows haughty and you forget the LORD your God, who took you out of the land of Egypt, out of the house of bondage. He who has led you through the great, terrible wilderness, a place of snakes, fiery serpents and scorpions, and thirst without water; He who brought forth water for you from the flinty rock. Who fed you manna in the desert, which your ancestors had never known, in order to afflict you and in order to test you, to benefit you in the end. Lest you say in your heart: "it is my own strength, the power of my own hand that has earned me all this wealth". Remember the LORD your God, for it is He who gives you the strength to earn wealth, in order to fulfill His covenant which He swore to your ancestors, as on this day.

The Torah scroll is lifted and the congregation says "This is the Torah" on page 372.

YISRAEL

לֹא עַל־הַלֶּחֶם לְבַדּוֹ יִחְיֶה הָאָדָם כִּי עַל־כָּל־מוֹצָא פִי־יהוה יִחְיֶה הָאָדָם: שִׂמְלָתְךָ לֹא בָלְתָה מֵעָלֶיךָ וְרַגְלְךָ לֹא בָצֵקָה זֶה אַרְבָּעִים שָׁנָה: וְיָדַעְתָּ עִם־לְבָבֶךָ כִּי כַּאֲשֶׁר יְיַסֵּר אִישׁ אֶת־בְּנוֹ יהוה אֱלֹהֶיךָ מְיַסְּרֶךָּ: וְשָׁמַרְתָּ אֶת־מִצְוֹת יהוה אֱלֹהֶיךָ לָלֶכֶת בִּדְרָכָיו וּלְיִרְאָה אֹתוֹ: כִּי יהוה אֱלֹהֶיךָ מְבִיאֲךָ אֶל־אֶרֶץ טוֹבָה אֶרֶץ נַחֲלֵי מָיִם עֲיָנֹת וּתְהֹמֹת יֹצְאִים בַּבִּקְעָה וּבָהָר: אֶרֶץ חִטָּה וּשְׂעֹרָה וְגֶפֶן וּתְאֵנָה וְרִמּוֹן אֶרֶץ־זֵית שֶׁמֶן וּדְבָשׁ: אֶרֶץ אֲשֶׁר לֹא בְמִסְכֵּנֻת תֹּאכַל־בָּהּ לֶחֶם לֹא־תֶחְסַר כֹּל בָּהּ אֶרֶץ אֲשֶׁר אֲבָנֶיהָ בַרְזֶל וּמֵהֲרָרֶיהָ תַּחְצֹב נְחֹשֶׁת: וְאָכַלְתָּ וְשָׂבָעְתָּ וּבֵרַכְתָּ אֶת־יהוה אֱלֹהֶיךָ עַל־הָאָרֶץ הַטֹּבָה אֲשֶׁר נָתַן־לָךְ: הִשָּׁמֶר לְךָ פֶּן־תִּשְׁכַּח אֶת־יהוה אֱלֹהֶיךָ לְבִלְתִּי שְׁמֹר מִצְוֹתָיו וּמִשְׁפָּטָיו וְחֻקֹּתָיו אֲשֶׁר אָנֹכִי מְצַוְּךָ הַיּוֹם: פֶּן־תֹּאכַל וְשָׂבָעְתָּ וּבָתִּים טוֹבִים תִּבְנֶה וְיָשָׁבְתָּ: וּבְקָרְךָ וְצֹאנְךָ יִרְבְּיֻן וְכֶסֶף וְזָהָב יִרְבֶּה־לָּךְ וְכֹל אֲשֶׁר־לְךָ יִרְבֶּה: וְרָם לְבָבֶךָ וְשָׁכַחְתָּ אֶת־יהוה אֱלֹהֶיךָ הַמּוֹצִיאֲךָ מֵאֶרֶץ מִצְרַיִם מִבֵּית עֲבָדִים: הַמּוֹלִיכְךָ בַּמִּדְבָּר הַגָּדֹל וְהַנּוֹרָא נָחָשׁ שָׂרָף וְעַקְרָב וְצִמָּאוֹן אֲשֶׁר אֵין־מָיִם הַמּוֹצִיא לְךָ מַיִם מִצּוּר הַחַלָּמִישׁ: הַמַּאֲכִלְךָ מָן בַּמִּדְבָּר אֲשֶׁר לֹא־יָדְעוּן אֲבֹתֶיךָ לְמַעַן עַנֹּתְךָ וּלְמַעַן נַסֹּתֶךָ לְהֵיטִבְךָ בְּאַחֲרִיתֶךָ: וְאָמַרְתָּ בִּלְבָבֶךָ כֹּחִי וְעֹצֶם יָדִי עָשָׂה לִי אֶת־הַחַיִל הַזֶּה: וְזָכַרְתָּ אֶת־יהוה אֱלֹהֶיךָ כִּי הוּא הַנֹּתֵן לְךָ כֹּחַ לַעֲשׂוֹת חָיִל לְמַעַן הָקִים אֶת־בְּרִיתוֹ אֲשֶׁר־נִשְׁבַּע לַאֲבֹתֶיךָ כַּיּוֹם הַזֶּה:

ישראל

The ספר תורה is lifted and the קהל say וְזֹאת הַתּוֹרָה on page 373.

HAFTARA

The Haftara blessings are not recited.

עוֹד הַיּוֹם This day he will halt at Nob; he will wave his hand, mountain   *Is. 10:32–*
of the daughter of Zion, hill of Jerusalem.   *12:6*

See, the sovereign LORD of hosts will lop off the boughs with an axe. The tall trees will be felled, the lofty ones laid low. He will cut down the forest thickets with an axe. Lebanon will fall before the Mighty One.

A shoot will grow from the stump of Jesse; from his roots a branch will bear fruit. The spirit of the LORD will rest on him – a spirit of

---

and so on. Rabbi Yosef Karo did not connect the seventh day of Pesaḥ to any festival. Recently, however, one of the greatest figures of the reestablishment of the State of Israel, Rabbi Amram Aburbeh, the Chief Rabbi of Petaḥ Tikva, renewed the dialogue begun in the sixteenth-century work: "In our time, we have been granted the knowledge that ו (the seventh day of Pesaḥ) corresponds to ע [according to the *Atbash* code]: the seventh day of Pesaḥ is יום העצמאות" (*Netivei Am*, vol. 1, Tel Aviv 5733, p. 187; vol. 2, Jerusalem 5726, p. 317).

Thus we can neatly connect the seventh day of Pesaḥ, the final day of the exodus from Egypt and the beginning of national freedom, to Yom HaAtzma'ut, the day that symbolizes national freedom as renewed in our generation.

Jews living outside of Israel, who observe an eighth day of Pesaḥ, read a passage from Isaiah 10 for the *Haftara* of this final day. Those who live in Israel "miss" this reading, as the extra day is not observed. Now, however, Yom HaAtzma'ut provides us with an opportunity to read this fitting passage, which speaks of both past and future redemption and expresses joyous gratitude for our ancestors' salvation as well as the salvation still to come. In the words of Isaiah, the poet laureate of hope: "On that day the LORD will reach out His hand a second time to reclaim the remnant that is left of His people," this time bringing them back not from one place of exile but "from the four quarters of the earth" (Isaiah 11:11–12) (see Rabbi J. Sacks, *The Koren Pesaḥ Maḥzor*, p. 607).

The congregations of the Religious Kibbutz Movement had the custom of reading this *Haftara* with all the accompanying blessings, but this was strongly opposed. Rabbi Shlomo Goren voiced his reservations about the blessings

הפטרה

The הפטרה blessings are not recited.

ישעיה
י:לב–יב:ו

עוֹד הַיּוֹם בְּנֹב לַעֲמֹד יְנֹפֵף יָדוֹ הַר בַּת־צִיּוֹן גִּבְעַת
יְרוּשָׁלָֽםִ:   הִנֵּה הָאָדוֹן יהוה צְבָאוֹת מְסָעֵף פֻּארָה
בְּמַעֲרָצָה וְרָמֵי הַקּוֹמָה גְּדֻעִים וְהַגְּבֹהִים יִשְׁפָּֽלוּ: וְנִקַּף סִבְכֵי
הַיַּֽעַר בַּבַּרְזֶל וְהַלְּבָנוֹן בְּאַדִּיר יִפּֽוֹל: וְיָצָא חֹֽטֶר מִגֵּֽזַע
יִשַׁי וְנֵֽצֶר מִשָּׁרָשָׁיו יִפְרֶה: וְנָחָה עָלָיו רֽוּחַ יהוה רֽוּחַ חָכְמָה וּבִינָה

HAFTARA WITHOUT BLESSINGS

It seems that no blessing should be read over the *Haftara*, as Maimonides ruled: "*Haftarot* from the books of the Prophets are only read on Shabbat, festivals, and Tisha B'Av" (Laws of Prayer 12:2). And our entire study is based on the similarity to Ḥanukka and Purim, as Yom HaAtzma'ut is likewise not a biblically ordained festival, of the same category that Maimonides intended. (Rabbi Ḥayyim David HaLevi, "Reading the Torah and the *Haftara* on Yom HaAtzma'ut, its Meaning and Laws," *Religion and State*, 5729)

THE HAFTARA OF YOM HAATZMA'UT

Rabbi Yosef Karo, writing in his *Shulḥan Arukh* (*Oraḥ Ḥayyim* 428:3), presents a connection between the days of the various festivals and the days of Pesaḥ, hidden in what is known as an *Atbash* (אתב״ש) acrostic (where the first letter of the alphabet, *alef*, corresponds to the last letter, *taf*; the second, *beit*, with the second-to-last, *shin*, and so on):

א׳ פסח – ת׳ (= תשעה באב – Tisha B'Av)

ב׳ פסח – ש׳ (= שבועות – Shavuot)

ג׳ פסח – ר׳ (= ראש השנה – Rosh HaShana)

ד׳ פסח – ק׳ (= קריאת התורה בשמחת תורה –

(The Torah Reading on Simḥat Torah outside of Israel

ה׳ פסח – צ׳ (= צום יום הכיפורים – The Fast of Yom Kippur)

ו׳ פסח – פ׳ (= פורים – Purim)

The first day of Pesaḥ always falls on the same day of the week as Tisha B'Av; the second day of Pesaḥ always falls on the same day of the week as Shavuot,

wisdom and understanding, a spirit of counsel and power, a spirit of knowledge and the fear of the LORD, and he will delight in the fear of the LORD. He will not judge by what his eyes see, or decide by what his ears hear; with justice he will judge the poor, and with equity defend the humble in the land. He will strike the earth with the rod of his mouth; with the breath of his lips he will slay the wicked. Justice will be his belt and faithfulness the sash around his waist. The wolf will live with the lamb, the leopard will lie down with the kid, the calf and the lion and the yearling together; and a little child will lead them. The cow will graze with the bear, their young will lie down together, and the lion will eat straw like the ox. An infant will play near the cobra's hole, and a young child put his hand into the viper's nest. They will neither harm nor destroy on all My holy mountain, for the earth will be full of the knowledge of the LORD as the waters cover the sea.

---

contrast the Rambam in his well-known *Iggeret Teiman* clearly asserts that *Mashiaḥ* will arrive after the conclusion of the war. An intermediate position suggests that *Mashiaḥ ben Yosef* will participate, and be killed, in the war while *Mashiaḥ ben David* will reign after the war, which will yield uncontested Jewish sovereignty.

This debate influences modern opinions which attempted to identify World War II as the war of Gog uMagog. Several Modern authorities claimed that the past war which included Nazi attempts to capture Jerusalem was the Gog uMagog experience. This position assumes the arrival of *Mashiaḥ after* the war. Casting World War II as Gog uMagog lends further foundation to the designation of the Modern State as a Messianic event.

Commenting on this war (as well as the redemptive role of Eliyahu) the Rambam (*Hilkhot Melakhim* 12:2) summarizes: "These events are concealed by our prophets and will not fully be deciphered until they occur." Due to uncertainties in the verses there are significant debates among the commentators. Ultimately, these sequences and events do not constitute basic religious tenets, and a person shouldn't engage seriously in these issues as primary religious topics. As discussed in the introduction to this siddur, redemptive consciousness demands that we thirst for redemption and study its general models, without presuming precise levels of accuracy, and without making apocalyptic thought too important in general religious discourse.

רוּחַ עֵצָה֙ וּגְבוּרָ֔ה רֻ֥וּחַ דַּ֖עַת וְיִרְאַ֣ת יְהֹוָֽה: וַהֲרִיח֖וֹ בְּיִרְאַ֣ת יְהֹוָ֑ה
וְלֹֽא־לְמַרְאֵ֤ה עֵינָיו֙ יִשְׁפּ֔וֹט וְלֹֽא־לְמִשְׁמַ֥ע אָזְנָ֖יו יוֹכִ֑יחַ: וְשָׁפַ֤ט
בְּצֶ֨דֶק֙ דַּלִּ֔ים וְהוֹכִ֥יחַ בְּמִישׁ֖וֹר לְעַנְוֵי־אָ֑רֶץ וְהִכָּה־אֶ֨רֶץ֙ בְּשֵׁ֣בֶט
פִּ֔יו וּבְר֥וּחַ שְׂפָתָ֖יו יָמִ֥ית רָשָֽׁע: וְהָ֥יָה צֶ֖דֶק אֵז֣וֹר מָתְנָ֑יו וְהָאֱמוּנָ֖ה
אֵז֥וֹר חֲלָצָֽיו: וְגָ֤ר זְאֵב֙ עִם־כֶּ֔בֶשׂ וְנָמֵ֖ר עִם־גְּדִ֣י יִרְבָּ֑ץ וְעֵ֨גֶל וּכְפִ֤יר
וּמְרִיא֙ יַחְדָּ֔ו וְנַ֥עַר קָטֹ֖ן נֹהֵ֥ג בָּֽם: וּפָרָ֤ה וָדֹב֙ תִּרְעֶ֔ינָה יַחְדָּ֖ו יִרְבְּצ֣וּ
יַלְדֵיהֶ֑ן וְאַרְיֵ֖ה כַּבָּקָ֥ר יֹֽאכַל־תֶּֽבֶן: וְשִֽׁעֲשַׁ֥ע יוֹנֵ֖ק עַל־חֻ֣ר פָּ֑תֶן
וְעַל֙ מְאוּרַ֣ת צִפְעוֹנִ֔י גָּמ֖וּל יָד֣וֹ הָדָֽה: לֹֽא־יָרֵ֥עוּ וְלֹֽא־יַשְׁחִ֖יתוּ
בְּכָל־הַ֣ר קָדְשִׁ֑י כִּֽי־מָלְאָ֣ה הָאָ֗רֶץ דֵּעָה֙ אֶת־יְהֹוָ֔ה כַּמַּ֖יִם לַיָּ֥ם

---

being part of the prayer service in the Religious Kibbutz congregations, and many other authorities encouraged the reading, but not its blessings.

Rabbi Goren ruled, however, that the congregations who had already instituted the custom of reciting the blessings over the *Haftara* could continue, because their custom had become established and there is no need to reverse it.

BL

THE GREAT WAR OF GOG AND MAGOG

Magog was one of the seven children of Yafet the son of Noaḥ. Several prophecies – primarily in the book of *Yeḥezkel* – describe a fierce war, spearheaded by the king of this nation, named Gog, who will construct a consortium of foreign powers aligned against the Jews and Yerushalayim. In part the war will be prompted by severe political upheaval, primarily within the world of Islam (*Yalkut Shimoni Yeshayahu* 60:499). A parallel narrative in *Ovadia* (1:11) portrays the empire of Edom (typically viewed as Western Christendom) as bystanders who are faulted for non-intervention on behalf of the Jewish people. After repeated efforts Gog meets with some success, but ultimately HaKadosh Barukh Hu defends the Jewish people through supernatural miracles, and this triumph closes history, while convincingly displaying the divine presence. Furthermore it formally ends the period of Jewish Exile; subsequent to the war Jews are no longer exiled from Israel.

There is interesting disagreement as to the role of *Mashiaḥ* in this war. Many assumed that *Mashiaḥ* would *precede* and participate in the war. By

On that day the stock of Jesse will stand as a banner for the peoples; nations will rally to him, and his place of rest will be glorious.

On that day the LORD will reach out His hand a second time to reclaim the remnant that is left of His people from Assyria, Lower Egypt, Pathros, Cush, Elam, Shinar, Hamath and the islands of the sea. He will raise a banner for the nations and gather the exiles of Israel; He will assemble the scattered people of Judah from the four quarters of the earth. Ephraim's jealousy will vanish, and Judah's harassment will end. Ephraim will not be jealous of Judah, nor will Judah be hostile toward Ephraim. They will swoop down on the slopes of Philistia to the west; together they will plunder the people to the east. Edom and Moab will be subject to them, and the Ammonites shall obey them. The LORD will dry up the gulf of the Egyptian sea; with a scorching wind He will sweep His hand over the Euphrates River. He will

---

night of Pesaḥ was referred to as *shimurim* (vigils): "Because the LORD kept vigil that night to bring them out of Egypt, on this night all the Israelites are to keep vigil to honor the LORD for the generations to come." (*Shemot* 12:42), affirming that the model of that evening is *reserved* for future historical redemption. Both specific events as well as general patterns of the liberation from Egypt will shape the final *geula*.

Casting the final *geula* as the *second* redemption omits the return from Bavel during the days of Ezra from the series. Though sovereignty in Israel was reestablished and the *Mikdash* was reconstructed, the return was flawed from the outset when only 42,000 Jews returned. Most remained in various host countries, in part because conditions in Israel were too harsh. Sadly the Jews who did return were conscious that this process would never recapture the triumphs of the First *Mikdash* and would soon dissolve. When envisioning a complete redemption Yeshayahu must invoke the first *geula,* rather than the more recent experience which would ultimately be more meaningful to the generations reading his prophecy.

Yirmiyahu predicts that when *Mashiaḥ* arrives people will no longer say, "As surely as the LORD lives, who brought the Israelites up out of Egypt," but they will say, "As surely as the LORD lives, who brought the descendants of Israel up out of the land of the north and out of all the countries where He had banished them" (*Yirmiyahu* 23:7–8), suggesting that the marvels of the Messianic Era will considerably surpass the miracles of Egypt, rendering the

מְכַסִּֽים׃   וְהָיָה בַּיּוֹם הַהוּא שֹׁרֶשׁ יִשַׁי אֲשֶׁר עֹמֵד לְנֵס

עַמִּים אֵלָיו גּוֹיִם יִדְרֹשׁוּ וְהָיְתָה מְנֻחָתוֹ כָּבוֹד׃   וְהָיָה ׀

בַּיּוֹם הַהוּא יוֹסִיף אֲדֹנָי ׀ שֵׁנִית יָדוֹ לִקְנוֹת אֶת־שְׁאָר עַמּוֹ אֲשֶׁר

יִשָּׁאֵר מֵאַשּׁוּר וּמִמִּצְרַֽיִם וּמִפַּתְרוֹס וּמִכּוּשׁ וּמֵעֵילָם וּמִשִּׁנְעָר

וּמֵחֲמָת וּמֵאִיֵּי הַיָּם׃ וְנָשָׂא נֵס לַגּוֹיִם וְאָסַף נִדְחֵי יִשְׂרָאֵל וּנְפֻצוֹת

יְהוּדָה יְקַבֵּץ מֵאַרְבַּע כַּנְפוֹת הָאָֽרֶץ׃ וְסָֽרָה קִנְאַת אֶפְרַיִם וְצֹרְרֵי

יְהוּדָה יִכָּרֵתוּ אֶפְרַיִם לֹא־יְקַנֵּא אֶת־יְהוּדָה וִיהוּדָה לֹא־יָצֹר

אֶת־אֶפְרָֽיִם׃ וְעָפוּ בְכָתֵף פְּלִשְׁתִּים יָמָּה יַחְדָּו יָבֹזּוּ אֶת־בְּנֵי־

קֶֽדֶם אֱדוֹם וּמוֹאָב מִשְׁלוֹחַ יָדָם וּבְנֵי עַמּוֹן מִשְׁמַעְתָּם׃ וְהֶחֱרִים

יהוה אֵת לְשׁוֹן יָם־מִצְרַיִם וְהֵנִיף יָדוֹ עַל־הַנָּהָר בַּעְיָם רוּחוֹ

A BANNER

The conventional function of the messianic banner is to summon worldwide Jewish exiles. In this particular context, *Mashiaḥ himself* acts as a flag for the Gentile nations who are seeking him: "On that day the Root of Jesse will stand as a banner for the peoples; the nations will rally to him, and his resting place will be glorious" (*Yeshayahu* 11:10). This image is repeated two verses later as he is described as raising a flag for all nations. This casts the *Mashiaḥ* as a universal teacher who educates a broader audience.

The content of his instruction is unclear, but presumably he purges other religions of pagan impurities, and reinforces commitment to the seven Noaḥide Laws. The phrase "the nations will rally to him" suggests the general interest in, and solicitation of, this instruction. The verse concludes by describing the worldwide honor and reverence which he will enjoy. Ironically a flagpole, which is often employed to mobilize soldiers to battle, will be utilized to gather various nations to a utopian state of peace centered upon *Yerushalayim*. The conversion of a military symbol into a peaceful one is consistent with the overall tone of the chapter, describing harmony between otherwise predatory animals.

יוֹסִיף אֲדֹנָי שֵׁנִית יָדוֹ לִקְנוֹת אֶת־שְׁאָר עַמּוֹ *The Lord will reach out His hand a second time to reclaim the remnant that is left of His people.* The prophecy that HaKadosh Barukh Hu will redeem His people a *second* time establishes the exodus from Egypt as a model and a precursor for our final redemption. The

break it up into seven streams so that people can cross over in sandals. There will be a highway for the remnant of His people that is left from Assyria, as there was for Israel when they came up from Egypt. In that day you will say: "I will praise You, O LORD. Although You were angry with me, Your anger has turned away and You have comforted me. Surely God is my salvation; I will trust and not be afraid. The LORD, the LORD, is my strength and my song; He has become my salvation." With joy you will draw water from the wells of salvation. In that day you will say: "Give thanks to the LORD, call on His name; make known among the nations what He has done, and proclaim that His name is exalted. Sing to the LORD, for He has done glorious things; let this be known to all the world. Shout aloud and sing for joy, people of Zion, for great is the Holy One of Israel among you."

---

offering of water symbolized the expectation of drawing divine knowledge, or *Ruaḥ HaKodesh*, even in a pre-messianic era. Our expectation is that our exposure to *Ruaḥ HaKodesh* will increase in the Messianic Era.

Rabbi Yitzḥak Abrabanel was born in the fifteenth century to a family which traced itself to the Davidic dynasty. A statesman, philosopher, and biblical commentator, he lived through the Spanish Inquisition and wrote extensively about the historical connotations of this event. Among his works is a messianic trilogy entitled *Migdol Yeshu'ot*, which outlines messianic expectations. One of the volumes, named *Maayanei Hayeshua* – based on this phrase – is a commentary on the book of Daniel. His thesis maintains that the prophecies of Daniel referred to a final redemption which hasn't yet occurred, rather than the return to Israel with Ezra and Neḥemya. Daniel dreams of four animals representing four empires which would rule the world in the pre-messianic era. The fourth animal symbolizes not just ancient Rome, but Christian Rome, and by extension the overall Christian world. This perspective debunked Christian claims that Daniel's eschatological prophecies had materialized, and *Mashiaḥ* had already arrived. This was an especially valuable lesson for a post-Inquisition Jewish world, still reeling from national persecution and mass conversion.

ATḤALTA DIGEULA

Rabbi Menachem Mendel of Kotzk – commonly referred to as the Kotzker Rebbe – was the unquestioned leader of Polish Ḥasidut during the turn of the

וְהִכָּ֨הוּ לְשִׁבְעָ֤ה נְחָלִים֙ וְהִדְרִ֣יךְ בַּנְּעָלִ֑ים: וְהָ֨יְתָ֤ה מְסִלָּה֙ לִשְׁאָ֣ר
עַמּ֔וֹ אֲשֶׁ֥ר יִשָּׁאֵ֖ר מֵאַשּׁ֑וּר כַּאֲשֶׁ֤ר הָֽיְתָה֙ לְיִשְׂרָאֵ֔ל בְּי֖וֹם עֲלֹת֥וֹ
מֵאֶ֥רֶץ מִצְרָֽיִם: וְאָֽמַרְתָּ֙ בַּיּ֣וֹם הַה֔וּא אֽוֹדְךָ֣ יהו֔ה כִּ֥י אָנַ֖פְתָּ בִּ֑י
יָשֹׁ֥ב אַפְּךָ֖ וּֽתְנַחֲמֵֽנִי: הִנֵּ֨ה אֵ֧ל יְשֽׁוּעָתִ֛י אֶבְטַ֖ח וְלֹ֣א אֶפְחָ֑ד כִּֽי־
עָזִּ֤י וְזִמְרָת֙ יָ֣הּ יהו֔ה וַֽיְהִי־לִ֖י לִֽישׁוּעָֽה: וּשְׁאַבְתֶּם־מַ֖יִם בְּשָׂשׂ֑וֹן
מִמַּעַיְנֵ֖י הַיְשׁוּעָֽה: וַֽאֲמַרְתֶּ֞ם בַּיּ֣וֹם הַה֗וּא הוֹד֤וּ לַֽיהוה֙ קִרְא֣וּ
בִשְׁמ֔וֹ הוֹדִ֥יעוּ בָֽעַמִּ֖ים עֲלִֽילֹתָ֑יו הַזְכִּ֕ירוּ כִּ֥י נִשְׂגָּ֖ב שְׁמֽוֹ: זַמְּר֣וּ יהו֔ה
כִּ֥י גֵא֖וּת עָשָׂ֑ה מוּדַ֥עַת זֹ֖את בְּכָל־הָאָֽרֶץ: צַֽהֲלִ֥י וָרֹ֖נִּי יוֹשֶׁ֣בֶת צִיּ֑וֹן
כִּֽי־גָד֥וֹל בְּקִרְבֵּ֖ךְ קְד֥וֹשׁ יִשְׂרָאֵֽל:

---

first redemption ancillary. This sentiment is also conveyed in our verse, in which "the LORD will reach out His hand a second time to reclaim the remnant that is left of His people," which also implies that the ultimate redemption will surpass the initial one. A well-known legal debate emerged between the Rabbis and Ben Azzai as to whether prayers in the Messianic period will even include a reference to the exodus. Even if we do continue to mention the exodus from Egypt, the experience will be dwarfed by our final redemption.

This image of a *"second time"* is incorporated into the conclusion of the *Musaf Kedusha* in which we say וְהוּא יַשְׁמִיעֵנוּ בְּרַחֲמָיו שֵׁנִית לְעֵינֵי כָּל חָי – He, in His compassion, will let us hear a second time in the presence of all that lives.

וּשְׁאַבְתֶּם־מַיִם בְּשָׂשׂוֹן מִמַּעַיְנֵי הַיְשׁוּעָה *With joy you will draw water from the wells of salvation.* The imagery of drawing water from a well of salvation is consistent with many prophecies portraying the spread of divine knowledge through the metaphor of swelling water. Perhaps the most familiar is the prophecy in which the knowledge of God disseminates across the globe "as the waters cover the sea" (ibid. 11:9). In typical water metaphors, the water spreads independently and naturally. In this image the Jewish people actively and joyously draw the water, or knowledge of God. The need to actively draw water from depths suggests access to deeper and previously inaccessible knowledge of HaKadosh Barukh Hu – perhaps even mystical knowledge.

The annual ceremony of *Siṃhat Beit HaSho'eva* was held on Sukkot, and involved celebrations culminating in pouring holy water on the altar. The phrase "*Sho'eva*" was patterned on this verse. The drawing and eventual

GOVERNMENT ——————— SHAḤARIT · YOM HAATZMA'UT · 388

The Prayer for the Welfare of the Canadian Government is on the next page.

PRAYER FOR THE WELFARE OF THE AMERICAN GOVERNMENT

The Leader says the following:

הַנּוֹתֵן תְּשׁוּעָה May He who gives salvation to kings and dominion to princes, whose kingdom is an everlasting kingdom, who delivers His servant David from the evil sword, who makes a way in the sea and a path through the mighty waters, bless and protect, guard and help, exalt, magnify and uplift the President, Vice President and all officials of this land. May the Supreme King of kings in His mercy put into their hearts and the hearts of all their counselors and officials, to deal kindly with us and all Israel. In their days and in ours, may Judah be saved and Israel dwell in safety, and may the Redeemer come to Zion. May this be His will, and let us say: Amen.

PRAYER FOR THE SAFETY OF THE AMERICAN MILITARY

The Leader says the following:

אַדִּיר בַּמָּרוֹם God on high who dwells in might, the King to whom peace belongs, look down from Your holy habitation and bless the soldiers of the American military forces who risk their lives for the sake of peace on earth. Be their shelter and stronghold, and let them not falter. Give them the strength and courage to thwart the plans of the enemy and end the rule of evil. May their enemies be scattered and their foes flee before them, and may they rejoice in Your salvation. Bring them back safely to their homes, as is written: "The LORD *Ps. 121* will guard you from all harm, He will guard your life. The LORD will guard your going and coming, now and for evermore." And may there be fulfilled for us the verse: "Nation shall not lift up sword against *Is. 2* nation, nor shall they learn war any more." Let all the inhabitants on earth know that sovereignty is Yours and Your name inspires awe over all You have created – and let us say: Amen.

---

eighteenth century. He once commented that if the nations awarded Israel to the Jewish people it would constitute *Atḥalta diGeula* – the first stage of our redemptive process.

The Prayer for the Welfare of the Canadian Government is on the next page.

תפילה לשלום המלכות

The שליח ציבור *says the following:*

הַנּוֹתֵן תְּשׁוּעָה לַמְּלָכִים וּמֶמְשָׁלָה לַנְּסִיכִים, מַלְכוּתוֹ מַלְכוּת כָּל
עוֹלָמִים, הַפּוֹצֶה אֶת דָּוִד עַבְדּוֹ מֵחֶרֶב רָעָה, הַנּוֹתֵן בַּיָּם דֶּרֶךְ
וּבְמַיִם עַזִּים נְתִיבָה, הוּא יְבָרֵךְ וְיִשְׁמֹר וְיִנְצֹר וְיַעֲזֹר וִירוֹמֵם וִיגַדֵּל
וִינַשֵּׂא לְמַעְלָה אֶת הַנָּשִׂיא וְאֶת מִשְׁנֵהוּ וְאֶת כָּל שָׂרֵי הָאָרֶץ
הַזֹּאת. מֶלֶךְ מַלְכֵי הַמְּלָכִים, בְּרַחֲמָיו יִתֵּן בְּלִבָּם וּבְלֵב כָּל יוֹעֲצֵיהֶם
וְשָׂרֵיהֶם לַעֲשׂוֹת טוֹבָה עִמָּנוּ וְעִם כָּל יִשְׂרָאֵל. בִּימֵיהֶם וּבְיָמֵינוּ
תִּוָּשַׁע יְהוּדָה, וְיִשְׂרָאֵל יִשְׁכֹּן לָבֶטַח, וּבָא לְצִיּוֹן גּוֹאֵל. וְכֵן יְהִי
רָצוֹן, וְנֹאמַר אָמֵן.

תפילה לשלום חיילי צבא ארצות הברית

The שליח ציבור *says the following:*

אַדִּיר בַּמָּרוֹם שׁוֹכֵן בִּגְבוּרָה, מֶלֶךְ שֶׁהַשָּׁלוֹם שֶׁלּוֹ, הַשְׁקִיפָה
מִמְּעוֹן קָדְשֶׁךָ, וּבָרֵךְ אֶת חַיָּלֵי צְבָא אַרְצוֹת הַבְּרִית, הַמְחָרְפִים
נַפְשָׁם בְּלֶכְתָּם לָשִׂים שָׁלוֹם בָּאָרֶץ. הֱיֵה נָא לָהֶם מַחֲסֶה וּמָעוֹז,
וְאַל תִּתֵּן לַמּוֹט רַגְלָם, חַזֵּק יְדֵיהֶם וְאַמֵּץ רוּחָם לְהָפֵר עֲצַת אוֹיֵב
וּלְהַעֲבִיר מֶמְשֶׁלֶת זָדוֹן, יָפֻצוּ אוֹיְבֵיהֶם וְיָנוּסוּ מְשַׂנְאֵיהֶם מִפְּנֵיהֶם,
וְיִשְׂמְחוּ בִישׁוּעָתֶךָ. הֲשִׁיבֵם בְּשָׁלוֹם אֶל בֵּיתָם, כַּכָּתוּב בְּדִבְרֵי
קָדְשֶׁךָ: יהוה יִשְׁמָרְךָ מִכָּל־רָע, יִשְׁמֹר אֶת־נַפְשֶׁךָ: יהוה יִשְׁמָר־ תהלים קכא
צֵאתְךָ וּבוֹאֶךָ, מֵעַתָּה וְעַד־עוֹלָם: וְקַיֵּם בָּנוּ מִקְרָא שֶׁכָּתוּב:
לֹא־יִשָּׂא גוֹי אֶל־גּוֹי חֶרֶב, וְלֹא־יִלְמְדוּ עוֹד מִלְחָמָה: וְיֵדְעוּ כָּל ישעיה ב
יוֹשְׁבֵי תֵבֵל כִּי לְךָ מְלוּכָה יָאָתָה, וְשִׁמְךָ נוֹרָא עַל כָּל מַה שֶּׁבָּרָאתָ.
וְנֹאמַר אָמֵן.

PRAYER FOR THE WELFARE OF THE CANADIAN GOVERNMENT

The Leader says the following:

הַנּוֹתֵן תְּשׁוּעָה May He who gives salvation to kings and dominion to princes, whose kingdom is an everlasting kingdom, who delivers His servant David from the evil sword, who makes a way in the sea and a path through the mighty waters, bless and protect, guard and help, exalt, magnify and uplift the Prime Minister and all the elected and appointed officials of Canada. May the Supreme King of kings in His mercy put into their hearts and the hearts of all their counselors and officials, to deal kindly with us and all Israel. In their days and in ours, may Judah be saved and Israel dwell in safety, and may the Redeemer come to Zion. May this be His will, and let us say: Amen.

PRAYER FOR THE SAFETY OF THE CANADIAN MILITARY FORCES

The Leader says the following:

אַדִּיר בַּמָּרוֹם God on high who dwells in might, the King to whom peace belongs, look down from Your holy habitation and bless the soldiers of the Canadian Forces who risk their lives for the sake of peace on earth. Be their shelter and stronghold, and let them not falter. Give them the strength and courage to thwart the plans of the enemy and end the rule of evil. May their enemies be scattered and their foes flee before them, and may they rejoice in Your salvation. Bring them back safely to their homes, as is written: "The *Ps. 121* LORD will guard you from all harm, He will guard your life. The LORD will guard your going and coming, now and for evermore." And may there be fulfilled for us the verse: "Nation shall not lift up *Is. 2* sword against nation, nor shall they learn war any more." Let all the inhabitants on earth know that sovereignty is Yours and Your name inspires awe over all You have created – and let us say: Amen.

תפילה לשלום המלכות

The שליח ציבור *says the following:*

הַנּוֹתֵן תְּשׁוּעָה לַמְּלָכִים וּמֶמְשָׁלָה לַנְּסִיכִים, מַלְכוּתוֹ מַלְכוּת כָּל
עוֹלָמִים, הַפּוֹצֶה אֶת דָּוִד עַבְדּוֹ מֵחֶרֶב רָעָה, הַנּוֹתֵן בַּיָּם דֶּרֶךְ
וּבְמַיִם עַזִּים נְתִיבָה, הוּא יְבָרֵךְ וְיִשְׁמֹר וְיִנְצֹר וְיַעֲזֹר וִירוֹמֵם וִיגַדֵּל
וִינַשֵּׂא לְמַעְלָה אֶת רֹאשׁ הַמֶּמְשָׁלָה וְאֶת כָּל שָׂרֵי הָאָרֶץ הַזֹּאת.
מֶלֶךְ מַלְכֵי הַמְּלָכִים, בְּרַחֲמָיו יִתֵּן בְּלִבָּם וּבְלֵב כָּל יוֹעֲצֵיהֶם
וְשָׂרֵיהֶם לַעֲשׂוֹת טוֹבָה עִמָּנוּ וְעִם כָּל יִשְׂרָאֵל. בִּימֵיהֶם וּבְיָמֵינוּ
תִּוָּשַׁע יְהוּדָה, וְיִשְׂרָאֵל יִשְׁכֹּן לָבֶטַח, וּבָא לְצִיּוֹן גּוֹאֵל. וְכֵן יְהִי
רָצוֹן, וְנֹאמַר אָמֵן.

תפילה לשלום חיילי צבא קנדה

The שליח ציבור *says the following:*

אַדִּיר בַּמָּרוֹם שׁוֹכֵן בִּגְבוּרָה, מֶלֶךְ שֶׁהַשָּׁלוֹם שֶׁלּוֹ, הַשְׁקִיפָה
מִמְּעוֹן קָדְשֶׁךָ, וּבָרֵךְ אֶת חַיְלֵי צְבָא קָנָדָה, הַמְּחָרְפִים נַפְשָׁם
בְּלֶכְתָּם לָשִׂים שָׁלוֹם בָּאָרֶץ. הֱיֵה נָא לָהֶם מַחֲסֶה וּמָעֹז, וְאַל תִּתֵּן
לַמּוֹט רַגְלָם, חַזֵּק יְדֵיהֶם וְאַמֵּץ רוּחָם לְהָפֵר עֲצַת אוֹיֵב וּלְהַעֲבִיר
מֶמְשֶׁלֶת זָדוֹן, יְפֻצּוּ אוֹיְבֵיהֶם וְיָנֻסוּ מְשַׂנְאֵיהֶם מִפְּנֵיהֶם, וְיִשְׂמְחוּ
בִישׁוּעָתֶךָ. הֲשִׁיבֵם בְּשָׁלוֹם אֶל בֵּיתָם, כַּכָּתוּב בְּדִבְרֵי קָדְשֶׁךָ:

תהלים קכא

יהוה יִשְׁמָרְךָ מִכָּל־רָע, יִשְׁמֹר אֶת־נַפְשֶׁךָ: יהוה יִשְׁמָר־צֵאתְךָ

ישעיה ב

וּבוֹאֶךָ, מֵעַתָּה וְעַד־עוֹלָם: וְקַיֵּם בָּנוּ מִקְרָא שֶׁכָּתוּב: לֹא־יִשָּׂא גוֹי
אֶל־גּוֹי חֶרֶב, וְלֹא־יִלְמְדוּ עוֹד מִלְחָמָה: וְיֵדְעוּ כָּל יוֹשְׁבֵי תֵבֵל כִּי
לְךָ מְלוּכָה יָאֵתָה, וְשִׁמְךָ נוֹרָא עַל כָּל מַה שֶׁבָּרֵאתָ. וְנֹאמַר אָמֵן.

PRAYER FOR THE STATE OF ISRAEL

The Leader says the following prayer:

אָבִינוּ שֶׁבַּשָּׁמַיִם Heavenly Father, Israel's Rock and Redeemer,
bless the State of Israel, the first flowering of our redemption.
Shield it under the wings of Your loving-kindness
and spread over it the Tabernacle of Your peace.
Send Your light and truth to its leaders, ministers and counselors,
and direct them with good counsel before You.

---

custom, in the Rabbis' Kaddish as well): "קדם אבוהון די בשמיא, Before our
Father in heaven."

It also features frequently in the Oral Law. In *Sota* (49a), it is stated, "Upon
whom can we rely? – Upon our Father in heaven." In *Berakhot* (32b) it says,
"Rabbi Elazar said: From the day that the Temple was destroyed, an iron wall
came between Israel and their Father in Heaven." This phrase conveys a unique
tension: "Our Father" is an expression of closeness; "in heaven" is an expression
of distance. Here, closeness and distance come together.   YR

הָגֵן עָלֶיהָ בְּאֶבְרַת חַסְדֶּךָ וּפְרֹשׂ עָלֶיהָ סֻכַּת שְׁלוֹמֶךָ *Shield it under the wings of Your*
loving-kindness and spread over it the Tabernacle of Your peace. The request
for protection is comprised of two parts. The expression "the wings of Your
loving-kindness" is original, appearing here for the first time in the prayer
service. God watches over His people today just as He watched over them
in the harsh desert of Sinai: "Like an eagle watches its nest and hovers over
its young" (*Devarim* 32:11) – at first it circles overhead protectively, and then
"spreads its wings to catch them" – if the eagle senses that its young are in
danger, it will "lift them onto its wings," protect them from any threat. The
term "loving-kindness" is used to suggest how God protects us out of divine
grace, a kindness bestowed even if those praying are not worthy of it.

The second part of this request, "and spread over it the Tabernacle of Your
peace" also appears in the second blessing after the Shema, "השכיבנו, Help
us lie down," a blessing for protection and deliverance. The *Etz Yosef* (a commentary cited in the prayer book *Otzar HaTefillot*) comments on this phrase,
explaining that the blessing for protection is not a prayer for a stable condition, but rather for an underlying foundation of redemption.   YR

וּשְׁלַח אוֹרְךָ וַאֲמִתְּךָ לְרָאשֶׁיהָ, שָׂרֶיהָ וְיוֹעֲצֶיהָ *Send Your light and truth to its leaders,*
ministers and counselors. After peace, principled leadership is the next thing

תפילה לשלום מדינת ישראל

The שליח ציבור *says the following prayer:*

אָבִינוּ שֶׁבַּשָּׁמַיִם, צוּר יִשְׂרָאֵל וְגוֹאֲלוֹ
בָּרֵךְ אֶת מְדִינַת יִשְׂרָאֵל, רֵאשִׁית צְמִיחַת גְּאֻלָּתֵנוּ.
הָגֵן עָלֶיהָ בְּאֶבְרַת חַסְדֶּךָ וּפְרֹשׂ עָלֶיהָ סֻכַּת שְׁלוֹמֶךָ
וּשְׁלַח אוֹרְךָ וַאֲמִתְּךָ לְרָאשֶׁיהָ, שָׂרֶיהָ וְיוֹעֲצֶיהָ
וְתַקְּנֵם בְּעֵצָה טוֹבָה מִלְּפָנֶיךָ.

THE PRAYER FOR THE STATE OF ISRAEL

The Jewish prayer book is a receptacle for the collective memory of the
Jewish people – all it has endured in the Land of Israel and outside of it;
the best of times, the worst of times; its finest hours, its lowest hours. The
commemoration of historical events is not only kept for its own sake, so it
will not fade from the national memory, but for the sake of education, to
provide examples of God's might and love for Israel through the acts He
has performed for them in the past, and what He will do in the future. The
mention of these great events justifies the praise, thanksgiving and requests
that comprise our prayers.

Our hopes and ideals for the identity of a Jewish State are summarized in
the requests of this prayer:

1. Peace.
2. Wise and principled leadership.
3. A strong and safeguarded defense force.
4. The ingathering of exiles.
5. A faithfulness and closeness to God and His commandments.
6. The coming of the Messiah and the final redemption.
7. The acceptance of God's revelation throughout the world.

The first section of the prayer, from the opening "Heavenly Father" until "everlasting joy to its inhabitants," is written in a poetic, contemporary style, in
stark contrast to the largely biblical and liturgical prose of the remainder.   YR

אָבִינוּ שֶׁבַּשָּׁמַיִם *Heavenly Father.* In the liturgy, this expression appears in two
prayers, besides the Prayer for the State. The Aramaic equivalent occurs frequently in the prayer service, appearing in Full Kaddish (and in Ashkenazic

Strengthen the hands of the defenders of our Holy Land;
grant them deliverance, our God,
and crown them with the crown of victory.
Grant peace in the land
and everlasting joy to its inhabitants.

As for our brothers, the whole house of Israel,
remember them in all the lands of our (*In Israel say:* their) dispersion,
and swiftly lead us (*In Israel say:* them) upright to Zion Your city,
and Jerusalem Your dwelling place,
as is written in the Torah of Moses Your servant:
"Even if you are scattered to the furthermost lands under the heavens,   *Deut. 30*
from there the LORD your God will gather you and take you back.

---

were multiple "classic candidates" to lead our people back from Bavel, yet
HaKadosh Barukh Hu selected a proverbial "vermin" to conduct this diminished redemption.

Despite the disappointment of this "foul" outstretched hand, the woman
ultimately awakens and follows her solicitor. Though the Jewish people
may have rightfully scorned this inferior redemptive experience, those that
did awaken responded with enthusiasm, fervor, and commitment. As the
Midrash comments, they announced "even though [you have sent inferior
leadership], we are ecstatic." The opportunity to return home was exhilarat-
ing, regardless of the caliber of leadership.

Our return to the Modern State was steered by leaders of vision, with a
profound sense of Jewish history and Jewish national identity. Many, however,
had abandoned the classic religious values and halakhic behavior which sits at
the heart of our covenant with HaKadosh Barukh Hu and our warrant to our
land. For many the flawed leadership invalidates the Zionist enterprise, and
debunks the belief that our return is divinely ordained. This scene reminds us
that sometimes God dispatches classic leadership to steward our redemption.
More often He chooses unlikely heroes to lead us back to our homeland. Just
because the outstretched hand isn't as fragrant as we would imagine or wish,
this does not invalidate its redemptive function.

אִם־יִהְיֶה נִדַּחֲךָ ... וְהֵיטִבְךָ וְהִרְבְּךָ מֵאֲבֹתֶיךָ *Even if you are scattered... and He will
make you more prosperous and numerous than your ancestors.* These verses are
taken from Deuteronomy 30, in which Moses describes the process of the

חַזֵּק אֶת יְדֵי מְגִנֵּי אֶרֶץ קָדְשֵׁנוּ
וְהַנְחִילֵם אֱלֹהֵינוּ יְשׁוּעָה וַעֲטֶרֶת נִצָּחוֹן תְּעַטְּרֵם
וְנָתַתָּ שָׁלוֹם בָּאָרֶץ וְשִׂמְחַת עוֹלָם לְיוֹשְׁבֶיהָ.

וְאֶת אַחֵינוּ כָּל בֵּית יִשְׂרָאֵל
פְּקָד נָא בְּכָל אַרְצוֹת פְּזוּרֵינוּ (בארץ ישראל: פְּזוּרֵיהֶם)
וְתוֹלִיכֵנוּ (בארץ ישראל: וְתוֹלִיכֵם) מְהֵרָה קוֹמְמִיּוּת לְצִיּוֹן עִירֶךָ
וְלִירוּשָׁלַיִם מִשְׁכַּן שְׁמֶךָ
כַּכָּתוּב בְּתוֹרַת מֹשֶׁה עַבְדֶּךָ:

דברים ל

אִם־יִהְיֶה נִדַּחֲךָ בִּקְצֵה הַשָּׁמָיִם
מִשָּׁם יְקַבֶּצְךָ יהוה אֱלֹהֶיךָ וּמִשָּׁם יִקָּחֶךָ:

---

we pray for, in recognition that without God's guidance, without His divine truth in the hearts of our leaders, nothing else in our list of requests can be achieved.

YR

THE DOOR OF HISTORY

The fifth chapter of *Shir HaShirim* portrays an earnest "knock on the door," soliciting a slumbering woman. This metaphor represents HaKadosh Barukh Hu imploring the Jewish people to return to their homeland. Most interpret this scene as a metaphor for the return of Ezra and the Jews from the Babylonian Exile. The woman – or in this case the Jewish people – is sluggish in answering the request. Unfortunately only 42,000 Jews returned to Israel to rebuild the *Mikdash*.

In the scene at the door, the "solicitor" becomes desperate and thrusts his hand through a gap in the door, hoping to actually establish contact with the lethargic resident of the home. Belatedly, the lazy woman answers, but her response is too late and the suitor has already left.

The image of a "hand thrust through a door" is a tantalizing illustration. Ḥazal remark (*Shir HaShirim Raba* chapter 5) that typically an alcove in a door houses vermin and rodents; a hand thrust through that alcove would consequently become putrid and reeking. As our return to Israel was brokered by a *Koresh* (a heathen king), it was less attractive than a conventional redemption spearheaded by righteous or even Jewish agents. There

The LORD your God will bring you
to the land your ancestors possessed and you will possess it;
and He will make you more prosperous
and numerous than your ancestors.
Then the LORD your God will open up your heart
and the heart of your descendants,
to love the LORD your God
with all your heart and with all your soul,
that you may live."

Unite our hearts to love and revere Your name
and observe all the words of Your Torah,
and swiftly send us Your righteous anointed one
of the house of David,
to redeem those who long for Your salvation.

Appear in Your glorious majesty over all the dwellers on earth,
and let all who breathe declare:
The LORD God of Israel is King and His kingship
has dominion over all. Amen, Selah.

THE BEGINNING OF REDEMPTION

Let us thank God that in His great mercy and kindness, we have merited
to see the first buds of the redemption in the form of the establishment
of the State of Israel.

God has shown us that we have a reached a time of favor, a time to come
to God with might, and help to build and establish our land and state with
holy purity. Israel's Torah, its laws and statutes, which were given to us at
Mount Sinai, are what have stood before us throughout our exile, and they
will stand before us to maintain and sustain the State of Israel. It is our duty
to observe them all the more in our Holy Land, so that we will merit the
dwelling of the Divine Presence in the State of Israel and the coming of
the righteous Messiah speedily in our time.

(From a proclamation, signed by two hundred rabbis, of the Mizraḥi
movement, HaPoel HaMizraḥi, and Agudat Yisrael, in the run-up to the
elections of the first Knesset, 1949, according to M.M. Kasher's *HaTekufa
HaGedola*, pp. 374–76.)

וֶהֱבִיאֲךָ יהוה אֱלֹהֶיךָ אֶל־הָאָרֶץ אֲשֶׁר־יָרְשׁוּ אֲבֹתֶיךָ וִירִשְׁתָּהּ
וְהֵיטִבְךָ וְהִרְבְּךָ מֵאֲבֹתֶיךָ:
וּמָל יהוה אֱלֹהֶיךָ אֶת־לְבָבְךָ וְאֶת־לְבַב זַרְעֶךָ
לְאַהֲבָה אֶת־יהוה אֱלֹהֶיךָ בְּכָל־לְבָבְךָ וּבְכָל־נַפְשְׁךָ
לְמַעַן חַיֶּיךָ:

וְיַחֵד לְבָבֵנוּ לְאַהֲבָה וּלְיִרְאָה אֶת שְׁמֶךָ
וְלִשְׁמֹר אֶת כָּל דִּבְרֵי תּוֹרָתֶךָ
וּשְׁלַח לָנוּ מְהֵרָה בֶּן דָּוִד מְשִׁיחַ צִדְקֶךָ
לִפְדּוֹת מְחַכֵּי קֵץ יְשׁוּעָתֶךָ.

וְהוֹפַע בַּהֲדַר גְּאוֹן עֻזֶּךָ עַל כָּל יוֹשְׁבֵי תֵבֵל אַרְצֶךָ
וְיֹאמַר כֹּל אֲשֶׁר נְשָׁמָה בְאַפּוֹ
יהוה אֱלֹהֵי יִשְׂרָאֵל מֶלֶךְ וּמַלְכוּתוֹ בַּכֹּל מָשָׁלָה
אָמֵן סֶלָה.

---

people's salvation when they come to be redeemed from exile. The first stage will be the ingathering of exiles; the second stage, their settling of the Land of Israel. The integration of these verses into the Prayer for the State is indicative of the fundamental message of this prayer. This is not another prayer for the welfare of the government, like those we recite for the countries of our dispersion. Rather, the ancient verses of God's promise of redemption are here woven into the very fabric of the prayer, a true redemption which can only be fulfilled in the Land of Israel.

YR

לִפְדּוֹת מְחַכֵּי קֵץ יְשׁוּעָתֶךָ *To redeem those who long for Your salvation.* The Gemara (*Shabbat* 31a) lists the questions a person will face during Final Judgment. The fourth question posed will be צפית לישועה – "did you await Redemption?" *Nusaḥ Sefarad* inserts this phraseology into the *berakha* of "*Et Tzemaḥ*" which describes awaiting redemption – "כִּי לִישׁוּעָתְךָ קִוִּינוּ כָּל הַיּוֹם וּמְצַפִּים לִישׁוּעָה".

The word "*meḥakei*" implies passive waiting or waiting with patience. The term "*tzipita*" implies *envisioning* Redemption.

PRAYER FOR ISRAEL'S DEFENSE FORCES

The Leader says the following prayer:

מִי שֶׁבֵּרַךְ May He who blessed our ancestors, Abraham, Isaac and Jacob, bless the members of Israel's Defense Forces and its security services who stand guard over our land and the cities of our God from the Lebanese border to the Egyptian desert, from the Mediterranean sea to the approach of the Aravah, and wherever else they are, on land, in air and at sea. May the LORD make the enemies who rise against us be struck down before them. May the Holy One, blessed be He, protect and deliver them from all trouble and distress, affliction and illness, and send blessing and success to all the work of their hands. May He subdue our enemies under them and crown them with deliverance and victory. And may there be fulfilled in them the verse, "It is the LORD your God who goes with you to fight for you against your enemies, to deliver you." And let us say: Amen. *Deut. 20*

---

fulfillment of a mitzva which is equated to the entire Torah. Even without complete performance of mitzvot, courageous performance of the great mitzva of rebuilding our land renders them partners in the divine redemptive process.

THE FOUR HISTORICAL OATHS TO GOD
In four places in *Shir HaShirim* the daughters of Jerusalem are sworn not to awaken or instigate the "love" until it is requested. The content of these oaths is unclear.

The Gemara in *Ketubot* records two oaths posed to the Jewish people, and one to the international community. The Jews were sworn not to forcibly return to Israel, nor to rebel against the Gentile nations. The Gentiles for their part were sworn not to excessively persecute the Jewish people. Taken literally, the two oaths directed to the Jewish people ban us from returning to Israel militarily. This reading forms a cornerstone of many anti-Zionist positions, which claim that our initiative is unholy since it violates the terms of this divine oath.

Responding to these claims, many different interpretations are offered. Some claim that since the Gentiles violated their end of the bargain by tormenting the Jews, we are relieved of our obligations. Still others believe that

מי שברך לחיילי צה״ל

The שליח ציבור *says the following prayer:*

מִי שֶׁבֵּרַךְ אֲבוֹתֵינוּ אַבְרָהָם יִצְחָק וְיַעֲקֹב הוּא יְבָרֵךְ אֶת חַיָּלֵי
צְבָא הַהֲגָנָה לְיִשְׂרָאֵל וְאַנְשֵׁי כֹחוֹת הַבִּטָּחוֹן, הָעוֹמְדִים עַל מִשְׁמַר
אַרְצֵנוּ וְעָרֵי אֱלֹהֵינוּ, מִגְּבוּל הַלְּבָנוֹן וְעַד מִדְבַּר מִצְרַיִם וּמִן הַיָּם
הַגָּדוֹל עַד לְבוֹא הָעֲרָבָה וּבְכָל מָקוֹם שֶׁהֵם, בַּיַּבָּשָׁה, בָּאֲוִיר וּבַיָּם.
יִתֵּן יהוה אֶת אוֹיְבֵינוּ הַקָּמִים עָלֵינוּ נִגָּפִים לִפְנֵיהֶם. הַקָּדוֹשׁ בָּרוּךְ
הוּא יִשְׁמֹר וְיַצִּיל אֶת חַיָּלֵינוּ מִכָּל צָרָה וְצוּקָה וּמִכָּל נֶגַע וּמַחֲלָה,
וְיִשְׁלַח בְּרָכָה וְהַצְלָחָה בְּכָל מַעֲשֵׂי יְדֵיהֶם. יַדְבֵּר שׂוֹנְאֵינוּ תַּחְתֵּיהֶם
וִיעַטְּרֵם בְּכֶתֶר יְשׁוּעָה וּבַעֲטֶרֶת נִצָּחוֹן. וִיקֻיַּם בָּהֶם הַכָּתוּב: כִּי
יהוה אֱלֹהֵיכֶם הַהֹלֵךְ עִמָּכֶם לְהִלָּחֵם לָכֶם עִם־אֹיְבֵיכֶם לְהוֹשִׁיעַ
אֶתְכֶם: וְנֹאמַר אָמֵן.

דברים כ

FULFILLING ONLY *ONE* MITZVA – LOVE FOR THE LAND OF ISRAEL

One of the great mysteries of our redemption is the secular nature of our State.
The founders of Zionism were largely those who had abandoned the classic
rituals and halakhot which are immutable to history. For so many this reality
indicates that our return isn't redemptive or divine.

An interesting comment of the Rambam reminds us of the value of even
one mitzva performed with dedication and passion. A well-known Gemara
(*Makkot* 24.) cites Rabbi Neḥunya ben HaKanna who claims that HaKadosh
Barukh Hu boosted the number of mitzvot He delivered to us to augment
our merits. The literal meaning suggests that a greater number of mitzvot
invites a more comprehensive religious experience, and by extension, superior rewards. Commenting on this statement the Rambam asserts that
the abundance of mitzvot offers opportunities for religious success even
for those who will only perform *selected* mitzvot. Inevitably, given the sheer
number of mitzva opportunities , even religious underperformers will excel
at *one* mitzva. Although ideally religious experience should be expressed
through comprehensive adherence, even performance of isolated mitzvot
is considerable.

The dedication and sacrifice which even secular Zionists have displayed,
and continue to display, on behalf of the struggle to return to Israel is a heroic

PRAYER FOR THOSE BEING HELD IN CAPTIVITY

If Israeli soldiers or civilians are being held in captivity, the Leader says the following:

מִי שֶׁבֵּרַךְ May He who blessed our ancestors, Abraham, Isaac and Jacob, Joseph, Moses and Aaron, David and Solomon, bless, protect and guard the members of Israel's Defense Forces missing in action or held captive, and other captives among our brethren, the whole house of Israel, who are in distress or captivity, as we, the members of this holy congregation, pray on their behalf. May the Holy One, blessed be He, have compassion on them and bring them out from darkness and the shadow of death; may He break their bonds, deliver them from their distress, and bring them swiftly back to their families' embrace. Give thanks to the Ps. 107 LORD for His loving-kindness and for the wonders He does for the children of men; and may there be fulfilled in them the verse: "Those redeemed by the LORD will return; they will enter Zion with singing, Is. 35 and everlasting joy will crown their heads. Gladness and joy will overtake them, and sorrow and sighing will flee away." And let us say: Amen.

PRAYER FOR FALLEN ISRAELI SOLDIERS

אֵל מָלֵא רַחֲמִים God, full of mercy, who dwells on high, grant fitting rest on the wings of the Divine Presence, in the heights of the holy, the pure and the brave, who shine like the radiance of heaven, to the souls of the holy ones who fought in any of Israel's battles, in clandestine operations and in Israel's Defense Forces, who fell in battle and sacrificed their lives for the consecration of God's name, for the people and the land, and for this we pray for the ascent of their souls. Therefore, Master of compassion, shelter them in the shadow of Your wings forever, and bind their souls in the bond of everlasting life. The LORD is their heritage; may the Garden of Eden be their resting place,

---

host countries and in turn be subjected to severe violence. God established a balanced new reality, that Jews would be relatively passive in pursuing redemption, while their host Gentile countries would, by and large, tolerate their presence. This indeed has been in force for much of history. Now that we believe the end of history has begun, we have every legal right to prompt the conclusion of this process and our return to Israel.

מי שברך לשבויים

If Israeli soldiers or civilians are being held in captivity, the שליח ציבור says the following:

מִי שֶׁבֵּרַךְ אֲבוֹתֵינוּ אַבְרָהָם יִצְחָק וְיַעֲקֹב, יוֹסֵף מֹשֶׁה וְאַהֲרֹן, דָּוִד
וּשְׁלֹמֹה, הוּא יְבָרֵךְ וְיִשְׁמֹר וְיִנְצֹר אֶת נְעֲדְרֵי צְבָא הַהֲגָנָה לְיִשְׂרָאֵל
וּשְׁבוּיָו, וְאֶת כָּל אַחֵינוּ הַנְּתוּנִים בְּצָרָה וּבְשִׁבְיָה, בַּעֲבוּר שֶׁכָּל
הַקָּהָל הַקָּדוֹשׁ הַזֶּה מִתְפַּלֵּל בַּעֲבוּרָם. הַקָּדוֹשׁ בָּרוּךְ הוּא יְמַלֵּא
רַחֲמִים עֲלֵיהֶם, וְיוֹצִיאֵם מֵחֹשֶׁךְ וְצַלְמָוֶת, וּמוֹסְרוֹתֵיהֶם יְנַתֵּק,
וּמִמְּצוּקוֹתֵיהֶם יוֹשִׁיעֵם, וִישִׁיבֵם מְהֵרָה לְחֵיק מִשְׁפְּחוֹתֵיהֶם. יוֹדוּ
לַיהוה חַסְדּוֹ וְנִפְלְאוֹתָיו לִבְנֵי אָדָם: וִיקַיֵּם בָּהֶם מִקְרָא שֶׁכָּתוּב:
וּפְדוּיֵי יהוה יְשֻׁבוּן, וּבָאוּ צִיּוֹן בְּרִנָּה, וְשִׂמְחַת עוֹלָם עַל־רֹאשָׁם,
שָׂשׂוֹן וְשִׂמְחָה יַשִּׂיגוּ, וְנָסוּ יָגוֹן וַאֲנָחָה: וְנֹאמַר אָמֵן.

תהלים קז
ישעיה לה

תפילת יזכור לחללי צה״ל

אֵל מָלֵא רַחֲמִים, שׁוֹכֵן בַּמְּרוֹמִים, הַמְצֵא מְנוּחָה נְכוֹנָה עַל כַּנְפֵי
הַשְּׁכִינָה, בְּמַעֲלוֹת קְדוֹשִׁים טְהוֹרִים וְגִבּוֹרִים, כְּזֹהַר הָרָקִיעַ
מַזְהִירִים, לְנִשְׁמוֹת הַקְּדוֹשִׁים שֶׁנִּלְחֲמוּ בְּכָל מַעַרְכוֹת יִשְׂרָאֵל,
בַּמַּחְתֶּרֶת וּבִצְבָא הַהֲגָנָה לְיִשְׂרָאֵל, וְשֶׁנָּפְלוּ בְּמִלְחַמְתָּם וּמָסְרוּ
נַפְשָׁם עַל קְדֻשַּׁת הַשֵּׁם, הָעָם וְהָאָרֶץ, בַּעֲבוּר שֶׁאָנוּ מִתְפַּלְּלִים
לְעִלּוּי נִשְׁמוֹתֵיהֶם. לָכֵן, בַּעַל הָרַחֲמִים יַסְתִּירֵם בְּסֵתֶר כְּנָפָיו
לְעוֹלָמִים, וְיִצְרֹר בִּצְרוֹר הַחַיִּים אֶת נִשְׁמוֹתֵיהֶם, יהוה הוּא נַחֲלָתָם,

we didn't violate any oath, since we returned to Israel through international authorization. Having settled the land, we were aggressively attacked by our Arab neighbors. Establishing an army was a defense mechanism, rather than a tool to enable our national reclamation of the Land of Israel. Finally, some claim that the oaths do not represent a normative system of mandates. When He exiled us, HaKadosh Barukh Hu established basic paradigms for history. Without these "realities," history would become too violent. Jews, perennially viewed as strangers and driven by redemptive fervor, would destabilize their

may they rest in peace, may their merit stand for all Israel, and may they receive their reward at the End of Days, and let us say: Amen.

IN MEMORY OF VICTIMS OF THE HOLOCAUST

אֵל מָלֵא רַחֲמִים God, full of mercy, Justice of widows and Father of orphans, please do not be silent and hold Your peace for the blood of Israel that was shed like water. Grant fitting rest on the wings of the Divine Presence, in the heights of the holy and the pure who shine and radiate light like the radiance of heaven, to the souls of the millions of Jews, men, women and children, who were murdered, slaughtered, burned, strangled, and buried alive, in the lands touched by the German enemy and its followers. They were all holy and pure; among them were great scholars and righteous individuals, cedars of Lebanon and noble masters of Torah, may the Garden of Eden be their resting place. Therefore, Master of compassion, shelter them in the shadow of Your wings forever, and bind their souls in the bond of everlasting life. The LORD is their heritage; may they rest in peace, and let us say: Amen.

RETURNING THE TORAH TO THE ARK

The Ark is opened. The Leader takes the Torah scroll and says:

יְהַלְלוּ Let them praise the name of the LORD,
    for His name alone is sublime.

Ps. 148

The congregation responds:

הוֹדוֹ His majesty is above earth and heaven.
    He has raised the horn of His people,
    for the glory of all His devoted ones,
    the children of Israel, the people close to Him.
    Halleluya!

---

of these systems "recites" praise to Him. The morning stars (*kokhvei or*) either sing actual (but inaudible) praise, or reflect His splendor in their planetary motion. Fire, snow, hail, and strong winds all follow the divinely installed

בְּגַן עֵדֶן תְּהֵא מְנוּחָתָם, וְיָנוּחוּ בְשָׁלוֹם עַל מִשְׁכְּבוֹתֵיהֶם וְתַעֲמֹד
לְכָל יִשְׂרָאֵל זְכוּתָם, וְיַעַמְדוּ לְגוֹרָלָם לְקֵץ הַיָּמִין, וְנֹאמַר אָמֵן.

אזכרה לקדושי השואה

אֵל מָלֵא רַחֲמִים, דִּין אַלְמָנוֹת וַאֲבִי יְתוֹמִים, אַל נָא תֶחֱשֶׁה
וְתִתְאַפַּק לְדַם יִשְׂרָאֵל שֶׁנִּשְׁפַּךְ כַּמָּיִם. הַמְצֵא מְנוּחָה נְכוֹנָה עַל
כַּנְפֵי הַשְּׁכִינָה, בְּמַעֲלוֹת קְדוֹשִׁים וּטְהוֹרִים, כְּזֹהַר הָרָקִיעַ מְאִירִים
וּמַזְהִירִים, לְנִשְׁמוֹתֵיהֶם שֶׁל רִבְבוֹת אַלְפֵי יִשְׂרָאֵל, אֲנָשִׁים וְנָשִׁים,
יְלָדִים וִילָדוֹת, שֶׁנֶּהֶרְגוּ וְנִשְׁחֲטוּ וְנִשְׂרְפוּ וְנֶחְנְקוּ וְנִקְבְּרוּ חַיִּים,
בָּאֲרָצוֹת אֲשֶׁר נָגְעָה בָּהֶן יַד הַצּוֹרֵר הַגֶּרְמָנִי וְגְרוּרָיו. כֻּלָּם קְדוֹשִׁים
וּטְהוֹרִים, וּבָהֶם גְּאוֹנִים וְצַדִּיקִים, אַרְזֵי הַלְּבָנוֹן אַדִּירֵי הַתּוֹרָה.
בְּגַן עֵדֶן תְּהֵא מְנוּחָתָם. לָכֵן, בַּעַל הָרַחֲמִים יַסְתִּירֵם בְּסֵתֶר כְּנָפָיו
לְעוֹלָמִים, וְיִצְרֹר בִּצְרוֹר הַחַיִּים אֶת נִשְׁמָתָם, יהוה הוּא נַחֲלָתָם,
וְיָנוּחוּ בְשָׁלוֹם עַל מִשְׁכָּבָם, וְנֹאמַר אָמֵן.

הכנסת ספר תורה

The ארון קודש *is opened. The* שליח ציבור *takes the* ספר תורה *and says:*

תהלים קמח

יְהַלְלוּ אֶת־שֵׁם יהוה, כִּי נִשְׂגָּב־שְׁמוֹ, לְבַדּוֹ

The קהל *responds:*

הוֹדוֹ עַל־אֶרֶץ וְשָׁמָיִם:
וַיָּרֶם קֶרֶן לְעַמּוֹ, תְּהִלָּה לְכָל־חֲסִידָיו
לִבְנֵי יִשְׂרָאֵל עַם קְרֹבוֹ, הַלְלוּיָהּ:

הוֹדוֹ עַל־אֶרֶץ וְשָׁמָיִם *His majesty is above earth and heaven.* The whole of chapter 148 of *Tehillim* acknowledges the majesty of HaKadosh Barukh Hu as discerned in the cosmos, nature, and the general human race. Each sub-element

As the Torah scroll is returned to the Ark, say:

לְדָוִד מִזְמוֹר A psalm of David. The earth is the Lᴏʀᴅ's and all it contains, *Ps. 24*
the world and all who live in it. For He founded it on the seas and
established it on the streams. Who may climb the mountain of the
Lᴏʀᴅ? Who may stand in His holy place? He who has clean hands and
a pure heart, who has not taken My name in vain, or sworn deceitfully.
He shall receive blessing from the Lᴏʀᴅ, and just reward from God,
his salvation. This is a generation of those who seek Him, the descendants of Jacob who seek Your presence, Selah! Lift up your heads, O
gates; be uplifted, eternal doors, so that the King of glory may enter.
Who is the King of glory? It is the Lᴏʀᴅ, strong and mighty, the Lᴏʀᴅ
mighty in battle. Lift up your heads, O gates; lift them up, eternal doors,
so that the King of glory may enter. Who is He, the King of glory? The
Lᴏʀᴅ of hosts, He is the King of glory, Selah!

As the Torah scroll is placed into the Ark, say:

וּבְנֻחֹה יֹאמַר When the Ark came to rest, Moses would say:
"Return, O Lᴏʀᴅ, to the myriad thousands of Israel." *Num. 10*
Advance, Lᴏʀᴅ, to Your resting place, You and Your mighty Ark. *Ps. 132*
Your priests are clothed in righteousness,
and Your devoted ones sing in joy.
For the sake of Your servant David,
do not reject Your anointed one.
For I give you good instruction; do not forsake My Torah. *Prov. 4*
It is a tree of life to those who grasp it, *Prov. 3*
and those who uphold it are happy.
Its ways are ways of pleasantness, and all its paths are peace.
‣ Turn us back, O Lᴏʀᴅ, to You, and we will return. *Lam. 5*
Renew our days as of old.

The Ark is closed.

---

a common "shifting" between the universal presence of God and His particular love for the Jewish people. The contrast between the universal and
cosmological sweep of HaKadosh Barukh Hu and His parochial interest
and concern for His nation amplifies the Divine love for the Jewish people.

As the ספר תורה is returned to the ארון קודש, say:

תהלים כד

לְדָוִד מִזְמוֹר, לַיהוה הָאָרֶץ וּמְלוֹאָהּ, תֵּבֵל וְיֹשְׁבֵי בָהּ: כִּי־הוּא עַל־יַמִּים יְסָדָהּ, וְעַל־נְהָרוֹת יְכוֹנְנֶהָ: מִי־יַעֲלֶה בְהַר־יהוה, וּמִי־יָקוּם בִּמְקוֹם קָדְשׁוֹ: נְקִי כַפַּיִם וּבַר־לֵבָב, אֲשֶׁר לֹא־נָשָׂא לַשָּׁוְא נַפְשִׁי וְלֹא נִשְׁבַּע לְמִרְמָה: יִשָּׂא בְרָכָה מֵאֵת יהוה, וּצְדָקָה מֵאֱלֹהֵי יִשְׁעוֹ: זֶה דּוֹר דֹּרְשָׁו, מְבַקְשֵׁי פָנֶיךָ, יַעֲקֹב, סֶלָה: שְׂאוּ שְׁעָרִים רָאשֵׁיכֶם, וְהִנָּשְׂאוּ פִּתְחֵי עוֹלָם, וְיָבוֹא מֶלֶךְ הַכָּבוֹד: מִי זֶה מֶלֶךְ הַכָּבוֹד, יהוה עִזּוּז וְגִבּוֹר, יהוה גִּבּוֹר מִלְחָמָה: שְׂאוּ שְׁעָרִים רָאשֵׁיכֶם, וּשְׂאוּ פִּתְחֵי עוֹלָם, וְיָבֹא מֶלֶךְ הַכָּבוֹד: מִי הוּא זֶה מֶלֶךְ הַכָּבוֹד, יהוה צְבָאוֹת הוּא מֶלֶךְ הַכָּבוֹד, סֶלָה:

As the ספר תורה is placed into the ארון קודש, say:

במדבר

וּבְנֻחֹה יֹאמַר, שׁוּבָה יהוה רִבְבוֹת אַלְפֵי יִשְׂרָאֵל:

תהלים קלב

קוּמָה יהוה לִמְנוּחָתֶךָ, אַתָּה וַאֲרוֹן עֻזֶּךָ: כֹּהֲנֶיךָ יִלְבְּשׁוּ־צֶדֶק, וַחֲסִידֶיךָ יְרַנֵּנוּ: בַּעֲבוּר דָּוִד עַבְדֶּךָ אַל־תָּשֵׁב פְּנֵי מְשִׁיחֶךָ:

משלי ד

כִּי לֶקַח טוֹב נָתַתִּי לָכֶם, תּוֹרָתִי אַל־תַּעֲזֹבוּ:

משלי ג

עֵץ־חַיִּים הִיא לַמַּחֲזִיקִים בָּהּ, וְתֹמְכֶיהָ מְאֻשָּׁר: דְּרָכֶיהָ דַרְכֵי־נֹעַם וְכָל־נְתִיבוֹתֶיהָ שָׁלוֹם:

איכה ה

‹ הֲשִׁיבֵנוּ יהוה אֵלֶיךָ וְנָשׁוּבָה, חַדֵּשׁ יָמֵינוּ כְּקֶדֶם:

The ארון קודש is closed.

rules of nature, and reflect His will. Kings and nations, young and old, all acknowledge His authority.

The chapter ends by recognizing that even though His glory suffuses heaven and earth, He chose to place Israel, *His nation,* as primary. This is

Some have the custom to touch the hand-tefillin at °, and the head-tefillin at °°.

אַשְׁרֵי Happy are those who dwell in Your House; they shall continue to praise You, Selah!

Ps. 84

Happy are the people for whom this is so; happy are the people whose God is the Lord.

Ps. 144

A song of praise by David.

Ps. 145

I will exalt You, my God, the King, and bless Your name for ever and all time. Every day I will bless You, and praise Your name for ever and all time. Great is the Lord and greatly to be praised; His greatness is unfathomable. One generation will praise Your works to the next, and tell of Your mighty deeds. On the glorious splendor of Your majesty I will meditate, and on the acts of Your wonders. They shall talk of the power of Your awesome deeds, and I will tell of Your greatness. They shall recite the record of Your great goodness, and sing with joy of Your righteousness. The Lord is gracious and compassionate, slow to anger and great in loving-kindness. The Lord is good to all, and His compassion extends to all His works. All Your works shall thank You, Lord, and Your devoted ones shall bless You. They shall talk of the glory of Your kingship, and speak of Your might. To make known to mankind His mighty deeds and the glorious majesty of His kingship. Your kingdom is an everlasting kingdom, and Your reign is for all generations. The Lord supports all who fall, and raises all who are bowed down. All raise their eyes to You in hope, and You give them their food in due season. °You open Your hand, °°and satisfy every living thing with favor. The Lord is righteous in all His ways, and kind in all He does. The Lord is close to all who call on Him, to all who call on Him in truth. He fulfills the will of those who revere Him; He hears their cry and saves them. The Lord guards all who love Him, but all the wicked He will destroy.
‣ My mouth shall speak the praise of the Lord, and all creatures shall bless His holy name for ever and all time.

We will bless the Lord now and for ever. Halleluya!

Ps. 115

Some have the custom to touch the תפילין של ראש at °°, and the תפילין של יד at °.

תהלים פד

אַשְׁרֵי יוֹשְׁבֵי בֵיתֶךָ, עוֹד יְהַלְלוּךָ סֶּלָה:

תהלים קמד

אַשְׁרֵי הָעָם שֶׁכָּכָה לּוֹ, אַשְׁרֵי הָעָם שֶׁיהוה אֱלֹהָיו:

תהלים קמה

תְּהִלָּה לְדָוִד

אֲרוֹמִמְךָ אֱלוֹהַי הַמֶּלֶךְ, וַאֲבָרְכָה שִׁמְךָ לְעוֹלָם וָעֶד:

בְּכָל־יוֹם אֲבָרְכֶךָּ, וַאֲהַלְלָה שִׁמְךָ לְעוֹלָם וָעֶד:

גָּדוֹל יהוה וּמְהֻלָּל מְאֹד, וְלִגְדֻלָּתוֹ אֵין חֵקֶר:

דּוֹר לְדוֹר יְשַׁבַּח מַעֲשֶׂיךָ, וּגְבוּרֹתֶיךָ יַגִּידוּ:

הֲדַר כְּבוֹד הוֹדֶךָ, וְדִבְרֵי נִפְלְאֹתֶיךָ אָשִׂיחָה:

וֶעֱזוּז נוֹרְאֹתֶיךָ יֹאמֵרוּ, וּגְדוּלָּתְךָ אֲסַפְּרֶנָּה:

זֵכֶר רַב־טוּבְךָ יַבִּיעוּ, וְצִדְקָתְךָ יְרַנֵּנוּ:

חַנּוּן וְרַחוּם יהוה, אֶרֶךְ אַפַּיִם וּגְדָל־חָסֶד:

טוֹב־יהוה לַכֹּל, וְרַחֲמָיו עַל־כָּל־מַעֲשָׂיו:

יוֹדוּךָ יהוה כָּל־מַעֲשֶׂיךָ, וַחֲסִידֶיךָ יְבָרְכוּכָה:

כְּבוֹד מַלְכוּתְךָ יֹאמֵרוּ, וּגְבוּרָתְךָ יְדַבֵּרוּ:

לְהוֹדִיעַ לִבְנֵי הָאָדָם גְּבוּרֹתָיו, וּכְבוֹד הֲדַר מַלְכוּתוֹ:

מַלְכוּתְךָ מַלְכוּת כָּל־עֹלָמִים, וּמֶמְשַׁלְתְּךָ בְּכָל־דּוֹר וָדֹר:

סוֹמֵךְ יהוה לְכָל־הַנֹּפְלִים, וְזוֹקֵף לְכָל־הַכְּפוּפִים:

עֵינֵי־כֹל אֵלֶיךָ יְשַׂבֵּרוּ, וְאַתָּה נוֹתֵן־לָהֶם אֶת־אָכְלָם בְּעִתּוֹ:

°פּוֹתֵחַ אֶת־יָדֶךָ, °°וּמַשְׂבִּיעַ לְכָל־חַי רָצוֹן:

צַדִּיק יהוה בְּכָל־דְּרָכָיו, וְחָסִיד בְּכָל־מַעֲשָׂיו:

קָרוֹב יהוה לְכָל־קֹרְאָיו, לְכֹל אֲשֶׁר יִקְרָאֻהוּ בֶאֱמֶת:

רְצוֹן־יְרֵאָיו יַעֲשֶׂה, וְאֶת־שַׁוְעָתָם יִשְׁמַע, וְיוֹשִׁיעֵם:

שׁוֹמֵר יהוה אֶת־כָּל־אֹהֲבָיו, וְאֵת כָּל־הָרְשָׁעִים יַשְׁמִיד:

‹ תְּהִלַּת יהוה יְדַבֶּר פִּי, וִיבָרֵךְ כָּל־בָּשָׂר שֵׁם קָדְשׁוֹ לְעוֹלָם וָעֶד:

תהלים קטו

וַאֲנַחְנוּ נְבָרֵךְ יָהּ מֵעַתָּה וְעַד־עוֹלָם, הַלְלוּיָהּ:

וּבָא לְצִיּוֹן גּוֹאֵל "A redeemer will come to Zion,   *Is. 59*
to those in Jacob who repent of their sins," declares the LORD.
"As for Me, this is My covenant with them," says the LORD.
"My spirit, that is on you, and My words I have placed in your
mouth will not depart from your mouth, or from the mouth of
your children, or from the mouth of their descendants from this
time on and for ever," says the LORD.

▸ You are the Holy One, enthroned on the praises of Israel.   *Ps. 22*
And (the angels) call to one another, saying, "Holy, holy, holy   *Is. 6*
is the LORD of hosts; the whole world is filled with His glory."
And they receive permission from one another, saying: *Targum*
"Holy in the highest heavens, home of His Presence; holy on earth,   *Yonatan*
the work of His strength; holy for ever and all time is the LORD of hosts;   *Is. 6*
the whole earth is full of His radiant glory."

▸ Then a wind lifted me up and I heard behind me the sound of a   *Ezek. 3*
great noise, saying, "Blessed is the LORD's glory from His place."
Then a wind lifted me up and I heard behind me   *Targum*
the sound of a great tempest of those who uttered praise, saying,   *Yonatan*
"Blessed is the LORD's glory from the place of the home of His Presence."   *Ezek. 3*

The LORD shall reign for ever and all time.   *Ex. 15*
The LORD's kingdom is established for ever and all time.   *Targum*
                                                                                    Onkelos
                                                                                    Ex. 15

---

him and lured him into a journey of self-discovery on his way to Israel. He
never arrived, but his initiative enabled Avraham's eventual arrival.

Rav Yosef Karo, in addition to redacting the *Shulḥan Arukh*, was a leading
mystic who had frequent encounters with an angel. He recorded these conversations in a sefer called *Maggid Meisharim*. In one of these conversations
the angel explained the divine strategy of dispatching *meraglim* (spies) to
explore the Land of Israel prior to conquest. A divinely waged war had no
need for reconnaissance missions. HaKadosh Barukh Hu planned that the
favorable reports about Israel would inspire national longing for the Land.
This longing would atone for the previous betrayal of the *Egel* (golden calf)

ישעיה נט

וּבָא לְצִיּוֹן גּוֹאֵל, וּלְשָׁבֵי פֶשַׁע בְּיַעֲקֹב, נְאֻם יהוה:

וַאֲנִי זֹאת בְּרִיתִי אוֹתָם, אָמַר יהוה

רוּחִי אֲשֶׁר עָלֶיךָ וּדְבָרַי אֲשֶׁר־שַׂמְתִּי בְּפִיךָ

לֹא־יָמוּשׁוּ מִפִּיךָ וּמִפִּי זַרְעֲךָ וּמִפִּי זֶרַע זַרְעֲךָ

אָמַר יהוה, מֵעַתָּה וְעַד־עוֹלָם:

תהלים כב
ישעיה ו

‹ וְאַתָּה קָדוֹשׁ יוֹשֵׁב תְּהִלּוֹת יִשְׂרָאֵל: וְקָרָא זֶה אֶל־זֶה וְאָמַר

קָדוֹשׁ, קָדוֹשׁ, קָדוֹשׁ, יהוה צְבָאוֹת, מְלֹא כָל־הָאָרֶץ כְּבוֹדוֹ:

תרגום
יונתן
ישעיה ו

וּמְקַבְּלִין דֵּין מִן דֵּין וְאָמְרִין, קַדִּישׁ בִּשְׁמֵי מְרוֹמָא עִלָּאָה בֵּית שְׁכִינְתֵּה

קַדִּישׁ עַל אַרְעָא עוֹבַד גְּבוּרְתֵּה, קַדִּישׁ לְעָלַם וּלְעָלְמֵי עָלְמַיָּא

יהוה צְבָאוֹת, מַלְיָא כָל אַרְעָא זִיו יְקָרֵהּ.

יחזקאל ג

‹ וַתִּשָּׂאֵנִי רוּחַ, וָאֶשְׁמַע אַחֲרַי קוֹל רַעַשׁ גָּדוֹל

בָּרוּךְ כְּבוֹד־יהוה מִמְּקוֹמוֹ:

תרגום
יונתן
יחזקאל ג

וּנְטָלַתְנִי רוּחָא, וּשְׁמָעִית בַּתְרַי קָל זִיעַ סַגִּיא, דִּמְשַׁבְּחִין וְאָמְרִין

בְּרִיךְ יְקָרָא דַיהוה מֵאֲתַר בֵּית שְׁכִינְתֵּה.

שמות טו

יהוה יִמְלֹךְ לְעֹלָם וָעֶד:

תרגום
אונקלוס
שמות טו

יהוה מַלְכוּתֵהּ קָאֵם לְעָלַם וּלְעָלְמֵי עָלְמַיָּא.

וּבָא לְצִיּוֹן גּוֹאֵל, וּלְשָׁבֵי פֶשַׁע בְּיַעֲקֹב *A redeemer will come to Zion, to those in Jacob who repent of their sins.* Typically the experience of *teshuva* is driven by internal religious conscience and personal moral character. However, the Land of Israel and its historical message can also stir *teshuva*.

The Torah describes the pilgrimage of Avraham's father to relocate to the Land of Israel: "And Teraḥ took Abram his son, and Lot the son of Ḥaran, his son's son, and Sarai his daughter-in-law, his son Abram's wife; and they went forth with them from Ur of the Chaldees, to go into the land of Canaan; and they came unto Ḥaran, and dwelt there" (*Bereshit* 11:31). As *Ḥazal* documented, Teraḥ was immersed in a world of paganism, yet the land called to

יהוה LORD, God of Abraham, Isaac and Yisrael, our ancestors, may *1 Chr. 29*
You keep this for ever so that it forms the thoughts in Your people's
heart, and directs their heart toward You. He is compassionate. He *Ps. 78*
forgives iniquity and does not destroy. Repeatedly He suppresses
His anger, not rousing His full wrath. For You, my LORD, are good *Ps. 86*
and forgiving, abundantly kind to all who call on You. Your righ- *Ps. 119*
teousness is eternally righteous, and Your Torah is truth. Grant *Mic. 7*
truth to Jacob, loving-kindness to Abraham, as You promised our
ancestors in ancient times. Blessed is my LORD for day after day *Ps. 68*
He burdens us [with His blessings]; God is our salvation, Selah!
The LORD of hosts is with us; the God of Jacob is our refuge, Selah! *Ps. 46*
LORD of hosts, happy is the one who trusts in You. LORD, save! May *Ps. 84*
                                                                    Ps. 20
the King answer us on the day we call.

בָּרוּךְ Blessed is He, our God, who created us for His glory, separating us from those who go astray; who gave us the Torah of truth,
planting within us eternal life. May He open our heart to His Torah,
imbuing our heart with the love and awe of Him, that we may do
His will and serve Him with a perfect heart, so that we neither toil
in vain nor give birth to confusion.

יְהִי רָצוֹן May it be Your will, O LORD our God and God of our ancestors, that we keep Your laws in this world, and thus be worthy to live,
see and inherit goodness and blessing in the Messianic Age and in
the life of the World to Come. So that my soul may sing to You and *Ps. 30*
not be silent. LORD, my God, for ever I will thank You. Blessed is *Jer. 17*
the man who trusts in the LORD, whose trust is in the LORD alone.
Trust in the LORD for evermore, for God, the LORD, is an everlast- *Is. 26*
ing Rock. ‣ Those who know Your name trust in You, for You, LORD, *Ps. 9*
do not forsake those who seek You. The LORD desired, for the sake *Is. 42*
of Israel's merit, to make the Torah great and glorious.

The Land possesses a unique ability to stir the hearts of Jews and draw their
attention back to HaKadosh Barukh Hu. Even for those who don't sense an
internal urge for religion, the Land can redirect their hearts.

יהוה אֱלֹהֵי אַבְרָהָם יִצְחָק וְיִשְׂרָאֵל אֲבֹתֵינוּ, שָׁמְרָה-זֹּאת לְעוֹלָם דברי הימים
א׳ כט

לְיֵצֶר מַחְשְׁבוֹת לְבַב עַמֶּךָ, וְהָכֵן לְבָבָם אֵלֶיךָ: וְהוּא רַחוּם יְכַפֵּר תהלים עח

עָוֹן וְלֹא-יַשְׁחִית, וְהִרְבָּה לְהָשִׁיב אַפּוֹ, וְלֹא-יָעִיר כָּל-חֲמָתוֹ: כִּי- תהלים פו

אַתָּה אֲדֹנָי טוֹב וְסַלָּח, וְרַב-חֶסֶד לְכָל-קֹרְאֶיךָ: צִדְקָתְךָ צֶדֶק תהלים קיט

לְעוֹלָם וְתוֹרָתְךָ אֱמֶת: תִּתֵּן אֱמֶת לְיַעֲקֹב, חֶסֶד לְאַבְרָהָם, אֲשֶׁר- מיכה ז

נִשְׁבַּעְתָּ לַאֲבֹתֵינוּ מִימֵי קֶדֶם: בָּרוּךְ אֲדֹנָי יוֹם יוֹם יַעֲמָס-לָנוּ, הָאֵל תהלים סח

יְשׁוּעָתֵנוּ סֶלָה: יהוה צְבָאוֹת עִמָּנוּ, מִשְׂגָּב לָנוּ אֱלֹהֵי יַעֲקֹב סֶלָה: תהלים מו

יהוה צְבָאוֹת, אַשְׁרֵי אָדָם בֹּטֵחַ בָּךְ: יהוה הוֹשִׁיעָה, הַמֶּלֶךְ יַעֲנֵנוּ תהלים פד
תהלים כ

בְיוֹם-קָרְאֵנוּ:

בָּרוּךְ הוּא אֱלֹהֵינוּ שֶׁבְּרָאָנוּ לִכְבוֹדוֹ, וְהִבְדִּילָנוּ מִן הַתּוֹעִים, וְנָתַן
לָנוּ תּוֹרַת אֱמֶת, וְחַיֵּי עוֹלָם נָטַע בְּתוֹכֵנוּ. הוּא יִפְתַּח לִבֵּנוּ בְּתוֹרָתוֹ,
וְיָשֵׂם בְּלִבֵּנוּ אַהֲבָתוֹ וְיִרְאָתוֹ וְלַעֲשׂוֹת רְצוֹנוֹ וּלְעָבְדוֹ בְּלֵבָב שָׁלֵם,
לְמַעַן לֹא נִיגַע לָרִיק וְלֹא נֵלֵד לַבֶּהָלָה.

יְהִי רָצוֹן מִלְּפָנֶיךָ יהוה אֱלֹהֵינוּ וֵאלֹהֵי אֲבוֹתֵינוּ, שֶׁנִּשְׁמֹר חֻקֶּיךָ
בָּעוֹלָם הַזֶּה, וְנִזְכֶּה וְנִחְיֶה וְנִרְאֶה וְנִירַשׁ טוֹבָה וּבְרָכָה, לִשְׁנֵי
יְמוֹת הַמָּשִׁיחַ וּלְחַיֵּי הָעוֹלָם הַבָּא. לְמַעַן יְזַמֶּרְךָ כָבוֹד וְלֹא יִדֹּם, תהלים ל

יהוה אֱלֹהָי, לְעוֹלָם אוֹדֶךָּ: בָּרוּךְ הַגֶּבֶר אֲשֶׁר יִבְטַח בַּיהוה, וְהָיָה ירמיה יז

יהוה מִבְטַחוֹ: בִּטְחוּ בַיהוה עֲדֵי-עַד, כִּי בְּיָהּ יהוה צוּר עוֹלָמִים: ישעיה כו

‹ וְיִבְטְחוּ בְךָ יוֹדְעֵי שְׁמֶךָ, כִּי לֹא-עָזַבְתָּ דֹרְשֶׁיךָ, יהוה: יהוה חָפֵץ תהלים ט
ישעיה מב

לְמַעַן צִדְקוֹ, יַגְדִּיל תּוֹרָה וְיַאְדִּיר:

_____

and enable national *teshuva*. Though God intended this program, He allowed
it to arise out of human initiative, so that this penitent process should be
sincere. Unfortunately the plan was thwarted by the toxic reports which the
meraglim conveyed.

FULL KADDISH

Leader: יִתְגַּדַּל Magnified and sanctified may His great name be,
in the world He created by His will.
May He establish His kingdom in your lifetime
and in your days,
and in the lifetime of all the house of Israel,
swiftly and soon –
and say: Amen.

All: May His great name be blessed
for ever and all time.

Leader: Blessed and praised,
glorified and exalted,
raised and honored,
uplifted and lauded be
the name of the Holy One,
blessed be He,
beyond any blessing,
song, praise and consolation
uttered in the world –
and say: Amen.

May the prayers and pleas of all Israel
be accepted by their Father in heaven –
and say: Amen.

May there be great peace from heaven,
and life for us and all Israel –
and say: Amen.

*Bow, take three steps back, as if taking leave of the Divine Presence,
then bow, first left, then right, then center, while saying:*

May He who makes peace in His high places,
make peace for us and all Israel –
and say: Amen.

On Yom HaZikaron, some communities add the prayers on page 4.

קדיש שלם

ש״ץ: יִתְגַּדַּל וְיִתְקַדַּשׁ שְׁמֵהּ רַבָּא (קהל: אָמֵן)

בְּעָלְמָא דִּי בְרָא כִרְעוּתֵהּ

וְיַמְלִיךְ מַלְכוּתֵהּ

בְּחַיֵּיכוֹן וּבְיוֹמֵיכוֹן וּבְחַיֵּי דְכָל בֵּית יִשְׂרָאֵל

בַּעֲגָלָא וּבִזְמַן קָרִיב

וְאִמְרוּ אָמֵן. (קהל: אָמֵן)

קהל וש״ץ: יְהֵא שְׁמֵהּ רַבָּא מְבָרַךְ לְעָלַם וּלְעָלְמֵי עָלְמַיָּא.

ש״ץ: יִתְבָּרַךְ וְיִשְׁתַּבַּח וְיִתְפָּאַר

וְיִתְרוֹמַם וְיִתְנַשֵּׂא וְיִתְהַדָּר וְיִתְעַלֶּה וְיִתְהַלָּל

שְׁמֵהּ דְּקֻדְשָׁא בְּרִיךְ הוּא (קהל: בְּרִיךְ הוּא)

לְעֵלָּא מִן כָּל בִּרְכָתָא וְשִׁירָתָא, תֻּשְׁבְּחָתָא וְנֶחֱמָתָא

דַּאֲמִירָן בְּעָלְמָא

וְאִמְרוּ אָמֵן. (קהל: אָמֵן)

תִּתְקַבַּל צְלוֹתְהוֹן וּבָעוּתְהוֹן דְּכָל יִשְׂרָאֵל

קֳדָם אֲבוּהוֹן דִּי בִשְׁמַיָּא

וְאִמְרוּ אָמֵן. (קהל: אָמֵן)

יְהֵא שְׁלָמָא רַבָּא מִן שְׁמַיָּא

וְחַיִּים, עָלֵינוּ וְעַל כָּל יִשְׂרָאֵל

וְאִמְרוּ אָמֵן. (קהל: אָמֵן)

Bow, take three steps back, as if taking leave of the Divine Presence,
then bow, first left, then right, then center, while saying:

עֹשֶׂה שָׁלוֹם בִּמְרוֹמָיו

הוּא יַעֲשֶׂה שָׁלוֹם עָלֵינוּ וְעַל כָּל יִשְׂרָאֵל

וְאִמְרוּ אָמֵן. (קהל: אָמֵן)

On יום הזיכרון, *some communities add the prayers on page 5.*

Stand while saying Aleinu. Bow at ˈ.

עָלֵֽינוּ It is our duty to praise the Master of all,
and ascribe greatness to the Author of creation,
who has not made us like the nations of the lands
nor placed us like the families of the earth;
who has not made our portion like theirs,
nor our destiny like all their multitudes.
(For they worship vanity and emptiness,
and pray to a god who cannot save.)
ˈBut we bow in worship and thank the Supreme King of kings,
the Holy One, blessed be He,
who extends the heavens and establishes the earth,
whose throne of glory is in the heavens above,
and whose power's Presence is in the highest of heights.
He is our God; there is no other.
Truly He is our King, there is none else,
as it is written in His Torah:
"You shall know and take to heart this day that the LORD is God,
in heaven above and on earth below.
There is no other."

Therefore, we place our hope in You, LORD our God,
that we may soon see the glory of Your power,
when You will remove abominations from the earth,
and idols will be utterly destroyed,
when the world will be perfected under the sovereignty of the Almighty,
when all humanity will call on Your name,
to turn all the earth's wicked toward You.
All the world's inhabitants will realize and know
that to You every knee must bow and every tongue swear loyalty.
Before You, LORD our God, they will kneel and bow down
and give honor to Your glorious name.
They will all accept the yoke of Your kingdom,
and You will reign over them soon and for ever.
For the kingdom is Yours, and to all eternity You will reign in glory,
as it is written in Your Torah: "The LORD will reign for ever and ever."

Stand while saying עָלֵינוּ. *Bow at* ײ.

עָלֵינוּ לְשַׁבֵּחַ לַאֲדוֹן הַכֹּל, לָתֵת גְּדֻלָּה לְיוֹצֵר בְּרֵאשִׁית
שֶׁלֹּא עָשָׂנוּ כְּגוֹיֵי הָאֲרָצוֹת, וְלֹא שָׂמָנוּ כְּמִשְׁפְּחוֹת הָאֲדָמָה
שֶׁלֹּא שָׂם חֶלְקֵנוּ כָּהֶם וְגוֹרָלֵנוּ כְּכָל הֲמוֹנָם.
(שֶׁהֵם מִשְׁתַּחֲוִים לְהֶבֶל וָרִיק וּמִתְפַּלְלִים אֶל אֵל לֹא יוֹשִׁיעַ.)
וַאֲנַחְנוּ כּוֹרְעִים וּמִשְׁתַּחֲוִים וּמוֹדִים
לִפְנֵי מֶלֶךְ מַלְכֵי הַמְּלָכִים, הַקָּדוֹשׁ בָּרוּךְ הוּא
שֶׁהוּא נוֹטֶה שָׁמַיִם וְיוֹסֵד אָרֶץ, וּמוֹשַׁב יְקָרוֹ בַּשָּׁמַיִם מִמַּעַל
וּשְׁכִינַת עֻזּוֹ בְּגָבְהֵי מְרוֹמִים.
הוּא אֱלֹהֵינוּ, אֵין עוֹד.
אֱמֶת מַלְכֵּנוּ, אֶפֶס זוּלָתוֹ

כַּכָּתוּב בְּתוֹרָתוֹ, וְיָדַעְתָּ הַיּוֹם וַהֲשֵׁבֹתָ אֶל־לְבָבֶךָ
כִּי יהוה הוּא הָאֱלֹהִים בַּשָּׁמַיִם מִמַּעַל וְעַל־הָאָרֶץ מִתָּחַת
אֵין עוֹד:

דברים ד

עַל כֵּן נְקַוֶּה לְּךָ יהוה אֱלֹהֵינוּ, לִרְאוֹת מְהֵרָה בְּתִפְאֶרֶת עֻזֶּךָ
לְהַעֲבִיר גִּלּוּלִים מִן הָאָרֶץ, וְהָאֱלִילִים כָּרוֹת יִכָּרֵתוּן
לְתַקֵּן עוֹלָם בְּמַלְכוּת שַׁדַּי.
וְכָל בְּנֵי בָשָׂר יִקְרְאוּ בִשְׁמֶךָ לְהַפְנוֹת אֵלֶיךָ כָּל רִשְׁעֵי אָרֶץ.
יַכִּירוּ וְיֵדְעוּ כָּל יוֹשְׁבֵי תֵבֵל
כִּי לְךָ תִּכְרַע כָּל בֶּרֶךְ, תִּשָּׁבַע כָּל לָשׁוֹן.
לְפָנֶיךָ יהוה אֱלֹהֵינוּ יִכְרְעוּ וְיִפֹּלוּ, וְלִכְבוֹד שִׁמְךָ יְקָר יִתֵּנוּ
וִיקַבְּלוּ כֻלָּם אֶת עֹל מַלְכוּתֶךָ
וְתִמְלֹךְ עֲלֵיהֶם מְהֵרָה לְעוֹלָם וָעֶד.
כִּי הַמַּלְכוּת שֶׁלְּךָ הִיא וּלְעוֹלְמֵי עַד תִּמְלֹךְ בְּכָבוֹד
כַּכָּתוּב בְּתוֹרָתֶךָ, יהוה יִמְלֹךְ לְעֹלָם וָעֶד:

שמות טו

▸ And it is said: "Then the Lord shall be King over all the earth; on that day the Lord shall be One and His name One."

Zech. 14

Some add:

Have no fear of sudden terror or of the ruin when it overtakes the wicked.

Prov. 3

Devise your strategy, but it will be thwarted; propose your plan, but it will not stand, for God is with us.

Is. 8

When you grow old, I will still be the same.

Is. 46

When your hair turns gray, I will still carry you.
I made you, I will bear you, I will carry you, and I will rescue you.

MOURNER'S KADDISH

The following prayer, said by mourners, requires the presence of a minyan.
A transliteration can be found on page 667.

Mourner: יִתְגַּדַּל Magnified and sanctified may His great name be,
in the world He created by His will.
May He establish His kingdom
in your lifetime and in your days,
and in the lifetime of all the house of Israel,
swiftly and soon – and say: Amen.

All: May His great name be blessed for ever and all time.

Mourner: Blessed and praised, glorified and exalted,
raised and honored, uplifted and lauded
be the name of the Holy One,
blessed be He,
beyond any blessing, song,
praise and consolation
uttered in the world – and say: Amen.

May there be great peace from heaven,
and life for us and all Israel – and say: Amen.

Bow, take three steps back, as if taking leave of the Divine Presence,
then bow, first left, then right, then center, while saying:
May He who makes peace in His high places,
make peace for us and all Israel – and say: Amen.

זכריה יד

‣ וְנֶאֱמַר, וְהָיָה יהוה לְמֶלֶךְ עַל־כָּל־הָאָרֶץ
בַּיּוֹם הַהוּא יִהְיֶה יהוה אֶחָד וּשְׁמוֹ אֶחָד:

Some add:

משלי ג

אַל־תִּירָא מִפַּחַד פִּתְאֹם וּמִשֹּׁאַת רְשָׁעִים כִּי תָבֹא:

ישעיה ח

עֻצוּ עֵצָה וְתֻפָר, דַּבְּרוּ דָבָר וְלֹא יָקוּם, כִּי עִמָּנוּ אֵל:

ישעיה מו

וְעַד־זִקְנָה אֲנִי הוּא, וְעַד־שֵׂיבָה אֲנִי אֶסְבֹּל אֲנִי עָשִׂיתִי וַאֲנִי אֶשָּׂא וַאֲנִי אֶסְבֹּל וַאֲמַלֵּט:

קדיש יתום

The following prayer, said by mourners, requires the presence of a מנין.
A transliteration can be found on page 667.

אבל: יִתְגַּדַּל וְיִתְקַדַּשׁ שְׁמֵהּ רַבָּא (קהל: אָמֵן)
בְּעָלְמָא דִּי בְרָא כִרְעוּתֵהּ
וְיַמְלִיךְ מַלְכוּתֵהּ
בְּחַיֵּיכוֹן וּבְיוֹמֵיכוֹן וּבְחַיֵּי דְכָל בֵּית יִשְׂרָאֵל
בַּעֲגָלָא וּבִזְמַן קָרִיב, וְאִמְרוּ אָמֵן. (קהל: אָמֵן)

קהל
ואבל: יְהֵא שְׁמֵהּ רַבָּא מְבָרַךְ לְעָלַם וּלְעָלְמֵי עָלְמַיָּא.

אבל: יִתְבָּרַךְ וְיִשְׁתַּבַּח וְיִתְפָּאַר
וְיִתְרוֹמַם וְיִתְנַשֵּׂא וְיִתְהַדָּר וְיִתְעַלֶּה וְיִתְהַלָּל
שְׁמֵהּ דְּקֻדְשָׁא בְּרִיךְ הוּא (קהל: בְּרִיךְ הוּא)
לְעֵלָּא מִן כָּל בִּרְכָתָא וְשִׁירָתָא, תֻּשְׁבְּחָתָא וְנֶחֱמָתָא
דַּאֲמִירָן בְּעָלְמָא, וְאִמְרוּ אָמֵן. (קהל: אָמֵן)

יְהֵא שְׁלָמָא רַבָּא מִן שְׁמַיָּא
וְחַיִּים, עָלֵינוּ וְעַל כָּל יִשְׂרָאֵל, וְאִמְרוּ אָמֵן. (קהל: אָמֵן)

Bow, take three steps back, as if taking leave of the Divine Presence,
then bow, first left, then right, then center, while saying:

עֹשֶׂה שָׁלוֹם בִּמְרוֹמָיו, הוּא יַעֲשֶׂה שָׁלוֹם עָלֵינוּ
וְעַל כָּל יִשְׂרָאֵל, וְאִמְרוּ אָמֵן. (קהל: אָמֵן)

THE DAILY PSALM

One of the following psalms is said on the appropriate day of the week as indicated.
After the psalm, the Mourner's Kaddish on page 416 is said.

Tuesday: Today is the third day of the week,
on which the Levites used to say this psalm in the Temple:

מִזְמוֹר לְאָסָף A psalm of Asaph. God stands in the divine assembly. Among *Ps. 82* the judges He delivers judgment. How long will you judge unjustly, show-ing favor to the wicked? Selah. Do justice to the weak and the orphaned. Vindicate the poor and destitute. Rescue the weak and needy. Save them from the hand of the wicked. They do not know nor do they understand. They walk about in darkness while all the earth's foundations shake. I once said, "You are like gods, all of you are sons of the Most High." But you shall die like mere men, you will fall like any prince. ‣ Arise, O Lord, judge the earth, for all the nations are Your possession. *Mourner's Kaddish (page 416)*

Wednesday: Today is the fourth day of the week,
on which the Levites used to say this psalm in the Temple:

אֵל־נְקָמוֹת God of retribution, Lord, God of retribution, appear! Rise up, *Ps. 94* Judge of the earth. Repay to the arrogant what they deserve. How long shall the wicked, Lord, how long shall the wicked triumph? They pour out insolent words. All the evildoers are full of boasting. They crush Your people, Lord, and oppress Your inheritance. They kill the widow and the stranger. They murder the orphaned. They say, "The Lord does not see. The God of Jacob pays no heed." Take heed, you most brutish people. You fools, when will you grow wise? Will He who implants the ear not hear? Will He who formed the eye not see? Will He who disciplines na-tions – He who teaches man knowledge – not punish? The Lord knows that the thoughts of man are a mere fleeting breath. Happy is the man whom You discipline, Lord, the one You instruct in Your Torah, giving him tranquility in days of trouble, until a pit is dug for the wicked. For the Lord will not forsake His people, nor abandon His heritage. Judgment shall again accord with justice, and all the upright in heart will follow it. Who will rise up for me against the wicked? Who will stand up for me against wrongdoers? Had the Lord not been my help, I would soon have dwelt in death's silence. When I thought my foot was slipping, Your loving-kindness, Lord, gave me support. When I was filled with anxiety,

שִׁיר שֶׁל יוֹם

One of the following psalms is said on the appropriate day of the week as indicated.
After the psalm, קדיש יתום on page 417 is said.

Tuesday הַיּוֹם יוֹם שְׁלִישִׁי בְּשַׁבָּת, שֶׁבּוֹ הָיוּ הַלְוִיִּם אוֹמְרִים בְּבֵית הַמִּקְדָּשׁ:

תהלים פב מִזְמוֹר לְאָסָף, אֱלֹהִים נִצָּב בַּעֲדַת־אֵל, בְּקֶרֶב אֱלֹהִים יִשְׁפֹּט: עַד־
מָתַי תִּשְׁפְּטוּ־עָוֶל, וּפְנֵי רְשָׁעִים תִּשְׂאוּ־סֶלָה: שִׁפְטוּ־דַל וְיָתוֹם,
עָנִי וָרָשׁ הַצְדִּיקוּ: פַּלְּטוּ־דַל וְאֶבְיוֹן, מִיַּד רְשָׁעִים הַצִּילוּ: לֹא יָדְעוּ
וְלֹא יָבִינוּ, בַּחֲשֵׁכָה יִתְהַלָּכוּ, יִמּוֹטוּ כָּל־מוֹסְדֵי אָרֶץ: אֲנִי־אָמַרְתִּי
אֱלֹהִים אַתֶּם, וּבְנֵי עֶלְיוֹן כֻּלְּכֶם: אָכֵן כְּאָדָם תְּמוּתוּן, וּכְאַחַד
הַשָּׂרִים תִּפֹּלוּ: ‹ קוּמָה אֱלֹהִים שָׁפְטָה הָאָרֶץ, כִּי־אַתָּה תִנְחַל
בְּכָל־הַגּוֹיִם: קדיש יתום (page 417)

Wednesday הַיּוֹם יוֹם רְבִיעִי בְּשַׁבָּת, שֶׁבּוֹ הָיוּ הַלְוִיִּם אוֹמְרִים בְּבֵית הַמִּקְדָּשׁ:

תהלים צד אֵל־נְקָמוֹת יהוה, אֵל נְקָמוֹת הוֹפִיעַ: הִנָּשֵׂא שֹׁפֵט הָאָרֶץ, הָשֵׁב
גְּמוּל עַל־גֵּאִים: עַד־מָתַי רְשָׁעִים, יהוה, עַד־מָתַי רְשָׁעִים יַעֲלֹזוּ:
יַבִּיעוּ יְדַבְּרוּ עָתָק, יִתְאַמְּרוּ כָּל־פֹּעֲלֵי אָוֶן: עַמְּךָ יהוה יְדַכְּאוּ,
וְנַחֲלָתְךָ יְעַנּוּ: אַלְמָנָה וְגֵר יַהֲרֹגוּ, וִיתוֹמִים יְרַצֵּחוּ: וַיֹּאמְרוּ לֹא
יִרְאֶה־יָּהּ, וְלֹא־יָבִין אֱלֹהֵי יַעֲקֹב: בִּינוּ בֹּעֲרִים בָּעָם, וּכְסִילִים מָתַי
תַּשְׂכִּילוּ: הֲנֹטַע אֹזֶן הֲלֹא יִשְׁמָע, אִם־יֹצֵר עַיִן הֲלֹא יַבִּיט: הֲיֹסֵר
גּוֹיִם הֲלֹא יוֹכִיחַ, הַמְלַמֵּד אָדָם דָּעַת: יהוה יֹדֵעַ מַחְשְׁבוֹת אָדָם,
כִּי־הֵמָּה הָבֶל: אַשְׁרֵי הַגֶּבֶר אֲשֶׁר־תְּיַסְּרֶנּוּ יָּהּ, וּמִתּוֹרָתְךָ תְלַמְּדֶנּוּ:
לְהַשְׁקִיט לוֹ מִימֵי רָע, עַד יִכָּרֶה לָרָשָׁע שָׁחַת: כִּי לֹא־יִטֹּשׁ יהוה
עַמּוֹ, וְנַחֲלָתוֹ לֹא יַעֲזֹב: כִּי־עַד־צֶדֶק יָשׁוּב מִשְׁפָּט, וְאַחֲרָיו כָּל־
יִשְׁרֵי־לֵב: מִי־יָקוּם לִי עִם־מְרֵעִים, מִי־יִתְיַצֵּב לִי עִם־פֹּעֲלֵי אָוֶן:
לוּלֵי יהוה עֶזְרָתָה לִּי, כִּמְעַט שָׁכְנָה דוּמָה נַפְשִׁי: אִם־אָמַרְתִּי

Your consolations soothed my soul. Can a corrupt throne be allied with You? Can injustice be framed into law? They join forces against the life of the righteous, and condemn the innocent to death. But the LORD is my stronghold, my God is the Rock of my refuge. He will bring back on them their wickedness, and destroy them for their evil deeds. The LORD our God will destroy them.

▸ Come, let us sing for joy to the LORD; let us shout aloud to the Rock of   *Ps. 95*
our salvation. Let us greet Him with thanksgiving, shout aloud to Him with songs of praise. For the LORD is the great God, the King great above all powers.

Mourner's Kaddish (page 416)

Thursday: Today is the fifth day of the week,
         on which the Levites used to say this psalm in the Temple:

לַמְנַצֵּחַ For the conductor of music. On the Gittit. By Asaph. Sing for joy   *Ps. 81*
to God, our strength. Shout aloud to the God of Jacob. Raise a song, beat the drum, play the sweet harp and lyre. Sound the shofar on the new moon, on our feast day when the moon is hidden. For it is a statute for Israel, an ordinance of the God of Jacob. He established it as a testimony for Joseph when He went forth against the land of Egypt, where I heard a language that I did not know. I relieved his shoulder of the burden. His hands were freed from the builder's basket. In distress you called and I rescued you. I answered you from the secret place of thunder; I tested you at the waters of Meribah, Selah! Hear, My people, and I will warn you. Israel, if you would only listen to Me! Let there be no strange god among you. Do not bow down to an alien god. I am the LORD your God who brought you out of the land of Egypt. Open your mouth wide and I will fill it. But My people would not listen to Me. Israel would have none of Me. So I left them to their stubborn hearts, letting them follow their own devices. If only My people would listen to Me, if Israel would walk in My ways, I would soon subdue their enemies, and turn My hand against their foes. Those who hate the LORD would cower before Him and their doom would last for ever. ▸ He would feed Israel with the finest wheat – with honey from the rock I would satisfy you.

Mourner's Kaddish (page 416)

*In Israel "Ein Keloheinu" through "Bless the LORD" (pages 422–426), is said.
Outside Israel continue with "I Believe" on page 426.*

מַטָּה רַגְלִי, חַסְדְּךָ יהוה יִסְעָדֵנִי: בְּרֹב שַׂרְעַפַּי בְּקִרְבִּי, תַּנְחוּמֶיךָ
יְשַׁעַשְׁעוּ נַפְשִׁי: הַיְחָבְרְךָ כִּסֵּא הַוּוֹת, יֹצֵר עָמָל עֲלֵי־חֹק: יָגוֹדּוּ
עַל־נֶפֶשׁ צַדִּיק, וְדָם נָקִי יַרְשִׁיעוּ: וַיְהִי יהוה לִי לְמִשְׂגָּב, וֵאלֹהַי
לְצוּר מַחְסִי: וַיָּשֶׁב עֲלֵיהֶם אֶת־אוֹנָם, וּבְרָעָתָם יַצְמִיתֵם, יַצְמִיתֵם
יהוה אֱלֹהֵינוּ:

תהלים צה
‹ לְכוּ נְרַנְּנָה לַיהוה, נָרִיעָה לְצוּר יִשְׁעֵנוּ: נְקַדְּמָה פָנָיו בְּתוֹדָה,
בִּזְמִרוֹת נָרִיעַ לוֹ: כִּי אֵל גָּדוֹל יהוה, וּמֶלֶךְ גָּדוֹל עַל־כָּל־אֱלֹהִים:

(page 417) קדיש יתום

Thursday הַיּוֹם יוֹם חֲמִישִׁי בְּשַׁבָּת, שֶׁבּוֹ הָיוּ הַלְוִיִּם אוֹמְרִים בְּבֵית הַמִּקְדָּשׁ:

תהלים פא
לַמְנַצֵּחַ עַל־הַגִּתִּית לְאָסָף: הַרְנִינוּ לֵאלֹהִים עוּזֵּנוּ, הָרִיעוּ לֵאלֹהֵי
יַעֲקֹב: שְׂאוּ־זִמְרָה וּתְנוּ־תֹף, כִּנּוֹר נָעִים עִם־נָבֶל: תִּקְעוּ בַחֹדֶשׁ
שׁוֹפָר, בַּכֵּסֶה לְיוֹם חַגֵּנוּ: כִּי חֹק לְיִשְׂרָאֵל הוּא, מִשְׁפָּט לֵאלֹהֵי
יַעֲקֹב: עֵדוּת בִּיהוֹסֵף שָׂמוֹ, בְּצֵאתוֹ עַל־אֶרֶץ מִצְרָיִם, שְׂפַת לֹא־
יָדַעְתִּי אֶשְׁמָע: הֲסִירוֹתִי מִסֵּבֶל שִׁכְמוֹ, כַּפָּיו מִדּוּד תַּעֲבֹרְנָה: בַּצָּרָה
קָרָאתָ וָאֲחַלְּצֶךָּ, אֶעֶנְךָ בְּסֵתֶר רַעַם, אֶבְחָנְךָ עַל־מֵי מְרִיבָה סֶלָה:
שְׁמַע עַמִּי וְאָעִידָה בָּךְ, יִשְׂרָאֵל אִם־תִּשְׁמַע־לִי: לֹא־יִהְיֶה בְךָ אֵל
זָר, וְלֹא תִשְׁתַּחֲוֶה לְאֵל נֵכָר: אָנֹכִי יהוה אֱלֹהֶיךָ, הַמַּעַלְךָ מֵאֶרֶץ
מִצְרָיִם, הַרְחֶב־פִּיךָ וַאֲמַלְאֵהוּ: וְלֹא־שָׁמַע עַמִּי לְקוֹלִי, וְיִשְׂרָאֵל
לֹא־אָבָה לִי: וָאֲשַׁלְּחֵהוּ בִּשְׁרִירוּת לִבָּם, יֵלְכוּ בְּמוֹעֲצוֹתֵיהֶם: לוּ
עַמִּי שֹׁמֵעַ לִי, יִשְׂרָאֵל בִּדְרָכַי יְהַלֵּכוּ: כִּמְעַט אוֹיְבֵיהֶם אַכְנִיעַ,
וְעַל־צָרֵיהֶם אָשִׁיב יָדִי: מְשַׂנְאֵי יהוה יְכַחֲשׁוּ־לוֹ, וִיהִי עִתָּם לְעוֹלָם:
‹ וַיַּאֲכִילֵהוּ מֵחֵלֶב חִטָּה, וּמִצּוּר, דְּבַשׁ אַשְׂבִּיעֶךָ:

(page 417) קדיש יתום

In אֶרֶץ יִשְׂרָאֵל, אֵין כֵּאלֹהֵינוּ through בָּרְכוּ (pages 423–427), is said.
In חוּץ לָאָרֶץ continue with אֲנִי מַאֲמִין on page 427.

In Israel the following through "Bless the Lord" on page 426, is said.

אֵין כֵּאלֹהֵינוּ There is none like our God, none like our Lord, none like our King, none like our Savior. Who is like our God? Like our Lord? Like our King? Like our Savior? We will thank our God, thank our Lord, thank our King, thank our Savior. Blessed is our God, blessed our Lord, blessed our King, blessed our Savior. You are our God, You are our Lord, You are our King, You are our Savior. You are He to whom our ancestors offered the fragrant incense.

פִּטּוּם הַקְּטֹרֶת The incense mixture consisted of balsam, onycha, galbanum and frankincense, each weighing seventy manehs; myrrh, cassia, spikenard and saffron, each weighing sixteen manehs; twelve manehs of costus, three of aromatic bark; nine of cinnamon; nine kabs of Carsina lye; three seahs and three kabs of Cyprus wine. If Cyprus wine was not available, old white wine might be used. A quarter of a kab of Sodom salt, and a minute amount of a smoke-raising herb. Rabbi Nathan says: Also a minute amount of Jordan amber. If one added honey to the mixture, he rendered it unfit for sacred use. If he omitted any one of its ingredients, he is guilty of a capital offence. *Keritot 6a*

Rabban Shimon ben Gamliel says: "Balsam" refers to the sap that drips from the balsam tree. The Carsina lye was used for bleaching the onycha to improve it. The Cyprus wine was used to soak the onycha in it to make it pungent. Though urine is suitable for this purpose, it is not brought into the Temple out of respect.

It was taught in the Academy of Elijah: Whoever studies [Torah] laws every day is assured that he will be destined for the World to Come, as it is said, "The ways of the world are His" – read not, "ways" [*halikhot*] but "laws" [*halakhot*]. *Megilla 28b* *Hab. 3*

Rabbi Elazar said in the name of Rabbi Ḥanina: The disciples of the sages increase peace in the world, as it is said, "And all your children shall be taught of the Lord, and great shall be the peace of your children [*banayikh*]." Read not *banayikh*, "your children," but *bonayikh*, "your builders." Those who love Your Torah have great peace; there is no stumbling block for them. May there be peace within your ramparts, prosperity in your palaces. For the sake of my brothers and friends, I shall say, "Peace be within you." For the sake of the House of the Lord our God, I will seek your good. ‣ May the Lord grant strength to His people; may the Lord bless His people with peace. *Berakhot 64a* *Is. 54* *Ps. 119* *Ps. 122* *Ps. 29*

In ארץ ישראל the following through בָּרְכוּ on page 427, is said.

אֵין כֵּאלֹהֵינוּ, אֵין כַּאדוֹנֵינוּ, אֵין כְּמַלְכֵּנוּ, אֵין כְּמוֹשִׁיעֵנוּ. מִי
כֵאלֹהֵינוּ, מִי כַאדוֹנֵינוּ, מִי כְמַלְכֵּנוּ, מִי כְמוֹשִׁיעֵנוּ. נוֹדֶה לֵאלֹהֵינוּ,
נוֹדֶה לַאדוֹנֵינוּ, נוֹדֶה לְמַלְכֵּנוּ, נוֹדֶה לְמוֹשִׁיעֵנוּ. בָּרוּךְ אֱלֹהֵינוּ, בָּרוּךְ
אֲדוֹנֵינוּ, בָּרוּךְ מַלְכֵּנוּ, בָּרוּךְ מוֹשִׁיעֵנוּ. אַתָּה הוּא אֱלֹהֵינוּ, אַתָּה
הוּא אֲדוֹנֵינוּ, אַתָּה הוּא מַלְכֵּנוּ, אַתָּה הוּא מוֹשִׁיעֵנוּ. אַתָּה הוּא
שֶׁהִקְטִירוּ אֲבוֹתֵינוּ לְפָנֶיךָ אֶת קְטֹרֶת הַסַּמִּים.

כריתות ו. פִּטּוּם הַקְּטֹרֶת: הַצֳּרִי, וְהַצִּפֹּרֶן, וְהַחֶלְבְּנָה, וְהַלְּבוֹנָה מִשְׁקַל שִׁבְעִים שִׁבְעִים
מָנֶה, מֹר, וּקְצִיעָה, שִׁבֹּלֶת נֵרְדְּ, וְכַרְכֹּם מִשְׁקַל שִׁשָּׁה עָשָׂר שִׁשָּׁה עָשָׂר מָנֶה,
הַקֹּשְׁטְ שְׁנֵים עָשָׂר, קִלּוּפָה שְׁלֹשָׁה, וְקִנָּמוֹן תִּשְׁעָה, בֹּרִית כַּרְשִׁינָה תִּשְׁעָה
קַבִּין, יֵין קַפְרִיסִין סְאִין תְּלָת וְקַבִּין תְּלָתָא, וְאִם אֵין לוֹ יֵין קַפְרִיסִין, מֵבִיא
חֲמַר חִוַּרְיָן עַתִּיק. מֶלַח סְדוֹמִית רֹבַע, מַעֲלֶה עָשָׁן כָּל שֶׁהוּא. רַבִּי נָתָן הַבַּבְלִי
אוֹמֵר: אַף כִּפַּת הַיַּרְדֵּן כָּל שֶׁהוּא, וְאִם נָתַן בָּהּ דְּבַשׁ פְּסָלָהּ, וְאִם חִסַּר אֶחָד
מִכָּל סַמָּנֶיהָ, חַיָּב מִיתָה.

רַבָּן שִׁמְעוֹן בֶּן גַּמְלִיאֵל אוֹמֵר: הַצֳּרִי אֵינוֹ אֶלָּא שְׂרָף הַנּוֹטֵף מֵעֲצֵי הַקְּטָף.
בֹּרִית כַּרְשִׁינָה שֶׁשָּׁפִין בָּהּ אֶת הַצִּפֹּרֶן כְּדֵי שֶׁתְּהֵא נָאָה, יֵין קַפְרִיסִין שֶׁשּׁוֹרִין
בּוֹ אֶת הַצִּפֹּרֶן כְּדֵי שֶׁתְּהֵא עַזָּה, וַהֲלֹא מֵי רַגְלַיִם יָפִין לָהּ, אֶלָּא שֶׁאֵין מַכְנִיסִין
מֵי רַגְלַיִם בַּמִּקְדָּשׁ מִפְּנֵי הַכָּבוֹד.

מגילה כח: תָּנָא דְּבֵי אֵלִיָּהוּ: כָּל הַשּׁוֹנֶה הֲלָכוֹת בְּכָל יוֹם, מֻבְטָח לוֹ שֶׁהוּא בֶּן עוֹלָם
חבקוק ג הַבָּא, שֶׁנֶּאֱמַר הֲלִיכוֹת עוֹלָם לוֹ: אַל תִּקְרֵי הֲלִיכוֹת אֶלָּא הֲלָכוֹת.

ברכות סד. אָמַר רַבִּי אֶלְעָזָר, אָמַר רַבִּי חֲנִינָא: תַּלְמִידֵי חֲכָמִים מַרְבִּים שָׁלוֹם בָּעוֹלָם,
ישעיה נד שֶׁנֶּאֱמַר וְכָל־בָּנַיִךְ לִמּוּדֵי יהוה, וְרַב שְׁלוֹם בָּנָיִךְ: אַל תִּקְרֵי בָּנָיִךְ, אֶלָּא
תהלים קכב בּוֹנָיִךְ. שָׁלוֹם רָב לְאֹהֲבֵי תוֹרָתֶךָ, וְאֵין־לָמוֹ מִכְשׁוֹל: יְהִי־שָׁלוֹם בְּחֵילֵךְ,
תהלים קיט שַׁלְוָה בְּאַרְמְנוֹתָיִךְ: לְמַעַן אַחַי וְרֵעָי אֲדַבְּרָה־נָּא שָׁלוֹם בָּךְ: לְמַעַן בֵּית
יהוה אֱלֹהֵינוּ אֲבַקְשָׁה טוֹב לָךְ: ◂ יהוה עֹז לְעַמּוֹ יִתֵּן, יהוה יְבָרֵךְ אֶת־
תהלים כט עַמּוֹ בַשָּׁלוֹם:

THE RABBIS' KADDISH

The following prayer, said by mourners, requires the presence of a minyan.
A transliteration can be found on page 666.

Mourner: יִתְגַּדַּל Magnified and sanctified may His great name be,
in the world He created by His will.
May He establish His kingdom in your lifetime
and in your days,
and in the lifetime of all the house of Israel,
swiftly and soon – and say: Amen.

All: May His great name be blessed for ever and all time.

Mourner: Blessed and praised, glorified and exalted,
raised and honored, uplifted and lauded be
the name of the Holy One,
blessed be He,
beyond any blessing,
song, praise and consolation
uttered in the world – and say: Amen.

To Israel, to the teachers,
their disciples and their disciples' disciples,
and to all who engage in the study of Torah,
in this (*in Israel add:* holy) place or elsewhere,
may there come to them and you
great peace, grace,
kindness and compassion,
long life, ample sustenance and deliverance,
from their Father in Heaven – and say: Amen.

May there be great peace from heaven,
and (good) life for us and all Israel – and say: Amen.

Bow, take three steps back, as if taking leave of the Divine Presence,
then bow, first left, then right, then center, while saying:
May He who makes peace in His high places,
in His compassion make peace
for us and all Israel – and say: Amen.

קדיש דרבנן

The following prayer, said by mourners, requires the presence of a מנין.
A transliteration can be found on page 666.

אבל: יִתְגַּדַּל וְיִתְקַדַּשׁ שְׁמֵהּ רַבָּא (קהל: אָמֵן)

בְּעָלְמָא דִּי בְרָא כִרְעוּתֵהּ

וְיַמְלִיךְ מַלְכוּתֵהּ

בְּחַיֵּיכוֹן וּבְיוֹמֵיכוֹן וּבְחַיֵּי דְכָל בֵּית יִשְׂרָאֵל

בַּעֲגָלָא וּבִזְמַן קָרִיב, וְאִמְרוּ אָמֵן. (קהל: אָמֵן)

קהל
ואבל: יְהֵא שְׁמֵהּ רַבָּא מְבָרַךְ לְעָלַם וּלְעָלְמֵי עָלְמַיָּא.

אבל: יִתְבָּרַךְ וְיִשְׁתַּבַּח וְיִתְפָּאַר וְיִתְרוֹמַם וְיִתְנַשֵּׂא

וְיִתְהַדָּר וְיִתְעַלֶּה וְיִתְהַלָּל

שְׁמֵהּ דְּקֻדְשָׁא בְּרִיךְ הוּא (קהל: בְּרִיךְ הוּא)

לְעֵלָּא מִן כָּל בִּרְכָתָא וְשִׁירָתָא, תֻּשְׁבְּחָתָא וְנֶחֱמָתָא

דַּאֲמִירָן בְּעָלְמָא, וְאִמְרוּ אָמֵן. (קהל: אָמֵן)

עַל יִשְׂרָאֵל וְעַל רַבָּנָן, וְעַל תַּלְמִידֵיהוֹן

וְעַל כָּל תַּלְמִידֵי תַלְמִידֵיהוֹן, וְעַל כָּל מָאן דְּעָסְקִין בְּאוֹרַיְתָא

דִּי בְאַתְרָא (בארץ ישראל: קַדִּישָׁא) הָדֵין וְדִי בְּכָל אֲתַר וַאֲתַר

יְהֵא לְהוֹן וּלְכוֹן שְׁלָמָא רַבָּא

חִנָּא וְחִסְדָּא, וְרַחֲמֵי, וְחַיֵּי אֲרִיכֵי, וּמְזוֹנֵי רְוִיחֵי

וּפֻרְקָנָא מִן קֳדָם אֲבוּהוֹן דִּי בִשְׁמַיָּא, וְאִמְרוּ אָמֵן. (קהל: אָמֵן)

יְהֵא שְׁלָמָא רַבָּא מִן שְׁמַיָּא

וְחַיִּים (טוֹבִים) עָלֵינוּ וְעַל כָּל יִשְׂרָאֵל, וְאִמְרוּ אָמֵן. (קהל: אָמֵן)

Bow, take three steps back, as if taking leave of the Divine Presence,
then bow, first left, then right, then center, while saying:

עֹשֶׂה שָׁלוֹם בִּמְרוֹמָיו

הוּא יַעֲשֶׂה בְרַחֲמָיו שָׁלוֹם

עָלֵינוּ וְעַל כָּל יִשְׂרָאֵל, וְאִמְרוּ אָמֵן. (קהל: אָמֵן)

In Israel, on days when the Torah is not read,
the person saying Kaddish adds:

Bless the LORD, the blessed One.

and the congregation responds:

Bless the LORD, the blessed One, for ever and all time.

All sing:

אֲנִי מַאֲמִין I believe
with perfect faith
in the coming of the Messiah,
and though he may delay,
I wait daily for his coming.

GOD'S MESSENGER

Rabbi Tzvi Yehuda HaKohen Kook placed a photo of Theodore Herzl on the bureau in his room among the other pictures of the greatest of rabbis, from the Vilna Gaon until his own father, Rabbi Abraham Isaac Kook. I have seen many photos of the rabbis, and many of Herzl, but I have never (until this very day) seen them together, only here in the room of Rabbi Tzvi Yehuda. When I gathered my courage and asked him, "What is the picture of Herzl doing among the photos of the rabbis?" he smiled and gave a lengthy reply, which concluded, "Perhaps some don't like it, but he was sent by God to begin taking us out of our exile." (Yoel Bin-Nun, *Nes Kibbutz Galuyot*, p. 251)

In ארץ ישראל, *on days when the* תורה *is not read,*
the person saying קדיש *adds:*

בָּרְכוּ אֶת יהוה הַמְבֹרָךְ.

and the קהל *responds:*

בָּרוּךְ יהוה הַמְבֹרָךְ לְעוֹלָם וָעֶד.

All sing:

אֲנִי מַאֲמִין בֶּאֱמוּנָה שְׁלֵמָה
בְּבִיאַת הַמָּשִׁיחַ
וְאַף עַל פִּי שֶׁיִּתְמַהְמֵהַּ
עִם כָּל זֶה אֲחַכֶּה לוֹ בְּכָל יוֹם שֶׁיָּבוֹא.

A DAY OF JOY AND THANKSGIVING

The fundamental turning point that occurred through God's compassion
for us, to save us and to redeem our souls with the declaration of our independence in the Land of Israel, obliges us to fulfill and to accept the day
of the Declaration of the State for all generations – the fifth of Iyar every
year – as a day of joy, the beginning of the redemption for the entire nation,
and to exempt this day from all of the mourning customs that apply during the Counting of the Omer, with instructions for a thanksgiving prayer
service that recounts the event. (The Decision of the Chief Rabbinate of
Israel, 8 Nisan 1949)

מנחה ליום העצמאות וליום ירושלים

MINḤA FOR YOM HAATZMA'UT
& YOM YERUSHALAYIM

Minḥa for Yom HaAtzma'ut
and Yom Yerushalayim

אַשְׁרֵי Happy are those who dwell in Your House;   *Ps. 84*
they shall continue to praise You, Selah!

Happy are the people for whom this is so;   *Ps. 144*
happy are the people whose God is the LORD.

A song of praise by David.   *Ps. 145*
I will exalt You, my God, the King, and bless Your name for
ever and all time. Every day I will bless You, and praise Your
name for ever and all time. Great is the LORD and greatly to be
praised; His greatness is unfathomable. One generation will
praise Your works to the next, and tell of Your mighty deeds.
On the glorious splendor of Your majesty I will meditate, and
on the acts of Your wonders. They shall talk of the power of
Your awesome deeds, and I will tell of Your greatness. They
shall recite the record of Your great goodness, and sing with
joy of Your righteousness. The LORD is gracious and compassionate, slow to anger and great in loving-kindness. The LORD
is good to all, and His compassion extends to all His works.
All Your works shall thank You, LORD, and Your devoted ones
shall bless You. They shall talk of the glory of Your kingship,
and speak of Your might. To make known to mankind His
mighty deeds and the glorious majesty of His kingship. Your
kingdom is an everlasting kingdom, and Your reign is for all
generations. The LORD supports all who fall, and raises all who
are bowed down. All raise their eyes to You in hope, and You
give them their food in due season. You open Your hand, and
satisfy every living thing with favor. The LORD is righteous in

מנחה ליום העצמאות
וליום ירושלים

תהלים פד

אַשְׁרֵי יוֹשְׁבֵי בֵיתֶךָ, עוֹד יְהַלְלוּךָ סֶּלָה:

תהלים קמד

אַשְׁרֵי הָעָם שֶׁכָּכָה לּוֹ, אַשְׁרֵי הָעָם שֶׁיהוה אֱלֹהָיו:

תהלים קמה

תְּהִלָּה לְדָוִד

אֲרוֹמִמְךָ אֱלוֹהַי הַמֶּלֶךְ, וַאֲבָרְכָה שִׁמְךָ לְעוֹלָם וָעֶד:

בְּכָל־יוֹם אֲבָרְכֶךָּ, וַאֲהַלְלָה שִׁמְךָ לְעוֹלָם וָעֶד:

גָּדוֹל יהוה וּמְהֻלָּל מְאֹד, וְלִגְדֻלָּתוֹ אֵין חֵקֶר:

דּוֹר לְדוֹר יְשַׁבַּח מַעֲשֶׂיךָ, וּגְבוּרֹתֶיךָ יַגִּידוּ:

הֲדַר כְּבוֹד הוֹדֶךָ, וְדִבְרֵי נִפְלְאֹתֶיךָ אָשִׂיחָה:

וֶעֱזוּז נוֹרְאֹתֶיךָ יֹאמֵרוּ, וּגְדוּלָּתְךָ אֲסַפְּרֶנָּה:

זֵכֶר רַב־טוּבְךָ יַבִּיעוּ, וְצִדְקָתְךָ יְרַנֵּנוּ:

חַנּוּן וְרַחוּם יהוה, אֶרֶךְ אַפַּיִם וּגְדָל־חָסֶד:

טוֹב־יהוה לַכֹּל, וְרַחֲמָיו עַל־כָּל־מַעֲשָׂיו:

יוֹדוּךָ יהוה כָּל־מַעֲשֶׂיךָ, וַחֲסִידֶיךָ יְבָרְכוּכָה:

כְּבוֹד מַלְכוּתְךָ יֹאמֵרוּ, וּגְבוּרָתְךָ יְדַבֵּרוּ:

לְהוֹדִיעַ לִבְנֵי הָאָדָם גְּבוּרֹתָיו, וּכְבוֹד הֲדַר מַלְכוּתוֹ:

מַלְכוּתְךָ מַלְכוּת כָּל־עֹלָמִים, וּמֶמְשַׁלְתְּךָ בְּכָל־דּוֹר וָדֹר:

סוֹמֵךְ יהוה לְכָל־הַנֹּפְלִים, וְזוֹקֵף לְכָל־הַכְּפוּפִים:

עֵינֵי־כֹל אֵלֶיךָ יְשַׂבֵּרוּ, וְאַתָּה נוֹתֵן־לָהֶם אֶת־אָכְלָם בְּעִתּוֹ:

פּוֹתֵחַ אֶת־יָדֶךָ, וּמַשְׂבִּיעַ לְכָל־חַי רָצוֹן:

all His ways, and kind in all He does. The LORD is close to all
who call on Him, to all who call on Him in truth. He fulfills
the will of those who revere Him; He hears their cry and saves
them. The LORD guards all who love Him, but all the wicked
He will destroy. ‣ My mouth shall speak the praise of the LORD,
and all creatures shall bless His holy name for ever and all time.

We will bless the LORD now and for ever. Halleluya!   *Ps. 115*

HALF KADDISH

Leader: יִתְגַּדַּל Magnified and sanctified
may His great name be,
in the world He created by His will.
May He establish His kingdom
in your lifetime and in your days,
and in the lifetime of all the house of Israel,
swiftly and soon –
and say: Amen.

All: May His great name be blessed
for ever and all time.

Leader: Blessed and praised,
glorified and exalted,
raised and honored,
uplifted and lauded
be the name of the Holy One,
blessed be He,
beyond any blessing,
song, praise and consolation
uttered in the world –
and say: Amen.

צַדִּיק יהוה בְּכָל־דְּרָכָיו, וְחָסִיד בְּכָל־מַעֲשָׂיו:

קָרוֹב יהוה לְכָל־קֹרְאָיו, לְכֹל אֲשֶׁר יִקְרָאֻהוּ בֶאֱמֶת:

רְצוֹן־יְרֵאָיו יַעֲשֶׂה, וְאֶת־שַׁוְעָתָם יִשְׁמַע, וְיוֹשִׁיעֵם:

שׁוֹמֵר יהוה אֶת־כָּל־אֹהֲבָיו, וְאֵת כָּל־הָרְשָׁעִים יַשְׁמִיד:

‹ תְּהִלַּת יהוה יְדַבֶּר־פִּי, וִיבָרֵךְ כָּל־בָּשָׂר שֵׁם קָדְשׁוֹ לְעוֹלָם וָעֶד:

וַאֲנַחְנוּ נְבָרֵךְ יָהּ מֵעַתָּה וְעַד־עוֹלָם, הַלְלוּיָהּ:

תהלים קטו

חצי קדיש

שׁ״ץ: יִתְגַּדַּל וְיִתְקַדַּשׁ שְׁמֵהּ רַבָּא (קהל אָמֵן)

בְּעָלְמָא דִּי בְרָא כִרְעוּתֵהּ

וְיַמְלִיךְ מַלְכוּתֵהּ

בְּחַיֵּיכוֹן וּבְיוֹמֵיכוֹן וּבְחַיֵּי דְכָל בֵּית יִשְׂרָאֵל

בַּעֲגָלָא וּבִזְמַן קָרִיב

וְאִמְרוּ אָמֵן. (קהל אָמֵן)

קהל יְהֵא שְׁמֵהּ רַבָּא מְבָרַךְ לְעָלַם וּלְעָלְמֵי עָלְמַיָּא.
וש״ץ:

שׁ״ץ: יִתְבָּרַךְ וְיִשְׁתַּבַּח וְיִתְפָּאַר וְיִתְרוֹמַם וְיִתְנַשֵּׂא

וְיִתְהַדָּר וְיִתְעַלֶּה וְיִתְהַלָּל

שְׁמֵהּ דְּקֻדְשָׁא בְּרִיךְ הוּא (קהל בְּרִיךְ הוּא)

לְעֵלָּא מִן כָּל בִּרְכָתָא וְשִׁירָתָא

תֻּשְׁבְּחָתָא וְנֶחֱמָתָא

דַּאֲמִירָן בְּעָלְמָא

וְאִמְרוּ אָמֵן. (קהל אָמֵן)

THE AMIDA

The following prayer, until "in former years" on page 458, is said silently, standing
with feet together. If there is a minyan, the Amida is repeated aloud by the Leader.
Take three steps forward and at the points indicated by ˙, bend the knees at the
first word, bow at the second, and stand straight before saying God's name.

When I proclaim the LORD's name, give glory to our God.   *Deut. 32*

O LORD, open my lips, so that my mouth may declare Your praise.   *Ps. 51*

PATRIARCHS

˙בָּרוּךְ Blessed are You, LORD our God and God of our fathers,
God of Abraham, God of Isaac and God of Jacob;
the great, mighty and awesome God, God Most High,
who bestows acts of loving-kindness and creates all,
who remembers the loving-kindness of the fathers
and will bring a Redeemer to their children's children
for the sake of His name, in love.
King, Helper, Savior, Shield:
˙Blessed are You, LORD, Shield of Abraham.

DIVINE MIGHT

אַתָּה גִּבּוֹר You are eternally mighty, LORD.
You give life to the dead and have great power to save.

In Israel: He causes the dew to fall.

He sustains the living with loving-kindness,
and with great compassion revives the dead.
He supports the fallen, heals the sick,
sets captives free,
and keeps His faith with those who sleep in the dust.
Who is like You, Master of might,
and to whom can You be compared,
O King who brings death and gives life,
and makes salvation grow?
Faithful are You to revive the dead.
Blessed are You, LORD, who revives the dead.

עמידה

The following prayer, until קְדֻשָּׁה *on page 459, is said silently, standing with feet together. If there is a* מִנְיָן, *the* עמידה *is repeated aloud by the* שְׁלִיחַ צִבּוּר. *Take three steps forward and at the points indicated by* ׳, *bend the knees at the first word, bow at the second, and stand straight before saying God's name.*

דברים לב

תהלים נא

כִּי שֵׁם יהוה אֶקְרָא, הָבוּ גֹדֶל לֵאלֹהֵינוּ:

אֲדֹנָי, שְׂפָתַי תִּפְתָּח, וּפִי יַגִּיד תְּהִלָּתֶךָ:

אבות

יבָּרוּךְ אַתָּה יהוה, אֱלֹהֵינוּ וֵאלֹהֵי אֲבוֹתֵינוּ

אֱלֹהֵי אַבְרָהָם, אֱלֹהֵי יִצְחָק, וֵאלֹהֵי יַעֲקֹב

הָאֵל הַגָּדוֹל הַגִּבּוֹר וְהַנּוֹרָא, אֵל עֶלְיוֹן

גּוֹמֵל חֲסָדִים טוֹבִים, וְקֹנֵה הַכֹּל, וְזוֹכֵר חַסְדֵי אָבוֹת

וּמֵבִיא גוֹאֵל לִבְנֵי בְנֵיהֶם לְמַעַן שְׁמוֹ בְּאַהֲבָה.

מֶלֶךְ עוֹזֵר וּמוֹשִׁיעַ וּמָגֵן.

יבָּרוּךְ אַתָּה יהוה, מָגֵן אַבְרָהָם.

גבורות

אַתָּה גִּבּוֹר לְעוֹלָם, אֲדֹנָי

מְחַיֵּה מֵתִים אַתָּה, רַב לְהוֹשִׁיעַ

בארץ ישראל: מוֹרִיד הַטָּל

מְכַלְכֵּל חַיִּים בְּחֶסֶד, מְחַיֵּה מֵתִים בְּרַחֲמִים רַבִּים

סוֹמֵךְ נוֹפְלִים, וְרוֹפֵא חוֹלִים, וּמַתִּיר אֲסוּרִים

וּמְקַיֵּם אֱמוּנָתוֹ לִישֵׁנֵי עָפָר.

מִי כָמוֹךָ, בַּעַל גְּבוּרוֹת, וּמִי דּוֹמֶה לָּךְ

מֶלֶךְ, מֵמִית וּמְחַיֶּה וּמַצְמִיחַ יְשׁוּעָה.

וְנֶאֱמָן אַתָּה לְהַחֲיוֹת מֵתִים.

בָּרוּךְ אַתָּה יהוה, מְחַיֵּה הַמֵּתִים.

When saying the Amida silently, continue with "You are holy" below.

KEDUSHA

> *During the Leader's Repetition, the following is said standing with feet together, rising on the toes at the words indicated by ⌃.*

Cong. then
Leader:
נְקַדֵּשׁ We will sanctify Your name on earth,
as they sanctify it in the highest heavens,
as is written by Your prophet,
"And they [the angels] call to one another saying: *Is. 6*

Cong. then
Leader:
⌃Holy, ⌃holy, ⌃holy is the LORD of hosts
the whole world is filled with His glory."
Those facing them say "Blessed – "

Cong. then
Leader:
⌃"Blessed is the LORD's glory from His place."   *Ezek. 3*
And in Your holy Writings it is written thus:

Cong. then
Leader:
⌃"The LORD shall reign for ever. He is your God, Zion,   *Ps. 146*
from generation to generation, Halleluya!"

Leader:
From generation to generation we will declare Your greatness,
and we will proclaim Your holiness for evermore.
Your praise, our God, shall not leave our mouth forever,
for You, God, are a great and holy King.
Blessed are You, LORD,
the holy God.

> *The Leader continues with "You grace humanity" below.*

HOLINESS

אַתָּה קָדוֹשׁ You are holy and Your name is holy,
and holy ones praise You daily, Selah!
Blessed are You, LORD, the holy God.

KNOWLEDGE

אַתָּה חוֹנֵן You grace humanity with knowledge
and teach mortals understanding.
Grace us with the knowledge, understanding
and discernment that come from You.
Blessed are You, LORD, who graciously grants knowledge.

When saying the עמידה *silently, continue with* אַתָּה קָדוֹשׁ *below*

קדושה

During the חזרת הש״ץ, *the following is said standing*
with feet together, rising on the toes at the words indicated by ‎ ‎.

קהל
then
ש״ץ

נְקַדֵּשׁ אֶת שִׁמְךָ בָּעוֹלָם, כְּשֵׁם שֶׁמַּקְדִּישִׁים אוֹתוֹ בִּשְׁמֵי מָרוֹם

ישעיהו

כַּכָּתוּב עַל יַד נְבִיאֶךָ: וְקָרָא זֶה אֶל־זֶה וְאָמַר

קהל
then
ש״ץ

‎קָדוֹשׁ, קָדוֹשׁ, קָדוֹשׁ, יהוה צְבָאוֹת, מְלֹא כָל־הָאָרֶץ כְּבוֹדוֹ:
לְעֻמָּתָם בָּרוּךְ יֹאמֵרוּ

יחזקאל ג

קהל
then
ש״ץ

‎בָּרוּךְ כְּבוֹד־יהוה מִמְּקוֹמוֹ:
וּבְדִבְרֵי קָדְשְׁךָ כָּתוּב לֵאמֹר

תהלים קמו

קהל
then
ש״ץ

‎יִמְלֹךְ יהוה לְעוֹלָם, אֱלֹהַיִךְ צִיּוֹן לְדֹר וָדֹר, הַלְלוּיָהּ:

ש״ץ:

לְדוֹר וָדוֹר נַגִּיד גָּדְלֶךָ, וּלְנֵצַח נְצָחִים קְדֻשָּׁתְךָ נַקְדִּישׁ
וְשִׁבְחֲךָ אֱלֹהֵינוּ מִפִּינוּ לֹא יָמוּשׁ לְעוֹלָם וָעֶד
כִּי אֵל מֶלֶךְ גָּדוֹל וְקָדוֹשׁ אָתָּה.
בָּרוּךְ אַתָּה יהוה, הָאֵל הַקָּדוֹשׁ.

The שליח ציבור *continues with* אַתָּה חוֹנֵן *below.*

קדושת השם

אַתָּה קָדוֹשׁ וְשִׁמְךָ קָדוֹשׁ
וּקְדוֹשִׁים בְּכָל יוֹם יְהַלְלוּךָ סֶּלָה.
בָּרוּךְ אַתָּה יהוה, הָאֵל הַקָּדוֹשׁ.

דעת

אַתָּה חוֹנֵן לְאָדָם דַּעַת, וּמְלַמֵּד לֶאֱנוֹשׁ בִּינָה.
חָנֵּנוּ מֵאִתְּךָ דֵּעָה בִּינָה וְהַשְׂכֵּל.
בָּרוּךְ אַתָּה יהוה, חוֹנֵן הַדָּעַת.

REPENTANCE

הֲשִׁיבֵנוּ Bring us back, our Father, to Your Torah.
Draw us near, our King, to Your service.
Lead us back to You in perfect repentance.
Blessed are You, LORD,
who desires repentance.

FORGIVENESS

Strike the left side of the chest at °.

סְלַח לָנוּ Forgive us, our Father, for we have °sinned.
Pardon us, our King, for we have °transgressed;
for You pardon and forgive.
Blessed are You, LORD,
the gracious One who repeatedly forgives.

REDEMPTION

רְאֵה Look on our affliction, plead our cause,
and redeem us soon for Your name's sake,
for You are a powerful Redeemer.
Blessed are You, LORD,
the Redeemer of Israel.

I am the LORD their God" (*Vayikra* 26:44). Our redemptive experience isn't limited to decisive shifts in history and supernatural homecomings to Israel. That our people have survived for close to two thousand years without a land is a great miracle of history. Throughout this period we faced unparalleled hatred and hostility. Without HaKadosh Barukh Hu *redeeming* us, we would long since have disappeared. When Shmuel the *Amora* taught the story of Esther, he introduced the discussion by citing the above verse. He reminded his students that even miraculous divine intervention which *doesn't* directly enable a return to Israel is a redemptive stage. Our ultimate return to Israel is an extension of the redemptive history we have experienced since we left Yerushalayim. Quantum leaps such as the formation of the modern State cannot be divorced from the larger dynamic of Jewish history throughout the ages.

תשובה

הֲשִׁיבֵנוּ אָבִינוּ לְתוֹרָתֶךָ
וְקָרְבֵנוּ מַלְכֵּנוּ לַעֲבוֹדָתֶךָ
וְהַחֲזִירֵנוּ בִּתְשׁוּבָה שְׁלֵמָה לְפָנֶיךָ.
בָּרוּךְ אַתָּה יהוה, הָרוֹצֶה בִּתְשׁוּבָה.

סליחה

Strike the left side of the chest at °.

סְלַח לָנוּ אָבִינוּ כִּי °חָטָאנוּ
מְחַל לָנוּ מַלְכֵּנוּ כִּי °פָשָׁעְנוּ
כִּי מוֹחֵל וְסוֹלֵחַ אָתָּה.
בָּרוּךְ אַתָּה יהוה, חַנּוּן הַמַּרְבֶּה לִסְלֹחַ.

גאולה

רְאֵה בְעָנְיֵנוּ, וְרִיבָה רִיבֵנוּ
וּגְאָלֵנוּ מְהֵרָה לְמַעַן שְׁמֶךָ
כִּי גּוֹאֵל חָזָק אָתָּה.
בָּרוּךְ אַתָּה יהוה, גּוֹאֵל יִשְׂרָאֵל.

גאולה *Redemption.* The seventh *berakha* of the *Shemoneh Esreh* is a prayer for redemption. Though the *berakha* itself asks for ultimate redemption, its conclusion may refer to non-messianic redemptions. Rashi (*Megilla* 17b) claims that the conclusion doesn't refer to our final redemption – those messianic events are addressed in subsequent *berakhot* regarding the rebuilding of Yerushalayim, reconstruction of the *Mikdash*, and revival of the Jewish monarchy. Instead this *berakha* addresses the innumerable moments in history when HaKadosh Barukh Hu protected the Jewish people.

When describing our expulsion from Israel, the Torah assures us "when they are in the land of their enemies, I will not spurn them, neither will I abhor them so as to destroy them utterly and break My covenant with them, for

HEALING

רְפָאֵנוּ Heal us, LORD, and we shall be healed.
Save us and we shall be saved,
for You are our praise.
Bring complete recovery for all our ailments,

The following prayer for a sick person may be said here:
May it be Your will, O LORD my God and God of my ancestors, that You
speedily send a complete recovery from heaven, a healing of both soul and
body, to the patient (*name*), son/daughter of (*mother's name*) among the
other afflicted of Israel.

---

for You, God, King, are a faithful and compassionate Healer.
Blessed are You, LORD, Healer of the sick of His people Israel.

PROSPERITY

בָּרֵךְ Bless this year for us, LORD our God,
and all its types of produce for good.
Grant blessing on the face of the earth,
and from its goodness satisfy us,
blessing our year as the best of years.
Blessed are You, LORD, who blesses the years.

---

toward Yerushalayim to explore the culture and religion of their hosts. Upon
arriving in Yerushalayim and witnessing the unified Jewish commitment to
monotheism, they were enchanted and chose to convert. Zevulun's business
acumen attracted fellow merchants to our culture and exposed them to the
beauty of our people and our religion.

We have fortunately witnessed a revival of this phenomenon. The State
of Israel has become, with God's help, an economic superpower attracting
investment from across the globe. Although the initial interest in our state
is commercial, the entire world is exposed to a democracy which respects
human rights and enjoys a rich cultural fabric. We have once again been able
to parlay our commercial success into historical and cultural influence. May
we merit witnessing this influence wielded on behalf of religious and moral
transformation as well.

רפואה

רְפָאֵנוּ יהוה וְנֵרָפֵא, הוֹשִׁיעֵנוּ וְנִוָּשֵׁעָה, כִּי תְהִלָּתֵנוּ אָתָּה
וְהַעֲלֵה רְפוּאָה שְׁלֵמָה לְכָל מַכּוֹתֵינוּ

The following prayer for a sick person may be said here:

יְהִי רָצוֹן מִלְּפָנֶיךָ יהוה אֱלֹהַי וֵאלֹהֵי אֲבוֹתַי, שֶׁתִּשְׁלַח מְהֵרָה רְפוּאָה שְׁלֵמָה
מִן הַשָּׁמַיִם רְפוּאַת הַנֶּפֶשׁ וּרְפוּאַת הַגּוּף לַחוֹלֶה/לַחוֹלָה *name of patient*
בֶּן/בַּת *mother's name* בְּתוֹךְ שְׁאָר חוֹלֵי יִשְׂרָאֵל.

כִּי אֵל מֶלֶךְ רוֹפֵא נֶאֱמָן וְרַחֲמָן אָתָּה.
בָּרוּךְ אַתָּה יהוה, רוֹפֵא חוֹלֵי עַמּוֹ יִשְׂרָאֵל.

ברכת השנים

בָּרֵךְ עָלֵינוּ יהוה אֱלֹהֵינוּ אֶת הַשָּׁנָה הַזֹּאת
וְאֶת כָּל מִינֵי תְבוּאָתָהּ, לְטוֹבָה
וְתֵן בְּרָכָה עַל פְּנֵי הָאֲדָמָה
וְשַׂבְּעֵנוּ מִטּוּבָהּ
וּבָרֵךְ שְׁנָתֵנוּ כַּשָּׁנִים הַטּוֹבוֹת.
בָּרוּךְ אַתָּה יהוה, מְבָרֵךְ הַשָּׁנִים.

THE ZEVULUN EFFECT

וְתֵן בְּרָכָה עַל פְּנֵי הָאֲדָמָה... וּבָרֵךְ שְׁנָתֵנוּ כַּשָּׁנִים הַטּוֹבוֹת *Grant blessing on the face of the earth... blessing our year as the best of years.* Economic prosperity is coveted to enable both national welfare and religious pursuits. However national economic prosperity can also advance our international agenda of reshaping the world in the image of God. The Midrash speaks of the tribe of Zevulun, whose members resided by the sea and were ocean farers. Their maritime commercial activity attracted many ancient traders from neighboring countries, who landed at the coastal sea-ports of Israel. Having docked, their curiosity about the Jewish people was stoked, and they traveled easterly

INGATHERING OF EXILES

תְּקַע Sound the great shofar for our freedom,
raise high the banner to gather our exiles,
and gather us together from the four quarters of the earth.
Blessed are You, LORD,
who gathers the dispersed of His people Israel.

JUSTICE

הָשִׁיבָה Restore our judges as at first,
and our counselors as at the beginning,
and remove from us sorrow and sighing.
May You alone, LORD,
reign over us with loving-kindness and compassion,
and vindicate us in justice.
Blessed are You, LORD,
the King who loves righteousness and justice.

וְהָסֵר מִמֶּנּוּ יָגוֹן וַאֲנָחָה *And remove from us sorrow and sighing.* This phrase seems out of place in this *berakha*, which otherwise speaks of the restoration of justice and the reconstruction of the Jewish political system. A variant version of this *berakha* (see Rabbi Barukh Epstein's commentary on *Tefilla, Barukh She'amar*) reads, "You should remove Yavan (Greece) and Edom (Rome)." Greece and Rome posed unique challenges to the Jewish people; they were the first organized and civilized cultures with which Judaism had to contend. Prior to these encounters Judaism had defeated pagan and heathen cultures, but Greece and subsequently Rome were enlightened, culturally advanced nations. Additionally they provided competent and equitable judicial systems which challenged the classic Jewish system.

The Gemara (*Gittin* 88b) derives a Biblical prohibition to litigate in a Gentile court. Generally Gentile courts were religious institutions, and suing in those forums was tantamount to subscribing to their theologies. The encounter with Greece and Rome undoubtedly provided a new and stiff challenge in general. Additionally the temptation to employ their judicial system could have been enticing. The phrase "remove Greece and Rome" is therefore perfectly consistent with the overall theme of the *berakha*: the restoration of Jewish judges and Jewish sovereignty.

קבוץ גלויות

תְּקַע בְּשׁוֹפָר גָּדוֹל לְחֵרוּתֵנוּ, וְשָׂא נֵס לְקַבֵּץ גָּלֻיּוֹתֵינוּ
וְקַבְּצֵנוּ יַחַד מֵאַרְבַּע כַּנְפוֹת הָאָרֶץ.
בָּרוּךְ אַתָּה יהוה, מְקַבֵּץ נִדְחֵי עַמּוֹ יִשְׂרָאֵל.

השבת המשפט

הָשִׁיבָה שׁוֹפְטֵינוּ כְּבָרִאשׁוֹנָה וְיוֹעֲצֵינוּ כְּבַתְּחִלָּה
וְהָסֵר מִמֶּנּוּ יָגוֹן וַאֲנָחָה
וּמְלֹךְ עָלֵינוּ אַתָּה יהוה לְבַדְּךָ בְּחֶסֶד וּבְרַחֲמִים
וְצַדְּקֵנוּ בַּמִּשְׁפָּט.
בָּרוּךְ אַתָּה יהוה, מֶלֶךְ אוֹהֵב צְדָקָה וּמִשְׁפָּט.

APPOINTING JUDGES IN THE LAND OF ISRAEL

The Torah instructs the stationing of courts "in all your towns which the
LORD your God is giving you, according to your tribes, and they shall judge
the people with righteous judgment" (*Devarim* 16:18). Ideally courts should
not be assembled ad hoc by litigants, but should be regionally instituted. As
the text suggests, this mitzva only applies in the Land of Israel. As the Rambam claims, there is no mitzva to organize courts in the Diaspora; if necessary
they can be convened to adjudicate disputes. By contrast the Land of Israel
should be landscaped with courts and judges. In Israel, judges play more than
a purely judicial role. They serve as role models to inspire moral behavior.
Furthermore the courts supervise religious conduct and instill the country
with the values necessary to build a morally and religiously suitable society.
The mitzva to settle the land isn't accomplished by merely living in the land.
The mitzva to settle also mandates that we construct a society characterized
by monotheism and morality, centered upon the *Mikdash* in Yerushalayim.
Some have claimed that this is the reason that the Rambam does not cite
"living in Israel" as one of the 613 commandments. As a meta-mitzva it trick-
les down to many sub-mitzvot, all of which are counted separately. Since it
subsumes so many secondary mitzvot it cannot be counted independently.
The fact that it *isn't* counted renders it *more* important, not less significant,
than mitzvot which are counted.

AGAINST INFORMERS

וְלַמַּלְשִׁינִים For the slanderers let there be no hope,
and may all wickedness perish in an instant.
May all Your people's enemies swiftly be cut down.
May You swiftly uproot, crush, cast down
and humble the arrogant swiftly in our days.
Blessed are You, Lord,
who destroys enemies and humbles the arrogant.

THE RIGHTEOUS

עַל הַצַּדִּיקִים To the righteous, the pious,
the elders of Your people the house of Israel,
the remnant of their scholars,
the righteous converts, and to us,
may Your compassion be aroused, Lord our God.
Grant a good reward to all who sincerely trust in Your name.
Set our lot with them,
so that we may never be ashamed, for in You we trust.
Blessed are You, Lord,
who is the support and trust of the righteous.

REBUILDING JERUSALEM

וְלִירוּשָׁלַיִם To Jerusalem, Your city,
may You return in compassion,
and may You dwell in it as You promised.
May You rebuild it rapidly in our days
as an everlasting structure,
and install within it soon the throne of David.
Blessed are You, Lord,
who builds Jerusalem.

בניין ירושלים *Rebuilding Jerusalem.* Though Yerushalayim has often lain desolate and unpopulated, Jews have always recognized it as the epicenter of past Jewish history, and the location which would one day regain its previous

ברכת המינים

וְלַמַּלְשִׁינִים אַל תְּהִי תִקְוָה

וְכָל הָרִשְׁעָה כְּרֶגַע תֹּאבֵד

וְכָל אוֹיְבֵי עַמְּךָ מְהֵרָה יִכָּרֵתוּ

וְהַזֵּדִים מְהֵרָה תְעַקֵּר וּתְשַׁבֵּר וּתְמַגֵּר וְתַכְנִיעַ בִּמְהֵרָה בְיָמֵינוּ.

בָּרוּךְ אַתָּה יהוה, שׁוֹבֵר אוֹיְבִים וּמַכְנִיעַ זֵדִים.

על הצדיקים

עַל הַצַּדִּיקִים וְעַל הַחֲסִידִים

וְעַל זִקְנֵי עַמְּךָ בֵּית יִשְׂרָאֵל

וְעַל פְּלֵיטַת סוֹפְרֵיהֶם, וְעַל גֵּרֵי הַצֶּדֶק, וְעָלֵינוּ

יֶהֱמוּ רַחֲמֶיךָ יהוה אֱלֹהֵינוּ

וְתֵן שָׂכָר טוֹב לְכָל הַבּוֹטְחִים בְּשִׁמְךָ בֶּאֱמֶת

וְשִׂים חֶלְקֵנוּ עִמָּהֶם

וּלְעוֹלָם לֹא נֵבוֹשׁ כִּי בְךָ בָּטָחְנוּ.

בָּרוּךְ אַתָּה יהוה, מִשְׁעָן וּמִבְטָח לַצַּדִּיקִים.

בנין ירושלים

וְלִירוּשָׁלַיִם עִירְךָ בְּרַחֲמִים תָּשׁוּב

וְתִשְׁכֹּן בְּתוֹכָהּ כַּאֲשֶׁר דִּבַּרְתָּ

וּבְנֵה אוֹתָהּ בְּקָרוֹב בְּיָמֵינוּ בִּנְיַן עוֹלָם

וְכִסֵּא דָוִד מְהֵרָה לְתוֹכָהּ תָּכִין.

בָּרוּךְ אַתָּה יהוה, בּוֹנֵה יְרוּשָׁלָיִם.

If this variant existed it was obviously censured at some point due to its being politically inflammatory. During the last millennia other segments of our prayer liturgy were altered or expurgated due to alleged blasphemies.

KINGDOM OF DAVID

אֶת צֶמַח May the offshoot of Your servant David soon flower,
and may his pride be raised high by Your salvation,
for we wait for Your salvation all day.
Blessed are You, LORD,
who makes the glory of salvation flourish.

RESPONSE TO PRAYER

שְׁמַע קוֹלֵנוּ Listen to our voice, LORD our God.
Spare us and have compassion on us,
and in compassion and favor accept our prayer,
for You, God, listen to prayers and pleas.
Do not turn us away, O our King,
empty-handed from Your presence,
for You listen with compassion
to the prayer of Your people Israel.
Blessed are You, LORD,
who listens to prayer.

Seventy years later German Jews were invited directly by Ezra to return to
Israel. They deferred his request by suggesting that Ezra return to the "cen-
tral Yerushalayim" while we will remain in the "smaller Yerushalayim." For
this crime of referring to *any* alternate location as Yerushalayim, German
Jews were destined to suffer disproportionately to Jews in other parts of the
Diaspora.

Unfortunately only approximately 42,000 Jews actually returned with
Ezra to launch the Second *Beit HaMikdash* era. Most remained in Bavel due
to their relative comfort. However the offense of referring to Germany as a
mini-Yerushalayim was intolerable.

MASHIAḤ AND SINNERS

Eliyahu the prophet identifies *Mashiaḥ* as sitting among the poor and dis-
eased, and attending to his bandages (*Sanhedrin* 98a). This image suggests
that one of his roles is to "suffer on behalf of the Jewish people and absorb

משיח בן דוד

אֶת צֶמַח דָּוִד עַבְדְּךָ מְהֵרָה תַצְמִיחַ
וְקַרְנוֹ תָּרוּם בִּישׁוּעָתֶךָ
כִּי לִישׁוּעָתְךָ קִוִּינוּ כָּל הַיּוֹם.
בָּרוּךְ אַתָּה יהוה, מַצְמִיחַ קֶרֶן יְשׁוּעָה.

שומע תפלה

שְׁמַע קוֹלֵנוּ יהוה אֱלֹהֵינוּ, חוּס וְרַחֵם עָלֵינוּ
וְקַבֵּל בְּרַחֲמִים וּבְרָצוֹן אֶת תְּפִלָּתֵנוּ
כִּי אֵל שׁוֹמֵעַ תְּפִלּוֹת וְתַחֲנוּנִים אֶתָּה
וּמִלְּפָנֶיךָ מַלְכֵּנוּ רֵיקָם אַל תְּשִׁיבֵנוּ
כִּי אַתָּה שׁוֹמֵעַ תְּפִלַּת עַמְּךָ יִשְׂרָאֵל בְּרַחֲמִים.
בָּרוּךְ אַתָּה יהוה, שׁוֹמֵעַ תְּפִלָּה.

---

lofty status. Halakhically, prayers are directed towards Yerushalayim which, as Yaakov recognized, constitutes a gateway to Heaven.

Though physically dislocated from Yerushalayim, Jewish hearts and imaginations always remain loyal to our "Great City." The Jerusalem Talmud (Ḥagiga 2:2) records a letter penned from the Jews of Yerushalayim to their brethren in Alexandria. At that point Alexandria had become one of the leading cultural and commercial centers of the ancient world, hosting a thriving Jewish community. Yet the letter opened with a message from the people of "The great city of Yerushalayim to the small town of Alexandria." Despite the empirical conditions, Jews always acknowledged the supremacy of Yerushalayim and its inevitable renewal.

An ominous account is provided by Rabbi Yehoshua Falk, the sixteenth-century super-commentator to the *Shulḥan Arukh*. He quotes a longstanding tradition that Jews were exiled to Germany *during the destruction of the First Beit HaMikdash*. We typically assume that Jews remained within the broader Mediterranean basin, with most being expelled to Bavel and Persia.

TEMPLE SERVICE

רְצֵה Find favor, LORD our God,
in Your people Israel and their prayer.
Restore the service to Your most holy House,
and accept in love and favor
the fire-offerings of Israel and their prayer.
May the service of Your people Israel
always find favor with You.
And may our eyes witness Your return
to Zion in compassion.
Blessed are You, LORD,
who restores His Presence to Zion.

---

of *Torah Shebikhtav* was the positioning of the *Sanhedrin* in a hall incorporated in the *Mikdash* complex. Before the *Torah Shebe'al Peh* was committed to text, the *Sanhedrin* played a more *creative* role in shaping the transmission of Torah. Their judicial role was secondary to their educational one. They convened within the *Mikdash*, which served as the channel for the ongoing delivery of Torah. If they depart the *Mikdash* they abdicate their distinctive status and operate as a common court.

The first descent of *Shekhina* to our world occurred at Sinai. Mass revelation didn't occur independently, but was bound to the delivery of the divine Torah. Rav Soloveitchik claimed that the *Mikdash* – as a shelter for the *Shekhina* – must maintain the original conditions of this first epiphany. For it to accurately re-create this event and contain the *Shekhina* it must also host the continuing evolution of Torah.

Similarly the priests who were tasked with supervising sacrifices and general *Mikdash* rituals were also Torah purveyors. When Moshe blesses the tribe of Levi and awards them with *Mikdash* responsibility he says, "They teach Yaakov Your rules and give Israel Your teachings. They burn incense for You to smell and sacrifice burnt offerings on Your altar" (*Devarim* 33:10). The first part of this verse describes the *Levi'im* as educators of Torah, while the conclusion portrays their *Mikdash* activities. The juxtaposition of these two phrases stresses the integration of Torah delivery and *Mikdash* rituals. In fact every *Sanhedrin* included *Kohanim* and *Levi'im* – without their

עבודה

רְצֵה יהוה אֱלֹהֵינוּ בְּעַמְּךָ יִשְׂרָאֵל, וּבִתְפִלָּתָם
וְהָשֵׁב אֶת הָעֲבוֹדָה לִדְבִיר בֵּיתֶךָ
וְאִשֵּׁי יִשְׂרָאֵל וּתְפִלָּתָם בְּאַהֲבָה תְקַבֵּל בְּרָצוֹן
וּתְהִי לְרָצוֹן תָּמִיד עֲבוֹדַת יִשְׂרָאֵל עַמֶּךָ.
וְתֶחֱזֶינָה עֵינֵינוּ בְּשׁוּבְךָ לְצִיּוֹן בְּרַחֲמִים.
בָּרוּךְ אַתָּה יהוה, הַמַּחֲזִיר שְׁכִינָתוֹ לְצִיּוֹן.

---

some of the affliction intended for them." This portrait is based on the verses in *Yeshayahu*, which provide the following description of *Mashiaḥ*:

> He was despised and rejected by mankind, a man of suffering, and familiar with pain. Like one from whom people hide their faces he was despised, and we held him in low esteem. Surely he took up our pain and bore our suffering, yet we considered him punished by God, stricken by him, and afflicted. (*Yeshayahu* 53:4–5)

The ensuing verses in this chapter suggest that he bears this suffering to atone for our sins, protect us from deserved punishment, and possibly even hasten the redemption. Completing the picture, the Midrash describes *Mashiaḥ* willingly accepting this fate on behalf of his beloved people.

Historically this assignment to *Mashiaḥ* was affected by broader religious thought. With the rise of Christianity and in particular the story of Jesus, the notion of a suffering *Mashiaḥ* was muted within general Jewish discourse. As *Ḥasidut* evolved, the concept of a great leader suffering on behalf of a common sinner became more prevalent. This Messianic image served as precedent for the notion that the torment of a devoted leader can both atone for the sins of the common Jew and mitigate punishment which would otherwise target him.

עבודה *Temple Service.* Classically the *Mikdash* is defined as an epicenter of ritual, and a facility of prayer. Yet the *Mikdash* was also the central conduit of Torah and its continuing evolution. An actual *Sefer Torah* was placed either within the *Aron* or next to it in the Inner Sanctum. Complementing this icon

THANKSGIVING

Bow at the first nine words.

מוֹדִים We give thanks to You,
for You are the LORD our God
and God of our ancestors
for ever and all time.
You are the Rock of our lives,
Shield of our salvation
from generation to generation.
We will thank You and
declare Your praise for our lives,
which are entrusted into Your hand;
for our souls,
which are placed in Your charge;
for Your miracles
which are with us every day;
and for Your wonders and favors
at all times, evening,
morning and midday.
You are good –
for Your compassion never fails.
You are compassionate –
for Your loving-kindnesses
never cease.
We have always
placed our hope in You.

During the Leader's Repetition, the congregation says quietly:
מוֹדִים We give thanks
to You, for You are
the LORD our God
and God of our ancestors,
God of all flesh,
who formed us
and formed the universe.
Blessings and thanks
are due to Your great
and holy name
for giving us life
and sustaining us.
May You continue
to give us life
and sustain us;
and may You gather our
exiles to Your holy courts,
to keep Your decrees,
do Your will and serve You
with a perfect heart,
for it is for us
to give You thanks.
Blessed be God to whom
thanksgiving is due.

A similar dual prayer is voiced at the conclusion of the *Shemoneh Esreh*, in which we pray for the rebuilding of the *Mikdash,* and that HaKadosh Barukh Hu should provide our measure of Torah, and that we should merit the opportunity to perform *avoda.*

הודאה

Bow at the first five words.

מוֹדִים אֲנַחְנוּ לָךְ

שָׁאַתָּה הוּא יהוה אֱלֹהֵינוּ

וֵאלֹהֵי אֲבוֹתֵינוּ לְעוֹלָם וָעֶד.

צוּר חַיֵּינוּ, מָגֵן יִשְׁעֵנוּ

אַתָּה הוּא לְדוֹר וָדוֹר.

נוֹדֶה לְּךָ וּנְסַפֵּר תְּהִלָּתֶךָ

עַל חַיֵּינוּ הַמְּסוּרִים בְּיָדֶךָ

וְעַל נִשְׁמוֹתֵינוּ הַפְּקוּדוֹת לָךְ

וְעַל נִסֶּיךָ שֶׁבְּכָל יוֹם עִמָּנוּ

וְעַל נִפְלְאוֹתֶיךָ וְטוֹבוֹתֶיךָ

שֶׁבְּכָל עֵת

עֶרֶב וָבֹקֶר וְצָהֳרָיִם.

הַטּוֹב, כִּי לֹא כָלוּ רַחֲמֶיךָ

וְהַמְרַחֵם, כִּי לֹא תַמּוּ חֲסָדֶיךָ

מֵעוֹלָם קִוִּינוּ לָךְ.

During the חזרת הש״ץ,
the קהל *says quietly:*

מוֹדִים אֲנַחְנוּ לָךְ
שָׁאַתָּה הוּא יהוה אֱלֹהֵינוּ
וֵאלֹהֵי אֲבוֹתֵינוּ
אֱלֹהֵי כָל בָּשָׂר
יוֹצְרֵנוּ, יוֹצֵר בְּרֵאשִׁית.
בְּרָכוֹת וְהוֹדָאוֹת
לְשִׁמְךָ הַגָּדוֹל וְהַקָּדוֹשׁ
עַל שֶׁהֶחֱיִיתָנוּ וְקִיַּמְתָּנוּ.
כֵּן תְּחַיֵּנוּ וּתְקַיְּמֵנוּ
וְתֶאֱסֹף גָּלֻיּוֹתֵינוּ
לְחַצְרוֹת קָדְשֶׁךָ
לִשְׁמֹר חֻקֶּיךָ
וְלַעֲשׂוֹת רְצוֹנֶךָ וּלְעָבְדְּךָ
בְּלֵבָב שָׁלֵם
עַל שֶׁאֲנַחְנוּ מוֹדִים לָךְ.
בָּרוּךְ אֵל הַהוֹדָאוֹת.

presence the judicial body would have been severed from the *Mikdash* core.

By requesting "Bring us back… to Your Torah. Draw us near… to Your service," we are restating the affiliation between renewed Torah study and reintroduced *Mikdash* ritual (conveyed by the term *avodatekha*). When the *Mikdash* is finally rebuilt, our *avoda* as well as our Torah study will be rejuvenated.

*At this point in the silent Amida it is permitted to add a rabbinically
formulated "Al HaNissim." The following was written by Rabbi Neria
(alternative versions can be found on pages 662–665).*

עַל הַנִּסִּים [We thank You also] for the miracles, the redemption, the mighty
deeds, the salvations, and the victories in battle which You performed for
our ancestors in those days, at this time.

When the armies of the Middle East rose up against Your people Israel
and sought to destroy, slay and exterminate the inhabitants of Your Land,
young and old, children and women, and among them those who had
survived the sword and were saved from the horror of Your enemies' flames,
one from a city, two from a family, hoping to find a resting place for the
soles of their feet in Your land that You had promised them; then You in
Your great compassion stood by us in our time of distress, thwarted their
counsel and frustrated their plans, raised us upright and established our
liberty, championed our cause, judged our claim, avenged our wrong,
delivered the strong into the hands of the weak, the many into the hands of
the few, the impure into the hands of the holy. You made for Yourself great
and holy renown in Your world, and for Your people Israel You performed

---

which mitzva performance is impossible, a person is excused based on the
ones (אונס) exemption. The same author, in a response, cites a different reason for his opposition to *aliya* – the danger of traveling to Israel. This practical concern of *Pikuaḥ Nefesh* (preservation of life) is more often cited in his
name, and was frequently implemented as an argument against immigration
to Israel (see *Pitḥei Teshuva Even HaEzer* 75:6).

Fortunately, in the modern State of Israel, most land-based mitzvot –
though complicated – can be strictly maintained. The mitzva which remains
a big challenge (at least at a national level) is *Shemitta*. Collapsing the entire
agricultural sector once every seven years is hardly feasible, and is certainly
not the preference of an industry which is still driven by many secular Jews.

This *Shemitta* challenge was even more overwhelming in the latter part of
the nineteenth century, as the first *moshavot* (agriculture-based communities)
were established. The first *moshavot* included Petaḥ Tikva, Rosh Pina, Rishon
LeTziyon, Zikhron Yaakov, Nes Tziyona and Reḥovot. As these were formed,
beginning in the year 1882, the first *Shemitta* of 1889 posed existential challenges; without a halakhic solution, the entire enterprise of Jewish settlement
would fail. The question was referred to halakhic authorities in Russia, many

At this point in the silent עמידה it is permitted to add a rabbinically
formulated עַל הַנִּסִּים. The following was written by Rabbi Neria
(alternative versions can be found on pages 662–665).

עַל הַנִּסִּים וְעַל הַפֻּרְקָן וְעַל הַגְּבוּרוֹת וְעַל הַתְּשׁוּעוֹת וְעַל הַמִּלְחָמוֹת
שֶׁעָשִׂיתָ לַאֲבוֹתֵינוּ בַּיָּמִים הָהֵם בַּזְּמַן הַזֶּה.

כְּשֶׁעָמְדוּ צִבְאוֹת עֲרָב עַל עַמְּךָ יִשְׂרָאֵל, וּבִקְשׁוּ לְהַשְׁמִיד לַהֲרֹג וּלְאַבֵּד אֶת
יוֹשְׁבֵי אַרְצֶךָ, מִנַּעַר וְעַד זָקֵן טַף וְנָשִׁים, וּבָהֶם עַם שְׂרִידֵי חֶרֶב אֲשֶׁר נִצְּלוּ מִתַּפַּת
הָאֵשׁ שֶׁל שׂוֹנְאֶיךָ, אֶחָד מֵעִיר וּשְׁנַיִם מִמִּשְׁפָּחָה, וְשָׁבוּ לִמְצֹא מָנוֹחַ לְכַף
רַגְלָם בְּאַרְצְךָ אֲשֶׁר הִבְטַחְתָּ לָהֶם. וְאַתָּה בְּרַחֲמֶיךָ הָרַבִּים עָמַדְתָּ לָנוּ
בְּעֵת צָרָתֵנוּ, הֵפַרְתָּ אֶת עֲצָתָם וְקִלְקַלְתָּ אֶת מַחֲשַׁבְתָּם, זָקַפְתָּ קוֹמָתֵנוּ
וְקוֹמַמְתָּ אֶת חֻרְבוֹתֵינוּ, רַבְתָּ אֶת רִיבֵנוּ, דַּנְתָּ אֶת דִּינֵנוּ, נָקַמְתָּ אֶת נִקְמָתֵנוּ,
מָסַרְתָּ רַבִּים בְּיַד מְעַטִּים, טְמֵאִים בְּיַד קְדוֹשִׁים, וְעָשִׂיתָ לְךָ שֵׁם גָּדוֹל
וְקָדוֹשׁ בְּעוֹלָמֶךָ, וּלְעַמְּךָ יִשְׂרָאֵל עָשִׂיתָ תְּשׁוּעָה גְדוֹלָה וּפֻרְקָן כְּהַיּוֹם הַזֶּה,

AL HANISSIM

For a discussion on the addition of *Al HaNissim* to the silent Amida, see
page 95.

HALAKHIC COMPLEXITY OF LIVING IN ISRAEL

From among the 613 mitzvot, some are classified as "*teluyot baAretz*," and only
apply in Israel. Living in Israel affords an encounter with additional mitzvot
which don't apply, or are practiced rabbinically, outside of Israel. The Gemara
(*Sota* 14a) depicts Moshe Rabbeinu's desperation to enter the Land of Israel
– in part because of the opportunity to fulfill additional mitzvot.

In a very provocative statement, one of the well-known twelfth-century
Tosafists argued *against* immigrating to Israel due to the added risk of halakhic infractions. His comments are cited in a Tosafot in *Ketubot* (110b) and
reflect a period of sparse and economically challenging Jewish settlement in
Israel. Under those conditions, many unique mitzvot of Israel were difficult
to maintain and he argued against *aliya*. Most authorities didn't accept his
opinion. Presumably, the importance of living in Israel would offset the potential halakhic hazards of life in Israel. Extra mitzvot, though challenging,
provide additional opportunities to fulfill divine will. Under conditions in

a great salvation and redemption as of this day. You subjugated peoples under us, nations beneath our feet, and You gave us our inheritance, the Land of Canaan to its borders, and returned us to the place of Your holy Sanctuary.

(In the same way, make us a miracle and a glorious wonder, thwart the counsel of our enemies, have us prosper in the pastures of our Land, and gather in our scattered ones from the four corners of the earth, and we will rejoice in the rebuilding of Your city and in the establishment of Your Sanctuary and in the flourishing of the pride of Your servant David, speedily in our days, and we will give thanks to Your great name.)

Continue with "For all these things."

וְעַל כֻּלָּם For all these things may Your name be blessed and exalted, our King, continually, for ever and all time.
Let all that lives thank You, Selah!
and praise Your name in truth,
God, our Savior and Help, Selah!
ˎBlessed are You, LORD,
whose name is "the Good"
and to whom thanks are due.

Barukh Hu instructs him to remain in Israel by employing an intriguing verb: "The LORD appeared to Yitzhak and said, 'Do not go down to Egypt; settle (*shekhon*) in the land where I tell you to live'" (*Bereshit* 26:2).

The verb *shekhon* directs Yitzhak to settle, but can also refer to the related noun *shekhuna*, society. His mission included not only remaining in the land, but also constructing permanent societies. We have records of his agricultural activity, but his interactions with coastal tribes of Pelishtim suggest a broader range of involvement. Many have commented on a third implication of the word *shekhon* – *Shekhina* or *Presence of God*. By securing communal life in Israel – as connoted by the term *shekhuna* – the actual *Shekhina* becomes entrenched.

What is implicit in the experiences of his predecessors is explicit in the account of Yaakov. After returning from his first exile in Lavan's house, he encounters his first opportunity to embed himself in the land and landscape

הִדְבַּרְתָּ עַמִּים תַּחְתֵּנוּ וּלְאֻמִּים תַּחַת רַגְלֵנוּ, וַתִּתֶּן לָנוּ אֶת נַחֲלָתֵנוּ, אֶרֶץ
כְּנַעַן לִגְבוּלוֹתֶיהָ, וַהֲחֵזַרְתָּנוּ אֶל מְקוֹם מִקְדַּשׁ הֵיכָלֶךָ.

(כֵּן עֲשֵׂה עִמָּנוּ נֵס וָפֶלֶא לְטוֹבָה, הָפֵר עֲצַת אוֹיְבֵינוּ, וְדַשְּׁנוּ בִּנְאוֹת אַרְצֶךָ,
וּנְפוּצוֹתֵינוּ מֵאַרְבַּע כַּנְפוֹת הָאָרֶץ תְּקַבֵּץ, וְנִשְׂמַח בְּבִנְיַן עִירֶךָ וּבְתִקּוּן
הֵיכָלֶךָ וּבִצְמִיחַת קֶרֶן לְדָוִד עַבְדֶּךָ בִּמְהֵרָה בְיָמֵינוּ, וְנוֹדֶה לְשִׁמְךָ הַגָּדוֹל).

Continue with וְעַל כֻּלָּם.

וְעַל כֻּלָּם יִתְבָּרַךְ וְיִתְרוֹמַם שִׁמְךָ מַלְכֵּנוּ תָּמִיד לְעוֹלָם וָעֶד.
וְכֹל הַחַיִּים יוֹדְוּךָ סֶלָה, וִיהַלְלוּ אֶת שִׁמְךָ בֶּאֱמֶת
הָאֵל יְשׁוּעָתֵנוּ וְעֶזְרָתֵנוּ סֶלָה.
בָּרוּךְ אַתָּה יהוה, הַטּוֹב שִׁמְךָ וּלְךָ נָאֶה לְהוֹדוֹת.

---

of whom suggested a *heter mekhira* as a loophole to circumvent *Shemitta*. By
selling the land to non-Jews, the land no longer possesses its sanctity, and
Shemitta laws do not apply. Many opposed this loophole, and refused to abide
by its leniencies. After his *aliya* in 1904, Rav Kook supported this halakhic
accommodation, and the institution of *heter mekhira* is commonly associated
with him even though it was developed decades before his arrival.

ESTABLISHING COMMUNITIES IN ISRAEL

A famous dispute between the Ramban and the Rambam surrounds the question of whether living in Israel is actually a formal mitzva. The *pasuk* which
the Ramban invokes to prove it is a mitzva, "Take possession of the land and
settle in it, for I have given you the land to possess" (*Bemidbar* 33:53), suggests
a compound mitzva. To completely fulfill the commandment, the land must
be conquered but also settled. Presumably all the conditions necessary for
viable living entail part of the mitzva.

All of the *Avot* were involved in developing the larger infrastructure necessary to create sustainable communities in Israel. Avraham establishes an
Eshel (*Bereshit* 21:33) which is generally assumed to be a retreat for weary
travelers as well as spiritual seekers. For his part Yitzḥak was instructed to
remain in Israel – in part to help build maintainable communities. HaKadosh

PEACE

שָׁלוֹם רָב Grant great peace to Your people Israel for ever,
for You are the sovereign LORD of all peace;
and may it be good in Your eyes
to bless Your people Israel
at every time, at every hour, with Your peace.
Blessed are You, LORD,
who blesses His people Israel with peace.

The following verse concludes the Leader's Repetition of the Amida.
Some also say it here as part of the silent Amida.

May the words of my mouth and the meditation of my heart   Ps. 19
find favor before You, LORD, my Rock and Redeemer.

---

flicts and military crusades. Unfortunately we have yet to merit international
acceptance of our historical role and our station in the Land of Israel. We have
been involuntarily compelled to once again be a nation of warriors battling
on behalf of HaKadosh Barukh Hu and our Land. This is not our ideal, nor
our dream for a messianic conclusion. The final Mishna in the entire Talmud
cites Rabbi Shimon ben Ḥalafta: "The greatest endowment God offers the
Jewish people is a state of peace, as the verse exclaims, 'The LORD gives
strength to His people; the LORD blesses His people with peace' (*Tehillim*
29:11)."

Not only is our religion predicated upon the pursuit of peace, but our
image of God is merciful and compassionate. Commenting on the fact
that to save a life, almost all prohibitions must be violated, the Rambam
says "this [prioritization of life] stresses that the agenda of the Torah isn't
vengeance or death, but compassion, kindness, and peace (*rahamim, hesed,
veshalom*).

Sadly the divine image has always been tarnished by those who indis-
criminately murder in the name of religion, and portray a god who is angry
and celebrates human suffering. This vandalizing of the divine image is
tantamount to heresy; distorting the true features of God is equivalent to
denying His presence.

As we struggle toward the messianic endpoint of universal peace we are required to lift a sword. This imposition cannot obscure our ultimate objective.

ברכת שלום

שָׁלוֹם רָב עַל יִשְׂרָאֵל עַמְּךָ תָּשִׂים לְעוֹלָם
כִּי אַתָּה הוּא מֶלֶךְ אָדוֹן לְכָל הַשָּׁלוֹם.
וְטוֹב בְּעֵינֶיךָ לְבָרֵךְ אֶת עַמְּךָ יִשְׂרָאֵל
בְּכָל עֵת וּבְכָל שָׁעָה בִּשְׁלוֹמֶךָ.
בָּרוּךְ אַתָּה יהוה, הַמְבָרֵךְ אֶת עַמּוֹ יִשְׂרָאֵל בַּשָּׁלוֹם.

The following verse concludes the חזרת הש״ץ.
Some also say it here as part of the silent עמידה.

תהלים יט יִהְיוּ לְרָצוֹן אִמְרֵי־פִי וְהֶגְיוֹן לִבִּי לְפָנֶיךָ, יהוה צוּרִי וְגֹאֲלִי:

---

of Israel. The Torah describes his first efforts: "He arrived safely at the city of Shekhem in Canaan and camped (*vayiḥan*) within sight of the city. For a hundred pieces of silver, he bought from the sons of Ḥamor, the father of Shekhem, the plot of ground where he pitched his tent" (*Bereshit* 33:18–19). The term *vayiḥan* (literally to collaborate) suggests behavior beyond legal acquisition. Ḥazal (*Bereshit Raba* 79:6) claim that he launched commercial activity with the local populations. The ensuing narrative of Dina's rape demonstrates how valued his trade was considered. The prospect of commercial interaction persuaded the residents of Shekhem to enter what would ultimately prove to be a failed union.

THE GIFT OF PEACE

Upon our first entry into the Land of Israel we were instructed to battle thirty-one pagan tribes. The land could not withstand the moral degeneracy and idolatrous confusion which were introduced by these barbaric races. The path to monotheism demanded their elimination or relocation. Once the presence of HaKadosh Barukh Hu was established, however, a period of peace and serenity was set to flourish. The Jewish redemptive narrative is not pivoted on warlike aggression toward our enemies or those who still fail to acknowledge the presence of God. Even the eschatological wars described by the prophets are defensive in nature, directed solely against our aggressors and generally waged primarily by God Himself.

Unlike many religious cultures, Judaism isn't pitched upon violent con-

אֱלֹהַי My God,

*Berakhot
17a*

guard my tongue from evil and my lips from deceitful speech.
To those who curse me, let my soul be silent;
may my soul be to all like the dust.
Open my heart to Your Torah and let my soul
pursue Your commandments.
As for all who plan evil against me,
swiftly thwart their counsel and frustrate their plans.

Act for the sake of Your name;
act for the sake of Your right hand;
act for the sake of Your holiness;
act for the sake of Your Torah.

That Your beloved ones may be delivered,

Ps. 60

save with Your right hand and answer me.

May the words of my mouth and the meditation of my heart

Ps. 19

find favor before You, LORD, my Rock and Redeemer.

Bow, take three steps back, then bow, first left, then right, then center, while saying:

May He who makes peace in His high places,
make peace for us and all Israel –
and say: Amen.

יְהִי רָצוֹן May it be Your will, LORD our God and God of our ancestors,
that the Temple be rebuilt speedily in our days,
and grant us a share in Your Torah.
And there we will serve You with reverence,
as in the days of old and as in former years.
Then the offering of Judah and Jerusalem

Mal. 3

will be pleasing to the LORD
as in the days of old and as in former years.

אֱלֹהַי

נְצֹר לְשׁוֹנִי מֵרָע וּשְׂפָתַי מִדַּבֵּר מִרְמָה

וְלִמְקַלְלַי נַפְשִׁי תִדֹּם, וְנַפְשִׁי כֶּעָפָר לַכֹּל תִּהְיֶה.

פְּתַח לִבִּי בְּתוֹרָתֶךָ, וּבְמִצְוֹתֶיךָ תִּרְדּוֹף נַפְשִׁי.

וְכָל הַחוֹשְׁבִים עָלַי רָעָה

מְהֵרָה הָפֵר עֲצָתָם וְקַלְקֵל מַחֲשַׁבְתָּם.

עֲשֵׂה לְמַעַן שְׁמֶךָ

עֲשֵׂה לְמַעַן יְמִינֶךָ

עֲשֵׂה לְמַעַן קְדֻשָּׁתֶךָ

עֲשֵׂה לְמַעַן תּוֹרָתֶךָ.

תהלים ס — לְמַעַן יֵחָלְצוּן יְדִידֶיךָ, הוֹשִׁיעָה יְמִינְךָ וַעֲנֵנִי:

תהלים יט — יִהְיוּ לְרָצוֹן אִמְרֵי־פִי וְהֶגְיוֹן לִבִּי לְפָנֶיךָ, יהוה צוּרִי וְגֹאֲלִי:

Bow, take three steps back, then bow, first left, then right, then center, while saying:

עֹשֶׂה שָׁלוֹם בִּמְרוֹמָיו

הוּא יַעֲשֶׂה שָׁלוֹם עָלֵינוּ וְעַל כָּל יִשְׂרָאֵל,

וְאִמְרוּ אָמֵן.

יְהִי רָצוֹן מִלְּפָנֶיךָ יהוה אֱלֹהֵינוּ וֵאלֹהֵי אֲבוֹתֵינוּ

שֶׁיִּבָּנֶה בֵּית הַמִּקְדָּשׁ בִּמְהֵרָה בְיָמֵינוּ,

וְתֵן חֶלְקֵנוּ בְּתוֹרָתֶךָ

וְשָׁם נַעֲבָדְךָ בְּיִרְאָה כִּימֵי עוֹלָם וּכְשָׁנִים קַדְמֹנִיּוֹת.

מלאכי ג — וְעָרְבָה לַיהוה מִנְחַת יְהוּדָה וִירוּשָׁלָ͏ִם כִּימֵי עוֹלָם וּכְשָׁנִים קַדְמֹנִיּוֹת:

FULL KADDISH

Leader: יִתְגַּדַּל Magnified and sanctified
may His great name be,
in the world He created by His will.
May He establish His kingdom
in your lifetime and in your days,
and in the lifetime of all the house of Israel,
swiftly and soon –
and say: Amen.

All: May His great name be blessed for ever and all time.

Leader: Blessed and praised,
glorified and exalted,
raised and honored,
uplifted and lauded be
the name of the Holy One,
blessed be He,
beyond any blessing,
song, praise and consolation
uttered in the world –
and say: Amen.

May the prayers and pleas of all Israel
be accepted by their Father in heaven –
and say: Amen.

May there be great peace from heaven,
and life for us and all Israel –
and say: Amen.

Bow, take three steps back, as if taking leave of the Divine Presence,
then bow, first left, then right, then center, while saying:
May He who makes peace in His high places,
make peace for us and all Israel –
and say: Amen.

קדיש שלם

ש״ץ: יִתְגַּדַּל וְיִתְקַדַּשׁ שְׁמֵהּ רַבָּא (קהל: אָמֵן)
בְּעָלְמָא דִּי בְרָא כִרְעוּתֵהּ
וְיַמְלִיךְ מַלְכוּתֵהּ
בְּחַיֵּיכוֹן וּבְיוֹמֵיכוֹן וּבְחַיֵּי דְּכָל בֵּית יִשְׂרָאֵל
בַּעֲגָלָא וּבִזְמַן קָרִיב
וְאִמְרוּ אָמֵן. (קהל: אָמֵן)

קהל
ושׁ״ץ: יְהֵא שְׁמֵהּ רַבָּא מְבָרַךְ לְעָלַם וּלְעָלְמֵי עָלְמַיָּא.

ש״ץ: יִתְבָּרַךְ וְיִשְׁתַּבַּח וְיִתְפָּאַר
וְיִתְרוֹמַם וְיִתְנַשֵּׂא וְיִתְהַדָּר וְיִתְעַלֶּה וְיִתְהַלָּל
שְׁמֵהּ דְּקֻדְשָׁא בְּרִיךְ הוּא (קהל: בְּרִיךְ הוּא)
לְעֵלָּא מִן כָּל בִּרְכָתָא וְשִׁירָתָא, תֻּשְׁבְּחָתָא וְנֶחֱמָתָא
דַּאֲמִירָן בְּעָלְמָא
וְאִמְרוּ אָמֵן. (קהל: אָמֵן)

תִּתְקַבֵּל צְלוֹתְהוֹן וּבָעוּתְהוֹן דְּכָל יִשְׂרָאֵל
קֳדָם אֲבוּהוֹן דִּי בִשְׁמַיָּא
וְאִמְרוּ אָמֵן. (קהל: אָמֵן)

יְהֵא שְׁלָמָא רַבָּא מִן שְׁמַיָּא
וְחַיִּים, עָלֵינוּ וְעַל כָּל יִשְׂרָאֵל
וְאִמְרוּ אָמֵן. (קהל: אָמֵן)

*Bow, take three steps back, as if taking leave of the Divine Presence,
then bow, first left, then right, then center, while saying:*

עֹשֶׂה שָׁלוֹם בִּמְרוֹמָיו
הוּא יַעֲשֶׂה שָׁלוֹם עָלֵינוּ וְעַל כָּל יִשְׂרָאֵל
וְאִמְרוּ אָמֵן. (קהל: אָמֵן)

Stand while saying Aleinu. Bow at ˙.

עָלֵינוּ It is our duty to praise the Master of all,
and ascribe greatness to the Author of creation,
who has not made us like the nations of the lands
nor placed us like the families of the earth;
who has not made our portion like theirs,
nor our destiny like all their multitudes.
(For they worship vanity and emptiness,
and pray to a god who cannot save.)
˙But we bow in worship and thank the Supreme King of kings,
the Holy One, blessed be He,
who extends the heavens and establishes the earth,
whose throne of glory is in the heavens above,
and whose power's Presence is in the highest of heights.
He is our God; there is no other.
Truly He is our King, there is none else,
as it is written in His Torah:
"You shall know and take to heart this day that the Lord is God,   *Deut. 4*
in heaven above and on earth below. There is no other."

Therefore, we place our hope in You, Lord our God,
that we may soon see the glory of Your power,
when You will remove abominations from the earth,
and idols will be utterly destroyed,
when the world will be perfected
under the sovereignty of the Almighty,
when all humanity will call on Your name,
to turn all the earth's wicked toward You.
All the world's inhabitants will realize and know
that to You every knee must bow and every tongue swear loyalty.
Before You, Lord our God, they will kneel and bow down
and give honor to Your glorious name.
They will all accept the yoke of Your kingdom,
and You will reign over them soon and for ever.
For the kingdom is Yours, and to all eternity You will reign in glory,
as it is written in Your Torah: "The Lord will reign for ever and ever."   *Ex. 15*

Stand while saying עָלֵינוּ. *Bow at* ·.

עָלֵינוּ לְשַׁבֵּחַ לַאֲדוֹן הַכֹּל, לָתֵת גְּדֻלָּה לְיוֹצֵר בְּרֵאשִׁית
שֶׁלֹּא עָשָׂנוּ כְּגוֹיֵי הָאֲרָצוֹת, וְלֹא שָׂמָנוּ כְּמִשְׁפְּחוֹת הָאֲדָמָה
שֶׁלֹּא שָׂם חֶלְקֵנוּ כָּהֶם וְגוֹרָלֵנוּ כְּכָל הֲמוֹנָם.
(שֶׁהֵם מִשְׁתַּחֲוִים לְהֶבֶל וָרִיק וּמִתְפַּלְלִים אֶל אֵל לֹא יוֹשִׁיעַ.)
וַאֲנַחְנוּ כּוֹרְעִים וּמִשְׁתַּחֲוִים וּמוֹדִים
לִפְנֵי מֶלֶךְ מַלְכֵי הַמְּלָכִים, הַקָּדוֹשׁ בָּרוּךְ הוּא
שֶׁהוּא נוֹטֶה שָׁמַיִם וְיוֹסֵד אָרֶץ
וּמוֹשַׁב יְקָרוֹ בַּשָּׁמַיִם מִמַּעַל, וּשְׁכִינַת עֻזּוֹ בְּגָבְהֵי מְרוֹמִים.
הוּא אֱלֹהֵינוּ, אֵין עוֹד.
אֱמֶת מַלְכֵּנוּ, אֶפֶס זוּלָתוֹ
כַּכָּתוּב בְּתוֹרָתוֹ
וְיָדַעְתָּ הַיּוֹם וַהֲשֵׁבֹתָ אֶל־לְבָבֶךָ   דברים ד
כִּי יהוה הוּא הָאֱלֹהִים בַּשָּׁמַיִם מִמַּעַל וְעַל־הָאָרֶץ מִתָּחַת, אֵין עוֹד:

עַל כֵּן נְקַוֶּה לְּךָ יהוה אֱלֹהֵינוּ, לִרְאוֹת מְהֵרָה בְּתִפְאֶרֶת עֻזֶּךָ
לְהַעֲבִיר גִּלּוּלִים מִן הָאָרֶץ, וְהָאֱלִילִים כָּרוֹת יִכָּרֵתוּן
לְתַקֵּן עוֹלָם בְּמַלְכוּת שַׁדַּי.
וְכָל בְּנֵי בָשָׂר יִקְרְאוּ בִשְׁמֶךָ לְהַפְנוֹת אֵלֶיךָ כָּל רִשְׁעֵי אָרֶץ.
יַכִּירוּ וְיֵדְעוּ כָּל יוֹשְׁבֵי תֵבֵל
כִּי לְךָ תִּכְרַע כָּל בֶּרֶךְ, תִּשָּׁבַע כָּל לָשׁוֹן.
לְפָנֶיךָ יהוה אֱלֹהֵינוּ יִכְרְעוּ וְיִפֹּלוּ, וְלִכְבוֹד שִׁמְךָ יְקָר יִתֵּנוּ
וִיקַבְּלוּ כֻלָּם אֶת עֹל מַלְכוּתֶךָ
וְתִמְלֹךְ עֲלֵיהֶם מְהֵרָה לְעוֹלָם וָעֶד.
כִּי הַמַּלְכוּת שֶׁלְּךָ הִיא וּלְעוֹלְמֵי עַד תִּמְלֹךְ בְּכָבוֹד
כַּכָּתוּב בְּתוֹרָתֶךָ, יהוה יִמְלֹךְ לְעֹלָם וָעֶד: שמות טו

▸ And it is said: "Then the LORD shall be King over all the earth;   *Zech. 14*
on that day the LORD shall be One and His name One."

Some add:

Have no fear of sudden terror or of the ruin when it overtakes the wicked.   *Prov. 3*

Devise your strategy, but it will be thwarted; propose your plan,   *Is. 8*
but it will not stand, for God is with us.

When you grow old, I will still be the same.   *Is. 46*
When your hair turns gray, I will still carry you.
I made you, I will bear you, I will carry you, and I will rescue you.

MOURNER'S KADDISH

The following prayer, said by mourners, requires the presence of a minyan.
A transliteration can be found on page 667.

Mourner: יִתְגַּדַּל Magnified and sanctified
may His great name be,
in the world He created by His will.
May He establish His kingdom
in your lifetime and in your days,
and in the lifetime of all the house of Israel,
swiftly and soon – and say: Amen.

All: May His great name be blessed for ever and all time.

Mourner: Blessed and praised, glorified and exalted,
raised and honored,
uplifted and lauded
be the name of the Holy One,
blessed be He,
beyond any blessing,
song, praise and consolation
uttered in the world – and say: Amen.

May there be great peace from heaven,
and life for us and all Israel – and say: Amen.

Bow, take three steps back, as if taking leave of the Divine Presence,
then bow, first left, then right, then center, while saying:

May He who makes peace in His high places,
make peace for us and all Israel – and say: Amen.

זכריה יד

◀ וְנֶאֱמַר, וְהָיָה יהוה לְמֶלֶךְ עַל־כָּל־הָאָרֶץ
בַּיּוֹם הַהוּא יִהְיֶה יהוה אֶחָד וּשְׁמוֹ אֶחָד:

Some add:

משלי ג
אַל־תִּירָא מִפַּחַד פִּתְאֹם וּמִשֹּׁאַת רְשָׁעִים כִּי תָבֹא:

ישעיה ח
עֻצוּ עֵצָה וְתֻפָר, דַּבְּרוּ דָבָר וְלֹא יָקוּם, כִּי עִמָּנוּ אֵל:

ישעיה מו
וְעַד־זִקְנָה אֲנִי הוּא, וְעַד־שֵׂיבָה אֲנִי אֶסְבֹּל אֲנִי עָשִׂיתִי וַאֲנִי אֶשָּׂא וַאֲנִי אֶסְבֹּל וַאֲמַלֵּט:

קדיש יתום

The following prayer, said by mourners, requires the presence of a מנין.
A transliteration can be found on page 667.

אבל
יִתְגַּדַּל וְיִתְקַדַּשׁ שְׁמֵהּ רַבָּא (קהל: אָמֵן)
בְּעָלְמָא דִּי בְרָא כִרְעוּתֵהּ
וְיַמְלִיךְ מַלְכוּתֵהּ
בְּחַיֵּיכוֹן וּבְיוֹמֵיכוֹן וּבְחַיֵּי דְּכָל בֵּית יִשְׂרָאֵל
בַּעֲגָלָא וּבִזְמַן קָרִיב, וְאִמְרוּ אָמֵן. (קהל: אָמֵן)

קהל
ואבל
יְהֵא שְׁמֵהּ רַבָּא מְבָרַךְ לְעָלַם וּלְעָלְמֵי עָלְמַיָּא.

אבל
יִתְבָּרַךְ וְיִשְׁתַּבַּח וְיִתְפָּאַר
וְיִתְרוֹמַם וְיִתְנַשֵּׂא וְיִתְהַדָּר וְיִתְעַלֶּה וְיִתְהַלָּל
שְׁמֵהּ דְּקֻדְשָׁא בְּרִיךְ הוּא (קהל: בְּרִיךְ הוּא)
לְעֵלָּא מִן כָּל בִּרְכָתָא וְשִׁירָתָא, תֻּשְׁבְּחָתָא וְנֶחֱמָתָא
דַּאֲמִירָן בְּעָלְמָא, וְאִמְרוּ אָמֵן. (קהל: אָמֵן)

יְהֵא שְׁלָמָא רַבָּא מִן שְׁמַיָּא
וְחַיִּים, עָלֵינוּ וְעַל כָּל יִשְׂרָאֵל, וְאִמְרוּ אָמֵן. (קהל: אָמֵן)

Bow, take three steps back, as if taking leave of the Divine Presence,
then bow, first left, then right, then center, while saying:

עֹשֶׂה שָׁלוֹם בִּמְרוֹמָיו
הוּא יַעֲשֶׂה שָׁלוֹם עָלֵינוּ
וְעַל כָּל יִשְׂרָאֵל, וְאִמְרוּ אָמֵן. (קהל: אָמֵן)

מעריב למוצאי
יום העצמאות ויום ירושלים

MA'ARIV FOR MOTZA'EI
YOM HAATZMA'UT & YOM YERUSHALAYIM

Ma'ariv for Motza'ei Yom HaAtzma'ut and Yom Yerushalayim

Before the Prayers the Leader says:

וְהוּא רַחוּם He is compassionate.　　　　　　　　　*Ps. 78*
He forgives iniquity and does not destroy.
Repeatedly He suppresses His anger, not rousing His full wrath.
Lord, save! May the King, answer us on the day we call.　　*Ps. 20*

BLESSINGS OF THE SHEMA

*The Leader says the following, bowing at "Bless," standing straight
at "the Lord"; the congregation, followed by the Leader, responds,
bowing at "Bless," standing straight at "the Lord":*

Leader: # BLESS
the Lord, the blessed One.

Congregation: Bless the Lord, the blessed One,
for ever and all time.

Leader: Bless the Lord, the blessed One,
for ever and all time.

בָּרוּךְ Blessed are You, Lord our God, King of the Universe,
who by His word brings on evenings,
by His wisdom opens the gates of heaven,
with understanding makes time change and the seasons rotate,
and by His will orders the stars in their constellations in the sky.
He creates day and night, rolling away the light before the darkness,
and darkness before the light.
▸ He makes the day pass and brings on night,
distinguishing day from night:
the Lord of hosts is His name.
May the living and forever enduring God rule over us for all time.
Blessed are You, Lord, who brings on evenings.

מעריב למוצאי
יום העצמאות ויום ירושלים

Before the תפילה *the* שליח ציבור *says:*

תהלים עח

וְהוּא רַחוּם, יְכַפֵּר עָוֹן וְלֹא־יַשְׁחִית
וְהִרְבָּה לְהָשִׁיב אַפּוֹ, וְלֹא־יָעִיר כָּל־חֲמָתוֹ:

תהלים כ

יהוה הוֹשִׁיעָה, הַמֶּלֶךְ יַעֲנֵנוּ בְיוֹם־קָרְאֵנוּ:

קריאת שמע וברכותיה

The שליח ציבור *says the following, bowing at* בָּרְכוּ, *standing straight at* ה'; *the* קהל, *followed by the* שליח ציבור, *responds, bowing at* בָּרוּךְ, *standing straight at* ה':

בָּרְכוּ :ש״ץ

יְ:

אֶת יהוה הַמְבֹרָךְ.

בָּרוּךְ יהוה הַמְבֹרָךְ לְעוֹלָם וָעֶד. :קהל

בָּרוּךְ יהוה הַמְבֹרָךְ לְעוֹלָם וָעֶד. :ש״ץ

בָּרוּךְ אַתָּה יהוה אֱלֹהֵינוּ מֶלֶךְ הָעוֹלָם
אֲשֶׁר בִּדְבָרוֹ מַעֲרִיב עֲרָבִים, בְּחָכְמָה פּוֹתֵחַ שְׁעָרִים
וּבִתְבוּנָה מְשַׁנֶּה עִתִּים וּמַחֲלִיף אֶת הַזְּמַנִּים
וּמְסַדֵּר אֶת הַכּוֹכָבִים בְּמִשְׁמְרוֹתֵיהֶם בָּרָקִיעַ כִּרְצוֹנוֹ.
בּוֹרֵא יוֹם וָלָיְלָה, גּוֹלֵל אוֹר מִפְּנֵי חֹשֶׁךְ וְחֹשֶׁךְ מִפְּנֵי אוֹר
‹ וּמַעֲבִיר יוֹם וּמֵבִיא לָיְלָה, וּמַבְדִּיל בֵּין יוֹם וּבֵין לָיְלָה
יהוה צְבָאוֹת שְׁמוֹ.
אֵל חַי וְקַיָּם תָּמִיד, יִמְלֹךְ עָלֵינוּ לְעוֹלָם וָעֶד.
בָּרוּךְ אַתָּה יהוה, הַמַּעֲרִיב עֲרָבִים.

אַהֲבַת עוֹלָם With everlasting love
have You loved Your people, the house of Israel.
You have taught us Torah and commandments,
decrees and laws of justice.
Therefore, LORD our God, when we lie down and when we rise up
we will speak of Your decrees, rejoicing in the words of Your Torah
and Your commandments for ever.
▸ For they are our life and the length of our days;
on them will we meditate day and night.
May You never take away Your love from us.
Blessed are You, LORD, who loves His people Israel.

The Shema must be said with intense concentration.
When not with a minyan, say:
God, faithful King!

The following verse should be said aloud, while covering the eyes with the right hand:

Listen, Israel: the LORD is our God, the LORD is One.

Deut. 6

Quietly: Blessed be the name of His glorious kingdom for ever and all time.

וְאָהַבְתָּ Love the LORD your God with all your heart, with all your soul, and with all your might. These words which I command you today shall be on your heart. Teach them repeatedly to your children, speaking of them when you sit at home and when you travel on the way, when you lie down and when you rise. Bind them as a sign on your hand, and they shall be an emblem between your eyes. Write them on the doorposts of your house and gates.

Deut. 6

וְהָיָה If you indeed heed My commandments with which I charge you today, to love the LORD your God and worship Him with all your heart and with all your soul, I will give rain in your land in its

Deut. 11

---

so that you may gather in your grain and your wine and your oil" (*Devarim* 11:14). Ostensibly, by describing a standard agricultural experience, the Torah sanctions a normal work routine. Given this lifestyle, Torah study is relegated

אַהֲבַת עוֹלָם בֵּית יִשְׂרָאֵל עַמְּךָ אָהֶבְתָּ
תּוֹרָה וּמִצְוֹת, חֻקִּים וּמִשְׁפָּטִים, אוֹתָנוּ לִמֵּדְתָּ
עַל כֵּן יהוה אֱלֹהֵינוּ בְּשָׁכְבֵנוּ וּבְקוּמֵנוּ נָשִׂיחַ בְּחֻקֶּיךָ
וְנִשְׂמַח בְּדִבְרֵי תוֹרָתֶךָ וּבְמִצְוֹתֶיךָ לְעוֹלָם וָעֶד
◄ כִּי הֵם חַיֵּינוּ וְאֹרֶךְ יָמֵינוּ, וּבָהֶם נֶהְגֶּה יוֹמָם וָלֵיְלָה. דָזָדָה
וְאַהֲבָתְךָ אַל תָּסִיר מִמֶּנּוּ לְעוֹלָמִים.
בָּרוּךְ אַתָּה יהוה, אוֹהֵב עַמּוֹ יִשְׂרָאֵל.

The שמע must be said with intense concentration.

When not with a מנין, say:

אֵל מֶלֶךְ נֶאֱמָן

The following verse should be said aloud, while covering the eyes with the right hand:

דברים ו

שְׁמַע יִשְׂרָאֵל, יהוה אֱלֹהֵינוּ, יהוה ׀ אֶחָֽד: דָזוּ

Quietly בָּרוּךְ שֵׁם כְּבוֹד מַלְכוּתוֹ לְעוֹלָם וָעֶד.

דברים ו

וְאָהַבְתָּ אֵת יהוה אֱלֹהֶיךָ, בְּכָל־לְבָבְךָ וּבְכָל־נַפְשְׁךָ וּבְכָל־מְאֹדֶךָ:
וְהָיוּ הַדְּבָרִים הָאֵלֶּה, אֲשֶׁר אָנֹכִי מְצַוְּךָ הַיּוֹם, עַל־לְבָבֶךָ: וְשִׁנַּנְתָּם
לְבָנֶיךָ וְדִבַּרְתָּ בָּם, בְּשִׁבְתְּךָ בְּבֵיתֶךָ וּבְלֶכְתְּךָ בַדֶּרֶךְ, וּבְשָׁכְבְּךָ
וּבְקוּמֶךָ: וּקְשַׁרְתָּם לְאוֹת עַל־יָדֶךָ וְהָיוּ לְטֹטָפֹת בֵּין עֵינֶיךָ:
וּכְתַבְתָּם עַל־מְזֻזוֹת בֵּיתֶךָ וּבִשְׁעָרֶיךָ:

דברים יא

וְהָיָה אִם־שָׁמֹעַ תִּשְׁמְעוּ אֶל־מִצְוֹתַי אֲשֶׁר אָנֹכִי מְצַוֶּה אֶתְכֶם
הַיּוֹם, לְאַהֲבָה אֶת־יהוה אֱלֹהֵיכֶם וּלְעָבְדוֹ, בְּכָל־לְבַבְכֶם וּבְכָל־
נַפְשְׁכֶם: וְנָתַתִּי מְטַר־אַרְצְכֶם בְּעִתּוֹ, יוֹרֶה וּמַלְקוֹשׁ, וְאָסַפְתָּ דְגָנֶךָ

AGRICULTURE IN THE LAND OF ISRAEL

A seminal debate about religious lifestyle and faith between Rabbi Yishmael
and Rabbi Shimon Bar Yoḥai surrounds the interpretation of the verse, "He
will give the rain for your land in its season, the early rain and the later rain,

season, the early and late rain; and you shall gather in your grain, wine and oil. I will give grass in your field for your cattle, and you shall eat and be satisfied. Be careful lest your heart be tempted and you go astray and worship other gods, bowing down to them. Then the LORD's anger will flare against you and He will close the heavens so that there will be no rain. The land will not yield its crops, and you will perish swiftly from the good land that the LORD is giving you. Therefore, set these, My words, on your heart and soul. Bind them as a sign on your hand, and they shall be an emblem between your eyes. Teach them to your children, speaking of them when you sit at home and when you travel on the way, when you lie down and when you rise. Write them on the doorposts of your house and gates, so that you and your children may live long in the land that the LORD swore to your ancestors to give them, for as long as the heavens are above the earth.

וַיֹּאמֶר The LORD spoke to Moses, saying: Speak to the Israelites *Num. 15* and tell them to make tassels on the corners of their garments for all generations. They shall attach to the tassel at each corner a thread of blue. This shall be your tassel, and you shall see it and remember all of the LORD's commandments and keep them,

---

concerns. It is an inherent mitzva to cultivate the land, and this cannot be ignored for the sake of total Torah study, in much the same way that other mitzvot cannot be neglected for Torah study. Emphatically he equates neglecting the development of the Land of Israel for Torah study to discarding the mitzva of *Tefillin* for Torah study. Just as the latter is unacceptable so is the former.

Furthermore, the religious import of agriculture is evidenced by the personal investment of Boaz, as narrated in the story of Rut. Despite his superior religious stature he was personally involved in the evening winnowing activity (see *Rut* 3:2). Additionally the Gemara in *Bava Batra* reports that Rabbi Yannai – a student of Rabbi Yehuda HaNasi and a leading Torah scholar of the third century – planted over four hundred vineyards. The personal participation of these great Torah scholars highlights the religious spirit of agricultural activity in the Land of Israel.

וְתִירֹשְׁךָ וְיִצְהָרֶךָ: וְנָתַתִּי עֵשֶׂב בְּשָׂדְךָ לִבְהֶמְתֶּךָ, וְאָכַלְתָּ וְשָׂבָעְתָּ: הִשָּׁמְרוּ לָכֶם פֶּן־יִפְתֶּה לְבַבְכֶם, וְסַרְתֶּם וַעֲבַדְתֶּם אֱלֹהִים אֲחֵרִים וְהִשְׁתַּחֲוִיתֶם לָהֶם: וְחָרָה אַף־יְהוָה בָּכֶם, וְעָצַר אֶת־הַשָּׁמַיִם וְלֹא־יִהְיֶה מָטָר, וְהָאֲדָמָה לֹא תִתֵּן אֶת־יְבוּלָהּ, וַאֲבַדְתֶּם מְהֵרָה מֵעַל הָאָרֶץ הַטֹּבָה אֲשֶׁר יְהוָה נֹתֵן לָכֶם: וְשַׂמְתֶּם אֶת־דְּבָרַי אֵלֶּה עַל־לְבַבְכֶם וְעַל־נַפְשְׁכֶם, וּקְשַׁרְתֶּם אֹתָם לְאוֹת עַל־יֶדְכֶם, וְהָיוּ לְטוֹטָפֹת בֵּין עֵינֵיכֶם: וְלִמַּדְתֶּם אֹתָם אֶת־בְּנֵיכֶם לְדַבֵּר בָּם, בְּשִׁבְתְּךָ בְּבֵיתֶךָ וּבְלֶכְתְּךָ בַדֶּרֶךְ, וּבְשָׁכְבְּךָ וּבְקוּמֶךָ: וּכְתַבְתָּם עַל־מְזוּזוֹת בֵּיתֶךָ וּבִשְׁעָרֶיךָ: לְמַעַן יִרְבּוּ יְמֵיכֶם וִימֵי בְנֵיכֶם עַל הָאֲדָמָה אֲשֶׁר נִשְׁבַּע יְהוָה לַאֲבֹתֵיכֶם לָתֵת לָהֶם, כִּימֵי הַשָּׁמַיִם עַל־הָאָרֶץ:

במדבר טו

וַיֹּאמֶר יְהוָה אֶל־מֹשֶׁה לֵּאמֹר: דַּבֵּר אֶל־בְּנֵי יִשְׂרָאֵל וְאָמַרְתָּ אֲלֵהֶם, וְעָשׂוּ לָהֶם צִיצִת עַל־כַּנְפֵי בִגְדֵיהֶם לְדֹרֹתָם, וְנָתְנוּ עַל־צִיצִת הַכָּנָף פְּתִיל תְּכֵלֶת: וְהָיָה לָכֶם לְצִיצִת, וּרְאִיתֶם אֹתוֹ וּזְכַרְתֶּם אֶת־כָּל־מִצְוֺת יְהוָה וַעֲשִׂיתֶם אֹתָם, וְלֹא תָתוּרוּ אַחֲרֵי

---

to spare time, which undoubtedly is limited. In a famous lament, Rabbi Shimon Bar Yoḥai observes that if a person follows a typical workload, when will Torah be studied? He contends that ideally a person should dedicate all his time to Torah study, and entrust others with material labor. The Gemara (*Berakhot* 35b) which cites this debate concludes that many attempted Bar Yoḥai's policy and failed, whereas those who practiced Rabbi Yishmael's program succeeded. Typically this conclusion implies that Rabbi Yishmael's approach is more practical, whereas Bar Yoḥai's represents an ideal which is elusive in the real world of practical considerations.

Commenting on this discussion, the Ḥatam Sofer (*Sukka* 36a) frames the debate as referring solely to life in Israel. Outside the Land even Rabbi Yishmael would agree to Bar Yoḥai's schedule of full Torah commitment, even at the cost of material investment. However, within the Land of Israel agricultural activity isn't a retreat from religious experience for practical

not straying after your heart and after your eyes, following your own sinful desires. Thus you will be reminded to keep all My commandments, and be holy to your God. I am the LORD your God, who brought you out of the land of Egypt to be your God. I am the LORD your God.

True –

The Leader repeats:
‣ The LORD your God is true –

וֶאֱמוּנָה – and faithful is all this,
and firmly established for us
that He is the LORD our God,
and there is none besides Him,
and that we, Israel, are His people.
He is our King, who redeems us from the hand of kings
and delivers us from the grasp of all tyrants.
He is our God, who on our behalf repays our foes
and brings just retribution on our mortal enemies;
who performs great deeds beyond understanding
and wonders beyond number;
who kept us alive, not letting our foot slip;   Ps. 66
who led us on the high places of our enemies,
raising our pride above all our foes;
who did miracles for us
and brought vengeance against Pharaoh;
who performed signs
and wonders in the land of Ham's children;
who smote in His wrath all the firstborn of Egypt,
and brought out His people Israel from their midst
into everlasting freedom;
who led His children through the divided Reed Sea,
plunging their pursuers and enemies into the depths.
When His children saw His might,
they gave praise and thanks to His name,

לְבַבְכֶם וְאַחֲרֵי עֵינֵיכֶם, אֲשֶׁר־אַתֶּם זֹנִים אַחֲרֵיהֶם: לְמַעַן תִּזְכְּרוּ
וַעֲשִׂיתֶם אֶת־כָּל־מִצְוֹתָי, וִהְיִיתֶם קְדֹשִׁים לֵאלֹהֵיכֶם: אֲנִי יהוה
אֱלֹהֵיכֶם, אֲשֶׁר הוֹצֵאתִי אֶתְכֶם מֵאֶרֶץ מִצְרַיִם, לִהְיוֹת לָכֶם
לֵאלֹהִים, אֲנִי יהוה אֱלֹהֵיכֶם:

אֱמֶת

The שליח ציבור repeats:

‹ יהוה אֱלֹהֵיכֶם אֱמֶת

וֶאֱמוּנָה כָּל זֹאת וְקַיָּם עָלֵינוּ
כִּי הוּא יהוה אֱלֹהֵינוּ וְאֵין זוּלָתוֹ
וַאֲנַחְנוּ יִשְׂרָאֵל עַמּוֹ.
הַפּוֹדֵנוּ מִיַּד מְלָכִים
מַלְכֵּנוּ הַגּוֹאֲלֵנוּ מִכַּף כָּל הֶעָרִיצִים.
הָאֵל הַנִּפְרָע לָנוּ מִצָּרֵינוּ
וְהַמְשַׁלֵּם גְּמוּל לְכָל אוֹיְבֵי נַפְשֵׁנוּ.
הָעוֹשֶׂה גְדוֹלוֹת עַד אֵין חֵקֶר, וְנִפְלָאוֹת עַד אֵין מִסְפָּר
הַשָּׂם נַפְשֵׁנוּ בַּחַיִּים, וְלֹא־נָתַן לַמּוֹט רַגְלֵנוּ:
הַמַּדְרִיכֵנוּ עַל בָּמוֹת אוֹיְבֵינוּ
וַיָּרֶם קַרְנֵנוּ עַל כָּל שׂוֹנְאֵינוּ.
הָעוֹשֶׂה לָּנוּ נִסִּים וּנְקָמָה בְּפַרְעֹה
אוֹתוֹת וּמוֹפְתִים בְּאַדְמַת בְּנֵי חָם.
הַמַּכֶּה בְעֶבְרָתוֹ כָּל בְּכוֹרֵי מִצְרָיִם
וַיּוֹצֵא אֶת עַמּוֹ יִשְׂרָאֵל מִתּוֹכָם לְחֵרוּת עוֹלָם.
הַמַּעֲבִיר בָּנָיו בֵּין גִּזְרֵי יַם סוּף
אֶת רוֹדְפֵיהֶם וְאֶת שׂוֹנְאֵיהֶם בִּתְהוֹמוֹת טִבַּע
וְרָאוּ בָנָיו גְּבוּרָתוֹ, שִׁבְּחוּ וְהוֹדוּ לִשְׁמוֹ

תהלים סו

‣ and willingly accepted His Sovereignty.
   Moses and the children of Israel
   then sang a song to You with great joy,
   and they all exclaimed:

   מִי־כָמֹכָה "Who is like You, Lord, among the mighty?   *Ex. 15*
   Who is like You, majestic in holiness,
   awesome in praises, doing wonders?"

‣ Your children beheld Your majesty
   as You parted the sea before Moses.
   "This is my God!" they responded, and then said:

   "The Lord shall reign for ever and ever."   *Ex. 15*

‣ And it is said,

   "For the Lord has redeemed Jacob and rescued him   *Jer. 31*
   from a power stronger than his own."

   Blessed are You, Lord, who redeemed Israel.

הַשְׁכִּיבֵנוּ Help us lie down, O Lord our God, in peace,
and rise up, O our King, to life.
Spread over us Your canopy of peace.
Direct us with Your good counsel,
and save us for the sake of Your name.
Shield us and remove from us every enemy,
plague, sword, famine and sorrow.
Remove the adversary from before and behind us.
Shelter us in the shadow of Your wings,
for You, God, are our Guardian and Deliverer;
You, God, are a gracious and compassionate King.
‣ Guard our going out and our coming in,
for life and peace, from now and for ever.
Blessed are You, Lord,
who guards His people Israel for ever.

‹ וּמַלְכוּתוֹ בְּרָצוֹן קִבְּלוּ עֲלֵיהֶם.

מֹשֶׁה וּבְנֵי יִשְׂרָאֵל, לְךָ עָנוּ שִׁירָה בְּשִׂמְחָה רַבָּה
וְאָמְרוּ כֻלָם

שמות טו

מִי־כָמֹכָה בָּאֵלִם יהוה

מִי כָּמֹכָה נֶאְדָּר בַּקֹּדֶשׁ

נוֹרָא תְהִלֹּת עֹשֵׂה פֶלֶא:

‹ מַלְכוּתְךָ רָאוּ בָנֶיךָ, בּוֹקֵעַ יָם לִפְנֵי מֹשֶׁה
זֶה אֵלִי עָנוּ, וְאָמְרוּ

שמות טו

יהוה יִמְלֹךְ לְעֹלָם וָעֶד:

‹ וְנֶאֱמַר

ירמיהו לא

כִּי־פָדָה יהוה אֶת־יַעֲקֹב, וּגְאָלוֹ מִיַּד חָזָק מִמֶּנּוּ:

בָּרוּךְ אַתָּה יהוה, גָּאַל יִשְׂרָאֵל.

הַשְׁכִּיבֵנוּ יהוה אֱלֹהֵינוּ לְשָׁלוֹם

וְהַעֲמִידֵנוּ מַלְכֵּנוּ לְחַיִּים

וּפְרֹשׂ עָלֵינוּ סֻכַּת שְׁלוֹמֶךָ

וְתַקְּנֵנוּ בְּעֵצָה טוֹבָה מִלְּפָנֶיךָ

וְהוֹשִׁיעֵנוּ לְמַעַן שְׁמֶךָ.

וְהָגֵן בַּעֲדֵנוּ, וְהָסֵר מֵעָלֵינוּ אוֹיֵב, דֶּבֶר וְחֶרֶב וְרָעָב וְיָגוֹן

וְהָסֵר שָׂטָן מִלְּפָנֵינוּ וּמֵאַחֲרֵינוּ, וּבְצֵל כְּנָפֶיךָ תַּסְתִּירֵנוּ

כִּי אֵל שׁוֹמְרֵנוּ וּמַצִּילֵנוּ אָתָּה

כִּי אֵל מֶלֶךְ חַנּוּן וְרַחוּם אָתָּה.

‹ וּשְׁמֹר צֵאתֵנוּ וּבוֹאֵנוּ לְחַיִּים וּלְשָׁלוֹם מֵעַתָּה וְעַד עוֹלָם.

בָּרוּךְ אַתָּה יהוה, שׁוֹמֵר עַמּוֹ יִשְׂרָאֵל לָעַד.

In Israel the service continues with Half Kaddish on page 480.

בָּרוּךְ Blessed be the LORD for ever. Amen and Amen.   *Ps. 89*

Blessed from Zion be the LORD   *Ps. 135*

who dwells in Jerusalem. Halleluya!

Blessed be the LORD, God of Israel,   *Ps. 72*

who alone does wondrous things.

Blessed be His glorious name for ever,

and may the whole earth be filled with His glory. Amen and Amen.

May the glory of the LORD endure for ever;   *Ps. 104*

may the LORD rejoice in His works.

May the name of the LORD be blessed now and for all time.   *Ps. 113*

For the sake of His great name   *1 Sam. 12*

the LORD will not abandon His people,

for the LORD vowed to make you a people of His own.

When all the people saw [God's wonders] they fell on their faces   *1 Kings 18*

and said: "The LORD, He is God; the LORD, He is God."

Then the LORD shall be King over all the earth;   *Zech. 14*

on that day the LORD shall be One and His name One.

May Your love, LORD, be upon us,   *Ps. 33*

as we have put our hope in You.

Save us, LORD our God, gather us   *Ps. 106*

and deliver us from the nations,

to thank Your holy name, and glory in Your praise.

All the nations You made shall come and bow before You, LORD,   *Ps. 86*

and pay honor to Your name,

for You are great and You perform wonders:

You alone are God.

We, Your people, the flock of Your pasture, will praise You for ever. *Ps. 79*

For all generations we will relate Your praise.

בָּרוּךְ Blessed is the LORD by day, blessed is the LORD by night.

Blessed is the LORD when we lie down;

blessed is the LORD when we rise.

For in Your hand are the souls of the living and the dead,

In ארץ ישראל the service continues with חצי קדיש on page 481.

תהלים פט	בָּרוּךְ יְהוה לְעוֹלָם, אָמֵן וְאָמֵן:
תהלים קלה	בָּרוּךְ יְהוה מִצִּיּוֹן, שֹׁכֵן יְרוּשָׁלָֽםִ, הַלְלוּיָהּ:
תהלים עב	בָּרוּךְ יְהוה אֱלֹהִים אֱלֹהֵי יִשְׂרָאֵל, עֹשֵׂה נִפְלָאוֹת לְבַדּוֹ:
	וּבָרוּךְ שֵׁם כְּבוֹדוֹ לְעוֹלָם
	וְיִמָּלֵא כְבוֹדוֹ אֶת־כָּל־הָאָֽרֶץ, אָמֵן וְאָמֵן:
תהלים קד	יְהִי כְבוֹד יְהוה לְעוֹלָם, יִשְׂמַח יְהוה בְּמַעֲשָׂיו:
תהלים קיג	יְהִי שֵׁם יְהוה מְבֹרָךְ מֵעַתָּה וְעַד־עוֹלָם:
שמואל א, יב	כִּי לֹא־יִטֹּשׁ יְהוה אֶת־עַמּוֹ בַּעֲבוּר שְׁמוֹ הַגָּדוֹל
	כִּי הוֹאִיל יְהוה לַעֲשׂוֹת אֶתְכֶם לוֹ לְעָם:
מלכים א, יח	וַיַּרְא כָּל־הָעָם וַיִּפְּלוּ עַל־פְּנֵיהֶם
	וַיֹּאמְרוּ, יְהוה הוּא הָאֱלֹהִים, יְהוה הוּא הָאֱלֹהִים:
זכריה יד	וְהָיָה יְהוה לְמֶֽלֶךְ עַל־כָּל־הָאָֽרֶץ
	בַּיּוֹם הַהוּא יִהְיֶה יְהוה אֶחָד וּשְׁמוֹ אֶחָד:
תהלים לג	יְהִי־חַסְדְּךָ יְהוה עָלֵֽינוּ, כַּאֲשֶׁר יִחַֽלְנוּ לָךְ:
תהלים קו	הוֹשִׁיעֵֽנוּ יְהוה אֱלֹהֵֽינוּ, וְקַבְּצֵֽנוּ מִן־הַגּוֹיִם
	לְהוֹדוֹת לְשֵׁם קָדְשֶֽׁךָ, לְהִשְׁתַּבֵּֽחַ בִּתְהִלָּתֶֽךָ:
תהלים פו	כָּל־גּוֹיִם אֲשֶׁר עָשִֽׂיתָ, יָבֽוֹאוּ וְיִשְׁתַּחֲווּ לְפָנֶֽיךָ, אֲדֹנָי
	וִיכַבְּדוּ לִשְׁמֶֽךָ:
	כִּי־גָדוֹל אַתָּה וְעֹשֵׂה נִפְלָאוֹת, אַתָּה אֱלֹהִים לְבַדֶּֽךָ:
תהלים עט	וַאֲנַֽחְנוּ עַמְּךָ וְצֹאן מַרְעִיתֶֽךָ, נוֹדֶה לְּךָ לְעוֹלָם
	לְדוֹר וָדֹר נְסַפֵּר תְּהִלָּתֶֽךָ:

בָּרוּךְ יְהוה בַּיּוֹם, בָּרוּךְ יְהוה בַּלָּֽיְלָה

בָּרוּךְ יְהוה בְּשָׁכְבֵּֽנוּ, בָּרוּךְ יְהוה בְּקוּמֵֽנוּ.

כִּי בְיָדְךָ נַפְשׁוֹת הַחַיִּים וְהַמֵּתִים.

[as it is written:] "In His hand is every living soul, *Job 12*
and the breath of all mankind."
Into Your hand I entrust my spirit: *Ps. 31*
You redeemed me, Lᴏʀᴅ, God of truth.
Our God in heaven, bring unity to Your name,
establish Your kingdom constantly
and reign over us for ever and all time.

יִרְאוּ May our eyes see, our hearts rejoice,
and our souls be glad in Your true salvation,
when Zion is told, "Your God reigns."
The Lᴏʀᴅ is King, the Lᴏʀᴅ was King,
the Lᴏʀᴅ will be King for ever and all time.
▸ For sovereignty is Yours, and to all eternity You will reign in glory,
for we have no king but You.
Blessed are You, Lᴏʀᴅ,
the King who in His constant glory will reign over us
and all His creation for ever and all time.

HALF KADDISH

Leader: יִתְגַּדֵּל Magnified and sanctified
may His great name be,
in the world He created by His will.
May He establish His kingdom
in your lifetime and in your days,
and in the lifetime of all the house of Israel,
swiftly and soon – and say: Amen.

All: May His great name be blessed for ever and all time.

Leader: Blessed and praised, glorified and exalted,
raised and honored, uplifted and lauded
be the name of the Holy One, blessed be He,
beyond any blessing, song, praise and consolation
uttered in the world – and say: Amen.

איוב יב

תהלים לא

אֲשֶׁר בְּיָדוֹ נֶפֶשׁ כָּל־חָי, וְרוּחַ כָּל־בְּשַׂר־אִישׁ:

בְּיָדְךָ אַפְקִיד רוּחִי, פָּדִיתָה אוֹתִי יהוה אֵל אֱמֶת:

אֱלֹהֵינוּ שֶׁבַּשָּׁמַיִם, יַחֵד שִׁמְךָ וְקַיֵּם מַלְכוּתְךָ תָּמִיד

וּמְלֹךְ עָלֵינוּ לְעוֹלָם וָעֶד.

יֵרָאוּ עֵינֵינוּ וְיִשְׂמַח לִבֵּנוּ, וְתָגֵל נַפְשֵׁנוּ בִּישׁוּעָתְךָ בֶּאֱמֶת

בֶּאֱמֹר לְצִיּוֹן מָלַךְ אֱלֹהָיִךְ.

יהוה מֶלֶךְ, יהוה מָלָךְ, יהוה יִמְלֹךְ לְעֹלָם וָעֶד.

‹ כִּי הַמַּלְכוּת שֶׁלְּךָ הִיא, וּלְעוֹלְמֵי עַד תִּמְלֹךְ בְּכָבוֹד

כִּי אֵין לָנוּ מֶלֶךְ אֶלָּא אָתָּה.

בָּרוּךְ אַתָּה יהוה

הַמֶּלֶךְ בִּכְבוֹדוֹ תָּמִיד, יִמְלֹךְ עָלֵינוּ לְעוֹלָם וָעֶד

וְעַל כָּל מַעֲשָׂיו.

חצי קדיש

ש״ץ
יִתְגַּדַּל וְיִתְקַדַּשׁ שְׁמֵהּ רַבָּא (קהל: אָמֵן)

בְּעָלְמָא דִּי בְרָא כִרְעוּתֵהּ

וְיַמְלִיךְ מַלְכוּתֵהּ

בְּחַיֵּיכוֹן וּבְיוֹמֵיכוֹן וּבְחַיֵּי דְכָל בֵּית יִשְׂרָאֵל

בַּעֲגָלָא וּבִזְמַן קָרִיב, וְאִמְרוּ אָמֵן. (קהל: אָמֵן)

קהל
וש״ץ:
יְהֵא שְׁמֵהּ רַבָּא מְבָרַךְ לְעָלַם וּלְעָלְמֵי עָלְמַיָּא.

ש״ץ:
יִתְבָּרַךְ וְיִשְׁתַּבַּח וְיִתְפָּאַר וְיִתְרוֹמַם וְיִתְנַשֵּׂא

וְיִתְהַדָּר וְיִתְעַלֶּה וְיִתְהַלָּל

שְׁמֵהּ דְּקֻדְשָׁא בְּרִיךְ הוּא (קהל: בְּרִיךְ הוּא)

לְעֵלָּא מִן כָּל בִּרְכָתָא וְשִׁירָתָא, תֻּשְׁבְּחָתָא וְנֶחֱמָתָא

דַּאֲמִירָן בְּעָלְמָא, וְאִמְרוּ אָמֵן. (קהל: אָמֵן)

THE AMIDA

The following prayer, until "in former years" on page 496, is said silently, standing with feet together. Take three steps forward and at the points indicated by ', bend the knees at the first word, bow at the second, and stand straight before saying God's name.

O Lord, open my lips,   *Ps. 51*
so that my mouth may declare Your praise.

PATRIARCHS

'בָּרוּךְ Blessed are You, Lord our God and God of our fathers,
God of Abraham, God of Isaac and God of Jacob;
the great, mighty and awesome God, God Most High,
who bestows acts of loving-kindness and creates all,
who remembers the loving-kindness of the fathers
and will bring a Redeemer to their children's children
for the sake of His name, in love.
King, Helper, Savior, Shield:
'Blessed are You, Lord,
Shield of Abraham.

DIVINE MIGHT

אַתָּה גִּבּוֹר You are eternally mighty, Lord.
You give life to the dead
and have great power to save.

In Israel: He causes the dew to fall.

He sustains the living with loving-kindness,
and with great compassion revives the dead.
He supports the fallen, heals the sick,
sets captives free,
and keeps His faith with those who sleep in the dust.
Who is like You, Master of might,
and to whom can You be compared,
O King who brings death and gives life,
and makes salvation grow?

עמידה

The following prayer, until קֶדְמֹנִיּוֹת *on page 497, is said silently, standing with feet*
together. Take three steps forward and at the points indicated by ׳, *bend the knees at*
the first word, bow at the second, and stand straight before saying God's name.

תהלים נא

אֲדֹנָי, שְׂפָתַי תִּפְתָּח, וּפִי יַגִּיד תְּהִלָּתֶךָ:

אבות

׳בָּרוּךְ אַתָּה יהוה, אֱלֹהֵינוּ וֵאלֹהֵי אֲבוֹתֵינוּ

אֱלֹהֵי אַבְרָהָם, אֱלֹהֵי יִצְחָק, וֵאלֹהֵי יַעֲקֹב

הָאֵל הַגָּדוֹל הַגִּבּוֹר וְהַנּוֹרָא, אֵל עֶלְיוֹן

גּוֹמֵל חֲסָדִים טוֹבִים, וְקֹנֵה הַכֹּל

וְזוֹכֵר חַסְדֵי אָבוֹת

וּמֵבִיא גוֹאֵל לִבְנֵי בְנֵיהֶם לְמַעַן שְׁמוֹ בְּאַהֲבָה.

מֶלֶךְ עוֹזֵר וּמוֹשִׁיעַ וּמָגֵן.

׳בָּרוּךְ אַתָּה יהוה, מָגֵן אַבְרָהָם.

גבורות

אַתָּה גִּבּוֹר לְעוֹלָם, אֲדֹנָי

מְחַיֵּה מֵתִים אַתָּה, רַב לְהוֹשִׁיעַ

בארץ ישראל: מוֹרִיד הַטָּל

מְכַלְכֵּל חַיִּים בְּחֶסֶד

מְחַיֵּה מֵתִים בְּרַחֲמִים רַבִּים

סוֹמֵךְ נוֹפְלִים, וְרוֹפֵא חוֹלִים, וּמַתִּיר אֲסוּרִים

וּמְקַיֵּם אֱמוּנָתוֹ לִישֵׁנֵי עָפָר.

מִי כָמוֹךָ, בַּעַל גְּבוּרוֹת, וּמִי דּוֹמֶה לָּךְ

מֶלֶךְ, מֵמִית וּמְחַיֶּה וּמַצְמִיחַ יְשׁוּעָה.

Faithful are You to revive the dead.
Blessed are You, Lord, who revives the dead.

HOLINESS

אַתָּה קָדוֹשׁ You are holy and Your name is holy,
and holy ones praise You daily, Selah!
Blessed are You,
Lord, the holy God.

KNOWLEDGE

אַתָּה חוֹנֵן You grace humanity with knowledge
and teach mortals understanding.
Grace us with the knowledge, understanding
and discernment that come from You.
Blessed are You, Lord,
who graciously grants knowledge.

REPENTANCE

הֲשִׁיבֵנוּ Bring us back, our Father, to Your Torah.
Draw us near, our King, to Your service.
Lead us back to You in perfect repentance.
Blessed are You, Lord,
who desires repentance.

FORGIVENESS

Strike the left side of the chest at °.
סְלַח לָנוּ Forgive us, our Father,
for we have °sinned.
Pardon us, our King,
for we have °transgressed;
for You pardon and forgive.
Blessed are You, Lord,
the gracious One who repeatedly forgives.

וְנֶאֱמָן אַתָּה לְהַחֲיוֹת מֵתִים.
בָּרוּךְ אַתָּה יהוה, מְחַיֵּה הַמֵּתִים.

קדושת השם
אַתָּה קָדוֹשׁ וְשִׁמְךָ קָדוֹשׁ
וּקְדוֹשִׁים בְּכָל יוֹם יְהַלְלוּךָ סֶּלָה.
בָּרוּךְ אַתָּה יהוה, הָאֵל הַקָּדוֹשׁ.

דעת
אַתָּה חוֹנֵן לְאָדָם דַּעַת
וּמְלַמֵּד לֶאֱנוֹשׁ בִּינָה.
חָנֵּנוּ מֵאִתְּךָ דֵּעָה בִּינָה וְהַשְׂכֵּל.
בָּרוּךְ אַתָּה יהוה, חוֹנֵן הַדָּעַת.

תשובה
הֲשִׁיבֵנוּ אָבִינוּ לְתוֹרָתֶךָ
וְקָרְבֵנוּ מַלְכֵּנוּ לַעֲבוֹדָתֶךָ
וְהַחֲזִירֵנוּ בִּתְשׁוּבָה שְׁלֵמָה לְפָנֶיךָ.
בָּרוּךְ אַתָּה יהוה, הָרוֹצֶה בִּתְשׁוּבָה.

סליחה
Strike the left side of the chest at °.
סְלַח לָנוּ אָבִינוּ כִּי °חָטָאנוּ
מְחַל לָנוּ מַלְכֵּנוּ כִּי °פָשָׁעְנוּ
כִּי מוֹחֵל וְסוֹלֵחַ אָתָּה.
בָּרוּךְ אַתָּה יהוה, חַנּוּן הַמַּרְבֶּה לִסְלֹחַ.

REDEMPTION

רְאֵה Look on our affliction,
plead our cause,
and redeem us soon for Your name's sake,
for You are a powerful Redeemer.
Blessed are You, LORD,
the Redeemer of Israel.

HEALING

רְפָאֵנוּ Heal us, LORD, and we shall be healed.
Save us and we shall be saved,
for You are our praise.
Bring complete recovery for all our ailments,

The following prayer for a sick person may be said here:
May it be Your will, O LORD my God and God of my ancestors, that You
speedily send a complete recovery from heaven, a healing of both soul and
body, to the patient (*name*), son/daughter of (*mother's name*) among the
other afflicted of Israel.

---

for You, God, King, are a faithful and compassionate Healer.
Blessed are You, LORD,
Healer of the sick of His people Israel.

PROSPERITY

בָּרֵךְ Bless this year for us, LORD our God,
and all its types of produce for good.

In a well-known essay titled *"Tzipita LiYeshua,"* the Ḥafetz Ḥayyim addresses this incongruity. These conflicting imageries could reflect different
potential historical narratives. Redemption can evolve from deep religious
resurgence or it may be prompted by comprehensive religious collapse. Unwilling to allow further complete disintegration, HaKadosh Barukh Hu may
be "compelled" to intervene and redeem humanity.

Furthermore, the surrounding religious bankruptcy severely challenges
the righteous, thereby augmenting the consequences of their devotion. This
"augmented righteousness" warrants divine redemption.

גאולה

רְאֵה בְעָנְיֵנוּ, וְרִיבָה רִיבֵנוּ, וּגְאָלֵנוּ מְהֵרָה לְמַעַן שְׁמֶךָ
כִּי גּוֹאֵל חָזָק אָתָּה.
בָּרוּךְ אַתָּה יהוה, גּוֹאֵל יִשְׂרָאֵל.

רפואה

רְפָאֵנוּ יהוה וְנֵרָפֵא, הוֹשִׁיעֵנוּ וְנִוָּשֵׁעָה, כִּי תְהִלָּתֵנוּ אָתָּה
וְהַעֲלֵה רְפוּאָה שְׁלֵמָה לְכָל מַכּוֹתֵינוּ

The following prayer for a sick person may be said here:

יְהִי רָצוֹן מִלְּפָנֶיךָ יהוה אֱלֹהַי וֵאלֹהֵי אֲבוֹתַי, שֶׁתִּשְׁלַח מְהֵרָה רְפוּאָה שְׁלֵמָה
מִן הַשָּׁמַיִם רְפוּאַת הַנֶּפֶשׁ וּרְפוּאַת הַגּוּף לַחוֹלֶה/לַחוֹלָה *name of patient*
בֶּן/בַּת *mother's name* בְּתוֹךְ שְׁאָר חוֹלֵי יִשְׂרָאֵל.

כִּי אֵל מֶלֶךְ רוֹפֵא נֶאֱמָן וְרַחֲמָן אָתָּה.
בָּרוּךְ אַתָּה יהוה, רוֹפֵא חוֹלֵי עַמּוֹ יִשְׂרָאֵל.

ברכת השנים

בָּרֵךְ עָלֵינוּ יהוה אֱלֹהֵינוּ אֶת הַשָּׁנָה הַזֹּאת
וְאֶת כָּל מִינֵי תְבוּאָתָהּ, לְטוֹבָה

RIGHTEOUS AND WICKED PEOPLE AND REDEMPTION
The Torah links redemption to religious revival and national penitence. Presumably heightened religious awareness and practice prompts redemption. If that religious energy is absent, redemption is delayed and its quality is adulterated. Religious debility is cast as a redemptive inhibitor, not a facilitator.

Yet Ḥazal describe a pre-messianic era in dramatic sinful and immoral imagery. A very poignant Gemara (*Sanhedrin* 97a) portrays the pre-messianic prevailing culture as insolent, disrespectful to elders, ignorant, contemptuous of those who are righteous, and generally dishonest and morally decadent. This depiction is obviously at odds with the Torah's description of a virtuous and moral pre-messianic generation.

Grant blessing on the face of the earth,
and from its goodness satisfy us,
blessing our year as the best of years.
Blessed are You, LORD,
who blesses the years.

INGATHERING OF EXILES

תְּקַע Sound the great shofar for our freedom,
raise high the banner to gather our exiles,
and gather us together from the four quarters of the earth.
Blessed are You, LORD,
who gathers the dispersed of His people Israel.

JUSTICE

הָשִׁיבָה Restore our judges as at first,
and our counselors as at the beginning,
and remove from us sorrow and sighing.
May You alone, LORD, reign over us
with loving-kindness and compassion,
and vindicate us in justice.
Blessed are You, LORD,
the King who loves righteousness and justice.

In either instance a singular and symbolic event launches a global phenomenon of liberation and return. In contrast, the conclusion of the *berakha* describes HaKadosh Barukh Hu as *actually* collecting those who have been thrust aside. Rashi comments (*Devarim* 30:3) that the process of ingathering is arduous, requiring God to literally relocate each *individual Jew* back to Israel. In the verse immediately preceding another prophecy about the heavenly shofar, Yeshayahu describes the strenuous nature of the final ingathering by prophesying that "You will be gathered one by one" (*Yeshayahu* 27:12).

HASHIVA SHOFTEINU
Ideally Jewish judges have been inspirited with *Semikha* – an uninterrupted "force" passed individually from Moshe to his students, and thereafter from

וְתֵן בְּרָכָה עַל פְּנֵי הָאֲדָמָה וְשַׂבְּעֵנוּ מִטּוּבָהּ
וּבָרֵךְ שְׁנָתֵנוּ כַּשָּׁנִים הַטּוֹבוֹת.
בָּרוּךְ אַתָּה יהוה, מְבָרֵךְ הַשָּׁנִים.

קבוץ גלויות

תְּקַע בְּשׁוֹפָר גָּדוֹל לְחֵרוּתֵנוּ, וְשָׂא נֵס לְקַבֵּץ גָּלֻיּוֹתֵינוּ
וְקַבְּצֵנוּ יַחַד מֵאַרְבַּע כַּנְפוֹת הָאָרֶץ.
בָּרוּךְ אַתָּה יהוה, מְקַבֵּץ נִדְחֵי עַמּוֹ יִשְׂרָאֵל.

השבת המשפט

הָשִׁיבָה שׁוֹפְטֵינוּ כְּבָרִאשׁוֹנָה, וְיוֹעֲצֵינוּ כְּבַתְּחִלָּה
וְהָסֵר מִמֶּנּוּ יָגוֹן וַאֲנָחָה
וּמְלֹךְ עָלֵינוּ אַתָּה יהוה לְבַדְּךָ בְּחֶסֶד וּבְרַחֲמִים
וְצַדְּקֵנוּ בַּמִּשְׁפָּט.
בָּרוּךְ אַתָּה יהוה, מֶלֶךְ אוֹהֵב צְדָקָה וּמִשְׁפָּט.

תְּקַע בְּשׁוֹפָר גָּדוֹל לְחֵרוּתֵנוּ, וְשָׂא נֵס לְקַבֵּץ גָּלֻיּוֹתֵינוּ... מְקַבֵּץ נִדְחֵי עַמּוֹ יִשְׂרָאֵל *Sound the great shofar for our freedom, raise high the banner to gather our exiles... who gathers the dispersed of His people Israel."* The opening phrase of the *berakha* describes a heavenly shofar being sounded to liberate the Jewish People. This image figures prominently in the *Tefilla* of Rosh HaShana, and in the symbolism of the shofar. The role of the shofar in liberating Jews from exile was already alluded to at *Har HaMoriya*, when the ram's horns were trapped in the shrubs. Jews would be similarly trapped in numerous historical "thickets" only to be finally emancipated when the horn of the shofar sounds.

Subsequently, the *berakha* describes a "pole" being raised to beckon the returning exiles. Both *Yeshayahu* (18:3) and *Yirmiyahu* (51:27) couple the image of a heavenly shofar with the raising of a pole to initiate the ingathering. The lofty pole provides a visual complement to the auditory solicitation of the shofar.

AGAINST INFORMERS

וְלַמַּלְשִׁינִים For the slanderers let there be no hope,
and may all wickedness perish in an instant.
May all Your people's enemies swiftly be cut down.
May You swiftly uproot, crush, cast down
and humble the arrogant swiftly in our days.
Blessed are You, LORD,
who destroys enemies and humbles the arrogant.

THE RIGHTEOUS

עַל הַצַּדִּיקִים To the righteous, the pious,
the elders of Your people the house of Israel,
the remnant of their scholars,
the righteous converts, and to us,
may Your compassion be aroused, LORD our God.
Grant a good reward to all who sincerely trust in Your name.
Set our lot with them, so that we may never be ashamed,
for in You we trust.
Blessed are You, LORD,
who is the support and trust of the righteous.

---

the verse "I will restore your leaders as in days of old, your rulers as at the
beginning" (*Yeshayahu* 1:26), which serves as the basis for this *berakha*. The
Rambam inferred that this process of rejuvenated learning yielding renewed
Semikha would occur *prior* to the arrival of the Mashiaḥ.

In the sixteenth century the first attempt to renew *Semikha* was carried
out in Tzefat, and nominated Rabbi Yaakov Beirav as the new head of the
Sanhedrin. He presented *Semikha* to four students, among them Rabbi Yosef
Karo, the eventual author of the *Shulḥan Arukh*. This movement was met with
stiff opposition, and eventually was suspended. Subsequent attempts were
made throughout the intervening years, but none succeeded. Some thought
was invested in renewing *Semikha* in the modern State of Israel in 1950, but
these initiatives were also opposed and eventually withdrawn. We still await
the fulfillment of this promise to restore our Judges with their original status
and authority.

ברכת המינים

וְלַמַּלְשִׁינִים אַל תְּהִי תִקְוָה

וְכָל הָרִשְׁעָה כְּרֶגַע תֹּאבֵד

וְכָל אוֹיְבֵי עַמְּךָ מְהֵרָה יִכָּרֵתוּ

וְהַזֵּדִים מְהֵרָה תְעַקֵּר וּתְשַׁבֵּר וּתְמַגֵּר וְתַכְנִיעַ בִּמְהֵרָה בְיָמֵינוּ.

בָּרוּךְ אַתָּה יהוה, שׁוֹבֵר אוֹיְבִים וּמַכְנִיעַ זֵדִים.

על הצדיקים

עַל הַצַּדִּיקִים וְעַל הַחֲסִידִים, וְעַל זִקְנֵי עַמְּךָ בֵּית יִשְׂרָאֵל

וְעַל פְּלֵיטַת סוֹפְרֵיהֶם, וְעַל גֵּרֵי הַצֶּדֶק, וְעָלֵינוּ

יֶהֱמוּ רַחֲמֶיךָ יהוה אֱלֹהֵינוּ

וְתֵן שָׂכָר טוֹב לְכָל הַבּוֹטְחִים בְּשִׁמְךָ בֶּאֱמֶת

וְשִׂים חֶלְקֵנוּ עִמָּהֶם

וּלְעוֹלָם לֹא נֵבוֹשׁ כִּי בְךָ בָטָחְנוּ.

בָּרוּךְ אַתָּה יהוה, מִשְׁעָן וּמִבְטָח לַצַּדִּיקִים.

---

student to student. Beyond mere knowledge, a judge requires this identity as a "*samukh*" to adjudicate most halakhic issues. In the absence of this condition judges are severely limited in the authority they wield and the scope of litigations they can settle. Our current day *Semikha* is a mere shadow of this original title, and merely entails recognition that a person has studied sufficient Torah that his teachings and rulings be considered genuinely. Since it was discontinued around the fourth century, we no longer enjoy actual *Semikha*.

Classic *Semikha* must be delivered in the Land of Israel, although once delivered the recipients enjoy authority even outside its borders. Most opinions claim that once this direct line of *Semikha* was interrupted it could not be re-established through purely human induction. The Rambam disagreed and asserted that if "all" the Torah scholars in Israel would agree upon one candidate, he could be vested with reinitiated *Semikha*, and be capable of transferring *Semikha* to his disciples. The Rambam based his position upon

REBUILDING JERUSALEM

וְלִירוּשָׁלַיִם To Jerusalem, Your city, may You return in compassion,
and may You dwell in it as You promised.
May You rebuild it rapidly in our days as an everlasting structure,
and install within it soon the throne of David.
Blessed are You, LORD, who builds Jerusalem.

KINGDOM OF DAVID

אֶת צֶמַח May the offshoot of Your servant David soon flower,
and may his pride be raised high by Your salvation,
for we wait for Your salvation all day.
Blessed are You, LORD, who makes the glory of salvation flourish.

RESPONSE TO PRAYER

שְׁמַע קוֹלֵנוּ Listen to our voice, LORD our God.
Spare us and have compassion on us,
and in compassion and favor accept our prayer,
for You, God, listen to prayers and pleas.
Do not turn us away, O our King,
empty-handed from Your presence,
for You listen with compassion to the prayer of Your people Israel.
Blessed are You, LORD, who listens to prayer.

---

the terrestrial city is restored with My Presence." The notion of a universal
Yerushalayim reinforces the city's role in spiritual and metaphysical affairs.
Events which occur in this city ripple in influence beyond its municipal
boundaries.

In modern times the emancipation of Yerushalayim has produced an additional unifying dynamic. The Soviet regime succeeded in crushing Jewish
identity for close to fifty years. Millions of Jews were barely aware of their
Jewish origin, and those that did know were either ashamed of their roots
or concealed them. The miraculous events of the Six Day War in 1967, and
primarily the unification of Yerushalayim, unleashed a resuscitated Jewish
identity across the Soviet Union and aroused a proud and indefatigable
movement of Jewish resistance. The heroism of these Prisoners of Zion
ultimately led to the release of Russian Jewry and to the immigration of

בניין ירושלים

וְלִירוּשָׁלַיִם עִירְךָ בְּרַחֲמִים תָּשׁוּב, וְתִשְׁכֹּן בְּתוֹכָהּ כַּאֲשֶׁר דִּבַּרְתָּ
וּבְנֵה אוֹתָהּ בְּקָרוֹב בְּיָמֵינוּ בִּנְיַן עוֹלָם
וְכִסֵּא דָוִד מְהֵרָה לְתוֹכָהּ תָּכִין.
בָּרוּךְ אַתָּה יהוה, בּוֹנֵה יְרוּשָׁלָיִם.

משיח בן דוד

אֶת צֶמַח דָּוִד עַבְדְּךָ מְהֵרָה תַצְמִיחַ, וְקַרְנוֹ תָּרוּם בִּישׁוּעָתֶךָ
כִּי לִישׁוּעָתְךָ קִוִּינוּ כָּל הַיּוֹם.
בָּרוּךְ אַתָּה יהוה, מַצְמִיחַ קֶרֶן יְשׁוּעָה.

שומע תפלה

שְׁמַע קוֹלֵנוּ יהוה אֱלֹהֵינוּ
חוּס וְרַחֵם עָלֵינוּ, וְקַבֵּל בְּרַחֲמִים וּבְרָצוֹן אֶת תְּפִלָּתֵנוּ
כִּי אֵל שׁוֹמֵעַ תְּפִלּוֹת וְתַחֲנוּנִים אָתָּה
וּמִלְּפָנֶיךָ מַלְכֵּנוּ רֵיקָם אַל תְּשִׁיבֵנוּ
כִּי אַתָּה שׁוֹמֵעַ תְּפִלַּת עַמְּךָ יִשְׂרָאֵל בְּרַחֲמִים.
בָּרוּךְ אַתָּה יהוה, שׁוֹמֵעַ תְּפִלָּה.

THE CITY OF UNITY

Yerushalayim is referred to as a city "that is closely bound together" (*Tehillim*
122:3). This phrase speaks to the ability of Yerushalayim to *unite*.

Historically Yerushalayim was a united city, in that it wasn't parceled
among the various tribes who divvied up the rest of the country (*Yoma* 12b).
Since it was a commonwealth, it was excluded for certain halakhot which
apply to classic residences in Israel. One example of this differentiation is
the fact that a house in Yerushalayim stricken with *tzara'at* does not become
ritually impure, since it doesn't qualify as a residence.

Rabbi Yoḥanan (*Ta'anit* 5a) took this reference of a "united city" to refer
to the link between the actual city and its celestial counterpart. HaKadosh
Barukh Hu announced, "I will only settle in the Heavenly Yerushalayim once

TEMPLE SERVICE

רְצֵה Find favor, Lᴏʀᴅ our God,
in Your people Israel and their prayer.
Restore the service to Your most holy House,
and accept in love and favor
the fire-offerings of Israel and their prayer.
May the service of Your people Israel
always find favor with You.
And may our eyes witness Your return to Zion in compassion.
Blessed are You, Lᴏʀᴅ,
who restores His Presence to Zion.

THANKSGIVING

Bow at the first nine words.

מוֹדִים We give thanks to You,
for You are the Lᴏʀᴅ our God and God of our ancestors
for ever and all time.
You are the Rock of our lives,
Shield of our salvation from generation to generation.
We will thank You and declare Your praise for our lives,
which are entrusted into Your hand;
for our souls, which are placed in Your charge;
for Your miracles which are with us every day;
and for Your wonders and favors at all times,
evening, morning and midday.
You are good – for Your compassion never fails.
You are compassionate – for Your loving-kindnesses never cease.
We have always placed our hope in You.
For all these things may Your name be blessed and exalted, our
King, continually, for ever and all time.
Let all that lives thank You, Selah! and praise Your name in truth,
God, our Savior and Help, Selah!
Blessed are You, Lᴏʀᴅ, whose name is "the Good"
and to whom thanks are due.

עבודה

רְצֵה יהוה אֱלֹהֵינוּ בְּעַמְּךָ יִשְׂרָאֵל, וּבִתְפִלָּתָם

וְהָשֵׁב אֶת הָעֲבוֹדָה לִדְבִיר בֵּיתֶךָ

וְאִשֵּׁי יִשְׂרָאֵל וּתְפִלָּתָם בְּאַהֲבָה תְקַבֵּל בְּרָצוֹן

וּתְהִי לְרָצוֹן תָּמִיד עֲבוֹדַת יִשְׂרָאֵל עַמֶּךָ.

וְתֶחֱזֶינָה עֵינֵינוּ בְּשׁוּבְךָ לְצִיּוֹן בְּרַחֲמִים.

בָּרוּךְ אַתָּה יהוה, הַמַּחֲזִיר שְׁכִינָתוֹ לְצִיּוֹן.

הודאה

Bow at the first five words.

יְמוֹדִים אֲנַחְנוּ לָךְ

שָׁאַתָּה הוּא יהוה אֱלֹהֵינוּ וֵאלֹהֵי אֲבוֹתֵינוּ לְעוֹלָם וָעֶד.

צוּר חַיֵּינוּ, מָגֵן יִשְׁעֵנוּ אַתָּה הוּא לְדוֹר וָדוֹר.

נוֹדֶה לְּךָ וּנְסַפֵּר תְּהִלָּתֶךָ, עַל חַיֵּינוּ הַמְּסוּרִים בְּיָדֶךָ

וְעַל נִשְׁמוֹתֵינוּ הַפְּקוּדוֹת לָךְ, וְעַל נִסֶּיךָ שֶׁבְּכָל יוֹם עִמָּנוּ

וְעַל נִפְלְאוֹתֶיךָ וְטוֹבוֹתֶיךָ שֶׁבְּכָל עֵת, עֶרֶב וָבֹקֶר וְצָהֳרָיִם.

הַטּוֹב, כִּי לֹא כָלוּ רַחֲמֶיךָ

וְהַמְרַחֵם, כִּי לֹא תַמּוּ חֲסָדֶיךָ

מֵעוֹלָם קִוִּינוּ לָךְ.

וְעַל כֻּלָּם יִתְבָּרַךְ וְיִתְרוֹמַם שִׁמְךָ מַלְכֵּנוּ תָּמִיד לְעוֹלָם וָעֶד.

וְכֹל הַחַיִּים יוֹדוּךָ סֶּלָה, וִיהַלְלוּ אֶת שִׁמְךָ בֶּאֱמֶת

הָאֵל יְשׁוּעָתֵנוּ וְעֶזְרָתֵנוּ סֶלָה.

יְבָּרוּךְ אַתָּה יהוה, הַטּוֹב שִׁמְךָ וּלְךָ נָאֶה לְהוֹדוֹת.

over one million Russian Jews to Israel. Only Yerushalayim maintained the
sway and influence to reawaken those Jews and reunite them with Jewish
History.

PEACE

שָׁלוֹם רָב Grant great peace to Your people Israel for ever,
for You are the sovereign Lᴏʀᴅ of all peace;
and may it be good in Your eyes to bless Your people Israel
at every time, at every hour, with Your peace.
Blessed are You, Lᴏʀᴅ, who blesses His people Israel with peace.

Some say the following verse:
May the words of my mouth and the meditation of my heart   *Ps. 19*
find favor before You, Lᴏʀᴅ, my Rock and Redeemer.

אֱלֹהַי My God,   *Berakhot*
                                                                 17a
guard my tongue from evil and my lips from deceitful speech.
To those who curse me, let my soul be silent;
may my soul be to all like the dust.
Open my heart to Your Torah
and let my soul pursue Your commandments.
As for all who plan evil against me,
swiftly thwart their counsel and frustrate their plans.
    Act for the sake of Your name; act for the sake of Your right hand;
     act for the sake of Your holiness; act for the sake of Your Torah.
That Your beloved ones may be delivered,   *Ps. 60*
save with Your right hand and answer me.
May the words of my mouth   *Ps. 19*
and the meditation of my heart find favor before You,
Lᴏʀᴅ, my Rock and Redeemer.

Bow, take three steps back, then bow, first left, then right, then center, while saying:
May He who makes peace in His high places,
make peace for us and all Israel – and say: Amen.

יְהִי רָצוֹן May it be Your will, Lᴏʀᴅ our God and God of our ancestors,
that the Temple be rebuilt speedily in our days, and grant us a share in Your Torah.
And there we will serve You with reverence,
as in the days of old and as in former years.
Then the offering of Judah and Jerusalem   *Mal. 3*
will be pleasing to the Lᴏʀᴅ as in the days of old and as in former years.

בברכת שלום

שָׁלוֹם רָב עַל יִשְׂרָאֵל עַמְּךָ תָּשִׂים לְעוֹלָם

כִּי אַתָּה הוּא מֶלֶךְ אָדוֹן לְכָל הַשָּׁלוֹם.

וְטוֹב בְּעֵינֶיךָ לְבָרֵךְ אֶת עַמְּךָ יִשְׂרָאֵל

בְּכָל עֵת וּבְכָל שָׁעָה בִּשְׁלוֹמֶךָ.

בָּרוּךְ אַתָּה יהוה, הַמְבָרֵךְ אֶת עַמּוֹ יִשְׂרָאֵל בַּשָּׁלוֹם.

Some say the following verse:

תהלים יט

יִהְיוּ לְרָצוֹן אִמְרֵי־פִי וְהֶגְיוֹן לִבִּי לְפָנֶיךָ, יהוה צוּרִי וְגֹאֲלִי:

ברכות יז

אֱלֹהַי

נְצֹר לְשׁוֹנִי מֵרָע וּשְׂפָתַי מִדַּבֵּר מִרְמָה

וְלִמְקַלְלַי נַפְשִׁי תִדֹּם, וְנַפְשִׁי כֶּעָפָר לַכֹּל תִּהְיֶה.

פְּתַח לִבִּי בְּתוֹרָתֶךָ, וּבְמִצְוֹתֶיךָ תִּרְדֹּף נַפְשִׁי.

וְכָל הַחוֹשְׁבִים עָלַי רָעָה

מְהֵרָה הָפֵר עֲצָתָם וְקַלְקֵל מַחֲשַׁבְתָּם.

עֲשֵׂה לְמַעַן שְׁמֶךָ, עֲשֵׂה לְמַעַן יְמִינֶךָ

עֲשֵׂה לְמַעַן קְדֻשָּׁתֶךָ, עֲשֵׂה לְמַעַן תּוֹרָתֶךָ.

תהלים ס

לְמַעַן יֵחָלְצוּן יְדִידֶיךָ, הוֹשִׁיעָה יְמִינְךָ וַעֲנֵנִי:

תהלים יט

יִהְיוּ לְרָצוֹן אִמְרֵי־פִי וְהֶגְיוֹן לִבִּי לְפָנֶיךָ, יהוה צוּרִי וְגֹאֲלִי:

Bow, take three steps back, then bow, first left, then right, then center, while saying:

עֹשֶׂה שָׁלוֹם בִּמְרוֹמָיו

הוּא יַעֲשֶׂה שָׁלוֹם עָלֵינוּ וְעַל כָּל יִשְׂרָאֵל, וְאִמְרוּ אָמֵן.

יְהִי רָצוֹן מִלְּפָנֶיךָ יהוה אֱלֹהֵינוּ וֵאלֹהֵי אֲבוֹתֵינוּ

שֶׁיִּבָּנֶה בֵּית הַמִּקְדָּשׁ בִּמְהֵרָה בְיָמֵינוּ, וְתֵן חֶלְקֵנוּ בְּתוֹרָתֶךָ

וְשָׁם נַעֲבָדְךָ בְּיִרְאָה כִּימֵי עוֹלָם וּכְשָׁנִים קַדְמֹנִיּוֹת.

מלאכי ג

וְעָרְבָה לַיהוה מִנְחַת יְהוּדָה וִירוּשָׁלָיִם כִּימֵי עוֹלָם וּכְשָׁנִים קַדְמֹנִיּוֹת:

FULL KADDISH

Leader: יִתְגַּדַּל Magnified and sanctified
may His great name be,
in the world He created by His will.
May He establish His kingdom
in your lifetime and in your days,
and in the lifetime of all the house of Israel,
swiftly and soon –
and say: Amen.

All: May His great name be blessed
for ever and all time.

Leader: Blessed and praised, glorified and exalted,
raised and honored,
uplifted and lauded be
the name of the Holy One,
blessed be He,
beyond any blessing, song,
praise and consolation
uttered in the world –
and say: Amen.

May the prayers and pleas of all Israel
be accepted by their Father in heaven –
and say: Amen.

May there be great peace from heaven,
and life for us and all Israel –
and say: Amen.

*Bow, take three steps back, as if taking leave of the Divine Presence,
then bow, first left, then right, then center, while saying:*
May He who makes peace in His high places,
make peace for us and all Israel –
and say: Amen.

קדיש שלם

ש״ץ יִתְגַּדַּל וְיִתְקַדַּשׁ שְׁמֵהּ רַבָּא (קהל: אָמֵן)
בְּעָלְמָא דִּי בְרָא כִרְעוּתֵהּ
וְיַמְלִיךְ מַלְכוּתֵהּ
בְּחַיֵּיכוֹן וּבְיוֹמֵיכוֹן וּבְחַיֵּי דְּכָל בֵּית יִשְׂרָאֵל
בַּעֲגָלָא וּבִזְמַן קָרִיב
וְאִמְרוּ אָמֵן. (קהל: אָמֵן)

קהל יְהֵא שְׁמֵהּ רַבָּא מְבָרַךְ לְעָלַם וּלְעָלְמֵי עָלְמַיָּא.
ושׁ״ץ:

ש״ץ יִתְבָּרַךְ וְיִשְׁתַּבַּח וְיִתְפָּאַר וְיִתְרוֹמַם וְיִתְנַשֵּׂא
וְיִתְהַדָּר וְיִתְעַלֶּה וְיִתְהַלָּל
שְׁמֵהּ דְּקֻדְשָׁא בְּרִיךְ הוּא (קהל: בְּרִיךְ הוּא)
לְעֵלָּא מִן כָּל בִּרְכָתָא וְשִׁירָתָא, תֻּשְׁבְּחָתָא וְנֶחֱמָתָא
דַּאֲמִירָן בְּעָלְמָא
וְאִמְרוּ אָמֵן. (קהל: אָמֵן)

תִּתְקַבַּל צְלוֹתְהוֹן וּבָעוּתְהוֹן דְּכָל יִשְׂרָאֵל
קֳדָם אֲבוּהוֹן דִּי בִשְׁמַיָּא
וְאִמְרוּ אָמֵן. (קהל: אָמֵן)

יְהֵא שְׁלָמָא רַבָּא מִן שְׁמַיָּא
וְחַיִּים, עָלֵינוּ וְעַל כָּל יִשְׂרָאֵל
וְאִמְרוּ אָמֵן. (קהל: אָמֵן)

*Bow, take three steps back, as if taking leave of the Divine Presence,
then bow, first left, then right, then center, while saying:*

עֹשֶׂה שָׁלוֹם בִּמְרוֹמָיו
הוּא יַעֲשֶׂה שָׁלוֹם עָלֵינוּ וְעַל כָּל יִשְׂרָאֵל
וְאִמְרוּ אָמֵן. (קהל: אָמֵן)

COUNTING OF THE OMER

The Omer is counted each night from the second night of Pesaḥ until the night before
Some say the following meditation before the blessing:

For the sake of the unification of the Holy One, blessed be He,
and His Divine Presence, in reverence and love,
to unify the name *Yod-Heh* with *Vav-Heh*
in perfect unity in the name of all Israel.

הִנְנִי I am prepared and ready to fulfill the positive commandment of Counting the Omer, as is written in the Torah, "You shall count seven complete weeks from the day following the [Pesaḥ] rest day, when you brought the Omer as a wave-offering. To the day after the seventh week you shall count fifty days. Then you shall present a meal-offering of new grain to the LORD." May the pleasantness of the LORD our God be upon us. Establish for us the work of our hands, O establish the work of our hands. *Lev. 23*

Ps. 90

---

phrase: "From the day after the Sabbath (ממחרת השבת), the day you brought the sheaf of the wave offering, count off seven full weeks" (*Vayikra* 23:15). The literal reading of this verse implies the scheduling of the *Omer* sacrifice on a Sunday – after the Shabbat. Within the context of the list of festivals this would establish the Sunday immediately after Pesaḥ as the date of *Korban Omer*. Consequently Shavuot would be scheduled seven weeks later – on a Sunday. The Gemara (*Menaḥot* 65b) reinterprets this verse to refer to the day *after* the fifteenth of Nisan (the first day of Pesaḥ). The *Omer* is offered on the sixteenth of Nisan, regardless of the day of the week on which this date occurs.

Rav Kook (*Ma'amarei Harai'a* Volume 1) asserted that the debate wasn't merely technical or exegetical, but concerned different views of the role of agriculture in the Land of Israel. Processing the *Omer* requires harvesting the grains the night before the sacrifice. If the sixteenth of Nisan falls on Shabbat, these preliminary ceremonies, as well as the eventual sacrifice, would necessarily override Shabbat. Unable to conceive of agricultural celebrations overriding Shabbat observance, the *Tzeddukim* interpreted the verse in a manner which would ensure that *Omer never* overrides Shabbat. By asserting that the *Omer* is always offered on Sunday, the scenario of agricultural activity and

סֵדֶר סְפִירַת הָעוֹמֶר

The עוֹמֶר *is counted each night from the second night of* פֶּסַח *until the night before* שָׁבוּעוֹת.
Some say the following meditation before the blessing:

לְשֵׁם יְחוּד קֻדְשָׁא בְּרִיךְ הוּא וּשְׁכִינְתֵּהּ בִּדְחִילוּ וּרְחִימוּ
לְיַחֵד שֵׁם י"ה בו"ה בְּיִחוּדָא שְׁלִים בְּשֵׁם כָּל יִשְׂרָאֵל.

הִנְנִי מוּכָן וּמְזֻמָּן לְקַיֵּם מִצְוַת עֲשֵׂה שֶׁל סְפִירַת הָעוֹמֶר. כְּמוֹ שֶׁכָּתוּב
בַּתּוֹרָה, וּסְפַרְתֶּם לָכֶם מִמָּחֳרַת הַשַּׁבָּת, מִיּוֹם הֲבִיאֲכֶם אֶת־עֹמֶר הַתְּנוּפָה, ויקרא כג
שֶׁבַע שַׁבָּתוֹת תְּמִימֹת תִּהְיֶינָה: עַד מִמָּחֳרַת הַשַּׁבָּת הַשְּׁבִיעִת תִּסְפְּרוּ
חֲמִשִּׁים יוֹם, וְהִקְרַבְתֶּם מִנְחָה חֲדָשָׁה לַיהוה: וִיהִי נֹעַם אֲדֹנָי אֱלֹהֵינוּ תהלים צ
עָלֵינוּ, וּמַעֲשֵׂה יָדֵינוּ כּוֹנְנָה עָלֵינוּ, וּמַעֲשֵׂה יָדֵינוּ כּוֹנְנֵהוּ:

THE *OMER KORBAN* AND THE MEANING OF AGRICULTURE IN THE LAND OF ISRAEL

The three *Regalim*, Pilgrimage Festivals, are based on important historical events which surrounded our original redemption. Additionally they are tracked to the agricultural cycle in Israel. At various stages of agricultural success we celebrate by ascending to Yerushalayim, performing sacrifices, and conducting a national holiday. Each holiday includes unique sacrifices to punctuate the particular stage of agricultural achievement.

Perhaps the most prominent agrarian *korban* is the *Omer* sacrifice, offered on the second day of Pesaḥ, and marking the first ripening of the earliest grains of barley. Launching the harvest season, this *korban* celebrated the initial yield.

During the Second Temple era a sect known as *Tzeddukim* seceded from mainstream Judaism in their denial of the Oral tradition. This powerful faction infiltrated many positions of influence, including the office of the High Priest. Tensions between this sect and the *Perushim*, who acknowledged the authority of the Oral tradition, often led to violent confrontations. One of the most contentious disputes surrounded the schedule of the *Omer* sacrifice. Discrepancies in this schedule would affect the date of Shavuot and the celebration of *Matan Torah*.

The Torah announces the date of the *Korban Omer* with an ambiguous

בָּרוּךְ Blessed are You, Lᴏʀᴅ our God, King of the Universe,
who has made us holy through His commandments,
and has commanded us about counting the Omer.

4 Iyar: Today is the nineteenth day,
        making two weeks and five days of the Omer.

5 Iyar: Today is the twentieth day,
        making two weeks and six days of the Omer.

6 Iyar: Today is the twenty-first day,
        making three weeks of the Omer.

7 Iyar: Today is the twenty-second day,
        making three weeks and one day of the Omer.

29 Iyar: Today is the forty-fourth day,
        making six weeks and two days of the Omer.

הָרַחֲמָן May the Compassionate One restore the Temple service
to its place speedily in our days.
Amen, Selah.

---

is framed with this prayer. Tosafot (*Megilla* 20b) elaborate that unlike most mitzvot, the mitzva of *Omer* has been completely suspended in the absence of the *Mikdash*. Though *korbanot* are obviously halted without an operating *Mikdash*, most non-*Mikdash* based mitzvot are either unaffected by the lack of *Mikdash* or only partially suspended. Mitzvot such as *Tzitzit* and *Tefillin* are unaffected, and apply equally with or without a *Mikdash*. Other mitzvot such as *Matza* and *Lulav* are qualitatively reduced in the absence of *Mikdash*, but not completely suspended.

The counting of the *Omer* is intended to calculate the interval between the *Omer* sacrifice and the *korban* of the *Shetei HaLeḥem*, two breads, scheduled on Shavuot. Without these *korbanot*, most claim that the mitzva of counting the *Omer* doesn't apply on a Biblical level. Our counting is merely a rabbinic institution to recall the lost mitzva of *Omer*. As this mitzva has suffered the greatest impact of *Ḥurban HaMikdash* it closes with a prayer for the rebuilding of the *Mikdash*.

בָּרוּךְ אַתָּה יהוה אֱלֹהֵינוּ מֶלֶךְ הָעוֹלָם
אֲשֶׁר קִדְּשָׁנוּ בְּמִצְוֹתָיו וְצִוָּנוּ עַל סְפִירַת הָעֹמֶר.

ד׳ באייר: הַיּוֹם תִּשְׁעָה עָשָׂר יוֹם

שֶׁהֵם שְׁנֵי שָׁבוּעוֹת וַחֲמִשָּׁה יָמִים בָּעֹמֶר.   הוד שבתפארת

ה׳ באייר: הַיּוֹם עֶשְׂרִים יוֹם

שֶׁהֵם שְׁנֵי שָׁבוּעוֹת וְשִׁשָּׁה יָמִים בָּעֹמֶר.   יסוד שבתפארת

ו׳ באייר: הַיּוֹם אֶחָד וְעֶשְׂרִים יוֹם

שֶׁהֵם שְׁלֹשָׁה שָׁבוּעוֹת בָּעֹמֶר.   מלכות שבתפארת

ז׳ באייר: הַיּוֹם שְׁנַיִם וְעֶשְׂרִים יוֹם

שֶׁהֵם שְׁלֹשָׁה שָׁבוּעוֹת וְיוֹם אֶחָד בָּעֹמֶר.   חסד שבנצח

כ״ט באייר: הַיּוֹם אַרְבָּעָה וְאַרְבָּעִים יוֹם

שֶׁהֵם שִׁשָּׁה שָׁבוּעוֹת וּשְׁנֵי יָמִים בָּעֹמֶר.   גבורה שבמלכות

הָרַחֲמָן הוּא יַחֲזִיר לָנוּ עֲבוֹדַת בֵּית הַמִּקְדָּשׁ לִמְקוֹמָהּ
בִּמְהֵרָה בְיָמֵינוּ
אָמֵן סֶלָה.

---

celebration overriding Shabbat was avoided. This view doesn't acknowledge the religious meaning of cultivating the Land of Israel. As development of the Land of Israel is bereft of religious content it cannot possibly set aside Shabbat observance.

The authentic *Perushi* position grants religious meaning not just to ritual and sacrifice but to developing the Land of Israel. Ceremonies which mark this process are suffused with spiritual content, and can take precedence over Shabbat observance.

הָרַחֲמָן הוּא יַחֲזִיר לָנוּ עֲבוֹדַת בֵּית הַמִּקְדָּשׁ *May the Compassionate One restore the Temple service.* The *Omer* recital is concluded with a unique prayer for the rebuilding of the *Mikdash* and the restoration of its rituals. No other mitzva

Some add:

לַמְנַצֵּחַ For the conductor of music. With stringed instruments. A psalm, a *Ps. 67* song. May God be gracious to us and bless us. May He make His face shine on us, Selah. Then will Your way be known on earth, Your salvation among all the nations. Let the peoples praise You, God; let all peoples praise You. Let nations rejoice and sing for joy, for You judge the peoples with equity, and guide the nations of the earth, Selah. Let the peoples praise You, God; let all peoples praise You. The earth has yielded its harvest. May God, our God, bless us. God will bless us, and all the ends of the earth will fear Him.

אָנָּא Please, by the power of Your great right hand,
     set the captive nation free.
Accept Your people's prayer. Strengthen us, purify us,
     You who are revered.
Please, Mighty One, guard like the pupil of the eye those
     who seek Your unity.
Bless them, cleanse them, have compassion on them,
     grant them Your righteousness always.
Mighty One, Holy One, in Your great goodness
     guide Your congregation.
Only One, Exalted One, turn to Your people,
     who proclaim Your holiness.
Accept our plea and heed our cry, You who know all secret thoughts.
     Blessed be the name of His glorious kingdom for ever and all time.

רִבּוֹנוֹ שֶׁל עוֹלָם Master of the Universe, You commanded us through Your servant Moses to count the Omer, to cleanse our carapaces and impurities, as You have written in Your Torah: "You shall count seven complete weeks *Lev. 23* from the day following the [Pesaḥ] rest day, when you brought the Omer as a wave-offering. To the day after the seventh week, you shall count fifty days." This is so that the souls of Your people Israel may be purified from their uncleanliness. May it also be Your will, LORD our God and God of our ancestors, that in the merit of the Omer count that I have counted today, there may be rectified any defect on my part in the counting of (*insert the appropriate sefira for each day*). May I be cleansed and sanctified with Your holiness on high, and through this may there flow a rich stream through all worlds, to rectify our lives, spirits and souls from any dross and defect, purifying and sanctifying us with Your sublime holiness. Amen, Selah.

Some add:

תהלים סז

לַמְנַצֵּחַ בִּנְגִינֹת, מִזְמוֹר שִׁיר: אֱלֹהִים יְחָנֵּנוּ וִיבָרְכֵנוּ, יָאֵר פָּנָיו אִתָּנוּ
סֶלָה: לָדַעַת בָּאָרֶץ דַּרְכֶּךָ, בְּכָל־גּוֹיִם יְשׁוּעָתֶךָ: יוֹדוּךָ עַמִּים אֱלֹהִים,
יוֹדוּךָ עַמִּים כֻּלָּם: יִשְׂמְחוּ וִירַנְּנוּ לְאֻמִּים, כִּי־תִשְׁפֹּט עַמִּים מִישֹׁר,
וּלְאֻמִּים בָּאָרֶץ תַּנְחֵם סֶלָה: יוֹדוּךָ עַמִּים אֱלֹהִים, יוֹדוּךָ עַמִּים כֻּלָּם:
אֶרֶץ נָתְנָה יְבוּלָהּ, יְבָרְכֵנוּ אֱלֹהִים אֱלֹהֵינוּ: יְבָרְכֵנוּ אֱלֹהִים, וְיִירְאוּ אוֹתוֹ
כָּל־אַפְסֵי־אָרֶץ:

אָנָּא, בְּכֹחַ גְּדֻלַּת יְמִינְךָ, תַּתִּיר צְרוּרָה.
קַבֵּל רִנַּת עַמְּךָ, שַׂגְּבֵנוּ, טַהֲרֵנוּ, נוֹרָא.
נָא גִבּוֹר, דּוֹרְשֵׁי יִחוּדְךָ כְּבָבַת שָׁמְרֵם.
בָּרְכֵם, טַהֲרֵם, רַחֲמֵם, צִדְקָתְךָ תָּמִיד גָּמְלֵם.
חֲסִין קָדוֹשׁ, בְּרֹב טוּבְךָ נַהֵל עֲדָתֶךָ.
יָחִיד גֵּאֶה, לְעַמְּךָ פְּנֵה, זוֹכְרֵי קְדֻשָּׁתֶךָ.
שַׁוְעָתֵנוּ קַבֵּל וּשְׁמַע צַעֲקָתֵנוּ, יוֹדֵעַ תַּעֲלוּמוֹת.
בָּרוּךְ שֵׁם כְּבוֹד מַלְכוּתוֹ לְעוֹלָם וָעֶד.

רִבּוֹנוֹ שֶׁל עוֹלָם, אַתָּה צִוִּיתָנוּ עַל יְדֵי מֹשֶׁה עַבְדְּךָ לִסְפֹּר סְפִירַת הָעֹמֶר,
כְּדֵי לְטַהֲרֵנוּ מִקְּלִפּוֹתֵינוּ וּמִטֻּמְאוֹתֵינוּ. כְּמוֹ שֶׁכָּתַבְתָּ בְּתוֹרָתֶךָ: וּסְפַרְתֶּם ויקרא כג
לָכֶם מִמָּחֳרַת הַשַּׁבָּת, מִיּוֹם הֲבִיאֲכֶם אֶת־עֹמֶר הַתְּנוּפָה, שֶׁבַע שַׁבָּתוֹת
תְּמִימֹת תִּהְיֶינָה: עַד מִמָּחֳרַת הַשַּׁבָּת הַשְּׁבִיעִת תִּסְפְּרוּ חֲמִשִּׁים יוֹם: כְּדֵי
שֶׁיִּטָּהֲרוּ נַפְשׁוֹת עַמְּךָ יִשְׂרָאֵל מִזֻּהֲמָתָם. וּבְכֵן יְהִי רָצוֹן מִלְּפָנֶיךָ יהוה
אֱלֹהֵינוּ וֵאלֹהֵי אֲבוֹתֵינוּ, שֶׁבִּזְכוּת סְפִירַת הָעֹמֶר שֶׁסָּפַרְתִּי הַיּוֹם, יְתַקֵּן
מַה שֶּׁפָּגַמְתִּי בִּסְפִירָה ספירה (*insert appropriate* ספירה *for each day*) וְאֶטָּהֵר וְאֶתְקַדֵּשׁ
בִּקְדֻשָּׁה שֶׁל מַעְלָה, וְעַל יְדֵי זֶה יֻשְׁפַּע שֶׁפַע רַב בְּכָל הָעוֹלָמוֹת, לְתַקֵּן
אֶת נַפְשׁוֹתֵינוּ וְרוּחוֹתֵינוּ וְנִשְׁמוֹתֵינוּ מִכָּל סִיג וּפְגָם, וּלְטַהֲרֵנוּ וּלְקַדְּשֵׁנוּ
בִּקְדֻשָּׁתְךָ הָעֶלְיוֹנָה, אָמֵן סֶלָה.

Stand while saying Aleinu. Bow at ˙.

עָלֵינוּ It is our duty to praise the Master of all,
and ascribe greatness to the Author of creation,
who has not made us like the nations of the lands
nor placed us like the families of the earth;
who has not made our portion like theirs,
nor our destiny like all their multitudes.
(For they worship vanity and emptiness,
and pray to a god who cannot save.)
˙But we bow in worship and thank the Supreme King of kings,
the Holy One, blessed be He,
who extends the heavens and establishes the earth,
whose throne of glory is in the heavens above,
and whose power's Presence is in the highest of heights.
He is our God; there is no other.
Truly He is our King, there is none else,
as it is written in His Torah: "You shall know and take to heart this day   *Deut. 4*
that the Lord is God, in heaven above and on earth below.
There is no other."

Therefore, we place our hope in You, Lord our God,
that we may soon see the glory of Your power,
when You will remove abominations from the earth,
and idols will be utterly destroyed,
when the world will be perfected under the sovereignty of the Almighty,
when all humanity will call on Your name,
to turn all the earth's wicked toward You.
All the world's inhabitants will realize and know
that to You every knee must bow and every tongue swear loyalty.
Before You, Lord our God, they will kneel and bow down
and give honor to Your glorious name.
They will all accept the yoke of Your kingdom,
and You will reign over them soon and for ever.
For the kingdom is Yours, and to all eternity You will reign in glory,
as it is written in Your Torah: "The Lord will reign for ever and ever."   *Ex. 15*
▸ And it is said: "Then the Lord shall be King over all the earth;   *Zech. 14*
on that day the Lord shall be One and His name One."

Stand while saying עָלֵינוּ. Bow at ˇ.

עָלֵינוּ לְשַׁבֵּחַ לַאֲדוֹן הַכֹּל, לָתֵת גְּדֻלָּה לְיוֹצֵר בְּרֵאשִׁית
שֶׁלֹּא עָשָׂנוּ כְּגוֹיֵי הָאֲרָצוֹת, וְלֹא שָׂמָנוּ כְּמִשְׁפְּחוֹת הָאֲדָמָה
שֶׁלֹּא שָׂם חֶלְקֵנוּ כָּהֶם וְגוֹרָלֵנוּ כְּכָל הֲמוֹנָם.
(שֶׁהֵם מִשְׁתַּחֲוִים לְהֶבֶל וָרִיק וּמִתְפַּלְלִים אֶל אֵל לֹא יוֹשִׁיעַ.)
ˇוַאֲנַחְנוּ כּוֹרְעִים וּמִשְׁתַּחֲוִים וּמוֹדִים
לִפְנֵי מֶלֶךְ מַלְכֵי הַמְּלָכִים, הַקָּדוֹשׁ בָּרוּךְ הוּא
שֶׁהוּא נוֹטֶה שָׁמַיִם וְיוֹסֵד אָרֶץ, וּמוֹשַׁב יְקָרוֹ בַּשָּׁמַיִם מִמַּעַל
וּשְׁכִינַת עֻזּוֹ בְּגָבְהֵי מְרוֹמִים.
הוּא אֱלֹהֵינוּ, אֵין עוֹד.
אֱמֶת מַלְכֵּנוּ, אֶפֶס זוּלָתוֹ
כַּכָּתוּב בְּתוֹרָתוֹ, וְיָדַעְתָּ הַיּוֹם וַהֲשֵׁבֹתָ אֶל־לְבָבֶךָ

דברים ד

כִּי יהוה הוּא הָאֱלֹהִים בַּשָּׁמַיִם מִמַּעַל וְעַל־הָאָרֶץ מִתָּחַת, אֵין עוֹד:

עַל כֵּן נְקַוֶּה לְךָ יהוה אֱלֹהֵינוּ, לִרְאוֹת מְהֵרָה בְּתִפְאֶרֶת עֻזֶּךָ
לְהַעֲבִיר גִּלּוּלִים מִן הָאָרֶץ, וְהָאֱלִילִים כָּרוֹת יִכָּרֵתוּן
לְתַקֵּן עוֹלָם בְּמַלְכוּת שַׁדַּי.
וְכָל בְּנֵי בָשָׂר יִקְרְאוּ בִשְׁמֶךָ לְהַפְנוֹת אֵלֶיךָ כָּל רִשְׁעֵי אָרֶץ.
יַכִּירוּ וְיֵדְעוּ כָּל יוֹשְׁבֵי תֵבֵל
כִּי לְךָ תִּכְרַע כָּל בֶּרֶךְ, תִּשָּׁבַע כָּל לָשׁוֹן.
לְפָנֶיךָ יהוה אֱלֹהֵינוּ יִכְרְעוּ וְיִפֹּלוּ, וְלִכְבוֹד שִׁמְךָ יְקָר יִתֵּנוּ
וִיקַבְּלוּ כֻלָּם אֶת עֹל מַלְכוּתֶךָ
וְתִמְלֹךְ עֲלֵיהֶם מְהֵרָה לְעוֹלָם וָעֶד.
כִּי הַמַּלְכוּת שֶׁלְּךָ הִיא וּלְעוֹלְמֵי עַד תִּמְלֹךְ בְּכָבוֹד
כַּכָּתוּב בְּתוֹרָתֶךָ, יהוה יִמְלֹךְ לְעֹלָם וָעֶד:

שמות טו

‣ וְנֶאֱמַר, וְהָיָה יהוה לְמֶלֶךְ עַל־כָּל־הָאָרֶץ

זכריה יד

בַּיּוֹם הַהוּא יִהְיֶה יהוה אֶחָד וּשְׁמוֹ אֶחָד:

Some add:

Have no fear of sudden terror or of the ruin when it overtakes the wicked.   *Prov. 3*

Devise your strategy, but it will be thwarted; propose your plan,   *Is. 8*
but it will not stand, for God is with us.

When you grow old, I will still be the same.   *Is. 46*
When your hair turns gray, I will still carry you.
I made you, I will bear you,
I will carry you, and I will rescue you.

MOURNER'S KADDISH

The following prayer, said by mourners, requires the presence of a minyan.
A transliteration can be found on page 667.

Mourner: יִתְגַּדַּל Magnified and sanctified may His great name be,
in the world He created by His will.
May He establish His kingdom
in your lifetime and in your days,
and in the lifetime of all the house of Israel,
swiftly and soon – and say: Amen.

All: May His great name be blessed for ever and all time.

Mourner: Blessed and praised,
glorified and exalted,
raised and honored,
uplifted and lauded
be the name of the Holy One,
blessed be He,
beyond any blessing, song,
praise and consolation
uttered in the world – and say: Amen.

May there be great peace from heaven,
and life for us and all Israel – and say: Amen.

Bow, take three steps back, as if taking leave of the Divine Presence,
then bow, first left, then right, then center, while saying:

May He who makes peace in His high places,
make peace for us and all Israel – and say: Amen.

Some add:

משלי ג
אַל־תִּירָא מִפַּחַד פִּתְאֹם וּמִשֹּׁאַת רְשָׁעִים כִּי תָבֹא:

ישעיה ח
עֻצוּ עֵצָה וְתֻפָר, דַּבְּרוּ דָבָר וְלֹא יָקוּם, כִּי עִמָּנוּ אֵל:

ישעיה מו
וְעַד־זִקְנָה אֲנִי הוּא, וְעַד־שֵׂיבָה אֲנִי אֶסְבֹּל
אֲנִי עָשִׂיתִי וַאֲנִי אֶשָּׂא וַאֲנִי אֶסְבֹּל וַאֲמַלֵּט:

קדיש יתום

The following prayer, said by mourners, requires the presence of a מנין.
A transliteration can be found on page 667.

אבל יִתְגַּדַּל וְיִתְקַדַּשׁ שְׁמֵהּ רַבָּא (קהל: אָמֵן)
בְּעָלְמָא דִּי בְרָא כִרְעוּתֵהּ
וְיַמְלִיךְ מַלְכוּתֵהּ
בְּחַיֵּיכוֹן וּבְיוֹמֵיכוֹן וּבְחַיֵּי דְכָל בֵּית יִשְׂרָאֵל
בַּעֲגָלָא וּבִזְמַן קָרִיב, וְאִמְרוּ אָמֵן. (קהל: אָמֵן)

קהל ואבל: יְהֵא שְׁמֵהּ רַבָּא מְבָרַךְ לְעָלַם וּלְעָלְמֵי עָלְמַיָּא.

אבל יִתְבָּרַךְ וְיִשְׁתַּבַּח וְיִתְפָּאַר
וְיִתְרוֹמַם וְיִתְנַשֵּׂא וְיִתְהַדָּר וְיִתְעַלֶּה וְיִתְהַלָּל
שְׁמֵהּ דְּקֻדְשָׁא בְּרִיךְ הוּא (קהל: בְּרִיךְ הוּא)
לְעֵלָּא מִן כָּל בִּרְכָתָא
וְשִׁירָתָא, תֻּשְׁבְּחָתָא וְנֶחֱמָתָא
דַּאֲמִירָן בְּעָלְמָא, וְאִמְרוּ אָמֵן. (קהל: אָמֵן)

יְהֵא שְׁלָמָא רַבָּא מִן שְׁמַיָּא
וְחַיִּים, עָלֵינוּ וְעַל כָּל יִשְׂרָאֵל, וְאִמְרוּ אָמֵן. (קהל: אָמֵן)

Bow, take three steps back, as if taking leave of the Divine Presence,
then bow, first left, then right, then center, while saying:

עֹשֶׂה שָׁלוֹם בִּמְרוֹמָיו, הוּא יַעֲשֶׂה שָׁלוֹם
עָלֵינוּ וְעַל כָּל יִשְׂרָאֵל, וְאִמְרוּ אָמֵן. (קהל: אָמֵן)

יום ירושלים

YOM YERUSHALAYIM

מעריב ליום ירושלים

MAʾARIV FOR YOM YERUSHALAYIM

Ma'ariv for Yom Yerushalayim

In Israel and some communities outside Israel the following
is said before Ma'ariv responsively, verse by verse:

A song of ascents. Of David. *Ps.* 122

I rejoiced when they said to me,
"Let us go to the House of the Lord."
Our feet stood within your gates, Jerusalem:
Jerusalem built as a city joined together.
There the tribes went up, the tribes of the Lord –
as a testimony to Israel – to give thanks to the name of the Lord.
For there the thrones of justice are set,
the thrones of the house of David.
Pray for the peace of Jerusalem:
"May those who love you prosper.
May there be peace within your ramparts,
tranquility in your citadels."
For the sake of my brothers and my friends,
I shall say, "Peace be within you."
For the sake of the House of the Lord our God,
I shall seek your good.

A song of ascents. Of David. *Ps.* 124

Had the Lord not been on our side – let Israel say it –
had the Lord not been on our side
when men rose up against us,
they would have swallowed us alive
when their anger raged against us.
The waters would have engulfed us;
the torrent would have swept over us;
over us would have swept the raging waters.
Blessed be the Lord who did not leave us as a prey for their teeth.
We escaped like a bird from the fowler's trap;
the trap broke and we escaped.
Our help is in the name of the Lord, Maker of heaven and earth.

מעריב ליום ירושלים

In ארץ ישראל and some communities in חוץ לארץ the following
is said before מעריב responsively, verse by verse:

תהלים קכב

שִׁיר הַמַּעֲלוֹת לְדָוִד

שָׂמַחְתִּי בְּאֹמְרִים לִי בֵּית יהוה נֵלֵךְ:

עֹמְדוֹת הָיוּ רַגְלֵינוּ, בִּשְׁעָרַיִךְ יְרוּשָׁלָ͏ִם:

יְרוּשָׁלַ͏ִם הַבְּנוּיָה, כְּעִיר שֶׁחֻבְּרָה־לָּהּ יַחְדָּו:

שֶׁשָּׁם עָלוּ שְׁבָטִים שִׁבְטֵי־יָהּ, עֵדוּת לְיִשְׂרָאֵל

לְהֹדוֹת לְשֵׁם יהוה:

כִּי שָׁמָּה יָשְׁבוּ כִסְאוֹת לְמִשְׁפָּט, כִּסְאוֹת לְבֵית דָּוִד:

שַׁאֲלוּ שְׁלוֹם יְרוּשָׁלָ͏ִם, יִשְׁלָיוּ אֹהֲבָיִךְ:

יְהִי־שָׁלוֹם בְּחֵילֵךְ, שַׁלְוָה בְּאַרְמְנוֹתָיִךְ:

לְמַעַן אַחַי וְרֵעָי, אֲדַבְּרָה־נָּא שָׁלוֹם בָּךְ:

לְמַעַן בֵּית־יהוה אֱלֹהֵינוּ, אֲבַקְשָׁה טוֹב לָךְ:

תהלים קכד

שִׁיר הַמַּעֲלוֹת לְדָוִד

לוּלֵי יהוה שֶׁהָיָה לָנוּ, יֹאמַר־נָא יִשְׂרָאֵל:

לוּלֵי יהוה שֶׁהָיָה לָנוּ, בְּקוּם עָלֵינוּ אָדָם:

אֲזַי חַיִּים בְּלָעוּנוּ, בַּחֲרוֹת אַפָּם בָּנוּ:

אֲזַי הַמַּיִם שְׁטָפוּנוּ, נַחְלָה עָבַר עַל־נַפְשֵׁנוּ:

אֲזַי עָבַר עַל־נַפְשֵׁנוּ, הַמַּיִם הַזֵּידוֹנִים:

בָּרוּךְ יהוה, שֶׁלֹּא נְתָנָנוּ טֶרֶף לְשִׁנֵּיהֶם:

נַפְשֵׁנוּ כְּצִפּוֹר נִמְלְטָה מִפַּח יוֹקְשִׁים

הַפַּח נִשְׁבָּר וַאֲנַחְנוּ נִמְלָטְנוּ:

עֶזְרֵנוּ בְּשֵׁם יהוה, עֹשֵׂה שָׁמַיִם וָאָרֶץ:

A song of ascents.

Ps. 132

LORD, remember David and all the hardship he endured.
He swore an oath to the LORD
 and made a vow to the Mighty One of Jacob:
"I will not enter my house, nor go to bed;
 I will not give sleep to my eyes or slumber to my eyelids,
 until I find a place for the LORD,
 a dwelling for the Mighty One of Jacob."
We heard of it in Efrat, we found it in the fields of Yaar.
Let us enter His dwelling, worship at His footstool.
Advance, LORD, to Your resting place, You and Your mighty Ark.
Your priests are robed in righteousness;
Your devoted ones sing for joy.
For the sake of Your servant David,
 do not reject Your anointed one.
The LORD swore to David a firm oath that He will not revoke:
"One of your own descendants I will set upon your throne.
If your sons keep My covenant and My decrees that I teach them,
 then their sons shall sit upon your throne for all time."

Alternatively, "*ohel*" (literally "tent") may be seen as referring to a tempo-rary structure, whereas "*mishkan*" implies a more permanent edifice. First Bilam admires the temporary "houses of God" which Jews would erect, he describes them as *ohalei Yaakov* – assigning to them the name of Jacob, repre-senting his struggle with his brother, and by extension the Jewish experience in exile. During this stage Jews valiantly erected impressive *Batei Kenesset* and *Batei Midrash*, but they were transient, and faded with time.

When Jewish history is revived, enduring structures can be assembled since the period of "*Yisrael*" has begun. *Yisrael* represents Jacob's triumph over his brother ("For you have wrestled with Angel and Man and *triumphed*" – *Bereshit* 32:28).

Although we haven't yet merited the construction of the Third *Beit HaMik-dash*, we have witnessed the rise of grand *Batei Midrash* and *Batei Kenesset*, which honor Torah and the Jewish people. The period of "*Yisrael*" has en-abled the construction of more permanent "*mishkenot*."

שִׁיר הַמַּעֲלוֹת

זְכוֹר־יהוה לְדָוִד אֵת כָּל־עֻנּוֹתוֹ:

אֲשֶׁר נִשְׁבַּע לַיהוה, נָדַר לַאֲבִיר יַעֲקֹב:

אִם־אָבֹא בְּאֹהֶל בֵּיתִי, אִם־אֶעֱלֶה עַל־עֶרֶשׂ יְצוּעָי:

אִם־אֶתֵּן שְׁנַת לְעֵינָי, לְעַפְעַפַּי תְּנוּמָה:

עַד־אֶמְצָא מָקוֹם לַיהוה, מִשְׁכָּנוֹת לַאֲבִיר יַעֲקֹב:

הִנֵּה־שְׁמַעֲנוּהָ בְאֶפְרָתָה, מְצָאנוּהָ בִּשְׂדֵי־יָעַר:

נָבוֹאָה לְמִשְׁכְּנוֹתָיו, נִשְׁתַּחֲוֶה לַהֲדֹם רַגְלָיו:

קוּמָה יהוה לִמְנוּחָתֶךָ, אַתָּה וַאֲרוֹן עֻזֶּךָ:

כֹּהֲנֶיךָ יִלְבְּשׁוּ־צֶדֶק, וַחֲסִידֶיךָ יְרַנֵּנוּ:

בַּעֲבוּר דָּוִד עַבְדֶּךָ, אַל־תָּשֵׁב פְּנֵי מְשִׁיחֶךָ:

נִשְׁבַּע־יהוה לְדָוִד

אֱמֶת לֹא־יָשׁוּב מִמֶּנָּה, מִפְּרִי בִטְנְךָ אָשִׁית לְכִסֵּא־לָךְ:

אִם־יִשְׁמְרוּ בָנֶיךָ בְּרִיתִי, וְעֵדֹתִי זוֹ אֲלַמְּדֵם

גַּם־בְּנֵיהֶם עֲדֵי־עַד, יֵשְׁבוּ לְכִסֵּא־לָךְ:

USING THE TERM *MISHKAN* TO DESCRIBE THE *MIKDASH*

Bilam employs the plural tense "*mishkenotekha*" to describe the Tabernacle. Ḥazal (*Shemot Raba* 31:10) interpret this as an allusion to the two Temples which served as "*mashkon*" or mortgages on behalf of the Jewish people. Instead of "collecting the debt" of their sins from the people, the two structures were appropriated, thereby sparing the nation itself harsher penalty.

The notion of *mashkon* also suggests a future return of the Creditor. Collateral is seized to enable future compensation or reconciliation. HaKadosh Barukh Hu didn't merely condemn the *Batei Mikdash*, but holds them as collateral to ensure future encounters with His beloved nation.

The Midrash suggests that the word "*ohel*" refers to a standing *Mikdash*, whereas "*mishkan*" refers to a wrecked *Mikdash*, which has been taken as collateral.

For the LORD has chosen Zion; He desired it for His home.
This is My resting place for all time;
here I will dwell, for that is My desire.
I will amply bless its store of food;
its poor I will satisfy with bread.
I will clothe its priests with salvation;
its loyal ones shall sing for joy.
There I will make David's dynasty flourish;
I will prepare a lamp for My anointed one.
I will clothe his enemies with shame,
but on him will be a shining crown.

It is customary to sing this psalm in the melody of HaTikva.

A song of ascents.   Ps. 126
When the LORD brought back the exiles of Zion
we were like people who dream.
Then were our mouths filled with laughter,
and our tongues with songs of joy.
Then was it said among the nations,
"The LORD has done great things for them."
The LORD did do great things for us and we rejoiced.
Bring back our exiles, LORD, like streams in a dry land.
May those who sowed in tears, reap in joy.
May one who goes out weeping, carrying a bag of seed,
come back with songs of joy, carrying his sheaves.

---

he laments living in comfortable residences while the actual site of the Divine Home has yet to be discovered. Though he didn't merit to actually construct the *Mikdash*, he did search relentlessly for its location, and purchased the land which would one day house it. In response to David's searching for the site, HaKadosh Barukh Hu declares that the "pursued" site was already chosen, and that God Himself covets the time when He will reside there.

The notion that HaKadosh Barukh Hu desires a human initiative in locating His Presence in Yerushalayim is already captured by a verse in *Devarim* (12:5) which instructs "לְשִׁכְנוֹ תִדְרְשׁוּ וּבָאתָ שָּׁמָּה – for His dwelling, to that place you must go." As the *Sifrei* translates, "Search for the location, and only after discovering it will God corroborate through prophetic signal."

כִּי־בָחַר יהוה בְּצִיּוֹן, אִוָּהּ לְמוֹשָׁב לוֹ:

זֹאת־מְנוּחָתִי עֲדֵי־עַד, פֹּה אֵשֵׁב כִּי אִוִּתִיהָ:

צֵידָהּ בָּרֵךְ אֲבָרֵךְ, אֶבְיוֹנֶיהָ אַשְׂבִּיעַ לָחֶם:

וְכֹהֲנֶיהָ אַלְבִּישׁ יֶשַׁע, וַחֲסִידֶיהָ רַנֵּן יְרַנֵּנוּ:

שָׁם אַצְמִיחַ קֶרֶן לְדָוִד, עָרַכְתִּי נֵר לִמְשִׁיחִי:

אוֹיְבָיו אַלְבִּישׁ בֹּשֶׁת, וְעָלָיו יָצִיץ נִזְרוֹ:

It is customary to sing this psalm in the melody of הַתִּקְוָה.

תהלים קכז

שִׁיר הַמַּעֲלוֹת

בְּשׁוּב יהוה אֶת־שִׁיבַת צִיּוֹן, הָיִינוּ כְּחֹלְמִים:

אָז יִמָּלֵא שְׂחוֹק פִּינוּ וּלְשׁוֹנֵנוּ רִנָּה

אָז יֹאמְרוּ בַגּוֹיִם הִגְדִּיל יהוה לַעֲשׂוֹת עִם־אֵלֶּה:

הִגְדִּיל יהוה לַעֲשׂוֹת עִמָּנוּ, הָיִינוּ שְׂמֵחִים:

שׁוּבָה יהוה אֶת־שְׁבִיתֵנוּ, כַּאֲפִיקִים בַּנֶּגֶב:

הַזֹּרְעִים בְּדִמְעָה בְּרִנָּה יִקְצֹרוּ:

הָלוֹךְ יֵלֵךְ וּבָכֹה נֹשֵׂא מֶשֶׁךְ־הַזָּרַע, בֹּא־יָבֹא בְרִנָּה נֹשֵׂא אֲלֻמֹּתָיו:

כִּי־בָחַר יהוה בְּצִיּוֹן, אִוָּהּ לְמוֹשָׁב לוֹ *For the* LORD *has chosen Zion; He desired it for His home.* This verse captures the preselection of Yerushalayim as the site of the *Mikdash.* By performing the historical covenants on this mountain, it was predestined to house the presence of the *Shekhina* and to become the national capital of the Jewish homeland.

Yet despite its prior appointment, its location wasn't directly revealed to man. HaKadosh Barukh Hu prefers that human beings discover Him and partner with Him in establishing His presence in the human realm. Avraham wasn't informed of the precise location of Israel, but was instructed to journey to the land which "I will show you." Even the directions to the *Akeda* didn't include a specific set of coordinates describing the mountain upon which to sacrifice his son. According to *Ḥazal,* Avraham inferred its location by noticing an "unusual" cloud-covering atop this mountain.

So it was for the founder of our nation and so it was for David HaMelekh in advancing the actual construction of the *Mikdash.* In Psalms Chapter 132

Some say:

וְהוּא רַחוּם **He is compassionate.**   *Ps. 78*
He forgives iniquity and does not destroy.
Repeatedly He suppresses His anger, not rousing His full wrath.
LORD, save! May the King, answer us on the day we call.   *Ps. 20*

BLESSINGS OF THE SHEMA

*The Leader says the following, bowing at "Bless," standing straight
at "the LORD"; the congregation, followed by the Leader, responds,
bowing at "Bless," standing straight at "the LORD":*

Leader: # BLESS
the LORD, the blessed One.

Congregation: Bless the LORD, the blessed One,
for ever and all time.

Leader: Bless the LORD, the blessed One,
for ever and all time.

בָּרוּךְ **Blessed are You,** LORD our God, King of the Universe,
who by His word brings on evenings,
by His wisdom opens the gates of heaven,
with understanding makes time change and the seasons rotate,
and by His will
orders the stars in their constellations in the sky.
He creates day and night,
rolling away the light before the darkness,
and darkness before the light.
‣ He makes the day pass and brings on night,
distinguishing day from night:
the LORD of hosts is His name.
May the living and forever enduring God rule over us for all time.
Blessed are You, LORD, who brings on evenings.

Some say:

וְהוּא רַחוּם, יְכַפֵּר עָוֹן וְלֹא־יַשְׁחִית
וְהִרְבָּה לְהָשִׁיב אַפּוֹ, וְלֹא־יָעִיר כָּל־חֲמָתוֹ:

יהוה הוֹשִׁיעָה, הַמֶּלֶךְ יַעֲנֵנוּ בְיוֹם־קָרְאֵנוּ:

קריאת שמע וברכותיה

The שליח ציבור *says the following, bowing at* בָּרְכוּ, *standing straight at* ה'; *the* קהל,
followed by the שליח ציבור, *responds, bowing at* בָּרוּךְ, *standing straight at* ה':

ש״ץ:

בָּרְכוּ

אֶת יהוה הַמְבֹרָךְ.

קהל: בָּרוּךְ יהוה הַמְבֹרָךְ לְעוֹלָם וָעֶד.

ש״ץ: בָּרוּךְ יהוה הַמְבֹרָךְ לְעוֹלָם וָעֶד.

בָּרוּךְ אַתָּה יהוה אֱלֹהֵינוּ מֶלֶךְ הָעוֹלָם
אֲשֶׁר בִּדְבָרוֹ מַעֲרִיב עֲרָבִים
בְּחָכְמָה פּוֹתֵחַ שְׁעָרִים
וּבִתְבוּנָה מְשַׁנֶּה עִתִּים וּמַחֲלִיף אֶת הַזְּמַנִּים
וּמְסַדֵּר אֶת הַכּוֹכָבִים בְּמִשְׁמְרוֹתֵיהֶם בָּרָקִיעַ כִּרְצוֹנוֹ.
בּוֹרֵא יוֹם וָלַיְלָה, גּוֹלֵל אוֹר מִפְּנֵי חֹשֶׁךְ וְחֹשֶׁךְ מִפְּנֵי אוֹר
‹ וּמַעֲבִיר יוֹם וּמֵבִיא לַיְלָה, וּמַבְדִּיל בֵּין יוֹם וּבֵין לַיְלָה
יהוה צְבָאוֹת שְׁמוֹ.
אֵל חַי וְקַיָּם תָּמִיד, יִמְלֹךְ עָלֵינוּ לְעוֹלָם וָעֶד.
בָּרוּךְ אַתָּה יהוה, הַמַּעֲרִיב עֲרָבִים.

אַהֲבַת עוֹלָם With everlasting love
have You loved Your people, the house of Israel.
You have taught us Torah and commandments,
decrees and laws of justice.
Therefore, LORD our God, when we lie down and when we rise up
we will speak of Your decrees, rejoicing in the words of Your Torah
and Your commandments for ever.
➤ For they are our life and the length of our days;
on them will we meditate day and night.
May You never take away Your love from us.
Blessed are You, LORD, who loves His people Israel.

The Shema must be said with intense concentration.
When not with a minyan, say:
God, faithful King!

The following verse should be said aloud, while covering the eyes with the right hand:

Listen, Israel: the LORD is our God, the LORD is One.

Deut. 6

Quietly: Blessed be the name of His glorious kingdom for ever and all time.

וְאָהַבְתָּ Love the LORD your God with all your heart, with all your soul, and with all your might. These words which I command you today shall be on your heart. Teach them repeatedly to your children, speaking of them when you sit at home and when you travel on the way, when you lie down and when you rise. Bind them as a sign on your hand, and they shall be an emblem between your eyes. Write them on the doorposts of your house and gates.

Deut. 6

וְהָיָה If you indeed heed My commandments with which I charge you today, to love the LORD your God and worship Him with all your heart and with all your soul, I will give rain in your land in its season, the early and late rain; and you shall gather in your grain, wine and oil. I will give grass in your field for your cattle, and you shall eat and be satisfied. Be careful lest your heart be tempted and

Deut. 11

אַהֲבַת עוֹלָם בֵּית יִשְׂרָאֵל עַמְּךָ אָהַבְתָּ,
תּוֹרָה וּמִצְוֹת, חֻקִּים וּמִשְׁפָּטִים, אוֹתָנוּ לִמַּדְתָּ.
עַל כֵּן יהוה אֱלֹהֵינוּ בְּשָׁכְבֵנוּ וּבְקוּמֵנוּ נָשִׂיחַ בְּחֻקֶּיךָ,
וְנִשְׂמַח בְּדִבְרֵי תוֹרָתֶךָ וּבְמִצְוֹתֶיךָ לְעוֹלָם וָעֶד.
‹ כִּי הֵם חַיֵּינוּ וְאֹרֶךְ יָמֵינוּ, וּבָהֶם נֶהְגֶּה יוֹמָם וָלָיְלָה.
וְאַהֲבָתְךָ אַל תָּסִיר מִמֶּנּוּ לְעוֹלָמִים.
בָּרוּךְ אַתָּה יהוה, אוֹהֵב עַמּוֹ יִשְׂרָאֵל.

The שמע must be said with intense concentration.
When not with a מנין, say:

אֵל מֶלֶךְ נֶאֱמָן

The following verse should be said aloud, while covering the eyes with the right hand:

שְׁמַע יִשְׂרָאֵל, יהוה אֱלֹהֵינוּ, יהוה ׀ אֶחָד:

דברים ו

Quietly בָּרוּךְ שֵׁם כְּבוֹד מַלְכוּתוֹ לְעוֹלָם וָעֶד.

וְאָהַבְתָּ אֵת יהוה אֱלֹהֶיךָ, בְּכָל־לְבָבְךָ וּבְכָל־נַפְשְׁךָ וּבְכָל־מְאֹדֶךָ: דברים ו
וְהָיוּ הַדְּבָרִים הָאֵלֶּה, אֲשֶׁר אָנֹכִי מְצַוְּךָ הַיּוֹם, עַל־לְבָבֶךָ: וְשִׁנַּנְתָּם
לְבָנֶיךָ וְדִבַּרְתָּ בָּם, בְּשִׁבְתְּךָ בְּבֵיתֶךָ וּבְלֶכְתְּךָ בַדֶּרֶךְ, וּבְשָׁכְבְּךָ
וּבְקוּמֶךָ: וּקְשַׁרְתָּם לְאוֹת עַל־יָדֶךָ וְהָיוּ לְטֹטָפֹת בֵּין עֵינֶיךָ:
וּכְתַבְתָּם עַל־מְזֻזוֹת בֵּיתֶךָ וּבִשְׁעָרֶיךָ:

וְהָיָה אִם־שָׁמֹעַ תִּשְׁמְעוּ אֶל־מִצְוֹתַי אֲשֶׁר אָנֹכִי מְצַוֶּה אֶתְכֶם דברים יא
הַיּוֹם, לְאַהֲבָה אֶת־יהוה אֱלֹהֵיכֶם וּלְעָבְדוֹ, בְּכָל־לְבַבְכֶם וּבְכָל־
נַפְשְׁכֶם: וְנָתַתִּי מְטַר־אַרְצְכֶם בְּעִתּוֹ, יוֹרֶה וּמַלְקוֹשׁ, וְאָסַפְתָּ דְגָנֶךָ
וְתִירֹשְׁךָ וְיִצְהָרֶךָ: וְנָתַתִּי עֵשֶׂב בְּשָׂדְךָ לִבְהֶמְתֶּךָ, וְאָכַלְתָּ וְשָׂבָעְתָּ:
הִשָּׁמְרוּ לָכֶם פֶּן יִפְתֶּה לְבַבְכֶם, וְסַרְתֶּם וַעֲבַדְתֶּם אֱלֹהִים אֲחֵרִים
וְהִשְׁתַּחֲוִיתֶם לָהֶם: וְחָרָה אַף־יהוה בָּכֶם, וְעָצַר אֶת־הַשָּׁמַיִם

you go astray and worship other gods, bowing down to them. Then the LORD's anger will flare against you and He will close the heavens so that there will be no rain. The land will not yield its crops, and you will perish swiftly from the good land that the LORD is giving you. Therefore, set these, My words, on your heart and soul. Bind them as a sign on your hand, and they shall be an emblem between your eyes. Teach them to your children, speaking of them when you sit at home and when you travel on the way, when you lie down and when you rise. Write them on the doorposts of your house and gates, so that you and your children may live long in the land that the LORD swore to your ancestors to give them, for as long as the heavens are above the earth.

וַיֹּאמֶר The LORD spoke to Moses, saying: Speak to the Israelites *Num. 15* and tell them to make tassels on the corners of their garments for all generations. They shall attach to the tassel at each corner a thread of blue. This shall be your tassel, and you shall see it and remember all of the LORD's commandments and keep them, not straying after your heart and after your eyes, following your own sinful desires. Thus you will be reminded to keep all My commandments, and be holy to your God. I am the LORD your God, who brought you out of the land of Egypt to be your God. I am the LORD your God.

True –

The Leader repeats:

‣ The LORD your God is true –

וֶאֱמוּנָה – and faithful is all this,
and firmly established for us
that He is the LORD our God,
and there is none besides Him,
and that we, Israel, are His people.
He is our King, who redeems us from the hand of kings
and delivers us from the grasp of all tyrants.

וְלֹא־יִהְיֶה מָטָר, וְהָאֲדָמָה לֹא תִתֵּן אֶת־יְבוּלָהּ, וַאֲבַדְתֶּם מְהֵרָה מֵעַל הָאָרֶץ הַטֹּבָה אֲשֶׁר יהוה נֹתֵן לָכֶם: וְשַׂמְתֶּם אֶת־דְּבָרַי אֵלֶּה עַל־לְבַבְכֶם וְעַל־נַפְשְׁכֶם, וּקְשַׁרְתֶּם אֹתָם לְאוֹת עַל־יֶדְכֶם, וְהָיוּ לְטוֹטָפֹת בֵּין עֵינֵיכֶם: וְלִמַּדְתֶּם אֹתָם אֶת־בְּנֵיכֶם לְדַבֵּר בָּם, בְּשִׁבְתְּךָ בְּבֵיתֶךָ וּבְלֶכְתְּךָ בַדֶּרֶךְ, וּבְשָׁכְבְּךָ וּבְקוּמֶךָ: וּכְתַבְתָּם עַל־מְזוּזוֹת בֵּיתֶךָ וּבִשְׁעָרֶיךָ: לְמַעַן יִרְבּוּ יְמֵיכֶם וִימֵי בְנֵיכֶם עַל הָאֲדָמָה אֲשֶׁר נִשְׁבַּע יהוה לַאֲבֹתֵיכֶם לָתֵת לָהֶם, כִּימֵי הַשָּׁמַיִם עַל־הָאָרֶץ:

במדבר טו

וַיֹּאמֶר יהוה אֶל־מֹשֶׁה לֵּאמֹר: דַּבֵּר אֶל־בְּנֵי יִשְׂרָאֵל וְאָמַרְתָּ אֲלֵהֶם, וְעָשׂוּ לָהֶם צִיצִת עַל־כַּנְפֵי בִגְדֵיהֶם לְדֹרֹתָם, וְנָתְנוּ עַל־צִיצִת הַכָּנָף פְּתִיל תְּכֵלֶת: וְהָיָה לָכֶם לְצִיצִת, וּרְאִיתֶם אֹתוֹ וּזְכַרְתֶּם אֶת־כָּל־מִצְוֹת יהוה וַעֲשִׂיתֶם אֹתָם, וְלֹא תָתוּרוּ אַחֲרֵי לְבַבְכֶם וְאַחֲרֵי עֵינֵיכֶם, אֲשֶׁר־אַתֶּם זֹנִים אַחֲרֵיהֶם: לְמַעַן תִּזְכְּרוּ וַעֲשִׂיתֶם אֶת־כָּל־מִצְוֹתָי, וִהְיִיתֶם קְדֹשִׁים לֵאלֹהֵיכֶם: אֲנִי יהוה אֱלֹהֵיכֶם, אֲשֶׁר הוֹצֵאתִי אֶתְכֶם מֵאֶרֶץ מִצְרַיִם, לִהְיוֹת לָכֶם לֵאלֹהִים, אֲנִי יהוה אֱלֹהֵיכֶם:

אֱמֶת

The שליח ציבור *repeats:*

‹ יהוה אֱלֹהֵיכֶם אֱמֶת

וֶאֱמוּנָה כָּל זֹאת וְקַיָּם עָלֵינוּ
כִּי הוּא יהוה אֱלֹהֵינוּ וְאֵין זוּלָתוֹ
וַאֲנַחְנוּ יִשְׂרָאֵל עַמּוֹ.
הַפּוֹדֵנוּ מִיַּד מְלָכִים
מַלְכֵּנוּ הַגּוֹאֲלֵנוּ מִכַּף כָּל הֶעָרִיצִים.

He is our God, who on our behalf repays our foes
and brings just retribution on our mortal enemies;
who performs great deeds beyond understanding
and wonders beyond number;
who kept us alive, not letting our foot slip;   *Ps. 66*
who led us on the high places of our enemies,
raising our pride above all our foes;
who did miracles for us
and brought vengeance against Pharaoh;
who performed signs and wonders
in the land of Ham's children;
who smote in His wrath all the firstborn of Egypt,
and brought out His people Israel from their midst
into everlasting freedom;
who led His children through the divided Reed Sea,
plunging their pursuers and enemies into the depths.
When His children saw His might,
they gave praise and thanks to His name,
▸ and willingly accepted His Sovereignty.
Moses and the children of Israel
then sang a song to You with great joy,
and they all exclaimed:

> מִי־כָמֹכָה "Who is like You, Lord, among the mighty?   *Ex. 15*
> Who is like You, majestic in holiness,
> awesome in praises, doing wonders?"

▸ Your children beheld Your majesty
as You parted the sea before Moses.
"This is my God!" they responded, and then said:

> "The Lord shall reign for ever and ever."   *Ex. 15*

▸ And it is said,

> "For the Lord has redeemed Jacob and rescued him   *Jer. 31*
> from a power stronger than his own."

Blessed are You, Lord, who redeemed Israel.

הָאֵל הַנִּפְרָע לָנוּ מִצָּרֵינוּ

וְהַמְשַׁלֵּם גְּמוּל לְכָל אוֹיְבֵי נַפְשֵׁנוּ.

הָעוֹשֶׂה גְדוֹלוֹת עַד אֵין חֵקֶר, וְנִפְלָאוֹת עַד אֵין מִסְפָּר

תהלים סו הַשָּׂם נַפְשֵׁנוּ בַּחַיִּים, וְלֹא־נָתַן לַמּוֹט רַגְלֵנוּ:

הַמַּדְרִיכֵנוּ עַל בָּמוֹת אוֹיְבֵינוּ

וַיָּרֶם קַרְנֵנוּ עַל כָּל שׂוֹנְאֵינוּ.

הָעוֹשֶׂה לָּנוּ נִסִּים וּנְקָמָה בְּפַרְעֹה

אוֹתוֹת וּמוֹפְתִים בְּאַדְמַת בְּנֵי חָם.

הַמַּכֶּה בְעֶבְרָתוֹ כָּל בְּכוֹרֵי מִצְרָיִם

וַיּוֹצֵא אֶת עַמּוֹ יִשְׂרָאֵל מִתּוֹכָם לְחֵרוּת עוֹלָם.

הַמַּעֲבִיר בָּנָיו בֵּין גִּזְרֵי יַם סוּף

אֶת רוֹדְפֵיהֶם וְאֶת שׂוֹנְאֵיהֶם בִּתְהוֹמוֹת טִבַּע

וְרָאוּ בָנָיו גְּבוּרָתוֹ, שִׁבְּחוּ וְהוֹדוּ לִשְׁמוֹ

‹ וּמַלְכוּתוֹ בְּרָצוֹן קִבְּלוּ עֲלֵיהֶם.

מֹשֶׁה וּבְנֵי יִשְׂרָאֵל, לְךָ עָנוּ שִׁירָה בְּשִׂמְחָה רַבָּה

וְאָמְרוּ כֻלָּם

שמות טו מִי־כָמֹכָה בָּאֵלִם יהוה

מִי כָּמֹכָה נֶאְדָּר בַּקֹּדֶשׁ

נוֹרָא תְהִלֹּת עֹשֵׂה פֶלֶא:

‹ מַלְכוּתְךָ רָאוּ בָנֶיךָ, בּוֹקֵעַ יָם לִפְנֵי מֹשֶׁה

זֶה אֵלִי עָנוּ, וְאָמְרוּ

שמות טו יהוה יִמְלֹךְ לְעֹלָם וָעֶד:

‹ וְנֶאֱמַר

ירמיהו לא כִּי־פָדָה יהוה אֶת־יַעֲקֹב, וּגְאָלוֹ מִיַּד חָזָק מִמֶּנּוּ:

בָּרוּךְ אַתָּה יהוה, גָּאַל יִשְׂרָאֵל.

הַשְׁכִּיבֵנוּ Help us lie down, O LORD our God, in peace,
and rise up, O our King, to life.
Spread over us Your canopy of peace.
Direct us with Your good counsel,
and save us for the sake of Your name.
Shield us and remove from us every enemy,
plague, sword, famine and sorrow.
Remove the adversary from before and behind us.
Shelter us in the shadow of Your wings,
for You, God, are our Guardian and Deliverer;
You, God, are a gracious and compassionate King.
▸ Guard our going out and our coming in,
for life and peace, from now and for ever.
Blessed are You, LORD, who guards His people Israel for ever.

In Israel the service continues with Half Kaddish on page 532.

בָּרוּךְ Blessed be the LORD for ever. Amen and Amen.   *Ps. 89*
Blessed from Zion be the LORD   *Ps. 135*
who dwells in Jerusalem. Halleluya!
Blessed be the LORD, God of Israel,   *Ps. 72*
who alone does wondrous things.
Blessed be His glorious name for ever,
and may the whole earth be filled with His glory. Amen and Amen.
May the glory of the LORD endure for ever;   *Ps. 104*
may the LORD rejoice in His works.
May the name of the LORD be blessed now and for all time.   *Ps. 113*
For the sake of His great name   *1 Sam. 12*
the LORD will not abandon His people,
for the LORD vowed to make you a people of His own.
When all the people saw [God's wonders] they fell on their faces   *1 Kings 18*
and said: "The LORD, He is God; the LORD, He is God."
Then the LORD shall be King over all the earth;   *Zech. 14*
on that day the LORD shall be One and His name One.

הַשְׁכִּיבֵנוּ יהוה אֱלֹהֵינוּ לְשָׁלוֹם

וְהַעֲמִידֵנוּ מַלְכֵּנוּ לְחַיִּים

וּפְרֹשׂ עָלֵינוּ סֻכַּת שְׁלוֹמֶךָ, וְתַקְּנֵנוּ בְּעֵצָה טוֹבָה מִלְּפָנֶיךָ

וְהוֹשִׁיעֵנוּ לְמַעַן שְׁמֶךָ.

וְהָגֵן בַּעֲדֵנוּ, וְהָסֵר מֵעָלֵינוּ אוֹיֵב, דֶּבֶר וְחֶרֶב וְרָעָב וְיָגוֹן

וְהָסֵר שָׂטָן מִלְּפָנֵינוּ וּמֵאַחֲרֵינוּ, וּבְצֵל כְּנָפֶיךָ תַּסְתִּירֵנוּ

כִּי אֵל שׁוֹמְרֵנוּ וּמַצִּילֵנוּ אָתָּה

כִּי אֵל מֶלֶךְ חַנּוּן וְרַחוּם אָתָּה.

‹ וּשְׁמֹר צֵאתֵנוּ וּבוֹאֵנוּ לְחַיִּים וּלְשָׁלוֹם מֵעַתָּה וְעַד עוֹלָם.

בָּרוּךְ אַתָּה יהוה, שׁוֹמֵר עַמּוֹ יִשְׂרָאֵל לָעַד.

In ארץ ישראל *the service continues with* חצי קדיש *on page 533.*

בָּרוּךְ יהוה לְעוֹלָם, אָמֵן וְאָמֵן:

בָּרוּךְ יהוה מִצִּיּוֹן, שֹׁכֵן יְרוּשָׁלָ͏ִם, הַלְלוּיָהּ:

בָּרוּךְ יהוה אֱלֹהִים אֱלֹהֵי יִשְׂרָאֵל, עֹשֵׂה נִפְלָאוֹת לְבַדּוֹ:

וּבָרוּךְ שֵׁם כְּבוֹדוֹ לְעוֹלָם

וְיִמָּלֵא כְבוֹדוֹ אֶת־כָּל־הָאָרֶץ, אָמֵן וְאָמֵן:

יְהִי כְבוֹד יהוה לְעוֹלָם, יִשְׂמַח יהוה בְּמַעֲשָׂיו:

יְהִי שֵׁם יהוה מְבֹרָךְ מֵעַתָּה וְעַד־עוֹלָם:

כִּי לֹא־יִטֹּשׁ יהוה אֶת־עַמּוֹ בַּעֲבוּר שְׁמוֹ הַגָּדוֹל

כִּי הוֹאִיל יהוה לַעֲשׂוֹת אֶתְכֶם לוֹ לְעָם:

וַיַּרְא כָּל־הָעָם וַיִּפְּלוּ עַל־פְּנֵיהֶם

וַיֹּאמְרוּ, יהוה הוּא הָאֱלֹהִים, יהוה הוּא הָאֱלֹהִים:

וְהָיָה יהוה לְמֶלֶךְ עַל־כָּל־הָאָרֶץ

בַּיּוֹם הַהוּא יִהְיֶה יהוה אֶחָד וּשְׁמוֹ אֶחָד:

May Your love, LORD, be upon us,
as we have put our hope in You.   *Ps. 33*

Save us, LORD our God, gather us   *Ps. 106*
and deliver us from the nations,
to thank Your holy name, and glory in Your praise.

All the nations You made shall come and bow before You, LORD,   *Ps. 86*
and pay honor to Your name,
for You are great and You perform wonders:
You alone are God.

We, Your people, the flock of Your pasture, will praise You for ever.   *Ps. 79*
For all generations we will relate Your praise.

בָּרוּךְ Blessed is the LORD by day, blessed is the LORD by night.
Blessed is the LORD when we lie down;
blessed is the LORD when we rise.
For in Your hand are the souls of the living and the dead,
[as it is written:] "In His hand is every living soul,   *Job 12*
and the breath of all mankind."
Into Your hand I entrust my spirit: *Ps. 31*
You redeemed me, LORD, God of truth.
Our God in heaven, bring unity to Your name,
establish Your kingdom constantly
and reign over us for ever and all time.

יִרְאוּ May our eyes see, our hearts rejoice,
and our souls be glad in Your true salvation,
when Zion is told, "Your God reigns."
The LORD is King, the LORD was King,
the LORD will be King for ever and all time.
▸ For sovereignty is Yours, and to all eternity You will reign in glory,
for we have no king but You.
Blessed are You, LORD,
the King who in His constant glory will reign over us
and all His creation for ever and all time.

תהלים לג

יְהִי־חַסְדְּךָ יהוה עָלֵינוּ, כַּאֲשֶׁר יִחַלְנוּ לָךְ:

תהלים קו

הוֹשִׁיעֵנוּ יהוה אֱלֹהֵינוּ, וְקַבְּצֵנוּ מִן־הַגּוֹיִם

לְהוֹדוֹת לְשֵׁם קָדְשֶׁךָ, לְהִשְׁתַּבֵּחַ בִּתְהִלָּתֶךָ:

תהלים פו

כָּל־גּוֹיִם אֲשֶׁר עָשִׂיתָ, יָבֹאוּ וְיִשְׁתַּחֲווּ לְפָנֶיךָ, אֲדֹנָי

וִיכַבְּדוּ לִשְׁמֶךָ:

כִּי־גָדוֹל אַתָּה וְעֹשֵׂה נִפְלָאוֹת, אַתָּה אֱלֹהִים לְבַדֶּךָ:

תהלים עט

וַאֲנַחְנוּ עַמְּךָ וְצֹאן מַרְעִיתֶךָ, נוֹדֶה לְךָ לְעוֹלָם

לְדוֹר וָדֹר נְסַפֵּר תְּהִלָּתֶךָ:

בָּרוּךְ יהוה בַּיּוֹם, בָּרוּךְ יהוה בַּלָּיְלָה

בָּרוּךְ יהוה בְּשָׁכְבֵנוּ, בָּרוּךְ יהוה בְּקוּמֵנוּ.

כִּי בְיָדְךָ נַפְשׁוֹת הַחַיִּים וְהַמֵּתִים.

איוב יב

אֲשֶׁר בְּיָדוֹ נֶפֶשׁ כָּל־חָי, וְרוּחַ כָּל־בְּשַׂר־אִישׁ:

תהלים לא

בְּיָדְךָ אַפְקִיד רוּחִי, פָּדִיתָה אוֹתִי יהוה אֵל אֱמֶת:

אֱלֹהֵינוּ שֶׁבַּשָּׁמַיִם, יַחֵד שִׁמְךָ וְקַיֵּם מַלְכוּתְךָ תָּמִיד

וּמְלֹךְ עָלֵינוּ לְעוֹלָם וָעֶד.

יִרְאוּ עֵינֵינוּ וְיִשְׂמַח לִבֵּנוּ

וְתָגֵל נַפְשֵׁנוּ בִּישׁוּעָתְךָ בֶּאֱמֶת

בֶּאֱמֹר לְצִיּוֹן מָלַךְ אֱלֹהָיִךְ.

יהוה מֶלֶךְ, יהוה מָלָךְ, יהוה יִמְלֹךְ לְעוֹלָם וָעֶד.

‹ כִּי הַמַּלְכוּת שֶׁלְּךָ הִיא, וּלְעוֹלְמֵי עַד תִּמְלֹךְ בְּכָבוֹד

כִּי אֵין לָנוּ מֶלֶךְ אֶלָּא אָתָּה.

בָּרוּךְ אַתָּה יהוה

הַמֶּלֶךְ בִּכְבוֹדוֹ תָּמִיד, יִמְלֹךְ עָלֵינוּ לְעוֹלָם וָעֶד, וְעַל כָּל מַעֲשָׂיו.

HALF KADDISH

Leader: יִתְגַּדַּל Magnified and sanctified
may His great name be,
in the world He created by His will.
May He establish His kingdom
in your lifetime and in your days,
and in the lifetime of all the house of Israel,
swiftly and soon –
and say: Amen.

All: May His great name be blessed for ever and all time.

Leader: Blessed and praised, glorified and exalted,
raised and honored,
uplifted and lauded
be the name of the Holy One,
blessed be He,
beyond any blessing,
song, praise and consolation
uttered in the world –
and say: Amen.

THE AMIDA

*The following prayer, until "in former years" on page 548, is said silently, standing with feet
together. Take three steps forward and at the points indicated by ˙, bend the knees at
the first word, bow at the second, and stand straight before saying God's name.*

O Lord, open my lips,
so that my mouth may declare Your praise.

Ps. 51

PATRIARCHS

בָּרוּךְ˙ Blessed are You, Lord our God and God of our fathers,
God of Abraham, God of Isaac and God of Jacob;
the great, mighty and awesome God, God Most High,

חצי קדיש

ש״ץ: יִתְגַּדַּל וְיִתְקַדַּשׁ שְׁמֵהּ רַבָּא (קהל: אָמֵן)
בְּעָלְמָא דִּי בְרָא כִרְעוּתֵהּ
וְיַמְלִיךְ מַלְכוּתֵהּ
בְּחַיֵּיכוֹן וּבְיוֹמֵיכוֹן וּבְחַיֵּי דְּכָל בֵּית יִשְׂרָאֵל
בַּעֲגָלָא וּבִזְמַן קָרִיב
וְאִמְרוּ אָמֵן. (קהל: אָמֵן)

קהל
ושׁ״ץ: יְהֵא שְׁמֵהּ רַבָּא מְבָרַךְ לְעָלַם וּלְעָלְמֵי עָלְמַיָּא.

ש״ץ: יִתְבָּרַךְ וְיִשְׁתַּבַּח וְיִתְפָּאַר וְיִתְרוֹמַם וְיִתְנַשֵּׂא
וְיִתְהַדָּר וְיִתְעַלֶּה וְיִתְהַלָּל
שְׁמֵהּ דְּקֻדְשָׁא בְּרִיךְ הוּא (קהל: בְּרִיךְ הוּא)
לְעֵלָּא מִן כָּל בִּרְכָתָא וְשִׁירָתָא, תֻּשְׁבְּחָתָא וְנֶחֱמָתָא
דַּאֲמִירָן בְּעָלְמָא
וְאִמְרוּ אָמֵן. (קהל: אָמֵן)

עמידה

The following prayer, until קַדְמוֹנִיּוֹת *on page 549, is said silently, standing with feet*
together. Take three steps forward and at the points indicated by ׳, bend the knees at
the first word, bow at the second, and stand straight before saying God's name.

תהלים נא

אֲדֹנָי, שְׂפָתַי תִּפְתָּח, וּפִי יַגִּיד תְּהִלָּתֶךָ:

אבות

יָּבָרוּךְ אַתָּה יהוה, אֱלֹהֵינוּ וֵאלֹהֵי אֲבוֹתֵינוּ
אֱלֹהֵי אַבְרָהָם, אֱלֹהֵי יִצְחָק, וֵאלֹהֵי יַעֲקֹב
הָאֵל הַגָּדוֹל הַגִּבּוֹר וְהַנּוֹרָא, אֵל עֶלְיוֹן

who bestows acts of loving-kindness and creates all,
who remembers the loving-kindness of the fathers
and will bring a Redeemer to their children's children
for the sake of His name, in love.
King, Helper, Savior, Shield:
▾Blessed are You, Lord,
Shield of Abraham.

DIVINE MIGHT

אַתָּה גִבּוֹר You are eternally mighty, Lord.
You give life to the dead
and have great power to save.

> *In Israel:* He causes the dew to fall.

He sustains the living with loving-kindness,
and with great compassion revives the dead.
He supports the fallen, heals the sick,
sets captives free,
and keeps His faith with those who sleep in the dust.
Who is like You, Master of might,
and to whom can You be compared,
O King who brings death and gives life,
and makes salvation grow?
Faithful are You to revive the dead.
Blessed are You, Lord,
who revives the dead.

HOLINESS

אַתָּה קָדוֹשׁ You are holy and Your name is holy,
and holy ones praise You daily, Selah!
Blessed are You,
Lord, the holy God.

גּוֹמֵל חֲסָדִים טוֹבִים, וְקוֹנֶה הַכֹּל

וְזוֹכֵר חַסְדֵי אָבוֹת

וּמֵבִיא גוֹאֵל לִבְנֵי בְנֵיהֶם לְמַעַן שְׁמוֹ בְּאַהֲבָה.

מֶלֶךְ עוֹזֵר וּמוֹשִׁיעַ וּמָגֵן.

יָּבָרוּךְ אַתָּה יהוה, מָגֵן אַבְרָהָם.

גבורות

אַתָּה גִבּוֹר לְעוֹלָם, אֲדֹנָי

מְחַיֵּה מֵתִים אַתָּה, רַב לְהוֹשִׁיעַ

בארץ ישראל: מוֹרִיד הַטָּל

מְכַלְכֵּל חַיִּים בְּחֶסֶד

מְחַיֵּה מֵתִים בְּרַחֲמִים רַבִּים

סוֹמֵךְ נוֹפְלִים, וְרוֹפֵא חוֹלִים, וּמַתִּיר אֲסוּרִים

וּמְקַיֵּם אֱמוּנָתוֹ לִישֵׁנֵי עָפָר.

מִי כָמוֹךָ, בַּעַל גְּבוּרוֹת

וּמִי דוֹמֶה לָךְ

מֶלֶךְ, מֵמִית וּמְחַיֶּה וּמַצְמִיחַ יְשׁוּעָה.

וְנֶאֱמָן אַתָּה לְהַחֲיוֹת מֵתִים.

בָּרוּךְ אַתָּה יהוה, מְחַיֵּה הַמֵּתִים.

קדושת השם

אַתָּה קָדוֹשׁ וְשִׁמְךָ קָדוֹשׁ

וּקְדוֹשִׁים בְּכָל יוֹם יְהַלְלוּךָ סֶּלָה.

בָּרוּךְ אַתָּה יהוה, הָאֵל הַקָּדוֹשׁ.

KNOWLEDGE

אַתָּה חוֹנֵן You grace humanity with knowledge
and teach mortals understanding.

On Motza'ei Shabbat say:

אַתָּה חוֹנַנְתָּנוּ You have graced us with the knowledge of Your Torah, and
taught us to perform the statutes of Your will. You have distinguished, LORD
our God, between sacred and profane, light and darkness, Israel and the
nations, and between the seventh day and the six days of work. Our Father,
our King, may the days approaching us bring peace; may we be free from
all sin, cleansed from all iniquity, holding fast to our reverence of You. And

---

Grace us with the knowledge, understanding
and discernment that come from You.
Blessed are You, LORD, who graciously grants knowledge.

REPENTANCE

הֲשִׁיבֵנוּ Bring us back, our Father, to Your Torah.
Draw us near, our King, to Your service.
Lead us back to You in perfect repentance.
Blessed are You, LORD, who desires repentance.

FORGIVENESS

Strike the left side of the chest at °.

סְלַח לָנוּ Forgive us, our Father,
for we have °sinned.
Pardon us, our King,
for we have °transgressed;
for You pardon and forgive.
Blessed are You, LORD, the gracious One who repeatedly forgives.

REDEMPTION

רְאֵה Look on our affliction,
plead our cause,
and redeem us soon for Your name's sake,
for You are a powerful Redeemer.
Blessed are You, LORD, the Redeemer of Israel.

דַעַת

אַתָּה חוֹנֵן לְאָדָם דַּעַת, וּמְלַמֵּד לֶאֱנוֹשׁ בִּינָה.

On מוצאי שבת say:

אַתָּה חוֹנַנְתָּנוּ לְמַדַּע תּוֹרָתֶךָ, וַתְּלַמְּדֵנוּ לַעֲשׂוֹת חֻקֵּי רְצוֹנֶךָ, וַתַּבְדֵּל
יהוה אֱלֹהֵינוּ בֵּין קֹדֶשׁ לְחֹל, בֵּין אוֹר לְחֹשֶׁךְ, בֵּין יִשְׂרָאֵל לָעַמִּים, בֵּין יוֹם
הַשְּׁבִיעִי לְשֵׁשֶׁת יְמֵי הַמַּעֲשֶׂה. אָבִינוּ מַלְכֵּנוּ, הָחֵל עָלֵינוּ הַיָּמִים הַבָּאִים
לִקְרָאתֵנוּ לְשָׁלוֹם, חֲשׂוּכִים מִכָּל חֵטְא וּמְנֻקִּים מִכָּל עָוֹן וּמְדֻבָּקִים בְּיִרְאָתֶךָ. וְ

חָנֵּנוּ מֵאִתְּךָ דֵּעָה בִּינָה וְהַשְׂכֵּל.
בָּרוּךְ אַתָּה יהוה, חוֹנֵן הַדָּעַת.

תְּשׁוּבָה

הֲשִׁיבֵנוּ אָבִינוּ לְתוֹרָתֶךָ
וְקָרְבֵנוּ מַלְכֵּנוּ לַעֲבוֹדָתֶךָ
וְהַחֲזִירֵנוּ בִּתְשׁוּבָה שְׁלֵמָה לְפָנֶיךָ.
בָּרוּךְ אַתָּה יהוה, הָרוֹצֶה בִּתְשׁוּבָה.

סְלִיחָה

Strike the left side of the chest at °.

סְלַח לָנוּ אָבִינוּ כִּי °חָטָאנוּ
מְחַל לָנוּ מַלְכֵּנוּ כִּי °פָשָׁעְנוּ
כִּי מוֹחֵל וְסוֹלֵחַ אָתָּה.
בָּרוּךְ אַתָּה יהוה, חַנּוּן הַמַּרְבֶּה לִסְלֹחַ.

גְּאוּלָה

רְאֵה בְעָנְיֵנוּ, וְרִיבָה רִיבֵנוּ
וּגְאָלֵנוּ מְהֵרָה לְמַעַן שְׁמֶךָ
כִּי גּוֹאֵל חָזָק אָתָּה.
בָּרוּךְ אַתָּה יהוה, גּוֹאֵל יִשְׂרָאֵל.

HEALING

רְפָאֵנוּ Heal us, LORD, and we shall be healed.

Save us and we shall be saved,

for You are our praise.

Bring complete recovery for all our ailments,

The following prayer for a sick person may be said here:

May it be Your will, O LORD my God and God of my ancestors, that You speedily send a complete recovery from heaven, a healing of both soul and body, to the patient (*name*), son/daughter of (*mother's name*) among the other afflicted of Israel.

---

for You, God, King, are a faithful and compassionate Healer.

Blessed are You, LORD,

Healer of the sick of His people Israel.

PROSPERITY

בָּרֵךְ Bless this year for us, LORD our God,

and all its types of produce for good.

Grant blessing on the face of the earth,

and from its goodness satisfy us,

blessing our year as the best of years.

Blessed are You, LORD,

who blesses the years.

INGATHERING OF EXILES

תְּקַע Sound the great shofar for our freedom,

raise high the banner to gather our exiles,

and gather us together

from the four quarters of the earth.

Blessed are You, LORD,

who gathers the dispersed of His people Israel.

רפואה

רְפָאֵנוּ יהוה וְנֵרָפֵא
הוֹשִׁיעֵנוּ וְנִוָּשֵׁעָה, כִּי תְהִלָּתֵנוּ אָתָּה
וְהַעֲלֵה רְפוּאָה שְׁלֵמָה לְכָל מַכּוֹתֵינוּ

The following prayer for a sick person may be said here:

יְהִי רָצוֹן מִלְּפָנֶיךָ יהוה אֱלֹהַי וֵאלֹהֵי אֲבוֹתַי, שֶׁתִּשְׁלַח מְהֵרָה רְפוּאָה שְׁלֵמָה
מִן הַשָּׁמַיִם רְפוּאַת הַנֶּפֶשׁ וּרְפוּאַת הַגּוּף לַחוֹלֶה/לַחוֹלָה name of patient
בֶּן/בַּת mother's name בְּתוֹךְ שְׁאָר חוֹלֵי יִשְׂרָאֵל.

כִּי אֵל מֶלֶךְ רוֹפֵא נֶאֱמָן וְרַחֲמָן אָתָּה.
בָּרוּךְ אַתָּה יהוה, רוֹפֵא חוֹלֵי עַמּוֹ יִשְׂרָאֵל.

ברכת השנים

בָּרֵךְ עָלֵינוּ יהוה אֱלֹהֵינוּ אֶת הַשָּׁנָה הַזֹּאת
וְאֶת כָּל מִינֵי תְבוּאָתָהּ, לְטוֹבָה
וְתֵן בְּרָכָה עַל פְּנֵי הָאֲדָמָה
וְשַׂבְּעֵנוּ מִטּוּבָהּ
וּבָרֵךְ שְׁנָתֵנוּ כַּשָּׁנִים הַטּוֹבוֹת.
בָּרוּךְ אַתָּה יהוה, מְבָרֵךְ הַשָּׁנִים.

קבוץ גלויות

תְּקַע בְּשׁוֹפָר גָּדוֹל לְחֵרוּתֵנוּ
וְשָׂא נֵס לְקַבֵּץ גָּלֻיּוֹתֵינוּ
וְקַבְּצֵנוּ יַחַד מֵאַרְבַּע כַּנְפוֹת הָאָרֶץ.
בָּרוּךְ אַתָּה יהוה, מְקַבֵּץ נִדְחֵי עַמּוֹ יִשְׂרָאֵל.

JUSTICE

הָשִׁיבָה Restore our judges as at first,
and our counselors as at the beginning,
and remove from us sorrow and sighing.
May You alone, LORD,
reign over us
with loving-kindness and compassion,
and vindicate us in justice.
Blessed are You, LORD,
the King who loves righteousness and justice.

AGAINST INFORMERS

וְלַמַּלְשִׁינִים For the slanderers let there be no hope,
and may all wickedness perish in an instant.
May all Your people's enemies swiftly be cut down.
May You swiftly uproot, crush, cast down
and humble the arrogant swiftly in our days.
Blessed are You, LORD,
who destroys enemies and humbles the arrogant.

THE RIGHTEOUS

עַל הַצַּדִּיקִים To the righteous, the pious,
the elders of Your people the house of Israel,
the remnant of their scholars,
the righteous converts, and to us,
may Your compassion be aroused,
LORD our God.
Grant a good reward to all
who sincerely trust in Your name.
Set our lot with them,
so that we may never be ashamed,
for in You we trust.
Blessed are You, LORD,
who is the support and trust of the righteous.

השבת המשפט

הָשִׁיבָה שׁוֹפְטֵינוּ כְּבָרִאשׁוֹנָה

וְיוֹעֲצֵינוּ כְּבַתְּחִלָּה

וְהָסֵר מִמֶּנּוּ יָגוֹן וַאֲנָחָה

וּמְלֹךְ עָלֵינוּ אַתָּה יהוה לְבַדְּךָ בְּחֶסֶד וּבְרַחֲמִים

וְצַדְּקֵנוּ בַּמִּשְׁפָּט.

בָּרוּךְ אַתָּה יהוה, מֶלֶךְ אוֹהֵב צְדָקָה וּמִשְׁפָּט.

ברכת המינים

וְלַמַּלְשִׁינִים אַל תְּהִי תִקְוָה

וְכָל הָרִשְׁעָה כְּרֶגַע תֹּאבֵד

וְכָל אוֹיְבֵי עַמְּךָ מְהֵרָה יִכָּרֵתוּ

וְהַזֵּדִים מְהֵרָה תְעַקֵּר וּתְשַׁבֵּר וּתְמַגֵּר וְתַכְנִיעַ בִּמְהֵרָה בְיָמֵינוּ.

בָּרוּךְ אַתָּה יהוה, שׁוֹבֵר אוֹיְבִים וּמַכְנִיעַ זֵדִים.

על הצדיקים

עַל הַצַּדִּיקִים וְעַל הַחֲסִידִים

וְעַל זִקְנֵי עַמְּךָ בֵּית יִשְׂרָאֵל

וְעַל פְּלֵיטַת סוֹפְרֵיהֶם

וְעַל גֵּרֵי הַצֶּדֶק, וְעָלֵינוּ

יֶהֱמוּ רַחֲמֶיךָ יהוה אֱלֹהֵינוּ

וְתֵן שָׂכָר טוֹב לְכָל הַבּוֹטְחִים בְּשִׁמְךָ בֶּאֱמֶת

וְשִׂים חֶלְקֵנוּ עִמָּהֶם

וּלְעוֹלָם לֹא נֵבוֹשׁ כִּי בְךָ בָּטָחְנוּ.

בָּרוּךְ אַתָּה יהוה, מִשְׁעָן וּמִבְטָח לַצַּדִּיקִים.

REBUILDING JERUSALEM

וְלִירוּשָׁלַיִם To Jerusalem, Your city, may You return in compassion,
and may You dwell in it as You promised.
May You rebuild it rapidly in our days
as an everlasting structure,
and install within it soon the throne of David.
Blessed are You, LORD, who builds Jerusalem.

KINGDOM OF DAVID

אֶת צֶמַח May the offshoot of Your servant David soon flower,
and may his pride be raised high by Your salvation,
for we wait for Your salvation all day.
Blessed are You, LORD, who makes the glory of salvation flourish.

RESPONSE TO PRAYER

שְׁמַע קוֹלֵנוּ Listen to our voice, LORD our God.
Spare us and have compassion on us,
and in compassion and favor accept our prayer,
for You, God, listen to prayers and pleas.
Do not turn us away, O our King,
empty-handed from Your presence,
for You listen with compassion
to the prayer of Your people Israel.
Blessed are You, LORD, who listens to prayer.

TEMPLE SERVICE

רְצֵה Find favor, LORD our God,
in Your people Israel and their prayer.
Restore the service to Your most holy House,
and accept in love and favor
the fire-offerings of Israel and their prayer.
May the service of Your people Israel always find favor with You.
And may our eyes witness
Your return to Zion in compassion.
Blessed are You, LORD, who restores His Presence to Zion.

בניין ירושלים

וְלִירוּשָׁלַיִם עִירְךָ בְּרַחֲמִים תָּשׁוּב

וְתִשְׁכֹּן בְּתוֹכָהּ כַּאֲשֶׁר דִּבַּרְתָּ

וּבְנֵה אוֹתָהּ בְּקָרוֹב בְּיָמֵינוּ בִּנְיַן עוֹלָם

וְכִסֵּא דָוִד מְהֵרָה לְתוֹכָהּ תָּכִין.

בָּרוּךְ אַתָּה יהוה, בּוֹנֵה יְרוּשָׁלָיִם.

משיח בן דוד

אֶת צֶמַח דָּוִד עַבְדְּךָ מְהֵרָה תַצְמִיחַ, וְקַרְנוֹ תָּרוּם בִּישׁוּעָתֶךָ

כִּי לִישׁוּעָתְךָ קִוִּינוּ כָּל הַיּוֹם.

בָּרוּךְ אַתָּה יהוה, מַצְמִיחַ קֶרֶן יְשׁוּעָה.

שומע תפלה

שְׁמַע קוֹלֵנוּ יהוה אֱלֹהֵינוּ

חוּס וְרַחֵם עָלֵינוּ, וְקַבֵּל בְּרַחֲמִים וּבְרָצוֹן אֶת תְּפִלָּתֵנוּ

כִּי אֵל שׁוֹמֵעַ תְּפִלּוֹת וְתַחֲנוּנִים אָתָּה

וּמִלְּפָנֶיךָ מַלְכֵּנוּ רֵיקָם אַל תְּשִׁיבֵנוּ

כִּי אַתָּה שׁוֹמֵעַ תְּפִלַּת עַמְּךָ יִשְׂרָאֵל בְּרַחֲמִים.

בָּרוּךְ אַתָּה יהוה, שׁוֹמֵעַ תְּפִלָּה.

עבודה

רְצֵה יהוה אֱלֹהֵינוּ בְּעַמְּךָ יִשְׂרָאֵל, וּבִתְפִלָּתָם

וְהָשֵׁב אֶת הָעֲבוֹדָה לִדְבִיר בֵּיתֶךָ

וְאִשֵּׁי יִשְׂרָאֵל וּתְפִלָּתָם בְּאַהֲבָה תְקַבֵּל בְּרָצוֹן

וּתְהִי לְרָצוֹן תָּמִיד עֲבוֹדַת יִשְׂרָאֵל עַמֶּךָ.

וְתֶחֱזֶינָה עֵינֵינוּ בְּשׁוּבְךָ לְצִיּוֹן בְּרַחֲמִים.

בָּרוּךְ אַתָּה יהוה, הַמַּחֲזִיר שְׁכִינָתוֹ לְצִיּוֹן.

THANKSGIVING

Bow at the first nine words.

מוֹדִים We give thanks to You,
for You are the LORD our God and God of our ancestors
for ever and all time.
You are the Rock of our lives,
Shield of our salvation from generation to generation.
We will thank You and declare Your praise for our lives,
which are entrusted into Your hand;
for our souls, which are placed in Your charge;
for Your miracles which are with us every day;
and for Your wonders and favors at all times,
evening, morning and midday.
You are good – for Your compassion never fails.
You are compassionate – for Your loving-kindnesses never cease.
We have always placed our hope in You.

> *At this point in the silent Amida it is permitted to add a rabbinically formulated "Al HaNissim." The following was written by Rabbi Neria (alternative versions can be found on pages 656–659).*
>
> עַל הַנִּסִּים [We thank You also] for the miracles, the redemption, the mighty deeds, the salvations, and the victories in battle which You performed for our ancestors in those days, at this time.
>
> When the armies of the Middle East rose up against Your people Israel and sought to destroy, slay and exterminate the inhabitants of Your Land, young and old, children and women, and among them those who had survived the sword and were saved from the horror of Your enemies' flames, one from a city, two from a family, hoping to find a resting place for the soles of their feet in Your land that You had promised them; then You in Your great compassion stood by us in our time of distress, thwarted their counsel and frustrated their plans, raised us upright and established our liberty, championed our cause, judged our claim, avenged our wrong, delivered the strong into the hands of the weak, the many into the hands of the few, the impure into the hands of the holy. You made for Yourself great and holy renown in Your world, and for Your people Israel You performed a great salvation and redemption as of this day. You subjugated peoples under us, nations beneath our feet, and You gave us our inheritance, the Land of Canaan to its borders, and returned us to the place of Your holy Sanctuary.

הודאה

Bow at the first five words.

מוֹדִים אֲנַחְנוּ לָךְ

שָׁאַתָּה הוּא יהוה אֱלֹהֵינוּ וֵאלֹהֵי אֲבוֹתֵינוּ לְעוֹלָם וָעֶד.

צוּר חַיֵּינוּ, מָגֵן יִשְׁעֵנוּ, אַתָּה הוּא לְדוֹר וָדוֹר.

נוֹדֶה לְּךָ וּנְסַפֵּר תְּהִלָּתֶךָ עַל חַיֵּינוּ הַמְּסוּרִים בְּיָדֶךָ

וְעַל נִשְׁמוֹתֵינוּ הַפְּקוּדוֹת לָךְ וְעַל נִסֶּיךָ שֶׁבְּכָל יוֹם עִמָּנוּ

וְעַל נִפְלְאוֹתֶיךָ וְטוֹבוֹתֶיךָ שֶׁבְּכָל עֵת, עֶרֶב וָבֹקֶר וְצָהֳרָיִם.

הַטּוֹב, כִּי לֹא כָלוּ רַחֲמֶיךָ, וְהַמְרַחֵם, כִּי לֹא תַמּוּ חֲסָדֶיךָ

מֵעוֹלָם קִוִּינוּ לָךְ.

At this point in the silent עמידה it is permitted to add a rabbinically formulated על הַנִּסִּים. The following was written by Rabbi Neria (alternative versions can be found on pages 656–659).

עַל הַנִּסִּים וְעַל הַפֻּרְקָן וְעַל הַגְּבוּרוֹת וְעַל הַתְּשׁוּעוֹת וְעַל הַמִּלְחָמוֹת שֶׁעָשִׂיתָ לַאֲבוֹתֵינוּ בַּיָּמִים הָהֵם בַּזְּמַן הַזֶּה.

כְּשֶׁעָמְדוּ צִבְאוֹת עֶרֶב עַל עַמְּךָ יִשְׂרָאֵל, וּבִקְשׁוּ לְהַשְׁמִיד לַהֲרֹג וּלְאַבֵּד אֶת יוֹשְׁבֵי אַרְצֶךָ, מִנַּעַר וְעַד זָקֵן טַף וְנָשִׁים, וּבָהֶם עַם שְׂרִידֵי חֶרֶב אֲשֶׁר נִצְּלוּ מִתַּפַּת הָאֵשׁ שֶׁל שׂוֹנְאֶיךָ, אֶחָד מֵעִיר וּשְׁנַיִם מִמִּשְׁפָּחָה, וְשָׁבְרוּ לִמְצֹא מָנוֹחַ לְכַף רַגְלָם בְּאַרְצְךָ אֲשֶׁר הִבְטַחְתָּ לָהֶם. וְאַתָּה בְּרַחֲמֶיךָ הָרַבִּים עָמַדְתָּ לָנוּ בְּעֵת צָרָתֵנוּ, הֵפַרְתָּ אֶת עֲצָתָם וְקִלְקַלְתָּ אֶת מַחֲשַׁבְתָּם, זָקַפְתָּ קוֹמָתֵנוּ וְקוֹמַמְתָּ אֶת חֵרוּתֵנוּ, רַבְתָּ אֶת רִיבֵנוּ, דַּנְתָּ אֶת דִּינֵנוּ, נָקַמְתָּ אֶת נִקְמָתֵנוּ, מָסַרְתָּ רַבִּים בְּיַד מְעַטִּים, טְמֵאִים בְּיַד קְדוֹשִׁים, וְעָשִׂיתָ לְּךָ שֵׁם גָּדוֹל וְקָדוֹשׁ בְּעוֹלָמֶךָ, וּלְעַמְּךָ יִשְׂרָאֵל עָשִׂיתָ תְּשׁוּעָה גְדוֹלָה וּפֻרְקָן כְּהַיּוֹם הַזֶּה, הִדְבַּרְתָּ עַמִּים תַּחְתֵּנוּ וּלְאֻמִּים תַּחַת רַגְלֵנוּ, וְנָתַתָּ לָנוּ אֶת נַחֲלָתֵנוּ, אֶרֶץ כְּנַעַן לִגְבוּלוֹתֶיהָ, וְהֶחֱזַרְתָּנוּ אֶל מְקוֹם מִקְדַּשׁ הֵיכָלֶךָ.

AL HANISSIM

For a discussion on the addition of *Al HaNissim* to the silent Amida, see page 95.

(In the same way, make us a miracle and a glorious wonder, thwart the counsel of our enemies, have us prosper in the pastures of our Land, and gather in our scattered ones from the four corners of the earth, and we will rejoice in the rebuilding of Your city and in the establishment of Your Sanctuary and in the flourishing of the pride of Your servant David, speedily in our days, and we will give thanks to Your great name.) *Continue with "For all these things."*

וְעַל כֻּלָּם For all these things may Your name be blessed and exalted, our King, continually, for ever and all time.
Let all that lives thank You, Selah! and praise Your name in truth, God, our Savior and Help, Selah!
ʼBlessed are You, Lord, whose name is "the Good"
and to whom thanks are due.

PEACE

שָׁלוֹם רָב Grant great peace to Your people Israel for ever,
for You are the sovereign Lord of all peace;
and may it be good in Your eyes to bless Your people Israel
at every time, at every hour, with Your peace.
Blessed are You, Lord, who blesses His people Israel with peace.

Some say the following verse:
May the words of my mouth and the meditation of my heart   Ps. 19
find favor before You, Lord, my Rock and Redeemer.

אֱלֹהַי My God,   Berakhot
guard my tongue from evil and my lips from deceitful speech.   17a
To those who curse me, let my soul be silent;
may my soul be to all like the dust.
Open my heart to Your Torah
and let my soul pursue Your commandments.
As for all who plan evil against me,
swiftly thwart their counsel and frustrate their plans.
    Act for the sake of Your name; act for the sake of Your right hand;
    act for the sake of Your holiness; act for the sake of Your Torah.
That Your beloved ones may be delivered,   Ps. 60
save with Your right hand and answer me.
May the words of my mouth and the meditation of my heart   Ps. 19
find favor before You, Lord, my Rock and Redeemer.

(כֵּן עֲשֵׂה עִמָּנוּ נֵס וָפֶלֶא לְטוֹבָה, הָפֵר עֲצַת אוֹיְבֵינוּ, וְדַשְּׁנֵנוּ בִּנְאוֹת אַרְצֶךָ,
וּנְפוּצוֹתֵינוּ מֵאַרְבַּע כַּנְפוֹת הָאָרֶץ תְּקַבֵּץ, וְנִשְׂמַח בְּבִנְיַן עִירֶךָ וּבְתִקּוּן הֵיכָלֶךָ
וּבִצְמִיחַת קֶרֶן לְדָוִד עַבְדֶּךָ בִּמְהֵרָה בְיָמֵינוּ, וְנוֹדֶה לְשִׁמְךָ הַגָּדוֹל).
Continue with וְעַל כֻּלָּם.

וְעַל כֻּלָּם יִתְבָּרַךְ וְיִתְרוֹמַם שִׁמְךָ מַלְכֵּנוּ תָּמִיד לְעוֹלָם וָעֶד.
וְכֹל הַחַיִּים יוֹדוּךָ סֶּלָה, וִיהַלְלוּ אֶת שִׁמְךָ בֶּאֱמֶת
הָאֵל יְשׁוּעָתֵנוּ וְעֶזְרָתֵנוּ סֶלָה.
בָּרוּךְ אַתָּה יהוה, הַטּוֹב שִׁמְךָ וּלְךָ נָאֶה לְהוֹדוֹת.

ברכת שלום
שָׁלוֹם רָב עַל יִשְׂרָאֵל עַמְּךָ תָּשִׂים לְעוֹלָם
כִּי אַתָּה הוּא מֶלֶךְ אָדוֹן לְכָל הַשָּׁלוֹם.
וְטוֹב בְּעֵינֶיךָ לְבָרֵךְ אֶת עַמְּךָ יִשְׂרָאֵל
בְּכָל עֵת וּבְכָל שָׁעָה בִּשְׁלוֹמֶךָ.
בָּרוּךְ אַתָּה יהוה, הַמְבָרֵךְ אֶת עַמּוֹ יִשְׂרָאֵל בַּשָּׁלוֹם.

Some say the following verse:

תהלים יט | יִהְיוּ לְרָצוֹן אִמְרֵי־פִי וְהֶגְיוֹן לִבִּי לְפָנֶיךָ, יהוה צוּרִי וְגֹאֲלִי:

ברכות יז | אֱלֹהַי
נְצֹר לְשׁוֹנִי מֵרָע וּשְׂפָתַי מִדַּבֵּר מִרְמָה
וְלִמְקַלְלַי נַפְשִׁי תִדֹּם, וְנַפְשִׁי כֶּעָפָר לַכֹּל תִּהְיֶה.
פְּתַח לִבִּי בְּתוֹרָתֶךָ, וּבְמִצְוֹתֶיךָ תִּרְדֹּף נַפְשִׁי.
וְכָל הַחוֹשְׁבִים עָלַי רָעָה, מְהֵרָה הָפֵר עֲצָתָם וְקַלְקֵל מַחֲשַׁבְתָּם.
עֲשֵׂה לְמַעַן שְׁמֶךָ, עֲשֵׂה לְמַעַן יְמִינֶךָ
עֲשֵׂה לְמַעַן קְדֻשָּׁתֶךָ, עֲשֵׂה לְמַעַן תּוֹרָתֶךָ.
תהלים ס | לְמַעַן יֵחָלְצוּן יְדִידֶיךָ, הוֹשִׁיעָה יְמִינְךָ וַעֲנֵנִי:
תהלים יט | יִהְיוּ לְרָצוֹן אִמְרֵי־פִי וְהֶגְיוֹן לִבִּי לְפָנֶיךָ, יהוה צוּרִי וְגֹאֲלִי:

Bow, take three steps back, then bow, first left, then right, then center, while saying:

May He who makes peace in His high places,
make peace for us and all Israel – and say: Amen.

יְהִי רָצוֹן May it be Your will, LORD our God and God of our ancestors,
that the Temple be rebuilt speedily in our days, and grant us a share in Your Torah.
And there we will serve You with reverence,
as in the days of old and as in former years.
Then the offering of Judah and Jerusalem   *Mal. 3*
will be pleasing to the LORD as in the days of old and as in former years.

> *After the Amida some sing:*
> That the Temple be rebuilt speedily in our days,
> and grant us a share in Your Torah.
> And may our eyes witness Your return to Zion in compassion.   *Ps. 122*
> Our feet stood within your gates, Jerusalem:
> Jerusalem built as a city joined together.

*On Yom Yerushalayim that falls on Motza'ei Shabbat, the
Leader continues with Half Kaddish below.*
On other evenings the Leader says Full Kaddish on page 554.

HALF KADDISH

Leader: יִתְגַּדַּל Magnified and sanctified may His great name be,
in the world He created by His will.
May He establish His kingdom
in your lifetime and in your days,
and in the lifetime of all the house of Israel,
swiftly and soon – and say: Amen.

All: May His great name be blessed for ever and all time.

Leader: Blessed and praised, glorified and exalted,
raised and honored,
uplifted and lauded be
the name of the Holy One,
blessed be He, beyond any blessing,
song, praise and consolation
uttered in the world – and say: Amen.

Bow, take three steps back, then bow, first left, then right, then center, while saying:

עֹשֶׂה שָׁלוֹם בִּמְרוֹמָיו
הוּא יַעֲשֶׂה שָׁלוֹם עָלֵינוּ וְעַל כָּל יִשְׂרָאֵל, וְאִמְרוּ אָמֵן.

יְהִי רָצוֹן מִלְּפָנֶיךָ יהוה אֱלֹהֵינוּ וֵאלֹהֵי אֲבוֹתֵינוּ
שֶׁיִּבָּנֶה בֵּית הַמִּקְדָּשׁ בִּמְהֵרָה בְיָמֵינוּ, וְתֵן חֶלְקֵנוּ בְּתוֹרָתֶךָ
וְשָׁם נַעֲבָדְךָ בְּיִרְאָה כִּימֵי עוֹלָם וּכְשָׁנִים קַדְמוֹנִיּוֹת.

מלאכי ג
וְעָרְבָה לַיהוה מִנְחַת יְהוּדָה וִירוּשָׁלַ͏ִם כִּימֵי עוֹלָם וּכְשָׁנִים קַדְמוֹנִיּוֹת:

After the עמידה *some sing:*

שֶׁיִּבָּנֶה בֵּית הַמִּקְדָּשׁ בִּמְהֵרָה בְיָמֵינוּ, וְתֵן חֶלְקֵנוּ בְּתוֹרָתֶךָ.
וְתֶחֱזֶינָה עֵינֵינוּ בְּשׁוּבְךָ לְצִיּוֹן בְּרַחֲמִים.
תהלים קכב
עֹמְדוֹת הָיוּ רַגְלֵינוּ בִּשְׁעָרַיִךְ יְרוּשָׁלָ͏ִם:
יְרוּשָׁלַ͏ִם הַבְּנוּיָה, כְּעִיר שֶׁחֻבְּרָה־לָּהּ יַחְדָּו:

On יום ירושלים *that falls on* מוצאי שבת, *the* שליח ציבור *continues with* חצי קדיש *below. On other evenings the* שליח ציבור *says* קדיש שלם *on page 555.*

חצי קדיש

ש״ץ: יִתְגַּדַּל וְיִתְקַדַּשׁ שְׁמֵהּ רַבָּא (קהל: אָמֵן)
בְּעָלְמָא דִּי בְרָא כִרְעוּתֵהּ
וְיַמְלִיךְ מַלְכוּתֵהּ
בְּחַיֵּיכוֹן וּבְיוֹמֵיכוֹן וּבְחַיֵּי דְכָל בֵּית יִשְׂרָאֵל
בַּעֲגָלָא וּבִזְמַן קָרִיב, וְאִמְרוּ אָמֵן. (קהל: אָמֵן)

קהל יְהֵא שְׁמֵהּ רַבָּא מְבָרַךְ לְעָלַם וּלְעָלְמֵי עָלְמַיָּא.
וש״ץ:

ש״ץ: יִתְבָּרַךְ וְיִשְׁתַּבַּח וְיִתְפָּאַר וְיִתְרוֹמַם וְיִתְנַשֵּׂא
וְיִתְהַדָּר וְיִתְעַלֶּה וְיִתְהַלָּל
שְׁמֵהּ דְּקֻדְשָׁא בְּרִיךְ הוּא (קהל: בְּרִיךְ הוּא)
לְעֵלָּא מִן כָּל בִּרְכָתָא וְשִׁירָתָא, תֻּשְׁבְּחָתָא וְנֶחֱמָתָא
דַּאֲמִירָן בְּעָלְמָא, וְאִמְרוּ אָמֵן. (קהל: אָמֵן)

"May the pleasantness" is said standing, and "You are the Holy One" is said sitting.

וִיהִי נֹעַם May the pleasantness of the LORD our God be upon us. Establish for us the work of our hands, O establish the work of our hands.   *Ps. 90*

יֹשֵׁב He who lives in the shelter of the Most High dwells in the shadow of the Almighty. I say of the LORD, my Refuge and Stronghold, my God in whom I trust, that He will save you from the fowler's snare and the deadly pestilence. With His pinions He will cover you, and beneath His wings you will find shelter; His faithfulness is an encircling shield. You need not fear terror by night, nor the arrow that flies by day; not the pestilence that stalks in darkness, nor the plague that ravages at noon. A thousand may fall at your side, ten thousand at your right hand, but it will not come near you. You will only look with your eyes and see the punishment of the wicked. Because you said, "The LORD is my Refuge," taking the Most High as your shelter, no harm will befall you, no plague come near your tent, for He will command His angels about you, to guard you in all your ways. They will lift you in their hands, lest your foot stumble on a stone. You will tread on lions and vipers; you will trample on young lions and snakes. [God says:] "Because he loves Me, I will rescue him; I will protect him, because he acknowledges My name. When he calls on Me, I will answer him; I will be with him in distress, I will deliver him and bring him honor. ▸ With long life I will satisfy him and show him My salvation.   *Ps. 91*
　　　　　With long life I will satisfy him and show him My salvation.

▸ You are the Holy One, enthroned on the praises of Israel.   *Ps. 22*
　And [the angels] call to one another, saying, "Holy, holy, holy   *Is. 6*
　is the LORD of hosts; the whole world is filled with His glory."

　And they receive permission from one another, saying: *Targum*
　"Holy in the highest heavens, home of His Presence; holy on earth,   *Yonatan*
　　the work of His strength; holy for ever and all time is the LORD of hosts;   *Is. 6*
　　the whole earth is full of His radiant glory."

▸ Then a wind lifted me up and I heard behind me the sound of a great   *Ezek. 3*
　noise, saying, "Blessed is the LORD's glory from His place."

　Then a wind lifted me up and I heard behind me   *Targum*
　　the sound of a great tempest of those who uttered praise, saying,   *Yonatan*
　"Blessed is the LORD's glory from the place of the home of His Presence."   *Ezek. 3*

וְאַתָּה קָדוֹשׁ is said standing, and וִיהִי נֹעַם is said sitting.

תהלים צ

וִיהִי נֹעַם אֲדֹנָי אֱלֹהֵינוּ עָלֵינוּ וּמַעֲשֵׂה יָדֵינוּ כּוֹנְנָה עָלֵינוּ וּמַעֲשֵׂה יָדֵינוּ כּוֹנְנֵהוּ:

תהלים צא

יֹשֵׁב בְּסֵתֶר עֶלְיוֹן, בְּצֵל שַׁדַּי יִתְלוֹנָן: אֹמַר לַיהוה מַחְסִי וּמְצוּדָתִי, אֱלֹהַי אֶבְטַח־בּוֹ: כִּי הוּא יַצִּילְךָ מִפַּח יָקוּשׁ, מִדֶּבֶר הַוּוֹת: בְּאֶבְרָתוֹ יָסֶךְ לָךְ, וְתַחַת־כְּנָפָיו תֶּחְסֶה, צִנָּה וְסֹחֵרָה אֲמִתּוֹ: לֹא־תִירָא מִפַּחַד לָיְלָה, מֵחֵץ יָעוּף יוֹמָם: מִדֶּבֶר בָּאֹפֶל יַהֲלֹךְ, מִקֶּטֶב יָשׁוּד צָהֳרָיִם: יִפֹּל מִצִּדְּךָ אֶלֶף, וּרְבָבָה מִימִינֶךָ, אֵלֶיךָ לֹא יִגָּשׁ: רַק בְּעֵינֶיךָ תַבִּיט, וְשִׁלֻּמַת רְשָׁעִים תִּרְאֶה: כִּי־אַתָּה יהוה מַחְסִי, עֶלְיוֹן שַׂמְתָּ מְעוֹנֶךָ: לֹא־תְאֻנֶּה אֵלֶיךָ רָעָה, וְנֶגַע לֹא־יִקְרַב בְּאָהֳלֶךָ: כִּי מַלְאָכָיו יְצַוֶּה־לָּךְ, לִשְׁמָרְךָ בְּכָל־דְּרָכֶיךָ: עַל־כַּפַּיִם יִשָּׂאוּנְךָ, פֶּן־תִּגֹּף בָּאֶבֶן רַגְלֶךָ: עַל־שַׁחַל וָפֶתֶן תִּדְרֹךְ, תִּרְמֹס כְּפִיר וְתַנִּין: כִּי בִי חָשַׁק וַאֲפַלְּטֵהוּ, אֲשַׂגְּבֵהוּ כִּי־יָדַע שְׁמִי: יִקְרָאֵנִי וְאֶעֱנֵהוּ, עִמּוֹ אָנֹכִי בְצָרָה, אֲחַלְּצֵהוּ וַאֲכַבְּדֵהוּ: ◂ אֹרֶךְ יָמִים אַשְׂבִּיעֵהוּ, וְאַרְאֵהוּ בִּישׁוּעָתִי: אֹרֶךְ יָמִים אַשְׂבִּיעֵהוּ, וְאַרְאֵהוּ בִּישׁוּעָתִי:

תהלים כב

◂ וְאַתָּה קָדוֹשׁ יוֹשֵׁב תְּהִלּוֹת יִשְׂרָאֵל: וְקָרָא זֶה אֶל־זֶה וְאָמַר

ישעיה ו

קָדוֹשׁ, קָדוֹשׁ, קָדוֹשׁ, יהוה צְבָאוֹת, מְלֹא כָל־הָאָרֶץ כְּבוֹדוֹ:

תרגום יונתן ישעיה ו

וּמְקַבְּלִין דֵּין מִן דֵּין וְאָמְרִין, קַדִּישׁ בִּשְׁמֵי מְרוֹמָא עִלָּאָה בֵּית שְׁכִינְתֵּהּ קַדִּישׁ עַל אַרְעָא עוֹבַד גְּבוּרְתֵּהּ, קַדִּישׁ לְעָלַם וּלְעָלְמֵי עָלְמַיָּא יהוה צְבָאוֹת, מַלְיָא כָל אַרְעָא זִיו יְקָרֵהּ.

יחזקאל ג

◂ וַתִּשָּׂאֵנִי רוּחַ, וָאֶשְׁמַע אַחֲרַי קוֹל רַעַשׁ גָּדוֹל בָּרוּךְ כְּבוֹד־יהוה מִמְּקוֹמוֹ:

תרגום יונתן יחזקאל ג

וּנְטָלַתְנִי רוּחָא, וּשְׁמָעִית בַּתְרַי קָל זִיעַ סַגִּיא, דִּמְשַׁבְּחִין וְאָמְרִין בְּרִיךְ יְקָרָא דַיהוה מֵאֲתַר בֵּית שְׁכִינְתֵּהּ.

The LORD shall reign for ever and all time.

Ex. 15

The LORD's kingdom is established for ever and all time.

Targum
Onkelos Ex. 15

יהוה LORD, God of Abraham, Isaac and Yisrael, our ancestors, may You keep this for ever so that it forms the thoughts in Your people's heart, and directs their heart toward You. He is compassionate. He forgives iniquity and does not destroy. Repeatedly He suppresses His anger, not rousing His full wrath. For You, my LORD, are good and forgiving, abundantly kind to all who call on You. Your righteousness is eternally righteous, and Your Torah is truth. Grant truth to Jacob, loving-kindness to Abraham, as You promised our ancestors in ancient times. Blessed is my LORD for day after day He burdens us [with His blessings]; God is our salvation, Selah! The LORD of hosts is with us; the God of Jacob is our refuge, Selah! LORD of hosts, happy is the one who trusts in You. LORD, save! May the King answer us on the day we call.

1 Chr. 29

Ps. 78

Ps. 86

Ps. 119

Micah 7

Ps. 68

Ps. 46

Ps. 84

Ps. 20

בָּרוּךְ Blessed is He, our God, who created us for His glory, separating us from those who go astray; who gave us the Torah of truth, planting within us eternal life. May He open our heart to His Torah, imbuing our heart with the love and awe of Him, that we may do His will and serve Him with a perfect heart, so that we neither toil in vain nor give birth to confusion.

יְהִי רָצוֹן May it be Your will, O LORD our God and God of our ancestors, that we keep Your laws in this world, and thus be worthy to live, see and inherit goodness and blessing in the Messianic Age and in the life of the World to Come. So that my soul may sing to You and not be silent. LORD, my God, for ever I will thank You. Blessed is the man who trusts in the LORD, whose trust is in the LORD alone. Trust in the LORD for evermore, for God, the LORD, is an everlasting Rock. ‣ Those who know Your name trust in You, for You, LORD, do not forsake those who seek You. The LORD desired, for the sake of Israel's merit, to make the Torah great and glorious.

Ps. 30

Jer. 17

Is. 26

Ps. 9

Is. 42

שמות טו
תרגום אונקלוס
שמות טו

יהוה יִמְלֹךְ לְעֹלָם וָעֶד:

יהוה מַלְכוּתֵהּ קָאֵם לְעָלַם וּלְעָלְמֵי עָלְמַיָּא.

דברי הימים
א' כט
תהלים עח

יהוה אֱלֹהֵי אַבְרָהָם יִצְחָק וְיִשְׂרָאֵל אֲבֹתֵינוּ, שָׁמְרָה־זֹּאת לְעוֹלָם
לְיֵצֶר מַחְשְׁבוֹת לְבַב עַמֶּךָ, וְהָכֵן לְבָבָם אֵלֶיךָ: וְהוּא רַחוּם יְכַפֵּר
עָוֹן וְלֹא־יַשְׁחִית, וְהִרְבָּה לְהָשִׁיב אַפּוֹ, וְלֹא־יָעִיר כָּל־חֲמָתוֹ:

תהלים פו
תהלים קיט

כִּי־אַתָּה אֲדֹנָי טוֹב וְסַלָּח, וְרַב־חֶסֶד לְכָל־קֹרְאֶיךָ: צִדְקָתְךָ
צֶדֶק לְעוֹלָם וְתוֹרָתְךָ אֱמֶת: תִּתֵּן אֱמֶת לְיַעֲקֹב, חֶסֶד לְאַבְרָהָם,

מיכה ז

אֲשֶׁר־נִשְׁבַּעְתָּ לַאֲבֹתֵינוּ מִימֵי קֶדֶם: בָּרוּךְ אֲדֹנָי יוֹם יוֹם יַעֲמָס־

תהלים סח

לָנוּ, הָאֵל יְשׁוּעָתֵנוּ סֶלָה: יהוה צְבָאוֹת עִמָּנוּ, מִשְׂגָּב לָנוּ אֱלֹהֵי

תהלים מו

יַעֲקֹב סֶלָה: יהוה צְבָאוֹת, אַשְׁרֵי אָדָם בֹּטֵחַ בָּךְ: יהוה הוֹשִׁיעָה,

תהלים פד
תהלים כ

הַמֶּלֶךְ יַעֲנֵנוּ בְיוֹם־קָרְאֵנוּ:

בָּרוּךְ הוּא אֱלֹהֵינוּ שֶׁבְּרָאָנוּ לִכְבוֹדוֹ, וְהִבְדִּילָנוּ מִן הַתּוֹעִים,
וְנָתַן לָנוּ תּוֹרַת אֱמֶת, וְחַיֵּי עוֹלָם נָטַע בְּתוֹכֵנוּ. הוּא יִפְתַּח לִבֵּנוּ
בְּתוֹרָתוֹ, וְיָשֵׂם בְּלִבֵּנוּ אַהֲבָתוֹ וְיִרְאָתוֹ וְלַעֲשׂוֹת רְצוֹנוֹ וּלְעָבְדוֹ
בְּלֵבָב שָׁלֵם, לְמַעַן לֹא נִיגַע לָרִיק וְלֹא נֵלֵד לַבֶּהָלָה.

יְהִי רָצוֹן מִלְּפָנֶיךָ יהוה אֱלֹהֵינוּ וֵאלֹהֵי אֲבוֹתֵינוּ, שֶׁנִּשְׁמֹר חֻקֶּיךָ
בָּעוֹלָם הַזֶּה, וְנִזְכֶּה וְנִחְיֶה וְנִרְאֶה וְנִירַשׁ טוֹבָה וּבְרָכָה, לִשְׁנֵי

תהלים ל

יְמוֹת הַמָּשִׁיחַ וּלְחַיֵּי הָעוֹלָם הַבָּא. לְמַעַן יְזַמֶּרְךָ כָבוֹד וְלֹא יִדֹּם,

ירמיה יז

יהוה אֱלֹהַי, לְעוֹלָם אוֹדֶךָּ: בָּרוּךְ הַגֶּבֶר אֲשֶׁר יִבְטַח בַּיהוה,

ישעיה כו

וְהָיָה יהוה מִבְטַחוֹ: בִּטְחוּ בַיהוה עֲדֵי־עַד, כִּי בְּיָהּ יהוה צוּר

תהלים ט

עוֹלָמִים: ◀ וְיִבְטְחוּ בְךָ יוֹדְעֵי שְׁמֶךָ, כִּי לֹא־עָזַבְתָּ דֹרְשֶׁיךָ, יהוה:

ישעיה מב

יהוה חָפֵץ לְמַעַן צִדְקוֹ, יַגְדִּיל תּוֹרָה וְיַאְדִּיר:

FULL KADDISH

Leader: יִתְגַּדַּל Magnified and sanctified may His great name be,
in the world He created by His will.
May He establish His kingdom
in your lifetime and in your days,
and in the lifetime of all the house of Israel,
swiftly and soon –
and say: Amen.

All: May His great name be blessed for ever and all time.

Leader: Blessed and praised,
glorified and exalted,
raised and honored,
uplifted and lauded be
the name of the Holy One,
blessed be He,
beyond any blessing,
song, praise and consolation
uttered in the world –
and say: Amen.

May the prayers and pleas of all Israel
be accepted by their Father in heaven –
and say: Amen.

May there be great peace from heaven,
and life for us and all Israel –
and say: Amen.

*Bow, take three steps back, as if taking leave of the Divine Presence,
then bow, first left, then right, then center, while saying:*

May He who makes peace in His high places,
make peace for us and all Israel –
and say: Amen.

קדיש שלם

ש״ץ: יִתְגַּדַּל וְיִתְקַדַּשׁ שְׁמֵהּ רַבָּא (קהל: אָמֵן)
בְּעָלְמָא דִּי בְרָא כִרְעוּתֵהּ
וְיַמְלִיךְ מַלְכוּתֵהּ
בְּחַיֵּיכוֹן וּבְיוֹמֵיכוֹן וּבְחַיֵּי דְכָל בֵּית יִשְׂרָאֵל
בַּעֲגָלָא וּבִזְמַן קָרִיב, וְאִמְרוּ אָמֵן. (קהל: אָמֵן)

קהל
ושץ: יְהֵא שְׁמֵהּ רַבָּא מְבָרַךְ לְעָלַם וּלְעָלְמֵי עָלְמַיָּא.

ש״ץ: יִתְבָּרַךְ וְיִשְׁתַּבַּח וְיִתְפָּאַר וְיִתְרוֹמַם וְיִתְנַשֵּׂא
וְיִתְהַדָּר וְיִתְעַלֶּה וְיִתְהַלָּל
שְׁמֵהּ דְּקֻדְשָׁא בְּרִיךְ הוּא (קהל: בְּרִיךְ הוּא)
לְעֵלָּא מִן כָּל בִּרְכָתָא
וְשִׁירָתָא, תֻּשְׁבְּחָתָא וְנֶחֱמָתָא
דַּאֲמִירָן בְּעָלְמָא, וְאִמְרוּ אָמֵן. (קהל: אָמֵן)

תִּתְקַבֵּל צְלוֹתְהוֹן וּבָעוּתְהוֹן דְּכָל יִשְׂרָאֵל
קֳדָם אֲבוּהוֹן דִּי בִשְׁמַיָּא, וְאִמְרוּ אָמֵן. (קהל: אָמֵן)

יְהֵא שְׁלָמָא רַבָּא מִן שְׁמַיָּא
וְחַיִּים, עָלֵינוּ וְעַל כָּל יִשְׂרָאֵל, וְאִמְרוּ אָמֵן. (קהל: אָמֵן)

Bow, take three steps back, as if taking leave of the Divine Presence,
then bow, first left, then right, then center, while saying:

עֹשֶׂה שָׁלוֹם בִּמְרוֹמָיו
הוּא יַעֲשֶׂה שָׁלוֹם עָלֵינוּ וְעַל כָּל יִשְׂרָאֵל
וְאִמְרוּ אָמֵן. (קהל: אָמֵן)

COUNTING OF THE OMER

Some say the following meditation before the blessing:

For the sake of the unification of the Holy One, blessed be He,
and His Divine Presence, in reverence and love,
to unify the name *Yod-Heh* with *Vav-Heh*
in perfect unity in the name of all Israel.

הִנְנִי I am prepared and ready
to fulfill the positive commandment
of Counting the Omer,
as is written in the Torah,
"You shall count seven complete weeks   *Lev. 23*
from the day following the [Pesaḥ] rest day,
when you brought the Omer as a wave-offering.
To the day after the seventh week you shall count fifty days.
Then you shall present a meal-offering of new grain to the LORD."
May the pleasantness of the LORD our God be upon us.   *Ps. 90*
Establish for us the work of our hands,
O establish the work of our hands.

בָּרוּךְ Blessed are You, LORD our God, King of the Universe,
who has made us holy through His commandments,
and has commanded us about counting the Omer.

Today is the forty-third day,
making six weeks and one day of the Omer.

הָרַחֲמָן May the Compassionate One
restore the Temple service to its place
speedily in our days. Amen, Selah.

Some add:

לַמְנַצֵּחַ For the conductor of music. With stringed instruments. A psalm, a   *Ps. 67*
song. May God be gracious to us and bless us. May He make His face shine
on us, Selah. Then will Your way be known on earth, Your salvation among
all the nations. Let the peoples praise You, God; let all peoples praise You.

סדר ספירת העומר

Some say the following meditation before the blessing:

לְשֵׁם יְחוּד קֻדְשָׁא בְּרִיךְ הוּא וּשְׁכִינְתֵּהּ בִּדְחִילוּ וּרְחִימוּ
לְיַחֵד שֵׁם י"ה בו"ה בְּיִחוּדָא שְׁלִים
בְּשֵׁם כָּל יִשְׂרָאֵל.

הִנְנִי מוּכָן וּמְזֻמָּן לְקַיֵּם מִצְוַת עֲשֵׂה שֶׁל סְפִירַת הָעֹמֶר.

כְּמוֹ שֶׁכָּתוּב בַּתּוֹרָה

וּסְפַרְתֶּם לָכֶם מִמָּחֳרַת הַשַּׁבָּת

ויקרא כג

מִיּוֹם הֲבִיאֲכֶם אֶת־עֹמֶר הַתְּנוּפָה

שֶׁבַע שַׁבָּתוֹת תְּמִימֹת תִּהְיֶינָה:

עַד מִמָּחֳרַת הַשַּׁבָּת הַשְּׁבִיעִת תִּסְפְּרוּ חֲמִשִּׁים יוֹם

וְהִקְרַבְתֶּם מִנְחָה חֲדָשָׁה לַיהוה:

תהלים צ

וִיהִי נֹעַם אֲדֹנָי אֱלֹהֵינוּ עָלֵינוּ

וּמַעֲשֵׂה יָדֵינוּ כּוֹנְנָה עָלֵינוּ

וּמַעֲשֵׂה יָדֵינוּ כּוֹנְנֵהוּ:

בָּרוּךְ אַתָּה יהוה אֱלֹהֵינוּ מֶלֶךְ הָעוֹלָם
אֲשֶׁר קִדְּשָׁנוּ בְּמִצְוֹתָיו וְצִוָּנוּ עַל סְפִירַת הָעֹמֶר.

הַיּוֹם שְׁלֹשָׁה וְאַרְבָּעִים יוֹם

חסד שבמלכות

שֶׁהֵם שִׁשָּׁה שָׁבוּעוֹת וְיוֹם אֶחָד בָּעֹמֶר.

הָרַחֲמָן הוּא יַחֲזִיר לָנוּ עֲבוֹדַת בֵּית הַמִּקְדָּשׁ לִמְקוֹמָהּ
בִּמְהֵרָה בְיָמֵינוּ, אָמֵן סֶלָה.

Some add:

תהלים סו

לַמְנַצֵּחַ בִּנְגִינֹת, מִזְמוֹר שִׁיר: אֱלֹהִים יְחָנֵּנוּ וִיבָרְכֵנוּ, יָאֵר פָּנָיו אִתָּנוּ סֶלָה:
לָדַעַת בָּאָרֶץ דַּרְכֶּךָ, בְּכָל־גּוֹיִם יְשׁוּעָתֶךָ: יוֹדוּךָ עַמִּים אֱלֹהִים, יוֹדוּךָ עַמִּים

Let nations rejoice and sing for joy, for You judge the peoples with equity,
and guide the nations of the earth, Selah. Let the peoples praise You, God;
let all peoples praise You. The earth has yielded its harvest. May God, our
God, bless us. God will bless us, and all the ends of the earth will fear Him.

אָנָּא Please, by the power of Your great right hand,
    set the captive nation free.
Accept Your people's prayer. Strengthen us, purify us,
    You who are revered.
Please, Mighty One, guard like the pupil of the eye
    those who seek Your unity.
Bless them, cleanse them, have compassion on them,
    grant them Your righteousness always.
Mighty One, Holy One, in Your great goodness
    guide Your congregation.
Only One, Exalted One, turn to Your people, who proclaim Your holiness.
Accept our plea and heed our cry, You who know all secret thoughts.
        Blessed be the name of His glorious kingdom for ever and all time.

רִבּוֹנוֹ שֶׁל עוֹלָם Master of the Universe, You commanded us through Your
servant Moses to count the Omer, to cleanse our carapaces and impurities,
as You have written in Your Torah: "You shall count seven complete weeks   *Lev. 23*
from the day following the [Pesaḥ] rest day, when you brought the Omer
as a wave-offering. To the day after the seventh week, you shall count fifty
days." This is so that the souls of Your people Israel may be purified from
their uncleanliness. May it also be Your will, LORD our God and God of our
ancestors, that in the merit of the Omer count that I have counted today,
there may be rectified any defect on my part in the counting of (*insert the
appropriate sefira for each day*). May I be cleansed and sanctified with Your
holiness on high, and through this may there flow a rich stream through
all worlds, to rectify our lives, spirits and souls from any dross and defect,
purifying and sanctifying us with Your sublime holiness. Amen, Selah.

*When Yom Yerushalayim falls on Motza'ei Shabbat the service continues on the next page.
On other days continue with "It is our duty" on page 566.*

כֻּלָּם: יִשְׂמְחוּ וִירַנְּנוּ לְאֻמִּים, כִּי־תִשְׁפֹּט עַמִּים מִישׁוֹר, וּלְאֻמִּים בָּאָרֶץ תַּנְחֵם סֶלָה: יוֹדוּךָ עַמִּים אֱלֹהִים, יוֹדוּךָ עַמִּים כֻּלָּם: אֶרֶץ נָתְנָה יְבוּלָהּ, יְבָרְכֵנוּ אֱלֹהִים אֱלֹהֵינוּ: יְבָרְכֵנוּ אֱלֹהִים, וְיִירְאוּ אוֹתוֹ כָּל־אַפְסֵי־אָרֶץ:

אָנָּא, בְּכֹחַ גְּדֻלַּת יְמִינְךָ, תַּתִּיר צְרוּרָה.
קַבֵּל רִנַּת עַמְּךָ, שַׂגְּבֵנוּ, טַהֲרֵנוּ, נוֹרָא.
נָא גִבּוֹר, דּוֹרְשֵׁי יִחוּדְךָ כְּבָבַת שָׁמְרֵם.
בָּרְכֵם, טַהֲרֵם, רַחֲמֵם, צִדְקָתְךָ תָּמִיד גָּמְלֵם.
חֲסִין קָדוֹשׁ, בְּרֹב טוּבְךָ נַהֵל עֲדָתֶךָ.
יָחִיד גֵּאֶה, לְעַמְּךָ פְּנֵה, זוֹכְרֵי קְדֻשָּׁתֶךָ.
שַׁוְעָתֵנוּ קַבֵּל וּשְׁמַע צַעֲקָתֵנוּ, יוֹדֵעַ תַּעֲלוּמוֹת.
בָּרוּךְ שֵׁם כְּבוֹד מַלְכוּתוֹ לְעוֹלָם וָעֶד.

רִבּוֹנוֹ שֶׁל עוֹלָם, אַתָּה צִוִּיתָנוּ עַל יְדֵי מֹשֶׁה עַבְדְּךָ לִסְפֹּר סְפִירַת הָעֹמֶר, כְּדֵי לְטַהֲרֵנוּ מִקְּלִפּוֹתֵינוּ וּמִטֻּמְאוֹתֵינוּ. כְּמוֹ שֶׁכָּתַבְתָּ בְּתוֹרָתֶךָ: וּסְפַרְתֶּם ויקרא כג לָכֶם מִמָּחֳרַת הַשַּׁבָּת, מִיּוֹם הֲבִיאֲכֶם אֶת־עֹמֶר הַתְּנוּפָה, שֶׁבַע שַׁבָּתוֹת תְּמִימֹת תִּהְיֶינָה: עַד מִמָּחֳרַת הַשַּׁבָּת הַשְּׁבִיעִת תִּסְפְּרוּ חֲמִשִּׁים יוֹם: כְּדֵי שֶׁיִּטַּהֲרוּ נַפְשׁוֹת עַמְּךָ יִשְׂרָאֵל מִזֻּהֲמָתָם. וּבְכֵן יְהִי רָצוֹן מִלְּפָנֶיךָ יהוה אֱלֹהֵינוּ וֵאלֹהֵי אֲבוֹתֵינוּ, שֶׁבִּזְכוּת סְפִירַת הָעֹמֶר שֶׁסָּפַרְתִּי הַיּוֹם, יְתֻקַּן מַה שֶׁפָּגַמְתִּי בִּסְפִירָה (for each day ספירה insert appropriate) וְאֶטָּהֵר וְאֶתְקַדֵּשׁ בִּקְדֻשָּׁה שֶׁל מַעְלָה, וְעַל יְדֵי זֶה יֻשְׁפַּע שֶׁפַע רַב בְּכָל הָעוֹלָמוֹת, לְתַקֵּן אֶת נַפְשׁוֹתֵינוּ וְרוּחוֹתֵינוּ וְנִשְׁמוֹתֵינוּ מִכָּל סִיג וּפְגָם, וּלְטַהֲרֵנוּ וּלְקַדְּשֵׁנוּ בִּקְדֻשָּׁתְךָ הָעֶלְיוֹנָה, אָמֵן סֶלָה.

When יום ירושלים falls on מוצאי שבת the service continues on the next page.
On other days continue with עָלֵינוּ on page 567.

BIBLICAL VERSES OF BLESSING

וְיִתֶּן־לְךָ May God give you dew from heaven and the richness of the earth, and *Gen. 27*
corn and wine in plenty. May peoples serve you and nations bow down to you.
Be lord over your brothers, and may your mother's sons bow down to you. A
curse on those who curse you, but a blessing on those who bless you.

וְאֵל שַׁדַּי May God Almighty bless you; may He make you fruitful and numer- *Gen. 28*
ous until you become an assembly of peoples. May He give you and your descendants the blessing of Abraham, that you may possess the land where you
are now staying, the land God gave to Abraham. This comes from the God of *Gen. 49*
your father – may He help you – and from the Almighty – may He bless you
with blessings of the heaven above and the blessings of the deep that lies below,
the blessings of breast and womb. The blessings of your father surpass the blessings of my fathers to the bounds of the endless hills. May they rest on the head
of Joseph, on the brow of the prince among his brothers. He will love you and *Deut. 7*
bless you and increase your numbers. He will bless the fruit of your womb and
the fruit of your land: your corn, your wine and oil, the calves of your herds
and the lambs of your flocks, in the land He swore to your fathers to give you.
You will be blessed more than any other people. None of your men or women
will be childless, nor any of your livestock without young. The Lord will keep
you free from any disease. He will not inflict on you the terrible diseases you
knew in Egypt, but He will inflict them on those who hate you.

הַמַּלְאָךְ May the angel who rescued me from all harm, bless these boys. May *Gen. 48*
they be called by my name and the names of my fathers Abraham and Isaac,
and may they increase greatly on the earth. The Lord your God has increased *Deut. 1*
your numbers so that today you are as many as the stars in the sky. May the
Lord, God of your fathers, increase you a thousand times, and bless you as
He promised you.

בָּרוּךְ You will be blessed in the city, and blessed in the field. You will be *Deut. 28*
blessed when you come in, and blessed when you go out. Your basket and
your kneading trough will be blessed. The fruit of your womb will be blessed,
and the crops of your land, and the young of your livestock, the calves of
your herds and the lambs of your flocks. The Lord will send a blessing on
your barns, and on everything you put your hand to. The Lord your God
will bless you in the land He is giving you. The Lord will open for you the
heavens, the storehouse of His bounty, to send rain on your land in season,
and to bless all the work of your hands. You will lend to many nations but
will borrow from none. For the Lord your God will bless you as He has *Deut. 15*

פסוקי ברכה

בראשית כז
וְיִתֶּן־לְךָ הָאֱלֹהִים מִטַּל הַשָּׁמַיִם וּמִשְׁמַנֵּי הָאָרֶץ, וְרֹב דָּגָן וְתִירֹשׁ: יַעַבְדוּךָ עַמִּים וְיִשְׁתַּחֲווּ לְךָ לְאֻמִּים, הֱוֵה גְבִיר לְאַחֶיךָ וְיִשְׁתַּחֲווּ לְךָ בְּנֵי אִמֶּךָ, אֹרְרֶיךָ אָרוּר וּמְבָרֲכֶיךָ בָּרוּךְ:

בראשית כח
וְאֵל שַׁדַּי יְבָרֵךְ אֹתְךָ וְיַפְרְךָ וְיַרְבֶּךָ, וְהָיִיתָ לִקְהַל עַמִּים: וְיִתֶּן־לְךָ אֶת־בִּרְכַּת אַבְרָהָם, לְךָ וּלְזַרְעֲךָ אִתָּךְ, לְרִשְׁתְּךָ אֶת־אֶרֶץ מְגֻרֶיךָ אֲשֶׁר־נָתַן

בראשית מט
אֱלֹהִים לְאַבְרָהָם: מֵאֵל אָבִיךָ וְיַעְזְרֶךָּ וְאֵת שַׁדַּי וִיבָרֲכֶךָּ, בִּרְכֹת שָׁמַיִם מֵעָל בִּרְכֹת תְּהוֹם רֹבֶצֶת תָּחַת, בִּרְכֹת שָׁדַיִם וָרָחַם: בִּרְכֹת אָבִיךָ גָּבְרוּ עַל־בִּרְכֹת הוֹרַי עַד־תַּאֲוַת גִּבְעֹת עוֹלָם, תִּהְיֶין לְרֹאשׁ יוֹסֵף וּלְקָדְקֹד

דברים ז
נְזִיר אֶחָיו: וַאֲהֵבְךָ וּבֵרַכְךָ וְהִרְבֶּךָ, וּבֵרַךְ פְּרִי־בִטְנְךָ וּפְרִי־אַדְמָתֶךָ, דְּגָנְךָ וְתִירֹשְׁךָ וְיִצְהָרֶךָ, שְׁגַר־אֲלָפֶיךָ וְעַשְׁתְּרֹת צֹאנֶךָ, עַל הָאֲדָמָה אֲשֶׁר־נִשְׁבַּע לַאֲבֹתֶיךָ לָתֶת לָךְ: בָּרוּךְ תִּהְיֶה מִכָּל־הָעַמִּים, לֹא־יִהְיֶה בְךָ עָקָר וַעֲקָרָה וּבִבְהֶמְתֶּךָ: וְהֵסִיר יהוה מִמְּךָ כָּל־חֹלִי, וְכָל־מַדְוֵי מִצְרַיִם הָרָעִים אֲשֶׁר יָדַעְתָּ, לֹא יְשִׂימָם בָּךְ, וּנְתָנָם בְּכָל־שֹׂנְאֶיךָ:

בראשית מח
הַמַּלְאָךְ הַגֹּאֵל אֹתִי מִכָּל־רָע יְבָרֵךְ אֶת־הַנְּעָרִים, וְיִקָּרֵא בָהֶם שְׁמִי וְשֵׁם
דברים א
אֲבֹתַי אַבְרָהָם וְיִצְחָק, וְיִדְגּוּ לָרֹב בְּקֶרֶב הָאָרֶץ: יהוה אֱלֹהֵיכֶם הִרְבָּה אֶתְכֶם, וְהִנְּכֶם הַיּוֹם כְּכוֹכְבֵי הַשָּׁמַיִם לָרֹב: יהוה אֱלֹהֵי אֲבוֹתֵכֶם יֹסֵף עֲלֵיכֶם כָּכֶם אֶלֶף פְּעָמִים, וִיבָרֵךְ אֶתְכֶם כַּאֲשֶׁר דִּבֶּר לָכֶם:

דברים כח
בָּרוּךְ אַתָּה בָּעִיר, וּבָרוּךְ אַתָּה בַּשָּׂדֶה: בָּרוּךְ אַתָּה בְּבֹאֶךָ, וּבָרוּךְ אַתָּה בְּצֵאתֶךָ: בָּרוּךְ טַנְאֲךָ וּמִשְׁאַרְתֶּךָ: בָּרוּךְ פְּרִי־בִטְנְךָ וּפְרִי אַדְמָתְךָ וּפְרִי בְהֶמְתֶּךָ, שְׁגַר אֲלָפֶיךָ וְעַשְׁתְּרוֹת צֹאנֶךָ: יְצַו יהוה אִתְּךָ אֶת־הַבְּרָכָה בַּאֲסָמֶיךָ וּבְכֹל מִשְׁלַח יָדֶךָ, וּבֵרַכְךָ בָּאָרֶץ אֲשֶׁר־יהוה אֱלֹהֶיךָ נֹתֵן לָךְ: יִפְתַּח יהוה לְךָ אֶת־אוֹצָרוֹ הַטּוֹב אֶת־הַשָּׁמַיִם, לָתֵת מְטַר־אַרְצְךָ בְּעִתּוֹ, וּלְבָרֵךְ אֵת כָּל־מַעֲשֵׂה יָדֶךָ, וְהִלְוִיתָ גּוֹיִם רַבִּים וְאַתָּה לֹא תִלְוֶה:

דברים טו
כִּי־יהוה אֱלֹהֶיךָ בֵּרַכְךָ כַּאֲשֶׁר דִּבֶּר־לָךְ, וְהַעֲבַטְתָּ גּוֹיִם רַבִּים וְאַתָּה

promised: you will lend to many nations but will borrow from none. You will
rule over many nations, but none will rule over you. Happy are you, Israel! *Deut. 33*
Who is like you, a people saved by the LORD? He is your Shield and Helper
and your glorious Sword. Your enemies will cower before you, and you will
tread on their high places.

מָחִיתִי I have wiped away your transgressions like a cloud, your sins like the *Is. 44*
morning mist. Return to Me for I have redeemed you. Sing for joy, O heavens,
for the LORD has done this; shout aloud, you depths of the earth; burst into
song, you mountains, you forests and all your trees, for the LORD has redeemed
Jacob, and will glory in Israel. Our Redeemer, the LORD of hosts is His name, *Is. 47*
the Holy One of Israel.

יִשְׂרָאֵל Israel is saved by the LORD with everlasting salvation. You will never *Is. 45*
be ashamed or disgraced to time everlasting. You will eat your fill and praise *Joel 2*
the name of the LORD your God, who has worked wonders for you. Never
again shall My people be shamed. Then you will know that I am in the midst
of Israel, that I am the LORD your God, and there is no other. Never again
will My people be shamed. You will go out in joy and be led out in peace. The *Is. 55*
mountains and hills will burst into song before you, and all the trees of the
field will clap their hands. Behold, God is my salvation, I will trust and not be *Is. 12*
afraid. The LORD, the LORD, is my strength and my song. He has become my
salvation. With joy you will draw water from the springs of salvation. On that
day you will say, "Thank the LORD, proclaim His name, make His deeds known
among the nations." Declare that His name is exalted. Sing to the LORD, for
He has done glorious things; let this be known throughout the world. Shout
aloud and sing for joy, you who dwell in Zion, for great in your midst is the
Holy One of Israel. On that day they will say, "See, this is our God; we set our *Is. 25*
hope in Him and He saved us. This is the LORD in whom we hoped; let us
rejoice and be glad in His salvation."

בֵּית Come, house of Jacob: let us walk in the light of the LORD. He will be the *Is. 2*
Is. 32
sure foundation of your times; a rich store of salvation, wisdom and knowledge – the fear of the LORD is a person's treasure. In everything he did, David *1 Sam. 18*
was successful, for the LORD was with him.

פָּדָה He redeemed my soul in peace from the battle waged against me, for the *Ps. 55*
sake of the many who were with me. The people said to Saul, "Shall Jonathan *1 Sam. 14*
die – he who has brought about this great deliverance in Israel? Heaven forbid!
As surely as the LORD lives, not a hair of his head shall fall to the ground, for he

לֹא תַעֲבֹט, וּמָשַׁלְתָּ בְּגוֹיִם רַבִּים וּבְךָ לֹא יִמְשֹׁלוּ: אַשְׁרֶיךָ יִשְׂרָאֵל, מִי כָמוֹךָ, עַם נוֹשַׁע בַּיהוה, מָגֵן עֶזְרֶךָ וַאֲשֶׁר־חֶרֶב גַּאֲוָתֶךָ, וְיִכָּחֲשׁוּ אֹיְבֶיךָ לָךְ, וְאַתָּה עַל־בָּמוֹתֵימוֹ תִדְרֹךְ:

דברים לג

מָחִיתִי כָעָב פְּשָׁעֶיךָ וְכֶעָנָן חַטֹּאותֶיךָ, שׁוּבָה אֵלַי כִּי גְאַלְתִּיךָ: רָנּוּ שָׁמַיִם כִּי־עָשָׂה יהוה, הָרִיעוּ תַּחְתִּיּוֹת אָרֶץ, פִּצְחוּ הָרִים רִנָּה, יַעַר וְכָל־עֵץ בּוֹ, כִּי־גָאַל יהוה יַעֲקֹב וּבְיִשְׂרָאֵל יִתְפָּאָר: גֹּאֲלֵנוּ, יהוה צְבָאוֹת שְׁמוֹ, קְדוֹשׁ יִשְׂרָאֵל:

ישעיה מד

ישעיה מז,
ישעיה

יִשְׂרָאֵל נוֹשַׁע בַּיהוה תְּשׁוּעַת עוֹלָמִים, לֹא־תֵבֹשׁוּ וְלֹא־תִכָּלְמוּ עַד־ עוֹלְמֵי עַד: וַאֲכַלְתֶּם אָכוֹל וְשָׂבוֹעַ, וְהִלַּלְתֶּם אֶת־שֵׁם יהוה אֱלֹהֵיכֶם אֲשֶׁר־עָשָׂה עִמָּכֶם לְהַפְלִיא, וְלֹא־יֵבֹשׁוּ עַמִּי לְעוֹלָם: וִידַעְתֶּם כִּי בְקֶרֶב יִשְׂרָאֵל אָנִי, וַאֲנִי יהוה אֱלֹהֵיכֶם וְאֵין עוֹד, וְלֹא־יֵבֹשׁוּ עַמִּי לְעוֹלָם: כִּי־ בְשִׂמְחָה תֵצֵאוּ וּבְשָׁלוֹם תּוּבָלוּן, הֶהָרִים וְהַגְּבָעוֹת יִפְצְחוּ לִפְנֵיכֶם רִנָּה, וְכָל־עֲצֵי הַשָּׂדֶה יִמְחֲאוּ־כָף: הִנֵּה אֵל יְשׁוּעָתִי אֶבְטַח, וְלֹא אֶפְחָד, כִּי־ עָזִּי וְזִמְרָת יָהּ יהוה, וַיְהִי־לִי לִישׁוּעָה: וּשְׁאַבְתֶּם־מַיִם בְּשָׂשׂוֹן, מִמַּעַיְנֵי הַיְשׁוּעָה: וַאֲמַרְתֶּם בַּיּוֹם הַהוּא, הוֹדוּ לַיהוה קִרְאוּ בִשְׁמוֹ, הוֹדִיעוּ בָעַמִּים עֲלִילֹתָיו, הַזְכִּירוּ כִּי נִשְׂגָּב שְׁמוֹ: זַמְּרוּ יהוה כִּי גֵאוּת עָשָׂה, מוּדַעַת זֹאת בְּכָל־הָאָרֶץ: צַהֲלִי וָרֹנִּי יוֹשֶׁבֶת צִיּוֹן, כִּי־גָדוֹל בְּקִרְבֵּךְ קְדוֹשׁ יִשְׂרָאֵל: וְאָמַר בַּיּוֹם הַהוּא, הִנֵּה אֱלֹהֵינוּ זֶה קִוִּינוּ לוֹ וְיוֹשִׁיעֵנוּ, זֶה יהוה קִוִּינוּ לוֹ, נָגִילָה וְנִשְׂמְחָה בִּישׁוּעָתוֹ:

ישעיה מה

יואל ב

ישעיה נה

ישעיה יב

ישעיה כה

בֵּית יַעֲקֹב לְכוּ וְנֵלְכָה בְּאוֹר יהוה: וְהָיָה אֱמוּנַת עִתֶּיךָ, חֹסֶן יְשׁוּעֹת חָכְמַת וָדָעַת, יִרְאַת יהוה הִיא אוֹצָרוֹ: וַיְהִי דָוִד לְכָל־דְּרָכָו מַשְׂכִּיל, וַיהוה עִמּוֹ:

ישעיה ב
ישעיה לב
שמואל א' יח,

פָּדָה בְשָׁלוֹם נַפְשִׁי מִקְּרָב־לִי, כִּי־בְרַבִּים הָיוּ עִמָּדִי: וַיֹּאמֶר הָעָם אֶל־ שָׁאוּל, הֲיוֹנָתָן יָמוּת אֲשֶׁר עָשָׂה הַיְשׁוּעָה הַגְּדוֹלָה הַזֹּאת בְּיִשְׂרָאֵל, חָלִילָה, חַי־יהוה אִם־יִפֹּל מִשַּׂעֲרַת רֹאשׁוֹ אַרְצָה, כִּי־עִם־אֱלֹהִים

תהלים נה
שמואל א' יד,

did this today with God's help." So the people rescued Jonathan and he did not
die. Those redeemed by the LORD shall return; they will enter Zion singing; *Is. 35*
everlasting joy will crown their heads. Gladness and joy will overtake them,
and sorrow and sighing will flee away.

הָפַכְתָּ You have turned my sorrow into dancing. You have removed my sack- *Ps. 30*
cloth and clothed me with joy. The LORD your God refused to listen to Balaam; *Deut. 23*
instead the LORD your God turned the curse into a blessing, for the LORD your
God loves you. Then maidens will dance and be glad; so too will young men *Jer. 31*
and old together; I will turn their mourning into gladness; I will give them
comfort and joy instead of sorrow.

בּוֹרֵא I create the speech of lips: Peace, peace to those far and near, says the *Is. 57*
LORD, and I will heal them. Then the spirit came upon Amasai, chief of the *1 Chr. 12*
captains, and he said: "We are yours, David! We are with you, son of Jesse!
Peace, peace to you, and peace to those who help you; for your God will help
you." Then David received them and made them leaders of his troop. And you *1 Sam. 25*
shall say: "To life! Peace be to you, peace to your household, and peace to all
that is yours!" The LORD will give strength to His people; the LORD will bless *Ps. 29*
His people with peace.

אָמַר Rabbi Yoḥanan said: Wherever you find the greatness of the Holy One, *Megilla 31a*
blessed be He, there you find His humility. This is written in the Torah, repeated in the Prophets, and stated a third time in the Writings. It is written in
the Torah: "For the LORD your God is God of gods and LORD of lords, the *Deut. 10*
great, mighty and awe-inspiring God, who shows no favoritism and accepts
no bribe." Immediately afterwards it is written, "He upholds the cause of
the orphan and widow, and loves the stranger, giving him food and clothing." It is repeated in the Prophets, as it says: "So says the High and Exalted *Is. 57*
One, who lives for ever and whose name is Holy: I live in a high and holy
place, but also with the contrite and lowly in spirit, to revive the spirit of
the lowly, and to revive the heart of the contrite." It is stated a third time in
the Writings: "Sing to God, make music for His name, extol Him who rides *Ps. 68*
the clouds – the LORD is His name – and exult before Him." Immediately
afterwards it is written: "Father of the orphans and Justice of widows, is God
in His holy habitation."

יְהִי May the LORD our God be with us, as He was with our ancestors. May *1 Kings 8*
He never abandon us or forsake us. You who cleave to the LORD your God *Deut. 4*
are all alive this day. For the LORD will comfort Zion, He will comfort all her *Is. 51*

ישעיה לה — עָשָׂה הַיּוֹם הַזֶּה, וַיִּפְדּוּ הָעָם אֶת־יוֹנָתָן וְלֹא־מֵת: וּפְדוּיֵי יהוה יְשֻׁבוּן וּבָאוּ צִיּוֹן בְּרִנָּה, וְשִׂמְחַת עוֹלָם עַל־רֹאשָׁם, שָׂשׂוֹן וְשִׂמְחָה יַשִּׂיגוּ, וְנָסוּ יָגוֹן וַאֲנָחָה:

תהלים ל — הָפַכְתָּ מִסְפְּדִי לְמָחוֹל לִי, פִּתַּחְתָּ שַׂקִּי, וַתְּאַזְּרֵנִי שִׂמְחָה: וְלֹא־אָבָה
דברים כג — יהוה אֱלֹהֶיךָ לִשְׁמֹעַ אֶל־בִּלְעָם, וַיַּהֲפֹךְ יהוה אֱלֹהֶיךָ לְּךָ אֶת־הַקְּלָלָה לִבְרָכָה, כִּי אֲהֵבְךָ יהוה אֱלֹהֶיךָ: אָז תִּשְׂמַח בְּתוּלָה בְּמָחוֹל, וּבַחֻרִים
ירמיה לא — וּזְקֵנִים יַחְדָּו, וְהָפַכְתִּי אֶבְלָם לְשָׂשׂוֹן, וְנִחַמְתִּים, וְשִׂמַּחְתִּים מִיגוֹנָם:

ישעיה נז — בּוֹרֵא נִיב שְׂפָתָיִם, שָׁלוֹם שָׁלוֹם לָרָחוֹק וְלַקָּרוֹב אָמַר יהוה, וּרְפָאתִיו:
דברי — וְרוּחַ לָבְשָׁה אֶת־עֲמָשַׂי רֹאשׁ הַשָּׁלִישִׁים, לְךָ דָוִיד וְעִמְּךָ בֶן־יִשַׁי, שָׁלוֹם
הימים א׳ יב — שָׁלוֹם לְךָ וְשָׁלוֹם לְעֹזְרֶךָ, כִּי עֲזָרְךָ אֱלֹהֶיךָ, וַיְקַבְּלֵם דָּוִיד וַיִּתְּנֵם בְּרָאשֵׁי
שמואל א׳ כה — הַגְּדוּד: וַאֲמַרְתֶּם כֹּה לֶחָי, וְאַתָּה שָׁלוֹם וּבֵיתְךָ שָׁלוֹם וְכֹל אֲשֶׁר־לְךָ
תהלים כט — שָׁלוֹם: יהוה עֹז לְעַמּוֹ יִתֵּן, יהוה יְבָרֵךְ אֶת־עַמּוֹ בַשָּׁלוֹם:

מגילה לא. — אָמַר רַבִּי יוֹחָנָן: בְּכָל מָקוֹם שֶׁאַתָּה מוֹצֵא גְדֻלָּתוֹ שֶׁל הַקָּדוֹשׁ בָּרוּךְ הוּא, שָׁם אַתָּה מוֹצֵא עַנְוְתָנוּתוֹ. דָּבָר זֶה כָּתוּב בַּתּוֹרָה, וְשָׁנוּי בַּנְּבִיאִים,
דברים י — וּמְשֻׁלָּשׁ בַּכְּתוּבִים. כָּתוּב בַּתּוֹרָה: כִּי יהוה אֱלֹהֵיכֶם הוּא אֱלֹהֵי הָאֱלֹהִים, וַאֲדֹנֵי הָאֲדֹנִים, הָאֵל הַגָּדֹל הַגִּבֹּר וְהַנּוֹרָא, אֲשֶׁר לֹא־יִשָּׂא פָנִים וְלֹא יִקַּח שֹׁחַד: וּכְתִיב בָּתְרֵהּ: עֹשֶׂה מִשְׁפַּט יָתוֹם וְאַלְמָנָה, וְאֹהֵב
ישעיה נז — גֵּר לָתֶת לוֹ לֶחֶם וְשִׂמְלָה: שָׁנוּי בַּנְּבִיאִים, דִּכְתִיב: כִּי כֹה אָמַר רָם וְנִשָּׂא שֹׁכֵן עַד וְקָדוֹשׁ שְׁמוֹ, מָרוֹם וְקָדוֹשׁ אֶשְׁכּוֹן, וְאֶת־דַּכָּא וּשְׁפַל־רוּחַ, לְהַחֲיוֹת רוּחַ שְׁפָלִים וּלְהַחֲיוֹת לֵב נִדְכָּאִים: מְשֻׁלָּשׁ בַּכְּתוּבִים,
תהלים סח — דִּכְתִיב: שִׁירוּ לֵאלֹהִים, זַמְּרוּ שְׁמוֹ, סֹלּוּ לָרֹכֵב בָּעֲרָבוֹת בְּיָהּ שְׁמוֹ, וְעִלְזוּ לְפָנָיו: וּכְתִיב בָּתְרֵהּ: אֲבִי יְתוֹמִים וְדַיַּן אַלְמָנוֹת, אֱלֹהִים בִּמְעוֹן קָדְשׁוֹ:

מלכים א׳ ח — יְהִי יהוה אֱלֹהֵינוּ עִמָּנוּ כַּאֲשֶׁר הָיָה עִם־אֲבֹתֵינוּ, אַל־יַעַזְבֵנוּ וְאַל־
דברים ד — יִטְּשֵׁנוּ: וְאַתֶּם הַדְּבֵקִים בַּיהוה אֱלֹהֵיכֶם, חַיִּים כֻּלְּכֶם הַיּוֹם: כִּי־נִחַם
ישעיה נא

ruins; He will make her wilderness like Eden, and her desert like a garden of
the LORD. Joy and gladness will be found there, thanksgiving and the sound
of singing. It pleased the LORD for the sake of [Israel's] righteousness to make   *Is. 42*
the Torah great and glorious.

שִׁיר הַמַּעֲלוֹת A song of ascents. Happy are all who fear the LORD, who walk in   *Ps. 128*
His ways. When you eat the fruit of your labor, happy and fortunate are you.
Your wife shall be like a fruitful vine within your house; your sons like olive
saplings around your table. So shall the man who fears the LORD be blessed.
May the LORD bless you from Zion; may you see the good of Jerusalem all
the days of your life; and may you live to see your children's children. Peace
be on Israel!

Some say the Havdala on page 574.

Stand while saying Aleinu. Bow at ˈ.
עָלֵינוּ It is our duty to praise the Master of all,
and ascribe greatness to the Author of creation,
who has not made us like the nations of the lands
nor placed us like the families of the earth;
who has not made our portion like theirs,
nor our destiny like all their multitudes.
(For they worship vanity and emptiness,
and pray to a god who cannot save.)
ˈBut we bow in worship
and thank the Supreme King of kings,
the Holy One, blessed be He,
who extends the heavens and establishes the earth,
whose throne of glory is in the heavens above,
and whose power's Presence is in the highest of heights.
He is our God; there is no other.
Truly He is our King, there is none else,
as it is written in His Torah:
"You shall know and take to heart this day   *Deut. 4*
that the LORD is God, in heaven above and on earth below.
There is no other."

ישעיה מב
יהוה צִיּוֹן, נִחַם כָּל־חָרְבֹתֶיהָ, וַיָּשֶׂם מִדְבָּרָהּ כְּעֵדֶן וְעַרְבָתָהּ כְּגַן־יהוה,
שָׂשׂוֹן וְשִׂמְחָה יִמָּצֵא בָהּ, תּוֹדָה וְקוֹל זִמְרָה: יהוה חָפֵץ לְמַעַן צִדְקוֹ,
יַגְדִּיל תּוֹרָה וְיַאְדִּיר:

תהלים קכח
שִׁיר הַמַּעֲלוֹת, אַשְׁרֵי כָּל־יְרֵא יהוה, הַהֹלֵךְ בִּדְרָכָיו: יְגִיעַ כַּפֶּיךָ כִּי
תֹאכֵל, אַשְׁרֶיךָ וְטוֹב לָךְ: אֶשְׁתְּךָ כְּגֶפֶן פֹּרִיָּה בְּיַרְכְּתֵי בֵיתֶךָ, בָּנֶיךָ כִּשְׁתִלֵי
זֵיתִים, סָבִיב לְשֻׁלְחָנֶךָ: הִנֵּה כִי־כֵן יְבֹרַךְ גָּבֶר יְרֵא יהוה: יְבָרֶכְךָ יהוה
מִצִּיּוֹן, וּרְאֵה בְּטוּב יְרוּשָׁלָ͏ִם, כֹּל יְמֵי חַיֶּיךָ: וּרְאֵה־בָנִים לְבָנֶיךָ, שָׁלוֹם
עַל־יִשְׂרָאֵל:

Some say the הבדלה on page 575.

Stand while saying עלינו. Bow at י.
עָלֵינוּ לְשַׁבֵּחַ לַאֲדוֹן הַכֹּל, לָתֵת גְּדֻלָּה לְיוֹצֵר בְּרֵאשִׁית
שֶׁלֹּא עָשָׂנוּ כְּגוֹיֵי הָאֲרָצוֹת, וְלֹא שָׂמָנוּ כְּמִשְׁפְּחוֹת הָאֲדָמָה
שֶׁלֹּא שָׂם חֶלְקֵנוּ כָּהֶם וְגֹרָלֵנוּ כְּכָל־הֲמוֹנָם.
(שֶׁהֵם מִשְׁתַּחֲוִים לְהֶבֶל וָרִיק וּמִתְפַּלְּלִים אֶל אֵל לֹא יוֹשִׁיעַ.)
וַאֲנַחְנוּ כּוֹרְעִים וּמִשְׁתַּחֲוִים וּמוֹדִים
לִפְנֵי מֶלֶךְ מַלְכֵי הַמְּלָכִים, הַקָּדוֹשׁ בָּרוּךְ הוּא
שֶׁהוּא נוֹטֶה שָׁמַיִם וְיוֹסֵד אָרֶץ
וּמוֹשַׁב יְקָרוֹ בַּשָּׁמַיִם מִמַּעַל
וּשְׁכִינַת עֻזּוֹ בְּגָבְהֵי מְרוֹמִים.
הוּא אֱלֹהֵינוּ, אֵין עוֹד.
אֱמֶת מַלְכֵּנוּ, אֶפֶס זוּלָתוֹ
דברים ד
כַּכָּתוּב בְּתוֹרָתוֹ, וְיָדַעְתָּ הַיּוֹם וַהֲשֵׁבֹתָ אֶל־לְבָבֶךָ
כִּי יהוה הוּא הָאֱלֹהִים בַּשָּׁמַיִם מִמַּעַל וְעַל־הָאָרֶץ מִתָּחַת
אֵין עוֹד:

Therefore, we place our hope in You, LORD our God,
that we may soon see the glory of Your power,
when You will remove abominations from the earth,
and idols will be utterly destroyed,
when the world will be perfected
under the sovereignty of the Almighty,
when all humanity will call on Your name,
to turn all the earth's wicked toward You.
All the world's inhabitants will realize and know
that to You every knee must bow and every tongue swear loyalty.
Before You, LORD our God, they will kneel and bow down
and give honor to Your glorious name.
They will all accept the yoke of Your kingdom,
and You will reign over them soon and for ever.
For the kingdom is Yours, and to all eternity You will reign in glory,
as it is written in Your Torah: "The LORD will reign for ever and ever."   *Ex. 15*
▸ And it is said: "Then the LORD shall be King over all the earth;   *Zech. 14*
on that day the LORD shall be One and His name One."

Some add:

Have no fear of sudden terror or of the ruin when it overtakes the wicked.   *Prov. 3*
Devise your strategy, but it will be thwarted; propose your plan,   *Is. 8*
but it will not stand, for God is with us.
When you grow old, I will still be the same.   *Is. 46*
When your hair turns gray, I will still carry you.
I made you, I will bear you, I will carry you, and I will rescue you.

MOURNER'S KADDISH

The following prayer, said by mourners, requires the presence of a minyan.
A transliteration can be found on page 667.

Mourner: יִתְגַּדַּל Magnified and sanctified may His great name be,
in the world He created by His will.
May He establish His kingdom
in your lifetime and in your days,
and in the lifetime of all the house of Israel,
swiftly and soon – and say: Amen.

עַל כֵּן נְקַוֶּה לְּךָ יהוה אֱלֹהֵינוּ, לִרְאוֹת מְהֵרָה בְּתִפְאֶרֶת עֻזֶּךָ
לְהַעֲבִיר גִּלּוּלִים מִן הָאָרֶץ, וְהָאֱלִילִים כָּרוֹת יִכָּרֵתוּן
לְתַקֵּן עוֹלָם בְּמַלְכוּת שַׁדַּי.
וְכָל בְּנֵי בָשָׂר יִקְרְאוּ בִשְׁמֶךָ לְהַפְנוֹת אֵלֶיךָ כָּל רִשְׁעֵי אָרֶץ.
יַכִּירוּ וְיֵדְעוּ כָּל יוֹשְׁבֵי תֵבֵל
כִּי לְךָ תִּכְרַע כָּל בֶּרֶךְ, תִּשָּׁבַע כָּל לָשׁוֹן.
לְפָנֶיךָ יהוה אֱלֹהֵינוּ יִכְרְעוּ וְיִפֹּלוּ, וְלִכְבוֹד שִׁמְךָ יְקָר יִתֵּנוּ
וִיקַבְּלוּ כֻלָּם אֶת עֹל מַלְכוּתֶךָ
וְתִמְלֹךְ עֲלֵיהֶם מְהֵרָה לְעוֹלָם וָעֶד.
כִּי הַמַּלְכוּת שֶׁלְּךָ הִיא וּלְעוֹלְמֵי עַד תִּמְלֹךְ בְּכָבוֹד

שמות טו

כַּכָּתוּב בְּתוֹרָתֶךָ, יהוה יִמְלֹךְ לְעֹלָם וָעֶד:

זכריה יד

◀ וְנֶאֱמַר, וְהָיָה יהוה לְמֶלֶךְ עַל־כָּל־הָאָרֶץ
בַּיּוֹם הַהוּא יִהְיֶה יהוה אֶחָד וּשְׁמוֹ אֶחָד:

Some add:

משלי ג

אַל־תִּירָא מִפַּחַד פִּתְאֹם וּמִשֹּׁאַת רְשָׁעִים כִּי תָבֹא:

ישעיה ח

עֻצוּ עֵצָה וְתֻפָר, דַּבְּרוּ דָבָר וְלֹא יָקוּם, כִּי עִמָּנוּ אֵל:

ישעיה מו

וְעַד־זִקְנָה אֲנִי הוּא, וְעַד־שֵׂיבָה אֲנִי אֶסְבֹּל
אֲנִי עָשִׂיתִי וַאֲנִי אֶשָּׂא וַאֲנִי אֶסְבֹּל וַאֲמַלֵּט:

קדיש יתום

The following prayer, said by mourners, requires the presence of a מנין.
A transliteration can be found on page 667.

אבל: יִתְגַּדַּל וְיִתְקַדַּשׁ שְׁמֵהּ רַבָּא (קהל: אָמֵן)
בְּעָלְמָא דִּי בְרָא כִרְעוּתֵהּ
וְיַמְלִיךְ מַלְכוּתֵהּ
בְּחַיֵּיכוֹן וּבְיוֹמֵיכוֹן וּבְחַיֵּי דְכָל בֵּית יִשְׂרָאֵל
בַּעֲגָלָא וּבִזְמַן קָרִיב, וְאִמְרוּ אָמֵן. (קהל: אָמֵן)

All: May His great name be blessed for ever and all time.

Mourner: Blessed and praised, glorified and exalted,
raised and honored,
uplifted and lauded
be the name of the Holy One,
blessed be He,
beyond any blessing,
song, praise and consolation
uttered in the world –
and say: Amen.

May there be great peace from heaven,
and life for us and all Israel –
and say: Amen.

Bow, take three steps back, as if taking leave of the Divine Presence,
then bow, first left, then right, then center, while saying:
May He who makes peace in His high places,
make peace for us and all Israel –
and say: Amen.

In Israel, the person saying Kaddish adds:
Bless the LORD, the blessed One.

and the congregation responds:
Bless the LORD, the blessed One, for ever and all time.

All sing:
אֲנִי מַאֲמִין I believe with perfect faith
in the coming of the Messiah,
and though he may delay,
I wait daily for his coming.

קהל
ואבל: יְהֵא שְׁמֵהּ רַבָּא מְבָרַךְ לְעָלַם וּלְעָלְמֵי עָלְמַיָּא.

אבל: יִתְבָּרַךְ וְיִשְׁתַּבַּח וְיִתְפָּאַר
וְיִתְרוֹמַם וְיִתְנַשֵּׂא וְיִתְהַדָּר וְיִתְעַלֶּה וְיִתְהַלָּל
שְׁמֵהּ דְּקֻדְשָׁא בְּרִיךְ הוּא (קהל: בְּרִיךְ הוּא)
לְעֵלָּא מִן כָּל בִּרְכָתָא
וְשִׁירָתָא, תֻּשְׁבְּחָתָא וְנֶחֱמָתָא
דַּאֲמִירָן בְּעָלְמָא, וְאִמְרוּ אָמֵן. (קהל: אָמֵן)

יְהֵא שְׁלָמָא רַבָּא מִן שְׁמַיָּא
וְחַיִּים, עָלֵינוּ וְעַל כָּל יִשְׂרָאֵל, וְאִמְרוּ אָמֵן. (קהל: אָמֵן)

Bow, take three steps back, as if taking leave of the Divine Presence,
then bow, first left, then right, then center, while saying:

עֹשֶׂה שָׁלוֹם בִּמְרוֹמָיו
הוּא יַעֲשֶׂה שָׁלוֹם עָלֵינוּ וְעַל כָּל יִשְׂרָאֵל, וְאִמְרוּ אָמֵן. (קהל: אָמֵן)

In ארץ ישראל, *the person saying* קדיש *adds:*
בָּרְכוּ אֶת יהוה הַמְבֹרָךְ.

and the קהל *responds:*
בָּרוּךְ יהוה הַמְבֹרָךְ לְעוֹלָם וָעֶד.

All sing:

אֲנִי מַאֲמִין בֶּאֱמוּנָה שְׁלֵמָה בְּבִיאַת הַמָּשִׁיחַ
וְאַף עַל פִּי שֶׁיִּתְמַהְמֵהַּ
עִם כָּל זֶה אֲחַכֶּה לּוֹ בְּכָל יוֹם שֶׁיָּבוֹא.

HATIKVA

The service continues with HaTikva.

כָּל עוֹד As long as in the heart, within,
A Jewish soul still yearns,
And onward, towards the ends of the east,
An eye still gazes toward Zion;

Our hope is not yet lost,
The hope of two thousand years,
To be a free people in our land,
The land of Zion and Jerusalem.

The transliteration of HaTikva:

Kol od balevav penima
Nefesh yehudi homiya,
Ulfa'atei mizraḥ, kadima,
Ayin letziyon tzofiya;

Od lo av'da tikvatenu,
Hatikva bat sh'not alpayim,
Lihyot am ḥofshi b'artzenu,
Eretz tziyon virushalayim.

התקווה

The service continues with התקווה.

כָּל עוֹד

בַּלֵּבָב פְּנִימָה
נֶפֶשׁ יְהוּדִי הוֹמִיָּה
וּלְפַאֲתֵי מִזְרָח, קָדִימָה
עַיִן לְצִיּוֹן צוֹפִיָּה

עוֹד לֹא אָבְדָה תִּקְוָתֵנוּ
הַתִּקְוָה בַּת שְׁנוֹת אַלְפַּיִם
לִהְיוֹת עַם חָפְשִׁי בְּאַרְצֵנוּ
אֶרֶץ צִיּוֹן וִירוּשָׁלַיִם.

HAVDALA AT HOME

On Motza'ei Shabbat, the Havdala is recited. When reciting the Havdala during the
Ma'ariv service some begin at "Please pay attention" others say the full Havdala.

Taking a cup of wine in the right hand, say:

הִנֵּה Behold, God is my salvation. I will trust and not be afraid.   *Is. 12*
The LORD, the LORD, is my strength and my song.
He has become my salvation.
With joy you will draw water from the springs of salvation.
Salvation is the LORD's; on Your people is Your blessing, Selah.   *Ps. 3*
The LORD of hosts is with us, the God of Jacob is our stronghold, Selah.   *Ps. 46*
LORD of hosts: happy is the one who trusts in You.   *Ps. 84*
LORD, save! May the King answer us on the day we call.   *Ps. 20*
For the Jews there was light and gladness, joy and honor –   *Esther 8*
so may it be for us.
I will lift the cup of salvation and call on the name of the LORD.   *Ps. 116*

When making Havdala for others, add:
Please pay attention, my masters.
Blessed are You, LORD our God, King of the Universe,
who creates the fruit of the vine.

Hold the spice box and say:
Blessed are You, LORD our God, King of the Universe,
who creates the various spices.

Smell the spices and put the spice box down.
Lift the hands toward the flame of the Havdala candle and say:
Blessed are You, LORD our God, King of the Universe,
who creates the lights of fire.

Holding the cup of wine again in the right hand, say:
בָּרוּךְ Blessed are You, LORD our God, King of the Universe, who
distinguishes between sacred and secular, between light and darkness,
between Israel and the nations, between the seventh day and the six
days of work. Blessed are You, LORD, who distinguishes between sacred
and secular.

סדר הבדלה בבית

On מוצאי שבת, the הבדלה is recited. When reciting the הבדלה during the
מעריב service some begin at סָבְרִי מָרָנָן others say the full הבדלה.

Taking a cup of wine in the right hand, say:

ישעיה יב

הִנֵּה אֵל יְשׁוּעָתִי אֶבְטַח, וְלֹא אֶפְחָד

כִּי־עָזִּי וְזִמְרָת יָהּ יהוה, וַיְהִי־לִי לִישׁוּעָה:

וּשְׁאַבְתֶּם־מַיִם בְּשָׂשׂוֹן, מִמַּעַיְנֵי הַיְשׁוּעָה:

תהלים ג

לַיהוה הַיְשׁוּעָה, עַל־עַמְּךָ בִרְכָתֶךָ סֶּלָה:

תהלים מו

יהוה צְבָאוֹת עִמָּנוּ, מִשְׂגָּב לָנוּ אֱלֹהֵי יַעֲקֹב סֶלָה:

תהלים פד

יהוה צְבָאוֹת, אַשְׁרֵי אָדָם בֹּטֵחַ בָּךְ:

תהלים כ

יהוה הוֹשִׁיעָה, הַמֶּלֶךְ יַעֲנֵנוּ בְיוֹם־קָרְאֵנוּ:

אסתר ח

לַיְּהוּדִים הָיְתָה אוֹרָה וְשִׂמְחָה וְשָׂשֹׂן וִיקָר: כֵּן תִּהְיֶה לָּנוּ.

תהלים קטז

כּוֹס־יְשׁוּעוֹת אֶשָּׂא, וּבְשֵׁם יהוה אֶקְרָא:

When making הבדלה for others, add:

סָבְרִי מָרָנָן

בָּרוּךְ אַתָּה יהוה אֱלֹהֵינוּ מֶלֶךְ הָעוֹלָם, בּוֹרֵא פְּרִי הַגָּפֶן.

Hold the spice box and say:

בָּרוּךְ אַתָּה יהוה אֱלֹהֵינוּ מֶלֶךְ הָעוֹלָם, בּוֹרֵא מִינֵי בְשָׂמִים.

Smell the spices and put the spice box down.
Lift the hands toward the flame of the הבדלה candle and say:

בָּרוּךְ אַתָּה יהוה אֱלֹהֵינוּ מֶלֶךְ הָעוֹלָם, בּוֹרֵא מְאוֹרֵי הָאֵשׁ.

Holding the cup of wine again in the right hand, say:

בָּרוּךְ אַתָּה יהוה אֱלֹהֵינוּ מֶלֶךְ הָעוֹלָם, הַמַּבְדִּיל בֵּין קֹדֶשׁ לְחֹל,
בֵּין אוֹר לְחֹשֶׁךְ, בֵּין יִשְׂרָאֵל לָעַמִּים, בֵּין יוֹם הַשְּׁבִיעִי לְשֵׁשֶׁת יְמֵי
הַמַּעֲשֶׂה. בָּרוּךְ אַתָּה יהוה, הַמַּבְדִּיל בֵּין קֹדֶשׁ לְחֹל.

שחרית ליום ירושלים

SHAḤARIT FOR YOM YERUSHALAYIM

The prayers begin on page 150 until after Hallel on page 350.

HALF KADDISH

Leader: יִתְגַּדַּל Magnified and sanctified
may His great name be,
in the world He created by His will.
May He establish His kingdom
in your lifetime and in your days,
and in the lifetime of all the house of Israel,
swiftly and soon –
and say: Amen.

All: May His great name be blessed for ever and all time.

Leader: Blessed and praised, glorified and exalted,
raised and honored, uplifted and lauded
be the name of the Holy One,
blessed be He,
beyond any blessing,
song, praise and consolation
uttered in the world –
and say: Amen.

*When Yom Yerushalayim falls on Monday, continue with the Reading
of the Torah below. On other days continue on page 598.*

REMOVING THE TORAH FROM THE ARK

Before taking the Torah out of the Ark, some add:

אֵין־כָּמוֹךָ There is none like You among the heavenly powers,   *Ps. 86*
LORD, and there are no works like Yours.
Your kingdom is an eternal kingdom,   *Ps. 145*
and Your dominion is for all generations.

The LORD is King, the LORD was King,
the LORD shall be King for ever and all time.
The LORD will give strength to His people;   *Ps. 29*
the LORD will bless His people with peace.

The prayers begin on page 151 until after הלל on page 351.

חצי קדיש

ש״ץ: יִתְגַּדַּל וְיִתְקַדַּשׁ שְׁמֵהּ רַבָּא (קהל: אָמֵן)

בְּעָלְמָא דִּי בְרָא כִרְעוּתֵהּ

וְיַמְלִיךְ מַלְכוּתֵהּ

בְּחַיֵּיכוֹן וּבְיוֹמֵיכוֹן וּבְחַיֵּי דְּכָל בֵּית יִשְׂרָאֵל

בַּעֲגָלָא וּבִזְמַן קָרִיב

וְאִמְרוּ אָמֵן. (קהל: אָמֵן)

קהל יְהֵא שְׁמֵהּ רַבָּא מְבָרַךְ לְעָלַם וּלְעָלְמֵי עָלְמַיָּא.
 וש״ץ:

ש״ץ: יִתְבָּרַךְ וְיִשְׁתַּבַּח וְיִתְפָּאַר וְיִתְרוֹמַם וְיִתְנַשֵּׂא

וְיִתְהַדָּר וְיִתְעַלֶּה וְיִתְהַלָּל

שְׁמֵהּ דְּקֻדְשָׁא בְּרִיךְ הוּא (קהל: בְּרִיךְ הוּא)

לְעֵלָּא מִן כָּל בִּרְכָתָא

וְשִׁירָתָא, תֻּשְׁבְּחָתָא וְנֶחֱמָתָא

דַּאֲמִירָן בְּעָלְמָא

וְאִמְרוּ אָמֵן. (קהל: אָמֵן)

When יום ירושלים falls on Monday, continue with the Reading of
the תורה below. On other days continue on page 599.

הוצאת ספר תורה

Before taking the תורה out of the ארון קודש, some add:

תהלים פו אֵין כָּמֽוֹךָ בָאֱלֹהִים, אֲדֹנָי, וְאֵין כְּמַעֲשֶׂיךָ:
תהלים קמה מַלְכוּתְךָ מַלְכוּת כָּל עֹלָמִים, וּמֶמְשַׁלְתְּךָ בְּכָל דּוֹר וָדֹר:

יהוה מֶֽלֶךְ, יהוה מָלָךְ, יהוה יִמְלֹךְ לְעֹלָם וָעֶד.
תהלים כט יהוה עֹז לְעַמּוֹ יִתֵּן, יהוה יְבָרֵךְ אֶת עַמּוֹ בַשָּׁלוֹם:

Father of compassion,
favor Zion with Your goodness; rebuild the walls of Jerusalem.
For we trust in You alone, King, God,
high and exalted, Master of worlds.

Ps. 51

The Ark is opened and the congregation stands. All say:

וַיְהִי בִּנְסֹעַ Whenever the Ark set out, Moses would say, "Arise, LORD, *Num. 10*
and may Your enemies be scattered. May those who hate You flee
before You." For the Torah shall come forth from Zion, and the *Is. 2*
word of the LORD from Jerusalem. Blessed is He who in His holiness gave the Torah to His people Israel.

Blessed is the name of the Master of the Universe. Blessed is Your crown and Your *Zohar,*
place. May Your favor always be with Your people Israel. Show Your people the *Vayak-hel*
salvation of Your right hand in Your Temple. Grant us the gift of Your good light, and
accept our prayers in mercy. May it be Your will to prolong our life in goodness. May I
be counted among the righteous, so that You will have compassion on me and protect
me and all that is mine and all that is Your people Israel's. You feed all; You sustain all;
You rule over all; You rule over kings, for sovereignty is Yours. I am a servant of the
Holy One, blessed be He, before whom and before whose glorious Torah I bow at
all times. Not in man do I trust, nor on any angel do I rely, but on the God of heaven
who is the God of truth, whose Torah is truth, whose prophets speak truth, and who
abounds in acts of love and truth. ‣ In Him I trust, and to His holy and glorious name I
offer praises. May it be Your will to open my heart to the Torah, and to fulfill the wishes
of my heart and of the hearts of all Your people Israel for good, for life, and for peace.

The Leader takes the Torah scroll in his right arm. Leader then congregation:
Listen, Israel: the LORD is our God, the LORD is One. *Deut. 6*

Leader then congregation:
One is our God; great is our Master; holy is His name.

The Leader takes the Torah scroll in his right arm, bows toward the Ark and says:
Magnify the LORD with me, and let us exalt His name together. *Ps. 34*

The Ark is closed. The Leader carries the Torah scroll to the bima and the congregation says:
לְךָ Yours, LORD, are the greatness and the power, the glory and the *1 Chr. 29*
majesty and splendor, for everything in heaven and earth is Yours.
Yours, LORD, is the kingdom; You are exalted as Head over all.

אַב הָרַחֲמִים, הֵיטִיבָה בִרְצוֹנְךָ אֶת־צִיּוֹן תִּבְנֶה חוֹמוֹת יְרוּשָׁלָיִם: כִּי בְךָ לְבַד בָּטָחְנוּ, מֶלֶךְ אֵל רָם וְנִשָּׂא, אֲדוֹן עוֹלָמִים.

The ארון קודש *is opened and the* קהל *stands. All say:*

וַיְהִי בִּנְסֹעַ הָאָרֹן וַיֹּאמֶר מֹשֶׁה, קוּמָה יְהוה וְיָפֻצוּ אֹיְבֶיךָ וְיָנֻסוּ מְשַׂנְאֶיךָ מִפָּנֶיךָ: כִּי מִצִּיּוֹן תֵּצֵא תוֹרָה וּדְבַר־יְהוה מִירוּשָׁלָיִם: בָּרוּךְ שֶׁנָּתַן תּוֹרָה לְעַמּוֹ יִשְׂרָאֵל בִּקְדֻשָּׁתוֹ.

בְּרִיךְ שְׁמֵהּ דְּמָרֵא עָלְמָא, בְּרִיךְ כִּתְרָךְ וְאַתְרָךְ. יְהֵא רְעוּתָךְ עִם עַמָּךְ יִשְׂרָאֵל לְעָלַם, וּפֻרְקַן יְמִינָךְ אַחֲזֵי לְעַמָּךְ בְּבֵית מַקְדְּשָׁךְ, וּלְאַמְטוֹיֵי לָנָא מִטּוּב נְהוֹרָךְ, וּלְקַבֵּל צְלוֹתָנָא בְּרַחֲמִין. יְהֵא רַעֲוָא קֳדָמָךְ דְּתוֹרִיךְ לָן חַיִּין בְּטִיבוּ, וְלֶהֱוֵי אֲנָא פְּקִידָא בְּגוֹ צַדִּיקַיָּא, לְמִרְחַם עֲלַי וּלְמִנְטַר יָתִי וְיַת כָּל דִּי לִי וְדִי לְעַמָּךְ יִשְׂרָאֵל. אַנְתְּ הוּא זָן לְכֹלָּא וּמְפַרְנֵס לְכֹלָּא, אַנְתְּ הוּא שַׁלִּיט עַל כֹּלָּא, אַנְתְּ הוּא דְּשַׁלִּיט עַל מַלְכַיָּא, וּמַלְכוּתָא דִּילָךְ הִיא. אֲנָא עַבְדָּא דְּקֻדְשָׁא בְּרִיךְ הוּא, דְּסָגִדְנָא קַמֵּהּ וּמִקַּמֵּי דִּיקָר אוֹרַיְתֵהּ בְּכָל עִדָּן וְעִדָּן. לָא עַל אֱנָשׁ רָחִיצְנָא וְלָא עַל בַּר אֱלָהִין סָמִיכְנָא, אֶלָּא בֵּאלָהָא דִשְׁמַיָּא, דְּהוּא אֱלָהָא קְשׁוֹט, וְאוֹרַיְתֵהּ קְשׁוֹט, וּנְבִיאוֹהִי קְשׁוֹט, וּמַסְגֵּא לְמֶעְבַּד טָבְוָן וּקְשׁוֹט. ◂ בֵּהּ אֲנָא רָחִיץ, וְלִשְׁמֵהּ קַדִּישָׁא יַקִּירָא אֲנָא אֵמַר תֻּשְׁבְּחָן. יְהֵא רַעֲוָא קֳדָמָךְ דְּתִפְתַּח לִבַּאי בְּאוֹרַיְתָא, וְתַשְׁלִים מִשְׁאֲלִין דְּלִבַּאי וְלִבָּא דְכָל עַמָּךְ יִשְׂרָאֵל לְטָב וּלְחַיִּין וְלִשְׁלָם.

The קהל *then* שליח ציבור *takes the* ספר תורה *in his right arm.*

שְׁמַע יִשְׂרָאֵל, יְהוה אֱלֹהֵינוּ, יְהוה אֶחָד:

The קהל *then* שליח ציבור

אֶחָד אֱלֹהֵינוּ, גָּדוֹל אֲדוֹנֵינוּ, קָדוֹשׁ שְׁמוֹ.

The שליח ציבור *takes the* ספר תורה *in his right arm, bows toward the* ארון קודש *and says:*

גַּדְּלוּ לַיהוה אִתִּי וּנְרוֹמְמָה שְׁמוֹ יַחְדָּו:

The ארון קודש *is closed. The* שליח ציבור *carries the* ספר תורה *to the* בימה *and the* קהל *says:*

לְךָ יְהוה הַגְּדֻלָּה וְהַגְּבוּרָה וְהַתִּפְאֶרֶת וְהַנֵּצַח וְהַהוֹד, כִּי־כֹל בַּשָּׁמַיִם וּבָאָרֶץ, לְךָ יְהוה הַמַּמְלָכָה וְהַמִּתְנַשֵּׂא לְכֹל לְרֹאשׁ:

רוֹמְמוּ Exalt the LORD our God and bow to His footstool; He is holy. *Ps. 99*
Exalt the LORD our God, and bow at His holy mountain, for holy is
the LORD our God.

אַב הָרַחֲמִים May the Father of compassion have compassion on the
people borne by Him. May He remember the covenant with the mighty
[patriarchs], and deliver us from evil times. May He reproach the evil
instinct in the people carried by Him, and graciously grant that we be
an everlasting remnant. May He fulfill in good measure our requests
for salvation and compassion.

The Torah scroll is placed on the bima and the Gabbai calls a Kohen to the Torah. .
May His kingship over us be soon revealed and made manifest. May He be gracious to
our surviving remnant, the remnant of His people the house of Israel in grace, loving-
kindness, compassion and favor, and let us say: Amen. Let us all render greatness to
our God and give honor to the Torah. *Let the Kohen come forward. Arise (*name*
son of *father's name*), the Kohen.

*If no Kohen is present, a Levi or Yisrael is called up as follows:
/As there is no Kohen, arise (*name* son of *father's name*) in place of a Kohen./

Blessed is He who, in His holiness, gave the Torah to His people Israel.

Congregation followed by the Gabbai:
You who cling to the LORD your God are all alive today.   *Deut. 4*

The appropriate Torah portions are to be found from page 588.

*The Reader shows the oleh the section to be read. The oleh touches the scroll at that place
with the tzitzit of his tallit, which he then kisses. Holding the handles of the scroll, he says:*

Oleh: Bless the LORD, the blessed One.

Cong: Bless the LORD, the blessed One, for ever and all time.

Oleh: Bless the LORD, the blessed One, for ever and all time.

Blessed are You, LORD our God, King of the Universe,
who has chosen us from all peoples and has given us His Torah.
Blessed are You, LORD, Giver of the Torah.

After the reading, the oleh says:

Oleh: Blessed are You, LORD our God, King of the Universe,
who has given us the Torah of truth,
planting everlasting life in our midst.
Blessed are You, LORD, Giver of the Torah.

רוֹמְמוּ יהוה אֱלֹהֵינוּ וְהִשְׁתַּחֲווּ לַהֲדֹם רַגְלָיו, קָדוֹשׁ הוּא: רוֹמְמוּ תהילים צט
יהוה אֱלֹהֵינוּ וְהִשְׁתַּחֲווּ לְהַר קָדְשׁוֹ, כִּי־קָדוֹשׁ יהוה אֱלֹהֵינוּ:

אַב הָרַחֲמִים הוּא יְרַחֵם עַם עֲמוּסִים, וְיִזְכֹּר בְּרִית אֵיתָנִים, וְיַצִּיל
נַפְשׁוֹתֵינוּ מִן הַשָּׁעוֹת הָרָעוֹת, וְיִגְעַר בְּיֵצֶר הָרַע מִן הַנְּשׂוּאִים, וְיָחֹן
אוֹתָנוּ לִפְלֵיטַת עוֹלָמִים, וִימַלֵּא מִשְׁאֲלוֹתֵינוּ בְּמִדָּה טוֹבָה יְשׁוּעָה
וְרַחֲמִים.

The כהן is placed on the שולחן and the גבאי calls a כהן to the תורה. The ספר תורה

וְתִגָּלֶה וְתֵרָאֶה מַלְכוּתוֹ עָלֵינוּ בִּזְמַן קָרוֹב, וְיָחֹן פְּלֵיטָתֵנוּ וּפְלֵיטַת עַמּוֹ בֵּית יִשְׂרָאֵל
לְחֵן וּלְחֶסֶד וּלְרַחֲמִים וּלְרָצוֹן וְנֹאמַר אָמֵן. הַכֹּל הָבוּ גֹדֶל לֵאלֹהֵינוּ וּתְנוּ כָבוֹד לַתּוֹרָה.
כֹּהֵן קְרַב, יַעֲמֹד (פלוני בֶּן פלוני) הַכֹּהֵן.*

*If no כהן is present, a לוי or ישראל is called up as follows:

/אֵין כָּאן כֹּהֵן, יַעֲמֹד (פלוני בֶּן פלוני) בִּמְקוֹם כֹּהֵן./

בָּרוּךְ שֶׁנָּתַן תּוֹרָה לְעַמּוֹ יִשְׂרָאֵל בִּקְדֻשָּׁתוֹ.

followed by the גבאי: קהל

וְאַתֶּם הַדְּבֵקִים בַּיהוה אֱלֹהֵיכֶם חַיִּים כֻּלְּכֶם הַיּוֹם: דברים ד

The appropriate תורה portions are to be found from page 589.

The קורא shows the עולה the section to be read. The עולה touches the ספר תורה at that place
with the ציצית of his טלית, which he then kisses. Holding the handles of the ספר תורה, he says:

עולה: בָּרְכוּ אֶת יהוה הַמְבֹרָךְ.

קהל: בָּרוּךְ יהוה הַמְבֹרָךְ לְעוֹלָם וָעֶד.

עולה: בָּרוּךְ יהוה הַמְבֹרָךְ לְעוֹלָם וָעֶד.
בָּרוּךְ אַתָּה יהוה, אֱלֹהֵינוּ מֶלֶךְ הָעוֹלָם
אֲשֶׁר בָּחַר בָּנוּ מִכָּל הָעַמִּים וְנָתַן לָנוּ אֶת תּוֹרָתוֹ.
בָּרוּךְ אַתָּה יהוה, נוֹתֵן הַתּוֹרָה.

After the קריאת התורה, the עולה says:

עולה: בָּרוּךְ אַתָּה יהוה אֱלֹהֵינוּ מֶלֶךְ הָעוֹלָם
אֲשֶׁר נָתַן לָנוּ תּוֹרַת אֱמֶת וְחַיֵּי עוֹלָם נָטַע בְּתוֹכֵנוּ.
בָּרוּךְ אַתָּה יהוה, נוֹתֵן הַתּוֹרָה.

One who has survived a situation of danger says:
Blessed are You, LORD our God, King of the Universe,
who bestows good on the unworthy,
who has bestowed on me much good.

The congregation responds:
Amen. May He who bestowed much good on you continue to bestow
on you much good, Selah.

After a Bar Mitzva boy has finished the Torah blessing, his father says aloud:
Blessed is He who has released me from the responsibility for this child.

FOR AN OLEH

May He who blessed our fathers, Abraham, Isaac and Jacob, bless (*name,
son of father's name*) who has been called up in honor of the All-Present, in
honor of the Torah, and in honor of Yom Yerushalayim. As a reward for this,
may the Holy One, blessed be He, protect and deliver him from all trouble
and distress, all infection and illness, and send blessing and success to all
the work of his hands, together with all Israel, his brethren, and let us say:
Amen.

FOR A SICK MAN

May He who blessed our fathers, Abraham, Isaac and Jacob, Moses and
Aaron, David and Solomon, bless and heal one who is ill, (*sick person's name,
son of mother's name*), on whose behalf (*name of the one making the offering*)
is making a contribution to charity. As a reward for this, may the Holy One,
blessed be He, be filled with compassion for him, to restore his health, cure
him, strengthen and revive him, sending him a swift and full recovery from
heaven to all his 248 organs and 365 sinews, amongst the other sick ones in
Israel, a healing of the spirit and a healing of the body, may healing be quick
to come – now, swiftly and soon, and let us say: Amen.

FOR A SICK WOMAN

May He who blessed our fathers, Abraham, Isaac and Jacob, Moses and
Aaron, David and Solomon, bless and heal one who is ill, (*sick person's
name, daughter of mother's name*), on whose behalf (*name of the one making
the offering*) is making a contribution to charity. As a reward for this, may
the Holy One, blessed be He, be filled with compassion for her, to restore
her health, cure her, strengthen and revive her, sending her a swift and full

One who has survived a situation of danger says:

בָּרוּךְ אַתָּה יהוה אֱלֹהֵינוּ מֶלֶךְ הָעוֹלָם הַגּוֹמֵל לְחַיָּבִים טוֹבוֹת שֶׁגְּמָלַנִי כָּל טוֹב.

The קהל *responds:*

אָמֵן. מִי שֶׁגְּמָלְךָ כָּל טוֹב הוּא יִגְמָלְךָ כָּל טוֹב, סֶלָה.

After a בר מצוה *has finished the* תורה *blessing, his father says aloud:*

בָּרוּךְ שֶׁפְּטָרַנִי מֵעָנְשׁוֹ שֶׁלָּזֶה.

מי שברך לעולה לתורה

מִי שֶׁבֵּרַךְ אֲבוֹתֵינוּ אַבְרָהָם יִצְחָק וְיַעֲקֹב, הוּא יְבָרֵךְ אֶת (פלוני בֶּן פלוני), בַּעֲבוּר שֶׁעָלָה לִכְבוֹד הַמָּקוֹם וְלִכְבוֹד הַתּוֹרָה וְלִכְבוֹד יוֹם יְרוּשָׁלַיִם. בִּשְׂכַר זֶה הַקָּדוֹשׁ בָּרוּךְ הוּא יִשְׁמְרֵהוּ וְיַצִּילֵהוּ מִכָּל צָרָה וְצוּקָה וּמִכָּל נֶגַע וּמַחֲלָה, וְיִשְׁלַח בְּרָכָה וְהַצְלָחָה בְּכָל מַעֲשֵׂה יָדָיו עִם כָּל יִשְׂרָאֵל אֶחָיו, וְנֹאמַר אָמֵן.

מי שברך לחולה

מִי שֶׁבֵּרַךְ אֲבוֹתֵינוּ אַבְרָהָם יִצְחָק וְיַעֲקֹב, מֹשֶׁה וְאַהֲרֹן דָּוִד וּשְׁלֹמֹה הוּא יְבָרֵךְ וִירַפֵּא אֶת הַחוֹלֶה (פלוני בֶּן פלונית) בַּעֲבוּר שֶׁ(פלוני בֶּן פלוני) נוֹדֵר צְדָקָה בַּעֲבוּרוֹ. בִּשְׂכַר זֶה הַקָּדוֹשׁ בָּרוּךְ הוּא יִמָּלֵא רַחֲמִים עָלָיו לְהַחֲלִימוֹ וּלְרַפְּאתוֹ וּלְהַחֲזִיקוֹ וּלְהַחֲיוֹתוֹ וְיִשְׁלַח לוֹ מְהֵרָה רְפוּאָה שְׁלֵמָה מִן הַשָּׁמַיִם לִרְמַ״ח אֵבָרָיו וּשְׁסָ״ה גִּידָיו בְּתוֹךְ שְׁאָר חוֹלֵי יִשְׂרָאֵל, רְפוּאַת הַנֶּפֶשׁ וּרְפוּאַת הַגּוּף וּרְפוּאָה קְרוֹבָה לָבוֹא, הַשְׁתָּא בַּעֲגָלָא וּבִזְמַן קָרִיב, וְנֹאמַר אָמֵן.

מי שברך לחולה

מִי שֶׁבֵּרַךְ אֲבוֹתֵינוּ אַבְרָהָם יִצְחָק וְיַעֲקֹב, מֹשֶׁה וְאַהֲרֹן דָּוִד וּשְׁלֹמֹה הוּא יְבָרֵךְ וִירַפֵּא אֶת הַחוֹלָה (פלונית בַּת פלונית) בַּעֲבוּר שֶׁ(פלוני בֶּן פלוני) נוֹדֵר צְדָקָה בַּעֲבוּרָהּ. בִּשְׂכַר זֶה הַקָּדוֹשׁ בָּרוּךְ הוּא יִמָּלֵא רַחֲמִים עָלֶיהָ לְהַחֲלִימָהּ וּלְרַפְּאתָהּ וּלְהַחֲזִיקָהּ וּלְהַחֲיוֹתָהּ וְיִשְׁלַח לָהּ מְהֵרָה רְפוּאָה

recovery from heaven to all her organs and sinews, amongst the other sick ones in Israel, a healing of the spirit and a healing of the body, may healing be quick to come – now, swiftly and soon, and let us say: Amen.

ON THE BIRTH OF A SON

May He who blessed our fathers, Abraham, Isaac and Jacob, Moses and Aaron, David and Solomon, Sarah, Rebecca, Rachel and Leah, bless the woman (*name*, daughter of *father's name*) who has given birth, and her son who has been born to her as an auspicious sign. Her husband, the child's father, is making a contribution to charity. As a reward for this, may father and mother merit to bring the child into the covenant of Abraham and to a life of Torah, to the marriage canopy and to good deeds, and let us say: Amen.

ON THE BIRTH OF A DAUGHTER

May He who blessed our fathers, Abraham, Isaac and Jacob, Moses and Aaron, David and Solomon, Sarah, Rebecca, Rachel and Leah, bless the woman (*name*, daughter of *father's name*) who has given birth, and her daughter who has been born to her as an auspicious sign; and may her name be called in Israel (*baby's name*, daughter of *father's name*). Her husband, the child's father, is making a contribution to charity. As a reward for this, may father and mother merit to raise her to a life of Torah, to the marriage canopy, and to good deeds, and let us say: Amen.

FOR A BAR MITZVA

May He who blessed our fathers, Abraham, Isaac and Jacob, bless (*name*, son of *father's name*) who has completed thirteen years and attained the age of the commandments, who has been called to the Torah to give praise and thanks to God, may His name be blessed, for all the good He has bestowed on him. May the Holy One, blessed be He, protect and sustain him and direct his heart to be perfect with God, to walk in His ways and keep the commandments all the days of his life, and let us say: Amen.

FOR A BAT MITZVA

May He who blessed our fathers, Abraham, Isaac and Jacob, Sarah, Rebecca, Rachel and Leah, bless (*name*, daughter of *father's name*) who has completed twelve years and attained the age of the commandments, and gives praise and thanks to God, may His name be blessed, for all the good He has bestowed on her. May the Holy One, blessed be He, protect and sustain her and direct her heart to be perfect with God, to walk in His ways and keep the commandments all the days of her life, and let us say: Amen.

שְׁלֵמָה מִן הַשָּׁמַיִם לְכָל אֵבָרֶיהָ וּלְכָל גִּידֶיהָ בְּתוֹךְ שְׁאָר חוֹלֵי יִשְׂרָאֵל, רְפוּאַת הַנֶּפֶשׁ וּרְפוּאַת הַגּוּף וּרְפוּאָה קְרוֹבָה לָבוֹא, הַשְׁתָּא בַּעֲגָלָא וּבִזְמַן קָרִיב, וְנֹאמַר אָמֵן.

מי שברך ליולדת בן

מִי שֶׁבֵּרַךְ אֲבוֹתֵינוּ אַבְרָהָם יִצְחָק וְיַעֲקֹב, מֹשֶׁה וְאַהֲרֹן דָּוִד וּשְׁלֹמֹה, שָׂרָה רִבְקָה רָחֵל וְלֵאָה הוּא יְבָרֵךְ אֶת הָאִשָּׁה הַיּוֹלֶדֶת (פלונית בת פלוני) וְאֶת בְּנָהּ שֶׁנּוֹלַד לָהּ לְמַזָּל טוֹב בַּעֲבוּר שֶׁבַּעְלָהּ וְאָבִיו נוֹדֵר צְדָקָה בַּעֲדָם. בִּשְׂכַר זֶה יִזְכּוּ אָבִיו וְאִמּוֹ לְהַכְנִיסוֹ בִּבְרִיתוֹ שֶׁל אַבְרָהָם אָבִינוּ וּלְגַדְּלוֹ לְתוֹרָה וּלְחֻפָּה וּלְמַעֲשִׂים טוֹבִים, וְנֹאמַר אָמֵן.

מי שברך ליולדת בת

מִי שֶׁבֵּרַךְ אֲבוֹתֵינוּ אַבְרָהָם יִצְחָק וְיַעֲקֹב, מֹשֶׁה וְאַהֲרֹן דָּוִד וּשְׁלֹמֹה, שָׂרָה רִבְקָה רָחֵל וְלֵאָה הוּא יְבָרֵךְ אֶת הָאִשָּׁה הַיּוֹלֶדֶת (פלונית בת פלוני) וְאֶת בִּתָּהּ שֶׁנּוֹלְדָה לָהּ לְמַזָּל טוֹב וְיִקָּרֵא שְׁמָהּ בְּיִשְׂרָאֵל (פלונית בת פלוני), בַּעֲבוּר שֶׁבַּעְלָהּ וְאָבִיהָ נוֹדֵר צְדָקָה בַּעֲדָן. בִּשְׂכַר זֶה יִזְכּוּ אָבִיהָ וְאִמָּהּ לְגַדְּלָהּ לְתוֹרָה וּלְחֻפָּה וּלְמַעֲשִׂים טוֹבִים, וְנֹאמַר אָמֵן.

מי שברך לבר מצווה

מִי שֶׁבֵּרַךְ אֲבוֹתֵינוּ אַבְרָהָם יִצְחָק וְיַעֲקֹב הוּא יְבָרֵךְ אֶת (פלוני בן פלוני) שֶׁמָּלְאוּ לוֹ שָׁלֹשׁ עֶשְׂרֵה שָׁנָה וְהִגִּיעַ לְמִצְוֹת, וְעָלָה לַתּוֹרָה, לָתֵת שֶׁבַח וְהוֹדָיָה לְהַשֵּׁם יִתְבָּרֵךְ עַל כָּל הַטּוֹבָה שֶׁגָּמַל אִתּוֹ. יִשְׁמְרֵהוּ הַקָּדוֹשׁ בָּרוּךְ הוּא וִיחַיֵּהוּ, וִיכוֹנֵן אֶת לִבּוֹ לִהְיוֹת שָׁלֵם עִם יהוה וְלָלֶכֶת בִּדְרָכָיו וְלִשְׁמֹר מִצְוֹתָיו כָּל הַיָּמִים, וְנֹאמַר אָמֵן.

מי שברך לבת מצווה

מִי שֶׁבֵּרַךְ אֲבוֹתֵינוּ אַבְרָהָם יִצְחָק וְיַעֲקֹב, שָׂרָה רִבְקָה רָחֵל וְלֵאָה, הוּא יְבָרֵךְ אֶת (פלונית בת פלוני) שֶׁמָּלְאוּ לָהּ שְׁתֵּים עֶשְׂרֵה שָׁנָה וְהִגִּיעָה לְמִצְוֹת, וְנוֹתֶנֶת שֶׁבַח וְהוֹדָיָה לְהַשֵּׁם יִתְבָּרֵךְ עַל כָּל הַטּוֹבָה שֶׁגָּמַל אִתָּהּ. יִשְׁמְרֶהָ הַקָּדוֹשׁ בָּרוּךְ הוּא וִיחַיֶּהָ, וִיכוֹנֵן אֶת לִבָּהּ לִהְיוֹת שָׁלֵם עִם יהוה וְלָלֶכֶת בִּדְרָכָיו וְלִשְׁמֹר מִצְוֹתָיו כָּל הַיָּמִים, וְנֹאמַר אָמֵן.

BEMIDBAR

The LORD spoke to Moses in the wilderness of Sinai in the Tent of *Num. 1:1–19*
Meeting, on the first day of the second month during the second year
of their Exodus from Egypt, saying: Count the heads of the entire
congregation of the children of Israel, their tribes according to their
ancestral houses; the head of every male shall be counted according
to the number of their names. Every eligible soldier in Israel, twenty
years of age and above – you and Aaron shall count them according to
their legions. With you will be the heads of each tribe, each of whom
is the head of his ancestral house. These are the names of these men LEVI
who shall stand with you: For [the tribe of] Reuben, Shamua ben
Zakur. For Simeon, Shelumiel ben Tzurishadai. For Judah, Nahshon
ben Aminadav. For Issachar, Netanel ben Tzuar. For Zebulun, Eliav
ben Helon. For the descendants of Joseph: For Ephraim, Elishama
ben Amihud; for Manasseh, Gamliel ben Pedah'tzur. For Benjamin,
Avidan ben Gidoni. For Dan, Ahiezer ben Amishadai. For Asher,
Pagiel ben Okhran. For Gad, Elyasaf ben De'uel. For Naftali, Ahira
ben Einan. These are the summoned men of the congregation, the
princes of the tribes of their patriarchs, all of them chiefs of the legions
of Israel. Moses and Aaron took these men who were designated by YISRAEL
name. And they gathered the entire congregation together on the first
day of the second month; they declared their lineage, that of each
family, that of each ancestral house. Each man's name was counted,
all who were twenty years of age and above, every head was counted.
Moses [carried out] all that the LORD had commanded, counting
them in the wilderness of Sinai.

NASO

The LORD spoke to Moses, saying: Count the heads of the sons of *Num.*
Gershon as well, according to their ancestral houses and their families. *4:21–37*
You shall count every man who is over thirty years of age and under the
age of fifty, every man eligible to serve, to perform work in the Tent of

במדבר

במדבר
א:א–יט

וַיְדַבֵּ֨ר יְהֹוָ֧ה אֶל־מֹשֶׁ֛ה בְּמִדְבַּ֥ר סִינַ֖י בְּאֹ֣הֶל מוֹעֵ֑ד בְּאֶחָד֩ לַחֹ֨דֶשׁ הַשֵּׁנִ֜י בַּשָּׁנָ֣ה הַשֵּׁנִ֗ית לְצֵאתָ֛ם מֵאֶ֥רֶץ מִצְרַ֖יִם לֵאמֹֽר: שְׂא֗וּ אֶת־רֹאשׁ֙ כׇּל־עֲדַ֣ת בְּנֵֽי־יִשְׂרָאֵ֔ל לְמִשְׁפְּחֹתָ֖ם לְבֵ֣ית אֲבֹתָ֑ם בְּמִסְפַּ֣ר שֵׁמ֔וֹת כׇּל־זָכָ֖ר לְגֻלְגְּלֹתָֽם: מִבֶּ֨ן עֶשְׂרִ֤ים שָׁנָה֙ וָמַ֔עְלָה כׇּל־יֹצֵ֥א צָבָ֖א בְּיִשְׂרָאֵ֑ל תִּפְקְד֥וּ אֹתָ֛ם לְצִבְאֹתָ֖ם אַתָּ֥ה וְאַהֲרֹֽן: וְאִתְּכֶ֣ם יִהְי֔וּ אִ֥ישׁ אִ֖ישׁ לַמַּטֶּ֑ה אִ֛ישׁ רֹ֥אשׁ לְבֵית־אֲבֹתָ֖יו הֽוּא:

לוי

*וְאֵ֨לֶּה שְׁמ֤וֹת הָֽאֲנָשִׁים֙ אֲשֶׁ֣ר יַֽעַמְד֣וּ אִתְּכֶ֔ם לִרְאוּבֵ֖ן אֱלִיצ֥וּר בֶּן־שְׁדֵיאֽוּר: לְשִׁמְע֕וֹן שְׁלֻמִיאֵ֖ל בֶּן־צוּרִֽישַׁדָּֽי: לִֽיהוּדָ֕ה נַחְשׁ֖וֹן בֶּן־עַמִּֽינָדָֽב: לְיִ֨שָּׂשכָ֔ר נְתַנְאֵ֖ל בֶּן־צוּעָֽר: לִזְבוּלֻ֕ן אֱלִיאָ֖ב בֶּן־חֵלֹֽן: לִבְנֵ֣י יוֹסֵ֔ף לְאֶפְרַ֕יִם אֱלִישָׁמָ֖ע בֶּן־עַמִּיה֑וּד לִמְנַשֶּׁ֕ה גַּמְלִיאֵ֖ל בֶּן־פְּדָהצֽוּר: לְבִ֨נְיָמִ֔ן אֲבִידָ֖ן בֶּן־גִּדְעֹנִֽי: לְדָ֕ן אֲחִיעֶ֖זֶר בֶּן־עַמִּֽישַׁדָּֽי: לְאָשֵׁ֕ר פַּגְעִיאֵ֖ל בֶּן־עׇכְרָֽן: לְגָ֕ד אֶלְיָסָ֖ף בֶּן־דְּעוּאֵֽל: לְנַפְתָּלִ֕י אֲחִירַ֖ע

קרואי
ישראל

בֶּן־עֵינָֽן: אֵ֚לֶּה קְרוּאֵ֣י הָֽעֵדָ֔ה נְשִׂיאֵ֖י מַטּ֣וֹת אֲבוֹתָ֑ם רָאשֵׁ֛י אַלְפֵ֥י יִשְׂרָאֵ֖ל הֵֽם: *וַיִּקַּ֥ח מֹשֶׁ֖ה וְאַהֲרֹ֑ן אֵ֚ת הָֽאֲנָשִׁ֣ים הָאֵ֔לֶּה אֲשֶׁ֥ר נִקְּב֖וּ בְּשֵׁמֽוֹת: וְאֵ֨ת כׇּל־הָֽעֵדָ֜ה הִקְהִ֗ילוּ בְּאֶחָד֙ לַחֹ֣דֶשׁ הַשֵּׁנִ֔י וַיִּתְיַֽלְד֥וּ עַל־מִשְׁפְּחֹתָ֖ם לְבֵ֣ית אֲבֹתָ֑ם בְּמִסְפַּ֣ר שֵׁמ֗וֹת מִבֶּ֨ן עֶשְׂרִ֥ים שָׁנָ֛ה וָמַ֖עְלָה לְגֻלְגְּלֹתָֽם: כַּֽאֲשֶׁ֛ר צִוָּ֥ה יְהֹוָ֖ה אֶת־מֹשֶׁ֑ה וַֽיִּפְקְדֵ֖ם בְּמִדְבַּ֥ר סִינָֽי:

נשא

במדבר
ד:כא–לו

וַיְדַבֵּ֥ר יְהֹוָ֖ה אֶל־מֹשֶׁ֥ה לֵּאמֹֽר: נָשֹׂ֗א אֶת־רֹ֛אשׁ בְּנֵ֥י גֵֽרְשׁ֖וֹן גַּם־הֵ֑ם לְבֵ֥ית אֲבֹתָ֖ם לְמִשְׁפְּחֹתָֽם: מִבֶּן֩ שְׁלֹשִׁ֨ים שָׁנָ֜ה וָמַ֗עְלָה עַ֛ד בֶּן־חֲמִשִּׁ֥ים שָׁנָ֖ה תִּפְקֹ֣ד אוֹתָ֑ם כׇּל־הַבָּא֙ לִצְבֹ֣א צָבָ֔א לַֽעֲבֹ֥ד עֲבֹדָ֖ה

Meeting. These are the duties of the family of Gershon: they shall work and they shall carry. They shall carry the curtains of the Tabernacle, LEVI the Tent of Meeting, its cover and the cover of tahash leather that is spread upon it, and the screen for the entrance of the Tent of Meeting. And the curtains of the courtyard and the screen for the entrance of the courtyard gate, which surrounds the Tabernacle and the altar, and their cords and all of the equipment belonging to their service; they shall do all they were commanded, and perform their work. All of the service of the sons of Gershon shall be performed according to the word of Aaron and his sons, all of their burden-carrying and their tasks; you shall hold them accountable for all of their charges. This shall be the task of the family of the sons of Gershon for the Tent of Meeting and their duties under Itamar son of Aaron the priest.

As for the sons of Merari, you shall count them according to their YISRAEL families and their ancestral houses. You shall count every man who is over thirty years of age and under the age of fifty, every man eligible to serve, to perform work in the Tent of Meeting. And this shall be their charge, the burden that they shall carry as a service to the Tent of Meeting: the beams of the Tabernacle, its bars and pillars and sockets. And the pillars surrounding the courtyard and their sockets and bars and cords and all of the equipment belonging to their service; you shall designate men by name to carry each of the vessels they are charged with. This shall be the duty of the family of the sons of Merari, their service for the Tent of Meeting under Itamar son of Aaron the priest.

Some extend the "Yisrael" portion:

And Moses and Aaron and the leaders of the congregation counted the descendants of Kehat according to their families and their ancestral houses. Every man over thirty years of age and under the age of fifty, every man eligible to serve, to perform worship in the Tent of Meeting. And their number according to their families was two thousand seven hundred and fifty. These were the counted of the families of Kehat, all who served in the Tent of Meeting, according to the orders of Moses and Aaron, following the word of the LORD to Moses.

בְּאֹהֶל מוֹעֵד: זֹאת עֲבֹדַת מִשְׁפְּחֹת הַגֵּרְשֻׁנִּי לַעֲבֹד וּלְמַשָּׂא:

לוי *וְנָשְׂאוּ אֶת־יְרִיעֹת הַמִּשְׁכָּן וְאֶת־אֹהֶל מוֹעֵד מִכְסֵהוּ וּמִכְסֵה

הַתַּחַשׁ אֲשֶׁר־עָלָיו מִלְמָעְלָה וְאֶת־מָסַךְ פֶּתַח אֹהֶל מוֹעֵד: וְאֵת

קַלְעֵי הֶחָצֵר וְאֶת־מָסַךְ ׀ פֶּתַח ׀ שַׁעַר הֶחָצֵר אֲשֶׁר עַל־הַמִּשְׁכָּן

וְעַל־הַמִּזְבֵּחַ סָבִיב וְאֵת מֵיתְרֵיהֶם וְאֶת־כָּל־כְּלֵי עֲבֹדָתָם וְאֵת כָּל־

אֲשֶׁר יֵעָשֶׂה לָהֶם וְעָבָדוּ: עַל־פִּי אַהֲרֹן וּבָנָיו תִּהְיֶה כָּל־עֲבֹדַת בְּנֵי

הַגֵּרְשֻׁנִּי לְכָל־מַשָּׂאָם וּלְכֹל עֲבֹדָתָם וּפְקַדְתֶּם עֲלֵהֶם בְּמִשְׁמֶרֶת

אֵת כָּל־מַשָּׂאָם: זֹאת עֲבֹדַת מִשְׁפְּחֹת בְּנֵי הַגֵּרְשֻׁנִּי בְּאֹהֶל מוֹעֵד

וּמִשְׁמַרְתָּם בְּיַד אִיתָמָר בֶּן־אַהֲרֹן הַכֹּהֵן:

ישראל *בְּנֵי מְרָרִי לְמִשְׁפְּחֹתָם לְבֵית־אֲבֹתָם תִּפְקֹד אֹתָם: מִבֶּן שְׁלֹשִׁים שָׁנָה

וָמַעְלָה וְעַד בֶּן־חֲמִשִּׁים שָׁנָה תִּפְקְדֵם כָּל־הַבָּא לַצָּבָא לַעֲבֹד

אֶת־עֲבֹדַת אֹהֶל מוֹעֵד: וְזֹאת מִשְׁמֶרֶת מַשָּׂאָם לְכָל־עֲבֹדָתָם

בְּאֹהֶל מוֹעֵד קַרְשֵׁי הַמִּשְׁכָּן וּבְרִיחָיו וְעַמּוּדָיו וַאֲדָנָיו: וְעַמּוּדֵי

הֶחָצֵר סָבִיב וְאַדְנֵיהֶם וִיתֵדֹתָם וּמֵיתְרֵיהֶם לְכָל־כְּלֵיהֶם וּלְכֹל

עֲבֹדָתָם וּבְשֵׁמֹת תִּפְקְדוּ אֶת־כְּלֵי מִשְׁמֶרֶת מַשָּׂאָם: זֹאת עֲבֹדַת

מִשְׁפְּחֹת בְּנֵי מְרָרִי לְכָל־עֲבֹדָתָם בְּאֹהֶל מוֹעֵד בְּיַד אִיתָמָר בֶּן־

אַהֲרֹן הַכֹּהֵן:

Some extend the ישראל portion:

וַיִּפְקֹד מֹשֶׁה וְאַהֲרֹן וּנְשִׂיאֵי הָעֵדָה אֶת־בְּנֵי הַקְּהָתִי לְמִשְׁפְּחֹתָם

וּלְבֵית אֲבֹתָם: מִבֶּן שְׁלֹשִׁים שָׁנָה וָמַעְלָה וְעַד בֶּן־חֲמִשִּׁים שָׁנָה

כָּל־הַבָּא לַצָּבָא לַעֲבֹדָה בְּאֹהֶל מוֹעֵד: וַיִּהְיוּ פְקֻדֵיהֶם לְמִשְׁפְּחֹתָם

אַלְפַּיִם שְׁבַע מֵאוֹת וַחֲמִשִּׁים: אֵלֶּה פְקוּדֵי מִשְׁפְּחֹת הַקְּהָתִי

כָּל־הָעֹבֵד בְּאֹהֶל מוֹעֵד אֲשֶׁר פָּקַד מֹשֶׁה וְאַהֲרֹן עַל־פִּי יְהוָה

בְּיַד־מֹשֶׁה:

HALF KADDISH

After the Reading of the Torah, the Reader says Half Kaddish:

Reader: יִתְגַּדַּל Magnified and sanctified
may His great name be,
in the world He created by His will.
May He establish His kingdom
in your lifetime and in your days,
and in the lifetime of all the house of Israel,
swiftly and soon –
and say: Amen.

All: May His great name be blessed for ever and all time.

Reader: Blessed and praised, glorified and exalted,
raised and honored,
uplifted and lauded
be the name of the Holy One,
blessed be He,
beyond any blessing,
song, praise and consolation
uttered in the world –
and say: Amen.

HAGBAHA AND GELILA

The Torah scroll is lifted and the congregation says:

וְזֹאת הַתּוֹרָה This is the Torah   *Deut. 4*
that Moses placed before the children of Israel,
at the Lord's commandment, by the hand of Moses.   *Num. 9*

Some add:
It is a tree of life to those who grasp it,   *Prov. 3*
and those who uphold it are happy.
Its ways are ways of pleasantness, and all its paths are peace.
Long life is at its right hand; at its left, riches and honor.
It pleased the Lord for the sake of [Israel's] righteousness,   *Is. 42*
to make the Torah great and glorious.

חצי קדיש

After the קריאת התורה, the קורא says חצי קדיש:

קורא: יִתְגַּדַּל וְיִתְקַדַּשׁ שְׁמֵהּ רַבָּא (קהל: אָמֵן)

בְּעָלְמָא דִּי בְרָא כִרְעוּתֵהּ

וְיַמְלִיךְ מַלְכוּתֵהּ

בְּחַיֵּיכוֹן וּבְיוֹמֵיכוֹן וּבְחַיֵּי דְכָל בֵּית יִשְׂרָאֵל

בַּעֲגָלָא וּבִזְמַן קָרִיב

וְאִמְרוּ אָמֵן. (קהל: אָמֵן)

קורא
וקהל: יְהֵא שְׁמֵהּ רַבָּא מְבָרַךְ לְעָלַם וּלְעָלְמֵי עָלְמַיָּא.

קורא: יִתְבָּרַךְ וְיִשְׁתַּבַּח וְיִתְפָּאַר וְיִתְרוֹמַם וְיִתְנַשֵּׂא

וְיִתְהַדָּר וְיִתְעַלֶּה וְיִתְהַלָּל

שְׁמֵהּ דְּקֻדְשָׁא בְּרִיךְ הוּא (קהל: בְּרִיךְ הוּא)

לְעֵלָּא מִן כָּל בִּרְכָתָא וְשִׁירָתָא

תֻּשְׁבְּחָתָא וְנֶחֱמָתָא

דַּאֲמִירָן בְּעָלְמָא

וְאִמְרוּ אָמֵן. (קהל: אָמֵן)

הגבהה וגלילה

The ספר תורה is lifted and the קהל says:

דברים ד

וְזֹאת הַתּוֹרָה אֲשֶׁר־שָׂם מֹשֶׁה לִפְנֵי בְּנֵי יִשְׂרָאֵל:

במדבר ט

עַל־פִּי יְהוָה בְּיַד־מֹשֶׁה:

Some add:

משלי ג

עֵץ־חַיִּים הִיא לַמַּחֲזִיקִים בָּהּ וְתֹמְכֶיהָ מְאֻשָּׁר:

דְּרָכֶיהָ דַרְכֵי־נֹעַם וְכָל־נְתִיבוֹתֶיהָ שָׁלוֹם:

אֹרֶךְ יָמִים בִּימִינָהּ בִּשְׂמֹאולָהּ עֹשֶׁר וְכָבוֹד:

ישעיה מב

יְהוָה חָפֵץ לְמַעַן צִדְקוֹ יַגְדִּיל תּוֹרָה וְיַאְדִּיר:

HAFTARA

The Haftara blessings are not recited.

I shall rejoice in the LORD , my soul shall exult in my God, for He has clothed me with garments of salvation, covered me with a cloak of righteousness, like a groom adorned with a turban, as a bride who dons her finery. For just as the land brings forth its greenery and a garden sprouts its seeds, so too shall the LORD God bring forth righteousness and glory in the presence of all the nations. For the sake of Zion I shall not be silent, and for the sake of Jerusalem I shall not remain still, until her righteousness shines out like the brightness of day and her salvation burns bright as a torch. And nations shall behold your righteousness; all kings will see your glory, and you [Zion] will be called by a new name, which will be pronounced by the LORD Himself. And you will be like a crown of splendor in the hand of the LORD, as a royal turban in the palm of your God. No longer shall you be called "Forsaken," and your land shall never again be called "Desolate"; instead, you shall be called "My Delight Is In Her" and your land shall be called "Possessed," for the LORD shall delight in you, and your land shall be possessed. As a young man possesses a maiden, so shall your children possess you, and as a groom rejoices over his bride, so shall your God rejoice over you. Upon your walls, Jerusalem, I have appointed watchmen; all day and all night, always – they shall never remain silent. You who utter the names of the LORD, do not remain silent! And do not allow Him to remain silent, until He establishes and makes Jerusalem the glory of all the land. The LORD has sworn by His right hand and by His mighty arm: Never shall I allow your harvest to be consumed by your enemies; never shall I allow foreigners to drink the wine you

Is. 61:10–63:9

THE BELOVED LAND

Rabbi Yeḥezkel Halberstam would say: "Whoever loves the Land of Israel – the land was made beloved for him. The Land of Israel unites the entire nation of Israel."

הפטרה

The הפטרה blessings are not recited.

ישעיה
סא:י–סג:ט

שׂוֹשׂ אָשִׂישׂ בַּיהוָה תָּגֵל נַפְשִׁי בֵּאלֹהַי כִּי הִלְבִּישַׁנִי בִּגְדֵי־יֶשַׁע מְעִיל צְדָקָה יְעָטָנִי כֶּחָתָן יְכַהֵן פְּאֵר וְכַכַּלָּה תַּעְדֶּה כֵלֶיהָ: כִּי כָאָרֶץ תּוֹצִיא צִמְחָהּ וּכְגַנָּה זֵרוּעֶיהָ תַצְמִיחַ כֵּן | אֲדֹנָי יְהוִה יַצְמִיחַ צְדָקָה וּתְהִלָּה נֶגֶד כָּל־הַגּוֹיִם: לְמַעַן צִיּוֹן לֹא אֶחֱשֶׁה וּלְמַעַן יְרוּשָׁלִַם לֹא אֶשְׁקוֹט עַד־יֵצֵא כַנֹּגַהּ צִדְקָהּ וִישׁוּעָתָהּ כְּלַפִּיד יִבְעָר: וְרָאוּ גוֹיִם צִדְקֵךְ וְכָל־מְלָכִים כְּבוֹדֵךְ וְקֹרָא לָךְ שֵׁם חָדָשׁ אֲשֶׁר פִּי יְהוָה יִקֳבֶנּוּ: וְהָיִית עֲטֶרֶת תִּפְאֶרֶת בְּיַד־יְהוָה וּצְנִיף מְלוּכָה בְּכַף־אֱלֹהָיִךְ: לֹא־יֵאָמֵר לָךְ עוֹד עֲזוּבָה וּלְאַרְצֵךְ לֹא־יֵאָמֵר עוֹד שְׁמָמָה כִּי לָךְ יִקָּרֵא חֶפְצִי־בָהּ וּלְאַרְצֵךְ בְּעוּלָה כִּי־חָפֵץ יְהוָה בָּךְ וְאַרְצֵךְ תִּבָּעֵל: כִּי־יִבְעַל בָּחוּר בְּתוּלָה יִבְעָלוּךְ בָּנָיִךְ וּמְשׂוֹשׂ חָתָן עַל־כַּלָּה יָשִׂישׂ עָלַיִךְ אֱלֹהָיִךְ: עַל־חוֹמֹתַיִךְ יְרוּשָׁלַםִ הִפְקַדְתִּי שֹׁמְרִים כָּל־הַיּוֹם וְכָל־הַלַּיְלָה תָּמִיד לֹא יֶחֱשׁוּ הַמַּזְכִּרִים אֶת־יְהוָה אַל־דֳּמִי לָכֶם: וְאַל־תִּתְּנוּ דֳמִי לוֹ עַד־יְכוֹנֵן וְעַד־יָשִׂים אֶת־יְרוּשָׁלַםִ תְּהִלָּה בָּאָרֶץ: נִשְׁבַּע יְהוָה בִּימִינוֹ וּבִזְרוֹעַ עֻזּוֹ אִם־אֶתֵּן אֶת־דְּגָנֵךְ עוֹד מַאֲכָל לְאֹיְבַיִךְ וְאִם־יִשְׁתּוּ בְנֵי־נֵכָר תִּירוֹשֵׁךְ אֲשֶׁר יָגַעַתְּ בּוֹ: כִּי מְאַסְפָיו יֹאכְלֻהוּ וְהִלְלוּ אֶת־יְהוָה וּמְקַבְּצָיו

וּצְנִיף

IN SPITE OF EVERYTHING – THE LAND OF ISRAEL

And even so, and in spite of everything – the Land of Israel; and as long as Israel's heart beats in the world, and as long as we hear "*Shema Yisrael*" in the world – the Land of Israel. (David Shimoni, in the wake of the 1929 Palestine Riots)

have toiled to produce. Rather, those who harvested it shall eat it and praise the LORD, and those who gathered [the grapes] shall drink [the wine] in My holy courtyards.

Pass through, pass through the gates; make way for the people; lay a road, lay a road here, remove all stones from the path; raise up a banner for the nations. For the LORD shall call out to the ends of the earth: "Tell the daughter of Zion, Behold, your Redeemer has come, his spoils [of war] are with him and his plunder goes before him." And they shall be called "The Holy People, the Redeemed of the LORD," and you shall be called "Sought After, a City No Longer Forsaken."

Who is this, coming from Edom, with crimson garments, from Botzra, wearing splendid garments, striding with His great strength? "It is I, who speaks righteously, who has great power to save." Why is your garment red, and your clothes as one who treads in a grape-vat? I tread the grape-press alone, no one from any nation was with Me; I trod upon them [My enemies] with My wrath and crushed them with My fury, until their blood oozed onto My clothes and all of My garments were soiled. For My heart is set upon a day of vengeance; the time of My redemption has arrived. I looked about, but there was no one to assist Me; I was astounded, but there was no one to rely on – so I worked salvation with My own arm, and it was My own fury that supported me. I trampled nations in My wrath and made them drunk with My fury, bringing their fortresses down to the ground.

I shall speak of the kindness of the LORD, [I shall tell of] the glories of the LORD, for all the LORD has done for us, the abundance of good He has done for the house of Israel, which He has bestowed upon them in His mercy and His great kindness. And He said: "Certainly they are My people, My children who shall not lie," and He became their Redeemer. In all of their troubles, He was troubled along with them; the angel of His countenance saved them – He Himself redeemed them in His love and His compassion, lifting them up and carrying them all the days of old.

יִשְׁתַּחֲווּ בְּחַצְרוֹת קָדְשִׁי: עִבְרוּ עִבְרוּ בַּשְּׁעָרִים
פַּנּוּ דֶּרֶךְ הָעָם סֹלּוּ סֹלּוּ הַמְסִלָּה סַקְּלוּ מֵאֶבֶן הָרִימוּ נֵס עַל־
הָעַמִּים: הִנֵּה יהוה הִשְׁמִיעַ אֶל־קְצֵה הָאָרֶץ אִמְרוּ לְבַת־
צִיּוֹן הִנֵּה יִשְׁעֵךְ בָּא הִנֵּה שְׂכָרוֹ אִתּוֹ וּפְעֻלָּתוֹ לְפָנָיו: וְקָרְאוּ
לָהֶם עַם־הַקֹּדֶשׁ גְּאוּלֵי יהוה וְלָךְ יִקָּרֵא דְרוּשָׁה עִיר לֹא
נֶעֱזָבָה: מִי־זֶה ׀ בָּא מֵאֱדוֹם חֲמוּץ בְּגָדִים מִבָּצְרָה
זֶה הָדוּר בִּלְבוּשׁוֹ צֹעֶה בְּרֹב כֹּחוֹ אֲנִי מְדַבֵּר בִּצְדָקָה רַב
לְהוֹשִׁיעַ: מַדּוּעַ אָדֹם לִלְבוּשֶׁךָ וּבְגָדֶיךָ כְּדֹרֵךְ בְּגַת: פּוּרָה ׀
דָּרַכְתִּי לְבַדִּי וּמֵעַמִּים אֵין־אִישׁ אִתִּי וְאֶדְרְכֵם בְּאַפִּי וְאֶרְמְסֵם
בַּחֲמָתִי וְיֵז נִצְחָם עַל־בְּגָדַי וְכָל־מַלְבּוּשַׁי אֶגְאָלְתִּי: כִּי יוֹם נָקָם
בְּלִבִּי וּשְׁנַת גְּאוּלַי בָּאָה: וְאַבִּיט וְאֵין עֹזֵר וְאֶשְׁתּוֹמֵם וְאֵין
סוֹמֵךְ וַתּוֹשַׁע לִי זְרֹעִי וַחֲמָתִי הִיא סְמָכָתְנִי: וְאָבוּס עַמִּים
בְּאַפִּי וַאֲשַׁכְּרֵם בַּחֲמָתִי וְאוֹרִיד לָאָרֶץ נִצְחָם: חַסְדֵי
יהוה ׀ אַזְכִּיר תְּהִלֹּת יהוה כְּעַל כֹּל אֲשֶׁר־גְּמָלָנוּ יהוה וְרַב־
טוּב לְבֵית יִשְׂרָאֵל אֲשֶׁר־גְּמָלָם כְּרַחֲמָיו וּכְרֹב חֲסָדָיו: וַיֹּאמֶר
אַךְ־עַמִּי הֵמָּה בָּנִים לֹא יְשַׁקֵּרוּ וַיְהִי לָהֶם לְמוֹשִׁיעַ: בְּכָל־
צָרָתָם ׀ לֹא צָר וּמַלְאַךְ פָּנָיו הוֹשִׁיעָם בְּאַהֲבָתוֹ וּבְחֶמְלָתוֹ
הוּא גְאָלָם וַיְנַטְּלֵם וַיְנַשְּׂאֵם כָּל־יְמֵי עוֹלָם:

לוֹ

THE END OF DAYS

At the end of days, the mountain of the LORD's Temple will be established
as the highest of the mountains; it will be exalted above the hills, and all
nations will stream to it. Many nations will come and say, Come, let us
go up to the mountain of the LORD, to the Temple of the God of Jacob.

The Prayer for the Welfare of the Canadian Government is on the next page.

PRAYER FOR THE WELFARE OF THE AMERICAN GOVERNMENT

The Leader says the following:

הַנּוֹתֵן תְּשׁוּעָה May He who gives salvation to kings and dominion to princes, whose kingdom is an everlasting kingdom, who delivers His servant David from the evil sword, who makes a way in the sea and a path through the mighty waters, bless and protect, guard and help, exalt, magnify and uplift the President, Vice President and all officials of this land. May the Supreme King of kings in His mercy put into their hearts and the hearts of all their counselors and officials, to deal kindly with us and all Israel. In their days and in ours, may Judah be saved and Israel dwell in safety, and may the Redeemer come to Zion. May this be His will, and let us say: Amen.

PRAYER FOR THE SAFETY OF THE AMERICAN MILITARY

The Leader says the following:

אַדִּיר בַּמָּרוֹם God on high who dwells in might, the King to whom peace belongs, look down from Your holy habitation and bless the soldiers of the American military forces who risk their lives for the sake of peace on earth. Be their shelter and stronghold, and let them not falter. Give them the strength and courage to thwart the plans of the enemy and end the rule of evil. May their enemies be scattered and their foes flee before them, and may they rejoice in Your salvation. Bring them back safely to their homes, as is written: "The Lord will guard you from all harm, He will guard your life. *Ps. 121* The Lord will guard your going and coming, now and for evermore." And may there be fulfilled for us the verse: "Nation shall *Is. 2* not lift up sword against nation, nor shall they learn war any more." Let all the inhabitants on earth know that sovereignty is Yours and Your name inspires awe over all You have created – and let us say: Amen.

The Prayer for the Welfare of the Canadian Government is on the next page.

תפילה לשלום המלכות (ארה"ב)

The ציבור שליח says the following:

הַנּוֹתֵן תְּשׁוּעָה לַמְּלָכִים וּמֶמְשָׁלָה לַנְּסִיכִים, מַלְכוּתוֹ מַלְכוּת כָּל
עוֹלָמִים, הַפּוֹצֶה אֶת דָּוִד עַבְדּוֹ מֵחֶרֶב רָעָה, הַנּוֹתֵן בַּיָּם דֶּרֶךְ וּבְמַיִם
עַזִּים נְתִיבָה, הוּא יְבָרֵךְ וְיִשְׁמֹר וְיִנְצֹר וְיַעֲזֹר וִירוֹמֵם וִיגַדֵּל וִינַשֵּׂא
לְמַעְלָה אֶת הַנָּשִׂיא וְאֶת מִשְׁנֵהוּ וְאֶת כָּל שָׂרֵי הָאָרֶץ הַזֹּאת. מֶלֶךְ
מַלְכֵי הַמְּלָכִים, בְּרַחֲמָיו יִתֵּן בְּלִבָּם וּבְלֵב כָּל יוֹעֲצֵיהֶם וְשָׂרֵיהֶם
לַעֲשׂוֹת טוֹבָה עִמָּנוּ וְעִם כָּל יִשְׂרָאֵל. בִּימֵיהֶם וּבְיָמֵינוּ תִּוָּשַׁע יְהוּדָה,
וְיִשְׂרָאֵל יִשְׁכֹּן לָבֶטַח, וּבָא לְצִיּוֹן גּוֹאֵל, וְכֵן יְהִי רָצוֹן, וְנֹאמַר אָמֵן.

תפילה לשלום חיילי צבא ארצות הברית

The ציבור שליח says the following:

אַדִּיר בַּמָּרוֹם שׁוֹכֵן בִּגְבוּרָה, מֶלֶךְ שֶׁהַשָּׁלוֹם שֶׁלּוֹ, הַשְׁקִיפָה מִמְּעוֹן
קָדְשְׁךָ, וּבָרֵךְ אֶת חַיָּלֵי צְבָא אַרְצוֹת הַבְּרִית, הַמְחָרְפִים נַפְשָׁם
בְּלֶכְתָּם לָשִׂים שָׁלוֹם בָּאָרֶץ. הֱיֵה נָא לָהֶם מַחֲסֶה וּמָעוֹז, וְאַל תִּתֵּן
לַמּוֹט רַגְלָם, חַזֵּק יְדֵיהֶם וְאַמֵּץ רוּחָם לְהָפֵר עֲצַת אוֹיֵב וּלְהַעֲבִיר
מֶמְשֶׁלֶת זָדוֹן, יָפוּצוּ אוֹיְבֵיהֶם וְיָנוּסוּ מְשַׂנְאֵיהֶם מִפְּנֵיהֶם, וְיִשְׂמְחוּ
בִּישׁוּעָתֶךָ. הֲשִׁיבֵם בְּשָׁלוֹם אֶל בֵּיתָם, כַּכָּתוּב בְּדִבְרֵי קָדְשֶׁךָ: יהוה
תהלים קכא
יִשְׁמָרְךָ מִכָּל־רָע, יִשְׁמֹר אֶת־נַפְשֶׁךָ: יהוה יִשְׁמָר־צֵאתְךָ וּבוֹאֶךָ,
מֵעַתָּה וְעַד־עוֹלָם: וְקַיֵּם בָּנוּ מִקְרָא שֶׁכָּתוּב: לֹא־יִשָּׂא גוֹי אֶל־גּוֹי
ישעיה ב
חֶרֶב, וְלֹא־יִלְמְדוּ עוֹד מִלְחָמָה: וְיֵדְעוּ כָּל יוֹשְׁבֵי תֵבֵל כִּי לְךָ מְלוּכָה
יָאֳתָה, וְשִׁמְךָ נוֹרָא עַל כָּל מַה שֶׁבָּרָאתָ. וְנֹאמַר אָמֵן.

He will teach us His ways, so that we may walk in His paths. The law will
go out from Zion, the word of the LORD from Jerusalem. (Isaiah 2:2–3)

PRAYER FOR THE WELFARE OF THE CANADIAN GOVERNMENT

The Leader says the following:

הַנּוֹתֵן תְּשׁוּעָה May He who gives salvation to kings and dominion to princes, whose kingdom is an everlasting kingdom, who delivers His servant David from the evil sword, who makes a way in the sea and a path through the mighty waters, bless and protect, guard and help, exalt, magnify and uplift the Prime Minister and all the elected and appointed officials of Canada. May the Supreme King of kings in His mercy put into their hearts and the hearts of all their counselors and officials, to deal kindly with us and all Israel. In their days and in ours, may Judah be saved and Israel dwell in safety, and may the Redeemer come to Zion. May this be His will, and let us say: Amen.

PRAYER FOR THE SAFETY OF THE CANADIAN MILITARY FORCES

The Leader says the following:

אַדִּיר בַּמָּרוֹם God on high who dwells in might, the King to whom peace belongs, look down from Your holy habitation and bless the soldiers of the Canadian Forces who risk their lives for the sake of peace on earth. Be their shelter and stronghold, and let them not falter. Give them the strength and courage to thwart the plans of the enemy and end the rule of evil. May their enemies be scattered and their foes flee before them, and may they rejoice in Your salvation. Bring them back safely to their homes, as is written: "The LORD will guard you from all harm, He will guard your life. The LORD will guard your going and coming, now and for evermore." And may there be fulfilled for us the verse: "Nation shall not lift up sword against nation, nor shall they learn war any more." Let all the inhabitants on earth know that sovereignty is Yours and Your name inspires awe over all You have created – and let us say: Amen. *Ps. 121* *Is. 2*

תפילה לשלום המלכות (קנדה)

The שליח ציבור says the following:

הַנּוֹתֵן תְּשׁוּעָה לַמְּלָכִים וּמֶמְשָׁלָה לַנְּסִיכִים, מַלְכוּתוֹ מַלְכוּת כָּל עוֹלָמִים, הַפּוֹצֶה אֶת דָּוִד עַבְדּוֹ מֵחֶרֶב רָעָה, הַנּוֹתֵן בַּיָּם דֶּרֶךְ וּבְמַיִם עַזִּים נְתִיבָה, הוּא יְבָרֵךְ וְיִשְׁמֹר וְיִנְצֹר וְיַעֲזֹר וִירוֹמֵם וִיגַדֵּל וִינַשֵּׂא לְמַעְלָה אֶת רֹאשׁ הַמֶּמְשָׁלָה וְאֶת כָּל שָׂרֵי הָאָרֶץ הַזֹּאת. מֶלֶךְ מַלְכֵי הַמְּלָכִים, בְּרַחֲמָיו יִתֵּן בְּלִבָּם וּבְלֵב כָּל יוֹעֲצֵיהֶם וְשָׂרֵיהֶם לַעֲשׂוֹת טוֹבָה עִמָּנוּ וְעִם כָּל יִשְׂרָאֵל. בִּימֵיהֶם וּבְיָמֵינוּ תִּוָּשַׁע יְהוּדָה, וְיִשְׂרָאֵל יִשְׁכֹּן לָבֶטַח, וּבָא לְצִיּוֹן גּוֹאֵל. וְכֵן יְהִי רָצוֹן, וְנֹאמַר אָמֵן.

תפילה לשלום חיילי צבא קנדה

The שליח ציבור says the following:

אַדִּיר בַּמָּרוֹם שׁוֹכֵן בִּגְבוּרָה, מֶלֶךְ שֶׁהַשָּׁלוֹם שֶׁלּוֹ, הַשְׁקִיפָה מִמְּעוֹן קָדְשְׁךָ, וּבָרֵךְ אֶת חַיָּלֵי צְבָא קָנָדָה, הַמְחָרְפִים נַפְשָׁם בְּלֶכְתָּם לָשִׂים שָׁלוֹם בָּאָרֶץ. הֱיֵה נָא לָהֶם מַחֲסֶה וּמָעוֹז, וְאַל תִּתֵּן לַמּוֹט רַגְלָם, חַזֵּק יְדֵיהֶם וְאַמֵּץ רוּחָם לְהָפֵר עֲצַת אוֹיֵב וּלְהַעֲבִיר מֶמְשֶׁלֶת זָדוֹן, יִפּוֹצוּ אוֹיְבֵיהֶם וְיָנוּסוּ מְשַׂנְאֵיהֶם מִפְּנֵיהֶם, וְיִשְׂמְחוּ בִּישׁוּעָתֶךָ.

תהלים קכא

הֲשִׁיבֵם בְּשָׁלוֹם אֶל בֵּיתָם, כַּכָּתוּב בְּדִבְרֵי קָדְשֶׁךָ: יהוה יִשְׁמָרְךָ מִכָּל רָע, יִשְׁמֹר אֶת נַפְשֶׁךָ: יהוה יִשְׁמָר צֵאתְךָ וּבוֹאֶךָ, מֵעַתָּה וְעַד עוֹלָם: וְקַיֵּם בָּנוּ מִקְרָא שֶׁכָּתוּב: לֹא יִשָּׂא גוֹי אֶל גּוֹי חֶרֶב,

ישעיה ב

וְלֹא יִלְמְדוּ עוֹד מִלְחָמָה: וְיֵדְעוּ כָּל יוֹשְׁבֵי תֵבֵל כִּי לְךָ מְלוּכָה יָאָתָה, וְשִׁמְךָ נוֹרָא עַל כָּל מַה שֶּׁבָּרָאתָ. וְנֹאמַר אָמֵן.

PRAYER FOR THE STATE OF ISRAEL

The Leader says the following prayer:

אָבִינוּ שֶׁבַּשָּׁמַיִם Heavenly Father, Israel's Rock and Redeemer,
bless the State of Israel, the first flowering of our redemption.
Shield it under the wings of Your loving-kindness
and spread over it the Tabernacle of Your peace.
Send Your light and truth
to its leaders, ministers and counselors,
and direct them with good counsel before You.

Strengthen the hands of the defenders of our Holy Land;
grant them deliverance, our God,
and crown them with the crown of victory.
Grant peace in the land
and everlasting joy to its inhabitants.

Several halakhot indicate that unlike any other item employed for a mitzva, a *sukka* resembles the *Mikdash* itself. The Gemara (*Sukka* 9a) likens a *sukka* to a sacrifice, in that it possesses sanctity, and unlike any other mitzva object, cannot be benefitted from. Furthermore, another Gemara (*Sukka* 43a) debates whether night residence is required to fulfill the mitzva of *Sukka*. Comparing habitation of the *sukka* to the continuous vigil of the *Kohanim* in the *Mikdash*, the Gemara rules that constant lodging in the *sukka* is necessary.

Finally a further Gemara (*Sukka* 5a) derives the requisite height of the *sukka* from the dimensions of the *Aron HaKodesh*. These halakhic discourses underscore the latent imagery of the aforementioned verse in *Tehillim*: Our *sukkot* are meant to embody a temporary and symbolic *Mikdash*.

By praying that HaKadosh Barukh Hu drape His *sukka* of peace upon us and Yerushalayim, we are not only praying for divine protection and the pursuit of global peace. We are additionally requesting the materialization of the absolute encounter with the *Shekhina* in Yerushalayim, heralded by the symbol of His *sukka*.

תפילה לשלום מדינת ישראל

The שליח ציבור *says the following prayer:*

אָבִֽינוּ שֶׁבַּשָּׁמַֽיִם, צוּר יִשְׂרָאֵל וְגוֹאֲלוֹ
בָּרֵךְ אֶת מְדִינַת יִשְׂרָאֵל, רֵאשִׁית צְמִיחַת גְּאֻלָּתֵֽנוּ.
הָגֵן עָלֶֽיהָ בְּאֶבְרַת חַסְדֶּֽךָ
וּפְרֹשׂ עָלֶֽיהָ סֻכַּת שְׁלוֹמֶֽךָ
וּשְׁלַח אוֹרְךָ וַאֲמִתְּךָ לְרָאשֶֽׁיהָ, שָׂרֶֽיהָ וְיוֹעֲצֶֽיהָ
וְתַקְּנֵם בְּעֵצָה טוֹבָה מִלְּפָנֶֽיךָ.

חַזֵּק אֶת יְדֵי מְגִנֵּי אֶֽרֶץ קָדְשֵֽׁנוּ
וְהַנְחִילֵם אֱלֹהֵֽינוּ יְשׁוּעָה וַעֲטֶֽרֶת נִצָּחוֹן תְּעַטְּרֵם
וְנָתַתָּ שָׁלוֹם בָּאָֽרֶץ
וְשִׂמְחַת עוֹלָם לְיוֹשְׁבֶֽיהָ.

PRAYER FOR THE STATE OF ISRAEL
For a discussion of this prayer see commentary on page 393.

A *SUKKA* OF PEACE
The phrase *sukkat shalom,* or *sukka* of peace, is a play on the term *sukkat shalem* – a *sukka* of *shalem* or perfection, which is incorporated in a verse in *Tehillim:* "His tabernacle is in Shalem; His dwelling place also is in Tziyon" (76:2). Sensing in this verse a *Sukka* erected in the vicinity of *Tziyon, Ḥazal* interpret the verse as follows: "Rabbi Berekhia said in the name of Rabbi Ḥelbo, 'Until it [Yerushalayim] is complete, God constructs a *sukka* and prays in it that He should witness the reconstruction of His House.'" We see then that a *sukka* is an image for a temporary Divine abode in a pre-messianic era. It serves as a microcosm for the ultimate encounter in the city of Yerushalayim. Until history is perfected (*shalem*) HaKadosh Barukh Hu suffices with a temporary encounter in a *sukka.*

As for our brothers, the whole house of Israel,
remember them in all the lands of our (*In Israel say:* their) dispersion,
and swiftly lead us (*In Israel say:* them) upright to Zion Your city,
and Jerusalem Your dwelling place,
as is written in the Torah of Moses Your servant:
"Even if you are scattered   *Deut. 30*
to the furthermost lands under the heavens,
from there the LORD your God will gather you and take you back.
The LORD your God will bring you
to the land your ancestors possessed and you will possess it;
and He will make you more prosperous
and numerous than your ancestors.
Then the LORD your God will open up your heart
and the heart of your descendants,
to love the LORD your God
with all your heart and with all your soul,
that you may live."

---

hundred meters – effectively double the recorded height of Adam. According
to a second opinion we will reach fifty meters – the stated height of the *Beit
HaMikdash.*

These suggested measurements for the height of a Jew in the messianic
period should be read figuratively. The Messianic Era will witness the restoration of the lost potential of fallen Man. One opinion suggests that the
restoration will recover the faculties enjoyed during the Temple era, forfeited
when the *Beit HaMikdash* was destroyed. The first opinion suggests that the
Messianic Era will enable the recovery of all potential lost after the fall into
sin in *Gan Eden.* Not only will Man recover that potential, he will increase
it twofold!

Though the verse speaks of the general experience of *komemiyut,* and the
Gemara interprets it as a messianic prophecy, this phrase in *Tefilla* designates
our return to our homeland as the context of *komemiyut.* Similarly, one of
the "*Haraḥamans*" in *Birkat HaMazon* paraphrases this verse, and prays that
we be steered with a *komemiyut* posture "*to our land.*"

וְאֶת אַחֵינוּ כָּל בֵּית יִשְׂרָאֵל

פְּקָד נָא בְּכָל אַרְצוֹת פְּזוּרֵינוּ (בארץ ישראל: פְּזוּרֵיהֶם)

וְתוֹלִיכֵנוּ (בארץ ישראל: וְתוֹלִיכֵם) מְהֵרָה קוֹמְמִיּוּת לְצִיּוֹן עִירֶךָ

וְלִירוּשָׁלַיִם מִשְׁכַּן שְׁמֶךָ

כַּכָּתוּב בְּתוֹרַת מֹשֶׁה עַבְדֶּךָ:

דברים ל

אִם־יִהְיֶה נִדַּחֲךָ בִּקְצֵה הַשָּׁמָיִם

מִשָּׁם יְקַבֶּצְךָ יהוה אֱלֹהֶיךָ וּמִשָּׁם יִקָּחֶךָ:

וֶהֱבִיאֲךָ יהוה אֱלֹהֶיךָ אֶל־הָאָרֶץ אֲשֶׁר־יָרְשׁוּ אֲבֹתֶיךָ וִירִשְׁתָּהּ

וְהֵיטִבְךָ וְהִרְבְּךָ מֵאֲבֹתֶיךָ:

וּמָל יהוה אֱלֹהֶיךָ אֶת־לְבָבְךָ וְאֶת־לְבַב זַרְעֶךָ

לְאַהֲבָה אֶת־יהוה אֱלֹהֶיךָ בְּכָל־לְבָבְךָ וּבְכָל־נַפְשְׁךָ

לְמַעַן חַיֶּיךָ:

קוֹמְמִיּוּת **Upright.** The term *komemiyut*, loosely translated as "upright with pride," is first introduced in *Parashat Beḥukotai*, where it describes the triumphant state of the Jewish people if they adhere to the Divine will. HaKadosh Barukh Hu promises to smash the slave-shackles which they bore in Egypt, thereby liberating them and making them upright with pride. Beyond the literal replacement of a stooped slave's posture with an erect freeman's stance, the term *komemiyut* connotes general national self-assurance and composure – as Rashi comments "*koma zekufa.*" Removing restraints is insufficient if a man can't stand upright, proud, and with dignity. This image of *komemiyut* evokes a previous description of the Jewish people departing Egypt "*beyad rama*" – literally with an exultant raised fist. These images reflect a national assurance, courage, and cultural confidence.

The Gemara (*Bava Batra* 95a) offers a different image of *komemiyut*. Sensing the word "*koma*" (story of a building) within the term *komemiyut*, the Gemara considers this phrase a prophecy for heightened stature during the messianic period. According to one opinion we will rise to a height of a

Unite our hearts to love and revere Your name
and observe all the words of Your Torah,
and swiftly send us Your righteous anointed one
of the house of David,
to redeem those who long for Your salvation.

Appear in Your glorious majesty over all the dwellers on earth,
and let all who breathe declare:
The LORD God of Israel is King and His kingship
has dominion over all.
Amen, Selah.

לִפְדּוֹת מְחַכֵּי קֵץ יְשׁוּעָתֶךָ *To redeem those who long for Your salvation.* The Gemara (*Sanhedrin* 97b) asserts that just as the Jewish people eagerly await redemption, similarly HaKadosh Barukh Hu awaits and yearns for it. The redemption is obstructed, however, by His *Midat HaDin* – Attribute of Judgment. This expression of a Divine desire to be reunited with His exiled people forms the cornerstone of *Shir HaShirim*. The story begins with rapturous scenes of original amorousness with God, as we were liberated from Egypt and received the Divine Word at *Har Sina*i. Yet it also depicts the great betrayal during the *Egel* (golden calf) debacle which condemned Jewish history. The past three thousand years have subjected both God and His nation to a great historical task to reunite and rekindle that original passion. Just as we clamor for Him, He craves that original state. This notion that HaKadosh Barukh Hu awaits the End of Days is consistent with the imagery of *Shir HaShirim*.

Furthermore, if He awaits the End of Days, but it is stymied by *Midat HaDin*, redemption is not a phenomenon which must be generated ex nihilo. It exists as part of our universe and is unnaturally thwarted. Our task of instigating redemption doesn't involve fashioning a new reality; it merely requires advancing a *suspended* reality. When the Torah begins by describing a primordial spirit hovering above the water prior to creation, *Ḥazal* interpret this as the soul of *Mashiaḥ*. Ironically the redemption of history *precedes* history itself. History was launched with a predetermined terminus. Though it may seem elusive, it is woven into the very fabric of our reality.

וְיַחֵד לְבָבֵנוּ לְאַהֲבָה וּלְיִרְאָה אֶת שְׁמֶךָ
וְלִשְׁמֹר אֶת כָּל דִּבְרֵי תוֹרָתֶךָ
וּשְׁלַח לָנוּ מְהֵרָה בֶן דָּוִד מְשִׁיחַ צִדְקֶךָ
לִפְדּוֹת מְחַכֵּי קֵץ יְשׁוּעָתֶךָ.

וְהוֹפַע בַּהֲדַר גְּאוֹן עֻזֶּךָ עַל כָּל יוֹשְׁבֵי תֵבֵל אַרְצֶךָ
וְיֹאמַר כֹּל אֲשֶׁר נְשָׁמָה בְאַפּוֹ
יהוה אֱלֹהֵי יִשְׂרָאֵל מֶלֶךְ וּמַלְכוּתוֹ בַּכֹּל מָשָׁלָה
אָמֵן סֶלָה.

When we lack a homeland and national sovereignty, we are bent and bowed. Even when Jews didn't suffer persecution they lived as outsiders. When Jews are settled in their homeland national pride surges, and as a consequence Jewish cultural expression is boosted. Even Jews who reside abroad experience *komemiyut* based on the recognition that we finally possess our homeland and national identity. This phrase was so resonant that Ben Gurion preferred to refer to the War of Independence as the War of *Komemiyut*, highlighting the role of the war in reawakening the sense of Jewish pride and identity after centuries of subjugation.

Not only does *komemiyut* fuel Jewish cultural expression, it also inspires religious achievement and Torah study. The fact that the extent of Torah study has experienced such a dramatic upsurge is directly linked to the *komemiyut* factor, as Torah growth is always driven by national identity.

Rav Kook asserted a metaphoric reading to the aforementioned Gemara. Though the different opinions debate the actual dimensions of a Messianic Jew, they both agree that he will be structured as *two* stories. These two stories represent the two facets of Jewish identity. Ideally we are fastened to land and location as the foundation of our national edifice. Even without this geographic grounding, a Jew always possessed the stability of being tethered to HaKadosh Barukh Hu and His Torah – a timeless upper story which is fastened to Heaven. Restoring land doesn't *create komemiyut*, it merely completes it.

PRAYER FOR ISRAEL'S DEFENSE FORCES

The Leader says the following prayer:

מִי שֶׁבֵּרַךְ May He who blessed our ancestors, Abraham, Isaac and Jacob, bless the members of Israel's Defense Forces and its security services who stand guard over our land and the cities of our God from the Lebanese border to the Egyptian desert, from the Mediterranean sea to the approach of the Aravah, and wherever else they are, on land, in air and at sea. May the LORD make the enemies who rise against us be struck down before them. May the Holy One, blessed be He, protect and deliver them from all trouble and distress, affliction and illness, and send blessing and success to all the work of their hands. May He subdue our enemies under them and crown them with deliverance and victory. And may there be fulfilled in them the verse, "It is the LORD your God   *Deut. 20* who goes with you to fight for you against your enemies, to deliver you." And let us say: Amen.

PRAYER FOR THOSE BEING HELD IN CAPTIVITY

If Israeli soldiers or civilians are being held in captivity, the Leader says the following:

מִי שֶׁבֵּרַךְ May He who blessed our ancestors, Abraham, Isaac and Jacob, Joseph, Moses and Aaron, David and Solomon, bless, protect and guard the members of Israel's Defense Forces missing in action or held captive, and other captives among our brethren, the whole house of Israel, who are in distress or captivity, as we, the members of this holy congregation, pray on their behalf. May the Holy One, blessed be He, have compassion on them and bring them out from darkness and the shadow of death; may He break their bonds, deliver them from their distress, and bring them swiftly back to their families' embrace. Give   *Ps. 107* thanks to the LORD for His loving-kindness and for the wonders He does for the children of men; and may there be fulfilled in them the verse: "Those redeemed by the LORD will return; they will enter Zion   *Is. 35* with singing, and everlasting joy will crown their heads. Gladness and joy will overtake them, and sorrow and sighing will flee away." And let us say: Amen.

On days that the Torah is not read continue with "Happy are those" on page 612.

מי שברך לחיילי צה״ל

The שְׁלִיחַ ציבור *says the following prayer:*

מִי שֶׁבֵּרַךְ אֲבוֹתֵינוּ אַבְרָהָם יִצְחָק וְיַעֲקֹב הוּא יְבָרֵךְ אֶת חַיָּלֵי
צְבָא הַהֲגָנָה לְיִשְׂרָאֵל וְאַנְשֵׁי כֹּחוֹת הַבִּטָּחוֹן, הָעוֹמְדִים עַל מִשְׁמַר
אַרְצֵנוּ וְעָרֵי אֱלֹהֵינוּ, מִגְּבוּל הַלְּבָנוֹן וְעַד מִדְבַּר מִצְרַיִם וּמִן הַיָּם
הַגָּדוֹל עַד לְבוֹא הָעֲרָבָה וּבְכָל מָקוֹם שֶׁהֵם, בַּיַּבָּשָׁה, בָּאֲוִיר וּבַיָּם.
יִתֵּן יהוה אֶת אוֹיְבֵינוּ הַקָּמִים עָלֵינוּ נִגָּפִים לִפְנֵיהֶם. הַקָּדוֹשׁ בָּרוּךְ
הוּא יִשְׁמֹר וְיַצִּיל אֶת חַיָּלֵינוּ מִכָּל צָרָה וְצוּקָה וּמִכָּל נֶגַע וּמַחֲלָה,
וְיִשְׁלַח בְּרָכָה וְהַצְלָחָה בְּכָל מַעֲשֵׂי יְדֵיהֶם. יַדְבֵּר שׂוֹנְאֵינוּ תַּחְתֵּיהֶם
וִיעַטְּרֵם בְּכֶתֶר יְשׁוּעָה וּבַעֲטֶרֶת נִצָּחוֹן. וִיקֻיַּם בָּהֶם הַכָּתוּב: כִּי
דברים כ
יהוה אֱלֹהֵיכֶם הַהֹלֵךְ עִמָּכֶם לְהִלָּחֵם לָכֶם עִם־אֹיְבֵיכֶם לְהוֹשִׁיעַ
אֶתְכֶם: וְנֹאמַר אָמֵן.

מי שברך לשבויים

If Israeli soldiers or civilians are being held in captivity, the שְׁלִיחַ ציבור *says the following:*

מִי שֶׁבֵּרַךְ אֲבוֹתֵינוּ אַבְרָהָם יִצְחָק וְיַעֲקֹב, יוֹסֵף מֹשֶׁה וְאַהֲרֹן,
דָּוִד וּשְׁלֹמֹה, הוּא יְבָרֵךְ וְיִשְׁמֹר וְיִנְצֹר אֶת נֶעְדְּרֵי צְבָא הַהֲגָנָה
לְיִשְׂרָאֵל וּשְׁבוּיָו, וְאֶת כָּל אַחֵינוּ הַנְּתוּנִים בְּצָרָה וּבְשִׁבְיָה, בַּעֲבוּר
שֶׁכָּל הַקָּהָל הַקָּדוֹשׁ הַזֶּה מִתְפַּלֵּל בַּעֲבוּרָם. הַקָּדוֹשׁ בָּרוּךְ הוּא
יִמָּלֵא רַחֲמִים עֲלֵיהֶם, וְיוֹצִיאֵם מֵחֹשֶׁךְ וְצַלְמָוֶת, וּמוֹסְרוֹתֵיהֶם
יְנַתֵּק, וּמִמְּצוּקוֹתֵיהֶם יוֹשִׁיעֵם, וִישִׁיבֵם מְהֵרָה לְחֵיק מִשְׁפְּחוֹתֵיהֶם.
תהלים קז
יוֹדוּ לַיהוה חַסְדּוֹ וְנִפְלְאוֹתָיו לִבְנֵי אָדָם: וִיקֻיַּם בָּהֶם מִקְרָא
ישעיה לה
שֶׁכָּתוּב: וּפְדוּיֵי יהוה יְשֻׁבוּן, וּבָאוּ צִיּוֹן בְּרִנָּה, וְשִׂמְחַת עוֹלָם
עַל־רֹאשָׁם, שָׂשׂוֹן וְשִׂמְחָה יַשִּׂיגוּ, וְנָסוּ יָגוֹן וַאֲנָחָה: וְנֹאמַר אָמֵן.

On days that the Torah is not read continue with אַשְׁרֵי *on page 613.*

RETURNING THE TORAH TO THE ARK

The Ark is opened. The Leader takes the Torah scroll and says:

יְהַלְלוּ Let them praise the name of the LORD,   *Ps. 148*

for His name alone is sublime.

The congregation responds:

הוֹדוֹ His majesty is above earth and heaven.

He has raised the horn of His people,

for the glory of all His devoted ones,

the children of Israel, the people close to Him.

Halleluya!

As the Torah scroll is returned to the Ark, say:

לְדָוִד מִזְמוֹר A psalm of David. The earth is the LORD's and all it contains,   *Ps. 24*
the world and all who live in it. For He founded it on the seas and established it on the streams. Who may climb the mountain of the LORD? Who
may stand in His holy place? He who has clean hands and a pure heart,
who has not taken My name in vain, or sworn deceitfully. He shall receive
blessing from the LORD, and just reward from God, his salvation. This is
a generation of those who seek Him, the descendants of Jacob who seek
Your presence, Selah! Lift up your heads, O gates; be uplifted, eternal
doors, so that the King of glory may enter. Who is the King of glory? It
is the LORD, strong and mighty, the LORD mighty in battle. Lift up your
heads, O gates; lift them up, eternal doors, so that the King of glory may
enter. Who is He, the King of glory? The LORD of hosts, He is the King
of glory, Selah!

As the Torah scroll is placed into the Ark, say:

וּבְנֻחֹה יֹאמַר When the Ark came to rest, Moses would say: "Return, O   *Num. 10*
LORD, to the myriad thousands of Israel." Advance, LORD, to Your resting   *Ps. 132*
place, You and Your mighty Ark. Your priests are clothed in righteousness,
and Your devoted ones sing in joy. For the sake of Your servant David,
do not reject Your anointed one. For I give you good instruction; do not   *Prov. 4*
forsake My Torah. It is a tree of life to those who grasp it, and those who   *Prov. 3*
uphold it are happy. Its ways are ways of pleasantness, and all its paths
are peace. ▸ Turn us back, O LORD, to You, and we will return. Renew   *Lam. 5*
our days as of old.

The Ark is closed.

הכנסת ספר תורה

The ארון קודש is opened. The שליח ציבור takes the ספר תורה and says:

יְהַלְלוּ אֶת־שֵׁם יהוה, כִּי־נִשְׂגָּב שְׁמוֹ, לְבַדּוֹ

תהלים קמח

The קהל responds:

הוֹדוֹ עַל־אֶרֶץ וְשָׁמָיִם:
וַיָּרֶם קֶרֶן לְעַמּוֹ
תְּהִלָּה לְכָל־חֲסִידָיו
לִבְנֵי יִשְׂרָאֵל עַם קְרֹבוֹ, הַלְלוּיָהּ:

As the ספר תורה is returned to the ארון קודש, say:

תהלים כד

לְדָוִד מִזְמוֹר, לַיהוה הָאָרֶץ וּמְלוֹאָהּ, תֵּבֵל וְיֹשְׁבֵי בָהּ: כִּי־הוּא עַל־
יַמִּים יְסָדָהּ, וְעַל־נְהָרוֹת יְכוֹנְנֶהָ: מִי־יַעֲלֶה בְהַר־יהוה, וּמִי־יָקוּם
בִּמְקוֹם קָדְשׁוֹ: נְקִי כַפַּיִם וּבַר־לֵבָב, אֲשֶׁר לֹא־נָשָׂא לַשָּׁוְא נַפְשִׁי
וְלֹא נִשְׁבַּע לְמִרְמָה: יִשָּׂא בְרָכָה מֵאֵת יהוה, וּצְדָקָה מֵאֱלֹהֵי יִשְׁעוֹ:
זֶה דּוֹר דֹּרְשָׁו, מְבַקְשֵׁי פָנֶיךָ, יַעֲקֹב, סֶלָה: שְׂאוּ שְׁעָרִים רָאשֵׁיכֶם,
וְהִנָּשְׂאוּ פִּתְחֵי עוֹלָם, וְיָבוֹא מֶלֶךְ הַכָּבוֹד: מִי זֶה מֶלֶךְ הַכָּבוֹד, יהוה
עִזּוּז וְגִבּוֹר, יהוה גִּבּוֹר מִלְחָמָה: שְׂאוּ שְׁעָרִים רָאשֵׁיכֶם, וּשְׂאוּ פִּתְחֵי
עוֹלָם, וְיָבֹא מֶלֶךְ הַכָּבוֹד: מִי הוּא זֶה מֶלֶךְ הַכָּבוֹד, יהוה צְבָאוֹת
הוּא מֶלֶךְ הַכָּבוֹד, סֶלָה:

As the ספר תורה is placed into the ארון קודש, say:

במדברי
תהלים קלב

וּבְנֻחֹה יֹאמַר, שׁוּבָה יהוה רִבְבוֹת אַלְפֵי יִשְׂרָאֵל: קוּמָה יהוה
לִמְנוּחָתֶךָ, אַתָּה וַאֲרוֹן עֻזֶּךָ: כֹּהֲנֶיךָ יִלְבְּשׁוּ־צֶדֶק, וַחֲסִידֶיךָ יְרַנֵּנוּ:

משלי ד

בַּעֲבוּר דָּוִד עַבְדֶּךָ אַל־תָּשֵׁב פְּנֵי מְשִׁיחֶךָ: כִּי לֶקַח טוֹב נָתַתִּי לָכֶם,

משלי ג

תּוֹרָתִי אַל־תַּעֲזֹבוּ: עֵץ־חַיִּים הִיא לַמַּחֲזִיקִים בָּהּ, וְתֹמְכֶיהָ מְאֻשָּׁר:

איכה ה

דְּרָכֶיהָ דַרְכֵי־נֹעַם וְכָל־נְתִיבֹתֶיהָ שָׁלוֹם: ◂ הֲשִׁיבֵנוּ יהוה אֵלֶיךָ וְנָשׁוּבָ,
חַדֵּשׁ יָמֵינוּ כְּקֶדֶם:

The ארון קודש is closed.

Some have the custom to touch the hand-tefillin at °, and the head-tefillin at °°.

אַשְׁרֵי Happy are those who dwell in Your House;   *Ps. 84*
they shall continue to praise You, Selah!
Happy are the people for whom this is so;   *Ps. 144*
happy are the people whose God is the LORD.

A song of praise by David.   *Ps. 145*

I will exalt You, my God, the King, and bless Your name for ever
and all time. Every day I will bless You, and praise Your name for
ever and all time. Great is the LORD and greatly to be praised;
His greatness is unfathomable. One generation will praise
Your works to the next, and tell of Your mighty deeds. On the
glorious splendor of Your majesty I will meditate, and on the
acts of Your wonders. They shall talk of the power of Your awesome deeds, and I will tell of Your greatness. They shall recite
the record of Your great goodness, and sing with joy of Your
righteousness. The LORD is gracious and compassionate, slow
to anger and great in loving-kindness. The LORD is good to all,
and His compassion extends to all His works. All Your works
shall thank You, LORD, and Your devoted ones shall bless You.
They shall talk of the glory of Your kingship, and speak of Your
might. To make known to mankind His mighty deeds and the
glorious majesty of His kingship. Your kingdom is an everlasting kingdom, and Your reign is for all generations. The LORD
supports all who fall, and raises all who are bowed down. All
raise their eyes to You in hope, and You give them their food
in due season. °You open Your hand, °°and satisfy every living
thing with favor. The LORD is righteous in all His ways, and
kind in all He does. The LORD is close to all who call on Him,
to all who call on Him in truth. He fulfills the will of those
who revere Him; He hears their cry and saves them. The LORD
guards all who love Him, but all the wicked He will destroy.
‣ My mouth shall speak the praise of the LORD, and all creatures shall bless His holy name for ever and all time.

We will bless the LORD now and for ever. Halleluya!   *Ps. 115*

Some have the custom to touch the תפילין של יד at °, and the תפילין של ראש at °°.

תהלים פד

אַשְׁרֵי יוֹשְׁבֵי בֵיתֶךָ, עוֹד יְהַלְלוּךָ סֶּלָה:

תהלים קמד

אַשְׁרֵי הָעָם שֶׁכָּכָה לּוֹ, אַשְׁרֵי הָעָם שֶׁיהוה אֱלֹהָיו:

תהלים קמה

תְּהִלָּה לְדָוִד

אֲרוֹמִמְךָ אֱלוֹהַי הַמֶּלֶךְ, וַאֲבָרְכָה שִׁמְךָ לְעוֹלָם וָעֶד:

בְּכָל־יוֹם אֲבָרְכֶךָ, וַאֲהַלְלָה שִׁמְךָ לְעוֹלָם וָעֶד:

גָּדוֹל יהוה וּמְהֻלָּל מְאֹד, וְלִגְדֻלָּתוֹ אֵין חֵקֶר:

דּוֹר לְדוֹר יְשַׁבַּח מַעֲשֶׂיךָ, וּגְבוּרֹתֶיךָ יַגִּידוּ:

הֲדַר כְּבוֹד הוֹדֶךָ, וְדִבְרֵי נִפְלְאֹתֶיךָ אָשִׂיחָה:

וֶעֱזוּז נוֹרְאֹתֶיךָ יֹאמֵרוּ, וּגְדוּלָּתְךָ אֲסַפְּרֶנָּה:

זֵכֶר רַב־טוּבְךָ יַבִּיעוּ, וְצִדְקָתְךָ יְרַנֵּנוּ:

חַנּוּן וְרַחוּם יהוה, אֶרֶךְ אַפַּיִם וּגְדָל־חָסֶד:

טוֹב־יהוה לַכֹּל, וְרַחֲמָיו עַל־כָּל־מַעֲשָׂיו:

יוֹדוּךָ יהוה כָּל־מַעֲשֶׂיךָ, וַחֲסִידֶיךָ יְבָרְכוּכָה:

כְּבוֹד מַלְכוּתְךָ יֹאמֵרוּ, וּגְבוּרָתְךָ יְדַבֵּרוּ:

לְהוֹדִיעַ לִבְנֵי הָאָדָם גְּבוּרֹתָיו, וּכְבוֹד הֲדַר מַלְכוּתוֹ:

מַלְכוּתְךָ מַלְכוּת כָּל־עֹלָמִים, וּמֶמְשַׁלְתְּךָ בְּכָל־דּוֹר וָדֹר:

סוֹמֵךְ יהוה לְכָל־הַנֹּפְלִים, וְזוֹקֵף לְכָל־הַכְּפוּפִים:

עֵינֵי־כֹל אֵלֶיךָ יְשַׂבֵּרוּ, וְאַתָּה נוֹתֵן־לָהֶם אֶת־אָכְלָם בְּעִתּוֹ:

°פּוֹתֵחַ אֶת־יָדֶךָ, °°וּמַשְׂבִּיעַ לְכָל־חַי רָצוֹן:

צַדִּיק יהוה בְּכָל־דְּרָכָיו, וְחָסִיד בְּכָל־מַעֲשָׂיו:

קָרוֹב יהוה לְכָל־קֹרְאָיו, לְכֹל אֲשֶׁר יִקְרָאֻהוּ בֶאֱמֶת:

רְצוֹן־יְרֵאָיו יַעֲשֶׂה, וְאֶת־שַׁוְעָתָם יִשְׁמַע, וְיוֹשִׁיעֵם:

שׁוֹמֵר יהוה אֶת־כָּל־אֹהֲבָיו, וְאֵת כָּל־הָרְשָׁעִים יַשְׁמִיד:

‹ תְּהִלַּת יהוה יְדַבֶּר פִּי, וִיבָרֵךְ כָּל־בָּשָׂר שֵׁם קָדְשׁוֹ לְעוֹלָם וָעֶד:

תהלים קטו

וַאֲנַחְנוּ נְבָרֵךְ יָהּ מֵעַתָּה וְעַד־עוֹלָם, הַלְלוּיָהּ:

וּבָא לְצִיּוֹן גּוֹאֵל "A redeemer will come to Zion, to those in Jacob who *Is. 59* repent of their sins," declares the LORD.

"As for Me, this is My covenant with them," says the LORD. "My spirit, that is on you, and My words I have placed in your mouth will not depart from your mouth, or from the mouth of your children, or from the mouth of their descendants from this time on and for ever," says the LORD.

▸ You are the Holy One, enthroned on the praises of Israel. And (the angels) *Ps. 22* call to one another, saying, "Holy, holy, holy is the LORD of hosts; the *Is. 6* whole world is filled with His glory."

And they receive permission from one another, saying: "Holy in the highest heavens, *Targum* home of His Presence; holy on earth, the work of His strength; holy for ever and all *Yonatan* time is the LORD of hosts; the whole earth is full of His radiant glory." *Is. 6*

▸ Then a wind lifted me up and I heard behind me the sound of a great noise, *Ezek. 3* saying, "Blessed is the LORD's glory from His place."

Then a wind lifted me up and I heard behind me the sound of a great tempest of those *Targum* who uttered praise, saying, "Blessed is the LORD's glory from the place of the home *Yonatan* of His Presence." *Ezek. 3*

The LORD shall reign for ever and all time. *Ex. 15*

The LORD's kingdom is established for ever and all time. *Targum Onkelos Ex. 15*

יהוה LORD, God of Abraham, Isaac and Yisrael, our ancestors, may You *1 Chr. 29* keep this for ever so that it forms the thoughts in Your people's heart, and directs their heart toward You. He is compassionate. He forgives iniquity *Ps. 78* and does not destroy. Repeatedly He suppresses His anger, not rousing His full wrath. For You, my LORD, are good and forgiving, abundantly *Ps. 86* kind to all who call on You. Your righteousness is eternally righteous, and *Ps. 119* Your Torah is truth. Grant truth to Jacob, loving-kindness to Abraham, as *Mic. 7* You promised our ancestors in ancient times. Blessed is my LORD for day *Ps. 68* after day He burdens us [with His blessings]; God is our salvation, Selah! The LORD of hosts is with us; the God of Jacob is our refuge, Selah! LORD *Ps. 46* *Ps. 84* of hosts, happy is the one who trusts in You. LORD, save! May the King *Ps. 20* answer us on the day we call.

בָּרוּךְ Blessed is He, our God, who created us for His glory, separating us from those who go astray; who gave us the Torah of truth, planting within us eternal life. May He open our heart to His Torah, imbuing our heart with the love and awe of Him, that we may do His will and serve Him with a perfect heart, so that we neither toil in vain nor give birth to confusion.

ישעיה נט

וּבָא לְצִיּוֹן גּוֹאֵל, וּלְשָׁבֵי פֶשַׁע בְּיַעֲקֹב, נְאֻם יְהוָה:

וַאֲנִי זֹאת בְּרִיתִי אוֹתָם, אָמַר יְהוָה, רוּחִי אֲשֶׁר עָלֶיךָ וּדְבָרַי אֲשֶׁר־
שַׂמְתִּי בְּפִיךָ, לֹא־יָמוּשׁוּ מִפִּיךָ וּמִפִּי זַרְעֲךָ וּמִפִּי זֶרַע זַרְעֲךָ, אָמַר יְהוָה,
מֵעַתָּה וְעַד־עוֹלָם:

תהלים כב
ישעיה ו

‣ וְאַתָּה קָדוֹשׁ יוֹשֵׁב תְּהִלּוֹת יִשְׂרָאֵל: וְקָרָא זֶה אֶל־זֶה וְאָמַר
קָדוֹשׁ, קָדוֹשׁ, קָדוֹשׁ, יְהוָה צְבָאוֹת, מְלֹא כָל־הָאָרֶץ כְּבוֹדוֹ:

תרגום
יונתן
ישעיה ו

וּמְקַבְּלִין דֵּין מִן דֵּין וְאָמְרִין, קַדִּישׁ בִּשְׁמֵי מְרוֹמָא עִלָּאָה בֵּית שְׁכִינְתֵּהּ, קַדִּישׁ
עַל אַרְעָא עוֹבַד גְּבוּרְתֵּהּ, קַדִּישׁ לְעָלַם וּלְעָלְמֵי עָלְמַיָּא, יְהוָה צְבָאוֹת, מַלְיָא כָל
אַרְעָא זִיו יְקָרֵהּ.

יחזקאל ג

‣ וַתִּשָּׂאֵנִי רוּחַ, וָאֶשְׁמַע אַחֲרַי קוֹל רַעַשׁ גָּדוֹל
בָּרוּךְ כְּבוֹד־יְהוָה מִמְּקוֹמוֹ:

תרגום
יונתן
יחזקאל ג

וּנְטָלַתְנִי רוּחָא, וּשְׁמָעִית בַּתְרַי קָל זִיעַ סַגִּיא, דִּמְשַׁבְּחִין וְאָמְרִין, בְּרִיךְ יְקָרָא דַיהוָה
מֵאֲתַר בֵּית שְׁכִינְתֵּהּ.

שמות טו
תרגום
אונקלוס
שמות טו

יְהוָה יִמְלֹךְ לְעֹלָם וָעֶד:
יְהוָה מַלְכוּתֵהּ קָאֵם לְעָלַם וּלְעָלְמֵי עָלְמַיָּא.

דברי הימים
א כט

יְהוָה אֱלֹהֵי אַבְרָהָם יִצְחָק וְיִשְׂרָאֵל אֲבֹתֵינוּ, שָׁמְרָה־זֹּאת לְעוֹלָם לְיֵצֶר

תהלים עח

מַחְשְׁבוֹת לְבַב עַמֶּךָ, וְהָכֵן לְבָבָם אֵלֶיךָ: וְהוּא רַחוּם יְכַפֵּר עָוֺן וְלֹא־

תהלים פו

יַשְׁחִית, וְהִרְבָּה לְהָשִׁיב אַפּוֹ, וְלֹא־יָעִיר כָּל־חֲמָתוֹ: כִּי־אַתָּה אֲדֹנָי טוֹב

תהלים קיט

וְסַלָּח, וְרַב־חֶסֶד לְכָל־קֹרְאֶיךָ: צִדְקָתְךָ צֶדֶק לְעוֹלָם וְתוֹרָתְךָ אֱמֶת:

מיכה ו

תִּתֵּן אֱמֶת לְיַעֲקֹב, חֶסֶד לְאַבְרָהָם, אֲשֶׁר־נִשְׁבַּעְתָּ לַאֲבֹתֵינוּ מִימֵי קֶדֶם:

תהלים סח

בָּרוּךְ אֲדֹנָי יוֹם יוֹם יַעֲמָס־לָנוּ, הָאֵל יְשׁוּעָתֵנוּ סֶלָה: יְהוָה צְבָאוֹת עִמָּנוּ,

תהלים פד
תהלים כ

מִשְׂגָּב לָנוּ אֱלֹהֵי יַעֲקֹב סֶלָה: יְהוָה צְבָאוֹת, אַשְׁרֵי אָדָם בֹּטֵחַ בָּךְ: יְהוָה
הוֹשִׁיעָה, הַמֶּלֶךְ יַעֲנֵנוּ בְיוֹם־קָרְאֵנוּ:

בָּרוּךְ הוּא אֱלֹהֵינוּ שֶׁבְּרָאָנוּ לִכְבוֹדוֹ, וְהִבְדִּילָנוּ מִן הַתּוֹעִים, וְנָתַן לָנוּ
תּוֹרַת אֱמֶת, וְחַיֵּי עוֹלָם נָטַע בְּתוֹכֵנוּ. הוּא יִפְתַּח לִבֵּנוּ בְּתוֹרָתוֹ, וְיָשֵׂם
בְּלִבֵּנוּ אַהֲבָתוֹ וְיִרְאָתוֹ וְלַעֲשׂוֹת רְצוֹנוֹ וּלְעָבְדוֹ בְּלֵבָב שָׁלֵם, לְמַעַן לֹא
נִיגַע לָרִיק וְלֹא נֵלֵד לַבֶּהָלָה.

יְהִי רָצוֹן May it be Your will, O LORD our God and God of our ancestors, that we keep Your laws in this world, and thus be worthy to live, see and inherit goodness and blessing in the Messianic Age and in the life of the World to Come. So that my soul may sing to You and not be silent. *Ps. 30* LORD, my God, for ever I will thank You. Blessed is the man who trusts *Jer. 17* in the LORD, whose trust is in the LORD alone. Trust in the LORD for *Is. 26* evermore, for God, the LORD, is an everlasting Rock. ▸ Those who know *Ps. 9* Your name trust in You, for You, LORD, do not forsake those who seek You. The LORD desired, for the sake of Israel's merit, to make the Torah *Is. 42* great and glorious.

FULL KADDISH

Leader: יִתְגַּדַּל Magnified and sanctified may His great name be,
in the world He created by His will.
May He establish His kingdom in your lifetime
and in your days,
and in the lifetime of all the house of Israel,
swiftly and soon – and say: Amen.

All: May His great name be blessed for ever and all time.

Leader: Blessed and praised, glorified and exalted,
raised and honored, uplifted and lauded be
the name of the Holy One, blessed be He,
beyond any blessing,
song, praise and consolation
uttered in the world – and say: Amen.

May the prayers and pleas of all Israel
be accepted by their Father in heaven – and say: Amen.

May there be great peace from heaven,
and life for us and all Israel – and say: Amen.

*Bow, take three steps back, as if taking leave of the Divine Presence,
then bow, first left, then right, then center, while saying:*
May He who makes peace in His high places,
make peace for us and all Israel – and say: Amen.

יְהִי רָצוֹן מִלְּפָנֶיךָ יהוה אֱלֹהֵינוּ וֵאלֹהֵי אֲבוֹתֵינוּ, שֶׁנִּשְׁמֹר חֻקֶּיךָ בָּעוֹלָם
הַזֶּה, וְנִזְכֶּה וְנִחְיֶה וְנִרְאֶה וְנִירַשׁ טוֹבָה וּבְרָכָה, לִשְׁנֵי יְמוֹת הַמָּשִׁיחַ וּלְחַיֵּי
הָעוֹלָם הַבָּא. לְמַעַן יְזַמֶּרְךָ כָבוֹד וְלֹא יִדֹּם, יהוה אֱלֹהַי, לְעוֹלָם אוֹדֶךָּ:
בָּרוּךְ הַגֶּבֶר אֲשֶׁר יִבְטַח בַּיהוה, וְהָיָה יהוה מִבְטַחוֹ: בִּטְחוּ בַיהוה עֲדֵי
עַד, כִּי בְּיָהּ יהוה צוּר עוֹלָמִים: ‹ וַיִּבְטְחוּ בְךָ יוֹדְעֵי שְׁמֶךָ, כִּי לֹא־עָזַבְתָּ
דֹרְשֶׁיךָ, יהוה: יהוה חָפֵץ לְמַעַן צִדְקוֹ, יַגְדִּיל תּוֹרָה וְיַאְדִּיר:

תהלים ל
ירמיה יז
ישעיה כו
תהלים ט

ישעיה מב

קדיש שלם

ש״ץ: יִתְגַּדַּל וְיִתְקַדַּשׁ שְׁמֵהּ רַבָּא (קהל: אָמֵן)
בְּעָלְמָא דִּי בְרָא כִרְעוּתֵהּ
וְיַמְלִיךְ מַלְכוּתֵהּ
בְּחַיֵּיכוֹן וּבְיוֹמֵיכוֹן וּבְחַיֵּי דְּכָל בֵּית יִשְׂרָאֵל
בַּעֲגָלָא וּבִזְמַן קָרִיב, וְאִמְרוּ אָמֵן. (קהל: אָמֵן)

קהל
ושׁ״ץ: יְהֵא שְׁמֵהּ רַבָּא מְבָרַךְ לְעָלַם וּלְעָלְמֵי עָלְמַיָּא.

שׁ״ץ: יִתְבָּרַךְ וְיִשְׁתַּבַּח וְיִתְפָּאַר
וְיִתְרוֹמַם וְיִתְנַשֵּׂא וְיִתְהַדָּר וְיִתְעַלֶּה וְיִתְהַלָּל
שְׁמֵהּ דְּקֻדְשָׁא בְּרִיךְ הוּא (קהל: בְּרִיךְ הוּא)
לְעֵלָּא מִן כָּל בִּרְכָתָא וְשִׁירָתָא, תֻּשְׁבְּחָתָא וְנֶחֱמָתָא
דַּאֲמִירָן בְּעָלְמָא, וְאִמְרוּ אָמֵן. (קהל: אָמֵן)

תִּתְקַבֵּל צְלוֹתְהוֹן וּבָעוּתְהוֹן דְּכָל יִשְׂרָאֵל
קֳדָם אֲבוּהוֹן דִּי בִשְׁמַיָּא, וְאִמְרוּ אָמֵן. (קהל: אָמֵן)

יְהֵא שְׁלָמָא רַבָּא מִן שְׁמַיָּא
וְחַיִּים, עָלֵינוּ וְעַל כָּל יִשְׂרָאֵל, וְאִמְרוּ אָמֵן. (קהל: אָמֵן)

Bow, take three steps back, as if taking leave of the Divine Presence,
then bow, first left, then right, then center, while saying:

עֹשֶׂה שָׁלוֹם בִּמְרוֹמָיו
הוּא יַעֲשֶׂה שָׁלוֹם עָלֵינוּ וְעַל כָּל יִשְׂרָאֵל, וְאִמְרוּ אָמֵן. (קהל: אָמֵן)

Stand while saying Aleinu. Bow at ˒.

עָלֵינוּ It is our duty to praise the Master of all,
and ascribe greatness to the Author of creation,
who has not made us like the nations of the lands
nor placed us like the families of the earth;
who has not made our portion like theirs,
nor our destiny like all their multitudes.
(For they worship vanity and emptiness,
and pray to a god who cannot save.)
˒But we bow in worship and thank the Supreme King of kings,
the Holy One, blessed be He,
who extends the heavens and establishes the earth,
whose throne of glory is in the heavens above,
and whose power's Presence is in the highest of heights.
He is our God; there is no other.
Truly He is our King, there is none else,
as it is written in His Torah:
"You shall know and take to heart this day that the LORD is God,   *Deut. 4*
in heaven above and on earth below. There is no other."

Therefore, we place our hope in You, LORD our God,
that we may soon see the glory of Your power,
when You will remove abominations from the earth,
and idols will be utterly destroyed,
when the world will be perfected under the sovereignty of the
Almighty,
when all humanity will call on Your name,
to turn all the earth's wicked toward You.
All the world's inhabitants will realize and know
that to You every knee must bow and every tongue swear loyalty.
Before You, LORD our God, they will kneel and bow down
and give honor to Your glorious name.
They will all accept the yoke of Your kingdom,
and You will reign over them soon and for ever.
For the kingdom is Yours, and to all eternity You will reign in glory,
as it is written in Your Torah: "The LORD will reign for ever and ever."   *Ex. 15*
˒ And it is said: "Then the LORD shall be King over all the earth;   *Zech. 14*
on that day the LORD shall be One and His name One."

Stand while saying עָלֵינוּ. Bow at ־.

עָלֵינוּ לְשַׁבֵּחַ לַאֲדוֹן הַכֹּל, לָתֵת גְּדֻלָּה לְיוֹצֵר בְּרֵאשִׁית

שֶׁלֹּא עָשֶׂנוּ כְּגוֹיֵי הָאֲרָצוֹת, וְלֹא שָׂמָנוּ כְּמִשְׁפְּחוֹת הָאֲדָמָה

שֶׁלֹּא שָׂם חֶלְקֵנוּ כָּהֶם וְגוֹרָלֵנוּ כְּכָל הֲמוֹנָם.

(שֶׁהֵם מִשְׁתַּחֲוִים לְהֶבֶל וָרִיק וּמִתְפַּלְּלִים אֶל אֵל לֹא יוֹשִׁיעַ.)

־וַאֲנַחְנוּ כּוֹרְעִים וּמִשְׁתַּחֲוִים וּמוֹדִים

לִפְנֵי מֶלֶךְ מַלְכֵי הַמְּלָכִים, הַקָּדוֹשׁ בָּרוּךְ הוּא

שֶׁהוּא נוֹטֶה שָׁמַיִם וְיוֹסֵד אָרֶץ, וּמוֹשַׁב יְקָרוֹ בַּשָּׁמַיִם מִמַּעַל

וּשְׁכִינַת עֻזּוֹ בְּגָבְהֵי מְרוֹמִים.

הוּא אֱלֹהֵינוּ, אֵין עוֹד.

אֱמֶת מַלְכֵּנוּ, אֶפֶס זוּלָתוֹ

כַּכָּתוּב בְּתוֹרָתוֹ

דברים ד

וְיָדַעְתָּ הַיּוֹם וַהֲשֵׁבֹתָ אֶל־לְבָבֶךָ

כִּי יְהֹוָה הוּא הָאֱלֹהִים בַּשָּׁמַיִם מִמַּעַל וְעַל־הָאָרֶץ מִתָּחַת, אֵין עוֹד:

עַל כֵּן נְקַוֶּה לְּךָ יְהֹוָה אֱלֹהֵינוּ, לִרְאוֹת מְהֵרָה בְּתִפְאֶרֶת עֻזֶּךָ

לְהַעֲבִיר גִּלּוּלִים מִן הָאָרֶץ, וְהָאֱלִילִים כָּרוֹת יִכָּרֵתוּן

לְתַקֵּן עוֹלָם בְּמַלְכוּת שַׁדַּי.

וְכָל בְּנֵי בָשָׂר יִקְרְאוּ בִשְׁמֶךָ לְהַפְנוֹת אֵלֶיךָ כָּל רִשְׁעֵי אָרֶץ.

יַכִּירוּ וְיֵדְעוּ כָּל יוֹשְׁבֵי תֵבֵל

כִּי לְךָ תִּכְרַע כָּל בֶּרֶךְ, תִּשָּׁבַע כָּל לָשׁוֹן.

לְפָנֶיךָ יְהֹוָה אֱלֹהֵינוּ יִכְרְעוּ וְיִפֹּלוּ, וְלִכְבוֹד שִׁמְךָ יְקָר יִתֵּנוּ

וִיקַבְּלוּ כֻלָּם אֶת עֹל מַלְכוּתֶךָ

וְתִמְלֹךְ עֲלֵיהֶם מְהֵרָה לְעוֹלָם וָעֶד.

כִּי הַמַּלְכוּת שֶׁלְּךָ הִיא וּלְעוֹלְמֵי עַד תִּמְלֹךְ בְּכָבוֹד

כַּכָּתוּב בְּתוֹרָתֶךָ, יְהֹוָה יִמְלֹךְ לְעֹלָם וָעֶד:

שמות טו

זכריה יד

־ וְנֶאֱמַר, וְהָיָה יְהֹוָה לְמֶלֶךְ עַל־כָּל־הָאָרֶץ

בַּיּוֹם הַהוּא יִהְיֶה יְהֹוָה אֶחָד וּשְׁמוֹ אֶחָד:

Some add:

Have no fear of sudden terror or of the ruin when it overtakes the wicked. *Prov. 3*

Devise your strategy, but it will be thwarted; propose your plan, *Is. 8*

but it will not stand, for God is with us. When you grow old, I will still be the same. *Is. 46*

When your hair turns gray, I will still carry you. I made you, I will bear you,

I will carry you, and I will rescue you.

MOURNER'S KADDISH

The following prayer, said by mourners, requires the presence of a minyan.
A transliteration can be found on page 667.

Mourner: יִתְגַּדַּל Magnified and sanctified may His great name be,

in the world He created by His will.

May He establish His kingdom

in your lifetime and in your days,

and in the lifetime of all the house of Israel,

swiftly and soon –

and say: Amen.

All: May His great name be blessed for ever and all time.

Mourner: Blessed and praised, glorified and exalted,

raised and honored, uplifted and lauded

be the name of the Holy One,

blessed be He,

beyond any blessing, song, praise and consolation

uttered in the world –

and say: Amen.

May there be great peace from heaven,

and life for us and all Israel –

and say: Amen.

Bow, take three steps back, as if taking leave of the Divine Presence,
then bow, first left, then right, then center, while saying:

May He who makes peace in His high places,

make peace for us and all Israel –

and say: Amen.

Some add:

משלי ג — אַל־תִּירָא מִפַּחַד פִּתְאֹם וּמִשֹּׁאַת רְשָׁעִים כִּי תָבֹא:

ישעיה ח — עֻצוּ עֵצָה וְתֻפָר, דַּבְּרוּ דָבָר וְלֹא יָקוּם, כִּי עִמָּנוּ אֵל:

ישעיה מו — וְעַד־זִקְנָה אֲנִי הוּא, וְעַד־שֵׂיבָה אֲנִי אֶסְבֹּל, אֲנִי עָשִׂיתִי וַאֲנִי אֶשָּׂא וַאֲנִי אֶסְבֹּל וַאֲמַלֵּט:

קדיש יתום

The following prayer, said by mourners, requires the presence of a מנין.
A transliteration can be found on page 667.

אבל — יִתְגַּדַּל וְיִתְקַדַּשׁ שְׁמֵהּ רַבָּא (קהל: אָמֵן)

בְּעָלְמָא דִּי בְרָא כִרְעוּתֵהּ

וְיַמְלִיךְ מַלְכוּתֵהּ

בְּחַיֵּיכוֹן וּבְיוֹמֵיכוֹן וּבְחַיֵּי דְּכָל בֵּית יִשְׂרָאֵל

בַּעֲגָלָא וּבִזְמַן קָרִיב, וְאִמְרוּ אָמֵן. (קהל: אָמֵן)

קהל ואבל: יְהֵא שְׁמֵהּ רַבָּא מְבָרַךְ לְעָלַם וּלְעָלְמֵי עָלְמַיָּא.

אבל — יִתְבָּרַךְ וְיִשְׁתַּבַּח וְיִתְפָּאַר

וְיִתְרוֹמַם וְיִתְנַשֵּׂא וְיִתְהַדָּר וְיִתְעַלֶּה וְיִתְהַלָּל

שְׁמֵהּ דְּקֻדְשָׁא בְּרִיךְ הוּא (קהל: בְּרִיךְ הוּא)

לְעֵלָּא מִן כָּל בִּרְכָתָא

וְשִׁירָתָא, תֻּשְׁבְּחָתָא וְנֶחֱמָתָא

דַּאֲמִירָן בְּעָלְמָא, וְאִמְרוּ אָמֵן. (קהל: אָמֵן)

יְהֵא שְׁלָמָא רַבָּא מִן שְׁמַיָּא

וְחַיִּים, עָלֵינוּ וְעַל כָּל יִשְׂרָאֵל, וְאִמְרוּ אָמֵן. (קהל: אָמֵן)

Bow, take three steps back, as if taking leave of the Divine Presence,
then bow, first left, then right, then center, while saying:

עֹשֶׂה שָׁלוֹם בִּמְרוֹמָיו

הוּא יַעֲשֶׂה שָׁלוֹם

עָלֵינוּ וְעַל כָּל יִשְׂרָאֵל, וְאִמְרוּ אָמֵן. (קהל: אָמֵן)

THE DAILY PSALM

One of the following psalms is said on the appropriate day of the week as indicated.
After the psalm, the Mourner's Kaddish on page 620 is said.

Sunday: Today is the first day of the week,
on which the Levites used to say this psalm in the Temple:

לְדָוִד מִזְמוֹר A psalm of David. The earth is the LORD's and all it contains, the *Ps. 24* world and all who live in it. For He founded it on the seas and established it on the streams. Who may climb the mountain of the LORD? Who may stand in His holy place? He who has clean hands and a pure heart, who has not taken My name in vain or sworn deceitfully. He shall receive a blessing from the LORD, and just reward from the God of his salvation. This is a generation of those who seek Him, the descendants of Jacob who seek Your presence, Selah! Lift up your heads, O gates; be uplifted, eternal doors, so that the King of glory may enter. Who is the King of glory? It is the LORD, strong and mighty, the LORD mighty in battle. Lift up your heads, O gates; lift them up, eternal doors, that the King of glory may enter. ‣ Who is He, the King of glory? The LORD of hosts, He is the King of glory, Selah!

Mourner's Kaddish (page 620)

Monday: Today is the second day of the week,
on which the Levites used to say this psalm in the Temple:

שִׁיר מִזְמוֹר A song. A psalm of the sons of Koraḥ. Great is the LORD and *Ps. 48* greatly to be praised in the city of God, on His holy mountain – beautiful in its heights, joy of all the earth, Mount Zion on its northern side, city of the great King. In its citadels God is known as a stronghold. See how the kings joined forces, advancing together. They saw, they were astounded, they panicked, they fled. There fear seized them, like the pains of a woman giving birth, like ships of Tarshish wrecked by an eastern wind. What we had heard, now we have seen, in the city of the LORD of hosts, in the city of our God. May God preserve it for ever, Selah! In the midst of Your Temple, God, we meditate on Your love. As is Your name, God, so is Your praise: it reaches to the ends of the earth. Your right hand is filled with righteousness. Let Mount Zion rejoice, let the towns of Judah be glad, because of Your judgments. Walk around Zion and encircle it. Count its towers, note its strong walls, view its citadels, so that you may tell a future generation ‣ that this is God, our God, for ever and ever. He will guide us for evermore.

Mourner's Kaddish (page 620)

שיר של יום

One of the following psalms is said on the appropriate day of the week as indicated.
After the psalm, קדיש יתום on page 621 is said.

Sunday הַיּוֹם יוֹם רִאשׁוֹן בְּשַׁבָּת, שֶׁבּוֹ הָיוּ הַלְוִיִּם אוֹמְרִים בְּבֵית הַמִּקְדָּשׁ:

תהלים כד לְדָוִד מִזְמוֹר, לַיהוה הָאָרֶץ וּמְלוֹאָהּ, תֵּבֵל וְיֹשְׁבֵי בָהּ: כִּי־הוּא עַל־
יַמִּים יְסָדָהּ, וְעַל־נְהָרוֹת יְכוֹנְנֶהָ: מִי־יַעֲלֶה בְהַר־יהוה, וּמִי־יָקוּם
בִּמְקוֹם קָדְשׁוֹ: נְקִי כַפַּיִם וּבַר־לֵבָב, אֲשֶׁר לֹא־נָשָׂא לַשָּׁוְא נַפְשִׁי,
וְלֹא נִשְׁבַּע לְמִרְמָה: יִשָּׂא בְרָכָה מֵאֵת יהוה, וּצְדָקָה מֵאֱלֹהֵי יִשְׁעוֹ:
זֶה דּוֹר דֹּרְשָׁו, מְבַקְשֵׁי פָנֶיךָ יַעֲקֹב סֶלָה: שְׂאוּ שְׁעָרִים רָאשֵׁיכֶם,
וְהִנָּשְׂאוּ פִּתְחֵי עוֹלָם, וְיָבוֹא מֶלֶךְ הַכָּבוֹד: מִי זֶה מֶלֶךְ הַכָּבוֹד, יהוה
עִזּוּז וְגִבּוֹר, יהוה גִּבּוֹר מִלְחָמָה: שְׂאוּ שְׁעָרִים רָאשֵׁיכֶם, וּשְׂאוּ פִּתְחֵי
עוֹלָם, וְיָבֹא מֶלֶךְ הַכָּבוֹד: ‹ מִי הוּא זֶה מֶלֶךְ הַכָּבוֹד, יהוה צְבָאוֹת
הוּא מֶלֶךְ הַכָּבוֹד סֶלָה: (page 621) קדיש יתום

Monday הַיּוֹם יוֹם שֵׁנִי בְּשַׁבָּת, שֶׁבּוֹ הָיוּ הַלְוִיִּם אוֹמְרִים בְּבֵית הַמִּקְדָּשׁ:

תהלים מח שִׁיר מִזְמוֹר לִבְנֵי־קֹרַח: גָּדוֹל יהוה וּמְהֻלָּל מְאֹד, בְּעִיר אֱלֹהֵינוּ, הַר־
קָדְשׁוֹ: יְפֵה נוֹף מְשׂוֹשׂ כָּל־הָאָרֶץ, הַר־צִיּוֹן יַרְכְּתֵי צָפוֹן, קִרְיַת מֶלֶךְ
רָב: אֱלֹהִים בְּאַרְמְנוֹתֶיהָ נוֹדַע לְמִשְׂגָּב: כִּי־הִנֵּה הַמְּלָכִים נוֹעֲדוּ,
עָבְרוּ יַחְדָּו: הֵמָּה רָאוּ כֵּן תָּמָהוּ, נִבְהֲלוּ נֶחְפָּזוּ: רְעָדָה אֲחָזָתַם שָׁם,
חִיל כַּיּוֹלֵדָה: בְּרוּחַ קָדִים תְּשַׁבֵּר אֳנִיּוֹת תַּרְשִׁישׁ: כַּאֲשֶׁר שָׁמַעְנוּ כֵּן
רָאִינוּ, בְּעִיר־יהוה צְבָאוֹת, בְּעִיר אֱלֹהֵינוּ, אֱלֹהִים יְכוֹנְנֶהָ עַד־עוֹלָם
סֶלָה: דִּמִּינוּ אֱלֹהִים חַסְדֶּךָ, בְּקֶרֶב הֵיכָלֶךָ: כְּשִׁמְךָ אֱלֹהִים כֵּן תְּהִלָּתְךָ
עַל־קַצְוֵי־אֶרֶץ, צֶדֶק מָלְאָה יְמִינֶךָ: יִשְׂמַח הַר־צִיּוֹן, תָּגֵלְנָה בְּנוֹת
יְהוּדָה, לְמַעַן מִשְׁפָּטֶיךָ: סֹבּוּ צִיּוֹן וְהַקִּיפוּהָ, סִפְרוּ מִגְדָּלֶיהָ: שִׁיתוּ
לִבְּכֶם לְחֵילָה, פַּסְּגוּ אַרְמְנוֹתֶיהָ, לְמַעַן תְּסַפְּרוּ לְדוֹר אַחֲרוֹן: ‹ כִּי זֶה
אֱלֹהִים אֱלֹהֵינוּ עוֹלָם וָעֶד, הוּא יְנַהֲגֵנוּ עַל־מוּת: (page 621) קדיש יתום

Wednesday: Today is the fourth day of the week,
on which the Levites used to say this psalm in the Temple:

אֵל־נְקָמוֹת God of retribution, Lord, God of retribution, appear! Rise up, *Ps. 94*
Judge of the earth. Repay to the arrogant what they deserve. How long shall
the wicked, Lord, how long shall the wicked triumph? They pour out insolent
words. All the evildoers are full of boasting. They crush Your people, Lord,
and oppress Your inheritance. They kill the widow and the stranger. They
murder the orphaned. They say, "The Lord does not see. The God of Jacob
pays no heed." Take heed, you most brutish people. You fools, when will you
grow wise? Will He who implants the ear not hear? Will He who formed the
eye not see? Will He who disciplines nations – He who teaches man knowledge – not punish? The Lord knows that the thoughts of man are a mere
fleeting breath. Happy is the man whom You discipline, Lord, the one You
instruct in Your Torah, giving him tranquility in days of trouble, until a pit is
dug for the wicked. For the Lord will not forsake His people, nor abandon
His heritage. Judgment shall again accord with justice, and all the upright in
heart will follow it. Who will rise up for me against the wicked? Who will
stand up for me against wrongdoers? Had the Lord not been my help, I would
soon have dwelt in death's silence. When I thought my foot was slipping, Your
loving-kindness, Lord, gave me support. When I was filled with anxiety, Your
consolations soothed my soul. Can a corrupt throne be allied with You? Can
injustice be framed into law? They join forces against the life of the righteous,
and condemn the innocent to death. But the Lord is my stronghold, my God
is the Rock of my refuge. He will bring back on them their wickedness, and
destroy them for their evil deeds. The Lord our God will destroy them.
‣ Come, let us sing for joy to the Lord; let us shout aloud to the Rock of our *Ps. 95*
salvation. Let us greet Him with thanksgiving, shout aloud to Him with songs
of praise. For the Lord is the great God, the King great above all powers.

Mourner's Kaddish (page 620)

Friday: Today is the sixth day of the week,
on which the Levites used to say this psalm in the Temple:

יהוה מָלָךְ The Lord reigns. He is robed in majesty. The Lord is robed, girded *Ps. 93*
with strength. The world is firmly established; it cannot be moved. Your
throne stands firm as of old; You are eternal. Rivers lift up, Lord, rivers lift
up their voice, rivers lift up their crashing waves. Mightier than the noise of
many waters, than the mighty waves of the sea is the Lord on high. ‣ Your
testimonies are very sure; holiness adorns Your House, Lord, for evermore.

Mourner's Kaddish (page 620)

הַיּוֹם יוֹם רְבִיעִי בְּשַׁבָּת, שֶׁבּוֹ הָיוּ הַלְוִיִּם אוֹמְרִים בְּבֵית הַמִּקְדָּשׁ: *Wednesday*

אֵל־נְקָמוֹת יהוה, אֵל נְקָמוֹת הוֹפִיעַ: הִנָּשֵׂא שֹׁפֵט הָאָרֶץ, הָשֵׁב גְּמוּל תהלים צד
עַל־גֵּאִים: עַד־מָתַי רְשָׁעִים, יהוה, עַד־מָתַי רְשָׁעִים יַעֲלֹזוּ: יַבִּיעוּ
יְדַבְּרוּ עָתָק, יִתְאַמְּרוּ כָּל־פֹּעֲלֵי אָוֶן: עַמְּךָ יהוה יְדַכְּאוּ, וְנַחֲלָתְךָ
יְעַנּוּ: אַלְמָנָה וְגֵר יַהֲרֹגוּ, וִיתוֹמִים יְרַצֵּחוּ: וַיֹּאמְרוּ לֹא יִרְאֶה־יָּהּ, וְלֹא־
יָבִין אֱלֹהֵי יַעֲקֹב: בִּינוּ בֹּעֲרִים בָּעָם, וּכְסִילִים מָתַי תַּשְׂכִּילוּ: הֲנֹטַע
אֹזֶן הֲלֹא יִשְׁמָע, אִם־יֹצֵר עַיִן הֲלֹא יַבִּיט: הֲיֹסֵר גּוֹיִם הֲלֹא יוֹכִיחַ,
הַמְלַמֵּד אָדָם דָּעַת: יהוה יֹדֵעַ מַחְשְׁבוֹת אָדָם, כִּי־הֵמָּה הָבֶל: אַשְׁרֵי
הַגֶּבֶר אֲשֶׁר־תְּיַסְּרֶנּוּ יָּהּ, וּמִתּוֹרָתְךָ תְלַמְּדֶנּוּ: לְהַשְׁקִיט לוֹ מִימֵי רָע,
עַד יִכָּרֶה לָרָשָׁע שָׁחַת: כִּי לֹא־יִטֹּשׁ יהוה עַמּוֹ, וְנַחֲלָתוֹ לֹא יַעֲזֹב:
כִּי־עַד־צֶדֶק יָשׁוּב מִשְׁפָּט, וְאַחֲרָיו כָּל־יִשְׁרֵי־לֵב: מִי־יָקוּם לִי עִם־
מְרֵעִים, מִי־יִתְיַצֵּב לִי עִם־פֹּעֲלֵי אָוֶן: לוּלֵי יהוה עֶזְרָתָה לִּי, כִּמְעַט
שָׁכְנָה דוּמָה נַפְשִׁי: אִם־אָמַרְתִּי מָטָה רַגְלִי, חַסְדְּךָ יהוה יִסְעָדֵנִי:
בְּרֹב שַׂרְעַפַּי בְּקִרְבִּי, תַּנְחוּמֶיךָ יְשַׁעַשְׁעוּ נַפְשִׁי: הַיְחָבְרְךָ כִּסֵּא הַוּוֹת,
יֹצֵר עָמָל עֲלֵי־חֹק: יָגוֹדּוּ עַל־נֶפֶשׁ צַדִּיק, וְדָם נָקִי יַרְשִׁיעוּ: וַיְהִי יהוה
לִי לְמִשְׂגָּב, וֵאלֹהַי לְצוּר מַחְסִי: וַיָּשֶׁב עֲלֵיהֶם אֶת־אוֹנָם, וּבְרָעָתָם
יַצְמִיתֵם, יַצְמִיתֵם יהוה אֱלֹהֵינוּ:

‹ לְכוּ נְרַנְּנָה לַיהוה, נָרִיעָה לְצוּר יִשְׁעֵנוּ: נְקַדְּמָה פָנָיו בְּתוֹדָה, בִּזְמִרוֹת תהלים צה
נָרִיעַ לוֹ: כִּי אֵל גָּדוֹל יהוה, וּמֶלֶךְ גָּדוֹל עַל־כָּל־אֱלֹהִים:

קדיש יתום *(page 621)*

הַיּוֹם יוֹם שִׁשִּׁי בְּשַׁבָּת, שֶׁבּוֹ הָיוּ הַלְוִיִּם אוֹמְרִים בְּבֵית הַמִּקְדָּשׁ *Friday*

יהוה מָלָךְ, גֵּאוּת לָבֵשׁ, לָבֵשׁ יהוה עֹז הִתְאַזָּר, אַף־תִּכּוֹן תֵּבֵל בַּל־ תהלים צג
תִּמּוֹט: נָכוֹן כִּסְאֲךָ מֵאָז, מֵעוֹלָם אָתָּה: נָשְׂאוּ נְהָרוֹת יהוה, נָשְׂאוּ
נְהָרוֹת קוֹלָם, יִשְׂאוּ נְהָרוֹת דָּכְיָם: מִקֹּלוֹת מַיִם רַבִּים, אַדִּירִים מִשְׁבְּרֵי־
יָם, אַדִּיר בַּמָּרוֹם יהוה: ‹ עֵדֹתֶיךָ נֶאֶמְנוּ מְאֹד, לְבֵיתְךָ נַאֲוָה־קֹדֶשׁ,
יהוה לְאֹרֶךְ יָמִים:

קדיש יתום *(page 621)*

In Israel the following through "Bless the LORD," *on page 630, is said.*

אֵין כֵּאלֹהֵינוּ There is none like our God, none like our LORD, none like our King, none like our Savior. Who is like our God? Like our LORD? Like our King? Like our Savior? We will thank our God, thank our LORD, thank our King, thank our Savior. Blessed is our God, blessed our LORD, blessed our King, blessed our Savior. You are our God, You are our LORD, You are our King, You are our Savior. You are He to whom our ancestors offered the fragrant incense.

פִּטוּם הַקְּטֹרֶת The incense mixture consisted of balsam, onycha, galbanum and frankincense, each weighing seventy manehs; myrrh, cassia, spikenard and saffron, each weighing sixteen manehs; twelve manehs of costus, three of aromatic bark; nine of cinnamon; nine kabs of Carsina lye; three seahs and three kabs of Cyprus wine. If Cyprus wine was not available, old white wine might be used. A quarter of a kab of Sodom salt, and a minute amount of a smoke-raising herb. Rabbi Nathan says: Also a minute amount of Jordan amber. If one added honey to the mixture, he rendered it unfit for sacred use. If he omitted any one of its ingredients, he is guilty of a capital offence. *Keritot 6a*

Rabban Shimon ben Gamliel says: "Balsam" refers to the sap that drips from the balsam tree. The Carsina lye was used for bleaching the onycha to improve it. The Cyprus wine was used to soak the onycha in it to make it pungent. Though urine is suitable for this purpose, it is not brought into the Temple out of respect.

It was taught in the Academy of Elijah: Whoever studies [Torah] laws every day is assured that he will be destined for the World to Come, as it is said, "The ways of the world are His" – read not, "ways" [*halikhot*] but "laws" [*halakhot*]. *Megilla 28b* / *Hab. 3*

Rabbi Elazar said in the name of Rabbi Ḥanina: The disciples of the sages increase peace in the world, as it is said, "And all your children shall be taught of the LORD, and great shall be the peace of your children [*banayikh*]." Read not *banayikh*, "your children," but *bonayikh*, "your builders." Those who love Your Torah have great peace; there is no stumbling block for them. May there be peace within your ramparts, prosperity in your palaces. For the sake of my brothers and friends, I shall say, "Peace be within you." For the sake of the House of the LORD our God, I will seek your good. ‣ May the LORD grant strength to His people; may the LORD bless His people with peace. *Berakhot 64a* / *Is. 54* / *Ps. 119* / *Ps. 122* / *Ps. 29*

In ארץ ישראל the following through בָּרְכוּ, on page 631, is said:

אֵין כֵּאלֹהֵינוּ, אֵין כַּאדוֹנֵינוּ, אֵין כְּמַלְכֵּנוּ, אֵין כְּמוֹשִׁיעֵנוּ. מִי
כֵאלֹהֵינוּ, מִי כַאדוֹנֵינוּ, מִי כְמַלְכֵּנוּ, מִי כְמוֹשִׁיעֵנוּ. נוֹדֶה לֵאלֹהֵינוּ,
נוֹדֶה לַאדוֹנֵינוּ, נוֹדֶה לְמַלְכֵּנוּ, נוֹדֶה לְמוֹשִׁיעֵנוּ. בָּרוּךְ אֱלֹהֵינוּ, בָּרוּךְ
אֲדוֹנֵינוּ, בָּרוּךְ מַלְכֵּנוּ, בָּרוּךְ מוֹשִׁיעֵנוּ. אַתָּה הוּא אֱלֹהֵינוּ, אַתָּה
הוּא אֲדוֹנֵינוּ, אַתָּה הוּא מַלְכֵּנוּ, אַתָּה הוּא מוֹשִׁיעֵנוּ. אַתָּה הוּא
שֶׁהִקְטִירוּ אֲבוֹתֵינוּ לְפָנֶיךָ אֶת קְטֹרֶת הַסַּמִּים.

כריתות ו

פִּטוּם הַקְּטֹרֶת: הַצֳּרִי, וְהַצִּפֹּרֶן, וְהַחֶלְבְּנָה, וְהַלְּבוֹנָה מִשְׁקַל שִׁבְעִים שִׁבְעִים
מָנֶה, מֹר, וּקְצִיעָה, שִׁבֹּלֶת נֵרְדְּ, וְכַרְכֹּם מִשְׁקַל שִׁשָּׁה עָשָׂר שִׁשָּׁה עָשָׂר מָנֶה,
הַקֹּשְׁטְ שְׁנֵים עָשָׂר, קִלּוּפָה שְׁלֹשָׁה, וְקִנָּמוֹן תִּשְׁעָה, בֹּרִית כַּרְשִׁינָה תִּשְׁעָה
קַבִּין, יֵין קַפְרִיסִין סְאִין תְּלָת וְקַבִּין תְּלָתָא, וְאִם אֵין לוֹ יֵין קַפְרִיסִין, מֵבִיא
חֲמַר חִוַּרְיָן עַתִּיק. מֶלַח סְדוֹמִית רֹבַע, מַעֲלֶה עָשָׁן כָּל שֶׁהוּא. רַבִּי נָתָן הַבַּבְלִי
אוֹמֵר: אַף כִּפַּת הַיַּרְדֵּן כָּל שֶׁהוּא, וְאִם נָתַן בָּהּ דְּבַשׁ פְּסָלָהּ, וְאִם חִסַּר אֶחָד
מִכָּל סַמָּנֶיהָ, חַיָּב מִיתָה.

רַבָּן שִׁמְעוֹן בֶּן גַּמְלִיאֵל אוֹמֵר: הַצֳּרִי אֵינוֹ אֶלָּא שְׂרָף הַנּוֹטֵף מֵעֲצֵי הַקְּטָף.
בֹּרִית כַּרְשִׁינָה שֶׁשָּׁפִין בָּהּ אֶת הַצִּפֹּרֶן כְּדֵי שֶׁתְּהֵא נָאָה, יֵין קַפְרִיסִין שֶׁשּׁוֹרִין
בּוֹ אֶת הַצִּפֹּרֶן כְּדֵי שֶׁתְּהֵא עַזָּה, וַהֲלֹא מֵי רַגְלַיִם יָפִין לָהּ, אֶלָּא שֶׁאֵין מַכְנִיסִין
מֵי רַגְלַיִם בַּמִּקְדָּשׁ מִפְּנֵי הַכָּבוֹד.

מגילה כח:

תָּנָא דְּבֵי אֵלִיָּהוּ: כָּל הַשּׁוֹנֶה הֲלָכוֹת בְּכָל יוֹם, מֻבְטָח לוֹ שֶׁהוּא בֶן עוֹלָם

חבקוק ג

הַבָּא, שֶׁנֶּאֱמַר הֲלִיכוֹת עוֹלָם לוֹ: אַל תִּקְרֵי הֲלִיכוֹת אֶלָּא הֲלָכוֹת.

ברכות סד.
ישעיה נד
תהלים קכב
תהלים קיט

אָמַר רַבִּי אֶלְעָזָר, אָמַר רַבִּי חֲנִינָא: תַּלְמִידֵי חֲכָמִים מַרְבִּים שָׁלוֹם בָּעוֹלָם,
שֶׁנֶּאֱמַר וְכָל־בָּנַיִךְ לִמּוּדֵי יהוה, וְרַב שְׁלוֹם בָּנָיִךְ: אַל תִּקְרֵי בָּנָיִךְ, אֶלָּא
בּוֹנָיִךְ. שָׁלוֹם רָב לְאֹהֲבֵי תוֹרָתֶךָ, וְאֵין־לָמוֹ מִכְשׁוֹל: יְהִי־שָׁלוֹם בְּחֵילֵךְ,
שַׁלְוָה בְּאַרְמְנוֹתָיִךְ: לְמַעַן אַחַי וְרֵעָי אֲדַבְּרָה־נָּא שָׁלוֹם בָּךְ: לְמַעַן בֵּית

תהלים כט

יהוה אֱלֹהֵינוּ אֲבַקְשָׁה טוֹב לָךְ: ◂ יהוה עֹז לְעַמּוֹ יִתֵּן, יהוה יְבָרֵךְ אֶת־
עַמּוֹ בַשָּׁלוֹם:

THE RABBIS' KADDISH

The following prayer, said by mourners, requires the presence of a minyan.
A transliteration can be found on page 666.

Mourner: יִתְגַּדַּל Magnified and sanctified may His great name be,
in the world He created by His will.
May He establish His kingdom in your lifetime
and in your days,
and in the lifetime of all the house of Israel,
swiftly and soon – and say: Amen.

All: May His great name be blessed for ever and all time.

Mourner: Blessed and praised, glorified and exalted,
raised and honored, uplifted and lauded be
the name of the Holy One,
blessed be He,
beyond any blessing,
song, praise and consolation
uttered in the world – and say: Amen.

To Israel, to the teachers,
their disciples and their disciples' disciples,
and to all who engage in the study of Torah,
in this (*in Israel add:* holy) place or elsewhere,
may there come to them and you
great peace, grace,
kindness and compassion,
long life, ample sustenance and deliverance,
from their Father in Heaven – and say: Amen.

May there be great peace from heaven,
and (good) life for us and all Israel – and say: Amen.

Bow, take three steps back, as if taking leave of the Divine Presence,
then bow, first left, then right, then center, while saying:
May He who makes peace in His high places,
in His compassion make peace
for us and all Israel – and say: Amen.

קדיש דרבנן

The following prayer, said by mourners, requires the presence of a מנין.
A transliteration can be found on page 666.

אבל יִתְגַּדַּל וְיִתְקַדַּשׁ שְׁמֵהּ רַבָּא (קהל: אָמֵן)
בְּעָלְמָא דִּי בְרָא כִרְעוּתֵהּ
וְיַמְלִיךְ מַלְכוּתֵהּ
בְּחַיֵּיכוֹן וּבְיוֹמֵיכוֹן וּבְחַיֵּי דְּכָל בֵּית יִשְׂרָאֵל
בַּעֲגָלָא וּבִזְמַן קָרִיב, וְאִמְרוּ אָמֵן. (קהל: אָמֵן)

קהל
ואבל
יְהֵא שְׁמֵהּ רַבָּא מְבָרַךְ לְעָלַם וּלְעָלְמֵי עָלְמַיָּא.

אבל יִתְבָּרַךְ וְיִשְׁתַּבַּח וְיִתְפָּאַר וְיִתְרוֹמַם וְיִתְנַשֵּׂא
וְיִתְהַדָּר וְיִתְעַלֶּה וְיִתְהַלָּל
שְׁמֵהּ דְּקֻדְשָׁא בְּרִיךְ הוּא (קהל: בְּרִיךְ הוּא)
לְעֵלָּא מִן כָּל בִּרְכָתָא וְשִׁירָתָא, תֻּשְׁבְּחָתָא וְנֶחֱמָתָא
דַּאֲמִירָן בְּעָלְמָא, וְאִמְרוּ אָמֵן. (קהל: אָמֵן)

עַל יִשְׂרָאֵל וְעַל רַבָּנָן, וְעַל תַּלְמִידֵיהוֹן
וְעַל כָּל תַּלְמִידֵי תַלְמִידֵיהוֹן, וְעַל כָּל מָאן דְּעָסְקִין בְּאוֹרַיְתָא
דִּי בְאַתְרָא (בארץ ישראל: קַדִּישָׁא) הָדֵין וְדִי בְכָל אֲתַר וַאֲתַר
יְהֵא לְהוֹן וּלְכוֹן שְׁלָמָא רַבָּא
חִנָּא וְחִסְדָּא, וְרַחֲמֵי, וְחַיֵּי אֲרִיכֵי, וּמְזוֹנֵי רְוִיחֵי
וּפֻרְקָנָא מִן קָדָם אֲבוּהוֹן דִּי בִשְׁמַיָּא, וְאִמְרוּ אָמֵן. (קהל: אָמֵן)

יְהֵא שְׁלָמָא רַבָּא מִן שְׁמַיָּא
וְחַיִּים (טוֹבִים) עָלֵינוּ וְעַל כָּל יִשְׂרָאֵל, וְאִמְרוּ אָמֵן. (קהל: אָמֵן)

Bow, take three steps back, as if taking leave of the Divine Presence,
then bow, first left, then right, then center, while saying:

עֹשֶׂה שָׁלוֹם בִּמְרוֹמָיו
הוּא יַעֲשֶׂה בְרַחֲמָיו שָׁלוֹם
עָלֵינוּ וְעַל כָּל יִשְׂרָאֵל, וְאִמְרוּ אָמֵן. (קהל: אָמֵן)

In Israel, on days when the Torah is not read,
the person saying Kaddish adds:

Bless the LORD, the blessed One.

and the congregation responds:

Bless the LORD, the blessed One, for ever and all time.

All sing:

אֲנִי מַאֲמִין I believe
with perfect faith
in the coming of the Messiah,
and though he may delay,
I wait daily for his coming.

In the War of Independence, great pains were taken to restore the nation's heart – the Old City and the Western Wall. You have merited to close the circle, to restore the nation's capital and its holy center. Many paratroopers, our best and oldest friends, have fallen in this difficult campaign. It was a daring and spirited battle, where you acted as a force that crushes all that meets its path without giving thought to its own wounds. You did not argue, you did not complain, you did not cry out. You only struggled forward – and you conquered. Jerusalem is yours forever. (Lt. Gen. Mordekhai "Motta" Gur, June 1967)

*In ארץ ישראל, on days when the תורה is not read,
the person saying קדיש adds:*

בָּרְכוּ אֶת יהוה הַמְבֹרָךְ.

and the קהל responds:

בָּרוּךְ יהוה הַמְבֹרָךְ לְעוֹלָם וָעֶד.

All sing:

אֲנִי מַאֲמִין בֶּאֱמוּנָה שְׁלֵמָה
בְּבִיאַת הַמָּשִׁיחַ
וְאַף עַל פִּי שֶׁיִּתְמַהְמֵהַּ
עִם כָּל זֶה אֲחַכֶּה לוֹ בְּכָל יוֹם שֶׁיָּבוֹא.

JERUSALEM, A CROWN OF GLORY

For two thousand years the Temple Mount was forbidden to the Jews. Until you came, you paratroopers, and returned it to the bosom of the nation. The Western Wall – where every heart beats – is in our hands once again.

Throughout our long history, many Jews have taken their lives in their hands in order to reach Jerusalem and live within it. Countless songs of yearning have expressed the deep longing for Jerusalem that throbs in the Jewish heart.

ברכות

GIVING THANKS

THE MEAL AND ITS BLESSINGS

On washing hands before eating bread:

Blessed are You, LORD our God, King of the Universe,
who has made us holy through His commandments,
and has commanded us about washing hands.

Before eating bread:

Blessed are You, LORD our God, King of the Universe,
who brings forth bread from the earth.

BIRKAT HAMAZON / GRACE AFTER MEALS

It is customary to sing this psalm to the melody of HaTikva:

שִׁיר הַמַּעֲלוֹת A song of ascents.   *Ps. 126*
When the LORD brought back the exiles of Zion
we were like people who dream.
Then were our mouths filled with laughter,
and our tongues with songs of joy.
Then was it said among the nations,
"The LORD has done great things for them."
The LORD did do great things for us and we rejoiced.
Bring back our exiles, LORD, like streams in a dry land.
May those who sowed in tears, reap in joy.
May one who goes out weeping, carrying a bag of seed,
come back with songs of joy, carrying his sheaves.

Some say:

תְּהִלַּת My mouth shall speak the praise of God,   *Ps. 145*
and all creatures shall bless His holy name
for ever and all time.
We will bless God now and for ever.   *Ps. 115*
Halleluya! Thank the LORD for He is good;   *Ps. 136*
His loving-kindness is for ever.
Who can tell of the LORD's mighty acts   *Ps. 106*
and make all His praise be heard?

סדר סעודה וברכותיה

On washing hands before eating bread:

בָּרוּךְ אַתָּה יהוה אֱלֹהֵינוּ מֶלֶךְ הָעוֹלָם
אֲשֶׁר קִדְּשָׁנוּ בְּמִצְוֹתָיו וְצִוָּנוּ עַל נְטִילַת יָדֵיִם.

Before eating bread:

בָּרוּךְ אַתָּה יהוה אֱלֹהֵינוּ מֶלֶךְ הָעוֹלָם
הַמּוֹצִיא לֶחֶם מִן הָאָרֶץ.

ברכת המזון

It is customary to sing this psalm to the melody of התקווה:

תהלים קכו

שִׁיר הַמַּעֲלוֹת
בְּשׁוּב יהוה אֶת־שִׁיבַת צִיּוֹן, הָיִינוּ כְּחֹלְמִים:
אָז יִמָּלֵא שְׂחוֹק פִּינוּ וּלְשׁוֹנֵנוּ רִנָּה
אָז יֹאמְרוּ בַגּוֹיִם הִגְדִּיל יהוה לַעֲשׂוֹת עִם־אֵלֶּה:
הִגְדִּיל יהוה לַעֲשׂוֹת עִמָּנוּ, הָיִינוּ שְׂמֵחִים:
שׁוּבָה יהוה אֶת־שְׁבִיתֵנוּ, כַּאֲפִיקִים בַּנֶּגֶב:
הַזֹּרְעִים בְּדִמְעָה בְּרִנָּה יִקְצֹרוּ:
הָלוֹךְ יֵלֵךְ וּבָכֹה נֹשֵׂא מֶשֶׁךְ־הַזָּרַע
בֹּא־יָבֹא בְרִנָּה נֹשֵׂא אֲלֻמֹּתָיו:

Some say:

תהלים קמה

תְּהִלַּת יהוה יְדַבֶּר פִּי
וִיבָרֵךְ כָּל־בָּשָׂר שֵׁם קָדְשׁוֹ לְעוֹלָם וָעֶד:

תהלים קטו
וַאֲנַחְנוּ נְבָרֵךְ יָהּ מֵעַתָּה וְעַד־עוֹלָם, הַלְלוּיָהּ:
תהלים קלו
הוֹדוּ לַיהוה כִּי־טוֹב, כִּי לְעוֹלָם חַסְדּוֹ:
תהלים קו
מִי יְמַלֵּל גְּבוּרוֹת יהוה, יַשְׁמִיעַ כָּל־תְּהִלָּתוֹ:

ZIMMUN / INVITATION

When three or more men say Birkat HaMazon together, the following zimmun is said.
When three or more women say Birkat HaMazon, substitute "Friends" for "Gentlemen."
The leader should ask permission from those with precedence to lead the Birkat HaMazon.

Leader Gentlemen, let us say grace.

Others May the name of the LORD be blessed from now and for ever. *Ps. 113*

Leader May the name of the LORD be blessed from now and for ever.
With your permission, (my father and teacher / my mother and
teacher / the Kohanim present / our teacher the Rabbi /
the master of this house / the mistress of this house)
my masters and teachers,
let us bless (*in a minyan:* our God,) the One
from whose food we have eaten.

Others Blessed be (*in a minyan:* our God,) the One
from whose food we have eaten, and by whose goodness we live.

*People present who have not taken part in the meal say:
**Blessed be (in a minyan: our God,) the One
whose name is continually blessed for ever and all time.

Leader Blessed be (*in a minyan:* our God,) the One
from whose food we have eaten, and by whose goodness we live.
Blessed be He, and blessed be His name.

BLESSING OF NOURISHMENT

בָּרוּךְ Blessed are You, LORD our God, King of the Universe,
who in His goodness feeds the whole world
with grace, kindness and compassion.
He gives food to all living things,
for His kindness is for ever.
Because of His continual great goodness,
we have never lacked food,
nor may we ever lack it, for the sake of His great name.
For He is God who feeds and sustains all, does good to all,
and prepares food for all creatures He has created.
Blessed are You, LORD, who feeds all.

סדר הזימון

When three or more men say ברכת המזון together, the following זימון is said.
When three or more women say ברכת המזון, substitute חֲבֵרוֹתַי for רַבּוֹתַי.
The leader should ask permission from those with precedence to lead the ברכת המזון.

Leader   רַבּוֹתַי, נְבָרֵךְ.

תהלים קיג   Others   יְהִי שֵׁם יהוה מְבֹרָךְ מֵעַתָּה וְעַד־עוֹלָם:

Leader   יְהִי שֵׁם יהוה מְבֹרָךְ מֵעַתָּה וְעַד־עוֹלָם:

בִּרְשׁוּת (אָבִי מוֹרִי / אִמִּי מוֹרָתִי / כֹּהֲנִים / מוֹרֵנוּ הָרַב /
בַּעַל הַבַּיִת הַזֶּה / בַּעֲלַת הַבַּיִת הַזֶּה)

מָרָנָן וְרַבָּנָן וְרַבּוֹתַי

נְבָרֵךְ (במנין: אֱלֹהֵינוּ) שֶׁאָכַלְנוּ מִשֶּׁלּוֹ.

Others   בָּרוּךְ (במנין: אֱלֹהֵינוּ) שֶׁאָכַלְנוּ מִשֶּׁלּוֹ וּבְטוּבוֹ חָיִינוּ.

People present who have not taken part in the meal say:

*בָּרוּךְ (במנין: אֱלֹהֵינוּ) וּמְבֹרָךְ שְׁמוֹ תָּמִיד לְעוֹלָם וָעֶד.

Leader   בָּרוּךְ (במנין: אֱלֹהֵינוּ) שֶׁאָכַלְנוּ מִשֶּׁלּוֹ וּבְטוּבוֹ חָיִינוּ.
בָּרוּךְ הוּא וּבָרוּךְ שְׁמוֹ.

ברכת הזן

בָּרוּךְ אַתָּה יהוה אֱלֹהֵינוּ מֶלֶךְ הָעוֹלָם
הַזָּן אֶת הָעוֹלָם כֻּלּוֹ בְּטוּבוֹ, בְּחֵן בְּחֶסֶד וּבְרַחֲמִים
הוּא נוֹתֵן לֶחֶם לְכָל בָּשָׂר, כִּי לְעוֹלָם חַסְדּוֹ.
וּבְטוּבוֹ הַגָּדוֹל, תָּמִיד לֹא חָסַר לָנוּ
וְאַל יֶחְסַר לָנוּ מָזוֹן לְעוֹלָם וָעֶד
בַּעֲבוּר שְׁמוֹ הַגָּדוֹל.
כִּי הוּא אֵל זָן וּמְפַרְנֵס לַכֹּל וּמֵטִיב לַכֹּל
וּמֵכִין מָזוֹן לְכָל בְּרִיּוֹתָיו אֲשֶׁר בָּרָא.
בָּרוּךְ אַתָּה יהוה, הַזָּן אֶת הַכֹּל.

BLESSING OF THE LAND

נוֹדֶה We thank You, LORD our God,
for having granted as a heritage to our ancestors
a desirable, good and spacious land;

SOME SCORNED THE STONES WHILE OTHERS GLORIFY

As disastrous as the *Egel* transgression was, HaKadosh Barukh Hu forgave the Jewish nation and was prepared to revive the original plan. However the fiasco of the *Meraglim* was less tolerable or forgivable, and the Jews were sent into a forty-year exile. Though He is willing to waive His own honor, God is less forgiving of slights to the Land of Israel. Recalling this failure, David HaMelekh claims, "Then they despised the pleasant land, having no faith in His promise" (*Tehillim* 106:24). The loathing of *Eretz Yisrael* was unpardonable.

Sanḥerev of Ashur was the most feared monarch of his day and faced off against Ḥizkiyahu during the siege of Yerushalayim. The Gemara (*Sanhedrin* 94b) asserts that he was rewarded with power and prestige, in part because he didn't mock the Land of Israel when he proposed to relocate the Jews to his own homeland. He offers them: "Make your peace with me... Then each of you will eat of his own vine... his own fig tree... drink the water of his own cistern, until I come and take you away to a land like your own land, a land of grain and wine... bread and vineyards... olive trees and honey" (*II Melakhim* 18:31–32). Since he acknowledged and broadcast the quality of Israel, he was empowered with glory.

Atoning for this scorn requires lavishing affection upon the Land of Israel. Reversing this disrespect is a vital precondition for redemption. David senses this prerequisite when he asserts, "our servants hold her stones dear and have pity on her dust. Nations will fear the name of the LORD, and all the kings of the earth will fear Your glory" (*Tehillim* 102:14–15). Until we covet the *stones and dirt* of Israel, redemption is delayed.

Ḥazal were highly sensitive to this expectation. The Gemara (*Ketubot* 113a) records that Rabbi Abba acted this out quite literally, by kissing the stones of Israel as he traveled through the border towns. Focusing on the dust, Rabbi Ḥanina ben Gamda actually rolled in the dirt of Israel. Rabbi Ḥanina wasn't satisfied with merely expressing his *personal* love; he cleaned the roads in Israel of any obstructions to assure that others would admire the Land as

ברכת הארץ
נוֹדֶה לְךָ, יהוה אֱלֹהֵינוּ
עַל שֶׁהִנְחַלְתָּ לַאֲבוֹתֵינוּ אֶרֶץ חֶמְדָּה טוֹבָה וּרְחָבָה

ברכת הארץ *Blessing of the land.* The second section of *Birkat HaMazon* was authored by Yehoshua, and addresses the gift of the Land of Israel. It details different features of the experience of receiving this divine gift. It reminds us that the Land is an appealing land (*Ḥemda Tova Ureḥava*), while reminding us that settling the land was the ultimate agenda for our emancipation from Egypt (*Ve'al SheHotzeitanu miEretz Mitzrayim*). The *berakha* stresses the covenantal nature of living in Israel by highlighting the personal covenants of *Brit Mila* (*Beritekha sheḤatamta bivsarenu*) and Torah (*Ve'al Toratekha shelimadtanu*).

The *berakha* concludes with a general blessing "upon the Land and its food." Thanking HaKadosh Barukh Hu for our food is a universal response, seemingly unrelated to the Land of Israel per se. In fact the first *berakha* of *Birkat HaMazon* expressed our appreciation for His sustaining all life. The second *berakha* restates this gratitude, and frames it within the appreciation of life in Israel.

One of the mistakes of the spies was the assumption that a divine covenant would operate only within supernatural circumstances. The Midrash comments, "they assumed that the Torah was delivered solely to consumers of manna." Unable to conceive of a covenant of Torah within normal human routine, they balked at the thought of entering Israel. As this passage would transition our nation from supernatural manna to natural food, they assumed it should be delayed or entirely suspended. This *berakha* reminds us of the objective of incorporating a covenant in the Land of Israel under natural conditions.

We have been absent from our land for close to two millennia and our connection to it was theoretical – in our hearts and prayers. This abstract encounter allows an "idealization" of life in Israel. It is sometimes difficult to appreciate sacred experiences when they are tethered to everyday routine. This *berakha* merges the Land of Israel as a covenant with the Land of Israel as a provider of food. The routine of the latter aspect doesn't dull the luster of the former.

for bringing us out, Lᴏʀᴅ our God, from the land of Egypt,
freeing us from the house of slavery;
for Your covenant which You sealed in our flesh;
for Your Torah which You taught us;
for Your laws which You made known to us;
for the life, grace and kindness You have bestowed on us;
and for the food by which You continually feed and sustain us,
every day, every season, every hour.

---

they were instructed to perform was circumcision. Due to health concerns
the mitzva was suspended under the dry and hazardous desert conditions. It
is unthinkable that a nation of uncircumcised Jews would lay claim to their
covenantal land.

Zekharia (9:11–12) reminds us of the indispensability of this mitzva in
facilitating our return to Israel: "As for you, because of the blood of My
covenant with you, I will free your prisoners from the waterless pit. Return
to your fortress, you prisoners of hope."

Furthermore an intriguing comment in the *Zohar* describes a mass "relocation" of the present residents of the land, to accommodate Jewish re-
population of their homeland. HaKadosh Barukh Hu evicts populations and
resettles [other] populations as He landscapes the country for His chosen
people. This population management occurs in response to our fulfillment
of the mitzva of *Mila*, which was so essential to the original Covenant of the
Land.

In his commentary to *Shir HaShirim*, the Ramban claims that this prophecy describes a pre-messianic stage in history in which general mitzva adherence has receded. Jewish conduct is likened to an empty cistern, because it
is devoid of mitzvot. Yet the prisoners will be returned to Israel based on the
merit of the "blood of My covenant" – a clear reference to the mitzva of *Mila*.

The comments of the Ramban have proven clairvoyant as we have returned
to our homeland. Unfortunately large segments of our population have yet to
embrace mitzvot in general; however *Mila* remains, by and large, a national
agenda. As we endeavor to fill our national cistern with renewed mitzva loyalty, the mitzva of *Mila* continues to buoy our presence in our Land.

וְעַל בְּרִיתְךָ שֶׁחָתַמְתָּ בִּבְשָׂרֵנוּ *For Your covenant which You sealed in our flesh.* Unlike most other mitzvot which are the unique province of the Jewish people,

וְעַל שֶׁהוֹצֵאתָנוּ יהוה אֱלֹהֵינוּ מֵאֶרֶץ מִצְרַיִם

וּפְדִיתָנוּ מִבֵּית עֲבָדִים

וְעַל בְּרִיתְךָ שֶׁחָתַמְתָּ בִּבְשָׂרֵנוּ

וְעַל תּוֹרָתְךָ שֶׁלִּמַּדְתָּנוּ

וְעַל חֻקֶּיךָ שֶׁהוֹדַעְתָּנוּ

וְעַל חַיִּים חֵן וָחֶסֶד שֶׁחוֹנַנְתָּנוּ

וְעַל אֲכִילַת מָזוֹן שָׁאַתָּה זָן וּמְפַרְנֵס אוֹתָנוּ תָּמִיד

בְּכָל יוֹם וּבְכָל עֵת וּבְכָל שָׁעָה.

---

well. Each had his own personal method for demonstrating his love for the Land of Israel and nullifying the insult of the *Meraglim*.

Centuries later Rabbi Yehuda HaLevi (*Kuzari* 5:27) highlighted this conduct. Ultimately he immigrated to Israel, and was able to demonstrably express his affection. In his well-known sonnet to Israel, *Tziyon Halo Tishali*, his love and regard for the actual land dominates the stanzas.

The Gemara (*Berakhot* 48b) claims that omitting the phrase "*Eretz Ḥemda Tova Ureḥava*" renders the *berakha* incomplete, and the *berakha* must be recited again. The central purpose of this *berakha* is to demonstrate our affection for the Land of Israel.

These legends have yielded the modern-day practice of kissing the ground of Israel upon first arrival. As we shower our land with affection, and reduce the insult of the *Meraglim*, we hasten the redemptive process.

THE MITZVA OF MILA

The Mitzva of *Mila* is conveyed to Avraham as part of a broader covenant which promises both nationhood and land: "I will establish ... an everlasting covenant between Me and you and ... the generations to come ... The whole land of Canaan ... I will give as an everlasting possession to you and your descendants ... As for you, you must keep My covenant ... Every male among you shall be circumcised" (*Bereshit* 17:7–10).

Apparently, this mitzva is pivotal in insuring our status as the people of God as well as our license to the Land of Israel. In fact when the Jews first entered Israel forty years after their departure from Egypt, the first mitzva

*At this point it is permitted to add a rabbinically formulated
"Al HaNissim." The following was written by Rabbi Neria
(alternative versions can be found on pages 662–665).*

עַל הַנִּסִּים [We thank You also] for the miracles, the redemption, the mighty deeds, the salvations, and the victories in battle which You performed for our ancestors in those days, at this time.

When the armies of the Middle East rose up against Your people Israel and sought to destroy, slay and exterminate the inhabitants of Your Land, young and old, children and women, and among them those who had survived the sword and were saved from the horror of Your enemies' flames, one from a city, two from a family, hoping to find a resting place for the soles of their feet in Your land that You had promised them; then You in Your great compassion stood by us in our time of distress, thwarted their counsel and frustrated their plans, raised us upright and established our liberty, championed our cause, judged our claim, avenged our wrong, delivered the strong into the hands of the weak, the many into the hands of the few, the impure into the hands of the holy. You made for Yourself great and holy renown in Your world, and for Your people Israel You performed a great salvation and redemption as of this day. You subjugated peoples under us, nations beneath our feet, and You gave us our inheritance, the Land of Canaan to its borders, and returned us to the place of Your holy Sanctuary.

(In the same way, make us a miracle and a glorious wonder, thwart the counsel of our enemies, have us prosper in the pastures of our Land, and gather in our scattered ones from the four corners of the earth, and we will rejoice in the rebuilding of Your city and in the establishment of Your Sanctuary and in the flourishing of the pride of Your servant David, speedily in our days, and we will give thanks to Your great name.) *Continue with "For all these things."*

generation of his descendants would inherit Israel, since the sins of the Emori still weren't severe enough to warrant their expulsion.

Jewish residency in Israel possesses metaphysical significance, and is therefore influenced by a multitude of variables. Our ascent to the land is intended to introduce moral and religious clarity to the entire planet. Those who practice, and thereby project even part of the message, secure a powerful anchor in our land. Their hold on Israel can be loosened due to their own moral and religious deterioration, or alternatively through our own progress and advance.

The struggle for Israel is not merely political or national, but has deep moral and religious underpinnings.

At this point it is permitted to add a rabbinically
formulated עַל הַנִּסִּים. *The following was written by Rabbi Neria*
(alternative versions can be found on pages 662–665).

עַל הַנִּסִּים וְעַל הַפֻּרְקָן וְעַל הַגְּבוּרוֹת וְעַל הַתְּשׁוּעוֹת וְעַל הַמִּלְחָמוֹת שֶׁעָשִׂיתָ
לַאֲבוֹתֵינוּ בַּיָּמִים הָהֵם בַּזְּמַן הַזֶּה.

כְּשֶׁעָמְדוּ צִבְאוֹת עֲרָב עַל עַמְּךָ יִשְׂרָאֵל, וּבִקְּשׁוּ לְהַשְׁמִיד לַהֲרֹג וּלְאַבֵּד אֶת
יוֹשְׁבֵי אַרְצֶךָ, מִנַּעַר וְעַד זָקֵן טַף וְנָשִׁים, וּבָהֶם עַם שְׂרִידֵי חֶרֶב אֲשֶׁר נִצְּלוּ מִתִּפַּת
הָאֵשׁ שֶׁל שׂוֹנְאֶיךָ, אֶחָד מֵעִיר וּשְׁנַיִם מִמִּשְׁפָּחָה, וְשַׁבְּרוּ לִמְצֹא מָנוֹחַ לְכַף
רַגְלָם בְּאַרְצְךָ אֲשֶׁר הִבְטַחְתָּ לָהֶם. וְאַתָּה בְּרַחֲמֶיךָ הָרַבִּים עָמַדְתָּ לָנוּ בְּעֵת
צָרָתֵנוּ, הֵפַרְתָּ אֶת עֲצָתָם וְקִלְקַלְתָּ אֶת מַחֲשַׁבְתָּם, זָקַפְתָּ קוֹמָתֵנוּ וְקוֹמַמְתָּ
אֶת חֻרְבוֹתֵנוּ, רַבְתָּ אֶת רִיבֵנוּ, דַּנְתָּ אֶת דִּינֵנוּ, נָקַמְתָּ אֶת נִקְמָתֵנוּ, מָסַרְתָּ רַבִּים
בְּיַד מְעַטִּים, טְמֵאִים בְּיַד קְדוֹשִׁים, וְעָשִׂיתָ לְךָ שֵׁם גָּדוֹל וְקָדוֹשׁ בְּעוֹלָמֶךָ,
וּלְעַמְּךָ יִשְׂרָאֵל עָשִׂיתָ תְּשׁוּעָה גְדוֹלָה וּפֻרְקָן כְּהַיּוֹם הַזֶּה, הִדְבַּרְתָּ עַמִּים
תַּחְתֵּנוּ וּלְאֻמִּים תַּחַת רַגְלֵנוּ, וְנָתַתָּ לָנוּ אֶת נַחֲלָתֵנוּ, אֶרֶץ כְּנַעַן לִגְבוּלוֹתֶיהָ,
וְהֶחֱזַרְתָּנוּ אֶל מְקוֹם מִקְדַּשׁ הֵיכָלֶךָ.

(כֵּן עֲשֵׂה עִמָּנוּ נֵס וָפֶלֶא לְטוֹבָה, הָפֵר עֲצַת אוֹיְבֵינוּ, וְדַשְּׁנֵנוּ בִּנְאוֹת אַרְצֶךָ,
וּנְפוּצוֹתֵינוּ מֵאַרְבַּע כַּנְפוֹת הָאָרֶץ תְּקַבֵּץ, וְנִשְׂמַח בְּבִנְיַן עִירֶךָ וּבְתִקּוּן הֵיכָלֶךָ,
וּבִצְמִיחַת קֶרֶן לְדָוִד עַבְדֶּךָ בִּמְהֵרָה בְיָמֵינוּ, וְנוֹדֶה לְשִׁמְךָ הַגָּדוֹל).

Continue with וְעַל כֻּלָּם.

the mitzva of *Mila* is performed by Muslims as well. In fact the mitzva was
delivered to Avraham before Yitzḥak was born, and Yishmael – father of
the Islamic nations – was the first child to be circumcised. This mitzva is so
potent in establishing presence in the Land of Israel that Muslims continue
to enjoy a hold in our Land.

The *Zohar* (*Va'era*) forecasts and laments the augmented Islamic presence
due to the merit of *Mila*: based on the merits of this mitzva, Muslims will
dominate the Land of Israel when it is "empty" – presumably a reference to
the period of Diaspora when Jews were absent. Subsequently they will stall
the full Jewish return to Israel until their merits expire.

The notion that Jewish acquisition of the land is stalled until local nations
"outlive" their welcome was already presented to Avraham in the original
covenant of *Berit Bein HaBetarim*. He was informed that only the fourth

וְעַל הַכֹּל For all this, Lᴏʀᴅ our God,
we thank and bless You.
May Your name be blessed continually
by the mouth of all that lives, for ever and all time –
for so it is written:
"You will eat and be satisfied,   *Deut. 8*
then you shall bless the Lᴏʀᴅ your God
for the good land He has given you."
Blessed are You, Lᴏʀᴅ,
for the land and for the food.

BLESSING FOR JERUSALEM

רַחֵם נָא Have compassion, please, Lᴏʀᴅ our God,
on Israel Your people,
on Jerusalem Your city,
on Zion the dwelling place of Your glory,
on the royal house of David Your anointed,
and on the great and holy House that bears Your name.
Our God, our Father,
tend us, feed us, sustain us and support us,
relieve us and send us relief, Lᴏʀᴅ our God,
swiftly from all our troubles.
Please, Lᴏʀᴅ our God, do not make us dependent
on the gifts or loans of other people,
but only on Your full, open, holy and generous hand
so that we may suffer neither shame nor humiliation
for ever and all time.

Israel as a "deer," and Ḥazal read multiple images into this metaphor. The
Gemara records a conversation between Rabbi Assi and Ulla in which the
former described an extensive population center contained in a relatively
small location. Responding to Ulla's astonishment at this report, Rabbi Assi
invoked the "deer" imagery: "Just as a deer skin naturally swells to contain
the flesh and organs, similarly the Land of Israel contracts and expands based
on her population" (*Gittin* 57a). The biblical boundaries of Israel extend to

וְעַל הַכֹּל, יהוה אֱלֹהֵינוּ
אֲנַחְנוּ מוֹדִים לָךְ וּמְבָרְכִים אוֹתָךְ
יִתְבָּרַךְ שִׁמְךָ בְּפִי כָּל חַי תָּמִיד לְעוֹלָם וָעֶד
כַּכָּתוּב: וְאָכַלְתָּ וְשָׂבָעְתָּ, וּבֵרַכְתָּ אֶת־יהוה אֱלֹהֶיךָ
עַל־הָאָרֶץ הַטֹּבָה אֲשֶׁר נָתַן־לָךְ:
בָּרוּךְ אַתָּה יהוה, עַל הָאָרֶץ וְעַל הַמָּזוֹן.

דברים ח

ברכת ירושלים

רַחֵם נָא, יהוה אֱלֹהֵינוּ
עַל יִשְׂרָאֵל עַמֶּךָ
וְעַל יְרוּשָׁלַיִם עִירֶךָ
וְעַל צִיּוֹן מִשְׁכַּן כְּבוֹדֶךָ
וְעַל מַלְכוּת בֵּית דָּוִד מְשִׁיחֶךָ
וְעַל הַבַּיִת הַגָּדוֹל וְהַקָּדוֹשׁ שֶׁנִּקְרָא שִׁמְךָ עָלָיו.
אֱלֹהֵינוּ, אָבִינוּ
רְעֵנוּ, זוּנֵנוּ, פַּרְנְסֵנוּ וְכַלְכְּלֵנוּ
וְהַרְוִיחֵנוּ, וְהַרְוַח לָנוּ יהוה אֱלֹהֵינוּ מְהֵרָה מִכָּל צָרוֹתֵינוּ.
וְנָא אַל תַּצְרִיכֵנוּ, יהוה אֱלֹהֵינוּ
לֹא לִידֵי מַתְּנַת בָּשָׂר וָדָם
וְלֹא לִידֵי הַלְוָאָתָם
כִּי אִם לְיָדְךָ הַמְּלֵאָה, הַפְּתוּחָה, הַקְּדוֹשָׁה וְהָרְחָבָה
שֶׁלֹּא נֵבוֹשׁ וְלֹא נִכָּלֵם לְעוֹלָם וָעֶד.

הַקְּדוֹשָׁה וְהָרְחָבָה *Holy and generous.* The land is described as sacred and broad, though the current State of Israel is a relatively narrow strip of land. *Hazal* were aware of the fluctuating size of Israel. *Yirmiyahu* (chapter 3) depicts

וּבְנֵה And may Jerusalem the holy city be rebuilt soon, in our time.
Blessed are You, LORD,
who in His compassion will rebuild Jerusalem. Amen.

BLESSING OF GOD'S GOODNESS

בָּרוּךְ Blessed are You, LORD our God, King of the Universe –
God our Father, our King, our Sovereign,
our Creator, our Redeemer, our Maker,
our Holy One, the Holy One of Jacob.
He is our Shepherd, Israel's Shepherd,
the good King who does good to all.
Every day He has done, is doing, and will do good to us.
He has acted, is acting, and will always act kindly toward us for ever,
granting us grace, kindness and compassion, relief and rescue,
prosperity, blessing, redemption and comfort,
sustenance and support,
compassion, life, peace and all good things,
and of all good things may He never let us lack.

---

messianic Land of Israel. In fact the Rambam (*Hilkhot Rotzei'aḥ veShemirat Nefesh* 8:40) claims that *Mashiaḥ* will designate three additional Cities of Refuge (*Arei Miklat*) in these territories.

Beyond this actual expansion, Ḥazal (*Pesikta Rabati* 1) speak of an exponential global expansion. *Yeshayahu* (66:23) speaks of a global pilgrimage to Yerushalayim. Recognizing the inability of the actual city of Yerushalayim to house the entire human race, the Midrash claims that the entire world will be *incorporated* into the Land of Israel. In a utopia which embraces the unquestioned authority of HaKadosh Barukh Hu, Yerushalayim emerges as the spiritual and political epicenter, while the entire world becomes a satellite of a greater Israel. This transformation may not occur in the classic manner of conquest or redrawing of boundaries. Potentially, as world peace pivoted on the divine kingdom materializes, borders dissolve and all of humanity attains *common* prosperity, with Yerushalayim and the Land of Israel as the source. In effect, boundaries vanish and the entire planet transforms into one "broad" Land of Israel in spirit.

וּבְנֵה יְרוּשָׁלַיִם עִיר הַקֹּדֶשׁ בִּמְהֵרָה בְיָמֵינוּ.
בָּרוּךְ אַתָּה יהוה, בּוֹנֵה בְרַחֲמָיו יְרוּשָׁלָיִם, אָמֵן.

ברכת הטוב והמטיב

בָּרוּךְ אַתָּה יהוה אֱלֹהֵינוּ מֶלֶךְ הָעוֹלָם
הָאֵל אָבִינוּ, מַלְכֵּנוּ, אַדִּירֵנוּ
בּוֹרְאֵנוּ, גּוֹאֲלֵנוּ, יוֹצְרֵנוּ, קְדוֹשֵׁנוּ, קְדוֹשׁ יַעֲקֹב
רוֹעֵנוּ, רוֹעֵה יִשְׂרָאֵל, הַמֶּלֶךְ הַטּוֹב וְהַמֵּיטִיב לַכֹּל
שֶׁבְּכָל יוֹם וָיוֹם
הוּא הֵיטִיב, הוּא מֵיטִיב, הוּא יֵיטִיב לָנוּ
הוּא גְמָלָנוּ, הוּא גוֹמְלֵנוּ, הוּא יִגְמְלֵנוּ לָעַד
לְחֵן וּלְחֶסֶד וּלְרַחֲמִים, וּלְרֶוַח, הַצָּלָה וְהַצְלָחָה
בְּרָכָה וִישׁוּעָה, נֶחָמָה, פַּרְנָסָה וְכַלְכָּלָה
וְרַחֲמִים וְחַיִּים וְשָׁלוֹם וְכָל טוֹב, וּמִכָּל טוּב לְעוֹלָם אַל יְחַסְּרֵנוּ.

areas which were never incorporated into Israel proper, affirming an expansion during the Messianic Era.

A different image to convey the potential expansion of Israel is that of a rolled-up scroll. In its condensed form, its true dimensions are indiscernible, and it appears diminutive. Once unraveled, its true size emerges. Similarly, the Land of Israel is composed of mountain ranges and rocky terrain which mask its actual size. Several messianic prophecies describe the flattening of Israel's topography – mountains are leveled into valleys, while lowlands are elevated. (See for example *Yeshayahu* 40:4). As the "scroll" of our land unfurls, its acreage expands. The actual boundaries of Israel reflect a condensed and contracted land mass.

Beyond the "flattening" effect, the messianic augmentation of Israel is aided by *actual* expansion. At the *Berit Bein HaBetarim* God promised Avraham the land of ten nations. However Yehoshua only conquered seven resident nations, with no mention of the land which had belonged to the Keini, Kenizi and Kadmoni tribes. Presumably these lands will be incorporated in the

ADDITIONAL REQUESTS

הָרַחֲמָן May the Compassionate One
    reign over us for ever and all time.

May the Compassionate One
    be blessed in heaven and on earth.

May the Compassionate One
    be praised from generation to generation,
    be glorified by us to all eternity,
    and honored among us for ever and all time.

May the Compassionate One
    grant us an honorable livelihood.

May the Compassionate One
    break the yoke from our neck and lead us upright to our land.

May the Compassionate One
    send us many blessings to this house
    and this table at which we have eaten.

May the Compassionate One
    send us Elijah the prophet –
    may he be remembered for good –
    to bring us good tidings of salvation and consolation.

May the Compassionate One
    bless the State of Israel, first flowering of our redemption.

May the Compassionate One
    bless the members of Israel's Defense Forces,
    who stand guard over our land.

A guest says:

יְהִי רָצוֹן May it be Your will that the master of this house shall not suffer shame in this world, nor humiliation in the World to Come. May all he owns prosper greatly, and may his and our possessions be successful and close to hand. Let not the Accuser hold sway over his deeds or ours, and may no thought of sin, iniquity or transgression enter him or us from now and for evermore.

בקשות נוספות

הָרַחֲמָן הוּא יִמְלֹךְ עָלֵינוּ לְעוֹלָם וָעֶד.

הָרַחֲמָן הוּא יִתְבָּרַךְ בַּשָּׁמַיִם וּבָאָרֶץ.

הָרַחֲמָן הוּא יִשְׁתַּבַּח לְדוֹר דּוֹרִים
וְיִתְפָּאַר בָּנוּ לָעַד וּלְנֵצַח נְצָחִים
וְיִתְהַדַּר בָּנוּ לָעַד וּלְעוֹלְמֵי עוֹלָמִים.

הָרַחֲמָן הוּא יְפַרְנְסֵנוּ בְּכָבוֹד.

הָרַחֲמָן הוּא יִשְׁבֹּר עֻלֵנוּ מֵעַל צַוָּארֵנוּ
וְהוּא יוֹלִיכֵנוּ קוֹמְמִיּוּת לְאַרְצֵנוּ.

הָרַחֲמָן הוּא יִשְׁלַח לָנוּ בְּרָכָה מְרֻבָּה בַּבַּיִת הַזֶּה
וְעַל שֻׁלְחָן זֶה שֶׁאָכַלְנוּ עָלָיו.

הָרַחֲמָן הוּא יִשְׁלַח לָנוּ אֶת אֵלִיָּהוּ הַנָּבִיא זָכוּר לַטּוֹב
וִיבַשֶּׂר לָנוּ בְּשׂוֹרוֹת טוֹבוֹת יְשׁוּעוֹת וְנֶחָמוֹת.

הָרַחֲמָן הוּא יְבָרֵךְ אֶת מְדִינַת יִשְׂרָאֵל
רֵאשִׁית צְמִיחַת גְּאֻלָּתֵנוּ.

הָרַחֲמָן הוּא יְבָרֵךְ אֶת חַיָּלֵי צְבָא הַהֲגָנָה לְיִשְׂרָאֵל
הָעוֹמְדִים עַל מִשְׁמַר אַרְצֵנוּ.

A guest says:

יְהִי רָצוֹן שֶׁלֹּא יֵבוֹשׁ בַּעַל הַבַּיִת בָּעוֹלָם הַזֶּה, וְלֹא יִכָּלֵם לָעוֹלָם
הַבָּא, וְיִצְלַח מְאֹד בְּכָל נְכָסָיו, וְיִהְיוּ נְכָסָיו וּנְכָסֵינוּ מֻצְלָחִים
וּקְרוֹבִים לָעִיר, וְאַל יִשְׁלֹט שָׂטָן לֹא בְּמַעֲשֵׂה יָדָיו וְלֹא בְּמַעֲשֵׂה
יָדֵינוּ. וְאַל יִזְדַּקֵּר לֹא לְפָנָיו וְלֹא לְפָנֵינוּ שׁוּם דְּבַר הִרְהוּר חֵטְא,
עֲבֵירָה וְעָוֹן, מֵעַתָּה וְעַד עוֹלָם.

הָרַחֲמָן May the Compassionate One bless –

When eating at one's own table, say (include the words in parentheses that apply):
me,
   (my wife/husband, / my father, my teacher /
   my mother, my teacher/ my children,)
and all that is mine,

A guest at someone else's table says (include the words in parentheses that apply):
the master of this house, him
   (and his wife, the mistress of this house / and his children,)
and all that is his,

Children at their parents' table say (include the words in parentheses that apply):
my father, my teacher, (master of this house,)
and my mother, my teacher, (mistress of this house,)
them, their household, their children,
and all that is theirs.

For all other guests, add:
and all the diners here,

אוֹתָנוּ – together with us and all that is ours.
Just as our forefathers
Abraham, Isaac and Jacob were blessed
in all, from all, with all,
so may He bless all of us together
with a complete blessing,
and let us say: Amen.

בַּמָרוֹם On high, may grace be invoked for them and for us,
as a safeguard of peace.
May we receive a blessing from the Lᴏʀᴅ
and a just reward from the God of our salvation,
and may we find grace and good favor
in the eyes of God and man.

הָרַחֲמָן הוּא יְבָרֵךְ

When eating at one's own table, say (include the words in parentheses that apply):

אוֹתִי

(וְאֶת אִשְׁתִּי / וְאֶת בַּעֲלִי / וְאֶת אָבִי מוֹרִי /

וְאֶת אִמִּי מוֹרָתִי / וְאֶת זַרְעִי)

וְאֶת כָּל אֲשֶׁר לִי.

A guest at someone else's table says (include the words in parentheses that apply):

אֶת בַּעַל הַבַּיִת הַזֶּה, אוֹתוֹ

(וְאֶת אִשְׁתּוֹ בַּעֲלַת הַבַּיִת הַזֶּה / וְאֶת זַרְעוֹ)

וְאֶת כָּל אֲשֶׁר לוֹ.

Children at their parents' table say (include the words in parentheses that apply):

אֶת אָבִי מוֹרִי (בַּעַל הַבַּיִת הַזֶּה)

וְאֶת אִמִּי מוֹרָתִי (בַּעֲלַת הַבַּיִת הַזֶּה)

אוֹתָם וְאֶת בֵּיתָם וְאֶת זַרְעָם

וְאֶת כָּל אֲשֶׁר לָהֶם

For all other guests, add:

וְאֶת כָּל הַמְסֻבִּין כָּאן

אוֹתָנוּ וְאֶת כָּל אֲשֶׁר לָנוּ כְּמוֹ שֶׁנִּתְבָּרְכוּ אֲבוֹתֵינוּ
אַבְרָהָם יִצְחָק וְיַעֲקֹב, בַּכֹּל, מִכֹּל, כֹּל, כֵּן יְבָרֵךְ אוֹתָנוּ כֻּלָּנוּ יַחַד בִּבְרָכָה שְׁלֵמָה.
וְנֹאמַר אָמֵן.

בַּמָּרוֹם יְלַמְּדוּ עֲלֵיהֶם וְעָלֵינוּ זְכוּת שֶׁתְּהֵא לְמִשְׁמֶרֶת שָׁלוֹם
וְנִשָּׂא בְרָכָה מֵאֵת יהוה וּצְדָקָה מֵאֱלֹהֵי יִשְׁעֵנוּ
וְנִמְצָא חֵן וְשֵׂכֶל טוֹב בְּעֵינֵי אֱלֹהִים וְאָדָם.

הָרַחֲמָן May the Compassionate One
make us worthy of the Messianic Age
and life in the World to Come.

_____

יְזַכֵּנוּ לִימוֹת הַמָּשִׁיחַ *Make us worthy of the Messianic Age.* A famed and provocative statement of Shmuel (*Berakhot* 34b) asserts that the Messianic Era
will not be apocalyptic, but will function "conventionally." The only modification will be the relief from *shibud malkhiyot* – foreign rule or governance.
The Rambam claimed that many apocalyptic visions were to be taken as
metaphor rather than narrative. The Messianic Era will mirror our familiar
reality, differing only in the restoration of Jewish sovereignty.

A more literal reading of messianic apocalyptic prophecies suggests that
its composition will be drastically different from our reality. Perhaps Shmuel's
statement refers to a preliminary messianic period in which "reality" is maintained while foreign oppression is alleviated. A subsequent apocalyptic era
emerges in the wake of more moderate political adjustments during the initial
period.

This position was adopted by Rabbi Tzvi Hirsh Kalisher, a leading nine-
teenth-century Rabbi, who dedicated his career to the resettlement of the
Land of Israel. He believed that the redemptive process would unfold gradually, and be initiated by human endeavor. By settling the Land, and fulfilling
the mitzvot of the Land, the process would be inaugurated. He actively cam-
paigned both with members of the Rothschild family as well as with Moses
Montefiore to raise funds for land purchase in Israel. Additionally, in 1860
he founded the first modern Zionist Organization known as Ḥevra LeYishuv
Eretz Yisrael, and traveled throughout Europe to secure endorsement for
his agenda. In 1862 he published his well-known *sefer*, *Derishat Tziyon*, in
which he outlines his positions of the pace and texture of redemption. He
also urged the renewal of *korbanot* and shared his halakhic positions with
his teachers – among them Rabbi Akiva Eiger, the leading Halakhist of his
generation, whose responses are included in the *sefer*.

Towards the end of his life, aged seventy-seven, in 1872, Rabbi Kalisher was
appointed rector of a school in Israel dedicated to implementing agricultural
halakhot. Sensing the opportunity to finally fulfill his lifelong dream, he
planned his *aliya*. However the imprisonment of his son – who had earlier
traveled to Israel to work on his father's agenda – physically weakened him

הָרַחֲמָן הוּא יְזַבֵּנוּ לִימוֹת הַמָּשִׁיחַ
וּלְחַיֵּי הָעוֹלָם הַבָּא

לִימוֹת הַמָּשִׁיחַ *The Messianic Age.* The term *Yemot HaMashiaḥ* is first employed by Shmuel in his statement cited in the Gemara (*Berakhot* 34b). The word *yemot* indicates a period or duration of time associated with *Mashiaḥ*. The phrase was subsequently employed by various Jewish thinkers in their description of the Messianic Era (see for example Rambam *Hilkhot Melakhim* 12:1). The terminology indicates that the messianic upheaval is not instantaneous, but part of a multi-staged process. Potentially, various stages in the messianic process may transpire *even before* the actual arrival of the *Mashiaḥ*. An intriguing timeline for the messianic arrival is provided by the Gemara (*Sanhedrin* 97a), which traces a seven-year messianic period, climaxing with the actual *Mashiaḥ* arriving only *after* the completion of the cycle. This image acknowledges messianic *events* occurring before the actual arrival of the *Mashiaḥ*.

The prospect of a multi-staged Messianic transformation also invites the possibility that the early phases may be incomplete, and redemptive gains partial. Furthermore, early stages of the process may be "natural," with latter stages more in line with apocalyptic prophecies. This is a core thesis of Rabbi Tzvi Hirsh Kalisher, who in his *sefer Derishat Tziyon* asserted that messianic events prior to the arrival the *Mashiaḥ* would be natural and political, while latter-stage messianic events, subsequent to the violent war of Gog and Magog, would be supernatural and apocalyptic. Naturally occurring events such as international repatriation of Israel to the Jews and the resettling of the Jewish population in Israel can be defined as messianic, even if they are encased in "natural" processes.

An additional indication of a multi-staged redemptive process composed of a preliminary "natural" stage stems from a verse in *Zekharia* (14:7). The description of a "day-long duration without daytime or nighttime" implies an extended period – commonly assumed to be a messianic "day" spanning decades or even centuries (Rashi for example assumes that it refers to a millennium). At the tail end of this period a supernatural or divine light develops. This imagery implies an earlier messianic period, absent of supernatural features, capped by the introduction of a second stage radiated by divine luminescence.

He gives great salvation to His king,   II Sam. 22
showing kindness to His anointed,
to David and his descendants for ever.
He who makes peace in His high places,
may He make peace for us and all Israel,
and let us say: Amen.

יְרֹאוּ Fear the Lord, you His holy ones;   Ps. 34
those who fear Him lack nothing.
Young lions may grow weak and hungry,
but those who seek the Lord lack no good thing.
Thank the Lord for He is good;   Ps. 118
His loving-kindness is for ever.
You open Your hand,   Ps. 145
and satisfy every living thing with favor.

Beyond the *general* message that redemption is staged, this *particular* image stresses gradual acquisition of sovereignty and military capability as developments of redemption. A fortress signals military capacity, but also political strength. Unlike the related images of sunrise and plant growth, the fortress image reminds us that we will gradually achieve military ability, as well as political sovereignty, as our *geula* evolves.

The same midrash which conjures the dual images of *magdil* and *migdol* also traces the gradual *political* rise of Mordekhai in Shushan. At first he merely lingered in the king's courtyard. Later he was robed in a nobleman's uniform and paraded on the king's horse. As the drama increases he is dressed in the full royal attire, and ultimately the Jewish people benefit from his new-found position: "The Jews had light and gladness and joy and honor" (*Esther* 8:16). Mordekhai's rise within the ranks of the Shushan political hierarchy serves as a model for gradual restoration of Jewish sovereignty.

Finally the fortress imagery *justifies* the gradual nature of redemption. Why does redemption evolve progressively rather than erupting all at once? The aforementioned midrash attributes this to our inability to fully appreciate, or process, the unfamiliar features of redemptive experience. After years of

שמואל ב׳ כב

מַגְדִּיל יְשׁוּעוֹת מַלְכּוֹ, וְעֹשֶׂה־חֶסֶד לִמְשִׁיחוֹ
לְדָוִד וּלְזַרְעוֹ עַד־עוֹלָם:
עֹשֶׂה שָׁלוֹם בִּמְרוֹמָיו
הוּא יַעֲשֶׂה שָׁלוֹם עָלֵינוּ וְעַל כָּל יִשְׂרָאֵל
וְאִמְרוּ אָמֵן.

תהלים לד

יְראוּ אֶת־יהוה קְדֹשָׁיו
כִּי־אֵין מַחְסוֹר לִירֵאָיו:
כְּפִירִים רָשׁוּ וְרָעֵבוּ
וְדֹרְשֵׁי יהוה לֹא־יַחְסְרוּ כָל־טוֹב:

תהלים קיח

הוֹדוּ לַיהוה כִּי־טוֹב, כִּי לְעוֹלָם חַסְדּוֹ:

תהלים קמה

פּוֹתֵחַ אֶת־יָדֶךָ, וּמַשְׂבִּיעַ לְכָל־חַי רָצוֹן:

---

and prevented his *aliya*. He passed away in 1874; the Kibbutz *Tirat Tzvi* is
named in his memory.

MAGDIL AND MIGDOL

The two related terms – *magdil* mentioned during weekday *Birkat HaMazon*
and *migdol* on Shabbat – are taken from *Tehillim* 18:51 and *II Shmuel* 22:51
respectively. These terms can also be translated as "fortress": "He is a fortress
of deliverance to His king, and shows loving-kindness to His anointed, to
David and his descendants forever."

In particular the term *migdol* describes an actual citadel, while the term
magdil portrays the *process of a fortress being constructed*. The Midrash (on
Tehillim 18:36) comments that the final product of redemption is conveyed
by the word *migdol*. However, as redemption evolves gradually, the various
partial stages are conveyed through the image of an "expanding" tower, still
under construction. Other images which convey the staged nature of redemption include the rising sun (see commentary on page 267) as well as a
blooming plant (see commentary on page 315).

Blessed is the person who trusts in the LORD,   Jer. 17
whose trust is in the LORD alone.
Once I was young, and now I am old,   Ps. 37
yet I have never watched a righteous man forsaken
or his children begging for bread.
The LORD will give His people strength.   Ps. 29
The LORD will bless His people with peace.

If Birkat HaMazon was made on a cup of wine,
then the blessing over wine is made and the majority of the cup is drunk,
after which Al HaMiḥya, on the next page, is said.

of the series of festivals which surround our historical destiny and the Land
of Israel. The Sefat Emet described it as a "preparation for building the
Mikdash; It restored Jewish pride and national vitality while stirring their
vision and facilitating the construction of the *Mikdash*." It is an example of
a pre-redemptive miracle, which generates national energy while providing
the momentum toward final redemption. He concludes his comments by
forecasting that "it is conceivable that a similar pattern will occur toward our
final redemption." Though we haven't yet merited some of the latter stages of
messianic evolution, the great marvels we have encountered in our homeland
have renewed a previously demoralized national spirit. The redemptive fervor
it has incited is unparalleled in our national history.

בָּרוּךְ הַגֶּבֶר אֲשֶׁר יִבְטַח בַּיהוה

וְהָיָה יהוה מִבְטַחוֹ:

נַעַר הָיִיתִי גַּם־זָקַנְתִּי

וְלֹא־רָאִיתִי צַדִּיק נֶעֱזָב

וְזַרְעוֹ מְבַקֶּשׁ־לָחֶם:

יהוה עֹז לְעַמּוֹ יִתֵּן, יהוה יְבָרֵךְ אֶת־עַמּוֹ בַשָּׁלוֹם:

If ברכת המזון *was made on a cup of wine,*
then בּוֹרֵא פְּרִי הַגֶּפֶן *is said and the majority of the cup is drunk,*
after which ברכה מעין שלוש, *on the next page, is said.*

"distance" from the *Shekhina*, we must be *eased* into contact and encounter. After centuries without national identity or institutions, we must slowly familiarize ourselves with the broader facets of governing a country. A fortress must be built gradually or else it will crumble. A *national redemptive* state must also evolve slowly and in stages.

PRE-REDEMPTIVE RENEWAL OF NATIONAL SPIRIT
The great miracle of Purim did not immediately or explicitly participate in our return to Israel. It occurred in a faraway location, apparently unrelated to our efforts to resettle the Land of Israel. Yet it was incorporated as part

BLESSING AFTER FOOD – AL HAMIḤYA

Grace after eating from the "seven species" of produce with which Israel is blessed: food made from the five grains (but not bread); wine or grape juice; grapes, figs, pomegranates, olives, or dates.

בָּרוּךְ Blessed are You, Lord our God, King of the Universe,

After grain products (but not bread or matza):	*After wine or grape juice:*	*After grapes, figs, olives, pomegranates or dates:*
for the nourishment and sustenance,	for the vine and the fruit of the vine,	for the tree and the fruit of the tree,

After grain products (but not bread or matza), and wine or grape juice:
for the nourishment and sustenance
and for the vine and the fruit of the vine,

and for the produce of the field; for the desirable, good and spacious land that You willingly gave as heritage to our ancestors, that they might eat of its fruit and be satisfied with its goodness. Have compassion, please, Lord our God, on Israel Your people, on Jerusalem, Your city, on Zion the home of Your glory, on Your altar and Your Temple. May You rebuild Jerusalem, the holy city swiftly in our time, and may You bring us back there, rejoicing in its rebuilding, eating from its fruit, satisfied by its goodness, and blessing You for it in holiness and purity. For You, God, are good and do good to all and we thank You for the land

After grain products (but not bread or matza):	*After wine or grape juice:*	*After grapes, figs, olives, pomegranates or dates:*
and for the nourishment. Blessed are You, Lord, for the land and for the nourishment.	and for the fruit of the vine. Blessed are You, Lord, for the land and for the fruit of the vine.	and for the fruit. Blessed are You, Lord, for the land and for the fruit.

After grain products (but not bread or matza), and wine or grape juice:
and for the nourishment and for the fruit of the vine. Blessed are You, Lord, for the land and for the nourishment and the fruit of the vine.

BLESSING AFTER FOOD – BOREH NEFASHOT

After food or drink that does not require Birkat HaMazon or Al HaMiḥya – such as meat, fish, dairy products, vegetables, beverages, or fruit other than grapes, figs, pomegranates, olives or dates – say:

בָּרוּךְ Blessed are You, Lord our God, King of the Universe, who creates the many forms of life and their needs. For all You have created to sustain the life of all that lives, blessed be He, Giver of life to the worlds.

ברכה מעין שלוש

Grace after eating from the "seven species" of produce with which Israel is blessed: food made from the five grains (but not bread); wine or grape juice; grapes, figs, pomegranates, olives, or dates.

בָּרוּךְ אַתָּה יהוה אֱלֹהֵינוּ מֶלֶךְ הָעוֹלָם, עַל

After grapes, figs, olives, *pomegranates or dates:*	*After wine or grape juice:*	*After grain products* *(but not bread or* מצה*):*
הָעֵץ וְעַל פְּרִי הָעֵץ	הַגֶּפֶן וְעַל פְּרִי הַגֶּפֶן	הַמִּחְיָה וְעַל הַכַּלְכָּלָה

After grain products (but not bread or מצה*), and wine or grape juice:*

הַמִּחְיָה וְעַל הַכַּלְכָּלָה וְעַל הַגֶּפֶן וְעַל פְּרִי הַגֶּפֶן

וְעַל תְּנוּבַת הַשָּׂדֶה וְעַל אֶרֶץ חֶמְדָּה טוֹבָה וּרְחָבָה, שֶׁרָצִיתָ וְהִנְחַלְתָּ
לַאֲבוֹתֵינוּ לֶאֱכֹל מִפִּרְיָהּ וְלִשְׂבֹּעַ מִטּוּבָהּ. רַחֵם נָא יהוה אֱלֹהֵינוּ עַל
יִשְׂרָאֵל עַמֶּךָ וְעַל יְרוּשָׁלַיִם עִירֶךָ וְעַל צִיּוֹן מִשְׁכַּן כְּבוֹדֶךָ וְעַל מִזְבְּחֶךָ
וְעַל הֵיכָלֶךָ. וּבְנֵה יְרוּשָׁלַיִם עִיר הַקֹּדֶשׁ בִּמְהֵרָה בְיָמֵינוּ, וְהַעֲלֵנוּ לְתוֹכָהּ
וְשַׂמְּחֵנוּ בְּבִנְיָנָהּ וְנֹאכַל מִפִּרְיָהּ וְנִשְׂבַּע מִטּוּבָהּ, וּנְבָרֶכְךָ עָלֶיהָ בִּקְדֻשָּׁה
וּבְטָהֳרָה. כִּי אַתָּה יהוה טוֹב וּמֵטִיב לַכֹּל, וְנוֹדֶה לְּךָ עַל הָאָרֶץ

After grapes, figs, olives, *pomegranates or dates:*	*After wine or grape juice:*	*After grain products* *(but not bread or* מצה*):*
וְעַל הַפֵּרוֹת.**	וְעַל פְּרִי הַגָּפֶן.*	וְעַל הַמִּחְיָה.
בָּרוּךְ אַתָּה יהוה עַל	בָּרוּךְ אַתָּה יהוה עַל	בָּרוּךְ אַתָּה יהוה עַל
הָאָרֶץ וְעַל הַפֵּרוֹת.**	הָאָרֶץ וְעַל פְּרִי הַגָּפֶן.*	הָאָרֶץ וְעַל הַמִּחְיָה.

After grain products (but not bread or מצה*), and wine or grape juice:*

וְעַל הַמִּחְיָה וְעַל פְּרִי הַגָּפֶן.*

בָּרוּךְ אַתָּה יהוה, עַל הָאָרֶץ וְעַל הַמִּחְיָה וְעַל פְּרִי הַגָּפֶן.*

If the wine is from אֶרֶץ יִשְׂרָאֵל, *then substitute* גַּפְנָהּ *for* הַגָּפֶן.
**If the fruit is from* אֶרֶץ יִשְׂרָאֵל, *then substitute* פֵּרוֹתֶיהָ *for* הַפֵּרוֹת.

בורא נפשות

After food or drink that does not require ברכת המזון *or* מעין שלוש – *such as meat, fish, dairy products, vegetables, beverages, or fruit other than grapes, figs, pomegranates, olives or dates – say:*

בָּרוּךְ אַתָּה יהוה אֱלֹהֵינוּ מֶלֶךְ הָעוֹלָם, בּוֹרֵא נְפָשׁוֹת רַבּוֹת וְחֶסְרוֹנָן עַל
כָּל מַה שֶּׁבָּרֵאתָ לְהַחֲיוֹת בָּהֶם נֶפֶשׁ כָּל חָי. בָּרוּךְ חֵי הָעוֹלָמִים.

BIRKAT KOHANIM IN ISRAEL

In Israel, the following is said by the Leader during the Repetition of the Amida when Kohanim bless the congregation. If there is more than one Kohen, a member of the congregation calls:

Kohanim!

The Kohanim respond:

Blessed are You, Lord our God, King of the Universe, who has made us holy with the holiness of Aaron, and has commanded us to bless His people Israel with love.

The Leader calls word by word, followed by the Kohanim:

יְבָרֶכְךָ May the LORD bless you and protect you. (*Cong:* Amen.) *Num. 6*
May the LORD make His face shine on you
and be gracious to you. (*Cong:* Amen.)
May the LORD turn His face toward you,
and grant you peace. (*Cong:* Amen.)

The Leader continues with "Grant peace" below.

The congregation says:

אַדִּיר Majestic One on high who dwells in power: You are peace and Your name is peace. May it be Your will to bestow on us and on Your people the house of Israel, life and blessing as a safeguard for peace.

The Kohanim say:

רִבּוֹנוֹ Master of the Universe: we have done what You have decreed for us. So too may You deal with us as You have promised us. Look down from Your holy dwelling place, from heaven, and bless Your people Israel and the land You have given us as You promised on oath to our ancestors, a land flowing with milk and honey. *Deut. 26*

The Leader continues:

שִׂים שָׁלוֹם Grant peace, goodness and blessing, grace, loving-kindness and compassion to us and all Israel Your people. Bless us, our Father, all as one, with the light of Your face, for by the light of Your face You have given us, LORD our God, the Torah of life and love of kindness, righteousness, blessing, compassion, life and peace. May it be good in Your eyes to bless Your people Israel at every time, in every hour, with Your peace. Blessed are You, LORD, who blesses His people Israel with peace.

The following verse concludes the Leader's Repetition of the Amida.

May the words of my mouth and the meditation of my heart *Ps. 19*
find favor before You, LORD, my Rock and Redeemer.

Continue with Hallel on page 326.

ברכת כהנים בארץ ישראל

In ארץ ישראל, *the following is said by the* שליח ציבור *during the* חזרת הש״ץ *when* כהנים say ברכת כהנים. *If there is more than one* כהן, *a member of the* קהל *calls:*

כֹּהֲנִים

The כהנים *respond:*

בָּרוּךְ אַתָּה יהוה אֱלֹהֵינוּ מֶלֶךְ הָעוֹלָם, אֲשֶׁר קִדְּשָׁנוּ בִּקְדֻשָׁתוֹ שֶׁל אַהֲרֹן וְצִוָּנוּ לְבָרֵךְ אֶת עַמּוֹ יִשְׂרָאֵל בְּאַהֲבָה.

The שליח ציבור *calls word by word, followed by the* כהנים:

במדברו

יְבָרֶכְךָ יהוה וְיִשְׁמְרֶךָ: קהל אָמֵן

יָאֵר יהוה פָּנָיו אֵלֶיךָ וִיחֻנֶּךָּ: קהל אָמֵן

יִשָּׂא יהוה פָּנָיו אֵלֶיךָ וְיָשֵׂם לְךָ שָׁלוֹם: קהל אָמֵן

The שליח ציבור *continues with* שִׂים שָׁלוֹם *below.*

The כהנים *say:*	*The* קהל *says:*

רִבּוֹנוֹ שֶׁל עוֹלָם, עָשִׂינוּ מַה שֶּׁגָּזַרְתָּ עָלֵינוּ, אַף אַתָּה עֲשֵׂה עִמָּנוּ כְּמוֹ שֶׁהִבְטַחְתָּנוּ. הַשְׁקִיפָה מִמְּעוֹן קָדְשְׁךָ מִן הַשָּׁמַיִם, וּבָרֵךְ אֶת עַמְּךָ אֶת יִשְׂרָאֵל, וְאֵת הָאֲדָמָה אֲשֶׁר נָתַתָּה לָנוּ, כַּאֲשֶׁר נִשְׁבַּעְתָּ לַאֲבֹתֵינוּ, אֶרֶץ זָבַת חָלָב וּדְבָשׁ:

דבריםכו

אַדִּיר בַּמָּרוֹם שׁוֹכֵן בִּגְבוּרָה, אַתָּה שָׁלוֹם וְשִׁמְךָ שָׁלוֹם. יְהִי רָצוֹן שֶׁתָּשִׂים עָלֵינוּ וְעַל כָּל עַמְּךָ בֵּית יִשְׂרָאֵל חַיִּים וּבְרָכָה לְמִשְׁמֶרֶת שָׁלוֹם.

The שליח ציבור *continues:*

שִׂים שָׁלוֹם טוֹבָה וּבְרָכָה, חֵן וָחֶסֶד וְרַחֲמִים עָלֵינוּ וְעַל כָּל יִשְׂרָאֵל עַמֶּךָ. בָּרְכֵנוּ אָבִינוּ כֻּלָּנוּ כְּאֶחָד בְּאוֹר פָּנֶיךָ, כִּי בְאוֹר פָּנֶיךָ נָתַתָּ לָּנוּ יהוה אֱלֹהֵינוּ, תּוֹרַת חַיִּים וְאַהֲבַת חֶסֶד, וּצְדָקָה וּבְרָכָה וְרַחֲמִים וְחַיִּים וְשָׁלוֹם. וְטוֹב בְּעֵינֶיךָ לְבָרֵךְ אֶת עַמְּךָ יִשְׂרָאֵל, בְּכָל עֵת וּבְכָל שָׁעָה בִּשְׁלוֹמֶךָ. בָּרוּךְ אַתָּה יהוה, הַמְבָרֵךְ אֶת עַמּוֹ יִשְׂרָאֵל בַּשָּׁלוֹם.

The following verse concludes the חזרת הש״ץ.

תהליםיט

יִהְיוּ לְרָצוֹן אִמְרֵי־פִי וְהֶגְיוֹן לִבִּי לְפָנֶיךָ, יהוה צוּרִי וְגֹאֲלִי:

Continue with הלל *on page 327.*

AL HANISSIM – ALTERNATIVE VERSIONS

Some communities add a version of Al HaNissim
to the Amida and Birkat HaMazon.

THE STANDARDIZED ALTERNATIVE VERSION OF AL HANISSIM
From *The Maḥzor of the Religious Kibbutz Movement*

עַל הַנִּסִּים וְעַל הַפֻּרְקָן וְעַל הַגְּבוּרוֹת וְעַל הַתְּשׁוּעוֹת וְעַל הַמִּלְחָמוֹת שֶׁעָשִׂיתָ
לַאֲבוֹתֵינוּ בַּיָּמִים הָהֵם בַּזְּמַן הַזֶּה.

אַתָּה הָאֵל עוֹרַרְתָּ אֶת לֵב אֲבוֹתֵינוּ לָשׁוּב לְהַר נַחֲלָתְךָ, לָשֶׁבֶת בָּהּ וּלְקוֹמֵם
אֶת הֲרִיסוֹתֶיהָ, אֶת אַדְמָתָהּ.

וּבְקוּם עָלֵינוּ אוֹיְבִים וַיִּתְנַכְּלוּ לָנוּ לְהַשְׁמִידֵנוּ, אַתָּה בִּגְבוּרָתְךָ הִפַּלְתָּ עֲלֵיהֶם
אֵימָתָה וָפַחַד וַיֵּעָזְבוּ אֶת כָּל אֲשֶׁר לָהֶם, וַיָּנוּסוּ בְּבֶהָלָה וּבְחִפָּזוֹן אֶל מִחוּץ
לִגְבוּלוֹת אַרְצֵנוּ. וּבְבוֹא עָלֵינוּ שִׁבְעָה גוֹיִם לְכַבֵּשׁ אֶת אַרְצֵנוּ וּלְשִׂימֵנוּ לְמַס
עוֹבֵד, אַתָּה בְּרַחֲמֶיךָ עָמַדְתָּ לִימִין צְבָא הַהֲגָנָה לְיִשְׂרָאֵל וּמָסַרְתָּ גִּבּוֹרִים
בְּיַד חַלָּשִׁים, וְרַבִּים בְּיַד מְעַטִּים, וּרְשָׁעִים בְּיַד צַדִּיקִים. וּבִזְרוֹעֲךָ הַנְּטוּיָה
עָזַרְתָּ לְבַחוּרֵי יִשְׂרָאֵל לְהַרְחִיב אֶת גְּבוּלוֹת מוֹשְׁבוֹתֵינוּ, וּלְהַעֲלוֹת אֶת
אַחֵינוּ מִמַּחֲנוֹת הַהֶסְגֵּר.

עַל הַכֹּל אֲנַחְנוּ מוֹדִים לָךְ.

בְּנֵה נָא אֶת עִיר קָדְשְׁךָ יְרוּשָׁלַיִם בִּירַת יִשְׂרָאֵל וּבָהּ תְּכוֹנֵן אֶת בֵּית מִקְדָּשְׁךָ
כִּימֵי שְׁלֹמֹה, וְכַאֲשֶׁר זִכִּיתָנוּ לִרְאוֹת אֶת רֵאשִׁית גְּאֻלָּתֵנוּ וּפְדוּת נַפְשֵׁנוּ, כֵּן
תְּחַיֵּנוּ וּתְחַזֵּינָה עֵינֵינוּ בִּגְאֻלַּת יִשְׂרָאֵל הַשְּׁלֵמָה, וְחַדֵּשׁ יָמֵינוּ כְּקֶדֶם, אָמֵן.

ALTERNATIVE VERSION OF AL HANISSIM
Source: *The Order of Prayers for Yom HaAtzma'ut* (3rd Edition),
(Religious Kibbutz Movement, 1976)

עַל הַנִּסִּים וְעַל הַפֻּרְקָן וְעַל הַגְּבוּרוֹת וְעַל הַתְּשׁוּעוֹת וְעַל הַמִּלְחָמוֹת שֶׁעָשִׂיתָ
לַאֲבוֹתֵינוּ בַּיָּמִים הָהֵם בַּזְּמַן הַזֶּה.

אַתָּה הָאֵל עוֹרַרְתָּ אֶת לֵב אֲבוֹתֵינוּ לָשׁוּב לְהַר נַחֲלָתְךָ לָשֶׁבֶת בָּהּ וּלְקוֹמֵם
אֶת הֲרִיסוֹתֶיהָ אֶת אַדְמָתָהּ. וּבְעֲמֹד עָלֵינוּ שִׁלְטוֹן רֶשַׁע וַיִּסְגֹּר אֶת שַׁעֲרֵי

אַרְצֵנוּ בִּפְנֵי אַחֵינוּ הַנִּמְלָטִים מֵחֶרֶב אוֹיֵב אַכְזָרִי, וַיְשִׁיבֵם בָּאֳנִיּוֹת לְאִיֵּי
הַיָּם וּלְחוֹפִים נִדָּחִים, אַתָּה בְּעֻזְּךָ מִגַּרְתָּ אֶת כִּסְאוֹ וַתְּשַׁחְרֵר אֶת הָאָרֶץ
מִיָּדוֹ. וּבְקוּם עָלֵינוּ אוֹיְבִים וַיִּתְנַכְּלוּ לָנוּ לְהַשְׁמִידֵנוּ אַתָּה בִּגְבוּרָתְךָ הִפַּלְתָּ
עֲלֵיהֶם אֵימָתָה וָפַחַד וַיַּעַזְבוּ אֶת כָּל אֲשֶׁר לָהֶם, וַיָּנוּסוּ בְּבֶהָלָה וּבְחִפָּזוֹן
אֶל מִחוּץ לִגְבוּלוֹת אַרְצֵנוּ. וּבְבוֹא עָלֵינוּ שִׁבְעָה גוֹיִים לִכְבֹּשׁ אֶת אַרְצֵנוּ
וּלְשׁוּמֵנוּ לְמַס עוֹבֵד, אַתָּה בְּרַחֲמֶיךָ עָמַדְתָּ לִימִין צְבָא הַהֲגָנָה לְיִשְׂרָאֵל
וּמָסַרְתָּ גִּבּוֹרִים בְּיַד חַלָּשִׁים וְרַבִּים בְּיַד מְעַטִּים וּרְשָׁעִים בְּיַד צַדִּיקִים.
וּבִזְרוֹעֲךָ הַנְּטוּיָה עָזַרְתָּ לְבַחוּרֵי יִשְׂרָאֵל לְהַרְחִיב אֶת גְּבוּלוֹת מוֹשְׁבוֹתֵינוּ,
וּלְהַעֲלוֹת אֶת אַחֵינוּ מִמַּחֲנוֹת הַהֶסְגֵּר.

עַל הַכֹּל אֲנַחְנוּ מוֹדִים לָךְ יהוה אֱלֹהֵינוּ בִּכְפִיפַת רֹאשׁ. וּבְיוֹם זֶה, יוֹם
חַגֵּנוּ וְשִׂמְחָתֵנוּ, אֲנַחְנוּ פּוֹרְשִׂים אֶת כַּפֵּינוּ לְפָנֶיךָ וּמִתְחַנְּנִים עַל אַחֵינוּ
הַפְּזוּרִים וְאוֹמְרִים: אָנָּא אָבִינוּ רוֹעֵנוּ. קַבְּצֵם בִּמְהֵרָה לִנְוֵה קָדְשְׁךָ וְהַשְׁכֵּן
אוֹתָם בּוֹ בְּשָׁלוֹם וְשַׁלְוָה וּבְהַשְׁקֵט וָבֶטַח. הַרְחֵב נָא אֶת גְּבוּלוֹת אַרְצֵנוּ
כַּאֲשֶׁר הִבְטַחְתָּ לַאֲבוֹתֵינוּ. לָתֵת לְזַרְעָם מִנְּהַר פְּרָת וְעַד נַחַל מִצְרָיִם.
בְּנֵה נָא אֶת עִיר קָדְשְׁךָ יְרוּשָׁלַיִם בִּירַת יִשְׂרָאֵל וּבָהּ תְּכוֹנֵן אֶת בֵּית
מִקְדָּשְׁךָ כִּימֵי שְׁלֹמֹה. וְכַאֲשֶׁר זִכִּיתָנוּ לִרְאוֹת אֶת רֵאשִׁית גְּאֻלָּתֵנוּ וּפְדוּת
נַפְשֵׁנוּ, כֵּן תְּחַיֵּינוּ וְתֶחֱזֶינָה עֵינֵינוּ בִּגְאֻלַּת יִשְׂרָאֵל הַשְּׁלֵמָה וְחַדֵּשׁ יָמֵינוּ
כְּקֶדֶם, אָמֵן.

ALTERNATIVE VERSION OF AL HANISSIM AS
AN EXPRESSION OF NATIONAL RENEWAL

Source: E.Z. Melamed, *Pirkei Minhag VeHalakha* (Jerusalem, 1960)

עַל הַנִּסִּים וְעַל הַפֻּרְקָן וְעַל הַגְּבוּרוֹת וְעַל הַתְּשׁוּעוֹת וְעַל הַמִּלְחָמוֹת שֶׁעָשִׂיתָ
לַאֲבוֹתֵינוּ בַּיָּמִים הָהֵם בַּזְּמַן הַזֶּה.

אַתָּה הָאֵל עוֹרַרְתָּ אֶת לֵב אֲבוֹתֵינוּ לָשׁוּב לְהַר נַחֲלָתְךָ לָשֶׁבֶת בָּהּ וּלְקוֹמֵם
אֶת הֲרִיסוֹתֶיהָ וְלַעֲבֹד אֶת אַדְמָתָהּ. וּבַעֲמֹד עָלֵינוּ שִׁלְטוֹן רֶשַׁע וַיִּסְגֹּר אֶת
שַׁעֲרֵי אַרְצֵנוּ בִּפְנֵי אַחֵינוּ הַנִּמְלָטִים מֵחֶרֶב אוֹיֵב אַכְזָרִי, וַיְשִׁיבֵם בָּאֳנִיּוֹת
לְאִיֵּי הַיָּם וּלְחוֹפִים נִדָּחִים, אַתָּה בְּעֻזְּךָ מִגַּרְתָּ אֶת כִּסְאוֹ וַתְּשַׁחְרֵר אֶת
הָאָרֶץ מִיָּדוֹ. וּבְקוּם עָלֵינוּ אוֹיְבִים מִבַּיִת וַיִּתְנַכְּלוּ לָנוּ לְהַשְׁמִידֵנוּ אַתָּה
בִּגְבוּרָתְךָ הִפַּלְתָּ עֲלֵיהֶם אֵימָתָה וָפַחַד וַיַּעַזְבוּ אֶת כָּל אֲשֶׁר לָהֶם, וַיָּנוּסוּ

בְּבֶהָלָה וּבְחִפָּזוֹן אֶל מִחוּץ לִגְבוּלוֹת אַרְצֵנוּ. וּבְבוֹא עָלֵינוּ שִׁבְעָה גוֹיִים לִכְבֹּשׁ אֶת אַרְצֵנוּ וּלְשׂוּמֵנוּ לְמַס עוֹבֵד, אַתָּה בְּרַחֲמֶיךָ עָמַדְתָּ לִימִין צְבָא הַהֲגָנָה לְיִשְׂרָאֵל וּמָסַרְתָּ גִבּוֹרִים בְּיַד חַלָּשִׁים וְרַבִּים בְּיַד מְעַטִים וּרְשָׁעִים בְּיַד צַדִּיקִים. וּבִזְרוֹעֲךָ הַנְּטוּיָה עָזַרְתָּ לְבַחוּרֵי יִשְׂרָאֵל לְהַרְחִיב אֶת גְּבוּלוֹת מוֹשְׁבוֹתֵינוּ, וּלְהַעֲלוֹת אֶת אַחֵינוּ מִמַּחֲנוֹת הַהֶסְגֵּר.

עַל הַכֹּל אֲנַחְנוּ מוֹדִים לָךְ יהוה אֱלֹהֵינוּ בִּכְפִיפַת רֹאשׁ. וּבְיוֹם זֶה, יוֹם חַגֵּנוּ וְשִׂמְחָתֵנוּ, אֲנַחְנוּ פּוֹרְשִׂים אֶת כַּפֵּינוּ לְפָנֶיךָ וּמִתְחַנְּנִים עַל אַחֵינוּ הַפְּזוּרִים וְאוֹמְרִים: אָנָּא אָבִינוּ רוֹעֵנוּ. קַבְּצֵם בִּמְהֵרָה לִנְוֵה קָדְשֶׁךָ וְהַשְׁכֵּן אוֹתָם בּוֹ בְּשָׁלוֹם וְשַׁלְוָה וּבְהַשְׁקֵט וָבֶטַח. הַרְחֵב נָא אֶת גְּבוּלוֹת אַרְצֵנוּ כַּאֲשֶׁר הִבְטַחְתָּ לַאֲבוֹתֵינוּ. לָתֵת לְזַרְעָם מִנְּהַר פְּרָת וְעַד נַחַל מִצְרַיִם. בְּנֵה נָא אֶת עִיר קָדְשֶׁךָ יְרוּשָׁלַיִם בִּירַת יִשְׂרָאֵל וּבָהּ תִּכּוֹנֵן אֶת בֵּית מִקְדָּשֶׁךָ כִּימֵי שְׁלֹמֹה. וְכַאֲשֶׁר זִכִּיתָנוּ לִרְאוֹת אֶת רֵאשִׁית גְּאֻלָּתֵנוּ וּפְדוּת נַפְשֵׁנוּ, כֵּן תְּחַיֵּנוּ וְתַחֲזֶינָה עֵינֵינוּ בִּגְאֻלַּת יִשְׂרָאֵל הַשְּׁלֵמָה וְחַדֵּשׁ יָמֵינוּ כְּקֶדֶם, אָמֵן.

ALTERNATIVE VERSION OF AL HANISSIM
Source: Kedem Synagogue, Tel Aviv, 1970s

עַל הַנִּסִּים וְעַל הַפֻּרְקָן וְעַל הַגְּבוּרוֹת וְעַל הַתְּשׁוּעוֹת וְעַל הַמִּלְחָמוֹת שֶׁעָשִׂיתָ לַאֲבוֹתֵינוּ בַּיָּמִים הָהֵם בַּזְּמַן הַזֶּה.

אַתָּה הָאֵל עוֹרַרְתָּ אֶת לֵב אֲבוֹתֵינוּ לָשׁוּב לְהַר נַחֲלָתְךָ לָשֶׁבֶת בָּהּ וּלְקוֹמֵם אֶת הֲרִיסוֹתֶיהָ וְאֶת אַדְמָתָהּ.

וּבְבוֹא עָלֵינוּ שִׁבְעָה גוֹיִים לִכְבֹּשׁ אֶת אַרְצֵנוּ וּלְשׂוּמֵנוּ לְמַס עוֹבֵד, אַתָּה בְּרַחֲמֶיךָ עָמַדְתָּ לִימִין צְבָא הַהֲגָנָה לְיִשְׂרָאֵל וּמָסַרְתָּ רְשָׁעִים בְּיַד צַדִּיקִים וְרַבִּים בְּיַד מְעַטִים.

עַל הַכֹּל אֲנַחְנוּ מוֹדִים לָךְ יהוה אֱלֹהֵינוּ. וּבְיוֹם זֶה, יוֹם חַגֵּנוּ וְשִׂמְחָתֵנוּ, אָנוּ פּוֹרְשִׂים אֶת כַּפֵּינוּ לְפָנֶיךָ עַל אַחֵינוּ הַפְּזוּרִים וְאוֹמְרִים: אָנָּא אָבִינוּ, קַבְּצֵם בִּמְהֵרָה לִנְוֵה קָדְשֶׁךָ וְהַשְׁכֵּן אוֹתָם בּוֹ בְּשָׁלוֹם וְשַׁלְוָה וּבְהַשְׁקֵט וָבֶטַח, וְכַאֲשֶׁר זִכִּיתָנוּ לִרְאוֹת אֶת רֵאשִׁית גְּאֻלָּתֵנוּ, כֵּן תְּחַיֵּנוּ וְתַחֲזֶינָה עֵינֵינוּ בִּגְאֻלַּת יִשְׂרָאֵל הַשְּׁלֵמָה וְחַדֵּשׁ יָמֵינוּ כְּקֶדֶם, אָמֵן.

ALTERNATIVE VERSION OF AL HANISSIM
(TO BE SAID DURING THE AMIDA)

Rabbi Meshulam Madar, Zikhron Ya'akov.
Source: A. Arendt, *Pirkei Meḥkar leYom HaAtzma'ut* (Ramat Gan, 1998)

עַל הַנִּסִּים וְעַל הַנִּפְלָאוֹת שֶׁעָשִׂיתָ לַאֲבוֹתֵינוּ בַּיָּמִים הָהֵם בַּזְּמַן הַזֶּה.
בִּימֵי הַוַּעַד הַלְאֻמִּי לְיִשְׂרָאֵל, בִּשְׁנַת חֲמֵשֶׁת אֲלָפִים וּשְׁבַע מֵאוֹת וּשְׁמוֹנֶה
לִבְרִיאַת הָעוֹלָם בְּהִתְחַדֵּשׁ מַלְכוּת יִשְׂרָאֵל, קָמוּ כָל מֶמְשְׁלוֹת עֵרֶב לְהִלָּחֵם
בָּנוּ, וְאַתָּה בְּרַחֲמֶיךָ הָרַבִּים עָמַדְתָּ לָנוּ בְּעֵת צָרוֹתֵינוּ וְהִרְחַבְתָּ אֶת גְּבוּלֵינוּ
וְכֹחַ וָעֹז לְהִלָּחֵם בָּהֶם נָתַתָּ לָנוּ, וְלַהֲדֹף אוֹתָם מִגְּבוּלוֹת אַרְצֵנוּ עָזַרְתָּ לָנוּ,
וְרַבְתָּ אֶת רִיבֵנוּ, וְנָקַמְתָּ אֶת נִקְמָתֵנוּ, וּמָסַרְתָּ רַבִּים בְּיַד מְעַטִּים, וְעָשִׂיתָ לָנוּ
תְּשׁוּעָה גְדוֹלָה וְנִסִּים וְנִפְלָאוֹת. וּכְשֵׁם שֶׁעָשִׂיתָ עִמָּנוּ נִסִּים וְנִפְלָאוֹת בַּיָּמִים
הָהֵם, כֵּן תַּעֲשֶׂה עִמָּנוּ בַּיָּמִים הָאֵלּוּ יְשׁוּעוֹת וְנֶחָמוֹת וְתַחֲזִירֵנוּ בִּתְשׁוּבָה
שְׁלֵמָה לְפָנֶיךָ וְנוֹדֶה לְשִׁמְךָ הַגָּדוֹל סֶלָה.

RABBIS' KADDISH

Mourner: Yitgadal ve-yitkadash shemeh raba. (*Cong:* Amen)
Be-alema di vera khir'uteh, ve-yamlikh malkhuteh,
be-hayyeikhon, uv-yomeikhon,
uv-hayyei de-khol beit Yisrael,
ba-agala uvi-zman kariv,
ve-imru Amen. (*Cong:* Amen)

All: Yeheh shemeh raba mevarakh le'alam ul-alemei alemaya.

Mourner: Yitbarakh ve-yishtabah ve-yitpa'ar ve-yitromam ve-yitnaseh
ve-yit-hadar ve-yit'aleh ve-yit-hallal
shemeh dekudsha, berikh hu. (*Cong:* Berikh hu)
Le-ela min kol birkhata
ve-shirata, tushbehata ve-nehemata, da-amiran be-alema,
ve-imru, Amen. (*Cong:* Amen)

Al Yisrael, ve-al rabanan,
ve-al talmideihon, ve-al kol talmidei talmideihon,
ve-al kol man de-asekin be-oraita
di be-atra (*In Israel:* kadisha) ha-dein ve-di be-khol atar va-atar,
yeheh lehon ul-khon shelama raba,
hina ve-hisda, ve-rahamei,
ve-hayyei arikhei, um-zonei re-vihei,
u-furkana min kodam avuhon di vish-maya,
ve-imru Amen. (*Cong:* Amen)

Yeheh shelama raba min shemaya
ve-hayyim (tovim) aleinu ve-al kol Yisrael,
ve-imru Amen. (*Cong:* Amen)

*Bow, take three steps back, as if taking leave of the Divine Presence,
then bow, first left, then right, then center, while saying:*
Oseh shalom bim-romav,
hu ya'aseh ve-rahamav shalom aleinu, ve-al kol Yisrael,
ve-imru Amen. (*Cong:* Amen)

MOURNER'S KADDISH

Mourner: Yitgadal ve-yitkadash shemeh raba. (*Cong:* Amen)
Be-alema di vera khir'uteh, ve-yamlikh malkhuteh,
be-ḥayyeikhon, uv-yomeikhon,
uv-ḥayyei de-khol beit Yisrael,
ba-agala uvi-zman kariv,
ve-imru Amen. (*Cong:* Amen)

All: Yeheh shemeh raba mevarakh le'alam ul-alemei alemaya.

Mourner: Yitbarakh ve-yishtabaḥ ve-yitpa'ar ve-yitromam ve-yitnaseh
ve-yit-hadar ve-yit'aleh ve-yit-hallal
shemeh dekudsha, berikh hu. (*Cong:* Berikh hu)
Le-ela min kol birkhata
ve-shirata, tushbeḥata ve-neḥemata, da-amiran be-alema,
ve-imru, Amen. (*Cong:* Amen)

Yeheh shelama raba min shemaya
ve-ḥayyim aleinu ve-al kol Yisrael,
ve-imru Amen. (*Cong:* Amen)

Bow, take three steps back, as if taking leave of the Divine Presence,
then bow, first left, then right, then center, while saying:

Oseh shalom bim-romav,
hu ya'aseh shalom aleinu, ve-al kol Yisrael,
ve-imru Amen. (*Cong:* Amen)

THE KRENGEL FAMILY WORLD MIZRACHI EDITION

מחזור קורן
ליום העצמאות וליום ירושלים

THE KOREN MAHZOR FOR
YOM HAATZMA'UT AND YOM YERUSHALAYIM

THE MAIDENBAUM AND ROTHENBERG ESSAYS

KOREN PUBLISHERS JERUSALEM

The Koren Maḥzor for Yom HaAtzma'ut and Yom Yerushalayim
Second Hebrew/English Edition, 2016
Nusaḥ Ashkenaz

Koren Publishers Jerusalem Ltd.
POB 4044, Jerusalem 9104001, ISRAEL
POB 8531, New Milford, CT 06776, USA

www.korenpub.com

The poem "On Jerusalem Day" on pages xxx–xxxii, with translation by Rabbi Pesach Tarlow,
is printed with the kind permission of the Maidenbaum family © Nathan Maidenbaum, 1977.

The creation of this Maḥzor was made possible with the generous support of
Torah Education in Israel.

Printed in the United States of America

Standard Size, Hardcover, ISBN 978 965 301 665 1
Compact Size, Hardcover, ISBN 978 965 301 824 2

YHASA2

WORLD MIZRACHI

*dedicates this page to our partners
in this wonderful project.*

To all at Koren Publishers Jerusalem
*for affording us this partnership opportunity;
your reinvigoration of the venerable Koren publishing house
in recent years is inspirational.*

*Our deepest gratitude to our friends and sponsors
from around the world, who appear in the dedication pages
and whose generosity has made this publication possible.*

A specific heartfelt thank you to

Zev Krengel

*for your generosity to this project and for your
outstanding leadership of the South African Jewish community,
and for the tireless efforts of you and your brother Avrom on many levels,
for the sake of Torah, Israel and the Jewish community.
How appropriate it is that this publication bears the Krengel name.*

Shalom and Iris Maidenbaum
and
Robert and Helene Rothenberg

*of New York,
for your generosity to this project and for your incredible
commitment to Torah learning, Israel and the Jewish People.
How fitting it is that the essay section bears
the Maidenbaum and Rothenberg names.*

Rav Doron Perez
Director-General

Kurt Rothschild
President

Harvey Blitz
Chairman

We would like to dedicate this Maḥzor
on the occasion of the marriage
of our daughter

Dr. Jessica Rachel Rothenberg

formerly of New York

to

Jeremy Ryan Ross

formerly of New Zealand.

Jessica and Jeremy are true Zionists who left "their land,
their places of birth and their parents' homes,"
to build independent, productive lives in the land of Israel,
contributing to their nation and to the land that they love.
They represent the brave future of the Jewish people
who will return from the four corners of the earth.
Jessica and Jeremy are an inspiration to us all.

We would also like to dedicate this Maḥzor
in memory of

Natan Schulsinger ז״ל

1922–2009

An orphan of the Holocaust who, as a member of the "Breicha,"
smuggled Jewish survivors on foot across
the Austrian/Italian Alps to board ships to Israel.
He then joined the Israeli Navy
upon his own arrival in Israel in 1948.

Robert and Helene Rothenberg

*It has been our honor to be involved in the publication of
this maḥzor commemorating Israel's 67th year of independence,
as well as the 48th anniversary of the reunification of Jerusalem.*

We wish to remember our dear parents,
Annette and Bernard Lanner ז״ל
and
Nathan and Esther Maidenbaum ל

In addition, we remember
Cantor Moshe Ehrlich ז״ל
*of Congregation Beth Sholom of Lawrence, New York
and a past president of Bnei Akiva, North America.*

We would also like to acknowledge
Rabbi Bernard Rosensweig
*Rabbi Emeritus of the Kew Gardens Synagogue Adath Yeshurun
in honor of the marriage of his grandson,* **Avigdor Rosensweig**
to our great-niece **Devorah Schreiber** *of Alon Shvut.*

We continue to be inspired by our Moreh d'Asra,
Rabbi Kenneth Hain
also of Congregation Beth Sholom.

אחרונים אחרונים חביבים
*we would like to thank our dear children,
who bring us constant joy and
are committed Zionists of the next generation.*

Shalom and Iris Maidenbaum

לזכר נשמת בנינו בכורינו היקר

Yaakov Levi Matanky
יעקב לוי ז״ל

בן הרב אריה ומרים אסתר מטנקי

שנקטף בדמי חייו

ב׳ מנחם אב תשס״ב

Yaakov ז״ל
dedicated his years
to inspiring his חניכים
in Bnei Akiva and Camp Moshava
towards a love of
ארץ ישראל לעם ישראל על פי תורת ישראל

May this מחזור *serve as a living tribute to his memory.*

שמאי אומר

עשה תורתך קבע

אמור מעט ועשה הרבה

והוי מקבל את כל האדם בסבר פנים יפות

(אבות ה:טו)

Rabbi Leonard and Margaret Matanky
and family

We remember
all the brave fallen soldiers
of the Israel Defense Forces
whose ultimate sacrifice affords us
the privilege of our precious
Medinat Yisrael.

Note to the Reader

For the full Maḥzor text, with translation and commentary,
please turn to the other end of this volume.

Contents

EDITOR'S PREFACE

For those of us who came of age after 1948, the State of Israel can seem to be a commonplace reality, its existence a simple fact. Yet when viewed from a broad perspective – historic, halakhic, and theological – it emerges as an extraordinary phenomenon, and one pregnant with implications for our future.

The essays collected here aim to provide the reader with this broad perspective. They address a wide variety of sources and ideas, from Tanakh to the present day, that highlight the religious significance of Israel. Some of the contributors view the State of Israel as having redemptive potential, while others view it as part of an active redemptive process. All, however, agree about its centrality to our lives and to our destinies as Jews.

Just as Shabbat reminds us of the wonder of Creation, and the ḥagim remind us of the marvel of God's providence, Yom HaAtzma'ut and Yom Yerushalayim remind us not to take for granted the miracle of Israel, and to seize the many opportunities it presents us. Since this collection intends to deepen and enhance our observance of Yom HaAtzma'ut and Yom Yerushalayim, it includes contributions only from writers who merited to celebrate these holidays, both contemporary and from the previous generation.

Many people were instrumental in bringing these essays to print. Special thanks to assistant editor Tomi Mager, proofreader Ita Olesker, and research assistant Rabbi Jonathan Ziring for their skill and professionalism, and to Yehudit Singer and World Mizrachi's Rabbi Doron Perez for their valuable suggestions.

We would most especially like to thank our distinguished contributors for their articles. In the case of authors who have ascended to *yeshiva shel ma'ala*, we are grateful to their families for allowing the republication of their essays. The contribution of an essay to this volume indicates the author's endorsement of the importance of Yom HaAtzma'ut and Yom Yerushalayim, not of the particular liturgical expression they should receive. Unless noted otherwise in the credits below, essays were written for this volume or for the original Hebrew version of the *Maḥzor Koren LeYom HaAtzma'ut* (Jerusalem, 2013).

❧ ❧ ❧

After two millennia of wandering and yearning, the Jewish people have returned to their homeland – a homeland that serves as a haven for Jews and a focus for Jewish identity, that enables the flourishing of Torah and the living of a holistic and integrated religious life. Perhaps the central challenge of our time is to shape our old-new home, to improve it and elevate it, so that, beyond all these, it will become a fountain of holiness, a beacon of justice, and a light unto the nations. This is a challenge and opportunity that calls out to each of us.

May we speedily behold the complete fulfillment of Isaiah's prophecy:

> For the Lord has comforted Zion, comforted all her ruins;
> He has made her wilderness like Eden, and her desert like the garden of the Lord;
> Joy and gladness shall abide there, thanksgiving and the sound of music...
> And the redeemed of the Lord shall return, and come with singing to Zion, crowned with everlasting joy;
> They shall obtain gladness and joy, and sorrow and sighing shall flee away. (51:3, 11)

Rabbi Reuven Ziegler
Jerusalem, 5775

CREDITS FOR REPUBLICATION AND TRANSLATION

Rabbi Tzvi Yehuda Kook *zt"l*: *Mitzpeh* Annual, 5713 (1953); reprinted in *LiNetivot Yisrael*, Beit El: MeAvnei HaMakom, 5762, 261–72. With thanks to MeAvnei HaMakom Publishers, Kiryat HaYeshiva Beit-El. Translated by Yoseif Bloch.

Rabbi Joseph B. Soloveitchik *zt"l*: Yom HaAtzma'ut 1956. Published as *"Kol Dodi Dofek"* in S. Federbusch, ed., *Torah UMelukha*, Jerusalem: Mossad Harav Kook, 1961, 11–44. English translation: Chapter 4 of *Kol Dodi Dofek: Listen – My Beloved Knocks*, New York: Yeshiva University, 2006, 31–42. With thanks to Prof. Haym Soloveitchik and Yeshiva University. Translated and annotated by David Z. Gordon.

Rabbi Shaul Yisraeli *zt"l*: Introduction to Rabbi Yisraeli's *Eretz Hemda*, Jerusalem: Mossad HaRav Kook, 1957. With thanks to the family of Rabbi Yisraeli and Mossad HaRav Kook. Translated by Yoseif Bloch.

Rabbi Nachum Rabinovitch: an address to the Rabbinical Council of America conference in Jerusalem, January, 1974. Published in *Tradition* 14:4 (Fall 1974), 20–28. With thanks to *Tradition* and the Rabbinical Council of America.

Rabbi Jonathan Sacks: *Future Tense*, London: Hodder and Stoughton, 2009, 131–53; US edition, New York: Schocken, 2010, 131–53. © 2009 Jonathan Sacks. Reproduced by permission of Hodder and Stoughton Limited and Random House LLC.

Rabbi Herschel Schachter: *Journal of Halacha and Contemporary Society*, vol. 8 (1984), 14–33. With thanks to the Rabbi Jacob Joseph School.

Rabbi Michael Rosensweig: From an address to the IPA Forum on Public Policy, January 1998.

Rabbi Yehuda Amital *zt"l*: Yom HaAtzma'ut 1994. From the Israel Koschitzky Virtual Beit Midrash. With thanks to the Amital family and Yeshivat Har Etzion. Adapted by Prof. Aviad Hacohen, translated by Kaeren Fish.

Rabbi Chaim Druckman: *LaZeman HaZeh*, Merkaz Shapira: Or Etzion, 2013, 263–72. With thanks to Yeshivat Or Etzion. Translated by Yoseif Bloch.

Rabbi Mordechai Greenberg: adapted from "*Tokfo shel Yom: LeMahuto shel Yom HaAtzma'ut*," Yeshivat Kerem B'Yavneh, 5758; reprinted in Rabbi Greenberg's *MiDarkhei HaKerem*, Yeshivat Kerem B'Yavneh, 5775, 363–84. With thanks to Yeshivat Kerem B'Yavneh. Translated by Meira Mintz.

Rabbi Eliyahu Sadan: *Vayehi Yadav Emuna*, 2nd ed., Eli: Yeshivat Bnei David, 2013, 162–65. With thanks to Yeshivat Bnei David. Translated by David Siegel.

Rabbi Yoel Bin-Nun: *Daf Kesher* 759 (29 Iyar 5760), Yeshivat Har Etzion. Translated by Sara Daniel.

Rabbi Mosheh Lichtenstein: "*Zekhor Lanu Brit Aharonim*," *Sinai* 129–130 (5762), 313–28; English: "The Religious Meaning of Yom HaAtzma'ut," *Alei Etzion* 14 (Adar 5766), 39–56. Translated by David Silverberg.

Rabbi Yitzhak Nissim *zt"l*: Yom Yerushalayim 1968. *LeDor UleDorot: Mivhar Ma'amarim UNe'umim shel HaRav Yitzhak Nissim*, ed. Rabbi Shmuel Katz, Jerusalem, 2013, 116–21. Translated by Sara Daniel.

Rabbi Shmuel Katz, Rabbi Benjamin Lau, Rabbi Yaakov Medan, Dr. Yoel Rappel: Translated by Sara Daniel.

INTRODUCTION
ISRAEL AND THE ART OF APPRECIATION

The establishment of the State of Israel and the reunification of Jerusalem are undoubtedly the most important events of salvation and deliverance in Jewish history since the time of Ḥanukka almost 2,200 years ago.

Miracles of Biblical Proportions

The remarkable reality of a sovereign State of Israel, only three years after the ovens of Auschwitz, and a united Jerusalem in which the Old City and Temple Mount fall under Jewish sovereignty for the first time since the Destruction in 70 CE, cannot be overstated. A handful of young pioneers and Holocaust survivors, and their descendants, overcame impossible political and military odds to defeat much larger and better trained national armies – "*delivering*," twice in nineteen years, "*the many into the hands of the few*." Now, after two thousand years, Israel has become a place of refuge for millions of Jewish exiles from over one hundred countries, speaking more than eighty languages. Hebrew has been revived from an ancient and static language of textual study into the living *lingua franca* of Jewish society. The Land of Israel itself has been transformed from an arid and barren backwater into a flourishing oasis of agriculture and an ecological marvel, home to a thriving and sustainable economy built from a bankrupt and starving old *Yishuv*. Israel, by its very existence, has facilitated a world with perhaps more Torah learners than at any other time in history. All this together creates a modern-day sovereign Israel and Jerusalem which stand at the center of Jewish religious, cultural, and political life. But perhaps more than anything, Israel has revived the spirit of a broken people, replacing despair with hope and faith, tragedy with triumph, and creating the belief in a bright future.

Complexity

The days of Yom HaAtzma'ut and Yom Yerushalayim were instituted by the Chief Rabbinate of Israel, and affirmed by all subsequent Chief Rabbinates, as days of great religious and halakhic significance. They are intended to be days of *Hallel* – praise and thanksgiving to Hashem in appreciation for these momentous times. Despite the seemingly undeniable miraculous nature of the events upon which these days are based, not everyone has embraced Yom HaAtzma'ut and Yom Yerushalayim in this spirit. One of the main reasons that many in the religious world have yet to do so is due to the complex spiritual, cultural, and political context in which Zionism and Israel were born. Many of the original and current protagonists in the story of Israel were and are distant from traditional Torah values, and at times even antagonistic toward them. In many ways, Zionism was developed from the ideological "isms" of the late-nineteenth century. Growing out of the cultural milieu of the Emancipation, *Haskala*, and Western, romantic nationalism, it is at times challenging to reconcile the aims of Zionism with Torah and Halakha. This complexity causes confusion for many, and creates doubt as to the appropriate spiritual context within which to place Israel's founding events, and hence how to relate to these days of deliverance.

The Dayeinu Song – Shifting Paradigms

I believe that the song *Dayeinu*, which appears in the Haggada and is sung spiritedly every year on the original night of deliverance for the Jewish people, *Leil HaSeder* – Seder night – is a most powerful guide to the art of appreciation and specifically to the appropriate attitude to the State of Israel in general and to Yom HaAtzma'ut and Yom Yerushalayim in particular. The reason is twofold. Firstly, this song forms the very first words of praise and gratitude that we utter at the Seder immediately after completing the story of the exodus from Egypt. As such, it forms the basis and foundation of Hallel – praise and thanksgiving to God for our original deliverance. Secondly, the song is all encompassing in nature. It reflects not only on the beginning of the journey to redemption, the exodus from Egypt and the theme of Pesaḥ, but on the entire journey of Jewish history, culminating in the building of the Temple in Jerusalem centuries later. It describes fifteen stages of this process of historical

redemption, and provides a critical insight into the process as a whole, and what our attitude at each stage should be.

The secret to revealing the profundity of this song lies in attempting to understand its apparent absurdity. A closer look at the song of *Dayeinu* reveals that many stanzas don't seem to make any logical sense at all. After each and every one of the fifteen stanzas, the Hebrew word *dayeinu* appears. In English, *dayeinu* means, "It would have been enough," It is the key phrase and chorus of the song.

If Hashem would have brought us out of Egypt and not split the sea, *dayeinu* – "It would have been enough."

If Hashem would have split the sea and not given us food and water in the desert, *dayeinu* – "It would have been enough." These are but two examples of the fifteen stages mentioned in the song.

Yet, this seems ludicrous. After all, if Hashem had brought us out of Egypt but not split the sea, surely we would all have died at the hands of the advancing Egyptian army.

If Hashem had split the sea but not given us food and water, surely we would all have died of starvation and heat exhaustion in the desert. It is abundantly clear that each individual stage is inherently incomplete without the continuation of the stage that follows. If the process of redemption had become "stuck" at any one of the fourteen stages following the exodus itself, it most certainly would *not* have been enough. The purpose of the redemption from Egypt would not have been achieved and the process would have been a failure.

An Attitude of Gratitude

The answer to this question is to understand the very essence of what gratitude and saying "thank you" is all about. In it lies the crux of the song and its relevance for us today. If our only focus in life is one of goal orientation, then we will never be able to feel appreciation for anything until we have achieved our goal. If we focus solely on the destination, we will find it exceptionally difficult to appreciate each stage of the journey. If the purpose of the *Dayeinu* song is to celebrate reaching the goal of redemption then indeed, it would *never* have been enough.

The *Dayeinu* song is about a different frame of mind – the mindset of gratitude and appreciation. When we focus on each stage of the process

itself and not on the end result, we can appreciate every small step. *When we see how far we have come as opposed to how far there is to go, what we have as opposed to what we still lack, we are able to feel deep gratitude irrespective of whether we have achieved our final aim or not.* The word *dayeinu* in this song means "it would have been enough *to say thank you.*" Hence, if Hashem had brought us out of Egypt but not split the sea, we would have thanked Him for this miraculous act, for this taste of freedom and dignity, regardless of what the future held. If Hashem had split the sea, but we had died of starvation and heat exhaustion soon afterward, we ought still to have thanked Him for having experienced the unparalleled marvel of the splitting of the sea and the work of divine justice against the Egyptian oppressors.

It is for this reason that Dayeinu also focuses on the final destination of the journey of redemption which began in Egypt – the arrival in the Land of Israel and the building of the Temple. This long and arduous journey, which wound itself through fifteen stages and 480 years until the building of the Temple in Solomon's time, should never prevent us from fully appreciating all Hashem has done for us every step of the way.

The Pesaḥ Pattern – Perfect Thanks in Imperfect Times

This then, is the essence of Hallel, saying *shira* and giving thanks. It is the ability to feel perfectly grateful in an imperfect situation. It requires a capacity to feel complete appreciation in a wholly incomplete reality. This is what gratitude and appreciation are about.

What is fascinating to contemplate is indeed just how imperfect our original deliverance from Egypt was. Our sages say that at least four-fifths of the Jewish people did not come out of Egypt and died in the plague of Darkness. While it is highly unlikely that this comment of the sages was meant as historical fact, it is clear that they wished to highlight the partial nature of the redemption.*

---

* The Midrash *Mekhilta* comments on the verse in Exodus (13:18) – "וחמושים עלו בני ישראל מארץ מצרים – And the Children of Israel went up armed out of the land of Egypt." Even though the word חמושים literally does mean armed (Joshua 1:14 and 4:12), the sages of the Midrash reflected on the additional meaning which comes from the number five, חמש. Rashi points out in his commentary to this verse one of the opinions mentioned in the midrash,

Furthermore, it was only three months from the day of salvation itself that *Bnei Yisrael* sinned with the Golden Calf, when only Moses' intense supplication saved them from annihilation. And it was barely a year later when the entire people of Israel chose to follow the ill advice of the ten spies and decided not to enter the Promised Land. This time, even Moses' heart-wrenching prayers could not prevent divine retribution. An entire generation died out in the desert, never achieving the aim of their redemption – entering into Eretz Yisrael.

The fact that so many died in Egypt, the subsequent horrific sins of the Golden Calf and the Spies, and the death of almost an entire generation, have never deterred us from celebrating Pesah. Indeed, since that very day until today we continue to celebrate the incomplete and imperfect redemption in the most perfect and complete way on *Leil HaSeder* and indeed throughout the week of Pesah.

Dayeinu is sung at a critical point in the Haggada narrative: immediately after we complete the story of the exodus and just before we begin Hallel. It is both our final reflection on the exodus and the opening lines of the Hallel that is about to follow. As such, it creates a crucial spiritual

that only one-fifth of the Children of Israel came out of Egypt, with the other four-fifths dying in the plague of Darkness. Amazingly, the midrash mentions two additional views that only one-fiftieth, or even more remarkably only one five-hundredth of the Children of Israel came out of Egypt. If we assume that there were around three million people who came out of Egypt, then according to the first view, twelve million remained behind. This would mean there were fifteen million Jews at the time. Even if this were feasible from a historic point of view, the other two points of view seem yet more unlikely, if not impossible – it would have meant that there were either half a billion Jews or 1.5 billion Jews! Additionally, it would mean that only a miniscule three million people came out while close to half a billion (or 1.5 billion) died in Egypt. This would have been a Shoah of unparalleled and unimaginable proportions. It seems, therefore, clear that the rabbis are not talking about historical facts, but rather philosophical insights into these occurrences. The central point of this midrash is not about the historical number of people, but rather to teach an important lesson about the nature of redemption. Perhaps it is that only small percentages merit seeing the light of redemption, while the vast majority of others lose themselves in either the darkness of exile or myopic philosophical vision.

paradigm within which to place our original exodus experience. It also forms a pivotal frame of reference to understand future processes of redemption.

This is a pertinent insight for us today. The State of Israel is, for many people, still distant from the ideal spiritual and moral state that it could become. There is no question that there is still a long journey ahead and so much more to pray for and to achieve. At the same time, this should never cloud our ability to appreciate the enormous accomplishments at every step of the way since the beginning of the Zionist endeavor; the establishment of the State, the reunification of Jerusalem, and the ongoing miracle that is the modern State of Israel. The Chief Rabbinate's designation of Yom HaAtzma'ut and Yom Yerushalayim as days of Hallel and thanksgiving capture the spirit of *Dayeinu* – to express heartfelt gratitude and appreciation for the enormity of the miracles that we have experienced, despite the fact that many stages of redemption still remain ahead.

May these great days live up to their designated aim – to be days of celebration and appreciation by all of *Klal Yisrael* for the era in which we are privileged to live. In a personal spirit of thanks, I have written a modern-day *Dayeinu* song in honor of Israel, which appears at the end of this article.

World Mizrachi and Koren

We at World Mizrachi feel honored to have partnered with Koren Publishers Jerusalem in the publication of this wonderful Maḥzor. Mizrachi was a significant partner in the founding of both the Zionist movement and the State of Israel; it was then, and remains today, the flagship of the Religious Zionist movement. Mizrachi – an acronym for two words, *merkaz ruḥani*, a spiritual center – has always committed itself to being a full and proactive partner in the Zionist enterprise and a constant reminder of its spiritual nature and destiny. How appropriate it is, therefore, that we have the privilege to be associated with this Yom HaAtzma'ut and Yom Yerushalayim Maḥzor which expresses our appreciation to Hashem for the remarkable times in which we live. What is unique about this publication is that it is not only a beautiful Maḥzor as part of the Koren Maḥzor series, but also a *sefer* containing articles by major rabbinic and educational leaders from across the religious Zionist world, both in Israel and

beyond. This incredible cadre of contributors anchors the place of Israel and Jerusalem in general, and Yom HaAtzma'ut and Yom Yerushalayim in particular, in Torah thought and halakhic life.

It is my sincere hope and prayer that this publication enhances the spiritual and religious significance of Yom HaAtzma'ut and Yom Yerushalayim throughout the Jewish world and contributes in the broadest possible way to the acceptance of these two days as our modern days of redemption and deliverance.

A MODERN-DAY DAYEINU SONG

IF Hashem had brought us back to the Land of Israel,
BUT not given us a sovereign state,
> DAYEINU – it would have been enough.

IF Hashem had given us a sovereign state and allowed us a taste of freedom and dignity for but a moment,
BUT we would have lost the War of Independence,
> DAYEINU – it would have been enough.

IF Hashem had helped us be victorious in the War of Independence,
BUT we would not have succeeded in building a viable country,
> DAYEINU – it would have been enough.

IF Hashem had helped us build a viable country,
BUT not brought back hundreds of thousands of Jews from Sephardic and Yemenite backgrounds,
> DAYEINU – it would have been enough.

IF Hashem had brought back hundreds of thousands of Jews from Sephardic and Yemenite backgrounds,
BUT not allowed us to win the Six-Day War,
> DAYEINU – it would have been enough.

IF Hashem had allowed us to win the Six-Day War,
BUT not given back to us the holy cities of Ḥevron, Beit El, Shilo, as well as the Golan Heights,
> DAYEINU – it would have been enough.

IF Hashem had given us Ḥevron, Beit El, Shilo, and the Golan Heights,
BUT not allowed us to liberate the Old City of Yerushalayim,
>> DAYEINU – it would have been enough.

IF Hashem had allowed us to liberate the Old City of Yerushalayim,
BUT not allowed us to rebuild her ruins,
>> DAYEINU – it would have been enough.

IF Hashem had allowed us to rebuild His Old City,
BUT not made Jerusalem into Israel's largest city with a population of over 800,000 people,
>> DAYEINU – it would have been enough.

IF Hashem had made Jerusalem Israel's largest city with a population of over 800,000 people,
BUT not allowed us to live with dignity in secure borders,
>> DAYEINU – it would have been enough.

IF Hashem had allowed us to live in secure borders,
BUT not created a strong and sustainable economy,
>> DAYEINU – it would have been enough.

IF Hashem had built for us a strong and sustainable economy,
BUT not ingathered the exiles from almost a hundred countries,
>> DAYEINU – it would have been enough.

IF Hashem had ingathered the exiles from almost a hundred countries,
BUT not allowed us to rebuild the Torah world in Israel with well over a hundred thousand men and women studying Torah full-time, perhaps the most in Jewish history,
>> DAYEINU – it would have been enough.

IF Hashem had rebuilt the Yeshiva and Torah world,
BUT not produced so many outstanding Torah scholars and leaders,
>> DAYEINU – it would have been enough.

IF Hashem had produced so many outstanding Torah scholars and leaders,
BUT not opened the gates of freedom to the oppressed Russian and Ethiopian Jews,
>> DAYEINU – it would have been enough.

IF Hashem had opened the gates of freedom to the oppressed Russian
and Ethiopian Jews,

BUT not made Israel's Jewish population soon-to-be larger than that of
world Jewry for the first time in 2,500 years,

DAYEINU – it would have been enough.

Rabbi Doron Perez
World Mizrachi
Jerusalem, 5775

NATHAN MAIDENBAUM, "ON JERUSALEM DAY"

My grandfather, Nathan Maidenbaum, ז״ל, was a dynamic and charismatic Torah scholar and Hebrew poet, as well as a self-made businessman. Born in Poland and educated in the Zionist schools of Tarbut and Mizrachi's Tachkemoni, his background provided him with the impetus to support Torah education and Zionism throughout his life. His proficiency in Tanakh and Hebrew literature, as well as his admiration for Zionist authors and poets such as Chaim Nachman Bialik and Uri Zvi Greenberg, inspired his own creative writing and literary contributions to *Hadoar* and *Panim el Panim*. Abba, as he was known to his children and grandchildren, was a kind, loving, and generous man with a cheerful disposition. He was steadfast in his support of Religious Zionism and among the first national vice presidents of Mizrachi in America. He was versatile in the sense that he maintained his religious convictions while navigating the challenges of succeeding in a secular world.

Although I was only ten years old when my grandfather passed away suddenly, he was an encouraging inspiration for my own rabbinical and Religious Zionist aspirations. Nathan Maidenbaum imbued his entire family with passionate Zionist values and was one of the "Master Builders" of Yeshiva University in New York, where I earned my rabbinical ordination, leading ultimately to my life's work today as a *reish metivta* at Yeshivat Har Etzion in Gush Etzion. I am proud to be fulfilling my grandfather's dream, living in Israel, in Gush Etzion, in the community of Alon Shvut, where I reside with my devoted wife, Aviva, and our dear children.

The poem which follows is one of Abba's last poetic endeavors, written two years prior to his untimely death in 1979. It was written in 1977 in honor of the tenth anniversary of Jerusalem's reunification. In his poem, written in Hebrew and translated into English, Abba articulates his

memorable and emotional first visit to Eretz Yisrael in 1947, and lovingly describes Yerushalayim alternately in emotional and historical contexts.

For more on the poem and to see the original handwritten poem by Nathan Maidenbaum with footnotes to Rabbi Pesach Tarlow's English translation, as well as acknowledgments by Prime Minister Menachem Begin and Professor Elie Wiesel, visit: www.yom-yerushalayim-nm.com.

With love and pride, I would like to acknowledge the significant contribution made to this publication by my aunt and uncle, Iris and Shalom Maidenbaum of Lawrence, New York.

Rabbi Doniel Schreiber
Alon Shvut, 5775

יום ב', כ"ח אייר תשל"ז   ב"ה

ליום "ירושלים"!

"זרים באו נחלתך", לפני שנות אלפיים,
נתצו חומותייך והרסו אותך, עיר הצדק, ירושלים!
בָּנַיִך עוּנו, חוללו והוגלו לכל אֲתָר וַאֲתָר.
נשארת אלמנה מבנים, כבושה בידי מושל זר.
שרידי גיבורי מצדה, קדשו נפשם אֱלֵי-קְרָב,
אַך נָפְלָה בקרבן, למאות שנים, בידי ישמעאל ונושאי-הצלב.

בכינו על נהרות כל הגלויות, זכרנו סבלך והכאב,
אַך בלבנו תמיד היית (כדברי ר' יהודה הלוי) המרכז והלֵב,
עָרגנו אֵלַיך, חָלמנו וארגנו חלומות, התפללנו תפילות:
"לירושלים עירך", שלוש פעמים ביום, השתפכנו בבכי ותפילות.
יתומים מאמא אוהבת, נשארנו בגלויות הרבה שנים!
עד שלפני כשלושים שנה, ב"ה, התקוממו גיבורינו – הבנים.

בפעם הראשונה דרכתי בחוצותייך ירושלים, לפני שלושים שנים.
ראיתיך דמועה, כואבת, נוגָה ובעצבות פנים.
אז גיבורי המחתרות חֵירפו נפשם, ובעוז שפתו דם,
נגד הכובשים, קלגסי זרים "הכַּלְניות" של בריטניה העם,
נראית לי אז כבולה ונתונה באזיקים,
וה-C.I.D., של הוד מלכותו הכתר הבריטי, בָּך מחזיקים!
ובימם ההם, הבריטי אָז היה בארץ עז,
נדכאנו מאד בעינוּיים אֲיומים, ולתקוות חֵירותנו בָּז.

רְאיתיך אז ירושלים! מפוצלת ובתוכה בְּוינגרד,
מוקפת אלפי חיילים וטנקים, של גנרל בַּרקר מכל עבר וְצַד.

בשנת תש"ח "אֵל נקמות הופיע" הָיינו דור ראשון לאתחלתא דגאולה.
בָּנַיִך ובנותייך התגייסו באהבת נפש לזו הפעולה,
אַך אחרי יום העצמאות, עדיין נשארת חֲצויה בְּפִגְיוֹן בַּגב,

עַל חוֹמוֹתַיִךְ, בְּכוֹנְנוֹת קְרָבִית, עָמְדוּ יְחִידוֹת לְגִיוֹנוֹת עֲרָב.
מִימִינֵךְ, גִּיסוֹת עֲבַדְלָה, וּבָאֶמְצַע הֶפְקֵר הָיָה הַשֶּׁטַח,
נָשָׂאנוּ עֵינֵינוּ מֵרָחוֹק לְ"כוֹתֶל" – בְּקָלוֹן, לַעַן וָמֶתַח...

לִפְנֵי עֶשֶׂר שָׁנִים בְּדִיוּק הִסְתָּעֲרוּ בָּנַיִךְ בִּגְבוּרָה וָלַהַב,
לִכְבּוֹשׁ "הָעִיר הָעַתִּיקָה", נִלְחֲמוּ בְּהַקְרָבָה עַצְמִית וּבְאַהַב
שִׁחְרְרוּ אוֹתָךְ מִשּׂוֹנְאַיִךְ, אֶחָדוּ גוּפָךְ הַפָּצוּעַ, "חוּבֶּרֶת יַחְדָּיו" "עִיר שֶׁכּוּלָךְ זָהָב".

נָעַם לִי כָּל בִּיקוּר בִּירוּשָׁלַיִם בְּכָל שָׁנָה בָּעֶרֶךְ,
דּוֹרֵךְ עַל אַדְמָתֶךְ, מִבַּית וְגַן עַד הַ"כּוֹתֶל" הַדֶּרֶךְ,
הַהַרְגָּשָׁה נִפְלָאָה, עִילָּאִית וֶאֱלוֹהִית הָאֲוִירָה,
אֵין כָּמוֹךְ לְיוֹפִי וָאוֹפִי – מִימֵי דָוִד, אֶת יְרוּשָׁלַיִם הַבִּירָה!
וַיֵּאָמֵר הַיּוֹם לָעוֹלָם "הַנָּאוֹר" וְ"לִידִידֵינוּ", שַׁגְרִירוּרֵי צַהַ"ל
נִשְׁבְּעוּ בְּדָמָם, שֶׁבִּירוּשָׁלַיִם לֹא נְוֹתֵר עַל רֶגֶב – אַף שַׁעַל!

לְעוֹלְמֵי־עַד תְּהִי שֶׁלָּנוּ! – מְאֻוחֶדֶת!
"קִרְיָה נֶאֱמָנָה" לָנוּ – בָּאֲצִילוּת נֶחְמֶדֶת!

— · —

כְּדִבְרֵי הַנָּבִיא הוֹשֵׁעַ, בְּהַפְטָרַת הַשָּׁבוּעַ,
כָּל לֵב יְהוּדִי אוֹמֵר לִירוּשָׁלַיִם:
"וְאֵרַשְׂתִּיךְ לִי לְעוֹלָם" בְּנִימָה נְעִימָה.

אַתְּ מְשׂוֹשׂ לִבֵּנוּ! תִּקְוֹת חַיֵּינוּ! אַתְּ לָנוּ כְּאִמָּא, אִמָּא.

נחום מ'

Monday, 28 Iyar, 5737

Foreigners came to Your inheritance, 2,000 years ago, smashed your walls and destroyed you, O city of righteousness, Jerusalem! Your children were tortured, defiled, and exiled to the ends of the earth. You remained a widow separated from your children, and crushed under foreign rule. The remnants of the heroes of Masada sacrificed their lives by the solemn oath of battle, but still you fell into Ishmaelite and Crusader hands for hundreds of years.

By the streams of our exile we wept, we remembered your suffering and pain.

But in our hearts (as Judah HaLevi once said) you were always the focal point and spiritual heart of the nation. We longed for you, we dreamt about you and wove dreams for you, we prayed for you. "For Jerusalem Your city," three times a day we poured out our hearts in tears and prayers. We have been orphans separated from a loving mother, left for centuries in exile. Until thirty years ago – thank God! – our brave young men rose up.

The first time I walked through your outskirts, O Jerusalem, some thirty years ago, I saw you bathed in tears, hurting, plaintive, and with a mournful countenance. Then the underground's valiant young men fought, without regard to personal safety, courageously losing their blood, against the conquerors, the British soldiers of occupation. You then appeared fettered and shackled while the soldiers of the C.I.D. – of the glorious crown of the British Empire – had you in their grasp. In those days, the British maintained their stronghold on the land; how depressed we were, our freedom being scorned, with little or no hope for our liberty.

I saw you then, Jerusalem! A divided city, and inside it Bevingrad, surrounded on every side by General Barker's thousands of soldiers and tanks. And in the year 5708, "God of vengeance, shine forth!" – we were the first generation of the Redemption. Then your sons and daughters gladly mobilized for the great event, but after the Day of Independence, you were still cut by a dagger in your back. On your walls stood the Arab Legions' units ready to do battle; on your right were Abdullah's columns. In the middle lay the empty expanse of No Man's Land and from afar we gazed at the Kotel with a mixture of disgrace, bitterness, and tension.

Exactly ten years ago, your sons, in an enthusiastic deed of glory, stormed and took the Old City. Fighting with self-sacrifice and love, they liberated you from your enemies and united your wounded body. Now joined together, you are whole – a Golden City.

For me each visit to Jerusalem is pleasant, as each year I trod your soil from Bayit Vegan to the Kotel, such a wondrous path of feelings – the air superb and Godly. There is none like you in beauty or character. From the time of David, you are Jerusalem the capital! And let it be told to the "civilized world" today and to "our friends" that by their blood the heroes of Tzahal have sworn that not one inch of Jerusalem shall ever be taken.

You will be ours, forever and a day! United!

"A Faithful City," for us you are a gracious divine inspiration!

As the Prophet Hosea said, in this week's Haftara, the heart of each Jew says to Jerusalem, "I will betroth You unto me forever."

In a note of joy with gleeful hearts you are the hope of our lives – you are as a mother to us, as a mother.

Translated by Rabbi Pesach Tarlow
on behalf of Nathan Maidenbaum

Eretz Yisrael and Medinat Yisrael

The Redemptive Vision

Rabbi Tzvi Yehuda Kook

I.

The vision of Israel's redemption is revealed in the words of the Torah and the Prophets, and further expounded and explicated in the Oral Torah and in the words of our sages and their successors, throughout all generations.

Exile is the destruction of the life of the nation, in that it is removed from its rightful place, as we say in our prayers, "We have been exiled from our land and distanced from our territory." Correspondingly, redemption, which is the nullification of exile, is the rejuvenation of the life of the nation, restoring its youth, as the Jewish people are once again connected to their rightful place. The first redemption culminates in a return to our *morasha*, our patrimony, the Land of Israel (Ex. 6:8). This parallels our other *morasha*, the Torah, which is given to "the congregation of Jacob" and is the guarantor of their salvation (Deut. 33:4).

Similarly, the final redemption ends with returning to this *morasha*, which exists forever; it replenishes and rejuvenates the Jewish people, uplifting their spirit and empowering their greatness. Just as the exile of the nation causes the overwhelming impurity of foreign lands to silence the song of God, the Divine Presence is also banished and displaced: "He was afflicted in all their afflictions" (Is. 63:9). This nullifies the Torah: "Since Israel have become exiled from their place, you can have no greater

neglect of the Torah than this" (*Ḥagiga* 5b), as the Torah could not be properly studied and applied, nor could it be spiritually incisive. In the Passover Haggada, we read the verse, "And the Egyptians did evil to us" (Deut. 26:6), which may be understood in the following way: the Egyptians made us evil (see *Olat Re'iya*; *Midrash HaGadol, Parashat Vayera*, "For I have known him") – in exile, we became deficient. The converse is true of redemption, the annulment of exile, which renews God's appearance from His place (see Ezek. 3:12), from the purity of the homeland, with all the delight of His song and the power of His word. It makes us exult, as we declare in the Haggada: "And there we shall sing a new song upon our redemption and upon the salvation of our souls. Blessed are You, O Lord, who has redeemed Israel!"

The starting point of any discussion regarding the realization of the vision of redemption is the sages' clear statement in the Jerusalem Talmud (*Berakhot* 1:1):

> Rabbi Ḥiyya the Great and Rabbi Shimon ben Ḥalafta were walking in the valley of Arbel at sunrise and they saw the dawn beginning to break. Rabbi Ḥiyya remarked: So is the redemption of Israel – [it proceeds] bit by bit (*kim'a kim'a*).

This teaching is quite clearly expressed in the words of the Torah and the Prophets as well. In both of them, we have whole passages that explain the plan of redemption and the ways of its fulfillment, fully elaborated upon and explained.

II.

It is explicit in the Torah that at the end of days, Israel will engage in repentance, but there are two terms used for this: returning unto (*ad*) God and returning to (*el*) God. The former appears in Deuteronomy 4:30 and 30:2. Let us consider the passage from chapter 30, which promises that after the first stirrings of repentance, the Jewish people will return to the land, the legacy of the patriarchs of yore, and they will exceed what their ancestors had:

> When all these blessings and curses I have set before you come upon you, and you take them to heart wherever the Lord your God

disperses you among the nations, and when you and your children *return unto the Lord your God* and obey Him with all your heart and with all your soul according to everything I command you today, then the Lord your God will restore your fortunes and have compassion on you and gather you again from all the nations where He scattered you. Even if you have been banished to the most distant land under the heavens, from there the Lord your God will gather you and bring you back. He will bring you to the land that belonged to your ancestors, and you will take possession of it. He will make you more prosperous and numerous than your ancestors. (Deut. 30:1–5)

At first the Jews return "unto" God, the first stirrings of repentance, and God will return them from exile. Two verses later (v. 7), we find the following: "The Lord your God will place all these curses upon your enemies who hate and persecute you." Finally, at the culmination of the passage, the Jews return to God: "If you obey the Lord your God and keep His commands and decrees that are written in this Book of the Law *and return to the Lord your God* with all your heart and with all your soul" (v. 10). The Torah then goes on to describe the nature of returning "to" God, whose practical meaning is fulfilling all the mitzvot, accompanied by a cornucopia of blessing that follows this reinforced observance. This complete repentance, the return "to" God, comes after the redemption of the ingathering of the exiles and the renewed inheritance of the land. This is a distinction between stages of repentance, return *ad* and then return *el.*

This appears in the Prophets as well. For example, Hosea calls, "Return, O Israel, *unto* the Lord your God, for you have stumbled in your sin. Take words with you and return *to* God" (14:2–3). Joel mentions the same: "Return *unto* me, with all your hearts, with fasting and crying and mourning; rend your hearts, not your garments and return *to* the Lord your God" (2:12–13). Amos laments five times, "'But you have not returned *unto* Me,' says the Lord" (4:6, 8–11). In the Book of Lamentations, Jeremiah says, "Let us search our ways and investigate, and let us return *unto* the Lord. Let us lift up our heart with our hands *to* God in the heavens" (3:40–41); the penultimate verse is "Restore us *to* You, O Lord, and we shall return; renew our days as of old" (5:21). And Isaiah says, "I have swept away your offenses like a cloud, your sins like

the morning mist. Return *to* Me, for I have redeemed you" (44:22) –
returning "to" God is preceded by redemption.

This may also be determined from the following Talmudic passage:

> Rabba contrasted two verses. It is written: "For Your mercy is great
> unto the heavens" (Ps. 57:11), whereas it is also written, "For Your
> mercy is great above the heavens" (108:5). How is this to be explained?
> Here ("above the heavens") it refers to those who act [properly] for its
> own sake; there ("unto the heavens") it refers to those who act with
> an ulterior motive. (*Pesaḥim* 50b)

Similarly, repentance out of fear, which is a lower level, is returning *unto*
God – until, up to but not including. Thus we find in Tractate *Yoma*:

> Rabbi Levi said: "Great is repentance, for it reaches up to the Throne
> of Glory, as it is said: 'Return, O Israel, unto the Lord your God.'" Said
> Rabbi Yoḥanan: "'Unto,' but not including."
>
> Indeed? Was it not Rabbi Yoḥanan who said: "Great is repentance,
> for it overrides a prohibition of the Torah, as it is said: 'But you have
> played the harlot with many lovers; and would you yet return to Me?
> says the Lord' (Jer. 3:1)."
>
> This concerns an individual, while that concerns the community.
> (*Yoma* 86a–b, according to the *Ein Yaakov* text)

Maharsha explains: "As far as the Throne of Glory, but not including it; in
other words, the angels and the archangels are the intermediaries. But did
not Rabbi Yoḥanan say, 'And would you yet return *to* Me?' This means all
the way to God, without any intermediary." However, "Repentance from
love is [all the way] to God" (*Olat Re'iya*, p. 335).

We may furthermore see the distinction in the translation of Onkelos,
who renders Deuteronomy 30:2, "When you and your children *return to
the service of the Lord your God*," and verse 10, "*And return before the Lord
your God*."

Maimonides (*Hilkhot Teshuva* 7:6) explains as follows:

> Great is repentance, for it draws one close to the Divine Presence,
> as Hosea states: "Return, O Israel, unto the Lord, your God" (14:2);

Amos states: "'But you have not returned unto Me,' says the Lord" (4:6); and Jeremiah states: "'If you will return, O Israel,' declares God, 'you will return to Me'" (4:1). Implied is that if you will return in repentance, you will cling to Me.

In the previous paragraph, Maimonides states as follows:

All the prophets commanded repentance, and Israel will only be redeemed through repentance. The Torah has already promised that, ultimately, Israel will repent toward the end of its exile and, immediately, it will be redeemed, as the Torah states: "When all these blessings and curses I have set before you come on you.... And when you and your children *return unto the Lord your God*...then the Lord your God will restore your fortunes..." (Deut. 30:1–3).

In *Akedat Yitzhak* (*Shaar HaMe'a*) we find the following:

It is stated, "Return unto the Lord your God," and redemption follows: "Then the Lord your God will restore your fortunes," followed in turn by repentance: "You will return and obey the voice of the Lord" (v. 8). After this act of repentance, "Then the Lord your God will make you most prosperous in all the work of your hands" (v. 9), and after that the repentance becomes even stronger: "and return to the Lord your God with all your heart and with all your soul," etc. This is complete repentance, and the culmination of perfection.

In *Orot HaTeshuva*, ch. 17, we see that the willing awakening of the nation to return to its land, to its nature, to its spirit, and to its character – all these contain the light of repentance.

In the Prophets (Ezek. 36), we find the same idea expressed, as we are told in *Sanhedrin* (98a):

Rabbi Abba also said: There can be no more manifest sign of redemption than this, as it says: "But you, O mountains of Israel, you shall shoot forth your branches, and yield your fruit to My people of Israel, for they are at hand to come" (Ezek. 36:8).

In verse 22, God says, "It is not for your sake, people of Israel, that I am going to do these things, but for the sake of My holy name," reminding one of the original redemption: "Not for your righteousness and for the straightness of your heart do you come to inherit the land" (Deut. 9:5–6).

Now we can see the sequence of the matter in Ezekiel 36. First of all, "For I will take you out of the nations; I will gather you from all the countries and bring you back into your own land" (v. 24). Then, "I will sprinkle clean water on you, and you will be clean; I will cleanse you from all your impurities and from all your idols" (v. 25). The next step is "I will give you a new heart and put a new spirit in you; I will remove from you your heart of stone and give you a heart of flesh" (v. 26). Finally, "And I will put My Spirit in you and move you to follow My decrees and be careful to keep My laws" (v. 27).

III.

Thus, this distinction is explained in the Torah, Prophets, *Targum* Onkelos, Maimonides, *Akedat Yitzḥak, Olat Re'iya,* and *Orot HaTeshuva* – distinguishing between returning unto God and returning to God, between repentance born of fear and repentance born of love, between the commencement of repentance and the culmination of repentance. This process of repentance dovetails with the opinion of Rabbi Yehoshua (see *Rishon LeTziyon* by Rabbi Tzvi Hirsch Kalischer, ch. 10), as opposed to that of Rabbi Eliezer, and we know the rule that that Halakha does not follow Rabbi Eliezer, especially when he disputes Rabbi Yehoshua. Their dispute is as follows:

> Rabbi Eliezer said: "If Israel repent, they will be redeemed; if not, they will not be redeemed."
>
> Rabbi Yehoshua said to him: "If they do not repent, will they not be redeemed? Rather, the Holy One, blessed be He, will set up a king over them, whose decrees shall be as cruel as Haman's; this will motivate Israel to engage in repentance, and he will thus bring them back to the right path." (*Sanhedrin* 97b)

Maharsha (ad loc.) explains that this is the distinction between willing repentance and compelled repentance, which comes from outside factors.

This is well explained and explored the great Kabbalist Rabbi Shlomo Eliashiv (*Hakdamot UShe'arim* 6:9):

> However, the future hope and greatest desires of all Israel – namely, the final destinies of the Messianic era and life in the World to Come – depend only on the covenant and not on our merit. This is the covenant of the patriarchs and Israel, and this covenant is inviolable, as Rabbeinu Tam says (*Tosafot, Shabbat* 58a, s.v. *UShmuel*) that the merit of the patriarchs has run out, but the covenant of the patriarchs has not run out. And thus it is explicit in the Torah at the end of the curses in Leviticus (26:44): "Yet in spite of this, when they are in the land of their enemies, I will not reject them or abhor them so as to destroy them completely, breaking my covenant with them; I am the Lord their God."
>
> This states explicitly that the covenant cannot be abrogated due to a sin, God forbid, as is clear in that passage, "upon the corpses of your idols" (Lev. 26:30) – though they are idolaters, the covenant is still in effect. The same covenant exists for every individual Jew as well, as Vilna Gaon writes in his commentary on *Parashat Nitzavim*: the Messianic era is not dependent on merits and actions at all. The same may be seen in *Sanhedrin* 97b, in the argument of Rabbi Eliezer and Rabbi Yehoshua. At its conclusion, Rabbi Eliezer is silent, as is explained there – thus, Rabbi Eliezer concedes to Rabbi Yehoshua that the future redemption does not depend on good deeds at all.
>
> And this is what Nahmanides writes in his commentary on *Parashat Ha'azinu*: the promise of redemption has no conditions attached to it of repentance and service, but it is promised to come in any case. This is what many verses in chapters 36 and 37 of Ezekiel teach, almost explicitly – namely, that the final redemption does not depend on repentance and good deeds at all; it is guaranteed to come in any case. Based on all this, we may say that the future redemption is not dependent on merits and acts at all.

Indeed, this is Rabbi Yehoshua's final conclusion; it is he whom the halakha follows against Rabbi Eliezer (*Sanhedrin* 97b). There is no doubt that Israel is delivered at the time of redemption not due to repentance and

good deeds – after all, in the end, Rabbi Eliezer is silent and concedes to him. Moreover, Rabbi Yohanan says that the Holy One, blessed be He, promises to Israel that a set end-time has been determined, whether they repent or not (*Shemot Raba*, ch. 25). In *Tikkunei Zohar Hadash*, the following is stated: "The end-time of the Holy One, blessed be He, is not dependent on their merits." Similar, *Or HaHayim* (Lev. 25:25) declares: "For the end of the exile comes even if Israel were to be utterly evil, God forbid."

Now, some may argue that Rabbi Eliezer does not concede the point; he merely does not respond. Granted, it is true that silence is not always concession in the language of the sages, as noted by Rabbi Reuven Margaliot in his essay "*Shetika LeHakhamim*" [reprinted in his *Mehkarim Bedarkei HaTalmud Vehidotav*, Jerusalem 1967, 90–96]. Nevertheless, this is the conclusion of the Tosafists (*Bava Batra* 62, s.v. *UModeh*): In most places where there is silence, there is concession (as with most sources cited by Rabbi Margaliot there).

Recently, I discovered a further analysis of Rabbi Eliezer's silent concession on *Sanhedrin* 98a, as revealed by what follows immediately afterward, the statement of Rabbi Abba. Rabbi Natan Friedlander, in *Yosef Hen* (Aderet, in his approbation there, notes that his father, Rabbi Binyamin, was also very much impressed by the ways and words of Rabbi Friedlander), pp. 54, writes as follows:

> The Talmud concludes there that Rabbi Eliezer was silent, and my master and teacher the sage Rabbi Yosef Zundel Salanter said to me that silence is considered concession, and the same is found in the Jerusalem Talmud (*Taanit* 1:1), that Rabbi Eliezer absented himself, as explained in *Korban HaEdah*, that he conceded; otherwise, why would the Talmud specifically have to conclude here that Rabbi Eliezer was silent, if not to tell us that he conceded to Rabbi Yehoshua? Indeed, he showed me that in *Pirkei DeRabbi Eliezer*, he concedes explicitly, so it turns out Rav is a lone opinion believing that redemption depends on repentance.

And after saying that Rabbi Eliezer fell silent, the Talmud then notes immediately: "Rabbi Abba also said: There can be no more manifest sign of redemption than this, as it says: 'But you, O mountains of Israel, you shall shoot forth your branches, and yield your fruit

to My people of Israel, for they are at hand to come' (Ezek. 36:8)." Rabbi Abba's statement refers to everything that came before, as if to say that repentance does not prevent redemption, nor does the end-time prevent it, for there is no other end-time than this manifest sign. When the time of favor arrives for Israel to come to the Holy Land, the inheritance of field and vineyard, and the land brings forth its yield in great abundance – this is the manifest end-time, and the generation in which the scion of David will come. (Earlier, the Talmud anonymously introduces Rabbi Abba with a conjunction, even though Rabbi Abba does not appear previously, to indicate that Rabbi Abba is, as it were, present throughout the preceding discussion, considering the words of all the aforementioned sages.) ...

IV.

The same statement made so clearly by the sages in the Jerusalem Talmud about the redemption of Israel, that it occurs bit by bit, dovetails with what is described by the Torah and Prophets and in the words of our great rabbis throughout the generations with regard to the spiritual-cultural aspects of redemption (namely, the process of repentance in relation to redemption). Yet in its original context, this statement in Y. *Berakhot* 1:1 refers to the practical and concrete aspects of redemption. As a proof-text, the Talmud cites a collection of verses from the Book of Esther, tracing the narrative. Mordecai at first is sitting at the king's gate, and then Haman takes the royal garb and mount to reward Mordecai at the behest of King Ahasuerus, but immediately afterwards, Mordecai returns to the king's gate. It is only after the dénouement that Mordecai leaves the king's presence "wearing royal garments of blue and white, a large crown of gold and a purple robe of fine linen," followed by: "For the Jews it was a time of happiness and joy, gladness and honor" (Est. 8:15–16).

It is from a basic toehold that redemption may proceed step by step; this represents the lowest level of salvation, not the absolute true sense of eradication of exile by emerging from it by virtue of full emancipation, but rather redemption *in the midst of* exile, among its specific travails, with the continuing overall status of being delayed in the Diaspora, of freedom *in the midst of* thralldom, for as the Talmud (*Megilla* 14a) notes, "We were still the slaves of Ahasuerus." As Rashi (*Megilla* 17b, s.v. *Athalta*) explains,

"The redemption for which we pray in the *Amida* is not redemption from exile, but redemption from constant distress. For the ingathering of the exiles, the rebuilding of Jerusalem, and the coming of the Messiah each have blessings of their own. Nevertheless, it is still termed redemption." This sets us on the proper path toward the ultimate goal of the redemption of Israel, in the truth of its perfection and absoluteness; namely, redemption *from* exile, redemption which is realized through the ingathering of the exiles, the rebuilding of Jerusalem, and the coming of the Messiah. From the level of redemption *within* exile, we can build up to the true, absolute redemption within the Land of Israel.

This true redemption, as it nullifies the "scattered and dispersed" status of the people, of its being in the lands of its enemies, brings it back to its original state of being "one nation in the land," in the territory which is unique to it, which belongs to it, which is appropriate to its universal and historic value. Just as the redemption fulfills the Torah and establishes the Divine Presence through the return of Israel to their place and their rebirth in it – as opposed to the great violation of the Torah and the awful exile of the Divine Presence amidst Israel's exile and the destruction of their existence through this – the redemptive return revivifies Israel and restores it to life, in the perfection of its truth, in the delight of the Lord and the light of His command, in the effective renewal of the settlement in the land and its inheritance. This settlement in the land, which fulfills the Torah and its commandments, is more than a mere mitzva; rather, it is "equal to all of the commandments in the Torah" (*Sifrei, Parashat Re'eh*). This is eloquently described by the father of Israel, Nahmanides, in his addenda to Maimonides' *Sefer HaMitzvot* (positive commandment no. 4), with regard to the mitzva to take possession of the land, "that we shall not leave it in the hands of any other nation or in desolation":

> The sages amplify this commandment of dwelling in the Land of Israel, saying that anyone who leaves it is an idolater, as it says (*Ketubot* 110b): "This is to tell you, that whoever lives outside the land may be regarded as one who worships idols. Similarly it was said in Scripture by David, 'For they have driven me out this day that I should not cleave to the inheritance of the Lord, saying: "Go, serve other gods"

(1 Sam. 26:19).'" And there are many other amplifications of this sort. This is all based on the positive command to take possession of the land and dwell in it, and it is binding on every one of us, even in the time of exile, as may be seen in the Talmud in many places, for they have said that dwelling in the Land of Israel is "equal to all of the commandments in the Torah."

Therefore, the true redemption – revealed in the dwelling in the land and Israel's rebirth in it – is the renewal of settlement of the land along with the ingathering of the exiles: "You shall shoot forth your branches, and yield your fruit to My people of Israel, for they are at hand to come." The true redemption appears at the apex of concrete development, in the land's being in our hands "that we shall not leave it in the hands of any other nation or in desolation," in our dominion and sovereignty over it, in our essence as a nation clinging to its sacred reality. Therefore, it is our political control, with all these internal and external expressions of its concretization, through which this mitzva of taking possession is revealed and fulfilled, which serves as the basis and root of continual dwelling in the land; these elements are the ones to practically fulfill, through our sovereignty, the act of redemption, and through them its vision becomes reality, and the word of the King of the Universe is brought to fruition.

The dedication to sanctifying God's name, which lies in the fulfillment of this lofty communal mitzva, with the occurrence of miracles and the glory of the victories emerging from it, adds to and completes the authority of our power and the mighty splendor of this glorious, unwavering reality. This reminds us of the talmudic discussion in *Berakhot* 20a: "Said R. Papa to Abaye: 'How is it that for the former generations miracles were performed and for us miracles are not performed?' He replied: 'The former generations used to be ready to sacrifice their lives for the sanctity of God's name; we do not sacrifice our lives for the sanctity of God's name.'" Only by a readiness to sanctify God's name may we merit the fulfillment of the psalmist's vision: "For God will save Zion and rebuild the cities of Judah. Then people will settle there and possess it; the children of His servants will inherit it, and those who love His name will dwell there" (Ps. 69:36–37).

V.

This bit-by-bit process, which characterizes Israel's practical and spiritual redemption, includes within it all of the delays and interruptions, as well as all of the failures and retreats, the complications and snags, along the way. This wondrous phenomenon is a halting process, and as long as its enlightenment is inchoate, as long as its power is not fully mature, as long as it is not fully formed and totally perfected, there is a place, amid the imperfection and incompletion, amid the deficiencies of enlightenment and empowerment, for all manner of defects and weaknesses, obscurity and corruption. These require redoubled efforts to strengthen and to repair, to elevate and to improve, to reach the glory and grandeur of lofty perfection. In the meantime, in the shadows of the steps of this process, until liberty has been fully realized, elements of subjugation remain; until repentance has been fully realized, elements of sinfulness remain; until renewal and purification have been fully realized, elements of the impurities, tarnishing, and corrosion of exile remain; until enlightenment has been fully realized, elements of confusing shadow and gloom remain. All of these surround and confound the essence of this great process. These demand and engender steadfastness and courage on the part of our partners in the holy enterprise of the commencement of our very blessed and brilliant culmination.

In the meantime, amid the marvelous and multifarious strides we take in the process of redemption, we also encounter obstacles and obscurities imported from foreign lands, causing internal and external problems of activity and intellect as they invade the land of our life and the legacy of our revivification. We must turn to the greatest storehouse of strength, the broad truth of our divine rebirth, our faith in the healing of our spirits when returning to our homeland: "The voice of your watchmen – they lift up their voice; together they sing for joy; for eye to eye they see the return of the Lord to Zion" (Is. 52:8). The lower eye, the contemporary perspective, struggling with our current difficulties of starting out, ethically and politically, must meet the upper eye, the historical perspective, which surveys the progress over generations in attaining renewal and rebirth. Perfecting the vision of the entire horizon of reality, the full vista of the overarching theme – including all the episodes of our redemption and the salvation of our soul – this is what gives us the solutions to our dreams and

our wars, what confirms the truth of their promise, what fulfills the song of our tongue and the development of our dialect. The logic of justice and the narrative of glory, the word of the truth and faith that belong to the Life-Giver of the World – these can be seen as chapters of our national narrative, as stages in the fulfillment of the age-old vision within the reality of our country and in the arrangement of our sovereignty, solving our disputes and enlightening our paths.

Once we comprehend this unambiguously, we may properly evaluate the activities and agendas of all the segments of our society; this strengthens loving brotherhood in Israel and understanding of its unique path. As these are strengthened, we will experience greater success in repair and elevation, in the formation of "a created nation that shall praise God" (Ps. 102:18) with the rebuilding of Jerusalem, the birth of a nation in joy and strength, the augmentation of the glorious splendor and the intensification of sanctifying God's name. This created nation has been rejuvenated and revitalized, with the exaltation of the Torah and the mitzvot, and the delight of the Rock of our salvation upon His people and His inheritance. The gaps and breaches of the halting movement of this redemptive process are filled with its great light, which continues to overflow from its full spring, until the day when the Messiah's face will be revealed, as it should and must be.

As we saw at the beginning, "Rabbi Ḥiyya remarked: So is the redemption of Israel – at first bit by bit, and as it proceeds, it gets faster and bigger" (Y. *Berakhot* 1:1). As Micah puts it, "Though I have fallen, I will rise; though I sit in darkness, the Lord will be my light" (7:8). Until we witness God's full goodness and compassion, we may rest assured in the sublime knowledge of this teaching of Rabbi Ḥiyya, that in the study hall of the yeshiva of heaven, the process is clarified, turning darkness into light and bitterness into sweetness (introduction to Zohar). The blessing is refined until it is ready to descend upon Jerusalem "as the dew that descended upon the mountains of Zion, for there the Lord commanded the blessing: Life forevermore" (Ps. 133:3).

Six Knocks

Rabbi Joseph B. Soloveitchik

Yom HaAtzma'ut 1956

Eight years ago, in the midst of a night of the terrors of Majdanek, Treblinka, and Buchenwald; in a night of gas chambers and crematoria; in a night of total Divine Self-concealment; in a night ruled by the devil of doubt and destruction who sought to sweep the Lover from her own tent into the Catholic Church; in a night of continuous searching for the Beloved – on that very night the Beloved appeared. The Almighty, who was hiding in His splendid sanctum, suddenly appeared and began to beckon at the tent of the Lover, who tossed and turned on her bed beset by convulsions and the agonies of hell. Because of the beating and knocking at the door of the mournful Lover (cf. Song of Songs 5:2), the State of Israel was born.

How many times did the Beloved knock on the door of the Lover? It appears to me that we can count at least six knocks.

First, the knock of the Beloved was heard in the political arena. From the point of view of international relations, no one will deny that the rebirth of the State of Israel, in a political sense, was an almost supernatural

17

occurrence. Both Russia and the Western nations supported the establishment of the State of Israel. This was perhaps the one resolution on which East and West concurred [during the Cold War era]. I am inclined to believe that the United Nations was especially created for this end – for the sake of fulfilling the mission that divine providence had placed upon it. It appears to me that one cannot point to any other concrete accomplishment on the part of the United Nations. Our Rabbis of blessed memory already expressed this view: At times rain falls on account of one individual and for one blade of grass (*Bereshit Raba* 66:2). I do not know who the representatives of the press, with their human eyes, saw to be the chairman in that fateful session of the General Assembly in which the creation of the State of Israel was decided, but he who looked carefully with his spiritual eye saw the true Chairman who conducted the proceedings – the Beloved. He knocked with His gavel on the lectern. Do we not interpret the passage "On that night the king could not sleep" (Est. 6:1) as meaning that the *King of the Universe* could not sleep? If Ahasuerus alone had been sleepless, the matter would not have been at all important, and salvation would not have arisen on that night. If, however, the King, the Master of the Universe, could not sleep, as it were, redemption would be born. If just anyone were to have opened the session of the United Nations, the State of Israel would not have been born. But it was the Beloved who rapped on the Chairman's lectern, and the miracle materialized. Listen! My Beloved knocks!

Second, the knock of the Beloved was heard on the battlefield. The tiny defense forces of [the State of] Israel defeated the mighty Arab armies. The miracle of "the many delivered into the hands of the few" materialized before our eyes, and an even greater miracle happened! God hardened the heart of Ishmael and commanded him to go into battle against the State of Israel. Had the Arabs not declared war on Israel and instead supported the Partition Plan, the State of Israel would have remained without Jerusalem, without a major portion of the Galilee, and without some areas of the Negev. If thousands of years ago Pharaoh had allowed the Children of Israel to leave immediately, as Moses had originally requested, Moses would have been bound by his word to return in three days. Pharaoh, however, hardened his heart and did not listen to Moses. "The Holy One then took Israel out with a mighty hand

and by an outstretched arm" (Deut. 4:34). Consequently, the force of the promise [that the Children of Israel would return to Egypt] was vitiated. No contract that is based upon mutuality of promise binds one side if the other party refuses to fulfill its obligations. Listen! My Beloved knocks!

Third, the Beloved also began to knock on the door of the tent of theology, and possibly this is the strongest beckoning. I have, on several occasions, emphasized in my remarks concerning the Land of Israel that the theological arguments of Christian theologians to the effect that the Holy One has taken away from the community of Israel its rights to the Land of Israel, and that all of the biblical promises relating to Zion and Jerusalem now refer in an allegorical sense to Christianity and the Christian Church, were all publicly shown to be false, baseless contentions by the establishment of the State of Israel. One must have a broad familiarity with theological literature from the time of Justin Martyr[1] down to the theologians of our own day to comprehend the full extent of this marvel by which the central axiom of Christian theology was shattered.

We should pay careful attention to the learned explanation of our secretary of state, Mr. Dulles (who served as the deacon of an Episcopalian Church), to a committee of the United States Senate that the Arabs hate the Jews because they killed the founder of their religion. This "explanation" possesses hidden and deep symbolic significance. I am not a psychiatrist and surely not a psychoanalyst, but I know how to study Talmud, and I remember well what our Rabbis of blessed memory said about Balaam: "From his blessings…you may learn what was in his heart" (*Sanhedrin* 105b). Sometimes, when a person speaks too much, something of the truth slips out. When one of the senators asked the secretary of state, "Why do the Arabs hate the Jews?" he really wanted

---

1. Justin Martyr (c. 100–165 CE), the author of one of the earliest anti-Jewish polemical tracts by a Christian theologian. See, e.g., *Dialogue with Trypho (the Jew)*, wherein Martyr tries to demonstrate that a New Covenant has superseded the old Covenant of God with the Jewish people and that the gentiles have been selected to replace Israel as God's chosen people. [Ed. note: All footnotes in this essay are by the translator, not by the author.]

to answer, "Personally, I too, as a Christian, have no great love for them, because they killed our messiah and consequently forfeited their portion of Abraham's heritage." An angel sat in the throat of the secretary, or a hook was put into it (as in the exegesis of the Rabbis of blessed memory on the phrase "and God put a word in Balaam's mouth" [Num. 23:5, *Sota* 10a]: "he put a hook in his mouth"), and instead of saying, "Our Lord" and "for myself," he let other words slip out: the "Arabs" and "Mohammed." In his subconscious he was terrified of the "awful" fact that the community of Israel rules over Zion and Jerusalem. I find satisfaction in reading about the State of Israel in the Catholic and Protestant newspapers. Despite themselves, they must mention the name of Israel when they report the news of Zion and Jerusalem, which we possess. I always have a special sense of satisfaction when I read in the paper that Israel's reaction is not as yet known because today is Saturday and government offices are closed, or when I read, on the eve of Passover, an item from the United Press that "Jews will sit down tonight to the Seder table in the hope that the miracles of Egypt will return and recur today." Listen! My Beloved knocks!

Fourth, the Beloved knocks in the heart of the youth which is assimilated and perplexed. The period of *hester panim*[2] in the beginning of the 1940s caused confusion among the Jewish masses and especially Jewish youth. Assimilation increased, and the urge to flee from Judaism and the Jewish people reached its apex. Fear, despair, and ignorance caused many to forsake the Jewish community and "climb aboard the ship," to flee to Tarshish from the presence of the Lord (Jonah 1:3), just as Jonah sought to flee God's presence. A seemingly unstoppable tidal wave stood over us and threatened to destroy us. Suddenly, the Beloved began to beckon to the hearts of the perplexed, and His beckoning, the establishment of the State of Israel, at least slowed the process of flight. Many who were once alienated are now bound to the Jewish state with ties of pride in its mighty accomplishments.

Many American Jews who were partially assimilated find themselves beset by hidden fear and concern for any crisis that the State of Israel

2. Lit. the "hiding of countenance." This is the notion of the removal of divine protection from the Jewish people.

passes through, and they pray for its well-being and welfare even though they are far from being totally committed to it. Even Jews who are hostile to the State of Israel must defend themselves from the strange charge of dual loyalty and proclaim daily and declare that they have no stake in the Holy Land. It is good for a Jew when he cannot ignore his Jewishness and is obliged to perpetually answer the questions, "Who are you?" and "What is your occupation?" (Jonah 1:8), even when extraordinary fear grips him and he does not have the strength or fortitude to answer with true pride, "I am a Jew, and I fear the Lord, the God of heaven" (Jonah 1:9). The unrelenting question of "Who are you?" ties him to the Jewish people. The very mention of the name Israel is a reminder to the fleeing Jew that he cannot escape from the community of Israel, in whose midst he has been enmeshed from birth. Everywhere we turn we hear the name "Israel." When we listen to a radio station, when we open a paper, when we participate in a debate on current events, we encounter the question of Israel; it is always a topic of public concern.

This phenomenon is extremely important for Jews who are afflicted with self-hatred and want to turn away from Judaism and run for their lives. They hide, like Jonah in his day, in the recesses of the ship and seek to "slumber" (Jonah 1:5). The Captain, however, does not permit them to ignore their fate. The shadow of Israel continuously chases after them. Random thoughts and paradoxical reflections arise from the subconscious of even the most confirmed assimilationist. And when a Jew begins to think, to reflect, when he is unable to sleep, it is impossible to know where his thoughts will take him and how his doubts will be expressed. Listen! My Beloved knocks!

The fifth knock of the Beloved is perhaps the most important. For the first time in the annals of our exile, divine providence has amazed our enemies with the astounding discovery that Jewish blood is not cheap! If the antisemites describe this phenomenon as being "an eye for an eye," we will agree with them. If we want to courageously defend our continued national and historical existence, we must, from time to time, interpret the verse of "an eye for an eye" literally. So many "eyes" were lost in the course of our bitter exile because we did *not* repay hurt for hurt. The time has come for us to fulfill the simple meaning of "an eye for an

eye" (Ex. 21:24). Of course, I am sure everyone recognizes that I am an adherent of the Oral Law, and from my perspective there is no doubt that the verse refers to monetary restitution, as defined by Halakha. However, with respect to the Mufti[3] and Nasser,[4] I would demand that we interpret the verse in accordance with its literal meaning – the taking of an actual eye! Pay no attention to the saccharine suggestions of known assimilationists and of some Jewish socialists who stand pat in their rebelliousness and think they are still living in Bialystok, Brest-Litovsk, and Minsk[5] of the year 1905, and openly declare that revenge is forbidden to the Jewish people in any place, at any time, and under all circumstances. "Vanity of vanities!" (Eccl. 1:2). Revenge is forbidden when it is pointless, but if one is aroused thereby to self-defense, it is the most elementary right of man to take his revenge.

The Torah has always taught that a man is permitted – indeed, has a sacred obligation – to defend himself. With the verse, "If a burglar is caught in the act of breaking in" (Ex. 22:1), the Torah establishes the halakha that one may defend not only one's life but his property as well. If the thief who comes to take the property of the householder is capable of killing the householder (should the householder not comply with his demands), the householder may rise up against the criminal and kill him. For good reason the Torah relates that two of its great heroes, Abraham and Moses, took sword in hand to defend their brethren: "And when Abraham heard that his kinsman was taken captive, he led forth his retainers" (Gen. 14:14); "And when Moses saw the Egyptian smite a Jew…he struck down the Egyptian" (Ex. 2:11–12). This behavior does not contradict the principle of loving-kindness and compassion. On the

---

3. Haj Amin Al-Husseini (1897–1974), who dominated the Arab nationalist movement in Palestine and led the anti-Jewish riots in 1921, 1929, and 1936. The Mufti collaborated with Hitler and led the Nazi coup in Iraq during World War II. Prior to the invasion by five Arab armies in May, 1948, he led the armed opposition to the future State of Israel.

4. Gammal Abdel Nasser (1918–1970), prime minister of Egypt (1954–1956), president of Egypt (1956–1970), led Egypt during the Suez Campaign (1956) and the Six-Day War (1967).

5. Russian cities where the Black Hundreds carried out pogroms against the Jews in 1905, accusing them of sympathy for the Japanese during the Russo-Japanese War.

contrary, a passive position, without self-defense, may sometimes lead to the most awesome brutality.

"And I will gain honor from Pharaoh, and all his hosts, his chariots, and his horsemen. And the Egyptians will know that I am the Lord" (Ex. 14:17–18). God did not seek honor and recognition. He wanted Pharaoh, Moses' contemporary, to know that he must pay a high price for his edict that "every male child born shall be cast into the river" (Ex. 1:22). His present desire is that the blood of Jewish children who were slain as they recited the eighteen benedictions of the daily [Amida] prayer shall also be avenged. When God smote the Egyptians, He sought to demonstrate that there will always be accountability for the spilling of Jewish blood. At present, it is necessary not only to convince the dictator of Egypt [Nasser], but the self-righteous Nehru,[6] the Foreign Office in London, and the sanctimonious members of the United Nations, that Jewish blood is not cheap. Therefore, how laughable it is when they try to persuade us to rely on the declaration of the three Great Powers guaranteeing the status quo.[7] We all know from experience what value can be attached to the pronouncements of the British Foreign Office and the so-called friendship of certain officials in our State Department.

In general, how absurd is the request that an entire people be dependent on the kindnesses of others and remain without the ability to defend itself. Public and private honor is dependent upon the possibility of defending one's life and one's honor. A people that cannot defend its freedom and tranquility is neither free nor independent. The third of the phrases of divine redemption is "And I shall redeem you with an outstretched hand and with great judgments" (Ex. 6:6). Thank God we have lived to see the day when, with the help of God, Jews have it within their power to defend themselves.

---

6. Jawaharlal Nehru (1889–1964), prime minister of the Republic of India (1947–1964).

7. Declaration of the United States, Britain, and France warning that "should the three Governments … find any one of these states [Israel or its Arab neighbors] contemplates violating the frontiers of the armistice lines they will … act both within and without the framework of the United Nations to prevent such a violation." See Howard M. Sachar, A History of Israel (New York, 1982), 458.

Let us not forget that the poison of Hitlerite antisemitism (which made Jews fair game to all) still permeates this generation, which looked with equanimity upon the horrible scene of the suffocation of millions in gas chambers as a normal event that need not be challenged. The antidote for this venom that poisoned minds and dulled hearts is the readiness of the State of Israel to defend the lives of its citizens. Listen! My Beloved knocks!

The sixth beckoning, of which we should also not lose sight, was heard at the time of the opening of the gates of the Land of Israel. A Jew escaping from an enemy's land now knows that he can find refuge in the land of his forefathers. This is a new phenomenon in the annals of our history. Up to now, when a Jewish population was uprooted, it wandered in the wilderness of the nations without finding shelter and habitation. The shutting of the gates in the face of the exiled caused total destruction for much of the Jewish people. Now the situation has changed. When any nation expels its Jewish minority, the exiled now direct their steps to Zion, and she, as a compassionate mother, absorbs them. We are all witnesses to the settlement of Oriental Jewry in Israel over the last several years. Who knows what would have been in store for these brothers of ours in the lands of their origin if not for the State of Israel, which brought them to her in planes and ships? Had Israel been born before the Hitlerian Holocaust, hundreds of thousands of Jews could have been saved from the gas chambers and the crematoria. The miracle of the state tarried somewhat, and in the wake of its delay, thousands and tens of thousands of Jews were taken to the slaughter. Now that the hour of *hester panim* has passed, however, the possibility exists for Jews who are pried from their homes to take root in the Holy Land. This should not be taken lightly. Listen! My Beloved knocks!

The Torah of Eretz Yisrael

Rabbi Shaul Yisraeli

Blessed is our God, who created us for His glory, and separated us from the wayward, and gave us the Torah of truth" (*Uva LeTziyon* prayer). The separation between Israel and the nations, which the sages count as one of the vast separations "between holy and mundane, between light and dark" (Havdala service), is expressed in every single aspect of the activities of life, both that of the individual and the community. This includes the connection of the nation to its unique land, in which "the eyes of the Lord your God are constantly present, from the year's beginning until year's end" (Deut. 11:12).

"He set the boundaries of peoples, to the number of the Children of Israel" (Deut. 32:8). This, according to the *Sifrei*, refers to national borders, so that no foreign entity would encroach upon the Land of Israel. On the one hand, as Rabbeinu Saadia Gaon puts it (*Emunot VeDeot*, third essay), "Our nation is no nation except through its *Torot*"; yet on the other hand, the essentials of these *Torot*, the Written Torah and the Oral Torah, are inextricably bound to this desirable land: "And He gave them the lands of the nations…that they might keep His statutes and observe His laws" (Ps. 105:44–45).

The sages have said that the Torah applies essentially when the Jewish people reside in their own land. Even those mitzvot that require physical action, such as tefillin and mezuza, apply outside of the Land of Israel only as "reminders," as explained by the *Sifrei* (*Parashat Ekev* 43:17): "So that they will not be new to you when you return." The connection between the Torah and the Land of Israel is felt most profoundly with those commandments that are specific to the land, since these apply nowhere else. These mitzvot are designed to form the character of the populace as an agricultural nation, living its life in the bosom of nature, plowing, sowing, and reaping. The people, however, are not influenced by being earth-bound; on the contrary, the people influence this earthly existence. The Talmudic term for ignoramus, *am haaretz*, literally means "people of the land," as Maimonides (*Commentary to the Mishna*, introduction to *Zera'im*) explains: these are people devoid of wisdom, dedicated only to cultivating the land. This is not the destiny of the Jewish people; rather, as the Talmud puts it (*Rosh HaShana* 35a), they are *am shebasadot*, the people in the fields, connected to Torah and prayer. The physical acts they perform are also tools for spirituality; even their "regular" food is eaten as if it were a holy portion from God's table.

This does not apply only to those who work themselves to death, as it were, in the tents of Torah; they are not the sole heirs of Torah and mitzvot. As Moses states: "You are standing this day *all of you* before the Lord your God: your heads, your tribes, your elders, and your officers, all the men of Israel, your children, your wives, and your stranger who is in the midst of your camp" (Deut. 29:9–10). Moreover, those mitzvot tied to a life of activity – plowing, reaping, and the like – cannot be fulfilled at all except by those who occupy themselves with such activities. Adam is placed in the Garden of Eden "to work it and to guard it" (Gen. 2:15); "to work it" simply means cultivation, while "to guard it" basically denotes protection. It is only on this basis that we can add another layer: "to work it" by performing the positive commandments, "and to guard it" by observing the prohibitions, as explained by the Zohar (vol. I, 27). This is the secret of the greatness of the Torah of truth: it encompasses all forms of life and is not confined to a cadre of uniquely gifted individuals. Indeed, the nation as a whole

becomes special: a treasure among the peoples, a kingdom of priests, a holy nation (Ex. 19:5–6).

"'And the gold of that land is good' (Gen. 2:12) – for there is no Torah like the Torah of the Land of Israel" (*Bereshit Raba* 16). The superiority of the Torah of the Land of Israel is not expressed in the subjects studied, nor in the method of study; indeed, the curriculum is the same, whether it is Torah studied inside or outside of Israel. Thus, the distinction between the Torah of the Land of Israel and the Torah of *Ḥutz LaAretz* ("Outside the Land") must be a difference in conceptualization and scope. The Zohar (*Zohar Ḥadash*, Ruth 210) states: "'Now this was the custom in former times in Israel upon redemption and upon exchange' (Ruth 4:7) – 'upon redemption,' this is the Jerusalem Talmud; 'upon exchange,' this is the Babylonian Talmud." The Babylonian Talmud is defined as "exchange" (*temura*) because it was the nation's replacement for losing its normal life. Torah outside of Israel was a substitute for customary features of national life. It was the ground beneath their feet when the literal ground was pulled out from under them, and it erected a wall of fire around the nation when its physical fortresses fell to the enemy. However, an "exchange" is only a temporary solution, an emergency measure, and therefore it cannot be regarded as good. This term "good" applies only to the Torah of the Land of Israel, which is defined as "redemption."

The Torah of the Land of Israel does not invalidate all the features of national life that characterize every other people; rather, it demands them: a state, an army, industry and labor, intellectual activities, agriculture. However, the Torah of the Land of Israel redeems these features of national life, giving them another meaning, and thus these elements themselves, which otherwise might subjugate people to physicality and materialism, are the tools for spiritual elevation. Isaiah (42:5) states: "Who gives soul to the people on it and spirit to those who walk in it," and the Talmud (*Ketubot* 111a) understands this as teaching that being in the Land of Israel guarantees one a portion in the World to Come. In the place of a war of the spirit against the body comes the resuscitation of the body: a soul is placed within it, and a spirit is given to it, a spirit of life.

Thus, the body is raised to rebirth, and the ways of the world (*halikhot*) turn into laws (*halakhot*) that ratify existence. It is a fulfillment of the verse: "In all your ways acknowledge Him, and He will make your paths straight" (Prov. 3:6).

✶✶✶

The Babylonian Talmud (*Gittin* 55b–56a) famously ascribes the destruction of Jerusalem to the incident of Bar Kamtza, [who is embarrassed at a feast in the presence of the sages and then puts a blemish in the animal that Caesar sends to the Temple in Jerusalem for an offering. The priests are about to offer the animal regardless, in order to avoid a diplomatic catastrophe, but Rabbi Zekharia ben Avkulas dissuades them. Rabbi Yoḥanan then concludes: "Through the humility of Rabbi Zekharia ben Avkulas our House has been destroyed, our Temple burnt, and we ourselves exiled from our land."] However, the version of this story written in the Land of Israel (*Eikha Raba* 4:3) differs. There Rabbi Zekharia ben Avkulas is blamed for a different type of inaction, namely, failure to halt the escalation of humiliation at the feast itself, when the host tells Bar Kamtza to leave:

> Said [Bar Kamtza to the host]: "Since I am here, let me stay, and I will pay you for whatever I eat and drink." He said, "I won't." "Then let me give you half the cost of the party." "No," said the other. "Then let me pay for the whole party." He still said, "Get out." Now, Rabbi Zekharia ben Avkulas was present, and he had the opportunity to protest but declined to do so. [The host] took [Bar Kamtza] by the hand and put him out. Said [Bar Kamtza], "Since the elders were sitting there peacefully, I will pay them back...." Said Rabbi Yose: "Through the humility of Rabbi Zekharia ben Avkulas our Temple has been burnt."

There is no question that Rabbi Zekharia's humility is basically a positive thing. It comes from his constant concern for self-perfection and dissatisfaction with what has been achieved. His is a view turned ever inward, continuous self-criticism that does not allow any room for directing others or being concerned with them. This worldview does not voice protest

when it is necessary or deal with setting things right. Perhaps it emerges from a certain disregard for a public that constantly thinks of the vanities of this world, for the ordinary people who are immersed in ethereal life and not eternal life: What, ask the scholars, do these trivialities have to do with us? Greatness is not to be expected of these people, so should we dedicate thought to them? Is this not a waste of our time, a distraction from Torah study? Rabbi Zekharia sits there, as do other rabbis, undoubtedly engaged in dispute over a matter of Torah. Their discussion is enjoyable and edifying, and they do not suspect or surmise that they are laying the groundwork for the destruction of the Temple.

Perhaps this is what Rabban Yoḥanan ben Zakkai meant when he said: "Grant me Yavne and its sages." Yavne was not chosen at random. As the Talmud reports: "A favorite saying of the rabbis of Yavne was: 'I am God's creature and my fellow is God's creature. My work is in the town and his work is in the country.... Will you say that I do much and he does little? We have learned: One may accomplish much or one may accomplish little; what matters is that one direct his heart to heaven'" (*Berakhot* 17a, see Rashi ad loc.). Among the sages of Yavne, Rabban Yoḥanan ben Zakkai founded an approach that was in direct opposition to that of Rabbi Zekharia ben Avkulas. According to this approach, the whole nation is a single entity, and there is no justification in seeking the perfection of the individual while rejecting the mission of maintaining a certain level of spirituality for the wider community. In the corporate framework of the nation, no one can be relinquished. Nor there is anyone who is entitled. "One may accomplish much or one may accomplish little; what matters is that one direct his heart to heaven." This means that there is no justification for isolation; instead, Torah scholars must forge close relationships with the people. Rabban Yoḥanan ben Zakkai recognized that only in this way could the nation be rebuilt, and there they kept the ember of the nation in its land burning bright, with Yavne and its sages.

Among the agricultural settlements of the Land of Israel, the Religious Zionist settlements of the "*Torah VaAvoda*" movement shine like sparkling diamonds. They constitute a unified body that keeps the Torah

and mitzvot, and are crowned with the glory of enjoying the fruits of their own labors. This is where the conditions for the realization of all the mitzvot in their entirety are being met; this is where the endeavor to revive the ideal of the Jewish farmer is made flesh, that of *am shebasadot*, "the people in the fields."

This revival of a form of life that had been snatched away from us certainly gives rise to many questions, as well as mistakes and missteps. This is the way of renewal. As the sages say: "A man does not fully understand the words of the Torah until he has stumbled in them" (*Gittin* 43a). We cannot be afraid of errors, just as we must not restrain criticism. What is important is that the critiques be faithful, not disingenuous or rejoicing in finding faults in others. Rather, criticism must be motivated by love, by pain, by a desire to fix things and a readiness to assist in repairing what is broken.

And before the criticism and the rebuke, there must be guidance. More than ever, the nation requires sages in the Land of Israel who can make halakha sweet, sages of Yavne who know that success requires collaboration with the community and who are ready to march arm-in-arm with the public in order to reliably support them, to guide and direct them to tranquil waters. Without doubt, this requires us to delve into the halakha in order to apply it to every area of life, formulating *halakhot* of society and *halakhot* of state, *halakhot* of the army, and *halakhot* of agriculture. We must clarify these *halakhot* and analyze the problems of the modern era to determine how they may be solved in the light of halakha.

The Religious Significance of Israel

Rabbi Nachum L. Rabinovitch

We have been through times of euphoria and bitter disillusionment and yet we have still not confronted, as Jews, the basic questions which the emergence of the State of Israel raises. From the perspective of history, a few decades are but a breathing space; nonetheless, as individuals whom Providence has planted in an era of unparalleled turmoil, we have only a single life span in which to come to terms with the challenges of our time and to respond in a manner that will be meaningful and fruitful.

Rightly may we lament the lack of explicit divine guidance at this crucial juncture. This does not, however, relieve us of the duty to decide and to act. It is the ineluctable predicament of man that his vision is restricted, his understanding limited, and his resources inadequate to master the currents of destiny. It is not that for which we can be held accountable. As believing Jews, committed to the concept of individual responsibility, we know that a human decision must be an act of faith, since we can never be completely certain that we have chosen the right. The only certainties are

31

that we may not escape the obligation to decide for ourselves, and that He above will ultimately make His will prevail.

To shrink from facing up to the perplexities and the demands of the historical situation is as much a renunciation of faith as the denial of history's God. In the words of Isaiah:

> Hear, you deaf, and look, you blind, that you may see. Who is blind but My servant? Or deaf, as My messenger that I send? Who is blind as he that is wholehearted and blind as the Lord's servant? Seeing many things, you observe not; opening the ears, he hears not.... You are My witnesses, says the Lord, and My servant whom I have chosen, that you may know and believe Me and understand, that I am He! (Is. 42:18–20; 43:10)

On the one hand, we must look with open eyes at the events that Providence brings to pass. On the other hand, we dare not fall prey to the temptation to see more than we have been shown and to hear more than has been said. The profound difficulties that beset such an approach are perhaps best described in context of the experience of our forebears during the Babylonian Exile and the Restoration:

> R. Joshua b. Levi said: Why were they called "Men of the Great Assembly?" Because they restored the crown of the divine attributes.
> Moses had come and said: "The great God, mighty and awesome." Then came Jeremiah and said: "Strangers are reveling in His Temple – where then is His awe?" Hence he omitted [in his prayer the attribute] "awesome."
> Daniel came and said: "Strangers are enslaving His sons – where is His might?" Hence he omitted [in his prayer the attribute] "mighty."
> But they [the Men of the Great Assembly] came and said: "Therein is manifest His awe: Surely, were it not for the awesome power of the Holy One blessed be He, how could one people endure among the nations!"
> But how could our teachers [Jeremiah and Daniel] abolish what Moses instituted? Said R. Elazar: Since they knew that the Holy One, blessed be He, is truthful, they would not lie about Him. (Yoma 69b)

R. Joshua b. Levi is concerned with a very fundamental theological question. The problem of the divine attributes did not originate with the

fierce confrontation between faith and philosophy in the Middle Ages. It is crucial to the religious experience as such. Thus we are told:

> A certain [prayer leader] went down before the ark in the presence of R. Ḥanina and said: "The great, the mighty, the awesome, the majestic, the strong, the powerful God." [R. Ḥanina] said to him: "Have you finished the praises of your Master? Even the first three, had it not been that Moses wrote them in the Law and the Men of the Great Assembly came and ordained them, we should not recite; and you say all this! It is as if a man had thousands of thousands of *denarii* of gold and people to praise his wealth would say he had a thousand. Would it not be an insult to him?" (*Megilla* 25)

How can the infinity of the Divine be circumscribed by words? How can transcendence be imprisoned in concepts? How can the ineffable be defined? Yet faith itself is not possible unless there are words that can echo the reverberations of the infinite, unless the immediate awareness of God's Fatherhood and Kingship gives rise to a conception of immanence that points beyond to the Unknowable and Unthinkable. Truly, no attributes can be predicated of Him who is above all understanding; yet if He chooses to seek out man and to summon him, it can only be within the realm of human experience, only in the manifestation of personal qualities.

What is faith other than the sure knowledge that the Divine Presence can touch man and that he, too, can reach out in response?

If God cares, then man too can shape history and give it purpose; if man is helpless and history is meaningless, then he mocks and blasphemes who claims it for Providence.

Thus Jeremiah and Daniel could not utter the Mosaic formula of praise. When the Sanctuary lovingly built and revered through centuries lay in ruins, when the people God Himself had chosen and made the bearers of His name were downtrodden and enslaved, when the enemy disported himself as conqueror of the God of Israel, He chose to hide His face. Where then were His might and His awe?

In our generation, more than any other, Jeremiah and Daniel would have recognized their own. We saw days which were "neither day nor night," when it seemed to every rational observer that the history of the

Jewish people was almost at its close. How perilously near to victory was Hitler and how imminent the "final solution" for all of us? Even our bloody annals of slaughter and martyrdom have no parallel to the enormity that was the Nazi era, when tenfold "the number who went forth from Egypt" were brutally destroyed.

When a million Jewish children were being turned into soap could a Jeremiah or a Daniel have pronounced the words "mighty and awesome"?

Then came the Men of the Great Assembly. Though the survivors of the Destruction had been pitifully few, and they and their descendants were reduced to abject spiritual poverty, yet they began to nourish the hope of Redemption. The restoration was, as recorded in the Bible,[1] a miserable affair. The *olim* were a minority among Babylonian Jews. Intellectually, religiously, and socially they were a poor lot. The area assigned to them for settlement was a small enclave surrounding the ruin that had been Jerusalem.

They were surrounded on all sides by enemies and subject to the arbitrary whims of their Persian overlords. Internally, they were hopelessly divided by social and religious strife – many of them had taken pagan wives and their children were not even Jews. Even when, after years of patient struggle, they finally succeeded in realizing the pinnacle of their aspirations and the Temple was consecrated, the old men among them wept in disillusionment and frustration, for it was but a shadow of the glory which they still remembered from their youth (Ezra 3:12).

All this the Men of the Great Assembly beheld. They saw that in the rebuilt Temple there was no *Shekhina*. There was no Holy Ark in the Holy of Holies and there were no Tablets of the Law. The Holy of Holies was absolutely empty. The High Priest did not possess the *Urim* and *Tumim*, nor was he anointed (*Yoma* 21b). Of course, no one even dared to mention the

---

1. See Ezra 2:64: "The whole congregation together was 42,360." Also, see ibid. 9:1–2: "The people of Israel and the priests and the Levites have not separated themselves from the peoples of the lands, doing according to their abominations, even the Canaanite, the Hittite, the Perizite, the Jebusite, the Ammonite, the Moabite, the Egyptian, and the Emorite. For they have taken their daughters for themselves and for their sons so that the holy seed have mingled themselves with the peoples of those lands: indeed the hand of the princes and rulers has been chief in this crime."

promised anointed king of the house of David; on the gate of the Temple Mount was engraved the emblem of Shushan – a firm reminder that the Emperor of Persia was king and on his precarious mercy depended the fragile security of the restored Jewish Commonwealth (*Menaḥot* 98a).

Yet the supremely important fact was the reality of Jewish survival. "All the nations had gathered to destroy them, but some reestablished themselves" (Rashi to *Yoma* 69b). "Surely, were it not for the awesome power of the Holy One blessed be He, how could one people endure among the nations?" (*Yoma* 69b).

This inexplicable fact, which flies in the face of all the apparent laws of history, gave the Men of the Great Assembly the courage to restore the divine crown to its pristine greatness. Moreover, this very fact itself, the reassertion of a near-autonomous Jewish polity, however small in dimensions, is the concrete manifestation of the divine greatness. To have witnessed the ingathering of the struggling exiles, to have seen their first halting steps in rebuilding the nation, to have felt the vigor of new hope surging through the "dry bones" (see Ezek. 37:1–4) is to experience the divine attributes of "these are the manifestations of His awesome greatness."

Nothing can explain the terrible God-forsakenness of the Holocaust years. It is not given to Man to understand "why dost Thou hide Thyself at times in trouble?" (Ps. 10:1). The man of faith is also the faithful man, and so he does not mock the Hiding God by false attributes. Nor can there be any recompense in this world for the rivers of blood shed to sanctify His name. In the face of the terrifying mystery of endless *Akedot*, when the heavens are shut fast against both heartrending pleas for pity and outraged demands for justice, the true believer can only "sit alone in silence ... and put his mouth in the dust" (Lam. 3:28–29).

The rebirth of Israel is not an indemnity for the unspeakable horrors of the Nazi era, and certainly not for the accumulated anguish of seventy-five generations of suffering.[2] The reestablishment of the Jewish state does not

---

2. *Rosh HaShana* 23a: "R. Yoḥanan also said: Alas for the idol-worshipers, since they have no means of remedy, as it says: 'For brass I will bring gold, and for iron I will bring silver, and for wood brass and for stones iron.' But what can he bring to replace R. Akiva and his companions?"

solve the dread perplexity of exile, nor does it spell the quick end of that persistent hatred of the Jew which is the mark of civilization unredeemed.

Is the State of Israel the long-awaited fulfillment of the prophecies? Surely, only a prophet call tell. Are the footsteps of the Messiah resounding over the hills? Who amongst us can presume to recognize the signs?

There is one simple, basic fact which is there for all the world to see. It is so utterly simple and so totally obvious that thousands of millions of people all over the globe know it and see it. Israel *is*, and it bears God's name, and it has restored God's crown!

In the light of this radical truth, all other questions take on a different meaning. In fact, it is only in virtue of this that they have any meaning at all, for he who "sits alone in silence" can ask no questions and give no answers.

The questions are, of course, manifold. Yet there is nothing wrong in the admission that we do not know all the answers.

The challenges are very great indeed. It has been pointed out that the existence of the state makes possible the fulfillment of two great aims of Torah: the ingathering of the exiles and the building of a just society. The achievement of these ends will require all the dedication and ingenuity that all Jews everywhere are capable of, and we hope that their accomplishment may initiate the Messianic era.

Yet it is imperative to recognize the basic truth that the religious significance of the State of Israel is not limited to its being the instrument for the attainment of religious ends or even to its being a stage in the process of redemption, as we pray for it to be.

In the case of an individual man, it is true that he can be instrumental in the fulfillment of commandments and as a link in the chain of history leading to the Redemption. Yet there is a higher metaphysical significance possessed by the individual, for he is an image of God. He is that, even if he tragically fails in his instrumental capacity, even if he falls into the abyss of crime beyond the hope of rehabilitation so that the death penalty must be exacted on him. Nonetheless, he commands respect as the image of God.[3]

---

3. Deuteronomy 21:23. See *Sanhedrin* 46b: "R. Meir said: A parable was stated: To what is this matter comparable? To two twin brothers [who lived] in one city; one was appointed king, and the other took to highway robbery. At the king's

Likewise, in the case of the collective Jewish people there is religious import in the very existence of Jewish self-determination besides its instrumental character. The Covenant is binding not only upon us: it also obligates Him who has chosen Israel to be His people and who has pledged Himself to be our God. Though it defies understanding, all our accumulated historical experience demonstrates the common fate in which the dignity of the Jewish people and the glory of our God are inextricably intertwined: "They were dispersed through the countries... wherever they came they profaned My holy name, in that men said of them, 'These are the people of the Lord, and yet they had to go out of His land'" (Ezek. 36:19–20).

We are prone to think of the twentieth century as the post-religious era. Indeed, in some ways that is so. Yet it is a grievous error to suppose that indifference to religion is all that widespread. The Nazis openly proclaimed their war against biblical religion and the God of Israel. So, of course, do the Communists. It is also painfully obvious that the restoration of Israel poses a theological dilemma for many Christians. As for Islam, the resurgence of fundamentalist zeal expresses itself unequivocally in repeated calls for a jihad against the Jews.

The epic of Israel reborn spells out the renewal of the crown of *our* God not only for us but for others as well!

The faithful man not only believes, he also testifies, and his testimony can be trusted to vindicate his belief. "You are My witnesses, saith the Lord, and I am God" (Is. 43:12.).[4] The sages explain: "If you are My witnesses, then I am God: but if you are not My witnesses, I am not!" (Sifri to Deut. 33:5). This is the ultimate paradox of faith! The revelation of God is really a disclosure only if we know it and bear witness to it. He is our Redeemer only if we hear the promise as a command: "He says to Jerusalem, 'Let it be inhabited' and to the cities of Judah 'Let them be built'" (Is. 44:26).

The sad truth is that we are afraid. We crave to believe but we are afraid to open our eyes to see the hard intractable reality of Israel under siege.

---

command they hanged him. But all who saw him exclaimed, 'The king is hanged!' whereupon the king issued a command and he was taken down."

4. It is important to bear in mind that this passage is part of a message to the Jews of the Diaspora who survived the exile and to whom Cyrus' declaration was addressed.

We are afraid to open our ears to hear the urgent summons to leave the Diaspora and settle the waste places and fill the land with Jews.

Two tasks face us now. One applies to Jews everywhere. It is to cultivate the understanding that true faith requires the mobilization of all our intellectual, spiritual, and physical resources for the security and the upbuilding of the state and the people of Israel. To let down our guard, to underestimate our enemies, or to overlook the immense obstacles – economic, social, political, and military – which beset us is not only dangerous folly, but it is, above all, a betrayal of our witness. The crown of God has been entrusted to us for safekeeping and we dare not foist the job on anybody else, even the Almighty Himself! The shape of Israeli society for generations to come is being determined now. It must and it can be permeated with Torah, not starry-eyed otherworldly faith but the kind of unswerving trust in the God of Israel which opens our eyes to see and to bear witness to His awesome deeds.

The second compelling imperative of our time is addressed to Jews in the *Golah*:

> Listen to me, O Jacob
> and Israel whom I called: …
> Go forth from Babylon,
> flee from Chaldea;
> Declare this with a shout of joy,
> proclaim it,
> send it forth to the end of the earth. (Is. 48:12, 20)

These words were intended for the generation of the Return with Zerubabel. Will we now heed and obey?[5]

---

5. Compare to *Yoma* 9b: "Said Resh Lakish to him: … It is written: 'If she be a wall, we will build upon her a turret of silver; if she be a door, we will enclose her with boards of cedar' (Song 8:9). Had you made yourself like a wall [i.e., in a single unit] and had all come up in the days of Ezra, you would have been compared to silver, which no rottenness can ever affect. Now that you have come up like doors [Rashi: as a gate with two doors, one open and one closed, since you came in halves], you are like cedarwood, over which rottenness prevails."

Israel, Gateway of Hope

Rabbi Jonathan Sacks

In 1871, my great-grandfather, Rabbi Arye Leib Frumkin, left his home in Kelm, Lithuania, to go live in Israel, following his father who had done so some twenty years earlier. One of his first acts was to begin writing a book, *The History of the Sages of Jerusalem*, a chronicle of the continuous Jewish presence in Jerusalem since Nahmanides arrived there in 1265, and he began reconstructing the community that had been devastated during the Crusades.

In 1881, pogroms broke out in over one hundred towns in Russia. In 1882 the notorious antisemitic May Laws were enacted, sending millions of Jews into flight to the West. Something happened to my great-grandfather as a result of these experiences. Evidently he realized that *aliya*, going to live in Israel, was no longer a matter of a pilgrimage of the few, but an urgent necessity to the many. He moved to one of the first agricultural settlements in the new Yishuv. It had been settled some three or four years earlier, but all the original farmers had contracted malaria and left. Some were now prepared to go back to work the land, but not to live there. It was, they believed, simply too much of a hazard to health.

He led the return and built the first house there. When the settlers began to succeed in taming the land, they were attacked by local Arabs, and in 1894 he decided that it was simply too dangerous to stay, and he moved to London. Eventually he returned and was buried there. On his gravestone it records that he had built the first house.

What fascinates me is the name the settlers gave to the village. I do not know why they decided on this particular name, but I have a guess. It was set in the Yarkon Valley, and when they discovered it was a malarial swamp, it appeared to them as "a valley of trouble." But they knew the Hebrew Bible, and they recalled a verse from the prophet Hosea in which God promised to turn the valley of trouble into a "gateway of hope" (2:18). That is the name they gave the village, today the sixth largest town in Israel: Petaḥ Tikva, the gateway of hope.

I tell this story because opposition to Israel is at the epicenter of the new antisemitism, the spread of which is one of the most significant events of my lifetime. Antisemitism is never harmless; it has always in the past been a prelude to tragedy. The new antisemitism, coming as it does within living memory of the Holocaust, almost defies belief. That Israel, alone among the 192 members of the United Nations, finds its very right to exist called into question, and that the United Nations itself, which voted in 1947 to bring Israel into existence, should be home to some of the worst assaults on its right to self-defense – are not phenomena that can be passed over in silence. A narrative is taking shape and a climate of opinion is being formed that are dangerous in the extreme, and they must be challenged.

It is often said that Israel was created at the expense of the local population to make amends for the Holocaust. Europe committed the crime; the Palestinians were forced to pay the price. That is simply untrue. As George Eliot's novel and my great-grandfather's story make clear, the return to Zion was being thought about and acted on long before the Holocaust. The Jewish attachment to Israel goes back long before the Balfour Declaration in 1917, ratified in 1922 by the League of Nations; before 1890, when the word "Zionism" was coined; before 1862, when Moses Hess wrote the first great document of secular Zionism, *Rome and Jerusalem*.

It goes back to the first recorded syllables of Jewish time, some four thousand years ago, when God told Abraham to leave his land,

his birthplace and his father's house and travel to "the land which I will show you." Seven times God promised the land to Abraham, once to Isaac, and three times to Jacob. The Book of Genesis ends with Joseph telling his brothers, "God will surely come to your aid and take you up out of this land to the land he promised on oath to Abraham, Isaac, and Jacob" (50:24). Exodus opens with God summoning Moses to lead the Israelites to the "land flowing with milk and honey" (3:8). The whole of the Pentateuch – in a sense the whole of Jewish history – is about the long, arduous journey to Israel, the Promised Land.

The Jewish connection with the land goes back, in other words, for twice as long as the entire history of Christianity, three times that of Islam. Benjamin Disraeli, who despite the fact that he had been baptized as a Christian retained enormous pride in his Jewish ancestry, said in reply to an insult by the Irish Catholic Daniel O'Connell, "Yes, I am a Jew, and when the ancestors of the right honorable gentleman were brutal savages in an unknown island, mine were priests in the Temple of Solomon." Disraeli was in fact a proto-Zionist and wrote two of the first Zionist novels, *Alroy* and *Tancred*.

WHY A LAND?

At the heart of Judaism is a mystery, or more precisely a proposition that successive generations have found it hard to understand. Why Israel? Why does the Hebrew Bible so resolutely and unerringly focus on this place, what Spinoza called a mere "strip of territory"? The God of Abraham is the God of the whole world, a God unbounded by space. Why then does He choose any particular space, let alone one so small and apparently unprepossessing?

The question "Why Israel?" is the geographical way of asking "Why the Jews?" The answer lies in the duality that defines Jewish faith and constitutes one of its most important contributions to civilization. Judaism embodies and exemplifies the necessary tension between the universal and the unique, between everywhere in general and somewhere in particular.

If there were only universals, the world would consist of empires, each claiming the totality of truth and each demonstrating that truth by attempting to conquer or convert everyone else. When, in 1532, Pizarro

and his Spanish troops massacred the Incas, seized their land, and took their vast treasures of gold, he told Atahualpa, ruler of the Incas:

> We come to conquer this land…that all may come to a knowledge of God and of His Holy Catholic Faith; and by reason of our good mission, God, the creator of heaven and earth and of all things in them, permits this, in order that you may know Him and come out from the bestial and diabolical life that you lead…. When you have seen the errors in which you live, you will understand the good that we have done you by coming to your land…. Our Lord permitted that your pride should be brought low and that no Indian should be able to offend a Christian.

If there is only one truth, and you have it, then others do not. They live in error. That has been the justification of many crimes in the course of history.

If, on the other hand, there are only particulars – only a multiplicity of cultures and ethnicities with no universal moral principles to bind them – then the natural state of the world is a ceaseless proliferation of warring tribes. That is the risk today, in a post-modern, morally relativist world with ethnic conflicts, violence, and terror scarring the face of many parts of the globe.

The Abrahamic covenant as understood by Judaism is the only principled way of avoiding these two scenarios. Jews belonged somewhere, not everywhere. Yet the God they worshipped was the God of everywhere, not just somewhere. So Jews were commanded to be neither an empire nor a tribe, harboring neither universal aspirations nor tribal belligerence. Theirs was to be a small land, but a significant one, for it was there, and there alone, that they were to live their destiny.

That destiny was to create a society that would honor the proposition that we are all created in the image and likeness of God. It would be a place in which the freedom of some would not lead to the enslavement of others. It would be the opposite of Egypt, whose bread of affliction and bitter herbs of slavery they were to eat every year on the festival of Passover, to remind them of what they were to avoid.

It would be the only nation in the world whose sovereign was God Himself, and whose constitution – the Torah – was His word. Philo, in first-century Alexandria, struggled to explain this to an audience that was either Greek or Roman, and to do so he had to invent a word: *theocracy*, literally, "rule by God." But since theocracy has come to mean rule by clerics, the better word is *nomocracy*, "the rule of law, not men."

Judaism is the code of a self-governing society. We tend to forget this, since Jews have lived in dispersion for two thousand years, without the sovereign power to govern themselves, and because modern Israel is a secular state. Judaism is a religion of redemption rather than salvation; it is about the shared spaces of our collective lives, not an interior drama of the soul – though Judaism, in the books of Psalms and Job, knows the interior drama as well.

The Jewish God is the God of love: You shall love the Lord your God with all your heart, all your soul, and all your might. You shall love your neighbor as yourself. And, you shall love the stranger. The Hebrew Bible is a book suffused with love – the love of God for humanity, and the love of a people for God. All its tense emotions of anger and jealousy are part of the story of that often unreciprocated love.

But because Judaism is also the code of a society, it is also about the social emotions: righteousness (*tzedek/tzedaka*), justice (*mishpat*), loving-kindness (*ḥesed*), and compassion (*raḥamim*). These structure the template of biblical law, which covers all aspects of the life of society, its economy, welfare systems, education, family life, employer-employee relations, the protection of the environment, and so on. The broad principles driving this elaborate structure, traditionally enumerated as 613 commands, are clear. No one should be left in dire poverty. No one should lack access to justice and the courts. No family should be without its share of the land. One day in seven, everyone should be free. One year in seven, all debts should be cancelled. One year in fifty, all land that had been sold should revert to its original owners. It was the nearest thing the ancient world had ever seen to an egalitarian society.

None of this was possible without a land. The sages said, "Whoever lives outside Israel is as if he had no God" (*Ketubot* 110b). Nahmanides in the thirteenth century said that "the main purpose of all the commands

is for those who live in the land of the Lord" (Commentary on the Torah, Deut. 11:18). These are mystical sentiments, but we can translate them into secular terms. Judaism is the constitution of a self-governing nation, the architectonics of a society dedicated to the service of God in freedom and dignity. Without a land and state, Judaism is a shadow of itself. God may still live in the heart, but not in the public square, in the justice of the courts, the morality of the economy, and the humanitarianism of everyday life.

Jews have lived in almost every country under the sun. *In four thousand years, only in Israel have they been able to live as a free, self-governing people.* Only in Israel have they been able to construct an agriculture, a medical system, an economic infrastructure, in the spirit of the Torah and its concern for freedom, justice, and the sanctity of life. Only in Israel can Jews today speak the Hebrew of the Bible as the language of everyday speech. Only there can they live Jewish time within a calendar structured according to the rhythms of the Jewish year. Only in Israel can Jews once again walk where the prophets walked, climb the mountains Abraham climbed and to which David lifted his eyes. Israel is the only place where Jews have been able to live Judaism in anything other than an edited edition, continuing the story their ancestors began.

That, not antisemitism, is why my great-grandfather travelled there to be part of the great rebuilding, and why George Eliot saw the return of Jews to Zion as the rebirth of this ancient people that had taught the world so much.

WHY THIS LAND?

Why there? The Bible doesn't say. We can only speculate. But implicit in the biblical narrative is an answer: Israel is a place from which it is impossible to build an empire. The geography is wrong. The Judean hills in one direction and the Sinai desert in the other block easy access to the surrounding lands. The coastal plain is narrow and in ancient times was open to easy attack from the sea.

The cradle of civilization was not there. It was in the alluvial plains of the Tigris-Euphrates valley and the rich, well-watered lands of the lower Nile. It was in Mesopotamia that the first city states were built, and in Egypt that the greatest and longest-lived of ancient empires had its base.

The normal movement of population is from poor countries to rich ones, and from more rudimentary to more advanced civilizations. The two great Jewish journeys, Abraham's from Ur of the Chaldees, and Moses and the Israelites' from Egypt, were in precisely the opposite direction. *At the heart of the Bible is a critique of empires.* It is there in its brief sketch of the Tower of Babel, whose builders had the hubris that they could, unaided, reach heaven. It is there in its fuller portrait of pharaonic Egypt, which first welcomed the Hebrews, then enslaved them.

Israel is a land of small towns and small farms, whose ideal is the modest utopia envisioned by the prophet Micah:

> Every man will sit under his own vine
> and under his own fig tree,
> and no one will make them afraid,
> for the Lord Almighty has spoken. (Mic. 4:4)

The Israelites never aspired to be an Egypt, a colossus, a superpower. To the contrary, in one of the most glorious passages in the Bible, Isaiah imagines a day when God will love Israel's enemies as He loves His own people:

> In that day there will be a highway from Egypt to Assyria. The Assyrians will go to Egypt and the Egyptians to Assyria. The Egyptians and Assyrians will worship together. In that day Israel will be the third, along with Egypt and Assyria, a blessing on the earth. The Lord Almighty will bless them, saying, "Blessed be Egypt My people, Assyria My handiwork, and Israel My inheritance." (Is. 19:23–25)

That is why it is so ironic that Israel should be called an imperialist power. Israel is the only nation to have ruled the land in the past four thousand years that has *not* been an empire and never sought to become one. Israel has been ruled by many empires: Egypt, Assyria, Babylon, Persia, Greece, Rome, the Byzantines, the Umayyad, the Abbasids, the Fatimids, the Crusaders, the Mamluks, and the Ottomans. The only non-imperial power to control the land was and is Israel.

This explains a much misunderstood sentence. It is sometimes said that the early Zionists claimed that Israel was "a land without a people, for a people without a land," thus ignoring the non-Jewish population resident there. That was not the original proposition, which was made by a Christian, Lord Shaftesbury, in 1843. He said, "There is a country *without a nation*; and God now in His wisdom and mercy, directs us to *a nation without a country*, His own once loved, nay still loved people, the sons of Abraham, of Isaac, and of Jacob." The meaning is that Israel was the only nation to create a nation-state within the land. At all other times, it existed as, at best, an administrative district within an empire whose base was elsewhere.

THE LAND THAT MAKES YOU LOOK TO HEAVEN

There is another intriguing footnote, within the Bible itself, as to why this land is different. In a masterstroke of delayed information, Moses tells the Israelites as they are almost within sight of the land that there is a qualification to the description he has given all along, that it is "a land flowing with milk and honey." It is a good land, but with one caveat:

> The land you are entering to take over is not like the land of Egypt, from which you have come, where you planted your seed and irrigated it by foot as in a vegetable garden. The land you are crossing the Jordan to take possession of is a land of mountains and valleys that drinks rain from heaven. It is a land the Lord your God cares for; the eyes of the Lord your God are continually on it from the beginning of the year to its end. (Deut. 11:10–12)

Israel is not the Nile delta or the Tigris-Euphrates valley. It is a land dependent on rain, and rain in that part of the world is not predictable. In a sense we knew this already: Abraham, Isaac, and Jacob all have to migrate temporarily because of drought and famine. We have merely lost sight of this during the narrative from Exodus to Deuteronomy, in which our focus has been on Egypt and the desert. But the passage intimates a correlation between geography and spirituality. Israel is a place where people look up to heaven in search of rain, not down to earth and its

natural water supply. It is a place where you have to pray, not one in which nature and its seasons are predictable.

That is part of a larger narrative. Because the terrain of Israel is such that it cannot become the base of an empire, it will constantly be at threat from larger and stronger neighboring powers. Israel will constantly find itself outnumbered. It will need to rely on exceptional courage from its soldiers, and unexpected tactics of war. That will take high national morale, which in turn will require from the people a sense of belonging to a just and inclusive society.

Commitment will be needed from every individual. They will need to feel that their cause is just and that they are fighting for something worth preserving. So the entire configuration of the Torah's social ethics, whose guardians were the prophets, is already implicit from the beginning, from the kind of geopolitical entity Israel is and will be. It would always be a small and highly vulnerable country, set in a strategic location at the junction of three continents: Europe, Africa, and Asia.

There is a metonymic moment at which this is hinted for the first time. It occurs in the first battle the Israelites have to fight for themselves, against the Amalekites after the crossing of the Red Sea:

> So Joshua fought the Amalekites as Moses had ordered, and Moses, Aaron, and Hur went to the top of the hill. As long as Moses held up his hands, the Israelites were winning, but whenever he lowered his hands, the Amalekites were winning. (Ex. 17:10–11)

The sages understood the symbolism. When the Israelites looked up, they won. When they looked down, they began to lose. Israel, within itself, would always seem to testify to something beyond itself. It would become, like no other, a holy land. Its history would contain a message significantly different from the usual laws of nations and their wars, in which victory goes to the strong, the weak are vanquished, great powers rise, bestride the narrow world like a colossus, and then decline, their place to be taken by another and younger power. Israel would survive, but it would do so against the odds. As with its agriculture, so with its battles: Israel is a people that must lift its eyes to heaven. As Ben-Gurion famously said: In Israel, to be a realist, you have to believe in miracles.

THE PERPETUAL JOURNEY

The journey to the land was never easy. Almost as soon as Abraham arrived, he was forced by famine to leave. Jacob and his family went into exile in Egypt, where, generations later, they were enslaved. In the days of Moses, the Israelites made the second great journey to the land. It should have taken a few weeks, but it lasted forty years. Moses himself died without entering it.

Centuries later, the Assyrians conquered the north, and then the Babylonians did the same to the south, destroying the Temple and taking many of the people captive. It might have been the end of Jewish history. But it was there that a great determination was born. In words engraved on the Jewish soul ever since, they vowed never to forget where they came from, the land to which God had first called them, the place they called home. Though they no longer lived in the land, the land lived on in them. By the waters of Babylon, they made a pledge:

> If I forget you, O Jerusalem,
> may my right hand forget its skill.
> May my tongue cling to the roof of my mouth
> if I do not remember you,
> if I do not consider Jerusalem
> my highest joy. (Ps. 137:5–6)

They came back, reorganized their society, rebuilt the Temple, and in the days of Ezra and Nehemiah solemnly renewed their covenant with God. They were conquered again, first by the Greeks, then by the Romans. As long as they were free to practice Judaism, they did not take up arms against their rulers, but they were not always free. That led to three rebellions, the first against the Seleucid Antiochus IV in the second century BCE, then against Rome in the first century CE, and a third time, under Bar Kokhba, in 132 CE.

The first revolt was successful, but the second and third were disastrous. The Temple was destroyed. Jerusalem was levelled to the ground and rebuilt as a Roman polis, Aelia Capitolina. Jews were forbidden to enter except on one day of the year, the Ninth of Av, when they mourned the loss of the Temple as if a close relative had died. The Hadrianic

persecutions, after the Bar Kokhba rebellion, were so draconian that the Talmud records an extraordinary statement that there were rabbis who took the view that Jews should no longer marry and have children, with the result that the Jewish people would cease to be (*Bava Batra* 60b). Slowly, Jewish life moved back to Babylon and elsewhere. The longest exile had begun.

Yet Israel remained the focus of Jewish hopes. Wherever Jews were, they built synagogues, each of which was a symbolic fragment of the Temple in Jerusalem. Wherever they were they prayed about Jerusalem, facing Jerusalem. They remembered it and wept for it, as the psalm had said, at every time of joy. They never relinquished their claim to the land, and there were places, especially in the north, from which they never left. The Jewish people were the circumference of a circle at whose center was the holy land and Jerusalem the holy city. For centuries they lived suspended between memory and hope, sustained by the promise that one day God would bring them back.

Throughout the Middle Ages until modern times, when they could, they returned. Judah HaLevi set sail to go there in 1140, though we do not know if he reached his destination. Maimonides and his family went there in 1165, though they were unable to stay in a land ravaged by the Crusaders and were eventually forced to leave and go to Egypt. Nahmanides went in 1267 and revived the Jewish community in Jerusalem.

In the fifteenth and sixteenth centuries exiles came from Spain and Portugal, turning the community in Safed into the world center of Jewish scholarship and mysticism. In the seventeenth century they came from the Ukraine after the massacres of 1648. In the eighteenth century, disciples of both the Baal Shem Tov and the Vilna Gaon made their way to the land. In the nineteenth century, as travel became easier, more Jews came.

In 1798 Napoleon began his campaign in the Middle East, landing first in Egypt, then in Palestine. With a strong sense of history, he realized that this could herald the return of Jews to the land from which they had been exiled for so long. Grandiloquently he called on them to take up the challenge. The campaign foundered and nothing came of the offer, but the possibility had been raised. Soon thereafter, the French historian Chateaubriand visited Jerusalem. There he found a tiny Jewish

community whose persistence filled him with awe. Speaking of the Jewish settlement, he wrote:

> It has seen Jerusalem destroyed seventeen times, yet there exists nothing in the world which can discourage it or prevent it from raising its eyes to Zion. He who beholds the Jews dispersed over the face of the earth, in keeping with the Word of God, lingers and marvels. But he will be struck with amazement, as at a miracle, who finds them still in Jerusalem and perceives even [those], who in law and justice are the masters of Judea, to exist as slaves and strangers in their own land; how despite all abuses they await the king who is to deliver them.... If there is anything among the nations of the world marked with the stamp of the miraculous, this, in our opinion, is that miracle.

It was the wave of European nationalism in the nineteenth century that led Jews, as it led non-Jews like George Eliot and Lord Shaftesbury, to believe that the time had come to re-establish a Jewish state. The first Jewish Zionists, in the mid-nineteenth century, were religious figures, Rabbis Yehuda Alkalai and Zvi Hirsch Kalischer, who heard, in the mood of the age, a divine call to reestablish themselves as a nation in their own land.

Soon, though, another force began to emerge: antisemitism. The first to detect it was the erstwhile colleague of Karl Marx, Moses Hess, whose tract *Rome and Jerusalem* (1862) was the first document of secular Zionism. This was followed by Judah Leib Pinsker's *Auto-Emancipation* after the 1881 Russian pogroms, and then Theodor Herzl's *The Jewish State* (1896) after the Dreyfus trial in France led him to conclude that Europe was now unsafe for Jews.

With Herzl, the longstanding program of *aliya* and settlement became a political movement. The "return to Zion," a dream as old as the prophets, had become Zionism. Its great achievement was the Balfour Declaration of 1917, a commitment on the part of the British government, by then the dominant power in the Middle East, to establish in Palestine a "national home for the Jewish people."

Then came 1933, and the rise to power of Hitler. No one who had read or heard his words could doubt the danger. Antisemitism was at the heart of his program, and laws against Jews among the first of his acts. Gradually,

inexorably, Jews were deprived of their rights, their jobs, their freedoms; they were spoken of as lice, vermin, a cancer in the body of the German nation that had to be surgically removed.

A major humanitarian catastrophe was in the making and everyone knew it. In July 1938, world leaders gathered in the French town of Evian to discuss ways of saving the Jews. None was forthcoming. Nation after nation shut its doors. Millions of Jews were in danger and there was nowhere they could go. Jews discovered that on the whole surface of the earth there was not an inch they could call home in the sense given by the poet Robert Frost as the place where, "when you have to go there, they have to let you in." From that moment a Jewish homeland, promised twenty years earlier, became a moral necessity.

As the smoke of war cleared in 1945, as the Russians entered Auschwitz and the British Bergen-Belsen, slowly people began to understand the enormity of what had happened. A third of world Jewry had gone up in flames. One and a half million children had been murdered, not just because of their faith, or their parent's faith, but because one of their grandparents had been a Jew. When the destruction was over, a pillar of cloud marked the place where Europe's Jews had once been, and a silence that consumed all words.

Even then, the Jewish situation remained tense. Refugee ships like the *Exodus*, carrying Holocaust survivors to Mandatory Palestine, were turned back. There was violence in the land. Britain turned to the United Nations, and on November 29, 1947, the historic vote for partition took place. It passed by thirty-three votes to thirteen with ten abstentions, among them Britain: one of the few occasions during the Cold War period that America and Russia voted together, both supporting the motion. There were to be two states, one Jewish, one Arab. Two thousand years of Jewish powerlessness were at an end. On the 5th of Iyar 5708, May 14, 1948, the State of Israel was proclaimed. The land promised to Abraham was to be theirs again.

CHOOSING LIFE

Since its establishment, Israel has done extraordinary things. It has absorbed immigrants from 103 countries, speaking 82 languages. It has turned a desolate landscape into a place of forests and fields. It has

developed some of the finest agricultural and medical techniques and created one of the world's most advanced high-tech economies. It has produced great poets and novelists, artists and sculptors, symphony orchestras, universities, and research institutes. It has presided over the rebirth of the great Talmudic academies destroyed in Eastern Europe during the Holocaust. Wherever in the world there is a humanitarian disaster, Israel, if permitted, is one of the first to send aid. It has shared its technologies with other developing countries. Under immense strain, it has sustained democracy, a free press, and an independent – some say, too independent – judiciary. Had my great-grandfather, or for that matter George Eliot, been able to see what it has achieved, they would hardly believe it. In truth, I hardly believe it when I read Jewish history and begin to understand what Jewish life was like when there was no Israel.

For me, more than anything else, Israel is living testimony to the power of Moses' command, "Choose life."

Twenty-six centuries ago, in exile in Babylon, the prophet Ezekiel had the most haunting of all prophetic visions. He saw a valley of dry bones, a heap of skeletons. God asked him, "Son of man, can these bones live?" Ezekiel replied, "God, You alone know" (37:3). Then the bones came together, grew flesh and skin, and began to breathe and live again. Then God said: "Son of man, these bones are the whole house of Israel. They say, 'Our bones are dried up. *Avda tikvatenu*, our hope is lost.' Therefore prophesy and say to them: 'This is what God says: My people, I am going to open your graves and bring you up from them; I will bring you back to the Land of Israel'" (37:11–12).

It was this passage that Naftali Herz Imber was alluding to in 1877, when he wrote in the song that was to become Israel's national anthem, "Hatikva," the phrase *od lo avda tikvatenu*, "Our hope is not yet lost." Little could he have known that seventy years later one-third of the Jewish people would become, in Auschwitz and Treblinka and Bergen-Belsen, a valley of dry bones. Who could have been blamed for saying, "Our bones are dried up, our hope is lost"?

Yet, a mere three years after standing eyeball to eyeball with the angel of death, the Jewish people, by proclaiming the State of Israel, made a momentous affirmation of life, as if they had heard across the centuries

the echo of God's words to Ezekiel: "I will bring you back to the Land of Israel."

And a day will come when the story of Israel in modern times will speak not just to Jews, but to all who believe in the power of the human spirit as it reaches out to God, as an everlasting symbol of the victory of life over death, hope over despair. Israel has taken a barren land and made it bloom again. It has taken an ancient language, the Hebrew of the Bible, and made it speak again. It has taken the West's oldest faith and made it young again. It has taken a shattered nation and made it live again.

More than a century ago a young Jew from Lithuania, my great-grandfather, built a house on land never before cultivated, and the settlers gave it a name from a verse in the Book of Hosea in which God said, "I will turn the valley of trouble into a gateway of hope." That remains the Jewish hope. Israel is the land of hope.

The Mitzva of Living in Eretz Yisrael

Rabbi Hershel Schachter

After the destruction of the First Temple, the prophet Jeremiah bewailed the neglect into which the Land of Israel had fallen: "She is Zion; there is no one who inquires after her" (Jer. 30:17). The Talmud understood this neglect to include an intellectual dimension, namely, a laxity in the study of laws pertaining to Eretz Yisrael. Therefore the Rabbis derived from the verse an obligation to delve into the *halakhot* of Eretz Yisrael: "From this we infer that Zion ought to be inquired after" (*Rosh HaShana* 30a). What follows is one attempt at "inquiring after Zion."

Interestingly, the mitzva of *yishuv Eretz Yisrael* – living in the land of Israel – is discussed in the *Even HaEzer* section of the *Shulḥan Arukh* (74:3–5), and even there merely as a tangential issue arising from a mishna in *Ketubot* (110b). The mishna rules that should one spouse desire to move to Israel while the other opposes the move to the point of divorce, it is the spouse who wants to go who is considered justified in his or her claim, and the other one is guilty of breaking up the marriage. In practical terms, this means that if the wife is the recalcitrant partner, she need not be paid

the sum to which her marriage contract, *ketuba*, entitles her in the event of divorce or the death of her husband. If the husband refuses to move, he must divorce his wife, if she so wishes, and pay her the amount of her *ketuba*. In the Gemara it is clear that the halakha sides with the spouse who wishes to go, because it is that spouse who is conforming to the mitzva of *yishuv Eretz Yisrael*.

THE MITZVA: BIBLICAL OR RABBINIC?

If *yishuv Eretz Yisrael* is a mitzva, what is its biblical source? The Ramban, on two occasions (Commentary to Numbers 33:55, and *Hashmatot* to Rambam's *Sefer HaMitzvot*, positive commandment no. 4), points to the same verse: "Conquer the land and dwell therein" (Num. 33:55). The first phrase is understood by Ramban as obligating the Jewish community collectively to take control of the government of Israel and "not leave it in the hands of another." The second phrase, "and dwell therein," legislates a positive commandment for each individual to live in the Land of Israel, even if the land is under foreign domination. These two mitzvot, according to Ramban, are applicable throughout history and are as relevant to our generation as to the generation led by Joshua bin Nun, who first entered Israel.

But it is Rambam's view on the issue that has most puzzled the later commentators. For although the Rambam in *Mishneh Torah* includes the various statements of the Gemara regarding living in Eretz Yisrael (see *Ishut* 13:19 and *Melakhim* 5:12), he nonetheless omits both *kibbush Eretz Yisrael* (conquering the land) and *yishuv Eretz Yisrael* (living in the land) from his enumeration of the 613 mitzvot. Does his silence mean that he does not consider living in Israel to be a mitzva? Alternatively, perhaps, Rambam considers it a mitzva, but refrains from counting it among the 613 due to some other reason peculiar to his methodology in selecting the mitzvot to be counted.

Some commentators[1] suggest that the Rambam considers *yishuv haAretz* to be a mitzva, but only on a rabbinic level, with the verse cited

---

1. *Sdei Ḥemed Maarekhet Eretz Yisrael* in the name of *Knesset HaGedola* to *Yoreh De'ah* 239; also *Ar'a DeRabbanan* quoting responsa of Rabbi David b. Zimri (Radvaz).

by Ramban operative only during the original conquest of Israel.[2] If this is indeed the Rambam's position, then there would actually be no change in our attitude toward the observance of the mitzva, for we are as scrupulous in our observance of rabbinic mitzvot as in those which are divinely ordained (*Yoreh De'ah* 2:454).

When Rabbi Avraham of Sochatshov, author of Responsa *Avnei Nezer*, was asked whether *yishuv haAretz* is a mitzva today, and if so, why the great hasidic rebbeim of Europe never moved to Israel, he penned a lengthy responsum analyzing the Rambam's approach. In fact, suggests the Avnei Nezer, even the Rambam agrees that living in Eretz Yisrael is a biblical commandment in force in all periods in history. His failure to count it in his listing of mitzvot is due to an extraneous technical reason. Whenever the Torah lists two mitzvot, with one designed to lead up to and facilitate the performance of the other, Rambam regards the listing of both as unnecessary repetition, and lists only the first of the two. For that reason, once the Rambam counts the mitzva of building the Tabernacle (*Sefer HaMitzvot*, positive commandment no. 20), whose purpose was to house the Ark of the Law, he sees no need to list the mitzva of building the Ark itself (Ex. 25:8, 10). And similarly, once he enumerated the mitzva of destroying the nations who impeded the Jewish conquest and settlement of Israel (*haharem taharimem*, Deut. 20:17; *Sefer HaMitzvot*, positive commandment no. 187), he no longer finds it necessary to count the actual conquest and settlement as separate mitzvot. Both of the above opinions agree that *yishuv Eretz Yisrael* is a mitzva according to the Rambam, and only differ as to whether its nature is biblical or rabbinic.

Rabbi Isaac de Leon, in his commentary *Megillat Esther* on the Rambam's *Sefer HaMitzvot* (commenting on Ramban's *Hashmatot*, positive commandment no. 4), opens the door to the most radical interpretation of the Rambam, by explaining that Rambam's failure to mention *kibbush* (conquest) and *yishuv Eretz Yisrael* indicates his view that they do not constitute mitzvot today. For, *Megillat Esther* explains, these mitzvot applied only in the days of Moses, Joshua, and David, before the Jewish

---

2. The Rambam would then be following the very rule he laid down in the first part of his *Sefer HaMitzvot* (*shoresh* 3) of not counting as a mitzva anything of a temporary nature – *horaat shaah*.

nation was exiled, and they will resume only in the days of Messiah, when the Jews will be returned to their land. So limited are these two commandments in their time of fulfillment that Rambam saw fit not to count them among the *Taryag* (613) mitzvot. The *Minḥat Elazar* wholeheartedly supports this understanding of the Rambam, which posits that *yishuv haAretz* is no longer a mitzva today.

The overwhelming majority of *aḥaronim*, however, reject the explanation of the *Megillat Esther* on several grounds. First, the Avnei Nezer points out that the Rambam himself counts the sacrificial rites as mitzvot, although these could only take place in the Temple. Clearly the fact that a mitzva cannot be performed at certain times in Jewish history in no way diminishes its status as a mitzva. The only time Rambam denies a commandment mitzva status is when the command was issued as a one-time occurrence, as, for example, when Moses was ordered to "raise his staff and stretch out his arm over the sea" (Ex. 14:16, 26) to part the waters [see footnote 2].

Furthermore, the contention of the *Megillat Esther* that in the days of Messiah a new mitzva, nonexistent for centuries, will be added to our observance, runs counter to a basic tenet of Judaism. We believe that the commandments of the Torah are eternal and will not be altered even in Messianic times.[3] This belief in the immutability of Torah forms part of Rambam's own thirteen principles of faith. In view of the difficulties inherent in the approach of the *Megillat Esther*, most *aḥaronim* conclude that *yishuv Eretz Yisrael* constitutes a biblical mitzva according to both Ramban and Rambam.

EXCEPTIONS AND EXEMPTIONS

Rabbeinu Chaim Cohen in *Tosafot* (*Ketubot* 110b) cites two reasons why the mitzva of living in the Land of Israel should not apply in his times. First, the journey to Israel and subsequent life there are fraught with danger; second, poverty and other difficulties will make it impossible to

---

3. The only law to be altered in the future was specified clearly in the Torah: When God expands the borders of Israel to include the territories of the Kini, Kenizi, and Kadmoni nations, three more cities of refuge will be added to the six already existing (Deut. 19:9).

observe the mitzvot connected to the land and will lead to the violation of those mitzvot. The Avnei Nezer dismisses both reasons, saying that they simply are no longer true.[4] Neither danger nor hardship is severe enough to excuse one from the mitzva of *yishuv haAretz*. If conditions were not a hindrance when the Avnei Nezer penned his responsum over a century ago, surely now they are no problem.

In Tractate *Bava Batra* (91a) the Talmud lists poverty as grounds for exemption from the mitzva. One who cannot make a comfortable living in Israel is not required to live there in penury. This rationale is cited by the *Pithei Teshuva* (*Even HaEzer* 75:3) and many other authorities, including Rabbi Shlomo Kluger[5] and the *Sand Ḥemed*.[6] In fact, as we shall see, the Avnei Nezer builds upon it his elaborate responsum explaining why *yishuv haAretz* was often neglected by Jewish leaders. It must be stressed, however, that a comfortable life in Israel does not mean a life with every luxury available in the Diaspora. Even if one's standard of living drops in Israel, it is not grounds for exemption unless the new style of life is indeed intolerable.

In Tractate *Avoda Zara* (13a), permission is granted to leave Israel in order to learn Torah or to marry. Although both Torah and prospective spouses are readily available in Israel, the Talmud recognizes that cases may arise where a person feels he can only lead a normal life learning from a particular rabbi or married to a particular person who resides outside Israel. *Tosafot* (ad loc.) present two opinions as to whether exemption from *yishuv haAretz* is limited to cases of these two important mitzvot – *talmud Torah* and marriage – or extends to any mitzva that one can perform only in *ḥutz laAretz*, outside the Land of Israel.

The common denominator of these cases is the opportunity to lead a normal life. One is not expected to live in Israel under abnormal and unbearable conditions. If living in Israel means a life of poverty, or a life devoid of the Torah or companionship of one's choice, then the obligation falls away.

---

4. See *Pithei Teshuva* to *Even HaEzer* 75:3, who cites the Responsa of Maharit as saying that the words of *Tosafot* were written by an erring student.
5. Responsa *HaElef Lekha Shlomo, Even HaEzer,* no. 118–20.
6. *Maarekhet Eretz Yisrael,* vol. 5, p. 11, sec. 9.

Stated differently, it may be said that Eretz Yisrael, being the *land* chosen and sanctified by God, is the natural and proper place for Jews, the *people* chosen and sanctified by Him. For individual Jews there may be extenuating circumstances, such as those outlined above, in which it becomes clear that their place is not in Israel. Based on this rationale, it has been suggested that the greatest scholars and leaders of the Diaspora may be permitted, or even obligated, to remain in *ḥutz laAretz*. Since their sphere of influence is in *galut*, and it is there that they will have the most beneficial effect in disseminating Torah, we cannot say that their place must be in Israel.[7]

Avnei Nezer seeks further justification for the failure of giants of Ḥasidut to immigrate to Israel in fulfillment of the mitzva. He finds that, given the nature and purpose of the mitzva, these hasidic leaders could not possibly have fulfilled it in their circumstances. To fully understand this point, we must first examine the nature of *mitzvat yishuv haAretz* as conceived by the Avnei Nezer.

THE NATURE OF THE MITZVA

Eretz Yisrael is described in the Torah as "the land upon which the eyes of God are always turned" (Deut. 11:12). The Talmud (*Taanit* 10a) interprets this added attention paid by God to Israel as denoting an extra measure of divine providence, or *hashgaḥa peratit*, bestowed by God only upon Israel and its inhabitants. One manifestation of this special *hashgaḥa* is the apportionment of rain, but it is really an all-around more intimate relationship that exists between God and His people living in the Land of Israel. This relationship is spelled out by the statement in the Talmud (*Taanit* 10a) that outside Israel a person receives his livelihood from God through an angel, but in Israel the sustenance is provided directly by God Himself. It is for this reason that Eretz Yisrael is called "the King's palace" (see Rabbi Yisakhar Teichtal, *Eim Habanim Semeiḥa* [Jerusalem, 5743], 157); although certainly God's dominion

---

7. This was told to me by the Ashkenazi Chief Rabbi of Israel, Rabbi Avraham Shapira. And so wrote Rabbi Chaim Ozer Grodzinski to Rabbi Kook (citing Responsa Maharam Schick, *Yoreh De'ah*), and Rabbi Joseph B. Soloveitchik was known to say this as well.

extends to the entire universe ("The whole earth is full of His glory," Is. 6:3), there exists a unique, more personal connection to God in His chosen land.[8]

In light of this aspect of Eretz Yisrael, the Avnei Nezer redefines the mitzva of *yishuv haAretz*. The Torah did not command us simply to be physically present in the Land of Israel. Rather, it required us to crave a closer personal relationship with God, one endowed with more *hashgaḥa peratit*. We are commanded to strive to live in Israel so that all our sustenance should come directly from God and not through any intermediary. When we live and work in Israel, our livelihood emanates from the hand of God.

Precisely for this reason, explains Avnei Nezer, most hasidic giants did not attempt to live in Eretz Yisrael. Having no source of income in Israel, these Rabbis would have been forced to subsist off of funds sent them by Hasidim from *outside Israel*. Thus, even in Israel, their livelihood would have come from the Diaspora, through the agency of an intermediary angel. They would not have fulfilled the purpose of *yishuv haAretz*; they would not have achieved closeness to God through directly receiving

---

8. Thus, even as there are gradations in the amount of divine protection afforded people, so too the amount of *hashgaḥa* varies depending upon location. Among people, the righteous will be both protected more and held accountable for more minor transgressions than will the average Jew, and the average Jew in turn is more clearly watched over than the wicked. And among lands, Israel is more closely supervised than *ḥutz laAretz*.

In supporting his point, the Avnei Nezer cites the midrashic story of how Jacob, upon returning to Israel from Laban's house, gathered all his material goods into one pile and presented them to Esau, in exchange for Esau's burial rights in the Cave of Makhpelah. On that occasion Jacob declared, "The possessions of *ḥutz laAretz* are not worth my having." The Avnei Nezer explains this statement to refer to the superiority of goods gained in Israel, directly from God, over those acquired while in *ḥutz laAretz*, in a more indirect manner. Only with the former does one fulfill *mitzvat yishuv haAretz*.

In a similar vein, we may understand the Talmudic dictum (*Ketubot* 110b): "He who lives in Israel is like one who has a God, and he who lives outside of Israel is like one who has none." In Israel, "the palace of the King," endowed with greater providence, one is truly more closely associated with God.

sustenance, for that only happens when one finds means of support from the Land itself.[9]

The view of the Avnei Nezer as to the nature of *mitzvat yishuv haAretz* is not, however, universally accepted. Another possibility is evident from the Gemara in *Sota* (14a), which asks why Moses, our teacher, so yearned to enter Israel. The Gemara queries rhetorically: Could it have been merely "to eat from its fruits and be satiated from its goodness"? The Gemara does not offer the obvious answer, that *yishuv haAretz* was certainly a mitzva in that generation, and Moses, craving a mitzva as a miser

---

9. Of course, then it was much more difficult to derive a source of income from within the Land. Today, in addition to its being easier to earn a living, the mere transfer of funds from outside of Israel to Israel helps the economy, and in that way achieves a partial fulfillment of *mitzvat yishuv haAretz*.

The Avnei Nezer further explains a story recounted in *Ketubot* 110b–111a. The talmudic sage Rabbi Zeira decided to emigrate from Babylonia to Israel, and therefore made a point of avoiding the presence of Rabbi Yehuda, who had forbidden the return to Israel from Bavel. Rabbi Yehuda derived his position from a verse in Jeremiah (27:22) referring to the vessels of the Temple during the time of the Babylonian exile: "They will be brought to Babylonia, and there they will remain, until the day on which I remember you." Rabbi Yehuda understood this verse to refer not only to vessels, but also people, and not only to the first exile, but also the second. Thus he derived a special law prohibiting by implication any return from Bavel. But how may a prophet introduce a new law, and especially one that contradicts the biblical command to live in Israel?

The Avnei Nezer resolves this difficulty based on *Berakhot* 57a. There Rabbi Zeira states that he didn't attempt the move to Israel until he saw barley in a dream. Barley is taken to be an auspicious token, because its Hebrew word, *se'ora*, is reminiscent of a verse in Isaiah (6:7), which speaks of atonement: *Vesar avonekha* – "Your sin has been removed." Only when Rabbi Zeira received a sign of his righteousness in a dream did he attempt to return from Bavel. This leads the Avnei Nezer to suggest that in Rabbi Zeira's view, Jeremiah never *forbade* returning from Bavel; he said only that people who will return will not succeed in settling the land and will have to leave again. There is no mitzva of *yishuv haAretz*, says the Avnei Nezer, unless one will have a *kelita tova* – a successful absorption process. Therefore Rabbi Zeira did not think at first that he would be able to fulfill the mitzva – surely the land would vomit him out because of his sins. Only when he had his encouraging dream did he realize that he was pure from sin and assured of a successful absorption in Israel, and he acted accordingly.

craves gold (see *Makkot* 10a), longed to fulfill yet another. Apparently taking into account the fact that the mitzva exists, the Gemara wants to know the *nature* of this mitzva that Moses was so eager to acquire. It answers that many mitzvot can be fulfilled only in the Land of Israel, and Moses desired the opportunity to fulfill all the mitzvot linked to the Land. The implication clearly is that the purpose of *yishuv haAretz* is to afford a person the chance of performing the *mitzvot hateluyot baAretz*, the commandments that can only be performed in Israel.

Tosafot on *Gittin* (2a) appear to share this view. They propose a contradiction between talmudic texts as to whether the city Acco is part of Eretz Yisrael, and conclude that in the days of Ezra only half of the city received the sanctification of the Land, with the accompanying obligations of tithes. Therefore only that half is part of Israel and is included in the mitzva of living in the Land of Israel. *Tosafot* clearly equate the obligation to fulfill the *mitzvot hateluyot baAretz* with the mitzva of *yishuv Eretz Yisrael*.

The Ritva (*Gittin* 2a), however, avoids *Tosafot's* question entirely by rejecting their premise. *Tosafot* were forced into their position when faced by one talmudic source (Mishna *Gittin* 2a) that denied to Acco *kedushat Eretz Yisrael* and another text (*Gittin* 76b) that established it a mitzva to live in Acco. By assuming that the mitzva of living in Israel can exist only concurrently with (and because of) *kedushat haAretz*, the *Tosafot* had to conclude that the two sources were discussing different halves of the city. The Ritva, however, denies the concept that living in Acco being a mitzva necessarily implies that the city had *kedushat haAretz* as well as *mitzvot hateluyot baAretz*. By divorcing the two issues, Ritva rejects the theory that the purpose of *yishuv Eretz Yisrael* is the fulfillment of the mitzvot linked to the land, saying that even were no such mitzvot to exist, one would still have to dwell in Eretz Yisrael, for it is the land chosen and beloved by God. Thus the Ritva's opinion would appear to concur with that of the Avnei Nezer that residence in Israel deepens the intimacy of one's relationship with God.

Based on the Ritva and the Avnei Nezer, we can suggest a novel interpretation of another statement made by the Gemara: "It is preferable to live in Eretz Yisrael, even in a city where most of the inhabitants are non-Jews, than to live outside of Israel, even in a city where most of the inhabitants are Jewish" (*Ketubot* 110b). Ostensibly the Gemara means that

although living in a city inhabited predominantly by non-Jews entails a degree of discomfort, one must bear the discomfort cheerfully for the sake of fulfilling the mitzva of *yishuv Eretz Yisrael*. In light of the Ritva and Avnei Nezer however, a new interpretation becomes possible.

Tosafot elsewhere in *Ketubot* (45b) state that although a city in Israel surrounded by a wall since the days of Joshua is endowed with added sanctity and, consequently, additional laws (see Mishna *Keilim* 1:7), nevertheless, when the city is inhabited by a majority of non-Jews, its special laws no longer apply. No source is cited by *Tosafot* for this statement, and many later commentators are baffled as to the origin of *Tosafot*'s rule. Rabbi Menachem Ziemba,[10] however, cites the *Biur HaGra* (*Oraḥ Ḥayyim* 688:2), who traces this law to a passage in the Jerusalem Talmud (*Megilla* 1:1) stating that a walled city inhabited by a majority of non-Jews is considered to be in a state of ruin – *beḥurbana* – and therefore loses its special sanctity and accompanying laws.

This may explain as well our original Gemara: One might have claimed that just as a city which is surrounded by a wall loses its special status when the majority of its population is non-Jewish, so too, any city in Eretz Yisrael should lose the sanctity of the Land of Israel when the majority of its population is non-Jewish; and since it would no longer have *mitzvot hateluyot baAretz*, there would be no mitzva to live in such a city. The Gemara comes to refute this presumption, saying that while that might have been so were the sole purpose of *yishuv haAretz* the fulfillment of *mitzvot hateluyot baAretz*, in fact there is a different purpose to the mitzva. That purpose is, as formulated by the Ritva and Avnei Nezer, to become closer to God in His Land, and this end is independent of *kedushat haAretz*.

Yet one obvious question on the approach of the Ritva and Avnei Nezer presents itself. If the purpose and nature of *yishuv haAretz* is to come closer to God, why doesn't the Gemara in *Sota* (14a) say so explicitly when it asks why Moses desired to enter the land? Instead of answering that Moses wanted to fulfill the mitzvot which can only be done in the land, the Gemara should have replied that he wanted to attain a more intimate relationship with God. To this, the Ritva and Avnei Nezer would answer that for Moses, with whom God communicated "face to

---

10. *Otzar HaSifrei* (Introduction to *Sifre Zuta*), p. 53.

face" (Deut. 34:10; also Num. 12:8), a closer relationship would have been impossible. Therefore, the Gemara asks, if the purpose of *yishuv haAretz* is closeness to God, and Moses had nothing more to gain in that area, why did he so desire to enter Israel? And the answer is given that there exists a *second* attraction to living in Israel, namely, the opportunity to fulfill the *mitzvot hateluyot baAretz*.[11]

HOW TO FULFILL THE MITZVA

Having ascertained the existence of a mitzva to live in Israel, we can examine the parameters of the mitzva. The Magen Avraham (*Oraḥ Ḥayyim* 248:15) presents two opinions as to whether one fulfills *mitzvat yishuv haAretz* even partially by visiting Israel.[12] The position that even a visit constitutes a partial fulfillment of the mitzva is based upon the statement in the Talmud (*Ketubot* 111a) that one who merely walks four cubits in Israel attains atonement for his sins.[13]

I once heard Rav Betzalel Zolti, the chief rabbi of Jerusalem, suggest in a public *shiur* in Jerusalem that this issue hinges upon a dispute between the Rambam and Raavad in *Hilkhot Avodat Kokhavim* 10:6. One interpretation given by the Gemara (*Avoda Zara* 20a) to the biblical prohibition of *lo teḥanem* (Deut. 7:2) is that we may not allow idolaters to live in Israel. The Rambam and Raavad disagree whether the prohibition includes merely visiting Israel. Rav Zolti assumed that the nature of the prohibition *lo teḥanem* is that whatever we Jews are commanded to do in the mitzva of *yishuv haAretz*, we are forbidden to allow an idolater to do. Thus, if we may not allow an idolater even to visit Israel, it may be

---

11. Along these lines, it is said of the Baal Shem Tov that although he lived outside of Israel, he did not sit in a *sukka* on Shemini Atzeret, thus following the custom of the Land of Israel, because a *tzaddik* is said to be on a level corresponding to Eretz Yisrael, even in *ḥutz laAretz*.

12. See also *Piskei Teshuva*, vol. 2, 73–74, where he suggests a distinction between visiting for less than thirty days, or for less than twelve months, as opposed to visiting for a longer time period. His distinctions are based on the Gemara in *Bava Batra* (7b–8a).

13. See also *Penei Yehoshua*, ibid., that such assurances always presuppose the good intentions and *teshuva* of the individual.

inferred that we ourselves can partially fulfill the mitzva of dwelling in the land by visiting Israel.

A man who wishes to live in Israel despite the objections of his wife must have pure motives, writes Rabbi Shlomo Kluger (Responsa *HaElef Lekha Shlomo, Even HaEzer* 119). Ordinarily we are guided by the Talmudic dictum: "One should always engage in Torah and mitzvot [even] for impure motives (*shelo lishmah*), for out of impure motives one will eventually reach pure motives" (*Pesaḥim* 50b and many other places). Yet we find occasional exceptions to this rule. The Mishna in *Avot* (2:2), for example, rules that those who occupy themselves with work for the community (*tzibbur*) should do so only if their motives are pure (*leshem Shamayim*). In other words, the Mishna ordains that in activities not explicitly required by the Torah – e.g., the writing of a *sefer*, staging of a demonstration, engaging in communal work – if one voluntarily gets involved, it must be for unclouded motives. A *sefer* should be written to enlighten others and prevent Torah from being forgotten, not in order to enhance the reputation of its author. Demonstrations and communal work must be done strictly for noble purposes. Similarly, on the rare occasions when the Torah permits performing a sin *lishmah*,[14] the license is limited to those with pure intentions.

Rabbi Shlomo Kluger groups *yishuv haAretz* in the same category, ruling that a man may divorce his wife without paying the amount of her *ketuba* only if his reason for wanting to live in Israel is to fulfill *mitzvat yishuv haAretz*. Accordingly, Rabbi Kluger disqualified the claim of a man who insisted on moving to Israel not for the sake of the mitzva but in order to better his financial prospects. This approach to *mitzvat yishuv haAretz* is quite unique.

LIMITATIONS

Opposition to the modern return to Zion has often based itself upon the now famous Talmudic passage of the *Shalosh Shevuot*, the "Three Oaths":

> What are these three oaths? One, that the Jews should not go up [to take the land] by force, and one that God made the Jews swear that

---

14. *Horayot* 10b and elsewhere. Regarding writing *ḥiddushei Torah shelo lishmah*, see Responsa *Meshiv Davar, Oraḥ Ḥayyim* 14.

they would not rebel against the nations of the world, and one that God made the nations swear that they would not enslave the Jews too much. (*Ketubot* 111a, based on Song of Songs 2:7, 3:5)

In expounding the verse, "I have made you swear, O daughter of Jerusalem," the Gemara relates that the Almighty administered three oaths. The time and nature of these oaths are not clear, but one of them entailed a commitment on the part of the Jews not to return and conquer Israel by force. Many *gedolim* in Europe took this to forbid any attempt at reestablishing the State of Israel before Messianic times. Numerous refutations have been offered to counter such an interpretation of the Gemara. First, it is noted that this passage, whatever its true meaning may be, is not cited by Rambam or the *Shulḥan Arukh*, and is therefore not halakhically binding upon us.

Beyond that, the Maharal of Prague (*Netzaḥ Yisrael*, ch. 24) demonstrates that the term *shevua* in its scriptural use need not mean literally "an oath."[15] Equating *shevua* with *brit* (covenant), the Maharal points out that *brit* need not always connote a formal covenant between two parties. If it were always to be taken literally, how could God be described as entering into a *brit* with salt (see *Sifrei*, Num. 18:19 and Rashi, Lev. 2:13) and bugs (*Nidda* 58b)? Rather *brit* and *shevua* indicate an unchanging fact of life, a strong tendency implanted by God in nature.[16] The Maharal explains that God never actually administered an oath to the Jewish people; He merely told us that a return to Zion would be impractical because by the laws of nature such a return would not work out. Any attempt at return, then, is not forbidden, but rather discouraged as futile. Should an attempt succeed, it clearly has triumphed over nature and is not in defiance of God's will.

Others suggest that the prohibition was against taking the Land *by force*. In view of the Balfour Declaration, the Partition Plan, and other actions taken by the world community in recognition of the State of Israel,

---

15. See the essay by Rabbi Shlomo Aviner on this topic, *Noam*, vol. 20, sec. 13.
16. See Ramban, Gen. 6:18–19, who develops the concept of *brit* as denoting something unconditional holding true regardless of future developments.

it is clear that the nations of the world voluntarily allowed us to return to Israel; our entry was not one of force.

Finally, it is pointed out that the same talmudic passage in *Ketubot* records that the Jews were not the only ones to swear.[17] God concurrently elicited an oath from the nations of the world not to be overzealous in persecuting the exiled Jews. Two thousand years of relentless oppression bear witness to the fact that the nations have failed to uphold their obligations under the *Shalosh Shevuot*. Consequently, we should no longer be bound by ours.

The *Minḥat Elazar* (vol. 5, no. 12) argues that since the expulsion from our land was intended as a punishment, we are not permitted to avoid God's wrath by ending the exile; rather, we must await redemption in the Diaspora, at a time of God's choosing. The foundations of this argument are very shaky. Surely Judaism does not forbid the attempt to avoid or curtail a punishment from God. Often sickness is a punishment inflicted on a person for his sins, and yet the Torah explicitly grants us license to seek a medical cure – *verapo yerapei* (Ex. 21:19) – from which we adduce the permission granted a physician to heal (*Bava Kamma* 85a).

Moreover, who is to say that the period of punishment has not elapsed? The very fact that an opportunity exists to return is proof that God no longer wishes to punish us. What further notification is necessary? In fact, failure on our part to recognize that the period of exile has ended can only be unwise and even dangerous. The Talmud (*Megilla* 29a) tells us that each time the Jewish people were exiled, the *Shekhina*, God's Spirit, followed them, and thus it too was in exile – *Shekhinta begaluta*. The significance of God's being in exile can best be understood by analogy to another law in the Talmud involving exile.

A person who kills accidentally is required by the Torah to flee to a city of refuge and reside there until the death of the High Priest (see Num. 35; Deut. 4:41–49, 19). At the same time, even while in exile, he is not expected to live a life of privation and hardship. From the phrase "and he shall live there" (Deut. 4:42), the Rabbis derive that the exiled man is to be provided with everything he needs to live a completely normal life (*Makkot* 10a). As

---

17. Rav Meir Simcha of Dvinsk, quoted in Rabbi Menaḥem Mendel Kasher's *Hatekufa Hagedola* (Jerusalem, 1969), 174.

Torah study is an essential element of life, the Mishna rules that "when a student is exiled, his teacher is exiled with him" (ibid.). The rebbi is required to open a yeshiva and provide a Torah atmosphere for his exiled student. It is in this manner that God accompanied us into exile; being Master and Teacher of the Jewish people, He followed his students into exile to provide them with spiritual guidance and divine protection.

But how long must the teacher remain in exile? Certainly when the High Priest dies and the student may return home, the teacher may return as well. And even if the student himself, having grown accustomed to his new surroundings, desires to remain, that need not hinder his rebbi from returning. Similarly, with the period of our exile at an end, God is free to return to His Land, even should we choose to tarry. He need no longer reside in exile for our benefit. The prospect of continuing to live in *galut*, with God's special protection removed, is frightening.

Finally, if we persist in staying in *galut* even when our punishment is over, we will be following the dangerous precedent set by the *eved nirtza*. A Hebrew slave who grows to enjoy the conditions of his servitude and refuses to go free at the end of his six-year term is made to undergo a *retzia* ceremony involving the piercing of his upper ear, after which he remains a slave until the Jubilee year (Ex. 21:5–6; Deut. 15:16–17). One interpretation given to explain the symbolism of piercing the ear is based upon the assumption that the slave was originally sold as a thief who, when apprehended, had no money with which to pay back his victim. "The ear which heard at Sinai 'Thou shalt not steal,' and yet [its owner] went out and stole, deserves to be pierced."[18] Rabbi Yehoshua Leib Diskin asks why, if the piercing is a punishment for the theft, is it not carried out immediately, but only after six years of servitude?[19] He answers that the true punishment for the theft is being sold into service for six years; no other punishment is ordinarily called for. But this particular thief, by displaying reluctance to go free after the six years are up, demonstrates that for him the servitude never constituted a punishment in the first place.

---

18. *Mekhilta*, quoted by Rashi, Ex. 21:6. Rashi also cites the rationale in a case of man who sold himself: "The ear which heard 'for unto Me are the Children of Israel slaves,' and yet [its owner] went out and acquired a master, deserves to be pierced."
19. *Ḥiddushei Maharil Diskin*, beginning of *Parashat Mishpatim*.

On the contrary, he revels in his new surroundings: "I love my master, my wife and children; I shall not go free" (Ex. 21:5). For such a man, to whom the punishment of the Torah means nothing, the Torah prescribes an additional punishment – the piercing of the ear.

One can argue that our presence in exile was a punishment, and, with our renewed access to Israel, that punishment is over. God forbid that we should sit back and willingly accept surroundings that are, essentially, meant as a punishment. God forbid that, by refusing to recognize the nature of one punishment, we bring upon ourselves another.

A NATIONAL OBLIGATION

Until now we have dealt with *mitzvat yishuv Eretz Yisrael* as derived, according to the Ramban, from the end of the verse, "Conquer the land and dwell therein." But, as noted above, a separate mitzva of the entire nation (*tzibbur*) to conquer Eretz Yisrael is learned by the Ramban from the first part of the verse. This mitzva, too, is conspicuously missing from the Rambam's enumeration of the 613 mitzvot. Moreover, the Rambam in his *Yad HaHazaka* doesn't even enumerate *mitzvat yishuv haAretz*. Here, then, there are more grounds for claiming that Rambam felt the mitzva to be applicable only when the Jews first entered Eretz Yisrael.

It is generally assumed, however, based on the Talmud Yerushalmi (*Moed Katan* 2:4), that this mitzva also applies throughout history, as the Ramban writes. The Yerushalmi offers a novel interpretation of a law cited in *Gittin* (8b), where the Gemara permits asking a non-Jew on Shabbat to write and sign the document necessary to purchase a house in Israel from its non-Jewish owner. Commentators speculate what precisely was the mitzva involved that made possible the suspension of the rabbinic prohibition of *amira lenokhri* (asking a gentile to do work on Shabbat). The *Tashbetz* (#21) suggests that it is *yishuv Eretz Yisrael*, settling in the land, that takes precedence over *amira lenokhri*. The Ramban (*Shabbat* 130b) and Rivash (#101), however, suggest that it is the mitzva of *kibbush Eretz Yisrael*, conquering the land, which carries the day. The Ramban writes that since *kibbush haAretz* is incumbent upon the Jewish people as a whole, it is classified as a *mitzva derabbim* (of the many) and, unlike ordinary mitzvot, a *mitzva derabbim* is of a higher priority than the prohibition of *amira lenokhri*.

The Yerushalmi supports the Rivash in saying that *kibbush haAretz* was the underlying reason for the law, and supports the Ramban in classifying *kibbush haAretz* as a mitzva for all generations. In explaining why one may instruct the non-Jew to violate Shabbat in order to buy a home in Israel, the Yerushalmi comments, "For Jericho, too, was conquered on the Sabbath." Clearly, the point being made is that buying a house from non-Jewish hands constitutes a partial conquering of the Land of Israel. For a genuine and complete mitzva of *kibbush haAretz*, such as the conquering of Jericho by Joshua, even biblical prohibitions are eased on Shabbat. For a partial fulfillment of *kibbush haAretz*, only rabbinic laws, such as *amira lenokhri*, are waived. Thus, without needing to classify *kibbush haAretz* as a *mitzva derabbim*, the Yerushalmi posits that this mitzva falls in the same category as sanctifying the new month (Mishna *Rosh HaShana* 22a) and the sacrificing of public offerings whose time of sacrifice is specified (*Pesaḥim* 66a). All of these mitzvot, by their very nature, take precedence over Shabbat. Moreover, since the law of the Gemara in *Gittin* (*amira lenokhri* to purchase land in Israel) did not apply only to a particular period in history, it is clear that the mitzva of *kibbush haAretz*, according to the Yerushalmi, applies equally to all times.

Conquering Israel by force clearly involves a fair amount of danger. One might have claimed that since *pikuaḥ nefesh* (preserving life) takes precedence over most mitzvot of the Torah, one need not participate in *kibbush haAretz* because of the element of life-threatening danger. The *Minḥat Ḥinukh* (mitzva 425), however, dispels any such thinking by pointing out that this mitzva, by its nature, incorporates danger; nevertheless, it was still commanded to the Jewish people. Any commandment that has danger woven into its very fabric cannot be suspended for considerations of *pikuaḥ nefesh*. (Of course this presupposes that the *kibbush* accomplished will be real and lasting. Only if military experts feel that waging war would be essential to secure or protect the safety of the state and its citizens would the mitzva apply, despite the accompanying loss of life.)

Rabbi Meir Simcha of Dvinsk, the Meshekh Ḥokhma (*Parashat Beḥukkotai*) cites the words of the famous midrash that the Jews merited redemption from Egypt because, throughout their exile and enslavement, they preserved their names, their language, and their unique dress (*Vayikra Raba* 32:5). In explaining the significance of these seemingly

trifling mitzvot, Rabbi Meir Simcha writes that although all mitzvot are equally important in the eyes of Jewish law and must all be observed, from a historical perspective some take on added significance. Outside Israel, it became historically very important that Jews retain their Hebrew names, tongue, and dress in order to combat the powerful forces of assimilation. In this manner, every period of history has its own mitzvot of the hour. Today, when every Jew settling in Israel contributes measurably to the security and economy of the state, and to the Jews in it, *yishuv Eretz Yisrael* may indeed be called a mitzva of the hour.[20]

20. The author wishes to thank Rabbi Moshe Rosenberg for his assistance in the preparation of this essay.

The Halakhic Centrality of Eretz Yisrael

Rabbi Michael Rosensweig

I.

The unique connection between the Jewish people and Eretz Yisrael is as old as Jewish history itself. Each of the *avot* (forefathers) of our nation had a special link to the land. Considering that their lives are paradigmatic, the link demands at least brief attention.

Abraham discovered the Divine Presence in the Diaspora. Yet, in his initial formal charge, he was asked to leave the security and comfort of his homeland in order to begin life anew in Eretz Yisrael. It is there that his children were destined to develop into a great nation. The Midrash likens the difficulty of this request, which entailed abandoning the past for an uncertain future in Israel, to the ultimate test of Abraham's commitment, the demand that he sacrifice his only child, Isaac, on Mt. Moriah (*Bereshit Raba* 39:11).

Significantly, Isaac, the first native-born Jew, had an even more intensive connection with Eretz Yisrael. He was forbidden under all circumstances to set foot outside the Land. Though in rabbinic thought, Isaac represents the theme of *gevura*, a certain heroic extreme, the typological implications of his idealistic commitment, and the symbolism represented by his status as the first connecting link in the nation's chain, are not to be dismissed.

The relationship to Eretz Yisrael of Jacob – the most balanced and prominent of the *avot* and the bearer of the quality of *tiferet* – is crucial. His divinely bestowed name, Yisrael, establishes him not only as the biological father of the twelve tribes, but as the embodiment of the qualities, goals, and aspirations of *Klal Yisrael* throughout the generations. Thus, his complex connection to Eretz Yisrael is particularly intriguing. His commitment to Eretz Yisrael is such that, when urged to leave the Land in order to protect himself from his vindictive brother, Jacob hesitated and even returned to Be'er Sheva, the location where his father was forbidden to exit, in the hope that he, too, would be similarly proscribed (*Bereshit Raba* 68:6; Ramban, Gen. 28:17). Despite his reluctance, his sojourn in the Diaspora and experiences with Laban were indispensable to his self-development as the future Yisrael. However, once his practical education was complete, it was equally crucial that he return to Eretz Yisrael. Jacob's life demonstrates that although Eretz Yisrael remains the place of ultimate spiritual fulfillment and the aspiration of all Jews, there are circumstances that justify life in the Diaspora (see *Avoda Zara* 13a, and *Tosafot*, s.v. *lilmod Torah*). Moreover, the Diaspora experience occasionally plays an important role in religious development. Yet it is important to note that, according to Ramban, when Jacob did spend significant time in the Diaspora, his own religious standards were affected by his habitat. Hence, only when residing within the confines of Eretz Yisrael did the laws of the Torah, like the prohibition to marry two sisters, apply prior to the Giving of the Torah. Jacob's link with Eretz Yisrael, then, was complex, even dialectical.

Indeed, the different models provided by the *avot* have resonated throughout Jewish history. While there were Jews and whole communities, like Isaac, which cleaved to the sanctity of Eretz Yisrael, there were many more communities that developed outside this ideal framework. Like Jacob, many Jews maintained an ongoing relationship with Eretz Yisrael, but not an exclusive one. Indeed, even when the option of life in Eretz Yisrael was available, it was often bypassed. The generation of Ezra, in which only a fraction of Jews returned to resettle the land, is a case in point – as is our own era, in which many Jews still choose to reside in the Diaspora though the opportunity to live in Israel is open to all.

A cursory survey of intellectual-cultural trends in Jewish history demonstrates that the contribution of the Diaspora frequently surpassed that of Eretz Yisrael. The legacy of the Babylonian Talmud; of the geonic centers in the early medieval period; of the various medieval schools of Qayrawan, Spain, Ashkenaz, and Provence; the scholarship of Italian Jewish communities in the sixteenth and seventeenth centuries; and the crucial contributions of eastern European Jews from the sixteenth century until the Holocaust and of Sephardic communities in Turkey, Morocco, and the Arab lands during this same era – all these unequivocally demonstrate the historical centrality of Diaspora Jewry. Indeed, even American Jewry, acknowledged to be relatively spiritually impoverished, has been blessed with halakhic leadership of the highest caliber in the past generation, with such world-renowned and influential figures as Rabbi Yosef Dov Soloveitchik, Rabbi Moshe Feinstein, Rabbi Aharon Kotler, and the Lubavitcher Rebbe, z"l. The impact of these *gedolim* on the world Jewish scene is undeniable. This brief sketch sufficiently negates the absurd claims and convoluted arguments of those Israeli revisionists who would minimize the significance of Jewish life outside of Eretz Yisrael.

At the same time, it is absolutely crucial to note that even as certain Diaspora communities flourished intellectually and religiously, the conviction of impermanence and irregularity, the ideal of the centrality of Eretz Yisrael (expressed so vividly by Rabbi Yehuda HaLevi's famous metaphor likening Eretz Yisrael to the heart of the Jewish body), the practical concern and special feeling of responsibility for its population (*Sifrei*, Deut. 15:6),[1] and the aspiration and even yearning for return never waned (see also *Berakhot* 30a and *Ketubot* 110b). It is necessary, then, to examine the role of Eretz Yisrael in various halakhic contexts in order to appreciate the halakhic value accorded to it in the larger scheme of Jewish life.

II.

The Mishna (*Kiddushin* 36b) asserts that any halakhic obligation relating to the land and its produce is limited to the soil of Eretz Yisrael. Included

---

1. However, compare this source to the parallel passages in Mekhilta, *Parashat Mishpatim* and *Bava Metzia* 71a.

in this classification are such obligations as *terumot, maasrot,* the laws of *Shemitta,* etc. The exclusion of the Diaspora from these obligations is eminently reasonable, as only the soil of Eretz Yisrael was endowed with special sanctity, *kedushat haAretz.*

Upon examination, however, it becomes evident that there are several important halakhic categories that are linked with – and some even completely restricted to – Eretz Yisrael, though they are completely unrelated to the soil or its produce. These broader applications of the uniqueness of Eretz Yisrael require justification, as the categories in question appear to be equally relevant, at times even indispensable, for a maximal Jewish life in the Diaspora. Moreover, if a group of *halakhot* unrelated to the Land and soil are nonetheless exclusive to Eretz Yisrael, what distinguishes them from the vast majority of halakhic obligations and categories that apply in all geographic settings?[2] Thus, the question of criterion – namely, understanding why certain mitzvot apply only in Eretz Yisrael – is the key to a proper evaluation of the interrelationship between Israel and the Diaspora.

In addition to the need to establish the conceptual basis for a highly select group of *halakhot* that are linked with Eretz Yisrael, it is also important to note and confront the implications of apparent historical and geographic inconsistencies in the definition of Eretz Yisrael itself. The Talmud records various views as to the initiation and endurance of *kedushat haAretz.* The soil of Eretz Yisrael was endowed with *kedusha* by the conquest of Joshua. It was only at this point that obligations like *terumot, maasrot,* and *Shemitta* were inaugurated. There is a general halakhic consensus that the destruction of the First Temple negated the initial conquest, thereby terminating the sanctity of the Land. Only in the era of Ezra, when a relatively small group ascended from Babylonia and resettled Eretz Yisrael, was *kedushat haAretz* restored. Halakhic authorities debate whether this second *kedusha* endured even past the destruction of the Second Temple. Rambam, for example, concludes that while

---

2. The formulation of *Sifrei* at the end of *Ekev,* which characterizes the application of personal halakhic obligations in the Diaspora as a form of *ḥinukh* that will ensure their proper implementation at the time when Jews return to Eretz Yisrael, looms larger in light of this problem. We shall later elaborate this theme.

the first *kedusha* of Joshua, brought about by conquest, was terminated, the *kedusha* of Ezra, associated with settlement, was enduring.[3]

In any case, there existed a period of limbo between the termination of Joshua's *kedusha* and the onset of Ezra's second *kedusha*. Furthermore, Ezra's resettlement was less extensive than Joshua's original conquest. Hence, even after the period of Ezra, there remained a geographic discrepancy between the two *kedushot*. While these historical and geographic factors are reflected in treatments of soil-related mitzvot like *terumot* and *Shemitta*, they inexplicably appear to be largely ignored in the broader applications of mitzvot of Eretz Yisrael. Only an analysis of the substance of these *halakhot* will yield the solution to this additional puzzle. It is to these specifics that we now turn our attention.

III.

The Talmud (*Sanhedrin* 11b, *Berakhot* 63b) establishes that the proclamation of a leap year should occur in Eretz Yisrael. However, there is an exception to this rule if the most prominent halakhic authority of the day resides in the Diaspora. Both the rule and the exception require clarification. Why is the determination of the calendar, a matter of national significance, limited to Eretz Yisrael? If Eretz Yisrael is indeed

---

3. Others conclude that even Ezra's *kedusha* was terminated. See, for example, Rashi on *Sanhedrin* 26a; *Sefer HaTeruma, Hilkhot Eretz Yisrael*.

Rambam's formulation in *Hilkhot Terumot* 1:5, which emphasizes this distinction between the two sanctifications, contains intriguing philosophical implications. A number of halakhists have suggested explanations for the distinction. See, for example, Radvaz ad loc.; Resp. Ḥatam Sofer, *Yoreh De'ah* 233, 234; and Rav Soloveitchik in his essay *Kol Dodi Dofek*. Though Rambam concludes that the second *kedusha* remains intact, he nevertheless rules that *terumot*, etc., are only rabbinic obligations in our era, inasmuch as the condition of the arrival of all, or at least a large representation of, *Klal Yisrael* is lacking. He develops this theme in *Hilkhot Terumot* 1:26. Rambam's entire presentation and his late introduction of this factor require elaboration. See, for example, Resp. Beit HaLevi 3:1; *Ḥiddushei R. Ḥayim HaLevi al HaRambam, Hilkhot Terumot* 1:10; ibid., *Hilkhot Shemitta* 12:16. The possibility that the presence of *Klal Yisrael* plays a role not only in the implementation of these obligations, but in determining a full measure of *kedushat haAretz*, is of great consequence in establishing the relationship between the Land and the nation.

necessary for this determination, how does the Diaspora location of the incomparable halakhic authority compensate for that requirement?

A further element demands clarification. *Tosafot* (*Sanhedrin* 11b) cites the Talmud Yerushalmi's contention that this exception can be demonstrated by the calendar proclamations of Ezekiel and others who resided outside of Eretz Yisrael. Minḥat Ḥinukh (no. 4) emphatically challenges the validity of these proofs. He notes that Ezekiel lived in the limbo period between the termination of the *kedushat haAretz* initiated by Joshua and the onset of Ezra's second sanctification of the soil of Eretz Yisrael. How can the capacity to proclaim the leap year in the Diaspora in an era in which there was an absence of *kedushat haAretz* provide a basis for a similar application in a period in which *kedushat haAretz* existed? The historical limbo, noted earlier, evidently does not alter this particular equation. Minḥat Ḥinukh himself suggests that perhaps the basis for calendar proclamations is *kedushat Yerushalayim*, which according to Rambam (*Hilkhot Beit HaBeḥira* 6:14–16) attained permanent status from the time of the first sanctification of Eretz Yisrael due to its special quality. Thus, the Yerushalmi's evidence from the period between the destruction of the First Temple and the time of Ezra is fully valid.

Rav Soloveitchik suggested a different and more fundamental approach. He challenged the very assumption of Minḥat Ḥinukh's critique and argued that one should distinguish between two completely different notions of *kedushat haAretz*. The entire talmudic discussion about the first and second *kedushot* and their respective endurance applies only to issues involving the soil and produce of Eretz Yisrael. With respect to these issues, there truly was a limbo period between the termination of one period of *kedusha* and the onset of the other, and there are locations included in the original conquest of Eretz Yisrael that were never reinvested with sanctity in the resettlement of Ezra. However, the enduring quality of the formal status of Eretz Yisrael – and its stature as a unique location endowed with special significance for all Jews – was never at issue once Jews conquered the land in the time of Joshua. Inasmuch as proclamation of the leap year is completely unrelated to the sanctity of the soil, the absence of that sanctity in the limbo period between the destruction of the First Temple and the resettlement of Ezra is irrelevant to the role of Eretz Yisrael in this context.

Rav Soloveitchik noted that the distinction between the sanctity of the soil (*kedushat Eretz Yisrael*) and the formal status of the Land of Israel (*shem Eretz Yisrael*) is relevant to two other issues that would otherwise be plagued by problematic geographic applications. An examination of these issues should not only further clarify this critical distinction, but also provide us with additional clues as to the criterion that underlies the surprising limitation of certain halakhic institutions to Eretz Yisrael.

Egla arufa, the special process outlined in the Torah (end of *Parashat Shofetim*) that follows the discovery of the corpse of an anonymous murder victim in the proximity of a Jewish community – in which, among other details, the city elders are obligated to proclaim their innocence in the matter – is also mysteriously confined to Eretz Yisrael. However, Rambam (*Hilkhot Rotze'aḥ* 10:1) notes that this law does apply to the other side of the Jordan River. Elsewhere, there are indications that the area on the other side of the Jordan, part of Joshua's original conquest, was not resettled in the time of Ezra.[4] Hence, an apparent geographic anomaly – paralleling the temporal discrepancy noted earlier – surfaces in this context. Rav Soloveitchik's distinction between the technical sanctity of the soil and the broader theme of Eretz Yisrael's special stature resolves this dilemma: *egla arufa* depends not on the former (which applies only on the western side of the Jordan), but on the latter (which applies also on the eastern side), for reasons we will soon clarify.

The Talmud (*Sanhedrin* 14a) establishes that *semikha*, classic rabbinic ordination that enables judges to adjudicate penalties and capital crimes, may be granted only in Eretz Yisrael.[5] Remarkably, the Talmud Bavli

---

4. See *Hilkhot Shemitta* 4:28. Actually, Rabad is more explicit on this point than Rambam. We should note that *Sifrei* on *Shofetim* includes the area on the other side of the Jordan River, *Ever HaYarden*, in the boundaries of Eretz Yisrael. However, while that reference is based on the biblical verses and the ideal boundaries of Eretz Yisrael, Rambam's work should reflect the later reality. Thus, his citation of the *Sifrei* is striking.

5. Classical *semikha* was granted by a court of three judges (Mishna *Sanhedrin* 2a), and it required the consent and participation of at least one who had attained this status himself. According to Rambam (*Hilkhot Sanhedrin* 4:3) the other two need not be *semukhim*, while Ramah demands that all three have attained this status. In any case, *semikha* represents an unbroken chain of tradition and authority dating

records no source for this mysterious exclusion of the Diaspora in a matter that is absolutely critical to the legal capacity and even autonomy of the Jewish court system.[6] The difficulty is compounded by the fact that the court system, once populated by *semukhim* (ordained judges) who received their ordination in Eretz Yisrael, applies with equal force in the Diaspora. This point is made unequivocally in the Mishna (*Makkot* 7a).

Moreover, when Rambam records the undisputed ruling that limits the granting of *semikha* to Eretz Yisrael, he adds an important geographic note (*Hilkhot Sanhedrin* 4:6); once again, the boundaries of the original conquest are applied in a post-Ezra era! The classical Maimonidean commentators note this apparent anomaly and offer various explanations. Not surprisingly, Minḥat Ḥinukh (no. 491), who equated the broad status of Eretz Yisrael with the technical status of the sanctity of its soil in the context of calendar proclamations, is particularly troubled by Rambam's expansion of ordination to Joshua's boundaries. However, Radvaz cites the view of R. Ashtori HaParḥi, a halakhist of the thirteenth century, who, like Rav Soloveitchik so many centuries later, distinguishes between the sanctity of the soil which dictates the status of the land's produce regarding issues of Shemitta, *terumot*, etc., and other *halakhot* that relate more broadly to the unique quality and status of Eretz Yisrael. These issues, including matters such as *semikha* and residence and burial in Eretz Yisrael, are not dependent on the technical sanctity of the soil, and therefore are not limited to the boundaries of Ezra's resettlement.

In his work *Kaftor VaFeraḥ* (ch. 10), R. Ashtori HaParḥi elaborates this distinction and traces the unique status of Eretz Yisrael as a location for the covenant between God and Abraham. While the geographic discrepancy has been satisfactorily resolved by the compelling distinction developed by *Kaftor VaFeraḥ* and Rav Soloveitchik, the very restriction

---

back to the time of Moses and Joshua. We shall later make brief reference to the Rambam's innovative and controversial suggestion of an alternative method of attaining this status.

6. Talmud Yerushalmi (*Bikkurim* 3:3) does cite a source for this exclusion based on a verse in Ezekiel (36:17). This source, however, raises more questions than it resolves. What does the general theme of dwelling in the land have to do with granting rabbinic ordination?

of these institutions to Eretz Yisrael, even in its broader scope, remains a curiosity.

Another halakhic context reflects the same distinction between two notions of the uniqueness of Eretz Yisrael, and provides us with yet another unanticipated instance of the centrality of Eretz Yisrael. The Torah establishes that if the majority of the population violates a halakhic prohibition that mandates a *korban* (sacrifice) because the Great Sanhedrin, the ultimate decisors of Jewish law, erred in their halakhic decision, one *korban* (namely, the *par he'elem davar shel tzibbur*) is brought for the entire community. However, if a majority did not fall prey to this error, each individual who did is obligated to provide his own sacrifice. The Talmud (*Horayot* 3a) defines the majority of the population in connection with this halakha not in terms of the overall world Jewish population, but on the basis of those Jews who reside specifically in Eretz Yisrael. The focus on the population of Eretz Yisrael is itself intriguing, since the fates of Diaspora Jews are no less affected by the error, and considering that when a majority of Israeli Jews are involved, one *korban* suffices for all world Jewry! Again, the question of the criterion for determining which mitzvot are restricted to Eretz Yisrael comes to the fore.

Furthermore, in keeping with the previous pattern, the question of the boundaries of Eretz Yisrael resurfaces. Minḥat Ḥinukh (no. 120) states with absolute conviction that while the verse (1 Kings 8:65) cited by the Talmud with reference to this *korban* refers specifically to the original boundaries of Eretz Yisrael at the time of the first conquest, an adjustment of the borders to reflect the reality of the post-Ezra era would be necessary in the subsequent application of this halakha. However, Rambam evidently does not acquiesce to such an adjustment. In his Commentary to the Mishna in Horayot, he explicitly applies the distinction between the sanctity of the soil and the broader stature of Eretz Yisrael, which eliminates this particular difficulty.

The notion that Eretz Yisrael has significance that transcends the obligation and capacity to accomplish specific imperatives relating to its produce or soil emerges clearly in Ramban's writings. While some Tosafists appear to limit the obligation to live in Eretz Yisrael to eras in which it is possible to implement *mitzvot hateluyot baAretz* (R. Ḥayim Cohen, *Tosafot, Ketubot* 110b), Ramban lists the obligation to settle in

Eretz Yisrael as one of the 613 commandments, and establishes the independence of this mitzva as well (Critique of *Sefer HaMitzvot*, positive commandments, *hashmatta* no. 4).

In his commentary on the Torah, Ramban makes numerous references to the centrality of Eretz Yisrael and to the special opportunity it provides for a more direct relationship between God and the Jewish people. He extensively develops the theme that only in Eretz Yisrael can Jews avoid mediation in their *avodat Hashem*.[7]

It comes as no surprise, then, that we should be able to trace to Ramban, as well, the disentanglement of the broader unique quality of Eretz Yisrael from the technical issue of the sanctity of its soil. Commenting on an apparent discrepancy as to the status of Acco, Ramban distinguishes between *kedushat karka* (sanctity of the soil), which was lacking in Acco as it was not resettled in Ezra's era, and *ḥibat Eretz Yisrael* (the affection for the Land of Israel), which applies unconditionally to all locations that were originally included in Joshua's conquest (see his comments in a *hashmatta* to his *ḥiddushim* on *Gittin* 2a). Ramban's unshakable conviction as to the unique quality of religious life in Eretz Yisrael, and the special opportunities it presents, had important impact on subsequent halakhists as well.[8] While Ramban's projection of Eretz Yisrael's transcendent and intrinsic significance is often contrasted with Rambam's less dramatic perspective,[9] we note that our previous analysis of the role of Eretz Yisrael

---

7. See, for example, Ramban's commentary on Leviticus 18:25. A general overview of Ramban's perspective can be gained from analyzing the various sections listed in the index of Rabbi Chavel's edition of his commentary. See also the chapter on this theme in C. Henoch's *Ramban KeḤoker UMekubal* (Jerusalem, 1982), 141–59. Ramban's comprehensive view is of great significance to our topic, but it demands an extensive treatment not appropriate for this particular presentation.

8. See, for example, several of the sections in Responsa of Rashba on matters dealt with in Ramban's Torah commentary. Ritva's adoption of Ramban's analysis of Acco (*Gittin* 2a) reflects this as well. Of course, some of Ramban's general orientation can be traced to R. Yehuda HaLevi, who in his *Kuzari* and other writings projects the almost mystical centrality of Eretz Yisrael in Judaism.

9. The extensive discussion regarding Rambam's omission of settling in Eretz Yisrael as one of the 613 commandments is a case in point. The contrast between Rambam's and Ramban's positions is sometimes characterized in terms of their respective

in the contexts of *semikha* and *egla arufa* focused on the more moderate Rambam's stance.

Indeed, one of the most ambitious formulations of the central role of Eretz Yisrael is to be found in one of the earliest rabbinic texts, the *Sifrei* (*Ekev*, 43). This passage establishes the ideal link between Eretz Yisrael and all mitzvot: "Even though I will exile you from the Land, continue [in the Diaspora] to be distinguished by mitzvot, so that when you return [to Eretz Yisrael] they will not be new to you." Commenting on the verse in *Ekev* (Deut. 11:18), Rashi and Ramban cite a version of the *Sifrei* that includes the specific examples of *tefillin* and *mezuza*.[10] Thus, the *Sifrei* feels compelled to justify the obligation to observe mitzvot in the Diaspora, and characterizes this obligation as a guarantee that Jews will remain immersed in the mitzvot so that they will be able to resume the ideal upon the return to Eretz Yisrael! While some dismiss this statement as hyperbole, or reinterpret its meaning so that it bears a more moderate message,[11] it remains an important piece of the puzzle in the effort to decipher the precise role of Eretz Yisrael in the general halakhic scheme.

The key to comprehending the selective centrality of Eretz Yisrael is to be found in another talmudic passage (*Sanhedrin* 43b). There, the Talmud asserts that *arevut*, the legal responsibility of every Jew for the actions of his fellow, came about only when Jews crossed into Eretz Yisrael. The crucial implication that emerges from this passage is that at that historic juncture, the collective entity of *Klal Yisrael*, even as it relates to individual behavior, was born.[12] Eretz Yisrael, the national headquarters of the Jewish people and the ideal setting in which Jewish life in all of its

---

rationalistic and mystical orientations. While this approach should not be summarily dismissed, it does not sufficiently take into account the halakhic nuances that stand at the core of these issues. The issue requires independent treatment.

10. Netziv in his commentary to *Sifrei* discusses the different versions of the text.

11. The Netziv suggests the possibility that the reference is only to *mitzvot hateluyot baAretz*. The comments attributed to Gra in *Kol Eliyahu* are particularly striking, as they reflect incredulity that this text can be accepted at face value.

12. The impact of *arevut* as described in this way is particularly reflected in the explanation by some halakhists that one can repeat a blessing on behalf of a fellow Jew who has not yet fulfilled his obligation on the basis of *arevut*, not only because all Jews are connected, but because the fulfillment of even one who has previously

manifold facets can flourish, is indispensable to the national destiny and sense of community that distinguishes *Klal Yisrael* as a nation.

Indeed, the formula of the previously-mentioned passage (*Horayot* 3a) regarding *par he'elem davar shel tzibbur* – "These [i.e., the inhabitants of Eretz Yisrael] are called *kahal*, and these [i.e., the inhabitants of the Diaspora] are not called *kahal*" – explicitly and dramatically captures this theme. It succinctly establishes that Jews can live in the Diaspora, achieve great accomplishments, and, as individuals and individual communities, they are surely obligated to observe the vast majority of the mitzvot, the primary means of Jewish religious expression. However, in matters relating to national destiny, with regard to issues pertaining to the theme of collective responsibility or representation, or where ideal structures are essential, Eretz Yisrael becomes an important ingredient, at times even a necessary condition.

IV.

If we now review those issues in which Eretz Yisrael plays a central role, we may easily perceive the underlying pattern and common thread.

The calculation and fixing of the calendar is certainly a prerogative of great national significance. Its symbolic value in terms of control over time and timing transcends the substantive issues that it dictates. It is surely no coincidence that some of the great controversies of Jewish history – between Karaites and Rabbinites, between R. Saadia and Aharon ben Meir, etc. – have erupted over the control of the calendar, and through it, the national community (see also the intriguing story related in *Berakhot* 63a–b). In explaining Rambam's view that the existence of the Great Sanhedrin was necessary for calendar calculation by means of the viewing method – although, as Ramban notes in his critique of this doctrine, this body did not function in its formal judicial role once it was removed from the *lishkat hagazit* in the Temple, an event that occurred well before the end of the period of visual calculation – Rav Soloveitchik has demonstrated that the real source of calendar authority resides with the totality of the nation. The function of the Great Sanhedrin in this context was not related to their

---

engaged in the observance remains incomplete until every member of the Jewish collective has joined in the observance. See *Rosh HaShana* 29a.

formal judicial status, which was indeed undermined by their relocation outside the Temple, but to their unique capacity to represent the interests of the entire nation in this determination.[13] Indeed, the Talmud (*Beitza* 17a) notes that, in contrast to Shabbat, the sanctity of other holidays is credited to *Klal Yisrael* precisely because they are fixed by calendar calculation, which is the special prerogative of the entire people.

Given this perspective, the centrality of Eretz Yisrael as the preferred source of calendar decisions, and the focus on the broader theme and borders of Eretz Yisrael rather than the narrower confines of *kedushat karka*, becomes compelling. Moreover, we can now appreciate the remaining qualification of this rule. Since the motif of Eretz Yisrael in this context is linked to the national representation of *Klal Yisrael*, the question of authentic, outstanding rabbinic leadership cannot be ignored. This factor, too, is critical in determining and embodying the interests of the entire nation, as the Torah perspective is an indispensable part of this equation. As noted, the role of rabbinic leadership in the form of the Great Sanhedrin was part of the initial process of visual sanctification of the months. Thus, the circumstances in which Eretz Yisrael is bereft of outstanding rabbinic leadership justifies an exception to the rule that proclamation of a leap year must take place in Eretz Yisrael.

Perhaps more than any other law, *egla arufa* exemplifies the ideal of collective responsibility between all Jews, and the particular role of the community and its elders in addressing that responsibility. As the Talmud and Midrash note (*Sota* 48b), it is unthinkable that the elders of the city were directly involved in the death of the anonymous victim. Yet the need to proclaim their innocence derives from a far more demanding standard of complicity and culpability. Specifically, they declare that they did not

---

13. Rambam's view and Ramban's critique are found in *Sefer HaMitzvot*, positive commandment 153. For Rav Soloveitchik's treatment of the issue, see "*Keviat Moadim al pi HaRe'iya ve'al pi HaHeshbon*" in his *Kovetz Ḥiddushei Torah* (Jerusalem, 1984), 47–65. This notion that the Great Sanhedrin functions occasionally as the representative of the entire nation has other important applications as well. See, for example, *Ḥiddushei HaGriz al HaRambam, Hilkhot Sanhedrin* 5:1, with regard to the appointment of a king. I have argued elsewhere ("*BeInyan Semikha uSemikhat Zekenim*," *Beit Yitzḥak* 21 [5749], 91–101) that the convergence of both the judicial and national representation motifs is the basis for the Sanhedrin's role.

turn away the traveler and deny him the shelter and protection that could have prevented his ultimate fate. It seems obvious, however, that while the theme of broader responsibility is conveyed by these expressions, it is not limited to them. The underlying principle of *egla arufa* is that the elders of the city, by personal example and by means of their influence, shape the spiritual-moral climate in which they reside. They are broadly accountable for the moral standards that prevail in the community at large, as reflected in all that transpires therein. This ambitious conception of community obligation and corporate responsibility, the ultimate communal form of *arevut*, is workable only in the one location that embodies these demanding themes, namely, Eretz Yisrael.

Rabbinic ordination is the basis not only for the authority of individual judges, but ultimately for that of the entire network of courts, linking lesser monetary courts, composed of three judges, to twenty-three-member courts with the capacity to adjudicate capital offenses and fines, and ultimately to the Great Sanhedrin of seventy-one. While the Mishna (*Makkot* 7a) does establish that this structure is effective in the Diaspora, it is the Eretz Yisrael root that enables the far-flung network to operate effectively.[14] There is no institution more essential to the autonomous, corporate-national life of the Jewish people than the court network. Its link to Eretz Yisrael, thus, becomes self-evident. This is reflected in the need for a functioning *Sanhedrin HaGadol* at the foot of the Temple. It also underlies the need for *semikha*, which provides judicial authority, to have its source in Eretz Yisrael. *Sefer HaḤinukh* (no. 491) even indicates that the mitzva to appoint judges is limited to Eretz Yisrael because *semikha* can be granted only there. His critics all note that this formulation is highly problematic, inasmuch as judges also adjudicate in the Diaspora. Probably *Sefer HaḤinukh* intends to underscore that the court system in the Diaspora, while effective, cannot fully duplicate its function in the autonomous and communally demanding climate afforded by life in Eretz Yisrael, the national headquarters of world

---

14. This view is strikingly dramatized by Ritva (*Makkot* 7a), who characterizes the operating mechanism of even those Diaspora courts that were populated by *semukhim* in terms of a form of representation of the authorities of Eretz Yisrael. The principle invoked by Ritva, "they are their emissaries," originally appears in the Talmud (*Bava Kamma* 84b) with regard to judges lacking *semikha*.

Jewry. In contrast to Diaspora communities, the obligation to appoint judges in Eretz Yisrael goes beyond the specific need to dispense justice when the need arises. The very presence of courts in communities projects the theme of justice as a central value, and exposes the community to the moral standards of its judges.

Indeed, the Talmud differentiates between Eretz Yisrael and Diaspora communities with respect to the scope of the obligation to appoint judges. While it is sufficient to set up courts in each broader jurisdiction in the Diaspora, it is necessary to establish a court presence in individual communities in Eretz Yisrael.[15] The link between *semikha* and Eretz Yisrael probably accented for the author of *Sefer HaḤinukh* the distinctive role of court appointment in Eretz Yisrael, as well.

We have previously noted that Talmud Bavli does not cite a source for the limitation of *semikha* to Eretz Yisrael. Our analysis indicates, however, that the limitation is grounded in broader themes relating to the court system and the uniqueness of Eretz Yisrael as the national headquarters of world Jewry, each of which is well documented.[16] Moreover, in this light, it should come as no surprise that Rambam, in another context (*Perush HaMishnayot* to *Bekhorot* 4:3), actually invokes the passage in *Horayot* regarding the communal sacrifice of *par he'elem davar shel tzibbur* as the foundation for this restriction of *semikha* to Eretz Yisrael! The two applications emerge as commonly based. Furthermore, Or Same'aḥ (*Sanhedrin* 4:6), without citing Rambam's explicit comment, anticipates this link with *Horayot* (3b) and even posits that this source, which explicitly includes the broader boundaries of Joshua's conquest, is the basis for Rambam's border expansion in the matter of *semikha*!

There is a further element in Rambam's doctrine that reinforces the patterns previously developed. In a celebrated and controversial passage, Rambam proposed an alternative method of attaining *semikha* after the uninterrupted chain of granters and recipients had been ruptured.

15. *Makkot* 7a. Ramban, in his commentary to *Shoftim*, discusses Rambam's position on this matter, and relates to some of these same themes. The status of establishing courts for *Bnei Noaḥ*, a parallel theme, is relevant to this issue as well.

16. This should also serve to explain the otherwise ambiguous Talmud Yerushalmi source cited in note 6 above.

He argued that the consensus of scholars in Eretz Yisrael could rein-stitute *semikha*.[17] This view again accents the theme of Eretz Yisrael as the embodiment of the national-corporate interests of *Klal Yisrael*. A consensus reached by its halakhic leadership compensates for a historical-chronological break in the chain of generations.

Many other institutions that are associated with the national destiny of *Klal Yisrael*, like prophecy, also bear a special link to Eretz Yisrael. The Talmud (*Bava Batra* 15a) asserts that the Men of the Great Assembly authored the Book of Ezekiel. Rashi and others indicate that Ezekiel him-self could not have transmitted his prophetic experiences in written form, inasmuch as he lived in the Diaspora. The fact that he lived in the historic era between the termination of Joshua's *kedushat karka* that resulted from the First Temple's destruction and the renewal of that *kedusha* at the time of Ezra is of no consequence, as we have previously demonstrated.

The special significance of residing in Eretz Yisrael, and even in return-ing to the national homeland upon death, can also be more fully appre-ciated against this background. Ramban, Rashbatz, *Kaftor VaFeraḥ*, and others have unequivocally demonstrated the independence of these themes from the narrower conception of *kedushat karka*.[18]

Moreover, while the vast majority of mitzvot apply in the Diaspora, undeniably the themes of collective responsibility and national destiny, which pervade many *halakhot*, can be more fully appreciated in the envi-ronment of Eretz Yisrael, in which these dimensions are enhanced. It is, thus, necessary for the *Sifrei* to urge that one remain immersed even in these motifs despite a measure of incongruity with Diaspora life.

V.

Armed with this perspective, we can now approach the biblical evi-dence. Precisely because Abraham is the father of the nation, his first

---

17. Rambam's view is expressed in *Hilkhot Sanhedrin* 4:11; *Perush HaMishnayot* San-hedrin 1:3; and *Perush HaMishnayot* Bekhorot 4:3. There are important subtleties that distinguish the presentations. I have analyzed these in the article published in *Beit Yitzḥak* 21, mentioned previously.

18. *Tashbetz*, vol. 3, no. 200, employs *Ever HaYarden* as a litmus test for many of these distinctions.

task was to establish his independence from his past life. The obligation to relocate in Eretz Yisrael – conjuring up the formidable image of the *Akeda* challenge, as both employ the words *lekh lekha* – was symptomatic of his commitment to a new national destiny (*Kaftor VaFerah* specifically accents this dimension). Furthermore, Abraham's relocation to Eretz Yisrael is undoubtedly consistent with his singular contribution as the exemplar of *hesed* and *arevut*, essential features of this new national and corporate destiny to be realized particularly in this special venue.

Isaac's link with Eretz Yisrael intensified beyond Abraham's because he represents the pure extreme of an ideal spiritual life; it can best be achieved in a unique setting that not only affords the opportunity for realization of all mitzvot, but whose religious climate persistently accents the theme of national aspiration and the demanding standards of *arevut* and community life. Personal pressures could not outweigh an extreme idealistic commitment that would typologically serve as an important counterweight to more pragmatic considerations for Jews throughout the generations.

Jacob-Israel captures the relationship with Eretz Yisrael in all of its multifarious complexity. His experience demonstrates the viability of a productive and creative Jewish life in the Diaspora, even the desirability of such an experience under certain circumstances. Moreover, Jacob's odyssey reflects the need to balance other values that occasionally justify compromising one ideal to safeguard others. Jacob's encounter with Laban also accents the ability to maintain principles in less than ideal environments. At the same time, his initial reservations about leaving Eretz Yisrael, his aspiration to return, his recognition that complacency regarding life in the Diaspora endangered his entire spiritual well-being, his decision to sacrifice in order to return, all constitute a definite blueprint for the entire nation that bears his name. Ramban's aforementioned view of the halakhic consequences attendant upon Jacob's respective status in the Diaspora and Eretz Yisrael dramatically underscores the centrality of Eretz Yisrael to all Jews, regardless of their permanent address.

The fact that the experiences of the *avot* all took place well in advance of the onset of technical *kedushat karka* actually enhances their relevance.

It is surely no coincidence that Ramban specifically invokes the *avot* in his initial presentation of the independent mitzva to settle in Eretz Yisrael.

VI.

We have seen that Eretz Yisrael has national-corporate significance that explains its central halakhic role even in issues not related to *kedushat karka*. This motif dictates that Eretz Yisrael be the focus of the unity and cooperation of world Jewry, not the source of friction and divisiveness that it often is. The export of Diaspora controversies like "Who Is a Jew?" to Israel is doubly disturbing when one considers that, beyond all the substantive damage, it subverts the very themes Eretz Yisrael embodies: nationhood and unity. While divisions do and will continue to exist, it is critical that an effort be made to de-emphasize these in favor of those areas in which a common front can be projected.

To the extent that Eretz Yisrael is a rallying point for world Jewry generally, and particularly in times of crisis, the halakhic theme of Eretz Yisrael's uniqueness is accented. It is necessary, however, that Jews close ranks not only against external enemies, but unite in order to enhance the spiritual and economic well-being of fellow Jews as well. With its emphasis on both of these dimensions, Operation Exodus, which resettled much of the Jewish population of the former Soviet Union, was a case in point. Eretz Yisrael's centrality demanded that, ideally, these Jews be directed to the State of Israel. The strengthening of the state, the need to ensure the continuing Jewish identification of this population, as well as the conviction that their best opportunity for a meaningful religious Jewish future lies with Eretz Yisrael, underlay efforts to encourage this *aliya*. Clearly these pragmatic factors, all of which represented a national agenda, fully dovetailed with the halakhic perspective.

The need to accent that which binds, rather than divides, is critical within the Orthodox community as well. Too much has been made of relatively less significant debates, on matters such as the saying of *Hallel* on Yom HaAtzma'ut, with or without a *berakha*, half or whole, with *Taḥanun* or without, etc. For that matter, the passions expressed over the terminology hardly seem to be worth fragmenting the Orthodox world. I am not suggesting that these are not symbolically and even halakhically important, nor am I suggesting that communities that feel strongly about

the rightness of their position should simply abandon their conviction for the sake of unity. However, I do think that the effort to find common formulae with a broader base of support should be made. Shifting the primary focus of Yom HaAtzma'ut observance away from ritual, and dedicating the day to rigorous study and appreciation of the rich character and significance of Eretz Yisrael reflected in Tanakh, halakha, and history, would, in addition to the obvious substantive benefits, also promote the unity theme of Eretz Yisrael itself by downplaying divisions and widening the day's appeal.

The tendency that unfortunately prevails in all segments of the Jewish community to distinguish oneself by exaggerating differences in order to carve out clear niches and distinct identities is singularly inappropriate with respect to Eretz Yisrael issues. Moreover, legitimate differences on these issues need to be put in proper perspective by all sides of the debate. More often than not, they pale into insignificance in light of the more urgent crises that we confront. The price paid for disunity needs to be offset by the value of the controversial issue. As part of the calculation, we need to evaluate not only the impact of fragmentation on other issues, but also to consider that the halakhic centrality of Eretz Yisrael itself derives from its national-communal unifying character.

"The Beginning of the Flowering of Our Redemption"

Rabbi Jacob J. Schacter

I t was not supposed to be this way. The unfolding of Jewish history in its final stages was meant to follow a certain expected trajectory and this did not fit. The narrative of our nation was a narrative of the alternating realities of exile and redemption, Temple, and destruction. After wandering in the desert, our forefathers arrived in the Promised Land and, after a number of centuries, the Temple was built. A few hundred years later, it was destroyed and the Jews went into exile. Exile ended, albeit after a brief period of time, with the building of the Second Temple. But this too was destroyed and, once again, the Jews went into exile, this time a long and bitter exile. And, for close to two millennia, the expectation was that this exile would end the same way the previous one did, with the building of the Temple, the Third and final Temple.[1] But this did not quite happen.

---

1. I write this aware of the fact that the reality of the early years of both the First and Second Temples was more complex and multilayered.

On the one hand, I submit that exile, as it had existed for some nineteen hundred years, came to an end with the founding of the State of Israel. *Blessed are You... who has kept us alive, sustained us, and brought us to this time.* No longer did helplessness, precariousness, or vulnerability fully define Jewish existence throughout the world. There was now a Jewish state, a Jewish homeland under the authority of Jews. Jewish pride, confidence, and power now defined much of Jewish existence. To make the point clear, imagine how different the Jewish world would look today if the State of Israel had been founded just ten years earlier, in 1938 instead of 1948. The State of Israel has, thank God, made an enormous difference not only for those Jews living in it but for Jews all over the world.

Yet, on the other hand, even its most fervent supporters recognize that the State of Israel has not brought about redemption. Indeed, final redemption seems very far off. "Only a part of the Jewish people has gathered together into a Jewish state, and only in certain areas of the country. Only some of the returnees observe the precepts of the Torah. Political and military strife has not vanished from the land. Peace is elusive and morality compromised. Universal redemption seems even more remote than before."[2]

Surely, the Jewish state today is not what our grandparents – and their grandparents – had in mind when they prayed for close to two millennia: "May our eyes witness Your return to Zion in mercy," or "May You return to Your city, Jerusalem, in mercy." In the scheme of Jewish historical expectations, the State of Israel is "the unexpected state."[3]

And so the question is clear. What is the religious status of this reality that is neither here nor there, neither exile nor redemption? "Does what has been achieved constitute a part of the process of final redemption, or is it an abortion of that process? Is this the beginning of the End, a step toward the fulfillment of the prophetic promises, or is it rather a violent betrayal of those promises in all their perfection?"[4]

2. Aviezer Ravitzky, *Messianism, Zionism, and Jewish Religious Radicalism* (Chicago, 1996), 1.
3. See Yosef Ḥayim Yerushalmi, "Israel, the Unexpected State: Messianism, Sectarianism, and the Zionist Revolution," in David N. Meyers and Alexander Kaye, eds., *The Faith of Fallen Jews: Yosef Hayim Yerushalmi and the Writing of Jewish History* (Waltham, 2014), 277–96.
4. Aviezer Ravitzky, *Messianism*, ibid.

Contemplating the possibility of a political return of the Jewish people
to the Land of Israel, the shapers of religious Zionist ideology in the nineteenth century framed their vision in redemptive terms. For example, Rabbi
Tzvi Hirsch Kalischer applied to the newly unfolding political development
of his time the age-old concept of redemption taking place step-by-step,
little by little, "*me'at me'at... le'at le'at.*"[5] In the same context, Rabbi Yehuda
Alkalai invoked the rabbinic image of "*kim'a kim'a.*"[6] Rabbi Yisrael Yehoshua
Trunk of Kutno wrote in 1891, and Rabbi Avraham Yitzhak HaCohen Kook
in 1913, that the gathering of Jews in Eretz Yisrael, then slowly under way,
was "*at'halta degeula*, the beginning of the redemption."[7] Ze'ev Yavetz, the
editor of *HaMizrah*, the official publication of the religious Zionist Mizrachi
movement, supported the Uganda Plan suggested by the British in 1903,
going so far as to consider it to be "*at'halta degeula.*"[8]

These sentiments, and there are many more such examples, only
grew in intensity as the practical establishment of a political state became
more and more realistic. Rabbi Isser Zalman Meltzer, one of the most
prominent rabbis of the Yishuv, favored the partition plan recommended
by the Peel Commission in July 1937, referring to it as "*at'halta degeula,*"
even though the amount of land it granted the Jews was only a fraction of
what they wanted.[9] One decade later, on December 21, 1947, a few months
before the founding of the State, the Ashkenazi Chief Rabbi of Eretz

---

5. Rabbi Tzvi Hirsch Kalischer, *Derishat Tzion* (Jerusalem, 1964), 88.

6. Rabbi Yehuda Alkalai, "Minhat Yehuda," in *Kitvei HaRav Yehuda Alkalai*, vol. 1
   (Jerusalem, 1974), 201–202. This phrase and the concept it represents appears
   multiple times in rabbinic literature. See, for example, *Midrash Shir HaShirim
   Raba* 6:10; *Midrash Esther Raba* 10:14; *Midrash Tanhuma, Devarim* 1; Yerushalmi,
   Berakhot 1:1, *Yoma* 3:2; *Midrash Tehillim* 18:36. See Rabbi Menahem M. Kasher,
   HaTekufa HaGedola (Jerusalem, 1969), 67–70.

7. For the rabbi of Kutno, see *Shu"t Yeshuot Malko, Yoreh De'ah* #66; for Rabbi Kook,
   see *Iggerot HaRaaya*, vol. 2 (Jerusalem, 1985), 176.

8. See Mordecai Eliav, "HaMizrah – Ketav HaEt HaRishon shel HaMizrahi," *Sinai*
   129–130 (2002), 41.

9. This was reported by Chief Rabbi Yitzhak Isaac HaLevi Herzog (who opposed
   the recommendation) at the eulogy he delivered for Rabbi Meltzer in 1953. See
   Rabbi Itamar Warhaftig, "Emdat Rabbanim BePolmos Halukat HaAretz (5697),"
   Tehumin 9 (1988), 270, n. 3. My thanks to Rabbi Shmuel Marcus for bringing this
   source to my attention.

Yisrael, Rabbi Yitzḥak Isaac HaLevi Herzog, wrote to the religious Zionist leader Shlomo Zalman Shragai: "Blessed be He that we have reached this stage, even though it is still only the beginning of the redemption, and perhaps only the beginning of the beginning."[10] The only religious or traditional categories available to these thinkers were redemptive images, which they invoked – again and again – while fully aware that a significant amount of limiting or tempering or hedging was fully in order. What is now unfolding, wrote Rabbi Herzog, is "only the beginning of the redemption," one step removed from redemption, "and perhaps only the beginning of the beginning," two steps removed.[11]

It is precisely this nuanced formulation, acknowledging the arrival of a form of redemption albeit with a double hedge – "the beginning of the beginning" – that made its way into the Prayer for the State of Israel, in the words "*reishit tzemiḥat geulatenu.*" The incipient State is described here as "the beginning of the flowering of our redemption." It surely was not recognized as "our redemption"; it was even understood as representing neither "the beginning of our redemption" nor "the flowering of our redemption." The best that can be asserted is that it is "the beginning of the flowering of our redemption," once again two steps removed from redemption. Engaged in a battle for its very survival that commenced even before the State was founded against a vastly stronger and more powerful enemy, it was manifestly obvious to the authors of this text that the State did not represent the final vision of redemption but, just as clearly, they asserted that the absolute miracle of a Jewish state in the Jewish homeland after two thousand years was surely to be understood and framed within the context of redemption, perceived as a process that was beginning to unfold.

---

10. *Barkai* 2 (1985), 223.

11. Note also the formulation used by Winston Churchill in the speech he delivered at the Lord Mayor's Day Luncheon in London on November 9, 1942, celebrating the British victory at the Battle of El Alamein: "Now this is not the end. It is not even the beginning of the end. But it is, perhaps, the end of the beginning." This victory was crucial for the safety of the Yishuv, stopping the advance of General Erwin Rommel which had threatened to destroy it and bringing an end to the "two hundred days of dread" there. It is possible, maybe even likely, that Chief Rabbi Herzog was aware of this speech. My thanks to Myron Chaitovsky for bringing it to my attention.

Much ink has been spilled in trying to determine who is responsible for authoring this particular formulation.[12] In addition, many have
searched for sources or precedents for it and, indeed, very similar ones are
found in the writings of Rabbi Avraham Yitzḥak HaCohen Kook in a number of places. In an essay written while still living in Boisk in 1901–1902,
just before his move to Jaffa, Rabbi Kook used the phrase, "*reishit tzemiḥat
yeshuat Yisrael*, the first flowering of the salvation of Israel," and in an
essay penned in 1919–1920 he included the phrase, "*reishit tzemiḥat geulat
ammenu*, the first flowering of the redemption of our people."[13] A number
of his letters also contain this kind of language, although no one has yet
found this identical phrase in his writings.[14] To be sure, there were many,
including Rabbi Joseph B. Soloveitchik, who saw the State in very positive terms but did not perceive it in any way as messianic or redemptive.[15]
But this is not the message of the Prayer for the State of Israel. Regardless
of who authored it, its meaning is crystal clear. The newly founded State

---

12. There is a growing secondary literature on this phrase and its implications, as
well as on other matters relevant to the Prayer for the State of Israel. The most
comprehensive is Joel Rappel, *The Convergence of Politics and Prayer: Jewish Prayers
for the Government and the State of Israel* (PhD thesis, Boston University, 2008).

13. See Rabbi Avraham Yitzḥak HaCohen Kook, *Maamarei HaRaaya: Kovetz
Maamarim* (Jerusalem, 1984), 321, 42. I have not found references to these formulations by Rabbi Kook cited in the secondary literature on this phrase. My
thanks to Dr. Shnayer Z. Leiman for bringing them to my attention several years
ago. For the latter phrase, see also Rabbi Moshe Tzevi Neriya, ed., *Mo'adei HaRaaya*
(Jerusalem, 1984), 388.

14. These are cited regularly in the literature. See *Iggerot HaRaaya* (Jerusalem, 1985),
vol. 2, 117, and vol. 3, 134: *reishit tzemiḥat yeshuatenu*; vol. 3, 130: *reishit hatza'ad shel
tzemiḥat keren yeshuat Yisrael*. For more examples, see Ephraim Yair, "HaTefilla
LiShlom HaMedina," in Simḥa Raz, ed., *Kovetz HaTziyonut HaDatit* (Jerusalem,
1997), 379.

15. Many have addressed Rabbi Soloveitchik's position. Among them see the article
based on a lecture by Rabbi Aharon Lichtenstein, "Rav Soloveitchik's Approach to
Zionism," *Alei Etzion* 14 (2006), 21–37, and Reuven Ziegler, *Majesty and Humility:
The Thought of Rabbi Joseph B. Soloveitchik* (Jerusalem and New York, 2012), 276–98.
See too the exchange between Rabbi Shubert Spero and Rabbi Norman Lamm
in *Shma* 4/73 (May 3, 1974); Rabbi Yehuda Amital, "Lishmoa Kol Bikhyo shel
Tinok," *Alon Shevut leBogerei Yeshivat Har Etzion* 1 (Tevet 5754), 85.

of Israel is placed squarely in the forefront of the redemptive unfolding of the Jewish people.[16]

But the clear redemptive focus and message of this prayer for the welfare of the State of Israel is not limited only to this most well-known phrase; indeed it is present in less explicit, albeit highly significant, ways throughout. I want to draw attention here to only a few examples:

- Some of the biblical verses included in their totality in this prayer (Deut. 30:4–5), as well as some biblical words and phrases that appear there, also carry explicit redemptive connotations that make this connection obvious.[17]

- The prayer begins with the words: "Rock of Israel and its Redeemer." The reference to God as "Rock of Israel" already appears in the Bible (II Sam. 23:3; Is. 30:29) and is most familiar from the last blessing of the *Shema* in the Morning Service. Its connection to redemption is clear from the fact that the paragraph that it begins ends with a reference to God as the "Redeemer of Israel."

But the connection is stronger than that. After listing a number of themes to be mentioned in the *emet veyatziv* prayer following the morning *Shema* (e.g., the exodus from Egypt, the kingship of God, the Splitting of the Sea and the Slaying of the Firstborn), the Talmud Yerushalmi states: "One must say: 'Rock of Israel and its Redeemer.'"[18] God is already described by this very title, "Rock of Israel and its Redeemer," in this early source. In fact, some recited this phrase as the text for the blessing of redemption in the Evening Service for Holidays, and texts reflecting the custom in Eretz Yisrael indicate that this was the

---

16. Note also the triple hedge in a document dated January 21, 1949, some eight months after the founding of the State: נודה לד׳ על שזכינו ברוב רחמיו וחסדיו לראות את הניצנים הראשונים של האתחלתא דגאולה עם הקמתה של מדינת ישראל, referring to the founding of the State of Israel as "the first buddings of the beginning of the redemption." See Rabbi Menaḥem M. Kasher, *HaTekufa HaGedola*, 374. For other formulations, see Rabbi Yitzḥak Dadon, ed., *At'ḥalta Hi* (Jerusalem, 2006).

17. See Gilad Strauss, "HaMekorot LiTefilla LiShlom HaMedina," *Shmaatin* 104–105 (1991), 87–88.

18. Yerushalmi, *Berakhot* 1:6.

case there all year round in the Morning and Evening Services as well.[19] Clearly, the reference to God as "Rock of Israel" is intimately linked with redemption.

- But, for me, the most striking and significant part of the prayer that reflects a clear messianic or redemptive message are the two phrases that appear toward the beginning: "Spread over it the Tabernacle of Your peace" and "Direct them with good counsel before You." It is clear that they both come from the *Hash-kivenu* prayer recited as part of every Evening Service. But why invoke *Hashkivenu* and, more significantly, why two phrases from this same prayer? Surely many other texts could have served as sources for passages that would have been eminently appropriate to have been included in the Prayer for the State of Israel!

The Abudarham cites Rabbi Avraham HaYarhi, who notes that the phrase, "Spread over it the Tabernacle of Your peace," in particular, has messianic connotations, citing the verses in Ezekiel (16:8): "I spread the hems of My garment over you," and in Ruth (3:9): "Spread your robe over your maidservant, for you are a redeemer."[20] However, the authors of this prayer may have wished to convey – via this double reference to *Hashkivenu* – a message based on a more familiar traditional text, a passage from the

---

19. See Levi Ginzberg, *Perushim VeHiddushim BiYerushalmi* (New York, 1941), 217; *Bah, Orah Hayyim* 66, s.v., *uma shekatav vehotem*; *Taz, Orah Hayyim* 66:6; *Magen Avraham, Orah Hayyim,* 236, beginning. See also Yitzhak Moshe Elbogen, *HaTefilla BeYisrael BeHitpat'hutah HaHistorit* (Tel Aviv, 1972), 200; Rabbi Shelomo Yosef Zevin, *LeOr HaHalakha* (Jerusalem, 2004), 283; *Encyclopedia Talmudit,* vol. 4, column 407.

The phrase, *"mitokh bittahon beTzur Yisrael,* with trust in the Rock of Israel," already appeared at the end of *Megillat HaAtzma'ut,* Israel's Declaration of Independence, in a well-known attempt to compromise between those who wanted an overt reference to God in the document and those who were opposed to it. It also begins the prayer composed by Chief Rabbis Herzog and Uziel in honor of the seventy-fifth birthday of Israel President Chaim Weizmann in 1949. See the text published in Rabbi Shmuel Katz, "MiMismakhei HaRabbanut HaRashit MiShenot Kum HaMedina," *Tehumin* 18 (1998), 490.

20. *Abudarham Hashalem* (Jerusalem, 1963), 141.

beginning of the first tractate of the Talmud. The Talmud (*Berakhot* 4b) cites the opinion of R. Yoḥanan that the obligation to juxtapose redemption and prayer also applies during the Evening Service. The Gemara then questions: What about *Hashkivenu*? Does that paragraph not create an interruption between redemption (the blessing of *Ga'al Yisrael*) and prayer (the *Amida*)? The Gemara answers that once *Hashkivenu* was instituted, it is simply an extension of redemption and therefore is not considered an interruption.

Indeed, the significance of this notion is very clear in our context. *Hashkivenu* has the halakhic status of a *geula arikhta*, a drawn-out redemption, which is precisely how the authors of this prayer saw the newly established State of Israel. For them it was the first step of an extended redemption. It was redemption, but only the *reishit* of the *tzemiḥat*, the beginning of the flowering of the redemption. What better source than *Hashkivenu* could have reflected this fundamental principle, which mirrored the role the nascent State was playing in the unfolding of Jewish destiny? Not one, but two phrases from this prayer were deliberately included, I believe, to make this point. Redemption takes a while to achieve; redemption is a process.[21]

For the authors of this prayer who composed it in Israel's infancy, the State was *reishit tzemiḥat geulatenu*. As we celebrate Yom HaAtzma'ut these many years later, may we merit that the *reishit* will turn into the *tzemiḥa* and the *tzemiḥa* will turn into *geulatenu*, speedily, in our days.

---

21. Shlomo Sukenik, *Konena Aleinu: BeInyan HaTefilla LiShlom HaMedina* (Jerusalem, n.d.), 21–22, already recognized the *geula arikhta* character of *Hashkivenu* but interpreted its significance in a different way. Rabbi Yaakov Ariel, "Geulat Layla – Geula Arikhta," in Rabbi Yehuda Shaviv, ed., *Ḥazon LaMoed* (Jerusalem, 1988), 95–96, interpreted this phrase as I did but did not apply it to the text of the *Tefilla LiShlom HaMedina*.

For more on the notion of redemption as a process, see my "Seeking Redemption in an Unredeemed World: Yosef at the Seder," in *And You Shall Transmit to Your Children: A Pesach Haggadah* (New York, 2014), 25–30.

Paradise Regained: Eretz Yisrael and the Garden of Eden

Dr. Yael Ziegler

Why does the Garden of Eden vanish after the third chapter of the Book of Genesis? After all, the Garden of Eden seems to be humankind's ideal setting, situated at the opening of the Bible to convey its preeminence. God places Adam in this Garden, which He has planted for the benefit of the newly created human. Brief though it may be, the biblical description depicts a lush, well-watered environment, rich with every delightful and tasty tree. A river that flows through the Garden waters its trees; the Garden thereby requires only minimal maintenance by man, who has been charged with its care: "And God took Adam, and placed him in the Garden of Eden to cultivate and guard it" (Gen. 2:15).

It is not only the Garden's beauty and delights that suggest its idyllic nature. The Torah's account of the Garden depicts a hierarchical and harmonious existence in which all parties know their role and act to facilitate human existence. Nature acts in harmony with man, serving

man's needs, as the land blossoms effortlessly. Animals are subordinate and unthreatening to man, and Adam rejects the possibility of partnering with animals: "And man did not find his helpmate who corresponds to him (*ezer kenegdo*)" (Gen. 2:20). Only woman is man's partner and helpmate, and he acknowledges her as his companion and mirror image.

The climax – and likely the objective – of this ideal lifestyle is the intimate, if subordinate, relationship between humans and God. Humans must obey God's instructions, which involve both positive commands (the cultivation of the Garden) and negative ones (avoiding the forbidden trees). Moreover, God's accessibility is a pivotal feature of this ideal setting: "And they heard the voice of God strolling about the Garden at the breezy time of the day" (Gen. 3:8). The pastoral environment, together with the harmony and hierarchy that prevail in the Garden, provide the ideal conditions in which man and woman can focus on their budding relationship with God.

Many midrashim highlight the depiction of the Garden as the ideal arena for the man-God relationship by interpreting Adam's tasks of "cultivating and working" the Garden (*le'ovdah uleshomrah*) as referring to purely spiritual activities. *Bereshit Raba* 16:4, for example, notes that these specific verbs are later employed in the context of Sabbath observance (e.g., Ex. 20:9, Deut. 5:12) and sacrifices (Ex. 3:12, Num. 28:2); therefore, it suggests that these verbs direct Adam to observe the Sabbath and to bring sacrifices. Similarly, *Pirkei DeRabbi Eliezer* 11 suggests that God employs these verbs to direct Adam to study Torah and to observe the commandments.

These midrashic readings may be attributed to several factors. First, as noted, these verbs are frequently used in later biblical passages to depict spiritual activity. Moreover, the verbs for toiling and guarding are presented with a feminine ending; therefore, they do not appear to be modifying the Garden, which is a masculine noun.[1] Finally, as Rav Soloveitchik notes in *The Lonely Man of Faith*, the second chapter

---

1. See Nahmanides' comment on Genesis 2:8. The dots in the final letters of the words *le'ovdah* and *leshomrah* (called a *mapik heh*) are evidence that these verbs modify a feminine noun. The Garden is a masculine noun, while Shabbat, Torah, and mitzvot are all feminine.

of Genesis depicts man as created to interact in the world not merely as an organic being, but primarily as a spiritual being. Adam's purpose is to develop a relationship with the divine. To this end, God creates a Garden and gives Adam instructions that assist him in his complex and mysterious task of achieving some manner of intimacy with the divine. On a final note, I suggest that even if one sense of the command is about cultivating the Garden, agricultural labors are themselves suitable preparation for spirituality. Farming the land requires patience, commitment, passion, responsibility, empathy, and mindfulness, all traits that facilitate the construction of a spiritual persona.

Harmony in the Garden does not last long. The snake, the woman, and the man each betray this harmonious existence and disobeys God's command. This has catastrophic results. Humans are banished from the Garden and banned from reentry: "And He expelled Adam, and He stationed east of the Garden of Eden the cherubim and the fiery revolving sword to guard the path to the tree of life" (Gen. 3:24). At this point in the biblical narrative, the Garden is lost irretrievably, along with its harmonious lifestyle. Outside the Garden, humans are doomed to contend with an implacable natural world that does not easily yield its fruit to man's labors. Enmity is decreed between woman and snake. Man is positioned to dominate woman, and the steady equilibrium between them is thrown into disarray. The most significant result of the expulsion from the Garden is the lost intimacy with God, whose presence in the Garden rendered Him accessible to the humans who dwelled there.

These shattering events should rightly be followed by an attempt to return to the Garden and reacquire its ideal pre-sin lifestyle. It is perplexing, therefore, that no biblical figure expresses an explicit desire to return to the elusive Garden (aside from Lot in Genesis 13:10, where the quest is plainly economic and not spiritual).[2]

Has the Garden been forsaken and forgotten? This is, in fact, not the case at all. Subsequent biblical narratives do indeed focus on the quest for the divinity, blessings, and harmony that held sway in the Garden – yet

---

2. Rabbi Mordekhai Breuer (*Pirkei Bereshit* [Alon Shevut, 5759], 120–21) suggests that rabbinic sources conflate the afterlife with the elusive Garden of Eden to ensure that the sublime Garden is not lost to humanity forever.

this search is no longer focused on the Garden of Eden, but rather on the Land of Israel. God allocates the Land of Israel to function as a substitute for Eden, as an ideal setting in which humans can serve God.

God promises that, given the right spiritual conditions, He will stroll among humans in the Land of Israel, just as He had in the Garden: "And I will place My residence in your midst.... And I will stroll in your midst" (Lev. 26:11–12; see Rashi there, and Nahmanides, Gen. 3:8). Israel is a land where nature is harnessed toward the supreme objective of human service of God. To this end, the land responds to the spiritual state of its inhabitants. When the nation of Israel obeys God, nature responds accordingly, the rain arrives in its proper season, and the land easily yields its fruit (e.g., Lev. 26:3–5, Deut. 11:13–15, Is. 1:19). Sinning, on the other hand, has a negative effect on the land that bears God's presence; the land reacts by refusing to provide produce, and, in the most extreme circumstances, actively disgorges its sinful inhabitants (Lev. 18:25–28, 19:22, 26:14–41). One passage promises that, in accordance with Israel's favorable conduct, all treacherous animals in the land of Israel will be suppressed (Lev. 26:6).[3] Thus, depending on Israel's obedience to God's commands, the land can secure the pre-sin harmonious conditions that held sway in the Garden of Eden. These conditions provide the idyllic environment best suited for serving God.[4]

Rabbi Mordekhai Sabato points out an extraordinary verbal linkage between the expulsion from the Garden, at the beginning of the Torah,

---

3. Nahmanides (Lev. 26:6, 12) explicitly notes the connection between this blessing and the return to the ideal conditions of the Garden of Eden. Rabbinic sources (e.g., *Sifra, Beḥukkotai* 1:2) record an argument as to whether the dangerous animals will be removed from the land or whether they will simply no longer represent a threat to humans. This latter position strongly recalls the relationship between Adam and the animals in Genesis 2:18–20. For similar portraits of the role of the animals in an ideal world, see Isaiah 11:6–9, 65:25.

4. The restoration of harmony and parity in the man-woman relationship occurs in the Song of Songs (e.g., 2:16, 6:3, and especially 7:11), whose setting in the Land of Israel as a replacement for the Garden of Eden is quite evident (see especially Song of Songs 4:12–5:1). For more on this idea, see my article, "HaHazara LeGan Eden BeShir HaShirim," in *BeHag HaMatzot*, ed. A. Bazak (Alon Shevut, 2015), 154–73.

and Moses' blessing to the Jewish people as they are about to enter the Land of Israel, at the end of the Torah.[5] The story of the Garden concludes with Adam's expulsion from the desirable Garden (*vayegaresh*, Gen. 3:24), while the Torah concludes with the expulsion of the enemy from the Land (*vayegaresh*, Deut. 33:27). The opening biblical story concludes with the installation of the fiery cherubs outside the Garden to prevent reentry (*vayashken*, Gen. 3:24), while the conclusion of the Torah uses the same word to promise the secure dwelling of Israel (*vayishkon*, Deut. 33:28). These parallels suggest that the tragic initial story of the Torah is remedied and finds closure in Israel's anticipated entrance into the Land of Israel, a land designed to reinstate the Eden-like environment originally given to humans.

Prophetic passages reveal the extent to which the Garden of Eden and the Land of Israel become interchangeable. Isaiah, for example, declares in his prophecy of the restoration of Zion that "The Lord has comforted Zion, comforted all her ruins; He has made her wilderness like Eden, and her desert like the garden of the Lord" (51:3). Ezekiel likewise prophesies that the ruined Land of Israel will be restored to the Garden of Eden (36:35; see also Joel 2:3). While one could argue that this is metaphoric language, designed to evoke the pastoral setting of Eden, it is certainly possible that these prophets recognize that the Land of Israel has been designated to replace Eden and its ideal pre-sin lifestyle.

God's accessibility in the Land of Israel is especially present within the Temple (e.g., I Kings 6:12–13). There, humans are tasked with the responsibility of toiling and guarding (*avoda* and *shemira*; e.g., Num. 18:7), just as Adam had been instructed in the Garden of Eden. For His part, God rests His glory within the Temple (e.g., II Chron. 7:1–3), recalling His presence in the Garden.[6] God's presence calls for man to be especially scrupulous

5. "Birth of a Nation: The Framing Statements of Moshe's Blessing," The Israel Koschitzky Virtual Beit Midrash, *Parashat HaShavua, VeZot HaBerakha*.

6. Some scholars posit that the floral motifs adorning the Temple (e.g., I Kings 6:18, 32) are designed to evoke the Garden. Intriguingly, *Midrash Tanhuma* 11 describes the Temple filled with trees that miraculously yield fruit. See also *Bemidbar Raba* 12:4. Poetic biblical passages allude to the Temple as a blossoming garden (e.g., Ps. 52:10, 92:13–14).

in his behavior, and expulsion is deemed an apt consequence for violation of the divine sanctity of the Temple, recalling the same consequence for disobedience in the Garden.[7]

God's presence is felt especially in the Holy of Holies, where His word emanates from between the golden cherubs (Num. 7:89). The cherubs feature centrally in the Temple, recurring throughout its architecture and tapestries, indicating its central role as a symbol that bears God's immanence (e.g., I Kings 6:32, 35; II Chron. 3:7, 14). These Temple cherubs offer a sharp contrast to the original biblical cherubs, the ones whose role was to block human reentry into the Garden after the expulsion.[8] The Temple cherubs welcome those who wish to experience God's presence, while the Garden cherubs were placed threateningly at its entrance (along with the fiery, turning sword) to thwart humans in this very quest. The Temple is both a *tikkun* (repair) for the expulsion from the Garden, as well as the ultimate setting for the restoration of Eden's spiritual conditions.[9] Thus, a midrash (*Pirkei DeRabbi Eliezer* 20) states that the gates to the Garden of Eden are to be found on the Temple Mount.

---

7. This expulsion is, of course, accompanied by the threat to destroy the Temple. See, for example, Jeremiah's prophecy in 7:3–15. *Bereshit Raba* 21:8 draws a parallel between the expulsion from Eden and the destruction of the Temple. See also *Eikha Raba* 1:1.

8. Significantly, the stated goal of the cherubs in Eden is to block human access to the "tree of life" (Gen. 3:24). In Proverbs 3:18, the tree of life refers to God's wisdom, that is, the Torah. Strikingly, the Temple cherubs seem likewise to hover protectively over the Ark that contains the stone tablets of the Ten Commandments (I Kings 8:7, 9). Nevertheless, the cherubs' role in the Temple is not to prevent human access to God's wisdom, but rather to disseminate it.

9. See, for example, Psalms 36:9, which draws a parallel between the Temple and Eden. Ezekiel (28:11–18) likewise conflates the Garden of Eden and the Temple (*Har Kodesh Elokim*). Moreover, Ezekiel 28:13 describes the Garden of Eden as the provenance of the precious stones of the high priest's breastplate (Ex. 28:17–20). The appearance of a cherub in Ezekiel's prophecy (28:14) only deepens the connection between these two places. Likewise, in his prophecy against Pharaoh, Ezekiel describes the trees of the Garden of Eden (31:7–9). Significantly, the trees that grow in that Garden are cedars and cypresses, the same types of wood that constitute the primary building materials of the Temple (I Kings 5:22).

One final question is in order. Why does God not return humankind to Eden, to the original sublime Garden? Why does God designate the Land of Israel as a substitute for the Garden? There is one critical difference between the new ideal setting and its previous incarnation: the Land of Israel has no rivers. This is not simply a technicality; it may be the key to understanding the need for a new environment in which to realize humanity's goals. Indeed, this absence of rivers, which translates into dependence upon rainfall, is specified as a defining feature of the Land of Israel: "For the land that you are coming to inherit is not like the land of Egypt.... [It is] a land of mountains and valleys; it soaks up water by the rains of heaven" (Deut. 11:10–11).[10] The dependence upon rain translates practically into dependence upon God, whose attention is consequently focused upon the land: "It is a land that the Lord your God seeks; His eyes are constantly upon it, from the beginning of the year to the end of the year" (Deut. 11:12).

What went wrong in the Garden of Eden? How can we ensure that a similar breakdown does not occur in the Land of Israel? Perhaps the presence of rivers, which enables humans to "water [the land] with [their] feet" (Deut. 11:10; that is, to create irrigation canals), causes humans to feel confident in their own prowess, their independent ability to ensure economic success. This leads to arrogance and is often a root cause of the human decision to cast off God's yoke. When people feel they can survive independently of God, they often lack motivation to obey His commands. This is a particularly relevant message for modern society, whose technological advancements have indeed frequently prompted people to reject God. Thus, the Land of Israel is designated to create a more suitable environment for the cultivation of a sense of dependence upon God.

10. The land of Egypt's most noteworthy feature, the one responsible for its prosperity, is the Nile River. Genesis 13:10 explicitly compares the land of Egypt to the "Garden of God" in terms of its well-irrigated conditions. It is also noteworthy that the maximal borders of the Land of Israel are *from* the river of Mesopotamia and up to – *but apparently not including* – the river of Egypt (see Gen. 15:18). In other words, the Land of Israel can encompass the territory between the two life-giving rivers of the Near East, but it cannot include these rivers themselves.

And yet, perhaps the supreme ideal still remains the one that prevailed in the Garden of Eden. Possibly, the model environment is one in which rivers flow through the land, creating an effortless, prosperous existence that nevertheless does not induce human arrogance. This vision, one that evokes the ideal end of days, may in fact be the one prophesied by Zechariah with reference to the currently riverless city of Jerusalem: "And it will be on that day, living waters will flow out of Jerusalem … in the summer and in the winter. And God shall be the King over the land; on that day God will be One, and His name will be One" (14:8–9).[11]

Contemporary life in the Land of Israel is no longer solely dependent on rainwater. Imports from foreign countries, desalination, and other modern technologies allow for the possibility of economic survival and even prosperity in modern Israel, whether or not rains arrive. In a sense, the Land of Israel today has reverted back to the situation of Eden. It is all too easy to enjoy the fruits of the Garden without perceiving God's role. In this context, Zechariah's vision takes on added significance, providing a model for maintaining a sense of dependence upon God despite favorable economic circumstances.

I close, then, with a fervent prayer that the inhabitants of modern Israel, who are privileged to have returned to the contemporary incarnation of the sublime Garden, will remain worthy of its blessings. May we recognize the enormity of the divine opportunity presented to us, and may we learn to discern God's role in providing the Land's bounty even when His direct intervention is not immediately apparent:

> And you will eat and be satiated, and celebrate the name of the Lord your God, who has done wonders for you, and My people will not be ashamed evermore. And you will know that I am in the midst of Israel and that I am the Lord your God. (Joel 2:26–27)

---

11. See also Ezekiel 47:1–13, where a water source emanates from the Temple and waters a huge tree. This depiction is reminiscent of the description of Eden. See also Joel 4:18, Isaiah 30:19, 30:25–26, 33:20–21, and Psalms 36:9, 46:5. One hint that the rivers of Eden will eventually reemerge in Jerusalem is that the Giḥon River flows from Eden (Gen. 2:13), and the Giḥon Spring is adjacent to Jerusalem (1 Kings 1:33, 38).

Yom HaAtzma'ut and Yom Yerushalayim

"It Is Wondrous in Our Eyes"

Rabbi Yehuda Amital

> *Thus says the Lord of hosts: Old men and old women shall yet again sit in the streets of Jerusalem, and every man with his staff in his hand because of his old age. And the streets of the city shall be full of boys and girls playing in its streets.*
>
> *Thus says the Lord of hosts: If it will be wondrous in the eyes of the remnant of this nation in those days, it will also be wondrous in My eyes, says the Lord of hosts.* (Zech. 8:4–6)

In this description by the prophet Zechariah, no exceptional or supernatural phenomenon is mentioned. There is no unique event, nor any description of awesome strength. All we have here, in effect, is a simple,

pastoral description of normal life. The grandfather and grandmother are sitting in Jerusalem, walking-sticks in hand, and the grandchildren are playing in the streets. Can it be that this very scene, according to the prophet, will be "wondrous in the eyes of the remnant of this nation"? Is it possible that such a natural scene prompts God to add, "It will also be wondrous in My eyes"?

Zechariah prophesied many great and inspiring events, but it is specifically here that "wondrousness" is mentioned. Moreover, Rabbi Akiva, the great *Tanna*, was able to look clearly, to smile, and to laugh at the very destruction of the Temple when he was reminded of this prophecy. The Talmud (*Makkot* 24b) recounts the story of Rabban Gamliel, Rabbi Elazar ben Azarya, and Rabbi Yehoshua, who were walking toward Jerusalem after the destruction of the Temple:

> When they reached Mt. Scopus, they tore their clothes. When they reached the Temple Mount, they saw a fox coming out of the place of the Holy of Holies. They began to cry, and Rabbi Akiva began to laugh. They said to him, "Why do you laugh?" He answered, "Why do you cry?" They said to him, "The place of which it is said, 'And the stranger who comes near will die' (Num. 1:51), now has foxes walking in it; shall we not cry?"
>
> He said to them, "For that reason I laugh. For it is written, 'I appoint for Myself faithful witnesses – Uriah HaKohen and Zechariah ben Yevarekhyahu' (Is. 8:2). What connection can there be between Uriah and Zechariah? After all, Uriah lived during the time of the First Temple, while Zechariah lived during the Second. But God made Zechariah's prophecy dependent on that of Uriah. Of Uriah it is written, 'Therefore because of you Zion shall be ploughed like a field' (Mic. 3:12), while in Zechariah we learn, 'Old men and old women shall yet again sit in the streets of Jerusalem.' Before the prophecy of Uriah was fulfilled, I was afraid that Zechariah's prophecy would never come true. Now that Uriah's prophecy has been fulfilled, Zechariah's prophecy will certainly be fulfilled as well."
>
> With that they said to him, "Akiva, you have comforted us; Akiva, you have comforted us."

But why did Rabbi Akiva mention specifically this prophecy of Zechariah? Did he not prophesy greater things than this? Was it not

Zechariah who said, "Sing and rejoice, O daughter of Zion, for I come and I will dwell in the midst of you ... and you shall know that the Lord of hosts has sent me to you" (2:14–15)? Why is this prophecy not mentioned? Did Zechariah's prophecies involve only boys and girls, old men and women? Did he not speak of God "giving victory to the tents of Judah first.... On that day shall the Lord defend the inhabitants of Jerusalem, and the feeblest among them shall be like David; and the house of David shall be like a divine being, like the angel of the Lord at their head" (12:7–8)? We could cite many other examples of Zechariah's inspiring prophecies. What is it, then, that makes this prophecy of old men and old women in Jerusalem, their walking-sticks in their hands, and of boys and girls playing in the streets, so special? Why does this prophecy bring comfort?

The suffering of exile was extraordinary. The entire country was emptied of its inhabitants; all were led away into captivity, young and old alike. But the prophet announces publicly: Life will return to its usual path. Life will be normal again! "Old men and old women shall yet again sit in the streets of Jerusalem ...."

A profound idea is contained here. Someone who lacks historical awareness – someone who sees only the present and is cut off from the past – is incapable of seeing the future; moreover, he perceives even the present in a distorted way. Rabbi Akiva, by contrast, was someone with historical perspective.

"Remember the days of old, understand the years of ages past. Ask your father and he shall expound to you, your elders – and they shall tell you" (Deut. 32:7). On Seder night, we discuss the story of the exodus from Egypt. We start with: "Originally our fathers were idol-worshippers, and now God has brought us near to His service, as it is written: 'And Joshua said to the nation: Your forefathers dwelt on the other side of the Jordan – Terah, the father of Abraham and the father of Naḥor – and they served other gods. And I took your father, Abraham, and I led him throughout the land of Canaan ....'" How is this connected to the exodus from Egypt? The answer is that a single event cannot be analyzed in isolation. The background to any event is broad. The exodus from Egypt cannot be understood without first understanding "Teraḥ, the father of Avraham ...."

Someone who does not understand the meaning of an entire nation being exiled from its land cannot understand the historical significance of

its return. The Land of Israel was entirely emptied of all her inhabitants. Has such a thing ever happened in history? A nation that was exiled from its land, and returns to it?

The prophet says, "Old men and old women shall yet again sit in the streets of Jerusalem." Once again there will be "boys and girls playing in its streets." Simple, normal life. Only someone with a deep historical awareness can understand the significance of such a scene. Miracles are one-time events. But Jews living a normal life in Eretz Yisrael, after seventy years of the Babylonian exile during which the country was empty and desolate – someone looking with historical perspective can only be astonished. Of him the prophet says, "If it will be wondrous in the eyes of the remnant of this nation in those days, it will also be wondrous in My eyes, says the Lord of hosts."

Normal life, that which other nations accept as a natural phenomenon, is perceived by us as a meta-historical one, a manifestation of the Divine. For them everything goes smoothly: "And Esau continued on his way to Se'ir" (Gen. 33:16); such is the way of the world. But "Jacob and his sons went down to Egypt" (Josh. 24:4). For us, every natural phenomenon becomes a supernatural one. For us, nothing is simple.

After two thousand years, children play in the streets of Israel, in the squares of Jerusalem! Can this be a natural phenomenon? After two thousand years?

For us, things have always been different. The connection between the nation of Israel and their land was created differently from that of any other nation. In the natural course of events, the connection between a nation and its land is created after people have lived in a certain area for a long time, have fought for it, have lived through shared experiences and troubles. Our connection to our land was created before the first Jew had set foot on it! "And God said to Abram, 'Go out of your country, from your birthplace, from your father's house, to the land which I shall show you'" (Gen. 12:1). It was then that the connection was formed. "The covenant which He made with Abraham, and His oath to Isaac, and He confirmed it to Jacob as a law, and to Israel as an everlasting covenant, saying: 'To you I will give the land of Canaan, the lot of your inheritance'; when they were few in number, a mere handful sojourning there" (Ps. 105:9–12). This was a unique event; it has no parallel in history.

Just as the connection between the nation of Israel and its land did not follow the natural order, so too the connection between the nation and the State of Israel was formed before the Jewish nation was in the land. Along came a Jew from an assimilated household, lacking any background in Judaism, lacking any familiarity with Jewish culture, and – using "Jewish intuition" alone – revealed what our Sages had long before understood: that Zion is the birthplace of all Jews, "both those actually born there as well as those who yearn to see it" (*Ketubot* 75a). Herzl intuitively understood that although there were almost no Jews living in Eretz Yisrael, nevertheless this would become the Jewish state. Is it generally acceptable for a nation to choose a place, go there, and create a state? Isn't a state usually created for those who already live in a place and not for the sake of those who will flock to it after it is created?

At the time of the Balfour Declaration, in 1917, how many Jews were living in the land? A few tens of thousands? Nevertheless, the declaration stated: "His Majesty's Government view with favor the establishment in Palestine of a national home for the Jewish people." A strange phenomenon. So too later, when Britain betrayed the Jewish nation by refusing to allow the survivors of Auschwitz and Majdanek entry into the land. The mighty Britain closed the doors. Certain of its policy, Britain made every effort to prevent the establishment of a Jewish state in Eretz Yisrael, and transferred the decision into the hands of the United Nations, fully confident that this body would leave control of the region in Britain's hands.

And then the unbelievable happened. A committee was formed and its recommendation was to create two states in Eretz Yisrael: a Jewish state and an Arab state. In order for such a resolution to be passed, a two-thirds majority of the UN was required. And the UN was clearly divided, with a cold war between East and West. Whatever one side supported, the other would reject. And even if the countries of the East and West would agree, what would be the position of Uruguay, Paraguay, and all the other little countries – how would they vote?

The family history of every ambassador from Uruguay and Paraguay was carefully investigated in the hope of finding a grandmother, a third cousin, anyone who served as a connection to Judaism. One of the delegates, Dr. Leo Cohen, told me that throughout the day of the UN vote

he walked around with a Book of Psalms in his hand, knowing that "Only a miracle could save us." To obtain a two-thirds majority!

I remember it well. On November 29, 1947, I was at Kibbutz Be'erot Yitzhak. We all listened intently to the voting on the radio: "Yes. No. Yes. No." And the miracle happened: two-thirds! An unprecedented event!

But what happened after that? Today we live in a "now" generation: Peace now, Moshiach now – everything must be now. We are incapable of imagining what tomorrow might bring. Everything is measured by the yardstick of what is happening today. Today is quiet – tomorrow will be too. Today there is terrorism – tomorrow it will continue. Today there is peace – tomorrow there will be peace. It is a generation with an impaired sense of history. There is no awareness of the past, and none of the future – only a sense of today, of now.

In 1948, it was a different generation, one with historical perspective. Recently we have suffered terrible terrorist attacks. Let me tell you something: During those few months, between the UN vote on November 29 and the Declaration of Statehood on May 14, there were seven car bombs here. One of them, on Ben-Yehuda Street, killed fifty Jews, and this in addition to the victims killed by marauders on the roads and by snipers in the *yishuvim*. I won't mention too much; I won't detail everything that happened here in Gush Etzion, all within five months. The Convoy of Thirty Five fell, the Nebi Daniel force lost fifteen victims, an attack on the high ground here brought another twelve to their deaths, and an attack on another convoy making its way to the Gush cost another ten lives.

And do you know how many victims fell here in Gush Etzion on the 3rd and 4th of Iyyar, 5708? More than one hundred and fifty. Just two days before the declaration of the state! During those five months, two hundred and forty victims fell in Gush Etzion alone. And despite it all, the establishment of the State of Israel was declared, and the next day everyone recited *Hallel* with great excitement. People danced in the streets. Had they gone mad?

It was the strong sense of history that prompted this. That generation knew and understood the significance of Jewish independence in Eretz Yisrael after two thousand years; it was a state meant not for the 600,000 Jews living there then, but for millions of Jews yet to come. Each person understood that he was fighting for the millions who would come to Israel.

What were the borders of that state? They did not include the Kotel. Nahariya was not ours, nor were Nazareth, Lod, Ramle, Ashkelon, Be'er Sheva. Jerusalem was an international city. What were they saying *Hallel* for?

They said *Hallel* for the sovereignty that had returned to Israel. They remembered the words of Maimonides in *Hilkhot Ḥanukka*, where he teaches that in the merit of the Hasmoneans, "Sovereignty returned to Israel for two hundred years" (3:1). They understood the significance of that sovereignty. There was a strong belief that "It was not by their sword that they took the land, nor their might that saved them, but rather Your right hand and Your arm, and the light of Your countenance, for You favored them" (Ps. 44:4). Without "You favored them," there is nothing.

I will not even go into how, on the day after the declaration of the state, I had to rush to finish reciting *Hallel* because I had been drafted. They began to invade from all sides: from Egypt, from Syria, from Jordan, from Lebanon; units even came from Iraq. How were we supposed to stand up to them, after the British had forbidden us to stockpile arms? All in all we were 600,000 Jews.

If, in Zechariah's time, normal life in Israel after seventy years of exile was considered wondrous, should we consider it natural after two thousand years of exile?

Three books of the Prophets – Haggai, Zechariah, and Malachi – and two from the Writings – Ezra and Nehemiah – deal with a time when a total of forty thousand Jews resided in Eretz Yisrael. Those were all who returned. Forty thousand. And today, thanks to God's grace, we have merited to see many millions of Jews in Israel!

Someone who cannot see the past will also be incapable of seeing the future and of perceiving God's hand "when God redeems the captivity of His nation" (Ps. 14:7). Can a nation rising out of the ashes of the Holocaust allow itself to ignore this?

True, most Jews today never saw all of this. They were born to a life of freedom. They never experienced living in bunkers, praying for the day when they could walk in the streets and look around without fear. Only someone who looks at the entire two thousand years and sees Jews being led into exile by Titus, sees the Crusades and pogroms – only someone

who sees all of this understands the meaning of Jewish independence. Along came the Jews after two thousand years and claimed their ownership of Eretz Yisrael. No such thing had ever happened before. It is no wonder that the Arabs cannot understand it – "What are you doing here? How long did you live in Eretz Yisrael, anyway?" If you do the calculations, you'll see that Jews lived in Yemen for longer.

"It is not by their sword that they took the land" (Ps. 44:4). Is it possible not to see the great hand of God?

Someone who sees only today, now, is disturbed by problems and questions. But someone with a feel for history knows, like Rabbi Akiva who saw a fox emerging out of the place of the Holy of Holies, that "old men and women shall yet again sit in the streets of Jerusalem."

The prophet Jeremiah says:

Thus says the Lord: Again there shall be heard in this place – which you say is desolate, empty of man and of beast; in the cities of Judea and in the streets of Jerusalem, which are deserted and without man, without inhabitant, and without animal – the voice of joy and the voice of gladness, the voice of the bridegroom and the voice of the bride, the voice of those who will say, "Praise the Lord of hosts, for the Lord is good, for His kindness is forever," when they bring thanksgiving offerings to God's house. For I shall return the captivity of the land as in former times, says the Lord. (33:10–12)

For our many sins, we have yet to merit seeing the "bringing of thanksgiving offerings to God's house." But the Men of the Great Assembly, when they composed the seven blessing recited at weddings, left out the end of the verse and changed it to read: "Again there shall be heard in the cities of Judea and in the streets of Jerusalem, the voice of joy and the voice of gladness, the voice of the bridegroom and the voice of the bride, *the joyous voice of bridegrooms emanating from the ḥuppa and that of the young men coming from their celebration.*" What are the "young men" here celebrating? Are they holding a *siyum*? Or simply having a party?

They are, in fact, the representatives of "normal life." A normal state of affairs involves young people coming out of parties, and it was them to whom

the Men of the Great Assembly referred. Are we blind to the fulfillment of this prophecy? Have we not participated in the joy of bridegrooms and brides in Jerusalem? Have we not danced in its streets? Have we not been witness to the joyous sounds of wedding parties emanating from the ḥuppa?

I have much in my heart that is waiting to be said. But for now let me just note three matters that require special emphasis in our times.

1. The need to strive for unity. God does not punish the community so long as it functions as a "community." A *midrash aggada* in the Yerushalmi (*Pe'ah* 1:1) asks: "How is it possible that in the generation of King David – where everyone, even the children, knew Torah – there were casualties when they went out to war, while in the days of King Ahab – a generation of idol-worshippers – they were always victorious when they went out to war?" The Gemara explains, "In the days of King David there was causeless hatred and informing. In the days of Ahab, despite the fact that they were idol-worshippers, they were united among themselves, and hence they were victorious in war." Unity is the first basic requirement, and we must guard it carefully.
2. The need to strengthen our appreciation of Jewish sovereignty.
3. The need to strengthen the moral foundation of our nation, to fight materialism, and to raise the moral, religious, Torah, and cultural level of the nation. We cannot focus all our energies on the fight for land and ignore these issues.

We have prevailed in worse times, and we shall prevail now. But we have to know that without a strong sense of history, we shall not be able to understand what is happening in Israel. If we fail to take our past into account, we will not understand the future, and even our appreciation of the present will be perverted.

Today let us all say, in the words of the Psalms:

I have faith in Your loving-kindness; my heart shall rejoice in Your salvation; I shall sing to the Lord for He has rendered me good. (13:6)

God has given me suffering – but has not left me to die! (118:18)

Open for me the gates of righteousness, I shall enter them and praise God.... I praise You for You have answered me, and have been my salvation. The stone which the builders despised has become the chief cornerstone. This is God's doing – it is wondrous in our eyes. This day God has made – let us rejoice and be glad in it! (118:19–24)

The Joy of Yom HaAtzma'ut

Rabbi Chaim Druckman

IS THE CELEBRATION STILL RELEVANT?

The prayer of *Hallel*, recited on Jewish holidays, includes verses from Psalm 118, which opens and concludes with the words, "O give thanks to the Lord, for He is good; for His steadfast love endures forever." Verse 24 of this psalm states: "This is the day the Lord has made; let us rejoice and be glad in it (*bo*)." The Zohar makes use of the ambiguity of the pronoun "*bo*" (which can refer to any masculine noun) to expound: "'*Bo*' – in the day; '*bo*' – in the Holy One, blessed be He" (Zohar Volume III 105a).

Thus, we celebrate Yom HaAtzma'ut with joy, praise, and gratitude, because "This is the day the Lord has made;" therefore, "rejoice and be glad *in Him*," in the Holy One, blessed be He. Our rejoicing on the day emanates from our joy in God, who has brought about this day.

And yet, in recent years, we hear people wondering if this celebration is still relevant. This question is asked out of deep, heartfelt pain in the midst of the difficult current reality, in which we, through our own actions, are chipping away at our own independence and damaging it. In light of this reality, we must confront a piercing question: Is it still relevant to celebrate our independence on Yom HaAtzma'ut?

121

CELEBRATING YOM HAATZMA'UT – A BIBLICAL OBLIGATION

The sages explain in the Talmud (*Megilla* 14a) that Purim was instituted based on an *a fortiori* argument from Passover: "If, for being delivered from slavery to freedom [in the exodus from Egypt], we chant *Hallel*, should we not do so all the more for being delivered from death to life [in the miracle of Purim]?"

Thus, Purim's status as a holiday is based on an *a fortiori* argument derived from the Torah's commandment regarding the holiday of Passover. On Passover we celebrate the Jewish people's liberation from slavery to freedom; on Purim, the salvation is so much greater and more significant: from death to life! All the more so should we celebrate this holiday!

In light of this passage, Rabbi Moshe Sofer (*Ḥatam Sofer*) rules that Purim's holiday status is biblical, since this status was derived by an *a fortiori* argument, the most basic of the principles by which the Torah is expounded. He notes that although the mitzvot of Purim were instituted by the sages, nevertheless, the essence of the holiday is a biblical obligation, and whoever does not celebrate this holiday violates a biblical command. However, if one celebrates the holiday, but not in the manner decreed by the sages, one violates only a rabbinical ruling. *Ḥatam Sofer* writes:

> Establishing a holiday on the day of a miracle is a biblical obligation, as it is an *a fortiori* argument from the Torah. In my humble opinion, the day of Purim and the days of Ḥanukka are from the Torah! However, what to do on them – whether to send portions of food or to light candles or to commemorate them in some other way – is of rabbinic origin. Whoever does nothing to commemorate the days of Ḥanukka and Purim violates a biblical positive command! (*Yoreh De'ah* 233)

In the early years of the State of Israel, Rabbi Meshulam Rath was asked to explain the halakhic position on designating Yom HaAtzma'ut as a holiday on which we recite *Hallel* and bless *Sheheḥeyanu* (Who has kept us alive). In his responsum, Rabbi Rath deals with these questions at length and in depth. As for the validity of the status of Yom HaAtzma'ut as a holiday, he determines:

It is obvious in our case, which is relevant to the entire community of Israel and includes deliverance from slavery to freedom (we were redeemed from the subjugation of kingdoms, and we have become free men and have achieved political independence) as well as deliverance from death to life (we were saved from the hands of our enemies who sought to exterminate us) – certainly we have an obligation to institute a holiday! (Responsa *Kol Mevaser* 1:21)

Thus, it is obvious that Yom HaAtzma'ut must be instituted as a holiday, because the establishment of the State of Israel constitutes *liberation* from slavery to freedom as well as *salvation* from death to life – both the liberation of Passover and the salvation of Purim.

According to the above, granting Yom HaAtzma'ut the status of a holiday, which includes joy and gratitude, is mandated by the Torah. Therefore, this is not dependent on our subjective feelings at all! The Torah's determination obligates us to rejoice, celebrate, and thank God, for our liberation and salvation.

THE MIRACLES OF 5708 (1948)
A. "The Many into the Hands of the Few"

On the eve of the declaration of independence of the State of Israel, the Arab countries declared that within a week, they intended to wipe out the entire Yishuv (Jewish population) in the Land of Israel. The Arab armies' proclamation, "We will drive you into the sea," was not a figure of speech, but rather a serious threat to invade the Land of Israel from the north, east, and south, so that the Mediterranean Sea to the west would be the Jews' last refuge.

The massacre in Kfar Etzion,[1] carried out one day before the declaration, would have been the fate of the entire Yishuv had we not defeated our enemies. Only six hundred thousand Jews were living then in the Land of Israel, surrounded by millions of Arabs. The Israel Defense Forces had not yet been established, and no serious weaponry was available; nev-

---

1. On the day before the declaration of the State of Israel, May 14, 1948, Arab tanks broke open the gates of Kibbutz Kfar Etzion and infiltrated it. The kibbutz fell into the hands of the enemy, who slaughtered almost all of the defenders.

ertheless, God delivered them into our hands. Is there a better example of "the many into the hands of the few"?

On Ḥanukka, we repeatedly recite the *Al HaNissim* prayer in which we thank God for delivering "the many into the hands of the few." The Ḥanukka miracle took place more than two thousand years ago – but this wondrous event has happened also in our time! God delivered the many into the hands of the few, and thus saved us from certain death and gave us the gift of our own lives – is it not appropriate that we thank Him for this?

B. The Heroism of the Decision

The heroism displayed on the battlefield began, in fact, with the declaration of independence itself. The Arab countries threatened to eradicate us should we dare to declare independence. The United States, which supported the establishment of a Jewish state when voting in the United Nations, proposed that it was nevertheless not the right time to declare independence; even within the Yishuv itself there existed conflicting views, so that in the end, the decision to declare the independence of the State of Israel passed with a majority of only two votes. This, in itself, is a miracle from heaven! Despite everything, our independence was declared and the State of Israel was established, which is an incomparable act of heroism.

The Talmud states:

> If a shepherd who was guarding his flock left it and entered the town, and then a wolf came and killed part of the flock, or a lion came and tore them to pieces, we do not say, "Had he been there, he could have saved them," but rather we take his measure: If he could have saved them, he is responsible; if not, he is exempt.
>
> But why so? Let us say to him, "Had you been there, the verse, 'Your servant slew both the lion and the bear' (1 Sam. 17:36) would have been fulfilled for you!" (*Bava Metzia* 106a)

Ostensibly, the claim could have been made against the shepherd who abandoned his flock that had he not been derelict in his duty, he might have experienced a miracle like the one which transpired for King David, who told Saul that when he was a shepherd, "Your servant slew both

the lion and the bear." The Tosafists explain (s.v. Mativ) that the miracle referenced here is "the spirit of heroism and the knowledge of warfare." In other words, when a person finds himself in a difficult situation and successfully exhibits "the spirit of heroism and the knowledge of warfare," this is a miracle from above, in that this person is able to figure out the proper ways to act and save himself in a time of peril. This is what happened to David, and it is certainly what happened to the Jewish people as well.

Like David who challenged Goliath, Israel boldly declared independence in the face of the entire world. Everything that transpired was due to the grace of God, emanating from the One "Who girds Israel with might," that went on to reveal itself on the battlefield as well.

C. Saving the Entirety of Israel

Not only was the Yishuv in Israel saved, but *Klal Yisrael* itself was saved. First of all, from a halakhic standpoint, the Jews living in the Land of Israel are considered *Klal Yisrael*. This is derived from Maimonides' formulation in *Sefer HaMitzvot*:

> Let us imagine, for example, that there would be no Jewish inhabitants in the Land of Israel. Now, God would never allow such a thing, since He has already promised that the signs of the nation shall never be utterly obliterated. (Positive #153)

In regard to this, Ḥatam Sofer points out:

> Based on this, it appears that if, God forbid, there would be no Jews left in the Land of Israel, even if there would still be Jews living outside of Israel, this would be classified as "destruction of the nation," God forbid. (*Yoreh De'ah* 234)

The elimination of all Jewish population from the Land of Israel constitutes destruction of the entire nation. God has promised us that such a thing will never transpire. Therefore, it is inconceivable that the Land of Israel could ever be empty of Jews.

However, it is not only according to Halakha that saving the Jewish population of the Land of Israel is considered saving *Klal Yisrael*, but also in terms of the reality at that time. What would have befallen the survivors of the Holocaust – those "brands plucked out of the fire" (cf. Zech. 3:2) – if the Arabs had put their vile scheme into effect and slaughtered the Jewish population of the Land of Israel? Had this happened, the Jews living in Arab lands would also have suffered a terrible and bitter fate. And what would have been the fate of the Jews of Ethiopia and the Jews of Russia? Indeed, the Jewish spark was rekindled in the Soviet Union only as a result of the establishment of the State of Israel, and it was truly revealed only after the Six-Day War.

In truth, it was not only these Jews, residing in lands of oppression and repression, who were saved by the miracle of the State of Israel; it was the Jews living in lands of peace and prosperity as well. I once heard from Rabbi Joseph B. Soloveitchik that as the Holocaust raged through Europe, many Christian missionaries in America called upon the Jews to embrace Christianity as their last hope for survival; otherwise, they would suffer the same fate as their fellow Jews in Europe. The horrors of the Holocaust were exploited by Christian theologians as a persuasive tactic; the end of the Jewish people was nigh, they claimed, because they had failed to accept the Christian savior. American Jews were faced with the threat of spiritual annihilation until the State of Israel was established, inspiring them and instilling in them pride for their people.

Similarly, I heard from the chief Rabbi of Tel Aviv, Rabbi Ḥayim David HaLevi, that during one of the years soon after the establishment of the State of Israel, he spent the High Holidays in South America. On Yom Kippur eve, the great synagogue was filled with people praying. When the prayer service ended, Rabbi HaLevi saw that the congregants filed out, got into their cars and drove away. Shocked, he asked those accompanying him about this bizarre tableau. They responded that these Jews were already several generations distant from Judaism; even their grandfathers had intermarried. "If so," asked Rabbi HaLevi, "I have another question: what brings them to the synagogue?!" The answer was as follows: "The establishment of the State of Israel has brought these Jews to once again identify with the Jewish people."

GRATITUDE

The rejoicing and thanksgiving on Yom HaAtzma'ut express gratitude to God not only for saving us, but also for the monumental gift that He gave us: the State of Israel.

The very fact that we have been granted independence, and that we are no longer subjugated to others, obligates us to give gratitude to God, lest we be ingrates; this is true despite the many problems which exist in the State of Israel.

Consider this parable: a man receives a vase for flowers from his friend, which is beautiful beyond compare, but one of the recipient's family members filled it with mud instead of flowers. Would anyone think that the recipient no longer has to thank the giver of this lovely gift? After all, it was someone in the recipient's family who filled it with mud – why should the giver suffer for that reason?

This is our situation as well. We received an incomparable gift from God – the State of Israel; we have merited what so many generations before us have not. Now, problems have sprung up, all of *our own* doing – is that any reason not to thank God? On the contrary! Our gratitude should arouse in us the desire to do better, to make certain that everything in the State of Israel is conducted in the correct and proper manner. Certainly, we must thank God for everything He has done for us.

Every year, for thousands of years, we have celebrated the Exodus of the Jews from Egypt on Passover. Does the fact that those same Jews sinned only a few months later with the Golden Calf keep us from celebrating Passover?

On Ḥanukka we celebrate God's miracles, as brought about by the Hasmoneans, whom Nahmanides (Gen. 49:10) termed "sublime saints." Does the fact that the Hasmonean dynasty later became Sadducees mean that we should stop celebrating Ḥanukka?

The same is true in our time. Should the problems *we* have brought about put an end to our gratitude to God for the great miracles He has wrought for us, for the redemption from subjugation which He has granted us, for the salvation from death to life which we have merited? Every single one of these elements is expressed in the happiness, praise, and thanksgiving of Yom HaAtzma'ut.

PAIN AND JOY IN THE LAND OF ISRAEL

In the *Shulḥan Arukh*, Rabbi Yosef Karo rules: "If one's father dies, one recites the blessing *'Dayan HaEmet'* (the True Judge); if one inherits money... one also recites the blessing *'Sheheḥeyanu'* (Who has kept us alive)."

There is no need to describe the terrible pain and agony of losing a parent; even if a parent were to leave his child a fortune, the pain of the parent's death would be deep and the sorrow over the loss would be overwhelming. Nevertheless, Halakha determines that if the parent leaves the child an inheritance, the child must recite two blessings. Not only does he recite *Dayan HaEmet*, declaring that God is the True Judge in deciding when to take his parent's life, but he also recites *Sheheḥeyanu*, a blessing usually recited in joy, associated with seasonal mitzvot and new acquisitions. Does this blessing invalidate the pain and loss of a parent's death? God forbid! But it does teach us a great lesson: In a situation where pain and joy are admixed, each one receives its due and is not nullified by the other (*Oraḥ Ḥayyim* 223:2).

There is a famous dispute in the *Shulḥan Arukh* regarding the obligation to recite the *Sheheḥeyanu* blessing on the mitzva of circumcision (*Yoreh De'ah* 265:7). Rabbi Yosef Karo rules that the blessing of *Sheheḥeyanu* is recited only when the father is the one performing the circumcision, but when the act of circumcision is performed by someone else, *Sheheḥeyanu* is not recited. In his gloss, Rabbi Moshe Isserles (the Rema) makes a different distinction: the *Sheheḥeyanu* is not recited even if the father is performing the circumcision, unless this is his firstborn son and the baby must be "redeemed" in a later ceremony; in such a case, the *Sheheḥeyanu* blessing is recited over the act of circumcision on the eighth day rather than at the redemption ceremony on the thirtieth day. The *Shakh* (ad loc. 17) writes that the custom is not to recite *Sheheḥeyanu* even in such a case.

One of the reasons traditionally given for the custom not to recite the blessing of *Sheheḥeyanu* on the mitzva of circumcision is "the pain of the infant" (see the Gra, ad loc.). And yet, Rabbi Yosef Karo cites Maimonides' view:

> According to Maimonides, the father always recites the blessing of *Sheheḥeyanu* for every circumcision, and this is how we practice in all of the communities of the Land of Israel, and in Syria, and in its environs, and in the Egyptian community.

Rabbi Karo stresses that the custom in the Land of Israel and its environs is to follow Maimonides and recite the blessing of *Sheheḥeyanu* on every act of circumcision. Why, in the Land of Israel, is "the pain of the infant" not a consideration? Do Israeli babies not feel pain? We must learn a great lesson from this: In the Land of Israel, the pain of the circumcision does not invalidate the great joy of the occasion! In the Land of Israel, when pain and joy co-exist, one does not nullify the other. Even when the pain is great, it does not blur the happiness, upon which one must indeed bless God, "Who has kept us alive, sustained us and brought us to this time."

SANCTIFICATION OF GOD'S NAME IS GREATER THAN DESECRATION OF GOD'S NAME

In the Jerusalem Talmud, Rabbi Abba bar Zemina is cited, expressing what ostensibly seems to be a bizarre sentiment: "Said Rabbi Abba bar Zemina in the name of Rabbi Hoshaya: Sanctification of God's name is greater than desecration of God's name" (*Kiddushin* 4:1). My master and teacher, Rabbi Tzvi Yehuda Kook *zt"l*, would ask about this passage: "What is novel about this? Did we need the Jerusalem Talmud to come and teach us that it is better to sanctify God's name than to desecrate it?"

My esteemed teacher explained that this passage refers to a single situation which embodies both the sanctification and the desecration of God's name. The Jerusalem Talmud teaches us that in such a situation we must not be afraid to take action which has both positive and negative elements, because *the positive side overpowers* the negative side. This is what "sanctification of God's name is greater than desecration of God's name" means – we must concentrate on the positive side of such an act.

Yes, the State of Israel has negative elements, but we must not let the negative overwhelm the positive. It is certainly relevant to celebrate Yom HaAtzma'ut, since the aspect of sanctifying God's name through the establishment of the State of Israel is greater than any negative aspects.

CELEBRATION AND HAPPINESS: UNDERSTANDING THE IMPORTANCE OF INDEPENDENCE

The obligation to celebrate and rejoice is not only an expression of gratitude, as we have explained, but is also required because ultimately,

celebration and rejoicing strengthen our independence and our determination to protect it.

Celebrating something demonstrates its importance. For example, if a person receives a diamond, the more valuable he knows it to be, the more he will put effort into guarding it and making sure that it does not become flawed. The same is true of our celebration and joy over our independence; this reinforces the importance of protecting our independence, safeguarding our country, taking pride in our homeland, and never compromising its principles. Celebrating Yom HaAtzma'ut is, in itself, a statement about the importance of our independence and our need to protect it.

Celebrating Yom HaAtzma'ut also reaffirms that we are capable of safeguarding our independence. Celebrating Yom HaAtzma'ut reminds us of the events of 1948, how we stood the few against the many, and were victorious by the grace of God, because we believed in the righteousness of our path and had faith in our future. The same powers which we had then still exist today, but they must be awakened and discovered, developed and nurtured.

This is the task of a person of faith, one who believes that everything which transpired in our generation is the work of God, part of a divine plan for the redemption of Israel. It is the task of one who believes that everything which has taken place over the past century, especially since the establishment of the State of Israel – the ingathering of the exiles and the return of the Land of Israel and Jerusalem to our hands – is part of a divine plan. Certainly, this divine plan cannot be halted; this is a mechanism which cannot be stopped. At most, its action can only be delayed. "Shall I bring to the birth and not cause to bring forth? says the Lord. Or shall I who cause to bring forth thereupon shut the womb? says your God" (Is. 66:9). Rashi (ad loc.) explains: "Will I bring a woman to the birth stool and not open her womb to bring out her fetus? That is to say, shall I commence a thing and not be able to complete it?"

One who believes that everything that has happened in our generation is not a coincidence, but rather is part of the divine plan for the redemption of Israel, will never despair; such a person is confident that this verse will be fulfilled: "For the Lord will not cast off His people, nor will He forsake His inheritance" (Ps. 94:14). Not only does such a person not

despair, he even understands that we are obligated to recognize this plan, to identify with it and to act according to it. We must bring the nation of Israel to true perception and clear vision, to the point that the entire nation becomes partner to the divine plan, working together with the Holy One, blessed be He, to bring it to fruition.

All this must be expressed in our great celebration and happiness on Yom HaAtzma'ut: "This is the day the Lord has made; let us rejoice and be glad in it!" (Ps. 118:24).

The Turning Point

Rabbi Mordechai Greenberg

JEWISH NATIONALISM

We have been celebrating Yom HaAtzma'ut for many decades, yet many still wonder what it is that we are happy about. After all, this day is supposed to express our political independence and our security, but full independence and security elude us! We remain vulnerable to acts of terror and susceptible to war; we face existential threats just as in previous generations, when we were in *galut*. What, then, is the special significance of this day?

At the root of the dispute about the significance of Yom HaAtzma'ut are differing outlooks on Jewish nationalism. Is there indeed a concept of nationalism in the Jewish worldview? One could argue that the main focus of Judaism is one's connection to God through the observance of Torah and mitzvot, and that nationality is irrelevant. A Jew can thus be a citizen of another nation – America, England, or any other – observe all the mitzvot of the Torah, and lack nothing. According to this view, there is little reason to yearn for a Jewish state.

There was a dispute in Hungary many years ago about this very point. On the national census form, there were separate sections for religion and nationality. The rabbis of the time argued regarding how to fill in the space for nationality: Should the Jews write that they were Jewish or Hungarian? Rav Moshe Shmuel Glasner maintained that it is heretical to enter one's religion as "Jewish" but his nationality as Hungarian or German. Indeed, he wrote, this is a *yehareg ve'al ya'avor* – an obligation for

which one must give up his life rather than transgress.[1] In the opinion of most authorities, *Am Yisrael* is indeed a "nation," and its members cannot belong to another nation.

In the second half of the nineteenth century, a wave of nationalism began spreading through Europe. In 1863, the Poles raised their national flag as a sign of rebellion. The following Shabbat, the Ḥiddushei HaRim sighed and said that he was concerned that there would now be a *kitrug*, a Heavenly allegation against the Jewish people. The Poles care so much about their nation and are willing to sacrifice their lives for it, he noted, while we are complacent in *galut*.[2]

What is Jewish nationalism? Some understand that it is fundamentally the same as all other nationalisms – the desire to have a land of one's own and the yearning to live there. The only thing that makes the Jewish people unique is that we also have the Torah. Others, however, argue that Jewish nationalism is essentially different. As Rav Kook defined it, Jewish nationalism is not dependent on the state; the basis of our nationality is divine and spiritual. As the Meshekh Ḥokhma (*Parashat Aḥarei Mot*) writes, "God does not designate His name on the individual, because the individual, without the connection to the *Klal*, is not the ultimate purpose."

Judaism rejects the famous principle articulated in the New Testament: "Render unto Caesar that which is Caesar's and unto God that which is God's." This is essentially the concept of separation of church and state. According to this worldview, religion is a private matter, one in which the state should not be involved. There is, however, a deeper implication of this idea – that ethical principles and the connection to God are not relevant to the political state and society, but only to the individual. An individual can separate himself from society and then live ethically if he so chooses. But a state has to contend with a host of social issues, inter-relations with other nations, politics, and wars. Politics is not ethical. A state cannot survive without breaching the bounds of moral conduct, and political issues therefore cannot be based on religious foundations.

The Jewish concept of the place of religion in society is the very antithesis of this idea. The Book of Kings states, "The queen of Sheba saw all

1. *Torah Umelukha*, ed. S. Federbusch (Jerusalem, 1961), 67.
2. *Ḥassidut Vetzion*, ed. S. Federbusch (Jerusalem, 1963), 48.

the wisdom of Solomon, the palace that he had erected ... and his burnt-offerings that he sacrificed (*ve'olato asher ya'aleh*) to the Temple of God, and she was overwhelmed" (1 Kings 10:4–5). According to one explanation of this verse, the queen of Sheba was impressed by the sheer number of sacrifices that King Solomon offered in the Temple on a daily basis. However, the Malbim and others refer to the parallel verse in 1 Chronicles (9:4), which refers to *aliyato asher ya'aleh* – a ramp or passageway that led from Solomon's palace to the Holy Temple. The queen of Sheba was impressed by the link between the Jewish king and his religion. The Jewish outlook is that nothing is divorced from spirituality; everything must be based on divine ideals and morality.

The meaning of this connection is that there is no social or political realm that is not based on justice and ethics. As a nation, we aspire to demonstrate that a political state can also observe the ways of God, without having sovereignty and political stability inhibit the nation's connection to God.

This is the uniqueness of the Jewish people: our religion and our nationhood are inextricably bound together. Rav Kook writes, "There exist in the world righteous people, philosophers, holy and Godly people, but there is no nation whose inherent soul cannot be fulfilled other than through the goal of the divine plan in the world – other than Israel" (*Orot*, 50). The Jewish people is the only nation that represents God in this world.

Our national goal is, as we say in *Aleinu*, "to perfect the world under the reign of God." How can this be accomplished? Certainly not by having the Israeli ambassador give a *musar* speech at the UN! Lofty concepts are not enough. The only way to achieve this goal is for Jews to have a state of their own and demonstrate that things can be different – by running their agriculture, their economy, and their army in an elevated, divine manner. The state is necessary to show the world that the moral demands presented by the Torah are possible to implement in real life – not only in the lives of individuals, which is obvious to all, but in the lives of a modern, technologically advanced nation. It is not enough to live under the rule of others and to live our personal lives according to the Torah. All elements of the government – the prime minister, the police force, the army – must take on a Jewish aspect in order to achieve our goal of modeling the ideal state.

THE DESTRUCTION OF NATIONALISM

"Because of our sins we were exiled from our land" – every young child knows this line from the Musaf prayer of festivals. But why do we deserve specifically this punishment for our sins? Why couldn't God have punished the Jewish people while they remained in their land? Why was Israel punished specifically with *galut* (exile)? Divine punishment is a direct consequence of sin, with the purpose of rectifying it. How did *galut* rectify the sins of the generations of the First and Second Temples?

Based on what we have said, it is possible to explain that the Jewish people failed to fulfill their mission during the thousand years of the two Temples. The people were truly righteous, but the government and social order were not based on justice and integrity, as clearly indicated by the relentless rebuke of the prophets. The punishment of *galut* indicates that at that moment, the mission of the Jewish people is too high an ideal. *Galut* dismantles the national framework, removing the nation from the land and thereby dividing the nation into individual communities and families – a nation of individuals – who can deal with only religious issues, instead of national ones. It is easier to achieve a moral, divine existence as individuals; once the individuals of the Jewish nation have regained their strength, they can rejoin together once again to fulfill the divine goal.

The exile of the Jewish people from the Land of Israel brought about the complete destruction of the land, and the nation was dispersed throughout the world. This led to "internal destruction" as well; the people no longer had the motivation to behave as a nation or to return to the land. The sentiment was that it was better to remain in exile under the shelter of the nations. Indeed, the *Haskala* took this outlook to be the hallmark of the "*Galut* Jew." However, this is not the true form of the Jew – only a temporary one.

In fact, this state of *galut* was necessary for our ultimate growth. Rav Kook explains that before the destruction, while we were still a nation among nations, we were negatively influenced by our neighbors to concern ourselves only with the material concerns of state. During *galut*, in contrast, we could only dream about our national goals. This is not a normal state; as the Maharal writes, every nation needs a country. Nevertheless, this respite was good for us; we strengthened our feelings of moral good, of spirit, and of religion (*Orot*, 52).

But in exile we remained, and once there, it was most difficult to extricate ourselves and return to our own state. Indeed, this explains Ḥazal's statement that the Jewish people took an "oath" not to return to the Land of Israel by force. The opponents of Zionism argued that this oath prohibits the Jewish people from returning to the Land of Israel until they receive permission to leave exile. But how is it possible that the nation took an oath contrary to an explicit mitzva? The halakha is that one cannot take an oath that goes against the oath that we took at Mt. Sinai! Nahmanides writes that it is a biblical commandment to live in the Land of Israel; how, then, could the Jewish people swear not to return?

The answer is that Ḥazal did not mean to say that the Jewish people took an actual oath; rather, we became so bound up in our exile that it was as if we had taken an oath not to leave *galut* (see *Akeidat Yitzḥak*, Deut. 23:13–14; in his *Epistle to Yemen*, Maimonides also seems to understand the oaths in this fashion). Divine providence arranged history so that the Jewish people could not rebel against the nations and return to Eretz Yisrael; the land was desolate, the ruling nations didn't allow it, and the Jews were afraid and had no motivation. The circumstances did not allow us to hasten the redemption.

In a similar vein, the Ohr Same'aḥ wrote that divine providence arranged that in San Remo (where the UN was at the time), the enlightened nations declared that Eretz Yisrael should belong to the Jewish people. Thus, "since the fear of the oath is removed," the mitzva of living in Eretz Yisrael returns in full force.[3] What does he mean by the "fear of the oath"? If there is an oath, why should our "fear" of it or lack thereof make any difference? Rather, there was no actual prohibition in the first place; it was just that divine providence prevented us from arousing ourselves to return to Eretz Yisrael prematurely, and now divine providence has released the chains binding us to *galut* so that we can return to fulfill our destiny – as a divine nation leading its national life in Eretz Yisrael.

THE SIGNS OF THE REDEMPTION

But how do we know that the time is now? Ḥazal gave us signs so that we would know when the time of the redemption has arrived. The effects of

---

3. Rabbi Menaḥem Mendel Kasher, *Hatekufa Hagedola* (Jerusalem, 1968), 174.

galut – the desolation of the land, the dispersion of the Jewish people, the opposition of the other nations, and our fear of them – are means to prevent us from returning to the land before we are ready. When the reality changes – when Eretz Yisrael is no longer desolate, when the Jews begin to band together, when the nations agree, and when the Jews regain courage to return to the land – these are signs that we are allowed to return.

The Talmud (*Sanhedrin* 98a) states that the clearest sign of the end of *galut* is when the land begins to bear fruit again, as the verse states: "But you, mountains of Israel, will give forth your branch and bear your fruit for My people of Israel, for they are soon to come" (Ezek. 36:8). The Maharsha explains that as long as the Jewish people are not present, Eretz Yisrael will not bear its fruit properly. Thus, when it begins to do so, it is a sign that the time of redemption is close and the Jewish people will return. The land giving forth her fruits and the ingathering of the exiles – "for they are soon to come" – are practical and obvious signs that the end of the *galut* is approaching, as these are the two foundations on which the nation is built: a unified nation in its land.

How do we define the "ingathering of the exiles"? How many Jews must be settled in Eretz Yisrael in order to know that the sign of "they are soon to come" has been fulfilled? The Vilna Gaon is reported to have said that if it were possible to bring 600,000 Jews to Eretz Yisrael, the *sitra aḥra* – the metaphysical forces of evil – would be overcome.[4] Rav Kook similarly wrote that when 600,000 Jews are settled in Eretz Yisrael, that will mark the beginning of the restoration of the land; we will then be guaranteed that the time had arrived when God would fulfill His word to establish us as a nation before Him, and that there will be no further destruction.[5] Indeed, in 1948, the UN's official report listed 625,000 Jews as living in Israel.[6]

---

4. R. Hillel of Shklov, *Kol HaTor*, ed. Rabbi M. M. Kasher (Jerusalem, 1968), chs. 1, 5.

5. *Olat Re'iya*, vol. 1 (Jerusalem, 1985), 388. This idea is based on a midrash on the verse: "She will dwell there as in the days of her youth, and as on the day of her ascent from the land of Egypt" (Hos. 2:17): "Just as they left Egypt with 600,000 and they entered the Land with 600,000, so too, in the time of the Messiah, they will be 600,000" (*Yalkut Shimoni*, Hosea 518).

6. Efraim Shmueli, *Toledot Ameinu Bazeman Haḥadash*, 7 (Tel Aviv, 1984), 159. Thirty years before, at the time of the Balfour Declaration, there were only 56,000 Jews in the country!

The signs that *Ḥazal* gave us to alert us to the time period in which our national destiny will be fulfilled have come to fruition. The land is ready for us, we are gathered together at long last, the nations allow it, and we finally have the motivation. The time has arrived for us to rebuild our ideal state in Eretz Yisrael.

THE SIGNIFICANCE OF THE DAY

What, then, is the significance of Yom HaAtzma'ut? How can we celebrate that we have a state when we still face so many challenges and threats?

The answer is that our celebration is not related only to the ideas of political independence and security. Rather, on this day we reached the turning point between *galut* and redemption. Rav Kook writes that the Jewish state is fundamentally different from all other countries, as its very essence contains the divine ideal: "This state is our state, *Medinat Yisrael*, the foundation of God's throne in the world, whose whole desire is that God be One and His Name One" (*Orot*, 160).[7]

The distance to be traveled is indeed still great, but we have crossed the barricade. The period of the exile is over and we are marching on the path toward redemption. We now have the ability to establish a state and to govern it according to the social system that God demands. We are once again able to join "Caesar and God" and to build a bridge to go to the House of God. Even if we are far from the ultimate goal, the roadblocks that divine providence placed before us for two thousand years have been removed. The powers that accumulated within us over the course of the lengthy *galut* have awakened and we have finally achieved our desire – establishing a Jewish state that will realize the divine idea in the life of the nation before the eyes of the entire world.

---

7. This passage marks the first time that the Jewish state is called "*Medinat Yisrael*," decades before the actual establishment of the State of Israel.

"The Foundation of God's Throne in the World"

Rabbi Eliezer Sadan

In *Orot* (160:6–7), his classic work of Jewish thought, Rabbi Abraham Isaac HaKohen Kook wrote that the State of Israel is "the foundation of God's throne in the world." Rabbi Kook's language alludes to the biblical passage: "Then Solomon sat on the throne of God as king instead of David his father, and prospered, and all Israel obeyed him" (1 Chron. 29:23).

Simply put, King Solomon sat on the throne of the Kingdom of Israel. Why, then, does the Bible refer to it as "the throne of God"? Although a royal throne is the place from which the monarch leads his people, the leadership emanating from the royal throne of Solomon was entirely a revelation of divine wisdom, a revelation of the divine idea which illuminates human life. The groundwork for the restoration of that divine kingdom is being set in our time by the establishment of the State of Israel.

The Torah of Israel governs not only the religious experience of individuals, but also the national life of the Jewish people in their entirety. The entire conduct of communal life, national life, political and social life – everything is illuminated and directed according to God's word. And

it becomes clear that the royal throne of Solomon is, in itself, the foundation of God's throne in the world, and that the monarchy of Solomon thus served as the vehicle through which divine leadership was made manifest and took effect in the world. In the reign of King Solomon, the fusion of divine will and Jewish national life reached its historical apex when the Temple was established in a period of peace and prosperity. That is the reason the Bible uses the expression "the throne of God" to characterize Solomon's monarchy. The only other place we find this expression in the Bible is in connection with the final redemption: "At that time they shall call Jerusalem the throne of God; and all the nations shall be gathered to it, to the name of the Lord, to Jerusalem" (Jer. 3:17). Over the course of history, there was only one period in which the Jewish nation realized its full potential – under the reign of Solomon, some 2800 years ago. The first flowering of the longed-for redemption is now unfolding in our own generation.

Solomon's reign set the precedent for the culmination of Jewish history in the final redemption. The period of David and Solomon was a glimpse into the future, a vision to inspire and guide all generations as they progress towards the accomplishment of our national ambition.

Moses opened his concluding address to the Jewish people with the ringing declaration: "The Lord our God spoke to us at Ḥorev, saying: …Behold I have set the land before you; go in and possess the land which the Lord swore to your fathers…" (Deut. 1:6–8). The Torah as a living reality can only be realized in the life of a nation established in its homeland. The world-redemptive mission of the Jewish people can only be accomplished by the nation as a whole, when living a vital and exemplary national life in the Land of Israel.

The Jewish people were not told at Sinai: "You shall be to Me a collection of dedicated scholars, a select group of saints and the righteous," but rather: "You shall be My own treasure from among all peoples…. You shall be to Me a kingdom of priests and a holy nation" (Ex. 19:5–6). We received the Torah in order that we become "a nation that knows God and serves Him" (*Guide of the Perplexed* III:51).

Maimonides asks why the patriarchs involved themselves extensively with mundane matters such as raising livestock, growing crops, digging wells and the like (ibid.). Would it not have been more appropriate for the progenitors of the nation to set up study halls and teach the word

of God? Does not such preoccupation with the mundane come at the expense of Torah study? Maimonides explains that from the moment God told Abraham, "Go from your country, from your kindred, and from your father's house, to the land that I will show you; and I will make of you a great nation" (Gen. 12:1), Abraham understood that his task was to establish a nation-state. A nation-state requires a land. Furthermore, a nation-state cannot function in its land without a vast physical infrastructure, comprising an army, economic system, agriculture, roads, etc. Concerned that the physical demands of national life would later conflict with the spiritual service of God, the patriarchs set a precedent for future generations, engaging in the routine tasks of the world while remaining fully conscious of God's presence.

Maharal observes that the Torah, which governs the life of the nation, was given not to the patriarchs but to the entire Jewish people (*Tiferet Yisrael* 17). Only when the Jewish people in their entirety assembled at Sinai could they receive the Torah. After they had encamped there and absorbed the Torah, God then told them: "You have dwelt long enough in this mountain…. Go in and possess the land which the Lord swore to your fathers, Abraham, Isaac, and Jacob, to give to them and to their seed after them" (Deut. 1:6–8). Many of the mitzvot of the Torah are operative only when the Jewish people dwell in the Land of Israel. The majority of these mitzvot are concerned with the administration of the nation as a whole and the regulation of social and public welfare. It was at Sinai that we were elected to be God's chosen people, entrusted with the historic, world-redemptive mission of the patriarchs: "And in you shall all the families of the earth be blessed" (Gen. 12:3).

Rabbi Kook foresaw that the State of Israel would lay the cornerstone for the reestablishment of God's throne in the world. He envisioned a new era of national growth and prosperity, progressing by stages until the inner essence of the Jewish people, now concealed, would finally be revealed in all its glory.

For the past two millennia, Jews have prayed three times a day for the restoration of God's kingdom:

> Restore our judges as at first and our counselors as at the beginning, and remove from us sorrow and sighing. May You alone, Lord, reign

over us with loving-kindness and compassion, and vindicate us in justice. Blessed are You, Lord, the King who loves righteousness and justice.

When the Messiah will ascend to the throne of the Kingdom of Israel, he will follow "the way of the Lord, to do righteousness and justice" (Gen. 18:19), by instituting a society based on the complementary values of loving kindness and compassion on the one hand, and righteousness and justice on the other. This model society will set a shining example for all of mankind, inspiring the nations of the world to follow its moral principles. Although noble and exalted *individuals* have arisen among the nations throughout history, the utopian transformation of mankind can come about only through the catalyst of an exemplary *nation*. How awe-inspiring for the world to behold a powerful, thriving nation whose multitudes work together harmoniously, in righteousness and justice, for the sake of a higher purpose! This is the age-old dream of mankind come true. The prophet Isaiah foretold mankind's response: "And many peoples shall go and say: Come, let us go up to the mountain of the Lord, to the house of the God of Jacob, and He will teach us of His ways, and we will walk in His paths: for out of Zion shall go forth the Law, and the word of God from Jerusalem" (Is. 2:2-3).

The reemergence of the Jewish State thus secures the foundation of the Torah of Israel. Moreover, in addition to what it means to contemporary Jews, the State of Israel represents an immense sanctification of God's name in the eyes of the nations. In particular, the reestablishment of the Jewish commonwealth puts the lie to the ideology that God has abandoned His chosen people for their "sin" of rejecting the Christian messiah, and has appointed the Church and its followers in their place. The Christians hijacked the texts of our Holy Scriptures and abused them in the service of their beliefs. For untold centuries, Christians persecuted and oppressed the Jews in the name of a vengeful God. And now – lo and behold! God in His compassion has brought His chosen people back to the Land of Israel. The Jewish State, thriving and prosperous, is the living refutation of their supersessionist beliefs.

Rabbi Kook taught that the redemption will unfold gradually, like the coming of the dawn, until its light finally blazes in the sky, dispelling the darkness forever. His vision is anchored in the words of the prophets. The

sweep of exile and return to the Land of Israel was foretold by the prophet Ezekiel in the following verses:

> I poured My fury upon them [the house of Israel] for the blood which they had shed upon the land, and because they had defiled it with their idols; and I scattered them among the nations, and they were dispersed through the countries; according to their way and according to their doings I judged them. And when they came into the nations where they came *they profaned My holy name, in that men said of them: These are the people of God, and they are gone forth out of His land.* (Ezek. 36:18–20)

The words of the prophet teach us that the very fact of exile is a desecration of God's name in the world.

> But *I had pity for My holy name*, which the house of Israel had profaned among the nations into which they came. (36:21)

Ezekiel teaches us that the profanation of God's name is intolerable and cannot endure forever.

> And *I will sanctify My great name*, which has been profaned among the nations, which you have profaned in their midst; and *the nations shall know that I am God, says the Lord God, when I shall be sanctified in you before their eyes.* For I will take you from among the nations and gather you out of all the countries, and will bring you into your own land. (36:23–24)

From these words of the prophet, we learn that God's name is sanctified by the fact that the return of His people to Zion is witnessed by the nations of the world. God exiled His people – as He warned; and God has now brought us back to the land of our forefathers for the sake of His name – as He promised. It is no coincidence that the Vatican was the only European state to refuse to recognize the State of Israel when it was established. The very existence of a Jewish state on Jewish national soil resoundingly contradicts the theological doctrine of the Catholic Church.

Ezekiel continues the prophecy of return by saying in God's name:

> I will then sprinkle clean water upon you, and you shall be clean;
> from all your impurities and from all your idols, will I cleanse you.
> (36:25)

The physical return to the Land of Israel *precedes* the spiritual return
of the Jewish people to the Covenant of Sinai. The State of Israel has
been established, the exiles are being gathered from the four corners
of the earth; and yet, our nation is still tainted by spiritual impurities
and blemishes. Spiritual purification is the next stage in the process of
redemption. Nonetheless, the reality of the reestablishment of a Jewish
commonwealth in the Land of Israel sanctifies God's name, which had
been desecrated by the very fact of our exile.

Ezekiel foretold that the physical return of the Jewish people to Zion
would take place before their spiritual return to Torah observance. In
this, he was following the precedent of the prophecy of exile and return
found in the text of the Torah. In *Parashat Nitzavim* it is written: "God
will turn your captivity and have compassion upon you, and will return
and gather you from all the peoples among which the Lord your God has
scattered you .... The Lord your God will bring you into the land that your
fathers possessed, and you shall possess it; and He will do you good and
multiply you more than your fathers" (Deut. 30:3-5). Thus far, we have
merited the ingathering of the exiles, possession of the Land of Israel,
and renewed national prosperity. It is only after the culmination of these
physical stages that the spiritual phase of the redemption will take place:
"The Lord your God will circumcise your heart and the hearts of your
children, to love the Lord your God with all your heart and with all your
soul, and become fully alive" (30:6).

A Psalm for the Day of Our Independence

Rabbi Yoel Bin-Nun

Psalm 107, which opens the fifth part of the Book of Psalms according to the Masoretic text, is recited by Sephardic communities on Pesaḥ, and its recital on Yom HaAtzma'ut was instituted by the Chief Rabbinate headed by Rabbi Yitzḥak Herzog and Rabbi Benzion Uziel. Its inclusion, I believe, captures the intentions of the psalmist, who wrote this hymn as a song of praise to celebrate the independence of the Jewish people and their return to their own land.

The psalm contains seven stanzas, which can be divided into three parts: the opening stanza, four middle stanzas, and two concluding stanzas. I will discuss each stanza in sequence.

STANZA 1 – A SONG OF THE INGATHERING OF EXILES

הֹדוּ לַה׳ כִּי־טוֹב, כִּי לְעוֹלָם חַסְדּוֹ:

יֹאמְרוּ גְּאוּלֵי ה׳, אֲשֶׁר גְּאָלָם מִיַּד־צָר:

וּמֵאֲרָצוֹת קִבְּצָם, מִמִּזְרָח וּמִמַּעֲרָב, מִצָּפוֹן וּמִיָּם:

Thank the Lord for He is good; His loving-kindness is forever.
Let those the Lord redeemed say this –
those He redeemed from the enemy's hand,
those He gathered from the lands,
from east and west, from north and south. (vv. 1–3)

In the opening of the psalm, the poet refers to "those the Lord redeemed ...
those He redeemed from the enemy's hand." Without further explanation,
the reader would no doubt attribute the mentioned redemption according to his or her own concept of redemption: the building of the Temple,
the resurrection of the dead, the appointment of a king, the Messiah's
arrival, or the sanctification of the world in God's name. However, none of
these options is mentioned here, and the psalmist immediately interprets
this redemption in reference to מֵאֲרָצוֹת קִבְּצָם – a massive ingathering of
the exiles.

Until recent times, the nation of Israel – in fact, the entire world – had
never seen an ingathering of exiles on a scale described by Psalm 107.
The Children of Israel left Egypt and Babylonia in a single group, and
headed in a single direction from one point of origin, not from the four
corners of the earth. Only in the latest ingathering of exiles, that of the
Zionist movement, has this psalm been fulfilled in all its might and
glory: Jews have gathered from the four corners of the earth, by desert,
sea, and air. In contrast to the prophecies of Isaiah, where the coming
of the Messiah, the "shoot that issues forth from the stump of Jesse"
(Is. 11:2), precedes the ingathering of exiles, "and the outcasts of Israel
shall be assembled, and the dispersed of Judah shall be gathered from
the four corners of the earth" (Is. 11:12), this psalm does not mention
the Messiah.

Like Deuteronomy's section on repentance – "Even if you are scattered to the furthermost lands under the heavens, from there the Lord
your God will gather you and take you back" (Deut. 30:4) – Psalm 107
seems to be a prophecy that explicitly refers to our time. Although both
believing and non-believing Jews may find it difficult to accept, the
words "those He gathered from the lands" describe the miracles of our
own time.

STANZA 2 – THE PATH OF THE REDEEMED

תָּעוּ בַמִּדְבָּר, בִּישִׁימוֹן דָּרֶךְ, עִיר מוֹשָׁב לֹא מָצָאוּ:
רְעֵבִים גַּם־צְמֵאִים, נַפְשָׁם בָּהֶם תִּתְעַטָּף:
וַיִּצְעֲקוּ אֶל־ה' בַּצַּר לָהֶם, מִמְּצוּקוֹתֵיהֶם יַצִּילֵם:
וַיַּדְרִיכֵם בְּדֶרֶךְ יְשָׁרָה, לָלֶכֶת אֶל־עִיר מוֹשָׁב:
יוֹדוּ לַה' חַסְדּוֹ, וְנִפְלְאוֹתָיו לִבְנֵי אָדָם:
כִּי־הִשְׂבִּיעַ נֶפֶשׁ שֹׁקֵקָה, וְנֶפֶשׁ רְעֵבָה מִלֵּא־טוֹב:

Some lost their way in desert wastelands,
finding no way to a city where they could live.
They were hungry and thirsty, and their spirit grew faint.
Then they cried out to the Lord in their trouble,
and He rescued them from their distress.
He led them by a straight path to a city where they could live.
 Let them thank the Lord for His loving-kindness
 and His wondrous deeds for humankind,
for He satisfies the thirsty and fills the hungry with good. (vv. 4–9)

The four stanzas that comprise the main body of the psalm (stanzas 2–5) describe four groups of "those the Lord redeemed": those who "lost their way in desert wastelands," those who "sat in darkness and the shadow of death," those who "came close to the gates of death," and "those who go to sea in ships." From these stanzas, Halakha derives that "four [kinds of people] must be thankful," and must recite the blessing of *HaGomel*, "Who bestows good things": people who have made a dangerous journey, released prisoners, those who have recovered from serious illness, and those who have crossed the sea and reached their destination (*Berakhot* 54b). From this halakhic perspective, the psalm can be read as relating to the millions of Jews who emigrated from Eastern Europe to escape persecution, those who crossed the seas hoping to find a foreign land that would harbor them, those liberated from concentration camps, who survived unimaginable privations and an almost total destruction of body and mind – all would qualify under the halakhic criteria of *Birkat HaGomel*, those whom God has redeemed.

Yet in their biblical context, the psalm's verses can also be interpreted specifically in relation to the path of redemption that leads to the Holy Land, the return to Israel. I picture those who journeyed through the desert on foot from Yemen and Iraq; those who "came out of Egypt" and traveled over hundreds of kilometers of burning wasteland; those who walked from Ethiopia and Sudan, leaving family behind and burying loved ones on the way, striving to reach the airplanes that would cross them over the Red Sea and the Mediterranean. I see these people in the words "lost their way in desert wastelands."

STANZAS 3 AND 4 – "FOR THEY HAD REBELLED AGAINST GOD'S WORDS AND DESPISED THE COUNSEL OF THE MOST HIGH"
Stanza 3

יֹשְׁבֵי חֹשֶׁךְ וְצַלְמָוֶת, אֲסִירֵי עֳנִי וּבַרְזֶל:
כִּי־הִמְרוּ אִמְרֵי־אֵל, וַעֲצַת עֶלְיוֹן נָאָצוּ:
וַיַּכְנַע בֶּעָמָל לִבָּם, כָּשְׁלוּ וְאֵין עֹזֵר:
וַיִּזְעֲקוּ אֶל־ה' בַּצַּר לָהֶם, מִמְּצֻקוֹתֵיהֶם יוֹשִׁיעֵם:
יוֹצִיאֵם מֵחֹשֶׁךְ וְצַלְמָוֶת, וּמוֹסְרוֹתֵיהֶם יְנַתֵּק:
יוֹדוּ לַה' חַסְדּוֹ, וְנִפְלְאוֹתָיו לִבְנֵי אָדָם:
כִּי־שִׁבַּר דַּלְתוֹת נְחֹשֶׁת, וּבְרִיחֵי בַרְזֶל גִּדֵּעַ:

Some sat in darkness and the shadow of death,
cruelly bound in iron chains,
for they had rebelled against God's words
and despised the counsel of the Most High.
He humbled their hearts with hard labor;
they stumbled, and there was none to help.
Then they cried to the Lord in their trouble,
and He saved them from their distress.
He brought them out from darkness and the shadow of death
and broke open their chains.
   Let them thank the Lord for His loving-kindness
   and His wondrous deeds for humankind,
for He shattered gates of bronze and broke their iron bars. (vv. 10–16)

STANZA 4

אֱוִלִים מִדֶּרֶךְ פִּשְׁעָם, וּמֵעֲוֹנֹתֵיהֶם יִתְעַנּוּ:
כָּל־אֹכֶל תְּתַעֵב נַפְשָׁם, וַיַּגִּיעוּ עַד־שַׁעֲרֵי מָוֶת:
וַיִּזְעֲקוּ אֶל־ה' בַּצַּר לָהֶם, מִמְּצֻקוֹתֵיהֶם יוֹשִׁיעֵם:
יִשְׁלַח דְּבָרוֹ וְיִרְפָּאֵם, וִימַלֵּט מִשְּׁחִיתוֹתָם:
יוֹדוּ לַה' חַסְדּוֹ, וְנִפְלְאוֹתָיו לִבְנֵי אָדָם:
וְיִזְבְּחוּ זִבְחֵי תוֹדָה וִיסַפְּרוּ מַעֲשָׂיו בְּרִנָּה:

Some were fools with sinful ways,
and suffered affliction because of their iniquities.
They found all food repulsive,
and came close to the gates of death.
Then they cried to the Lord in their trouble,
and He saved them from their distress.
He sent His word and healed them;
He rescued them from their destruction.
Let them thank the Lord for His loving-kindness
and His wondrous deeds for humankind.
Let them sacrifice thanksgiving-offerings
and tell His deeds with songs of joy. (vv. 17–22)

In order to discover the meaning of these stanzas, we can turn to a chiastic parallelism in the central verses of the psalm. While stanzas 2 and 5 describe the journey of the ingathering of the exiles, the third and fourth stanzas depict those who did not take that path, thus remaining in exile. These central stanzas are wrought with stronger, more emphatic expressions: a "cry" (צעקה) becomes a "scream" (זעקה), "rescue" (הצלה) becomes "salvation" (ישועה) – all this, of course, in the wake of a grave crisis.

The language of the verses anticipates the horrors of the concentration camps: "darkness and the shadow of death" and "gates of death." These images were manifested in the death camps of the Nazis and the Gulag camps of the Soviet Union. These horrifying visions were foreseen by the psalmist as he wrote of those who "sat in darkness and the shadow of death, cruelly bound in iron chains." Never before have the words "They

found all food repulsive, and came close to the gates of death" been fulfilled in so gruesome a reality. Of course, the psalmist is only describing
those who survived this reality, rather than those who perished – perhaps
he could not; perhaps he did not wish to; perhaps there is a limit to the
prophetic vision of the psalms, and the psalmist could not anticipate a
holocaust of such profoundly horrific depth.[1]

There are various reasons why so few joined the redemptive return to
Zion. Many openly and consciously refused the divine summons – among
them great people who did not believe that this was, indeed, a divine summons. America had already closed its gates in the 1920's after accepting
three million Jewish immigrants, there was a belief that Arab riots "made
Palestine too dangerous for Jews," and even those anxious to make the
journey were often thwarted by the limited quotas of Jewish immigration
set by the British Mandate. Some of those who wanted to come, like my
grandfather, may his blood be avenged, were too late. My grandfather,
whose name I bear, was murdered in the Rohatyn ghetto on the day
before Shavuot eve, 1943. Few saw what was coming.

STANZA 5 – "THOSE WHO GO TO SEA IN SHIPS"

יוֹרְדֵי הַיָּם בָּאֳנִיּוֹת, עֹשֵׂי מְלָאכָה בְּמַיִם רַבִּים:
הֵמָּה רָאוּ מַעֲשֵׂי ה', וְנִפְלְאוֹתָיו בִּמְצוּלָה:
וַיֹּאמֶר, וַיַּעֲמֵד רוּחַ סְעָרָה, וַתְּרוֹמֵם גַּלָּיו:
יַעֲלוּ שָׁמַיִם, יֵרְדוּ תְהוֹמוֹת, נַפְשָׁם בְּרָעָה תִתְמוֹגָג:
יָחוֹגּוּ וְיָנוּעוּ כַּשִּׁכּוֹר, וְכָל־חָכְמָתָם תִּתְבַּלָּע:
וַיִּצְעֲקוּ אֶל־ה' בַּצַּר לָהֶם, וּמִמְּצוּקֹתֵיהֶם יוֹצִיאֵם:
יָקֵם סְעָרָה לִדְמָמָה, וַיֶּחֱשׁוּ גַּלֵּיהֶם:
וַיִּשְׂמְחוּ כִי־יִשְׁתֹּקוּ, וַיַּנְחֵם אֶל־מְחוֹז חֶפְצָם:
יוֹדוּ לַה' חַסְדּוֹ, וְנִפְלְאוֹתָיו לִבְנֵי אָדָם:
וִירֹמְמוּהוּ בִּקְהַל־עָם, וּבְמוֹשַׁב זְקֵנִים יְהַלְלוּהוּ:

---

1. "Even the holy spirit that rests on the prophets is of certain measure" (Lev. Rabba
15:2). See also Rabbi A. Y. Kook, *Orot, Orot HaTeḥiya*, 18.

Those who go to sea in ships,
plying their trade in the mighty waters,
have seen the works of the Lord,
His wondrous deeds in the deep.
He spoke and stirred up a tempest that lifted high the waves.
They rose to the heavens and plunged down to the depths;
their souls melted in misery.
They reeled and staggered like drunkards;
all their skill was to no avail.
Then they cried to the Lord in their trouble,
and He brought them out of their distress.
He stilled the storm to a whisper,
and the waves of the sea grew calm.
They rejoiced when all was quiet,
then He guided them to their destination.
    Let them thank the Lord for His loving-kindness
    and His wondrous deeds for humankind.
Let them exalt Him in the assembly of the people
and praise Him in the council of the elders. (vv. 23–32)

In this stanza, the psalmist turns back to the redeemed who are immigrating to the Land of Israel, this time via the sea. In comparison with the other stanzas, here the descriptions of distress and salvation are more numerous and extend over many verses. In the Masoretic version of the text, some of the verses of this stanza are bracketed by the letter *nun* (נ) in reverse, which according to the sages signifies a "passage that is out of place" (*Shabbat* 115b–116a). Indeed, it is as though the psalmist has taken an earlier psalm describing the salvation of seafarers and incorporated its verses into this psalm of redemption.

The distinctive features of this stanza indicates the significance that the psalmist ascribes to the seafarers' salvation. The ingathering of the exiles via the sea is unprecedented and unique to the redemption described in this psalm. While reading this stanza, one is reminded of the ships of the *Maapilim* – the illegal immigrant organizations of *Aliya Bet* – ships of redemption packed with the survivors of the camps, witnesses to the horrors of the previous verses. These ships, often built for cargo and other

purposes, were crammed instead with passengers at ten to twenty times
their intended capacity, and they sailed illegally to Israel. The British
government attempted to stop these ships and eventually put an end to
such passage.

STANZA 6 – REDEMPTION FOR A
TROUBLED LAND AND ITS PEOPLE

Those who make their way across the desert and the sea will find their
destination, the Land of Israel, to be a desolate and deserted place:

יָשֵׂם נְהָרוֹת לְמִדְבָּר, וּמֹצָאֵי מַיִם לְצִמָּאוֹן:
אֶרֶץ פְּרִי לִמְלֵחָה, מֵרָעַת יֹשְׁבֵי בָהּ:
יָשֵׂם מִדְבָּר לַאֲגַם־מַיִם, וְאֶרֶץ צִיָּה לְמֹצָאֵי מָיִם:
וַיּוֹשֶׁב שָׁם רְעֵבִים, וַיְכוֹנְנוּ עִיר מוֹשָׁב:
וַיִּזְרְעוּ שָׂדוֹת, וַיִּטְּעוּ כְרָמִים, וַיַּעֲשׂוּ פְּרִי תְבוּאָה:
וַיְבָרֲכֵם וַיִּרְבּוּ מְאֹד, וּבְהֶמְתָּם לֹא יַמְעִיט:

> He turns rivers into a desert, springs of water into parched land,
> fruitful land into a salt marsh,
>   because of the wickedness of its inhabitants.
> He turns the desert into pools of water,
> parched land into flowing springs;
> He brings the hungry to live there,
>   they build themselves a town in which to live.
> They sow fields and plant vineyards that yield a fruitful harvest;
> He blesses them, and they increase greatly,
>   their herds do not decrease. (vv. 33–38)

The stanza opens with a description of the rivers and water sources that
have dried up and become a parched desert. This stark vision recalls Mark
Twain's description in his book *Innocents Abroad*. The first immigrants to
Israel landed in a malarial wasteland of thorns and swamp. They made
the land bloom, repaired its water supplies, built communities, planted
vineyards, plowed fields, and raised animals. This was an agricultural
revolution, "*haketz hameguleh*," an indication of the beginning of redemption (see *Sanhedrin* 98a).

STANZA 7 – "THE UPRIGHT SEE AND REJOICE"

וַיִּמְעֲטוּ וַיָּשֹׁחוּ, מֵעֹצֶר רָעָה וְיָגוֹן:
שֹׁפֵךְ בּוּז עַל־נְדִיבִים, וַיַּתְעֵם בְּתֹהוּ לֹא־דָרֶךְ:
וַיְשַׂגֵּב אֶבְיוֹן מֵעוֹנִי, וַיָּשֶׂם כַּצֹּאן מִשְׁפָּחוֹת:
יִרְאוּ יְשָׁרִים וְיִשְׂמָחוּ, וְכָל־עַוְלָה קָפְצָה פִּיהָ:
מִי־חָכָם וְיִשְׁמָר־אֵלֶּה, וְיִתְבּוֹנְנוּ חַסְדֵי ה':

Though they had been few
and brought low by oppression, adversity and sorrow.
He pours contempt on nobles
and makes them wander in a pathless waste.
He lifts the destitute from poverty
and enlarges their families like flocks.
The upright see and rejoice,
but the mouth of all wrongdoers is stopped.
Whoever is wise, let him lay these things to heart,
and reflect on the loving-kindness of the Lord. (vv. 39–43)

The descriptions in this stanza are painted in broad strokes – deterioration and disaster. Once again, the Masoretic text incorporates a reversed *nun*, which, as mentioned above, signifies the possible appropriation of an earlier text. In this case, we can posit that the text in question is the Book of Job, which also features the words, "He pours contempt on nobles and makes them wander in a pathless waste." Job also complains about the corruption among the leadership, but he places the blame on God, who has allowed this situation to unfold:

To Him belong strength and insight; both deceived and deceiver are His. He leads rulers away stripped and makes fools of judges. He takes off the shackles put on by kings and ties a loincloth around their waist. He leads priests away stripped and overthrows officials long established. He silences the lips of trusted advisers and takes away the discernment of elders. *He pours contempt on nobles* and disarms the mighty. He reveals the deep things of darkness and brings utter darkness into the light. He makes nations great, and destroys them;

He enlarges nations, and disperses them. He deprives the leaders of the earth of their reason; He *makes them wander in a pathless waste.* They grope in darkness with no light; He makes them stagger like drunkards. (Job 12:16–25)

Psalm 107 highlights the verse "He pours contempt on nobles..." by surrounding it with the parallel structure of the phrases, "they had been... brought low" and "He lifts the destitute," together with "they had been few" and "enlarges their families." We all know families who are more like large tribes, whose family reunions fill halls – who are all descended from a single refugee who arrived from a war-torn Europe as the only surviving member of their family.

As a foil to the corruption of the "nobles," the psalm concludes with the praise of those "upright" and "wise" individuals, those who "see" the kindness of God and understand the obligation to thank Him.

In all my years at Yeshivat Mercaz HaRav, Rabbi Tzvi Yehuda HaKohen Kook, of blessed memory, would open his Yom HaAtzma'ut sermon with the two concluding verses of this psalm. I only understood their full significance when I studied the psalm for the first time, many years ago at Yeshivat Har Etzion in Alon Shevut. Rabbi Tzvi Yehuda would begin with an obvious question: Why does the psalmist refer to those who meditate on God's kindness as "the upright" (ישרים) and not "the righteous" (צדיקים)? His answer was based on the famous passage from the Talmud, which interprets the verse in Zechariah as referring to the righteous in the World to Come:

> Why is it written: "Who has despised the day of small things"? What causes the tables of the righteous to be despoiled in the World to Come? The smallness [of faith] which was in them, for they did not trust in the Holy One, blessed be He. (*Sota* 48b)

Rabbi Tzvi Yehuda would marvel at this verse: How can the Talmud refer to people who do not trust in God as "righteous"? Righteous people

who are not "believers"? His answer was unequivocal: indeed, there are righteous people who are not believers. There are righteous people with true virtues, people of righteous inner character, who indeed do not meditate upon God's kindness. The special individuals the psalm is referring to, the "upright," are the ones who do praise God for His goodness, even when everyone else is complaining.[2]

Rabbi Tzvi Yehuda was one of these "upright" people. On the eve of the Six-Day War, he gave a famous speech about how his soul was torn as he heard the announcement of the UN partition plan in 1947: a Jewish state would be founded, but only on part of the Land of Israel. Although he was completely devoted to the Land of Israel in its entirety, each hill and every furrow of earth, he knew how to praise God for His kindness in endowing His people with a state:

> Where is our Shekhem? How can we forget it?
> Where is our Hebron? How can we forget it?
> And where is our Jericho? How can we forget it?
> And where is our other side of the Jordan? How can we forget it?
> And where is each and every furrow of the soil of our homeland? ... I could not rejoice then.
> [Rabbi Harlap and I sat] in horrified silence, until we eventually recovered, and declared, as one: "This is the Lord's doing, it is wondrous in our eyes!"

Although he had not prayed for a state that divided the land, he understood that this was a divine decision, and rejoiced with all his being: "This is the Lord's doing, it is wondrous in our eyes." In his eulogy of Rabbi Tzvi Yehuda in Yeshivat Har Etzion, Rabbi Yehuda Amital said that many people are concerned with the Land of Israel, but one only person was concerned for the sanctity of the State of Israel – Rabbi Tzvi Yehuda.

While some upright individuals can see the kind hand of God and rejoice, others see only despair. Despair is as old as Zionism, as old as

---

2. In this context, Rabbi Tzvi Yehuda Kook would relate the words of the Netziv (Rabbi Naftali Tzvi Yehuda Berlin) in the introduction to his commentary on Genesis, that the patriarchs were "upright."

the Jewish people. It is the shadow of faith. Despair can be read in the poetry of Bialik and the writings of Brenner; in Chaim Weizmann's call, "People of Israel – Where Are You?"; in Herzl's Farewell Letter; in the mournful lyrics of Rachel Bluwstein during the famine of 1927; in the ominous, fearful reports that preceded the Six-Day War. It is no easy task to meditate upon God's kindness. Even Moses, the greatest of prophets, asked "Why have You sent me?" (Ex. 5:22), and begged God, "Please kill me" (Num. 11:15), when faced with the crises that paved the path to redemption.

Psalm 107, a song of the ingathering of exiles, is also wrought with difficulties and pain. It does not depict a rapid overnight redemption, but rather a process similar to the exodus from Egypt, which unfolded over the course of 480 years until the Temple was finally built. Nowadays, we are not experiencing a fraction of the anguish and suffering that was endured by the previous generation and the generation before that. On the fifth of Iyar, 1948, the psalmist's vision was fulfilled: for the very first time, ships were officially admitted to the docks of Haifa, ships filled with survivors of the Holocaust and refugees from all over the world. This is the vision of Psalm 107, and this is the opening of the evening prayers for Yom HaAtzma'ut, the day that commemorates the renewal of the independence of the Jewish state in the Land of Israel.

May it be God's will that we merit to sing the song of redemption, the song of the upright, to recognize and meditate upon the kindness of God.

Holiday of the Renewal of the Covenant

Rabbi Mosheh Lichtenstein

Various attempts have been made in recent years to examine the status of Yom HaAtzma'ut in order to lend it religious significance. The heart wants to sing, the soul senses the enormity of the event, but the mind insists on understanding the unique status of this day. Not surprisingly, the explanations that have been given reflect the basic spiritual outlooks of their authors. This essay will attempt to address this question by utilizing the categories drawn from the teachings of my revered grandfather, Rav Yosef Dov HaLevi Soloveitchik, *zt"l*.

WHY ESTABLISH A HOLIDAY?

In our days, as in the time of the Hasmoneans, *Am Yisrael* arose in its land as "the few against the many, the weak against the mighty." In both instances, the Almighty granted us victory over our foes in the merit of the self-sacrifice and persistence of those fighting on behalf of the Jewish

people. It would seem, therefore, that there is no need to look any further to find a basis for commemorating Yom HaAtzma'ut. Clearly, however, there is much more to the issue.

In order to examine one aspect of the religious significance of the establishment of a Jewish state in our generation, and of the festival marking this event, I would like to assess it through the prism of Ḥanukka and Purim. A close examination of the nature of these holidays will help us comprehend the meaning of Yom HaAtzma'ut.[1]

Ḥazal established for us two festivals commemorating wonders and miracles God performed for our ancestors. At first glance, the reason for the establishment of these holidays is clear. Both in Ahasuerus's Shushan and during the time of the Hellenistic monarch Antiochus, the Jews faced a very real threat to their existence. Whether the threat was directed toward their physical existence – "to destroy, kill, and eradicate young and old, children and women, on a single day" – or whether it involved spiritual persecution intended "to make them forget Your Torah and violate the statutes of Your will," in both cases harsh decrees were issued against the Jews. The nation feared for its very existence, but the Almighty intervened and rescued them from harm. This is the straightforward reading of the verses toward the end of *Megillat Esther* (9:20–28) and in the text of *Al HaNissim*, the section that is added to our prayer service on Purim. As for Ḥanukka, the historical background to this holiday is already presented in the Gemara (*Shabbat* 21b), and it adds to the events related in *Al HaNissim* the story of the miracle of the oil.

Nevertheless, the deeper meaning of Ḥanukka and Purim requires further clarification. Many miracles occurred throughout Jewish history, as recorded in both the Scriptures and the oral tradition, but we never hear of these events warranting the establishment of festivals. Are we obliged to observe a holiday to commemorate the collapse of the walls of Jericho, or the descent of crystal stones from the heavens during the time of Joshua? Neither do we find any requirement to commemorate the miracles that occurred in the Temple.

---

1. For greater detail regarding Ḥanukka and Purim, see my article, "'*VehaYamim HaEileh Nizkarim VeNaasim*' – *Pirsumei Nisa UBrit BeḤanukka VePurim*," in *Ketonet Yosef: Studies in Memory of R. Yosef Wanefsky* (New York, 2002), 236–70.

The same applies to miraculous military triumphs. Throughout history, in virtually every generation, there have been those who have arisen to destroy us, and the Almighty rescued us from their hands. Ḥanukka and Purim are far from the only instances where the Almighty fought on our behalf. Ḥazal asked in *Pesaḥim* (117a), "This *Hallel* – who [initially] recited it?" They replied, "The prophets among them established that Israel should recite it over every incident and every crisis that might befall them – when they are redeemed, they recite it over their redemption." The obligation to recite *Hallel* applies whenever God rescues us; it is not limited to Ḥanukka and Purim. But, as opposed to the obligation of *Hallel*, the establishment of a special holiday to be observed for all time occurred only twice: on Ḥanukka and Purim.

The question thus arises: If so many miracles were performed for our forefathers and no festivals were instituted in response, and if we were rescued from danger so many times without establishing a festival in commemoration, what is unique about the miracles of Ḥanukka and Purim that warranted the establishment of these holidays? In fact, we know of several occasions recorded in *Megillat Taanit* when the Jewish people were saved from danger, and *Ḥazal* commemorated these events only by forbidding eulogies and fasts on these days (see *Taanit* 17b–18b; *Rosh HaShana* 18b–19b). Although we can easily understand the prohibitions against eulogies and fasting on Ḥanukka and Purim within the framework of *Megillat Taanit*, we must still search for an explanation for the eternally binding establishment of these festivals. Seemingly, the military victory and the miracle themselves do not warrant the establishment of a *Yom Tov*.

One might suggest that in terms of the nationwide scope of the danger and the sheer magnitude of the ultimate redemption, these two events have no equal. Still, it appears that the answer to our question lies elsewhere, in a factor other than the actual miracle and salvation. These festivals are days of *brit* (covenant); the essential nature of these days relates to the covenant established between *Am Yisrael* and the Almighty. *Ḥazal* (*Shabbat* 88a) comment that *Bnei Yisrael* "accepted it [the Torah] once again during the time of Ahasuerus"; likewise, we might say that "they accepted it once again during the time of Matityahu."

PASSOVER – "I WILL TAKE YOU TO BE MY PEOPLE"

To further develop this notion, let us turn our attention to Passover, the first of all the festivals. Here, too, the holiday does not serve to commemorate the miracles that occurred at the Sea of Reeds, but rather involves the election of Israel and the covenant established between them and God. This becomes clear from an examination of the four "expressions of redemption" God uses when promising to release the Jewish people from bondage:

> Say, therefore, to the Children of Israel: I am the Lord. I will free (*vehotzeiti*) you from the labors of the Egyptians and deliver (*vehitzalti*) you from their bondage. I will redeem (*vegaalti*) you with an outstretched arm and through extraordinary chastisements. And I will take (*velakaḥti*) you to be My people, and I will be your God. And you shall know that I, the Lord, am your God who freed you from the labors of the Egyptians. (Ex. 6:6–7)

God informs Moses not only of the release from bondage and the yoke of the Egyptian slavery (*vehotzeiti, vehitzalti, vegaalti*), but also of Israel's election as the Almighty's nation (*velakaḥti*). These two promises involve two different, intrinsically unrelated concepts. The Israelites could have become the chosen nation without achieving freedom, and, conversely, God could have freed them without designating them as His people. In assessing the nature of Passover, we must determine which of these motifs forms the basis of the various mitzvot performed on this festival.

It would appear that the festival stems primarily from the nation's entry into the covenant and their election as God's people – the realization of "*velakaḥti*." The Children of Israel left Egypt on the morning of the fifteenth of Nissan, but their rescue was not complete until seven days later, when Pharaoh and his army drowned at sea. Yet *Am Yisrael's* election and entry into a covenant with God occurred on the night of the fifteenth. They placed upon their doorframes the covenantal blood of the Paschal Lamb and performed the other mitzvot associated with the paschal offering that night, even before their departure from Egypt. These mitzvot thus result not from the nation's freedom from Egypt, but rather from the covenant. Herein lies the importance and centrality of

the paschal offering, and this is what renders the obligation to recall the exodus, one of the fundamental aspects of Judaism. *Am Yisrael*'s entry into the covenant, rather than their freedom, lends this event its singular importance.[2]

The essential nature of the festivals involves the relationship established between man and God, and the fact that man comes to the Temple on the festival to stand before God. This closeness between man and God lies at the heart of the *yamim tovim*. Thus, Sukkot, which does not commemorate any rescue or salvation, but rather represents our closeness with God, is included among the festivals; conversely, other days when the Jews were saved from calamity did not become national holidays.

Several halakhic factors express this principle. First, the three pilgrimage festivals are inextricably bound with sacrificial offerings. In fact, one could say that the purpose of these three festivals is the bringing of offerings and appearing before God in the Temple courtyard. Therefore, particular significance is afforded even to sacrificing voluntary offerings on these holidays (see Lev. 23:37–8, Num. 29:39). Sacrifice both creates and expresses a condition of standing before God, which gives the day festive status; and festive status creates and expresses a condition of standing before God, which mandates offerings. These are two sides of the same coin.

The status of the *kohen gadol* with respect to the laws of mourning also testifies to the connection between the sanctity of the festivals and the concept of standing before God. The straightforward reading of the Gemara in *Moed Katan* (14b) indicates that a *kohen gadol* does not observe the mourning laws upon the death of a relative because for him, every day has the status of a festival. Needless to say, the "festival" observed by a *kohen gadol* every day throughout the year cannot possibly relate to the

---

2. In truth, both aspects of Passover – the salvation from slavery and the election as God's people – come to dual expression in many of the mitzvot of Passover. One may distinguish, in this vein, between the offering of the paschal sacrifice and its consumption; the two openings of the Haggada: "We were slaves" and "Our ancestors were idolaters"; differing aspects of *ḥametz* and matza (see R. Yose HaGelili's opinion on the paschal sacrifice in Egypt, *Pesaḥim* 28b, and *Tosafot Pesaḥim* 36b s.v. *mei peirot*); and other elements that we cannot discuss here.

exodus from Egypt and *Am Yisrael*'s rescue from crisis. Rather, the festive status of the *kohen gadol* stems from the fact that he constantly stands before God, and his daily existence thus resembles the rest of the nation's experience during the three pilgrimage festivals.[3]

ḤANUKKA AND PURIM

In light of all this, we may argue that the primary theme of Ḥanukka and Purim, too, relates not to the actual miracle or rescue from danger, but rather to the accompanying *brit*. What sets these two events apart from other instances of salvation is that they also featured the establishment of a covenant between *Am Yisrael* and the Almighty. On these two occasions, there arose the need for a renewed covenant due to a challenge posed to the initial covenant of Sinai, calling into question its ongoing validity.

Both Ḥanukka and Purim mark historic turning points when *Am Yisrael* confronted new, unfamiliar circumstances that led them to question the significance of the covenant of Sinai. The Purim story concerns the nation's encounter with exile. In the wake of the Temple's destruction and the Jews' exile to Babylonia, a school of thought developed that viewed the initial covenant as null and void. This resulted primarily from the reality of exile itself and the sense among many that the exile reflected God's annulment of the covenant.[4] Quite possibly, many among

---

3. The Rav *zt"l*, explaining the obligation of rejoicing on the festivals, developed the connection between the festivals and the experience of standing before God by analyzing the Gemara's discussion of mourning on the festivals. See his *UVikkashtem MiSham*, second half of note 19 [*And From There You Shall Seek* (Jersey City, 2008), 195–98].

4. See *Sifrei*, Num. 15:41: "What is taught by the repetition of the words, 'I am the Lord your God'? It is so that Israel shall not say, 'Why did the Almighty issue to us the commandments? Is it not for us to perform them and receive reward? Then we will not perform them and we will not receive reward!' It is just as Israel said to Ezekiel, as it is written, 'Certain elders came to me…and sat down before me' (Ezek. 20:1). They said to him, 'Ezekiel, if a slave is sold by his master, does he not leave his possession?' He said to them, 'Yes.' They said to him, 'Since the Almighty has sold us to the nations of the world, we have left His possession.' He said to them, 'If a slave's master sold him on condition that he would return, does he leave his possession?' [As it is written,] 'And what you have in mind shall never come to pass – when you say: We will be like the nations, like the families of the lands,

the nation held the pagan belief that God's domain was limited to the Land of Israel, and thus the covenant no longer applied once the Jews left.

Ezekiel fought against these beliefs even in the first generation of the exile, but the phenomenon spread and became further entrenched, to the point where, during the time of Ahasuerus, the nation almost abrogated the covenant completely. A new generation arose in Shushan that never knew the Land of Israel. The people's dislocation from its land now combined with the modern, cosmopolitan society of Shushan, which warmly welcomed the Jews as equal citizens. A new theory now spread throughout the Jewish community, claiming that the Torah may have well suited their lives in the old country, in the traditional society led by *kohanim* and prophets, when they were surrounded on all sides by cruel, pagan nations. But in the modern, liberal, technologically advanced empire of Persia, the Torah lifestyle, which sets the Jews apart from the rest of society, has no place. The new reality, they claimed, warranted assimilation and acculturation, which necessarily entailed an abrogation of the Sinaitic covenant.

Mordecai and Esther worked to reaffirm the covenant in opposition to these claims. The old man Mordecai, a Jerusalemite driven to Babylon by Nebuchadnezzar, and Esther, a young woman born in Persia and fully integrated in Persian culture while remaining committed to Torah, joined forces to affirm the validity and relevance of the covenant in all places, at all times. Not only did a war against the Jews' enemies erupt in Shushan, but a far more essential drama unfolded, as well: the reaffirmation of the covenant and its application to Jewish life in exile. The primary theme of Purim is the rejection of the process of assimilation and the renewed acceptance of the covenant of the Torah: "They accepted it once again during the time of Ahasuerus" (*Shabbat* 88b). Thus, we commemorate on Purim not only our miraculous salvation from Haman's plan to destroy the Jews, but also the renewal of the covenant in the face of the spiritual danger of total assimilation.

Whereas Purim marks the first encounter with exile, which resulted in the claim of the covenant's irrelevance to exilic reality, Ḥanukka marks the

---

worshipping wood and stone. As I live – declares the Lord God – I will reign over you with a strong hand, and with an outstretched arm, and with overflowing fury' (Ezek. 20:32–33)."

challenge stemming from the Jews' first encounter with secular wisdom. The Jews' exposure to Greek-Hellenistic culture was their first contact with a highly sophisticated international cultural system. Here, too, a movement arose that argued for the adoption of the Greeks' cultural achievements at the expense of the Sinaitic covenant. As was the case in Shushan, the proponents of assimilation did not necessarily deny the Torah's significance to previous generations. They rather questioned the need for its observance after the Jews' exposure to the wisdom of the nations.

We might describe their argument as follows: So long as *Bnei Yisrael* were surrounded by pagan "barbarians" (as the Greeks called the pagans), the Torah helped them progress morally and culturally beyond the other ancient peoples. It effectively achieved the goal it set for itself: to keep the Jews away from the abominable practices of the surrounding nations and have them live a more noble existence. But the Torah was necessary only when the alternative was Canaanite culture, before the Jews were introduced to the sophisticated scholarship of the Greeks. Once, however, Greek philosophy and culture infiltrated into the Land of Israel, the Jews no longer had any need for the Torah and a relationship with the God of Israel.

Matityahu and his sons, like Mordecai and Esther in Persia, waved the banner of the renewal of the covenant. They triggered a process of reaffirmation of the *brit*'s relevance to the new and changing circumstances that the Jews now confronted.

It turns out, then, that on Ḥanukka, too, we celebrate both the triumph of the few over the many, as well as the renewal of the covenant in the time of Matityahu. We have thus answered our question of why we celebrate the miracle of Ḥanukka but do not observe a festival to commemorate other miracles. The festival of Ḥanukka is a festival of the *brit*, rather than a festival of a miracle. On Ḥanukka we commemorate not the miracle per se, but rather the reaffirmation of the covenant that accompanied it.

To explain the function of the miracle within the framework of the covenant, we must take note of the basic difference between the covenants established in the times of Mordecai and Matityahu, on the one hand, and the covenant of Sinai, on the other. The covenant of Sinai began, as did the Exodus, with the Almighty summoning the Children

of Israel to become His people. When *Am Yisrael* encamp at the foot of Mount Sinai, God says to Moses: "Now then, if you will obey Me faithfully and keep My covenant, you shall be My treasured possession among all the peoples. Indeed, all the earth is Mine, but you shall be to Me a kingdom of priests and a holy nation" (Ex. 19:5–6). The Torah then continues, "Moses came and summoned the elders of the people and put before them all that the Lord had commanded him. All the people answered as one, saying, 'All that the Lord has spoken we will do.' And Moses brought back the people's words to the Lord" (Ex. 19:7–8). God initiates this covenant by turning to the Children of Israel and inviting them to establish this *brit*. Ḥazal extend this notion even further with the famous image of God suspending the mountain over the Children of Israel, as if forcing the covenant upon them (*Shabbat* 88a).

In Shushan and Modi'in, by contrast, the covenant was established by the people's initiative, rather than by God's. As it was the nation who initially sought to abrogate the covenant, the renewal of the covenant likewise had to come from them. Esther's call, "Go and assemble!" and Matityahu's cry of "Who is for the Lord – follow me!" and the nation's positive response, constitute the renewal and reaffirmation of the covenant with God. The miracle in both cases served as a signal from above that the Almighty accepted their initiative and joined in a covenant with them. In other words, the miracle was the pipeline through which the Almighty conveyed His positive response to the nation's invitation that He re-establish His covenant with them.[5]

RENEWAL OF *BRIT AVOT*

Until now, everything I said was based upon an analysis of sources, either from the Tanakh or Ḥazal, and I relied upon these sources in reaching conclusions. However, I approach this next section, an attempt to understand the events of more recent times, with fear and trembling. In

---

5. The question of whether the laws in *Megillat Taanit* applying to Ḥanukka and Purim are still binding revolves around the question of whether Ḥanukka and Purim nowadays are strictly celebrations of the covenant, or whether they continue to mark the nation's salvation as well. See my article (referred to above, note 1), "*VehaYamim HaEileh*," 257–59.

this undertaking, one can no longer rely on scriptural texts or Ḥazal's authority, but rather only on one's best judgment. I hope and pray that I will neither stumble nor err in this analysis, especially in light of the particular gravity of the topic at hand.

Over the course of over two millennia of exile and encounters with foreign peoples, these two covenants of Ḥanukka and Purim sufficed as the basis of our nation's existence in the Diaspora. They allowed us to withstand every upheaval in every time and place, and no new festivals were established. One generation followed another, and we enjoyed the secure support of the covenants of Ḥanukka and Purim.

However, in the first half of the twentieth century, as a result of the historical and spiritual conditions that came into being, the covenant between Israel and our Father in Heaven once again faced existential danger. The days of Shushan and Modi'in returned. The relevance of the previous covenants was put to the test, and the need arose once again to reaffirm the *brit*. As in the earlier instances, now too a process of the covenant's renewal became necessary in response to the new forces that threatened to destroy it.

The first challenge to the covenant came from the secularist movement and the widespread abandonment of the Torah that came upon us like a tidal wave in the twentieth century.[6] True, the encounter with "enlightenment" and general culture is the theme of Ḥanukka, and thus no renewal of the covenant was necessary for the encounter itself – but this time, the results of the encounter were far more widespread. As opposed to the time of the Hasmoneans, this period witnessed a process of abrogation of the covenant by an enormous percentage of the nation. Throughout the generations, our nation has never seen a situation of such widespread neglect of the covenant of Sinai. Without trying to determine

6. I discuss here the events of the early twentieth century, and not the nineteenth century, when the process began to unfold, because my interest here is in the covenant between Israel and God, and not the process of secularization itself. The significant point is not the beginning of the process, when secularization was the lot of only certain influential individuals and groups, but rather the stage at which secularization became a widespread phenomenon and a dominant force. In any event, the precise date is not important for our purposes.

the scope of Torah observance in earlier generations, suffice it to say that a situation where public debate and the basic axioms of Jewish society are entirely detached from Jewish tradition, as the Torah is perceived to be the possession of a small minority of the nation, is unique to modern times.

The cries of the Jews who remained loyal to Torah fell upon deaf ears, and their efforts were largely to no avail. As secularization continued to intensify, the fear of the Jewish people's complete abrogation of the Torah, as well as of the Almighty's rejection of His nation, became ever more real. The Jewish people's connection to God – and its very identity as a nation – was in danger of being lost. Indeed, to our great sorrow, various ideologies emerged that encouraged this end.

And so, the Jewish people once again confronted a situation that endangered the *brit*; therefore, they faced the dire need for the reaffirmation of its significance even in the modern era. Thankfully, in spite of the unprecedented wave of secularization, *Am Yisrael* did not lose its identity; the connection between the Jew and his Judaism did not disappear, and *Am Yisrael* did not entirely assimilate amid the gentile nations. The covenant was reinstated through the Zionist movement. Of course, it was not the Sinaitic covenant, *brit Sinai*, that Zionism reaccepted; unfortunately, the Zionism of Herzl, Weizmann, and Ben-Gurion did not return to the covenant of Sinai or make any attempt to revive it. Rather, Zionism brought back to life the covenant of the patriarchs, *brit avot*.

The sanctity of *Am Yisrael* and its connection to God rests upon two pillars: the covenant of the patriarchs and the covenant of Sinai. The first focuses on our national identity as *Am Yisrael* and is based upon God's promise to Abraham: "I will uphold My covenant between Me and you, and your offspring to come, as an everlasting covenant throughout the ages, to be God to you and to your offspring to come. I assign the land you sojourn in to you and your offspring to come, all the land of Canaan, as an everlasting holding, and I will be their God" (Gen. 17:7–8). The second covenant relates to the acceptance of the Torah and was conveyed to our forefathers at Sinai, in the verses cited earlier: "Now then, if you will obey Me faithfully and keep My covenant, you shall be My treasured possession among all the peoples. Indeed, all the earth is Mine, but you shall be to Me a kingdom of priests and a holy nation" (Ex. 19:5–6). Through our return

to the land and newfound connection to our Jewish past, the covenant of the patriarchs was reinstated. Obviously, Zionism did not invent the notion of the *brit avot* or give birth to the concept of connecting with the Jewish past. Just as the historic and religious efforts of Mordecai and Esther, of Matityahu and Judah Maccabee, did not invent any new covenant but rather reaffirmed the old covenant under new circumstances, so too we may credit Zionism with a similar achievement. Under new historical and spiritual conditions, it renewed the status of *Am Yisrael* as a nation with a past, present, and future, as a single national entity. It thereby reinstated the covenant of the patriarchs in the new realities of the modern era.

Let us not underestimate this monumental accomplishment. National identity is under assault in a cosmopolitan world. Liberalism and rationalism encourage individualism, not national identity; the more liberal the approach, the more the element of national identity fades away (and often disappears altogether). Communism similarly pointed to economic status as the sole means of identity, thereby eliminating the national component, as it called to all workers in the world to unite at the expense of their national identities. In a world in which all these "isms" operated simultaneously and won the enthusiastic approval of large segments of the Jewish people, the emphasis on the unity and singularity of *Am Yisrael* as a nation indeed qualifies as a renewal of the covenant.

To this we must add a second component, as well: the land. "I will remember My covenant with Jacob; I will remember also My covenant with Isaac, and also My covenant with Abraham; and I will remember the land" (Lev. 26:42). In addressing Jewish national identity, the covenant of the patriarchs is inextricably bound to the land.[7] The return to the land and its redemption from other peoples marked a significant historic shift from the previous millennia of exile. The Jews once again could live as a nation; the descendants of Abraham no longer needed to live in isolated pockets, but rather as a nation dwelling in its homeland. If the relocation from Jerusalem to Shushan necessitated a renewal of the covenant due to the new reality, then the return to Jerusalem likewise

7. See Rabbi Joseph B. Soloveitchik, *Ḥamesh Derashot* (Jerusalem, 1974), 90–92.

requires reestablishing the covenant in light of the new reality – the ingathering of the exiles.

True, the value of *brit avot* in the absence of Torah is hardly self-evident. After all, the covenant with Abraham is geared toward the establishment of a nation that observes the Torah and exemplifies its values, as the Torah explicitly testifies: "For I have singled him out, that he may instruct his children and his posterity to keep the way of the Lord by doing what is just and right" (Gen. 18:19). Perhaps, then, we cannot speak at all about this covenant's renewal without "keeping the way of the Lord," and we therefore cannot acknowledge any meaningful shift from the past in the abstract national identity championed by the Zionist movement. Indeed, many leading rabbis disregarded the Zionist enterprise entirely, on the assumption that we can afford no religious significance to a Jewish identity that lacks Torah.

However, Religious Zionism and its thinkers came along and asserted the religious significance of national Jewish identity. Isaiah's prophecy (44:5), "One shall say, 'I am the Lord's'; another shall use the name of Jacob," was perceived as representative of two basic, independently valuable principles. Identifying oneself with "Jacob" is of intrinsic significance, even if we do not perceive some underlying, unbeknownst yearning for the covenant of Sinai on the part of the secular community, and even without acknowledging a deep, concealed desire for the world of Torah and mitzvot.[8] Religious Zionism saw in national identity itself a meaningful religious quality. The bond between the nation and its land is an outgrowth of the covenant with Abraham, and this covenant is confirmed and continued by his descendants who return to their land. Specifically due to the abandonment of the covenant of Sinai, the covenant of the patriarchs now took on even greater meaning and importance.

---

8. Maimonides, in his responsum to Ovadya the proselyte (*Teshuvot HaRambam*, Blau edition, responsum 293), indeed interprets this verse as expressing two principles. However, he took this in a somewhat different direction, emphasizing the convert's status as one who "calls in the name of God," rather than highlighting that there are Jews whose identity derives solely from their attachment to Jacob.

THE HOLOCAUST AND THE COVENANT

The prophet Jeremiah writes in one of his most celebrated prophecies:

> Thus said the Lord: The people who escaped from the sword found favor in the wilderness, when Israel was marching toward tranquility.... Again you shall plant vineyards on the hills of Samaria; men shall plant and live to enjoy them. For the day is coming when watchmen shall proclaim on the heights of Ephraim: Come, let us go up to Zion, to the Lord our God....
>
> I will bring them in from the north land, gather them from the ends of the earth – the blind and the lame among them, those with child and those in labor – in a vast throng they shall return here. They shall come with weeping, and with compassion will I guide them. I will lead them to streams of water, by a level road where they will not stumble. For I am ever a Father to Israel; Ephraim is My firstborn.
>
> Hear the word of the Lord, O nations, and tell it in the isles afar. Say: He who scattered Israel will gather them and will guard them as a shepherd his flock. For the Lord will ransom Jacob, redeem him from one too strong for him. They shall come and shout on the heights of Zion, radiant over the bounty of the Lord – over new grain and wine and oil, and over sheep and cattle. They shall fare like a watered garden; they shall never languish again. Then shall maidens dance gaily, young men and old alike. I will turn their mourning to joy; I will comfort them and cheer them in their grief. I will give the priests their fill of fatness, and My people shall enjoy My full bounty, declares the Lord....
>
> Thus said the Lord: Restrain your voice from weeping, your eyes from shedding tears. For there is a reward for your labor, declares the Lord: they shall return from the enemy's land. And there is hope for your future, declares the Lord: your children shall return to their country. (Jer. 31:1–16)

Underlying these famous verses is the basic assumption that there is religious significance and value to finding "tranquility" for the "people who escaped from the sword." Bringing the survivors to their homeland amidst crying and compassion, leading them to streams of life-giving waters, as they enjoy the full bounty of God – all these are objectives proclaimed by

the Almighty through His prophets. The message of comfort delivered by Jeremiah, the prophet of the destruction, is, first and foremost, "Jacob shall again have calm and quiet with none to trouble him" (Jer. 30:10).

The very reality of a tranquil existence, accompanied by joy and consolation, constitutes a religious value, for two reasons. First, granting respite and calm to an embittered, depressed soul, and relieving it of its troubles, involves concern for the suffering and misfortune of others – a form of *gemilut ḥasadim* that the Almighty performs for His creatures. *Ḥazal* remarked that "the Torah begins with kindness and ends with kindness" (*Sota* 14a), and they enumerate many expressions of God's kindness (clothing Adam and Eve, visiting Abraham when he was ailing, comforting Isaac after his father's death, and burying Moses).

Second, the "bounty of the Lord" contains within it the message that the Almighty has not dissociated Himself from His people. They should never conclude in light of the calamities that befall them that He has forsaken them and rejected them. The prophet describes here not merely mercy and compassion one feels toward strangers, but rather a parent's affection for his child: "For I am ever a Father to Israel; Ephraim is My firstborn."

We learn from Jeremiah's prophecy that had the State of Israel come into being only to provide "tranquility" for the Holocaust survivors – this reason alone would have sufficed. Had they merely come to the land and seen the fulfillment of the promise, "I will turn their mourning to joy; I will comfort them and cheer them from their grief," this itself would have justified the state's existence from a religious perspective and rendered its establishment a meaningful event and the fulfillment of Jeremiah's prophecy.[9] Just as *Ḥazal* linked this prophecy to the story of the *Akeda*

---

9. I have been told that my grandfather, Rav Soloveitchik *zt"l*, emphasized a similar point by citing other verses that underscore this notion in an especially striking manner. As he banged on the table, the Rav cited the following verses from II Kings (14:23–28) and applied them to David Ben-Gurion:

In the fifteenth year of King Amazia son of Joash of Judah, King Jeroboam son of Joash of Israel became king in Shomron – for forty-one years. He did what was displeasing to the Lord; he did not depart from all the sins that Jeroboam son of Nebat had caused Israel to commit. It was he who restored the territory of Israel from Levo Chamat to the sea of the Arava, in accordance with the promise that the Lord, the God of Israel, had made through His servant,

by designating it as the *haftara* for the second day of Rosh HaShana, so may we draw an association between these words of consolation and the many "*akedot*" our generation has experienced.

But this does not explain the full religious significance of the establishment of the state with respect to the years of horror and destruction that preceded it. The connection between the Holocaust and the establishment of the Jewish state is much deeper than simply the granting of tranquility to those who escaped from the sword. It relates not merely to a respite for the survivors, but to the renewal of the covenant that was threatened by this unthinkable tragedy. In the last section, we pointed to secularization as the first factor that threatened the covenant in the modern era. The second factor that brought into question the continued validity of the covenant was the Holocaust. I refer not to the theological problem of evil, but rather to the existential sense that we were totally abandoned by God, resulting from our false hopes for salvation and unanswered pleas for mercy.[10] The feeling of helplessness in the face of the arrogant, ruthless legions of evil yielded a sense of complete detachment between the Almighty and His world. The silence of the King of kings as the enemy slaughtered His people brought about serious doubts concerning His relationship to the world and to His nation.[11]

---

the prophet Jonah son of Amittai from Gat-Ḥefer. For the Lord saw the very bitter plight of Israel ... and with none to help Israel. And the Lord resolved not to blot out the name of Israel from under heaven; and He delivered them through Jeroboam son of Joash. The other events of Jeroboam's reign, and all his actions and exploits, how he fought and recovered Damascus and Ḥamat for Judah in Israel, are recorded in the Annals of the King of Israel.

10. By no means do I intend to belittle the theological problem; rather, I do not view it as a focal point of our discussion, for two reasons. First, I believe that in most instances, the presentation of organized, structured reflections and fully developed theological analyses occurred only after enough time had elapsed to allow the events to be digested and there was enough geographic distance to allow disconnection from the dread and terror. The initial confrontation occurred on the existential level, not the theological level. Second, I am not certain that the theological discussion would yield different results from the classic answers given to explain evil throughout the ages, whatever they may be.

11. Thus, for example, Simon Wiesenthal spoke of his sense that God was "on leave" as an obvious, existential truth in his life at that time. See his book *The Sunflower* (New York, 1976), 7–9.

It hardly would have surprised us had the survivors scattered through-out the earth and distanced themselves as far as possible from places where Jews face danger. Considering the ordeal they had endured, we would have accepted this decision sympathetically. Had they washed away their Jewish identity rather than fought for it, we most certainly would have viewed this as a natural response to the unspeakable suffering they had experienced. Their mere return to normal life and building families would have represented to us the failure of the plot devised by our foes, and the survivors' triumph over the oppressors. The understandable desire to live peaceful lives and enjoy a "normal" existence after the years of horror would have very likely scattered the Jewish people throughout the world among the gentiles.

We might have expected the feeling of abandonment and neglect by God, combined with the desire for tranquility and normalcy, to cause the Jewish people to distance themselves from Jewish identity.[12] Such a response would have endangered the covenant. If the covenant with the patriarchs formed the single thread connecting *Am Yisrael* to God in the wake of the wave of secularization that overcame the nation, then the loss of this covenant, of Jewish identity, would have meant our complete detachment from the Almighty, Heaven forbid.

But this is not what happened. Rather than scatter to the four corners of the earth, to remote lands whose inhabitants had never heard of the Jewish people, many survivors headed specifically toward the Land of the Patriarchs. Unfortunately, these survivors were not greeted by the joy of grain, wine, and oil, but rather by a bloody war. Among the fallen heroes of Kfar Etzion were survivors of the ghettos; the battalion that fought at Latrun included former concentration camp inmates. Through this remarkable display of self-sacrifice, they reaffirmed the relevance of the

---

12. Rabbi Yona Immanuel *zt"l*, a Holocaust survivor, recounts how in the summer of 1945 he heard missionaries use this very argument – with unparalleled gall – in their efforts to prey on the souls of survivors and lead them away from Judaism: "The priests were especially interested in sick Jewish patients. They helped them and tried to influence them to convert to Christianity, saying, 'You've suffered enough'; 'You deserve to live more serene lives'...'Here we offer you everything – studies and a secure future'..." (*Yesupar LeDor* [Jerusalem, 1994], 188).

covenant and their connection to *Am Yisrael* and its heritage, in spite of all they had been through.

The self-sacrifice of the Holocaust survivors joined with the selfless devotion of the population in Eretz Yisrael, who fought for the land and thereby reinstated the covenant whose validity had been challenged by secularization and persecution. Just as the Jews of Shushan and Modi'in renewed their commitment to the *brit*, so did a similar renewal occur throughout the Land of Israel when the Jewish state was declared. Its significance, then, and the significance of Yom HaAtzma'ut which commemorates this event, extends beyond the specific achievement of establishing a national entity in the land of our fathers, or a national home for the Jewish people. Its significance stems from the reinstating of the covenant of the patriarchs in the modern world. We might add that even in the Diaspora, the establishment of the State of Israel brought about a revival of Jewish identity or, in other words, a revival of the *brit avot*.

This renewal of the covenant, more than anything else, lends meaning and significance to Yom HaAtzma'ut and turns it into an exalted day of celebration. What lies at the heart of this festival is neither the establishment of the national entity nor the claims of the beginning of the redemption ("the footsteps of the Messiah"), but rather the renewal of the covenant on the part of the founding generation of the State of Israel.

But our discussion cannot end here. First, we must address the famous distinction drawn by my teacher and grandfather, Rav Soloveitchik *zt"l*, between two aspects of the covenant: *brit goral* (covenant of fate) and *brit yi'ud* (covenant of destiny).[13] The former refers to a historical reality forced upon one, whereas the latter describes one's conscious decision to accept this reality and lend it meaning. Undoubtedly, many among the founding generation of 1948 perceived these events as a result of the *brit goral*. But it is equally certain that many, many others looked upon this historical reality as their *yi'ud* – their willingly chosen destiny. They expressed this by their willingness to sacrifice their lives. It is perhaps this self-sacrifice that establishes the founding of the state as a conscious acceptance of the *brit avot*, in whose merit we were deserving of national revival.[14]

---

13. He develops this idea most famously in his work *Kol Dodi Dofek*.
14. These words continue to be relevant as we face new waves of deadly violence. Likewise, the challenge to transform fate to destiny is among our most important tasks today.

Second, despite the equation drawn above between Ḥanukka and Purim, on the one hand, and Yom HaAtzma'ut, on the other, one critical and painful distinction remains: namely, the connection to the covenant of the Torah. We can speak all we want in praise of the covenant of the patriarchs, but we may never overlook the absence of the most basic point of connection between the Almighty and His creatures. There is a clear difference between Shushan and Modi'in, when a rabbinic scholar from the Sanhedrin or a *kohen gadol* led the nation to a renewed acceptance of the Torah, and the modern State of Israel, where the secular political leadership, however infused with Jewish identity, has no ambition of affirming the covenant of Sinai, but rather chooses to ignore it.[15] The second half of the renewed covenant still awaits us, the moment when we will have the privilege of declaring in unison, as one person with a single heart, Ruth's timeless words: "Your nation is my nation, and your God is my God!"

---

15. Neither can we ignore the fact that we have witnessed over recent years an unfortunate decline in commitment to the covenant of the patriarchs, the connection to the Land of Israel, and so on. This might be the result of our particular historical circumstances, or perhaps the covenant of the patriarchs cannot last long without being connected to Torah. In any case, as the connection to *brit Avot* weakens, the covenant of Torah becomes even more essential.

Yom HaAtzma'ut: Personal Reflections on Diaspora Observance

Dr. Erica Brown

Celebrating Israel's Independence Day in the Diaspora is a little bit like making a birthday party where the guest of honor fails to show up. It cannot be otherwise. If the commemoration takes place at a distance – if you are not physically in Israel – then the larger piece of the national equation will, by definition, be compromised. Having said that, it is important to acknowledge that some Diaspora communities and Jewish organizations – synagogues, JCCs, and youth groups – are better at making it a holiday than others, and a few moments of reflection on "best practices" may stimulate the development of more positive and content-rich programs and experiences. Such reflection may also lead to a larger conversation specifically about Religious Zionism outside of Israel and the tenuous and sometimes dangerous relationship between religion and nationalism.

MARKING INDEPENDENCE IN ISRAEL

Independence Day celebrations are relatively new for many countries. Our globe has changed radically in the past century. After World War II, many European countries relinquished political power over their colonies across Asia and Africa. Thirty-four new countries have been placed on world maps since 1990. In a list of over two hundred countries that celebrate an independence day annually, most – like Israel – were established in the twentieth century, and most of those in the second half of the century. There are a few outliers. Portugal has commemorated its independence day on December 1 since 1640. Swedish celebrations on June 6 have been marked since 1523. Japan is among the earliest, dating all the way back to 660 BCE. Most countries have much later dates because the establishment of independent statehood is a relatively modern concept.

According to Benedict Anderson, author of *Imagined Communities*, countries establish such dates in part because they need to mark a boundary not only in place but also in time. Determining a calendar date to mark independence gives a polity or political entity the status of a country among the family of nations, a place free from the tyranny of military occupation or persecution, set apart from surrounding countries, distinct, unique, and worthy of note. For most countries, independence is a function of internationally recognized boundaries and an organized economy and currency. It implies formal and structural oversight of education, transportation, and other public services and utilities, security and protection for its inhabitants, some aspects of culture, and – most importantly – independent and unchallenged sovereignty. The achievement of such practical and lofty goals should not go unnoticed by its citizens.

A date to celebrate independence may be chosen because it marks an event of broad and obvious national significance, or it may be more arbitrary. The date's importance may simply lie in the virtue of establishing a calendar presence and a holiday, to embed in the consciousness of its citizens a growing sense of belonging, the baby steps on the road to nationhood. Often such days are fraught with controversy, and Israel's day of independence is no exception; competing national narratives can make one person's celebration into another's day of mourning, as is the case in modern-day Israel.

For us as Jews, who characterize commitment through a powerful meld of faith, culture, history, language, ritual, and ethnicity, establishing our own independence day is not a statement of newness as a people but the adding of another layer – a national presence – to an already rich identity. Obviously, Israel Independence Day – Yom HaAtzma'ut – should be an occasion featuring communal events and celebrations of joy and substance along a nationalist theme. Beyond barbeques, car flags, special TV shows, fireworks, and plastic hammers, Israel uses a host of events to give the day meaning. Many IDF bases are open to the public. Israel's president opens his home to honor 120 outstanding soldiers, and there is an official ceremony the night of Independence Day on Mount Herzl. Twelve torches are lit, one for each of the twelve tribes, taking a modern occasion and extending its reach back across the sands of time to the Israelites' earliest wilderness days. The Israel Prize, Israel's most important civilian honor, is also awarded on Yom HaAtzma'ut.

These national rituals showcase Israel's achievements and heroes, its important current national sites, and its nod to history, as if to say that we may have achieved statehood in 1948 but we became a people long before. Perhaps the most outward way this is achieved is through the *Ḥidon HaTanakh*, the famous Bible Contest open to teenagers across the globe, which is held every Yom HaAtzma'ut. The tie-in of the day to mastery of the Bible is not accidental. It roots modern Israel in its most ancient references in a sacred text that has transcended time; in a sweep of succession, it suggests that children are both the inheritors of this magnificent enterprise and the future leaders who will emerge from pages of old to take on the contemporary challenges of statehood, armed with song and verse.

All of this activity is truncated in the Diaspora and often pitifully reduced to slight changes in the prayer service, among those who pray at all. Jewish day schools and congregational schools of the Zionist ilk may dress the halls with flags and pictures and dress themselves in blue and white, but the sense of national pride and the day as a platform for events of significance are, of course, not the norm. It is one of the days – a day among a host of days – where celebrating in the Diaspora feels like reading a postcard from a close friend who longs for your presence: "Wish you were here."

THE VOID IN COMMEMORATION

This raises an honest dilemma for Jewish educators and Jewish organizations. If one fails to celebrate Yom HaAtzma'ut in the Diaspora out of ideological differences, laziness, or lack of creativity, it is a slap in the face to this transformational turning point in the development of our people; it is a diminishment of the spiritual and national center that Israel is for world Jewry, whether as relief and refuge, or as the place where Jews can express their Judaism fully and autonomously. If, on the other hand, one does mark the day while living in another country, how can the national element be appropriately marked in the absence of a state-wide focus? An Israeli friend who was teaching for a few years in an American Jewish day school told me he laughed when some teachers walked in on Yom HaAtzma'ut wearing *kova'ei tembel* (Israeli kibbutz-style hats) and serving falafel balls. "We mostly eat shawarma now, and no one would be caught dead in one of those hats," he insisted. Is it possible that outside Israel we have frozen time to a period of Zionism that feels more idealistic, nostalgic, and comfortable, but that to an Israeli would seem stale or even foreign?

Outside of Israel, those who regard themselves as Religious Zionists have an additional particular challenge. While I annually attend a beautiful and meaningful Yom HaAtzma'ut celebration in our area day school and am always moved, I am also struck by how the prayer service feels hollow, a hodgepodge of *tefillot* pulled from a variety of holidays across the Jewish calendar year. This imposter service seems to miss entirely the vastness and complexity of what modern Israel has come to be in the religious mind-set, where it is no longer a mythic aspiration but a real place with its politics and its controversies, its share of domestic and foreign woes, and its immense accomplishments as a start-up nation full of innovation and with global reach. Instead of celebrating Israel on this day, the prayer service seems to narrow it and make it less significant than it should be. The way that Yom HaAtzma'ut is observed outside of Israel often lacks the creative spark that characterizes so much of what happens inside the country today.

I am not questioning the intention of those who originally put together this blend of Shabbat, Yom Kippur, and Rosh Ḥodesh practices. No doubt they too wanted the day to feel rooted in tradition and part

of the holiday calendar, and by using prayer that is central to holy days, they were elevating the status of Yom HaAtzma'ut. In the early 1950s, the chief rabbinate of Israel wanted to bring sanctity to what was otherwise a purely national celebration. What better way to achieve this than to cut and paste from the siddur and the maḥzor? But the prayers as they are currently organized fail to move me precisely because they are not specifically for this day alone. The appropriation of these texts from their original contexts makes me feel each year that this is a pretend holiday, especially outside of Israel, where the prayer service takes on greater significance because the national observance is so muted. Since Yom HaAtzma'ut in the Diaspora is not celebrated everywhere the eye can see, those of us who are Religious Zionists feel we need to say the *tefillot* a bit louder so that God can hear them. This brings into greater focus the fact that these prayers feel a little shabby in this setting, leftovers from other days. The pages we use are photocopied. Their edges are bent and ripped.

Those of us who take prayer seriously are usually moved by the unique prayers said on special days. *Tefillat Tal* and *Akdamot*, the *Musaf* for Yom Kippur and *Ḥad Gadya*, are belted out loudly because we know Shavuot, Yom Kippur, and Passover come around infrequently. In the 1950s, when the chief rabbinate decreed Yom HaAtzma'ut a minor religious festival in addition to its national status, they declared that *Hallel* should be recited to honor this day and place it among a constellation of holy days, much the way the Talmud records attempts to observe military triumphs of old as national days of significance, though most of these are lost to us now. But in limiting the *Hallel* to a set of psalms without a blessing, they were also hedging. They were telling us that this day resonated in our history as an outburst of joy on the timeline of Jewish history that could only be of a divine and miraculous nature, and then undermined it all by removing the blessing from its recitation. This may explain why Rabbi Shlomo Goren, in 1973, insisted on the recitation of the blessing, ramping up the status of the day, despite objections from Rabbis Ovadia Yosef and Joseph Soloveitchik. In questioning the canonization of these prayers, neither scholar was demeaning the significance of the Jewish state as much as questioning whether or not it was too early to conclude that this national dream also achieved the religious aspirations associated with it.

Most Religious Zionist day schools and Modern Orthodox synagogues have stayed in the "safe" zone and recite *Hallel* without the blessing. It is in this moment, the moment in the Diaspora where we begin *Hallel* without a blessing, that we realize how contradictory and confusing these days are for Religious Zionists outside of Israel. We lack the national festive atmosphere and citizenship. We lack prayers constructed especially for the day, and we lack the blessing that tells us this is a truly holy day. Without the strong national elements, the religious dimensions, which are somewhat weak, feel weaker still.

WHAT SHOULD WE DO?
There are practical ways to address some of these problems.

- Fly to Israel for Yom HaAtzma'ut. While this is an expensive and less likely option, I believe that all Jews should experience Israel's Independence Day in Israel at least once. One day alone will expose the wide abyss between the regions' celebrations of Yom HaAtzma'ut and possibly stimulate more serious thinking about its observance in the Diaspora.
- Find sacred texts – like parts of Deuteronomy 8 – that celebrate the uniqueness of Israel and include them in the service while preserving the basic formulation.
- Create song contests, events, and award ceremonies that mimic what happens in Israel to some degree, to beef up the nationalistic element.
- Use the day annually to stimulate study and facilitated conversation about Israeli politics, history, and culture, instead of variations on the same *daglanut* or flag-waving dances that can feel tired and repetitive.
- Revisit the curriculum or typical programing and structure of Yom HaAtzma'ut in schools and Jewish centers and ask where it can be more lively, more intellectually robust, more engaging, more creative. Use more Hebrew language.
- Create opportunities to discuss Jewish peoplehood, Jewish identity, and what it means to have a truly global Jewish community. What continues to unite us and what challenges our solidarity?

- Think of ways to harness technology to possibly join Israelis celebrating in Israel in "real time."
- Find out how expat Israelis in your local community celebrate Yom HaAtzma'ut. Often they hold their own celebrations. Try to partner with them on programming and community-wide conversations.

Using just one of these steps as a platform for change can offer a more inviting and engaging celebration.

GLOBAL UNITY

Yom HaAtzma'ut should be a time for reflection on how Israel is the center that disseminates the psychic bonds connecting our entire global Jewish family, as Isaiah said: "For out of Zion shall come forth Torah and the word of the Lord from Jerusalem" (2:3). Orthodox day schools spend very little time defining peoplehood as a feeling or a construct, demonstrating examples of it, or finding ways to strengthen it. School-age children rarely have opportunities to articulate what being Jewish means to them. We often mistakenly assume that a deep Jewish identity is on offer for day school children if only they would take their Jewish studies more seriously. If anything, we tend to use Israel's Memorial and Independence Days to highlight only religious Israelis who serve our country, died for it, or take joy in its festivities. This limits the reach of Zionism and Judaism to a perilously narrow purview.

Again, we turn to Benedict Anderson to rethink our connections across the ocean and across time:

I propose the following definition of the nation: it is an imagined political community – and imagined as both inherently limited and sovereign. It is imagined because the members of even the smallest nation will never know most of their fellow-members, meet them, or even hear of them, yet in the minds of each lives the image of their communion.... Communities are to be distinguished, not by their falsity/genuineness, but by the style in which they are imagined.... Finally, [the nation] is imagined as a community, because, regardless of the actual inequality and exploitation that

may prevail in each, the nation is conceived as a deep, horizontal comradeship.[1]

In an interview with Anderson, a writer asked him if he was actually nationalistic in an age where nationalism has become threatening and frightening at times. His answer? "Yes, absolutely. I must be the only one writing about nationalism who doesn't think it ugly... I actually think that nationalism can be an attractive ideology. I like its Utopian elements."[2]

Michael Billig, another widely-read scholar on the subject, writes that it is a banal mysticism that binds us to a homeland, "that special place which is more than a place, more than a geophysical area."[3] Israel is for many of us that special place which is more than a place. Our celebration of Israel should also be more than just a same-old, same-old disconnected religious nod to an Israel of yore, or a big anniversary party with a guest list limited by geography. Yom HaAtzma'ut needs to be a global restatement of our commitment to a country that deepens Jewish identity for us all. If our celebrations cannot be genuinely nationalistic outside of Israel's borders, then at least they can be more fun, more fresh, more educational, and more transformative.

1. *Imagined Communities: Reflections on the Origin and Spread of Nationalism* (London, 1983), 6.
2. http://www.uio.no/english/research/interfaculty-research-areas/culcom/news/2005/anderson.html
3. *Banal Nationalism* (London, 1995), 175.

Establishing a Holiday: The Chief Rabbinate and Yom HaAtzma'ut

Rabbi Shmuel Katz

One of the boldest, most important, and most meaningful decisions that the Chief Rabbinate has made since its establishment, took place in the month of Nissan in the year 5709 (1949), when it instituted Yom HaAtzma'ut as a day of religious significance, praise, and thanksgiving to God, as an obligation for all generations!

When this decision was made, Israel's chief rabbis were Rabbi Yitzchak HaLevi Herzog and Rabbi Ben-Zion Meir Hai Uziel. The two worked together in full harmony and mutual admiration and respect. Their worldviews with regard to the redemption process that had unfolded over the last few generations, the spiritual value of the state's establishment, and the obligation to participate in the nation's joys and sorrows, allowed them to guide this most meaningful of processes.

FUNDAMENTAL QUESTIONS

The Chief Rabbinate could neither relate to nor voice its opinion about Yom HaAtzma'ut until the government and Knesset made its decisions. On 13 Adar, 5709, the government chose 5 Iyar as the national "State Day," which would be celebrated annually as a national holiday. This decision was published in the national media and became known to all. On 12 Nissan, the government proposed the "Independence Day Law" for debate in the Knesset. This was the first official debate regarding the character of the day. The members of the Knesset were almost unanimous in their desire that this day should be of traditional Jewish significance like the rest of the Jewish festivals, rather than a regular day. At the end of that same day, it was decided that a Knesset committee would determine this question, but due to time constraints these decisions were passed to the government, together with a suggestion most relevant to our topic at hand: "In regard to the declaration of the festival and its content, the committee has also proposed that this issue be discussed with the *Honorable Chief Rabbis*" (italics mine).

Thus, the organization of this national festival was passed from the legislative branch to the executive branch – to the government itself. On 27 Nissan the "governmental committee" publicized the program for Yom HaAtzma'ut, which made no mention of the synagogue or any customs regarding a festive meal. The following day, Prime Minister David Ben-Gurion issued special instructions with regard to public transport, post office opening hours, restaurants, and places of entertainment – all purely technical – which failed to contribute to the festive atmosphere of the day as it was to be celebrated within the family, community, or nation. The special proclamation issued in honor of the first Independence Day was completely devoid of any religious content, and the absence of God's name or any biblical verses was very pronounced. How did the chief rabbis prepare for this historic day? What had they to propose to the aforementioned governmental committee? What guidelines did they offer to the spiritual leaders and the public with regard to the forthcoming holiday?

Rabbi Herzog and Rabbi Uziel were faced with new and difficult halakhic questions that no rabbi in Israel or the Diaspora had faced before, and all this took place less than a month before the state's first National Independence Day. Now the Chief Rabbinate was given the opportunity to fulfill at least part of its vision – to form the religious character of the

new Jewish state by giving religious-spiritual guidelines to the new Jewish festival – something that had not been done since the destruction of the Second Temple!

The chief rabbis and the Rabbinate needed to address several fundamental questions:

1. Is the Chief Rabbinate authorized to establish a festival for future generations? And if so, are they authorized to obligate the Jews in the Diaspora as well?
2. Is there religious significance to a one-time historical event such as the establishment of a Jewish state, even if it is not run according to the Torah, and its government does not observe the Torah and its commandments?
3. Is it halakhically appropriate to join the Knesset in its decision making, and to choose the fifth of Iyar in particular? Perhaps Yom HaAtzma'ut should have been celebrated on the last day of the War of Independence?
4. Which passages should be added to the prayer service on this day? Is it appropriate to recite *Hallel*, with or without a blessing?
5. Can new prayers be composed in honor of this day, in order to best express its atmosphere?
6. Does Yom HaAtzma'ut overrule the recital of *Taḥanun* in the daily prayer service, the *Selikhot* recited on Mondays and Thursdays after Pesaḥ, and the mourning customs of *Sefirat HaOmer*?

From the very first year, there were various opinions and multiple disputes in regard to these questions. I now wish to discuss the considerations, deliberations, and the decision-making process of Rabbi Herzog, Rabbi Uziel, and the Rabbinate council, which ultimately led to the formation of the spiritual and religious character of Yom HaAtzma'ut and the prayer service that is followed by many until this very day.

INITIAL GUIDELINES

The first document I found concerning the Rabbinate's decisions about Yom HaAtzma'ut is a letter that Rabbi Herzog and Rabbi Uziel sent to the extended Rabbinate council on 8 Nissan, 5709. The letter, sent only three

weeks after the government's announcement that the fifth of Iyar would serve as a national holiday, expressed the chief rabbis' clear opinions in regard to the many questions they had been asked:

> The fundamental turning point in God's compassion on us, the declaration of our independence in the Land, which saved us and redeemed our souls, obligates us *to uphold and keep this day of the fifth of Iyar, the day of the declaration of the State of Israel, for all generations, as a day of joy of the beginning of the redemption for all of Israel,* and to exempt the day of this great miracle from all customs of mourning of the Omer period, and to add thanksgiving prayers and sermons about this great event during the time of the Minha prayer in synagogues (italics mine).

The preparations for the Pesah holiday seem to have prevented the Rabbinate council's gathering in Jerusalem for a proper discussion of the topic, which led the chief rabbis to ask for their immediate approval in order to announce their decision to the public before Yom HaAtzma'ut. Note the following regarding the above declaration:

1. The chief rabbis consider the day of the declaration of the state – the fifth of Iyar – as "the beginning of the redemption." This perspective is the starting point of all their decisions in regard to this day, despite the fact that this opinion was not shared by the entire council.
2. The holiday was fixed for the generations and for all of Israel, even those in the Diaspora, regardless of how the State's religious and spiritual character will unfold in the years to come, and how much Torah and mitzvot will be fulfilled by its citizens in the future.
3. In order for Yom HaAtzma'ut's greatness and unique festive spirit to be publicized as a crucial turning point in Israel's history, the chief rabbis decided to cancel the mourning customs of the Omer period. This decision proved to be the center of a heated debate for years to come.
4. The Chief Rabbinate did not yet propose a specific prayer service for this day. At this stage, they merely emphasized that the Minha prayer should be recited with special festivity.

I have not found any documents that testify to the council's reply; it may have been given by telephone. I did, however, find a proclamation that the Chief Rabbinate prepared for the public, "with the knowledge of the extended council and the Rabbinate offices in Israel," in anticipation of "State Day" (as of yet, the holiday had no official name). This time, the Chief Rabbinate's guidelines were more detailed:

1. *Taḥanun* is not be said during Shaḥarit and Minḥa, and there are to be no eulogies on this day.
2. During the Minḥa prayer, before *Ashrei*, when the Ark is opened, the prayer leader will recite a prayer for the fallen soldiers of the IDF. After the repetition of the silent prayer, *Hallel* is to be recited without its blessings before and after, and the rabbi should give a special sermon in honor of the day.
3. Charity should be given as it is on Purim.
4. The public should celebrate with festive meals, accompanied by both *zemirot* and sacred poems by poets such as Rabbi Yehuda HaLevi between courses, as well as chapters of Psalms: 30, 144, 146, 149, and 150.
5. These meals have the status of *seudot mitzva* – meals that are a mitzva in themselves.

From this document, several important details can be inferred:

1. There are no guidelines for the evening prayers of the festival.
2. The recitation of *Hallel* was originally intended for the Minḥa prayer – which is not the case with any other festival! I can only assume that this surprising instruction came in order to allow people who worked during the day to participate in a festive prayer service after working hours.
3. There is no mention of the mourning customs of the Omer period here.
4. These guidelines seem to be an attempt to lend this day the same status as rabbinically ordained festivals: Ḥanukka and Purim.
5. There are precise guidelines as to which chapters of Psalms should be recited at the festive meal.

This proclamation, it seems, was not made public.

ḤAREDI OPPOSITION

On 11 Nissan, a short, surprising passage was published in the media in the name of the Chief Rabbinate, without waiting for the official decision of the Knesset, who only convened on this subject the following day:

> "State Day," the fifth of Iyar, which falls during the Omer period, during which certain customs of mourning are observed, will have the same status *as Lag BaOmer*, and according to the decision of the Chief Rabbinate, [on the fifth of Iyar] *all celebrations, weddings, haircuts, etc., are permitted* (italics mine).

This announcement pleased many of the Chief Rabbinate's supporters, one of whom said: "This halakhic ruling is an event in the life of the Torah. It proves in what esteem Torah Judaism and its highest authority, the Chief Rabbinate, hold the day of the establishment of the state." However, this joy did not last long. It seems that this bold, sweeping decision – to equate this day with Lag BaOmer – aggravated many within the council and outside of it, mostly within the *ḥaredi* community. After making inquiries in the Chief Rabbinate of Tel Aviv, and with Rabbi Herzog himself, the *Agudat Yisrael* journal announced that this information was inaccurate, and the subject was still under debate. It also demanded the agreement of all rabbinic authorities in both Israel and the Diaspora before a final decision could be reached, in order to prevent dissent within the Torah-observant community and the desecration of God's name. This demand was not met due to lack of time, especially given the fact that unanimous agreement would not be reached in any case.

Rabbi Herzog and Rabbi Uziel reckoned that, as the highest halakhic authority in the state, the Chief Rabbinate had the power to decide this matter itself, even considering that such a decision had ramifications for the entire community in all its different sectors, in Israel and the Diaspora.

The extended Chief Rabbinate council did not convene for an emergency meeting until 18 Nissan, during Ḥol HaMoed Pesaḥ (meetings were not usually held at all during Ḥol HaMoed). The protocol testifies to the reservations about this decision, with clarification that when the Old City

of Jerusalem will once again be under Israeli rule, the Chief Rabbinate will debate whether the mourning customs of the Omer will be canceled on this day. Concerning the festive character of the day and its thanksgiving prayers, it was decided that:

1. *Taḥanun* is not to be recited on this day.
2. During the morning prayers, *Hallel* is to be recited without a blessing, a memorial service is to be held for those who fell during the War of Independence, and a blessing is to be recited for the state.
3. A meal of festivity and song is to be held, and presents should be given to the poor.

These definitions show fundamental changes: *Hallel* (still without blessings) is to be recited during the *morning prayers*, and there is an important addition: the Prayer for the Welfare of the State. When this decision was published, further changes were made: there was no mention of the Prayer for the Welfare of the State; the mention of the fallen soldiers was moved to the Minḥa prayer service; and it was emphasized that the festive meal has the status of a *seudat mitzva*. Concerning marriage and haircuts on this day, it was decided that "the Chief Rabbinate will make considerations *when the entire holy city of Jerusalem, old and new as one, will be restored to Israel.*"

THE FORMATION OF THE PRAYER SERVICE

These guidelines were too general and too brief to enhance the festive atmosphere of the synagogue prayers. Indeed, on the 30 Nissan, the national papers published a detailed prayer service: "Prayer and Thanksgiving for Independence Day," which listed additional prayers to be recited on this day and the special festive customs to be fulfilled. This service included familiar passages of prayer from other festivals in an attempt to project the festive atmosphere of the established festivals onto this new day, and also expressed that this day is only the "beginning of the redemption," and we must continue to believe in the full redemption and the coming of the Messiah. These additions did not contain any blessings, so that there would be no halakhic questions concerning the utterance of God's name.

This message, which was published in the name of the Chief Rabbinate, seemed to imply that they were the ones who created the new prayer service, but this was not the case. Careful research has revealed that rabbis associated with the social-political organization HaPo'el HaMizrachi, who were not satisfied with the Chief Rabbinate's guidelines published after Pesaḥ, were the ones who compiled the service. In a letter to the Chief Rabbinate, they requested that the Chief Rabbinate lend their authority to the proposed prayer service as the universal prayer service for the new festival. In the event of insufficient time to hold a meeting on the subject, they would settle for the Chief Rabbinate's authorization of the service as an optional program, so that local rabbis would be able to publicize the service in their communities.

The rabbi of Kfar HaRo'eh, Rabbi Shaul Yisraeli, and his neighbor, Rabbi Moshe Tzvi Neriah, the head of the Bnei Akiva yeshiva there, seem to be the ones who compiled most of the service's content. Rabbi Yisraeli met with Rabbi Uziel in order to obtain his approval. Rabbi Uziel deleted several passages from the original proposed service, including: "*Hineni mukhan umezuman*, I am prepared and ready to hear the sound of the shofar on the day of Israel's independence"; "Sound the great shofar for our freedom ... blessed is He who gathers the dispersed of His people Israel"; the blessing, with *shem umalkhut* (God's name and kingship, i.e. a full blessing), "He who performed miracles for us in those days and at this time"; and a Torah reading from Deuteronomy 30:1–20, over which three people were to say blessings. Rabbi Yisraeli made two additions in his own handwriting: in the evening prayers, "He who performed miracles for our forefathers *and for us*"; and in the morning prayers, "We are obligated to thank and praise ... and we will say a new song before Him, Hallelujah." After the service was edited and corrected, it was sent to the newspapers for publication.

THE AUTHORITY OF THE DAY

In order that the religious community accept the Chief Rabbinate's confirmation of the Knesset's decision to institute the fifth of Iyar as a festival, there was a need to justify the importance of this day – 5 Iyar, 5708 – from the point of view of Halakha and *emuna*, faith. After all, this day did not mark any particular victory; on the contrary, the declaration

of statehood caused the armies of the surrounding countries to attack the newborn state the very next day. Before the first anniversary of Israeli independence, Rabbi Herzog was in the United States, and Rabbi Uziel, therefore, took on this important mission. He issued a special proclamation in honor of the first Independence Day of the state:

"On this day, you became a people unto the Lord your God!" (Deut. 27:9) – these words are worthy to be said on this day, the day of the declaration of our independent state in the Land of Israel. For on this day, we have shaken loose the yoke of submission to foreign rule in the Land of Israel, which took the form of the [British] Mandate, which desired to strangle [Israel] to death, and from the threat of war from the surrounding nations, who wished to enslave us forever. This bold declaration, which all nations of the earth scorned, rendered the entire nation of Israel, in the Land [of Israel] and in the Diaspora, into an independent, autonomous nation in its own land and in all areas of its life; gave courage and lion-strength to the army of God – that is, the Israeli army – in its fight for redemption, when they prevailed against all those who rose up against us; opened the gates of our Land, the portion of God, to the nation of Israel from wherever it was scattered and exiled; and awarded the nation of Israel its honored place amongst the nations…. *This day is a festival for Israel, who dwell in their Land, and for all those scattered throughout the Diaspora, for our generation and for all generations,* to thank the Lord for His kindness and to praise Him with song, joy, thanksgiving, and glory – "This is the day the Lord made; let us rejoice and be glad in it" (italics mine).

Rabbi Uziel's uplifting words clarify several important points regarding the nature of the day. In his opinion, Yom HaAtzma'ut's importance and halakhic significance – and its institution on this particular date – is derived from the following factors:

1. the lifting of the yoke of foreign domination and obtaining independent rule over the Land of Israel, together with the authority of the British Mandate in the Land ending at the midnight of that same Shabbat;

2. victory in the fierce war that ensued in the Land, the victory of few over many, rescue from death, and overcoming the danger of annihilation;

3. the courage of the nation's leaders to declare the establishment of the state on that day, despite the dangers it entailed, which transformed the nation of Israel – including those outside its borders – into an independent, autonomous nation;

4. the opening of the gates of the land on this day to Jews from all over the world, and especially to the survivors of the Holocaust, indicating that this day marked a kind of ending to the exile;

5. the achievement of an honorable place among the nations, after years of humiliation throughout their long exile, which culminated in the Holocaust;

Yom HaAtzma'ut, therefore, is also a festival for the Jews of the Diaspora, for from the day independence was declared, all Jews are able to move to the Land of Israel whenever they want, especially in times of trouble. Furthermore, for all these reasons, Yom HaAtzma'ut is a festival for all time and all generations to come!

These inspiring words were written on 28 Nissan, but for whatever reason they were not published until the very morning of Yom HaAtzma'ut itself, on 5 Iyar. If they had been published just a few days before, they certainly would have contributed to the anticipation of this festival and lifted the spirits of the general public, clarifying the greatness of the day to all. This statement was signed by Rabbi Uziel himself, not by the Chief Rabbinate, and it effectively served as a counterbalance to the government's statement, which did not at all relate to the religious-spiritual aspect of the day.

THE FIRST CELEBRATION

Celebratory prayers of thanks were held on the eve of the festival all over the country. The synagogues were bursting with thousands of people. A special ceremony was held in Jerusalem, organized by the Military Rabbinate, the religious services branch of the IDF, and the Ministry of Religion. This event opened with a thanksgiving ceremony for "the resurrection of Israel and the Ark's return from the battlefield to Jerusalem."

A special procession of IDF rabbis and soldiers marched forth, led by two Torah scrolls, a giant seal of the State of Israel, a royal flag emblazoned with the names of all the kings of Judah, the national flag, and the flags of the twelve tribes of Israel. Myriads of celebrating Jews accompanied the procession with song and dance through the streets of the capital, arriving at the Yeshurun Synagogue, where thousands gathered for the thanksgiving prayers.

The prayer service began with the opening of the Ark by Rabbi Uziel, who wore a golden badge of honor from his inauguration as Sephardic chief rabbi. After a festive evening prayer service, the chief rabbi of the IDF, Rabbi Shlomo Goren, read a parchment scroll inscribed with a special prayer compiled in honor of the first Yom HaAtzma'ut. Rabbi Uziel gave a speech; afterwards, the verses "When you come to war" (Num. 10:9–10) and "This very day they will halt at Nob" (Is. 10–12) were read out, and a memorial prayer was recited in honor of those who fell in the War of Independence. This service differed slightly from the order of prayers that the Chief Rabbinate itself proposed.

The next morning, an impressive military parade marched through Jerusalem, with Rabbi Uziel seated in a place of honor. A similar parade that was to be held in Tel Aviv was canceled because of the sheer numbers of the crowd and the vast multitudes that thronged the streets. Rabbi Herzog was the main speaker at the mass gathering held in honor of Yom HaAtzma'ut in Madison Square Garden in New York. His moving speech made a lasting impression on the 200,000 people who came to hear him.

The Song of Ascent

Rabbi Binyamin Lau

WHEN THE LORD BROUGHT BACK THE
EXILES OF ZION, WE WERE AS DREAMERS

For thousands of years, the people of Israel couldn't return home. Dwelling on foreign soil – the punishment of exile – had long since become a bitter yet familiar way of life.

This perpetual temporary state can already be traced back to Jacob's family's descent to Egypt. Joseph brought his brothers and father to the land of Goshen during the years of famine. While the famine soon passed, the Children of Israel did not return to the land promised to Abraham, Isaac, and Jacob, but rather settled comfortably: "And Israel dwelled in the land of Egypt, in the land of Goshen, and they took possession of it and were fruitful and multiplied greatly" (Gen. 47:27).

This verse seems laconic, but it stifles a scream. The phrase, "*vaye'aḥazu vah*, they took possession," conveys the human ability to adapt to new conditions, to become acclimatized to something, even if it does not belong to them. The possession of Goshen never should have taken place – Israel should have left Egypt and returned to their homeland when the famine ended. But they became entrenched in this new land, possessed by it, as Rabbi Tzaddok HaKohen of Lublin depicts: "They became possessed, suffused by the 'husk' of Egypt, like an unborn child in its mother's womb" (*Pri Tzaddik, Parashat VaYeḥi* 2).

This image illuminates the significance of Israel's sojourn in Egypt and their exodus from that place. One of the greatest everyday miracles is the miracle of birth – the stirring of the unborn child within its mother before its entrance into the world. The child's arrival is anticipated from the moment of its conception, but until the moment of birth, it dwells within its mother. If the child lingers too long within its mother, medical intervention is employed. So, too, in the exodus from Egypt, when Israel did not leave at the proper time, God intervened, performing a Caesarean of sorts: "And He brought Israel out from among them" (Ps. 136:11).

This pattern has since repeated itself countless times in Israel's history. We are forced into a certain situation; with time, we adapt ourselves to that situation, until it becomes bearable and even desirable. Before the destruction of the First Temple, myriads of Judeans were exiled to Babylonia with King Jeconiah (597 BCE). The prophet Jeremiah sent letters to the exiled Judeans, urging them to get settled in Babylonia, for the period of exile would span seventy years. Jeremiah's prophecy was a reaction to the proactive messianic factions who sought to arouse their fellow Jews' nationalism in an attempt to rebel against the Babylonian Empire. These parties harbored the illusion that Babylonia would soon fall and the Jews would shortly return to their independent homeland once more. Jeremiah, by contrast, prophesied:

> Thus says the Lord of hosts, the God of Israel, to all those I carried into exile from Jerusalem to Babylonia: Build houses and settle down; plant gardens and eat what they produce. Marry and have sons and daughters; find wives for your sons and give your daughters in marriage, so that they too may have sons and daughters. Increase in number there; do not decrease. Also, seek the peace and prosperity of the city to which I have carried you into exile. Pray to the Lord for it, because if it prospers, you too will prosper. (Jer. 29:4–7)

It seems that Jeremiah's prophecy succeeded; Judean society flourished in Babylonia. The Jewish nation was once again granted that curse of a blessing: "And they took possession of it and were fruitful and multiplied greatly" (Gen. 47:27).

In the middle of the sixth century BCE, the head of the new world empire, Cyrus of Persia, rose to power and changed the policy of the nations under his rule. Assyria (and Babylonia after it) had achieved power by exiling nations and creating an immigrant culture. The sense of displacement ensured the power of the ruling empire, for the immigrants were engrossed in their daily struggle to survive, with no time or energy left for rebellion. Cyrus's approach was different; he believed in allowing administrative and cultural freedom to the nations he conquered, and expressed his dominion through garrisons posted in every conquered city and the collection of taxes, which ensured the economic well-being of his empire. Cyrus's Declaration announced a change in Judah's status, and directed the Jews back to their own land:

> In the first year of Cyrus, king of Persia, in order to fulfill the word of the Lord spoken by Jeremiah, the Lord moved the heart of Cyrus, king of Persia, to make a proclamation throughout his realm and also to put it in writing. Thus says Cyrus, king of Persia: The Lord, the God of heaven, has given me all the kingdoms of the earth, and He has appointed me to build a Temple for Him at Jerusalem in Judah. Any of His people among you may go up to Jerusalem in Judah and build the Temple of the Lord, the God of Israel, the God who is in Jerusalem, and may their God be with them. (Ezra 1:1–3)

The days of the first Return to Zion were a time of hope for redemption. The prophets felt that God had returned to Zion, as expressed in Zechariah's prophecy:

> Rejoice and be glad, Daughter Zion. For I am coming, and I will live among you, declares the Lord. Many nations will be joined with the Lord in that day and will become My people. I will live among you and you will know that the Lord Almighty has sent me to you. The Lord will inherit Judah as His portion in the holy land and will again choose Jerusalem. Be still before the Lord, all mankind, because He has roused Himself from His holy dwelling. (Zech. 2:14–17)

This prophecy paints an optimistic picture. "Here He stands, behind our wall, gazing through the windows, glimpsing through every gap" (Song 2:9). We have awoken, hearing and sharing the tidings of redemption. But the first Return to Zion was a small affair, a mere fraction of the exiles returning to their homeland. That selfsame people who had wept by the rivers of Babylon were now finding it difficult to uproot themselves from its banks, possessed by the land they had taken possession of. Mother Babylon had welcomed them into her womb, warm and nurturing; they did not wish to leave her comforts and return to the desolated earth of Judah and Jerusalem. Few heeded the tidings of redemption and returned home. Most of the exiles, the strongest, most established members of society, continued to pray for the Return to Zion, but remained in Babylonia.

The period of the Second Temple saw a few years of independence during the time of the Hasmoneans, but Judea was mostly under foreign dominion. After the destruction of the Second Temple, there was a spark of national pride that flared into a rebellion led by Bar Kokhba. The reactions of the spiritual leaders of this time were mixed. The students of Rabbi Yoḥanan ben Zakkai focused only on Israel's spiritual legacy as expressed in Torah study and acts of kindness. Others, headed by Rabbi Akiva, argued as well for Israel's independence and their right to throw off the yoke of foreign nations. Nowadays, it is difficult to assess the balance of power that supported or rejected the rebellion, but there is no question as to its outcome. Hadrian's wrath led to destruction on a scale unprecedented in Israel's history – unprecedented and unmatched, until the Holocaust of the generation before our very own.

The blood of the rebels flowed like water, saturating the soil upon which they sought independence, all cries of national independence silenced by Hadrian's bloody edicts. Many left their homeland, and the *yeshivot* in Babylonia grew stronger and more central, until they became the new spiritual center of the Jewish people – a New Jerusalem.

In the third century BCE, a Torah scholar by the name of Rabbi Shimon ben Lakish sat in Tiberias and cried out about Israel's shame at her children's refusal to return to her. Interpreting the verse in the Song of Songs (8:9), he said: "'If she were a wall, we would build a silver watchtower; if a door, we would bar her with boards of cedar': If you had been a wall and you had all returned in the days of Ezra – you would have

been compared to silver, which does not rot; but because you returned like doors, you have been compared to cedar, which does rot" (*Yoma* 9b).

Rabbi Shimon's cry reflected what could have been Israel's reality if they had only heeded the voice of their Beloved that echoed in Cyrus's Declaration. The "wall" symbolizes a unified return to Zion, a universal rejection of exile. Doors open and close. There are many doors, but only one wall. Israel was supposed to have returned as a wall, as one united power, one person with one heart. But it chose to be a "door" – weak, divided, opening and closing. This choice, in Rabbi Shimon's eyes, led to the rotting of the cedar door.

At the end of the eleventh century, Rabbi Yehuda HaLevi lived in Muslim Spain, surrounded by Jews entrenched in the enlightened culture of the Spanish court, prosperous members of the local economy. In his classic work *Kuzari*, Rabbi HaLevi paints the Land of Israel in romantic colors, expressing the unique connection of Israel to its land. Then the king of the Khazars asks him this question: If Israel, this special land, is destined for you and your people, then what are you all doing here, in Spain? The author answers:

> You have indeed shamed me, O King of the Khazars. It is this sin that prevented the fulfillment of the divine promise with regard to the Second Temple, namely: "Rejoice and be glad, daughter of Zion" (Zech. 2:10). Divine providence was ready to restore everything as it had been at first, if they had all willingly consented to return. But only a part of the nation was ready to do so, while the majority and the aristocracy remained in Babylonia, preferring dependence and slavery, and unwilling to leave their houses and their affairs. (*Kuzari* II:24)

What heartache. What a sense of missed opportunity, matched only by the depth of the yearning, the longing for redemption. The people did not stir – once again, dashing all hope. Rabbi Yehuda HaLevi traces a line from the days of the Babylonian exile to his very own time: 1,500 years of Jewish history. He reads Cyrus's Declaration as a divine invitation to return to Zion: "Divine providence was ready to restore everything as it had been at first." There was a moment to seize the opportunity for Israel's return to its land, accompanied by divine grace – but most Jews chose to

stay in comfortable exile, "unwilling to leave their houses and their affairs." Today, says Rabbi Yehuda HaLevi, we are no less susceptible to the lures of foreign soil. The exiled Jew's prayer to return to Jerusalem and Israel is but the "nightingale's chatter" (ibid.).

For thousands of years, Jews in exile managed to establish wonderful communities, magnificent synagogues, education systems for their children, and networks of mutual aid. As the years passed, the communities only grew and flourished, and gradually, the Land of Israel was forgotten. Lips still uttered the prayer, "And may our eyes witness Your return to Zion," but these words no longer echoed in the hearts of their utterers. The dwellers of darkness had grown accustomed to the gloom, and only an external light could remind them of their true home.

Every few generations, the Beloved knocks on the door of His lover, and calls out to her: "Open for me" (Song 5:2). It is up to us to hear this knocking, to open the door before our Beloved slips away. Song of Songs expresses the sense of missed opportunity, of great loss: "I open for my beloved – but he has slipped away, gone" (5:6).

This tragedy replayed itself at the beginning of the reawakening of Zion at the start of the nineteenth century. The people were slumbering, and the "voice of the turtledove" rang out, seeking to rouse the hearts of the nation to return home. Some heeded the call and came: students of the Baal Shem Tov; students of the Vilna Gaon; students of the Ḥatam Sofer and students of the Or HaḤayyim HaKadosh from Morocco; some Jews from North Africa and from the east. They sensed that the time was ripe and understood that "If not now – when?" (*Avot* 1:14).

But many others refused to hear the call, and would have no hand in the Return to Zion. The Zionist movement rebelled against this Diasporic slumber, shaking itself awake in order to seize the moment. Spiritual leaders such as Rabbi Tzvi Hirsch Kalischer, Rabbi Shmuel Mohilever, Rabbi Yehuda Alkalai, and others, were harbingers of the national awakening in a spiritual-religious sense. Yet, like in the days of Cyrus, few were roused from their slumber. For every Jew who reached the holy shores, over fifty reached the shores of America – the golden land of opportunity. Zionism was hardly considered. Most of the Second Aliya consisted of immigrants who were not interested in the voice of God, but rather filled with the

zeitgeist of national identity, seeking to create New Jews and new types of Jewish life in Eretz Yisrael.

The renewed Return to Zion was received with mixed feelings. The religious world felt that this new spirit of nationalism had nothing to do with religion, and this was only confirmed by the secular Zionist rejection of the "old ways." Figures of national rebellion from Jewish history became sources of inspiration: the militant Maccabees, Bar Kokhba. In contrast, Jewish leaders had always portrayed the Maccabees in a more spiritual light and downplayed the story of Bar Kokhba's failed rebellion.

Rabbi Abraham Isaac Kook was almost alone in his approach to the nationalism of this generation. He sought to adopt the nationalistic movement as a manifestation of Israel's redemption. In his view, nationalism was rooted in religion, and religion would bloom anew along with the blossoming of nationalism. Near the time of his immigration to Israel in 1904, he was asked to eulogize Theodore Herzl. His riveting words powerfully set forth the connection between a national-political awakening and a national-spiritual awakening based on Torah. The rebuilding of Zion unfolded gradually, as anticipated by our sages: "*kim'a kim'a* – little by little" (*Y. Berakhot* 1:1). In our time, God did not redeem us overnight, but gradually, little by little, in small groups like springs in the desert.

Just a few years before the Bilu pioneers arrived in 1867, the American author Mark Twain visited Palestine. In his work *Innocents Abroad*, also referred to as "The Great Pleasure Excursion," he describes: "A desolation is here that not even imagination can grace with the pomp of life and action .... There was hardly a tree or a shrub anywhere .... Palestine sits in sackcloth and ashes." This was how the land looked before the establishment of Petah Tikva. For us, the generation that has witnessed only a flourishing, bustling land, it is almost impossible to grasp the momentum of this change. We have been born into the reality of the Land of Israel greeting her returning children with open arms, as Rabbi Abba says in *Sanhedrin* (98a): "There can be no more manifest sign of redemption than this: 'But you, O mountains of Israel, you shall shoot forth your branches, and yield your fruit to my people of Israel, for they are at hand to come' (Ezek. 36:8)." The prophet Ezekiel teaches that when Israel's children are stirred to return to the land, the land

itself will welcome them and bloom once more – and only then will redemption arise.

Yet the people still did not flock to Zion like "a wall." The people immigrated in dribs and drabs, a door opening here and there, settling the land inch by inch – but the Beloved's knock had yet to echo. Even the Balfour Declaration failed to stir the Jews in Europe. Only after the tragedy of the Holocaust, which almost wiped out our nation, did Israel hear the knock anew. Suddenly, after the body of the nation was ravaged by the Holocaust, the State of Israel burst forth. Ezekiel's vision of the dry bones was fulfilled before our very eyes in all its ghastly glory: "Thus says the Lord God: Behold, I am opening up your graves, and I shall raise you up from your graves, My people, and I shall bring you to the soil of Israel" (Ezek. 37:12).

The State of Israel, which opened its gates to each and every Jew (in accordance with the Law of Return), is the fulfillment of the dream nurtured throughout history. Today, when the majority of the Jewish people lives in Israel, most of the Torah world revolves around centers of study in Israel, and the identity of every Jew of the Diaspora is somehow connected to Israel, the miraculous historical process unfolding in our own time can no longer be denied. The establishment of the State of Israel is the resurrection of the Jewish nation. When we recite chapter 107 in Psalms: "God's redeemed will say," it is our own redemption we are praising.

WHEN THEY ARE REDEEMED – *HALLEL* IS RECITED FOR THEIR REDEMPTION

The obligation to give thanks for the redemption from crisis is the first stage of serving God. In a talmudic discussion that explores *Hallel*'s proper place in the prayer service, the sages present differing opinions as to the event which originally inspired the recital of *Hallel*:

Rabbi Eliezer says: Moses and Israel recited it when they stood at the sea…

Rabbi Yehuda says: Joshua and Israel recited it when the kings of Canaan stood against them…

Rabbi Elazar HaModai says: Deborah and Barak recited it when Sisera stood against them…

Rabbi Elazar ben Azarya says: Hezekiah and his associates recited it when Sennacherib stood against them…

Rabbi Akiva says: Hananiah, Mishael, and Azariah recited it when the wicked Nebuchadnezzar stood against them…

Rabbi Yose HaGelili says: Mordecai and Esther recited it when the wicked Haman stood against them…

And the sages say: The prophets among them instituted that Israel should recite it at every occasion and every crisis, may it not befall Israel, and when they are redeemed, [*Hallel*] is recited upon their redemption. (*Pesaḥim* 117a)

All of biblical history is compacted within this mishnaic dispute. The gratitude that floods the heart brings forth song. Only a stubbornly closed heart and closed eyes will prevent a person who recognizes God's hand in the world from offering joyous song for the divine salvation of millions from death.

One of the most difficult passages in the Talmud is the midrashic discussion that claims, as opposed to the passage above, that King Hezekiah *failed* to recite *Hallel* after his salvation from the threat of Sennacherib. The midrash is based on the verse from Isaiah, which poetically describes the future king who will sit on David's throne and lead Israel to long-awaited messianic tranquility for all eternity. This verse contains a linguistic curiosity: "Of the greatness of his government and peace there will be no end" (Is. 9:6). The Hebrew word לְמַרְבֵּה, meaning "of the greatness," is not written with a normal *mem*, but with a "final *mem*," the form the letter takes when it concludes a word – לסרבה. The midrash explains that this anomaly expresses how Isaiah hoped that this prophecy was a song of redemption for Hezekiah's reign, but his hopes were dashed, and the window of opportunity for the establishment of an everlasting kingdom was closed. Thus Bar Kappara (a third-century sage of the Land of Israel) describes the bitterness of the missed opportunity:

Bar Kappara from Tzippori interpreted: Why is the letter *mem* in the middle of a word usually open, while this is closed? The Holy One, blessed be He, wanted to make Hezekiah the Messiah, and Sennacherib Gog and Magog. The Attribute of Judgment said before

the Holy One, blessed be He: "Master of the world! David, king of Israel, sang many songs and praises before You – and You did not make him the Messiah; Hezekiah, for whom You performed all these miracles, did not sing before You – *him* you will make the Messiah?" Because of that, it was closed. (*Sanhedrin* 94a)

Bar Kappara calls King Hezekiah to account for the great miracle he experienced during Sennacherib's conquest, when all hovered on the brink of destruction and salvation arose at the very last moment. Assyria's attack on Israel in Hezekiah's time was one of the gravest conquests Israel had ever experienced. The Book of Isaiah opens with a depiction of Israel during this conquest: "Your land is wasteland, your cities burned with fire" (1:7). Jerusalem was besieged, and hope had almost faded away. The words of Rabshakeh, carrying Sennacherib's message to Hezekiah, broke the spirits of the people standing on the walls, and their weeping echoed through the desolate streets.

Suddenly – salvation, a miracle from heaven! The Assyrian army disappears overnight – retreating back to its own borders, leaving Jerusalem unscathed. Bar Kappara noted that after this great miracle, no reaction from the king is mentioned in the text. Perhaps he was grieving over the destruction of the cities of the plains and the deaths of myriads of his subjects; perhaps he was busy with the reconstruction of Jerusalem after the siege. In any case, Bar Kappara's words convey an important message relating to the recital of *Hallel*. Reciting *Hallel* is not to be reserved for a complete, messianic redemption alone; rather, *Hallel* is recited out of recognition that God has intervened and saved His people from destruction and death. Hezekiah's failure to sing a song of praise thus revoked his right to become the Messiah. The chance was lost; the *mem* was closed.

Several decades have passed since the War of Independence, and the sheer greatness of the hour and the magnitude of the salvation God provided during its battles has faded from memory. Moments before we were plunged into crisis, every neighboring Arab state announced the imminent liquidation of the "Zionist entity" from the Land of Israel. Indeed, many brave soldiers of Israel fell in combat, giving their lives for their people and land; but against all odds, the nation of Israel triumphed, holding onto its rightful inheritance. Following the establishment of the

state, the Israel Defense Forces were born, thus transforming the Jewish nation into a mighty force that will not suffer physical or mental oppression at the hand of its enemies.

Numerous dubious arguments have been made against the obligation to thank and praise God for all the good and blessing He has bestowed upon us. But these evasive claims cannot possibly counter the magnitude of the miracle, and the correspondingly great duty to thank Him. The Talmud (*Megilla* 14a) fixes the festival of Purim using an *a fortiori* argument: "If we give praise for [the transition] from slavery to freedom, how much more so for the [transition from] death to life!"

Based on this passage, the Ḥatam Sofer (Responsa 1, 208) held that Purim is in fact a Torah-ordained festival, for it is fundamentally based on one of the main principles by which the Torah is expounded. By the principle of *a fortiori*, we too, are required to recite *Hallel* on Yom HaAtzma'ut with true, uninhibited, unconditional joy. Thus ruled Rabbi Meshulam Rath in his responsa *Kol Mevaser* (1:21): The establishment of the State of Israel obligates us to proclaim a festival, for it marks salvation from death.

Some attempt to sabotage the festive joy by focusing upon certain shadows and complexities in the shining aura of the State of Israel. The process of a people readjusting to life upon their rightful land is certainly a long, arduous process. There is still a long way to go in the social and economic realm; there are many gaps to be bridged, many wrongs to be righted. We must strive to achieve equal rights for minorities, to strengthen the bond between the people and its Torah, and to create profound connections between all sectors of our people. Some express frustration at the political complications that are inconsistent with the great vision of a united people dwelling in all parts of the Promised Land.

But these shadows do not have the power to dim the great, divine light of the Holy Land. We have the duty to repair, but not to belittle what has been achieved. Stains are not removed by cutting them off a garment; shadows are not lifted by dimming the lights. Our skies will shine brighter only if we bring more light into our lives, with the hope that God will continue to shine His light upon us and Zion. "For with You is the fountain of life; in Your light, we see light" (Ps. 36:10).

Acknowledging God's Hand in History

Rabbi David Milston

I am the Lord your God, who brought you out from the land of Egypt, from the house of bondage" (Ex. 20:2). Many of our commentators have questioned this opening statement of the Ten Commandments. Why does the Almighty choose to introduce Himself as the Redeemer from Egypt, and not as the Creator of the Universe? Surely creation itself overrides specific miraculous events, even if they were essential for *Am Yisrael*. The most obvious answer is that the lessons resulting from the exodus from Egypt teach us fundamental principles in faith that cannot be derived from the creation of the world. But how so?

Let us begin by suggesting that the exile in Egypt was not just the physical exile of a people, but also the exile of an idea. If that is true, then we can also propose that the redemption of the people also served as the redemption of that idea.

When our patriarch Abraham discovered the Almighty, the novelty of his theological thesis was not only that God created the world, but that the very God who created everything continues to create on an ongoing basis.

211

Fundamental to Abrahamic belief is an actively involved God, who was, is, and will be a constant Creator, as we say every morning immediately prior to *Keriat Shema*: "In His goodness, He renews every day, continuously, the work of creation."

When the descendants of our founding father were enslaved and oppressed in Egypt, the theological essence of who they were and what they stood for, to a large extent, went into hibernation. Even if the people believed in themselves, the aggressive education of the masses as effected by Abraham is conspicuous in its absence. It would appear that their main aim was to survive slavery, to get out alive; if they could achieve that, they could then revive their ideology and spread the word.

As the Almighty, through the medium of Moses, our teacher, prepared to redeem the nation, He simultaneously organized the revival of their philosophy. In truth, the two objectives are interdependent; as we read in Exodus 3:12, the people are being freed in order that they formally accept the worship of God at Mt. Sinai.

The fact that the theological principles of *Am Yisrael* were hardly known while they were in Egypt is plainly evident from the first meeting between Moses and Pharaoh. When Moses initially approached Pharaoh as a representative of God and the nation, Pharaoh's immediate response was to question Moses regarding the Almighty: Who is this God, that I should adhere to His directives (Ex. 5:2)? Either Pharaoh denied God's existence entirely, or he was of the opinion that the Creator indeed exists, but He is not the slightest bit interested in the comings and goings of this world.

It seems clear that the objective of at least nine of the ten plagues was not to free the oppressed masses – that could have been achieved in a miraculous moment – but rather to redeem the Abrahamic idea from its exile, as Scripture itself testifies: "In order that they know that I am God in the midst of the land" (Ex. 8:18). Indeed, in their commentaries to the Haggada, both Maharal and Abrabanel explain the three *simanim* that Rabbi Yehuda gives for the ten plagues by invoking the idea that most if not all of the plagues had the objective of educating Egypt and the world about the Almighty.

Once we accept that there are two parallel liberations taking place – the freedom of a nation, and the revival of Abrahamic theology – we can

perhaps suggest that Passover is in essence a celebration of the former, while Shavuot is a celebration of the latter, remembering of course that you cannot have one without the other.

If this is the case, then it is clear that the opening words to the Ten Commandments are not referring to the physical freeing of *Am Yisrael*, but rather to a fundamental definition of God Himself. God did not simply create the world; He is actively involved in everything that transpires in the world as well. It was the Lord Himself who freed the nation from slavery. It is as if He is saying, "I am not simply God the original creator; I am God the active ruler of the universe." Thus, the exodus represents a further definition of God the Creator.

Though there are differences of opinions within Jewish philosophy regarding the demarcation lines that distinguish between the free choice of man, on the one hand, and divine providence and God's active involvement in the world, on the other, all are agreed that ongoing divine involvement in the world is fundamental to Judaism.

In days of old, when our nation was spiritually worthy, we had prophets and prophetesses who would pass on the word of God. We knew what was going to happen (if we chose to ignore our prophets' directives) at least on a national level, and to a large degree we knew why we had been punished in the aftermath of disaster. Once prophecy ceased, however, our already limited understanding of the Almighty became even more diminished. Of course, the fact that in our times we understand little of God's ways does not mean that God is not involved in the world, neither does it mean that events have no reason; rather, we simply have no clue, because we have no prophecy.

In these seemingly endless years of exile, the believing Jew is required to trust totally in the Almighty without possessing an inkling of why things are truly happening and when our final redemption will come. This reality has led many a believer to fall by the wayside during the last two millennia. While the harsh truisms of exile have expressed themselves in every way possible, the demand for the regular Jew simply to keep going, unconditionally, when nothing even remotely makes sense, has become increasingly more difficult. Perhaps if Isaiah were alive today, preaching to us publicly, it would make it easier for us all to keep the faith despite the eternal, unanswered questions that plague us. We do, of course, have the

Tanakh, and we are enthused and encouraged by the prophets therein, but the onus is now upon us to understand their message in a contemporary context, to internalize it, and move forward relentlessly.

But where do we draw the line? There are those who have presumed to take upon themselves the role of the prophets; they never hesitate to explain why things have happened, what is happening now, and what will happen in the future. This is, in my humble opinion, a very dangerous, and often hurtful and insensitive, approach to life. Even when the turn of events seems to fit logically with our theories, it does not mean that our explanation is the correct one. We can, perhaps, conjecture to ourselves about ourselves (though obviously not in definitive terms), but who are we to declare in absolute terms why things happened in the past and how the path of redemption will develop in the present and future?

So we have a paradox: On the one hand, God's ongoing activism in our world is fundamental to our belief, while on the other hand, we have no real tools to definitively understand what is happening and why.

It is with these thoughts in mind that I would like to address Yom HaAtzma'ut.

When we look at the events of the last one hundred years, certainly in the context of the past two millennia, we can see that something very special is going on. I know that in the past there have been false messiahs, but nothing in our exilic history remotely compares to what has occurred over the last ten decades, for good and for bad. To ignore these events, it seems to me, is to ignore the Almighty Himself.

The Holocaust is an unparalleled tragedy not just in the annals of Jewish history, but in the history of the world. I have been studying this terrible period for over twenty-five years, yet the more I delve into it, the less I understand. Each time I visit Poland, I leave even more astounded by the absolute evil of Nazi Germany and its more-than-willing allies, and even more in awe of the spirit of the victims who were murdered and the survivors who overcame the seemingly impossible. I cannot accept that this man-made hell can be fully explained. It is not just another historical event. Even if we can learn things about human nature in an attempt to try and ensure that history does not repeat itself, to even endeavor at philosophical and theological comprehension in this sphere is, at least to my mind, pointless, maybe even forbidden. The enormity of the Holocaust

ultimately leaves it beyond our grasp. I humbly accept my limitations, and glean what I can, with the knowledge that I will never really understand. Remember – yes; honor – definitely; learn specific lessons – that too; but fully comprehend – never.

I cannot understand the Holocaust and the evil therein, but I must not – and will not – ignore it. There are no legitimate human answers that can possibly explain these terrible years, so I look up to the Heavens, understanding my limitations, and strengthen my religious resolve through prayer and supplication. I do not understand, but I believe. I immerse myself in reading about the Holocaust not with the objective of philosophical comprehension, but because I never want to forget the millions of my brothers and sisters who were savagely destroyed, because I truly believe that God is involved in the world, and because I know that there is something massively significant taking place even though I don't know exactly what it is and what it means.

And when we move from the incomprehensible evil of the Second World War to the unbelievable wonders of 1948, 1967, and the here and now, I have the exact same fundamental feelings, though they understandably trigger a very different response.

The emergence of the State of Israel, in the context of the years that preceded independence, is equally beyond my comprehension. I understand how politically, in the aftermath of the Holocaust, the United Nations would feel it necessary to grant the Jewish people a homeland. What I cannot understand is how that decision materialized. How does a small, unarmed nation pick itself up after a third of her people have been murdered, and establish independence when all of the surrounding neighbors, without exception, deny her right to exist? How do unarmed civilians wage war against established armies who attack her from the north, the south, and the east? How does a country on the verge of destruction in the late spring months of 1967, in five and a half days, overcome the enemy and return after two thousand years of exile to the holy cities of Jerusalem and Hebron? To this very day I am astounded by our existence. There are 150 million people in and around the Middle East who don't want us here, yet we are here. The ongoing miracle of Israel is a phenomenon that I live and breathe every day. Yet, once again, I don't understand it. On the one hand, I can see the prophecies of Isaiah and Zechariah realizing

themselves at every juncture, but I can also see that we are a long way from complete redemption.

Surely to ignore the events that have transpired between 1948 and now is verging on heresy! Can a believing Jew, after two thousand years of exile, after the unparalleled destruction of the Holocaust, ignore the reality that is the State of Israel?

I do not understand the Holocaust, but it demands from me, as a believing Jew, to turn to God in prayer and supplication. I also don't understand the wonders which we continue to experience daily, but can I ignore them? Surely every believing Jew must acknowledge and turn to God with eternal gratitude and joy! How can this day, after all we have been through, not be a festival for everyone? Do we not believe in the God who brought us out of Egypt? Do we not believe that the Almighty is involved at all times? The same God who brought us out of Egypt has brought us back home after two thousand years, so how can we not acknowledge this? The facts are facts, and they are undeniable. We are back home, despite everything. Even if we do not know for certain that final redemption knocks at the door, who can close their eyes to the obvious?

Those of us who sing on Seder night "Next year in Jerusalem"; those of us who pray three times a day for the return to Zion; those of us who are constantly waiting for the Messiah – can we possibly turn a blind eye when a miracle like this stares us in the face, even though we don't understand the ways of God? As the Almighty knocks impatiently at our door, are we really going to tell Him that we are too tired to get dressed and open up? Are we going to let this window of opportunity disappear? How can we continue to chant "Next year in Jerusalem" in the same way as we did a hundred years ago? Jerusalem is ours – it is not a dream anymore, nor is it an unanswered prayer. It is real!

There is a famous midrash in *Pesikta Rabbati* (36): "Our Rabbis have taught that when the Messianic king reveals himself, and is standing on the roof of the Temple, he will say to the gathered people: Oh humble ones, the time of your redemption has arrived, and if you do not believe me, see my light that shines upon you."

A few years ago, on the last day of Passover, I attended a *seudat Mashiaḥ*. One of the speakers, Rabbi Karov of Karnei Shomron, noted something

extraordinary about this midrash: It describes a reality where the Messiah is standing on the roof of the Temple, and yet from his message, we can see that there are still many people who don't believe. How can that be?

Perhaps the *Pesikta Rabbati* is alluding to the reality that we ourselves live in today. After years of exile, we have come home; we have won wars that we should never have won; we have seen Jews return from the Soviet Union, from Morocco, from Western Europe, from the Southern Hemisphere, from North America, from Ethiopia! Are these not prophecies being fulfilled? Can a religious Jew who believes in God's involvement in this world turn a blind eye? Have we not been waiting for this forever?

True, as I said before, we have no prophets today, but we have the prophets of Tanakh; we cannot be sure that what they describe is what we are seeing, but surely there is a very good chance that it is, and we should at least try to make this work. We have never been so close. Is there not ample reason to celebrate after all we have gone through? Is this not the most powerful way to recognize the God who brought us out of Egypt, the active God?

Surely there can be no better time to mark renewed redemption than in the holy days that fall between Passover and Shavuot. Indeed, it seems to be no coincidence that our contemporary physical liberation, marked by Yom HaAtzma'ut, is contiguous to the festival of Passover, whereas our celebration of the liberation of our holy city of Jerusalem falls just a week before the spiritual climax of Shavuot.

We must remember that the mourning phase that coincides with this time in our yearly calendar cannot fundamentally override the festive theme that always existed at this time, a period of time that Nahmanides referred to as the Ḥol HaMoed that separates Passover from Shavuot. This is perhaps why it is much more acceptable to say *Sheheḥeyanu* during this time, despite the numerous customs of mourning that do apply, than it is to recite this blessing during the Three-Week period of mourning.

These days are essentially festive, and I have often wondered whether there is something fundamentally wrong with a religious approach that suggests that it is prohibited to celebrate this day because it falls in the mourning stages that coincide with the Omer. Do we honestly think that Rabbi Akiva (whose students were the ones who died in the epidemic that is the original source of our mourning during this period), who at

the end of *Makkot* (24b) refers to the verses in Zechariah (8:4–6) with hope, would mourn on this day if he lived now and saw those very same prophecies coming true before his eyes? If we suspended mourning on Lag BaOmer because an epidemic ceased, surely there is ample reason to suspend mourning on Yom HaAtzma'ut.

I acknowledge that we do not know for certain, but we have the Tanakh, we have our reality, and we have two thousand years of suffering and hope behind us. If we are not to stand up now, realize what we have, and ultimately act on our beliefs, then when?

I only ask of others what I ask of myself: Do not let this day pass without deep introspection. What is happening in the world and in Israel is the work of the Almighty. If we truly believe, we must surely act on those beliefs. If we truly await the Messiah, then surely what we see are the clearest signs since the destruction of the Second Temple. It is time to act! Let us remember the words of Motta Gur: *Har HaBayit beyadeinu* – "The Temple Mount is in our hands!" Redemption is in our hands. It appears that the Almighty is knocking at the door, and the religious community must lead the people to the door. It is up to us; there is simply nothing more important.

"Next year in Jerusalem" need not be a prayer. It should be a plan of action.

"For Great Is the Day of Jerusalem"

Rishon LeZion, Chief Rabbi Yitzḥak Nissim

Yom Yerushalayim 1968

Since the day that we were exiled from our homeland, there has been no time as important for our people, no time that saw the nation of Israel's situation change so drastically, as this past year. God gave strength and insight, courage and stamina to the Israeli army, who went out to defend the nation's homeland. They fought off those who rose against us and redeemed a portion of Israel that was in foreign hands. The entire course of events and actions, those of our enemies included, how they arose and how they took place in time and space, how the true unity of a scattered and dispersed nation came to light – all these could not have transpired through human force alone, but only by He who is the true shaper of all that comes to pass.

Cut off from Jerusalem, we had been like orphans. Our disconnection seems to have had no small influence over our estrangement from Jewish values, for we had been unable to imbibe the divine abundance that rains

down upon Jerusalem. We have given up our very lives, and it is as if all past generations and all future generations gave their lives up, together with us, in order to free the city from its yoke. The words of the prophet Jeremiah were fulfilled:

> Thus says the Lord: Cries of fear are heard – terror, not peace. Ask and see: Can a man bear children? Then why do I see every strong man with his hands on his stomach like a woman in labor, every face turned deathly pale? How awful that day will be! No other will be like it. It will be a time of trouble for Jacob, but he will be saved out of it.
>
> On that day, declares the Lord of hosts, I will break the yoke off their necks and will tear off their bonds; no longer will foreigners enslave them. Instead, they will serve the Lord their God and David their king, whom I will raise up for them. So do not be afraid, Jacob My servant; do not be dismayed, Israel, declares the Lord. I will surely save you out of a distant place, your descendants from the land of their exile. Jacob will again have peace and security, and no one will make him afraid. (Jer. 30:5–10)

The heavens fought through us, and we emerged victorious. The Temple Mount is in our hands, yet it is not in our hands. It is once again within the borders of the State of Israel, but on the other hand, we see the mountain, but we will not go up. Not that we cannot do so, but we hold ourselves back, for we will not lightly set our feet upon that holiest of places.

The Temple is the table of our Father in Heaven, and Zion, the source of our life, is the wedding hall. We have entered the hall, we have reached the table, but we do not appear before Him. We have done all that is humanly possible and now it is all in the hands of Heaven. For this is what we believe: the Holy One, blessed be He, will build it Himself. And there is no greater sorrow than this, that the sons who had been banished from their father's table, have now reached it and see him, but do not draw near. This sorrow is felt more deeply now, after the great victory, for it is more tangible and more obvious.

The nation has given its heart and poured its pure blood into the city, the selfsame city God's eyes are always watching, the selfsame city that unites the hearts of all of Israel. Not only does this city strengthen

and fortify the entire kingdom of Israel, it also symbolizes the exaltation of Israel; it is able to instill unadulterated faith into every heart, able to endow every Jew with an abundance of holiness and purity.

Zion is the eternal dwelling place of the Divine Presence. Following its destruction, and particularly when we were unable to go up and be seen there by the Divine Presence, it was as if a great barrier arose and separated between us and the Divine Presence. And now, when Jerusalem has been restored to its children, all barriers have fallen. Sanctity can once again emanate from Jerusalem to the people and breathe new spirit into them, believers and non-believers alike. A marked change has come into our lives, which expresses itself less in action than in a certain intoxication, a certain wonder, an aspect of thought that is not yet properly formed or revealed in all its depth. This change opens the heart to listen and to hear, to ask and to accept things which, until now, were not readily heard or admitted.

This change in values is the continuation of what came before. There have been times when many found little delight in Judaism, times of detachment and flight, assimilation and rejection of Israel's heritage, and pursuit of general human desires. Eventually, these desires were dulled and their oppositional force weakened. Moreover, despite the occasional sideways glance, the yearning to become part of the Jewish system grew stronger. The greatest turning point came during the great days of the Six-Day War.

The great flame of these "six days of creation" lit up the hearts of all of Israel. At that moment, the dichotomic tendency of the Jewish nation to divide the centers of the Jewish world into two, one within Israel and one without, which threatened to endanger the spirit of the nation by implying that the center in the Diaspora is parallel and comparable to Jerusalem – something which, God forbid, could have divided the nation into Jews and Israelis – was as if it had never been, and it passed away from the world. From the power of this great miracle, a miracle within a miracle occurred, and those who were on the brink of defining themselves as rivals to the center of Jerusalem arose and moved to Jerusalem. The perception of Jerusalem as the center of Torah and Judaism once seemed tentative, hesitant, given to change, accepted at will, and rejected at will; there is no doubt that this has completely changed.

Never before have the Torah leaders in the Diaspora felt so connected and devoted to Jerusalem, and this is one of the greatest achievements of those tumultuous six days. Not only do they feel obligated to deepen and strengthen their connection to Jerusalem and its sages and scholars, they also feel the need to visit the city and be inspired by its holiness. Those who are distant have grown closer; those who were close have become closer still. They feel the weight of the responsibility and the need to return to Zion; they sense that separation from the heart of the nation is as if a body is disconnected from its heart.

And for those who ask how Jerusalem can remain in our hands when all the surrounding nations are deliberating, making decisions, threats, and extortions from every angle, a clear answer can be found in the Radak's commentary on a verse in Psalms: "Jerusalem is surrounded by mountains like the Lord surrounds His people, now and forever" (125:2). He writes: "Even though Jerusalem is surrounded by mountains, she has no strength, and the nations rule over her. And she will have no strength until the nation of God shall be within her, for then He will surround His people, His name shall be a greater strength for her than the mountains, and the enemy shall never rule her again." This obvious solution is Israel's ascent to Jerusalem and its rebuilding in every direction, particularly that portion which had been under enemy rule and could not be reached, that which is the heart and soul of the nation.

Therefore, we must say things as they are, in all their harshness. Our victory will not be a victory until we inhabit Jerusalem and extend Israel's borders to the rest of the cities of our ancestors from which we have been exiled.

The prayer "Next Year in Jerusalem" was, until the Six Day War, a pure and honest prayer. All who said it hoped for it with all their heart and soul. But now, when the time of Jerusalem's redemption has come – now that Israel's borders have been extended and the road is paved and open to every person of Israel – can this prayer possibly have the same meaning, the same great truth, the same yearning? Can it still quicken the heartbeat of every Jew in every godless land?

Before Jerusalem's liberation, when we uttered these words they expressed the great desire to return to Zion, the source of our life and the dwelling place of the Divine Presence. We gave no thought to obstacles

on our side. But now, when the road is open before us, how can we leave our families and our property? What shall we eat, what shall we drink, and where can we stay?

How will we live out our lives? Will we truly be able to adjust to new circumstances? How will we become accustomed to new living conditions? These questions have replaced the pure, simple yearning when life in the holy city was but a sweet, abstract dream.

Let us consider the first days of our nation, the redemption of the Israelites from the slavery in Egypt. The nation enslaved in Egypt cried out and prayed for its release, begged to leave the house of slavery. Its redemption was paved with trials. God brought ten plagues upon Pharaoh until he agreed to let the people go – and even then, he changed his mind. The greatest act of salvation was at the splitting of the sea – the nation of Israel walked through on dry land, the water a wall on either side, while Pharaoh and his army were drowned in its depths. These trials befell the enemy, those who were delaying redemption. After the enemy had been taken care of, certain trials befell the Jewish nation itself. The nation wanted to be redeemed without a redemption process. They did not wish to pass through the harsh wilderness, but to reach their portions and be secure without undergoing a process of distillation and refinement, without obtaining the right to be redeemed.

Herein lays the similarity between the exodus of our ancestors and our own time.

However, we must not overlook the differences between the generation of the wilderness – the generation that left Egypt – and our generation, who Providence guided to redeem the Land. There has never been a time of martyrdom, strength, and might like our generation, the era of the Israeli Defense Forces. Who can compare to their courage, power, and stamina? They fought for the existence of their very souls upon holy ground, and in their might and merit an entire nation was able to return to a Land that had been denied to them for two thousand years. How will we repay them if we fail to retain their legacy, if we do not settle every part of the Land, build on every holy corner?

There are certain great matters that require a majority of the Jewish people to be dwelling in the Land of Israel. There cannot be a Sanhedrin unless the majority of Israel can be found in the Land of Israel, as

Maimonides teaches us (*Laws of Sanhedrin* 4:11), and the reinstallment of judges necessarily precedes the redemption, as it says: "I will restore your judges as in days of old, your advisors as at the beginning. Afterward you will be called the City of Righteousness, the Faithful City. Zion will be delivered with justice, her penitent ones with righteousness" (Is. 1:26–27). Israel will not be complete until the ingathering of exiles, until most of the nation will be found within the Land.

Will we, God forbid, have to face another forty years of wilderness until the Land is properly settled? Will Israel once again have to endure trials and tribulations until it returns to its Land? God has sworn to us that He will restore the people to their Land, and indeed God has given us the Land – will we return to it against our will, or in joy and gladness? Do we not long for the fulfillment of Isaiah's vision: "Those the Lord has rescued will return, and they will enter Zion with singing; everlasting joy will crown their heads, gladness and joy will overtake them, and sorrow and sighing will flee away" (Is. 51:11)? Having the majority of the nation within its borders will unleash a spiritual awakening. The miracles and events that have come to pass have increased, and will increase, the strength of faith, and will knit the hearts of the nation together as one. Israel's profound moral depth will be revealed even among those of our people who seem empty, as our sages said that they, too, are filled with good deeds as a pomegranate is filled with seeds (*Megilla* 6a).

Given our new situation, it is doubtful whether a person's Judaism is complete unless he himself returns to the Land of Israel and fulfills the commandment of living in the Land. Now there is nothing to prevent a Jew from doing so. The gates have opened and the roads have been paved. And how much more so does this apply to our spiritual leaders, for if they fail to do so, the words of the sages apply: "Their guilt is on your heads" (Deut. 1:13), for they serve as role models for the masses. And if they ask, "How can we abandon our flock?" – we see that when they are offered new positions, they readily move from place to place.

The redemption of Jerusalem is the redemption of the people, and the miracle of the six days is the miracle of the entire nation, even of those in the Diaspora. If, God forbid, Israel's enemies had prevailed, it would have affected the Jews all over the world. Our brothers in the Diaspora are our true brothers in joy and sorrow, and they have a part in our victory. Like

us, then, they are bound by the holy obligation of settling Jerusalem and the entire Land.

Three times a day, we say to God: "From generation to generation we will thank You and declare our praise for our lives, which are entrusted into Your hand; for our souls, which are placed in Your charge; for Your miracles, which are with us every day; and for Your wonders and favors at all times, evening and morning and midday." These miracles, which take place every day, are hidden, while the miracles we were granted in Jerusalem's redemption are revealed and obvious to all.

For a revealed miracle performed for all of Israel, we are required to give thanks. The liberation of Jerusalem moves us to celebrate, praise, and glorify the name of the Lord for the miracles and wonders He performs for us. It is therefore a positive commandment to celebrate and commemorate this day with praise and thanksgiving.

> If our mouths were as full of song as the sea, and our tongue with jubilation as its myriad waves, if our lips were full of praise like the spacious heavens … still we could not thank You enough, Lord our God and God of our ancestors, or bless Your name … for the miracles and wonders You have performed for us. … You redeemed us from Egypt, Lord our God, and freed us from the house of bondage. … You delivered us from the sword … until now Your mercies have helped us. (*Nishmat* prayer)

May You, our God, never abandon us while we inhabit Jerusalem and gather her children within her. Just as we have been granted to take part in the fulfillment of our prophets' visions, please let the rest of their words be fulfilled as well. As Zechariah says:

> Thus says the Lord: I will return to Zion and dwell in Jerusalem. Then Jerusalem will be called the Faithful City, and the mountain of the Lord Almighty will be called the Holy Mountain…. Thus says the Lord of hosts: I will save My people from the countries of the east and the west. I will bring them back to live in Jerusalem; they will be My people, and I will be faithful and righteous to them as their God. (Zech. 8:3, 7–8)

And Isaiah says:

> You who bring good news to Zion, go up on a high mountain. You who bring good news to Jerusalem, lift up your voice with a shout, lift it up, do not be afraid; say to the towns of Judah, "Here is your God!" ...He tends his flock like a shepherd: He gathers the lambs in his arms and carries them close to his heart. (Is. 40:9–11)

May it be God's will that Isaiah's prophecy be fulfilled in our time.

Yom Yerushalayim

Rabbi Berel Wein

It is strange for this elderly Jew to have to write an article about the importance and meaning of Jerusalem. If there ever was anything in Jewish life that was self-understood – axiomatic and integral to Jewish societal and personal life and consciousness – it was the centrality of Jerusalem to the Jewish soul. "Next year in Jerusalem!" was not simply an expression of hope, prayer, and longing, but a symbol of Jewish defiance and continuity. In Jewish thought and society, Jerusalem, not Rome, is the Eternal City; Jerusalem, not Paris, is the City of Lights. The great Rabbi Meir Simḥa HaCohen of Dvinsk, at the beginning of the twentieth century, wrote prophetically: "Woe to those who somehow think that Berlin is Jerusalem!"

Jerusalem may have had many imitators, but it had no replacements. Jerusalem remained the heart of the Jewish people just as Rabbi Yehuda HaLevi of twelfth-century Spain insisted that the people of Israel was the heart of all humanity – the strongest of all human organs and the most vulnerable of all the organs of the body. The metaphor that all of the life-blood of Jewish life is pumped throughout the Jewish world by the heart of Jerusalem was self-understood in past Jewish generations. It needed no explanation or repetition, no reinforcement or defensive justification.

When the Jewish people as a whole were physically and politically separated from Jerusalem, Jerusalem was not just a memory or nostalgia; it remained a real and an imposing presence in Jewish life and thought. If to some individual Jews it became just another imaginary place because of its distant location and unattractive reality – an old, poverty-ridden, dilapidated, small, and backwater city buried in the expanse of the Ottoman Empire – in the core Jewish soul, the reality of the city lived and thrived.

Over the past three centuries, Jews slowly have made their way back home to Jerusalem. Under terrible physical trials of privation, persecution, and derision, the Jewish community in Jerusalem grew. By the middle of the nineteenth century, Jews constituted the majority population in the city. They began to settle outside of the walls of the Old City and establish new neighborhoods. The ancient mother city responded to the return of its children to its holy precincts, and Jerusalem became alive again.

After the restoration of Jewish sovereignty in parts of the Land of Israel, Jerusalem became the capital of the State of Israel. Its population grew exponentially, and the building cranes became ubiquitous all over the areas of the city's expanded boundaries. After the Six-Day War, it was united, and again the Western Wall and its adjacent Temple Mount became the center of the Jewish world. A new special day was added to the Jewish calendar to mark the rebirth of the physical Jerusalem in Jewish life and prayer. The Jewish population grew, and the building of the infrastructure of the city continued apace. The mixed blessings of automobile traffic and constant construction projects affect all Jerusalemites, but they only serve to highlight the unimagined change in the face of the city that occurred over the last century. Jerusalem reborn is the miracle of our times.

But much of the world resents Jerusalem's revival. The United Nations wants it to become an "international city," though the rebuilding of the city worked, and there never has been such successful city management in all of human history. No one really seemed to notice the hard fortunes of the city until the Jews began to remake history there. The Muslim world especially, little concerned with the fate and fortunes of the city until the Jews began to arrive and rebuild it, wants it to be exclusively Muslim dominated and populated. The United States State Department does not

recognize united Jerusalem as being part of Israel, let alone as its capital city. And all of the latent and obvious antisemitism that still poisons the Western world is directed against Israel and Jerusalem. In their frustration, jealousy, and misplaced religious fervor, Muslims encourage and perpetrate violence in Jerusalem and publicly celebrate the killing of its innocent inhabitants. The attitude seems to be, "Better no Jerusalem than a Jewish Jerusalem." Jerusalem has always been a flash point as its key place in history and faiths make it a sensitive issue. Today, to a great extent, Jerusalem is the one issue that drives the world's thoughts and policies.

Jerusalem possesses the eternal quality of focusing human attention to think about holiness, closeness, and the struggle for faith. This view of what Jerusalem is all about makes the celebration of Yom Yerushalayim the necessary Jewish response to the opposition and enmity of the world to Jerusalem – to a Jewish Jerusalem. Yom Yerushalayim is the proper response of Jews to everything that is currently going on in the world. Rejoice in the fact that our generations have lived to see Jerusalem rebuilt in body and spirit, beauty and strength. Walk its streets and breathe its air; see its visions and bask in its memories. Appreciate the gifts that the Lord has granted us, and express one's thanks for living in such a momentous and historic time. That is what Yom Yerushalayim represents. That is why it is so special and sacred. That is why it is worthy of commemoration and celebration.

The Temple Mount: Heart of Israel

Rabbi Yaakov Medan

The Day of Jerusalem's Liberation, *Yom Ḥerut Yerushalayim*, preserves the immortal words of Motta Gur, the commander of the reserve paratrooper brigade that recaptured the Old City. These words, uttered at 10:30 on the morning of 28 Iyar, were ones that the nation of Israel had anticipated for two thousand years: "*Har HaBayit beyadeinu* – The Temple Mount is in our hands." Let us briefly sketch the history leading up to these words.

Mt. Moriah (the Temple Mount) and the Temple that stood upon it are the heart and soul of Israel. According to rabbinic literature, and in its wake Maimonides' *Hilkhot Beit HaBeḥira*, this mountain was singled out by God from the very time of creation. According to the prophet Ezekiel, the Garden of Eden stood upon this mountain, until Adam and Eve sinned and the Divine Presence departed.

Yet the main point that the Torah conveys about Mt. Moriah is that it is the location of the *Akeda*, the pinnacle of love between God and His people. There, Abraham chooses to fulfill God's request to sacrifice his

son, binding what is nearest and dearest to him for the sake of his devotion. There, his God tells him that He will never permit him to raise a hand against Isaac, and there God swears that He will bless his seed and watch over them forever.

The location of Mt. Moriah seems to have slipped out of the consciousness of the next generations – even our forefather Jacob makes no reference to it – but it returns in full force in King David's time when a deadly plague sweeps the kingdom. Like Abraham's knife outstretched over his bound son, an angel of death's sword is outstretched over Jerusalem, and once again, God's voice rings out to the bearer of death: "Enough, now withdraw your hand" (1 Chron. 21:15). King David then insists upon purchasing the mountain, which served as Ornan's threshing floor, for its full worth, and builds an altar upon the site, thus saving his people from certain disaster. The text also hints that this act invokes Abraham's merit for the binding of his son, and this merit brings the plague to an end.

From then on, Mt. Moriah became the heart of Israel, the epicenter of their connection with their Father in Heaven. King David dearly wished to build a Temple on this mountain, but he was not granted this honor; his son Solomon built it in his place. The mountain and the Temple upon it became a site of pilgrimage, the nation's destination three times a year. Three times a year, the entire people would gather to seek God's Presence; there they would experience true unity and brotherhood; there they understood that the true goal of their hearts was one: to restore God's glorious Presence to His world after it had departed from the Garden following the sin.

The mountain and the Temple upon it were not intended only as a site of sacrifice, though offerings are a precious and important mitzva. The Temple was above all a place of encounter between the nation and the Divine Presence. For without this encounter, what is our purpose in life? Encounter between the human and the Divine is the very purpose of existence – the most beautiful, the most yearned for, the most coveted of human experiences. No other pleasure, no amount of riches, can compare! No other goal, no other concept, is higher than this; no depth is more profound, and no light shines like its light!

The climax of this encounter is described in the Torah: "And when Moses came to the Tent of Meeting to speak with Him, and he heard

the Voice speaking to him above the curtain of atonement over the Ark of the Covenant, from between the two *Keruvim*, He spoke to him" (Num. 7:89). From the center of the Sanctuary, from the Holy of Holies, from between the two *Keruvim*, God's voice is heard by Moses. From there flows the spring of prophecy that carries God's word to His people. Once the Temple and the *Keruvim* were lost, so was prophecy, and we stand humbled and lost before the Omnipresent, for we no longer hear His words. The offerings were chiefly intended to atone for and redeem the individual and the nation so that they would become worthy of standing before God and hearing His word. The offerings, sacrificed in the Temple courtyard, prepared the people for entering deeper inside.

The Temple experienced hard times as well as good. Some years were stained by atrocity, by abominations that took place in the holy city of Jerusalem and throughout the beloved Land. We were no longer worthy, and the God's Temple was destroyed together with the holy city and the beloved Land. In time, God took us out of exile by means of King Cyrus of Persia's declaration, which paved the way back to Zion and to building the Second Temple (Ezra ch. 1). King Cyrus, ruler of an empire, declared that God had instructed him to build a Temple for Him in Jerusalem. In other words, the return to Zion was born out of the need to rebuild God's Temple in Jerusalem, and for that purpose the first of the exiles returned home.

Flavius Josephus, the great historian of the Second Temple period, in his works *Antiquities of the Jews* and *The History of the Jewish Wars against the Romans*, uses moving, poignant words to describe the profound esteem in which the Temple was held by the Jews of the Holy Land and the Diaspora, and the extent of its role as the heart of Israel. He describes how myriads of Jews did not hesitate to martyr themselves in the struggle against the emperor Caligula, who wanted to contaminate the Temple with an image of himself. Eventually, the emperor's messenger was deterred from committing such an abomination.

Due to our sins, the Second Temple was also destroyed, but the yearning for the mountain and the Temple that once stood upon it did not cease. The emperor Hadrian turned Jerusalem into a pagan city and placed idols where God's Sanctuary had stood; this was among the factors that led to the Bar Kokhba revolt, a fierce struggle that engaged half of the

armed forces of the Roman Empire and ended in horrific slaughter. Yet the yearning for the Temple and the Temple Mount only increased, and it was translated into the central theme of Israel's prayers throughout the generations of exile. Jews continued to take desperate measures to pray in the vicinity of the holy mountain.

Skipping over eighteen hundred years of yearning and longing, of prayer soaked with tears, we will now focus upon two scenes that transpired in our own time. On the eve of *Shabbat Parashat Balak*, the 10th of Tammuz 5708 (1948), the forces of the Irgun and the Leḥi, which had already been absorbed into the IDF but remained independently active in Jerusalem, attempted to penetrate the Old City from three different directions. The commander of the operation, General David Shaltiel, a secular Jew and a self-affirmed heretic in his youth, concealed a young lamb among his equipment, with plans to sacrifice it upon the Temple Mount as an offering to God once their mission had succeeded (L. Collins and D. Lapierre, *O Jerusalem* [New York, 1988], 425; N. Shragai, *Temple of Dispute* [Jerusalem, 1995], 15). But the operation failed.

The second of the scenes is the more familiar image of the paratroopers in the Six-Day War triumphant in their successful mission to liberate the Old City of Jerusalem. In his book *The Battle for Jerusalem* (New York, 1978), 363, Lt. Gen. Motta Gur writes:

> The consummation for which we had fought so hard – Mount Moriah, Abraham and Isaac, the Temple, the Zealots, the Maccabees, Bar-Kokhba, the wars against the Romans and Greeks. Thoughts of our long history churned in our minds. We were at the Temple Mount. The Temple Mount was ours.

In a military parade upon the mount, he said: "For two millennia, no Jew could enter the Temple Mount…. And then you came, you paratroopers, and you restored the Mount to the bosom of the nation" (ibid., 379). Eli Landau, a paratrooper officer and journalist, wrote at the time: "For two thousand years, the Jewish people have waited for the moment that they learn that the site of the Temple… this holy hill, is indeed in our hands once more. Millions of Jews from all over the world will once again be able to make pilgrimage to the Mountain of God."

We cannot overlook another aspect of the Day of Jerusalem's Liberation, well documented in Moshe Natan's book *The War over Jerusalem* (Jerusalem, 1968), 311–12:

> Legend tells us that when the young priests saw the Temple go up in flame, they seized the Temple keys and climbed up to the Sanctuary roof. Standing there in desperate clusters, they turned to God, and flung the keys to His house heavenward. Then they flung themselves into the flames that consumed the Sanctuary. At that moment, the image of a hand descended from the heavens and caught the airborne keys.
>
> On Wednesday, 27 Iyar, 5767, the paratroopers who saw the Western Wall from afar felt as if the keys had been returned to them, and they are clutching them in their hands, clutching them tightly.

Standing at the Western Wall, the chief rabbi of the IDF, Rabbi Shlomo Goren, a Torah scroll in his arm and a shofar to his lips, said the *Shehekheyanu* blessing, followed by the blessing "Comforter of Zion and Rebuilder of Jerusalem." Together with the paratroopers and Rabbi Goren, the entire nation – glued to their radios as the tears streamed down their cheeks – accepted the yoke of Heaven for one moment, just as they had nearly 3,300 years before at Mount Sinai.

The Glory of Jerusalem

Dr. Yoel Rappel

A connection that is both emotional and psychological, historical and religious, literary and poetic, links the Jewish people to Jerusalem, the city of Zion. "Yom Yerushalayim," Jerusalem Day, is a new festival in the Jewish calendar, yet prophets and poets, authors and exegetes, preachers and pilgrims, sages and scholars, have all given expression to the centrality of Jerusalem and the yearning of Jews from all corners of the earth for the beauty of the Golden City. The psalmist describes Jerusalem as it was on the three festivals of pilgrimage, when hundreds of thousands flocked to the city and the Temple at its heart:

> A song of ascents to David,
> I rejoiced when they said to me,
> Let us go to the House of God.
> Our feet were standing at your gates, Jerusalem.
> Jerusalem built up, like a city knit together.
> That is where the tribes go up,
> The tribes of the Lord,
> To give praise to the Lord's name. (Ps. 122:1–4)

The pilgrims swore, "If I forget thee, O Jerusalem, may my right hand wither" (Ps. 137:5). To this ancient vow, we add the prayer: "To Jerusalem, Your city, may You return in compassion, and may You dwell in it as You promised. May You rebuild it rapidly in our days as an everlasting structure" (*Amida* prayer). Two hundred and one centuries after King David established the city as the capital of his kingdom, one of the greatest poets of Spain, Rabbi Yehuda HaLevi, arrived in Jerusalem and sang: "Beautiful in its heights, joy of all the earth, city of the Great King. For you my soul has yearned from farthest west!"

The supreme status of Jerusalem in all forms of Jewish art is faithfully expressed in the words of Abraham Habermann, also known as Heiman HaYerushalmi (*Nitzotzot HaGeula*, Jerusalem, 1950): "Poets sing of the beauty, grace, and glory of every city. And every poet sings about Jerusalem, and whoever does not sing about Jerusalem – is not a poet."

Jerusalem today is a glorious city, the legendary subject of the psalmist: "Joy of all the earth, Mount Zion on its northern side, city of the Great King" (Ps. 48:3). Though the city of Jerusalem is barely a speck upon the world map, the heart and eye of every Jew turns to it. Abba Issi, in the name of Shmuel HaKatan, said:

This world is like a person's eye,
The white part is the ocean that surrounds the whole world,
The iris is the world,
The pupil is Jerusalem,
The face reflected in the pupil is the Temple,
May it be rebuilt swiftly, in our days, and in the days of all of Israel, Amen.
(*Derekh Eretz Zuta* 9)

In every time and generation, Jews have preserved the memory of Jerusalem through their actions and prayers. The loyalty and devotion to Jerusalem is expressed through the prayers, customs, and ceremonies that accompany a person from his birth until his last day.

Three times a day, a person recites the prayer "To Jerusalem, Your city, may You return in compassion," his face turned toward Jerusalem. Every meal is followed by the words, "And rebuild the city of Jerusalem swiftly

in our days" (Grace after Meals). As Yom Kippur ends, and at the end of the Pesaḥ Seder, every Jew cries out in song: "Next year in Jerusalem!" Under the wedding canopy, the groom breaks a glass in commemoration of the destruction of Jerusalem and the Temple. Some have the custom of sprinkling ashes upon the groom's head, as it is written: "To provide for those who grieve in Zion – to bestow on them a crown of beauty instead of ashes" (Is. 61:3). In the final blessing of the seven marriage blessings, all sing, "There will yet be heard in the cities of Judah and the streets of Jerusalem the sound of joy and the sound of gladness."

It is also written, "When a person whitewashes his home, let him leave a small place in commemoration of Jerusalem; when a women dons her jewelry, let her leave one piece off in commemoration of Jerusalem, as it says, 'If I forget thee, O Jerusalem, may my right hand wither'" (Mishna *Bava Batra* 2:6). When Jews pray, they face Jerusalem:

> If he is outside of Israel – let him direct his heart to Israel, as it says: "And they shall pray to You via their Land" (1 Kings 8:48).
> If he is in Israel – let him direct his heart to Jerusalem, as it says: "And they will pray to You through the city You have chosen" (8:44).
> If he is in Jerusalem, let him direct his heart to the Temple, as it says, "And they shall pray to this house" (11 Chron. 6:32).
> If he is near the Temple, let him direct his heart to the Holy of Holies, as it says: "And they shall pray to this place" (1 Kings 8:35).
> If he is standing in the Holy of Holies, let him direct his heart to the Ark ... all of Israel direct their hearts to one place. (*Berakhot* 30a)

Whoever is living the dream of generations past and is granted, as is our generation, to pray in Jerusalem, is fulfilling the words of the Midrash: "Whoever is praying in Jerusalem is essentially praying before the Heavenly Throne, for the gates of Heaven are there, and an opening is open to hear prayer" (*Midrash Shoḥer Tov* 91).

The vow to Jerusalem has been imprinted upon the souls, thoughts, and actions of millions of Jews throughout every exile. Every generation, countless Jews dreamed of reaching Jerusalem, of witnessing its rebuilding and renewal. The State of Israel's visionary, Benjamin Ze'ev (Theodore) Herzl, managed to set this dream in motion. During his visit

to the land in 1898, he passed through the city. The sights he saw depressed him deeply, and in his journal he writes:

> If the day shall come to pass when Jerusalem is ours, and if it will still be in my power to take action, my first deed will be to purify you, and all that is unholy I will command to clear away.... I shall empty the nests of filth, I shall burn the ruins that are not holy with fire, and I shall have the shops transferred to another place...the new Jerusalem shall dwell upon the hillsides; a refining, polishing hand shall transform it into a gemstone.

Seventy years after Herzl's visit, the paratroopers of the IDF reconquered East Jerusalem and reunited the two halves of the city. "The entire nation was amazed, and many even wept to hear the news of the reconquest of the Old City," said Chief of Staff Yitzchak Rabin when he received an honorary doctorate from the Hebrew University of Jerusalem. About the paratroopers' battle, he added: "The sense of salvation and connection created by the paratroopers reached straight into the heart of Jewish history, shattered the husks of shame and toughness, and awakened deep wells of emotion and exaltation."

Twenty five years after the reunification of the city, the "Jerusalem Covenant" was signed. The leaders of the state signed a treaty, just as the leaders and the people had done in the days of the Return to Zion following the Babylonian exile. Through this pact, the leaders of the State of Israel pledged:

> We enter into this covenant and write: We shall bind you to us forever; we shall bind you to us with faithfulness, with righteousness and justice, with steadfast love and compassion. We love you, O Jerusalem, with eternal love, under siege and when liberated from the yoke of oppressors. We have been martyred for you; we have yearned for you; we have clung to you. Forevermore our home shall be within you.

On Eagles' Wings: Yom Yerushalayim, Shavuot, and Their Meaning Today

Rabbi Doron Perez

AN UNFORGETTABLE NIGHT

Many people say that this night was the most memorable of their entire lives, etched into their consciousness forever. It was the first Shavuot to take place at the Kotel in nineteen years, and the first to take place under Jewish sovereign control in almost two thousand years. Only a few days after the liberation of the Old City during the Six-Day War, over 200,000 Jews made their way through its ancient alleyways to gather in the small but recently cleared plaza at the foot of the Wall. They came not as foreigners to someone else's Jerusalem, but as rightful owners to the heart of their national and spiritual home. These 200,000 people, emissaries of *Klal Yisrael*, experienced a *Matan Torah* with a sense of dignity, redemptive spirit, and destiny that had not been experienced for almost two millennia. In 1948, the Jewish people had been revived from the dead and began to form their collective national body. Now their soul, Jerusalem, had been restored. A new era had dawned.

Both the brevity of this war and its timing are quite remarkable. The day that the Kotel and the Temple Mount returned to Jewish sovereign

control, 28 Iyar, the third day of the war, is exactly one week before Shavuot. This day was designated by the Chief Rabbinate of Israel as Yom Yerushalayim. A few days later, on Shabbat, the second of Sivan, the war ended. It was at that very time, three thousand years before, that the Jewish people had arrived at the foot of Mt. Sinai to prepare to receive the Torah. This confluence of timing could never have been anticipated by anyone who lived through this period.

The war began, amidst much tension and fear, with mounting armies on the Egyptian and Syrian borders. Early Monday morning, June 5, Israel launched a pre-emptive strike against this threat. Wars usually last weeks, months, and often years or even decades. Incredibly, only six short days later, the war was over and Israel had tripled her size and, most importantly, the Jewish people had returned to the Old City and the Temple Mount. The timing of the war is imbued with enormous spiritual significance. The purpose of this article is to explore this significance of the close proximity between Yom Yerushalayim and Shavuot by drawing on both biblical and rabbinic literature.

IN THOSE DAYS AT THIS TIME

I find it extraordinary that the time the war ended, the beginning of Sivan, is the very same time three thousand years earlier that the Jewish people arrived in the Sinai desert. They began their preparations for receiving the Torah and the experience of hearing the *Aseret HaDibbrot* – the Ten Statements – directly from God. The opening verses of Chapter 19 of Exodus record this explicitly:

> In the third month [Sivan] after the Children of Israel went out of the land of Egypt, on that day they came to the wilderness of Sinai, for they departed from Refidim and came to the desert of Sinai and had encamped in the wilderness; and Israel camped before the mountain. And Moses went up to God, and the Lord called out to him from the mountain, saying: "Thus shall you say to the house of Jacob and tell the Children of Israel."

These verses describe the arrival of the Jewish people after more than forty days of trekking from Egypt to the Sinai desert and the foot of

Mt. Sinai. It is here that they encamped, as described in the Midrash, "as one man with one heart." They stood with a singular unity and with great anticipation to receive the Torah, our value system and law book. On that day, Moses ascended the mountain and was called upon by God to share His message with the Jewish people. What clearly emerges from these verses is the fact that the arrival at Sinai on Rosh Ḥodesh Sivan initiated a six-day spiritual preparation period before receiving the Torah on the sixth day of the month.

What was the message that God gave Moses for the Jewish people in order to prepare them for receiving the Torah? The verses continue:

> You have seen what I did to Egypt and how I carried you on eagles' wings and brought you to Myself. Now, therefore, if you will obey My voice and keep My Covenant, then you will be My own treasure from among the people, for all the earth is Mine; and you shall be to Me a kingdom of priests and a holy nation. These are the things that you must tell the Jewish people. (Ex. 19:4–6)

God's opening words to the Jewish people at the foot of Mt. Sinai recall that the Jewish people themselves had seen with their own eyes the miracles that He had performed in Egypt. He had carried them out on eagles' wings and redeemed them from slavery, from the clutches of the most powerful regime of that era. They had lived through this experience themselves. Rashi explains the significance of this personal experience:

> "You have seen": It is not a tradition that you have, and I did not send you a verbal account, nor did I have testimony presented to you by witnesses, but rather you, with your own eyes, saw what I did to Egypt.

The earth-shattering and revealed miracles of the exodus created out of the natural order the supernatural: deliverance of the strong into the hands of the weak and the many into the hands of the few; deliverance in the face of destruction, and the possibility of future life in the face of a seemingly certain death. The fact that the Jewish people themselves witnessed these miracles, through direct personal experience, creates a spiritual context for the preparations for *Matan Torah*, lending validity,

authenticity, vigor, and relevance to the revealed Word of God and His values. The God of Israel is not an untried and untested abstract spiritual entity hiding in the heavens. Rather, He is a Living God, involved intimately in human affairs, who has proven Himself to His people beyond any doubt in their own personal lives.

It was this very theme that Rabbi Yechezkel Levenstein, the famed Mashgiaḥ of the Ponevezh Yeshiva, drew upon when he shared a stirring *shiur* with his students immediately after the Six-Day War. Here is an excerpt of his words:

> "You have seen" (Ex. 19:4): It is not a tradition that we have…but rather something our own eyes saw recently, and this can serve for us a strong introduction and preparation to the receiving of the Torah. We saw with our own eyes open miracles. We saw God's closeness to us. It can be said that we merited this through the promise "that even though you will be dispersed in the land of your enemies, I will not despise you and be disgusted with you to destroy you" (Lev. 26:44). As it says in the Haggada, "It is that [promise that] stood for our forefathers and for us." … We saw with our own eyes what God, the protector of Israel, did for us, according to what the soldiers who experienced it have testified. (Quoted in Rabbi Menaḥem Mendel Kasher, *HaTekufa HaGedola* [Jerusalem, 1968], 2)

Rabbi Levenstein points out clearly that the enormity of the open miracles that we experienced during the Six-Day War and the fact that they were experienced on a first-hand, personal basis, serve as both an introduction to and preparation for Shavuot – the receiving of the Torah. After all, how could one live through this war and be indifferent to God's miracles? The breathtaking and lightning brevity of this war, with its remarkable achievements, transpired only a few short days before Shavuot. God's guiding hand seemed as clear in 1967 as it was three thousand years before at the original *Matan Torah*.

THE GOD OF ABRAHAM OR THE GOD OF ARISTOTLE?

One of the greatest of our medieval thinkers, Rabbi Yehuda HaLevi, makes a critical point in his seminal work, the *Kuzari* (1:25), regarding the significance of the miracles of *Yetziat Mitzrayim* and their relationship

to *Matan Torah*. Rabbi HaLevi poses a fundamental question regarding the very first statement of the *Aseret HaDibbrot*. In this statement, God famously introduces Himself, so to speak, to the Children of Israel at the foot of Mt. Sinai: "I am the Lord your God who brought you out of the land of Egypt, out of the house of bondage" (Ex. 20:1).

Why does God introduce Himself as the God who brought us out of Egypt and not the God who created heaven and earth? After all, the exodus seems to pale into insignificance in the face of the power of the Omnipotent God who created the entire cosmos. Surely, creating the universe *ex nihilo* is far more impressive than redeeming one small people at one particular point in history from one particular country. Rabbi HaLevi responds to this conundrum with a fundamental of Jewish faith. As awe-inspiring as the Creation of the world is, it transpired thousands of years before Mt. Sinai and was but a memory of the distant past. It is possible, as maintained by many of the Greek philosophers, that after the world was created it was then abandoned. God may be the Omnipotent power of Creation, but that does not presuppose in any way that He is involved in human affairs, in human history, and the lot of His people. By introducing Himself, maintains Rabbi HaLevi, as "the Lord your God who brought you out of the land of Egypt, out of the house of bondage," God has proven to His people that nothing could be further from the truth.

Indeed, He was and is involved in every way in human affairs, despite the feeling that He is occasionally distant. He cares about the course of human history and the pivotal role that the descendants of Abraham, Isaac, and Jacob, His people Israel, play in the unfolding of the human drama. He will not let them sink into oblivion and be crushed by the weight of Egyptian cruelty or any other dictatorial regime, but will redeem them, whether they deserve it or not – not only for their own sake, but for the sake of the moral and spiritual future of His world.

He proved to them that when all seemed lost, that nothing could possibly be done in the natural order to redeem His people, He would, if necessary, transcend the natural order and perform open miracles to realign His people with their destiny. The laws of nature exist to serve Him and His people's mission, and not the other way around. The laws of nature would not be unbreakable shackles to snuff out His spiritual purpose. *Bnei Yisrael*, who stood at Mt. Sinai, had experienced this in person. This was not only a God of the abstract-thinking philosophers,

but a God experienced in the realm of practical human life. They had lived through, seen, and experienced for themselves the awesome power, care, and concern of God. He became not only a powerful divine force, but a personal spiritual redeemer. They experienced this in a direct and undeniable fashion. He was now known to them unequivocally as the God who had brought them out of Egypt, out of the house of bondage. He was not only a distant King of a faraway heavenly palace, but also a loving and caring Father, intimately guiding and caring for His beloved children.

SIX DAYS IN JUNE: THE EAGLE SOARS AGAIN

Just as the Children of Israel had experienced directly God's open miracles and the miraculous feeling of soaring out of Egypt on the protective wings of an eagle, so too did the Jewish people in the modern era, in 1967, feel a similar sense of redemption. They had escaped near destruction at the hands of powerful and fully mechanized armies trained by the best Soviet military minds and equipped with their finest weaponry. Prime Minister Levi Eshkol stuttered in his radio address a few weeks before the war, not knowing how it would turn out. Rabbi Zalman Melamed, *Rosh Yeshiva* of Yeshivat Beit El, who was then an army chaplain, would later reveal to us, his students, at our Yom Yerushalayim festive meal, that the army Chief Rabbinate believed there were not enough spaces in Israel's cemeteries to bury the expected dead. They expected between 50,000 and 150,000 deaths and had begun converting parks into new potential cemeteries. He himself was sent to the beautiful Yarkon Park in Tel Aviv to do just that.

The Jewish State was only nineteen years old in 1967, and many of Israel's neighbors felt the time of her destruction had arrived. One hundred thousand Egyptian soldiers, and many thousands of tanks, crossed through the Sinai Peninsula towards Israel's border. The Straits of Tiran had been closed off and Israel was feeling isolated. Foreign Minister Abba Eban traveled around the world trying to gain the support of the leading Western nations, but almost no political or military support was forthcoming. The world would sit back once again and let Israel fight alone. The imminent danger was apparent. Rabbis from around the world have mentioned that more people came to pray in their synagogues on the day the war broke out than came on Yom Kippur. No one could have anticipated that in less than a week the war would be over, Judea, Samaria, and Gaza would be under Israeli sovereign control and the Kotel and Old

City would return to Jewish hands for the first time in two thousand years. Fifty thousand expected dead would be less than seven hundred and the world would marvel at the hand of God protecting His people.

It is not surprising that the 200,000 people who made their way to the Kotel a few days later for Shavuot indeed felt that God was carrying them on eagles' wings. Our celebrations of *Matan Torah* that year, and all subsequent celebrations since 6 Sivan 5727 (1967), are different from the Shavuot celebrations of the preceding two thousand years. Just as the Jewish people experienced open miracles and God's involvement in history in Egypt in biblical times, so too have we experienced them in modern times. It is with a sense of dignity, redemptive spirit, and destiny that we experience Shavuot today. It is with a feeling that the people have returned to their appropriate place in human history – building a collective society in their homeland, the land of Abraham, Isaac, and Jacob, and that they can begin once again to aspire to be "a light unto the nations." Once again we are being propelled on eagles' wings to fulfill our unique destiny.

SURVIVING OR THRIVING?

It is true that between the years 70 CE and 1948, the period of exile and dispersion, we have also witnessed an incredible miracle – that of the survival of the Jewish people against impossible odds. The Jewish people had soared on eagles' wings from imminent destruction to a new era of redemption. Both Rabbi Yechiel Michel Epstein, in his monumental halakhic work *Arukh HaShulḥan* (*Oraḥ Ḥayyim* 1:10), as well as Rabbi Yaakov Emden (introduction to his commentary on the *Siddur, Beit El*), have pointed out that the phenomenon of the survival of the Jewish people throughout their – at times – horrific *galut* of the last two thousand years is a truly remarkable miracle. Rabbi Emden goes so far as to say that it is perhaps even greater than the miracles of the exodus from Egypt. Surviving dispersion to over one hundred countries with very little to practically unite us; banishment from almost every European nation; hardly ever being able to legally own land; living through the harrowing crusades, Chmielnicki massacres, and the unthinkable Shoah, to name but a few trials – is nothing short of mind-boggling. The fact that we not only survived physically, but clung with unbending commitment to our Torah during these times despite separation of communities, is miraculous beyond words. This is undeniably true.

There is, however, one critical distinguishing factor between the miracles of the last two thousand years and the recent miracles that we experienced in 1948, 1967, and beyond. The former were miracles of a people struggling to survive, and the modern are miracles of a people beginning to thrive. Those were hidden miracles that could only be seen with the perspective of history; these are open miracles, overtly clear to all who dare to see them. Those were miracles during times of tragedy and difficulty; these are miracles at a time of triumph and redemption. It is true that the survival of the Jewish people through the Egyptian slavery is remarkable. It is the liberation from Egypt, though, which forms the foundation of our redemption and the focus of God's open miracles. It was only after being freed from slavery that we were able to march hopefully towards Mt. Sinai and the receiving of the Torah. These occurrences form the foundation of the national and spiritual pilgrimage festivals of Pesaḥ and Shavuot – of the physical freedom of our people and the revelation of our divine mission and destiny.

How blessed we are to live in an era when, between Pesaḥ and Shavuot, we are able to celebrate two modern days of deliverance, Yom HaAtzma'ut and Yom Yerushalayim. Yom HaAtzma'ut, so soon after Pesaḥ and so similar to it, is the day we received national freedom, thereafter being able to return as free people to our historic homeland. Yom Yerushalayim, only one week before Shavuot and so similar to it, is the day we returned to our holiest site, further tapping into our spiritual destiny. The Jewish people and the Torah world are not only surviving, but they are thriving as almost never before. The Shavuot experience since 1967 is now an inherently different collective experience. In the modern era, the Jewish people have experienced and the entire world has witnessed the awesome might of the God of Abraham, Isaac, and Jacob, and His eternal care and concern for His people, Israel, and their unique spiritual and moral mission. He has once again brought them to the forefront of world affairs to be a blessing to His world and a beacon of light to all nations. We have soared on eagles' wings into a new era of spiritual context, relevance, dignity, and destiny.

May we appreciate the enormity of the times that we live in, and may we commit and recommit to every element of God's Holy Torah and Halakha, which gently guide us through the personal and collective challenges of everyday life.

Epilogue:
A Reawakening

Rabbi Benji Levy

Imagine a student, sitting in the front and center seat of a massive lecture theatre, staring wide-eyed at the teacher giving the lesson of a lifetime. Immediately after the class, the student is asked to recount what was taught and responds, "My mind was elsewhere." Perhaps this is what King David meant when he wrote in the prophetic past, "When the LORD brought back the exiles of Zion we were like people who dream" (Psalms 126:1).

Daydreamers.

At the brink of annihilation, the Jewish people experienced a triumph deemed impossible by virtually any reasonable estimation. We witnessed the fulfillment of a two-millennia-old vision: a moment too miraculous to be anything but a dream. And as *Yehudim* – Jews whose namesake means gratitude, we must call out and respond. Respond with joy, respond with good deeds, and respond with gratitude in prayer and thanksgiving. Crafted from a clear view in the front row of Jewish history, this Maḥzor embodies exactly that – a reawakening.

I believe that it is no coincidence that the famous picture epitomizing the reunification of Jerusalem at the Kotel is that of Rabbi Shlomo Goren blowing the *shofar*. Yom Yerushalayim in 1967 heralded a miraculous awakening for the Jewish nation of biblical proportions, alongside other legendary *shofar* blasts such as the giving of the Torah at Sinai (Exodus 19:19) which transformed the moral landscape of civilization forever, or the announcement of the Jubilee year (Leviticus 25:9), introducing one of the most decisive statements about freedom ever made. Isaiah saw the *shofar* as the instrument of reunification, captivating the hearts and minds of those lost in exile (Isaiah 27:13), and this was the same sound heard on that fateful day next to the iconic ancient stones of the Western Wall.

Throughout our personal lives and throughout our collective history, God provides us with many wake-up calls. Maimonides explains that the call of the *shofar* serves as a communal alarm-clock of sorts, crying out the eternal message: "Awake sleepers from your sleep; rouse yourselves, slumberers from your slumber…" (*Mishneh Torah, Hilkhot Teshuva* 3:4). While we may daydream throughout the year, the *shofar* serves as our alarm clock, shocking us from our stupor with a raw sound that penetrates the heart.

This Maḥzor answers the call of the *shofar* with style, sophistication, and unity at its very core. Maimonides highlights unity of worship as the reason for fixed prayer, providing common expression to those unable to articulate their praise (*Mishneh Torah, Hilkhot Tefilla* 1:4). The Talmud highlights the purpose of praying toward Israel and specifically Jerusalem as ensuring that "all Jews are directing their hearts to a single place" (*Berakhot* 30a). This unity is encapsulated within this Maḥzor, and it goes one step further with the essays and commentaries of great contemporary thinkers to color the pages and add meaning to the prayers. The creation of this unique work highlights modern miracles in our ancient homeland, *Eretz Yisrael*, illuminated through *Torat Yisrael*, and uniting *Am Yisrael*, like "one person with one heart" (Rashi, Exodus 19:1).

The word *maḥzor* means "cycle." Seasons and cycles represent continuity and consistency, rigid in structure but renewed in style. This Maḥzor represents the newest cycle in the oldest relationship between the

Jewish people and our ancestral homeland. While each year the words are the
same, we will be different. The traditional
text is punctuated with fresh interpretations in light of the unique period in
which we find ourselves. This is the secret
of our people, finding the youth in our
ancient story.

Each time we turn this page and close
this book, let us continue to write the
next one in the narrative of our nation. May we be inspired through this
reawakening to connect to the unity of time, place, and prayer, heed the
primal call of our modern *shofar*, and be guided by the moral compass
of our Torah.

And may our eyes witness Your return to Zion in compassion.
Blessed are You, LORD, who restores His Presence to Zion.

Sydney, Australia
Kislev 5775 / December 2014